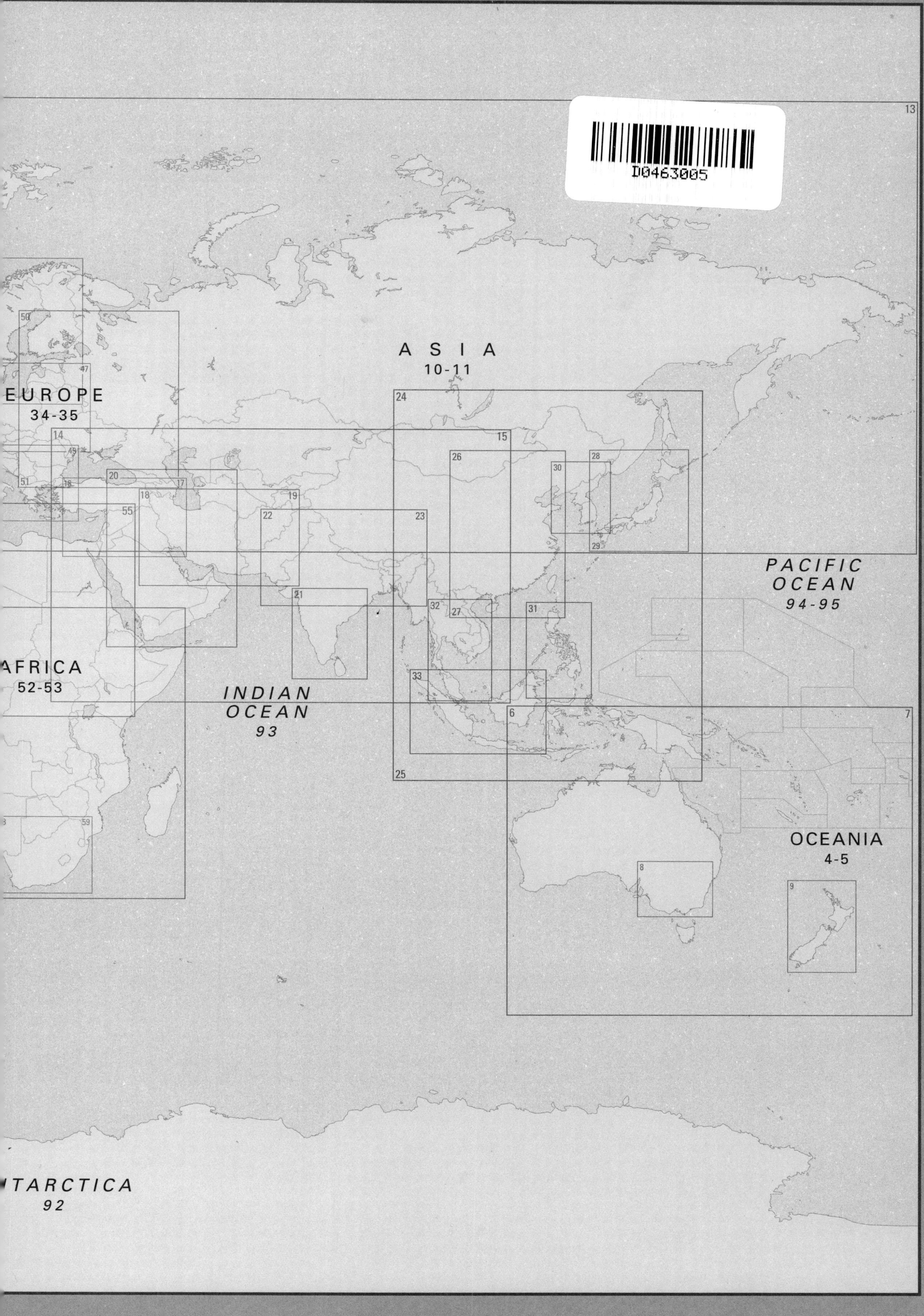

13

ASIA
10-11

EUROPE
34-35

PACIFIC
OCEAN
94-95

AFRICA
52-53

INDIAN
OCEAN
93

OCEANIA
4-5

ANTARCTICA
92

THE TIMES
ATLAS
OF THE
WORLD

SECOND FAMILY EDITION

TIMES Ⓣ **BOOKS**

RANDOM HOUSE

WORLD INFORMATION

Copyright © 1997 by Times Books
Maps copyright © 1997 by Bartholomew

All rights reserved under International and Pan-American Copyright Conventions. Published in the United States by Times Books, a division of Random House, Inc., New York. Published in Great Britain by Times Books, London, as *The Times Atlas of the World, New Generation Edition*. An earlier edition of this work was published in 1992.

The contents of this edition of *The Times Atlas of the World, Second Family Edition* are believed correct at the time of printing. Nevertheless, the publisher can accept no responsibility for errors or omissions, for changes in the detail given, or for any expense or loss thereby caused.

Library of Congress Cataloging-in-Publication Data

The Times atlas of the world.
—Second family ed.
p. cm.
Rev. and updated ed. of: The New York Times atlas of the world.
—New family ed. 1992, c1992.

Includes index.
ISBN 0-8129-2949-7
1. Atlases. I. Times Books (Firm)
II. Title: Times atlas of the world
G1021.   1997 <G&M>
912—do20

Random House website address:
http://www.randomhouse.com/

Printed in Italy

98765432

First U.S. edition

COUNTRY-FINDER

ATLAS OF THE WORLD

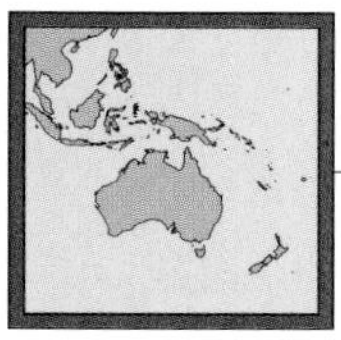

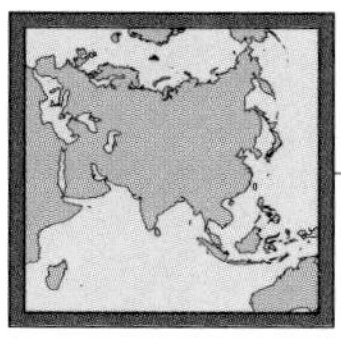

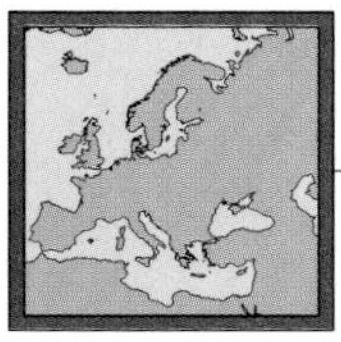

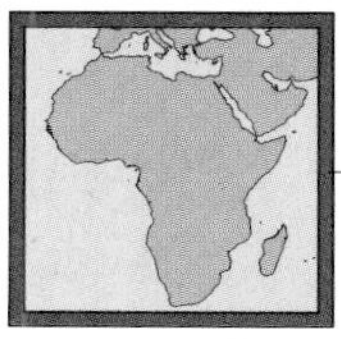

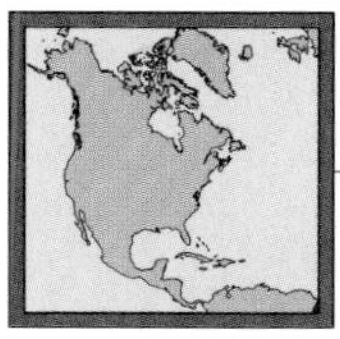

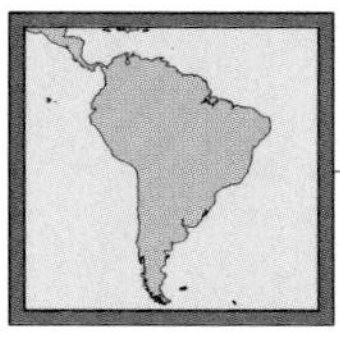

IN THIS GUIDE to States and Territories all independent states and major territories appear. The states and territories are arranged in alphabetical order using the same English-language conventional name form as is used on the maps. The name of the capital city is given in either its local form or in English-language form, whichever is more commonly used and understood. This reflects the names on the maps where alternative forms are also shown in brackets.

The statistics used for the area and population, and as the basis for languages and religions, are from the latest available sources. The information for the internal divisions in federal states may be for a less recent date than that for the entire country, but are the latest available.

The order of the different languages and religions reflects their relative importance within the country; generally all languages and religions with over one or two per cent speakers or adherents are mentioned.

For independent states membership of the following international organizations is shown by the abbreviations below. Territories are not shown as having separate membership of these international organizations.

ASEAN	Association of Southeast Asian Nations
CARICOM	Caribbean Community
CIS	Commonwealth of Independent States
COMM.	Commonwealth
EU	European Union
NAFTA	North American Free Trade Area
OAU	Organization of African Unity
OECD	Organization for Economic Cooperation and Development
OPEC	Organization of Petroleum Exporting Countries
SADC	Southern African Development Community
UN	United Nations

AFGHANISTAN
Status : REPUBLIC
Area : 652,225 sq km (251,825 sq mls)
Population : 20,141,000
Capital : KĀBUL
Language : DARI, PUSHTU, UZBEK, TURKMEN
Religion : SUNNI MUSLIM, SHI'A MUSLIM
Currency : AFGHANI
Organizations : UN

MAP PAGE: 19

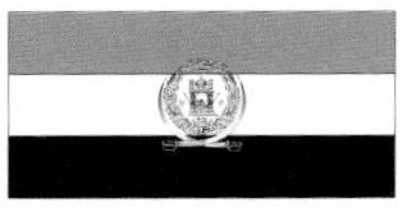

A LANDLOCKED COUNTRY in central Asia, Afghanistan borders Pakistan, Iran, Turkmenistan, Uzbekistan, Tajikistan and China. Its central highlands are bounded by the Hindu Kush to the north and desert to the south and west. Most farming is on the plains round Kabul, the most populated area, and in the far northeast. The climate is dry, with extreme temperatures. Civil war has disrupted the rural-based economy. Exports include dried fruit, nuts, carpets, wool, hides and cotton.

ALBANIA
Status : REPUBLIC
Area : 28,748 sq km (11,100 sq mls)
Population : 3,645,000
Capital : TIRANA
Language : ALBANIAN (GHEG, TOSK DIALECTS), GREEK
Religion : SUNNI MUSLIM, GREEK ORTHODOX, R.CATHOLIC
Currency : LEK
Organizations : UN

MAP PAGE: 49

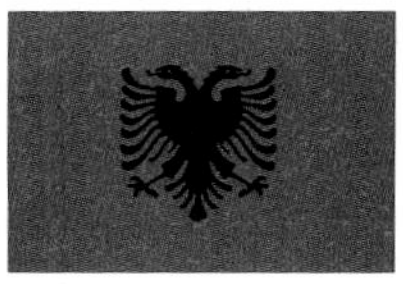

A LBANIA LIES IN the western Balkans of south Europe, on the Adriatic Sea. It is mountainous, with coastal plains which support half the population. The economy is based mainly on agriculture and mining, chiefly chromite. The fall of communism brought reform and foreign aid for the ailing economy.

ALGERIA
Status : REPUBLIC
Area : 2,381,741 sq km (919,595 sq mls)
Population : 28,548,000
Capital : ALGIERS
Language : ARABIC, FRENCH, BERBER
Religion : SUNNI MUSLIM, R.CATHOLIC
Currency : DINAR
Organizations : OAU, OPEC, UN

MAP PAGE: 54-55

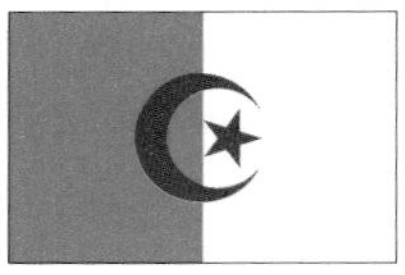

A LGERIA IS ON the Mediterranean coast of North Africa. The second largest country in Africa, it extends southwards from the coast into the Sahara Desert. Over 85 per cent of the land area is a dry sandstone plateau, cut by valleys and rocky mountains, including the Hoggar Massif in the southeast. Though hot, arid and largely uninhabited, the region contains oil and gas reserves. To the north lie the Atlas Mountains, enclosing the grassland of the Chott Plateau. The mountains separate the arid south from the narrow coastal plain which has a Mediterranean climate and is well suited to agriculture. Most people live on the plain and on the fertile northern slopes of the Atlas. Hydrocarbons have been the mainstay of the economy. Though reserves are dwindling, oil, natural gas and related products still account for over 90 per cent of export earnings. Other industries produce building materials, food products, iron, steel and vehicles. Agriculture employs a quarter of the workforce, producing mainly food crops. Political unrest including Islamic militancy in the early 1990s weakened the economy.

AMERICAN SAMOA
Status : US TERRITORY
Area : 197 sq km (76 sq mls)
Population : 56,000
Capital : PAGO PAGO
Language : SAMOAN, ENGLISH
Religion : PROTESTANT, R.CATHOLIC
Currency : US DOLLAR

MAP PAGE: 5

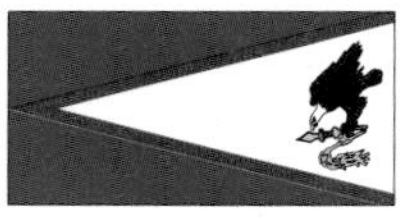

L YING IN THE South Pacific Ocean, American Samoa consists of five islands and two coral atolls. The main island is Tutuila.

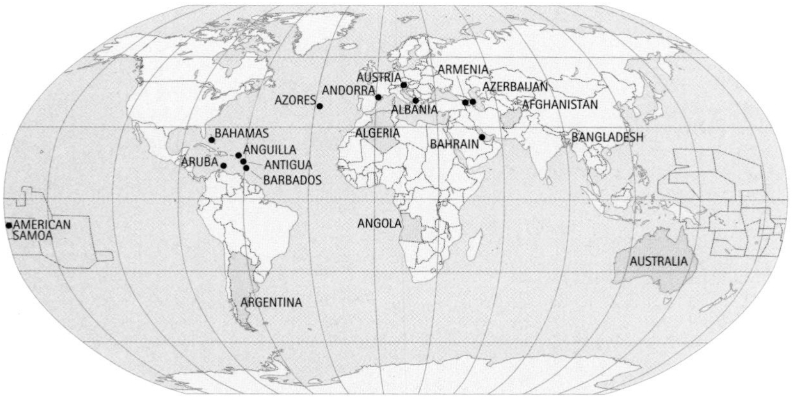

ANDORRA
Status : PRINCIPALITY
Area : 465 sq km (180 sq mls)
Population : 68,000
Capital : ANDORRA LA VELLA
Language : CATALAN, SPANISH, FRENCH
Religion : R.CATHOLIC
Currency : FRENCH FRANC, SPANISH PESETA
Organizations : UN

MAP PAGE: 45

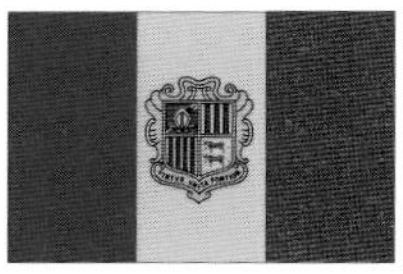

A LANDLOCKED STATE in southwest Europe, Andorra nestles in the Pyrenees between France and Spain. It consists of deep valleys and gorges, surrounded by mountains. Winter lasts six months, with heavy snowfalls; spring and summer are warm. One-third of the population lives in the capital. Tourism (about 12 million visitors a year), trade and banking are the main activities. Livestock, tobacco and timber are also important. Exports include clothing, mineral water, cattle, electrical equipment, and paper and paper products.

ANGOLA
Status : REPUBLIC
Area : 1,246,700 sq km (481,354 sq mls)
Population : 11,072,000
Capital : LUANDA
Language : PORTUGUESE, MANY LOCAL LANGUAGES
Religion : R.CATHOLIC, PROTESTANT, TRAD.BELIEFS
Currency : KWANZA
Organizations : OAU, SADC, UN

MAP PAGE: 56-57

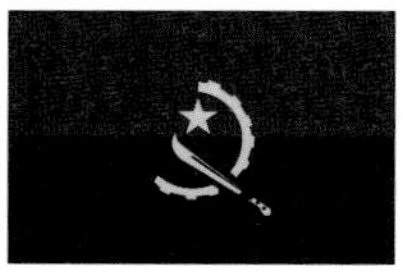

A NGOLA LIES ON the Atlantic coast of southern central Africa. Its northern province, Cabinda, is separated from the rest of the country by part of Zaire. Much of Angola is high plateau, with a fertile coastal plain where most people live. The climate is equatorial in the north but desert in the south. Over half the workforce are farmers, growing cassava, maize, bananas, coffee, cotton and sisal. Angola is rich in minerals. Oil and diamonds account for 90 per cent of exports. Civil war has slowed economic development.

ANGUILLA
Status : UK TERRITORY
Area : 155 sq km (60 sq mls)
Population : 8,000
Capital : THE VALLEY
Language : ENGLISH
Religion : PROTESTANT, R.CATHOLIC
Currency : E. CARIB. DOLLAR

MAP PAGE: 83

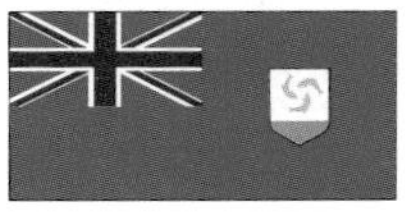

A NGUILLA LIES AT the northern end of the Leeward Islands in the Caribbean Sea. Tourism and fishing are the basis of the economy.

ANTIGUA AND BARBUDA
Status : MONARCHY
Area : 442 sq km (171 sq mls)
Population : 66,000
Capital : ST JOHN'S
Language : ENGLISH, CREOLE
Religion : PROTESTANT, R.CATHOLIC
Currency : E. CARIB. DOLLAR
Organizations : CARICOM, COMM., UN

MAP PAGE: 83

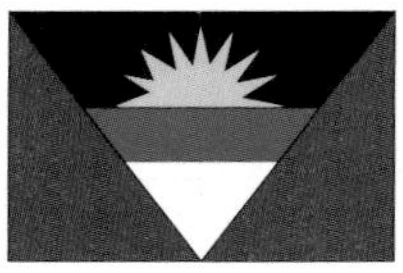

T HE STATE COMPRISES Antigua, Barbuda and Redonda, three of the Leeward Islands in the eastern Caribbean. Antigua, the largest and most populous, is mainly hilly scrubland, with many beaches and a warm, dry climate. The economy relies heavily on tourism.

ARGENTINA
Status : REPUBLIC
Area : 2,766,889 sq km (1,068,302 sq mls)
Population : 34,768,000
Capital : BUENOS AIRES
Language : SPANISH, ITALIAN, AMERINDIAN LANGUAGES
Religion : R.CATHOLIC, PROTESTANT, JEWISH
Currency : PESO
Organizations : UN

MAP PAGE: 88

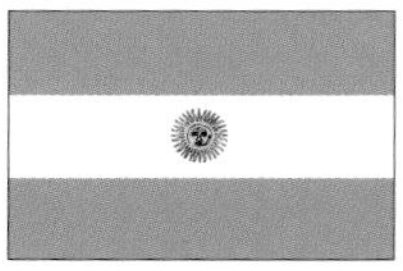

A RGENTINA OCCUPIES ALMOST the whole of the southern part of South America, from Bolivia to Cape Horn and from the Andes to the Atlantic Ocean. The second largest South American state has four geographical regions: the subtropical forests and swampland of the Chaco in the north; the temperate fertile plains or Pampas in the centre, which support most of the farming and the bulk of the population; the wooded foothills and valleys of the Andes in the west; and the cold, semi-arid plateaux of Patagonia, south of the Colorado river. Farming was the making of Argentina and still plays an important part in terms of export earnings. Beef, mutton and wool are the main produce but grains, sugarcane, soybeans, oilseeds and cotton are also important. Industry now makes the biggest contribution to the economy. Oil and gas are being produced and some mineral resources, chiefly iron ore, are being exploited. Manufacturing has expanded to include not only food processing but also textiles, motor vehicles, steel products, iron and steel, industrial chemicals and machinery.

ARMENIA
Status : REPUBLIC
Area : 29,800 sq km (11,506 sq mls)
Population : 3,599,000
Capital : YEREVAN
Language : ARMENIAN, AZERI, RUSSIAN
Religion : ARMENIAN ORTHODOX, R.CATHOLIC, SHI'A MUSLIM
Currency : DRAM
Organizations : CIS, UN

MAP PAGE: 17

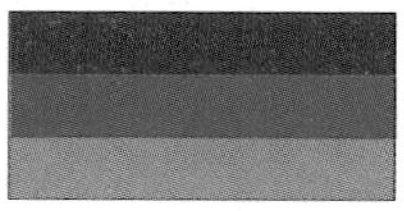

A LANDLOCKED STATE in southwest Asia, Armenia is in southwest Transcaucasia and borders Georgia, Azerbaijan, Iran and Turkey. It is mountainous, with a central plateau-basin, and dry, with warm summers and cold winters. One-third of the population lives in Yerevan. War over Nagorno-Karabakh, the majority-Armenian enclave in Azerbaijan, has crippled the economy. Manufacturing and mining were the main activities. Agriculture was also important, producing mostly grapes (for brandy), vegetables, wheat and tobacco.

ARUBA
Status : NETHERLANDS TERRITORY
Area : 193 sq km (75 sq mls)
Population : 70,000
Capital : ORANJESTAD
Language : DUTCH, PAPIAMENTO, ENGLISH
Religion : R.CATHOLIC, PROTESTANT
Currency : FLORIN

MAP PAGE: 83

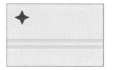

T HE MOST SOUTHWESTERLY of the islands in the Lesser Antilles, Aruba lies just off the coast of Venezuela. Tourism and offshore finance are the most important activities.

AUSTRALIA
Status : FEDERATION
Area : 7,682,300 sq km (2,966,153 sq mls)
Population : 18,054,000
Capital : CANBERRA
Language : ENGLISH, ITALIAN, GREEK, ABORIGINAL LANGUAGES
Religion : PROTESTANT, R.CATHOLIC, ORTHODOX, ABORIGINAL
Currency : DOLLAR
Organizations : COMM., OECD, UN

MAP PAGE: 6-7

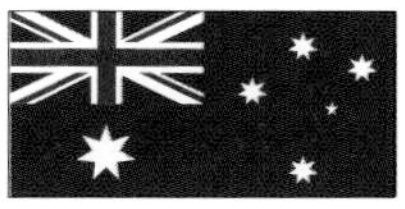

A USTRALIA, THE WORLD'S sixth largest country, occupies the smallest, flattest and driest continent. The western half of the continent is mostly arid plateaux, ridges and vast deserts. The central-eastern area comprises lowlands of river systems draining into Lake Eyre, while to the east is the Great Dividing Range, a belt of ridges and plateaux running from Queensland to Tasmania. Climatically more than two-thirds of the country is arid or semi-arid. The north is tropical monsoon: the south is subtropical in the west, temperate in the east. A majority of Australia's highly urbanized population lives in cities along on the east, southeast and southwest coasts. Australia is richly endowed with natural resources. It has vast mineral deposits and various sources of energy. Over 50 per cent of the land is suitable for livestock rearing, though only 6 per cent can be used for crop growing. Forests cover 18 per cent of the land and fishing grounds off the coasts are teeming with marine life. Agriculture was the main sector of the economy, but its contribution to national income has fallen in recent years, as other sectors have grown. Sheep-rearing is still the main activity and Australia is the world's leading wool producer. It is also a major beef exporter and wheat grower. Wool, wheat, meat (beef and mutton), sugar and dairy products account for a third of export earnings. Minerals have overtaken agricultural produce as an export earner. As well as being among the world's leading producers of iron and coal, bauxite, nickel and uranium, Australia also exploits lead, gold, silver, zinc and copper ores, tungsten and gems. Its is a major producer of coal; petroleum and natural gas are also being exploited. Manufacturing and processing has shifted from being based on agricultural produce (chiefly

food processing and textiles) to being based on mineral production. The main products are: iron and steel, construction materials, petrochemicals, motor vehicles, electrical goods. Along with manufacturing, trade and services are the key growth sectors of the economy. Tourism is a major foreign exchange earner, with 1.5 million visitors a year.

AUSTRALIAN CAPITAL TERRITORY
Status : FEDERAL TERRITORY
Area: 2,400 sq km (927 sq mls)
Population: 299,000
Capital: CANBERRA

NEW SOUTH WALES
Status: STATE
Area: 801,600 sq km (309,499 sq mls)
Population: 6,009,000
Capital: SYDNEY

NORTHERN TERRITORY
Status: TERRITORY
Area: 1,346,200 sq km (519,771 sq mls)
Population: 168,000
Capital: DARWIN

QUEENSLAND
Status: STATE
Area: 1,727,200 sq km (666,876 sq mls)
Population: 3,113,000
Capital: BRISBANE

SOUTH AUSTRALIA
Status: STATE
Area: 984,000 sq km (379,925 sq mls)
Population: 1,462,000
Capital: ADELAIDE

TASMANIA
Status: STATE
Area: 67,800 sq km (26,178 sq mls)
Population: 472,000
Capital: HOBART

VICTORIA
Status: STATE
Area: 227,600 sq km (87,877 sq mls)
Population: 4,462,000
Capital: MELBOURNE

WESTERN AUSTRALIA
Status: STATE
Area: 2,525,000 sq km (974,908 sq mls)
Population: 1,678,000
Capital: PERTH

AUSTRIA
Status : REPUBLIC
Area : 83,855 sq km (32,377 sq mls)
Population : 8,053,000
Capital : VIENNA
Language : GERMAN, SERBO-CROAT, TURKISH
Religion : R.CATHOLIC, PROTESTANT
Currency : SCHILLING
Organizations : EU, OECD, UN

MAP PAGE: 46

A LANDLOCKED STATE in central Europe, Austria borders the Czech Republic, Italy, Slovenia, Hungary, Germany, Switzerland and Liechtenstein. Two-thirds of the country, from the Swiss border to eastern Austria, lies within the Alps, with the low mountains of the Bohemian Massif to the north. The only lowlands are in the east. The Vienna Basin and Danube river valley in the northeast contain almost all the agricultural land and most of the population. Austria also has a large forested area, minerals, chiefly iron ore, and fast-flowing rivers for hydroelectric power. The climate varies according to altitude, but in general summers are warm and winters cold

with heavy snowfalls. Industry is the mainstay of the economy. Manufactures include machinery, iron and steel, electrical goods, chemicals, food products, vehicles, and paper products. Agricultural output covers 90 per cent of food needs. Crops include cereals, fruit (chiefly grapes) and vegetables as well as silage, sugar beet and rapeseed. Dairy and timber products are exported. With 15 million visitors a year, tourism is a major industry.

AZERBAIJAN
Status : REPUBLIC
Area : 86,600 sq km (33,436 sq mls)
Population : 7,499,000
Capital : BAKU
Language : AZERI, ARMENIAN, RUSSIAN, LEZGIAN
Religion : SHI'A MUSLIM, SUNNI MUSLIM, RUSSIAN AND ARMENIAN
Currency : MANAT
Organizations : CIS, UN

MAP PAGE: 17

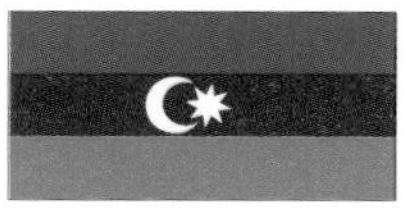

A ZERBAIJAN IS IN east Transcaucasia, southwest Asia, on the Caspian Sea. Its region of Nakhichevan is separated from the rest of the country by part of Armenia. It has mountains in the northeast and west, valleys in the centre and a coastal plain. The climate is continental. It is rich in energy and mineral resources. Oil production onshore and offshore is the main industry and the basis of heavy industries. Agriculture is still important, with cotton and tobacco the main cash crops. War with Armenia has reduced output.

AZORES
Status : PORTUGUESE TERRITORY
Area : 2,247 sq km (868 sq mls)
Population : 237,800
Capital : PONTA DELGADA
Language : PORTUGUESE
Religion : R.CATHOLIC, PROTESTANT
Currency : PORT. ESCUDO

MAP PAGE: 34

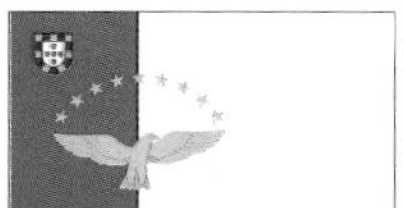

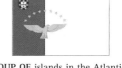

A GROUP OF islands in the Atlantic Ocean around 1500 kilometres (1000 miles) west of Portugal.

THE BAHAMAS
Status : MONARCHY
Area : 13,939 sq km (5,382 sq mls)
Population : 278,000
Capital : NASSAU
Language : ENGLISH, CREOLE, FRENCH CREOLE
Religion : PROTESTANT, R.CATHOLIC
Currency : DOLLAR
Organizations : CARICOM, COMM., UN

MAP PAGE: 83

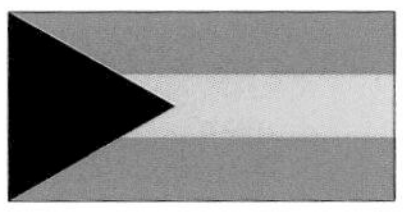

T HE BAHAMAS IS an archipelago of about 700 islands and 2,400 cays in the northern Caribbean between the Florida coast of the USA and Haiti. Twenty-two islands are inhabited, and two thirds of the population live on the main island of New Providence. The climate is warm for much of the year, with heavy rainfall in the summer. Tourism is the islands' main industry. Banking, insurance and ship registration are also major foreign exchange earners. Exports include oil transhipments, chemicals, pharmaceuticals, crayfish and rum.

BAHRAIN
Status : MONARCHY
Area : 691 sq km (267 sq mls)
Population : 586,000
Capital : AL MANĀMAH
Language : ARABIC, ENGLISH
Religion : SHI'A MUSLIM, SUNNI MUSLIM, CHRISTIAN
Currency : DINAR
Organizations : UN

MAP PAGE: 18

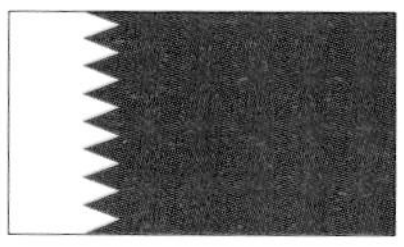

B AHRAIN'S 33 ARID islands lie in a bay in The Gulf, southwest Asia, off the coasts of Saudi Arabia and Qatar. Bahrain Island, the largest, has irrigated areas in the north where most people live. Oil is the main sector of the economy. Banking is also strong.

BANGLADESH
Status : REPUBLIC
Area : 143,998 sq km (55,598 sq mls)
Population : 120,433,000
Capital : DHAKA
Language : BENGALI, BIHARI, HINDI, ENGLISH, LOCAL LANGUAGES
Religion : SUNNI MUSLIM, HINDU, BUDDHIST, CHRISTIAN
Currency : TAKA
Organizations : COMM., UN

MAP PAGE: 23

T HE SOUTH ASIAN state of Bangladesh is in the northeast of the Indian subcontinent, on the Bay of Bengal. It consists almost entirely of the low-lying alluvial plains and deltas of the Ganges and Brahmaputra rivers. The southwest is swampy, with mangrove forests in the delta area. The north, northeast and southeast have low forested hills. With a cultivable area of 70 per cent and few other natural resources, Bangladesh has a strong agricultural base, engaging two-thirds of the workforce. Food crops include rice, wheat, fruit and pulses; cash crops include jute, sugar cane, oilseeds, spices and tea. The main industries produce fertilizers, iron and steel, paper and glass as well as agricultural, marine and timber products. Exports include garments, raw and manufactured jute, fish and prawns, leather and tea. Bangladesh faces problems of overpopulation, low world commodity prices and the vagaries of climate. Floods and cyclones during the summer monsoon season often destroy crops. As a result, the country relies on foreign aid and remittances from its workers abroad.

BARBADOS
Status : MONARCHY
Area : 430 sq km (166 sq mls)
Population : 264,000
Capital : BRIDGETOWN
Language : ENGLISH, CREOLE (BAJAN)
Religion : PROTESTANT, R.CATHOLIC
Currency : DOLLAR
Organizations : UN, COMM., CARICOM

MAP PAGE: 83

T HE MOST EASTERLY of the Caribbean islands, Barbados is small and densely populated, with a fairly flat terrain, white-sand beaches and a tropical climate. The economy is based on tourism, financial services, light industries and sugar production.

BELARUS

Status: REPUBLIC
Area: 207,600 sq km (80,155 sq mls)
Population: 10,141,000
Capital: MINSK
Language: BELORUSSIAN, RUSSIAN, UKRAINIAN
Religion: BELORUSSIAN ORTHODOX, R.CATHOLIC
Currency: ROUBLE
Organizations: CIS, UN

MAP PAGE: 47

BELARUS IS A landlocked state in east Europe, bounded by Lithuania, Latvia, Russia, Ukraine and Poland. Belarus consists of low hills and forested plains, with many lakes, rivers and, in the south, extensive marshes. It has a continental climate. Agriculture contributes a third of national income, with beef cattle and grains as the major products. Manufacturing produces a range of items, from machinery and crude steel to computers and watches. Output has fallen since the ending of cheap Soviet energy supplies and raw materials.

BELGIUM

Status: MONARCHY
Area: 30,520 sq km (11,784 sq mls)
Population: 10,113,000
Capital: BRUSSELS
Language: DUTCH (FLEMISH), FRENCH, GERMAN (ALL OFFICIAL), ITALIAN
Religion: R.CATHOLIC, PROTESTANT
Currency: FRANC
Organizations: EU, OECD, UN

MAP PAGE: 42

BELGIUM LIES ON the North Sea coast of west Europe. Beyond low sand dunes and a narrow belt of reclaimed land are fertile plains which extend to the Sambre-Meuse river valley from where the land rises to the forested Ardennes plateau in the southeast. Belgium has mild winters and cool summers. It is densely populated and has a highly urbanized population. The economy is based on trade, industry and services. With few mineral resources, Belgium imports raw materials for processing and manufacture, and exports semi-finished and finished goods. Metal working, machine building, food processing and brewing, chemical production, iron and steel, and textiles are the major industries. External trade is equivalent to over 70 per cent of national income. Exports include cars, machinery, chemicals, foodstuffs and animals, iron and steel, diamonds, textiles and petroleum products. The agricultural sector is small, but provides for most food needs and a tenth of exports. A large services sector reflects Belgium's position as the home base for over 800 international institutions.

BELIZE

Status: MONARCHY
Area: 22,965 sq km (8,867 sq mls)
Population: 217,000
Capital: BELMOPAN
Language: ENGLISH, CREOLE, SPANISH, MAYAN
Religion: R.CATHOLIC, PROTESTANT, HINDU
Currency: DOLLAR
Organizations: CARICOM, COMM., UN

MAP PAGE: 82

BELIZE IS ON the Caribbean coast of central America and includes cays and a large barrier reef offshore. Belize's coastal areas are flat and swampy; the north and west are hilly, and the southwest contains the Maya mountain range. Jungle covers about half of the country. The climate is tropical, but tempered by sea breezes. A third of the population lives in the capital. The economy is based primarily on agriculture, forestry and fishing. Exports include sugar, clothing, citrus concentrates, bananas and lobsters.

BENIN

Status: REPUBLIC
Area: 112,620 sq km (43,483 sq mls)
Population: 5,561,000
Capital: PORTO-NOVO
Language: FRENCH, FON, YORUBA, ADJA, LOCAL LANGUAGES
Religion: TRAD.BELIEFS, R.CATHOLIC, SUNNI MUSLIM
Currency: CFA FRANC
Organizations: OAU, UN

MAP PAGE: 54

BENIN IS IN west Africa, on the Gulf of Guinea. The Atakora range lies in the northwest; the Niger plains in the northeast. To the south are plateaux, then a fertile plain and finally an area of lagoons and sandy coast. The climate is tropical in the north, but equatorial in the south. The economy is based mainly on agriculture and transit trade. Agricultural products, chiefly cotton, coffee, cocoa beans and oil palms, account for two thirds of export earnings. Oil, produced offshore, is also a major export.

BERMUDA

Status: UK TERRITORY
Area: 54 sq km (21 sq mls)
Population: 63,000
Capital: HAMILTON
Language: ENGLISH
Religion: PROTESTANT, R.CATHOLIC
Currency: DOLLAR

MAP PAGE: 83

IN THE ATLANTIC Ocean to the east of the USA, Bermuda is a group of small islands. The climate is warm and humid. The economy is based on tourism, insurance and shipping.

BHUTAN

Status: MONARCHY
Area: 46,620 sq km (18,000 sq mls)
Population: 1,638,000
Capital: THIMPHU
Language: DZONGKHA, NEPALI, ASSAMESE, ENGLISH
Religion: BUDDHIST, HINDU
Currency: NGULTRUM, INDIAN RUPEE
Organizations: UN

MAP PAGE: 23

BHUTAN NESTLES IN the eastern Himalayas of south Asia, between China and India. It is mountainous in the north, with fertile valleys in the centre, where most people live, and forested lowlands in the south. The climate ranges between permanently cold in the far north and subtropical in the south. Most of the working population is involved in livestock raising and subsistence farming, though fruit and cardamon are exported. Electricity, minerals, timber and cement are the main exports. Bhutan relies heavily on aid.

BOLIVIA

Status: REPUBLIC
Area: 1,098,581 sq km (424,164 sq mls)
Population: 7,414,000
Capital: LA PAZ
Language: SPANISH, QUECHUA, AYMARA
Religion: R.CATHOLIC, PROTESTANT, BAHA'I
Currency: BOLIVIANO
Organizations: UN

MAP PAGE: 86-87

A LANDLOCKED STATE in central South America, Bolivia borders Brazil, Paraguay, Argentina, Chile and Peru. Most Bolivians live in the high plateau within the Andes ranges. The lowlands range between dense Amazon forest in the northeast and semi-arid grasslands in the southeast. Bolivia is rich in minerals, and sales (chiefly zinc, tin, silver and gold) generate half of export income. Natural gas and timber are also exported. Subsistence farming predominates, though sugar, soya beans and, unofficially, coca are exported.

BOSNIA–HERZEGOVINA

Status: REPUBLIC
Area: 51,130 sq km (19,741 sq mls)
Population: 4,484,000
Capital: SARAJEVO
Language: SERBO-CROAT
Religion: SUNNI MUSLIM, SERBIAN ORTHODOX, R.CATHOLIC, PROTESTANT
Currency: DINAR
Organizations: UN

MAP PAGE: 48-49

BOSNIA–HERZEGOVINA LIES IN the western Balkans of south Europe, on the Adriatic Sea. It is mountainous, with ridges crossing the country northwest-southeast. The main low-

lands are around the Sava valley in the north. Summers are warm, but winters can be very cold. Civil war has ruined the economy, which was based on agriculture, sheep rearing and forestry. All production has ceased, the currency is worthless and only the black economy operates. Much of the population relies on UN relief.

BOTSWANA

Status: REPUBLIC
Area: 581,370 sq km (224,468 sq mls)
Population: 1,456,000
Capital: GABORONE
Language: ENGLISH (OFFICIAL), SETSWANA, SHONA, LOCAL LANGUAGES
Religion: TRAD.BELIEFS, PROTESTANT, R.CATHOLIC
Currency: PULA
Organizations: COMM., OAU, SADC, UN

MAP PAGE: 57

BOTSWANA, A LANDLOCKED state in south Africa, borders South Africa, Namibia, Zambia and Zimbabwe. Over half of the country lies within the upland Kalahari desert, with swamps to the north and salt-pans to the northeast. Most people live near the eastern border. The climate is subtropical, but drought-prone. The economy was founded upon cattle rearing, and beef is an important export, but now it is based on mining and industry. Diamonds account for 80 per cent of export earnings. Copper-nickel matte is also exported.

BRAZIL

Status: REPUBLIC
Area: 8,511,965 sq km (3,286,488 sq mls)
Population: 155,822,000
Capital: BRASÍLIA
Language: PORTUGUESE, GERMAN, JAPANESE, ITALIAN, AMERINDIAN LANGUAGES
Religion: R.CATHOLIC, SPIRITIST, PROTESTANT
Currency: REAL
Organizations: UN

MAP PAGE: 86-88

BRAZIL, IN EASTERN South America, covers almost half of the continent - making it the world's fifth largest country - and borders ten countries and the Atlantic Ocean. The northwest contains the vast Amazon Basin, backed by the Guiana Highlands. The centre west is largely a vast plateau of savannah and rock escarpments. The northeast is mostly semi-arid plateaux, while the east and south contain the rugged mountains and fertile valleys of the Brazilian Highlands and narrow, fertile coastal plains. The Amazon basin is hot, humid and wet; the rest of Brazil is cooler and drier, with seasonal variations. The northeast is drought-prone. Most Brazilians live in urban areas along the coast and on the central plateau, chiefly São Paulo, Rio de Janeiro and Salvador. Brazil is well endowed with minerals and energy resources. Over 50 per cent of the land is forested and 7 per cent is cultivated. Agriculture employs a quarter of the workforce. Brazil is the world's largest producer of coffee and a leading producer of sugar, cocoa, soya beans and beef. Timber production and fish catches are also important. Brazil is a major producer of iron, bauxite and manganese ores, zinc, copper, tin, gold and diamonds as well as oil and coal. Manufacturing contributes a quarter of national income. Industrial products include food, machinery, iron and steel, textiles, cars, pharmaceuticals, chemicals, refined oil, metal products and paper products. The main exports are machinery, metallic ores, cars, metal products, coffee beans, soya products, electrical and electronic goods, and

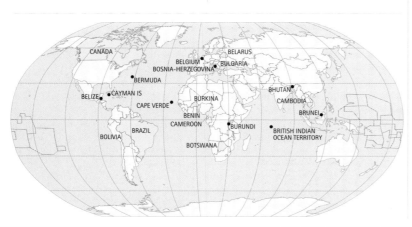

orange juice. Despite its natural wealth and one of the largest economies in the world, Brazil has a large external debt and growing poverty gap.

BRITISH INDIAN OCEAN TERRITORY
Status: UK TERRITORY
Area: 60 sq km (23 sq mls)
Population: 3,100

MAP PAGE: 10

THE TERRITORY CONSISTS of the Chagos Archipelago in the middle of the Indian Ocean. The islands are uninhabited apart from the joint British-US military base on Diego Garcia.

BRUNEI
Status: MONARCHY
Area: 5,765 sq km (2,226 sq mls)
Population: 285,000
Capital: BANDAR SERI BEGAWAN
Language: MALAY, ENGLISH, CHINESE
Religion: SUNNI MUSLIM, BUDDHIST, CHRISTIAN
Currency: DOLLAR (RINGGIT)
Organizations: ASEAN, COMM., UN

MAP PAGE: 33

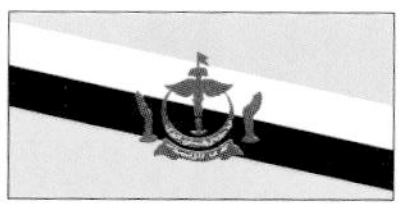

THE SOUTHEAST ASIAN state of Brunei lies on the northwest coast of the island of Borneo, on the South China Sea. Its two enclaves are surrounded inland by Malaysia. The western part is hilly with a narrow coastal plain which supports some crops and most of the population. The eastern part is mountainous and more forested. Tropical rainforest covers over two thirds of Brunei. The economy is dominated by the oil and gas industries.

BULGARIA
Status: REPUBLIC
Area: 110,994 sq km (42,855 sq mls)
Population: 8,402,000
Capital: SOFIA
Language: BULGARIAN, TURKISH, ROMANY, MACEDONIAN
Religion: BULGARIAN ORTHODOX, SUNNI MUSLIM
Currency: LEV
Organizations: UN

MAP PAGE: 49

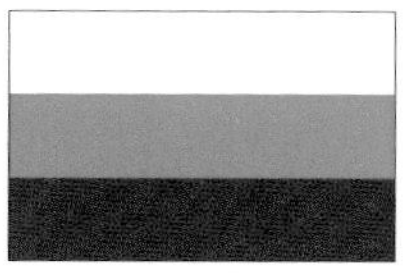

BULGARIA, IN SOUTH Europe, borders Romania, Yugoslavia, Macedonia, Greece, Turkey and the Black Sea. The Balkan Mountains separate the Danube plains in the north from the Rhodope massif and the lowlands in the south. The climate is subject to regional variation. The economy is based on agriculture and manufacturing, chiefly machinery, consumer goods, chemicals and metals. Disruption of Soviet-dominated trade has reduced output.

BURKINA
Status: REPUBLIC
Area: 274,200 sq km (105,869 sq mls)
Population: 10,200,000
Capital: OUAGADOUGOU
Language: FRENCH, MORE (MOSSI), FULANI, LOCAL LANGUAGES
Religion: TRAD.BELIEFS, SUNNI MUSLIM, R.CATHOLIC
Currency: CFA FRANC
Organizations: OAU, UN

MAP PAGE: 54

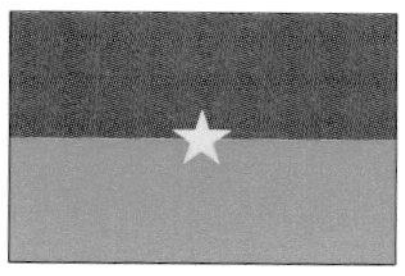

BURKINA, A LANDLOCKED country in west Africa, borders Mali, Niger, Benin, Togo, Ghana and Côte d'Ivoire. The north of Burkina lies in the Sahara and is arid. The south is mainly semi-arid savannah. Rainfall is erratic and droughts are common. Settlements centre on the country's rivers. Livestock rearing and farming are the main activities. Cotton, livestock, groundnuts and some minerals are exported. Burkina relies heavily on aid.

BURUNDI
Status: REPUBLIC
Area: 27,835 sq km (10,747 sq mls)
Population: 5,982,000
Capital: BUJUMBURA
Language: KIRUNDI (HUTU, TUTSI), FRENCH
Religion: R.CATHOLIC, TRAD.BELIEFS, PROTESTANT, SUNNI MUSLIM
Currency: FRANC
Organizations: OAU, UN

MAP PAGE: 56

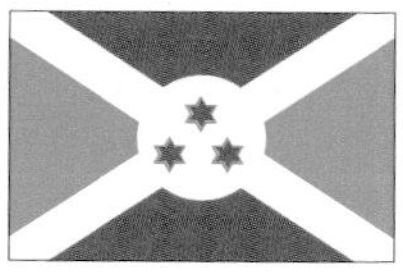

THE DENSELY POPULATED east African state of Burundi borders Rwanda, Zaire, Tanzania and Lake Tanganyika. It is hilly with high plateaux and a tropical climate. Burundi depends upon subsistence farming, coffee exports and foreign aid.

CAMBODIA
Status: MONARCHY
Area: 181,000 sq km (69,884 sq mls)
Population: 9,836,000
Capital: PHNUM PENH
Language: KHMER, VIETNAMESE
Religion: BUDDHIST, R.CATHOLIC, SUNNI MUSLIM
Currency: RIEL
Organizations: UN

MAP PAGE: 32

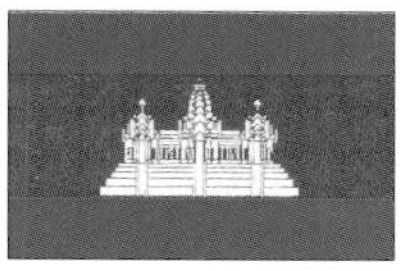

CAMBODIA LIES IN southeast Asia, on the Gulf of Thailand. It consists of the Mekong river basin, with the Tonle Sap (Great Lake) at its centre. To the north, northeast and east are plateaux and to the southwest are mountains. The climate is tropical monsoon, with forests covering half the land. Most people live on the plains and are engaged in farming (chiefly rice growing), fishing and forestry. Devastated by civil war, Cambodia is dependent on aid.

CAMEROON
Status: REPUBLIC
Area: 475,442 sq km (183,569 sq mls)
Population: 13,277,000
Capital: YAOUNDÉ
Language: FRENCH, ENGLISH, FANG, BAMILEKE, MANY LOCAL LANGUAGES
Religion: TRAD.BELIEFS, R.CATHOLIC, SUNNI MUSLIM, PROTESTANT
Currency: CFA FRANC
Organizations: OAU, UN, COMM.

MAP PAGE: 54-55

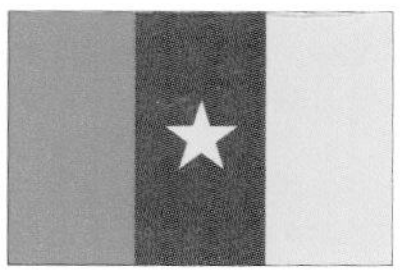

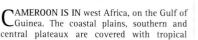

CAMEROON IS IN west Africa, on the Gulf of Guinea. The coastal plains, southern and central plateaux are covered with tropical forest. The northern lowlands are semi-arid savannah, and the western highlands, around Mount Cameroon, support a range of crops. A majority of Cameroonians are farmers. Cocoa, coffee and cotton are the main cash crops, though crude oil, sawn wood and logs account for over half of export earnings.

CANADA
Status: FEDERATION
Area: 9,970,610 sq km (3,849,674 sq mls)
Population: 29,606,000
Capital: OTTAWA
Language: ENGLISH, FRENCH, AMERINDIAN LANGUAGES, INUKTITUT (ESKIMO)
Religion: R.CATHOLIC, PROTESTANT, GREEK ORTHODOX, JEWISH
Currency: DOLLAR
Organizations: COMM., NAFTA, OECD, UN

MAP PAGE: 62-63

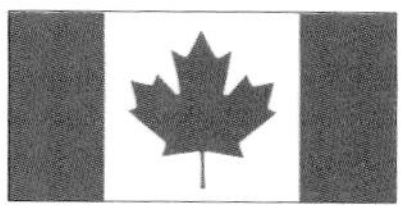

THE WORLD'S SECOND largest country, Canada covers the northern two-fifths of North America and has coastlines on the Atlantic, Arctic and Pacific Oceans. On the west coast, the Cordilleran region contains coastal mountains, interior plateaux and the Rocky Mountains. To the east lie the fertile prairies. Further east, covering about half the total land area, is the Canadian, or Laurentian, Shield, fairly flat U-shaped lowlands around the Hudson Bay extending to Labrador. The Shield is bordered to the south by the fertile Great Lakes-St Lawrence lowlands. In the far north climatic conditions are polar. In general, however, Canada has a continental climate. Winters are long and cold with heavy snowfalls, while summers are hot with light to moderate rainfall. Most Canadians live in the south, chiefly in the southeast, in the urban areas of the Great Lakes-St Lawrence basin, principally Toronto and Montreal. Canada is well endowed with minerals, energy resources, forests and rich coastal waters. Only 5 per cent of land is classified as arable, but that is still a large area. Canada is among the world's leading exporter of wheat. Other major agricultural exports are apples, beef cattle, potatoes, oilseeds and feed grain. Canada is also a leading exporter of wood from its vast coniferous forests, and fish and seafood from its rich Atlantic and Pacific fishing grounds. It is a top producer of iron ore, uranium, nickel, copper, zinc and other minerals, as well as crude oil and natural gas. Its abundant raw materials are the basis of for manufacturing industries. The principal ones are car manufacture, food processing, chemical production, lumber, woodpulp and paper making, oil refining, iron and steel, and metal refining. Canada is an important trading nation. External trade is equivalent to about 30 per cent of national income. Exports include cars, crude materials, minerals fuels (chiefly oil and gas), food (chiefly wheat), newsprint, lumber, wood pulp, industrial machinery and aluminium. Canada has an important banking and insurance sector.

ALBERTA
Status: PROVINCE
Area: 661,190 sq km (255,287 sq mls)
Population: 2,672,000
Capital: EDMONTON

BRITISH COLUMBIA
Status: PROVINCE
Area: 947,800 sq km (365,948 sq mls)
Population: 3,570,000
Capital: VICTORIA

MANITOBA
Status: PROVINCE
Area: 649,950 sq km (250,947 sq mls)
Population: 1,117,000
Capital: WINNIPEG

NEW BRUNSWICK
Status: PROVINCE
Area: 73,440 sq km (28,355 sq mls)
Population: 751,000
Capital: FREDERICTON

NEWFOUNDLAND
Status: PROVINCE
Area: 405,720 sq km (156,649 sq mls)
Population: 581,000
Capital: ST JOHN'S

NORTHWEST TERRITORIES
Status: TERRITORY
Area: 3,426,320 sq km (1,322,910 sq mls)
Population: 63,000
Capital: YELLOWKNIFE

NOVA SCOTIA
Status: PROVINCE
Area: 55,490 sq km (21,425 sq mls)
Population: 925,000
Capital: HALIFAX

ONTARIO
Status: PROVINCE
Area: 1,068,580 sq km (412,581 sq mls)
Population: 10,795,000
Capital: TORONTO

PRINCE EDWARD ISLAND
Status: PROVINCE
Area: 5,660 sq km (2,158 sq mls)
Population: 132,000
Capital: CHARLOTTETOWN

QUEBEC
Status: PROVINCE
Area: 1,540,680 sq km (594,860 sq mls)
Population: 7,226,000
Capital: QUÉBEC

SASKATCHEWAN
Status: PROVINCE
Area: 652,330 sq km (251,866 sq mls)
Population: 1,002,000
Capital: REGINA

YUKON TERRITORY
Status: TERRITORY
Area: 483,450 sq km (186,661 sq mls)
Population: 33,000
Capital: WHITEHORSE

CAPE VERDE
Status: REPUBLIC
Area: 4,033 sq km (1,557 sq mls)
Population: 392,000
Capital: PRAIA
Language: PORTUGUESE, PORTUGUESE CREOLE
Religion: R.CATHOLIC, PROTESTANT, TRAD.BELIEFS
Currency: ESCUDO
Organizations: OAU, UN

MAP PAGE: 54

CAPE VERDE COMPRISES ten semi-arid volcanic islands and five islets off the coast of west Africa. The economy is based on fishing and subsistence farming, but relies on workers' remittances and foreign aid.

CAYMAN ISLANDS
Status: UK TERRITORY
Area: 259 sq km (100 sq mls)
Population: 31,000
Capital: GEORGE TOWN
Language: ENGLISH
Religion: PROTESTANT, R.CATHOLIC
Currency: DOLLAR

MAP PAGE: 83

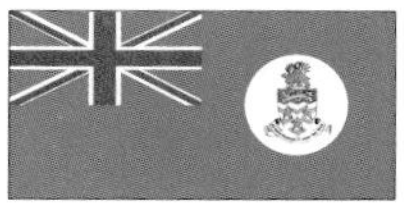

IN THE CARIBBEAN, northwest of Jamaica, there are three main islands: Grand Cayman, Little Cayman and Cayman Brac. They form one of the world's major offshore financial centres, though tourism is also important.

CENTRAL AFRICAN REPUBLIC
Status: REPUBLIC
Area: 622,436 sq km (240,324 sq mls)
Population: 3,315,000
Capital: BANGUI
Language: FRENCH, SANGO, BANDA, BAYA, LOCAL LANGUAGES
Religion: PROTESTANT, R.CATHOLIC, TRAD. BELIEFS, SUNNI MUSLIM
Currency: CFA FRANC
Organizations: OAU, UN

MAP PAGE: 56

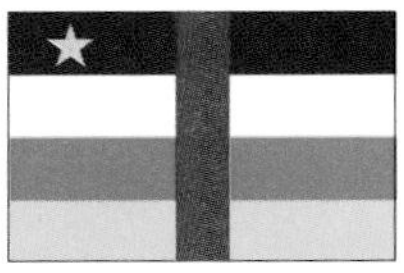

THE LANDLOCKED CENTRAL African Republic borders Chad, Sudan, Zaire, Congo and Cameroon. Most of the country is savannah plateaux, drained by the Ubangi and Chari river systems, with mountains to the north and west. The climate is hot with high rainfall. Most of the population live in the south and west, and a majority of the workforce is involved in subsistence farming. Some cotton, coffee, tobacco and timber are exported. However, diamonds and some gold account for more than half of export earnings.

CHAD
Status: REPUBLIC
Area: 1,284,000 sq km (495,755 sq mls)
Population: 6,361,000
Capital: NDJAMENA
Language: ARABIC, FRENCH, MANY LOCAL LANGUAGES
Religion: SUNNI MUSLIM, TRAD.BELIEFS, R.CATHOLIC
Currency: CFA FRANC
Organizations: OAU, UN

MAP PAGE: 55

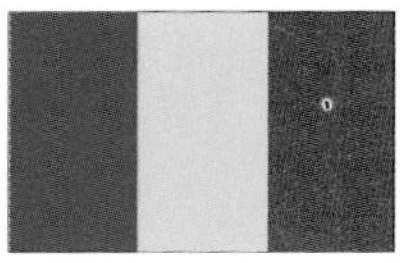

CHAD IS A landlocked state of central Africa, bordered by Libya, Sudan, Central African Republic, Niger, Nigeria and Cameroon. It consists of plateaux, the Tibesti massif in the north and Lake Chad basin in the west. Climatic conditions range between desert in the north and tropical forest in the southwest. Most people live in the south and near Lake Chad. Farming and cattle herding are the main activities, cattle and raw cotton the chief exports. Impoverished by civil war and drought, Chad relies upon foreign aid.

CHILE
Status: REPUBLIC
Area: 756,945 sq km (292,258 sq mls)
Population: 14,210,000
Capital: SANTIAGO
Language: SPANISH, AMERINDIAN LANGUAGES
Religion: R.CATHOLIC, PROTESTANT
Currency: PESO
Organizations: UN

MAP PAGE: 88

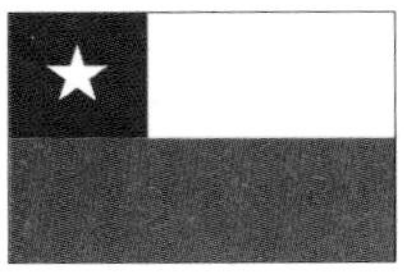

CHILE HUGS THE Pacific coast of the southern half of South America. Between the High Andes in the east and the lower coastal ranges is a central valley, with a mild climate, where most Chileans live. To the north is arid desert, to the south is cold, wet forested grassland. Chile is a leading exporter of copper, and is rich in other minerals and nitrates. Agriculture, forestry and fishing are important activities. Timber products, chemicals products and other manufactures account for a third of exports.

CHINA
Status: REPUBLIC
Area: 9,560,900 sq km (3,691,484 sq mls)
Population: 1,221,462,000
Capital: BEIJING
Language: CHINESE (MANDARIN OFFICIAL), MANY REGIONAL LANGUAGES
Religion: CONFUCIAN, TAOIST, BUDDHIST, SUNNI MUSLIM, R.CATHOLIC
Currency: YUAN
Organizations: UN

MAP PAGE: 15, 24-25

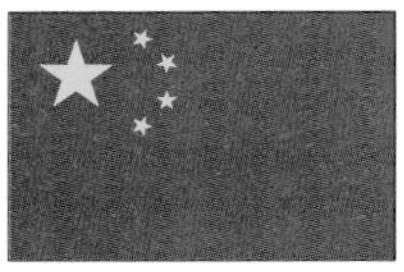

CHINA, THE WORLD'S third largest country, occupies almost the whole of east Asia, borders fourteen states and has coastlines on the Yellow, East China and South China seas. It has an amazing variety of landscapes. The southwest contains the high Tibetan plateau, flanked by the Himalayas and Kunlun mountains. The northwest is mountainous with arid basins and extends from the Tien Shan and Altai ranges and vast Taklimakan desert in the west to the Mongolian plateau and Gobi desert in the centre-east. Eastern China is predominantly lowland and is divided broadly into the basins of the Huang He (Yellow River) in the north, Chang Jiang (Yangtze) in the centre and Xi Jiang (Pearl River) in the southeast. The main exceptions are the Manchurian uplands, loess plateau, Qin Ling range, southeast mountains and the Yunnan plateau in the far south. Climatic conditions and vegetation are as diverse as the topography. Northern China has an extreme continental climate, much of the country experiences temperate conditions, while the southwest enjoys a moist, warm subtropical climate. More than 70 per cent of China's huge population live in rural areas, chiefly in the northern part of the eastern lowlands and along the coast. Agriculture and livestock rearing involves two thirds of the working population. China is the world's largest producer of rice, wheat, soya beans and sugar and is self-sufficient in cereals, fish and livestock. Cotton, soya bean and oilseeds are the major cash crops. China is rich in coal, oil, natural gas and many minerals, chiefly iron ore, wolfram (tungsten ore), tin and phosphates. Industrial and agricultural production were given a boost by the economic reforms of the 1980s which introduced a degree of private enterprise. Industry also benefited from the setting up of joint ventures and the inflow of foreign investment. The major industries produce iron and steel, machinery, textiles, processed foods, chemicals and building materials. China's chief exports are textiles and clothing, petroleum and products, machinery and transport equipment, agricultural products, metal products, iron and steel.

ANHUI (ANHWEI)
Status: PROVINCE
Area: 139,000 sq km (53,668 sq miles)
Population: 58,340,000
Capital: HEFEI

BEIJING (PEKING)
Status: MUNICIPALITY
Area: 16,800 sq km (6,487 sq miles)
Population: 11,020,000
Capital: BEIJING

FUJIAN (FUKIEN)
Status: PROVINCE
Area: 121,400 sq km (46,873 sq miles)
Population: 31,160,000
Capital: FUZHOU

GANSU (KANSU)
Status: PROVINCE
Area: 453,700 sq km (175,175 sq miles)
Population: 23,140,000
Capital: LANZHOU

GUANGDONG (KWANGTUNG)
Status: PROVINCE
Area: 178,000 sq km (68,726 sq miles)
Population: 65,250,000
Capital: GUANGZHOU

GUANGXI ZHUANG (KWANGSI CHUANG)
Status: AUTONOMOUS REGION
Area: 236,000 sq km (91,120 sq miles)
Population: 43,800,000
Capital: NANNING

GUIZHOU (KWEICHOW)
Status: PROVINCE
Area: 176,000 sq km (67,954 sq miles)
Population: 33,610,000
Capital: GUIYANG

HAINAN
Status: PROVINCE
Area: 34,000 sq km (13,127 sq miles)
Population: 6,860,000
Capital: HAIKOU

HEBEI (HOPEI)
Status: PROVINCE
Area: 187,700 sq km (72,471 sq miles)
Population: 62,750,000
Capital: SHIJIAZHUANG

HEILONGJIANG (HEILUNGKIANG)
Status: PROVINCE
Area: 454,600 sq km (175,522 sq miles)
Population: 36,080,000
Capital: HARBIN

HENAN (HONAN)
Status: PROVINCE
Area: 167,000 sq km (64,479 sq miles)
Population: 88,620,000
Capital: ZHENGZHOU

HONG KONG
Status: SPECIAL ADMINISTRATIVE REGION
Area: 1,075 sq km (415 sq mls)
Population: 6,190,000
Capital: HONG KONG
Language: CHINESE (CANTONESE, MANDARIN), ENGLISH
Religion: BUDDHIST, TAOIST, PROTESTANT
Currency: DOLLAR

HUBEI (HUPEI)
Status: PROVINCE
Area: 185,900 sq km (71,776 sq miles)
Population: 55,800,000
Capital: WUHAN

HUNAN
Status: PROVINCE
Area: 210,000 sq km (81,081 sq miles)
Population: 62,670,000
Capital: CHANGSHA

JIANGSU (KIANGSU)
Status: PROVINCE
Area: 102,600 sq km (39,614 sq miles)
Population: 69,110,000
Capital: NANJING

JIANGXI (KIANGSI)
Status: PROVINCE
Area: 166,900 sq km (64,440 sq miles)
Population: 39,130,000
Capital: NANCHANG

JILIN (KIRIN)
Status: PROVINCE
Area: 187,000 sq km (72,201 sq miles)
Population: 25,320,000
Capital: CHANGCHUN

LIAONING
Status: PROVINCE
Area: 147,400 sq km (56,911 sq miles)
Population: 40,160,000
Capital: SHENYANG

NEI MONGOL (INNER MONGOLIA)
Status: AUTONOMOUS REGION
Area: 1,183,000 sq km (456,759 sq miles)
Population: 22,070,000
Capital: HOHHOT

NINGXIA HUI (NINGHSIA HUI)
Status: AUTONOMOUS REGION
Area: 66,400 sq km (25,637 sq miles)
Population: 4,870,000
Capital: YINCHUAN

QINGHAI (TSINGHAI)
Status: PROVINCE
Area: 721,000 sq km (278,380 sq miles)
Population: 4,610,000
Capital: XINING

SHAANXI (SHENSI)
Status: PROVINCE
Area: 205,600 sq km (79,383 sq miles)
Population: 34,050,000
Capital: XI'AN

SHANDONG (SHANTUNG)
Status: PROVINCE
Area: 153,300 sq km (59,189 sq miles)
Population: 86,100,000
Capital: JINAN

SHANGHAI
Status: MUNICIPALITY
Area: 6,300 sq km (2,432 sq miles)
Population: 13,450,000
Capital: SHANGHAI

SHANXI (SHANSI)
Status: PROVINCE
Area: 156,300 sq km (60,348 sq miles)
Population: 29,790,000
Capital: TAIYUAN

SICHUAN (SZECHWAN)
Status: PROVINCE
Area: 569,000 sq km (219,692 sq miles)
Population: 109,980,000
Capital: CHENGDU

TIANJIN (TIENTSIN)
Status: MUNICIPALITY
Area: 11,300 sq km (4,363 sq miles)
Population: 9,200,000
Capital: TIANJIN

XIZANG (TIBET)
Status: AUTONOMOUS REGION
Area: 1,228,400 sq km (474,288 sq miles)
Population: 2,280,000
Capital: LHASA

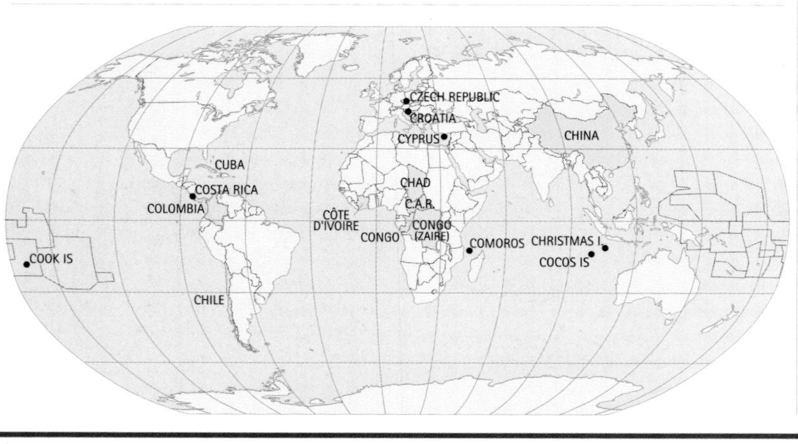

XINJIANG UYGUR (SINKIANG UIGHUR)
Status: AUTONOMOUS REGION
Area: 1,600,000 sq km (617,763 sq miles)
Population: 15,810,000
Capital: ÜRÜMQI

YUNNAN
Status: PROVINCE
Area: 394,000 sq km (152,124 sq miles)
Population: 38,320,000
Capital: KUNMING

ZHEJIANG (CHEKIANG)
Status: PROVINCE
Area: 101,800 sq km (39,305 sq miles)
Population: 42,360,000
Capital: HANGZHOU

CHRISTMAS ISLAND
Status: AUSTRALIAN TERRITORY
Area: 135 sq km (52 sq mls)
Population: 2,000
Capital: THE SETTLEMENT
Language: ENGLISH
Religion: BUDDHIST, SUNNI MUSLIM, PROTESTANT, R.CATHOLIC
Currency: AUSTR. DOLLAR

MAP PAGE: 25

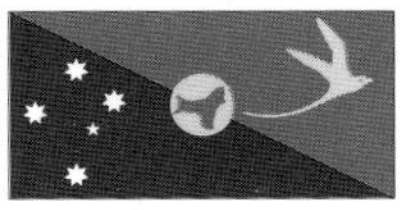

COCOS ISLANDS
Status: AUSTRALIAN TERRITORY
Area: 14 sq km (5 sq mls)
Population: 1,000
Capital: HOME ISLAND
Language: ENGLISH
Religion: SUNNI MUSLIM, CHRISTIAN
Currency: AUSTR. DOLLAR

MAP PAGE: 25

THE COCOS ISLANDS are two separate coral atolls in the east of the Indian Ocean between Sri Lanka and Australia. Most of the population live on West Island and Home Island.

COLOMBIA
Status: REPUBLIC
Area: 1,141,748 sq km (440,831 sq miles)
Population: 35,099,000
Capital: BOGOTÁ
Language: SPANISH, AMERINDIAN LANGUAGES
Religion: R.CATHOLIC, PROTESTANT
Currency: PESO
Organizations: UN

MAP PAGE: 86

A STATE IN northwest South America, Colombia has coastlines on the Pacific Ocean and the Caribbean Sea. Behind coastal plains lie three ranges of the Andes, separated by high valleys and plateaux where most Colombians live. To the southeast are the prairies and then the jungle of the Amazon. Colombia has a tropical climate, though temperatures vary with altitude. Only 5 per cent of land can be cultivated, but a range of crops are grown. Coffee (Colombia is the world's second largest producer), sugar, bananas, cotton and flowers are exported. Petroleum and its products are the main export. Coal, nickel, gold, silver, platinum and emeralds (Colombia is the world's largest producer) are mined. Industry involves mainly processing minerals and agricultural produce. In spite of government efforts to stop the drugs trade, coca growing and cocaine smuggling are rife.

COMOROS
Status: REPUBLIC
Area: 1,862 sq km (719 sq mls)
Population: 653,000
Capital: MORONI
Language: COMORIAN, FRENCH, ARABIC
Religion: SUNNI MUSLIM, R.CATHOLIC
Currency: FRANC
Organizations: OAU, UN

MAP PAGE: 57

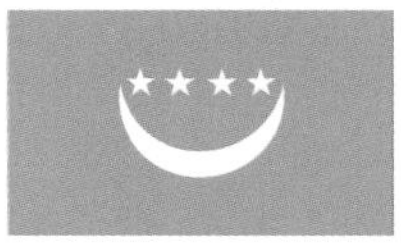

THE STATE COMPRISES three volcanic islands Grande Comore, Anjouan and Mohéil and some coral atolls in the Indian Ocean, off the east African coast. The tropical islands are mountainous, with poor soil. Subsistence farming predominates, but vanilla, cloves and ylang-ylang (an essential oil) are exported.

CONGO
Status: REPUBLIC
Area: 342,000 sq km (132,047 sq mls)
Population: 2,590,000
Capital: BRAZZAVILLE
Language: FRENCH (OFFICIAL), KONGO, MONOKUTUBA, LOCAL LANGUAGES
Religion: R.CATHOLIC, PROTESTANT, TRAD. BELIEFS, SUNNI MUSLIM
Currency: CFA FRANC
Organizations: OAU, UN

MAP PAGE: 56

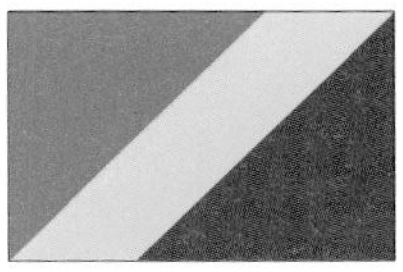

CONGO, IN CENTRAL Africa, is for the most part forest or savannah-covered plateaux drained by the Ubangi-Congo river systems. Sand dunes and lagoons line the short Atlantic coast. The climate is hot and tropical. Most Congolese live in the southern third of the country. Oil is the main source of export revenue. Diamonds, lead, zinc and gold are also mined. Hardwoods are the second biggest export earner. Half of the workforce are farmers, growing food crops and cash crops including sugar, coffee, cocoa and oil palms.

CONGO (ZAIRE)
Status: REPUBLIC
Area: 2,345,410 sq km (905,568 sq mls)
Population: 43,901,000
Capital: KINSHASA
Language: FRENCH, LINGALA, SWAHILI, KONGO, MANY LOCAL LANGUAGES
Religion: R.CATHOLIC, PROTESTANT, SUNNI MUSLIM, TRAD. BELIEFS
Currency: ZAÏRE
Organizations: OAU, UN

MAP PAGE: 56-57

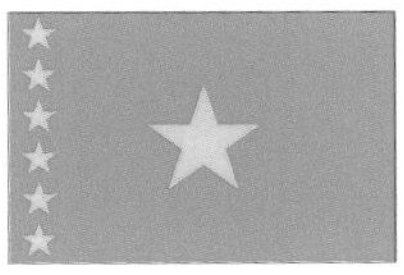

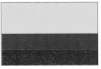

THE CENTRAL AFRICAN state of Congo consists of the basin of the Congo river flanked by plateaux, with high mountain ranges to the north and east and a short Atlantic coastline to the west. The climate is tropical with rainforest close to the Equator and savannah to the north and south. Congo has fertile land that grows a range of food crops and cash crops, chiefly coffee. It has vast mineral resources, copper and diamonds being the most important. However economic mismanagement and political turmoil have ruined the economy.

COOK ISLANDS
Status: NEW ZEALAND TERRITORY
Area: 293 sq km (113 sq mls)
Population: 19,000
Capital: AVARUA
Language: ENGLISH, MAORI
Religion: PROTESTANT, R.CATHOLIC
Currency: DOLLAR

MAP PAGE: 5

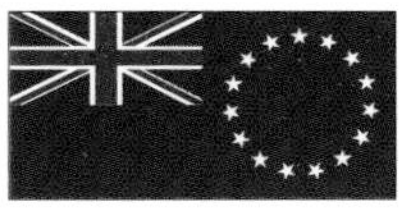

COSTA RICA
Status: REPUBLIC
Area: 51,100 sq km (19,730 sq mls)
Population: 3,333,000
Capital: SAN JOSÉ
Language: SPANISH
Religion: R.CATHOLIC, PROTESTANT
Currency: COLÓN
Organizations: UN

MAP PAGE: 83

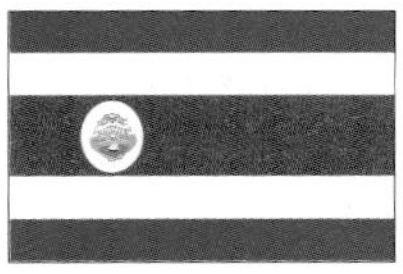

COSTA RICA HAS coastlines on the Caribbean Sea and Pacific Ocean. From the tropical coastal plains the land rises to mountains and a temperate central plateau where most people live. Farming is the main activity and exports include bananas, coffee, sugar, flowers and beef. There is some mining and a strong manufacturing sector, producing a range of goods from clothing (the main export) and electrical components to food products and cement.

CÔTE D'IVOIRE
Status: REPUBLIC
Area: 322,463 sq km (124,504 sq mls)
Population: 14,230,000
Capital: YAMOUSSOUKRO
Language: FRENCH (OFFICIAL), AKAN, KRU, GUR, LOCAL LANGUAGES
Religion: TRAD.BELIEFS, SUNNI MUSLIM, R.CATHOLIC
Currency: CFA FRANC
Organizations: OAU, UN

MAP PAGE: 54

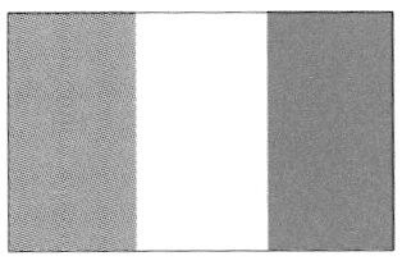

CÔTE D'IVOIRE (IVORY Coast) is in west Africa, on the Gulf of Guinea. In the north are plateaux and savannah, in the south are low undulating plains and rainforest, with sandbars and lagoons on the coast. Temperatures are warm, and rainfall is heavier in the south. Most of the workforce is engaged in farming. Côte d'Ivoire is a major producer of cocoa and coffee, and agricultural products (including cotton and timber) are the main export. Gold and diamonds are mined and some oil is produced offshore.

CROATIA
Status: REPUBLIC
Area: 56,538 sq km (21,829 sq mls)
Population: 4,495,000
Capital: ZAGREB
Language: SERBO-CROAT
Religion: R.CATHOLIC, ORTHODOX, SUNNI MUSLIM
Currency: KUNA
Organizations: UN

MAP PAGE: 48-49

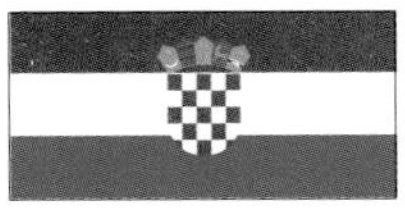

THE SOUTH EUROPEAN state of Croatia has a long coastline on the Adriatic Sea and many offshore islands. Coastal areas have a Mediterranean climate, inland is colder and wetter. Croatia was strong agriculturally and industrially, but secessionist and ethnic conflict, the loss of markets and the loss of tourist revenue have caused economic difficulties.

CUBA
Status: REPUBLIC
Area: 110,860 sq km (42,803 sq mls)
Population: 11,041,000
Capital: HAVANA
Language: SPANISH
Religion: R.CATHOLIC, PROTESTANT
Currency: PESO
Organizations: UN

MAP PAGE: 83

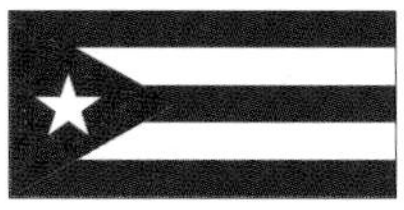

CUBA COMPRISES THE island of Cuba, the largest island in the Caribbean, and many islets and cays. A fifth of Cubans live in and around Havana. Sugar, with molasses and rum, account for two thirds of export earnings. Severe recession followed the disruption of traditional trade with east Europe and the ending of Russian subsidies.

CYPRUS
Status: REPUBLIC
Area: 9,251 sq km (3,572 sq mls)
Population: 742,000
Capital: NICOSIA
Language: GREEK, TURKISH, ENGLISH
Religion: GREEK (CYPRIOT) ORTHODOX, SUNNI MUSLIM
Currency: POUND
Organizations: COMM., UN

MAP PAGE: 16

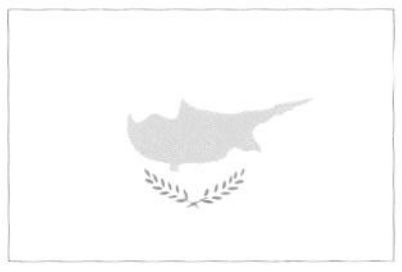

THE MEDITERRANEAN ISLAND of Cyprus has hot summers and mild winters. The economy of the Greek south is based mainly on specialist agriculture and tourism, though shipping and offshore banking are also major sources of income. The Turkish north depends upon agriculture, tourism and aid from Turkey.

CZECH REPUBLIC
Status: REPUBLIC
Area: 78,864 sq km (30,450 sq mls)
Population: 10,331,000
Capital: PRAGUE
Language: CZECH, MORAVIAN, SLOVAK
Religion: R.CATHOLIC, PROTESTANT
Currency: KORUNA
Organizations: UN, OECD

MAP PAGE: 46-47

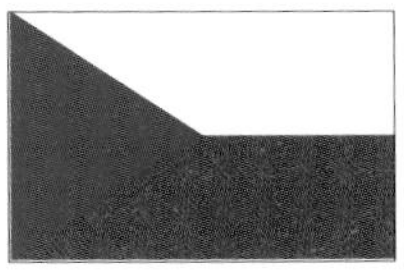

THE LANDLOCKED CZECH Republic in central Europe consists of rolling countryside, wooded hills and fertile valleys. The climate is temperate, but summers are warm and winters fairly cold. The country has substantial reserves of coal and lignite, timber and some minerals, chiefly iron ore, graphite, garnets and silver. It is highly industrialized and major manufactures include industrial machinery, consumer goods, cars, iron and steel, chemicals and glass. Since separation from Slovakia in January 1993, trade between the two countries has declined, exacerbating the difficulties the economy was already experiencing from the introduction of a free-market economy. There is, however, a growing tourist industry.

DENMARK

Status: MONARCHY
Area: 43,075 sq km (16,631 sq mls)
Population: 5,228,000
Capital: COPENHAGEN
Language: DANISH
Religion: PROTESTANT, R.CATHOLIC
Currency: KRONE
Organizations: EU, OECD, UN

MAP PAGE: 37

THE KINGDOM OF Denmark in north Europe occupies the Jutland Peninsula and nearly 500 islands in and between the North and Baltic seas. The country is low-lying, with a mixture of fertile and sandy soils, and long, indented coastlines. The climate is cool and temperate, with rainfall throughout the year. A fifth of the population lives in Greater Copenhagen on the largest of the islands, Zealand. Denmark's main natural resource is its agricultural potential; two thirds of the total area is fertile farmland or pasture. Agriculture, forestry and fishing are all important sectors of the economy. The chief agricultural products are cheese and other dairy products, beef and bacon, much of which is exported. Some oil and natural gas is produced from fields in the North Sea. Manufacturing, largely based on imported raw materials, now accounts for over half of exports. The main industries are iron and metal working, food processing and brewing, chemicals and engineering. Exports include machinery, food, chemicals, furniture, fuels and energy, and transport equipment.

DJIBOUTI

Status: REPUBLIC
Area: 23,200 sq km (8,958 sq mls)
Population: 577,000
Capital: DJIBOUTI
Language: SOMALI, FRENCH, ARABIC, ISSA, AFAR
Religion: SUNNI MUSLIM, R.CATHOLIC
Currency: FRANC
Organizations: OAU, UN

MAP PAGE: 56

DJIBOUTI LIES IN northeast Africa, on the Gulf of Aden. It consists mostly of low-lying desert, with some areas below sea level and a mountainous area to the north. Temperatures are high and rainfall is low. Most people live in the coastal strip. There is some camel, sheep and goat herding, and cattle, hides and skins are the main exports. With few natural resources, the economy is based on services and trade. The deep-water port and the railway line to Addis Ababa account for about two thirds of national income.

DOMINICA

Status: REPUBLIC
Area: 750 sq km (290 sq mls)
Population: 71,000
Capital: ROSEAU

Language: ENGLISH, FRENCH CREOLE
Religion: R.CATHOLIC, PROTESTANT
Currency: E. CARIB. DOLLAR, POUND STERLING, FRENCH FRANC
Organizations: CARICOM, COMM., UN

MAP PAGE: 83

DOMINICA IS THE most northerly of the Windward Islands in the eastern Caribbean. It is mountainous and forested, with a coastline of steep cliffs, and features geysers and hot springs. The climate is tropical and rainfall abundant. A quarter of Dominicans live in the capital. The economy is based on agriculture, with bananas (the major export), coconuts and citrus fruits the most important crops. There is some forestry, fishing and mining. Manufactured exports include soap, coconut oil, rum and bottled water. Tourism is growing.

DOMINICAN REPUBLIC

Status: REPUBLIC
Area: 48,442 sq km (18,704 sq mls)
Population: 7,915,000
Capital: SANTO DOMINGO
Language: SPANISH, FRENCH CREOLE
Religion: R.CATHOLIC, PROTESTANT
Currency: PESO
Organizations: UN

MAP PAGE: 83

THE STATE OCCUPIES the eastern two thirds of the Caribbean island of Hispaniola. It has a series of mountain ranges, including the highest peaks in the region, fertile valleys and a large coastal plain in the east. The climate is hot tropical, with heavy rainfall. A third of the population lives in the capital. Sugar, coffee and cocoa are the main cash crops. Bauxite, nickel (the main export), gold and silver are mined, and there is some light industry. Tourism is the main foreign exchange earner.

ECUADOR

Status: REPUBLIC
Area: 272,045 sq km (105,037 sq mls)
Population: 11,460,000
Capital: QUITO
Language: SPANISH, QUECHUA, AMERINDIAN LANGUAGES
Religion: R.CATHOLIC, PROTESTANT
Currency: SUCRE
Organizations: UN

MAP PAGE: 86

ECUADOR IS IN northwest South America, on the Pacific coast. It consists of a broad coastal plain, the high ranges of the Andes and the forested upper Amazon basin to the east. The climate is tropical, moderated by altitude. Most people live on the coast or in the mountain valleys. Ecuador is one of the continent's

leading oil producers. Mineral reserves include gold, silver, zinc and copper. Most of the workforce depends on agriculture. Ecuador is the world's leading producer of bananas. Shrimps, coffee and cocoa are also exported.

EGYPT

Status: REPUBLIC
Area: 1,000,250 sq km (386,199 sq mls)
Population: 59,226,000
Capital: CAIRO
Language: ARABIC, FRENCH
Religion: SUNNI MUSLIM, COPTIC CHRISTIAN
Currency: POUND
Organizations: OAU, UN

MAP PAGE: 55

EGYPT, ON THE eastern Mediterranean coast of North Africa, is low-lying, with areas below sea level in the west, and in the Qattara depression, and mountain ranges along the Red Sea coast and in the Sinai peninsula. It is a land of desert and semi-desert, except for the Nile valley, where 99 per cent of Egyptians live, about half of them in towns. The summers are hot, the winters mild and rainfall is negligible. Less than 4 per cent of land (chiefly around the Nile floodplain and delta) is cultivated, but farming employs half the workforce and contributes a sixth of exports. Cotton is the main cash crop. Rice, fruit and vegetables are exported, but Egypt imports over half its food needs. It has major reserves of oil and natural gas, phosphates, iron ore, manganese and nitrates. Oil and its products account for half of export earnings. Manufactures include cement, fertilizers, textiles, electrical goods, cars and processed foods. Workers' remittances, Suez canal tolls and tourist receipts are major sources of income, though attacks on tourists by Islamic militants has reduced the latter.

EL SALVADOR

Status: REPUBLIC
Area: 21,041 sq km (8,124 sq mls)
Population: 5,768,000
Capital: SAN SALVADOR
Language: SPANISH
Religion: R.CATHOLIC, PROTESTANT
Currency: COLÓN
Organizations: UN

MAP PAGE: 82

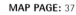

A DENSELY POPULATED state on the Pacific coast of central American, El Salvador has a coastal plain and volcanic mountain ranges that enclose a plateau where most people live. The coast is hot, with heavy summer rainfall, the highlands are cooler. Coffee (the chief export), sugar and cotton are main cash crops. Shrimps are also exported. Manufactures include processed foods, cosmetics, pharmaceuticals, textiles and clothing.

EQUATORIAL GUINEA

Status: REPUBLIC
Area: 28,051 sq km (10,831 sq mls)
Population: 400,000
Capital: MALABO
Language: SPANISH, FANG
Religion: R.CATHOLIC, TRAD.BELIEFS
Currency: CFA FRANC
Organizations: OAU, UN

MAP PAGE: 54

THE STATE CONSISTS of Rio Muni, an enclave on the Atlantic coast of central Africa, and the islands of Bioco, Annobón and Corisco group. Most people live on the coastal plain and upland plateau of the mainland; the capital is on the fertile volcanic island of Bioco. The climate is hot, humid and wet. Cocoa and timber are the main exports, but the economy depends heavily upon foreign aid.

ERITREA

Status: REPUBLIC
Area: 117,400 sq km (45,328 sq mls)
Population: 3,531,000
Capital: ASMARA
Language: TIGRINYA, ARABIC, TIGRE, ENGLISH
Religion: SUNNI MUSLIM, COPTIC CHRISTIAN
Currency: ETHIOPIAN BIRR
Organizations: OAU, UN

MAP PAGE: 56

ERITREA, ON THE Red Sea coast of northeast Africa, consists of high plateau in the north and a coastal plain that widens to the south. The coast is hot, inland is cooler. Rainfall is unreliable. The agricultural-based economy has suffered from 30 years of war and occasional poor rains. Coffee and cotton were the main cash crops, though food crops were important to reduce food aid.

ESTONIA

Status: REPUBLIC
Area: 45,200 sq km (17,452 sq mls)
Population: 1,530,000
Capital: TALLINN
Language: ESTONIAN, RUSSIAN
Religion: PROTESTANT, RUSSIAN ORTHODOX
Currency: KROON
Organizations: UN

MAP PAGE: 37

ESTONIA IS IN north Europe, on the Gulf of Finland and Baltic Sea. The land, one third of which is forested, is generally low-lying, with many lakes. The climate is temperate. About one third of Estonians live in Tallinn. Forests and oil-shale deposits are the main natural resources. Agriculture is limited to live-stock and dairy farming. Industries include timber, furniture production, shipbuilding, leather, fur and food processing.

ETHIOPIA

Status: REPUBLIC
Area: 1,133,880 sq km (437,794 sq mls)
Population: 56,677,000
Capital: ADDIS ABABA
Language: AMHARIC, OROMO, LOCAL LANGUAGES
Religion: ETHIOPIAN ORTHODOX, SUNNI MUSLIM, TRAD.BELIEFS
Currency: BIRR
Organizations: OAU, UN

MAP PAGE: 56

ETHIOPIA, IN NORTHEAST Africa, borders Eritrea, Djibouti, Somalia, Kenya and Sudan. The western half is a mountainous region traversed by the Great Rift Valley. To the east is mostly arid plateaus. The highlands are warm with summer rainfall, though droughts occur; the east is hot and dry. Most people live in the

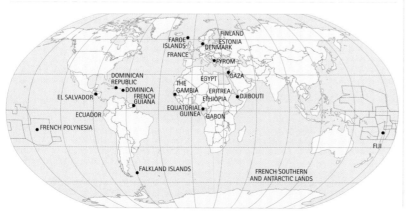

centre-north. Secessionist wars have hampered economic development. Subsistence farming is the main activity, though droughts have led to famine. Coffee is the main export and there is some light industry.

FALKLAND ISLANDS

Status: UK TERRITORY
Area: 12,170 sq km (4,699 sq mls)
Population: 2,000
Capital: STANLEY
Language: ENGLISH
Religion: PROTESTANT, R.CATHOLIC
Currency: POUND

MAP PAGE: 88

LYING IN THE southwest Atlantic Ocean, northeast of Cape Horn, the Falklands consists of two main islands, West Falkland and East Falkland, where most of the population live, and many smaller islands. The economy is based on sheep farming and the sale of fishing licences, though oil has been discovered offshore.

FAROE ISLANDS

Status: DANISH TERRITORY
Area: 1,399 sq km (540 sq mls)
Population: 47,000
Capital: TÓRSHAVN
Language: DANISH, FAEROESE
Religion: PROTESTANT
Currency: DANISH KRONE

MAP PAGE: 36

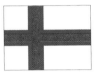

A SELF GOVERNING territory, the Faeroes lie in the north Atlantic Ocean between the UK and Iceland. The islands benefit from the Gulf Stream which has a moderating effect on the climate. The economy is based on deep-sea fishing and sheep farming.

FIJI

Status: REPUBLIC
Area: 18,330 sq km (7,077 sq mls)
Population: 784,000
Capital: SUVA
Language: ENGLISH, FIJIAN, HINDI
Religion: PROTESTANT, HINDU, R.CATHOLIC, SUNNI MUSLIM
Currency: DOLLAR
Organizations: UN

MAP PAGE: 7

FIJI COMPRISES TWO main islands, of volcanic origin and mountainous, and over 300 smaller islands in the South Pacific Ocean. The climate is tropical and the economy is based on agriculture (chiefly sugar, the main export), fishing, forestry, gold mining and tourism.

FINLAND

Status: REPUBLIC
Area: 338,145 sq km (130,559 sq mls)
Population: 5,108,000
Capital: HELSINKI
Language: FINNISH, SWEDISH
Religion: PROTESTANT, FINNISH (GREEK) ORTHODOX
Currency: MARKKA
Organizations: EU, OECD, UN

MAP PAGE: 36-37

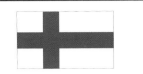

FINLAND IS IN north Europe, on the Gulf of Bothnia and the Gulf of Finland. It is low-lying apart from mountainous areas in the northwest. Forests cover 70 per cent of the land area, lakes and tundra over 20 per cent. Only 8 per cent is cultivated. Summers are short and warm, and winters are long and severe, particularly in the north. Most people live in the southern third of the country, along the coast or near the many lakes. Timber is the main resource and products of the forest-based industries account for a third of exports. Finland has a large fishing industry and its agricultural sector produces enough cereals and dairy products to cover domestic needs. It has some mineral deposits, chiefly zinc, copper, nickel, gold and silver. Finland is a highly industrialised country, though it must import most of the raw materials. Apart from the timber and related industries, it has important metal working, shipbuilding and engineering industries. Other industries produce chemicals, pharmaceuticals, plastics, rubber, textiles, electronic equipment, glass and ceramics.

F.Y.R.O.M. (MACEDONIA)

Status: REPUBLIC
Area: 25,713 sq km (9,928 sq mls)
Population: 2,163,000
Capital: SKOPJE
Language: MACEDONIAN, ALBANIAN, SERBO-CROAT, TURKISH, ROMANY
Religion: MACEDONIAN ORTHODOX, SUNNI MUSLIM, R.CATHOLIC
Currency: DENAR
Organizations: UN

MAP PAGE: 49

FYROM, FORMERLY THE Yugoslav republic of Macedonia, is a landlocked state of south Europe, bordered by Yugoslavia, Bulgaria, Greece and Albania. Lying within the south Balkans, it is a rugged country, traversed north-south by the Vardar valley. It has fine, hot summers, but very cold winters. The economy is based on industry, mining and, to a lesser degree, agriculture. But conflict with Greece and UN sanctions against Yugoslavia have reduced trade, caused economic difficulties and discouraged investment.

FRANCE

Status: REPUBLIC
Area: 543,965 sq km (210,026 sq mls)
Population: 58,143,000
Capital: PARIS
Language: FRENCH, FRENCH DIALECTS, ARABIC, GERMAN (ALSATIAN), BRETON
Religion: R.CATHOLIC, PROTESTANT, SUNNI MUSLIM
Currency: FRANC
Organizations: EU, OECD, UN

MAP PAGE: 44

FRANCE LIES IN southwest Europe, with coastlines on the North Sea, Atlantic Ocean and Mediterranean Sea; it includes the Mediterranean island of Corsica. Northern and western regions consist mostly of flat or rolling countryside, and include the major lowlands of the Paris basin, the Loire valley and the Aquitaine basin, drained by the Seine, Loire and Garonne river systems respectively. The centre-south is dominated by the Massif Central. Eastwards, beyond the fourth major lowland area of the Rhône-Saône valley, are the Alps and the Jura mountains. In the south-west, the Pyrenees form a natural border with Spain. The climate of northern parts is temper-

ate and wet, but in the centre and east it is continental, with warmer summers and milder winters. Along the south coast a Mediterranean climate prevails, with hot, dry summers and mild winters with some rainfall. Some 75 per cent of the population live in towns, but Greater Paris is the only major conurbation, with a sixth of the French population. Rich soil, a large cultivable area and contrasts in temperature and relief have given France a strong and varied agricultural base. It is a major producer of both fresh and processed food and the world's second largest exporter of agricultural products, after the USA. Major exports include cereals (chiefly wheat), dairy products, wines and sugar. France has relatively few mineral resources, though iron ore, potash salts, zinc and uranium are mined. It has coal reserves, some oil and natural gas, but it relies mainly for its energy needs on nuclear and hydroelectric power and imported fuels. France is the world's fourth largest industrial power after the USA, Japan and Germany. Heavy industries include iron, steel and aluminium production and oil refining. Other major industries are food processing, motor vehicles, aerospace, chemicals and pharmaceuticals, telecommunications, computers and armaments as well as luxury goods, fashion and perfumes. The main exports are machinery, agricultural products, cars and other transport equipment. France has a strong services sector and tourism is a major source of revenue and employment.

FRENCH GUIANA

Status: FRENCH TERRITORY
Area: 90,000 sq km (34,749 sq mls)
Population: 147,000
Capital: CAYENNE
Language: FRENCH, FRENCH CREOLE
Religion: R.CATHOLIC, PROTESTANT
Currency: FRENCH FRANC

MAP PAGE: 87

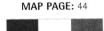

FRENCH GUIANA, ON the northeast coast of South America, is densely forested and is mountainous in the south. The climate is tropical with high rainfall. Most people live in the coastal strip and most workers are involved in subsistence farming, though sugar is exported. Livestock rearing and fishing are also important. Timber and mineral resources are largely unexploited and industry is limited. French Guiana depends upon French aid.

FRENCH POLYNESIA

Status: FRENCH TERRITORY
Area: 3,265 sq km (1,261 sq mls)
Population: 220,000
Capital: PAPEETE
Language: FRENCH, POLYNESIAN LANGUAGES
Religion: PROTESTANT, R.CATHOLIC, MORMON
Currency: PACIFIC FRANC

MAP PAGE: 5

EXTENDING OVER A vast area of the southeast Pacific Ocean, French Polynesia comprises more than 130 islands and coral atolls. The main island groups are the Marquesas, the Tuamotu Archipelago and the Society Islands. The capital, Papeete, is on Tahiti in the Society Islands. The climate is subtropical and the economy is based on tourism.

FRENCH SOUTHERN AND ANTARCTIC LANDS

Status: FRENCH TERRITORY
Area: 7,781 sq km (3,004 sq mls)

MAP PAGE: 3

THIS TERRITORY INCLUDES Crozet Island, Kerguelen, Amsterdam Island and St Paul Island. All are uninhabited apart from scientific research staff. In accordance with the Antarctic Treaty, French territorial claims in Antarctica have been suspended.

GABON

Status: REPUBLIC
Area: 267,667 sq km (103,347 sq mls)
Population: 1,320,000
Capital: LIBREVILLE
Language: FRENCH, FANG, LOCAL LANGUAGES
Religion: R.CATHOLIC, PROTESTANT, TRAD.BELIEFS
Currency: CFA FRANC
Organizations: OAU, UN

MAP PAGE: 56

GABON, ON THE Atlantic coast of central Africa consists of low plateaus, with a coastal plain lined by lagoons and mangrove swamps. The climate is tropical and rainforests cover 75 per cent of the land. Half of the population lives in towns, chiefly Libreville and Port Gentil. The economy is heavily dependent on mineral resources, mainly oil but also manganese and uranium. Timber, chiefly okoumé, is exported. Agriculture is mainly at subsistence level, but oil palms, bananas, sugarcane and rubber are grown.

THE GAMBIA

Status: REPUBLIC
Area: 11,295 sq km (4,361 sq mls)
Population: 1,118,000
Capital: BANJUL
Language: ENGLISH (OFFICIAL), MALINKE, FULANI, WOLOF
Religion: SUNNI MUSLIM, PROTESTANT
Currency: DALASI
Organizations: COMM., OAU, UN

MAP PAGE: 54

THE GAMBIA, ON the coast of west Africa, occupies a strip of land along the lower Gambia River. Sandy beaches are backed by mangrove swamps, beyond which is savannah. The climate is tropical, with rainfall in the summer. Over 70 per cent of Gambians are farmers, growing chiefly groundnuts (the main export) but also seed cotton, oil palms and food crops. Livestock rearing and fishing are important, while manufacturing is limited. Re-exports, mainly from Senegal, and tourism are major sources of income.

GAZA

Status: AUTONOMOUS REGION
Area: 363 sq km (140 sq mls)
Population: 756,000
Capital: GAZA
Language: ARABIC
Religion: SUNNI MUSLIM, SHI'A MUSLIM
Currency: ISRAELI SHEKEL

MAP PAGE: 16

GAZA IS A narrow strip of land on the southeast corner of the Mediterranean Sea, between Egypt and Israel. The territory has limited autonomy from Israel. The economy is based on agriculture and remittances from work in Israel.

GEORGIA

Status: REPUBLIC
Area: 69,700 sq km (26,911 sq mls)
Population: 5,457,000
Capital: T'BILISI
Language: GEORGIAN, RUSSIAN, ARMENIAN, AZERI, OSSETIAN, ABKHAZ
Religion: GEORGIAN ORTHODOX, RUSSIAN ORTHODOX, SHI'A MUSLIM
Currency: LARI
Organizations: CIS, UN

MAP PAGE: 51

GEORGIA IS IN northwest Transcaucasia, southwest Asia, on the Black Sea. Mountain ranges in the north and south flank the Kura and Rioni valleys. The climate is generally mild, but subtropical along the coast. Agriculture is important, with tea, grapes, citrus fruits and tobacco the major crops. Mineral resources include manganese, coal and oil, and the main industries are iron and steel, oil refining and machine building. However, economic activity has been seriously affected by separatist wars and political unrest.

GERMANY

Status: REPUBLIC
Area: 357,868 sq km (138,174 sq mls)
Population: 81,642,000
Capital: BERLIN
Language: GERMAN, TURKISH
Religion: PROTESTANT, R.CATHOLIC, SUNNI MUSLIM
Currency: MARK
Organizations: EU, OECD, UN

MAP PAGE: 46

THE WEST EUROPEAN state of Germany borders nine countries and has coastlines on the North and Baltic seas. It includes the southern part of the Jutland peninsula and Frisian islands. Behind the indented coastline and covering about one third of the country is the north German plain, a region of fertile farmland and sandy heaths drained by the country's major rivers. The central highlands are a belt of forested hills and plateaus which stretches from the Eifel region in the west to the Erzgebirge (Ore mountains) along the border with the Czech Republic. Farther south the land rises to the Swabian and Jura mountains, with the high rugged and forested Black Forest in the southwest and the Bavarian plateau and Alps to the southeast. The climate is temperate, with continental conditions in eastern areas where winters are colder. Rainfall is evenly spread throughout the year. Divided in 1945 after defeat in the second world war, Germany was reunified in 1990, barely a year after the collapse of communism in eastern Europe. It had been thought that west Germany, the world's third largest industrial economy and second largest exporter, would easily absorb east Germany, less than half the size and with a quarter of the population. But the initial cost of unification was high. The overhaul of east

German industry led to 30 per cent unemployment there, while the high level of investment and the rising social security bill led to tax increases in the west. In addition unification coincided with recession in the west German economy and rising unemployment, which created social tensions. However, by 1994 there were signs that the economy was pulling out of the recession. Germany lacks minerals and other industrial raw materials, with the exception of lignite and potash. It has a small agricultural base, though a few products (chiefly wines and beers) enjoy an international reputation. It is predominantly an industrial economy, dominated by the mechanical and engineering, iron and steel, chemical, pharmaceutical, motor, textile and high-tech industries. It also has a large service sector, with tourism, banking and finance being important.

BADEN-WÜRTTEMBERG

Status: STATE
Area: 35,751 sq km (13,804 sq miles)
Population: 10,344,009
Capital: STUTTGART

BAYERN
(BAVARIA)

Status: STATE
Area: 70,554 sq km (27,241 sq miles)
Population: 12,014,674
Capital: MÜNCHEN

BERLIN

Status: STATE
Area: 889 sq km (343 sq miles)
Population: 3,467,322
Capital: BERLIN

BRANDENBURG

Status: STATE
Area: 29,056 sq km (11,219 sq miles)
Population: 2,545,511
Capital: POTSDAM

BREMEN

Status: STATE
Area: 404 sq km (156 sq miles)
Population: 678,731
Capital: BREMEN

HAMBURG

Status: STATE
Area: 755 sq km (292 sq miles)
Population: 1,708,528
Capital: HAMBURG

HESSEN
(HESSE)

Status: STATE
Area: 21,114 sq km (8,152 sq miles)
Population: 6,016,251
Capital: WIESBADEN

MECKLENBURG-VORPOMMERN
(MECKLENBURG-WEST POMERANIA)

Status: STATE
Area: 23,559 sq km (9,096 sq miles)
Population: 1,829,587
Capital: SCHWERIN

NIEDERSACHSEN
(LOWER SAXONY)

Status: STATE
Area: 47,351 sq km (18,282 sq miles)
Population: 7,795,149
Capital: HANNOVER

NORDRHEIN-WESTFALEN
(NORTH RHINE-WESTPHALIA)

Status: STATE
Area: 34,070 sq km (13,155 sq miles)
Population: 17,908,473
Capital: DÜSSELDORF

RHEINLAND-PFALZ
(RHINELAND-PALATINATE)

Status: STATE
Area: 19,849 sq km (7,664 sq miles)
Population: 3,983,282
Capital: MAINZ

SAARLAND

Status: STATE
Area: 2,570 sq km (992 sq miles)
Population: 1,083,119
Capital: SAARBRÜCKEN

SACHSEN
(SAXONY)

Status: STATE
Area: 18,341 sq km (7,081 sq miles)
Population: 4,557,210
Capital: DRESDEN

SACHSEN-ANHALT
(SAXONY-ANHALT)

Status: STATE
Area: 20,607 sq km (7,956 sq miles)
Population: 2,731,463
Capital: MAGDEBURG

SCHLESWIG-HOLSTEIN

Status: STATE
Area: 15,731 sq km (6,074 sq miles)
Population: 2,730,595
Capital: KIEL

THÜRINGEN
(THURINGIA)

Status: STATE
Area: 16,251 sq km (6,275 sq miles)
Population: 2,496,685
Capital: ERFURT

GHANA

Status: REPUBLIC
Area: 238,537 sq km (92,100 sq mls)
Population: 17,453,000
Capital: ACCRA
Language: ENGLISH (OFFICIAL), HAUSA, AKAN, LOCAL LANGUAGES
Religion: PROTESTANT, R.CATHOLIC, SUNNI MUSLIM, TRAD. BELIEFS
Currency: CEDI
Organizations: COMM., OAU, UN

MAP PAGE: 54

A WEST AFRICAN STATE on the Gulf of Guinea, Ghana is a land of plains and low plateaux covered with savannah and, in the west, rainforest. In the east is the Volta basin. The climate is tropical, with high rainfall in the south, where most people live. Ghana is a major producer of cocoa. Timber is also an important commodity. Bauxite, gold, diamonds and manganese ore are mined, and there are a number of industries around Tema.

GIBRALTAR

Status: UK TERRITORY
Area: 6.5 sq km (2.5 sq mls)
Population: 28,000
Capital: GIBRALTAR
Language: ENGLISH, SPANISH
Religion: R.CATHOLIC, PROTESTANT, SUNNI MUSLIM
Currency: POUND

MAP PAGE: 45

GIBRALTAR LIES ON the south coast of Spain at the western entrance to the Mediterranean Sea. The economy depends on tourism, offshore banking and entrepôt trade.

GREECE

Status: REPUBLIC
Area: 131,957 sq km (50,949 sq mls)
Population: 10,458 ,000
Capital: ATHENS
Language: GREEK, MACEDONIAN
Religion: GREEK ORTHODOX, SUNNI MUSLIM
Currency: DRACHMA
Organizations: EU, OECD, UN

MAP PAGE: 49

GREECE OCCUPIES THE southern part of the Balkan Peninsula of south Europe and many islands in the Ionian, Aegean and Mediterranean Seas. The islands make up over one fifth of its area. Mountains and hills cover much of the country. The most important lowlands are the plains of Thessaly in the centre-east and Salonica in the northeast. Summers are hot and dry. Winters are mild and wet, colder in the north with heavy snowfalls in the mountains. One third of Greeks live in the Athens area. Agriculture involves one quarter of the workforce and exports include citrus fruits, raisins, wine, olives and olive oil. A variety of ores and minerals are mined and a wide range of manufactures are produced including food and tobacco products, textiles, clothing, chemical products and metal products. Tourism is an important industry and there is a large services sector. Tourism, shipping and remittances from Greeks abroad are major foreign exchange earners. The war in former Yugoslavia and UN embargo on trade to Serbia have lost Greece an important market and regular trade route.

GREENLAND

Status: DANISH TERRITORY
Area: 2,175,600 sq km (840,004 sq mls)
Population: 58,000
Capital: NUUK
Language: GREENLANDIC, DANISH
Religion: PROTESTANT
Currency: DANISH KRONE

MAP PAGE: 63

SITUATED TO THE northeast of North America between the Atlantic and Arctic Oceans, Greenland is the largest island in the world. It has a polar climate and over 80 per cent of the land area is permanent ice-cap. The economy is based on fishing and fish processing.

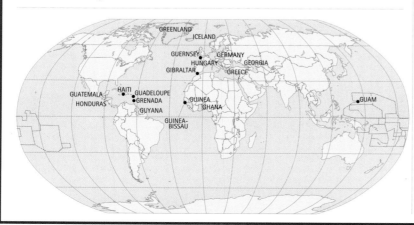

GRENADA

Status: MONARCHY
Area: 378 sq km (146 sq mls)
Population: 92,000
Capital: ST GEORGE'S
Language: ENGLISH, CREOLE
Religion: R.CATHOLIC, PROTESTANT
Currency: E. CARIB. DOLLAR
Organizations: CARICOM, COMM., UN

MAP PAGE: 83

THE CARIBBEAN STATE comprises Grenada, the most southerly of the Windward Islands, and the southern Grenadines. Grenada has wooded hills, beaches in the southwest, a warm climate and good rainfall. Agriculture is the main activity, with bananas, nutmeg and cocoa the main exports. Tourism and manufacturing are important. Grenada relies on grant aid.

GUADELOUPE

Status: FRENCH TERRITORY
Area: 1,780 sq km (687 sq mls)
Population: 428,000
Capital: BASSE TERRE
Language: FRENCH, FRENCH CREOLE
Religion: R.CATHOLIC, HINDU
Currency: FRENCH FRANC

MAP PAGE: 83

GUADELOUPE, IN THE Caribbean's Leeward group, consists of two main islands, Basse Terre and Grande Terre, connected by a bridge, and a few outer islands. The climate is tropical, but moderated by trade winds. Bananas, sugar and rum, tourism and French aid are the main sources of foreign exchange.

GUAM

Status: US TERRITORY
Area: 541 sq km (209 sq mls)
Population: 149,000
Capital: AGANA
Language: CHAMORRO, ENGLISH, TAGALOG
Religion: R.CATHOLIC
Currency: US DOLLAR

MAP PAGE: 25

LYING AT THE south end of the North Mariana Islands in the Western Pacific Ocean, Guam has a humid tropical climate. The island has a large US military base and the economy relies on that and tourism which is beginning to develop.

GUATEMALA

Status: REPUBLIC
Area: 108,890 sq km (42,043 sq mls)
Population: 10,621,000
Capital: GUATEMALA
Language: SPANISH, MAYAN LANGUAGES
Religion: R.CATHOLIC, PROTESTANT
Currency: QUETZAL
Organizations: UN

MAP PAGE: 82

THE MOST POPULOUS country in Central America after Mexico, Guatemala has a long Pacific and a short Caribbean coastline. Northern areas are lowland tropical forests. To the south lie mountain ranges with some active volcanoes, then the Pacific coastal plain. The climate is hot tropical in the lowlands, cooler in the highlands, where most people live. Farming is the main activity, coffee, sugar and bananas are the main exports. There is some mining and manufacturing (chiefly clothing and textiles). Tourism is important. Guerrilla activity is rife in certain areas.

GUERNSEY

Status: UK TERRITORY
Area: 78 sq km (30 sq mls)
Population: 64,000
Capital: ST PETER PORT
Language: ENGLISH, FRENCH
Religion: PROTESTANT, R.CATHOLIC
Currency: POUND

MAP PAGE: 44

ONE OF THE Channel Islands lying off the west coast of the Cherbourg peninsula in northern France.

GUINEA

Status: REPUBLIC
Area: 245,857 sq km (94,926 sq mls)
Population: 6,700,000
Capital: CONAKRY
Language: FRENCH, FULANI, MALINKE, LOCAL LANGUAGES
Religion: SUNNI MUSLIM, TRAD.BELIEFS, R.CATHOLIC
Currency: FRANC
Organizations: OAU, UN

MAP PAGE: 54

GUINEA IS IN west Africa, on the Atlantic Ocean. The coastal plains are lined with mangrove swamps. Inland are the Fouta Djallon mountains and plateaux. To the east are savannah plains drained by the upper Niger river system, while to the southeast are mountains. The climate is tropical, with high coastal rainfall. Agriculture is the main activity, with coffee, bananas and pineapples the chief cash crops. Bauxite, alumina, iron ore, gold and diamonds are the main exports, but Guinea relies upon foreign aid.

GUINEA-BISSAU

Status: REPUBLIC
Area: 36,125 sq km (13,948 sq mls)
Population: 1,073,000
Capital: BISSAU
Language: PORTUGUESE, PORTUGUESE CREOLE, LOCAL LANGUAGES
Religion: TRAD.BELIEFS, SUNNI MUSLIM, R.CATHOLIC
Currency: CFA FRANC
Organizations: OAU, UN

MAP PAGE: 54

GUINEA-BISSAU, ON THE Atlantic coast of west Africa, includes the Bijagos Archipelago. The mainland coast is swampy and contains many estuaries. Inland are forested plains and to the east are savannah plateaux. The climate is tropical. The economy is based mainly on subsistence farming. There is some fishing, but little industry. Forestry and mineral resources are largely unexploited. The main exports are cashews, groundnuts, oil palms and their products. Donors largely suspended support in 1991 because of payment arrears.

GUYANA

Status: REPUBLIC
Area: 214,969 sq km (83,000 sq mls)
Population: 835,000
Capital: GEORGETOWN
Language: ENGLISH, CREOLE, HINDI, AMERINDIAN LANGUAGES
Religion: PROTESTANT, HINDU, R.CATHOLIC, SUNNI MUSLIM
Currency: DOLLAR
Organizations: CARICOM, COMM., UN

MAP PAGE: 86-87

GUYANA, ON THE northeast coast of South America, consists of the densely forested highlands in the west, and the savannah uplands of the southwest. A lowland coastal belt supports crops and most of the population. The generally hot, humid and wet conditions are modified along the coast by sea breezes. The economy is based on agriculture, mining, forestry and fishing. Sugar, bauxite, gold and rice are the main exports. Other exports are shrimps and timber.

HAITI

Status: REPUBLIC
Area: 27,750 sq km (10,714 sq mls)
Population: 7,180,000
Capital: PORT-AU-PRINCE
Language: FRENCH, FRENCH CREOLE
Religion: R.CATHOLIC, PROTESTANT, VOODOO
Currency: GOURDE
Organizations: UN

MAP PAGE: 83

HAITI, OCCUPYING THE western third of the Caribbean island of Hispaniola, is a mountainous state, with small coastal plains and a central valley. The climate is tropical, hottest in coastal areas. Haiti has few natural resources, is overpopulated and relies on exports of local manufactures and coffee, and remittances from workers abroad. Political unrest and UN sanctions from 1991 to 1994 hit the economy badly.

HONDURAS

Status: REPUBLIC
Area: 112,088 sq km (43,277 sq mls)
Population: 5,953,000
Capital: TEGUCIGALPA
Language: SPANISH, AMERINDIAN LANGUAGES
Religion: R.CATHOLIC, PROTESTANT
Currency: LEMPIRA
Organizations: UN

MAP PAGE: 82-83

HONDURAS, IN CENTRAL America, is a mountainous and forested country with lowland areas along its long Caribbean and short Pacific coasts. Coastal areas are hot and humid with heavy summer rainfall, inland is cooler and drier. Most people live in the central valleys. Coffee and bananas are the main exports, along with shrimps, lead, zinc and timber. Industry involves mainly agricultural processing. Honduras depends on foreign aid.

HUNGARY

Status: REPUBLIC
Area: 93,030 sq km (35,919 sq mls)
Population: 10,225,000
Capital: BUDAPEST
Language: HUNGARIAN, ROMANY, GERMAN, SLOVAK
Religion: R.CATHOLIC, PROTESTANT
Currency: FORINT
Organizations: UN, OECD

MAP PAGE: 46-49

A LANDLOCKED COUNTRY in central Europe, Hungary borders Austria, Slovakia, Ukraine, Romania, Yugoslavia, Croatia and Slovenia. The Danube river flows north-south through central Hungary. To the east lies a great plain, flanked by highlands in the north. To the west low mountains and Lake Balaton separate a small plain and southern uplands. The climate is continental, with warm summers and cold winters. Rainfall is fairly evenly distributed thoughout the year. Half the population lives in urban areas, and one fifth lives in Budapest. Hungary has a predominantly industrial economy. The main industries produce metals, machinery, transport equipment (chiefly buses), textiles, chemicals and food products. Some minerals and energy reources are exploited, chiefly bauxite, coal and natural gas. Farming remains important, though output has fallen. Fruit, vegetables, cigarettes and wine are the main agricultural exports. Tourism is an important foreign exchange earner. Progress towards creating a market economy has been proved slow.

ICELAND

Status: REPUBLIC
Area: 102,820 sq km (39,699 sq mls)
Population: 269,000
Capital: REYKJAVIK
Language: ICELANDIC
Religion: PROTESTANT, R.CATHOLIC
Currency: KRÓNA
Organizations: OECD, UN

MAP PAGE: 36

THE NORTHWEST EUROPEAN island of Iceland lies in the Atlantic Ocean, near the Arctic Circle. It consists mainly of a plateau of basalt lava flows. Some of its 200 volcanoes are active, and there are geysers and hot springs, but one tenth of the country is covered by ice caps. Only coastal lowlands can be cultivated and settled, and over half the population lives in the Reykjavik area. The climate is fairly mild, moderated by the North Atlantic Drift and southwesterly winds. The mainstay of the economy is fishing and fish processing, which account for 80 per cent of exports. Agriculture involves mainly sheep and dairy farming. Iceland is self-sufficient in meat and dairy products, and exports wool and sheepskins. Diatomite is the only mineral resource but hydro-electric and geothermal energy resources are considerable. The main industries produce aluminium, ferro-silicon, electrical equipment, books, fertilizers, textiles and clothing. Tourism is growing in importance.

INDIA

Status: REPUBLIC
Area: 3,287,263 sq km (1,269,219 sq mls)
Population: 935,744,000
Capital: NEW DELHI
Language: HINDI, ENGLISH (OFFICIAL), MANY REGIONAL LANGUAGES
Religion: HINDU, SUNNI MUSLIM, SIKH, CHRISTIAN, BUDDHIST, JAIN
Currency: RUPEE
Organizations: COMM., UN

MAP PAGE: 14-15

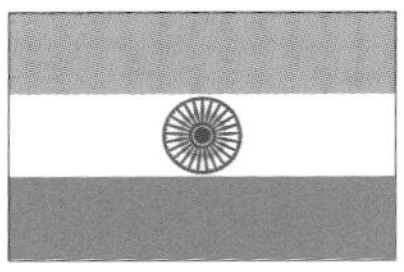

MOST OF THE South Asian state of India occupies a peninsula that juts out into the Indian Ocean between the Arabian Sea and Bay of Bengal. The heart of the peninsula is the Deccan plateau, bordered on either side by ranges of hills, the Western Ghats and the lower Eastern Ghats, which fall away to narrow coastal plains. To the north is a broad plain, drained by the Indus, Ganges and Brahmaputra rivers and their tributaries. The plain is intensively farmed and is the most populous region. In the west is the Thar Desert. The Himalayas form India's northern border, together with parts of the Karakoram and Hindu Kush ranges in the northwest. The climate shows marked seasonal variation: the hot season from March to June; the monsoon season from June to October; and the cold season from November to February. Rainfall ranges between heavy in the northeast Assam region and negligible in the Thar Desert, while temperatures range from very cold in the Himayalas to tropical heat over much of the south. India is among the ten largest economies in the world. It has achieved a high degree of self-sufficiency and its involvement in world trade is relatively small, though growing. Agriculture, forestry and fishing account for one third of national output and two thirds of employment. Much of the farming is on a subsistence basis and involves mainly rice and wheat growing. India is a major world producer of tea, sugar, jute, cotton and tobacco. Livestock is raised mainly for dairy products and hides. India has substantial reserves of coal, oil and natural gas and many minerals including iron, manganese and copper ores, bauxite, diamonds and gold. The manufacturing sector is large and diverse. The main manufactures are chemicals and chemical products, textiles, iron and steel, food products, electrical goods and transport equipment. The main exports are diamonds, clothing, chemicals and chemical products, textiles, leather and leather goods, iron ore, fish products, electronic goods and tea. However, with a huge population - the second largest in the world - India receives foreign aid to support its balance of payments.

INDONESIA

Status: REPUBLIC
Area: 1,919,445 sq km (741,102 sq mls)
Population: 194,564,000
Capital: JAKARTA
Language: INDONESIAN (OFFICIAL), MANY LOCAL LANGUAGES
Religion: SUNNI MUSLIM, PROTESTANT, R.CATHOLIC, HINDU, BUDDHIST
Currency: RUPIAH
Organizations: ASEAN, OPEC, UN

MAP PAGE: 25

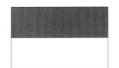

INDONESIA, THE LARGEST and most populous country in southeast Asia, consists of 13,677 islands extending along the Equator between the Pacific and Indian oceans. Sumatra, Java, Sulawesi, Kalimantan (two thirds of Borneo) and Irian Jaya (western New Guinea) make up 90 per cent of the land area. Most of Indonesia is mountainous and covered with rainforest or mangrove swamps, and there are over 300 volcanoes, some still active. Two thirds of the population live in the lowland areas of Java and Madura. In general the climate is tropical monsoon. Indonesia is rich in energy resources, minerals, forests and fertile soil. It is among the world's top producers of rice, palm oil, tea, coffee, rubber and tobacco. It is the world's leading exporter of natural gas and a major exporter of oil and timber. In recent years manufacturing output has risen. A range of goods are produced including textiles, clothing, cement, fertilizer and vehicles. Tourism has also increased. However, given its huge population, Indonesia remains a relatively poor country.

IRAN

Status: REPUBLIC
Area: 1,648,000 sq km (636,296 sq mls)
Population: 67,283,000
Capital: TEHRĀN
Language: FARSI (PERSIAN), AZERI, KURDISH, REGIONAL LANGUAGES
Religion: SHI'A MUSLIM, SUNNI MUSLIM, BAHA'I, CHRISTIAN, ZOROASTRIAN
Currency: RIAL
Organizations: OPEC, UN

MAP PAGE: 18-19

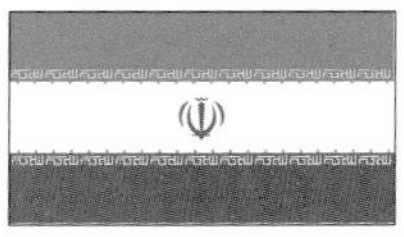

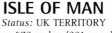

IRAN IS IN southwest Asia, on The Gulf, the Gulf of Oman and Caspian Sea. Eastern Iran is high plateaux country, with large salt pans and a vast sand desert. In the west the Zagros Mountains form a series of ridges, while to the north lie the Elburz Mountains. Most farming and settlement is on the narrow plain along the Caspian Sea and the foothills of the north and west. The climate is one of extremes, with hot summers and very cold winters. Most of the light rainfall is in the winter months. Agriculture involves one quarter of the workforce. Wheat is the main crop but fruit (chiefly dates) and pistachio nuts are grown for export. Fishing in the Caspian Sea is important and caviar is exported. Petroleum (the main export) and natural gas are Iran's leading natural resources. There are also reserves of coal, iron ore, copper ore and other minerals. Manufactures include carpets, clothing, food products, construction materials, chemicals, vehicles, leather goods and metal products. The 1979 revolution and 1980-88 war with Iraq slowed economic development.

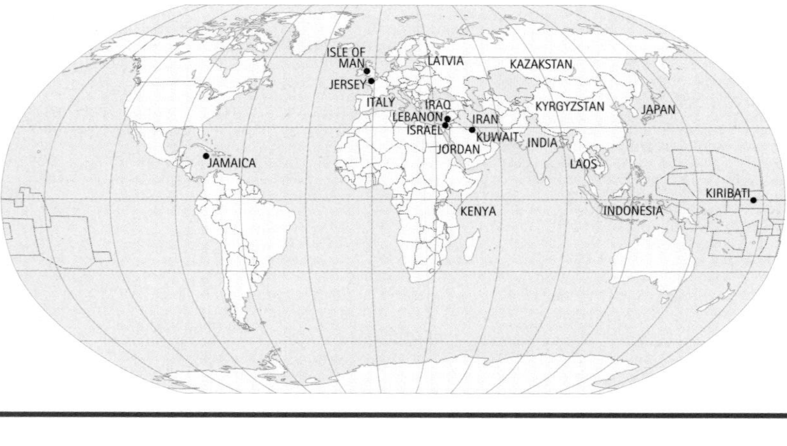

IRAQ

Status: REPUBLIC
Area: 438,317 sq km (169,235 sq mls)
Population: 20,449,000
Capital: BAGHDĀD
Language: ARABIC, KURDISH, TURKMEN
Religion: SHI'A MUSLIM, SUNNI MUSLIM, R.CATHOLIC
Currency: DINAR
Organizations: OPEC, UN

MAP PAGE: 17

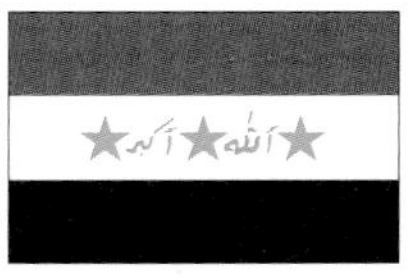

IRAQ, WHICH LIES on the northwest shores of The Gulf in southwest Asia, has at its heart the lowland valley of the Tigris and Euphrates rivers. In the southeast where the two rivers join are marshes and the Shatt al Arab waterway. Northern Iraq is hilly, rising to the Zagros Mountains, while western Iraq is desert. Summers are hot and dry, while winters are mild with light though unreliable rainfall. The Tigris-Euphrates valley contains most of the arable land and population, including one in five who live in Baghdad. One third of the workforce is involved in agriculture, with dates, cotton, wool, hides and skins exported in normal times. However, the 1980-88 war with Iran, defeat in the 1991 Gulf war and international sanctions have ruined the economy and caused considerable hardship. Petroleum and natural gas sales, which had accounted for 98 per cent of export earnings, were severely restricted. Much of the infrastructure was dam aged and industrial output - which had included petroleum products, cement, steel, textiles, bitumen and pharmaceuticals - was reduced.

ISLE OF MAN

Status: UK TERRITORY
Area: 572 sq km (221 sq mls)
Population: 72 ,000
Capital: DOUGLAS
Language: ENGLISH
Religion: PROTESTANT, R.CATHOLIC
Currency: POUND

MAP PAGE: 38

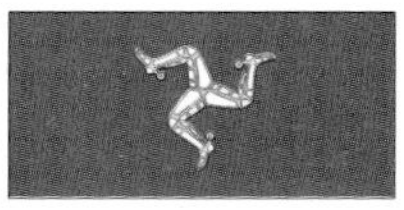

ISRAEL

Status: REPUBLIC
Area: 20,770 sq km (8,019 sq mls)
Population: 5,545,000
Capital: JERUSALEM
Language: HEBREW, ARABIC, YIDDISH, ENGLISH, RUSSIAN
Religion: JEWISH, SUNNI MUSLIM, CHRISTIAN, DRUZE
Currency: SHEKEL
Organizations: UN

MAP PAGE: 16

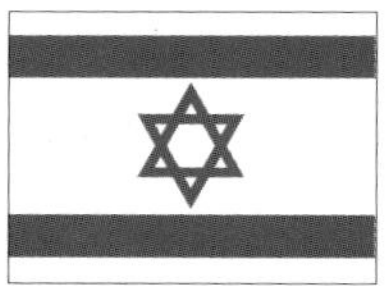

ISRAEL LIES ON the Mediterranean coast of southwest Asia. Beyond the coastal plain of Sharon are the hills and valleys of Judea and Samaria with the Galilee highlands to the north. In the east is the rift valley, which extends from Lake Tiberias to the Gulf of Aqaba and contains the Jordan river and Dead Sea. In the south is the Negev, a triangular semi-desert plateau. Most people live on the coastal plain or in northern and central areas. Much of Israel has warm summers and mild winters, during which most rain falls. Southern Israel is hot and dry. Agricultural production was boosted by the inclusion of the West Bank of the Jordan in 1967. Citrus fruit, vegetables and flowers are exported. Mineral resources are few but potash, bromine and some oil and gas are produced. Manufacturing makes the largest contribution to the economy. Israel produces finished diamonds, textiles, clothing and food products as well as chemical and metal products, military and transport equipment, electrical and electronic goods. Tourism and foreign aid are important to the economy.

ITALY

Status: REPUBLIC
Area: 301,245 sq km (116,311 sq mls)
Population: 57,187,000
Capital: ROME
Language: ITALIAN, ITALIAN DIALECTS
Religion: R.CATHOLIC
Currency: LIRA
Organizations: EU, OECD, UN

MAP PAGE: 48

MOST OF THE south European state of Italy occupies a peninsula that juts out into the Mediterranean Sea. It includes the main islands of Sicily and Sardinia and about 70 smaller islands in the surrounding seas. Italy is mountainous and dominated by two high ranges: the Alps, which form its northern border; and the Apennines, which run almost the full length of the peninsula. Many of Italy's mountains are of volcanic origin and its two active volcanoes are Vesuvius near Naples and Etna on Sicily. The main lowland area is the Po river valley in the northeast, which is the main agricultural and industrial area and is the most populous region. Italy has a Mediterranean climate with warm, dry summers and mild winters. Sicily and Sardinia are warmer and drier than the mainland. Northern Italy experiences colder, wetter winters, with heavy snow in the Alps. Italy's natural resources are limited. Only about 20 per cent of the land is suitable for cultivation. Some oil, natural gas and coal are produced, but most fuels and minerals used by industry must be imported. Italy has a fairly diversified economy. Agriculture flourishes, with cereals, wine, fruit (including olives) and vegetables the main crops. Italy is the world's largest wine producer. Cheese is also an important product. However, Italy is a net food importer. The north is the centre of Italian industry, especially around Turin, Milan and Genoa, while the south is largely agricultural with production based on smaller, less mechanized farms. Thus average income in the north is much higher than that in the south. Another feature of the Italian economy is the size of the state sector, which is much larger than that of other European Union countries. Italy's leading manufactures include industrial and office equipment, domestic appliances, cars, textiles, clothing, leather goods, chemicals and metal products and its famous brand names include Olivetti, Fiat and Benetton. Italy has a strong service sector. With over 25 million visitors a year, tourism is a major employer and accounts for 5 per cent of national income. Finance and banking are also important.

JAMAICA

Status: MONARCHY
Area: 10,991 sq km (4,244 sq mls)
Population: 2,530,000
Capital: KINGSTON
Language: ENGLISH, CREOLE
Religion: PROTESTANT, R.CATHOLIC, RASTAFARIAN
Currency: DOLLAR
Organizations: CARICOM, COMM., UN

MAP PAGE: 83

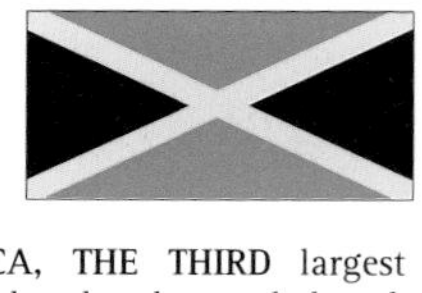

JAMAICA, THE THIRD largest Caribbean island, has beaches and densely populated coastal plains traversed by hills and plateaux rising to the forested Blue Mountains in the east. The climate is tropical, cooler and wetter on high ground. The economy is based on tourism, agriculture, mining and light manufacturing. Bauxite, alumina, sugar and bananas are the main exports. Jamaica depends on foreign aid.

JAPAN

Status: MONARCHY
Area: 377,727 sq km (145,841 sq mls)
Population: 125,197,000
Capital: TŌKYŌ
Language: JAPANESE
Religion: SHINTOIST, BUDDHIST, CHRISTIAN
Currency: YEN
Organizations: OECD, UN

MAP PAGE: 28-29

JAPAN, WHICH LIES in the Pacific Ocean off the coast of east Asia, consists of four main islands - Hokkaido, Honshu, Shikoku and Kyushu - which extend northeast-southwest over 1,600 km (995 miles). It includes more than 3,000 smaller volcanic islands in the surrounding Sea of Japan, East China Sea and Pacific Ocean. The central island of Honshu occupies 60 per cent of the total land area and contains 80 per cent of the population, mostly in the east-central Kanto plain which includes Tokyo, Kawasaki and Yokohama. Behind the long and deeply indented coastline, nearly three quarters of Japan is mountainous and heavily forested. The most rugged range crosses Honshu and includes the country's highest point, Mount Fuji, which reaches a height of 3,776 m (12,388 ft). Japan has over 60 active volcanoes, and is subject to frequent major earthquakes, monsoons, typhoons and tidal waves. The climate is generally temperate maritime, with warm summers and mild winters, except in western Hokkaido and northwest Honshu, where the winters are very cold with heavy snow. Rain falls mainly in June and July, and typhoons sometimes occur in September. Japan has few natural resources. It has a limited land area of which only 14 per cent is suitable for cultivation, and production of its few industrial raw materials (chiefly coal, oil, natural gas and copper) is insufficient for its industry. Most raw materials must be imported, including about 90 per cent of energy requirements. Yet, in a fairly short space of time, Japan has become the world's second largest industrial economy. Its economic success is based on manufacturing, which employs one third of the workforce and accounts for one third of national output. Japan has a range of heavy and light industries centred mainly round the major ports of Yokohama, Osaka and Tokyo. It is the world's largest manufacturer of cars, motorcycles and merchant ships, and a major producer of steel, textiles, chemicals and cement. It is a leading producer of many consumer durables, such as washing machines, and electronic equipment, chiefly office equipment and computers. Recent years have seen the spread of Japanese business overseas, with many industrial plants sited in the European Union and the USA. Japan has a strong service sector, banking and finance are particularly important and Tokyo is one of the world's major stock exchanges. Owing to intensive agricultural production, Japan is 70 per cent self-sufficient in food. The main food crops are rice, barley, fruit, wheat and soya beans. Livestock raising (chiefly cattle, pigs and chickens) and fishing are also important. Japan has one of the largest fishing fleets in the world. In spite of its forestry resources, Japan has to import timber as well as food.

JERSEY

Status: UK TERRITORY
Area: 116 sq km (45 sq mls)
Population: 87,000
Capital: ST HELIER
Language: ENGLISH, FRENCH
Religion: PROTESTANT, R.CATHOLIC
Currency: POUND

MAP PAGE: 44

ONE OF THE Channel Islands lying off the west coast of the Cherbourg peninsula in northern France.

JORDAN

Status: MONARCHY
Area: 89,206 sq km (34,443 sq mls)
Population: 5,439,000
Capital: 'AMMĀN
Language: ARABIC
Religion: SUNNI MUSLIM, CHRISTIAN, SHI'A MUSLIM
Currency: DINAR
Organizations: UN

MAP PAGE: 16-17

JORDAN, IN SOUTHWEST Asia, has a short coastline on the Gulf of Aqaba. Much of Jordan is rocky desert plateaux. In the west, behind a belt of hills, the land falls below sea level to the Dead Sea and Jordan river. Much of Jordan is hot and dry, the west is cooler and wetter and most people live in the northwest. Phosphates, potash, fertilizers, pharmaceuticals, fruit and vegetables are the main exports. Jordan relies upon tourism, workers' remittances and foreign aid, all of which were affected by the 1991 Gulf crisis.

KAZAKSTAN

Status: REPUBLIC
Area: 2,717,300 sq km (1,049,155 sq mls)
Population: 16,590,000
Capital: ALMATY
Language: KAZAKH, RUSSIAN, GERMAN, UKRAINIAN, UZBEK, TATAR
Religion: SUNNI MUSLIM, RUSSIAN ORTHODOX, PROTESTANT
Currency: TANGA
Organizations: CIS, UN

MAP PAGE: 12

STRETCHING ACROSS CENTRAL Asia, Kazakstan covers a vast area of steppe land and semi-desert. The land is flat in the west rising to mountains in the southeast. The climate is continental and mainly dry. Agriculture and livestock rearing are the main activities, with cotton and tobacco the main cash crops. Kazakstan is very rich in minerals, such as oil, natural gas, coal, iron ore, chromium, gold, lead and zinc. Mining, metallurgy, machine building and food processing are major industries.

KENYA

Status: REPUBLIC
Area: 582,646 sq km (224,961 sq mls)
Population: 30,522,000
Capital: NAIROBI
Language: SWAHILI (OFFICIAL), ENGLISH, MANY LOCAL LANGUAGES
Religion: R.CATHOLIC, PROTESTANT, TRAD.BELIEFS
Currency: SHILLING
Organizations: COMM., OAU, UN

MAP PAGE: 56

KENYA IS IN east Africa, on the Indian Ocean. Beyond the coastal plains the land rises to plateaux interrupted by volcanic mountains. The Rift Valley runs northwest of Nairobi to Lake Turkana. Most people live in central Kenya. Conditions are tropical on the coast, semi-desert in the north and savannah in the south. Agricultural products, chiefly tea and coffee, provide half export earnings. Light industry is important. Tourism is the main foreign exchange earner; oil refining and re-exports for landlocked neighbours are others.

KIRIBATI

Status: REPUBLIC
Area: 717 sq km (277 sq mls)
Population: 79,000
Capital: BAIRIKI
Language: I-KIRIBATI (GILBERTESE), ENGLISH
Religion: R.CATHOLIC, PROTESTANT, BAHA'I, MORMON
Currency: AUSTR. DOLLAR
Organizations: COMM.

MAP PAGE: 7

KIRIBATI COMPRISES 32 coral islands in the Gilbert, Phoenix and Line groups and the volcanic island of Banaba, which straddle the Equator in the Pacific Ocean. Most people live on the Gilbert islands, and the capital, Bairiki, is on Tarawa, one of the Gilbert Islands. The climate is hot, wetter in the north. Kiribati depends on subsistence farming and fishing. Copra and fish exports and licences for foreign fishing fleets are the main foreign exchange earners.

KUWAIT

Status: MONARCHY
Area: 17,818 sq km (6,880 sq mls)
Population: 1,691,000
Capital: KUWAIT
Language: ARABIC
Religion: SUNNI MUSLIM, SHI'A MUSLIM, OTHER MUSLIM, CHRISTIAN, HINDU
Currency: DINAR
Organizations: OPEC, UN

MAP PAGE: 17

KUWAIT LIES ON the northwest shores of The Gulf in southwest Asia. It is mainly low-lying desert, with irrigated areas along the Bay of Kuwait where most people live. Summers are hot and dry, winters are cool with some rainfall. The oil industry, which accounts for 80 per cent of exports, has largely recovered from the damage caused by Iraq in 1991. Income is also derived from extensive overseas investments.

KYRGYZSTAN

Status: REPUBLIC
Area: 198,500 sq km (76,641 sq mls)
Population: 4,668,000
Capital: BISHKEK
Language: KIRGHIZ, RUSSIAN, UZBEK
Religion: SUNNI MUSLIM, RUSSIAN ORTHODOX
Currency: SOM
Organizations: CIS, UN

MAP PAGE: 14-15

A LANDLOCKED CENTRAL Asian state, Kyrgyzstan is rugged and mountainous, lying in the western Tien Shan range. Most people live in the valleys of the north and west. Summers are hot and winters cold. Agriculture (chiefly livestock farming) is the main activity. Coal, gold, antimony and mercury are produced. Manufactures include machinery, metals and food products. Disruption of Russian-dominated trade has caused economic problems.

LAOS

Status: REPUBLIC
Area: 236,800 sq km (91,429 sq mls)
Population: 4,882,000
Capital: VIENTIANE
Language: LAO, LOCAL LANGUAGES
Religion: BUDDHIST, TRAD.BELIEFS, R.CATHOLIC, SUNNI MUSLIM
Currency: KIP
Organizations: UN

MAP PAGE: 25

A LANDLOCKED COUNTRY in southeast Asia, Laos borders Vietnam, Cambodia, Thailand, Myanmar and China. Forested mountains and plateaux predominate. The climate is tropical monsoon. Most people live in the Mekong valley and the low plateau in the south, and grow food crops, chiefly rice. Electricity, timber, coffee and tin are exported. Foreign aid and investment and the opium trade are important.

LATVIA

Status: REPUBLIC
Area: 63,700 sq km (24,595 sq mls)
Population: 2,515,000
Capital: RĪGA
Language: LATVIAN, RUSSIAN
Religion: PROTESTANT, R.CATHOLIC, RUSSIAN ORTHODOX
Currency: LAT
Organizations: UN

MAP PAGE: 37

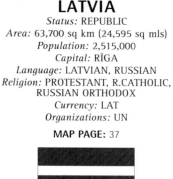

LATVIA IS IN north Europe, on the Baltic Sea and Gulf of Riga. The land is flat near the coast but hilly with woods and lakes inland. Latvia has a modified continental climate. One third of the people live in Riga. Crop and livestock farming are important. Industry is varied but specialist products include telephones, diesel trains, buses and paper. Latvia has few natural resources. Economic priorities are creating a market economy and reducing economic dependence on Russia.

LEBANON

Status: REPUBLIC
Area: 10,452 sq km (4,036 sq mls)
Population: 3,009,000
Capital: BEIRUT
Language: ARABIC, FRENCH, ARMENIAN
Religion: SHI'A, SUNNI AND OTHER MUSLIM, PROTESTANT, R.CATHOLIC
Currency: POUND
Organizations: UN

MAP PAGE: 16

LEBANON LIES ON the Mediterranean coast of southwest Asia. Beyond the coastal strip, where most people live, are two parallel mountain ranges, separated by the Bekaa Valley. In general the climate is Mediterranean. Civil war crippled the traditional sectors of banking, commerce and tourism, but some fruit production and light industry survived. Reconstruction is under way.

LESOTHO

Status: MONARCHY
Area: 30,355 sq km (11,720 sq mls)
Population: 2,050,000
Capital: MASERU
Language: SESOTHO, ENGLISH, ZULU
Religion: R.CATHOLIC, PROTESTANT, TRAD.BELIEFS
Currency: LOTI
Organizations: COMM., OAU, SADC, UN

MAP PAGE: 59

LESOTHO IS A landlocked state surrounded by the Republic of South Africa. It is a mountainous country lying within the Drakensberg range. Most people live in the western lowlands and southern Orange and Caledon river valleys. In general Lesotho has hot moist summers and cool, dry winters, with lower temperatures in the mountains. Subsistence farming and herding are the main activities. Exports include livestock, vegetables, wool and mohair. The economy depends heavily on South Africa for transport links and employment.

LIBERIA

Status: REPUBLIC
Area: 111,369 sq km (43,000 sq mls)
Population: 2,760,000
Capital: MONROVIA
Language: ENGLISH, CREOLE, MANY LOCAL LANGUAGES
Religion: TRAD. BELIEFS, SUNNI MUSLIM, PROTESTANT, R.CATHOLIC
Currency: DOLLAR
Organizations: OAU, UN

MAP PAGE: 54

LIBERIA IS ON the Atlantic coast of west Africa. Beyond the coastal belt of sandy beaches and mangrove swamps the land rises to a forested plateau, with highlands along the Guinea border. A quarter of the population lives along the coast. The climate is hot with heavy rainfall. The 1989-93 civil war ruined the economy. Before the war exports included iron ore, diamonds and gold along with rubber, timber and coffee. Ship registration was a major foreign exchange earner. Liberia now relies on foreign aid.

LIBYA

Status: REPUBLIC
Area: 1,759,540 sq km (679,362 sq mls)
Population: 5,407,000
Capital: TRIPOLI
Language: ARABIC, BERBER
Religion: SUNNI MUSLIM, R.CATHOLIC
Currency: DINAR
Organizations: OAU, OPEC, UN

MAP PAGE: 54-55

LIBYA LIES ON the Mediterranean coast of north Africa. The desert plains and hills of the Sahara dominate the landscape and the climate is hot and dry. Most people live in cities near the coast, where the climate is cooler with moderate rainfall. Farming and herding, chiefly in the northwest, are important but the main industry is oil, which accounts for about 95 per cent of export earnings. There is some heavy industry. In 1993 the UN imposed economic sanctions because of alleged sponsorship of terrorism.

LIECHTENSTEIN

Status: MONARCHY
Area: 160 sq km (62 sq mls)
Population: 31,000
Capital: VADUZ
Language: GERMAN
Religion: R.CATHOLIC, PROTESTANT
Currency: SWISS FRANC
Organizations: UN

MAP PAGE: 46

A LANDLOCKED STATE between Switzerland and Austria in central Europe, Liechtenstein occupies the floodplains of the upper Rhine valley and part of the Austrian Alps. It has a temperate climate with cool winters. Dairy farming is important, but manufacturing is dominant. Major products include precision instruments, dentistry equipment, pharmaceuticals, ceramics and textiles. There is also some metal working. Finance, chiefly banking, is very important. Tourism and postal stamps provide additional revenue.

LITHUANIA

Status: REPUBLIC
Area: 65,200 sq km (25,174 sq mls)
Population: 3,715,000
Capital: VILNIUS
Language: LITHUANIAN, RUSSIAN, POLISH
Religion: R.CATHOLIC, PROTESTANT, RUSSIAN ORTHODOX
Currency: LITAS
Organizations: UN

MAP PAGE: 37

LITHUANIA IS IN north Europe, on the eastern shores of the Baltic Sea. It is mainly lowland with many lakes, small rivers and marshes. The climate is generally temperate. About 15 per cent of people live in Vilnius. Agriculture, fishing and forestry are important, but manufacturing dominates the economy. The main products are processed foods, light industrial goods, machinery and metalworking equipment. Progress towards a market economy is slow. The economy remains heavily dependent on Russia.

LUXEMBOURG

Status: MONARCHY
Area: 2,586 sq km (998 sq mls)
Population: 410,000
Capital: LUXEMBOURG
Language: LETZEBURGISH, GERMAN, FRENCH, PORTUGUESE
Religion: R.CATHOLIC, PROTESTANT
Currency: FRANC
Organizations: EU, OECD, UN

MAP PAGE: 42

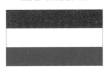

LUXEMBOURG, A LANDLOCKED country in west Europe, borders Belgium, France and Germany. The hills and forests of the Ardennes dominate the north, with rolling pasture to the south, where the main towns, farms and industries are found. Summers are warm and winters mild, though colder in the north. The iron and steel industry is still important, but light industries (including textiles, chemicals and food products) are growing. Luxembourg is a major banking centre and the home base of key European Union institutions.

MACAU

Status: PORTUGUESE TERRITORY
Area: 17 sq km (7 sq mls)
Population: 418,000
Capital: MACAU
Language: CANTONESE, PORTUGUESE
Religion: BUDDHIST, R.CATHOLIC, PROTESTANT
Currency: PATACA

MAP PAGE: 27

AN ENCLAVE ON the south coast of China, Macau consists of an area of the mainland and the two islands of Taipa and Coloane. The territory is scheduled to revert to China in 1999.

MADAGASCAR

Status: REPUBLIC
Area: 587,041 sq km (226,658 sq mls)
Population: 14,763,000
Capital: ANTANANARIVO
Language: MALAGASY, FRENCH
Religion: TRAD.BELIEFS, R.CATHOLIC, PROTESTANT, SUNNI MUSLIM
Currency: FRANC
Organizations: OAU, UN

MAP PAGE: 57

MADAGASCAR AND ADJACENT islets lie off the east coast of south Africa. The world's fourth largest island is in the main a high plateau with a coastal strip to the east and scrubby plain to the west. The climate is tropical with heavy rainfall in the north and east. Most people live on the plateau. Exports include coffee, vanilla, cloves, sugar and shrimps. The main industries are agricultural processing, textile manufacturing, oil refining and mining (chiefly chromite). Tourism and foreign aid are important.

MADEIRA

Status: PORTUGUESE TERRITORY
Area: 794 sq km (307 sq mls)
Population: 253,000
Capital: FUNCHAL
Language: PORTUGUESE
Religion: R.CATHOLIC, PROTESTANT
Currency: PORT. ESCUDO

MAP PAGE: 54

AN ISLAND GROUP in the Atlantic Ocean to the southwest of Portugal. Tourism is important to the economy.

MALAWI

Status: REPUBLIC
Area: 118,484 sq km (45,747 sq mls)
Population: 9,788,000
Capital: LILONGWE
Language: CHICHEWA, ENGLISH, LOMWE
Religion: PROTESTANT, R.CATHOLIC, TRAD. BELIEFS, SUNNI MUSLIM
Currency: KWACHA
Organizations: COMM., OAU, SADC, UN

MAP PAGE: 57

LANDLOCKED MALAWI IN central Africa is a narrow hilly country at the southern end of the East African Rift Valley. One fifth of the country is covered by Lake Malawi, which lies above sea level. Most people live in the southern regions. The climate is mainly subtropical with varying rainfall. The economy is predominantly agricultural. Tobacco, tea and sugar are the main exports. Manufacturing involves mainly chemicals, textiles and agricultural products. Malawi relies heavily on foreign aid.

MALAYSIA

Status: FEDERATION
Area: 332,665 sq km (128,442 sq mls)
Population: 20,140,000
Capital: KUALA LUMPUR
Language: MALAY, ENGLISH, CHINESE, TAMIL, LOCAL LANGUAGES
Religion: SUNNI MUSLIM, BUDDHIST, HINDU, CHRISTIAN, TRAD. BELIEFS
Currency: DOLLAR (RINGGIT)
Organizations: ASEAN, COMM., UN

MAP PAGE: 33

THE FEDERATION OF Malaysia, in southeast Asia, comprises two regions, separated by the South China Sea. Peninsular Malaysia occupies the southern Malay peninsula, which has a chain of mountains dividing the eastern coastal strip from the wider plains to the west. To the east, the states of Sabah and Sarawak in the north of the island of Borneo are mainly rainforest-covered hills and mountains with mangrove swamps along the coast. Both regions have a tropical climate with heavy rainfall. About 80 per cent of the population lives in Peninsular Malaysia, mainly on the coasts. The country is rich in natural resources. It is the world's largest producer of tin, palm oil, pepper and tropical hardwoods, and a major producer of natural rubber, coconut and cocoa. It also has vast reserves of minerals and fuels. However high economic growth in recent years has come from manufacturing which now provides most exports and involves mainly processing industries, electronics assembly and engineering (chiefly car production). With over 7 million visitors a year, tourism is also a major industry.

PENINSULAR MALAYSIA

Status: DIVISION
Area: 131,585 sq km (50,805 sq mls)
Population: 14,942,697
Capital: KUALA LUMPUR

SABAH

Status: STATE
Area: 76,115 sq km (29,388 sq mls)
Population: 1,583,726
Capital: KOTA KINABALU

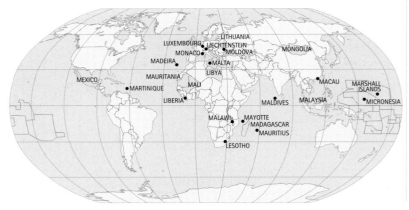

16

SARAWAK
Status: STATE
Area: 124,965 sq km (48,249 sq mls)
Population: 1,708,737
Capital: KUCHING

MALDIVES
Status: REPUBLIC
Area: 298 sq km (115 sq mls)
Population: 254,000
Capital: MALE
Language: DIVEHI (MALDIVIAN)
Religion: SUNNI MUSLIM
Currency: RUFIYAA
Organizations: COMM., UN

MAP PAGE: 15

THE MALDIVE ARCHIPELAGO comprises 1,190 coral atolls (202 of which are inhabited), in the Indian Ocean, southwest of India. The climate is hot, humid and monsoonal. The islands depend mainly on fishing and fish processing, light manufacturing (chiefly clothing) and tourism.

MALI
Status: REPUBLIC
Area: 1,240,140 sq km (478,821 sq mls)
Population: 10,795,000
Capital: BAMAKO
Language: FRENCH, BAMBARA, MANY LOCAL LANGUAGES
Religion: SUNNI MUSLIM, TRAD.BELIEFS, R.CATHOLIC
Currency: CFA FRANC
Organizations: OAU, UN

MAP PAGE: 54

A LANDLOCKED STATE in west Africa, Mali is low-lying, rising to mountains in the northeast. Northern regions lie within the Sahara desert. To the south, around the Niger river, are marshes and savannah grassland. Rainfall is unreliable. Most people live along the Niger and Senegal rivers. Exports include cotton and groundnuts. Some gold is produced. Mali relies heavily on foreign aid.

MALTA
Status: REPUBLIC
Area: 316 sq km (122 sq mls)
Population: 371,000
Capital: VALLETTA
Language: MALTESE, ENGLISH
Religion: R.CATHOLIC
Currency: LIRA
Organizations: COMM., UN

MAP PAGE: 48

THE ISLANDS OF Malta and Gozo lie in the Mediterranean Sea, off the coast of south Italy. Malta, the main island, has low hills and an indented coastline. Two thirds of the population lives in the Valletta area. The islands have hot, dry summers and mild winters. The main industries are tourism, ship building and repair, and export manufacturing (chiefly clothing). Vegetables, flowers, wine and tobacco are also exported.

MARSHALL ISLANDS
Status: REPUBLIC
Area: 181 sq km (70 sq mls)
Population: 56,000
Capital: DALAP-ULIGA-DARRIT
Language: MARSHALLESE, ENGLISH
Religion: PROTESTANT, R.CATHOLIC
Currency: US DOLLAR
Organizations: UN

MAP PAGE: 4

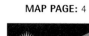

THE MARSHALL ISLANDS consist of over 1,000 atolls, islands and islets, within two chains, in the North Pacific Ocean. The main atolls are Majuro (home to half the population), Kwajalein, Jaluit, Enewetak and Bikini. The climate is tropical with heavy autumn rainfall. The islands depend on farming, fishing, tourism, financial services, and US aid and rent for a missile base.

MARTINIQUE
Status: FRENCH TERRITORY
Area: 1,079 sq km (417 sq mls)
Population: 379,000
Capital: FORT-DE-FRANCE
Language: FRENCH, FRENCH CREOLE
Religion: R.CATHOLIC, PROTESTANT, HINDU, TRAD.BELIEFS
Currency: FRENCH FRANC

MAP PAGE: 83

MARTINIQUE, ONE OF the Caribbean's Windward Islands, has volcanic peaks in the north, a populous central plain, and hills and beaches in the south. The tropical island depends on fruit growing (chiefly bananas), oil refining, rum distilling, tourism and French aid.

MAURITANIA
Status: REPUBLIC
Area: 1,030,700 sq km (397,955 sq mls)
Population: 2,284,000
Capital: NOUAKCHOTT
Language: ARABIC, FRENCH, LOCAL LANGUAGES
Religion: SUNNI MUSLIM
Currency: OUGUIYA
Organizations: OAU, UN

MAP PAGE: 54

MAURITANIA IS ON the Atlantic coast of northwest Africa and lies almost entirely within the Sahara desert. Oases and a fertile strip along the Senegal river to the south are the only areas suitable for cultivation. The climate is generally hot and dry. A quarter of Mauritanians live in Nouakchott. Livestock rearing and subsistence farming are important. The economy is heavily dependent on iron ore mining and fishing, which together account for 90 per cent of export earnings, and foreign aid.

MAURITIUS
Status: REPUBLIC
Area: 2,040 sq km (788 sq mls)
Population: 1,122,000
Capital: PORT LOUIS
Language: ENGLISH, FRENCH CREOLE, HINDI, INDIAN LANGUAGES
Religion: HINDU, R.CATHOLIC, SUNNI MUSLIM, PROTESTANT
Currency: RUPEE
Organizations: COMM., OAU, UN, SADC

MAP PAGE: 53

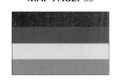

THE STATE COMPRISES Mauritius, Rodrigues and some 20 small islands in the Indian Ocean, east of Madagascar. The main island of Mauritius is volcanic in origin and has a coral coast rising to a central plateau. Most people live on the west side of the island. The climate is warm and humid. Mauritius depends mainly on sugar production, light manufacturing (chiefly clothing) and tourism.

MAYOTTE
Status: FRENCH TERRITORY
Area: 373 sq km (144 sq mls)
Population: 110,000
Capital: DZAOUDZI
Language: MAHORIAN (SWAHILI), FRENCH
Religion: SUNNI MUSLIM, R.CATHOLIC
Currency: FRENCH FRANC

MAP PAGE: 57

LYING IN THE Indian Ocean off the east coast of Central Africa, Mayotte is part of the Comoros Archipelago, but remains a French Territory.

MEXICO
Status: REPUBLIC
Area: 1,972,545 sq km (761,604 sq mls)
Population: 90,487,000
Capital: MÉXICO
Language: SPANISH, MANY AMERINDIAN LANGUAGES
Religion: R.CATHOLIC, PROTESTANT
Currency: PESO
Organizations: NAFTA, OECD, UN

MAP PAGE: 82

THE LARGEST COUNTRY in central America, Mexico extends southwards from the USA to Guatemala and Belize, and from the Pacific Ocean to the Gulf of Mexico. The greater part of the country is high plateaux flanked by the western and eastern Sierra Madre mountain ranges. The principal lowland is the Yucatán peninsula in the southeast. The climate varies with latitude and altitude: hot and humid in the lowlands, warm in the plateaux and cool with cold winters in the mountains. The north is arid, while the far south has heavy rainfall. Mexico City is one of the world's largest conurbations and the centre of trade and industry. Agriculture involves a quarter of the workforce and exports include coffee, fruit and vegetables. Shrimps are also exported and timber production is important for allied industries. Mexico is rich in minerals, including copper, zinc, lead and sulphur, and is the world's leading producer of silver. It is one of the world's largest producers of oil, from vast oil and gas resources in the Gulf of Mexico. The oil and petrochemical industries are still the mainstay, but a variety of manufactures are now produced including iron and steel, motor vehicles, textiles and electronic goods. Tourism is growing in importance.

FEDERATED STATES OF MICRONESIA
Status: REPUBLIC
Area: 701 sq km (271 sq mls)
Population: 105,000
Capital: PALIKIR
Language: ENGLISH, TRUKESE, POHNPEIAN, LOCAL LANGUAGES
Religion: PROTESTANT, R.CATHOLIC
Currency: US DOLLAR
Organizations: UN

MAP PAGE: 4

MICRONESIA COMPRISES 607 atolls and islands in the Carolines group in the North Pacific Ocean. A third of the population lives on Pohnpei. The climate is tropical with heavy

rainfall. Fishing and subsistence farming are the main activities. Copra and fish are the main exports. Income also derives from tourism and the licensing of foreign fishing fleets. The islands depend on US aid.

MOLDOVA
Status: REPUBLIC
Area: 33,700 sq km (13,012 sq mls)
Population: 4,432,000
Capital: CHIŞINĂU
Language: ROMANIAN, RUSSIAN, UKRAINIAN, GAGAUZ
Religion: MOLDOVAN ORTHODOX, RUSSIAN ORTHODOX
Currency: LEU
Organizations: CIS, UN

MAP PAGE: 47

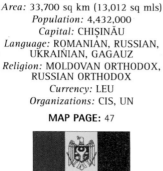

MOLDOVA IS IN east Europe, sandwiched between Romania and Ukraine. It consists of hilly steppe land, drained by the Prut and Dnestr rivers; the latter provides access to the Black Sea through Ukrainian territory. Moldova has long hot summers and mild winters. The economy is mainly agricultural, with tobacco, wine and fruit the chief products. Food processing and textiles are the main industries. Ethnic tension, which erupted into civil war in 1992, has slowed economic reform.

MONACO
Status: MONARCHY
Area: 2 sq km (0.8 sq ml)
Population: 32,000
Capital: MONACO
Language: FRENCH, MONEGASQUE, ITALIAN
Religion: R.CATHOLIC
Currency: FRENCH FRANC
Organizations: UN

MAP PAGE: 44

THE PRINCIPALITY, IN south Europe, occupies a rocky peninsula and a strip of land on France's Mediterranean coast. It depends on service industries (chiefly tourism, banking and finance) and light industry.

MONGOLIA
Status: REPUBLIC
Area: 1,565,000 sq km (604,250 sq mls)
Population: 2,410,000
Capital: ULAANBAATAR
Language: KHALKA (MONGOLIAN), KAZAKH, LOCAL LANGUAGES
Religion: BUDDHIST, SUNNI MUSLIM, TRAD.BELIEFS
Currency: TUGRIK
Organizations: UN

MAP PAGE: 24

MONGOLIA IS A landlocked country in east Asia between Russia and China. Much of it is high steppe land, with mountains and lakes in the west and north. In the south is the Gobi desert. Mongolia has long, cold winters and short, mild summers. A quarter of the population lives in the capital. Mongolia is rich in minerals and fuels. Copper accounts for half export earnings. Livestock breeding and agricultural processing are important. The demise of the Soviet Union caused economic problems and Mongolia depends on foreign aid.

MONTSERRAT

Status: UK TERRITORY
Area: 100 sq km (39 sq mls)
Population: 11,000
Capital: PLYMOUTH
Language: ENGLISH
Religion: PROTESTANT, R.CATHOLIC
Currency: E. CARIB. DOLLAR
Organizations: CARICOM

MAP PAGE: 83

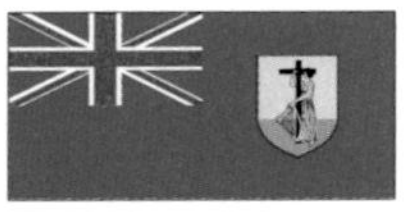

MOROCCO

Status: MONARCHY
Area: 446,550 sq km (172,414 sq mls)
Population: 27,111,000
Capital: RABAT
Language: ARABIC, BERBER, FRENCH,
SPANISH
Religion: SUNNI MUSLIM, R.CATHOLIC
Currency: DIRHAM
Organizations: UN

MAP PAGE: 54

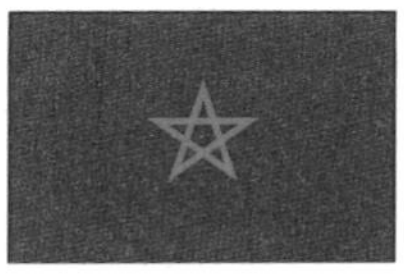

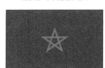

LYING IN THE northwest corner of Africa, Morocco has both Atlantic and Mediterranean coasts. The Atlas ranges separate the arid south and disputed Western Sahara from the fertile regions of the west and north, which have a milder climate. Most Moroccans live on the Atlantic coastal plain. The economy is based mainly on agriculture, phosphate mining and tourism. Manufacturing (chiefly textiles and clothing) and fishing are important.

MOZAMBIQUE

Status: REPUBLIC
Area: 799,380 sq km (308,642 sq mls)
Population: 17,423,000
Capital: MAPUTO
Language: PORTUGUESE, MAKUA,
TSONGA, MANY LOCAL LANGUAGES
Religion: TRAD.BELIEFS, R.CATHOLIC,
SUNNI MUSLIM
Currency: METICAL
Organizations: OAU, SADC, UN, COMM.

MAP PAGE: 57

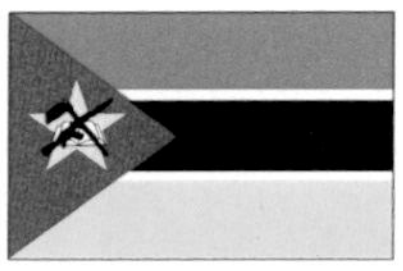

MOZAMBIQUE LIES ON the east coast of southern Africa. The land is mainly a savannah plateau drained by the Zambezi and other rivers, with highlands to the north. Most people live on the coast or in the river valleys. In general the climate is tropical with winter rainfall, but droughts occur. Reconstruction began in 1992 after 16 years of civil war. The economy is based on agriculture and trade. Exports include shrimps, cashews, cotton and sugar, but Mozambique relies heavily on aid.

MYANMAR

Status: REPUBLIC
Area: 676,577 sq km (261,228 sq mls)
Population: 46,527,000
Capital: YANGON
Language: BURMESE, SHAN, KAREN,
LOCAL LANGUAGES
Religion: BUDDHIST, SUNNI MUSLIM,
PROTESTANT, R.CATHOLIC
Currency: KYAT
Organizations: UN

MAP PAGE: 24-25

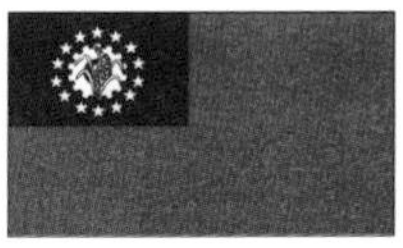

MYANMAR IS IN southeast Asia, on the Bay of Bengal and Andaman Sea. Most people live in the valley and delta of the Irrawaddy river, which is flanked on three sides by mountains and high plateaus. The climate is hot and monsoonal, and rainforest covers much of the land. Most people depend on agriculture. Exports include teak and rice. Myanmar is rich in oil and gemstones. Political unrest has affected economic development.

NAMIBIA

Status: REPUBLIC
Area: 824,292 sq km (318,261 sq mls)
Population: 1,540,000
Capital: WINDHOEK
Language: ENGLISH, AFRIKAANS,
GERMAN, OVAMBO
Religion: PROTESTANT, R.CATHOLIC
Currency: DOLLAR
Organizations: COMM., OAU, SADC, UN

MAP PAGE: 57

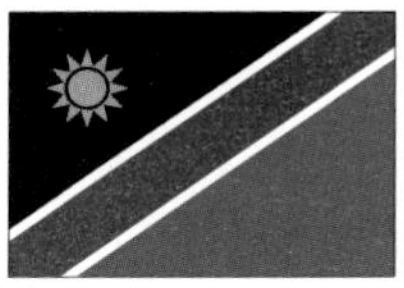

NAMIBIA LIES ON the Atlantic coast of southern Africa. Mountain ranges separate the coastal Namib Desert from the interior plateau, bordered to the south and east by the Kalahari desert. Namibia is hot and dry, but some summer rain falls in the north which supports crops, herds and most of the population. The economy is based mainly on agriculture and diamond and uranium mining. Fishing is increasingly important.

NAURU

Status: REPUBLIC
Area: 21 sq km (8 sq mls)
Population: 11,000
Capital: YAREN
Language: NAURUAN, GILBERTESE,
ENGLISH
Religion: PROTESTANT, R.CATHOLIC
Currency: AUSTR. DOLLAR
Organizations: COMM.

MAP PAGE: 7

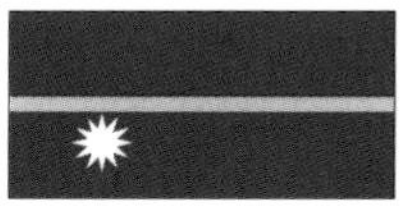

NAURU IS A coral island in the South Pacific Ocean, with a fertile coastal strip, a barren central plateau and a tropical climate. The economy is based on phosphate mining, but reserves are near exhaustion.

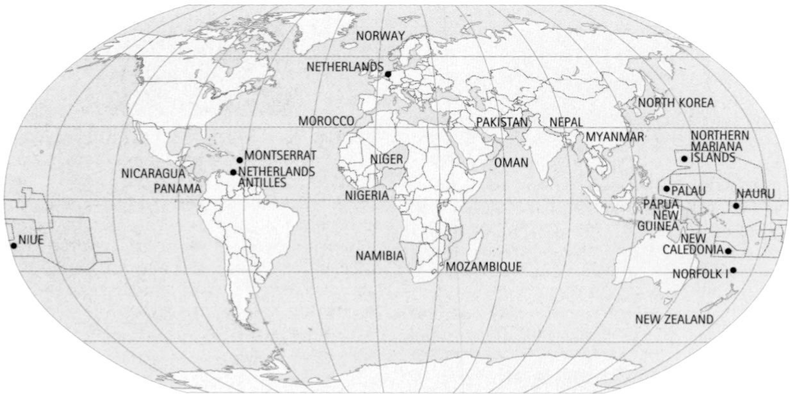

NEPAL

Status: MONARCHY
Area: 147,181 sq km (56,827 sq mls)
Population: 21,918,000
Capital: KATHMANDU
Language: NEPALI, MAITHILI,
BHOJPURI, ENGLISH,
MANY LOCAL LANGUAGES
Religion: HINDU, BUDDHIST,
SUNNI MUSLIM
Currency: RUPEE
Organizations: UN

MAP PAGE: 22-23

THE SOUTH ASIAN country of Nepal lies in the southern Himalayas between India and China. High mountains (including Everest) dominate northern Nepal. Most people live in the temperate central valleys and subtropical southern plains. The economy is based largely on agriculture and forestry. Manufacturing (chiefly textiles) and tourism are important. Nepal relies upon foreign aid.

NETHERLANDS

Status: MONARCHY
Area: 41,526 sq km (16,033 sq mls)
Population: 15,451,000
Capital: AMSTERDAM/THE HAGUE
Language: DUTCH, FRISIAN, TURKISH
Religion: R.CATHOLIC, PROTESTANT,
SUNNI MUSLIM
Currency: GUILDER
Organizations: EU, OECD, UN

MAP PAGE: 42

THE NETHERLANDS LIES on the North Sea coast of west Europe. Apart from hills in the far southeast, the land is flat and low-lying, much of it below sea level. The coastal region contains the delta of five rivers and polders (reclaimed land), protected by sand dunes, dikes and canals. The climate is temperate, with cool summers and mild winters. Rainfall is spread evenly throughout the year. The Netherlands is a densely populated country, with the majority of people living in the western Amsterdam-Rotterdam-The Hague area. Horticulture and dairy farming are important activities, with exports of eggs, butter and cheese. The Netherlands is Europe's leading producer and exporter of natural gas from reserves in the North Sea, but otherwise lacks raw materials. The economy is based mainly on international trade and manufacturing industry. Industrial sites are centred mainly around   the port of Rotterdam. The chief industries produce food products, chemicals, machinery, electric and electronic goods and transport equipment. Financial services and tourism are important.

NETHERLANDS ANTILLES

Status: NETHERLANDS TERRITORY
Area: 800 sq km (309 sq mls)
Population: 205,000
Capital: WILLEMSTAD
Language: DUTCH, PAPIAMENTO
Religion: R.CATHOLIC, PROTESTANT
Currency: GUILDER

MAP PAGE: 83

THE TERRITORY COMPRISES two separate island groups: Curaçao and Bonaire off the northern coast of South America, and Saba, Sint Eustatius and the southern part of Sint Maarten in the northern Lesser Antilles.

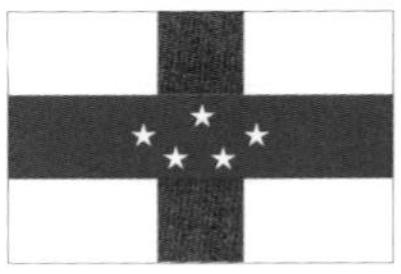

NEW CALEDONIA

Status: FRENCH TERRITORY
Area: 19,058 sq km (7,358 sq mls)
Population: 186,000
Capital: NOUMÉA
Language: FRENCH,
LOCAL LANGUAGES
Religion: R.CATHOLIC, PROTESTANT,
SUNNI MUSLIM
Currency: PACIFIC FRANC

MAP PAGE: 7

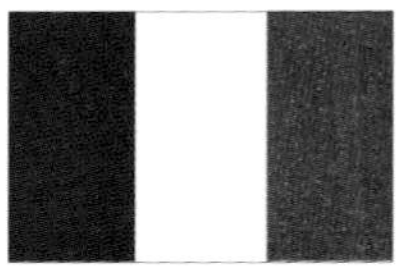

AN ISLAND GROUP, lying in the southwest Pacific, with a sub-tropical climate. The economy is based on nickel mining, tourism and agriculture.

NEW ZEALAND

Status: MONARCHY
Area: 270,534 sq km (104,454 sq mls)
Population: 3,542,000
Capital: WELLINGTON
Language: ENGLISH, MAORI
Religion: PROTESTANT, R.CATHOLIC
Currency: DOLLAR
Organizations: COMM., OECD, UN

MAP PAGE: 9

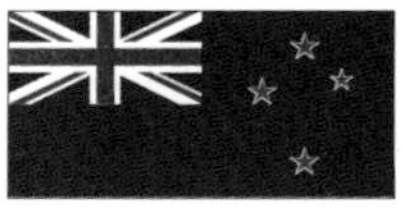

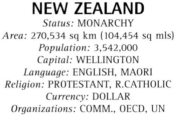

NEW ZEALAND, IN Australasia, comprises two main islands separated by the narrow Cook Strait, and a number of smaller islands. North Island, where three quarters of the population lives, has mountain ranges, broad fertile valleys and a volcanic central plateau with hot springs and two active volcanoes. South Island is also mountainous, with the Southern Alps running its entire length. The only major lowland area is the Canterbury Plains in the east. The climate is generally temperate, though South Island has cooler winters with upland snow. Rainfall is distributed throughout the year. Farming is the mainstay of the economy. New Zealand is one of the world's leading producers of meat (beef, lamb and mutton), wool and dairy products. Specialist foods, such as kiwi fruit, and fish are also important. Coal, oil and natural gas are produced, but hydroelectric and geothermal power provide much of the country's energy needs. Other industries produce timber, wood pulp, iron, aluminium, machinery and chemicals. Tourism is the largest foreign exchange earner.

NICARAGUA

Status: REPUBLIC
Area: 130,000 sq km (50,193 sq mls)
Population: 4,539,000
Capital: MANAGUA
Language: SPANISH,
AMERINDIAN LANGUAGES
Religion: R.CATHOLIC, PROTESTANT
Currency: CÓRDOBA
Organizations: UN

MAP PAGE: 82-83

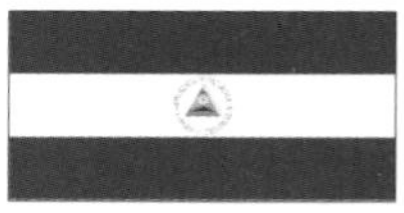

NICARAGUA LIES AT the heart of Central America, with both Pacific and Caribbean coasts. Mountain ranges separate the east, which is largely jungle, from the more developed western regions, which include Lake Nicaragua and some active volcanoes. The highest land is in the north. The climate is tropical. The economy is largely agricultural.

Traditional exports include cotton, coffee, bananas and gold. The aid-dependent economy has suffered from civil war (1978-89) and US sanctions.

NIGER

Status: REPUBLIC
Area: 1,267,000 sq km (489,191 sq mls)
Population: 9,151,000
Capital: NIAMEY
Language: FRENCH (OFFICIAL), HAUSA, FULANI, LOCAL LANGUAGES
Religion: SUNNI MUSLIM, TRAD.BELIEFS
Currency: CFA FRANC
Organizations: OAU, UN

MAP PAGE: 54-55

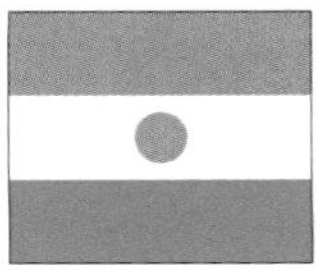

A LANDLOCKED STATE of west Africa, Niger lies mostly within the Sahara desert, but with savannah land in the south and Niger valley. The Air massif dominates central regions. Much of the country is hot and dry. The south has some summer rainfall, though droughts occur. The economy depends on subsistence farming and herding, uranium exports and foreign aid.

NIGERIA

Status: REPUBLIC
Area: 923,768 sq km (356,669 sq mls)
Population: 111,721,000
Capital: ABUJA
Language: ENGLISH, CREOLE, HAUSA, YORUBA, IBO, FULANI
Religion: SUNNI MUSLIM, PROTESTANT, R.CATHOLIC, TRAD. BELIEFS
Currency: NAIRA
Organizations: COMM., OAU, OPEC, UN

MAP PAGE: 54-55

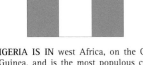

NIGERIA IS IN west Africa, on the Gulf of Guinea, and is the most populous country in the African continent. The Niger delta dominates coastal areas, fringed with sandy beaches, mangrove swamps and lagoons. Inland is a belt of rainforest that gives way to woodland or savannah on high plateaus. The far north is the semi-desert edge of the Sahara. The climate is tropical with heavy summer rainfall in the south but low rainfall in the north. Most people live in the coastal lowlands or in western Nigeria. About half the workforce is involved in agriculture, mainly growing subsistence crops, and Nigeria is virtually self-sufficient in food. Cocoa and rubber are the only significant export crops. The economy is heavily dependent on vast oil resources in the Niger delta and shallow offshore waters, which account for about 90 per cent of export earnings. Nigeria also has natural gas reserves and some mineral deposits, but these are as yet largely undeveloped. Industry involves mainly oil refining, chemicals (chiefly fertilizer), agricultural processing, textiles, steel manufacture and vehicle assembly. Economic mismanagement in the oil boom of the 1970s and political instability have left Nigeria with a heavy debt, poverty and rising unemployment.

NIUE

Status: NEW ZEALAND TERRITORY
Area: 258 sq km (100 sq mls)
Population: 2,000
Capital: ALOFI
Language: ENGLISH, POLYNESIAN (NIUEAN)
Religion: PROTESTANT, R.CATHOLIC
Currency: NZ DOLLAR

MAP PAGE: 7

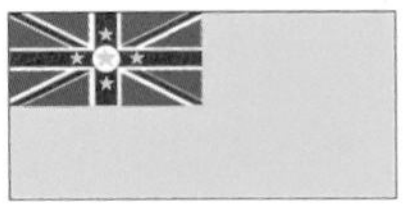

NORFOLK ISLAND

Status: AUSTRALIAN TERRITORY
Area: 35 sq km (14 sq mls)
Population: 2,000
Capital: KINGSTON
Language: ENGLISH
Religion: PROTESTANT, R.CATHOLIC
Currency: AUSTR. DOLLAR

MAP PAGE: 7

NORTH KOREA

Status: REPUBLIC
Area: 120,538 sq km (46,540 sq mls)
Population: 23,917,000
Capital: P'YŎNGYANG
Language: KOREAN
Religion: TRAD.BELIEFS, CHONDOIST, BUDDHIST, CONFUCIAN, TAOIST
Currency: WON
Organizations: UN

MAP PAGE: 30

OCCUPYING THE NORTHERN half of the Korean peninsula in east Asia, North Korea is a rugged and mountainous country. The principal lowlands and the main agricultural areas are the Pyongyang and Chaeryong plains in the southwest. More than half the population lives in urban areas, mainly on the coastal plains, which are wider along the Yellow Sea to the west than the Sea of Japan to the east. North Korea has a continental climate, with cold, dry winters and hot, wet summers. About half the workforce is involved in agriculture, mainly growing food crops on cooperative farms. A variety of minerals and ores, chiefly iron ore, are mined and are the basis of the country's heavy industry. Exports include minerals (chiefly lead, magnesite and zinc) and metal products (chiefly iron and steel). North Korea depends heavily on aid, but has suffered since support from Russia and China was ended in in 1991 and 1993 respectively. Agricultural, mining and maufacturing output have fallen. Living standards are much lower than in South Korea from which it was separated in 1945.

NORTHERN MARIANA ISLANDS

Status: US TERRITORY
Area: 477 sq km (184 sq mls)
Population: 47,000
Capital: SAIPAN
Language: ENGLISH, CHAMORRO, TAGALOG, LOCAL LANGUAGES
Religion: R.CATHOLIC, PROTESTANT
Currency: US DOLLAR

MAP PAGE: 24-25

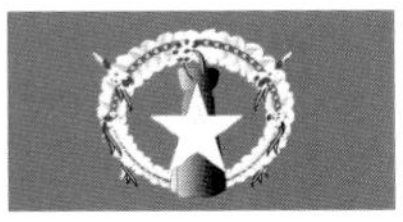

A CHAIN OF islands in the Western Pacific Ocean, tourism is increasingly important to the economy.

NORWAY

Status: MONARCHY
Area: 323,878 sq km (125,050 sq mls)
Population: 4,360,000
Capital: OSLO
Language: NORWEGIAN
Religion: PROTESTANT, R.CATHOLIC
Currency: KRONE
Organizations: OECD, UN

MAP PAGE: 36-37

A COUNTRY OF NORTH Europe, Norway stretches along the north and west coasts of Scandinavia, from the Arctic Ocean to the North Sea. Its extensive coastline is indented

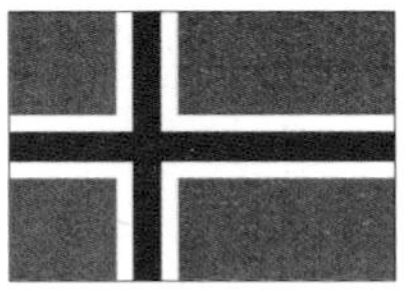

with fjords and fringed with many islands. Inland, the terrain is mountainous, with coniferous forests and lakes in the south. The only major lowland areas are along the southern North Sea and Skagerrak coasts, where most people live. The climate on the west coast is modified by the North Atlantic Drift. Inland, summers are warmer and winters are colder. Norway has vast petroleum and natural gas resources in the North Sea. It is west Europe's leading producer of oil and gas, which account for over 40 per cent of export earnings. Related industries include engineering (such as oil and gas platforms) and petrochemicals. More traditional industries process local raw materials: fish, timber and minerals. Agriculture is limited, but fishing and fish farming are important. Norway is the world's leading exporter of salmon. Merchant shipping and tourism are major sources of foreign exchange.

OMAN

Status: MONARCHY
Area: 309,500 sq km (119,499 sq mls)
Population: 2,163,000
Capital: MUSCAT
Language: ARABIC, BALUCHI, FARSI, SWAHILI, INDIAN LANGUAGES
Religion: IBADHI MUSLIM, SUNNI MUSLIM
Currency: RIAL
Organizations: UN

MAP PAGE: 20

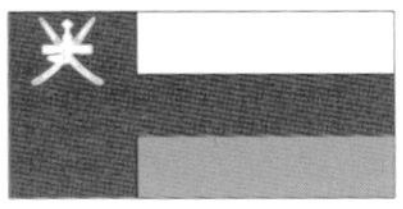

THE SULTANATE OF southwest Asia occupies the southeast coast of Arabia and an enclave north of the United Arab Emirates. Oman is a desert land, with mountains in the north and south. The climate is hot and mainly dry. Most people live on the coastal strip on the Gulf of Oman. The majority depends on farming and fishing, but the oil and gas industries dominate the economy. Copper is mined.

PAKISTAN

Status: REPUBLIC
Area: 803,940 sq km (310,403 sq mls)
Population: 129,808,000
Capital: ISLAMABAD
Language: URDU (OFFICIAL), PUNJABI, SINDHI, PUSHTU, ENGLISH
Religion: SUNNI MUSLIM, SHI'A MUSLIM, CHRISTIAN, HINDU
Currency: RUPEE
Organizations: COMM., UN

MAP PAGE: 14-15

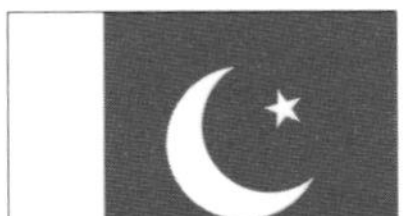

PAKISTAN IS IN the northwest part of the Indian subcontinent in south Asia, on the Arabian Sea. Eastern and southern Pakistan are dominated by the great basin drained by the Indus river system. It is the main agricultural area and contains most of the population. To the north the land rises to the mountains of the Karakoram and part of the Hindu Kush and Himalayas. The west is semi-desert plateaus and mountain ranges. The climate ranges between dry desert and polar ice cap. However, temperatures are generally warm and rainfall is monsoonal. Agriculture is the main sector of the economy, employing about half the workforce and accounting for over two thirds of export earnings. Cultivation is based on extensive irrigation schemes. Pakistan is one of the world's leading producers of cotton and an important exporter of rice. However, much of the country's food needs must be imported. Pakistan produces natural gas and has a variery of mineral deposits including coal and gold,

but they are little developed. The main industries are textiles and clothing manufacture and food processing, with fabrics and ready-made clothing the leading exports. Pakistan also produces leather goods, fertilizers, chemicals, paper and precision instruments. The country depends heavily upon foreign aid and remittances from Pakistanis working abroad.

PALAU

Status: REPUBLIC
Area: 497 sq km (192 sq mls)
Population: 17,000
Capital: KOROR
Language: PALAUAN, ENGLISH
Religion: R.CATHOLIC, PROTESTANT, TRAD.BELIEFS
Currency: US DOLLAR
Organizations: UN

MAP PAGE: 25

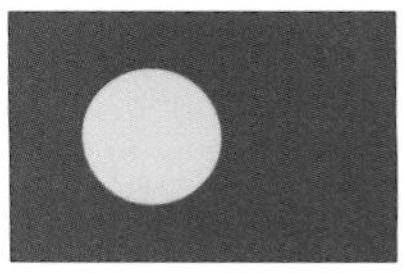

PALAU COMPRISES OVER 300 islands in the western Carolines group of the North Pacific Ocean. Two thirds of the people live on Koror. The climate is tropical. Palau depends on farming, fishing, tourism and US aid.

PANAMA

Status: REPUBLIC
Area: 77,082 sq km (29,762 sq mls)
Population: 2,631,000
Capital: PANAMÁ
Language: SPANISH, ENGLISH CREOLE, AMERINDIAN LANGUAGES
Religion: R.CATHOLIC, PROTESTANT, SUNNI MUSLIM, BAHA'I
Currency: BALBOA
Organizations: UN

MAP PAGE: 83

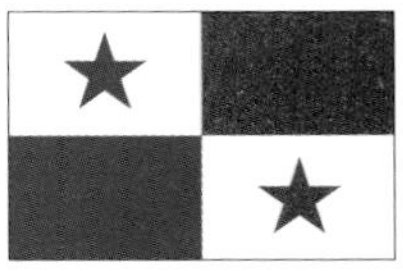

PANAMA IS THE most southerly state in Central America and has Pacific and Caribbean coasts. It is hilly, with mountains in the west and jungle near the Colombian border. The climate is tropical. Most people live on the drier Pacific side. The economy is based mainly on services related to the canal, shipping, banking and tourism. Exports include bananas, shrimps, sugar and petroleum products.

PAPUA NEW GUINEA

Status: MONARCHY
Area: 462,840 sq km (178,704 sq mls)
Population: 4,074,000
Capital: PORT MORESBY
Language: ENGLISH, TOK PISIN (PIDGIN), LOCAL LANGUAGES
Religion: PROTESTANT, R.CATHOLIC, TRAD.BELIEFS
Currency: KINA
Organizations: COMM., UN

MAP PAGE: 6

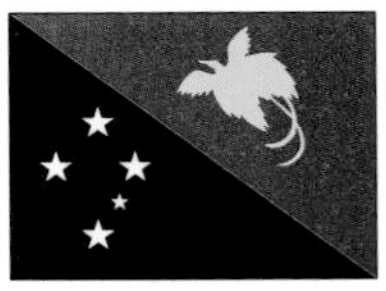

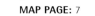

PAPUA NEW GUINEA, in Australasia, occupies the eastern half of New Guinea and includes many island groups. Papua New Guinea has a forested and mountainous interior, bordered by swampy plains, and a tropical monsoon climate. Most of the workforce are farmers. Timber, copra, coffee and cocoa are important, but exports are dominated by minerals, chiefly copper and gold. The country depends on foreign aid.

PARAGUAY

Status: REPUBLIC
Area: 406,752 sq km (157,048 sq mls)
Population: 4,828,000
Capital: ASUNCIÓN
Language: SPANISH, GUARANÍ
Religion: R.CATHOLIC, PROTESTANT
Currency: GUARANÍ
Organizations: UN

MAP PAGE: 88

PARAGUAY IS A landlocked country in central South America, bordering Bolivia, Brazil and Argentina. The river Paraguay separates a sparsely populated western zone of marsh and flat alluvial plains from a more developed, hilly and forested region to the east. The climate is subtropical. The mainstay of the economy is agriculture and agricultural processing. Exports include cotton, soya bean and edible oil products, timber and meat. The largest hydro-electric dam in the world is at Itaipú on the river Paraná.

PERU

Status: REPUBLIC
Area: 1,285,216 sq km (496,225 sq mls)
Population: 23,560,000
Capital: LIMA
Language: SPANISH, QUECHUA, AYMARA
Religion: R.CATHOLIC, PROTESTANT
Currency: SOL
Organizations: UN

MAP PAGE: 86

PERU LIES ON the Pacific coast of South America. Most people live on the coastal strip and the slopes of the high Andes. East of the Andes is high plateau country and the Amazon rainforest. The coast is temperate with low rainfall, while the east is hot, humid and wet. Agriculture involves one third of the workforce. Sugar, cotton, coffee and, illegally, coca are the main cash crops. Fishmeal and timber are also important, but copper, zinc, lead, gold, silver, petroleum and its products are the main exports.

PHILIPPINES

Status: REPUBLIC
Area: 300,000 sq km (115,831 sq mls)
Population: 70,267,000
Capital: MANILA
Language: ENGLISH, FILIPINO (TAGALOG), CEBUANO
Religion: R.CATHOLIC, AGLIPAYAN, SUNNI MUSLIM, PROTESTANT
Currency: PESO
Organizations: ASEAN, UN

MAP PAGE: 31

THE PHILIPPINES, IN southeast Asia, consists of 7,100 islands and atolls lying between the South China Sea and the Pacific

Ocean. The islands of Luzon and Mindanao occupy two thirds of the land area. They and nine other fairly large islands are mountainous and forested. There are ten active volcanoes and earthquakes are common. Most people live in the intermontane plains on the larger islands or on the coastal strips. The climate is hot and humid with heavy monsoonal rainfall. Coconuts, sugar, pineapples and bananas are the main agricultural exports. Fish and timber are also important. The Philippines produces copper, gold, silver, chromium and nickel as well as oil, though geothermal power is also used. The main industries process raw materials and produce electrical and electronic equipment and components, footwear and clothing, textiles and furniture. Tourism is being encouraged. Foreign aid and remittances from workers abroad are important to the economy, which faces problems of high population growth rate and high unemployment.

PITCAIRN ISLANDS

Status: UK TERRITORY
Area: 45 sq km (17 sq mls)
Population: 71
Capital: ADAMSTOWN
Language: ENGLISH
Religion: PROTESTANT
Currency: DOLLAR

MAP PAGE: 5

AN ISLAND GROUP in the southeast Pacific Ocean consisting of Pitcairn Island and three uninhabited islands. It was originally settled by mutineers from HMS Bounty.

POLAND

Status: REPUBLIC
Area: 312,683 sq km (120,728 sq mls)
Population: 38,588,000
Capital: WARSAW
Language: POLISH, GERMAN
Religion: R.CATHOLIC, POLISH ORTHODOX
Currency: ZŁOTY
Organizations: UN, OECD

MAP PAGE: 46-47

POLAND LIES ON the Baltic coast of central Europe. The Oder and Vistula deltas dominate the coast, fringed with sand dunes. Inland much of Poland is low-lying (part of the North European plain), with woods and lakes. In the south the land rises to the Sudeten and western Carpathian mountains which form the borders with the Czech Republic and Slovakia respectively. The climate is continental, with warm summers and cold winters. Conditions are milder in the west and on the coast. A third of the workforce is involved in agriculture, forestry and fishing. Agricultural exports include livestock products and sugar. The

economy is heavily industrialized, with mining and manufacturing accounting for 40 per cent of national income. Poland is one of the world's major producers of coal. It also produces copper, zinc, lead, nickel, sulphur and natural gas. The main industries are ship building, car manufacture, metal and chemical production. The transition to a market economy has resulted in 15 per cent unemployment and economic hardship.

PORTUGAL

Status: REPUBLIC
Area: 88,940 sq km (34,340 sq mls)
Population: 10,797,000
Capital: LISBON
Language: PORTUGUESE
Religion: R.CATHOLIC, PROTESTANT
Currency: ESCUDO
Organizations: EU, OECD, UN

MAP PAGE: 45

PORTUGAL LIES IN the western part of the Iberian peninsula in southwest Europe, has an Atlantic coastline and is flanked by Spain to the north and east. North of the river Tagus are mostly highlands with forests of pine and cork. South of the river is undulating lowland. The climate in the north is cool and moist, influenced by the Atlantic Ocean. The south is warmer, with dry, mild winters. Most Portuguese live near the coast, with one third of the total population in Lisbon and Oporto. Agriculture, fishing and forestry involve 12 per cent of the workfork. Wines, tomatoes, citrus fruit, cork (Portugal is the world's largest producer) and sardines are important exports. Mining and manufacturing are the main sectors of the economy. Portugal produces pyrite, kaolin, zinc, tungsten and other minerals. Export manufactures include textiles, clothing and footwear, electrical machinery and transport equipment, cork and wood products, and chemicals. Service industries, chiefly tourism and banking, are important to the economy as are remittances from workers abroad.

PUERTO RICO

Status: US TERRITORY
Area: 9,104 sq km (3,515 sq mls)
Population: 3,674,000
Capital: SAN JUAN
Language: SPANISH, ENGLISH
Religion: R.CATHOLIC, PROTESTANT
Currency: US DOLLAR

MAP PAGE: 83

THE CARIBBEAN ISLAND of Puerto Rico has a forested, hilly interior, coastal plains and a tropical climate. Half the population lives in the San Juan area. The economy is based on export manufacturing (chiefly chemicals and electronics), tourism and agriculture.

QATAR

Status: MONARCHY
Area: 11,437 sq km (4,416 sq mls)
Population: 551,000
Capital: DOHA
Language: ARABIC, INDIAN LANGUAGES
Religion: SUNNI MUSLIM, CHRISTIAN, HINDU
Currency: RIYAL
Organizations: OPEC, UN

MAP PAGE: 18

THE EMIRATE OCCUPIES a peninsula that extends northwards from east-central Arabia into The Gulf in southwest Asia. The

peninsula is flat and barren with sand dunes and salt pans. The climate is hot and mainly dry. Most people live in the Doha area. The economy is heavily dependent on petroleum, natural gas and the oil-refining industry. Income also comes from overseas investment.

REPUBLIC OF IRELAND

Status: REPUBLIC
Area: 70,282 sq km (27,136 sq mls)
Population: 3,582,000
Capital: DUBLIN
Language: ENGLISH, IRISH
Religion: R.CATHOLIC, PROTESTANT
Currency: PUNT
Organizations: EU, OECD, UN

MAP PAGE: 41

A STATE IN northwest Europe, the Irish republic occupies some 80 per cent of the island of Ireland in the Atlantic Ocean. It is a lowland country of wide valleys, lakes and peat bogs, with isolated mountain ranges around the coast. The west coast is rugged and indented with many bays. The climate is mild due to the North Atlantic Drift and rainfall is plentiful, though highest in the west. Nearly 60 per cent of people live in urban areas, Dublin and Cork being the main cities. Agriculture, the traditional mainstay, involves mainly the production of livestock, meat and dairy products, which account for about 20 percent of exports. Manufactured goods form the bulk of exports. The main industries are electronics, pharmaceuticals and engineering as well as food processing, brewing and textiles. Natural resources include petroleum, natural gas, peat, lead and zinc. Services industries are expanding, with tourism a major foreign exchange earner. The economy could benefit from peace in Northern Ireland, which is part of the United Kingdom.

RÉUNION

Status: FRENCH TERRITORY
Area: 2,551 sq km (985 sq mls)
Population: 653,000
Capital: ST-DENIS
Language: FRENCH, FRENCH CREOLE
Religion: R.CATHOLIC
Currency: FRENCH FRANC

MAP PAGE: 53

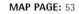

THE INDIAN OCEAN island of Réunion is mountainous, with coastal lowlands and a warm climate. It depends heavily on sugar, tourism and French aid. Some uninhabited islets to the east are administered from Réunion.

ROMANIA

Status: REPUBLIC
Area: 237,500 sq km (91,699 sq mls)
Population: 22,680,000
Capital: BUCHAREST
Language: ROMANIAN, HUNGARIAN
Religion: ROMANIAN ORTHODOX, R.CATHOLIC, PROTESTANT
Currency: LEU
Organizations: UN

MAP PAGE: 47. 49

ROMANIA LIES ON the Black Sea coast of east Europe. Mountains separate the Transylvanian plateau from the populous plains of the east and south and the Danube delta. The climate is continental. Romania is rich in fuels and metallic ores. Mining and manufacturing (chiefly metallurgy and machine building) predominate but agriculture is

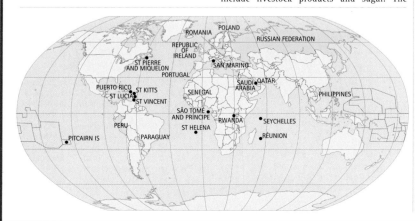

important. Pre-1989 mismanagement and economic reforms of the 1990s have caused hardship.

RUSSIAN FEDERATION

Status: REPUBLIC
Area: 17,075,400 sq km (6,592,849 sq mls)
Population: 148,141,000
Capital: MOSCOW
Language: RUSSIAN, TATAR, UKRAINIAN, LOCAL LANGUAGES
Religion: RUSSIAN ORTHODOX, SUNNI MUSLIM, OTHER CHRISTIAN, JEWISH
Currency: ROUBLE
Organizations: CIS, UN

MAP PAGE: 12-13

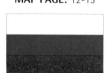

RUSSIA OCCUPIES MUCH of east Europe and all of north Asia, and is the world's largest state, nearly twice the size of the USA. It borders thirteen countries to the west and south and has long coastlines on the Arctic and Pacific oceans to the north and east. European Russia, which lies west of the Ural mountains, is part of the North European plain. To the south the land rises to uplands and the Caucasus Mountains on the border with Georgia and Azerbaijan. East of the Urals lies the flat Siberian plain. Much of central Siberia is plateaux. In the south is Lake Baikal, the world's deepest lake, and the Altai and Sayan ranges on the border with Azerbaijan and Mongolia. Eastern Siberia is rugged and mountainous with active volcanoes, notably in the Kamchatka peninsula. Russia's major rivers are the Volga in the west and the Ob, Yenisey, Lena and Amur in Siberia. The climate and vegetation range between Arctic tundra in the north and semi-arid steppe towards the Black and Caspian Sea coasts in the south. In general, the climate is continental with extreme temperatures. The majority of the population (the sixth largest in the world), industry and agriculture are concentrated in European Russia, but there has been increased migration to Siberia to exploit its vast natural resources. The economy is heavily dependent on exploitation of its raw materials and heavy industry. Russia has a wealth of mineral resources, though they are often difficult to exploit because of the climate. It is one of the world's leading producers of petroleum, natural gas and coal as well as iron and manganese ores, platinum, potash, asbestos and many precious and rare metals. Mining provides important exports and is the basis of heavy industry. Russia is a major producer of steel and machinery such as tractors, motor vehicles and generators, as well as chemicals and textiles. Other light industries are less important to the economy. Forests cover about 40 per cent of the land area and supply an important timber, paper and pulp industry. About 8 per cent of land is suitable for cultivation. However farming is generally inefficient and much of food needs, especially grains, must be imported. Fishing is important and Russia operates a large fleet throughout the world. Economic reforms begun in the late 1980s to liberalize the economy met with mixed success, largely because of political unrest. The transition to a free market economy, which was speeded up in the 1990s has been painful, with rising unemployment.

RWANDA

Status: REPUBLIC
Area: 26,338 sq km (10,169 sq mls)
Population: 7,952,000
Capital: KIGALI
Language: KINYARWANDA, FRENCH, ENGLISH
Religion: R.CATHOLIC, TRAD.BELIEFS, PROTESTANT, SUNNI MUSLIM
Currency: FRANC
Organizations: OAU, UN

MAP PAGE: 56

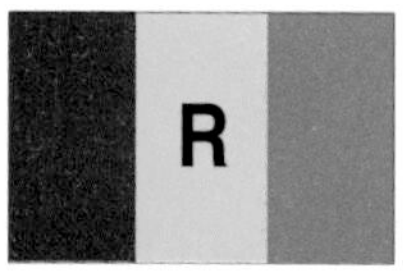

A DENSELY POPULATED and landlocked state in east Africa, Rwanda consists mainly of mountains and plateaux to the east of the Rift Valley. The climate is warm with a summer dry season. Rwanda depends upon subsistence farming, coffee and tea exports, light industry and foreign aid, but the 1990-93 civil war and ethnic conflict have devastated the country.

ST HELENA

Status: UK TERRITORY
Area: 411 sq km (159 sq mls)
Population: 7,000
Capital: JAMESTOWN
Language: ENGLISH
Religion: PROTESTANT, R.CATHOLIC
Currency: POUND STERLING

MAP PAGE: 53

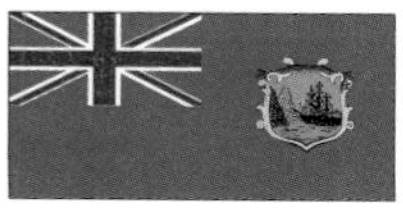

ST HELENA AND its dependencies, Ascension and Tristan da Cunha are isolated island groups lying in the south Atlantic Ocean. Ascension is over 1000 kilometres (620 miles) northwest of St Helena and Tristan da Cunha over 2000 kilometres (1240 miles) to the south.

ST KITTS-NEVIS

Status: MONARCHY
Area: 261 sq km (101 sq mls)
Population: 42,000
Capital: BASSETERRE
Language: ENGLISH, CREOLE
Religion: PROTESTANT, R.CATHOLIC
Currency: E. CARIB. DOLLAR
Organizations: CARICOM, COMM., UN

MAP PAGE: 83

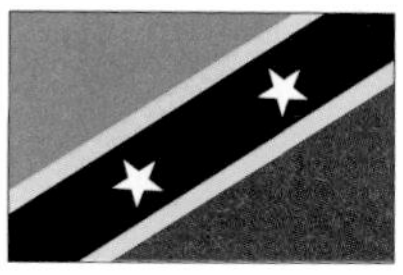

ST KITTS-NEVIS are in the Leeward group in the Caribbean Sea. Both volcanic islands are mountainous and forested with sandy beaches and a warm, wet climate. Some 75 per cent of the population lives on St Kitts. Agriculture is the main activity, with sugar, molasses and sea island cotton the main products. Tourism and manufacturing (chiefly garments and electronic components) are important.

ST LUCIA

Status: MONARCHY
Area: 616 sq km (238 sq mls)
Population: 145,000
Capital: CASTRIES
Language: ENGLISH, FRENCH CREOLE
Religion: R.CATHOLIC, PROTESTANT
Currency: E. CARIB. DOLLAR
Organizations: CARICOM, COMM., UN

MAP PAGE: 83

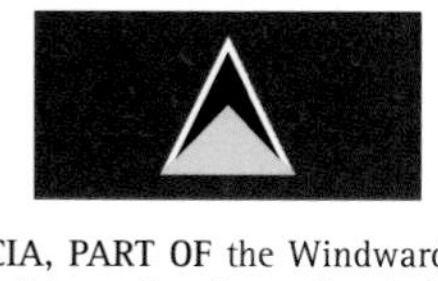

ST LUCIA, PART OF the Windward group in the Caribbean Sea, is a volcanic island with forested mountains, hot springs, sandy beaches and a wet tropical climate. Agriculture is the main activity, with bananas accounting for over half export earnings. Tourism, agricultural processing and manufacturing (chiefly garments, cardboard boxes and electronic components) are increasingly important.

ST PIERRE AND MIQUELON

Status: FRENCH TERRITORY
Area: 242 sq km (93 sq mls)
Population: 6,000
Capital: ST-PIERRE
Language: FRENCH
Religion: R.CATHOLIC
Currency: FRENCH FRANC

MAP PAGE: 67

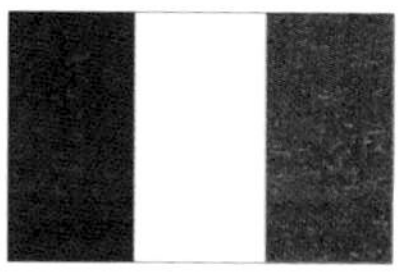

A GROUP OF islands off the south coast of Newfoundland in eastern Canada.

ST VINCENT AND THE GRENADINES

Status: MONARCHY
Area: 389 sq km (150 sq mls)
Population: 111,000
Capital: KINGSTOWN
Language: ENGLISH, CREOLE
Religion: PROTESTANT, R.CATHOLIC
Currency: E. CARIB. DOLLAR
Organizations: CARICOM, COMM., UN

MAP PAGE: 83

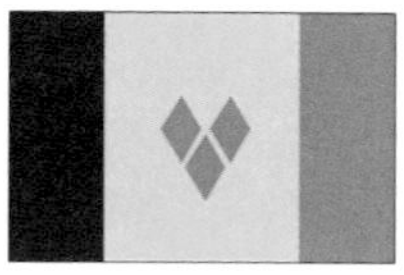

ST VINCENT, WHOSE TERRITORY includes 32 islets and cays in the Grenadines, is in the Windward Islands group in the Caribbean Sea. St Vincent is forested and mountainous, with an active volcano, Mount Soufrière. The climate is tropical and wet. The economy is based mainly on agriculture and tourism. Bananas account for about half export earnings. Arrowroot is also important.

SAN MARINO

Status: REPUBLIC
Area: 61 sq km (24 sq mls)
Population: 25,000
Capital: SAN MARINO
Language: ITALIAN
Religion: R.CATHOLIC
Currency: ITALIAN LIRA
Organizations: UN

MAP PAGE: 48

LANDLOCKED SAN MARINO lies on the slopes of Mt Titano in northeast Italy. It has a mild climate. A third of the people live in the capital. There is some agriculture and light industry, but most income comes from tourism and postage stamp sales.

SÃO TOMÉ AND PRÍNCIPE

Status: REPUBLIC
Area: 964 sq km (372 sq mls)
Population: 127,000
Capital: SÃO TOMÉ
Language: PORTUGUESE, PORTUGUESE CREOLE
Religion: R.CATHOLIC, PROTESTANT
Currency: DOBRA
Organizations: OAU, UN

MAP PAGE: 54

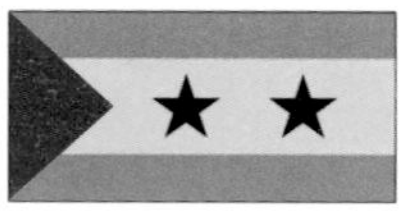

THE TWO MAIN islands and adjacent islets lie off the coast of west Africa in the Gulf of Guinea. São Tomé is the larger island and supports over 90 per cent of the population. Both São Tomé and Príncipe are mountainous and tree-covered, and have a hot and humid climate. The economy is heavily dependent on cocoa, which accounts for over 90 per cent of export earnings.

SAUDI ARABIA

Status: MONARCHY
Area: 2,200,000 sq km (849,425 sq mls)
Population: 17,880,000
Capital: RIYADH
Language: ARABIC
Religion: SUNNI MUSLIM, SHI'A MUSLIM
Currency: RIYAL
Organizations: OPEC, UN

MAP PAGE: 20

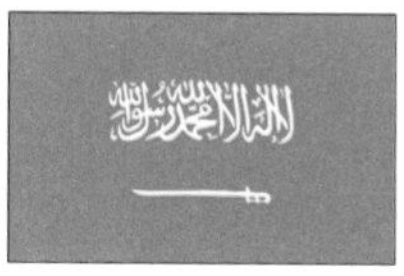

SAUDI ARABIA OCCUPIES most of the Arabian peninsula in southwest Asia. The terrain is desert or semi-desert plateaux, which rise to mountains running parallel to the Red Sea in the west and slope down to plains in the southeast and along The Gulf in the east. Most people live in urban areas, one third in the cities of Riyadh, Jiddah and Mecca. Summers are hot, winters are warm and rainfall is low. Saudi Arabia has the world's largest reserves of oil and gas, located in the northeast, both onshore and in The Gulf. Crude oil and refined products account for over 90 per cent of export earnings. Other industries and irrigated agrculture are being encouraged, but most food and raw materials are imported. Saudi Arabia has important banking and commercial interests. Each year 2 million pilgrims visit Islam's holiest cities, Mecca and Medina, in the west.

SENEGAL

Status: REPUBLIC
Area: 196,720 sq km (75,954 sq mls)
Population: 8,347,000
Capital: DAKAR
Language: FRENCH (OFFICIAL), WOLOF, FULANI, LOCAL LANGUAGES
Religion: SUNNI MUSLIM, R.CATHOLIC, TRAD.BELIEFS
Currency: CFA FRANC
Organizations: OAU, UN

MAP PAGE: 54

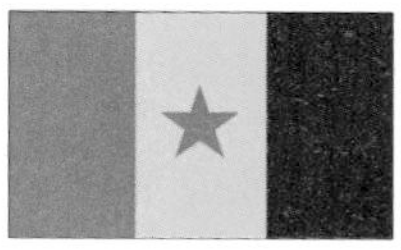

SENEGAL LIES ON the Atlantic coast of west Africa. The north is arid semi-desert, while the south is mainly fertile savannah bushland. The climate is tropical with summer rains, though droughts occur. One fifth of the population lives in Dakar. Groundnuts, phosphates and fish are the main resources. There is some oil refining and Dakar is a major port. Senegal relies heavily on aid.

SEYCHELLES

Status: REPUBLIC
Area: 455 sq km (176 sq mls)
Population: 75,000
Capital: VICTORIA
Language: SEYCHELLOIS (SESELWA, FRENCH CREOLE), ENGLISH
Religion: R.CATHOLIC, PROTESTANT
Currency: RUPEE
Organizations: COMM., OAU, UN

MAP PAGE: 53

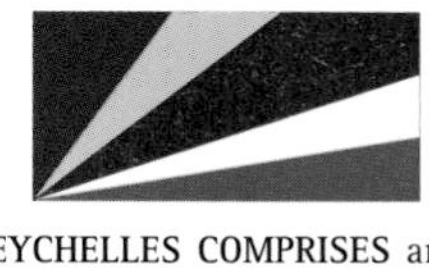

THE SEYCHELLES COMPRISES an archipelago of 115 granitic and coral islands in the western Indian Ocean. The main island, Mahé, contains about 90 per cent of the population. The climate is hot and humid with heavy rainfall. The economy is based mainly on tourism, transit trade, and light manufacturing, with fishing and agriculture (chiefly copra, cinnamon and tea) also important.

SIERRA LEONE
Status: REPUBLIC
Area: 71,740 sq km (27,699 sq mls)
Population: 4,509,000
Capital: FREETOWN
Language: ENGLISH, CREOLE, MENDE, TEMNE, LOCAL LANGUAGES
Religion: TRAD. BELIEFS, SUNNI MUSLIM, PROTESTANT, R.CATHOLIC
Currency: LEONE
Organizations: COMM., OAU, UN

MAP PAGE: 54

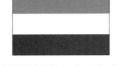

SIERRA LEONE LIES on the Atlantic coast of west Africa. Its coast is heavily indented and lined with mangrove swamps. Inland is a forested area rising to savannah plateaux, with the mountains to the northeast. The climate is tropical and rainfall is heavy. Most of the workforce is involved in subsistence farming. Cocoa and coffee are the main cash crops, but rutile (titanium ore), bauxite and diamonds are the main exports. Civil war and economic decline have caused serious difficulties.

SINGAPORE
Status: REPUBLIC
Area: 639 sq km (247 sq mls)
Population: 2,987,000
Capital: SINGAPORE
Language: CHINESE, ENGLISH, MALAY, TAMIL
Religion: BUDDHIST, TAOIST, SUNNI MUSLIM, CHRISTIAN, HINDU
Currency: DOLLAR
Organizations: ASEAN, COMM., UN

MAP PAGE: 32

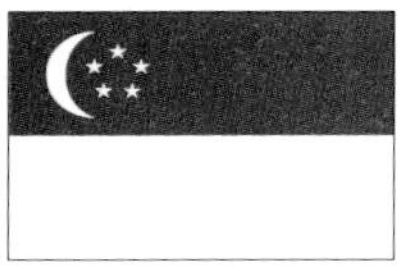

THE STATE COMPRISES the main island of Singapore and 57 other islands, lying off the southern tip of the Malay Peninsula in southeast Asia. A causeway links Singapore to the mainland across the Johor Strait. Singapore is generally low-lying and includes land reclaimed from swamps. It is hot and humid, with heavy rainfall throughout the year. There are fish farms and vegetable gardens in the north and east of the island, but most food needs must be imported. Singapore also lacks mineral and energy resources. Manufacturing industries and services are the main sectors of the economy. Their rapid development has fuelled the nation's impressive economic growth over the last three decades to become the richest of Asia's four 'little dragons'. The main industries include electronics, oil refining, chemicals, pharmaceuticals, ship building and repair, iron and steel, food processing and textiles. Singapore is a major financial centre. Its port is one of the world's largest and busiest and acts as an entrepot for neighbouring states. Tourism is also important.

SLOVAKIA
Status: REPUBLIC
Area: 49,035 sq km (18,933 sq mls)
Population: 5,364,000
Capital: BRATISLAVA
Language: SLOVAK, HUNGARIAN, CZECH
Religion: R.CATHOLIC, PROTESTANT, ORTHODOX
Currency: KORUNA
Organizations: UN

MAP PAGE: 46-47

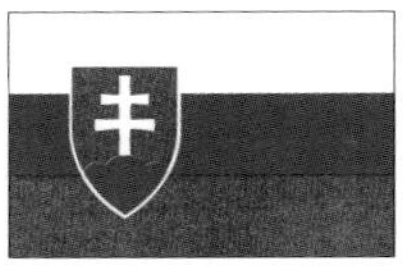

A LANDLOCKED COUNTRY in central Europe, Slovakia borders the Czech Republic, Poland, Ukraine, Hungary and Austria. Slovakia is mountainous along the border with Poland in the north, but low-lying along the plains of the Danube in the southwest. The climate is continental. Slovakia is the smaller, less populous and less developed part of former Czechoslovakia. With few natural resources, uncompetitive heavy industry and loss of federal subsidies, the economy has suffered economic difficulties.

SLOVENIA
Status: REPUBLIC
Area: 20,251 sq km (7,819 sq mls)
Population: 1,984,000
Capital: LJUBLJANA
Language: SLOVENE, SERBO-CROAT
Religion: R.CATHOLIC, PROTESTANT
Currency: TÓLAR
Organizations: UN

MAP PAGE: 48

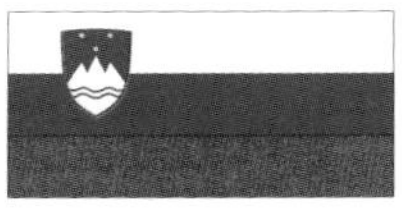

SLOVENIA LIES IN the northwest Balkans of south Europe and has a short coastline on the Adriatic Sea. It is mountainous and hilly, with lowlands on the coast and in the Sava and Drava river valleys. The climate is generally continental, but Mediterranean nearer the coast. Dairy farming, mercury mining, light manufacturing and tourism are the main activities. Conflict in the other former Yugoslav states, which has affected tourism and international trade, has caused serious economic problems.

SOLOMON ISLANDS
Status: MONARCHY
Area: 28,370 sq km (10,954 sq mls)
Population: 378,000
Capital: HONIARA
Language: ENGLISH, SOLOMON ISLANDS PIDGIN, MANY LOCAL LANGUAGES
Religion: PROTESTANT, R.CATHOLIC
Currency: DOLLAR
Organizations: COMM., UN

MAP PAGE: 7

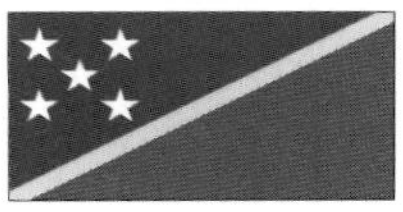

THE STATE CONSISTS of the southern Solomon, Santa Cruz and Shortland islands in Australasia. The six main islands are volcanic, mountainous and forested, though Guadalcanal, the most populous, has a large area of flat land. The climate is generally hot and humid. Subsistence farming and fishing predominate. Exports include fish, timber, copra and palm oil. The islands depend on foreign aid.

SOMALIA
Status: REPUBLIC
Area: 637,657 sq km (246,201 sq mls)
Population: 9,250,000
Capital: MOGADISHU
Language: SOMALI, ARABIC (OFFICIAL)
Religion: SUNNI MUSLIM
Currency: SHILLING
Organizations: OAU, UN

MAP PAGE: 56

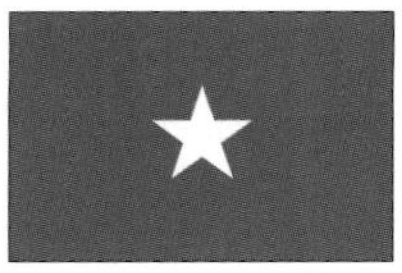

SOMALIA IS IN the Horn of northeast Africa, on the Gulf of Aden and Indian Ocean. It consists of a dry scrubby plateau, rising to highlands in the north. The climate is hot and dry, but coastal areas and the Jubba and Shebele river valleys support crops and the bulk of the population. Subsistence farming and herding are the main activities. Exports include livestock and bananas. Drought and war have ruined the economy.

SOUTH AFRICA
Status: REPUBLIC
Area: 1,219,080 sq km (470,689 sq mls)
Population: 41,244,000
Capital: PRETORIA/CAPE TOWN
Language: AFRIKAANS, ENGLISH, NINE LOCAL LANGUAGES (ALL OFFICIAL)
Religion: PROTESTANT, R.CATHOLIC, SUNNI MUSLIM, HINDU
Currency: RAND
Organizations: COMM., OAU, SADC, UN

MAP PAGE: 58-59

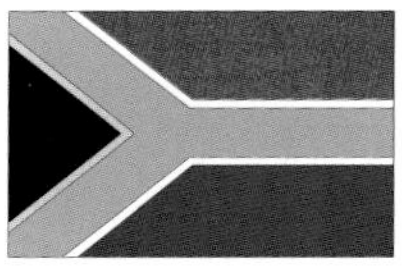

SOUTH AFRICA OCCUPIES most of the southern part of Africa. It borders five states, surrounds Lesotho and has a long coastline on the Atlantic and Indian oceans. Much of the land is a vast plateau, covered with grassland or bush and drained by the Orange and Limpopo river systems. A fertile coastal plain rises to mountain ridges in the south and east, including Table Mountain near Cape Town and the Drakensberg range in the east. Gauteng is the most populous province, with Johannesburg and Pretoria its main cities. South Africa has warm summers and mild winters. Most of the country has rainfall in summer, but the coast around Cape Town has winter rains. South Africa is the largest and most developed economy in Africa, though wealth is unevenly distributed. Agriculture provides one third of exports, including fruit, wine, wool and maize. South Africa is rich in minerals. It is the world's leading producer of gold, which accounts for one third of export earnings. Coal, diamonds, platinum, uranium, chromite and other minerals are also mined. The main industries process minerals and agricultural produce, and manufacture chemical products, motor vehicles, electrical equipment and textiles. Financial services are also important.

SOUTH KOREA
Status: REPUBLIC
Area: 99,274 sq km (38,330 sq mls)
Population: 44,851,000
Capital: SEOUL
Language: KOREAN
Religion: BUDDHIST, PROTESTANT, R.CATHOLIC, CONFUCIAN, TRADITIONAL
Currency: WON
Organizations: UN, OECD

MAP PAGE: 30

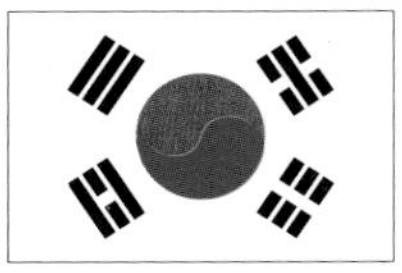

THE STATE CONSISTS of the southern half of the Korean Peninsula in east Asia and many islands lying off the western and southern coasts in the Yellow Sea. The terrain is mountainous, though less rugged than that of North Korea. Population density is high and most people live on the western coastal plains and in the Han basin in the northwest and Naktong basin in the southeast. South Korea has a continental climate, with hot, wet summers and dry, cold winters. Arable land is limited by the mountainous terrain, but because of intensive farming South Korea is nearly self-sufficient in food. Sericulture is important as is fishing, which contributes to exports. South Korea has few mineral resources, except for coal and tungsten. It is one of Asia's four 'little dragons' (Hong Kong, Singapore and Taiwan being the others), which have achieved high economic growth based mainly on export manufacturing. In South Korea industry is dominated by a few giant conglomerates, such as Hyundai and Samsung. The main manufactures are cars, electronic and electrical goods, ships, steel, chemicals, and toys as well as textiles, clothing, footwear and food products. Banking and other financial services are increasingly important.

SPAIN
Status: MONARCHY
Area: 504,782 sq km (194,897 sq mls)
Population: 39,210,000
Capital: MADRID
Language: SPANISH, CATALAN, GALICIAN, BASQUE
Religion: R.CATHOLIC
Currency: PESETA
Organizations: EU, OECD, UN

MAP PAGE: 45

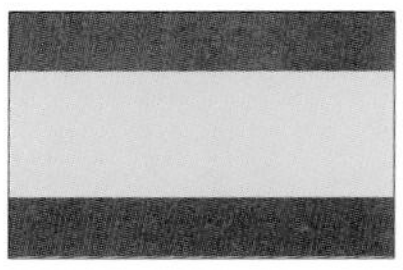

SPAIN OCCUPIES THE greater part of the Iberian peninsula in southwest Europe, with coastlines on the Atlantic Ocean (Bay of Biscay and Gulf of Cadiz) and Mediterranean Sea. It includes the Balearic and Canary island groups in the Mediterranean and Atlantic, and two enclaves in north Africa. Much of the mainland is a high plateau, the Meseta, drained by the Duero, Tagus and Guadiana rivers. The plateau is interrupted by a low mountain range and bounded to the east and north also by mountains, including the Pyrenees which form the border with France and Andorra. The main lowland areas are the Ebro basin in the northeast, the eastern coastal plains and the Guadalquivir basin in the southwest. Three quarters of the population lives in urban areas, chiefly Madrid and Barcelona, which alone contain one quarter of the population. The plateau experiences hot summers and cold winters. Conditions are cooler and wetter to the north, though warmer and drier to the south. Agriculture involves about 10 per cent of the workforce and fruit, vegetables and wine are exported. Fishing is an important industry and Spain has a large fishing fleet. Mineral resources include iron, lead, copper and mercury. Some oil is produced, but Spain has to import most energy needs. The economy is based mainly on manufacturing and services. Manufacturing industries account for one third of national income and are based mainly around Madrid and Barcelona. The principal products are machinery and transport equip-

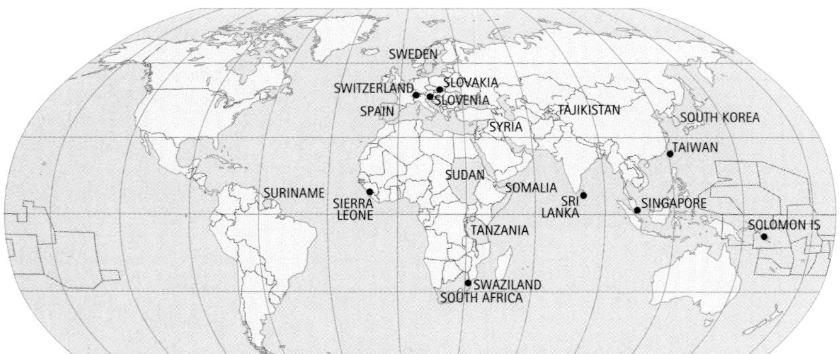

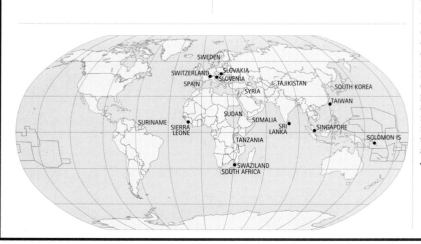

ment. Spain is a leading manufacturer of motor vehicles (SEAT). Other manufactures are agricultural products, chemicals, steel and other metals, paper products, wood and cork products, clothing and footwear, and textiles. With some 50 million visitors a year, tourism is a major industry, accounting for 10 per cent of national income and employing about the same percentage of the workforce. Banking and commerce are also important.

SRI LANKA
Status: REPUBLIC
Area: 65,610 sq km (25,332 sq mls)
Population: 18,354,000
Capital: COLOMBO
Language: SINHALESE, TAMIL, ENGLISH
Religion: BUDDHIST, HINDU,
SUNNI MUSLIM, R.CATHOLIC
Currency: RUPEE
Organizations: COMM., UN

MAP PAGE: 21

SRI LANKA LIES in the Indian Ocean off the southeast coast of India in south Asia. It has rolling coastal plains with mountains in the centre-south. The climate is hot and monsoonal and most people live on the west coast. Manufactures (chiefly textiles and clothing), tea, rubber, copra and gems are exported. The economy relies on aid and workers' remittances. Tourism has been damaged by separatist activities.

SUDAN
Status: REPUBLIC
Area: 2,505,813 sq km (967,500 sq mls)
Population: 28,098,000
Capital: KHARTOUM
Language: ARABIC, DINKA, NUBIAN,
BEJA, NUER, LOCAL LANGUAGES
Religion: SUNNI MUSLIM, TRAD.
BELIEFS, R.CATHOLIC, PROTESTANT
Currency: DINAR
Organizations: OAU, UN

MAP PAGE: 55

AFRICA'S LARGEST COUNTRY, Sudan is in northeast Africa, on the Red Sea. It lies within the Upper Nile basin, much of which is arid plain but with swamps to the south. Mountains lie to the northeast and south. The climate is hot and arid with light summer rainfall, though droughts occur. Most people live along the Nile and are farmers and herders. Cotton, gum arabic, livestock and other agricultural products are exported. In southern Sudan civil war has ruined the economy.

SURINAME
Status: REPUBLIC
Area: 163,820 sq km (63,251 sq mls)
Population: 423,000
Capital: PARAMARIBO
Language: DUTCH, SURINAMESE
(SRANAN TONGO), ENGLISH, HINDI,
JAVANESE
Religion: HINDU, R.CATHOLIC,
PROTESTANT, SUNNI MUSLIM
Currency: GUILDER
Organizations: CARICOM, UN

MAP PAGE: 87

SURINAME, ON THE Atlantic coast of northern South America, consists of a swampy coastal plain (where most people live), central plateaux and the Guiana Highlands. The climate is tropical and rainforest covers much of the land. Bauxite mining is the main industry.

Alumina and aluminium are the chief exports, with shrimps, rice, bananas and timber. Suriname depends on Dutch aid.

SWAZILAND
Status: MONARCHY
Area: 17,364 sq km (6,704 sq mls)
Population: 908,000
Capital: MBABANE
Language: SWAZI (SISWATI), ENGLISH
Religion: PROTESTANT, R.CATHOLIC,
TRAD.BELIEFS
Currency: EMALANGENI
Organizations: COMM., OAU, SADC, UN

MAP PAGE: 59

LANDLOCKED SWAZILAND IN southern Africa lies between Mozambique and South Africa. Savannah plateaux descend from mountains in the west towards hill country in the east. The climate is subtropical, temperate in the mountains. Subsistence farming predominates. Asbestos, coal and diamonds are mined. Exports include sugar, fruit and wood pulp. Tourism and workers' remittances are important.

SWEDEN
Status: MONARCHY
Area: 449,964 sq km (173,732 sq mls)
Population: 8,831,000
Capital: STOCKHOLM
Language: SWEDISH
Religion: PROTESTANT, R.CATHOLIC
Currency: KRONA
Organizations: EU, OECD, UN

MAP PAGE: 36-37

SWEDEN, THE LARGEST and most populous of the Scandinavian countries, occupies the eastern part of the peninsula in north Europe and borders the North and Baltic Seas and Gulf of Bothnia. Forested mountains cover the northern half of the country, part of which lies within the Arctic Circle. Southwards is a lowland lake region, where most of the population lives. Farther south is an upland region, and then a fertile plain at the tip of the peninsula. Sweden has warm summers and cold winters, though the latter are longer and more severe in the north and milder in the far south. Sweden's natural resources include coniferous forests, mineral deposits and water resources. There is little agriculture, though some dairy products, meat, cereals and vegetables are produced in the south. The forests supply timber for export and for the important pulp, paper and furniture industries. Sweden is one of the world's leading producers of iron ore. Copper, zinc, lead, uranium and other metallic ores are also mined. Mineral industries, chiefly iron and steel, are the basis for the production of a range of products, but chiefly machinery and transport equipment of which cars and trucks (Volvo and Saab) are the most important export. Sweden also manufactures chemicals, electrical goods (Electrolux) and telecommunications equipment (Ericsson). Like their Scandinavian neighbours, Swedes enjoy a high standard of living.

SWITZERLAND
Status: FEDERATION
Area: 41,293 sq km (15,943 sq mls)
Population: 7,040,000
Capital: BERN
Language: GERMAN, FRENCH, ITALIAN,
ROMANSCH
Religion: R.CATHOLIC, PROTESTANT
Currency: FRANC
Organizations: OECD

MAP PAGE: 46

SWITZERLAND IS A landlocked country of southwest Europe that is surrounded by France, Germany, Austria, Liechtenstein and Italy. It is also Europe's most mountainous country. The southern half of the nation lies within the Alps, while the northwest is dominated by the Jura mountains. The rest of the land is a high plateau, which contains the bulk of the population and economic activity. The climate varies greatly, depending on altitude and relief, but in general summers are mild and winters are cold with heavy snowfalls. Switzerland has one of the highest standards of living in the world. Yet it has few mineral resources and, owing to its mountainous terrain, agriculture is based mainly on dairy and stock farming. Most food and industrial raw materials have to be imported. Manufacturing makes the largest contribution to the economy and though varied is specialist in certain products. Engineering is the most important industry, producing precision instruments such as scientific and optical instruments, watches and clocks, and heavy machinery such as turbines and generators. Other industries produce chemicals, pharmaceuticals, metal products, textiles, clothing and food products (cheese and chocolate). Banking and other financial services are very important and Zurich is one of the world's leading banking cities. Tourism and international organisations based in Switzerland are also major foreign currency earners.

SYRIA
Status: REPUBLIC
Area: 185,180 sq km (71,498 sq mls)
Population: 14,186,000
Capital: DAMASCUS
Language: ARABIC, KURDISH,
ARMENIAN
Religion: SUNNI MUSLIM,
OTHER MUSLIM, CHRISTIAN
Currency: POUND
Organizations: UN

MAP PAGE: 16-17

SYRIA IS IN southwest Asia, on the Mediterranean Sea. Behind the coastal plain lies a range of hills and then a plateau cut by the Euphrates river. Mountains flank the borders with Lebanon and Israel, east of which is desert. The climate is Mediterranean in coastal regions, hotter and drier inland. Most Syrians live on the coast or in the river valleys. Cotton, cereals and fruit are important, but the main exports are petroleum and its products, textiles and chemicals. Syria receives support from Gulf states.

TAIWAN
Status: REPUBLIC
Area: 36,179 sq km (13,969 sq mls)
Population: 21,211,000
Capital: T'AI-PEI
Language: CHINESE (MANDARIN
OFFICIAL, FUKIEN, HAKKA),
LOCAL LANGUAGES
Religion: BUDDHIST, TAOIST,
CONFUCIAN, CHRISTIAN
Currency: DOLLAR

MAP PAGE: 27

THE EAST ASIAN state consists of the island of Taiwan, separated from mainland China by the Taiwan Strait, and several much smaller islands. Much of Taiwan itself is mountainous and forested. Densely populated coastal plains in the west contain the bulk of the population and most economic activity. Taiwan has a tropical monsoon climate, with warm, wet summers and mild winters. Agriculture is highly productive. Taiwan is virtually self-sufficient in food and exports some products. Coal, oil and natural gas are produced and a few minerals are mined but none of them are of great significance to the economy. Taiwan depends heavily on imports of raw materials and exports of manufactured goods. The latter is equivalent to 50 per cent of national income. The country's main manufactures are electrical and electronic goods, including television sets, watches, personal computers and calculators. Other products include clothing, footwear (chiefly track shoes), textiles and toys. In contrast to mainland China, Taiwan has enjoyed considerable prosperity.

TAJIKISTAN
Status: REPUBLIC
Area: 143,100 sq km (55,251 sq mls)
Population: 5,836,000
Capital: DUSHANBE
Language: TAJIK, UZBEK, RUSSIAN
Religion: SUNNI MUSLIM
Currency: ROUBLE
Organizations: CIS, UN

MAP PAGE: 14-15

LANDLOCKED TAJIKISTAN IN central Asia is a mountainous country, occupying the western Tien Shan and part of the Pamir ranges. In less mountainous western areas summers are warm though winters are cold. Most activity is in the Fergana basin. Agriculture is the main sector of the economy, chiefly cotton growing and cattle breeding. Mineral and fuel deposits include lead, zinc, uranium and oil. Textiles and clothing are the main manufactures. Civil war has damaged the economy, which depends heavily on Russian support.

TANZANIA
Status: REPUBLIC
Area: 945,087 sq km (364,900 sq mls)
Population: 30,337,000
Capital: DODOMA
Language: SWAHILI, ENGLISH,
NYAMWEZI, MANY LOCAL
LANGUAGES
Religion: R.CATHOLIC, SUNNI MUSLIM,
TRAD. BELIEFS, PROTESTANT
Currency: SHILLING
Organizations: COMM., OAU, SADC, UN

MAP PAGE: 56-57

TANZANIA LIES ON the coast of east Africa and includes Zanzibar in the Indian Ocean. Most of the mainland is a savannah plateau lying east of the great Rift Valley. In the north are Mount Kilimanjaro and the Serengeti National Park. The climate is tropical and most people live on the narrow coastal plain or in the north. The economy is mainly agricultural. Coffee, cotton and sisal are the main exports, with cloves from Zanzibar. Agricultural processing and diamond mining are the main industries, though tourism is growing. Tanzania depends heavily on aid.

THAILAND

Status: MONARCHY
Area: 513,115 sq km (198,115 sq mls)
Population: 59,401,000
Capital: BANGKOK
Language: THAI, LAO, CHINESE, MALAY, MON-KHMER LANGUAGES
Religion: BUDDHIST, SUNNI MUSLIM
Currency: BAHT
Organizations: ASEAN, UN

MAP PAGE: 32

A COUNTRY IN southeast Asia, Thailand borders Myanmar, Laos, Cambodia and Malaysia and has coastlines on the Gulf of Thailand and Andaman Sea. Central Thailand is dominated by the Chao Phraya river basin, which contains Bangkok, the only major urban centre, and most economic activity. To the east is a dry plateau drained by tributaries of the Mekong river, while to the north, west and south, extending halfway down the Malay peninsula, are forested hills and mountains. Many small islands line the coast. The climate is hot, humid and monsoonal. About half the workforce is involved in agriculture. Thailand is the world's leading exporter of rice and rubber, and a major exporter of maize and tapioca. Fish and fish processing are important. Thailand produces natural gas, some oil and lignite, metallic ores (chiefly tin and tungsten) and gemstones. Manufacturing is the largest contributor to national income, with electronics, textiles, clothing and footwear, and food processing the main industries. With over 5 million visitors a year, tourism is the major source of foreign exchange.

TOGO

Status: REPUBLIC
Area: 56,785 sq km (21,925 sq mls)
Population: 4,138,000
Capital: LOMÉ
Language: FRENCH, EWE, KABRE, MANY LOCAL LANGUAGES
Religion: TRAD. BELIEFS, R.CATHOLIC, SUNNI MUSLIM, PROTESTANT
Currency: CFA FRANC
Organizations: OAU, UN

MAP PAGE: 54

T OGO IS A long narrow country in west Africa with a short coastline on the Gulf of Guinea. The interior consists of plateaux rising to mountainous areas. The climate is tropical, drier inland. Agriculture is the mainstay of the economy. Cotton, coffee and cocoa are exported, but phosphates are the main exports. Oil refining and food processing are the main industries. Lomé is an entrepôt trade centre.

TOKELAU

Status: NEW ZEALAND TERRITORY
Area: 10 sq km (4 sq mls)
Population: 2,000
Language: ENGLISH, TOKELAUAN

Religion: PROTESTANT, R.CATHOLIC
Currency: NZ DOLLAR

MAP PAGE: 7

TONGA

Status: MONARCHY
Area: 748 sq km (289 sq mls)
Population: 98,000
Capital: NUKU'ALOFA
Language: TONGAN, ENGLISH
Religion: PROTESTANT, R.CATHOLIC, MORMON
Currency: PA'ANGA
Organizations: COMM.

MAP PAGE: 7

T ONGA COMPRISES SOME 170 islands in the South Pacific Ocean, northeast of New Zealand. The three main groups are Tongatapu (where 60 per cent of Tongans live), Ha'apai and Vava'u. The climate is warm with good rainfall and the economy relies heavily on agriculture. Exports include coconut products, root crops, bananas and vanilla. Fishing, tourism and light industry are increasingly important.

TRINIDAD AND TOBAGO

Status: REPUBLIC
Area: 5,130 sq km (1,981 sq mls)
Population: 1,306,000
Capital: PORT OF SPAIN
Language: ENGLISH, CREOLE, HINDI
Religion: R.CATHOLIC, HINDU, PROTESTANT, SUNNI MUSLIM
Currency: DOLLAR
Organizations: CARICOM, COMM., UN

MAP PAGE: 83

T RINIDAD, THE MOST southerly Caribbean island, lies off the Venezuelan coast. It is hilly in the north, with a populous central plain. Tobago, to the northeast, is smaller, more mountainous and less developed. The climate is tropical. Oil and petrochemicals dominate the economy. Asphalt is also important. Sugar, fruit, cocoa and coffee are produced. Tourism is important on Tobago.

TUNISIA

Status: REPUBLIC
Area: 164,150 sq km (63,379 sq mls)
Population: 8,896,000
Capital: TUNIS
Language: ARABIC, FRENCH
Religion: SUNNI MUSLIM
Currency: DINAR
Organizations: OAU, UN

MAP PAGE: 54-55

T UNISIA IS ON the Mediterranean coast of north Africa. The north is mountainous with valleys and coastal plains, where most people live. Beyond a central area of salt pans are Saharan plains. The north has a Mediterranean climate, the south is hot and arid. Oil and phosphates are the main resources. Olive oil, citrus fruit and textiles are also exported. Tourism is important.

TURKEY

Status: REPUBLIC
Area: 779,452 sq km (300,948 sq mls)
Population: 61,644,000
Capital: ANKARA
Language: TURKISH, KURDISH
Religion: SUNNI MUSLIM, SHI'A MUSLIM
Currency: LIRA
Organizations: OECD, UN

MAP PAGE: 16-17

T URKEY OCCUPIES THE Asia Minor peninsula of southwest Asia and has coastlines on the Black, Mediterranean and Aegean seas. It includes eastern Thrace, which is in south Europe and separated from the rest of the country by the Bosporus, Sea of Marmara and Dardanelles. The Asian mainland consists of the semi-arid Anatolian plateau, flanked to the north, south and east by mountains. Over 40 per cent of Turks live in central Anatolia and the Marmara and Aegean coastal plains. The coast has a Mediterranean climate, but inland conditions are more extreme with hot, dry summers and cold, snowy winters. Agriculture involves about half the workforce and exports include cotton, tobacco, fruit, nuts and livestock. Turkey is one of the world's major producers of chrome. Coal and lignite, petroleum, iron ore and boron are also exploited. Apart from food products, the main manufactures are textiles (the chief export), iron and steel, vehicles and chemicals. With over 7 million visitors a year, tourism is a major industry. Remittances by workers aboard are also important.

TURKMENISTAN

Status: REPUBLIC
Area: 488,100 sq km (188,456 sq mls)
Population: 4,099,000
Capital: ASHGABAT
Language: TURKMEN, RUSSIAN
Religion: SUNNI MUSLIM
Currency: MANAT
Organizations: CIS, UN

MAP PAGE: 14

T URKMENISTAN, IN CENTRAL Asia, lies mainly within the desert plains of the Kara Kum. Most people live on the fringes: the foothills of the Kopet Dag in the south, Amudarya valley in the north and Caspian Sea plains in the west. The climate is dry with extreme temperatures. The economy is based mainly on irrigated agriculture, chiefly cotton growing. Turkmenistan is rich in oil, natural gas (the main export) and minerals.

TURKS AND CAICOS ISLANDS

Status: UK TERRITORY
Area: 430 sq km (166 sq mls)
Population: 14,000
Capital: GRAND TURK
Language: ENGLISH
Religion: PROTESTANT
Currency: US DOLLAR

MAP PAGE: 83

T HE STATE CONSISTS of 40 or so low-lying islands and cays in the northern Caribbean. Only eight islands are inhabited, two fifths of people living on Grand Turk and Salt Cay. The climate is tropical. The islands depend on fishing, tourism and offshore banking.

TUVALU

Status: MONARCHY
Area: 25 sq km (10 sq mls)
Population: 10,000
Capital: FONGAFALE
Language: TUVALUAN, ENGLISH (OFFICIAL)
Religion: PROTESTANT
Currency: DOLLAR
Organizations: COMM.

MAP PAGE: 7

T UVALU COMPRISES NINE coral atolls in the South Pacific Ocean. One third of the population lives on Funafuti and most people depend on subsistence farming and fishing. The islands export copra, stamps and clothing, but rely heavily on UK aid.

UGANDA

Status: REPUBLIC
Area: 241,038 sq km (93,065 sq mls)
Population: 19,848,000
Capital: KAMPALA
Language: ENGLISH, SWAHILI (OFFICIAL), LUGANDA, MANY LOCAL LANGUAGES
Religion: R.CATHOLIC, PROTESTANT, SUNNI MUSLIM, TRAD. BELIEFS
Currency: SHILLING
Organizations: COMM., OAU, UN

MAP PAGE: 56

A LANDLOCKED COUNTRY in east Africa, Uganda consists of a savannah plateau with mountains and lakes. It includes part of Lake Victoria from which the Nile flows northwards to Sudan. The climate is warm and wet. Most people live in the southern half of the country. Agriculture dominates the economy. Coffee is the main export, with some cotton and tea. Uganda relies heavily on aid.

UKRAINE

Status: REPUBLIC
Area: 603,700 sq km (233,090 sq mls)
Population: 51,639,000
Capital: KIEV
Language: UKRAINIAN, RUSSIAN, REGIONAL LANGUAGES
Religion: UKRAINIAN ORTHODOX, R.CATHOLIC
Currency: HRYVNIA
Organizations: CIS, UN

MAP PAGE: 51

U KRAINE LIES ON the Black Sea coast of east Europe. Much of the land is steppe, generally flat and treeless, but with rich black soil and drained by the river Dnieper. Along the border with Belarus are forested, marshy plains. The only uplands are the Carpathian mountains in the west and smaller ranges on the Crimean peninsula. Summers are warm and winters are

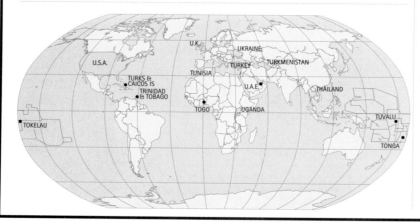

cold, with milder conditions in the Crimea. About a quarter of the population lives in the mainly industrial provinces of Donetsk, Kiev and Dnepropetrovsk. The Ukraine is rich in natural resources: fertile soil, substantial mineral deposits and forests. Agriculture, livestock raising and viticulture are important, but mining and manufacturing predominate, contributing over 40 per cent of national income. Coal mining, iron and steel production, engineering and chemicals are the main industries. Output has fallen and few state enterprises have been privatized since Ukraine became independent in 1991.

UNITED ARAB EMIRATES
(UAE)
Status: FEDERATION
Area: 77,700 sq km (30,000 sq mls)
Population: 2,314,000
Capital: ABU DHABI
Language: ARABIC (OFFICIAL), ENGLISH, HINDI, URDU, FARSI
Religion: SUNNI MUSLIM, SHI'A MUSLIM, CHRISTIAN
Currency: DIRHAM
Organizations: OPEC, UN

MAP PAGE: 20

THE UAE IS in east-central Arabia, southwest Asia. Six emirates lie on The Gulf while the seventh, Fujairah, fronts the Gulf of Oman. Most of the land is flat desert with sand dunes and salt pans. The only hilly area is in the northeast. Three emirates - Abu Dhabi, Dubai and Sharjah - contain 85 per cent of the population. Summers are hot and winters are mild with occasional rainfall in coastal areas. Fruit and vegetables are grown in oases and irrigated areas. The state's wealth is based on hydrocarbons, mainly within Abu Dhabi, but with smaller supplies in Dubai, Sharjah and Ras al Khaimah. Dubai is a thriving entrepot trade centre.

ABU DHABI
Status: EMIRATE
Area: 64,750 sq km (25,000 sq miles)
Population: 800,000

AJMAN
Status: EMIRATE
Area: 260 sq km (100 sq miles)
Population: 76,000

DUBAI
Status: EMIRATE
Area: 3,900 sq km (1,506 sq miles)
Population: 500,000

FUJAIRAH
Status: EMIRATE
Area: 1,170 sq km (452 sq miles)
Population: 63,000

RAS AL KHAIMAH
Status: EMIRATE
Area: 1,690 sq km (653 sq miles)
Population: 130,000

SHARJAH
Status: EMIRATE
Area: 2,600 sq km (1,004 sq miles)
Population: 314,000

UMM AL QAIWAIN
Status: EMIRATE
Area: 780 sq km (301 sq miles)
Population: 27,000

UNITED KINGDOM
(UK)
Status: MONARCHY
Area: 244,082 sq km (94,241 sq mls)
Population: 58,258,000
Capital: LONDON
Language: ENGLISH, SOUTH INDIAN LANGUAGES, CHINESE, WELSH, GAELIC
Religion: PROTESTANT, R.CATHOLIC, MUSLIM, SIKH, HINDU, JEWISH
Currency: POUND
Organizations: COMM., EU, OECD, UN

MAP PAGE: 34

A COUNTRY OF northwest Europe, the United Kingdom occupies the island of Great Britain, part of Ireland and many small adjacent islands in the Atlantic Ocean. Great Britain comprises the countries of England, Scotland and Wales. England covers over half the land area and supports over four-fifths of the population, chiefly in the southeast region. The landscape is flat or rolling with some uplands, notably the Cheviot Hills on the Scottish border, the Pennines in the centre-north and the Cumbrian mountains in the northwest. Scotland consists of southern uplands, central lowlands, highlands (which include the UK's highest peak) and islands. Wales is a land of mountains and river valleys. Northern Ireland contains uplands, plains and the UK's largest lake, Lough Neagh. The climate is mild, wet and variable. The UK has few mineral deposits, but has important energy resources. Over 40 per cent of land is suitable for grazing, over 25 per cent is cultivated, and 10 per cent is forested. Agriculture involves mainly sheep and cattle raising and dairy farming, with crop and fruit growing in the east and southeast. Productivity is high, but about one third of food needs must be imported. Both forestry and fishing are also important. The UK produces petroleum and natural gas from reserves in the North Sea and is self-sufficient in energy in net terms. It also has reserves of coal, though the coal industry has contracted in recent years. Manufacturing accounts for over 20 per cent of national income and relies heavily on imported raw materials. Major manufactures are food and drinks, motor vehicles and parts, aerospace equipment, machinery, electronic and electrical equipment, and chemicals and chemical products. However, the economy is dominated by service industries, including banking, insurance, finance, business services, retail and catering. London is one of the world's major banking, financial and insurance capitals. Tourism is a major industry, with over 18 million visitors a year. International trade is also important, equivalent to a third of national income and the UK has a large merchant fleet.

ENGLAND
Status: CONSTITUENT COUNTRY
Area: 130,423 sq km (50,357 sq miles)
Population: 48,532,700
Capital: LONDON

NORTHERN IRELAND
Status: CONSTITUENT REGION
Area: 14,121 sq km (5,452 sq miles)
Population: 1,631,800
Capital: BELFAST

SCOTLAND
Status: CONSTITUENT COUNTRY
Area: 78,772 sq km (30,414 sq miles)
Population: 5,120,200
Capital: EDINBURGH

WALES
Status: PRINCIPALITY
Area: 20,766 sq km (8,018 sq miles)
Population: 2,906,500
Capital: CARDIFF

UNITED STATES OF AMERICA
(USA)
Status: REPUBLIC
Area: 9,809,386 sq km (3,787,425 sq mls)
Population: 263,034,000
Capital: WASHINGTON D.C.
Language: ENGLISH, SPANISH, AMERINDIAN LANGUAGES
Religion: PROTESTANT, R.CATHOLIC, SUNNI MUSLIM, JEWISH, MORMON
Currency: DOLLAR
Organizations: NAFTA, OECD, UN

MAP PAGE: 70-71

THE USA COMPRISES 48 contiguous states in North America, bounded by Canada and Mexico, and the states of Alaska, to the northwest of Canada, and Hawaii, in the Pacific Ocean. The populous eastern states consist of the Atlantic coastal plain (which includes the Florida peninsula and the Gulf of Mexico coast) and the Appalachian mountains. The central states form a vast interior plain drained by the Mississippi-Missouri river system. To the west lie the Rocky Mountains, separated from the Pacific coastal ranges by the intermontane plateaux. The coastal ranges, which are prone to earthquakes, extend northwards into Alaska. Hawaii is a group of some 20 volcanic islands. Climatic conditions range between arctic in Alaska to desert in the intermontane plateaux. Most of the USA is temperate, though the interior has continental conditions. The USA has abundant natural resources. It has major reserves minerals and energy resources. About 20 per cent of the land can be used for crops, over 25 per cent is suitable for livestock rearing and over 30 per cent is forested. The USA has the largest economy in the world, which is based mainly on manufacturing and services. Though agriculture accounts for only about 2 per cent national income, productivity is high and the USA is a net exporter of food, chiefly grains and fruit. Major industrial crops include cotton, tobacco and sugarbeet. Livestock rearing, forestry and fishing are also important. Mining is well developed. The USA produces iron ore, bauxite, copper, lead, zinc, phosphate and many other minerals. It is a major producer of coal, petroleum and natural gas, though being the world's biggest energy user it must import significant quanities of petroleum and its products. Manufacturing is well diversified. The main products are: iron, steel and aluminium metals and products, machinery, transport equipment (chiefly motor vehicles and aircraft), electrical and electronic goods, food products, chemicals, textiles and clothing. Tourism is a major foreign currency earner. Other important service industries are banking and finance, and Wall Street in New York is a major stock exchange.

ALABAMA
Status: STATE
Area: 135,775 sq km (52,423 sq miles)
Population: 4,273,084
Capital: MONTGOMERY

ALASKA
Status: STATE
Area: 1,700,130 sq km (656,424 sq miles)
Population: 607,007
Capital: JUNEAU

ARIZONA
Status: STATE
Area: 295,274 sq km (114,006 sq miles)
Population: 4,428,068
Capital: PHOENIX

ARKANSAS
Status: STATE
Area: 137,741 sq km (53,182 sq miles)
Population: 2,509,793
Capital: LITTLE ROCK

CALIFORNIA
Status: STATE
Area: 423,999 sq km (163,707 sq miles)
Population: 31,878,234
Capital: SACRAMENTO

COLORADO
Status: STATE
Area: 269,618 sq km (104,100 sq miles)
Population: 3,822,676
Capital: DENVER

CONNECTICUT
Status: STATE
Area: 14,359 sq km (5,544 sq miles)
Population: 3,274,238
Capital: HARTFORD

DISTRICT OF COLUMBIA
Status: FEDERAL DISTRICT
Area: 176 sq km (68 sq miles)
Population: 543,213
Capital: WASHINGTON

DELAWARE
Status: STATE
Area: 6,446 sq km (2,489 sq miles)
Population: 724,842
Capital: DOVER

FLORIDA
Status: STATE
Area: 170,312 sq km (65,758 sq miles)
Population: 14,399,985
Capital: TALLAHASSEE

GEORGIA
Status: STATE
Area: 153,951 sq km (59,441 sq miles)
Population: 7,353,225
Capital: ATLANTA

HAWAII
Status: STATE
Area: 28,314 sq km (10,932 sq miles)
Population: 1,183,723
Capital: HONOLULU

IDAHO
Status: STATE
Area: 216,456 sq km (83,574 sq miles)
Population: 1,189,251
Capital: BOISE

ILLINOIS
Status: STATE
Area: 150,007 sq km (57,918 sq miles)
Population: 11,846,544
Capital: SPRINGFIELD

INDIANA
Status: STATE
Area: 94,327 sq km (36,420 sq miles)
Population: 5,840,528
Capital: INDIANAPOLIS

IOWA
Status: STATE
Area: 145,754 sq km (56,276 sq miles)
Population: 2,851,792
Capital: DES MOINES

KANSAS
Status: STATE
Area: 213,109 sq km (82,282 sq miles)
Population: 2,572,150
Capital: TOPEKA

KENTUCKY
Status: STATE
Area: 104,664 sq km (40,411 sq miles)
Population: 3,883,723
Capital: FRANKFORT

LOUISIANA
Status: STATE
Area: 134,273 sq km (51,843 sq miles)
Population: 4,350,579
Capital: BATON ROUGE

USA
continued

MAINE
Status: STATE
Area: 91,652 sq km (35,387 sq miles)
Population: 1,243,316
Capital: AUGUSTA

MARYLAND
Status: STATE
Area: 32,134 sq km (12,407 sq miles)
Population: 5,071,604
Capital: ANNAPOLIS

MASSACHUSETTS
Status: STATE
Area: 27,337 sq km (10,555 sq miles)
Population: 6,092,352
Capital: BOSTON

MICHIGAN
Status: STATE
Area: 250,737 sq km (96,810 sq miles)
Population: 9,594,350
Capital: LANSING

MINNESOTA
Status: STATE
Area: 225,181 sq km (86,943 sq miles)
Population: 4,657,758
Capital: ST PAUL

MISSISSIPPI
Status: STATE
Area: 125,443 sq km (48,434 sq miles)
Population: 2,716,115
Capital: JACKSON

MISSOURI
Status: STATE
Area: 180,545 sq km (69,709 sq miles)
Population: 5,358,692
Capital: JEFFERSON CITY

MONTANA
Status: STATE
Area: 380,847 sq km (147,046 sq miles)
Population: 879,372
Capital: HELENA

NEBRASKA
Status: STATE
Area: 200,356 sq km (77,358 sq miles)
Population: 1,652,093
Capital: LINCOLN

NEVADA
Status: STATE
Area: 286,367 sq km (110,567 sq miles)
Population: 1,603,163
Capital: CARSON CITY

NEW HAMPSHIRE
Status: STATE
Area: 24,219 sq km (9,351 sq miles)
Population: 1,162,481
Capital: CONCORD

NEW JERSEY
Status: STATE
Area: 22,590 sq km (8,722 sq miles)
Population: 7,987,933
Capital: TRENTON

NEW MEXICO
Status: STATE
Area: 314,937 sq km (121,598 sq miles)
Population: 1,713,407
Capital: SANTA FE

NEW YORK
Status: STATE
Area: 141,090 sq km (54,475 sq miles)
Population: 18,184,774
Capital: ALBANY

NORTH CAROLINA
Status: STATE
Area: 139,396 sq km (53,821 sq miles)
Population: 7,322,870
Capital: RALEIGH

NORTH DAKOTA
Status: STATE
Area: 183,123 sq km (70,704 sq miles)
Population: 643,539
Capital: BISMARCK

OHIO
Status: STATE
Area: 116,104 sq km (44,828 sq miles)
Population: 11,172,782
Capital: COLUMBUS

OKLAHOMA
Status: STATE
Area: 181,048 sq km (69,903 sq miles)
Population: 3,300,902
Capital: OKLAHOMA CITY

OREGON
Status: STATE
Area: 254,819 sq km (98,386 sq miles)
Population: 3,203,735
Capital: SALEM

PENNSYLVANIA
Status: STATE
Area: 119,290 sq km (46,058 sq miles)
Population: 12,056,112
Capital: HARRISBURG

RHODE ISLAND
Status: STATE
Area: 4,002 sq km (1,545 sq miles)
Population: 990,225
Capital: PROVIDENCE

SOUTH CAROLINA
Status: STATE
Area: 82,898 sq km (32,007 sq miles)
Population: 3,698,746
Capital: COLUMBIA

SOUTH DAKOTA
Status: STATE
Area: 199,742 sq km (77,121 sq miles)
Population: 732,405
Capital: PIERRE

TENNESSEE
Status: STATE
Area: 109,158 sq km (42,146 sq miles)
Population: 5,319,654
Capital: NASHVILLE

TEXAS
Status: STATE
Area: 695,673 sq km (268,601 sq miles)
Population: 19,128,261
Capital: AUSTIN

UTAH
Status: STATE
Area: 219,900 sq km (84,904 sq miles)
Population: 2,000,494
Capital: SALT LAKE CITY

VERMONT
Status: STATE
Area: 24,903 sq km (9,615 sq miles)
Population: 588,654
Capital: MONTPELIER

VIRGINIA
Status: STATE
Area: 110,771 sq km (42,769 sq miles)
Population: 6,675,451
Capital: RICHMOND

WASHINGTON
Status: STATE
Area: 184,674 sq km (71,303 sq miles)
Population: 5,532,939
Capital: OLYMPIA

WEST VIRGINIA
Status: STATE
Area: 62,758 sq km (24,231 sq miles)
Population: 1,825,754
Capital: CHARLESTON

WISCONSIN
Status: STATE
Area: 169,652 sq km (65,503 sq miles)
Population: 5,159,795
Capital: MADISON

WYOMING
Status: STATE
Area: 253,347 sq km (97,818 sq miles)
Population: 481,400
Capital: CHEYENNE

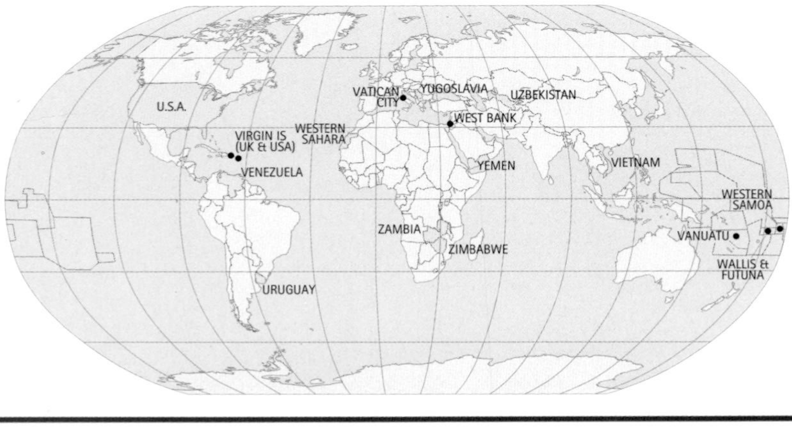

URUGUAY
Status: REPUBLIC
Area: 176,215 sq km (68,037 sq mls)
Population: 3,186,000
Capital: MONTEVIDEO
Language: SPANISH
Religion: R.CATHOLIC, PROTESTANT, JEWISH
Currency: PESO
Organizations: UN

MAP PAGE: 91

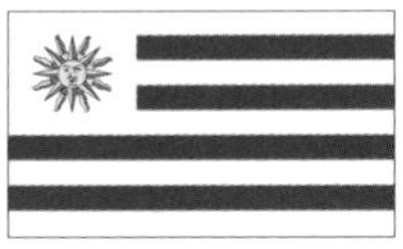

URUGUAY, ON THE Atlantic coast of central South America, is a low-lying land of prairies. The coast and the River Plate estuary in the south are fringed with lagoons and sand dunes. Almost half the population lives in Montevideo. Uruguay has warm summers and mild winters. The economy was founded on cattle and sheep ranching, and meat, wool and hides are major exports. The main industries produce food products, textiles, petroleum products, chemicals and transport equipment. Offshore banking and tourism are important.

UZBEKISTAN
Status: REPUBLIC
Area: 447,400 sq km (172,742 sq mls)
Population: 22,843,000
Capital: TASHKENT
Language: UZBEK, RUSSIAN, TAJIK, KAZAKH
Religion: SUNNI MUSLIM, RUSSIAN ORTHODOX
Currency: SOM
Organizations: CIS, UN

MAP PAGE: 14

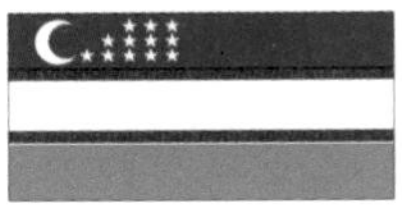

A REPUBLIC OF central Asia, Uzbekistan borders the Aral Sea and five countries. It consists mainly of the flat desert of the Kyzyl Kum, which rises eastwards towards the mountains of the western Pamirs. Most settlement is in the Fergana basin. The climate is dry and arid. The economy is based mainly on irrigated agriculture, chiefly cotton production. Industry specializes in fertilizers and machinery for cotton harvesting and textile manufacture. Uzbekistan is rich in minerals and has the largest gold mine in the world.

VANUATU
Status: REPUBLIC
Area: 12,190 sq km (4,707 sq mls)
Population: 169,000
Capital: PORT VILA
Language: ENGLISH, BISLAMA (ENGLISH CREOLE), FRENCH (ALL OFFICIAL)
Religion: PROTESTANT, R.CATHOLIC, TRAD.BELIEFS
Currency: VATU
Organizations: COMM., UN

MAP PAGE: 7

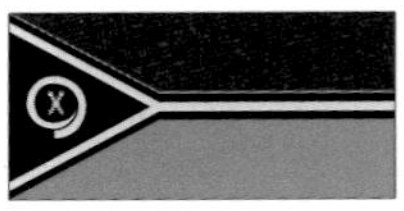

VANUATU OCCUPIES AN archipelago of some 80 islands in Oceania. Many of the islands are mountainous, of volcanic origin and densely forested. The climate is tropical with heavy rainfall. Half the population lives on the main islands of Efate, Santo and Tafea, and the majority of people live by farming. Copra, beef, seashells, cocoa and timber are the main exports. Tourism is growing and foreign aid is important.

VATICAN CITY
Status: ECCLESIASTICAL STATE
Area: 0.4 sq km (0.2 sq ml)
Population: 1,000
Language: ITALIAN
Religion: R.CATHOLIC
Currency: ITALIAN LIRA

MAP PAGE: 48

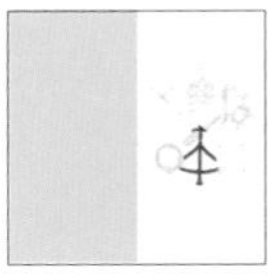

THE WORLD'S SMALLEST sovereign state, the Vatican City occupies a hill to the west of the river Tiber in the Italian capital, Rome. It is the headquarters of the Roman Catholic church and income comes from investments, voluntary contributions and tourism.

VENEZUELA
Status: REPUBLIC
Area: 912,050 sq km (352,144 sq mls)
Population: 21,644,000
Capital: CARACAS
Language: SPANISH, AMERINDIAN LANGUAGES
Religion: R.CATHOLIC, PROTESTANT
Currency: BOLÍVAR
Organizations: OPEC, UN

MAP PAGE: 89

VENEZUELA IS IN northern South America, on the Caribbean Sea. Its coast is much indented, with the oil-rich area of Lake Maracaibo at the western end and the swampy Orinoco delta in the east. Mountain ranges run parallel to the coast then turn southwestwards to form the northern extension of the Andes chain. Central Venezuela is lowland grasslands drained by the Orinoco river system, while to the south are the Guiana Highlands which contain the Angel Falls, the world's highest waterfall. About 85 per cent of the population lives in towns, mostly in the coastal mountain areas. The climate is tropical, with summer rainfall. Temperatures are lower in the mountains. Venezuela is an important oil producer, and sales account for about 75 per cent of export earnings. Bauxite, iron ore and gold are also mined and manufactures include aluminium, iron and steel, textiles, timber and wood products, and petrochemicals. Farming is important, particularly cattle ranching and dairy farming. Coffee, cotton, maize, rice and sugarcane are major crops.

VIETNAM
Status: REPUBLIC
Area: 329,565 sq km (127,246 sq mls)
Population: 74,545,000
Capital: HA NÔI
Language: VIETNAMESE, THAI, KHMER, CHINESE, MANY LOCAL LANGUAGES
Religion: BUDDHIST, TAOIST, R.CATHOLIC, CAO DAI, HOA HAO
Currency: DONG
Organizations: UN, ASEAN

MAP PAGE: 24-25

VIETNAM EXTENDS ALONG the east coast of the Indochina peninsula in southeast Asia, with the South China Sea to the east and south. The Red River (Song-koi) delta lowlands in the north are separated from the huge Mekong delta in the south by narrow coastal plains backed by the generally rough mountainous and forested terrain of the Annam highlands. Most people live in the river deltas. The climate is tropical, with summer monsoon rains. Over three quarters of the workforce is involved in agriculture, forestry and fishing. Rice growing is the main activity, and Vietnam is the world's third largest rice exporter, after the USA and Thailand. Coffee, tea and rubber are the main cash crops. The north is fairly rich in minerals including some oil, coal, iron ore, manganese, apatite and gold. The food processing and textile industries are important, but the steel, oil and gas and car industries are growing rapidly. The 1992 economic reform programme, inflow of foreign investment and the 1994 lifting of the US trade embargo are boosting an economy which suffered from decades of war and strife.

VIRGIN ISLANDS (UK)
Status: UK TERRITORY
Area: 153 sq km (59 sq mls)
Population: 19,000
Capital: ROAD TOWN
Language: ENGLISH
Religion: PROTESTANT, R.CATHOLIC
Currency: US DOLLAR

MAP PAGE: 83

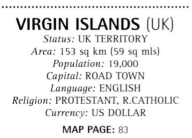

THE CARIBBEAN TERRITORY comprises four main islands and some 36 islets at the eastern end of the Virgin Islands group. Apart from the flat coral atoll of Anegada, the islands are volcanic in origin and hilly. The climate is subtropical and tourism is the main industry.

VIRGIN ISLANDS (USA)
Status: US TERRITORY
Area: 352 sq km (136 sq mls)
Population: 105,000
Capital: CHARLOTTE AMALIE
Language: ENGLISH, SPANISH
Religion: PROTESTANT, R.CATHOLIC
Currency: US DOLLAR

MAP PAGE: 83

THE TERRITORY CONSISTS of three main islands and some 50 islets in the Caribbean's western Virgin Islands. The islands are mostly hilly and of volcanic origin and the climate is subtropical. The economy is based on tourism, with some manufacturing on St Croix.

WALLIS AND FUTUNA
Status: FRENCH TERRITORY
Area: 274 sq km (106 sq mls)
Population: 14,000
Capital: MATA-UTU
Language: FRENCH, POLYNESIAN (WALLISIAN, FUTUNIAN)
Religion: R.CATHOLIC
Currency: PACIFIC FRANC

MAP PAGE: 7

THE SOUTH PACIFIC territory comprises the volcanic islands of the Wallis archipelago and Hoorn Islands. The climate is tropical. The islands depend upon subsistence farming, the sale of licences to foreign fishing fleets, workers' remittances and French aid.

WEST BANK
Status: TERRITORY
Area: 5,860 sq km (2,263 sq mls)
Population: 1,219,000
Language: ARABIC, HEBREW
Religion: SUNNI MUSLIM, JEWISH, SHI'A MUSLIM, CHRISTIAN

MAP PAGE: 16

THE TERRITORY CONSISTS of the west bank of the river Jordan and parts of Judea and Samaria in southwest Asia. The land was annexed by Israel in 1967, but the Jericho area was granted self-government under an agreement between Israel and the PLO in 1993.

WESTERN SAHARA
Status: TERRITORY
Area: 266,000 sq km (102,703 sq mls)
Population: 283,000
Capital: LAÂYOUNE
Language: ARABIC
Religion: SUNNI MUSLIM
Currency: MOROCCAN DIRHAM

MAP PAGE: 54

SITUATED ON THE northwest coast of Africa, the territory of Western Sahara is controlled by Morocco.

WESTERN SAMOA
Status: MONARCHY
Area: 2,831 sq km (1,093 sq mls)
Population: 171,000
Capital: APIA
Language: SAMOAN, ENGLISH
Religion: PROTESTANT, R.CATHOLIC, MORMON
Currency: TALA
Organizations: COMM., UN

MAP PAGE: 7

WESTERN SAMOA CONSISTS of two main mountainous and forested islands and seven small islands in the South Pacific Ocean. Seventy per cent of people live on Upolu. The climate is tropical. The economy is based on agriculture, with some fishing and light manufacturing. Traditional exports are coconut products, timber, taro, cocoa and fruit, but cyclones in recent years devastated the coconut palms. Tourism is increasing, but the islands depend upon workers' remittances and foreign aid.

YEMEN
Status: REPUBLIC
Area: 527,968 sq km (203,850 sq mls)
Population: 14,501,000
Capital: ŞAN'Ā
Language: ARABIC
Religion: SUNNI MUSLIM, SHI'A MUSLIM
Currency: DINAR, RIAL
Organizations: UN

MAP PAGE: 20

YEMEN OCCUPIES THE southwestern Arabian Peninsula, on the Red Sea and Gulf of Aden. Beyond the Red Sea coastal plain the land rises to a mountain range then descends to desert plateaux. Much of Yemen is hot and arid, but rainfall in the west supports crops and most settlement. Farming and fishing are the main activities, with cotton the main cash crop. Oil production is increasingly important. Remittances from workers abroad are the main foreign exchange earner.

YUGOSLAVIA
Status: REPUBLIC
Area: 102,173 sq km (39,449 sq mls)
Population: 10,544,000
Capital: BELGRADE
Language: SERBO-CROAT, ALBANIAN, HUNGARIAN
Religion: SERBIAN ORTHODOX, MONTENEGRIN ORTHODOX, SUNNI MUSLIM
Currency: DINAR
Organizations: UN

MAP PAGE: 49

THE SOUTH EUROPEAN state comprises only two of the former Yugoslav republics: the large and populous but landlocked Serbia and the much smaller Montenegro on the Adriatic Sea. The landscape is for the most part rugged, mountainous and forested. Northern Serbia (including the formerly autonomous province of Vojvodina) is low-lying, drained by the Danube river system. The climate is Mediterranean on the coast, continental inland. War and economic sanctions have ruined Serbia's economy and damaged that of Montenegro.

ZAIRE

see CONGO page 9

MAP PAGE: 124-125

ZAMBIA
Status: REPUBLIC
Area: 752,614 sq km (290,586 sq mls)
Population: 9,373,000
Capital: LUSAKA
Language: ENGLISH, BEMBA, NYANJA, TONGA, MANY LOCAL LANGUAGES
Religion: PROTESTANT, R.CATHOLIC, TRAD. BELIEFS, SUNNI MUSLIM
Currency: KWACHA
Organizations: COMM., OAU, SADC, UN

MAP PAGE: 57

A LANDLOCKED STATE in central Africa, Zambia borders seven countries. It is dominated by high savannah plateaux and flanked by the Zambezi river in the south. Most people live in the central Copperbelt. The climate is tropical with a rainy season from November to May. Agriculture, which involves 70 per cent of the workforce, is mainly at subsistence level. Copper is still the mainstay of the economy, though reserves are declining. Lead, zinc, cobalt and tobacco are also exported. Manufacturing and tourism are important.

ZIMBABWE
Status: REPUBLIC
Area: 390,759 sq km (150,873 sq mls)
Population: 11,526,000
Capital: HARARE
Language: ENGLISH (OFFICIAL), SHONA, NDEBELE
Religion: PROTESTANT, R.CATHOLIC, TRAD.BELIEFS
Currency: DOLLAR
Organizations: COMM., OAU, SADC, UN

MAP PAGE: 57

ZIMBABWE, A LANDLOCKED state in southern central Africa, consists of high plateaux flanked by the Zambezi river valley and Lake Kariba in the north and the Limpopo in the south. Climatic conditions are temperate because of altitude. Most people live in central Zimbabwe. Tobacco, cotton, sugar, tea, coffee and beef are produced for export as are a variety of minerals including gold, nickel, asbestos and copper. Manufacturing provides a wide range of goods. Tourism is a major foreign exchange earner.

GEOGRAPHICAL STATISTICS

MOUNTAINS

m		ft
4,509	MT WILHELM	14,793
4,073	MT VICTORIA	13,364
4,000	MT HAGEN	13,124
3,754	MT COOK	12,316
2,230	MT KOSCIUSKO	7,316

INLAND WATERS

sq km		sq miles
0–8,900	LAKE EYRE	0–3,435
0–5,780	LAKE TORRENS	0–2,230
0–4,770	LAKE GAIRDNER	0–1,840
0–2,410	LAKE FROME	0–930

ISLANDS

sq km		sq miles
808,510	NEW GUINEA	312,085
757,050	BORNEO	292,220
189,040	CELEBES (Sulawesi)	72,970
150,460	SOUTH ISLAND	58,080
134,045	JAVA	51,740
114,690	NORTH ISLAND	44,270
68,330	TASMANIA	26,375
36,500	NEW BRITAIN	14,090
33,915	TIMOR	13,090

RIVERS

km		miles
3,750	MURRAY-DARLING	2,330
1,480	LACHLAN	920
840	FLINDERS	520
820	GASCOYNE	510
650	VICTORIA	400

DRAINAGE BASINS

sq km		sq miles
910,000	MURRAY-DARLING	351,000
108,000	FLINDERS	42,000
85,000	LACHLAN	33,000
80,000	GASCOYNE	31,000
78,000	VICTORIA	30,000

MAXIMUM WATER DEPTHS

m		ft
9,175	CORAL SEA	30,102
7,440	BANDA SEA	24,409
6,220	CELEBES SEA	20,410
5,514	SOUTH CHINA SEA	18,091
4,570	TASMAN SEA	14,993
3,310	TIMOR SEA	10,860

SEE MAPS pages 4–9, 33

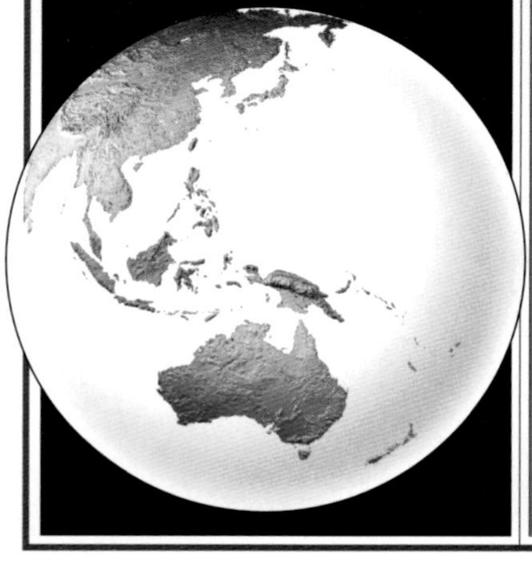

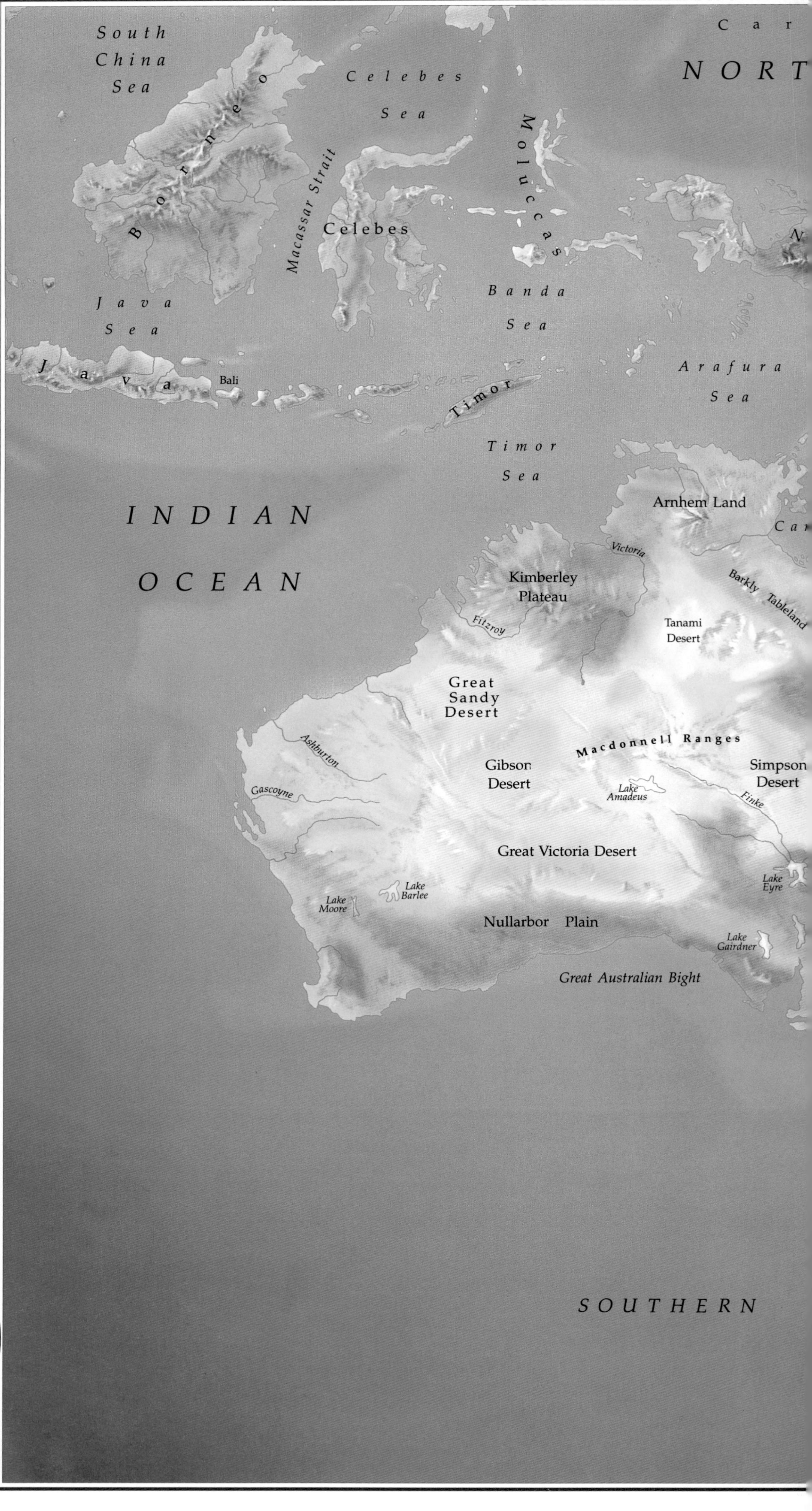

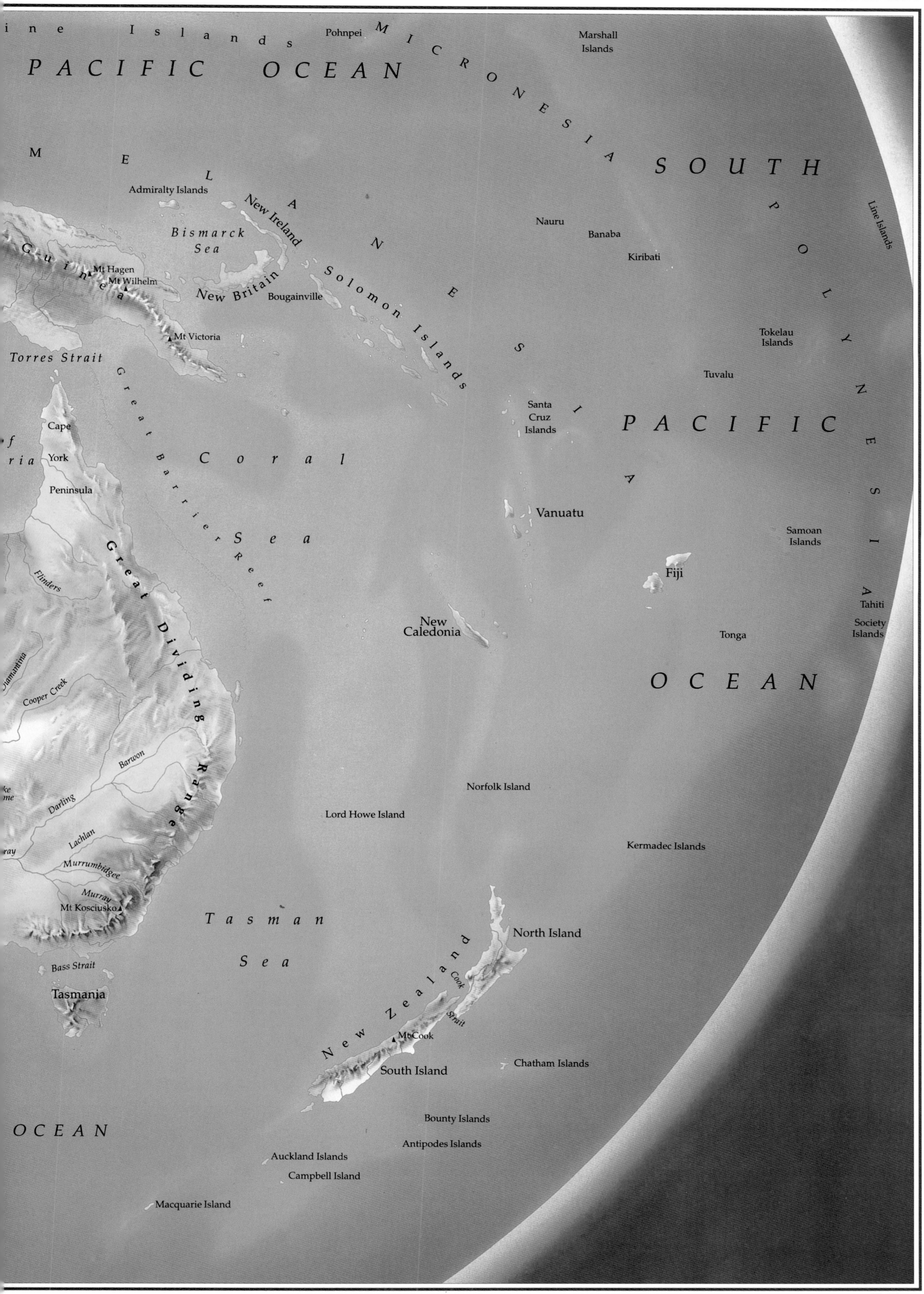

ine Islands Pohnpei MICRONESIA Marshall
Islands

PACIFIC   OCEAN

SOUTH

M M E L A N

Admiralty Islands

Bismarck
Sea

Guinea Mt Hagen Mt Wilhelm New Britain Bougainville New Ireland Solomon Islands

Nauru

Banaba

Kiribati

Line Islands

Tokelau
Islands

Mt Victoria

Torres Strait

Great Barrier Reef

Coral

Sea

Cape
York
Peninsula

ria

f

Flinders

Great Dividing Range

Diamantina

Cooper Creek

Barwon

Darling

Lachlan

Murrumbidgee

ke
me

ray

Murray

Mt Kosciusko

Tasman

Sea

Bass Strait

Tasmania

New Zealand

Cook
Strait

Mt Cook

South Island

Santa
Cruz
Islands

Vanuatu

New
Caledonia

Norfolk Island

Lord Howe Island

North Island

POLYNESIA

Tuvalu

PACIFIC

Samoan
Islands

Fiji

Tonga

OCEAN

Kermadec Islands

Chatham Islands

OCEAN

Bounty Islands

Antipodes Islands

Auckland Islands

Campbell Island

Macquarie Island

Tahiti
Society
Islands

©Bartholomew

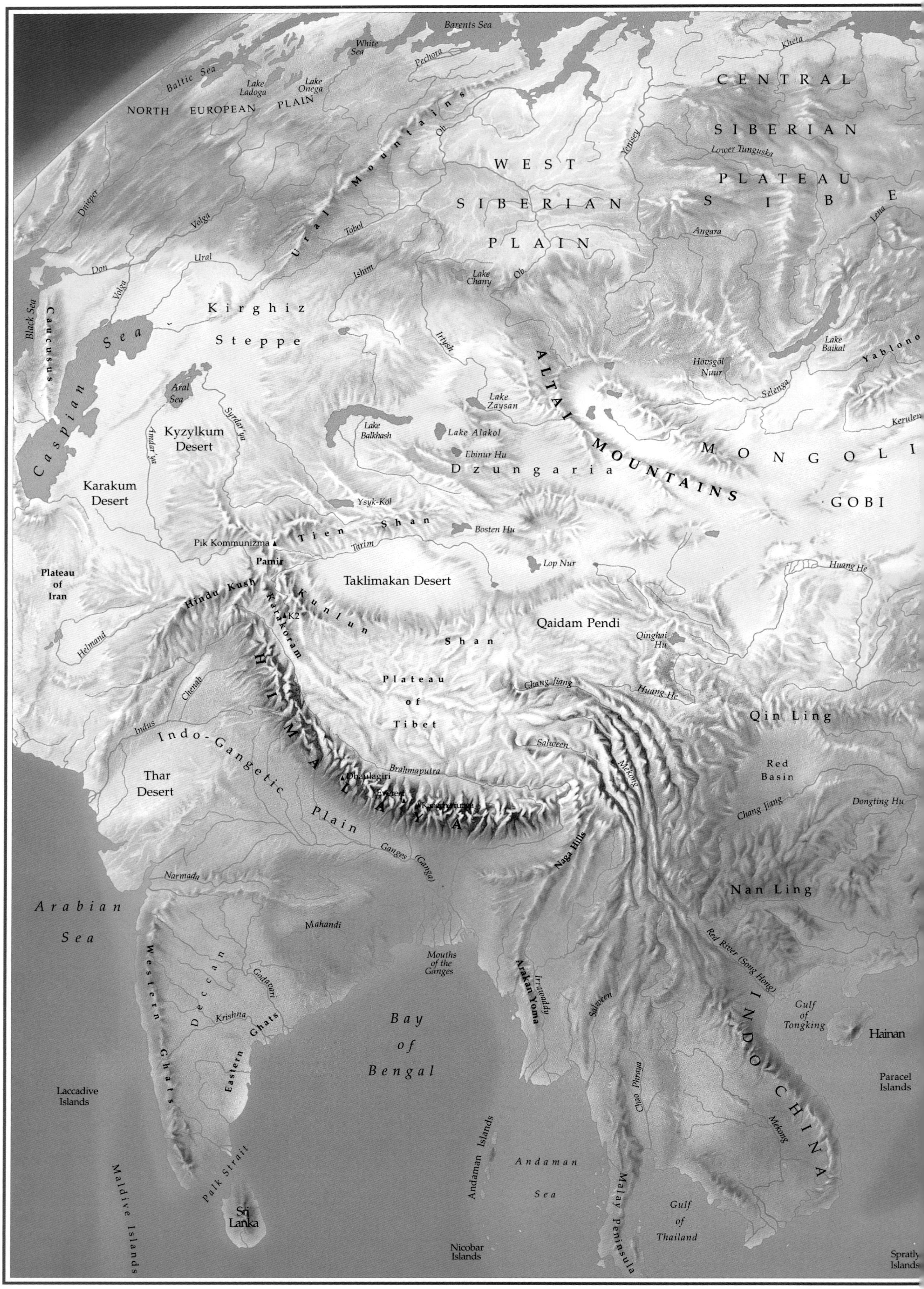

Barents Sea

Kheta

White Sea

Baltic Sea

Pechora

CENTRAL

Lake Ladoga

Lake Onega

NORTH EUROPEAN PLAIN

SIBERIAN

Ob

WEST

Volga

Tobol

SIBERIAN

PLATEAU

Dnieper

Ural Mountains

Lower Tunguska

S I B E

Don

Ural

Ishim

PLAIN

Angara

Lena

Volga

Lake Chany

Ob

Caucasus

Black Sea

Kirghiz

Irtysh

Hövsgöl Nuur

Lake Baikal

Yablono

Caspian Sea

Steppe

Lake Zaysan

Aral Sea

Lake Balkhash

Lake Alakol

Selenga

Kerulen

Kyzylkum Desert

Amdar'ya

Syrdar'ya

Ebinur Hu

M O N G O L I

Karakum Desert

Ysyk-Köl

D z u n g a r i a

ALTAI MOUNTAINS

GOBI

Plateau of Iran

Pik Kommunizma ▲

Tien Shan

Tarim

Bosten Hu

Pamir

Taklimakan Desert

Lop Nur

Huang He

Hindu Kush

Karakoram

Kunlun

Qaidam Pendi

Qinghai Hu

Helmand

K2 ▲

Shan

Qin Ling

Chenab

H I M A L A Y A

Plateau of Tibet

Chang Jiang

Huang He

Indus

Red Basin

Indo-Gangetic

Dhaulagiri ▲

Brahmaputra

Salween

Mekong

Chang Jiang

Dongting Hu

Thar Desert

Everest ▲

Plain

▲ Kanchenjunga

Ganges (Ganga)

Naga Hills

Narmada

Ganges

Nan Ling

Arabian Sea

Mahandi

Red River (Song Hong)

Western Ghats

Deccan

Godavari

Mouths of the Ganges

Arakan Yoma

Irrawaddy

I N D O C H I N A

Krishna

Eastern Ghats

Bay of Bengal

Salween

Gulf of Tongking

Hainan

Laccadive Islands

Chao Phraya

Paracel Islands

Andaman Islands

Andaman Sea

Mekong

Palk Strait

Malay Peninsula

Maldive Islands

Sri Lanka

Gulf of Thailand

Nicobar Islands

Spratly Islands

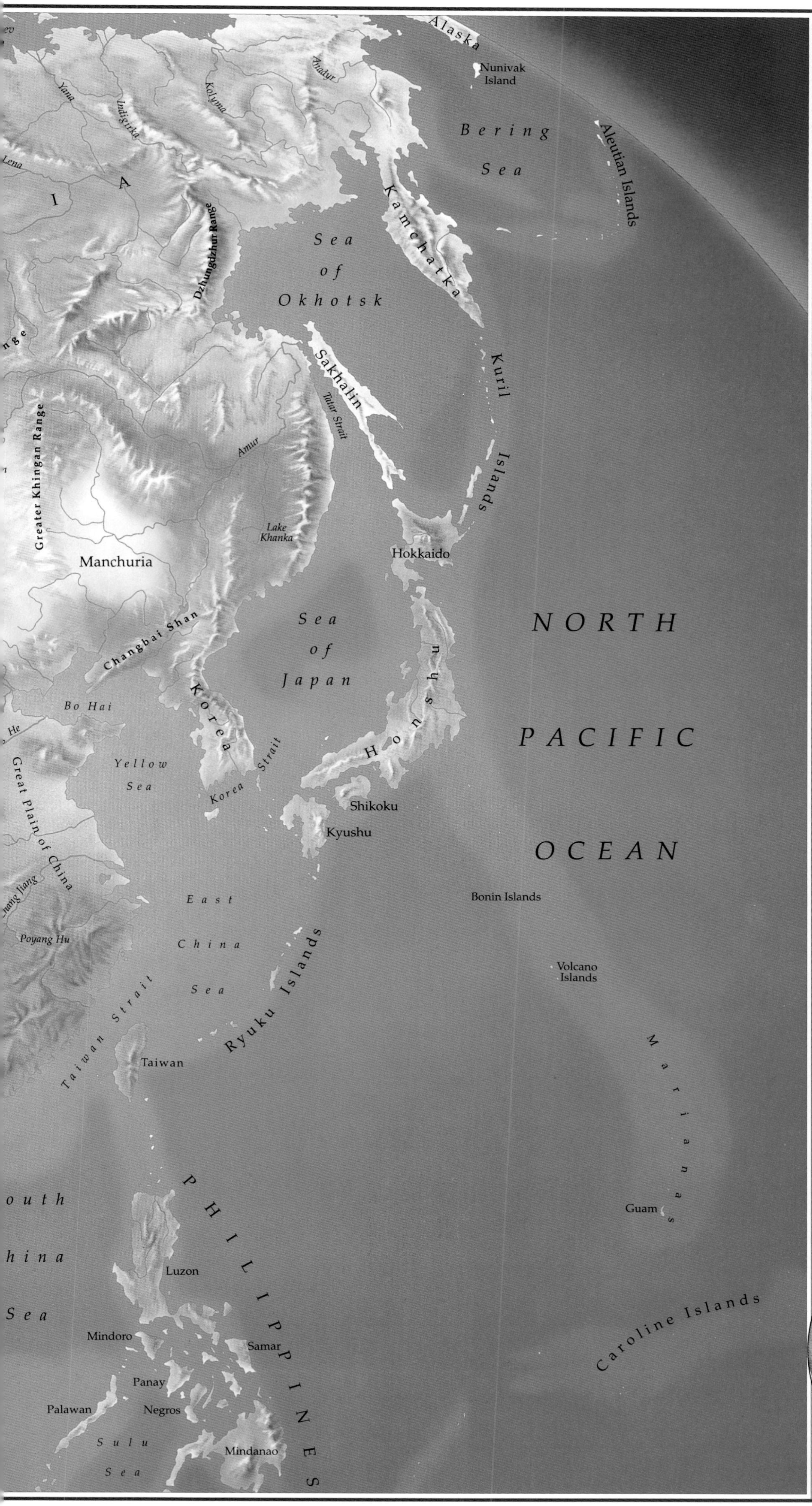

GEOGRAPHICAL STATISTICS

MOUNTAINS

m		ft
8,848	EVEREST	29,028
8,611	K2	28,251
8,598	KANGCHENJUNGA	28,210
8,172	DHAULAGIRI	26,811
7,495	PIK KOMMUNIZMA	24,590

INLAND WATERS

sq km		sq miles
371,000	CASPIAN SEA	143,205
30,500	LAKE BAIKAL	11,775
17,400	LAKE BALKHASH (Ozero Balkhash)	6,715
6,200	YSYK-KÖL	2,395

ISLANDS

sq km		sq miles
104,690	LUZON	40,410
94,630	MINDANAO	36,530
65,610	SRI LANKA	25,325
35,990	TAIWAN	13,890
34,000	HAINAN	13,125

RIVERS

km		miles
6,380	CHANG JIANG (Yangtze)	3,964
5,570	OB–IRTYSH	3,461
5,464	HUANG HE	3,395
4,425	MEKONG	2,750
4,416	AMUR (Heilong Jiang)	2,744
4,400	LENA	2,734
4,090	YENISEY	2,541

DRAINAGE BASINS

sq km		sq miles
2,700,000	YENISEY	1,042,000
2,430,000	OB–IRTYSH	938,000
2,420,000	LENA	934,000
1,840,000	AMUR (Heilong Jiang)	710,000
1,175,000	CHANG JIANG (Yangtze)	454,000
980,000	HUANG HE	378,000

MAXIMUM WATER DEPTHS

m		ft
3,743	SEA OF JAPAN	12,280
3,475	SEA OF OKHOTSK	11,401
2,999	EAST CHINA SEA	9,839
91	YELLOW SEA	299

SEE MAPS pages 10–32

©Bartholomew

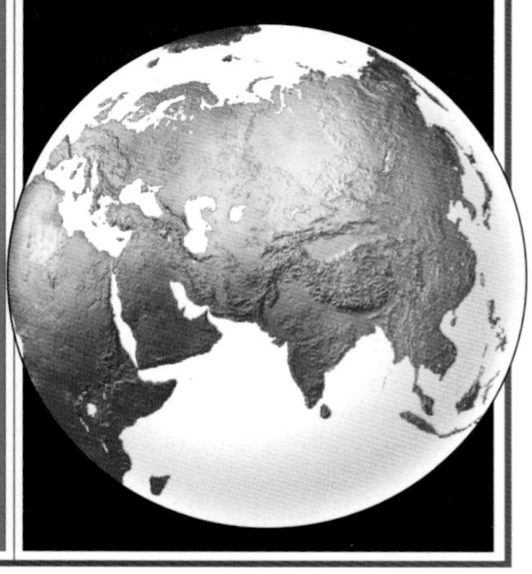

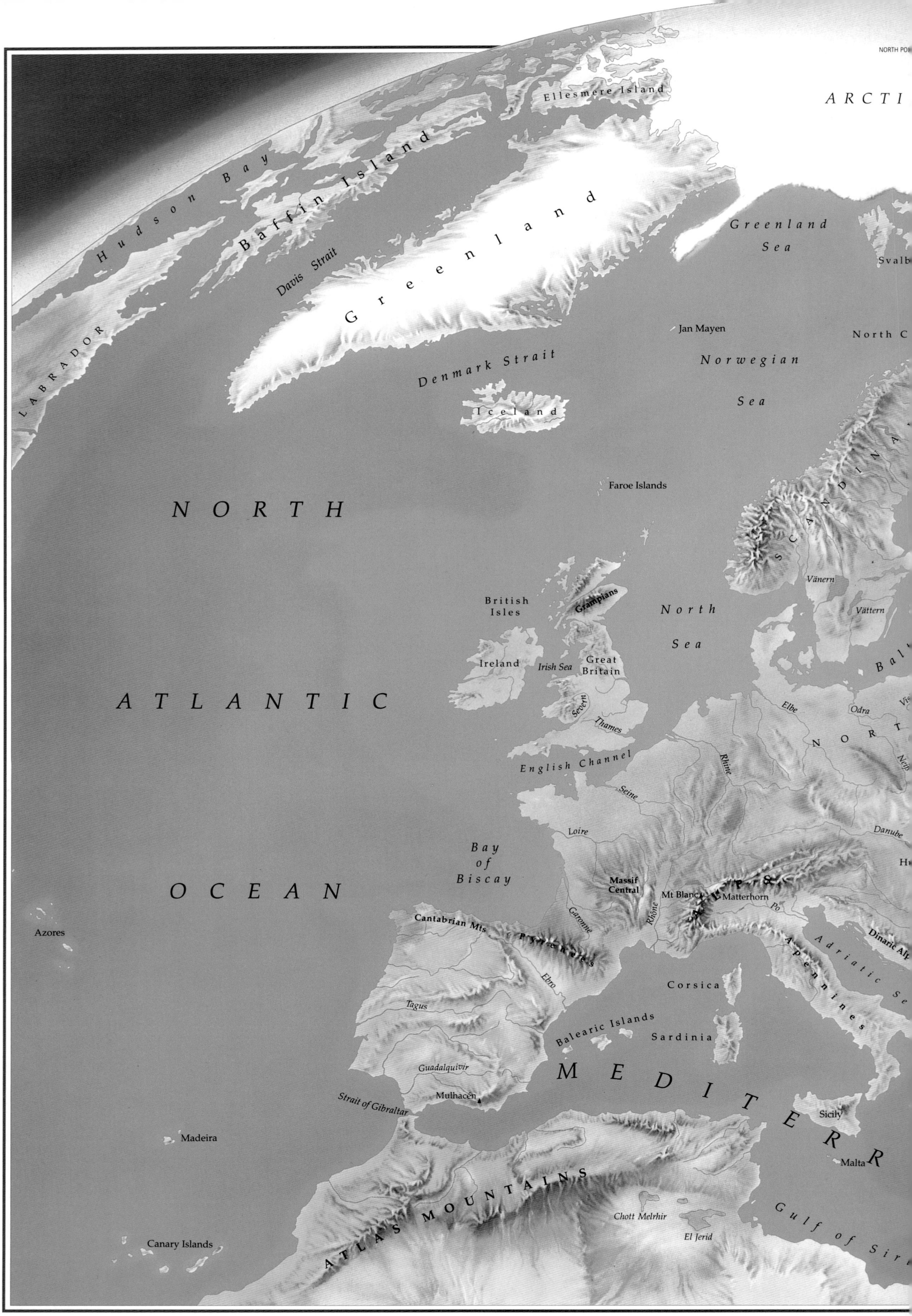

NORTH PO

A R C T I

Ellesmere Island

*Greenland
Sea*

Svalb

North C

Jan Mayen

Hudson Bay

Baffin Island

G r e e n l a n d

Davis Strait

Norwegian

Sea

LABRADOR

Denmark Strait

Iceland

Faroe Islands

N O R T H

SCANDINA

Vänern

British
Isles

Grampians

North

Sea

Vättern

A T L A N T I C

Ireland

Irish Sea

Great
Britain

Bal

Elbe

Odra

Vis

Severn

N O R

Thames

Rhine

Nei

English Channel

O C E A N

*Bay
of
Biscay*

Seine

Loire

Danube

H

**Massif
Central**

Rhône

Mt Blanc

Matterhorn

Po

Azores

Garonne

Dinaric Alp

Cantabrian Mts

P Y R E N E E S

Adriatic Se

Ebro

Apennines

Corsica

Tagus

Balearic Islands

Sardinia

Guadalquivir

M E D I T E R R

Strait of Gibraltar

Mulhacén

Sicily

Madeira

Malta

ATLAS MOUNTAINS

Chott Melrhir

Gulf of Sir

Canary Islands

El Jerid

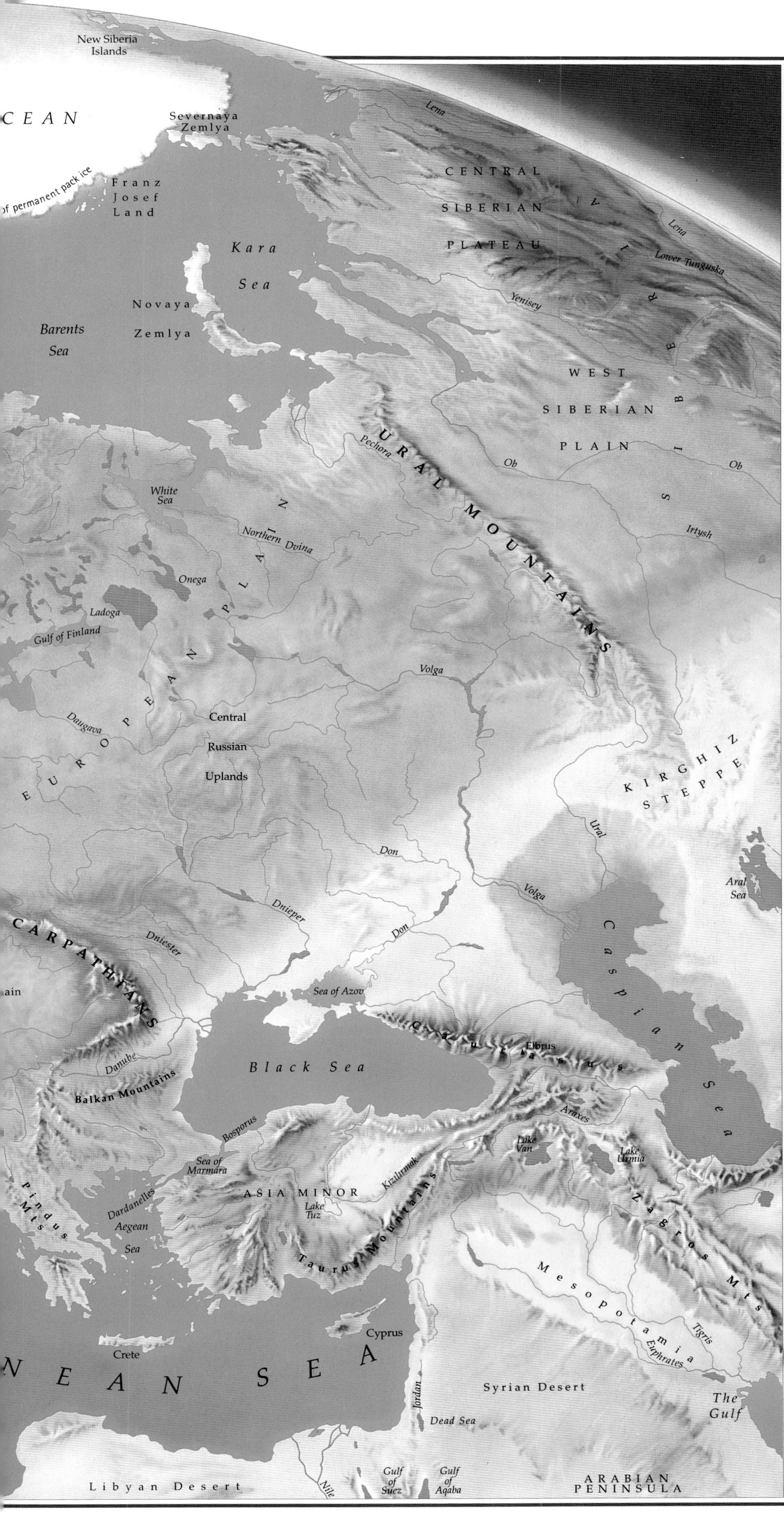

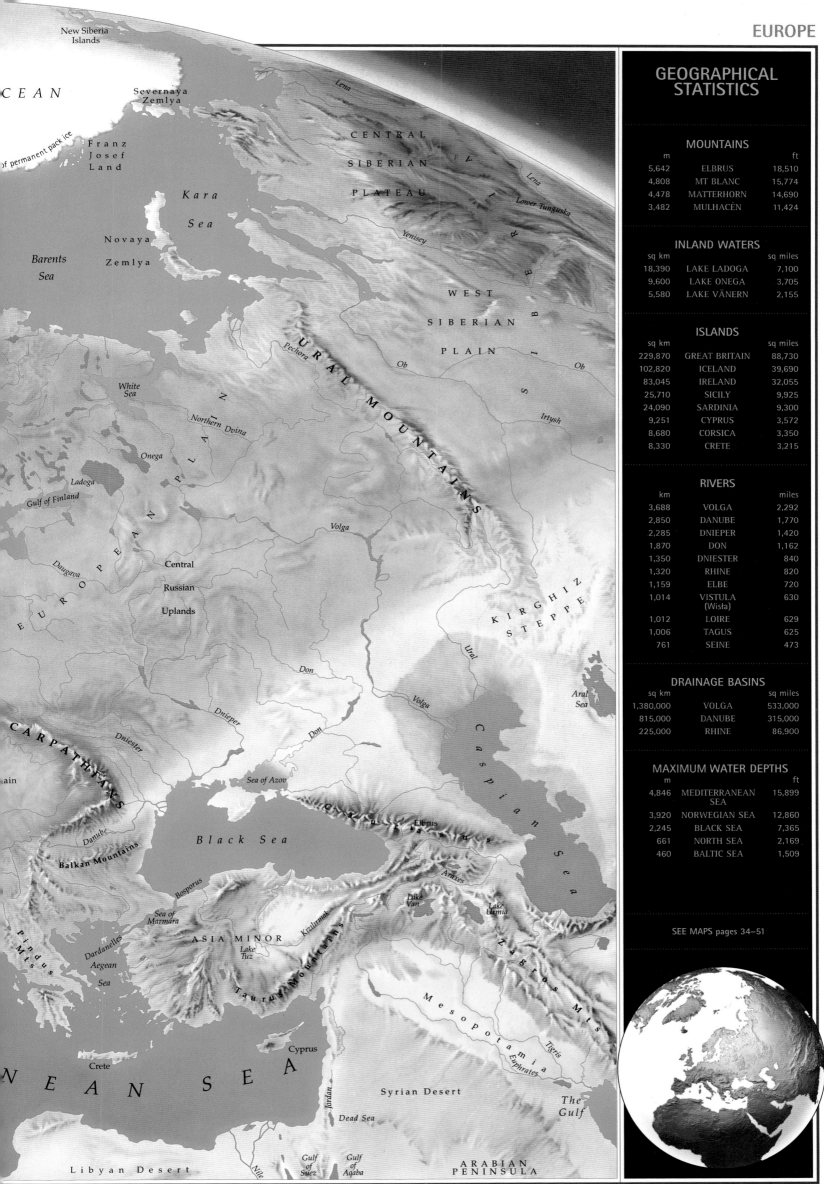

GEOGRAPHICAL STATISTICS

MOUNTAINS

m		ft
5,642	ELBRUS	18,510
4,808	MT BLANC	15,774
4,478	MATTERHORN	14,690
3,482	MULHACÉN	11,424

INLAND WATERS

sq km		sq miles
18,390	LAKE LADOGA	7,100
9,600	LAKE ONEGA	3,705
5,580	LAKE VÄNERN	2,155

ISLANDS

sq km		sq miles
229,870	GREAT BRITAIN	88,730
102,820	ICELAND	39,690
83,045	IRELAND	32,055
25,710	SICILY	9,925
24,090	SARDINIA	9,300
9,251	CYPRUS	3,572
8,680	CORSICA	3,350
8,330	CRETE	3,215

RIVERS

km		miles
3,688	VOLGA	2,292
2,850	DANUBE	1,770
2,285	DNIEPER	1,420
1,870	DON	1,162
1,350	DNIESTER	840
1,320	RHINE	820
1,159	ELBE	720
1,014	VISTULA (Wisła)	630
1,012	LOIRE	629
1,006	TAGUS	625
761	SEINE	473

DRAINAGE BASINS

sq km		sq miles
1,380,000	VOLGA	533,000
815,000	DANUBE	315,000
225,000	RHINE	86,900

MAXIMUM WATER DEPTHS

m		ft
4,846	MEDITERRANEAN SEA	15,899
3,920	NORWEGIAN SEA	12,860
2,245	BLACK SEA	7,365
661	NORTH SEA	2,169
460	BALTIC SEA	1,509

SEE MAPS pages 34–51

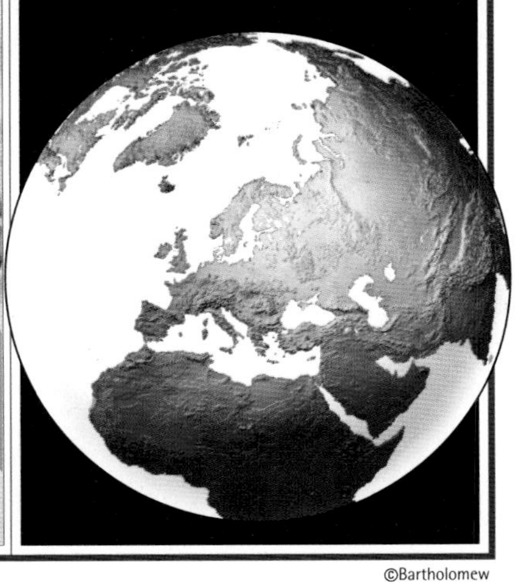

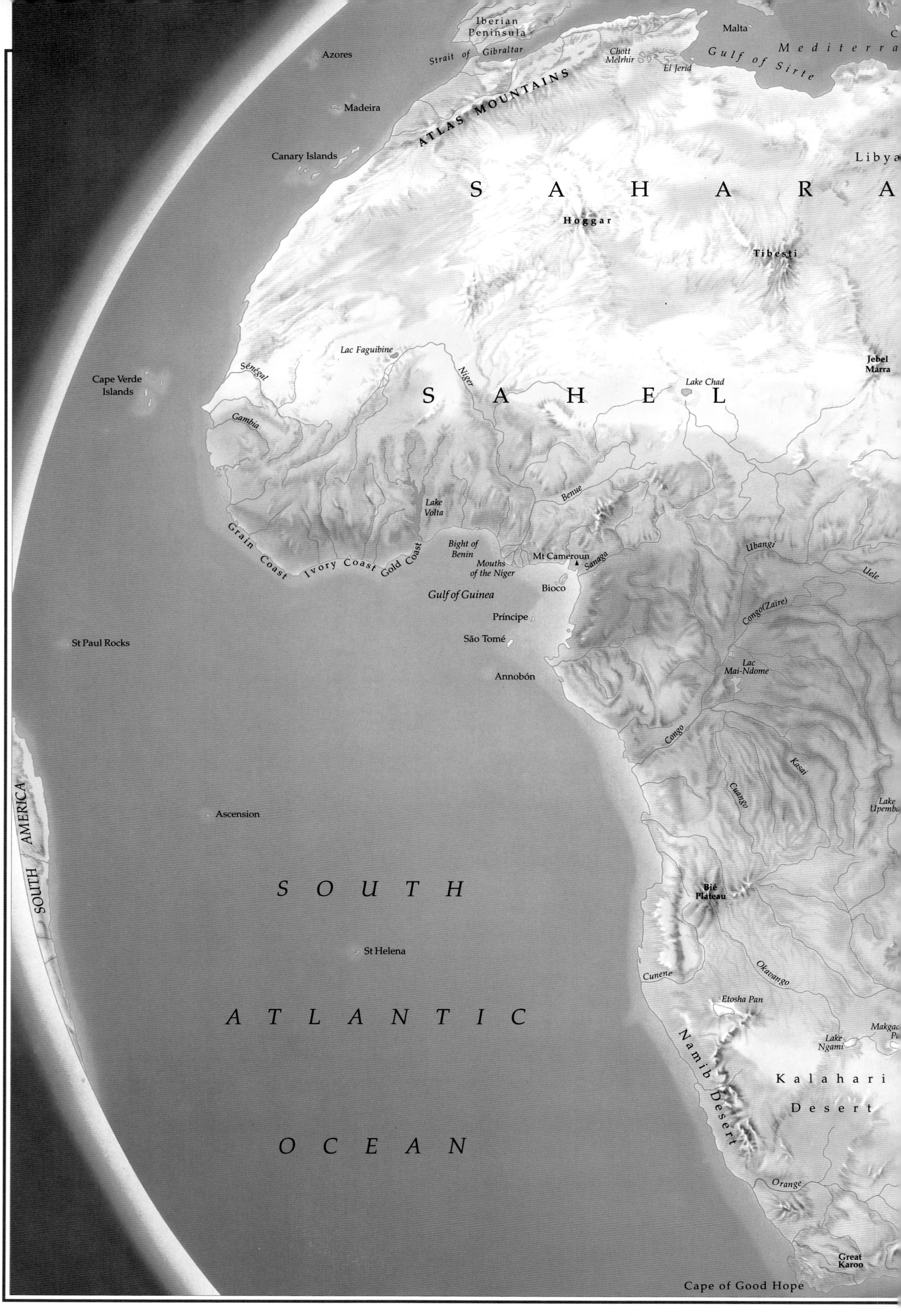

Iberian
Peninsula

Malta

Azores

Strait of Gibraltar

Chott
Melrhir

El Jerid

Gulf of Sirte

Mediterra

ATLAS MOUNTAINS

Madeira

Libya

Canary Islands

S A H A R A

Hoggar

Tibesti

Lac Faguibine

Jebel
Marra

Cape Verde
Islands

Sénégal

Niger

S A H E L

Lake Chad

Gambia

Benue

Lake
Volta

Grain Coast

Ivory Coast

Gold Coast

Bight of
Benin

Ubangi

Mouths
of the Niger

Mt Cameroun

Sanaga

Uele

Gulf of Guinea

Bioco

Congo (Zaïre)

St Paul Rocks

Príncipe

São Tomé

Annobón

Lac
Mai-Ndome

Congo

Kasai

Ascension

Cuango

Lake
Upemba

SOUTH AMERICA

S O U T H

Bié
Plateau

St Helena

A T L A N T I C

Cunene

Okavango

Etosha Pan

Makgad
Pa

Lake
Ngami

K a l a h a r i

Namib Desert

D e s e r t

O C E A N

Orange

Great
Karoo

Cape of Good Hope

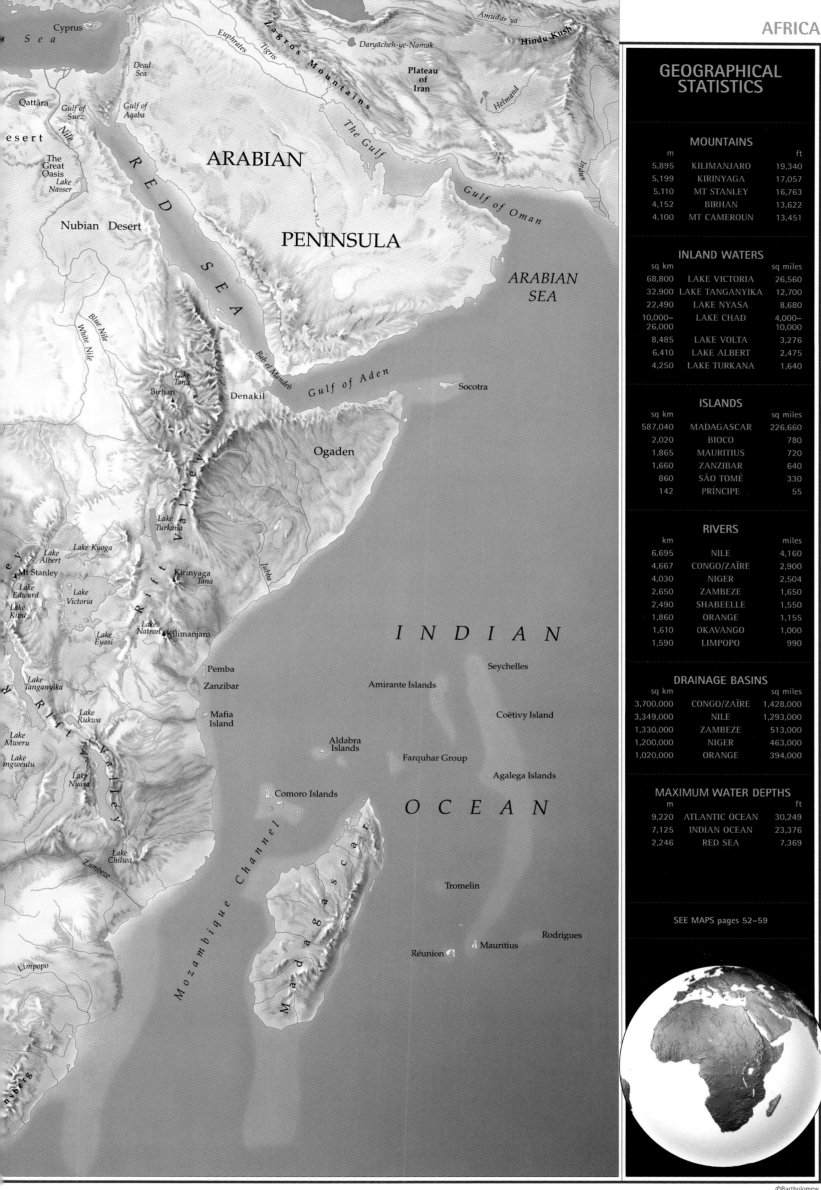

ARABIAN

PENINSULA

ARABIAN
SEA

RED SEA

Nubian Desert

Nile

Blue Nile
White Nile

Lake
Tana
Birhan

Denakil

Bab el Mandeb

Gulf of Aden

Socotra

Ogaden

Lake
Turkana

Rift Valley

Kirinyaga
Tana

Jubba

Lake Kyoga
Lake
Albert
Mt Stanley
Lake
Edward
Lake
Kivu
Lake
Victoria
Lake
Eyasi
Lake
Natron
Kilimanjaro

Lake
Tanganyika

Rift Valley

Lake
Rukwa

Lake
Mweru

Lake
mgweulu

Lake
Nyasa

Pemba
Zanzibar

Mafia
Island

Aldabra
Islands

Comoro Islands

Seychelles

Amirante Islands

Coëtivy Island

Farquhar Group

Agalega Islands

INDIAN

OCEAN

Mozambique Channel

Madagascar

Zambeze

Lake
Chilwa

Limpopo

nsberg

Tromelin

Rodrigues

Réunion   Mauritius

Cyprus   Sea

Dead
Sea

Qattâra

Gulf of
Suez
Gulf of
Aqaba

The
Great
Oasis
Lake
Nasser

esert

Nile

Euphrates
Tigris

Zagros Mountains

Daryācheh-ye-Namak

The Gulf

Plateau
of
Iran

Helmand

Amudar'ya

Hindu Kush

Indus

Gulf of Oman

SEE MAPS pages 52–59

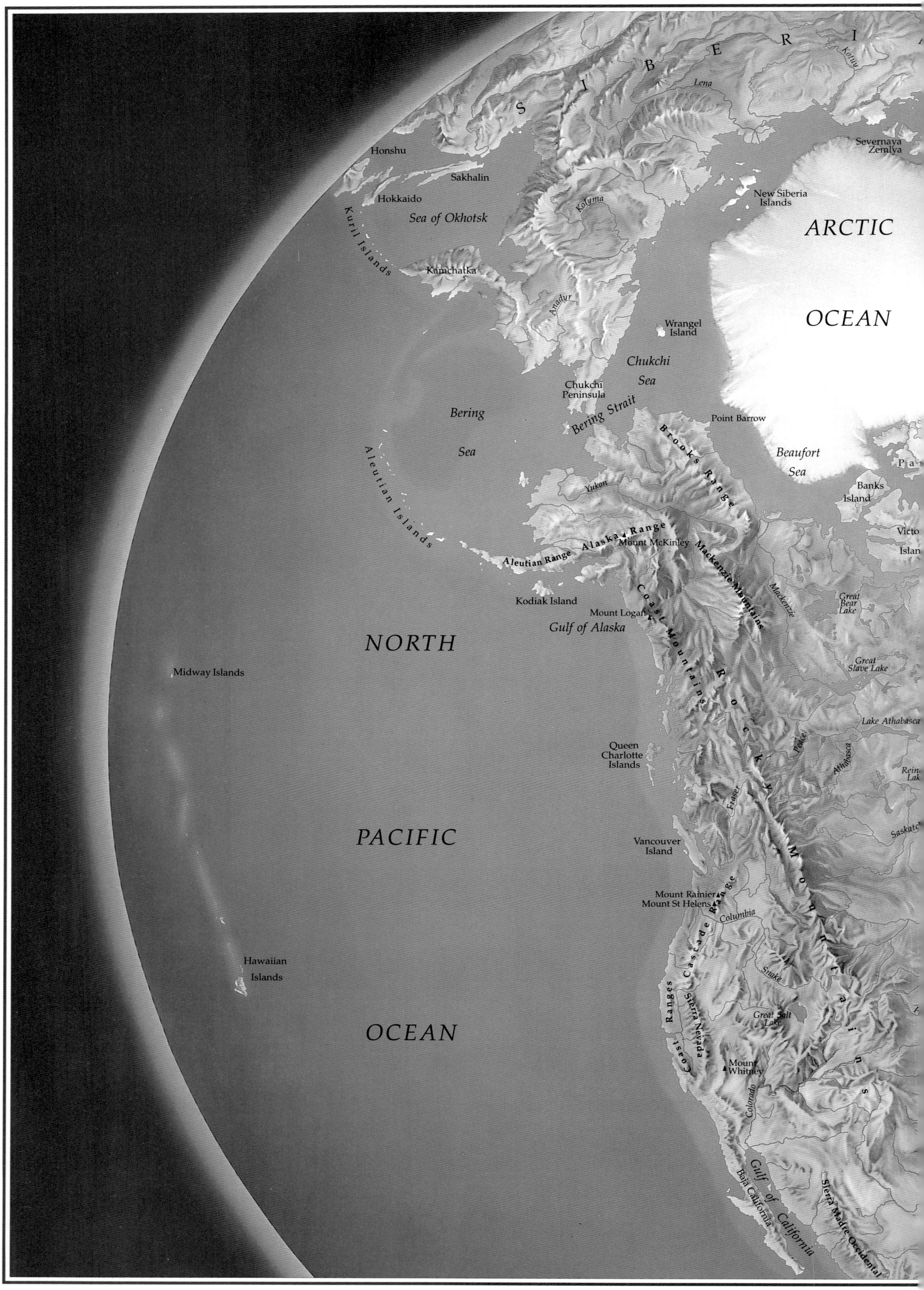

S I B E R I

Lena

Kolyma

Honshu

Sakhalin

Hokkaido

Sea of Okhotsk

Kuril Islands

Kamchatka

Anadyr

Severnaya
Zemlya

New Siberia
Islands

ARCTIC

OCEAN

Wrangel
Island

*Chukchi
Sea*

Chukchi
Peninsula

Bering Strait

Point Barrow

*Beaufort
Sea*

P a

Banks
Island

Bering

Sea

Brooks Range

Yukon

Aleutian Islands

Alaska Range

Mount McKinley

Aleutian Range

Mackenzie Mountains

Mackenzie

Great
Bear
Lake

Victo

Islan

Kodiak Island

Mount Logan

Gulf of Alaska

Coast Mountains

Great
Slave Lake

NORTH

Midway Islands

Lake Athabasca

R o c k y

Queen
Charlotte
Islands

Platte

Athabasca

Rein
Lak

PACIFIC

Vancouver
Island

Fraser

M o u n t a i n s

Saskatc

Mount Rainier
Mount St Helens

Cascade Range

Columbia

Coast Ranges

Sierra Nevada

Snake

Great Salt
Lake

*HAWAIIAN
Islands*

Mount
Whitney

OCEAN

Colorado

Coast Ranges

Gulf of California

Baja California

Sierra Madre Occidental

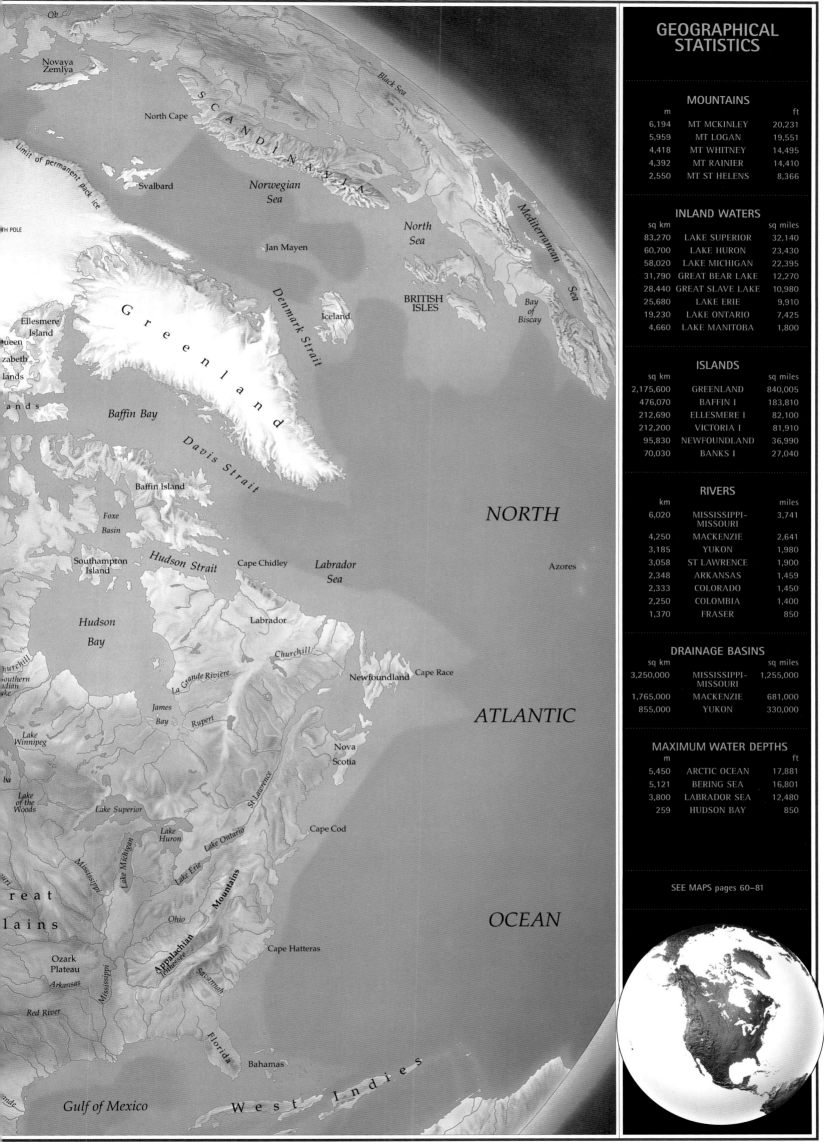

Ob

Novaya
Zemlya

North Cape

SCANDINAVIA

Limit of permanent pack ice

Svalbard

Norwegian
Sea

Black Sea

Mediterranean Sea

NORTH POLE

Jan Mayen

North
Sea

BRITISH
ISLES

Bay
of
Biscay

Ellesmere
Island

Greenland

Iceland

Denmark Strait

Queen
Elizabeth
Islands

Baffin Bay

Davis Strait

Foxe
Basin

Baffin Island

Southampton
Island

Hudson Strait

Cape Chidley

Labrador
Sea

NORTH

Azores

Hudson
Bay

Churchill

Southern
Indian
Lake

La Grande Rivière

Labrador

Churchill

Newfoundland

Cape Race

ATLANTIC

James
Bay

Rupert

Nova
Scotia

Lake
Winnipeg

Lake
of the
Woods

Lake Superior

St Lawrence

Cape Cod

Lake
Huron

Lake Michigan

Lake Ontario

Lake Erie

OCEAN

Mississippi

Great

Plains

Ohio

Mountains

Ozark
Plateau

Appalachian

Tennessee

Cape Hatteras

Arkansas

Mississippi

Savannah

Red River

Florida

Bahamas

West Indies

Gulf of Mexico

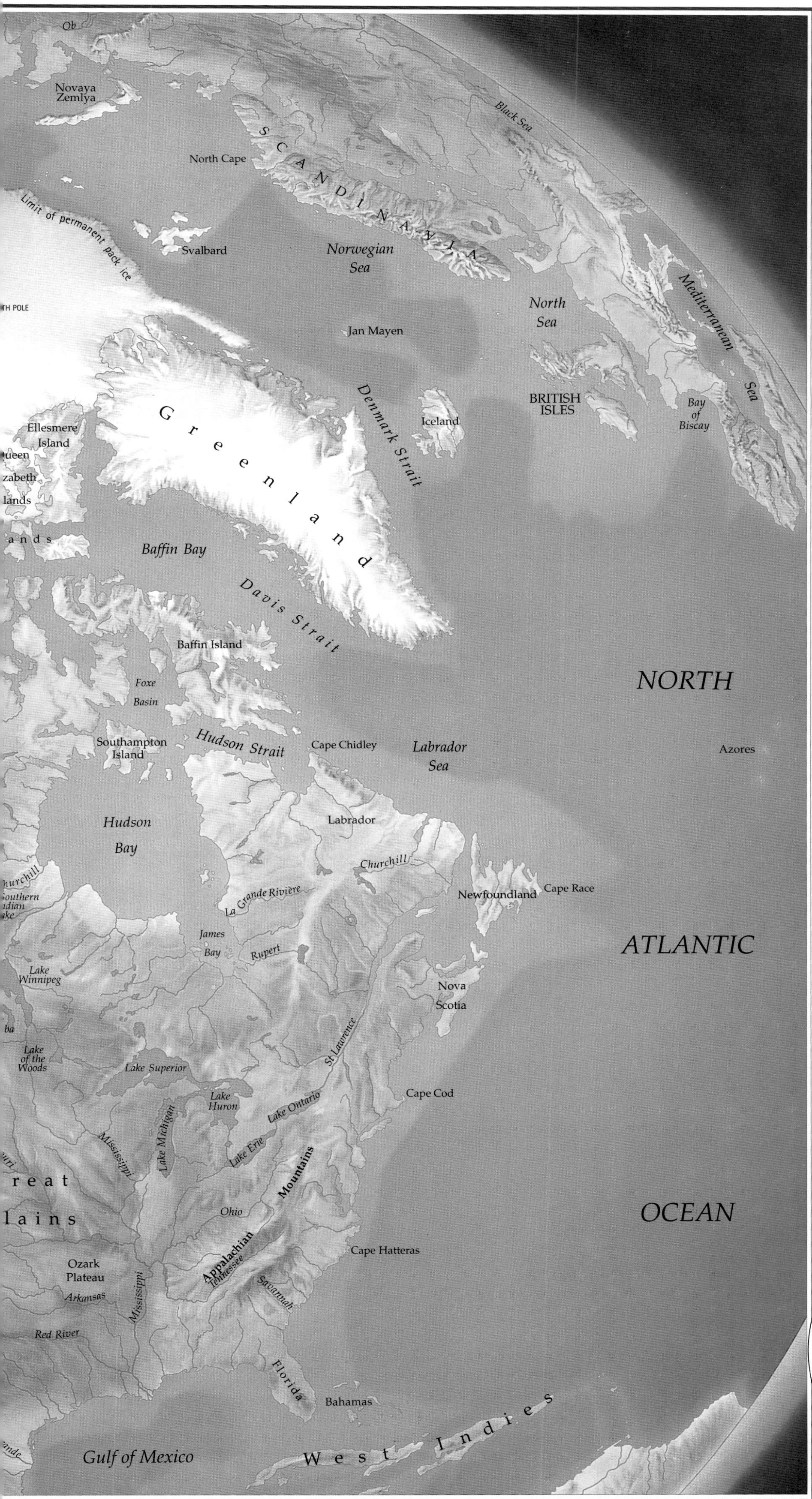

GEOGRAPHICAL STATISTICS

MOUNTAINS

m		ft
6,194	MT MCKINLEY	20,231
5,959	MT LOGAN	19,551
4,418	MT WHITNEY	14,495
4,392	MT RAINIER	14,410
2,550	MT ST HELENS	8,366

INLAND WATERS

sq km		sq miles
83,270	LAKE SUPERIOR	32,140
60,700	LAKE HURON	23,430
58,020	LAKE MICHIGAN	22,395
31,790	GREAT BEAR LAKE	12,270
28,440	GREAT SLAVE LAKE	10,980
25,680	LAKE ERIE	9,910
19,230	LAKE ONTARIO	7,425
4,660	LAKE MANITOBA	1,800

ISLANDS

sq km		sq miles
2,175,600	GREENLAND	840,005
476,070	BAFFIN I	183,810
212,690	ELLESMERE I	82,100
212,200	VICTORIA I	81,910
95,830	NEWFOUNDLAND	36,990
70,030	BANKS I	27,040

RIVERS

km		miles
6,020	MISSISSIPPI-MISSOURI	3,741
4,250	MACKENZIE	2,641
3,185	YUKON	1,980
3,058	ST LAWRENCE	1,900
2,348	ARKANSAS	1,459
2,333	COLORADO	1,450
2,250	COLOMBIA	1,400
1,370	FRASER	850

DRAINAGE BASINS

sq km		sq miles
3,250,000	MISSISSIPPI-MISSOURI	1,255,000
1,765,000	MACKENZIE	681,000
855,000	YUKON	330,000

MAXIMUM WATER DEPTHS

m		ft
5,450	ARCTIC OCEAN	17,881
5,121	BERING SEA	16,801
3,800	LABRADOR SEA	12,480
259	HUDSON BAY	850

SEE MAPS pages 60–81

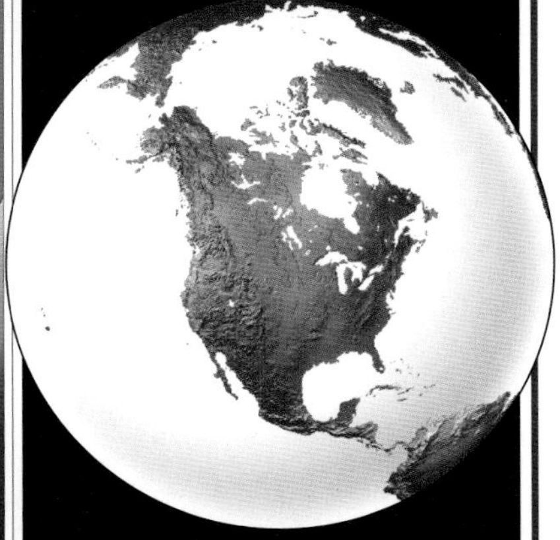

GEOGRAPHICAL STATISTICS

MOUNTAINS

m		ft
6,768	HUASCARAN	22,205
6,388	ANCOHUMA	20,958
6,310	CHIMBORAZO	20,702
5,896	COTOPAXI	19,344
5,452	POPOCATÉPETL	17,887
2,810	RORAIMA	9,219

INLAND WATERS

sq km		sq miles
8,340	LAKE TITICACA	3,220
8,270	LAKE NICARAGUA	3,190
1,340	LAKE POOPO	520

ISLANDS

sq km		sq miles
114,525	CUBA	44,205
78,460	HISPANIOLA	30,285
10,990	JAMAICA	4,245
8,895	PUERTO RICO	3,435

RIVERS

km		miles
6,516	AMAZON	4,049
3,200	MADEIRA	1,990
3,000	PURUS	1,860
2,900	SÃO FRANCISCO	1,800
2,870	RIO GRANDE	1,785
2,500	ORINOCO	1,555
2,200	ARAGUAIA	1,370
2,100	XINGU	1,300
2,000	NEGRO	1,240
1,700	PARNAÍBA	1,060
1,609	MARAÑON	1,000
1,550	MAGDALENA	963
1,350	CAUCA	840

DRAINAGE BASINS

sq km		sq miles
7,050,000	AMAZON	2,721,000
1,000,000	NEGRO	386,000
945,000	ORINOCO	365,000
623,000	SÃO FRANCISCO	241,000
260,000	MAGDALENA	100,000

MAXIMUM WATER DEPTHS

m		ft
11,022	PACIFIC OCEAN	36,161
7,100	CARIBBEAN SEA	23,294
4,377	GULF OF MEXICO	14,360

SEE MAPS pages 82–87, 89–90

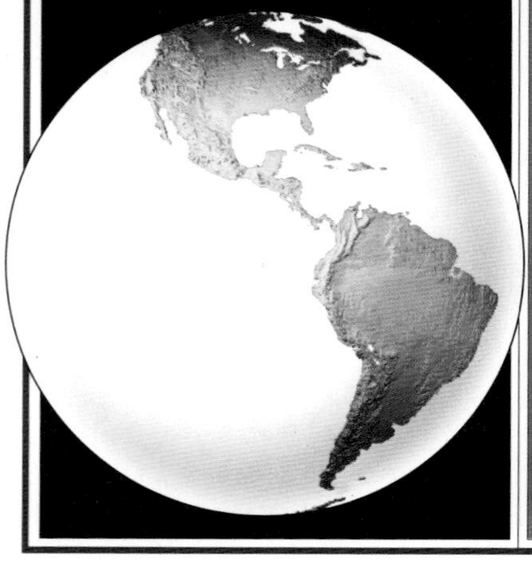

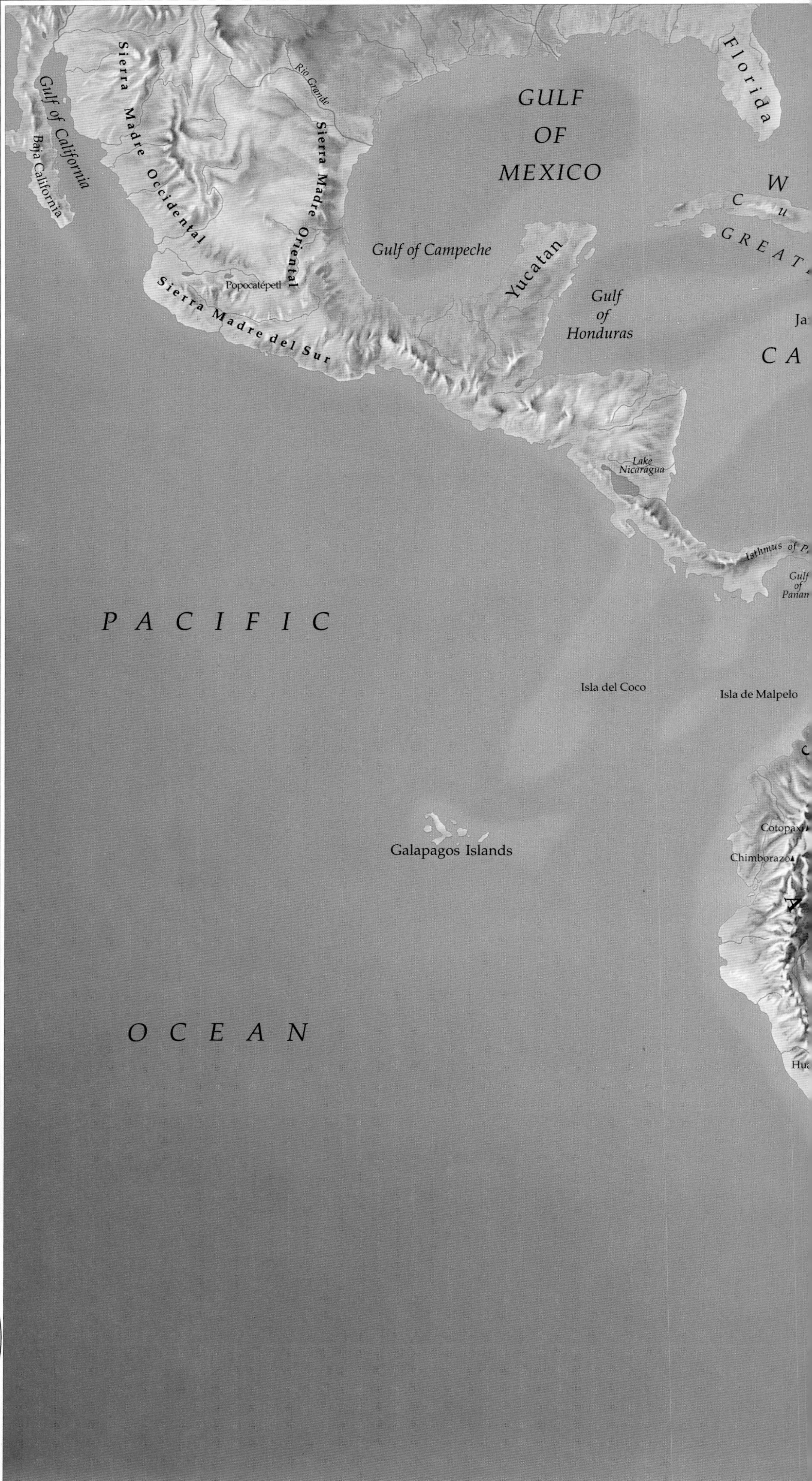

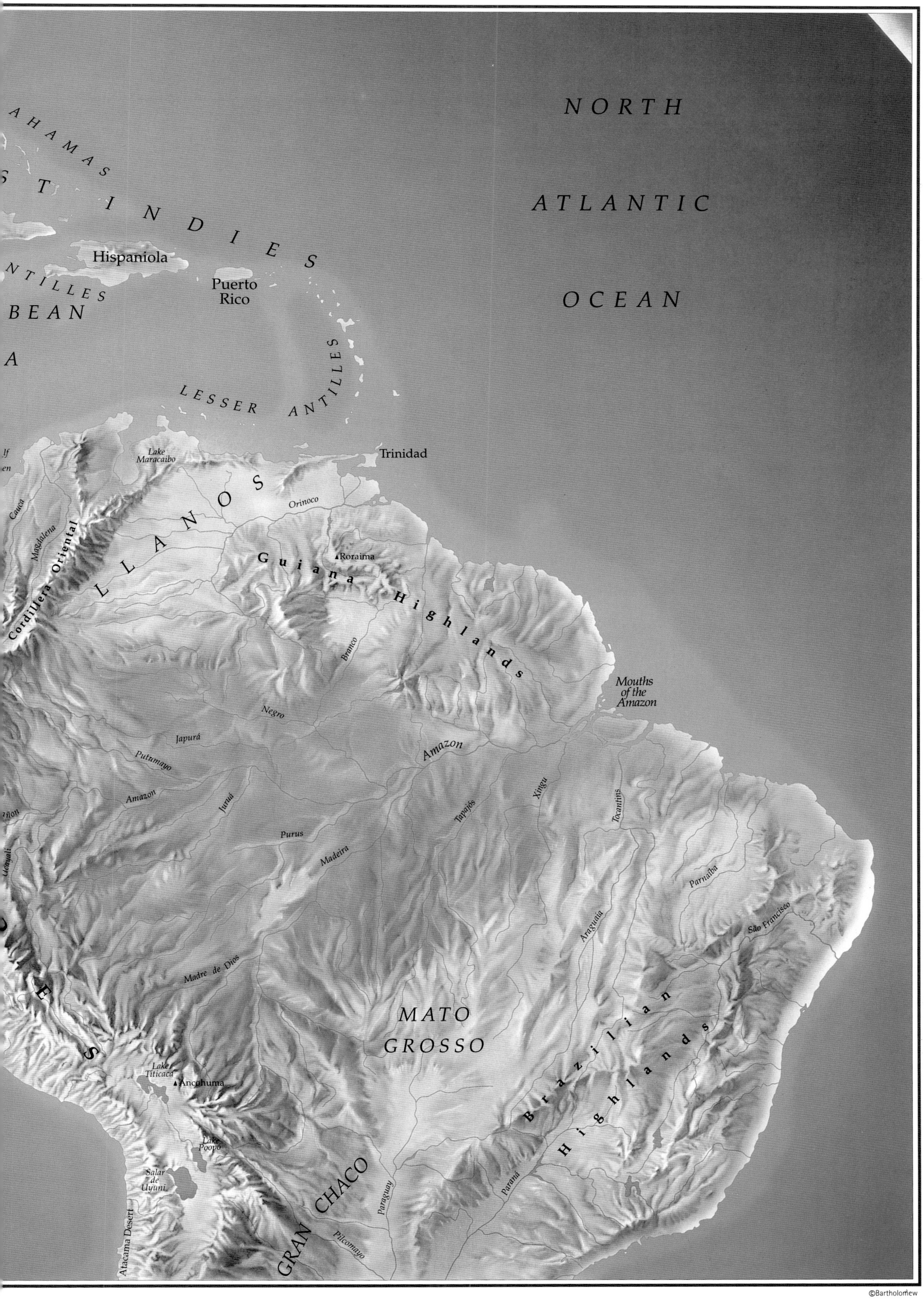

NORTH

ATLANTIC

OCEAN

BAHAMAS

WEST INDIES

Hispaniola

Puerto
Rico

ANTILLES

CARIBBEAN

LESSER ANTILLES

Trinidad

Lake
Maracaibo

Cauca

Magdalena

Cordillera Oriental

LLANOS

Orinoco

Guiana ▲Roraima
Highlands

Branco

Mouths
of the
Amazon

Negro

Japurá

Amazon

Putumayo

Amazon

Juruá

Purus

Madeira

Xingu

Tapajós

Tocantins

Parnaíba

Araguaia

São Francisco

Madre de Dios

MATO
GROSSO

Ucayali

Lake
Titicaca ▲Ancohuma

Lake
Poopó

Salar
de
Uyuni

Atacama Desert

GRAN CHACO

Pilcomayo

Paraguay

Paraná

Brazilian
Highlands

©Bartholomew

GEOGRAPHICAL STATISTICS

MOUNTAINS

m		ft
6,960	ACONCAGUA	22,834
6,908	OJOS DEL SALADO	22,664
4,897	VINSON MASSIF	16,066
4,528	MT KIRKPATRICK	14,856
4,181	MT SIDLEY	13,718
3,794	MT EREBUS	12,447

ISLANDS

sq km		sq miles
47,000	TIERRA DEL FUEGO	18,140
12,175	FALKLAND IS	4,700
3,760	SOUTH GEORGIA	1,450

RIVERS

km		miles
4,500	PARANÁ	2,800
2,600	PARAGUAY	1,615
2,200	URUGUAY	1,370
1,500	SALADO	930
1,100	PILCOMAYO	680
810	CHUBUT	500

DRAINAGE BASINS

sq km		sq miles
3,100,000	PARANÁ	1,197,000
1,100,000	PARAGUAY	425,000
800,000	SALADO	309,000
307,000	URUGUAY	119,000

ANTARCTICA

The continental area is
13,340,000 sq km (5,149,000 sq miles).

Ice sheet permanently covers 98% of this,
of which 87% lies on continental rock,
whilst 11% is floating ice shelves.

The total volume of ice is
30,000,000 cu km (7,000,000 cu miles)
with the greatest thickness being
4,700 m (15,420 ft) in east Antarctica.

SEE MAPS pages 88, 91–92

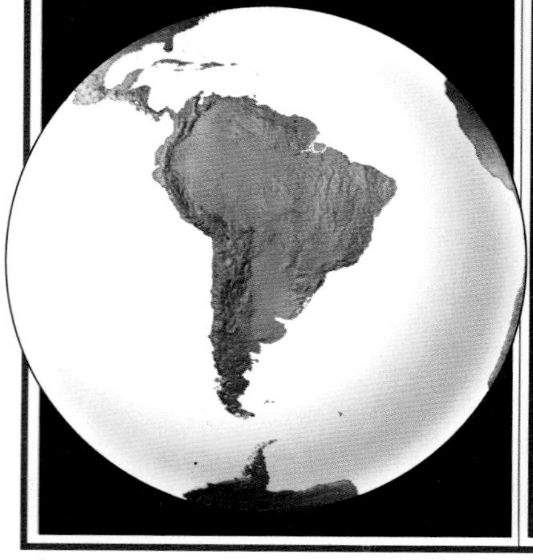

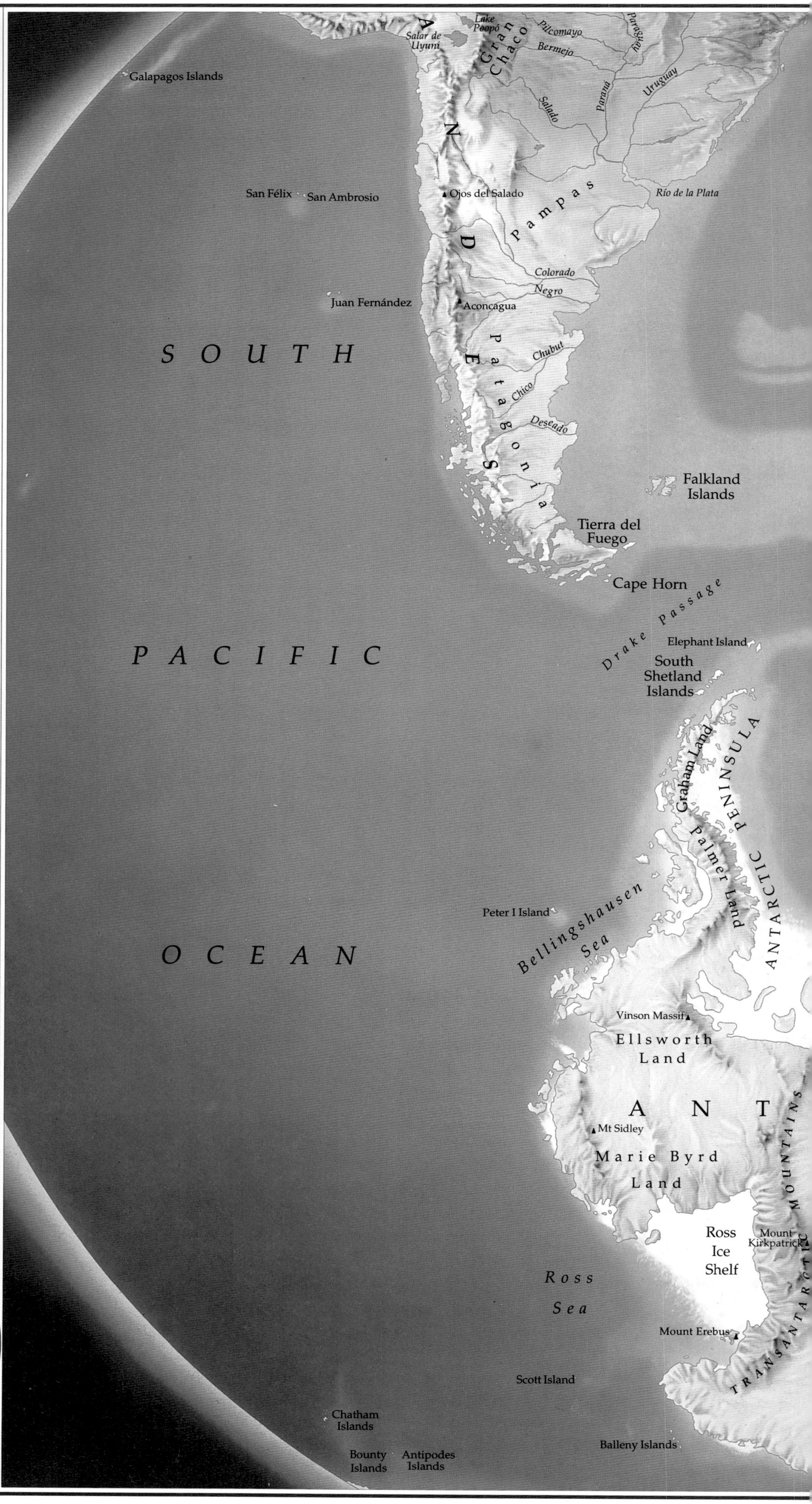

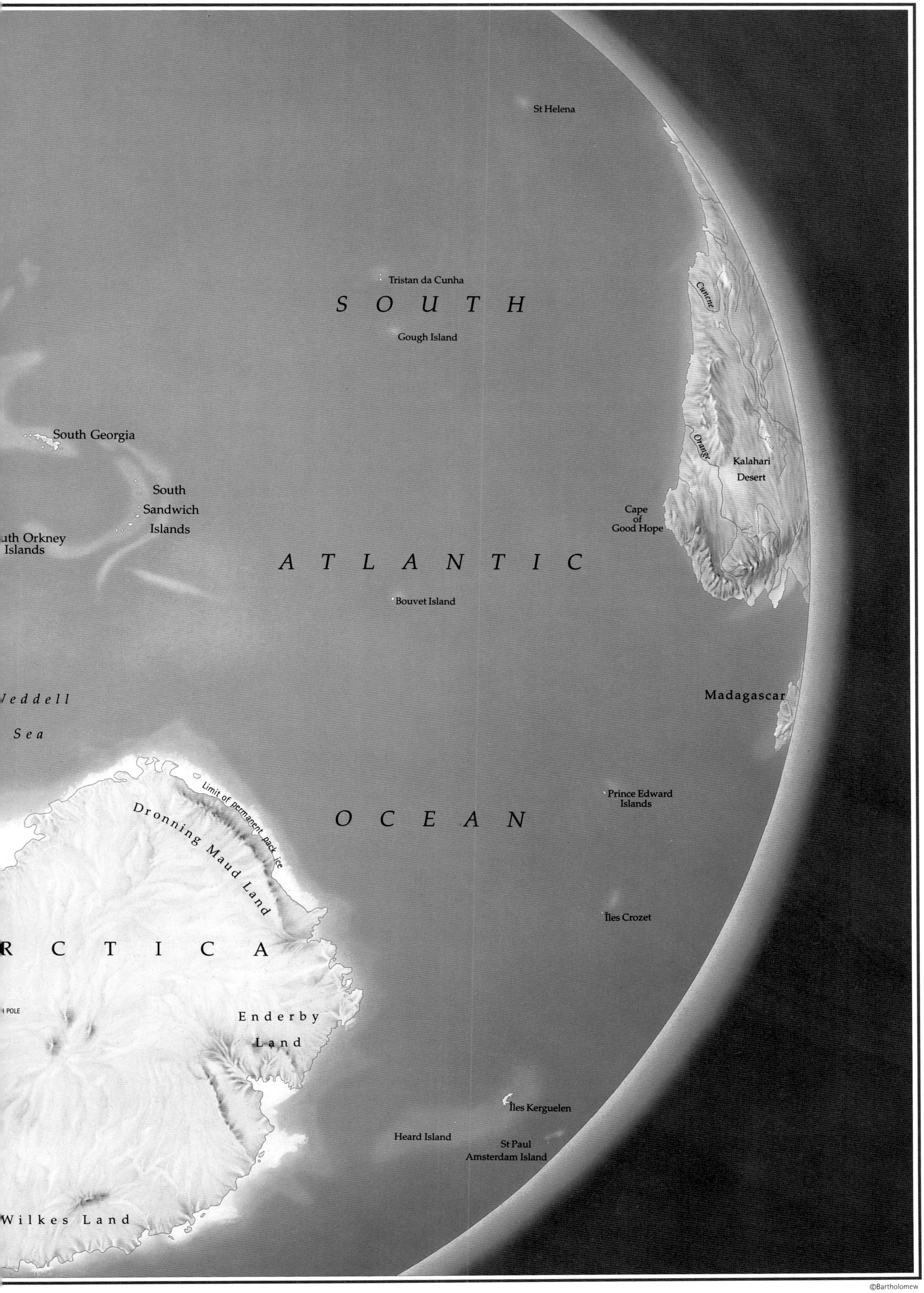

St Helena

Tristan da Cunha

S O U T H

Gough Island

Cunene

South Georgia

Orange

South
Sandwich
Islands

Kalahari
Desert

uth Orkney
Islands

A T L A N T I C

Cape
of
Good Hope

Bouvet Island

Madagascar

eddell

Sea

Prince Edward
Islands

Limit of permanent pack ice

O C E A N

Dronning Maud Land

Îles Crozet

R C T I C A

POLE

Enderby
Land

Îles Kerguelen

Heard Island

St Paul
Amsterdam Island

Wilkes Land

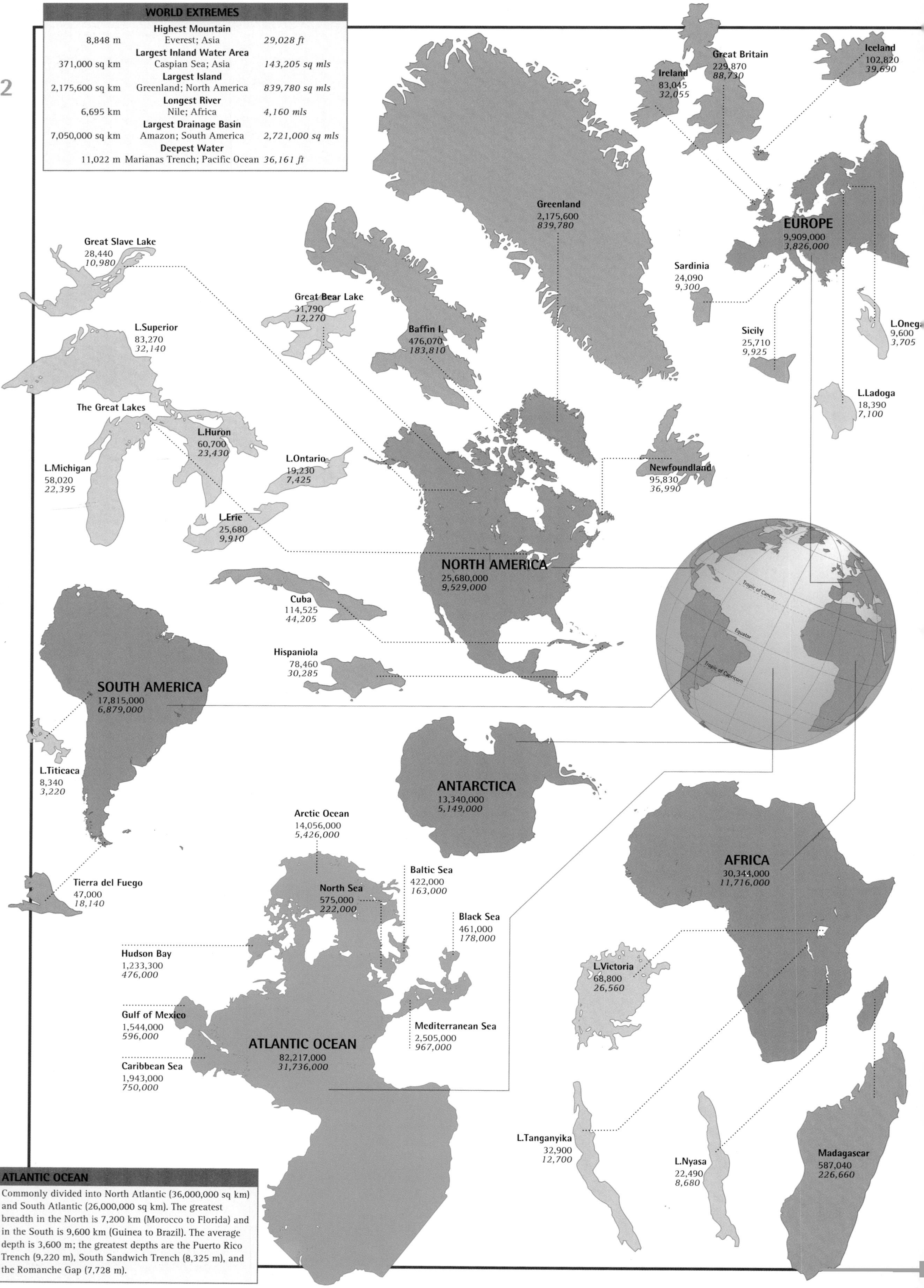

WORLD EXTREMES

Highest Mountain
8,848 m   Everest; Asia   29,028 ft
Largest Inland Water Area
371,000 sq km   Caspian Sea; Asia   143,205 sq mls
Largest Island
2,175,600 sq km   Greenland; North America   839,780 sq mls
Longest River
6,695 km   Nile; Africa   4,160 mls
Largest Drainage Basin
7,050,000 sq km   Amazon; South America   2,721,000 sq mls
Deepest Water
11,022 m Marianas Trench; Pacific Ocean   36,161 ft

ATLANTIC OCEAN

Commonly divided into North Atlantic (36,000,000 sq km) and South Atlantic (26,000,000 sq km). The greatest breadth in the North is 7,200 km (Morocco to Florida) and in the South is 9,600 km (Guinea to Brazil). The average depth is 3,600 m; the greatest depths are the Puerto Rico Trench (9,220 m), South Sandwich Trench (8,325 m), and the Romanche Gap (7,728 m).

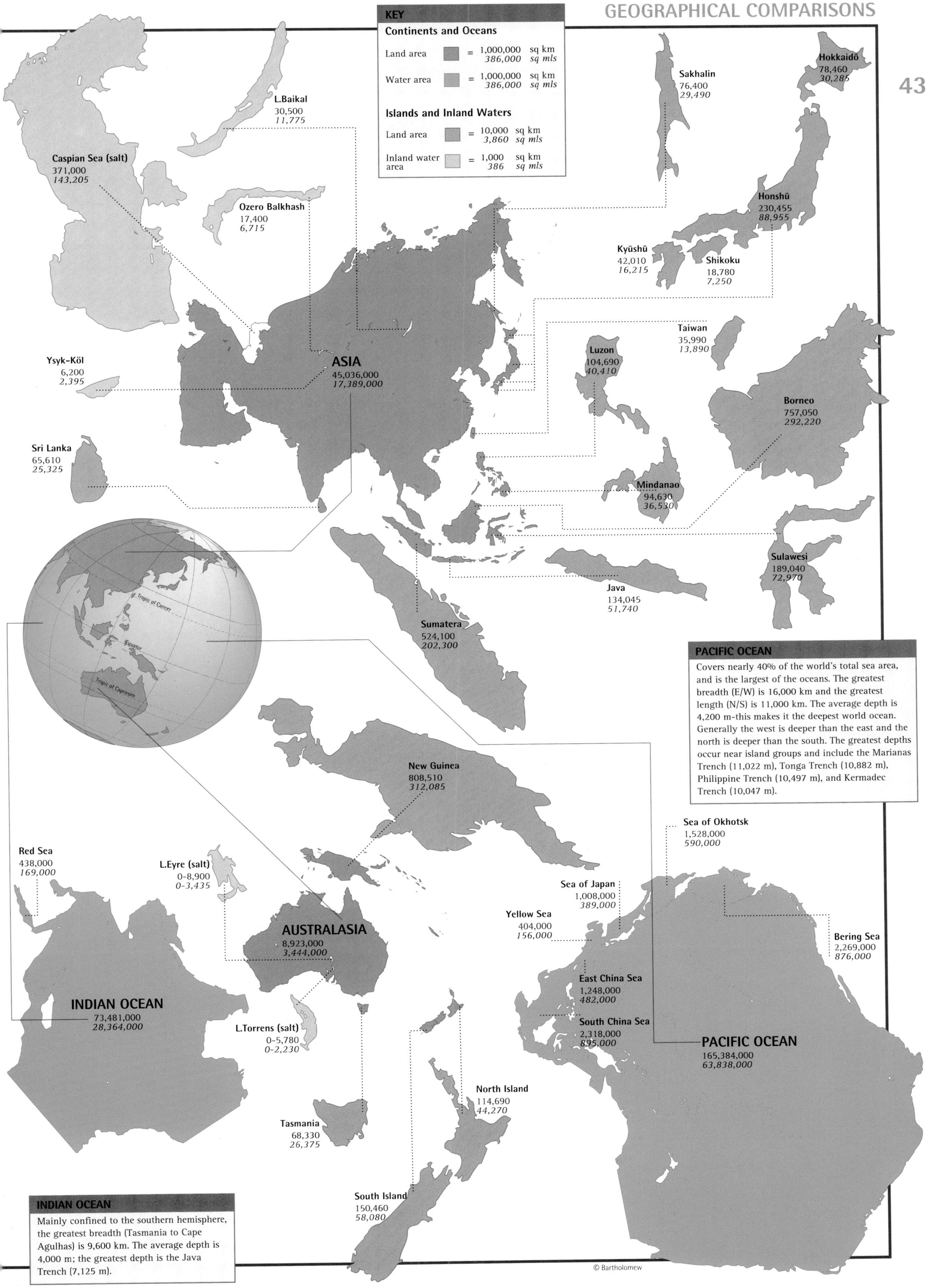

KEY

Continents and Oceans

Land area = 1,000,000 sq km
386,000 sq mls

Water area = 1,000,000 sq km
386,000 sq mls

Islands and Inland Waters

Land area = 10,000 sq km
3,860 sq mls

Inland water area = 1,000 sq km
386 sq mls

L.Baikal
30,500
11,775

Caspian Sea (salt)
371,000
143,205

Ozero Balkhash
17,400
6,715

Ysyk-Köl
6,200
2,395

ASIA
45,036,000
17,389,000

Sri Lanka
65,610
25,325

Sumatera
524,100
202,300

Sakhalin
76,400
29,490

Hokkaidō
78,460
30,285

Honshū
230,455
88,955

Kyūshū
42,010
16,215

Shikoku
18,780
7,250

Taiwan
35,990
13,890

Luzon
104,690
40,410

Borneo
757,050
292,220

Mindanao
94,630
36,530

Sulawesi
189,040
72,970

Java
134,045
51,740

New Guinea
808,510
312,085

PACIFIC OCEAN

Covers nearly 40% of the world's total sea area, and is the largest of the oceans. The greatest breadth (E/W) is 16,000 km and the greatest length (N/S) is 11,000 km. The average depth is 4,200 m-this makes it the deepest world ocean. Generally the west is deeper than the east and the north is deeper than the south. The greatest depths occur near island groups and include the Marianas Trench (11,022 m), Tonga Trench (10,882 m), Philippine Trench (10,497 m), and Kermadec Trench (10,047 m).

Red Sea
438,000
169,000

L.Eyre (salt)
0-8,900
0-3,435

AUSTRALASIA
8,923,000
3,444,000

INDIAN OCEAN
73,481,000
28,364,000

L.Torrens (salt)
0-5,780
0-2,230

Sea of Okhotsk
1,528,000
590,000

Sea of Japan
1,008,000
389,000

Yellow Sea
404,000
156,000

Bering Sea
2,269,000
876,000

East China Sea
1,248,000
482,000

South China Sea
2,318,000
895,000

PACIFIC OCEAN
165,384,000
63,838,000

North Island
114,690
44,270

Tasmania
68,330
26,375

South Island
150,460
58,080

INDIAN OCEAN

Mainly confined to the southern hemisphere, the greatest breadth (Tasmania to Cape Agulhas) is 9,600 km. The average depth is 4,000 m; the greatest depth is the Java Trench (7,125 m).

© Bartholomew

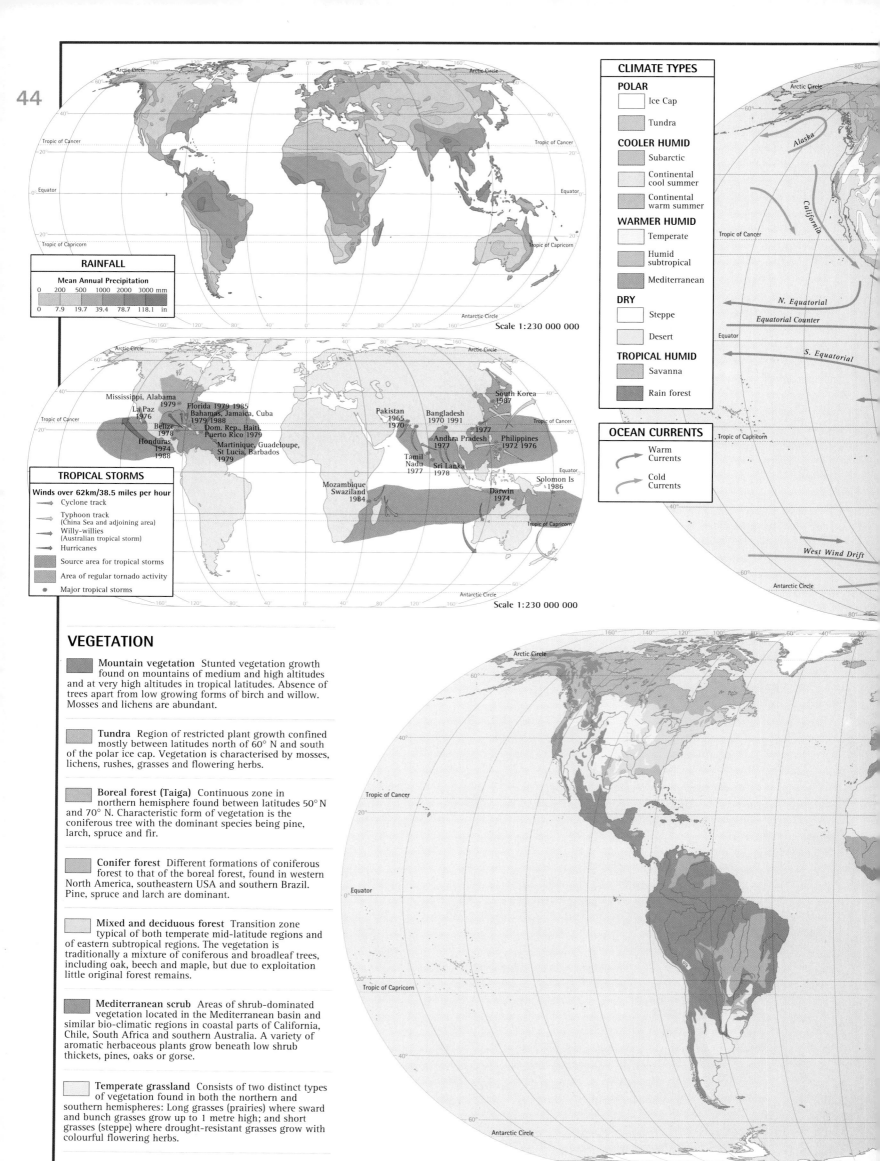

CLIMATE TYPES

POLAR

Ice Cap

Tundra

COOLER HUMID

Subarctic

Continental cool summer

Continental warm summer

WARMER HUMID

Temperate

Humid subtropical

Mediterranean

DRY

Steppe

Desert

TROPICAL HUMID

Savanna

Rain forest

OCEAN CURRENTS

Warm Currents

Cold Currents

Alaska

California

N. Equatorial

Equatorial Counter

S. Equatorial

West Wind Drift

RAINFALL

Mean Annual Precipitation

0	200	500	1000	2000	3000 mm
0	7.9	19.7	39.4	78.7	118.1 in

Scale 1:230 000 000

TROPICAL STORMS

Winds over 62km/38.5 miles per hour

→ Cyclone track

→ Typhoon track (China Sea and adjoining area)

→ Willy-willies (Australian tropical storm)

→ Hurricanes

Source area for tropical storms

Area of regular tornado activity

• Major tropical storms

Mississippi, Alabama 1979
La Paz 1976
Belize 1978
Honduras 1974 1988
Florida 1979 1985
Bahamas, Jamaica, Cuba 1979/1988
Dom. Rep., Haiti, Puerto Rico 1979
Martinique, Guadeloupe, St Lucia, Barbados 1979
South Korea 1987
Pakistan 1965 1970
Bangladesh 1970 1991
1977
Andhra Pradesh 1977
Philippines 1972 1976
Tamil Nadu 1977
Sri Lanka 1978
Mozambique Swaziland 1984
Darwin 1974
Solomon Is 1986

Scale 1:230 000 000

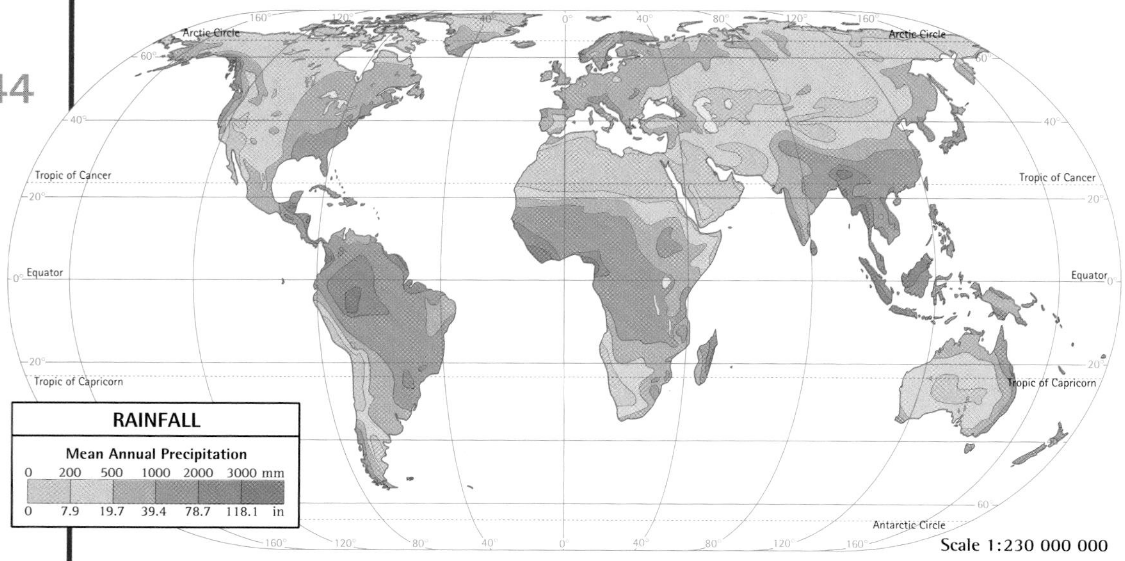

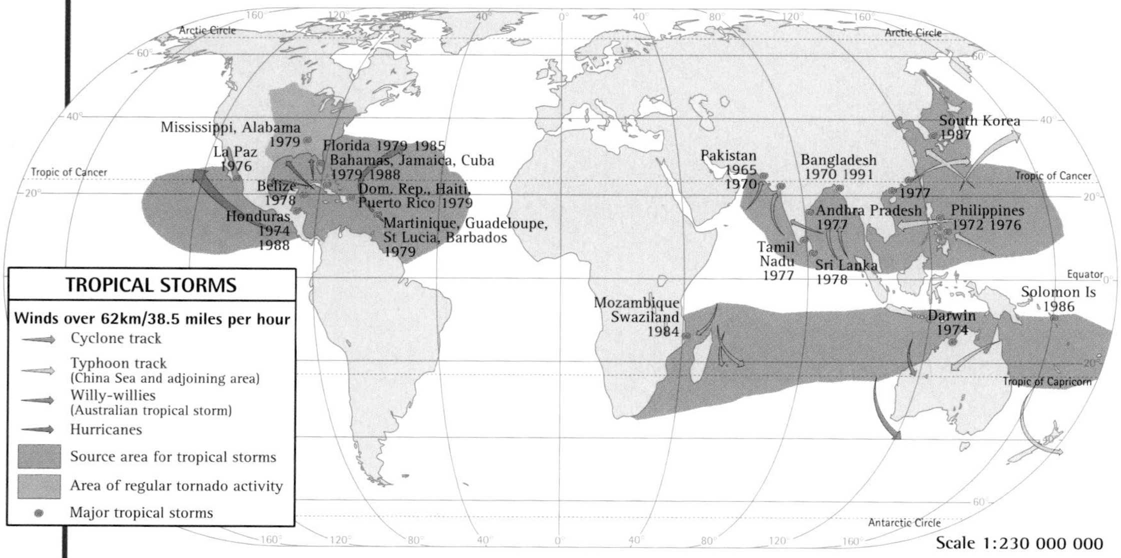

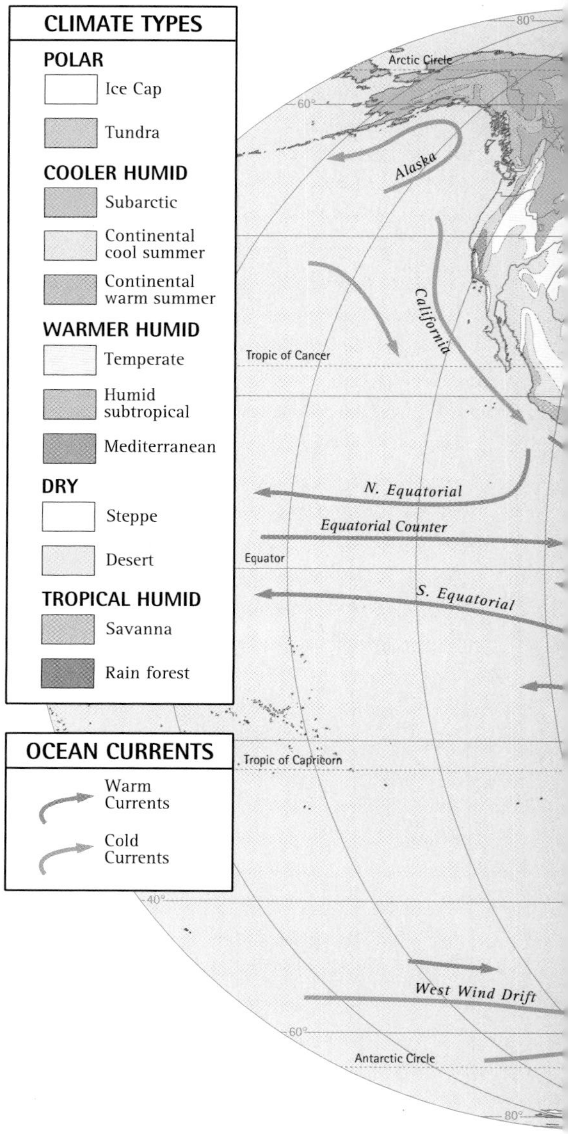

VEGETATION

Mountain vegetation Stunted vegetation growth found on mountains of medium and high altitudes and at very high altitudes in tropical latitudes. Absence of trees apart from low growing forms of birch and willow. Mosses and lichens are abundant.

Tundra Region of restricted plant growth confined mostly between latitudes north of 60° N and south of the polar ice cap. Vegetation is characterised by mosses, lichens, rushes, grasses and flowering herbs.

Boreal forest (Taiga) Continuous zone in northern hemisphere found between latitudes 50° N and 70° N. Characteristic form of vegetation is the coniferous tree with the dominant species being pine, larch, spruce and fir.

Conifer forest Different formations of coniferous forest to that of the boreal forest, found in western North America, southeastern USA and southern Brazil. Pine, spruce and larch are dominant.

Mixed and deciduous forest Transition zone typical of both temperate mid-latitude regions and of eastern subtropical regions. The vegetation is traditionally a mixture of coniferous and broadleaf trees, including oak, beech and maple, but due to exploitation little original forest remains.

Mediterranean scrub Areas of shrub-dominated vegetation located in the Mediterranean basin and similar bio-climatic regions in coastal parts of California, Chile, South Africa and southern Australia. A variety of aromatic herbaceous plants grow beneath low shrub thickets, pines, oaks or gorse.

Temperate grassland Consists of two distinct types of vegetation found in both the northern and southern hemispheres: Long grasses (prairies) where sward and bunch grasses grow up to 1 metre high; and short grasses (steppe) where drought-resistant grasses grow with colourful flowering herbs.

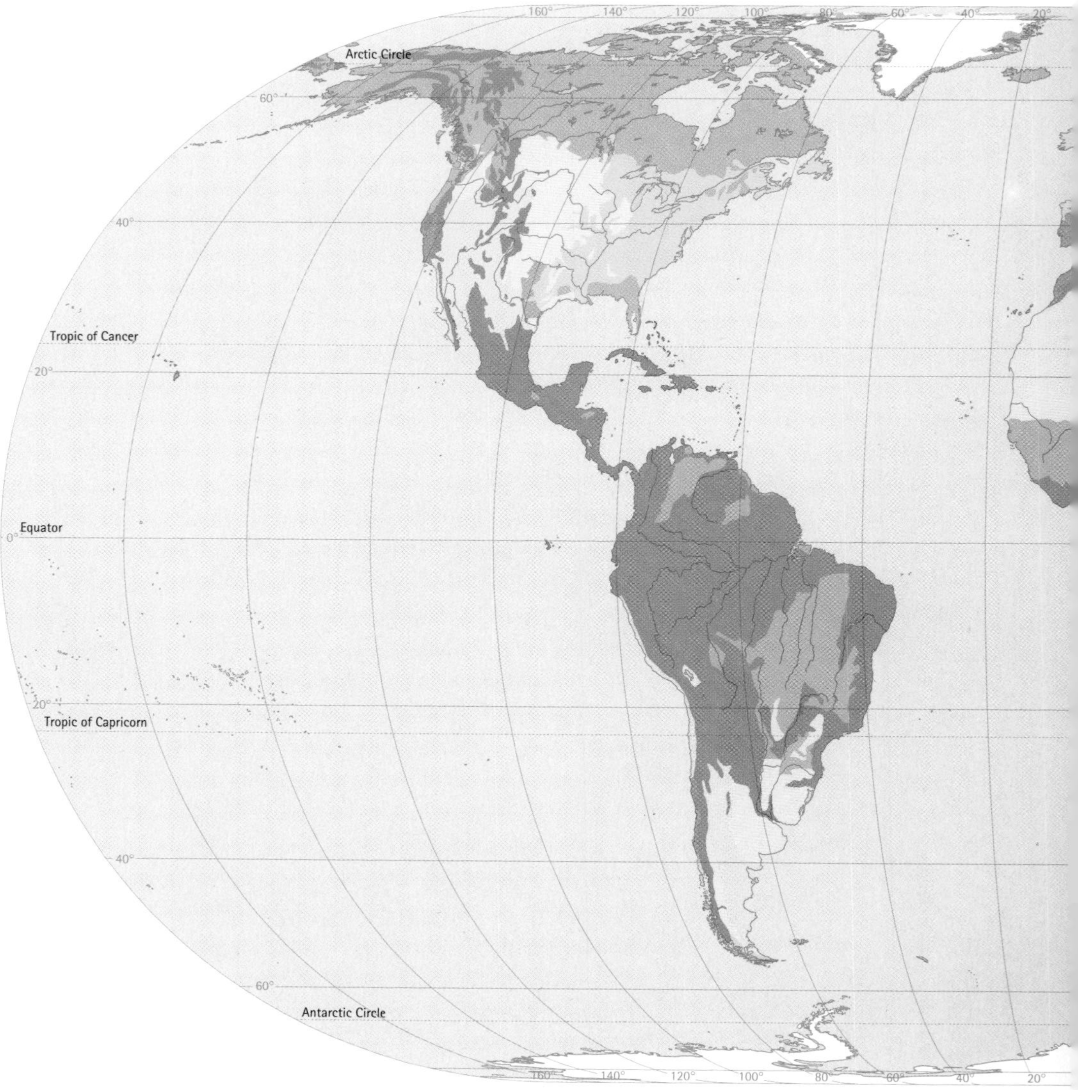

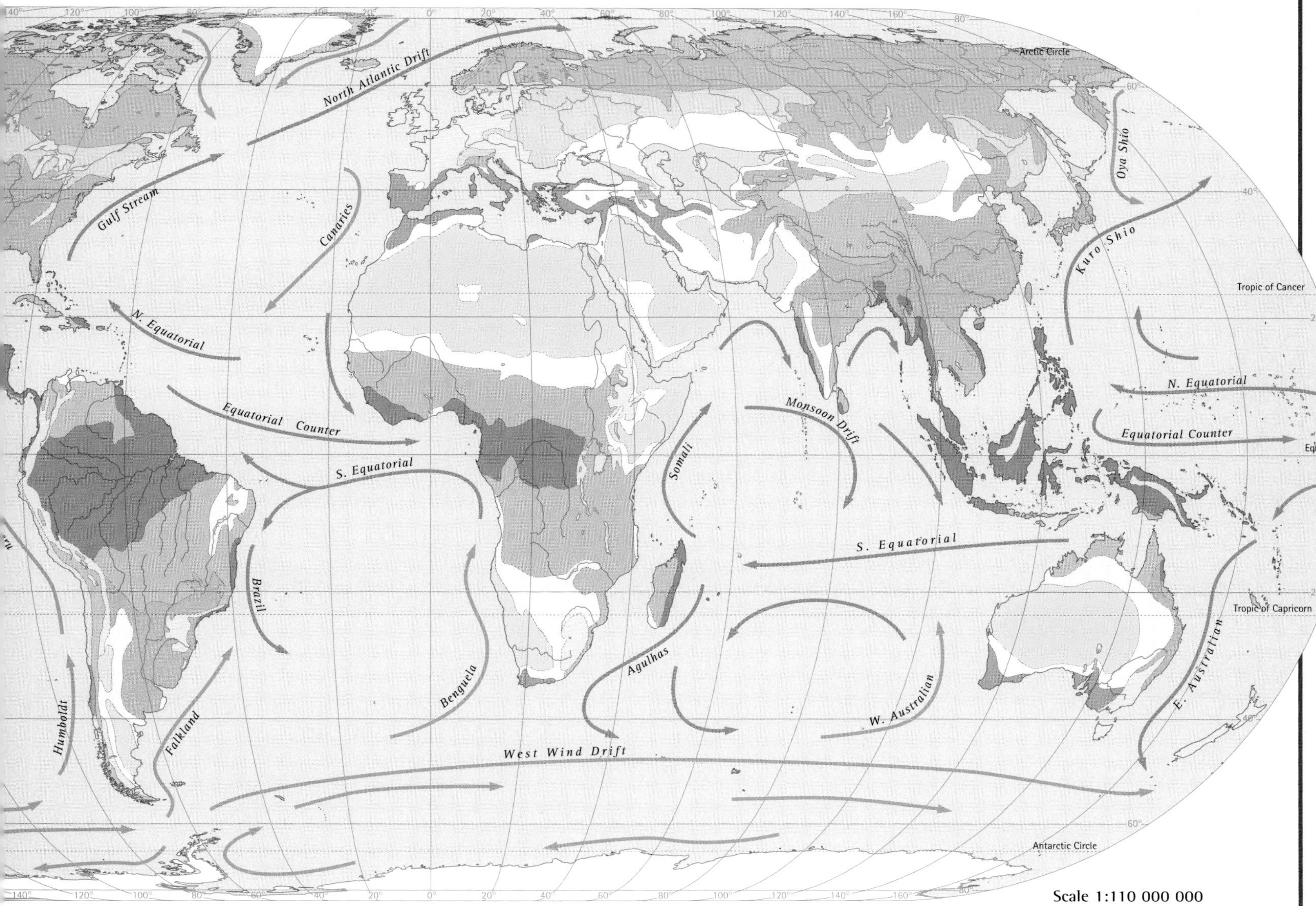

Scale 1:110 000 000

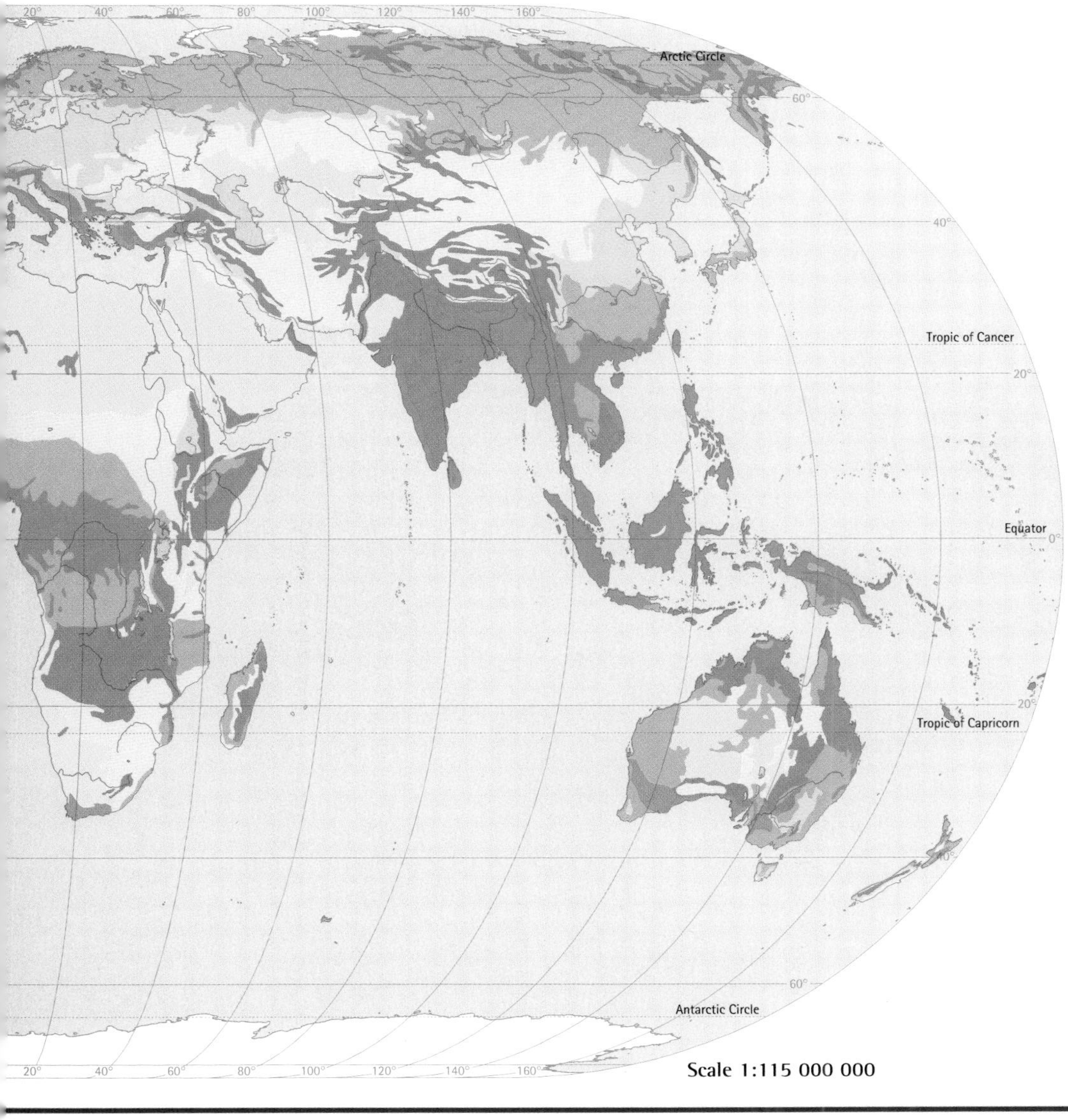

Scale 1:115 000 000

Savanna Grassland found in the tropics to the north and south of the tropical rain forests of South America and Africa and around the desert fringes of Australia. Grasses are interspersed with scattered thorn bushes or deciduous trees such as acacia in Africa and eucalypts in Australia.

Tropical rain forest (Selva) Dense forest located in tropical areas of high rainfall and continuous high temperature, particularly Central America, northern South America, west-central Africa and Southeast Asia. Up to three tree layers grow above a variable shrub layer.

Monsoon forest Deciduous forest mostly occuring in eastern India, parts of Southeast Asia and northern and northeastern Australia, growing in association with the monsoon climate.

Dry tropical forest and scrub Forest and scrub found in Central and South America, Africa, the Indian sub-continent and Australia. Thorny scrub and low to medium-sized semi-deciduous trees characterise the forest areas, whilst in the scrub areas the trees are replaced by low-growing widely spaced shrubs, bushes and succulents.

Sub-tropical forest Hardleaf evergreen forests growing between latitudes 15° to 40° north and south of the equator in China, Japan, Australia, New Zealand and South Africa.

Desert vegetation Limited vegetation growth in the harsh, dry conditions of desert areas. Xerophytic shrubs, grasses and cacti adapt themselves by relying on the chance occurrence of rain, storing water when it is available in short bursts and limiting water loss.

Ice cap and ice shelf Areas of permanent ice cap around the north and south poles. The intense cold, dry weather and the ice cover render these regions almost lifeless. In Antarctica, tiny patches of land free of ice have a cover of mosses and lichens which provide shelter for some insects and mites.

URBAN AGGLOMERATIONS

The populations given below are for selected urban agglomerations. These are defined as adjacent areas of settlement inhabited at urban levels of residential density, without regard to administrative boundaries.

Oceania

3,590,000	Sydney *Australia*
3,094,000	Melbourne *Australia*
1,450,000	Brisbane *Australia*
1,220,000	Perth *Australia*
1,039,000	Adelaide *Australia*
945,000	Auckland *New Zealand*

Asia

26,836,000	Tōkyō *Japan**
15,093,000	Bombay *India*
15,082,000	Shanghai *China*
12,362,000	Beijing *China*
11,673,000	Calcutta *India*
11,641,000	Seoul *S. Korea*
11,500,000	Jakarta *Indonesia*
10,687,000	Tianjin *China*
10,601,000	Ōsaka-Kōbe *Japan*
9,882,000	Delhi *India*
9,863,000	Karachi *Pakistan*
9,280,000	Manila-Quezon City *Philippines*
7,832,000	Dhaka *Bangladesh*
6,830,000	Tehrān *Iran*
6,566,000	Bangkok *Thailand*
5,906,000	Madras *India*
5,574,000	Hong Kong *China*
5,343,000	Hyderabad *India*
5,310,000	Shenyang *China*
5,085,000	Lahore *Pakistan*
4,749,000	Bangalore *India*
4,478,000	Baghdād *Iraq*
4,399,000	Wuhan *China*
4,082,000	Pusan *S. Korea*
4,056,000	Guangzhou *China*
3,851,000	Yangon *Myanmar*
3,688,000	Ahmadabad *India*
3,555,000	Hồ Chi Minh *Vietnam*
3,525,000	Chongqing *China*
3,417,000	T'ai-pei *Taiwan*
3,401,000	Chengdu *China*
3,303,000	Harbin *China*
3,283,000	Xi'an *China*
3,196,000	Nagoya *Japan*
3,132,000	Dalian *China*
3,019,000	Jinan *China*
2,977,000	Bandung *Indonesia*
2,965,000	Nanjing *China*
2,940,000	Pune *India*
2,848,000	Singapore *Singapore*
2,826,000	Ankara *Turkey*
2,742,000	Surabaya *Indonesia*
2,704,000	Kita-Kyūshū *Japan*
2,576,000	Riyadh *Saudi Arabia*
2,523,000	Changchun *China*
2,502,000	Taiyuan *China*
2,470,000	P'yŏngyang *N. Korea*
2,432,000	Taegu *S. Korea*
2,356,000	Kanpur *India*
2,288,000	Tashkent *Uzbekistan*
2,222,000	Medan *Indonesia*
2,052,000	Damascus *Syria*
2,034,000	Kābul *Afghanistan*
2,031,000	İzmir *Turkey*
2,029,000	Lucknow *India*
2,011,000	Mashhad *Iran*
1,999,000	Zhengzhou *China*
1,942,000	Kunming *China*
1,921,000	Tel Aviv-Yafo *Israel*
1,875,000	Faisalabad *Pakistan*
1,855,000	Aleppo *Syria*
1,853,000	Baku *Azerbaijan*
1,792,000	Guiyang *China*
1,726,000	Kao-hsiung *Taiwan*
1,676,000	Peshawar *Pakistan*
1,643,000	Ürümqi *China*
1,581,000	Hangzhou *China*
1,563,000	Beirut *Lebanon*
1,498,000	Nanning *China*
1,469,000	Novosibirsk *Rus.Fed.*
1,353,000	T'bilisi *Georgia*
1,305,000	Yerevan *Armenia*
1,262,000	Almaty *Kazakstan*
1,247,000	Ha Nôi *Vietnam*
1,238,000	Kuala Lumpur *Malaysia*
1,187,000	'Ammān *Jordan*

Europe

9,469,000	Paris *France*
9,233,000	Moscow *Rus.Fed.*
7,817,000	İstanbul *Turkey*
7,335,000	London *U.K.*
6,481,000	Essen *Germany*
5,111,000	St Petersburg *Rus.Fed.*
4,251,000	Milan *Italy*
4,072,000	Madrid *Spain*
3,693,000	Athens *Greece*
3,606,000	Frankfurt am Main *Germany*
3,552,000	Katowice *Poland*
3,317,000	Berlin *Germany*
3,012,000	Naples *Italy*
2,984,000	Cologne *Germany*
2,931,000	Rome *Italy*
2,819,000	Barcelona *Spain*
2,809,000	Kiev *Ukraine*
2,625,000	Hamburg *Germany*
2,316,000	Warsaw *Poland*
2,302,000	Birmingham *U.K.*
2,277,000	Manchester *U.K.*
2,090,000	Bucharest *Romania*
2,060,000	Vienna *Austria*
2,017,000	Budapest *Hungary*
1,863,000	Lisbon *Portugal*
1,766,000	Minsk *Belarus*
1,680,000	Kharkiv *Ukraine*
1,545,000	Stockholm *Sweden*
1,454,000	Nizhniy Novgorod *Rus.Fed.*
1,413,000	Yekaterinburg *Rus.Fed.*
1,405,000	Belgrade *Yugoslavia*
1,384,000	Sofia *Bulgaria*
1,326,000	Copenhagen *Denmark*
1,311,000	Lyons *France*
1,230,000	Dnipropetrovs'k *Ukraine*
1,225,000	Prague *Czech Rep.*
1,109,000	Amsterdam *Netherlands*

Africa

10,287,000	Lagos *Nigeria*
9,656,000	Cairo *Egypt*
4,214,000	Kinshasa *Congo (Zaire)*
3,702,000	Algiers *Algeria*
3,577,000	Alexandria *Egypt*
3,289,000	Casablanca *Morocco*
3,272,000	Tripoli *Libya*
2,797,000	Abidjan *Côte d'Ivoire*
2,671,000	Cape Town *S. Africa*
2,429,000	Khartoum *Sudan*
2,227,000	Maputo *Mozambique*
2,209,000	Addis Ababa *Ethiopia*
2,207,000	Luanda *Angola*
2,079,000	Nairobi *Kenya*
2,037,000	Tunis *Tunisia*
1,986,000	Dakar *Senegal*
1,849,000	Johannesburg *S. Africa*
1,734,000	Dar es Salaam *Tanzania*
1,687,000	Accra *Ghana*
1,578,000	Rabat *Morocco*
1,322,000	Douala *Cameroon*
1,044,000	Harare *Zimbabwe*

North America

16,329,000	New York *U.S.A.*
15,643,000	México *Mexico*
12,410,000	Los Angeles *U.S.A.*
6,846,000	Chicago *U.S.A.*
4,483,000	Toronto *Canada*
4,304,000	Philadelphia *U.S.A.*
4,111,000	Washington D.C. *U.S.A.*
3,866,000	San Francisco *U.S.A.*
3,725,000	Detroit *U.S.A.*
3,612,000	Dallas *U.S.A.*
3,447,000	Miami-Fort Lauderdale *U.S.A.*
3,320,000	Montréal *Canada*
3,166,000	Houston *U.S.A.*
3,165,000	Guadalajara *Mexico*
2,842,000	Boston *U.S.A.*
2,806,000	Monterrey *Mexico*
2,716,000	San Diego *U.S.A.*
2,580,000	Santo Domingo *Dominican Republic*
2,464,000	Atlanta *U.S.A.*
2,353,000	Phoenix *U.S.A.*
2,241,000	Havana *Cuba*
2,239,000	Minneapolis *U.S.A.*
2,009,000	St Louis *U.S.A.*
1,969,000	Baltimore *U.S.A.*
1,939,000	Seattle *U.S.A.*
1,905,000	Tampa *U.S.A.*
1,823,000	Vancouver *Canada*
1,692,000	Cleveland *U.S.A.*
1,692,000	Pittsburg *U.S.A.*
1,682,000	Norfolk *U.S.A.*
1,611,000	Denver *U.S.A.*
1,266,000	Port-au-Prince *Haiti*
1,101,000	San Juan *Puerto Rico*
946,000	Guatemala *Guatemala*

South America

16,417,000	São Paulo *Brazil*
10,990,000	Buenos Aires *Argentina*
9,888,000	Rio de Janeiro *Brazil*
7,452,000	Lima *Peru*
5,614,000	Bogotá *Colombia*
5,065,000	Santiago *Chile*
3,899,000	Belo Horizonte *Brazil*
3,349,000	Porto Alegre *Brazil*
3,168,000	Recife *Brazil*
2,959,000	Caracas *Venezuela*
2,819,000	Salvador *Brazil*
2,660,000	Fortaleza *Brazil*
1,778,000	Brasília *Brazil*
1,769,000	Cali *Colombia*
1,717,000	Guayaquil *Ecuador*
1,607,000	Campinas *Brazil*
1,600,000	Maracaibo *Venezuela*
1,326,000	Montevideo *Uruguay*
1,294,000	Córdoba *Argentina*
1,246,000	La Paz *Bolivia*
1,244,000	Quito *Ecuador*

*includes Yokohama, Kawasaki, Chiba, and other adjacent towns and cities.

Source: United Nations. World urbanization prospects: the 1994 revision: estimates and projections of urban and rural populations and of urban agglomerations.

Eckert IV Projection

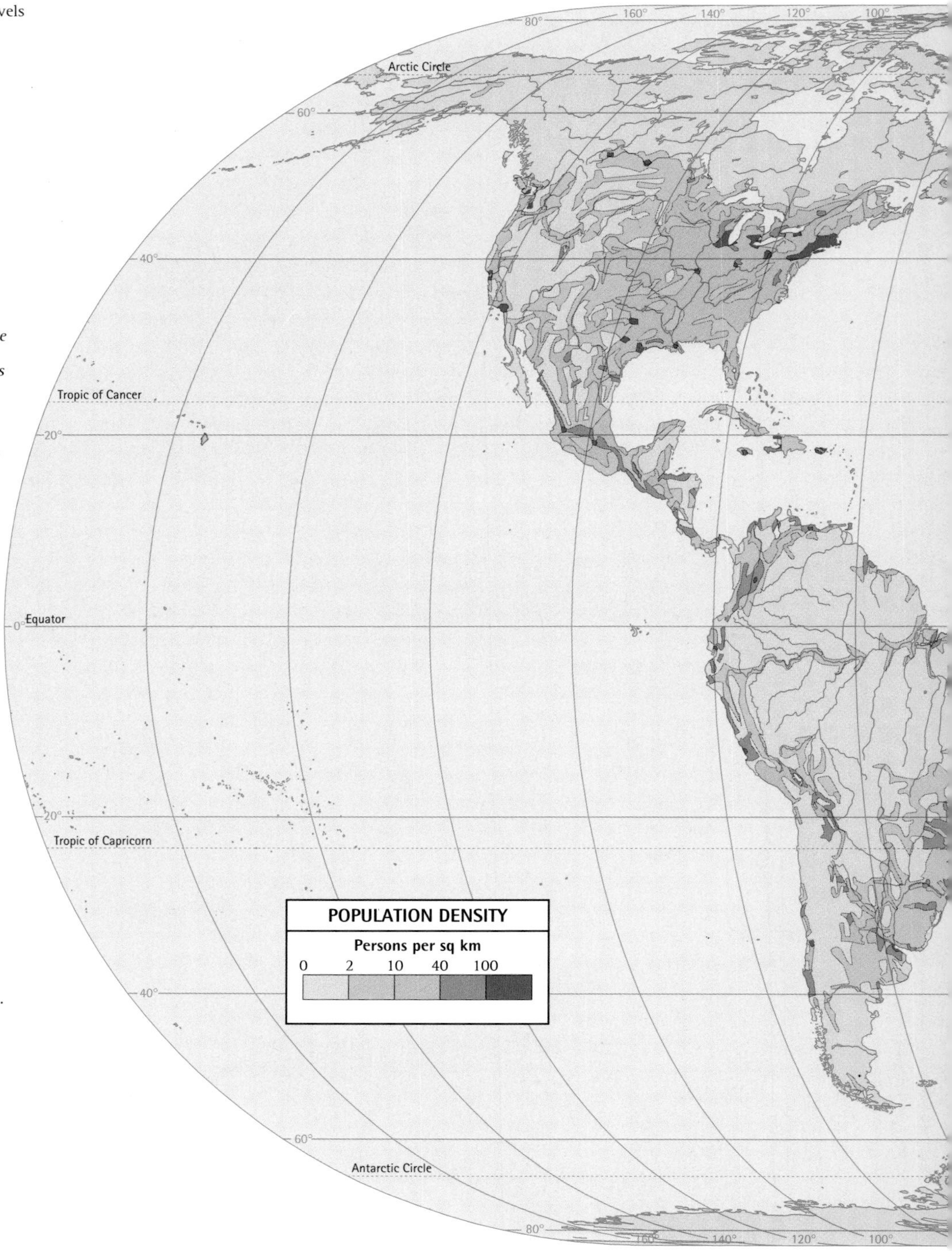

POPULATION DENSITY

Persons per sq km

0	2	10	40	100

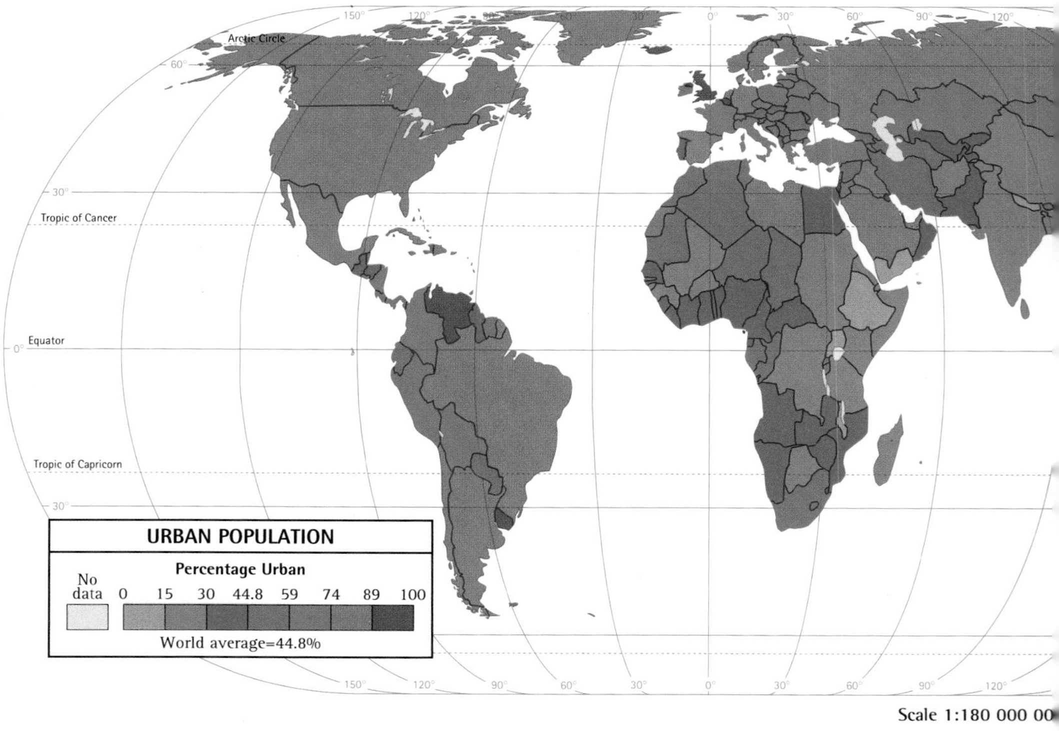

URBAN POPULATION

Percentage Urban

No data	0	15	30	44.8	59	74	89	100

World average=44.8%

Scale 1:180 000 000

Scale 1 : 90 000 000

POPULATION CHANGE

Percentage Population Change

No data -6.0 0 1.0 1.5 2.2 3.0 6.0

Statistics for 1990-95

Scale 1:180 000 000

© Bartholomew

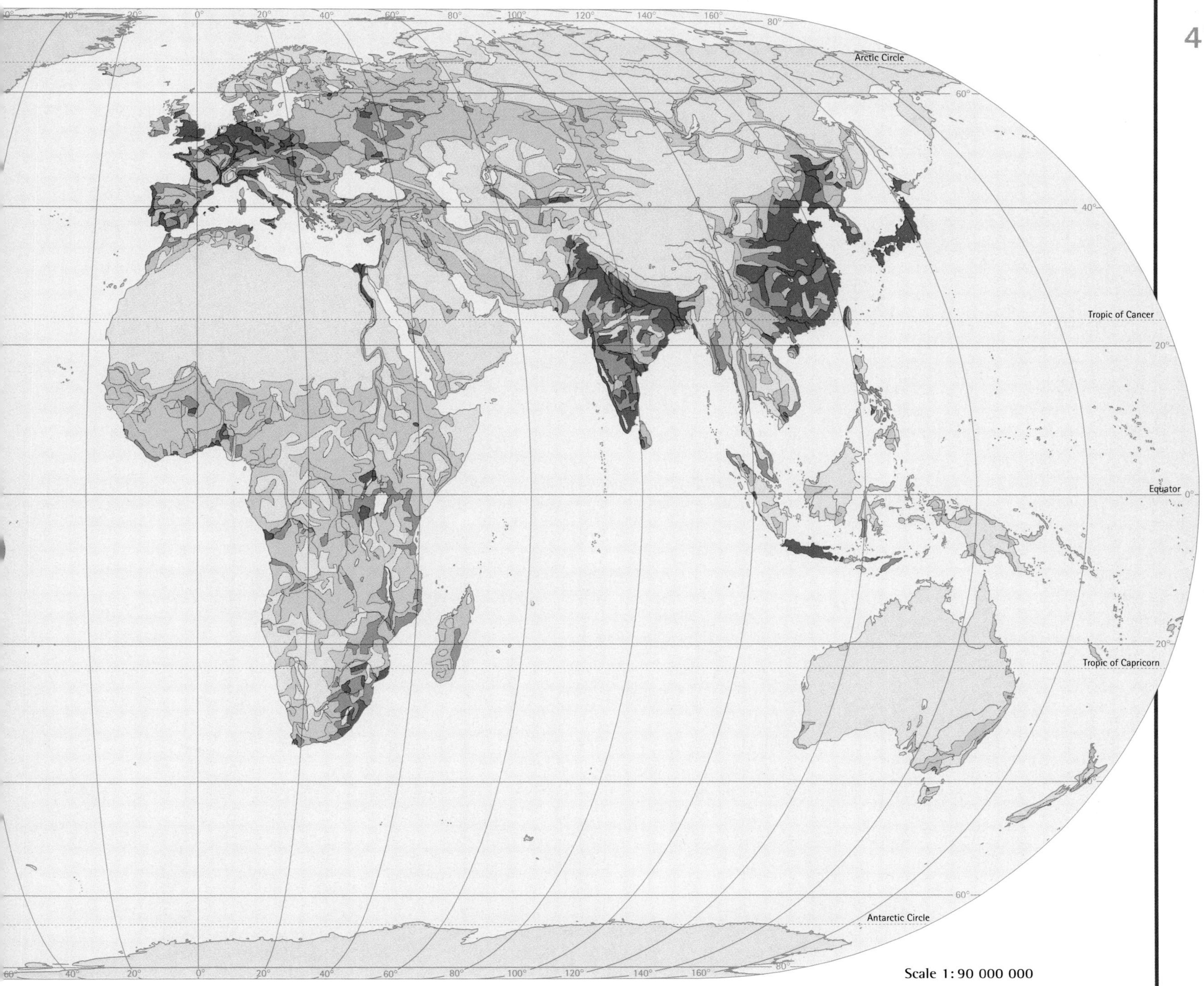

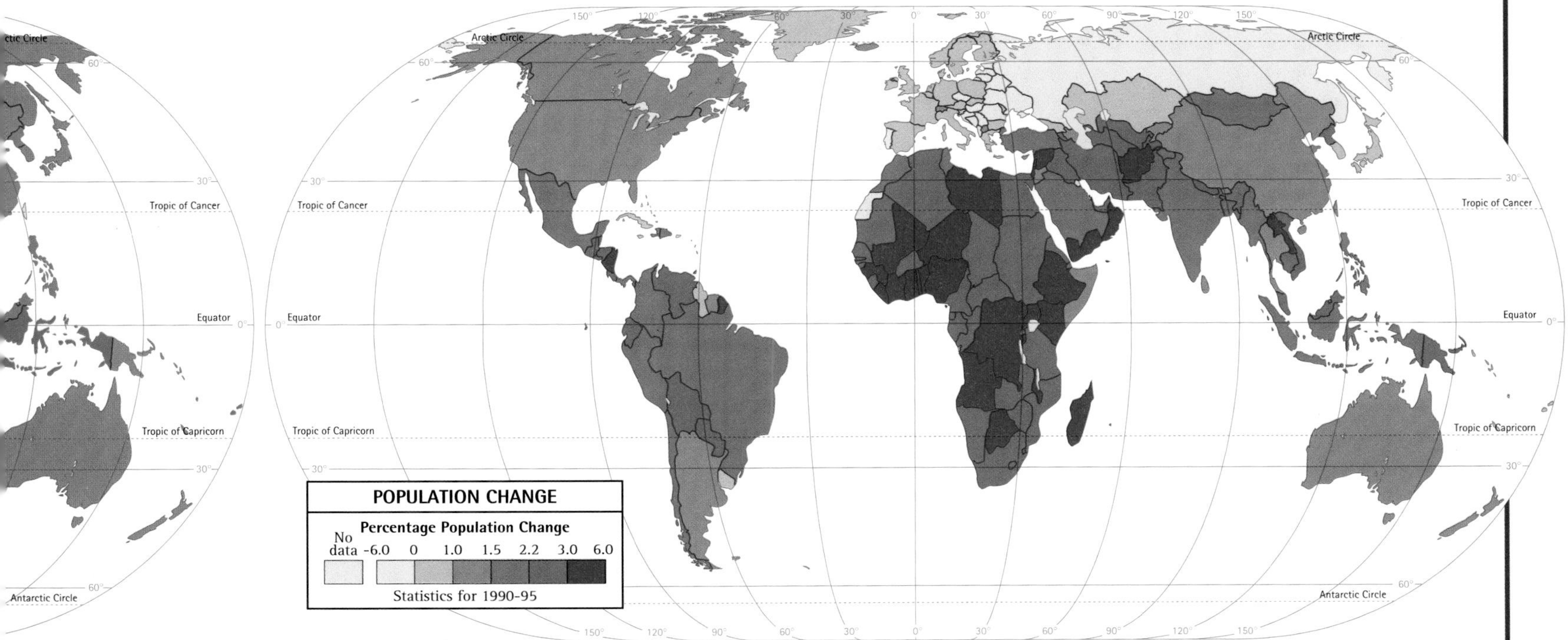

48

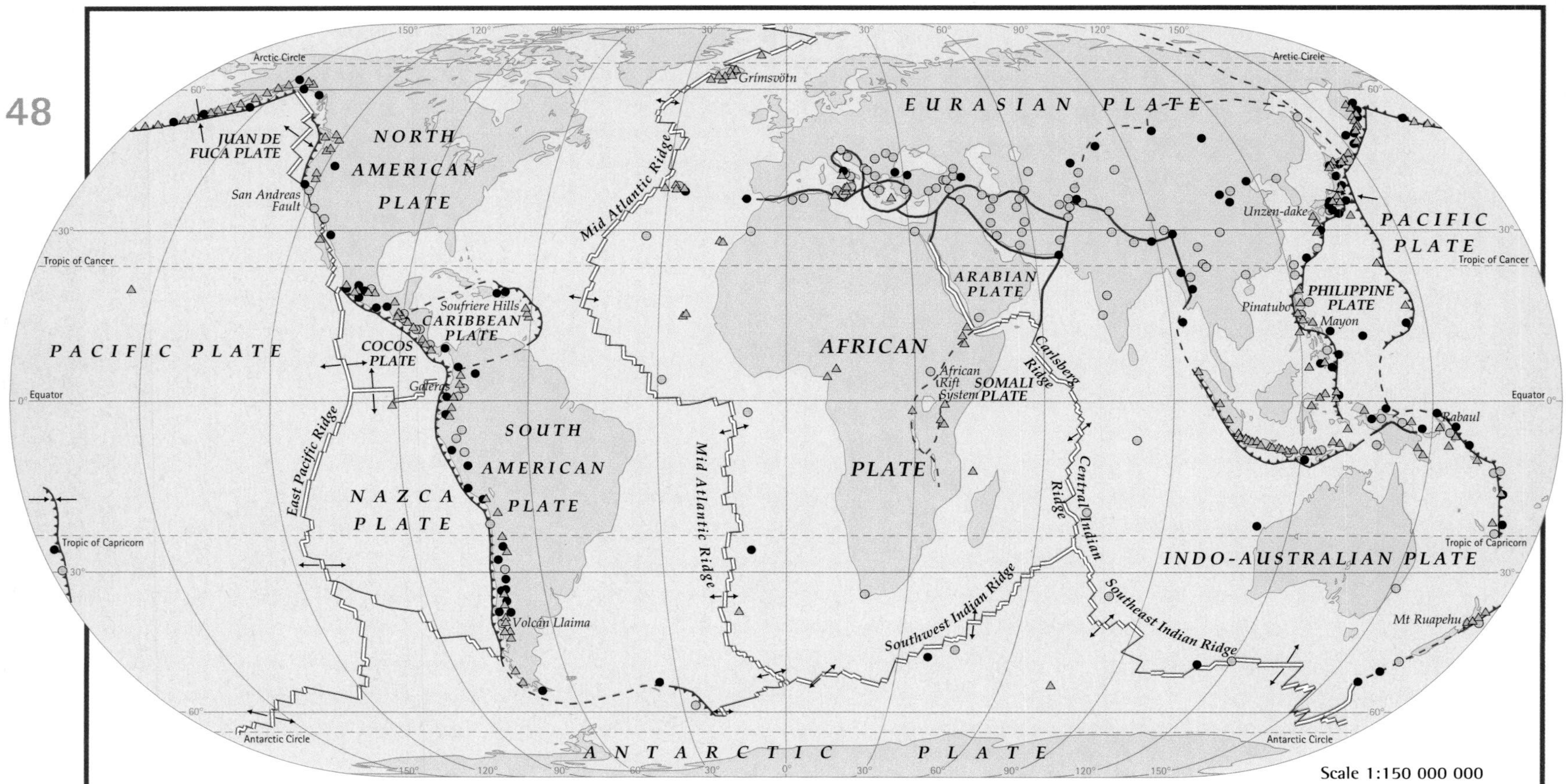

Scale 1:150 000 000

Major earthquakes since 1992

Year	Location	Force (Richter Scale)	Fatalities
1992	Kyrgyzstan	7.5	50
	Flores, Indonesia	7.5	2,500
	Erzincan, Turkey	6.8	500
	Cairo, Egypt	5.9	550
1993	Northern Japan	7.8	185
	Maharashtra, India	6.4	9,700
1994	Northern Bolivia	8.3	10
	Kuril Islands, Japan	8.3	10
1995	Kôbe, Japan	7.2	5,200
	Sakhalin, Rus. Fed.	7.6	2,500
1996	Biak, Indonesia	7.5	100
1997	Baluchistan, Pakistan	7.3	100
	Khorasan, Iran	7.1	2,400

EARTHQUAKES and VOLCANOES

〜〜〜 **Plate boundary and subduction zone**
Where a continental plate meets an oceanic plate, or where two oceanic plates collide, causing one plate to descend beneath the other, the process is known as subduction and forms deep ocean trenches.

—— **Plate boundary and collision zone**
Where two continental plates collide, the edge of one plate wedges under the other and throws up rocks from the continental crust which buckle and produce chains of fold mountains.

⊔ **Plate boundary and ocean ridge**
Where two oceanic plates drift apart their edges lift to form a ridge. Magma rises through the rift in the crust and cools to form new crust, creating mid-ocean ridges on the ocean floor.

– – – **Plate boundary uncertain**

● **High magnitude earthquake** (over 7.8 Richter scale)

○ **Lesser magnitude earthquake**

△ **Active volcano**

Major volcanic eruptions since 1991

Year	Location
1991	Pinatubo, Philippines
	Unzen-dake, Japan
1993	Mayon, Philippines
	Galeras, Columbia
1994	Volcán Llaima, Chile
	Rabaul, Papau New Guinea
1996	Soufriere Hills, Montserrat
	Mt Ruapehu, New Zealand
	Grimsvötn, Iceland

ENERGY

△	Oil
▲	Gas
■	Coal
■	Lignite
○	Uranium
●	Hydro

OIL RESERVES 1995 (thousand million tonnes): 11.7 · 11.4 · 2.3 · 7.8 · 89.2 · 9.8 · 6.1

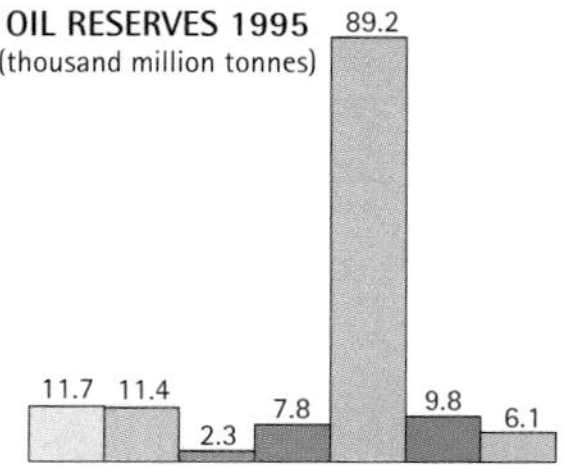

NATURAL GAS RESERVES 1995 (trillion cubic metres): 8.4 · 5.7 · 5.5 · 56.0 · 45.2 · 9.4 · 9.5

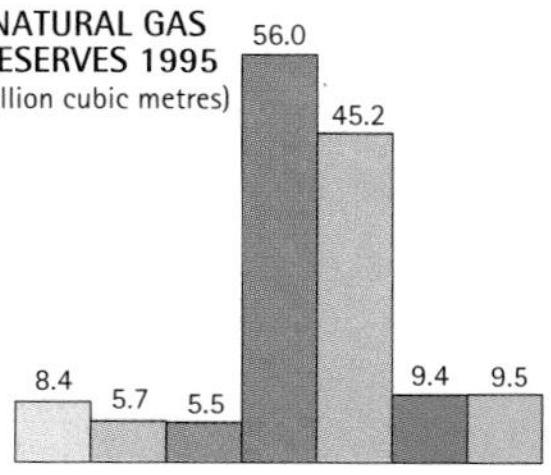

COAL RESERVES 1995 (thousand million tonnes): 250.4 · 10.2 · 156.7 · 241.0 · 61.9 · 311.5

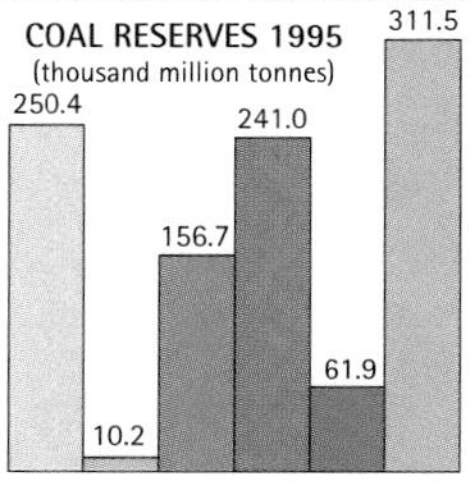

North America
South and Central America
Europe
Former Soviet Union
Middle East
Africa
Asia and Australasia

Scale 1:150 000 000

© Bartholomew

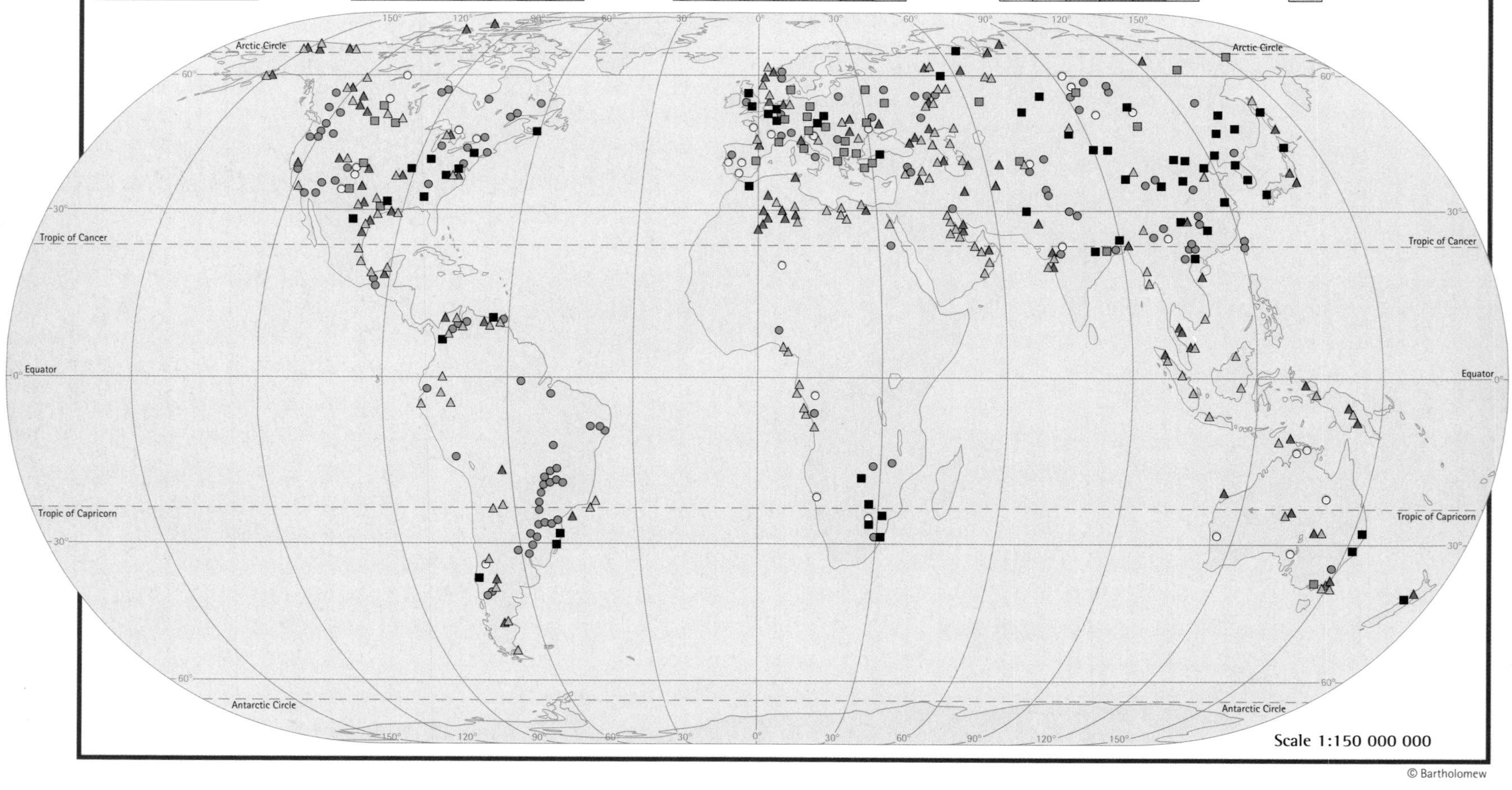

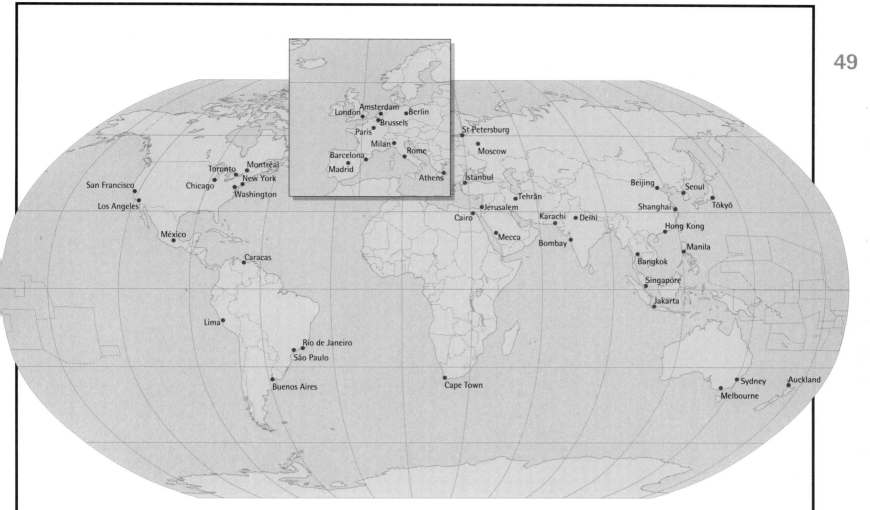

Contents

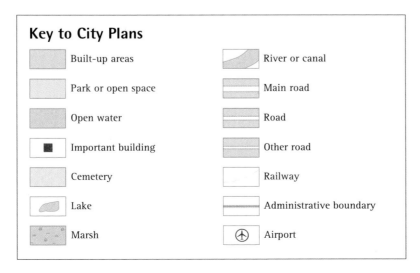

Key to City Plans

	Built-up areas		River or canal
	Park or open space		Main road
	Open water		Road
	Important building		Other road
	Cemetery		Railway
	Lake		Administrative boundary
	Marsh		Airport

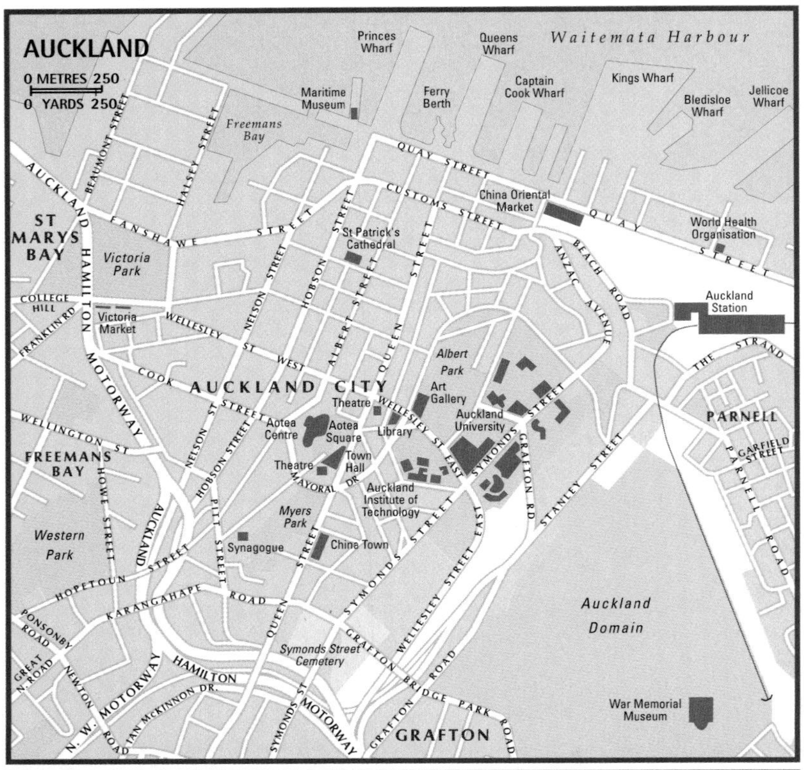

AUCKLAND

0 METRES 250
0 YARDS 250

Princes Wharf
Queens Wharf
Waitemata Harbour
Ferry Berth
Captain Cook Wharf
Kings Wharf
Bledisloe Wharf
Jellicoe Wharf
Maritime Museum
Freemans Bay
ST MARYS BAY
Victoria Park
China Oriental Market
World Health Organisation
St Patrick's Cathedral
Auckland Station
THE STRAND
Victoria Market
AUCKLAND CITY
Albert Park
Art Gallery
Auckland University
PARNELL
Theatre
Aotea Centre
Library
Aotea Square
Theatre
Town Hall
Auckland Institute of Technology
Myers Park
Synagogue
China Town
Auckland Domain
Symonds Street Cemetery
War Memorial Museum
GRAFTON

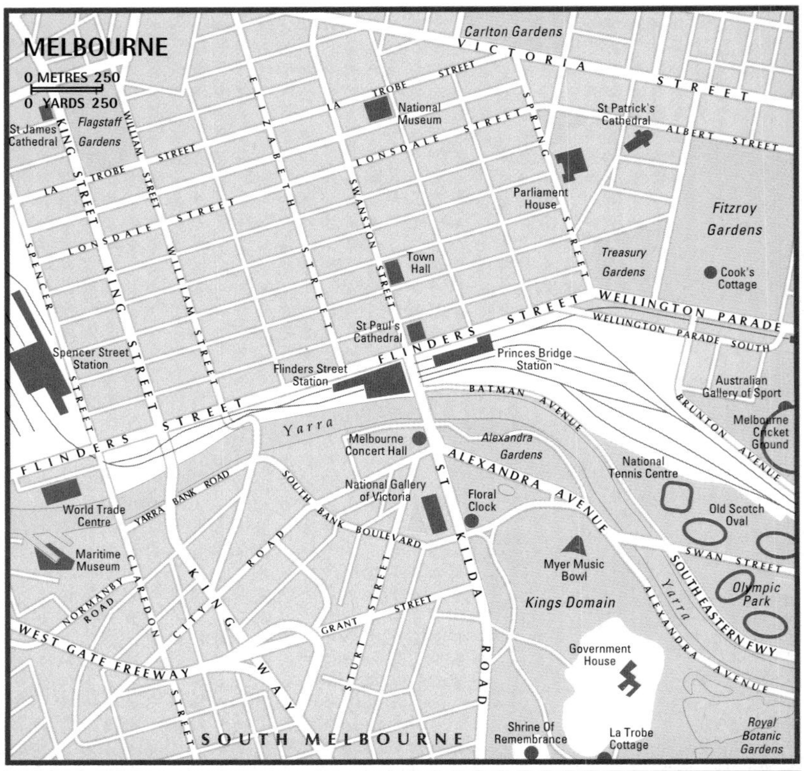

MELBOURNE

0 METRES 250
0 YARDS 250

Carlton Gardens
VICTORIA STREET
ALBERT STREET
National Museum
St Patrick's Cathedral
St James Cathedral
Flagstaff Gardens
LONSDALE STREET
Parliament House
Fitzroy Gardens
Town Hall
Treasury Gardens
Cook's Cottage
WELLINGTON PARADE
St Paul's Cathedral
FLINDERS STREET
Spencer Street Station
Flinders Street Station
Princes Bridge Station
Australian Gallery of Sport
BATMAN AVENUE
Yarra
Melbourne Cricket Ground
Melbourne Concert Hall
Alexandra Gardens
National Tennis Centre
World Trade Centre
National Gallery of Victoria
Floral Clock
Old Scotch Oval
Maritime Museum
Myer Music Bowl
Olympic Park
Kings Domain
WEST GATE FREEWAY
Government House
Shrine Of Remembrance
La Trobe Cottage
SOUTH MELBOURNE
Royal Botanic Gardens

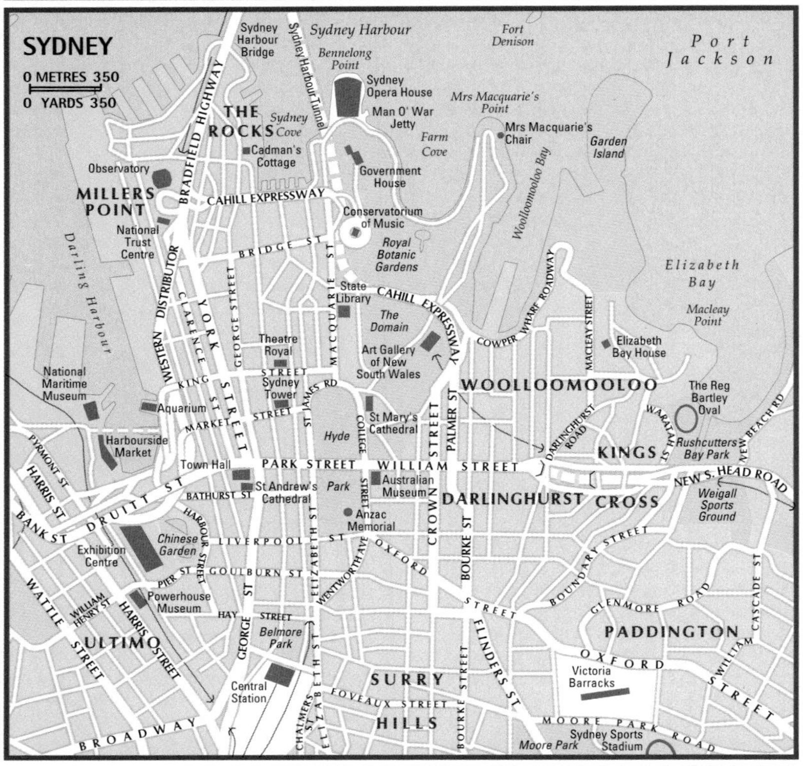

SYDNEY

0 METRES 350
0 YARDS 350

Sydney Harbour Bridge
Sydney Harbour
Bennelong Point
Fort Denison
Port Jackson
Sydney Harbour Tunnel
Sydney Opera House
Man O' War Jetty
Mrs Macquarie's Point
THE ROCKS
Sydney Cove
Cadman's Cottage
Observatory
Government House
Mrs Macquarie's Chair
Farm Cove
Garden Island
MILLERS POINT
CAHILL EXPRESSWAY
Conservatorium of Music
Royal Botanic Gardens
Elizabeth Bay
National Trust Centre
Woolloomooloo Bay
Elizabeth Bay House
BRIDGE ST
State Library
The Domain
Macleay Point
National Maritime Museum
Art Gallery of New South Wales
COWPER WHARF ROADWAY
Theatre Royal
Sydney Tower
WOOLLOOMOOLOO
The Reg Bartley Oval
Aquarium
St Mary's Cathedral
Rushcutters Bay Park
Harbourside Market
Hyde Park
KINGS CROSS
NEW S. HEAD ROAD
Town Hall
PARK STREET
WILLIAM STREET
Chinese Garden
St Andrew's Cathedral
Australian Museum
DARLINGHURST
Weigall Sports Ground
Exhibition Centre
Powerhouse Museum
PADDINGTON
ULTIMO
Belmore Park
OXFORD STREET
Victoria Barracks
Central Station
SURRY HILLS
BROADWAY
MOORE PARK ROAD
Sydney Sports Stadium
Moore Park

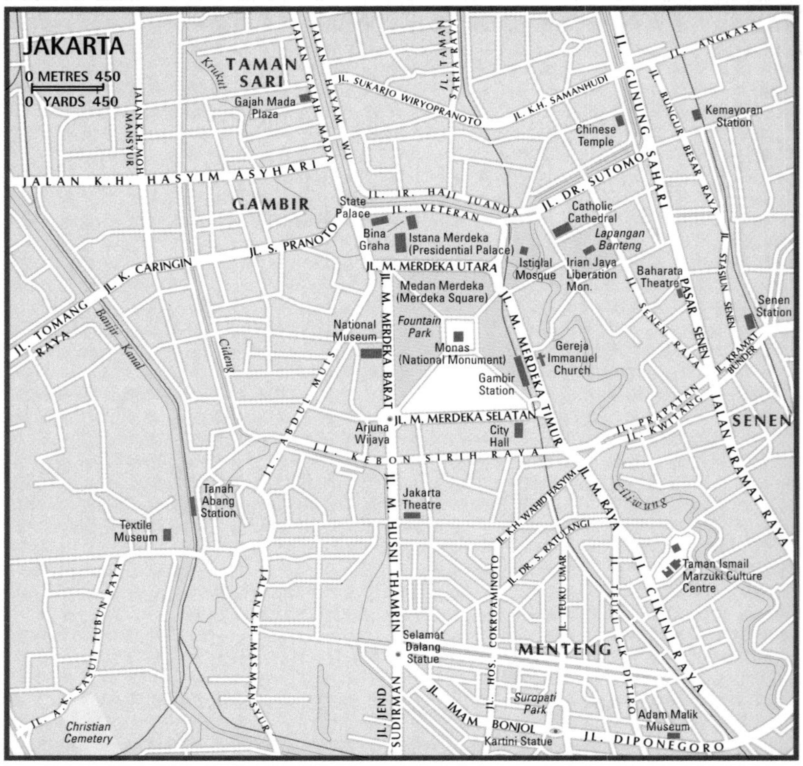

JAKARTA

0 METRES 450
0 YARDS 450

TAMAN SARI
Gajah Mada Plaza
Chinese Temple
Kemayoran Station
GAMBIR
State Palace
Catholic Cathedral
Bina Graha
Istana Merdeka (Presidential Palace)
Lapangan Banteng
Istiqlal Mosque
Irian Jaya Liberation Mon.
Baharata Theatre
Medan Merdeka (Merdeka Square)
National Museum
Monas (National Monument)
Gereja Immanuel Church
Senen Station
Fountain Park
Gambir Station
Arjuna Wijaya
City Hall
SENEN
Tanah Abang Station
Jakarta Theatre
Textile Museum
MENTENG
Taman Ismail Marzuki Culture Centre
Selamat Datang Statue
Suropati Park
Adam Malik Museum
Christian Cemetery
Kartini Statue
BONJOL
JL. DIPONEGORO

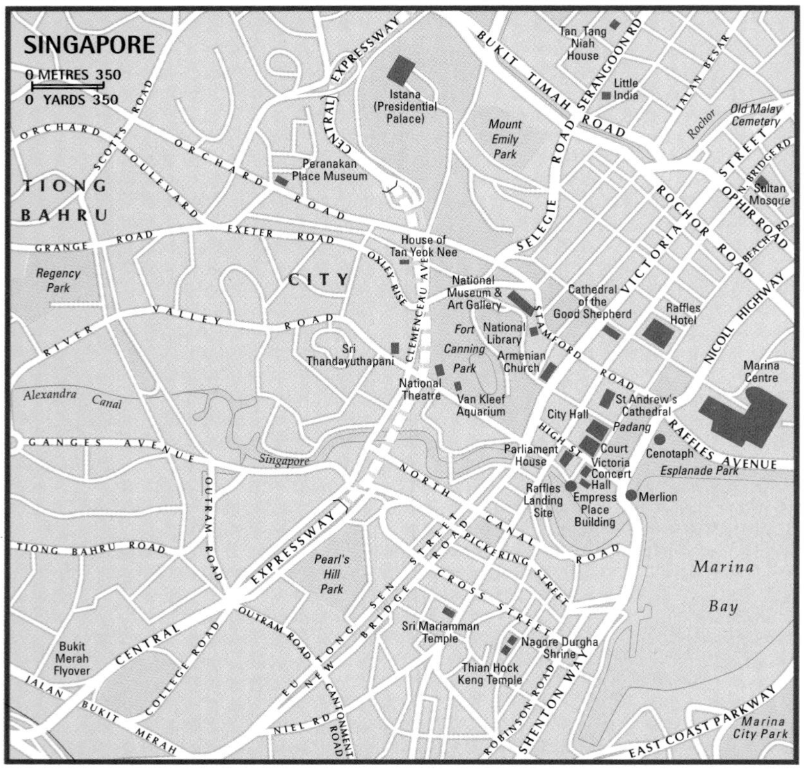

SINGAPORE

0 METRES 350
0 YARDS 350

Tan Teng Niah House
BUKIT TIMAH ROAD
Little India
Istana (Presidential Palace)
Old Malay Cemetery
Mount Emily Park
Rochor
Paranakan Place Museum
Sultan Mosque
TIONG BAHRU
House of Tan Yeok Nee
CITY
Regency Park
National Museum & Art Gallery
Cathedral of the Good Shepherd
Raffles Hotel
Fort Canning
National Library
Sri Thandayuthapani
Armenian Church
Marina Centre
National Theatre
Van Kleef Aquarium
St Andrew's Cathedral
City Hall
Padang
Parliament House
Court
Alexandra Canal
Victoria Concert Hall
Cenotaph
Esplanade Park
Raffles Landing Site
Empress Place Building
Merlion
Pearl's Hill Park
Marina Bay
Bukit Merah Flyover
Sri Mariamman Temple
Nagore Durgha Shrine
Thian Hock Keng Temple
Marina City Park
EAST COAST PARKWAY

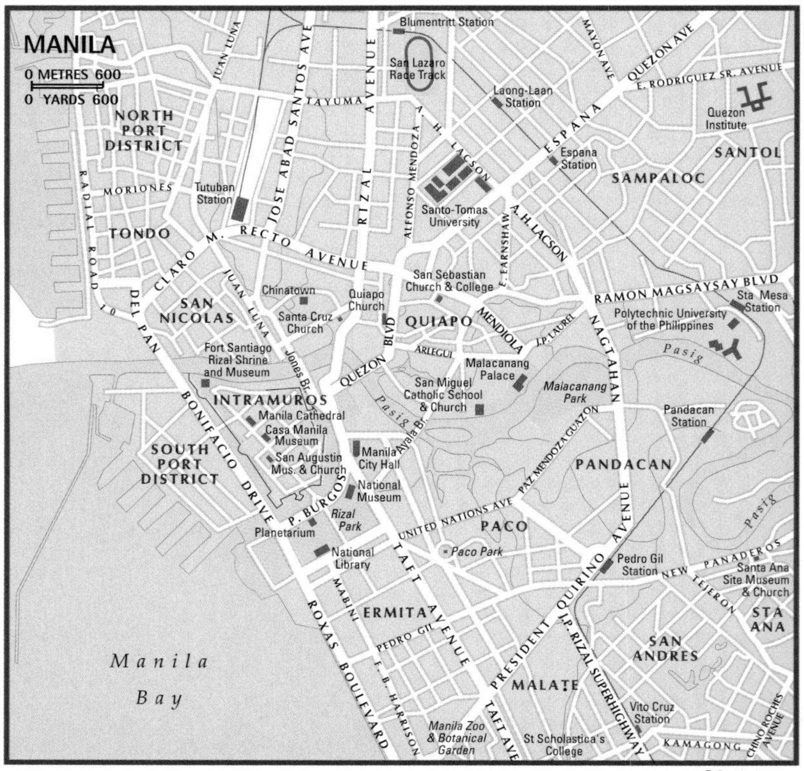

MANILA

0 METRES 600
0 YARDS 600

Blumentritt Station
San Lazaro Race Track
QUEZON AVE
Laong-Laan Station
Quezon Institute
NORTH PORT DISTRICT
Espana Station
SANTOL
Santo-Tomas University
SAMPALOC
Tutuban Station
San Sebastian Church & College
TONDO
RECTO AVENUE
Sta Mesa Station
Chinatown
RAMON MAGSAYSAY BLVD
SAN NICOLAS
Santa-Cruz Church
Polytechnic University of the Philippines
QUIAPO
Fort Santiago
Rizal Shrine and Museum
Malacanang Palace
Malacanang Park
INTRAMUROS
San Miguel Catholic School & Church
Pandacan Station
Manila Cathedral
PANDACAN
Casa Manila
San Agustin Mus. & Church
Manila City Hall
SOUTH PORT DISTRICT
National Museum
PACO
Rizal Park
Paco Park
Pedro Gil Station
Planetarium
National Library
Santa Ana Site Museum & Church
ERMITA
ROXAS BOULEVARD
SAN ANDRES
Manila Bay
MALATE
STA ANA
Manila Zoo & Botanical Garden
St Scholastica's College
Vito Cruz Station

© Bartholomew

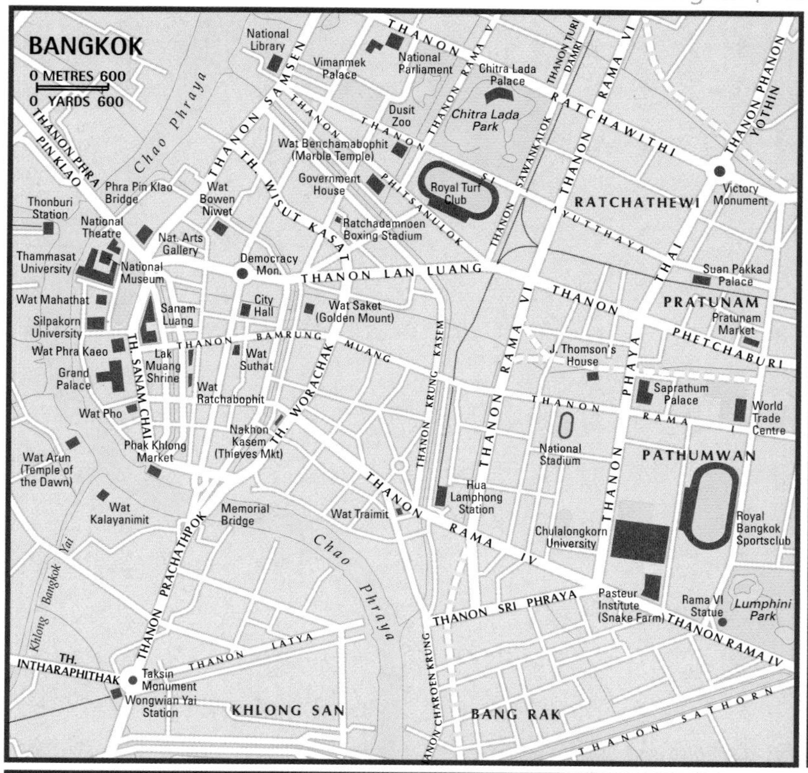

BANGKOK

0 METRES 600
0 YARDS 600

National Library
Vimanmek Palace
National Parliament
Chitra Lada Palace
THANON SAMSEN
THANON DIN DAENG
RAMA V
THANON PHAHON YOTHIN
Chao Phraya
Dusit Zoo
Chitra Lada Park
THANON PHRA PIN KLAO
THANON RATCHAWITHI
Wat Benchamabophit (Marble Temple)
RATCHATHEWI
Victory Monument
Thonburi Station
Phra Pin Klao Bridge
Wat Bowen Niwet
Government House
THANON PHITSANULOK
AYUTTHAYA
THANON RAMA VI
THANON PHAYA THAI
Nat. Arts Gallery
Ratchadamnoen Boxing Stadium
National Theatre
National Museum
Democracy Mon.
THANON LAN LUANG
PRATUNAM
Suan Pakkad Palace
Thammasat University
City Hall
Wat Saket (Golden Mount)
THANON PHETCHABURI
Pratunam Market
Wat Mahathat
Sanam Luang
THANON BAMRUNG MUANG
J. Thomson's House
Silpakorn University
Lak Muang Shrine
Wat Suthat
THANON RAMA I
Saprathum Palace
Wat Phra Kaeo
Wat Ratchabophit
THANON WORACHAK
World Trade Centre
Grand Palace
Phak Khlong Market
Nakhon Kasem (Thieves Mkt)
Wat Pho
Wat Traimit
PATHUMWAN
Wat Arun (Temple of the Dawn)
Memorial Bridge
National Stadium
Wat Kalayanimit
Hua Lamphong Station
Chulalongkorn University
Royal Bangkok Sportsclub
Chao Phraya
THANON PHRA CHATHIPROK
THANON SRI PHRAYA
Pasteur Institute (Snake Farm)
Rama VI Statue
Lumphini Park
TH. INTHARAPHITHAK
Taksin Monument
Wongwian Yai Station
THANON LATYA
THANON CHAROEN KRUNG
THANON RAMA IV
KHLONG SAN
BANG RAK
THANON SATHORN

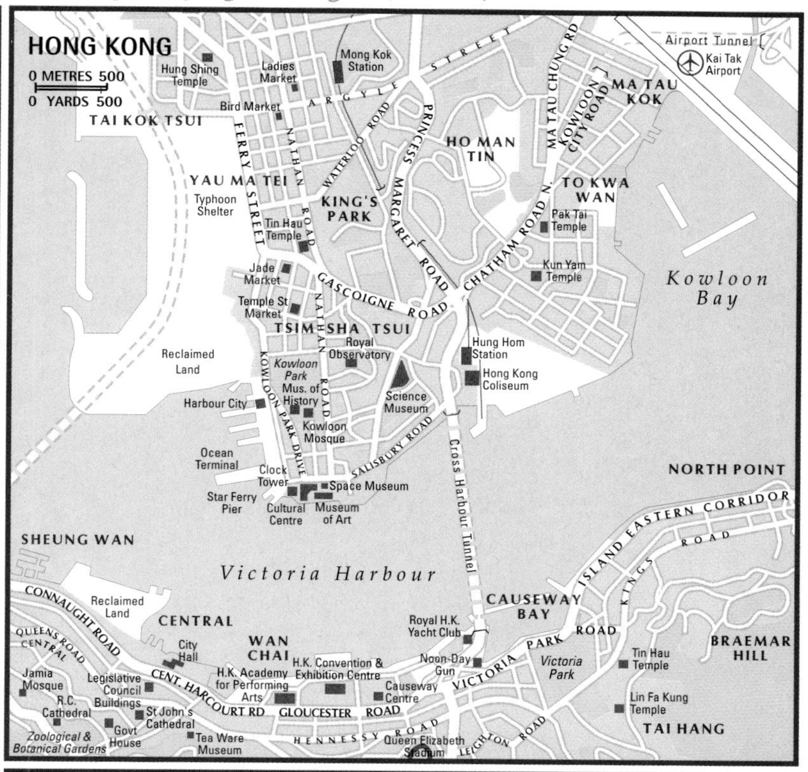

HONG KONG

0 METRES 500
0 YARDS 500

TAI KOK TSUI
Hung Shing Temple
Ladies Market
Mong Kok Station
ARGYLE STREET
Airport Tunnel
Kai Tak Airport
MA TAU KOK
Bird Market
NATHAN ROAD
WATERLOO ROAD
PRINCESS MARGARET ROAD
MA TAU CHUNG RD
KOWLOON CITY RD
YAU MA TEI
KING'S PARK
HO MAN TIN
TO KWA WAN
FERRY STREET
Typhoon Shelter
Tin Hau Temple
Jade Market
GASCOIGNE ROAD
CHATHAM ROAD N
Pak Tai Temple
Kun Yam Temple
TSIM SHA TSUI
Temple St Market
Royal Observatory
Kowloon Bay
Reclaimed Land
Kowloon Park Mus. of History
Hung Hom Station
Harbour City
Kowloon Mosque
Science Museum
Hong Kong Coliseum
Ocean Terminal
Clock Tower
Space Museum
Star Ferry Pier
Cultural Centre
Museum of Art
NORTH POINT
SHEUNG WAN
ISLAND EASTERN CORRIDOR
KINGS ROAD
Victoria Harbour
Reclaimed Land
CONNAUGHT ROAD
CENTRAL
City Hall
WAN CHAI
Royal H.K. Yacht Club
CAUSEWAY BAY
Noon-Day Gun
Victoria Park
Tin Hau Temple
BRAEMAR HILL
QUEENS ROAD CENTRAL
Jamia Mosque
R.C. Cathedral
Legislative Council Buildings
St John's Cathedral
CENT. HARCOURT RD
H.K. Academy for Performing Arts
H.K. Convention & Exhibition Centre
Causeway Centre
VICTORIA PARK ROAD
Lin Fa Kung Temple
TAI HANG
Zoological & Botanical Gardens
Govt House
Tea Ware Museum
GLOUCESTER ROAD
Queen Elizabeth Stadium
HENNESSY ROAD
LEIGHTON ROAD

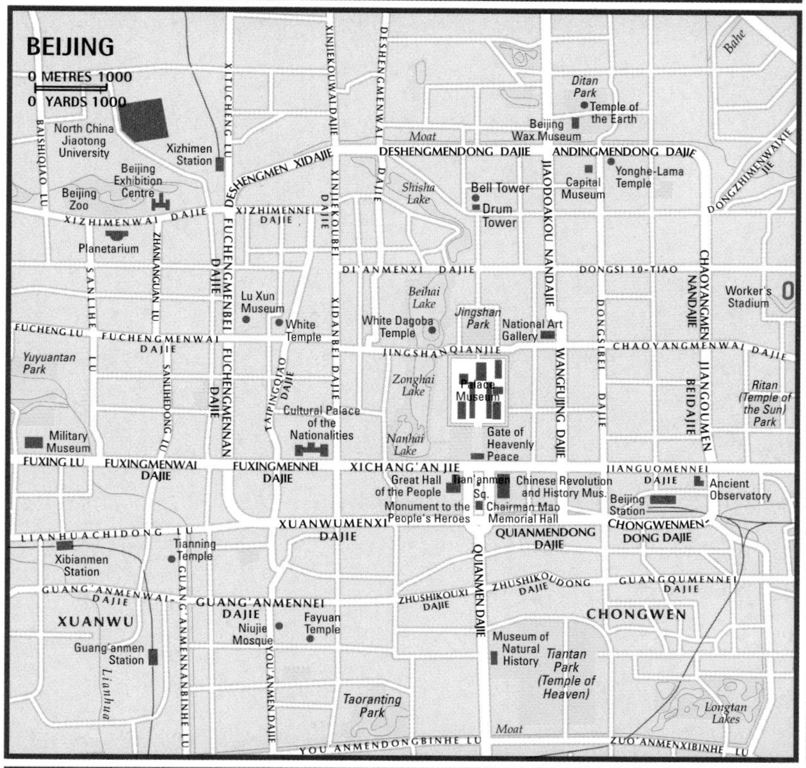

BEIJING

0 METRES 1000
0 YARDS 1000

XINJIEKOUWAIDAJIE
DESHENGMEN XIDAJIE
Baihe
Ditan Park
Temple of the Earth
North China Jiaotong University
BAISHIQIAO LU
Xizhimen Station
Beijing Wax Museum
Beijing Exhibition Centre
DESHENGMENDONG DAJIE
ANDINGMENDONG DAJIE
Yonghe-Lama Temple
DONGZHIMENWAIHAJIE
Beijing Zoo
XIZHIMENNEI DAJIE
Shisha Lake
Bell Tower
Capital Museum
Planetarium
ZHANGZIZHONG LU
Drum Tower
JIAODAOKOU NANDAJIE
CHAOYANGMEN NANDAJIE
FUCHENG LU
Lu Xun Museum
DI ANMENXI DAJIE
DONGSI 10-TIAO
Worker's Stadium
Yuyuantan Park
White Temple
Beihai Lake
Jingshan Park
National Art Gallery
FUCHENGMENNEI DAJIE
White Dagoba Temple
WANGFUJING DAJIE
FUCHENGMENWAI DAJIE
SANLIHEDONG LU
Zhonghai Lake
Palace Museum
JINGSHANQIANJIE
Ritan (Temple of the Sun) Park
FUXING LU
FUXINGMENWAI DAJIE
FUXINGMENNEI DAJIE
Cultural Palace of the Nationalities
Nanhai Lake
XICHANG'AN JIE
Gate of Heavenly Peace
JIANGUOMENNEI DAJIE
Military Museum
Great Hall of the People
Tian'anmen Sq
Chinese Revolution and History Mus.
Ancient Observatory
LIANHUACHIDONG LU
Monument to the People's Heroes
Chairman Mao Memorial Hall
Beijing Station
JIANGUOMENNEI DAJIE
Xibanmen Station
XUANWUMENXI DAJIE
QIANMENDONG DAJIE
CHONGWENMEN DONG DAJIE
GUANG'ANMENWAI DAJIE
Tianning Temple
GUANG'ANMENNEI DAJIE
QUANMEN DAJIE
ZHUSHIKOUXI DAJIE
ZHUSHIKOUDONG DAJIE
GUANGQUMENNEI DAJIE
XUANWU
Fayuan Temple
Niujie Mosque
Museum of Natural History
Tiantan Park (Temple of Heaven)
CHONGWEN
Guang'anmen Station
Lianhua
Taoranting Park
YOU ANMENDONGBINHE LU
ZUO ANMENXIBINHE LU
Longtan Lakes
Moat

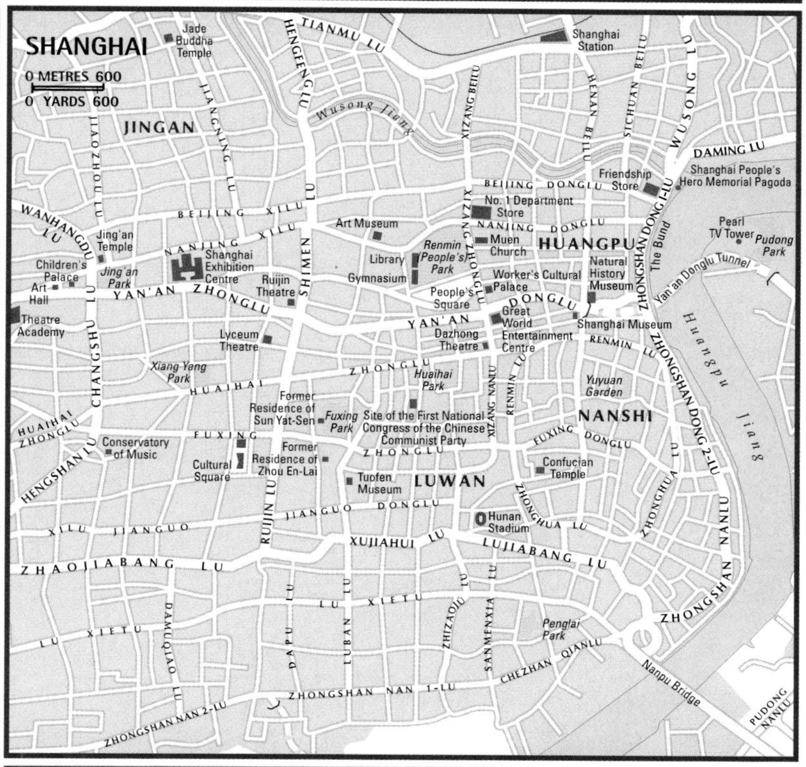

SHANGHAI

0 METRES 600
0 YARDS 600

Jade Buddha Temple
TIANMU LU
Shanghai Station
HENGFENG LU
JIANGNING LU
WUSONG RD
DAMING LU
JINGAN
Wuson River
WANHANGDU LU
Jing'an Temple
Art Museum
BEIJING DONGLU
NANJING DONGLU
Friendship Store
Shanghai People's Hero Memorial Pagoda
Children's Palace
Shanghai Exhibition Centre
No. 1 Department Store
Muen Church
HUANGPU
Pearl TV Tower
Pudong Park
CHANGSHU LU
Art Hall
NANJING XILU
Library
Renmin People's Park
Worker's Cultural Palace
Natural History Museum
The Bund
YAN'AN ZHONGLU
Ruijin Theatre
Gymnasium
People's Square
Great World Entertainment Centre
Shanghai Museum
Huangpu Jiang
Theatre Academy
Jing'an Park
YAN'AN
Dazhong Theatre
HUAIHAI ZHONGLU
Xiang Yang Park
Lyceum Theatre
Huaihai Park
Fuxing Park
RENMIN
YAN'AN DONGLU Tunnel
HENGSHAN LU
Conservatory of Music
FUXING ZHONGLU
Former Residence of Sun Yat-Sen
Site of the First National Congress of the Chinese Communist Party
Yuyuan Garden
NANSHI
Cultural Square
Former Residence of Zhou En-Lai
Tupfen Museum
LUWAN
Confucian Temple
ZHONGSHAN DONG 2-LU
XILU JIANGUO
JIANGUO
Hunan Stadium
XUJIAHUI LU
LUJIABANG LU
ZHAOJIABANG LU
FUXING
Penglai Park
LU XIETU
ZHONGSHAN NAN 1-LU
ZHONGSHAN NAN 2-LU
Nanpu Bridge
PUDONG NANLU

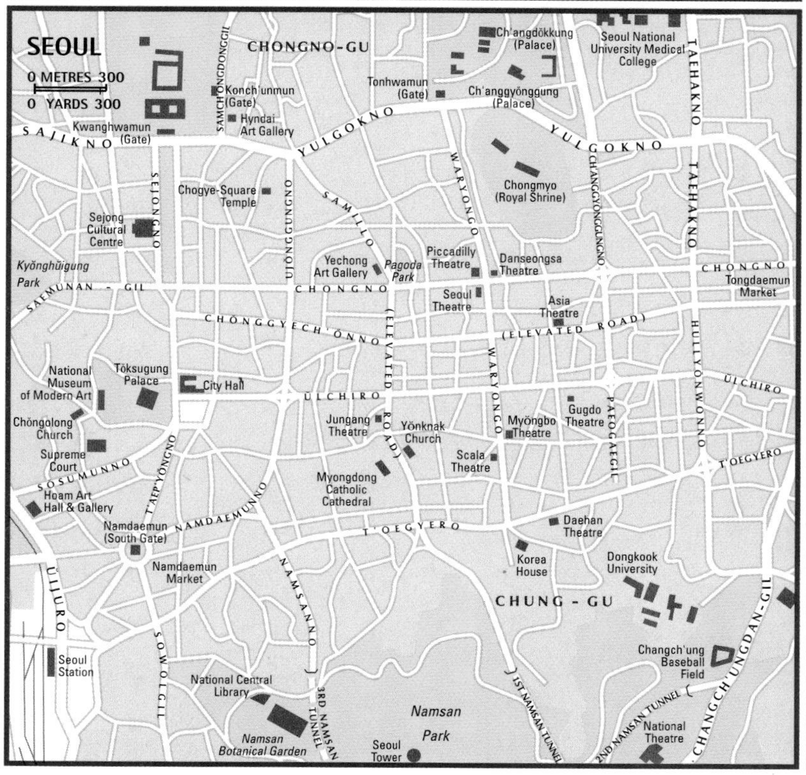

SEOUL

0 METRES 300
0 YARDS 300

CHONGNO-GU
Ch'angdokkung (Palace)
Seoul National University Medical College
Tonhwamun (Gate)
Konch'unmun (Gate)
Kwanghwamun (Gate)
Hyundai Art Gallery
Ch'anggyonggung (Palace)
TAEHAKNO
SAJIKNO
YULGOKNO
YULGOKNO
Chogye Square Temple
Chongmyo (Royal Shrine)
SAMILLO
Kyonghuigung Park
Yechong Art Gallery
Pagoda Park
Piccadilly Theatre
Danseongsa Theatre
CHONGNO
Tongdaemun Market
National Museum of Modern Art
Seoul Theatre
Asia Theatre
Chongolong Church
Toksugung Palace
City Hall
Jungang Theatre
Yonknak Church
Myongbo Theatre
Gugdo Theatre
Supreme Court
ULCHIRO
Scala Theatre
Myongdong Catholic Cathedral
Hoam Art Hall & Gallery
Namdaemun (South Gate)
Daehan Theatre
Korea House
Dongkook University
Namdaemun Market
CHUNG-GU
Changch'ung Baseball Field
Seoul Station
National Central Library
National Theatre
Namsan Tunnel
Namsan Botanical Garden
Namsan Park
Seoul Tower

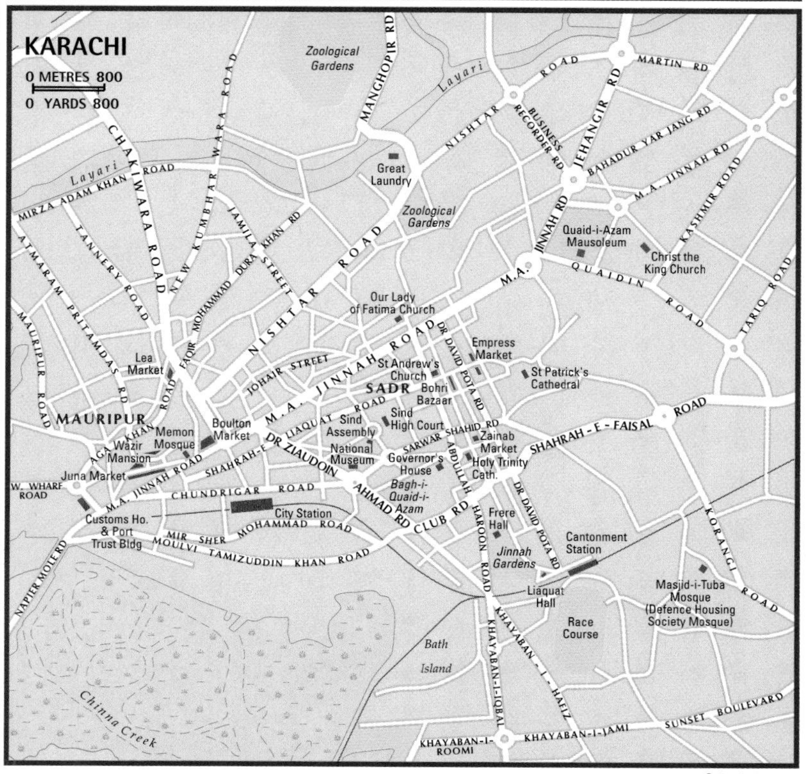

KARACHI

0 METRES 800
0 YARDS 800

Zoological Gardens
MANGHOPIR RD
NISHTAR ROAD
MARTIN RD
Layari
BUSINESS RECORDER RD
JEHANGIR RD
M.A. JINNAH RD
Great Laundry
CHANIWARA ROAD
Layari
MIRZA ADAM KHAN ROAD
Zoological Gardens
Quaid-i-Azam Mausoleum
KASHMIR ROAD
Christ the King Church
TANNERY ROAD
LAWRENCE ROAD
Our Lady of Fatima Church
M.A.
QUAIDIN ROAD
MAURIPUR
Lea Market
St Andrew's Church
Empress Market
St Patrick's Cathedral
SADR
Memon Mosque
Boulton Market
Sind Assembly
Sind High Court
National Museum
SHAHRAH-E-FAISAL
Wazir Mansion
Juna Market
Governor's House
DR ZIAUDDIN AHMAD RD
CLUB RD
Zainab Market
Holy Trinity Cath.
W. WHARF ROAD
Customs Ho. & Port Trust Bldg
City Station
CHUNDRIGAR ROAD
Bagh-i-Quaid-i-Azam
Frere Hall
Jinnah Gardens
Cantonment Station
NAPIER MOLE RD
Mir Sher Mohammad Road
MOULVI TAMIZUDDIN KHAN ROAD
KHAYABAN-I-ROOMI
Liaquat Hall
Race Course
Bath Island
Masjid-i-Tuba Mosque (Defence Housing Society Mosque)
China Creek
SUNSET BOULEVARD
KHAYABAN-I-JAMI

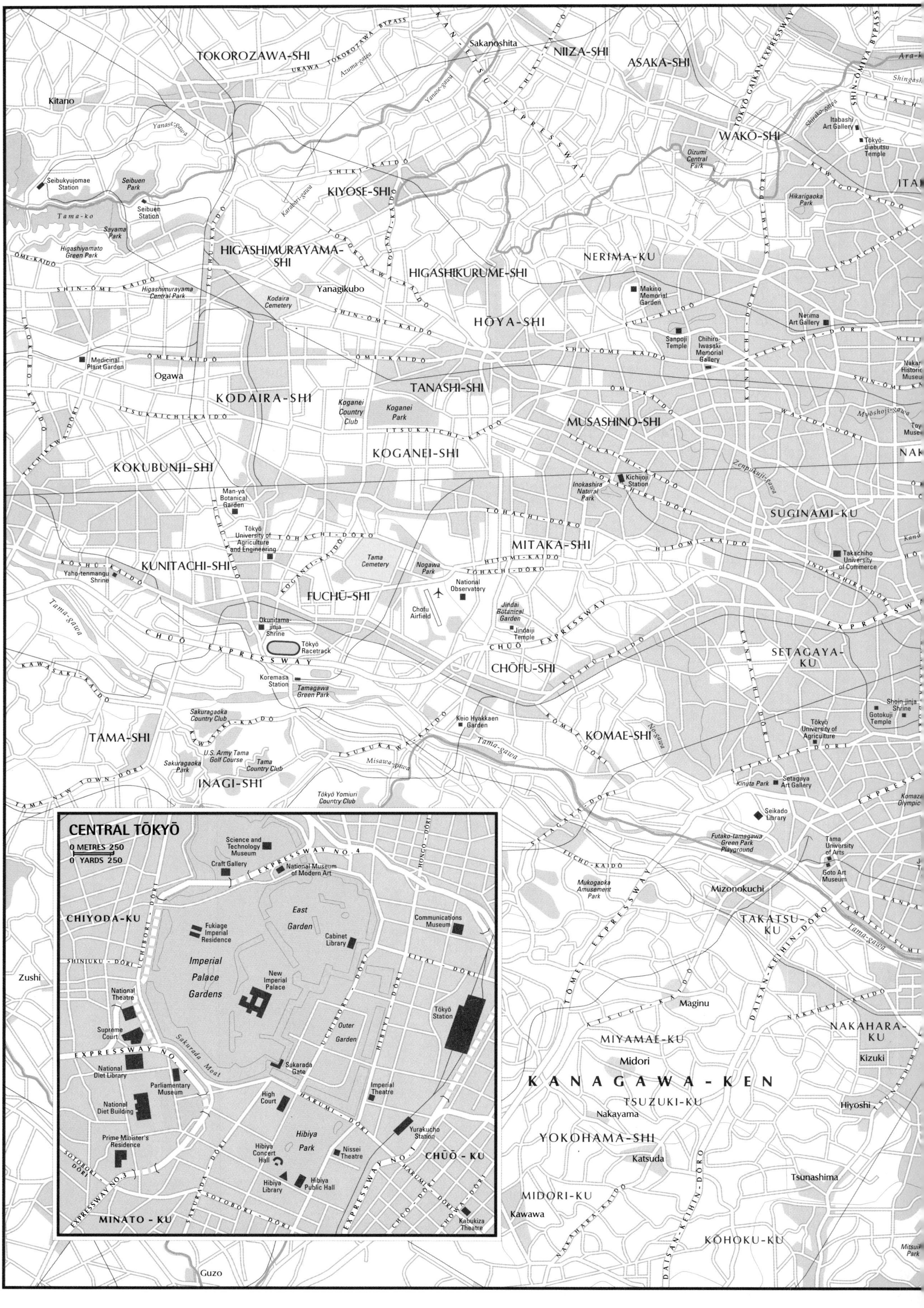

Kitano

TOKOROZAWA-SHI

NIIZA-SHI
ASAKA-SHI
WAKŌ-SHI
Sakanoshita

Seibukyujomae
Station
Seibuen
Park
Tama-ko
Sayama
Park
Seibuen
Station

Itabashi
Art Gallery
Tōkyō-
daibutsu
Temple

Higashiyamato
Green Park

Oizumi
Central
Park

Hikarigaoka
Park

KIYOSE-SHI

NERIMA-KU

HIGASHIMURAYAMA-
SHI

HIGASHIKURUME-SHI

Makino
Memorial
Garden

Nerima
Art Gallery

SHIN-ŌME KAIDO

Higashimurayama
Central Park

Kodaira
Cemetery

Yanagikubo

HŌYA-SHI

Sanpoji
Temple

Chihiro-
Iwasaki
Memorial
Gallery

Nakano
Historical
Museum

Medicinal
Plant Garden

ŌME-KAIDO

ŌME-KAIDO

TANASHI-SHI

Ogawa

KODAIRA-SHI

Koganei
Country
Club
Koganei
Park

MUSASHINO-SHI

Toy
Museum

ITSUKAICHI-KAIDO

KOGANEI-SHI

Inokashira
Natural
Park

Kichijoji
Station

SUGINAMI-KU

KOKUBUNJI-SHI

Man-yo
Botanical
Garden

TOHACHI-DORO

Takachiho
University
of Commerce

Tōkyō
University of
Agriculture
and Engineering

HITOMI-KAIDO

Yaho-tenmangu
Shrine

KUNITACHI-SHI

Tama
Cemetery

Nogawa
Park

National
Observatory

MITAKA-SHI

Jindai
Botanical
Garden

SETAGAYA-
KU

FUCHŪ-SHI

Chofu
Airfield

Jindaiji
Temple

CHŪO   EXPRESSWAY

Okunitama-
jinja
Shrine

Tōkyō
Racetrack

CHŌFU-SHI

Shoin-jinja
Shrine

Koremasa
Station

Tamagawa
Green Park

Keio Hyakkaen
Garden

KOMAE-SHI

Gotokuji
Temple

Tōkyō
University of
Agriculture

Sakuragaoka
Country Club

Tama-gawa

Kinuta Park

Setagaya
Art Gallery

TAMA-SHI

U.S. Army Tama
Golf Course

Tama
Country
Club

Misawa-gawa

Seikado
Library

Komazawa
Olympic

Sakuragaoka
Park

INAGI-SHI

Tōkyō Yomiuri
Country Club

Futako-tamagawa
Green Park
Playground

Tama
University
of Arts

Mukogaoka
Amusement
Park

Goto Art
Museum

Mizonokuchi

TAKATSU-
KU

Zushi

NAKAHARA-
KU

Maginu

Midori

Kizuki

KANAGAWA-KEN

TSUZUKI-KU

Nakayama

Hiyoshi

YOKOHAMA-SHI

Katsuda

MIDORI-KU

Kawawa

Tsunashima

KŌHOKU-KU

Mitsui

Guzo

CENTRAL TŌKYŌ

0 METRES 250
0 YARDS 250

Science and
Technology
Museum

Craft Gallery

National Museum
of Modern Art

EXPRESSWAY NO. 4

CHIYODA-KU

East
Garden

Communications
Museum

Fukiage
Imperial
Residence

Cabinet
Library

SHINJUKU - DORI

Imperial
Palace
Gardens

New
Imperial
Palace

National
Theatre

Supreme
Court

Outer
Garden

Tōkyō
Station

National
Diet Library

Sakurada
Gate

Parliamentary
Museum

National
Diet Building

High
Court

Imperial
Theatre

Prime Minister's
Residence

Hibiya
Park

Yurakucho
Station

Hibiya
Concert
Hall

Nissei
Theatre

CHŪO - KU

Hibiya
Library

Hibiya
Public Hall

MINATO - KU

Kabukiza
Theatre

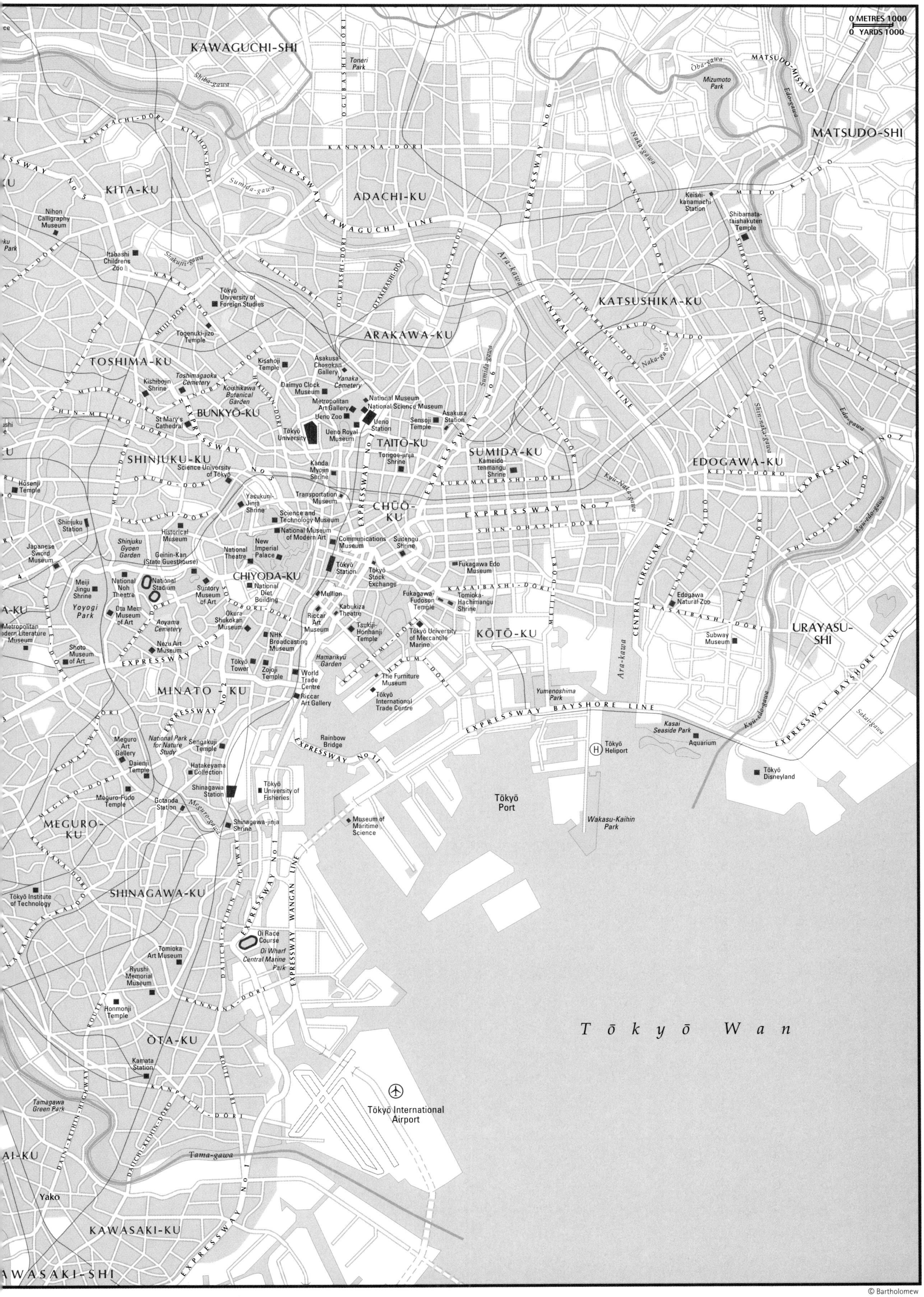

0 METRES 1000
0 YARDS 1000

KAWAGUCHI-SHI

MATSUDO-MISATO

MATSUDO-SHI

Toneri
Park

Mizumoto
Park

Ōba-gawa

Edo-gawa

Shiba-gawa

KITA-KU

Shakujii-gawa

ADACHI-KU

Sumida-gawa

KATSUSHIKA-KU

EXPRESSWAY KAWAGUCHI LINE

CENTRAL CIRCULAR LINE

MITO-KAIDO

Keisei-
kanamachi
Station

Shibamata-
taishakuten
Temple

Nihon
Calligraphy
Museum

Itabashi
Childrens
Zoo

Tōkyō University of
Foreign Studies

Togenuki-jizo
Temple

ARAKAWA-KU

Ara-kawa

Naka-gawa

TOSHIMA-KU

Kisshōji
Temple

Asakusa-
Chosokan
Gallery

Yanaka
Cemetery

EDOGAWA-KU

Edo-gawa

Kishibōjin
Shrine

Toshimagaoka
Cemetery

Daimyo Clock
Museum

BUNKYŌ-KU

Koishikawa
Botanical
Garden

Metropolitan
Art Gallery

National Museum

National Science Museum

Asakusa
Station

Sumida-gawa

KEIYO-DORO

St Mary's
Cathedral

Ueno Zoo

Ueno
Station

Sensōji
Temple

SUMIDA-KU

Tōkyō
University

Ueno Royal
Museum

TAITŌ-KU

Torigoe-jinja
Shrine

Kameido-
tenmangu
Shrine

SHINJUKU-KU

Science University
of Tōkyō

Kanda
Myojin
Shrine

KURAMAEBASHI-DORI

Hōsenji
Temple

Transportation
Museum

Yasukuni-
Jinja
Shrine

Science and
Technology Museum

CHŪŌ-
KU

EXPRESSWAY NO 7

Shinjuku
Station

Historical
Museum

National Museum
of Modern Art

Communications
Museum

Suitengu
Shrine

SHIN-OHASHI-DORI

Kyū-Nakagawa

Japanese
Sword
Museum

Shinjuku
Gyoen
Garden

Geinin-Kan
(State Guesthouse)

National
Theatre

New
Imperial
Palace

Fukagawa Edo
Museum

Edogawa
Natural Zoo

Meiji Jingu
Shrine

National
Stadium

Suntory
Museum
of Art

CHIYODA-KU

Tōkyō
Station

Tōkyō
Stock Exchange

Fukagawa-
Fudoson
Temple

Tomioka-
Hachimangu
Shrine

URAYASU-
SHI

Sakai-gawa

Yoyogi
Park

National Noh
Theatre

Ota Mem
Museum
of Art

Aoyama
Cemetery

National
Diet
Building

Okura
Shukokan
Museum

Mullion

Riccar
Art
Museum

Kabukiza
Theatre

KŌTŌ-
KU

Subway
Museum

Metropolitan
Modern Literature
Museum

NHK
Broadcasting
Museum

Nezu Art
Museum

Tsukiji-
Honhanji
Temple

Tōkyō University of
Mercantile Marine

Ara-kawa

Shoto
Museum of Art

EXPRESSWAY NO 3

Tōkyō
Tower

Zojoji
Temple

Hamarikyū
Garden

MINATO-KU

World
Trade
Centre

The Furniture
Museum

Yumenoshima
Park

Riccar
Art Gallery

Tōkyō
International
Trade Centre

EXPRESSWAY BAYSHORE LINE

Kasai
Seaside Park

Aquarium

Meguro
Art
Gallery

National Park
for Nature
Study

Sengakuji
Temple

Rainbow
Bridge

Tōkyō
Heliport

Tōkyō
Disneyland

Daienji
Temple

Hatakeyama
Collection

EXPRESSWAY No 11

Meguro-Fudo
Temple

Shinagawa
Station

Tōkyō
Port

MEGURO-KU

Gotanda
Station

Tōkyō University
of Fisheries

Shinagawa-jinja
Shrine

Wakasu-Kaihin
Park

Museum of
Maritime
Science

Tōkyō Institute
of Technology

SHINAGAWA-KU

Oi Race
Course

Oi Wharf
Central Marine
Park

Tōkyō Wan

Tomioka
Art Museum

Ryushi
Memorial
Museum

Honmonji
Temple

ŌTA-KU

Kamata
Station

Tamagawa
Green Park

Tōkyō International
Airport

Tama-gawa

KAWASAKI-KU

Yako

KAWASAKI-SHI

© Bartholomew

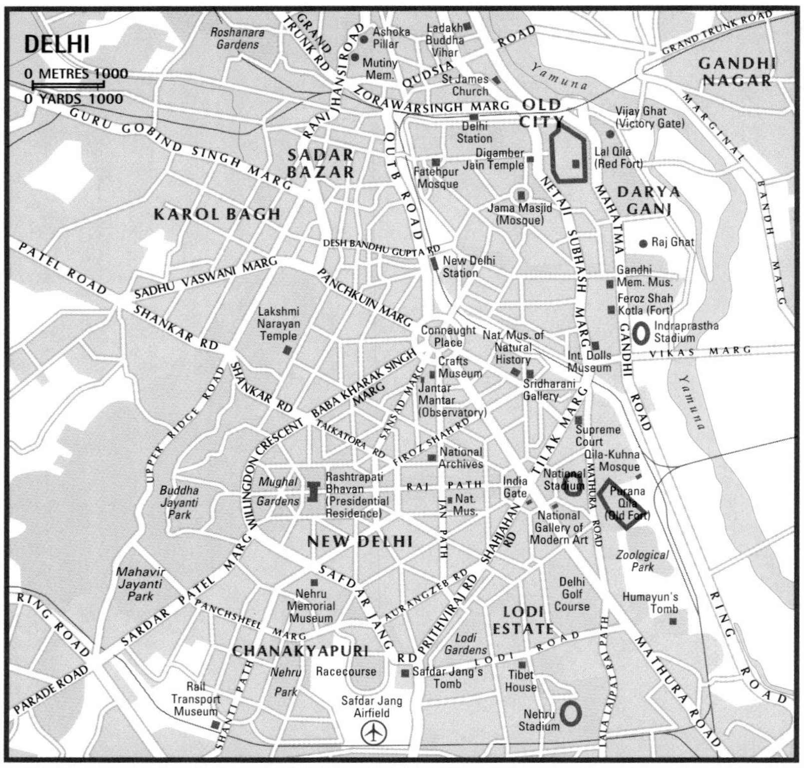

DELHI

0 METRES 1000
0 YARDS 1000

Roshanara Gardens · Ashoka Pillar · Ladakh Buddha Vihar · GRAND TRUNK ROAD · St James Church · GANDHI NAGAR
Mutiny Mem · OLD CITY
SADAR BAZAR · Delhi Station · Digamber Jain Temple · Vijay Ghat (Victory Gate) · Lal Qila (Red Fort) · DARYA GANJ
KAROL BAGH · Fatehpur Mosque · Jama Masjid (Mosque)
Lakshmi Narayan Temple · New Delhi Station · Gandhi Mem. Mus. · Feroz Shah Kotla (Fort) · Indraprastha Stadium · VIKAS MARG
Connaught Place · Nat. Mus. of Natural History · Int Dolls Museum
Buddha Jayanti Park · Mughal Gardens · Crafts Museum · Sridharani Gallery · Jantar Mantar (Observatory)
Rashtrapati Bhavan (Presidential Residence) · National Archives · Supreme Court · Qila-Kuhna Mosque · Purana Qila (Old Fort)
NEW DELHI · RAJ PATH · India Gate · Nat. Mus. · National Stadium · National Gallery of Modern Art
Mahavir Jayanti Park · Nehru Memorial Museum · Delhi Golf Course · Zoological Park
CHANAKYAPURI · Racecourse · Nehru Park · LODI ESTATE · Safdar Jang's Tomb · Lodi Gardens · Tibet House · Humayun's Tomb
Rail Transport Museum · Safdar Jang Airfield · Nehru Stadium

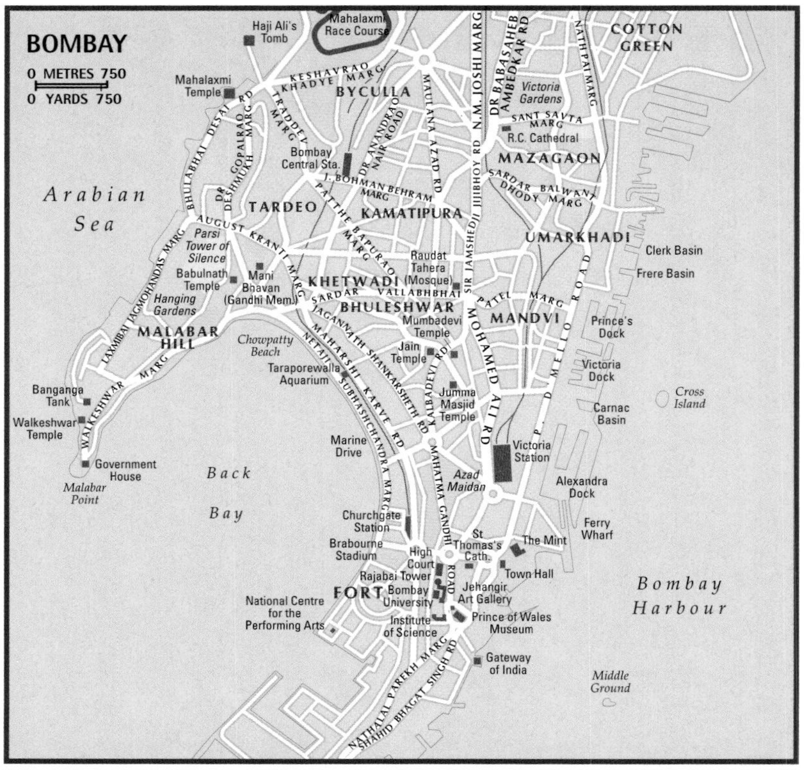

BOMBAY

0 METRES 750
0 YARDS 750

Haji Ali's Tomb · Mahalaxmi Race Course · COTTON GREEN
Mahalaxmi Temple · BYCULLA · Victoria Gardens
Parsi Tower of Silence · Bombay Central Sta. · MAZAGAON · R.C. Cathedral
TARDEO · KAMATIPURA · Clerk Basin · Frere Basin
Raudat Tahera (Mosque) · UMARKHADI
Babulnath Temple · Mani Bhavan (Gandhi Mem) · KHETWADI · MANDVI · Prince's Dock
Hanging Gardens · BHULESHWAR · Mumbadevi Temple · Victoria Station · Victoria Dock · Carnac Basin
MALABAR HILL · Chowpatty Beach · Jain Temple · Cross Island
Banganga Tank · Taraporewalla Aquarium · Jumma Masjid Temple · Alexandra Dock
Walkeshwar Temple · Marine Drive · Azad Maidan · Ferry Wharf
Government House · Churchgate Station · St Thomas's Cath. · The Mint
Malabar Point · Back Bay · Brabourne Stadium · Town Hall · Bombay Harbour
Rajabai Tower · High Court · Jehangir Art Gallery · FORT
National Centre for the Performing Arts · Bombay University · Prince of Wales Museum
Institute of Science · Gateway of India · Middle Ground

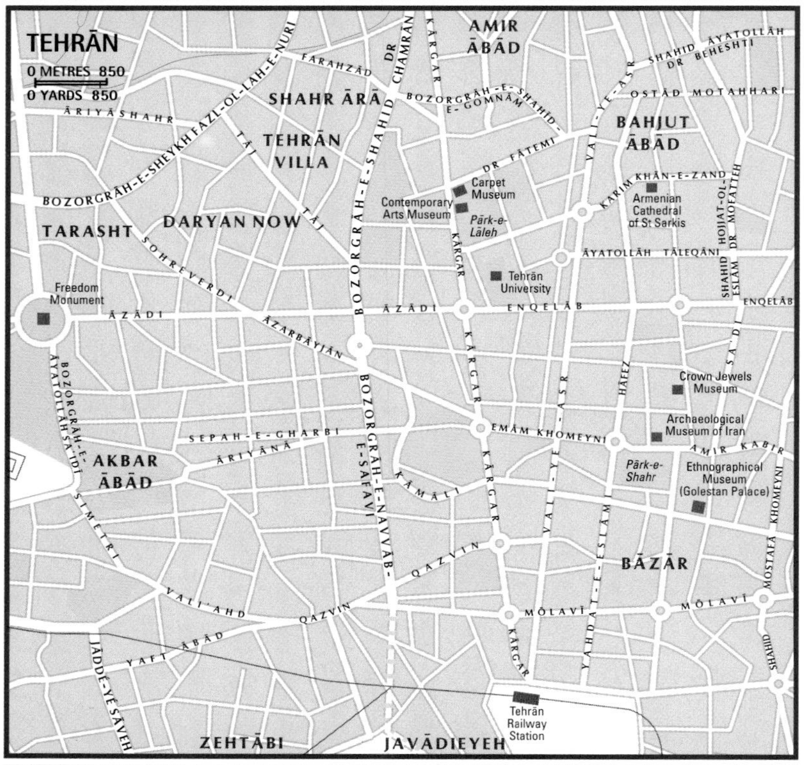

TEHRĀN

0 METRES 850
0 YARDS 850

AMIR ĀBĀD
SHAHR ĀRĀ
TEHRĀN VILLA · Contemporary Arts Museum · BAHJUT ĀBĀD
TARASHT · Park-e-Laleh · Armenian Cathedral of St Sarkis
DARYAN NOW · Carpet Museum
Freedom Monument · Tehran University
Crown Jewels Museum
Archaeological Museum of Iran
AKBAR ĀBĀD · EMĀM KHOMEYNI · Park-e-Shahr · Ethnographical Museum (Golestan Palace)
BĀZĀR
Tehrān Railway Station
ZEHTĀBI · JAVĀDIEYEH

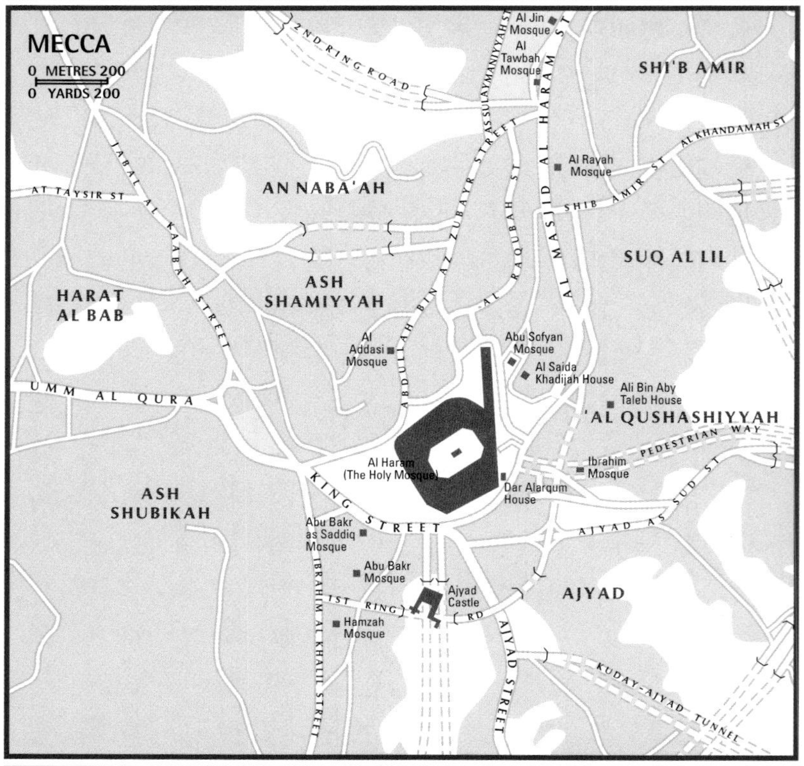

MECCA

0 METRES 200
0 YARDS 200

Al Jin Mosque · Al Tawbah Mosque · SHI'B AMIR
AN NABA'AH · Al Rayah Mosque
ASH SHAMIYYAH · SUQ AL LIL
HARAT AL BAB · Abu Sofyan Mosque · 'AL QUSHASHIYYAH
Al Addasi Mosque · Al Saida Khadijah House · Ali Bin Aby Taleb House
Al Haram (The Holy Mosque) · Ibrahim Mosque
UMM AL QURA · Dar Alarqum House
ASH SHUBIKAH · Abu Bakr as Saddiq Mosque · AJYAD
Abu Bakr Mosque · Ajyad Castle
Hamzah Mosque

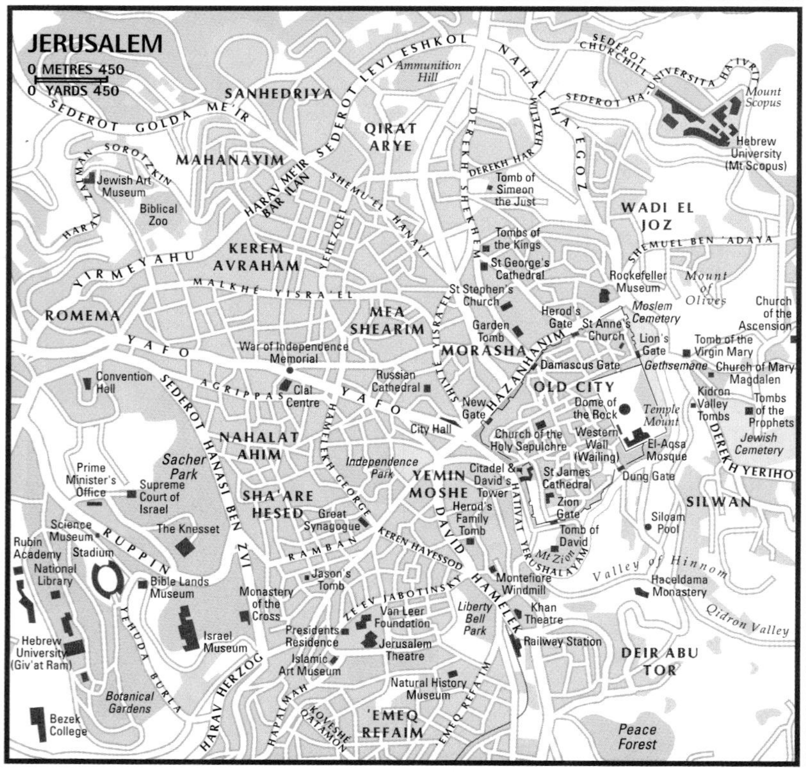

JERUSALEM

0 METRES 450
0 YARDS 450

SANHEDRIYA · Ammunition Hill · Mount Scopus
QIRAT ARYE · Hebrew University (Mt Scopus)
MAHANAYIM · Tomb of Simeon the Just
Jewish Art Museum · Biblical Zoo · Tombs of the Kings · WADI EL JOZ
KEREM AVRAHAM · St George's Cathedral · Rockefeller Museum · Mount of Olives · Church of the Ascension
ROMEMA · St Stephen's Church · Moslem Cemetery · Herod's Gate · St Anne's Church
MEA SHEARIM · War of Independence Memorial · Garden Tomb · Lion's Gate · Tomb of the Virgin Mary · Church of Mary Magdalen
Russian Cathedral · Damascus Gate · Gethsemane
Convention Hall · Clal Centre · City Hall · New Gate · MORASHA · Kidron Valley
Dome of the Rock · Temple Mount · Tombs of the Prophets
NAHALAT AHIM · Independence Park · OLD CITY · Western Wall (Wailing) · Jewish Cemetery
Prime Minister's Office · Supreme Court of Israel · Church of the Holy Sepulchre · El-Aqsa Mosque
Sacher Park · YEMIN MOSHE · Citadel & David's Tower · SILWAN
SHA'ARE HESED · The Knesset · Great Synagogue · Herod's Family Tomb · Zion Gate · Dung Gate
Science Museum · Rubin Academy · Van Leer Foundation · Jason's Tomb · Tomb of David · Siloam Pool
National Library · Bible Lands Museum · Monastery of the Cross · Liberty Bell Park · Khan Theatre · Montefiore Windmill · Tomb of Zechariah
Israel Museum · Presidents Residence · Jerusalem Theatre · St Andrew's · Haceldama Monastery
Hebrew University (Giv'at Ram) · Islamic Art Museum · Natural History Museum · Valley of Hinnom · DEIR ABU TOR
Botanical Gardens · Bezek College · EMEQ REFAIM · Peace Forest

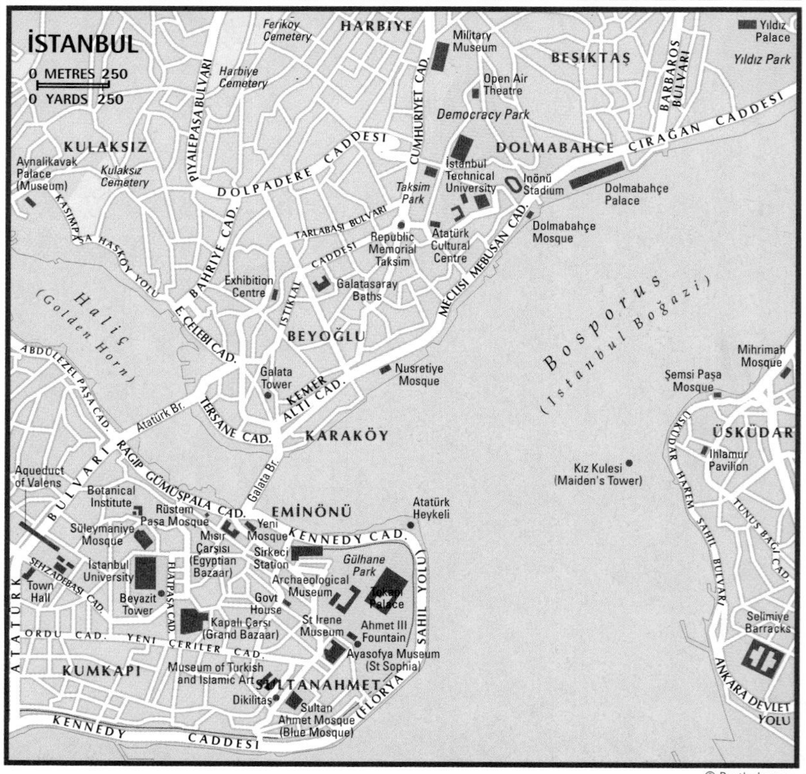

İSTANBUL

0 METRES 250
0 YARDS 250

Feriköy Cemetery · HARBIYE · Military Museum · Yıldız Palace
BEŞIKTAŞ · Barbaros Bulvarı · Yıldız Park
KULAKSIZ · Open Air Theatre · Democracy Park
Aynalıkavak Palace (Museum) · İstanbul Technical University · DOLMABAHÇE · İnönü Stadium · Dolmabahçe Palace
Kulaksız Cemetery · Taksim Park · Atatürk Cultural Centre · Dolmabahçe Mosque
Republic Memorial Taksim · Galatasaray Baths
Haliç (Golden Horn) · Exhibition Centre · BEYOĞLU · Galata Tower · Nusretiye Mosque
Bosporus (İstanbul Boğazi)
Galata Tower · KARAKÖY · Mihrimah Mosque
Aqueduct of Valens · Botanical Institute · Şemsi Paşa Mosque
ÜSKÜDAR · Kız Kulesi (Maiden's Tower) · İhlamur Pavilion
Rüstem Paşa Mosque · EMINÖNÜ · Yeni Mosque · Sirkeci Station · Gülhane Park
Süleymaniye Mosque · Kapalı Çarşı (Grand Bazaar) · Archaeological Museum · Atatürk Heykeli
İstanbul University · Govt House · Topkapı Palace
Town Hall · Beyazıt Tower · St Irene Museum · Ahmet III Fountain
KUMKAPI · Kapalı Çarşı (Grand Bazaar) · Ayasofya Museum (St Sophia)
Museum of Turkish and Islamic Arts · SULTANAHMET
Sultan Ahmet Mosque (Blue Mosque) · Selimiye Barracks
KENNEDY CADDESI · ANKARA DEVLET YOLU

© Bartholomew

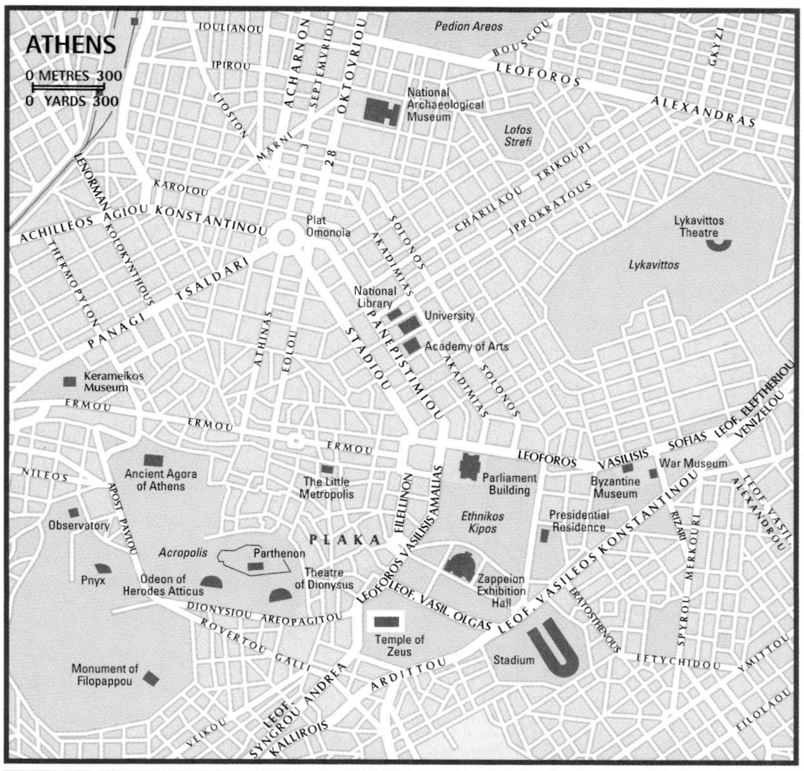

ATHENS
0 METRES 300
0 YARDS 300
Pedion Areos
National Archaeological Museum
LEOFOROS ALEXANDRAS
Lofos Strefi
Plat Omonoia
Lykavittos Theatre
Lykavittos
National Library
University
Academy of Arts
Kerameikos Museum
ERMOU
Ancient Agora of Athens
The Little Metropolis
Parliament Building
LEOFOROS VASILISIS SOFIAS
War Museum
Byzantine Museum
Ethnikos Kipos
Presidential Residence
Observatory
PLAKA
Acropolis
Parthenon
Pnyx
Odeon of Herodes Atticus
Theatre of Dionysus
Zappeion Exhibition Hall
Temple of Zeus
Stadium
Monument of Filopappou
ARDITTOU
LEOF. SYNGROU
KALLIROIS

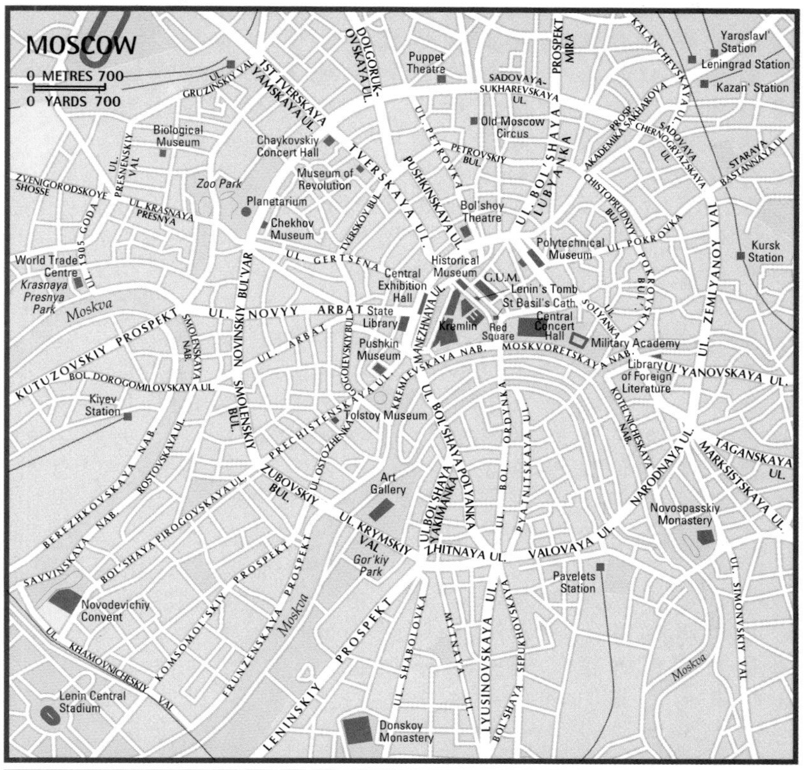

MOSCOW
0 METRES 700
0 YARDS 700
Puppet Theatre
Yaroslavl' Station
Leningrad Station
Kazan' Station
Biological Museum
Chaykovskiy Concert Hall
Old Moscow Circus
Zoo Park
Museum of Revolution
Planetarium
Bol'shoy Theatre
Chekhov Museum
Polytechnical Museum
Kursk Station
World Trade Centre
Krasnaya Presnya Park
Central Exhibition Hall
Historical Museum
G.U.M.
Lenin's Tomb
St Basil's Cath.
State Library
Kremlin
Red Square
Central Concert Hall
Military Academy
Pushkin Museum
Library of Foreign Literature
Kiyev Station
Tolstoy Museum
UL. NOVYY ARBAT
KUTUZOVSKIY PROSPEKT
Art Gallery
Gor'kiy Park
Novospasskiy Monastery
Novodevichiy Convent
Pavelets Station
Moskva
Lenin Central Stadium
Donskoy Monastery
LENINSKIY PROSPEKT

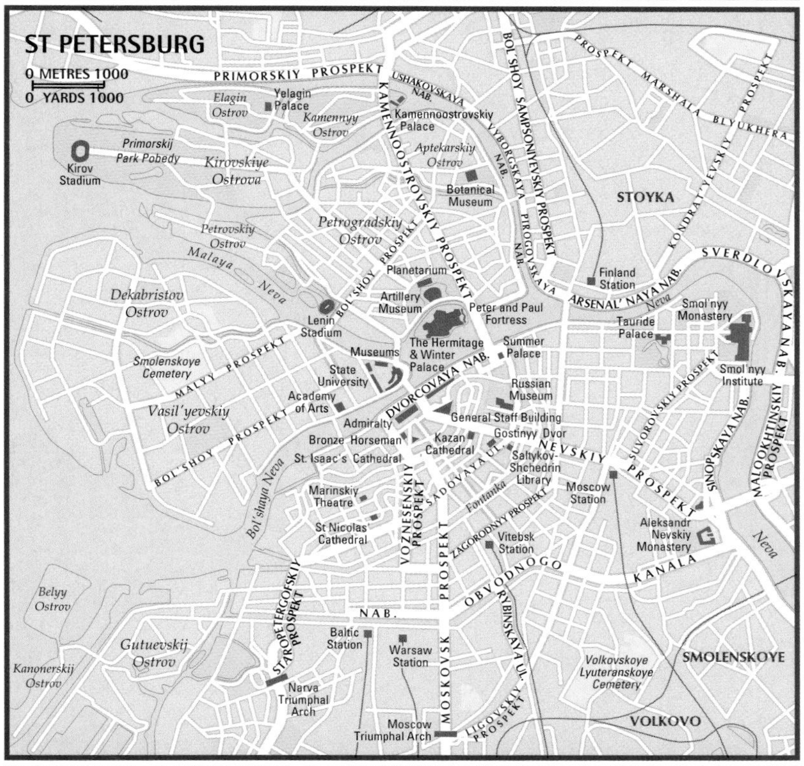

ST PETERSBURG
0 METRES 1000
0 YARDS 1000
PRIMORSKIY PROSPEKT
Elagin Ostrov
Yelagin Palace
Kamennyy Ostrov
Kamennoostrovskiy Palace
Primorskij Park Pobedy
Kirov Stadium
Kirovskie Ostrova
Aptekarskiy Ostrov
Botanical Museum
STOYKA
Petrovskiy Ostrov
Petrogradskiy Ostrov
Malaya Neva
Dekabristov Ostrov
Planetarium
Finland Station
Artillery Museum
Lenin Stadium
Peter and Paul Fortress
Smol'nyy Monastery
Tauride Palace
Summer Palace
Museums
The Hermitage & Winter Palace
Smolenskoye Cemetery
State University
Academy of Arts
Smol'nyy Institute
Russian Museum
Vasil'yevskiy Ostrov
Admiralty
General Staff Building
Bronze Horseman
Kazan' Cathedral
Gostinyy Dvor
St. Isaac's Cathedral
Saltykov-Shchedrin Library
NEVSKIY PROSPEKT
Mariinskiy Theatre
Moscow Station
St Nicolas' Cathedral
Aleksandr Nevskiy Monastery
Vitebsk Station
Belyy Ostrov
OBVODNOGO KANALA
Baltic Station
Warsaw Station
Gutuevskij Ostrov
Kanonerskij Ostrov
Volkovskoye Lyuteranskoye Cemetery
SMOLENSKOYE
Narva Triumphal Arch
Moscow Triumphal Arch
VOLKOVO
MOSKOVSKIY PROSPEKT

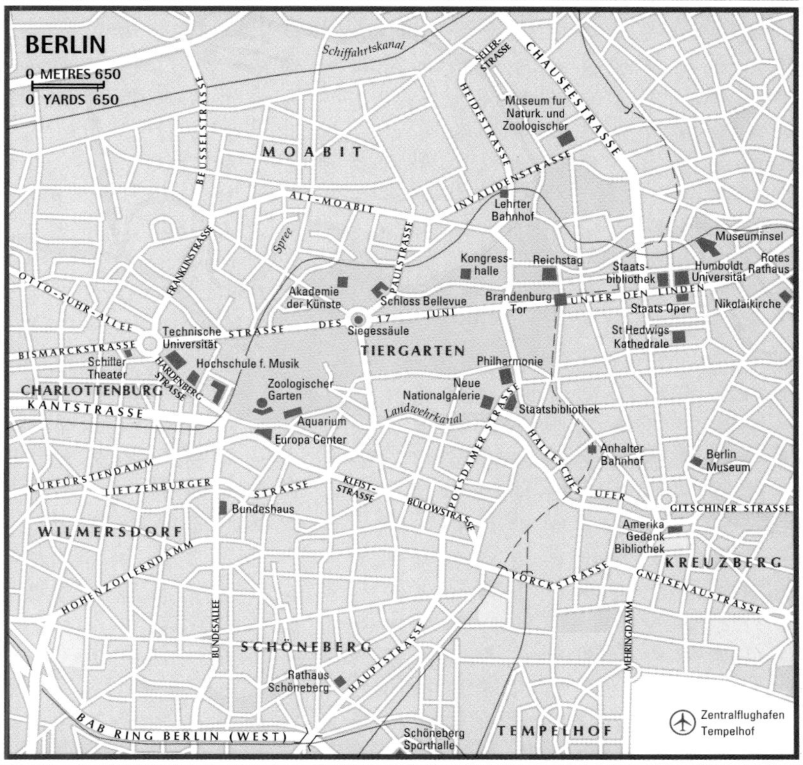

BERLIN
0 METRES 650
0 YARDS 650
Schiffahrtskanal
Museum fur Naturk. und Zoologischer
MOABIT
ALT-MOABIT
INVALIDENSTRASSE
Lehrter Bahnhof
Museuminsel
Kongress-halle
Reichstag
Staats-bibliothek
Humboldt Universität
Rotes Rathaus
Akademie der Künste
Schloss Bellevue
Brandenburg Tor
UNTER DEN LINDEN
Staats Oper
Nikolaikirche
Technische Universität
STRASSE DES 17 JUNI
Siegessäule
St Hedwigs Kathedrale
BISMARCKSTRASSE
Schiller Theater
Hochschule f. Musik
TIERGARTEN
Philharmonie
CHARLOTTENBURG
KANTSTRASSE
Zoologischer Garten
Neue Nationalgalerie
Staatsbibliothek
Aquarium
Europa Center
Landwehrkanal
Anhalter Bahnhof
Berlin Museum
KURFÜRSTENDAMM
Bundeshaus
GITSCHINER STRASSE
WILMERSDORF
Amerika Gedenk Bibliothek
KREUZBERG
SCHÖNEBERG
Rathaus Schöneberg
BAB RING BERLIN (WEST)
Schöneberg Sporthalle
TEMPELHOF
Zentralflughafen Tempelhof

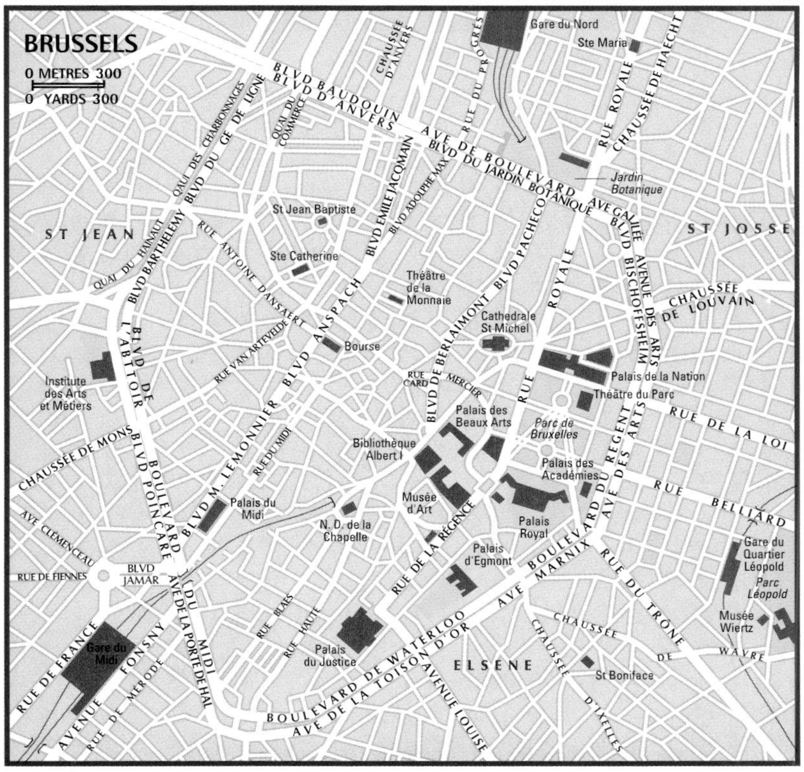

BRUSSELS
0 METRES 300
0 YARDS 300
Gare du Nord
Ste Marie
BLVD BAUDOUIN
BLVD D'ANVERS
RUE ROYALE
CHAUSSÉE DE HAECHT
Jardin Botanique
ST JEAN
St Jean Baptiste
ST JOSSE
Ste Catherine
Théâtre de la Monnaie
CHAUSSÉE DE LOUVAIN
Cathedrale St Michel
Bourse
Palais de la Nation
Théâtre du Parc
Institute des Arts et Metiers
Palais des Beaux Arts
Parc de Bruxelles
RUE DE LA LOI
Bibliothèque Albert I
Palais des Académies
CHAUSSÉE DE MONS
Palais du Midi
Musée d'Art
RUE BELLIARD
N. D. de la Chapelle
Palais Royal
Gare du Quartier Léopold
Parc Léopold
Palais d'Egmont
BLVD JAMAR
RUE DE FIENNES
Musée Wiertz
Gare du Midi
Palais du Justice
ELSENE
St Boniface
BOULEVARD DE WATERLOO
AVENUE LOUISE

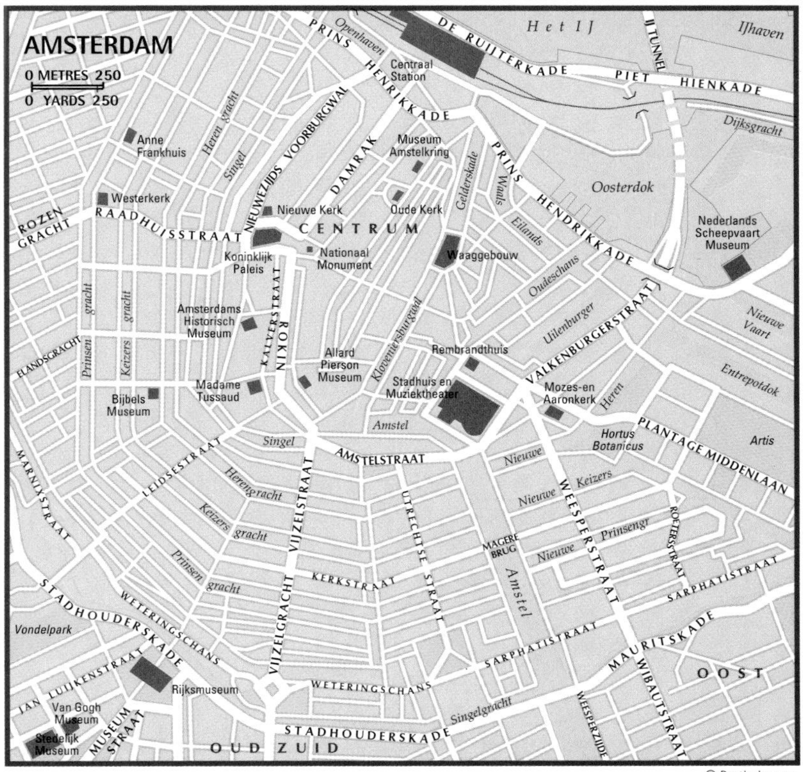

AMSTERDAM
0 METRES 250
0 YARDS 250
Het IJ
IJhaven
DE RUIJTERKADE
Centraal Station
PIET HIENKADE
PRINS HENDRIKKADE
Anne Frankhuis
Museum Amstelkring
DAMRAK
Westerkerk
Oosterdok
Nieuwe Kerk
Oude Kerk
RAADHUISSTRAAT
CENTRUM
Nederlands Scheepvaart Museum
Nationaal Monument
Koninklijk Paleis
Waaggebouw
Amsterdams Historisch Museum
Rembrandthuis
Allard Pierson Museum
Stadhuis en Muziektheater
VALKENBURGERSTRAAT
Bijbels Museum
Madame Tussaud
Mozes-en Aaronkerk
Amstel
Hortus Botanicus
PLANTAGE MIDDENLAAN
Artis
AMSTELSTRAAT
KERKSTRAAT
Magere Brug
SARPHATISTRAAT
Vondelpark
STADHOUDERSKADE
Rijksmuseum
WETERINGSCHANS
MAURITSKADE
OOST
Van Gogh Museum
Stedelijk Museum
MUSEUMSTRAAT
OUD ZUID

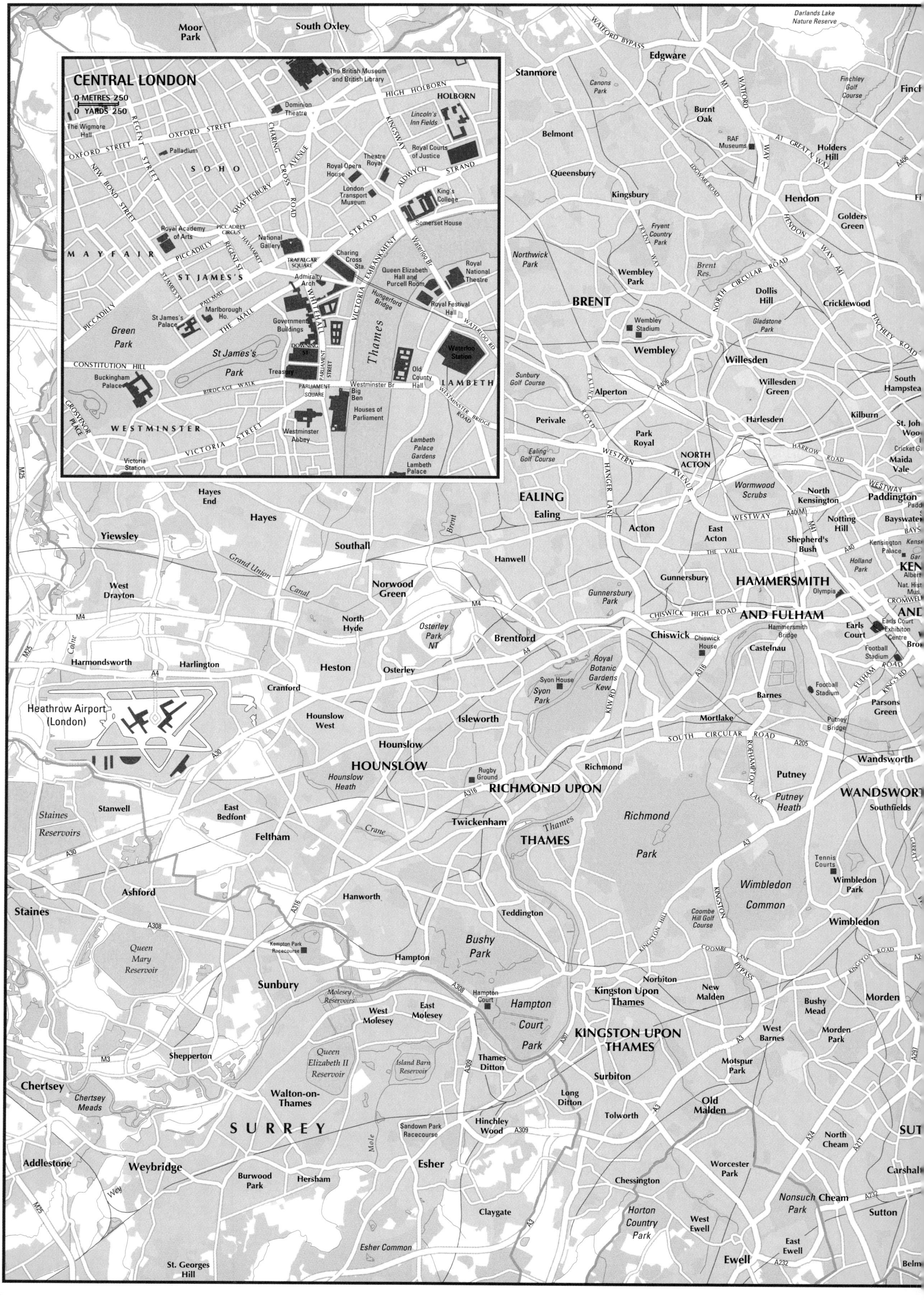

CENTRAL LONDON

0 METRES 250
0 YARDS 250

The Wigmore Hall

OXFORD STREET

REGENT STREET

NEW BOND STREET

The British Museum and British Library

Dominion Theatre

OXFORD STREET

HIGH HOLBORN

HOLBORN

SOHO

CHARING CROSS AVENUE

KINGSWAY

Lincoln's Inn Fields

Palladium

Royal Courts of Justice

Theatre Royal

ALDWYCH

STRAND

Royal Opera House

SHAFTESBURY AVENUE

London Transport Museum

King's College

HAYMARKET

REGENT STREET

Royal Academy of Arts

PICCADILLY CIRCUS

National Gallery

STRAND

Somerset House

MAYFAIR

PICCADILLY

St JAMES'S

TRAFALGAR SQUARE

Charing Cross Sta.

VICTORIA EMBANKMENT

Waterloo Br.

Royal National Theatre

ST JAMES'S STREET

Admiralty Arch

WHITEHALL

Queen Elizabeth Hall and Purcell Room

PICCADILLY

PALL MALL

St James's Palace

Marlborough Ho.

THE MALL

Government Buildings

Hungerford Bridge

Royal Festival Hall

Green Park

CONSTITUTION HILL

Buckingham Palace

St James's Park

DOWNING ST

Thames

Old County Hall

LAMBETH

Treasury

PARLIAMENT STREET

Waterloo Station

GROSVENOR PLACE

BIRDCAGE WALK

PARLIAMENT SQUARE

Westminster Br.
Big Ben

WATERLOO RD

WESTMINSTER

Westminster Abbey

Houses of Parliament

WESTMINSTER BRIDGE ROAD

VICTORIA STREET

VICTORIA STREET

Lambeth Palace Gardens
Lambeth Palace

M25

Victoria Station

Darlands Lake Nature Reserve

WATFORD BYPASS

Edgware

Moor Park

South Oxley

Stanmore

Finchley Golf Course

Finch

Canons Park

Burnt Oak

Belmont

RAF Museums

A1 GREAT N

Holders Hill

M1

WATFORD

A41

Queensbury

Kingsbury

EDGWAREROAD

Hendon

HENDON WAY

Golders Green

Kingsbury

Fryent Country Park

Northwick Park

FRYENT WAY

NORTH CIRCULAR ROAD

Dollis Hill

Cricklewood

BRENT

Brent Res.

FINCHLEY ROAD

Wembley Park

Wembley Stadium

Gladstone Park

Willesden

Wembley

Willesden Green

South Hampstea

Sunbury Golf Course

EALING ROAD

Harlesden

Kilburn

St. Joh Woo

Alperton

Park Royal

Cricket G

Perivale

A406

NORTH ACTON

Maida Vale

Ealing Golf Course

WESTERN AVENUE

HARROW ROAD

WESTWAY

Paddington

EALING

HANGER LANE

Wormwood Scrubs

North Kensington

A40(M)

Padd

Ealing

Brent

Acton

East Acton

A41

Notting Hill

Bayswate

Hanwell

THE VALE

Shepherd's Bush

A40

Kensington Palace

Kens

BAYS

Southall

M4

Gunnersbury

HAMMERSMITH

Holland Park

KEN

Grand Union Canal

Gunnersbury Park

Nat. Hist. Mus.

Albert

Norwood Green

CHISWICK HIGH ROAD

AND FULHAM

Olympia

AND

West Drayton

North Hyde

Chiswick

Hammersmith Bridge

CROMWELL

Yiewsley

M4

Osterley Park NT

Brentford

A4

Chiswick House

Castelnau

Earls Court

Earls Court Exhibition Centre

Bro

M4

Harmondsworth

Harlington

Heston

Osterley

Royal Botanic Gardens Kew

Barnes

Football Stadium

Football Stadium

KINGS RD

Cranford

Syon House

KEW RD

Parsons Green

Heathrow Airport (London)

Hounslow West

Syon Park

FULHAM ROAD

Putney Bridge

Isleworth

Mortlake

SOUTH CIRCULAR ROAD

A205

Wandsworth

A30

Hounslow

Rugby Ground

Richmond

ROEHAMPTON LANE

Putney

Staines Reservoirs

HOUNSLOW

A316

RICHMOND UPON

Richmond Park

Putney Heath

WANDSWORT

Hounslow Heath

Southfields

Stanwell

East Bedfont

Twickenham

Thames

A3

CARTR

WANDSWORTH

Crane

THAMES

Tennis Courts

Feltham

Wimbledon Park

Ashford

Hanworth

Teddington

KINGSTON HILL

Wimbledon Common

Wimbledon

Staines

A308

Coombe Hill Golf Course

A316

Bushy Park

KINGSTON LANE

Queen Mary Reservoir

Kempton Park Racecourse

COOMBE LANE

KINGSTON ROAD

Hampton

A2

Sunbury

Molesey Reservoirs

A308

Hampton Court

Norbiton

New Malden

Bushy Mead

Morden

West Molesey

East Molesey

Hampton Court Park

Kingston Upon Thames

West Barnes

Morden Park

Shepperton

M3

Queen Elizabeth II Reservoir

Island Barn Reservoir

Thames Ditton

KINGSTON UPON THAMES

Motspur Park

Chertsey

Walton-on-Thames

A309

Surbiton

Old Malden

North Cheam

SUT

Addlestone

SURREY

Mole

Sandown Park Racecourse

Hinchley Wood

A309

Long Ditton

Tolworth

A3

Worcester Park

Carshal

Chertsey Meads

Weybridge

Burwood Park

Hersham

Esher

Chessington

West Ewell

Sutton

St. Georges Hill

Wey

Claygate

Esher Common

Horton Country Park

Nonsuch Cheam Park

A232

Ewell

A24

East Ewell

Belm

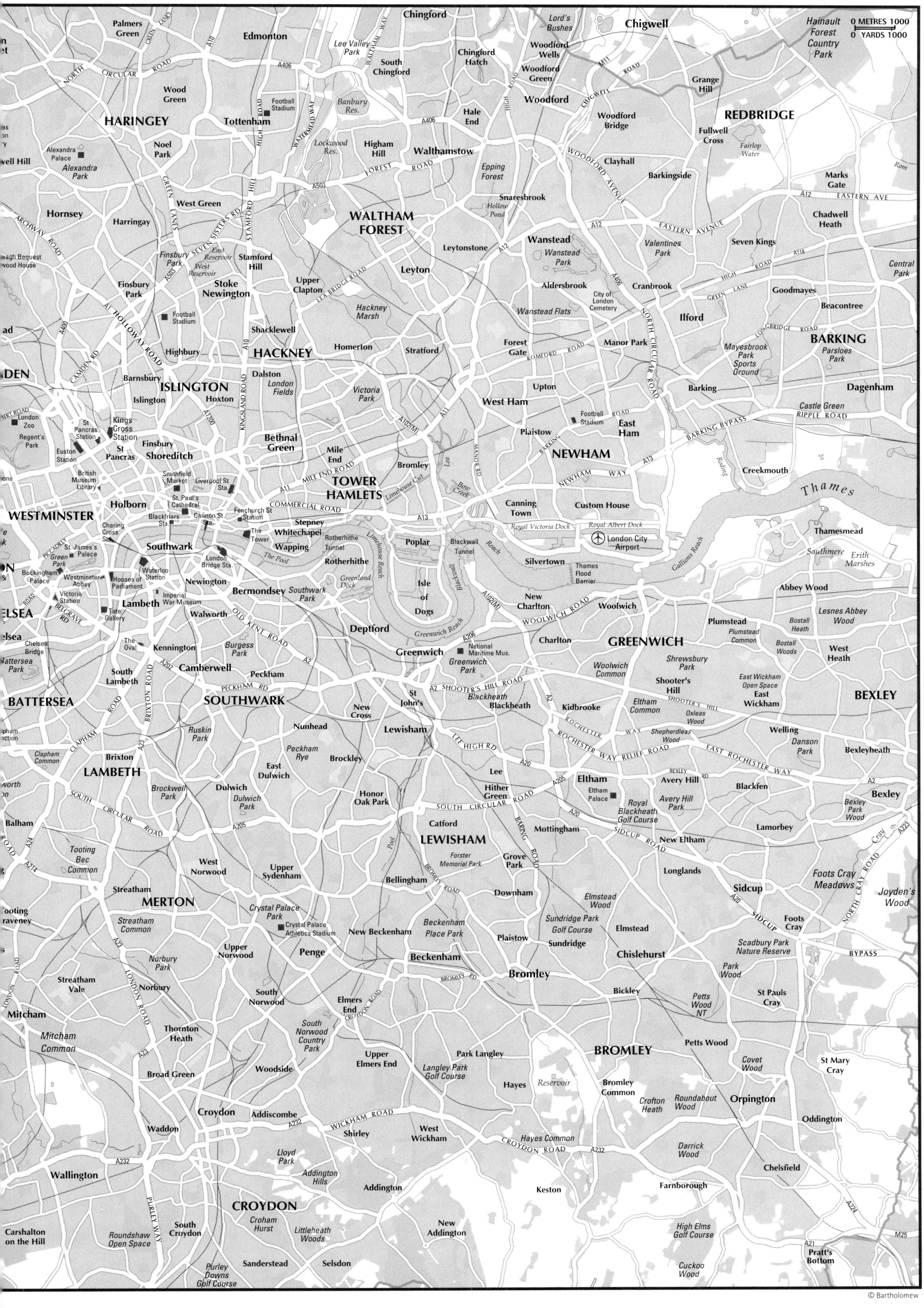
0 METRES 1000
0 YARDS 1000
Palmers Green
Edmonton
Chingford
Lee Valley Park
South Chingford
Chingford Hatch
Lord's Bushes
Chigwell
Woodford Wells
Woodford Green
Hainault Forest Country Park
Grange Hill
NORTH CIRCULAR ROAD
Wood Green
Football Stadium
Banbury Res.
Hale End
Woodford
Woodford Bridge
REDBRIDGE
Fullwell Cross
Fairlop Water
HARINGEY
Tottenham
Alexandra Palace
Alexandra Park
Noel Park
Lockwood Res.
Higham Hill
Walthamstow
Epping Forest
Clayhall
Barkingside
Marks Gate
FOREST ROAD
Snaresbrook
Hollow Pond
A12 EASTERN AVE
Chadwell Heath
Hornsey
Harringay
West Green
WALTHAM FOREST
EASTERN AVENUE
Wanstead
Wanstead Park
Valentines Park
Seven Kings
Finsbury Park
East Reservoir
West Reservoir
Stamford Hill
Leytonstone
Leyton
Central Park
Stoke Newington
Upper Clapton
LEA BRIDGE ROAD
Aldersbrook
City of London Cemetery
Cranbrook
HIGH ROAD
GREEN LANE
Goodmayes
Beacontree
Hackney Marsh
Wanstead Flats
Ilford
Shacklewell
Forest Gate
ROMFORD ROAD
Manor Park
LONGBRIDGE ROAD
BARKING
Parsloes Park
Highbury
HACKNEY
Homerton
Stratford
NORTH CIRCULAR ROAD
Mayesbrook Park Sports Ground
Dalston
London Fields
Victoria Park
Barnsbury
ISLINGTON
Islington
Hoxton
Upton
Barking
Dagenham
West Ham
Football Stadium
East Ham
Castle Green
RIPPLE ROAD
London Zoo
St Pancras Station
Kings Cross Station
Regent's Park
Euston Station
St Pancras
Finsbury
Shoreditch
Bethnal Green
Mile End
Plaistow
BARKING BYPASS
NEWHAM
Bromley
MILE END ROAD
Creekmouth
British Museum Library
Smithfield Market
Liverpool St Sta.
TOWER HAMLETS
Limehouse Cut
Bow Creek
NEWHAM WAY
Thames
Holborn
St. Paul's Cathedral
COMMERCIAL ROAD
Canning Town
Custom House
WESTMINSTER
Blackfriars Sta.
Cannon St Sta.
Fenchurch St Station
Charing Cross Sta.
Stepney
The Tower
Whitechapel
Wapping
Royal Victoria Dock
Royal Albert Dock
Thamesmead
London City Airport
Poplar
Blackwall Tunnel
St. James's Palace
Green Park
Southwark
Rotherhithe Tunnel
The Pool
Rotherhithe
Limehouse Reach
Silvertown
Southmere
Erith Marshes
Thames Flood Barrier
Gallions Reach
Buckingham Palace
Westminster Abbey
Houses of Parliament
Waterloo Station
London Bridge Sta.
Newington
Greenland Dock
Isle of Dogs
Blackwall Reach
New Charlton
Woolwich
Abbey Wood
Victoria Station
Imperial War Museum
Bermondsey
Southwark Park
WOOLWICH ROAD
Plumstead
Plumstead Common
Bostall Heath
Lesnes Abbey Wood
Tate Gallery
Lambeth
Walworth
OLD KENT ROAD
Deptford
Greenwich Reach
Chelsea Bridge
Battersea Park
The Oval
Kennington
Burgess Park
National Maritime Mus.
Greenwich
Greenwich Park
Charlton
GREENWICH
Bostall Woods
West Heath
Camberwell
Peckham
PECKHAM RD
South Lambeth
Woolwich Common
Shrewsbury Park
East Wickham Open Space
BATTERSEA
SOUTHWARK
SHOOTER'S HILL ROAD
Blackheath
St John's
Shooter's Hill
East Wickham
BEXLEY
New Cross
Kidbrooke
Eltham Common
Oxleas Wood
Nunhead
Lewisham
ROCHESTER WAY
Shepherdleas Wood
Welling
Ruskin Park
Clapham Common
Peckham Rye
Brockley
LEE HIGH RD
ROCHESTER WAY RELIEF ROAD
EAST ROCHESTER WAY
Danson Park
Bexleyheath
Brixton
LAMBETH
East Dulwich
Lee
Eltham
BEXLEY RD
Avery Hill
Blackfen
Dulwich
Brockwell Park
Honor Oak Park
Hither Green
Eltham Palace
Royal Blackheath Golf Course
Avery Hill Park
Bexley
Bexley Park Wood
Dulwich Park
SOUTH CIRCULAR ROAD
Catford
Balham
Mottingham
SIDCUP ROAD
Lamorbey
LEWISHAM
New Eltham
Tooting Bec Common
Forster Memorial Park
Grove Park
BARING ROAD
West Norwood
Upper Sydenham
Longlands
Foots Cray Meadows
Streatham
Bellingham
Downham
Sidcup
Joyden's Wood
MERTON
Crystal Palace Park
Elmstead Wood
Crystal Palace Athletics Stadium
Streatham Common
New Beckenham
Beckenham Place Park
Sundridge Park Golf Course
Elmstead
Foots Cray
NORTH CRAY ROAD
SIDCUP BYPASS
Plaistow
Sundridge
Scadbury Park Nature Reserve
Upper Norwood
Penge
Chislehurst
Norbury Park
Beckenham
Streatham Vale
Norbury
Bromley
Park Wood
LONDON ROAD
BROMLEY RD
Bickley
St Pauls Cray
South Norwood
Elmers End
CROYDON ROAD
Petts Wood NT
Mitcham
Mitcham Common
Thornton Heath
South Norwood Country Park
Petts Wood
BROMLEY
Park Langley
Upper Elmers End
Covet Wood
St Mary Cray
Woodside
Langley Park Golf Course
Broad Green
Hayes
Reservoir
Bromley Common
Crofton Heath
Roundabout Wood
Orpington
Croydon
Addiscombe
Oddington
Waddon
WICKHAM ROAD
Shirley
West Wickham
Hayes Common
CROYDON ROAD
Darrick Wood
Lloyd Park
Chelsfield
Wallington
Addington Hills
Addington
Farnborough
Keston
CROYDON
PURLEY WAY
Croham Hurst
Littleheath Woods
New Addington
High Elms Golf Course
Carshalton on the Hill
Roundshaw Open Space
South Croydon
Pratt's Bottom
Purley Downs Golf Course
Sanderstead
Selsdon
Cuckoo Wood

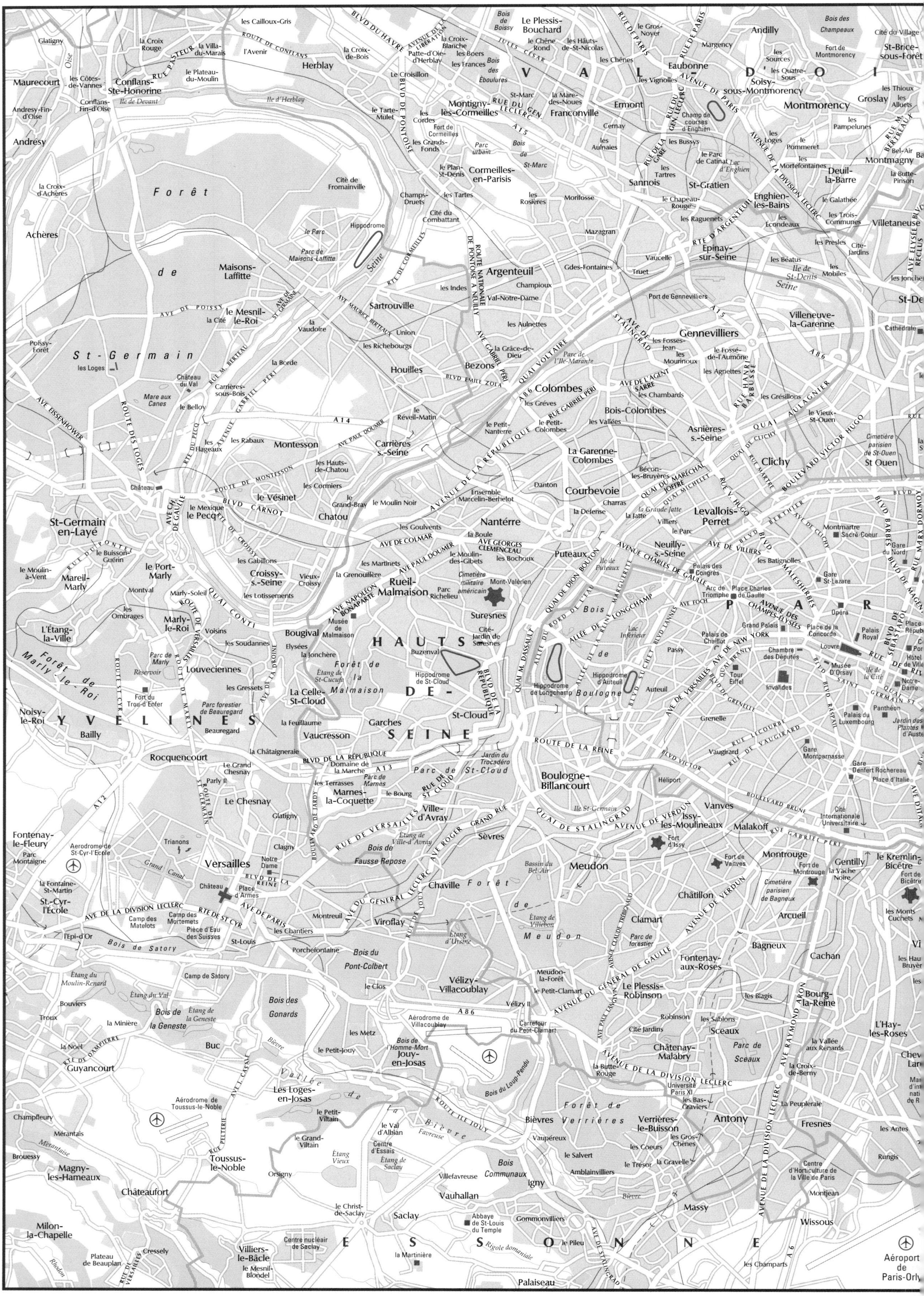
VAL-D'OISE
HAUTS-DE-SEINE
YVELINES
ESSONNE
PARIS
Forêt de St-Germain
Forêt de Marly-le-Roi
Herblay
Maurecourt
Conflans-Ste-Honorine
Andrésy
Achères
Maisons-Laffitte
Sartrouville
le Mesnil-le-Roi
Houilles
Montesson
Carrières-s.-Seine
le Vésinet
le Pecq
Chatou
St-Germain-en-Laye
Mareil-Marly
le Port-Marly
Croissy-s.-Seine
Rueil-Malmaison
Nantérre
Bougival
Louveciennes
Marly-le-Roi
L'Étang-la-Ville
Noisy-le-Roi
Bailly
Rocquencourt
le Chesnay
Versailles
St.-Cyr-l'École
Fontenay-le-Fleury
Guyancourt
Magny-les-Hameaux
Châteaufort
Milon-la-Chapelle
Toussus-le-Noble
Villiers-le-Bâcle
Saclay
Vauhallan
Igny
Bièvres
Jouy-en-Josas
les Loges-en-Josas
Buc
Vélizy-Villacoublay
Viroflay
Chaville
Sèvres
Meudon
Ville-d'Avray
Marnes-la-Coquette
Vaucresson
Garches
St-Cloud
Suresnes
La Celle-St-Cloud
Puteaux
Courbevoie
La Garenne-Colombes
Colombes
Bois-Colombes
Argenteuil
Bezons
Cormeilles-en-Parisis
Montigny-lès-Cormeilles
Franconville
Le Plessis-Bouchard
Ermont
Eaubonne
Sannois
St-Gratien
Soisy-sous-Montmorency
Montmorency
Andilly
Groslay
St-Brice-sous-Forêt
Enghien-les-Bains
Epinay-sur-Seine
Deuil-la-Barre
Montmagny
Villetaneuse
Villeneuve-la-Garenne
Gennevilliers
Asnières-s.-Seine
Clichy
St Ouen
Levallois-Perret
Neuilly-s.-Seine
Bois de Boulogne
Boulogne-Billancourt
Issy-les-Moulineaux
Vanves
Malakoff
Montrouge
Gentilly
le Kremlin-Bicêtre
Châtillon
Clamart
Bagneux
Arcueil
Cachan
Fontenay-aux-Roses
Le Plessis-Robinson
Bourg-la-Reine
Sceaux
Châtenay-Malabry
L'Hay-les-Roses
Antony
Fresnes
Verrières-le-Buisson
Massy
Wissous
Palaiseau
Aéroport de Paris-Orly
Aérodrome de Toussus-le-Noble
Aérodrome de Villacoublay
Aérodrome de St-Cyr-l'École
Seine
A 13
A 14
A 15
A 86
A 12
A 6

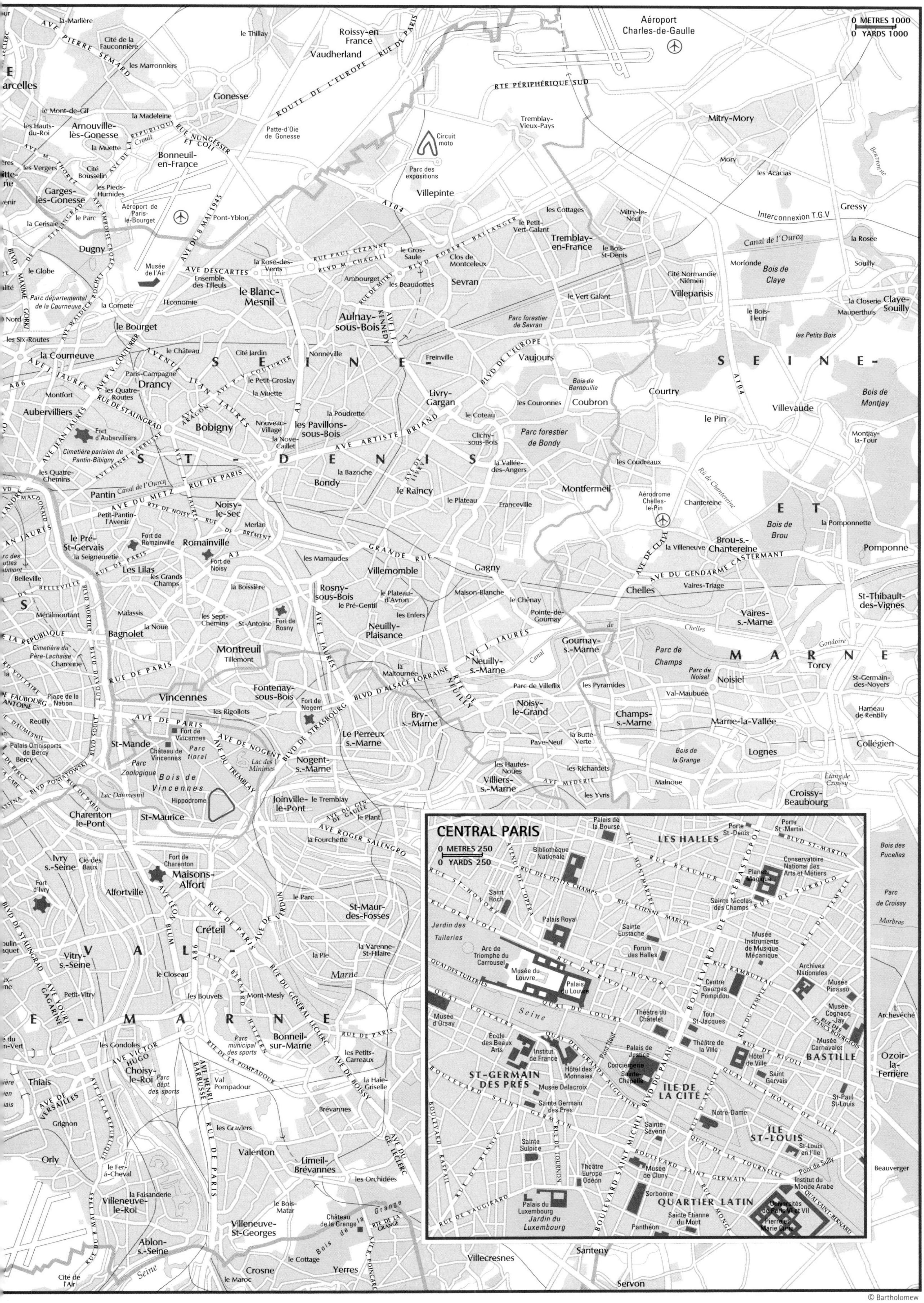
0 METRES 1000
0 YARDS 1000
Aéroport Charles-de-Gaulle
Roissy-en France
Vaudherland
le Thillay
la Marlière
Cité de la Fauconnière
les Marronniers
Sarcelles
Gonesse
RUE DE PARIS
ROUTE DE L'EUROPE
RTE PÉRIPHÉRIQUE SUD
Tremblay-Vieux-Pays
Mitry-Mory
Mory
les Acacias
Beuvronne
Gressy
le Mont-de-Gif
la Madeleine
les Hauts-du-Roi
Arnouville-lès-Gonesse
la Muette
Bonneuil-en-France
Patte-d'Oie de Gonesse
Circuit moto
Parc des expositions
Villepinte
les Vergers
Cité Bousselin
Garges-lès-Gonesse
les Pieds-Humides
Aéroport de Paris-le-Bourget
Pont-Yblon
A104
les Cottages
Mitry-le-Neuf
Interconnexion T.G.V
la Cerisaie
le Parc
le Petit-Vert-Galant
Tremblay-en-France
le Bois-St-Denis
Canal de l'Ourcq
la Rosée
Dugny
Musée de l'Air
AVE DU 8 MAI 1945
la Rose-des-Vents
RUE PAUL CÉZANNE
BLVD M. CHAGALL
le Gros-Saule
BLVD ROBERT BALLANGER
Clos de Montceleux
Morfonde
Bois de Claye
Souilly
le Globe
AVE DESCARTES
Ensemble des Tilleuls
Ambourget
les Beaudottes
Sevran
Cité Normandie Niémen
Villeparisis
Parc départemental de la Courneuve
la Comète
l'Économie
le Blanc-Mesnil
le Vert Galant
la Closerie
Claye-Souilly
Mauperthuis
le Bourget
Aulnay-sous-Bois
Parc forestier de Sevran
le Bois-Fleuri
les Six-Routes
les Petits Bois
la Courneuve
le Château
Cité Jardin
Nonneville
Freinville
BLVD DE L'EUROPE
Vaujours
Paris-Campagne
Drancy
les Quatre-Routes
le Petit-Groslay
la Muette
SEINE-ST-DENIS
Bois de Bernouille
Coubron
Courtry
Bois de Montjay
Montfort
Aubervilliers
la Poudrette
Livry-Gargan
les Couronnes
Villevaude
le Pin
Bobigny
Fort d'Aubervilliers
Nouveau-Village
les Pavillons-sous-Bois
le Coteau
Parc forestier de Bondy
Montjay-la-Tour
la Nove-Caillet
AVE ARISTIDE BRIAND
Clichy-sous-Bois
Cimetière parisien de Pantin-Bibigny
la Vallée-des-Angers
les Coudreaux
les Quatre-Chemins
la Bazoche
Bondy
le Raincy
Montfermeil
Rû de Chantereine
Pantin
RUE DE PARIS
Noisy-le-Sec
le Plateau
Franceville
Aérodrome Chelles-le-Pin
Chantereine
Petit-Pantin-l'Avenir
Merlan
SEINE-ET-MARNE
Bois de Brou
la Pomponnette
le Pré-St-Gervais
Fort de Romainville
Romainville
GRANDE RUE
la Villeneuve
Brou-s.-Chantereine
Pomponne
la Seigneurerie
Fort de Noisy
les Marnaudes
AVE DU GENDARME CASTERMANT
Les Lilas
les Grands Champs
Villemomble
Gagny
Chelles
Vaires-Triage
Belleville
la Boissière
Rosny-sous-Bois
le Plateau-d'Avron
Maison-Blanche
le Chênay
St-Thibault-des-Vignes
Ménilmontant
Malassis
les Sept-Chemins
St-Antoine
Fort de Rosny
le Pré-Gentil
les Enfers
Pointe-de-Gournay
Vaires-s.-Marne
Bagnolet
la Noue
Neuilly-Plaisance
Cimetière du Père-Lachaise
Charonne
Montreuil
Tillemont
Gournay-s.-Marne
Parc de Champs
Torcy
Neuilly-s.-Marne
la Maltournée
Parc de Noisiel
Noisiel
St-Germain-des-Noyers
Place de la Nation
Vincennes
Fontenay-sous-Bois
Fort de Nogent
BLVD D'ALSACE LORRAINE
Parc de Villeflix
les Pyramides
Val-Maubuée
Reuilly
les Rigollots
BLVD DE STRASBOURG
Bry-s.-Marne
Noisy-le-Grand
Champs-s.-Marne
Hameau de Rentilly
Marne-la-Vallée
Palais Omnisports de Bercy
Bercy
St-Mande
Fort de Vincennes
Château de Vincennes
Parc floral
Le Perreux s.-Marne
la Butte-Verte
Pave-Neuf
Lognes
Bois de la Grange
Collégien
Parc Zoologique
Bois de Vincennes
Lac des Minimes
Nogent-s.-Marne
les Hautes-Noues
les Richardets
Villiers-s.-Marne
Malnoue
Étang de Croissy
Lac Daumesnil
Hippodrome
Joinville-le-Pont
le Tremblay
les Yvris
Croissy-Beaubourg
Charenton le-Pont
St-Maurice
le Plant
la Fourchette
AVE ROGER SALENGRO
Ivry s.-Seine
Cité des Baux
Fort de Charenton
Maisons-Alfort
Bois des Pucelles
Fort d'Ivry
Alfortville
le Parc
St-Maur-des-Fosses
Parc de Croissy
Morbras
Créteil
Vitry-s.-Seine
la Pie
la Varenne-St-Hilaire
VAL-DE-MARNE
le Closeau
Marne
Petit-Vitry
les Bouvets
Mont-Mesly
L'Archevêché
Bonneuil-sur-Marne
les Gondoles
Parc municipal des sports
Choisy-le-Roi
Parc dépt. des sports
Val Pompadour
les Petits-Carreaux
Ozoir-la-Ferrière
Thiais
la Haie-Griselle
Brévannes
Grignon
les Gravliers
Orly
Valenton
Limeil-Brévannes
le Fer-à-Cheval
les Orchidées
la Faisanderie
Villeneuve-le-Roi
le Bois-Matar
Château de la Grange
Villeneuve-St-Georges
Bois de la Grange
Ablon-s.-Seine
Beauverger
Villecresnes
Santeny
Cité de l'Air
Seine
le Cottage
Crosne
le Maroc
Yerres
Servon
CENTRAL PARIS
0 METRES 250
0 YARDS 250
Palais de la Bourse
LES HALLES
Porte St-Denis
Porte St-Martin
BLVD ST-MARTIN
Bibliothèque Nationale
RUE RÉAUMUR
Conservatoire National des Arts et Métiers
Planetarium Magique
RUE DES PETITS CHAMPS
RUE DE TURBIGO
Saint Roch
RUE ÉTIENNE MARCEL
Sainte Nicolas des Champs
RUE ST-HONORÉ
Palais Royal
Jardin des Tuileries
Sainte Eustache
Musée Instruments de Musique Mécanique
Arc de Triomphe du Carrousel
Forum des Halles
RUE RAMBUTEAU
Archives Nationales
Musée du Louvre
Palais du Louvre
RUE DE RIVOLI
Centre Georges Pompidou
Musée Picasso
QUAI DES TUILERIES
QUAI DU LOUVRE
Théâtre du Châtelet
Tour St-Jacques
Musée Cognacq Jay
RUE FRANCS BOURGEOIS
Musée d'Orsay
QUAI VOLTAIRE
Seine
Pont Neuf
Palais de Justice
Théâtre de la Ville
Musée Carnavalet
BASTILLE
École des Beaux Arts
Institut de France
Conciergerie
Sainte-Chapelle
Hôtel de Ville
Saint Gervais
ST-GERMAIN DES PRÉS
Hôtel des Monnaies
ÎLE DE LA CITÉ
St-Paul St-Louis
Musée Delacroix
BOULEVARD SAINT GERMAIN
Sainte Germain des Pres
Notre-Dame
ÎLE ST-LOUIS
Sainte-Séverin
Sainte Sulpice
St-Louis en l'Île
Pont de Sully
Théâtre Europe Odéon
Musée de Cluny
Institut du Monde Arabe
Sorbonne
QUARTIER LATIN
Universités de Paris VI et VII
Palais du Luxembourg
Jardin du Luxembourg
Sainte Étienne du Mont
Pierre et Marie Curie
Panthéon
BOULEVARD SAINT MICHEL
BOULEVARD RASPAIL
RUE DE VAUGIRARD
QUAI SAINT-BERNARD

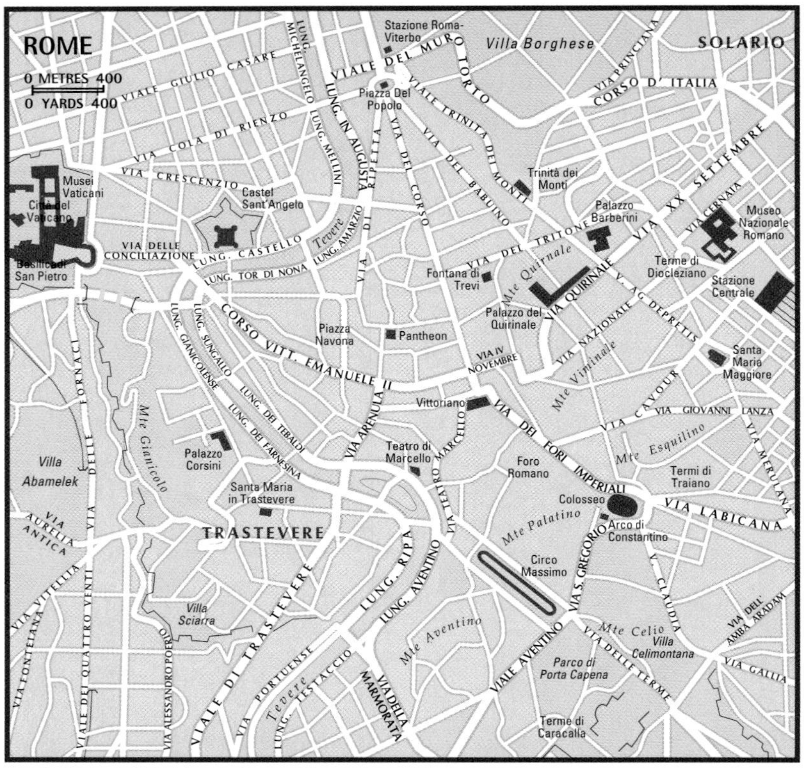
ROME
0 METRES 400
0 YARDS 400
Stazione Roma-Viterbo
Villa Borghese
SOLARIO
Piazza Del Popolo
CORSO D'ITALIA
VIA COLA DI RIENZO
Musei Vaticani
Città del Vaticano
Castel Sant'Angelo
Trinità dei Monti
Palazzo Barberini
Museo Nazionale Romano
VIA DELLE CONCILIAZIONE
Basilica di San Pietro
Fontana di Trevi
Terme di Diocleziano
Stazione Centrale
Palazzo del Quirinale
Piazza Navona
Pantheon
CORSO VITT. EMANUELE II
Santa Maria Maggiore
Vittoriano
VIA DEI FORI IMPERIALI
VIA CAVOUR
Mte Gianicolo
Palazzo Corsini
Teatro di Marcello
Foro Romano
Mte Esquilino
Termi di Traiano
Villa Abamelek
Santa Maria in Trastevere
Colosseo
Arco di Constantino
VIA LABICANA
TRASTEVERE
Mte Palatino
Circo Massimo
Villa Sciarra
VIALE DI TRASTEVERE
Mte Aventino
Mte Celio
Villa Celimontana
Parco di Porta Capena
Terme di Caracalla
Tevere

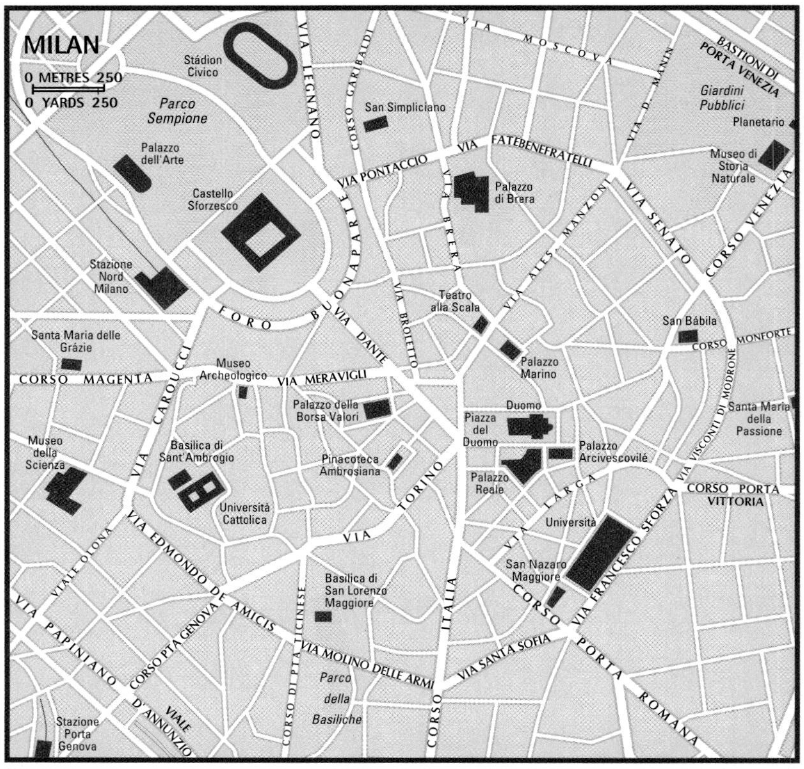
MILAN
0 METRES 250
0 YARDS 250
Stadion Civico
Parco Sempione
San Simpliciano
Giardini Pubblici
Planetario
Museo di Storia Naturale
Palazzo dell'Arte
Castello Sforzesco
Palazzo di Brera
Stazione Nord Milano
FORO BUONAPARTE
Teatro alla Scala
San Bàbila
Santa Maria delle Gràzie
Palazzo Marino
CORSO MAGENTA
Museo Archeologico
VIA MERAVIGLI
Palazzo della Borsa Valori
Duomo
Piazza del Duomo
Santa Maria della Passione
Museo della Scienza
Basilica di Sant'Ambrogio
Pinacoteca Ambrosiana
Palazzo Reale
Palazzo Arcivescovile
CORSO PORTA VITTORIA
Università Cattolica
Università
San Nazaro Maggiore
Basilica di San Lorenzo Maggiore
VIA FRANCESCO SFORZA
CORSO PORTA ROMANA
Parco della Basiliche
Stazione Porta Genova

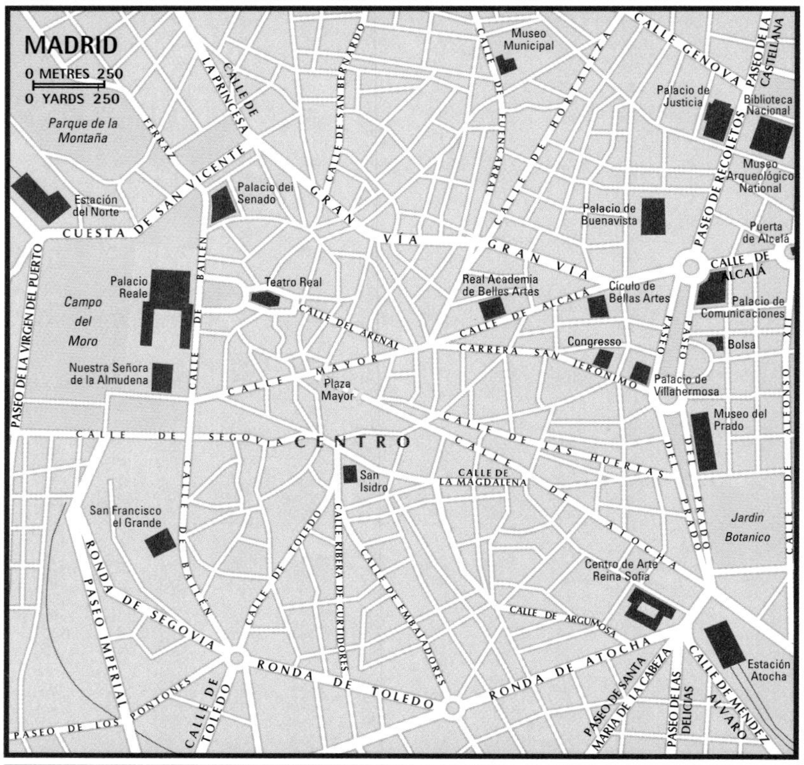
MADRID
0 METRES 250
0 YARDS 250
Museo Municipal
CALLE GENOVA
PASEO DE LA CASTELLANA
Palacio de Justicia
Biblioteca Nacional
Parque de la Montaña
Museo Arqueológico Nacional
Estación del Norte
Palacio del Senado
Palacio de Buenavista
CUESTA DE SAN VICENTE
GRAN VIA
Puerta de Alcalá
CALLE DE ALCALÁ
Palacio Reale
Teatro Real
Real Academia de Belles Artes
Cículo de Bellas Artes
Palacio de Comunicaciones
Campo del Moro
Congresso
Bolsa
Nuestra Señora de la Almudena
CALLE MAYOR
Plaza Mayor
Palacio de Villahermosa
Museo del Prado
CENTRO
CALLE DE SEGOVIA
San Isidro
CALLE DE LA MAGDALENA
San Francisco el Grande
Jardín Botanico
Centro de Arte Reina Sofía
RONDA DE SEGOVIA
PASEO IMPERIAL
RONDA DE TOLEDO
RONDA DE ATOCHA
Estación Atocha
PASEO DE LA VIRGEN DEL PUERTO

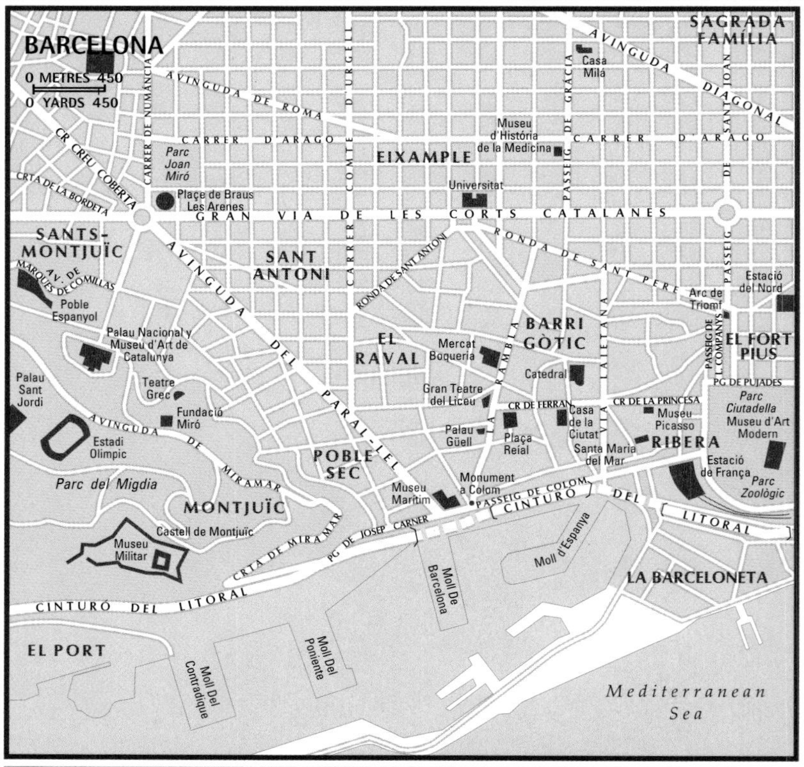
BARCELONA
0 METRES 450
0 YARDS 450
SAGRADA FAMÍLIA
Casa Milà
AVINGUDA DIAGONAL
Museu d'Història de la Medicina
CARRER D'ARAGO
EIXAMPLE
Parc Joan Miró
Plaça de Braus Les Arenes
Universitat
GRAN VIA DE LES CORTS CATALANES
SANTS-MONTJUÏC
SANT ANTONI
Arc de Triomf
Estació del Nord
Poble Espanyol
Palau Nacional y Museu d'Art de Catalunya
BARRI GÒTIC
EL RAVAL
Mercat Boqueria
EL FORT PIUS
Catedral
Palau Sant Jordi
Teatre Grec
Gran Teatre del Liceu
Fundació Miró
Casa de la Ciutat
Museu Picasso
Parc Ciutadella
Museu d'Art Modern
Estadi Olímpic
Palau Güell
Plaça Reial
Santa Maria del Mar
RIBERA
POBLE SEC
Parc del Migdia
MONTJUÏC
Museu Maritim
Monument a Colom
Estació de França
Parc Zoològic
Castell de Montjuïc
Museu Militar
Moll D'Espanya
LA BARCELONETA
Moll De Barcelona
CINTURÓ DEL LITORAL
EL PORT
Moll Del Contradique
Moll Del Ponent
Mediterranean Sea

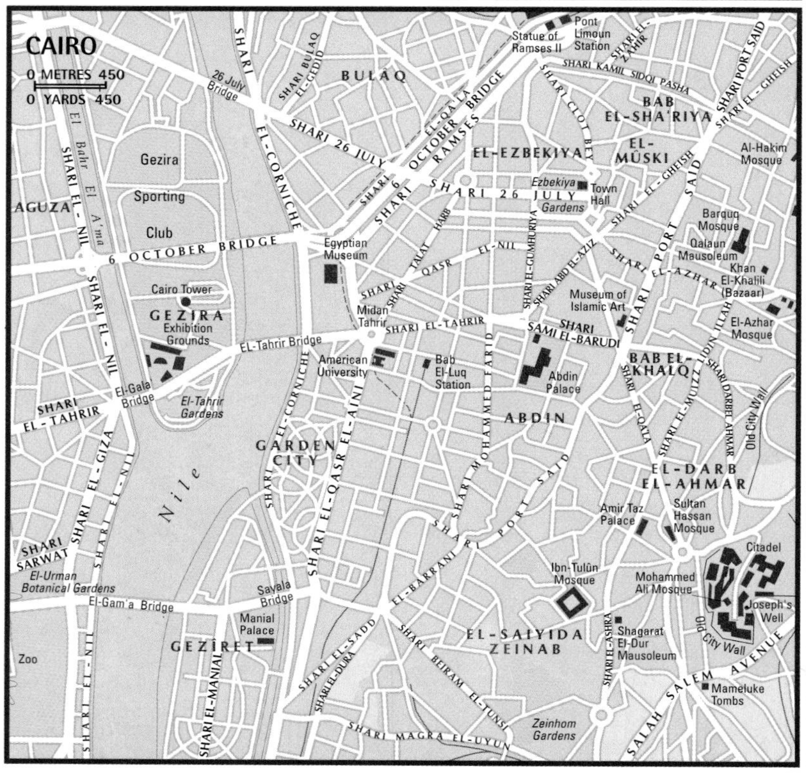
CAIRO
0 METRES 450
0 YARDS 450
Pont Limoun Station
Statue of Ramses II
BULAQ
26 July Bridge
SHARI 26 JULY
BAB EL-SHA'RIYA
Gezira Sporting Club
EL-EZBEKIYA
EL-MÜSKI
Al-Hakim Mosque
AGUZA
Ezbekiya Gardens
Town Hall
6 OCTOBER BRIDGE
Egyptian Museum
Barquq Mosque
Qalaun Mausoleum
Khan El-Khalili (Bazaar)
Cairo Tower
GEZIRA Exhibition Grounds
Midan Tahrir
Museum of Islamic Art
El-Azhar Mosque
EL-Tahrir Bridge
American University
Bab El-Luq Station
Abdin Palace
BAB EL-KHALQ
El-Gala Bridge
El-Tahrir Gardens
SHARI EL-TAHRIR
ABDIN
GARDEN CITY
Old City Wall
Nile
EL-DARB EL-AHMAR
Amir Taz Palace
Sultan Hassan Mosque
Citadel
SHARI SARWAT
El-Urman Botanical Gardens
El-Gam'a Bridge
Ibn-Tulün Mosque
Mohammed Ali Mosque
Joseph's Well
Savala Bridge
Manial Palace
GEZIRET
EL-SAIYIDA ZEINAB
Shagarat El-Dur Mausoleum
Zoo
Mameluke Tombs
Zeinhom Gardens
SHARI SALAH SALEM

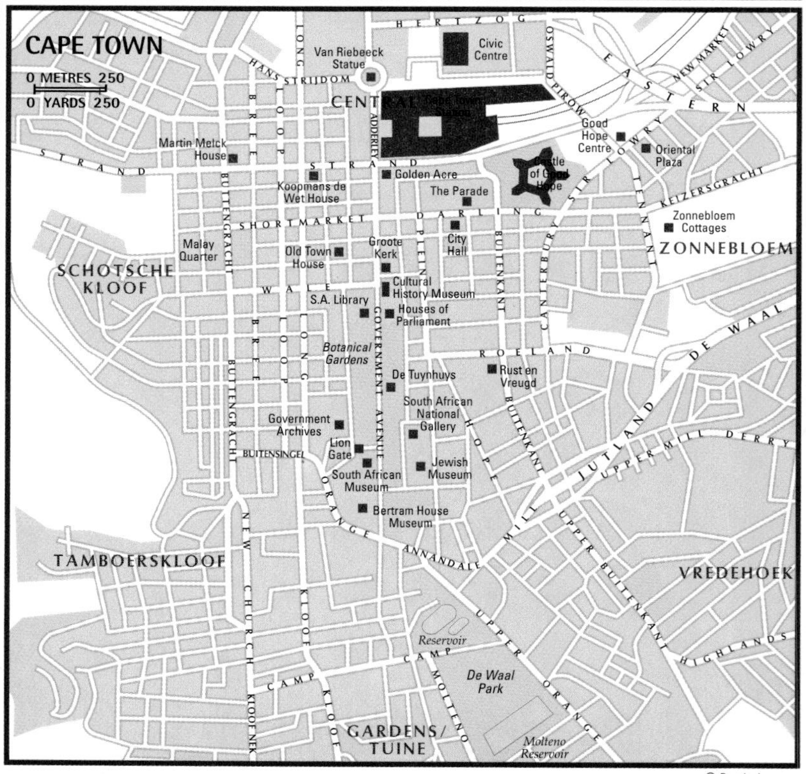
CAPE TOWN
0 METRES 250
0 YARDS 250
HERTZOG
Van Riebeeck Statue
Civic Centre
CENTRAL
Martin Melck House
STRAND
Good Hope Centre
Oriental Plaza
Castle of Good Hope
Koopmans de Wet House
Golden Acre
The Parade
DARLING
Zonnebloem Cottages
Malay Quarter
Groote Kerk
City Hall
ZONNEBLOEM
SCHOTSCHE KLOOF
Old Town House
Cultural History Museum
S.A. Library
Houses of Parliament
Botanical Gardens
De Tuynhuys
Rust en Vreugd
South African National Gallery
Government Archives
Lion Gate
Jewish Museum
South African Museum
Bertram House Museum
TAMBOERSKLOOF
VREDEHOEK
Reservoir
De Waal Park
GARDENS/TUINE
Molteno Reservoir

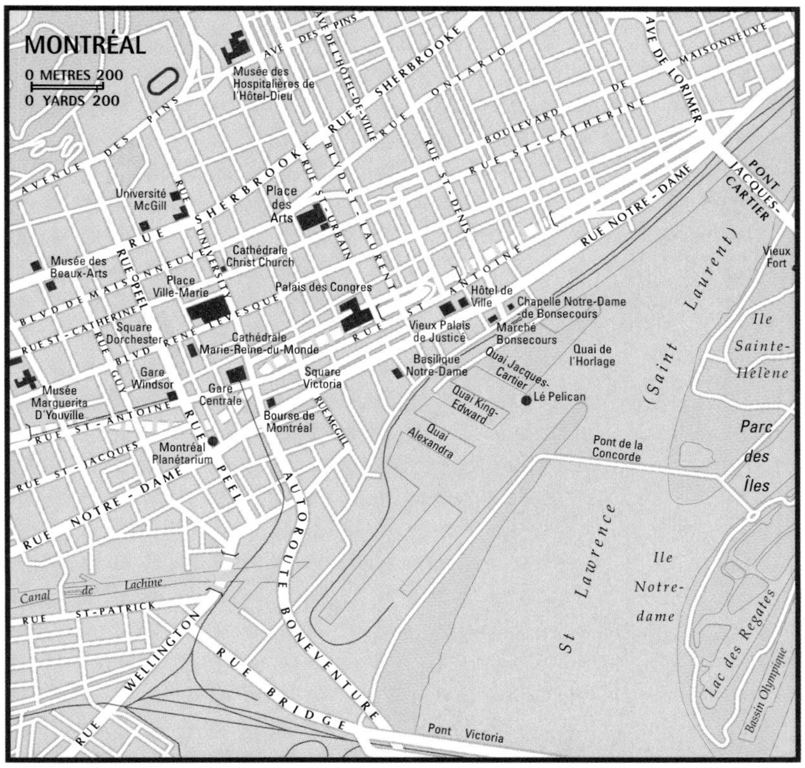
MONTRÉAL
0 METRES 200
0 YARDS 200
Musée des Hospitalières de l'Hôtel-Dieu
Université McGill
Place des Arts
Musée des Beaux-Arts
Cathédrale Christ Church
Place Ville-Marie
Palais des Congres
Square Dorchester
Cathédrale Marie-Reine-du-Monde
Gare Windsor
Gare Centrale
Musée Marguerita D'Youville
Square Victoria
Bourse de Montréal
Montréal Planétarium
Hôtel de Ville
Chapelle Notre-Dame -de Bonsecours
Marché Bonsecours
Vieux Palais de Justice
Basilique Notre-Dame
Quai de l'Horloge
Quai Jacques-Cartier
Lé Pelican
Quai King-Edward
Quai Alexandra
Pont de la Concorde
Pont Jacques-Cartier
Vieux Fort
Ile Sainte-Hélène
Parc des Îles
Ile Notre-dame
Lac des Regates
Bassin Olympique
St Lawrence
(Saint Laurent)
Pont Victoria
Canal de Lachine
RUE SHERBROOKE
RUE ST-CATHERINE
RUE NOTRE-DAME
RUE ST-ANTOINE
RUE ST-JACQUES
RUE ST-PATRICK
RUE WELLINGTON
RUE BRIDGE
AUTOROUTE BONEVENTURE
AVE DES PINS
AVE DE LORIMER
BLVD DE MAISONNEUVE
RUE ONTARIO
BOULEVARD RENÉ-LÉVESQUE

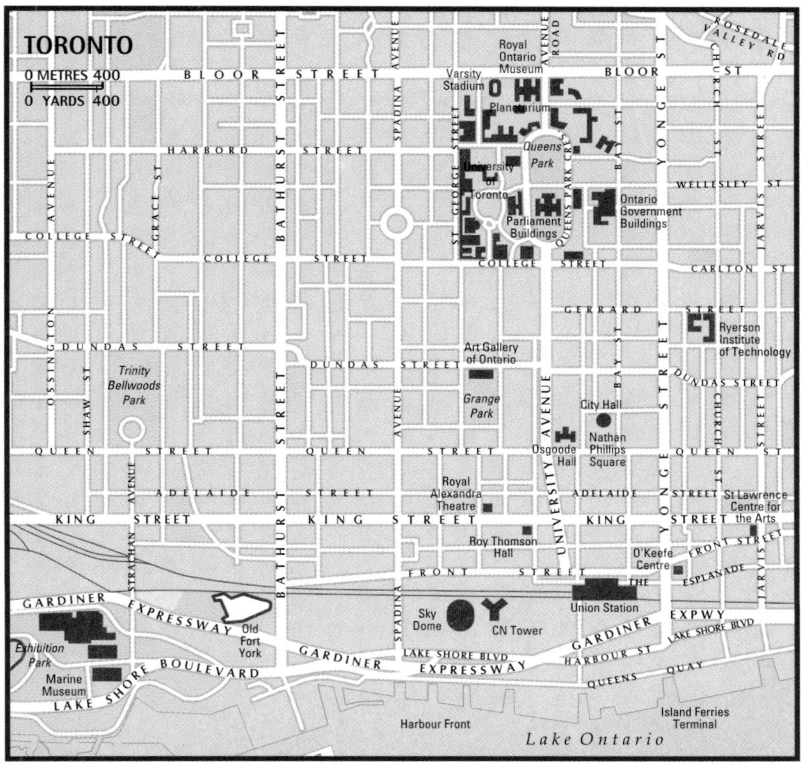
TORONTO
0 METRES 400
0 YARDS 400
BLOOR STREET
HARBORD STREET
COLLEGE STREET
GERRARD STREET
DUNDAS STREET
QUEEN STREET
ADELAIDE STREET
KING STREET
FRONT STREET
GARDINER EXPRESSWAY
LAKE SHORE BOULEVARD
BATHURST STREET
SPADINA AVENUE
UNIVERSITY AVENUE
YONGE STREET
JARVIS STREET
CHURCH STREET
BAY STREET
OSSINGTON AVENUE
SHAW ST
STRACHAN AVENUE
ROSEDALE VALLEY RD
WELLESLEY ST
CARLTON ST
ESPLANADE
QUEENS QUAY
HARBOUR ST
Royal Ontario Museum
Varsity Stadium
Planetarium
Queens Park
University of Toronto
Parliament Buildings
Ontario Government Buildings
Ryerson Institute of Technology
Art Gallery of Ontario
Grange Park
Trinity Bellwoods Park
City Hall
Osgoode Hall
Nathan Phillips Square
Royal Alexandra Theatre
Roy Thomson Hall
St Lawrence Centre for the Arts
O'Keefe Centre
Union Station
Sky Dome
CN Tower
Old Fort York
Exhibition Park
Marine Museum
Harbour Front
Island Ferries Terminal
Lake Ontario

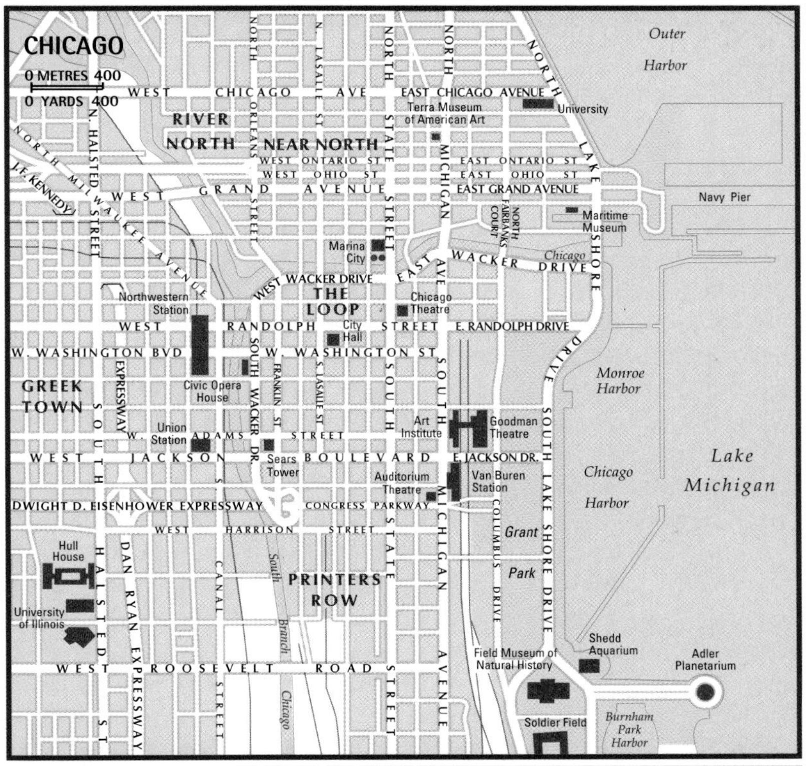
CHICAGO
0 METRES 400
0 YARDS 400
RIVER NORTH
NEAR NORTH
THE LOOP
GREEK TOWN
PRINTERS ROW
WEST CHICAGO AVE
EAST CHICAGO AVENUE
WEST ONTARIO ST
EAST ONTARIO ST
WEST OHIO ST
EAST OHIO ST
WEST GRAND AVENUE
EAST GRAND AVENUE
WACKER DRIVE
WEST WACKER DRIVE
WEST RANDOLPH STREET
E. RANDOLPH DRIVE
W. WASHINGTON BVD
W. WASHINGTON ST
WEST ADAMS STREET
WEST JACKSON BOULEVARD
E. JACKSON DR.
DWIGHT D. EISENHOWER EXPRESSWAY
CONGRESS PARKWAY
WEST HARRISON STREET
WEST ROOSEVELT ROAD
NORTH LASALLE ST
NORTH STATE STREET
NORTH MICHIGAN AVENUE
SOUTH MICHIGAN AVENUE
SOUTH STATE STREET
SOUTH LAKE SHORE DRIVE
SOUTH HALSTED ST
DAN RYAN EXPRESSWAY
Terra Museum of American Art
University
Navy Pier
Maritime Museum
Marina City
Northwestern Station
Chicago Theatre
City Hall
Civic Opera House
Union Station
Sears Tower
Art Institute
Goodman Theatre
Auditorium Theatre
Van Buren Station
Hull House
University of Illinois
Grant Park
Monroe Harbor
Chicago Harbor
Lake Michigan
Outer Harbor
Field Museum of Natural History
Shedd Aquarium
Adler Planetarium
Soldier Field
Burnham Park Harbor

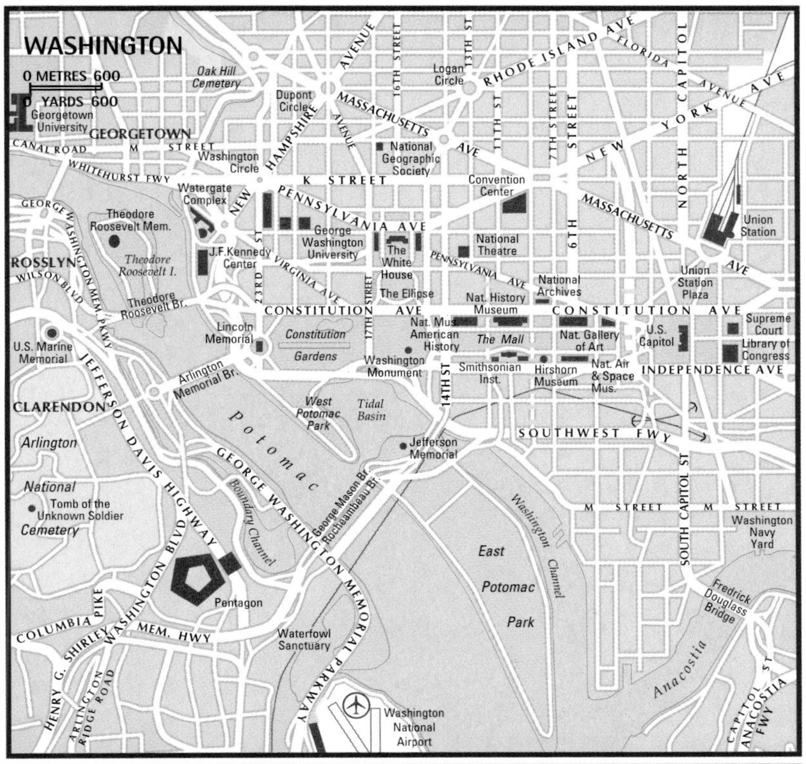
WASHINGTON
0 METRES 600
0 YARDS 600
Oak Hill Cemetery
Georgetown University
GEORGETOWN
Dupont Circle
Logan Circle
Washington Circle
National Geographic Society
Convention Center
Watergate Complex
Theodore Roosevelt Mem.
Theodore Roosevelt I.
ROSSLYN
J.F.Kennedy Center
George Washington University
The White House
The Ellipse
National Theatre
National Archives
Union Station
Union Station Plaza
Nat. History Museum
Nat. Mus. American History
The Mall
Nat. Gallery of Art
U.S. Capitol
Supreme Court
Library of Congress
Lincoln Memorial
Constitution Gardens
Washington Monument
Smithsonian Inst.
Hirshorn Museum
Nat. Air & Space Mus.
U.S. Marine Memorial
Arlington Memorial Br.
CLARENDON
Arlington
National Cemetery
Tomb of the Unknown Soldier
West Potomac Park
Tidal Basin
Jefferson Memorial
Potomac
Boundary Channel
Pentagon
East Potomac Park
Washington Channel
Washington Navy Yard
Fredrick Douglass Bridge
Anacostia
Waterfowl Sanctuary
Washington National Airport
MASSACHUSETTS AVE
RHODE ISLAND AVE
FLORIDA AVENUE
NEW YORK AVE
NEW HAMPSHIRE AVENUE
PENNSYLVANIA AVE
VIRGINIA AVE
K STREET
M STREET
CONSTITUTION AVE
INDEPENDENCE AVE
SOUTHWEST FWY
JEFFERSON DAVIS HIGHWAY
GEORGE WASHINGTON MEMORIAL PARKWAY
COLUMBIA PIKE
SHIRLEY MEM. HWY
NORTH CAPITOL
SOUTH CAPITOL STREET
WHITEHURST FWY
CANAL ROAD
WILSON BLVD
16TH STREET
14TH ST
17TH STREET

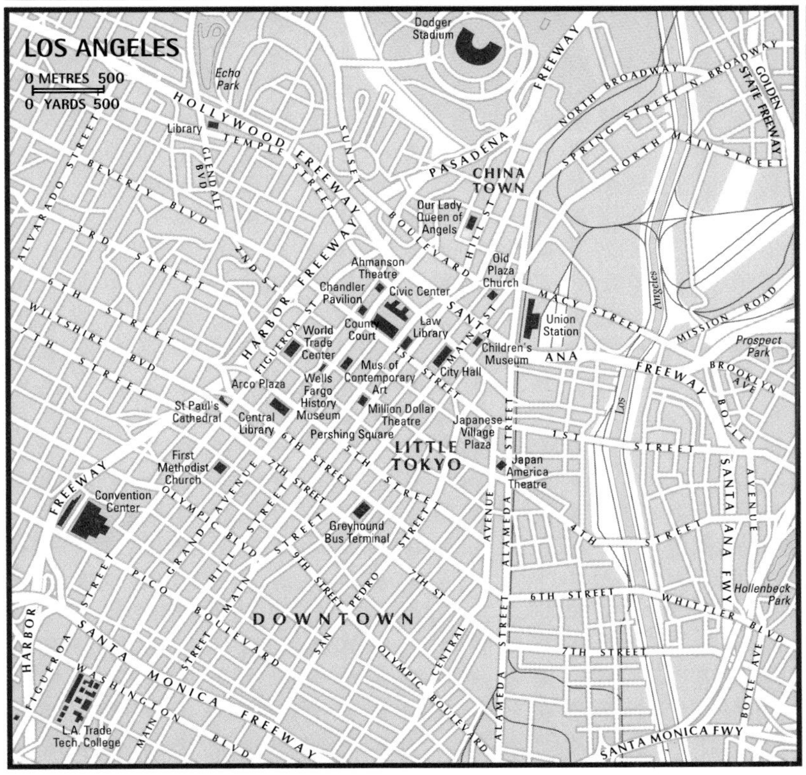
LOS ANGELES
0 METRES 500
0 YARDS 500
Dodger Stadium
Echo Park
Library
CHINA TOWN
Our Lady Queen of Angels
Old Plaza Church
Ahmanson Theatre
Chandler Pavilion
Civic Center
County Court
Law Library
City Hall
Union Station
Children's Museum
World Trade Center
Mus. of Contemporary Art
Arco Plaza
Wells Fargo History Museum
Million Dollar Theatre
Central Library
Pershing Square
St Paul's Cathedral
Japanese Village Plaza
LITTLE TOKYO
Japan America Theatre
First Methodist Church
Convention Center
Greyhound Bus Terminal
DOWNTOWN
Prospect Park
Hollenbeck Park
L.A. Trade Tech. College
HOLLYWOOD FREEWAY
HARBOR FREEWAY
PASADENA FREEWAY
GOLDEN STATE FREEWAY
SANTA MONICA FREEWAY
SANTA ANA FWY
SANTA MONICA FWY
SUNSET BLVD
OLYMPIC BLVD
WASHINGTON BLVD
PICO BLVD
BEVERLY BLVD
MISSION ROAD
WHITTIER BLVD
ALAMEDA STREET
CENTRAL AVENUE
GRAND AVENUE
FIGUEROA STREET
MACY STREET
N. BROADWAY
NORTH MAIN STREET
SAN PEDRO ST

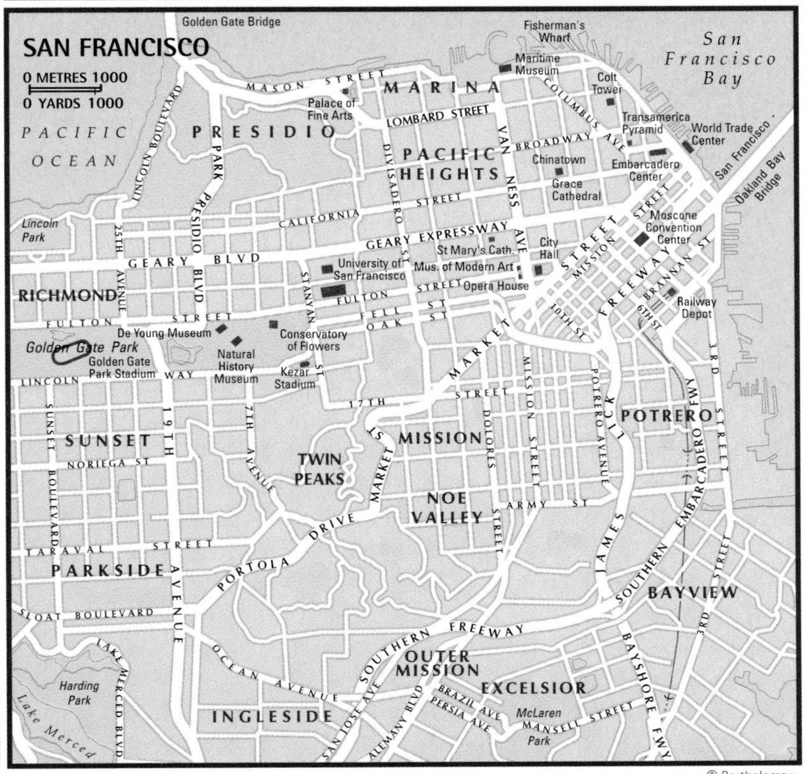
SAN FRANCISCO
0 METRES 1000
0 YARDS 1000
Golden Gate Bridge
Fisherman's Wharf
Maritime Museum
San Francisco Bay
Coit Tower
Transamerica Pyramid
World Trade Center
San Francisco-Oakland Bay Bridge
PACIFIC OCEAN
PRESIDIO
MARINA
Palace of Fine Arts
PACIFIC HEIGHTS
Chinatown
Grace Cathedral
Embarcadero Center
Moscone Convention Center
Lincoln Park
St Mary's Cath.
City Hall
University of San Francisco
Mus. of Modern Art
Opera House
RICHMOND
Railway Depot
Golden Gate Park
De Young Museum
Golden Gate Park Stadium
Natural History Museum
Conservatory of Flowers
Kezar Stadium
SUNSET
TWIN PEAKS
MISSION
NOE VALLEY
POTRERO
PARKSIDE
BAYVIEW
Harding Park
Lake Merced
INGLESIDE
OUTER MISSION
EXCELSIOR
McLaren Park
MASON STREET
LOMBARD STREET
GEARY EXPRESSWAY
GEARY BLVD
CALIFORNIA STREET
FULTON STREET
MARKET STREET
VAN NESS AVE
PORTOLA DRIVE
SOUTHERN FREEWAY
BAYSHORE BLVD
SLOAT BOULEVARD
LINCOLN WAY
NORIEGA ST
19TH AVENUE
SUNSET BLVD

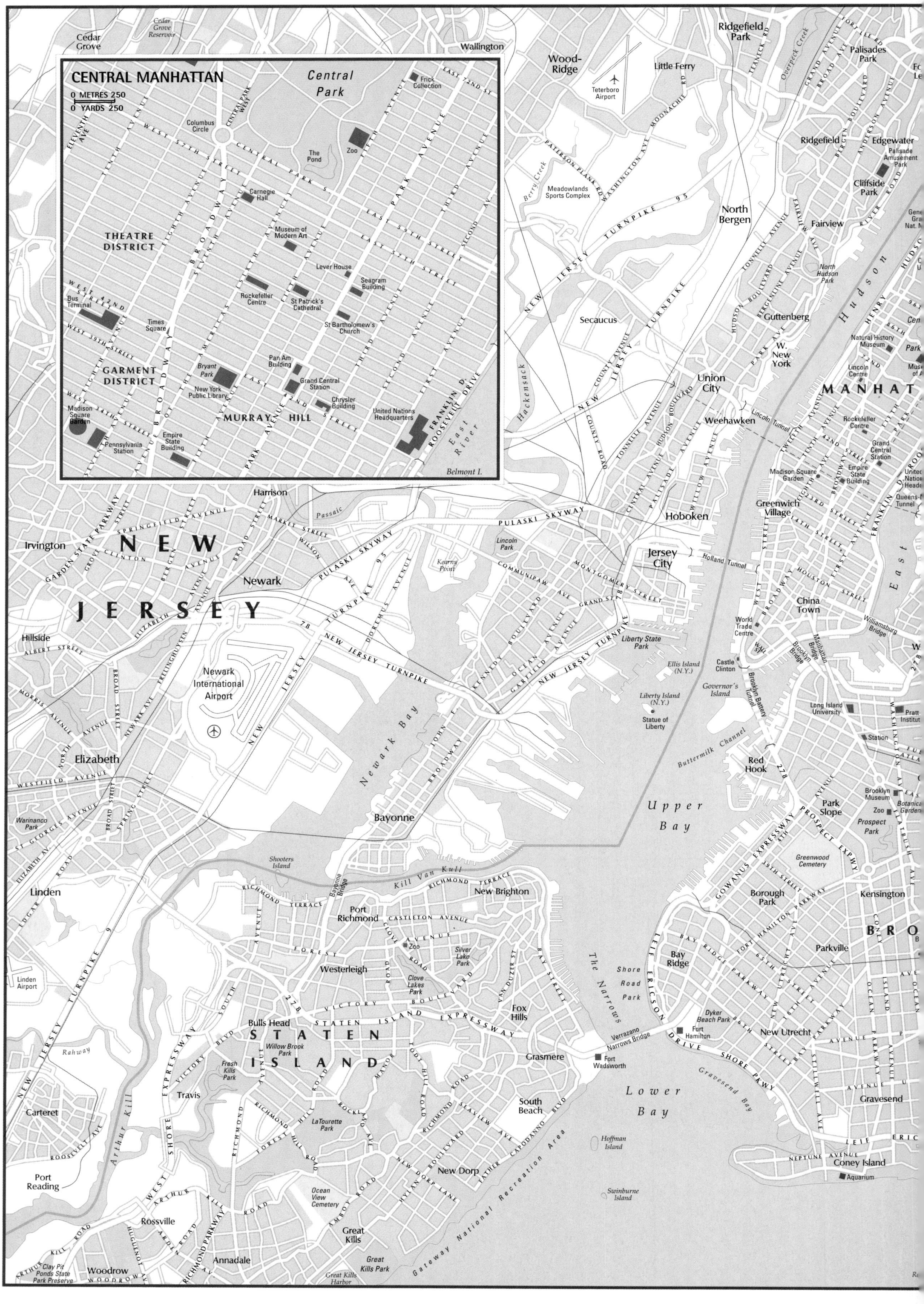

CENTRAL MANHATTAN

0 METRES 250
0 YARDS 250

Cedar Grove Reservoir

Central Park

Frick Collection

EAST 72ND ST

Columbus Circle

CENTRAL PARK SOUTH

The Pond

Zoo

ELEVENTH AVE

TENTH AVENUE

NINTH AVENUE

WEST 57TH STREET

EIGHTH AVENUE

BROADWAY

SEVENTH AVENUE

CENTRAL PARK S

AVENUE OF THE AMERICAS

FIFTH AVENUE

MADISON AVENUE

PARK AVENUE

LEXINGTON AVENUE

THIRD AVENUE

SECOND AVENUE

FIRST AVENUE

Carnegie Hall

Museum of Modern Art

EAST 55TH STREET

Lever House

Seagram Building

THEATRE DISTRICT

Rockefeller Centre

St Patrick's Cathedral

St Bartholomew's Church

WEST 42ND

Bus Terminal

Times Square

Pan Am Building

Grand Central Station

Chrysler Building

WEST 35TH STREET

Bryant Park

New York Public Library

GARMENT DISTRICT

MURRAY HILL

United Nations Headquarters

FRANKLIN D. ROOSEVELT DRIVE

Madison Square Garden

Pennsylvania Station

Empire State Building

WEST 34TH STREET

SEVENTH AVENUE

BROADWAY

FIFTH AVENUE

MADISON AVE

PARK AVENUE

THIRD AVENUE

East River

Belmont I.

Cedar Grove

Wallington

Wood-Ridge

Ridgefield Park

Little Ferry

Palisades Park

Teterboro Airport

NEW JERSEY TURNPIKE

MOONACHIE

Ridgefield

Edgewater

Palisade Amusement Park

Cliffside Park

PATERSON PLANK RD

WASHINGTON AVE

Berry Creek

Meadowlands Sports Complex

95

North Bergen

Fairview

Gene Gra Nat. M

Hackensack

Secaucus

NEW COUNTY AVENUE

NEW JERSEY TURNPIKE

COUNTY ROAD

PATERSON PLANK RD

HUDSON AVENUE

PALISADE AVENUE

BERGENLINE AVENUE

FAIRVIEW AVENUE

Guttenberg

W. New York

North Hudson Park

Natural History Museum

Hudson River

HENRY HUDSON PARKWAY

Cen

Union City

Weehawken

Lincoln Tunnel

Lincoln Centre

Mus of A

MANHAT

Harrison

Passaic

Hoboken

Rockefeller Centre

TWELFTH AVENUE

ELEVENTH AVENUE

Madison Square Garden

Empire State Building

Grand Central Station

United Nations Headq

Queens-f Tunnel

N E W

Pulaski Skyway

Lincoln Park

Jersey City

Holland Tunnel

FRANKLIN

Greenwich Village

EAST

Irvington

Newark

GARDEN STATE PARKWAY

SPRINGFIELD AVENUE

CLINTON

BERGEN STREET

GROVE

BROAD STREET

MARKET STREET

WILSON

PULASKI SKYWAY

COMMUNIPAW

MONTGOMERY STREET

HOUSTON STREET

BROADWAY

China Town

J E R S E Y

Kearny Point

AVE

DOREMUS AVENUE

COMMUNIPAW AVE

GRAND ST

NEW JERSEY TURNPIKE

Liberty State Park

World Trade Centre

WALL ST

Williamsburg Bridge

Hillside

ALBERT STREET

ELIZABETH

FRELINGHUYSEN

78

KENNEDY BOULEVARD

OCEAN AVENUE

GARFIELD AVENUE

Ellis Island (N.Y.)

Castle Clinton

Brooklyn Bridge

Manhattan Bridge

Long Island University

Pratt Institut

MORRIS AVENUE

NORTH AVENUE

NEW JERSEY TURNPIKE

Newark International Airport

NEW JERSEY

JOHN F. KENNEDY BOULEVARD

Liberty Island (N.Y.)

Statue of Liberty

Governor's Island

Brooklyn Battery Tunnel

Station

Elizabeth

WESTFIELD AVENUE

Newark Bay

Broadway

Upper Bay

Red Hook

Buttermilk Channel

Park Museum

Zoo

Botanica Garden

ST GEORGES AVENUE

SOUTH

BROAD STREET

SPRING STREET

Warinanco Park

Bayonne

278

Park Slope

Prospect Park

GOWANUS EXPRESSWAY

Greenwood Cemetery

PROSPECT EXPWY

Linden

Shooters Island

Bayonne Bridge

Kill Van Kull

RICHMOND TERRACE

New Brighton

39TH STREET

BAY RIDGE AVENUE

Borough Park

Kensington

B R O

EDGAR ROAD

LINDEN

Linden Airport

9

RICHMOND TERRACE

Port Richmond

CASTLETON AVENUE

Zoo

CLOVE ROAD

Silver Lake Park

The Narrows

Shore Road Park

LEIF ERICSON DRIVE

FORT HAMILTON PARKWAY

Bay Ridge

Parkville

NEW JERSEY TURNPIKE

ARTHUR KILL ROAD

WEST SHORE EXPRESSWAY

RICHMOND TERRACE

FOREST

Westerleigh

Clove Lakes Park

VANDUZER ST

BAY STREET

Fox Hills

STATEN ISLAND EXPRESSWAY

13TH AVENUE

Dyker Beach Park

Fort Hamilton

New Utrecht

OCEAN PARKWAY

VICTORY

Bulls Head

Willow Brook Park

VICTORY BLVD

STATEN ISLAND

BOULEVARD

MANOR ROAD

TODT HILL ROAD

RICHMOND ROAD

South Beach

Grasmere

Verrazano Narrows Bridge

Fort Wadsworth

Lower Bay

SHORE PKWY

Gravesend

Gravesend Bay

ERIC

Carteret

Rahway

Travis

FRESH KILL

Fresh Kills Park

LaTourette Park

RICHMOND HILL ROAD

FOREST HILL ROAD

ROCKLAND AVE

SEAVIEW AVE

New Dorp

NEW DORP LANE

FATHER CAPODANNO

Hoffman Island

Gateway National Recreation Area

NEPTUNE AVENUE

Coney Island

Port Reading

Rossville

WOODROW

Annadale

HYLAN BOULEVARD

AMBOY ROAD

Ocean View Cemetery

Great Kills

Swinburne Island

Aquarium

Clay Pit Ponds State Park Preserve

ARTHUR KILL ROAD

KILL ROAD

Woodrow

Great Kills Park

Great Kills Harbor

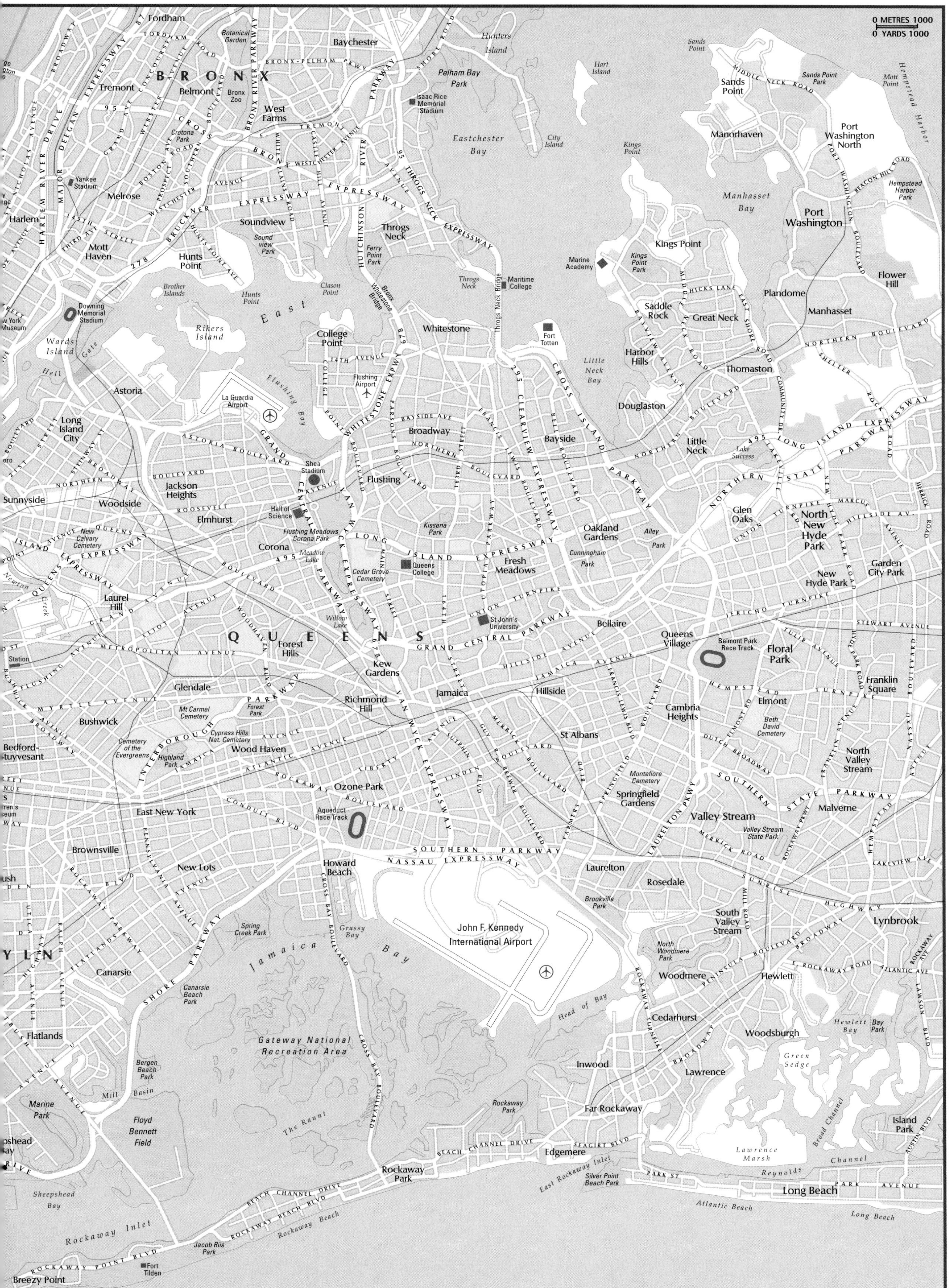

0 METRES 1000
0 YARDS 1000

BRONX

Fordham
Belmont
Bronx Zoo
Botanical Garden
Tremont
West Farms
Baychester
Hunters Island
Pelham Bay Park
Isaac Rice Memorial Stadium
Hart Island
City Island
Sands Point
Sands Point Park
Mott Point
Manorhaven
Port Washington North
Kings Point
Eastchester Bay
Soundview
Sound view Park
Throgs Neck
Ferry Point Park
Bronx Whitestone Bridge
Maritime College
Throgs Neck
Throgs Neck Bridge
Marine Academy
Kings Point
Kings Point Park
Saddle Rock
Great Neck
Port Washington
Manhasset Bay
Plandome
Manhasset
Harbor Hills
Thomaston
Hempstead Harbor Park
Flower Hill
Melrose
Harlem
Mott Haven
Hunts Point
Brother Islands
Hunts Point
Clason Point
Downing Memorial Stadium
New York Museum
Wards Island
Hell Gate
Rikers Island
East River
College Point
14TH AVENUE
Whitestone
Fort Totten
Little Neck Bay
Douglaston
Astoria
La Guardia Airport
Flushing Bay
Flushing Airport
Bayside Ave
Bayside
Little Neck
Glen Oaks
North New Hyde Park
Garden City Park
Long Island City
Sunnyside
Woodside
Jackson Heights
Elmhurst
Shea Stadium
Hall of Science
Corona
Flushing Meadows Corona Park
Meadow Lake
Flushing
Broadway
Northern Boulevard
Kissena Park
Fresh Meadows
Oakland Gardens
Alley Park
Cunningham Park
Lake Success
New Hyde Park
New Calvary Cemetery
Laurel Hill
Cedar Grove Cemetery
Queens College
Willow Lake
Forest Hills
Kew Gardens
St John's University
Union Turnpike
Bellaire
Queens Village
Belmont Park Race Track
Floral Park
Franklin Square
Elmont
Beth David Cemetery
QUEENS
Glendale
Mt Carmel Cemetery
Forest Park
Richmond Hill
Jamaica
Hillside
Cambria Heights
North Valley Stream
Bushwick
Bedford-Stuyvesant
Cemetery of the Evergreens
Highland Park
Cypress Hills Nat Cemetery
Wood Haven
St Albans
Montefiore Cemetery
Springfield Gardens
Valley Stream
Malverne
Ozone Park
East New York
Brownsville
New Lots
Howard Beach
Aqueduct Race Track
Laurelton
Rosedale
Brookville Park
South Valley Stream
Valley Stream State Park
Lynbrook
Canarsie
Spring Creek Park
Grassy Bay
John F. Kennedy International Airport
North Woodmere Park
Woodmere
Hewlett
Flatlands
Canarsie Beach Park
Jamaica Bay
Head of Bay
Cedarhurst
Woodsburgh
Hewlett Bay Park
Marine Park
Bergen Beach Park
Mill Basin
Floyd Bennett Field
Gateway National Recreation Area
The Raunt
Inwood
Lawrence
Green Sedge
Lawrence Marsh
Sheepshead Bay
Rockaway Inlet
Rockaway Point Blvd
Jacob Riis Park
Fort Tilden
Breezy Point
Rockaway Park
Edgemere
Far Rockaway
Rockaway Park
Silver Point Beach Park
Beach Channel Drive
Reynolds Channel
Long Beach
Atlantic Beach
Island Park

© Bartholomew

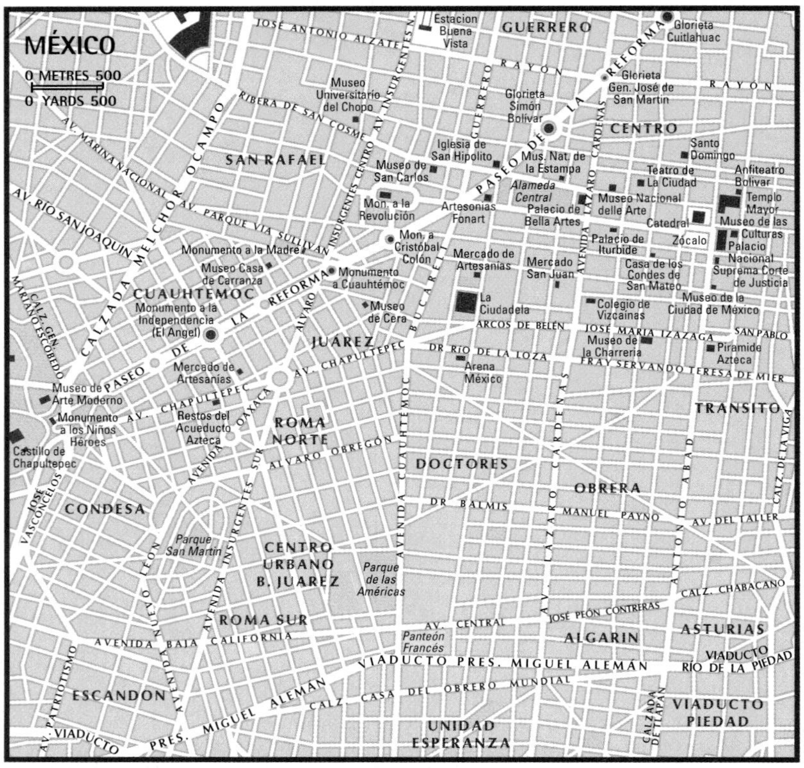

64

MÉXICO

LIMA

RIO DE JANEIRO

SÃO PAULO

BUENOS AIRES

CARACAS

© Bartholomew

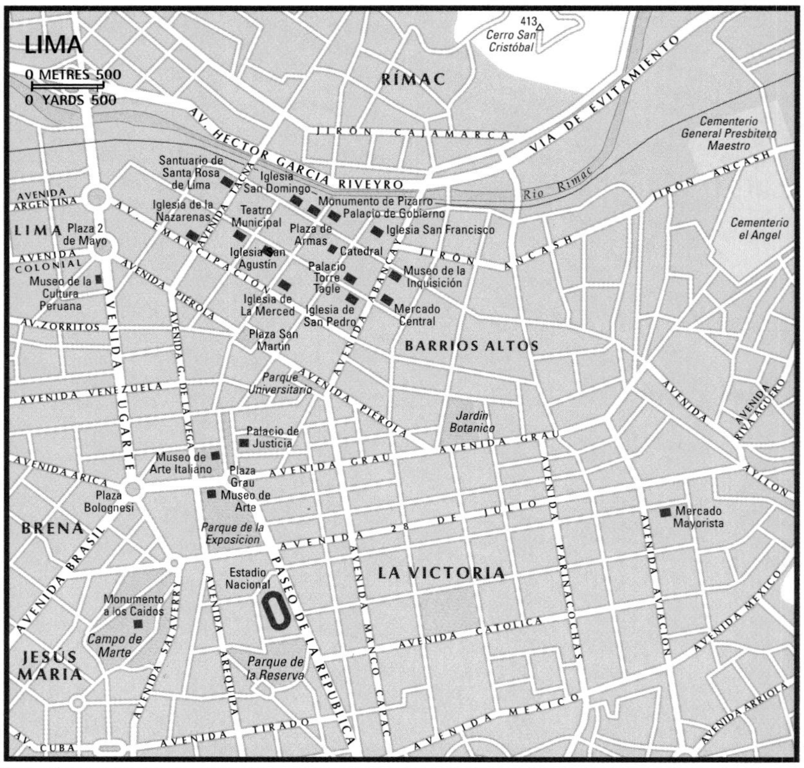

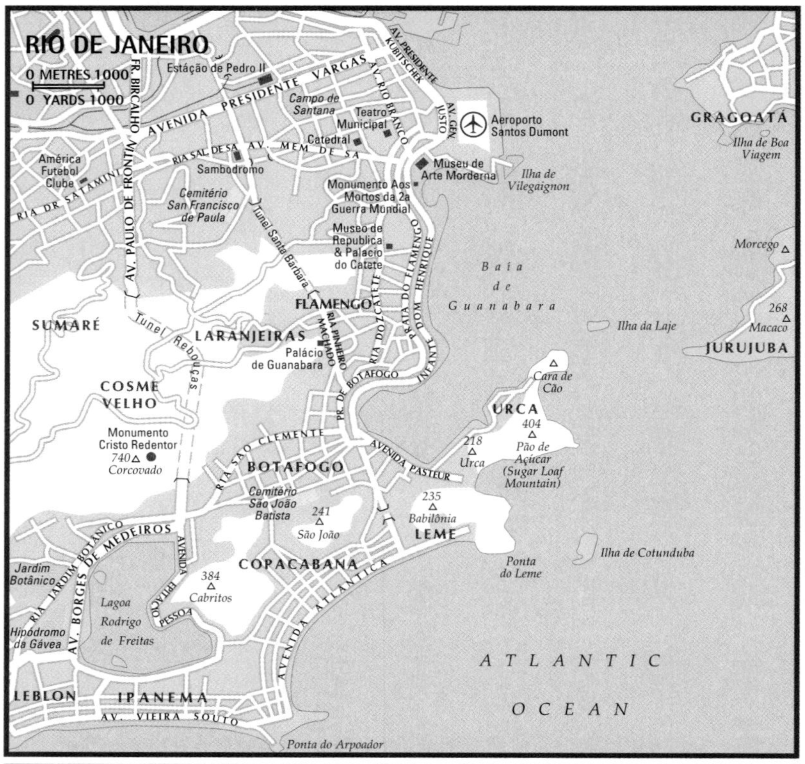

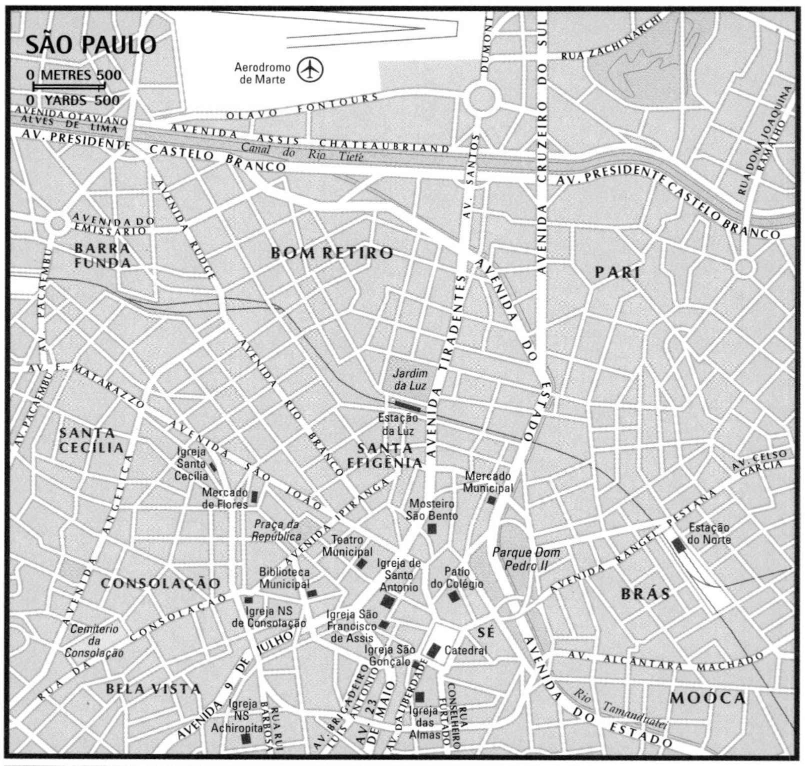

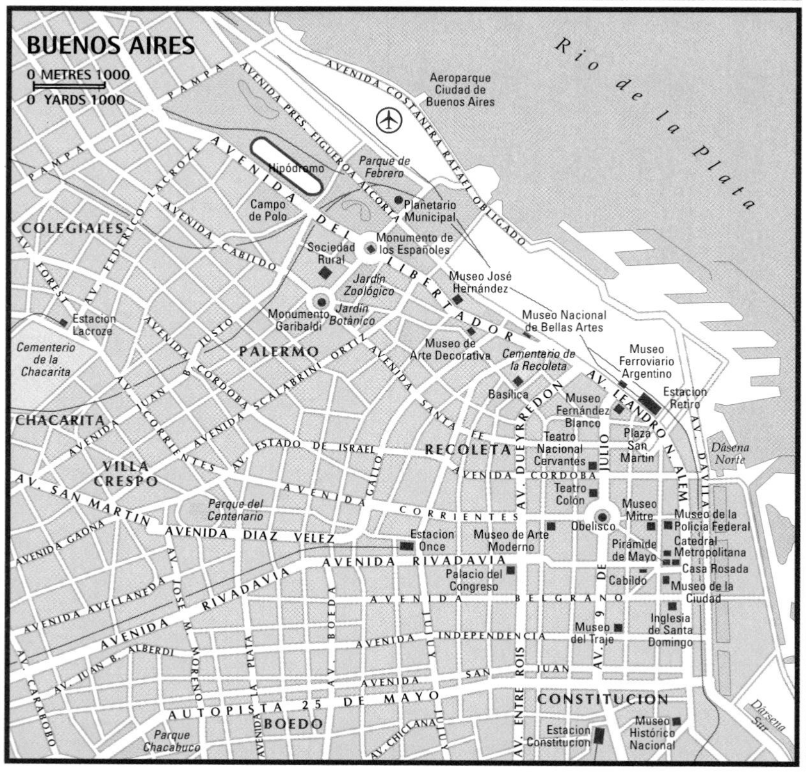

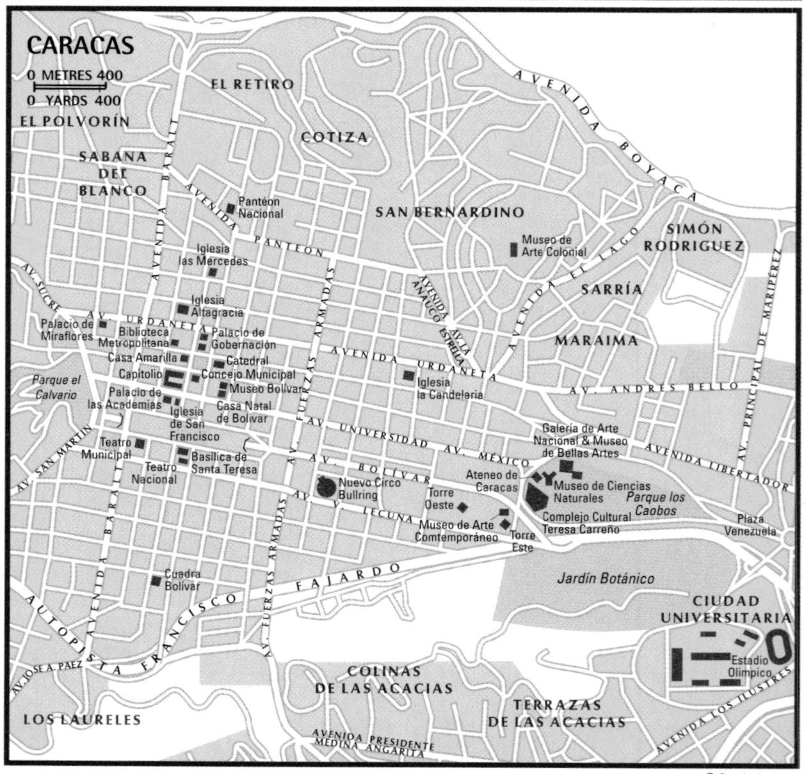

RELIEF

Contour intervals used in layer colouring

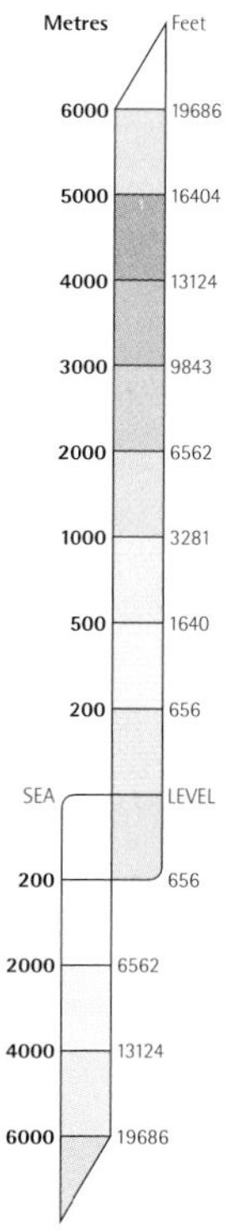

Metres	Feet
6000	19686
5000	16404
4000	13124
3000	9843
2000	6562
1000	3281
500	1640
200	656
SEA	LEVEL
200	656
2000	6562
4000	13124
6000	19686

Additional bathymetric contour layers are shown at scales greater than 1:2 million. These are labelled on an individual basis.

213 △ Summit
height in metres

PHYSICAL FEATURES

- Freshwater lake
- Seasonal freshwater lake
- Saltwater lake *or* Lagoon
- Seasonal saltwater lake
- Dry salt lake *or* Saltpan
- Marsh
- River
- Waterfall
- Dam *or* Barrage
- Seasonal river *or* Wadi
- Canal
- Flood dyke
- Reef
- Volcano
- Lava field
- Sandy desert
- Rocky desert
- Oasis
- Escarpment
- Mountain pass 923 *height in metres*
- Ice cap *or* Glacier

COMMUNICATIONS

- Motorway
- Motorway *under construction*
- Motorway tunnel

Motorways are classified separately at scales greater than 1:5 million. At smaller scales motorways are classified with main roads.

- Main road
- Main road *under construction*
- Main road tunnel
- Other road
- Other road *under construction*
- Other road tunnel
- Track
- Main railway
- Main railway *under construction*
- Main railway tunnel
- Other railway
- Other railway *under construction*
- Other railway tunnel
- ⊕ Main airport
- ✈ Other airport

BOUNDARIES

- International
- International *disputed*
- Ceasefire line
- Main administrative (U.K.)
- Main administrative
- Main administrative *through water*

OTHER FEATURES

- National park
- Reserve
- Ancient wall
- ∴ Historic *or* Tourist site
- Urban area

SETTLEMENTS

POPULATION	NATIONAL CAPITAL	ADMINISTRATIVE CAPITAL	CITY OR TOWN
Over 5 million	▣ **Beijing**	⊙ **Tianjin**	⊙ **New York**
1 to 5 million	▣ **Seoul**	⊙ **Lagos**	⊙ **Barranquilla**
500000 to 1 million	▣ **Bangui**	◎ **Douala**	◎ **Memphis**
100000 to 500000	□ Wellington	○ Mansa	○ Mara
50000 to 100000	□ Port of Spain	○ Lubango	○ Arecibo
10000 to 50000	□ Malabo	○ Chinhoyi	○ El Tigre
Less than 10000	□ Roseau	○ Áti	○ Soledad

STYLES OF LETTERING

COUNTRY NAME	MAIN ADMINISTRATIVE NAME	AREA NAME	MISCELLANEOUS NAME	PHYSICAL NAME
CANADA	XINJIANG UYGUR ZIZHIQU	PATAGONIA	Charles de Gaulle Airport	*Long Island*
SUDAN	MAHARASHTRA	KALIMANTAN	Rocky Mountains Forest Reserve	*LAKE ERIE*
TURKEY	KENTUCKY	ARTOIS	Disneyland Paris	*ANDES*
LIECHTENSTEIN	BRANDENBURG	PENINSULAR MALAYSIA	Great Wall	*Rio Grande*

2

GREENLAND

RUS. FED. U.S.A. Arctic Circle
Anchorage
Nuuk Reykjavik ICELAND

C A N A D A
Edmonton
Vancouver Winnipeg
Seattle Ottawa Montreal
Chicago Detroit Boston
Denver Pittsburgh New York
San Francisco Washington D.C. Philadelphia

UNITED
KINGD
REP. OF
IRELAND
Dublin

UNITED
STATES
OF AMERICA
Los Angeles
Dallas
Houston
Monterrey
Miami THE BAHAMAS
Nassau

PORTUGAL
Lisbon
Azores
(Portugal)
FRA
Rabat
MOROC

MEXICO
Guadalajara
México Havana
Belmopan BELIZE
GUATEMALA
Guatemala HONDURAS
San Salvador Tegucigalpa
EL SALVADOR NICARAGUA
Managua
COSTA RICA
San José PANAMA
PANAMA

Tropic of Cancer
CUBA
Kingston HAITI DOMINICAN
JAMAICA Port-au- REP.
Prince Puerto
Rico
(USA) San Juan

TRINIDAD & TOBAGO
Caracas Port of Spain
VENEZUELA
Georgetown Paramaribo
GUY. Cayenne
Bogotá SUR. FR. GU.
COLOMBIA

Laâyoune
Western
Sahara

MAURITANIA
Nouakchott
CAPE VERDE SENEGAL
Dakar Bamako
THE GAMBIA Bissau
GUINEA-BISSAU GUINEA
Conakry
Freetown C
SIERRA LEONE Yamous
Monrovia
LIBERIA

PACIFIC

OCEAN

Equator
Galapagos Is
(Ecuador)
Quito
ECUADOR

ATLANT

Recife

OCEAN

Hawaiian
Islands
(USA)

KIRIBATI

Marquesas
Is
(France)

French
Polynesia
W. Society Is
SAMOA (France)
American Tuamoto Is
Samoa Tahiti
Cook
Islands
(NZ)

PERU
Lima

BRAZIL

Brasília

BOLIVIA
La Paz
Sucre
PARAGUAY
Asunción

Belo Horizonte

Rio de Janeiro
São Paulo

TONGA

Tropic of Capricorn

Pitcairn
Islands
(UK)

Easter I.
(Chile)

CHILE

Santiago
Buenos
Aires

ARGENTINA

URUGUAY
Montevideo

Falkland Islands
(UK)

South Georgia
(UK)

South
Sandwich
Islands
(UK)

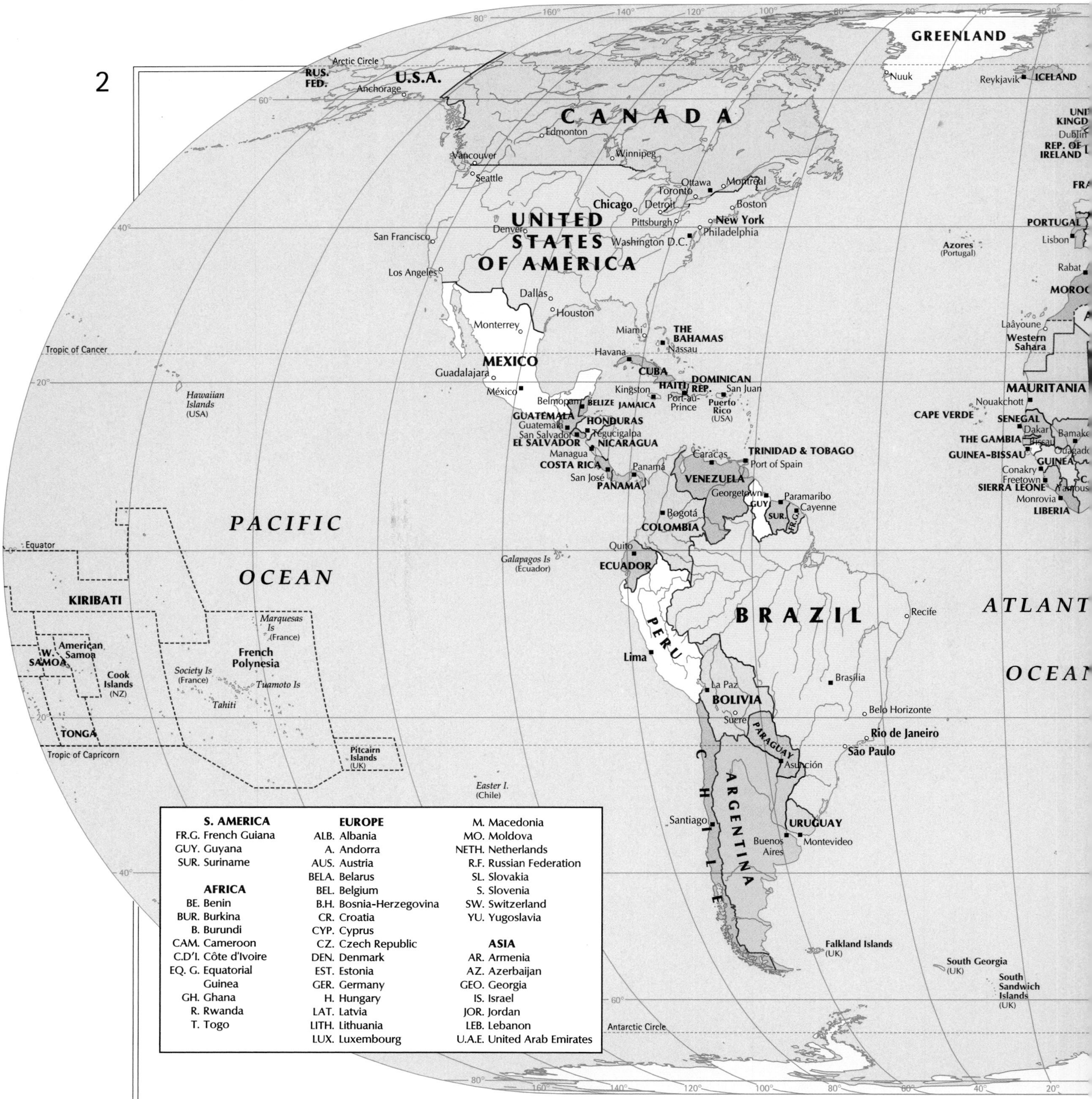

S. AMERICA	EUROPE	M. Macedonia
FR.G. French Guiana	ALB. Albania	MO. Moldova
GUY. Guyana	A. Andorra	NETH. Netherlands
SUR. Suriname	AUS. Austria	R.F. Russian Federation
	BELA. Belarus	SL. Slovakia
AFRICA	BEL. Belgium	S. Slovenia
BE. Benin	B.H. Bosnia-Herzegovina	SW. Switzerland
BUR. Burkina	CR. Croatia	YU. Yugoslavia
B. Burundi	CYP. Cyprus	
CAM. Cameroon	CZ. Czech Republic	**ASIA**
C.D'I. Côte d'Ivoire	DEN. Denmark	AR. Armenia
EQ. G. Equatorial	EST. Estonia	AZ. Azerbaijan
Guinea	GER. Germany	GEO. Georgia
GH. Ghana	H. Hungary	IS. Israel
R. Rwanda	LAT. Latvia	JOR. Jordan
T. Togo	LITH. Lithuania	LEB. Lebanon
	LUX. Luxembourg	U.A.E. United Arab Emirates

Antarctic Circle

Eckert IV Projection

TIME COMPARISONS

Time varies around the world due to the earth's rotation causing different parts of the world to be in light or darkness at any one time. To account for this, the world is divided into twenty-four Standard Time Zones based on 15° intervals of longitude.

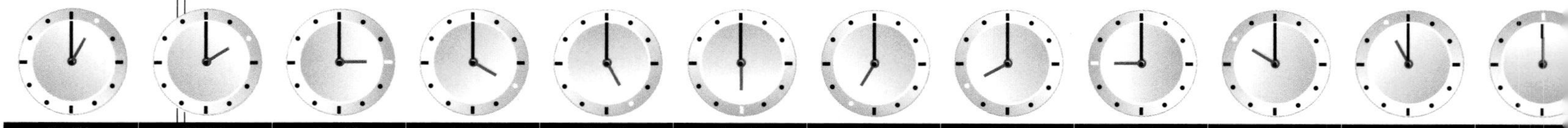

01:00	02:00	03:00	04:00	05:00	06:00	07:00	08:00	09:00	10:00	11:00	12:00
W. Samoa Am. Samoa	Cook Is Hawaiian Is Society Is Tahiti	Anchorage Pitcairn Is	Vancouver Seattle San Francisco Los Angeles	Edmonton Denver Easter I.	Winnipeg Chicago Dallas Houston Monterrey México San Salvador San José	Ottawa Toronto New York Philadelphia Washington D.C. Miami Havana Bogotá Quito Lima	Puerto Rico Caracas La Paz Sucre Asunción	Nuuk Recife Brasília Rio de Janeiro São Paulo Montevideo Buenos Aires	South Georgia S. Sandwich Is	Azores Cape Verde	Reykjav Dubli Londo Raba Nouakch Daka Freetov Accra

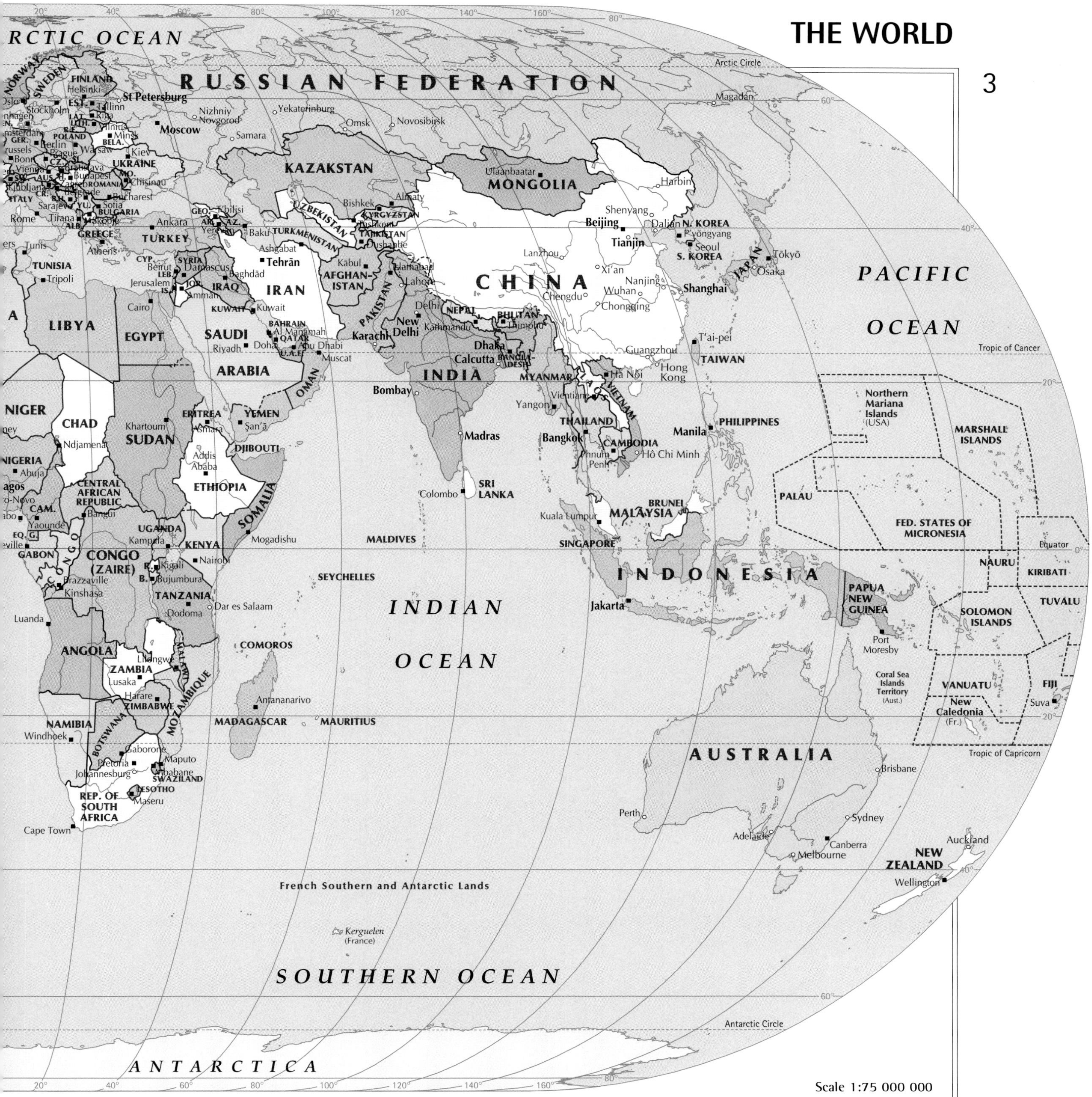

Scale 1:75 000 000

The table below gives examples of times observed at different parts of the world when it is 12 noon in the zone at the Greenwich Meridian (0° longitude). Daylight Saving Time, normally one hour ahead of local Standard Time, observed by certain countries for parts of the year, is not considered.

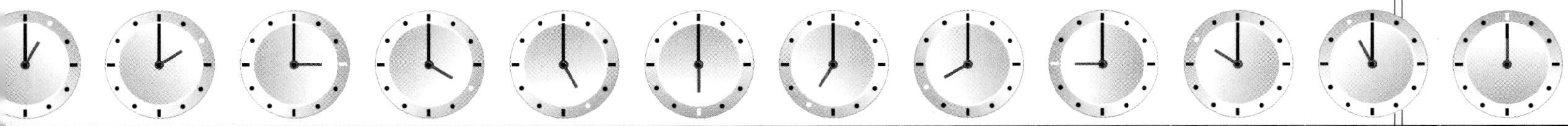

3:00	14:00	15:00	16:00	17:00	18:00	19:00	20:00	21:00	22:00	23:00	24:00
Oslo Berlin Paris Madrid Rome Algiers Abuja nshasa uanda	Helsinki Minsk Kiev Ankara Jerusalem Cairo Kigali Harare Pretoria Cape Town	St Petersburg Moscow Baghdād Doha Riyadh Addis Ababa Mogadishu Dodoma Antananarivo	T'bilisi Yerevan Baku Abu Dhabi Muscat Seychelles Mauritius	Yekaterinburg Ashgabat Bishkek Tashkent Islamabad Karachi	Omsk Almaty Thimpu Dhaka	Ha Nôi Vientiane Bangkok Phnum Penh Hô Chi Minh Jakarta	Ulaanbaatar Beijing T'ai-pei Hong Kong Manila Kuala Lumpur Singapore Perth	P'yŏngyang Seoul Tōkyō Ōsaka Palau	Port Moresby Brisbane Sydney Canberra Melbourne	Magadan Solomon Is Vanuatu New Caledonia	Marshall Is Tuvalu Fiji Auckland Wellington

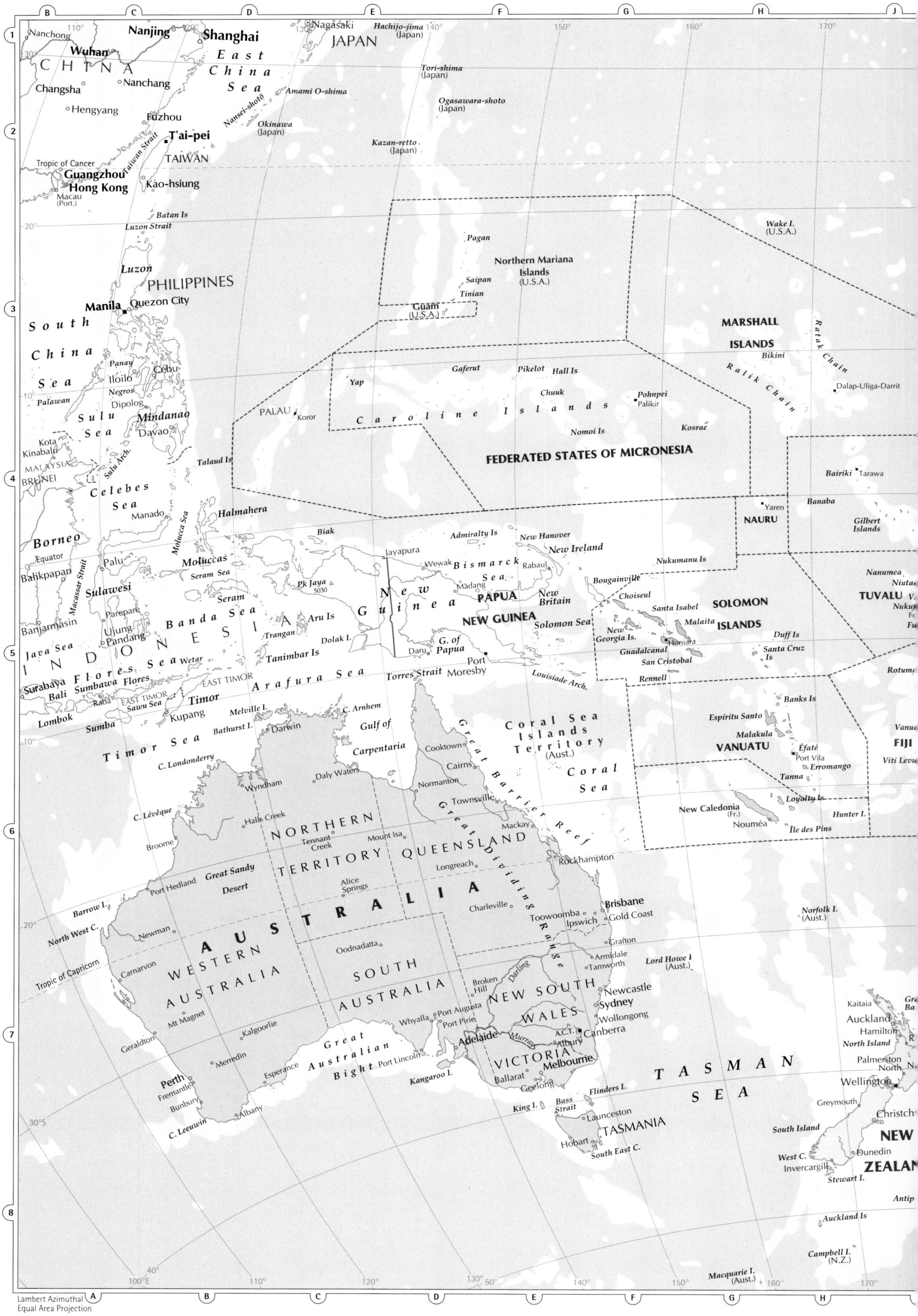

4

B · C · D · E · F · G · H · J

1

Nanchong   Nanjing   Shanghai   Nagasaki   Hachijo-jima   (Japan)
110°   130°   JAPAN   140°
Wuhan   *E a s t*
C H I N A   *C h i n a*
Changsha   Nanchang   *S e a*   Tori-shima   (Japan)   150°   160°   170°
Hengyang   Fuzhou   Amami O-shima

2

T'ai-pei   Okinawa   (Japan)   Ogasawara-shoto   (Japan)
TAIWAN   Kazan-retto   (Japan)
Tropic of Cancer   Guangzhou   Wake I.   (U.S.A.)
Hong Kong   Kao-hsiung   Pagan
Macau   (Port.)   Batan Is   20°   Northern Mariana   Islands   (U.S.A.)
Luzon Strait   Saipan

3

Luzon   PHILIPPINES   Tinian   Guam   (U.S.A.)   MARSHALL   Ratak Chain
Manila   Quezon City   ISLANDS
S o u t h   Bikini   Dalap-Uliga-Darrit
Gaferut   Pikelot   Hall Is   *Ralik Chain*
C h i n a   Panay   Chuuk
Iloilo   Cebu   Yap   Pohnpei   Palikir
S e a   Negros   10°   PALAU   Koror   *C a r o l i n e   I s l a n d s*   Kosrae
Palawan   Dipolog   Nomoi Is
Sulu   Mindanao   FEDERATED STATES OF MICRONESIA   Bairiki   Tarawa
Kota   *S e a*   Davao   Banaba
Kinabalu   Talaud Is   Gilbert   Islands
MALAYSIA   Yaren   NAURU
BRUNEI   4   *C e l e b e s*   Halmahera   Admiralty Is   New Hanover   Nanumea
S e a   Manado   Biak   New Ireland   Niutao
Borneo   Jayapura   Wewak   *B i s m a r c k*   Rabaul   TUVALU   Nukua
Equator   Palu   *Moluccas*   *S e a*   Nukumanu Is   Fu
Balikpapan   Molucca Sea   Pk Jaya   Madang   *New*   Bougainville
Macassar Strait   Seram Sea   5030   *N e w*   PAPUA   *Britain*   Choiseul   Santa Isabel   SOLOMON
Sulawesi   Seram   Aru Is   *G u i n e a*   NEW GUINEA   New   Malaita   ISLANDS
Parepare   *B a n d a   S e a*   Trangan   Solomon Sea   Georgia Is   Honiara   Duff Is
Banjarmasin   Ujung   Tanimbar Is   Daru   G. of   Guadalcanal   Santa Cruz
Pandang   5   Dolak I.   Papua   San Cristobal   Is
Java Sea   I N D O N E S I A   *F l o r e s*   *S e a* Wetar   Torres Strait   Port   Louisiade Arch.   Rennell   Rotuma
Surabaya   EAST TIMOR   *Arafura   Sea*   Moresby
Bali   Sumbawa   Flores   Timor Sea   Banks Is
Lombok   Raba   *Sawu Sea*   Timor   EAST TIMOR   C. Arnhem   Espíritu Santo   Vanu
Sumba   Kupang   Melville I.   Gulf of   *Coral Sea*   Malakula
Bathurst I.   Darwin   10°   *Islands*   VANUATU   Port Vila   FIJI
T i m o r   S e a   Carpentaria   *Territory*   Éfaté   Viti Levu
C. Londonderry   Cooktown   (Aust.)   Erromango
Wyndham   Daly Waters   Cairns   *C o r a l*   Tanna
C. Lévêque   Halls Creek   Normanton   *S e a*   Loyalty Is
6   Broome   NORTHERN   Townsville   New Caledonia   Hunter I.
Tennant   Mount Isa   (Fr.)   Île des Pins
Great Sandy   Creek   Mackay   Nouméa
Port Hedland   *Desert*   *TERRITORY*   QUEENSLAND   Rockhampton
Newman   Alice   Longreach   Norfolk I.
Barrow I.   20°   Springs   (Aust.)
North West C.   A U S T R A L I A   Charleville   Brisbane
Tropic of Capricorn   Oodnadatta   Toowoomba   Gold Coast
Carnarvon   WESTERN   SOUTH   Ipswich
Mt Magnet   AUSTRALIA   AUSTRALIA   Grafton
Broken   Darling   Armidale   Lord Howe I.
Hill   Tamworth   (Aust.)
7   Kalgoorlie   Whyalla   Port Augusta   NEW SOUTH   Newcastle
Geraldton   Port Pirie   WALES   Sydney
Great   Adelaide   A.C.T.   Canberra   Wollongong
Merredin   *Australian*   Murray   Albury
Esperance   Port Lincoln   VICTORIA   Kaitaia   Gr
Perth   *Bight*   Melbourne   Auckland   Ba
Fremantle   Kangaroo I.   Ballarat   Geelong   Hamilton
Bunbury   Flinders I.   *T A S M A N*   North Island
Albany   King I.   Bass   *S E A*   Palmerston
C. Leeuwin   30°S   Strait   Launceston   Greymouth   Wellington
Hobart   TASMANIA   Christ
South East C.   South Island   NEW
West C.   ZEALAN
Dunedin
Invercargill   Stewart I.

8   Antip
Auckland Is
Campbell I.   (N.Z.)
Macquarie I.   (Aust.)
40°   50°   160°   170°
100°E   110°   120°   130°   140°   150°

A · B · C · D · E · F · G · H

Lambert Azimuthal
Equal Area Projection

Metres   Feet
SEA   LEVEL
200   656
3000   9843

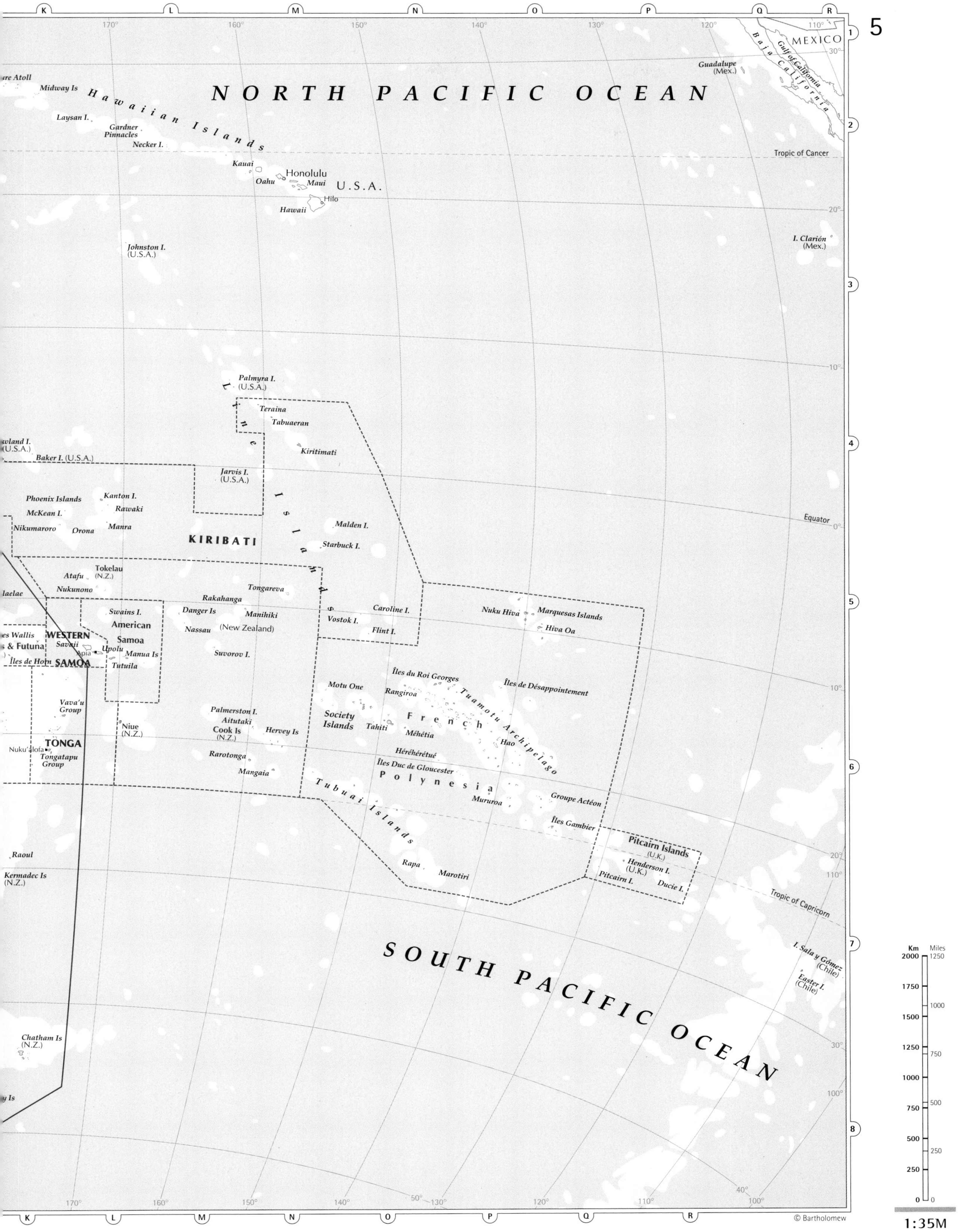

NORTH PACIFIC OCEAN

Hawaiian Islands

re Atoll
Midway Is
Laysan I.
Gardner
Pinnacles
Necker I.
Kauai
Oahu Honolulu
Maui
Hawaii Hilo
U.S.A.

Johnston I.
(U.S.A.)

Guadalupe
(Mex.)

MEXICO

Gulf of California

Baja California

Tropic of Cancer

I. Clarión
(Mex.)

Palmyra I.
(U.S.A.)
Teraina
Tabuaeran
Kiritimati
Jarvis I.
(U.S.A.)

owland I.
(U.S.A.)
Baker I. (U.S.A.)
Phoenix Islands
McKean I.
Nikumaroro Orona
Kanton I.
Rawaki
Manra
Malden I.
Starbuck I.

Line Islands

KIRIBATI

Atafu Tokelau
Nukunono (N.Z.)
aelae
Swains I.
es Wallis **WESTERN**
s & Futuna Savai'i
Îles de Horn **SAMOA**
Upolu
Apia
American
Samoa
Manua Is
Tutuila
Tongareva
Rakahanga
Danger Is Manihiki
Nassau (New Zealand)
Suvorov I.
Caroline I.
Vostok I.
Flint I.
Nuku Hiva Marquesas Islands
Hiva Oa

Îles du Roi Georges
Motu One Rangiroa
Îles de Désappointement

Vava'u
Group
Niue
(N.Z.)
Palmerston I.
Aitutaki
Cook Is
(N.Z.)
Hervey Is
Society
Islands
Tahiti
Méhétia
Hao
Nuku'alofa **TONGA**
Tongatapu
Group
Rarotonga
Mangaia
Hérehérétué
Îles Duc de Gloucester
Mururoa
Groupe Actéon
Îles Gambier

French
Tuamotu Archipelago

Polynesia

Tubuai Islands

Raoul
Kermadec Is
(N.Z.)
Rapa
Marotiri
Pitcairn Islands
(U.K.)
Henderson I.
(U.K.)
Pitcairn I. Ducie I.

Tropic of Capricorn

I. Sala y Gómez
(Chile)
Easter I.
(Chile)

Chatham Is
(N.Z.)

SOUTH PACIFIC OCEAN

y Is

© Bartholomew

1:35M

Km	Miles
2000	1250
1750	1000
1500	
1250	750
1000	500
750	
500	250
250	
0	0

6

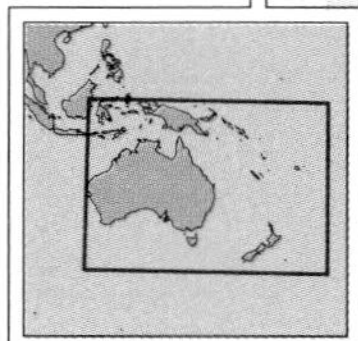

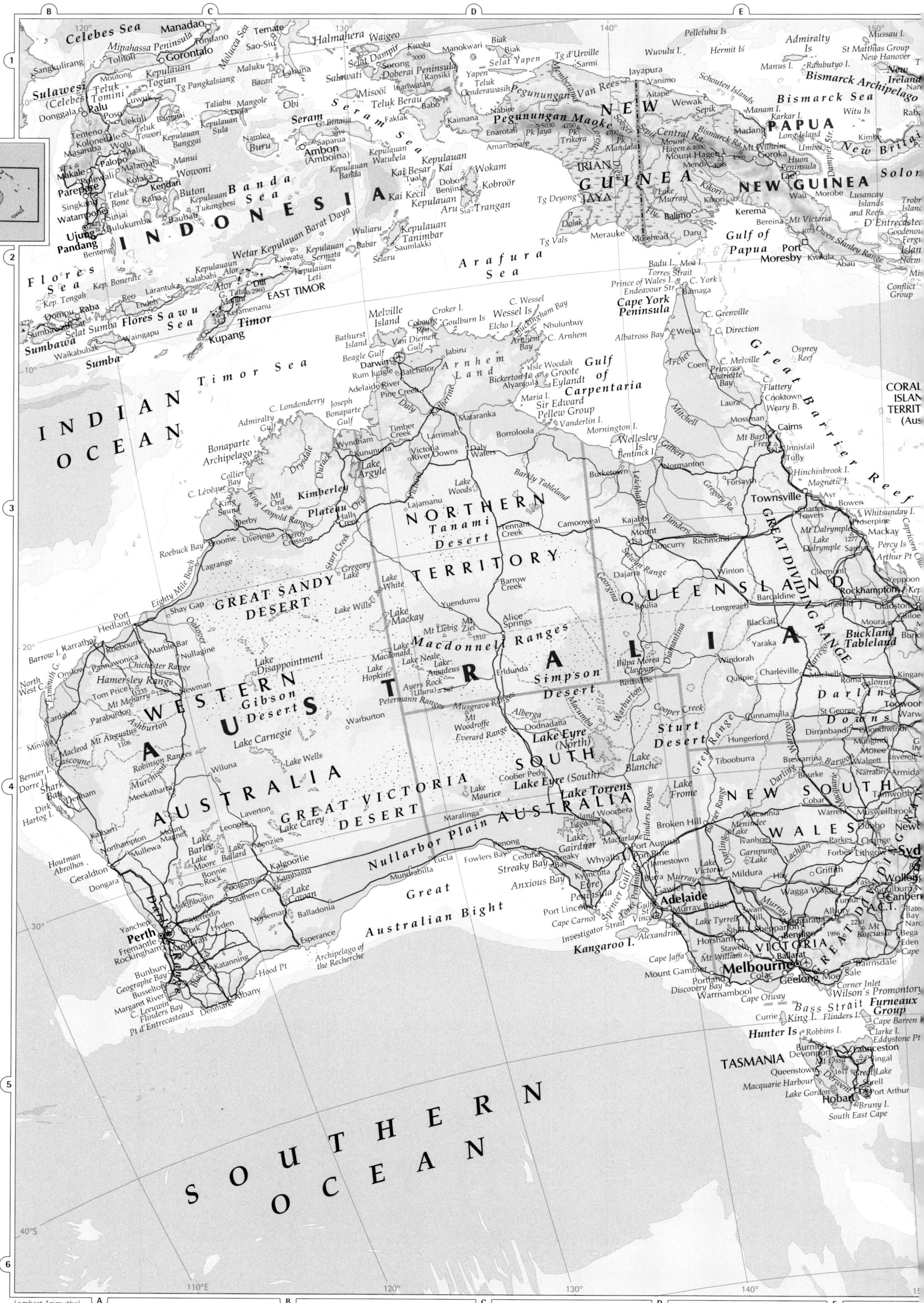

Celebes Sea
Manadao
Minahassa Peninsula
Gorontalo
Ternate
Halmahera
Waigeo
Biak
Manokwari
Selat Yapen
Sarmi
Jayapura
Vanimo
Wewak
Madang
Admiralty Is
Manus I.
Bismarck Sea
Bismarck Archipelago
New Ireland
St Matthias Group
New Hanover
Sulawesi (Celebes)
Teluk Tomini
Kepulauan Togian
Tg Pangkalsiang
Maluku
Obi
Seram
Ambon (Amboina)
Buru
Teluk Berau
Seram Sea
Pegunungan Maoke
Pegunungan Van Rees
NEW GUINEA
PAPUA NEW GUINEA
IRIAN JAYA
Pk Jaya
Central Ra.
Mount Hagen
Lae
Banda Sea
INDONESIA
Kepulauan Kai
Kepulauan Aru
Kepulauan Tanimbar
Tg Vals
Merauke
Daru
Gulf of Papua
Port Moresby
Ujung Pandang
Kendari
Buton
Flores Sea
Sumbawa
Flores
Sumba
Sawu Sea
Timor
Kupang
Dili
EAST TIMOR
Arafura Sea
Timor Sea
INDIAN OCEAN
Melville Island
Bathurst Island
Darwin
Arnhem Land
Groote Eylandt
Gulf of Carpentaria
Cape York Peninsula
Torres Strait
Coral Sea
Great Barrier Reef
Cairns
Townsville
Mackay
Rockhampton
Bonaparte Archipelago
Kimberley Plateau
Derby
Broome
Eighty Mile Beach
Port Hedland
Karratha
GREAT SANDY DESERT
Tanami Desert
NORTHERN TERRITORY
QUEENSLAND
GREAT DIVIDING RANGE
Alice Springs
Macdonnell Ranges
Simpson Desert
Ayers Rock (Uluru)
WESTERN AUSTRALIA
Gibson Desert
AUSTRALIA
Hamersley Range
Shark Bay
Carnarvon
Geraldton
Lake Carnegie
GREAT VICTORIA DESERT
SOUTH AUSTRALIA
Lake Eyre (North)
Lake Eyre (South)
Lake Torrens
Lake Gairdner
Nullarbor Plain
Great Australian Bight
Kalgoorlie
Perth
Fremantle
Albany
Esperance
Eucla
Port Augusta
Adelaide
Kangaroo I.
Spencer Gulf
Broken Hill
NEW SOUTH WALES
Darling Downs
VICTORIA
Melbourne
Bass Strait
King I.
Flinders I.
TASMANIA
Hobart
Launceston
SOUTHERN OCEAN
Sturt Desert
Mount Isa
Longreach
Barkly Tableland
Hunter Is
Furneaux Group

Lambert Azimuthal Equal Area Projection

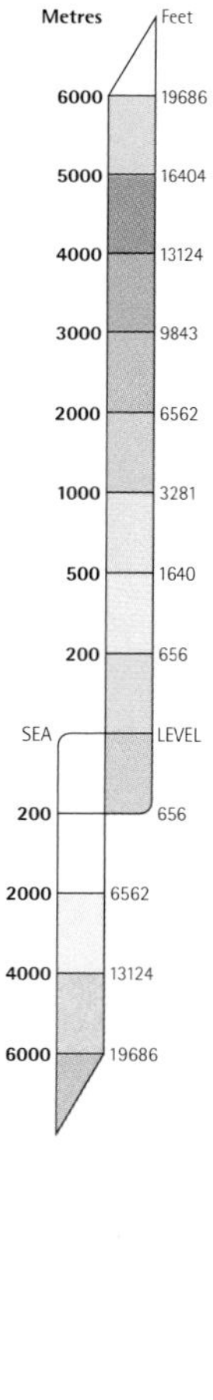

Metres
Feet
6000
19686
5000
16404
4000
13124
3000
9843
2000
6562
1000
3281
500
1640
200
656
SEA
LEVEL
200
656
2000
6562
4000
13124
6000
19686

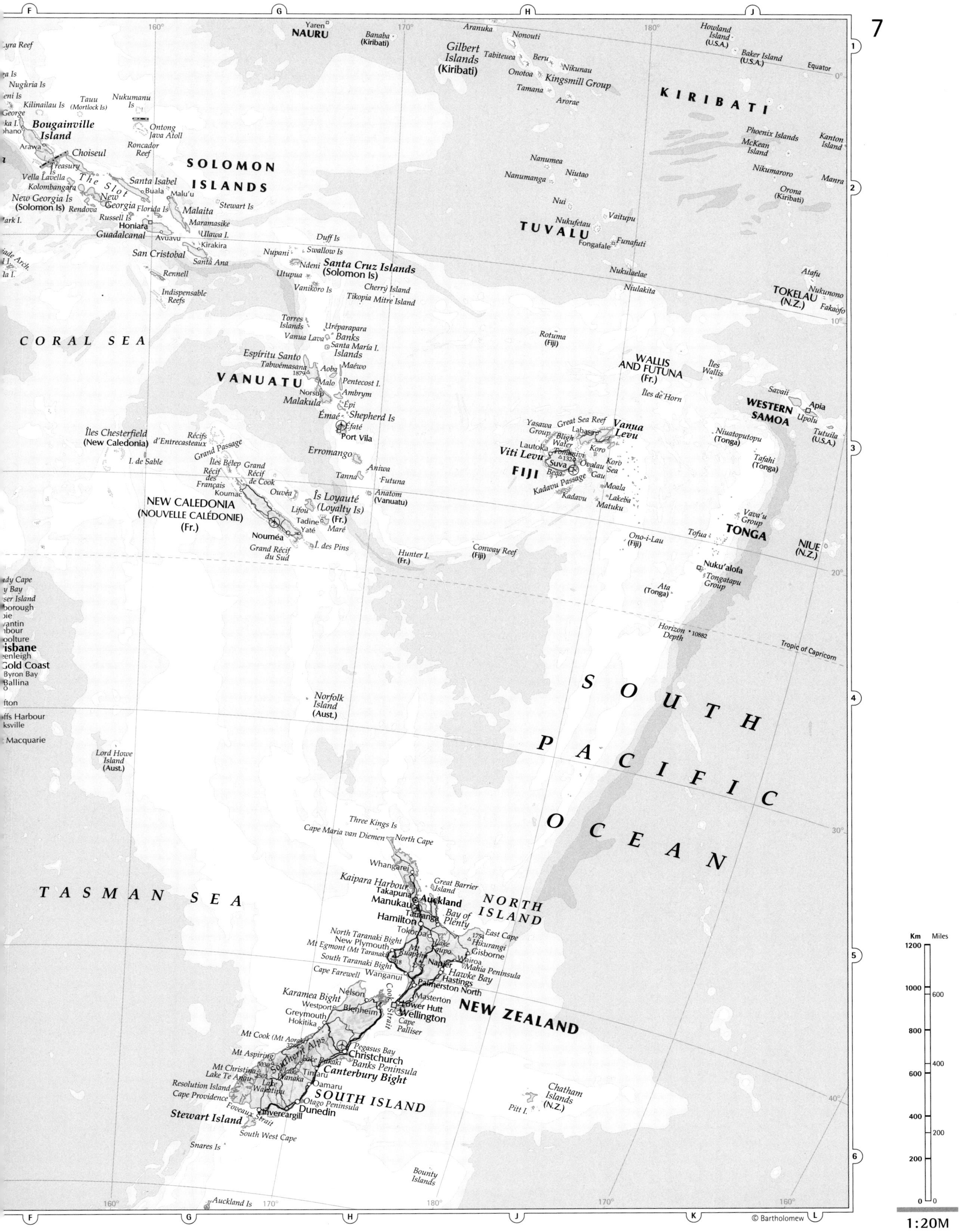

NAURU
Yaren

Banaba
(Kiribati)

Aranuka
Nonouti

Howland
Island
(U.S.A.)

Baker Island
(U.S.A.)

Equator

Gilbert
Islands
(Kiribati)

Tabiteuea
Beru
Nikunau
Onotoa
Tamana
Arorae

Tabiteuea
Nukunau
Kingsmill Group

K I R I B A T I

Phoenix Islands

Kanton
Island

McKean
Island

Nikumaroro

Manra

Orona
(Kiribati)

Nanumea
Niutao

Nanumanga

Nui

Nukufetau
Vaitupu

TUVALU

Fongafale Funafuti

Atafu

Nukulaelae

Niulakita

TOKELAU
(N.Z.)

Nukunono
Fakaofo

Lyra Reef

Nuguria Is

Kilinailau Is
*Tauu
(Mortlock Is)*
*Nukumanu
Is*

*Ontong
Java Atoll*

**Bougainville
Island**

Arawa
*Treasury
Is*
Choiseul

The Slot
Santa Isabel
Vella Lavella
*New
Georgia*
Kolombangara
Buala
Malu'u
*New Georgia
(Solomon Is)*
Rendova
Florida Is
Malaita
Russell Is
Maramasike
Honiara
Avuavu
Ulawa I.
Guadalcanal
Kirakira

**SOLOMON
ISLANDS**

Stewart Is

San Cristobal
Santa Ana
Rennell

Nupani
Swallow Is
Duff Is

Ndeni
Santa Cruz Islands
(Solomon Is)

Utupua
Cherry Island
Vanikoro Is
Tikopia Mitre Island

*Indispensable
Reefs*

*Torres
Islands*
Uréparapara
Vanua Lava
**Banks
Islands**
Santa María I.

C O R A L   S E A

*Rotuma
(Fiji)*

*Îles
Wallis*

**WALLIS
AND FUTUNA**
(Fr.)

Savaii
Apia

**WESTERN
SAMOA**
Upolu

*Tutuila
(U.S.A.)*

Îles de Horn

Espíritu Santo
*Tabwémasana
1879*
Aoba
Maéwo

VANUATU
Malo
Pentecost I.
Norsup
Ambrym
Malakula
Épi
Émaé
Shepherd Is
Éfaté
Port Vila

*Yasawa
Group*
Great Sea Reef
**Vanua
Levu**
Labasa
*Bligh
Water*
Lautoka
*Tomaniivi
1324*
Koro

*Niuatoputopu
(Tonga)*

*Tafahi
(Tonga)*

*Îles Chesterfield
(New Caledonia)*

*Récifs
d'Entrecasteaux*

Viti Levu
*Koro
Sea*
Suva
Ovalau
Gau
FIJI
Beqa

Îles Bélep
Grand Passage
*Grand
Récif
de Cook*
*Récif
des
Français*
I. de Sable

Erromango

Aniwa
Tanna
Futuna

*Anatom
(Vanuatu)*

Kadavu Passage
Moala
Lakeba
Kadavu
Matuku

*Vava'u
Group*

NEW CALEDONIA
(NOUVELLE CALÉDONIE)
(Fr.)

Koumac
Ouvéa
*Îs Loyauté
(Loyalty Is)*
Lifou
(Fr.)
Tadine
Maré
Nouméa
Yaté
Î. des Pins
*Grand Récif
du Sud*

*Hunter I.
(Fr.)*

*Conway Reef
(Fiji)*

*Ono-i-Lau
(Fiji)*

Nuku'alofa
Tofua

TONGA

NIUE
(N.Z.)

*Tongatapu
Group*

*Ata
(Tonga)*

*Norfolk
Island
(Aust.)*

S O U T H

P A C I F I C

O C E A N

*Horizon
Depth* •10882

Tropic of Capricorn

T A S M A N   S E A

*Lord Howe
Island
(Aust.)*

Three Kings Is
Cape Maria van Diemen
North Cape

Whangarei
Kaipara Harbour
Takapuna
*Great Barrier
Island*
Auckland
Manukau
Tauranga
Hamilton
*Bay of
Plenty*

**NORTH
ISLAND**

East Cape
Hicurangi
Gisborne

North Taranaki Bight
New Plymouth
Mt Egmont (Mt Taranaki)
South Taranaki Bight
Tokoroa
*Lake
Taupo*
Rotorua
Napier
Wairoa
Mahia Peninsula
Hawke Bay
Wanganui
Hastings
Palmerston North

Cape Farewell
Karamea Bight
Nelson
Masterton
Lower Hutt
Westport
Blenheim
Wellington
Greymouth
Cook Strait
*Cape
Palliser*
Hokitika

NEW ZEALAND

Mt Cook (Mt Aoraki)
Mt Aspiring
Southern Alps
Pegasus Bay
Christchurch
Banks Peninsula
Mt Christina
Lake Pukaki
Lake Te Anau
Lake Wanaka
Timaru
Canterbury Bight
Oamaru
Resolution Island
*Lake
Wakatipu*
Cape Providence
Otago Peninsula
SOUTH ISLAND
Invercargill
Dunedin
Stewart Island
Foveaux Strait
South West Cape

*Chatham
Islands
(N.Z.)*

Pitt I.

Snares Is

Auckland Is

*Bounty
Islands*

© Bartholomew

1:20M

Km   Miles
1200

1000

800

600

400

200

0

8

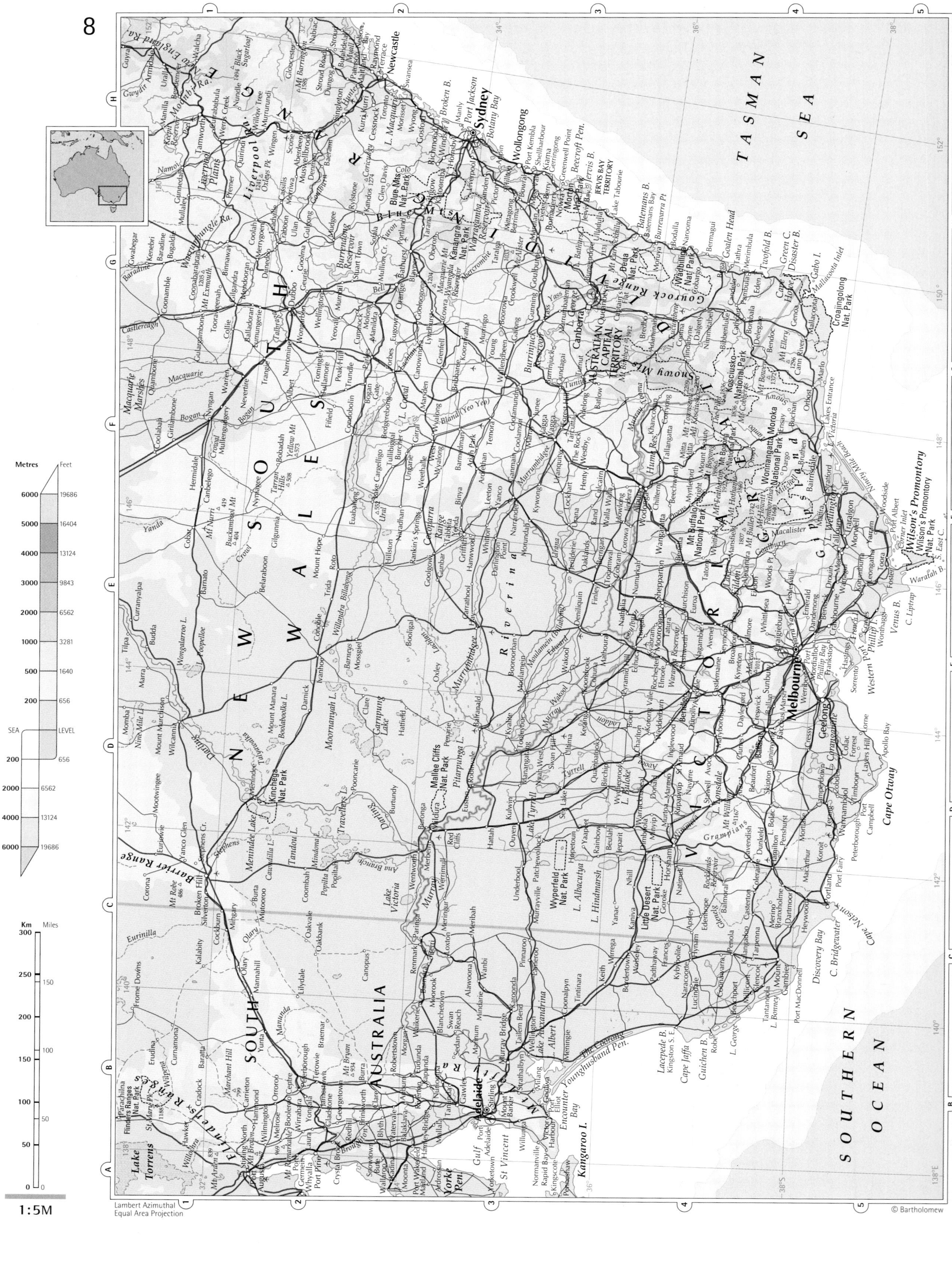

1:5M

Lambert Azimuthal
Equal Area Projection

© Bartholomew

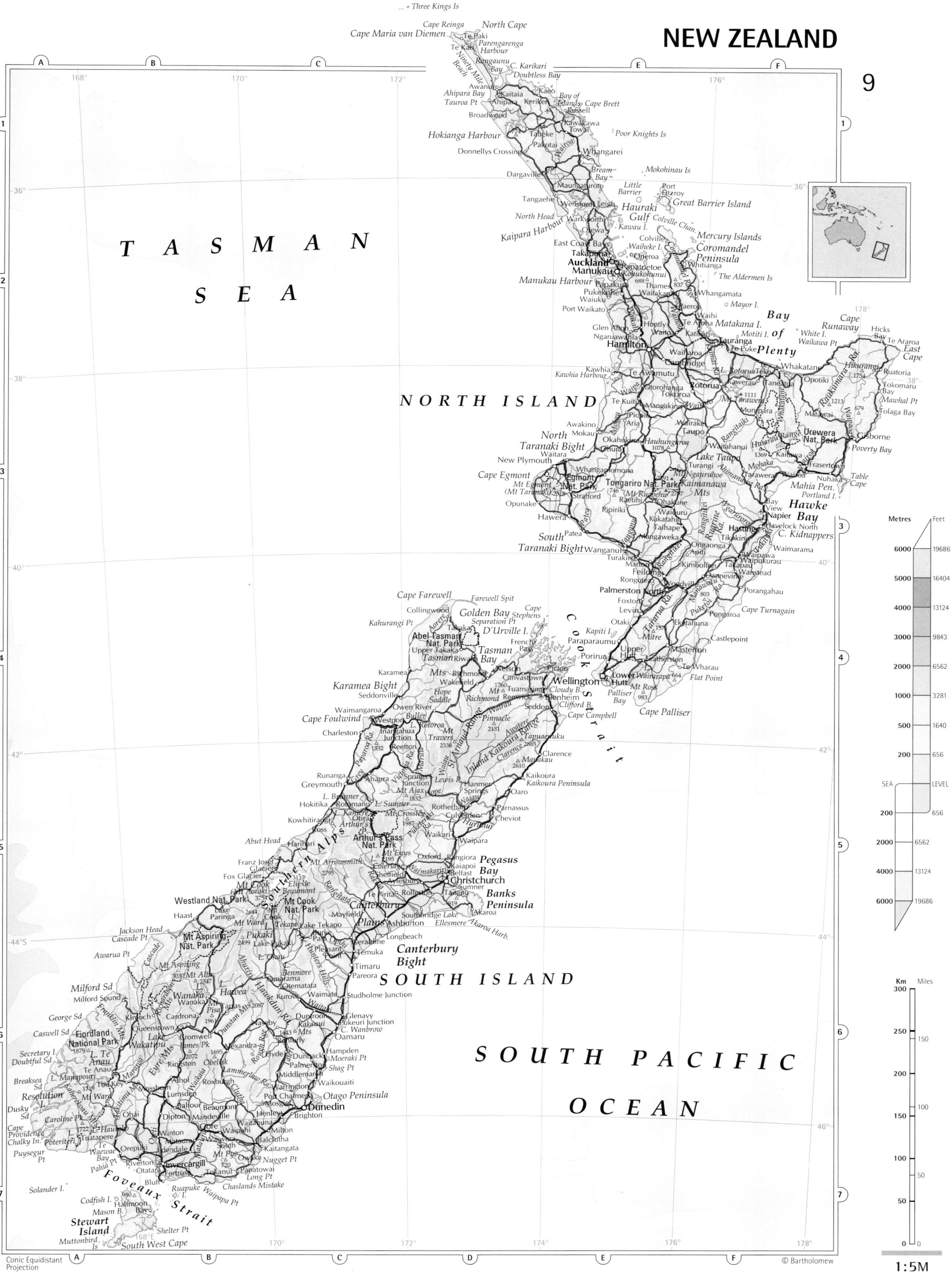

TASMAN SEA

SOUTH PACIFIC OCEAN

NORTH ISLAND

SOUTH ISLAND

Three Kings Is

Cape Reinga
North Cape
Cape Maria van Diemen
Te Paki
Parengarenga Harbour
C. Karikari
Doubtless Bay
Kaeo
Rangaunu Bay
Kaitaia
Ahipara
Keriken
Bay of Islands
Cape Brett
Russell
Tauroa Pt
Ahipara Bay
Awanui
Kawakawa Town
Broadwood
Poor Knights Is
Hokianga Harbour
Taheke
Whangarei
Donnellys Crossing
Pakotai
Bream Bay
Mokohinau Is
Dargaville
Maumaruroto
Tangaehu
Little Barrier
Port Fitzroy
Great Barrier Island
North Head
Wellsford
Leigh
Hauraki Gulf
Colville Chan.
Kaipara Harbour
Warkworth
Kawau I.
East Coast Bays
Takapuna
Waiheke I.
Colville
Mercury Islands
Auckland
Oneroa
Coromandel Peninsula
Manukau
Papatoetoe
Kohukohunui
Whitianga
Manukau Harbour
688
Whangamata
Papakura
Waiuku
Pukekohe
Thames
837
The Aldermen Is
Port Waikato
Waifakaruru
Mayor I.
Bay of Plenty
Cape Runaway
Hicks Bay
Te Araroa
East Cape
Glen Afton
Huntly
Te Aroha
Matakana I.
White I.
Waikawa Pt
Ngaruawahia
Katikati
Tauranga
Hamilton
Cambridge
Te Puke
Whakatane
Ruatoria
Hikurangi 1754
Kawhia
Te Awamutu
Rotorua
Tanwera
Opotiki
Hikurangi Ra
Kawhia Harbour
Tokoroa
Rotorua
Murupara
Matawai
Tolaga Bay
Awakino
Piopio
Mangakino
1111
Urewera Nat. Park
Gisborne
North Taranaki Bight
Mokau
Okahukura
Haununga
Taupo
Waitahanui
Poverty Bay
New Plymouth
Ohura
1078
Lake Taupo
Mohaka
Waitara
Whangamomona
Turangi
Kaiwaka
Cape Egmont
Mt Egmont
Egmont Nat. Park
Tongariro Nat. Park
Kaimanawa Mts
Bay View
Napier
Stratford
Mt Ruapehu 2797
Hawke Bay
(Mt Taranaki) 2518
Raetihi
Ohakune
Hastings
Opunake
Havelock North
Hawera
Pipiriki
Kakatahi
Waiouru
Tikokino
C. Kidnappers
South Taranaki Bight
Patea
Taihape
Waimarama
Wanganui
Mangaweka
Apiti
Waipawa
Ongaonga
Kimbolton
Takapau
Waipukurau
Turakina
Feilding
Dannevirke
Waipawa
Marton
Rongotea
Woodville
Porangahau
Palmerston North
Foxton
Cape Turnagain
Levin
Pongaroa
Otaki
Eketahuna
Castlepoint
Paraparaumu
Kapiti I.
Masterton
Cape Farewell
Farewell Spit
Cape Stephens
Mitre
Collingwood
Separation Pt
Kahurangi Pt
Golden Bay
Takaka
D'Urville I.
French Pass
Upper Hutt
Carterton
Abel Tasman Nat. Park
Tasman Mts
Upper Takaka
Tasman Bay
Featherston
Flat Point
Karamea
Riwaka
Nelson
Picton
Lower Wainarapa
Cook Strait
Karamea Bight
Richmond
Canvastown
Wellington
Te Wharau
Seddonville
Wakefield
Mt
1760
Tuamarina
Cloudy B.
Palliser Bay
Cape Palliser
Waimangaroa
Hope Saddle
Richmond
Renwick
Blenheim
Mt Ross
Owen River
Richmond Range
Seddon
Clifford B.
983
Westport
Buller
Cape Foulwind
Inangahua Junction
Pinnacle
Cape Campbell
Charleston
2336
Mt Travers
Spenser Mts
Amuri
Clarence
2885
Reefton
Pinnacle 2131
Inland Kaikoura Range
Tapuaenuku
Runanga
Springs Junction
Lewis Pass
Clarence
Manakau 2610
Greymouth
Ahaura
Hanmer Springs
Kaikoura
L. Brunner
Mt Ajax
1932
Hope
Rotomanu
Hokitika
L. Sumner
Rotherham
Oaro
Kowhitirangi
L. Kaniere
Waiau
Parnassus
Ross
Otira
Mt Crossley
Culverden
Cheviot
Arthur's Pass
1997
Puketeraki Ra
Waikari
Abut Head
Arthur's Pass Nat. Park
Hurunui
Waipara
Harihari
Waikari
Oxford
Pegasus Bay
Franz Josef Glacier
Mt Arrowsmith
Rangiora
Fox Glacier
Mt Euys
Kaiapoi
Belfast
Mt Cook
2795
Sheffield
Christchurch
Westland Nat. Park
Eldelston
Sumner
Haast
Aoraki
Karmakariri
Banks Peninsula
Paringa
Mt Cook
Te Pirita
Rolleston
Akaroa
Mt Ward
2644
Southern Alps
Mayfield
Taitapu
Mt Cook Nat. Park
Cook
Southbridge
Lake
Jackson Head
Rakaia
Te Pirita
Canterbury
Ellesmere
Akaroa Harb.
Cascade Pt
Mt Aspiring
3027 Mt Alba
Pukaki
Plains
Southbridge
Awarua Pt
Mt Aspiring Nat. Park
2499
Lake Pukaki
Ashburton
Longbeach
Canterbury Bight
Milford Sd
Tekapo
Mt Pleasant
Temuka
Milford Sound
Wanaka
L. Hawea
Kurow
Geraldine
Timaru
George Sd
Kinloch
Wanaka
Pisa
Fairlie
Hunters Hills
Pareora
Caswell Sd
Fiordland National Park
Queenstown
Lake Wakatipu
Cromwell
Hawkdun Ra
Studholme Junction
Secretary I.
1879
Te Anau
Cardrona
Alexandra
Ranfurly
Kakanui Mts
Oamaru
Doubtful Sd
L. Te Anau
Kingston
Hyde
Dunback
Hampden
Breaksea Sd
Eyre Mts
Lumsden
Clyde
Roxburgh
Middlemarch
Moeraki Pt
Resolution I.
Ward
Garvie Mts
Lammerlaw Ra
Warrington
Shag Pt
Dusky Sd
Caroline Pk
Dipton
Mandeville
Waikouaiti
Caswell
Ohai
Winton
Clutha
Milton
Port Chalmers
Mosgiel
Otago Peninsula
Cape Providence
Riverton
Invercargill
Gore
Waipahi
Balclutha
Dunedin
Chalky In.
Te Waewae Bay
Orepuki
Edendale
Kaitangata
Brighton
Puysegur Pt
Pahia
Otatara
Mt Pye
Owaka
Nugget Pt
Solander I.
Waimatuku
Waikawa
Ruapuke I.
Chaslands Mistake
Foveaux Strait
Bluff
Waipapa Pt
Codfish I.
Halfmoon Bay
Shelter Pt
Stewart Island
Mason B.
South West Cape
Muttonbird Is

Conic Equidistant Projection

© Bartholomew

1:5M

Metres	Feet
6000	19686
5000	16404
4000	13124
3000	9843
2000	6562
1000	3281
500	1640
200	656
SEA	LEVEL
200	656
2000	6562
4000	13124
6000	19686

Km	Miles
300	
250	150
200	
150	100
100	50
50	
0	0

10

North Pole

ARCTIC OCEAN

Franz Josef Land

O. Komsomolets
Severnaya Zemlya
O. Oktyabr'skoy Revolyutsii
O. Bolshevik

Spitsbergen (Nor.)

Svalbard (Nor.)

Novaya Zemlya

Kara Sea

Nordkapp

Barents Sea

Murmansk

White Sea

Archangel

Norwegian Sea

Faroe Islands (Den.)

Arctic Circle

Gulf of Bothnia

SWEDEN

NORWAY

Helsinki

Lake Onega
Lake Ladoga

St Petersburg

RUSSIAN FED.
(in Europe)

Salekhard

Norilsk

Surgut

Ob'

Nizhnyaya Tunguska

Yenisey

Bratsk

PORT.
SPAIN
Madrid
Balearic Is
Barcelona
Corsica
Sardinia

Bay of Biscay

IRELAND
Dublin
REP. OF
UNITED KINGDOM
Edinburgh
London
English Channel
The Hague
Amsterdam
NETH.
FRANCE
Paris
Lyon
BEL.
LUX.
GERMANY
Bonn
Hamburg
München
Rhine
Berlin
Copenhagen
DENMARK

North Sea

Oslo
Stockholm
Baltic Sea
ESTONIA
Tallinn
LATVIA
Riga
LITHUANIA
Vilnius
Minsk
BELARUS

Moscow

Nizhniy Novgorod

Perm

Yekaterinburg

Ural Mountains

Chelyabinsk

Omsk

Tomsk

Krasnoyarsk

Novosibirsk

Yenisey

Novokuznetsk

Mediterranean Sea
Tunis
Sicily
MALTA
Tyrrhenian Sea
Naples
Rome
ITALY
Milan
Turin
Genoa
Corsica
SWITZ.
Munich
Vienna
Ljubljana
AUSTRIA
SLOVENIA
Zagreb
CZECH REP.
Prague
Bratislava
SLOVAKIA
HUNGARY
Budapest
CROATIA
Sarajevo
BOSNIA
YUGO.
Danube
Belgrade
ROMANIA
Bucharest
Warsaw
POLAND

Kiev
UKRAINE
Chisinau
MOLDOVA
Odesa

Kharkiv

Rostov-na-Donu

Sea of Azov

Volgograd

Saratov

Samara

Kazan

Ural'sk

Orenburg

Aktyubinsk

Pavlodar

Karaganda

KAZAKSTAN

Aral Sea

Ozero Balkhash

Almaty

Tacheng

Altai Mts

MON

Barnaul

Tirana
ALBANIA
MACE.
Skopje
BULGARIA
Sofia
GREECE
Athens
Aegean Sea
Ionian Sea
Crete

Istanbul
Izmir
Ankara
TURKEY
Kayseri
Adana
Antalya
Samsun

Black Sea

Caucasus
GEORGIA
Tbilisi
ARMENIA
Yerevan
AZERBAIJAN
Baku

Caspian Sea

Astrakhan

Volga

Ural

CYPRUS
Nicosia
LEBANON
Beirut
SYRIA
Aleppo
Damascus
ISRAEL
Amman
Jerusalem
JORDAN
IRAQ
Baghdad
Mosul
Tigris
Euphrates
Basra

Tabriz

Tehrān

IRAN

Esfahan

Ahvāz

Mashhad

TURKMENISTAN

Ashgabat

UZBEKISTAN

Tashkent

Samarkand

Dushanbe

TAJIKISTAN

Bishkek

KYRGYZSTAN

Tien Shan

Kashi

Ürümqi

Yumen

XINJIANG

Hotan

EGYPT
Cairo
Nile
Alexandria
Port Said
Tropic of Cancer
L. Nasser

Red Sea

Medina
Mecca
Jeddah
SAUDI ARABIA
Riyadh

Kuwait
KUWAIT
The Gulf
BAHRAIN
Al Manāmah
QATAR
Doha
Abu Dhabi
U.A.E.
Dubai

Shīrāz
Kermān
Zāhedān

Herāt
Kābul
AFGHANISTAN
Islamabad
Kandahār
Quetta

K2

Rub' al Khālī

Gulf of Oman

Muscat

OMAN

Lahore
Ludhiana
PAKISTAN
Indus
Karachi
Hyderabad

XIZANG

Mt Everest 8848
HIMALAYA
Delhi
New Delhi
Jaipur
Kanpur
NEPAL
Kathmandu
Darjeeling
Thimphu
BHUTAN

Brahmaputra

Shillong

SUDAN
Port Sudan

ERITREA
Asmara

NORTH YEMEN
San'a
SOUTH YEMEN
Aden

Gulf of Aden

ARABIAN SEA

Ahmadabad
Jabalpur
Nagpur
Pune
Bombay
INDIA
Hyderabad
Vijayawada

Varanasi
Ganges
BANGLA-DESH
Dhaka
Chittagong
Mandalay
MYANMAR (BURMA)
Yangon

DJIBOUTI
Djibouti
ETHIOPIA
Addis Ababa

SOMALIA
Mogadishu

Socotra (Yemen)

Laccadive Is (India)

Bangalore
Madras

BAY OF BENGAL

Andaman Islands (India)

Equator

Trivandrum

Colombo
SRI LANKA

Nicobar Islands (India)

MALDIVES
Male

SEYCHELLES

INDIAN OCEAN

Aldabra Is
COMOROS
Amirante Islands
Mahé

Gan
Addu Atoll

British Indian Ocean Terr.
Chagos Archipelago

Metres
SEA
LEVEL
Feet

200 — 656

3000 — 9843

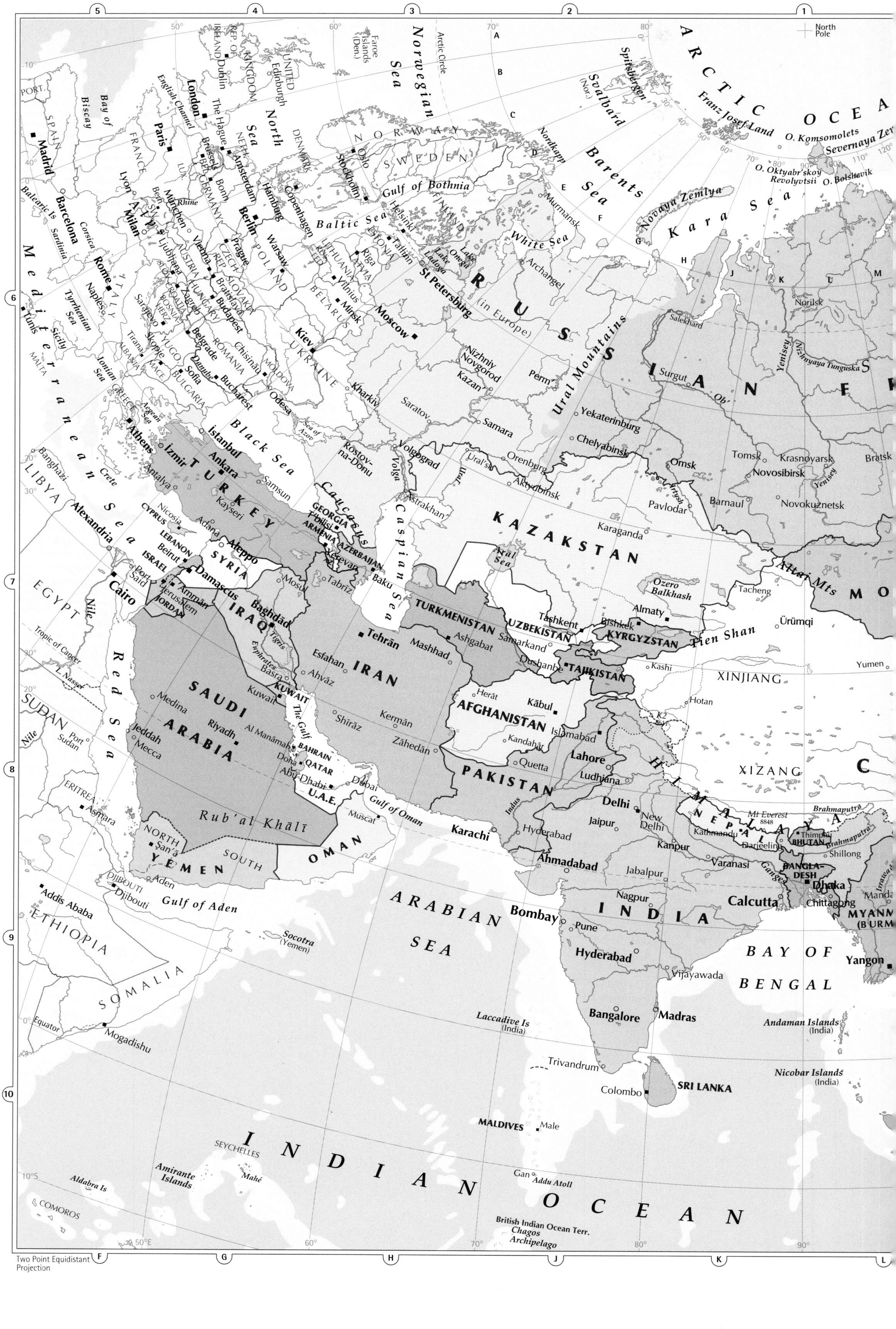

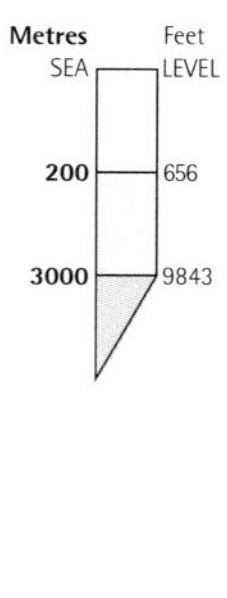

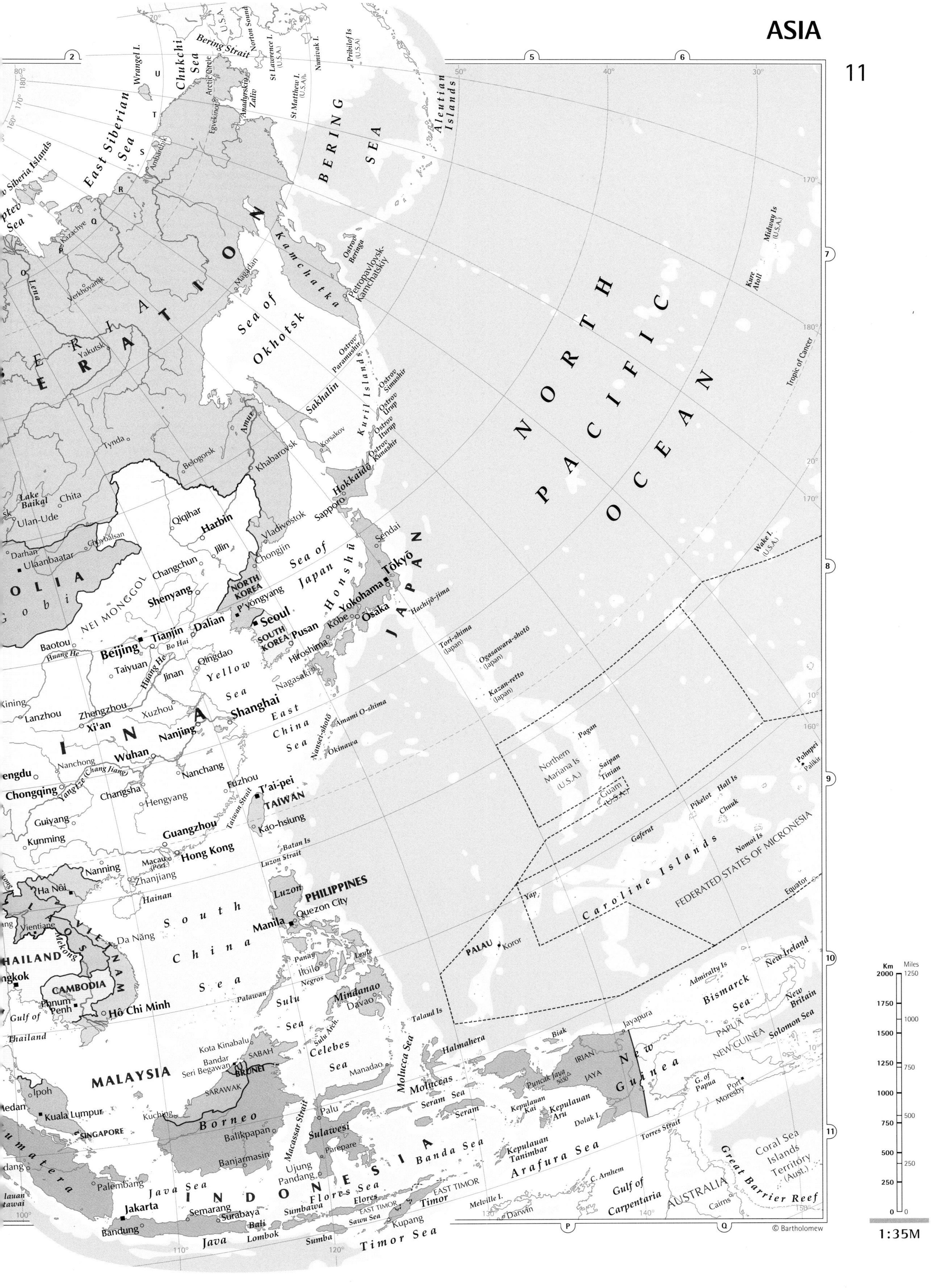
Wrangel I.
Chukchi Sea
Bering Strait
East Siberian Sea
Arctic Circle
Anadyrskiy Zaliv
St Lawrence I. (U.S.A.)
Norton Sound
Nunivak I.
Pribilof Is (U.S.A.)
St Matthew I. (U.S.A.)
BERING SEA
Aleutian Islands
Egvekinot
Ambarchik
Laptev Sea
Kazachye
Verkhoyansk
Lena
Yakutsk
Magadan
Kamchatka
Ostrov Beringa
Petropavlovsk-Kamchatskiy
Sea of Okhotsk
Ostrov Paramushir
Ostrov Simushir
Ostrov Urup
Ostrov Iturup
Ostrov Kunashir
Kuril Islands
Sakhalin
Korsakov
Amur
Tynda
Belogorsk
Khabarovsk
Hokkaido
Sapporo
Lake Baikal
Chita
Ulan-Ude
Qiqihar
Harbin
Jilin
Vladivostok
Choybalsan
Darhan
Ulaanbaatar
Changchun
Chongjin
NORTH KOREA
P'yongyang
Shenyang
NEI MONGGOL
Gobi
Sea of Japan
Honshū
Sendai
Tōkyō
Yokohama
Ōsaka
Kōbe
JAPAN
Hachijō-jima
Seoul
SOUTH KOREA
Pusan
Hiroshima
Nagasaki
Baotou
Huang He
Beijing
Tianjin
Dalian
Bo Hai
Qingdao
Taiyuan
Jinan
Yellow Sea
Xining
Lanzhou
Zhengzhou
Xuzhou
Xi'an
Shanghai
Nanjing
Wuhan
East China Sea
Nansei-shotō
Amami O-shima
Okinawa
Tori-shima (Japan)
Ogasawara-shotō (Japan)
Kazan-retto (Japan)
Chengdu
Nanchong
Chang Jiang (Yangtze)
Chongqing
Changsha
Nanchang
Fuzhou
T'ai-pei
TAIWAN
Taiwan Strait
Kao-hsiung
Hengyang
Guiyang
Kunming
Guangzhou
Hong Kong
Macau (Port.)
Zhanjiang
Nanning
Batan Is
Luzon Strait
Luzon
PHILIPPINES
Quezon City
Manila
Hainan
Ha Nôi
Vientiane
Mekong
LAOS
VIETNAM
THAILAND
Bangkok
CAMBODIA
Phnum Penh
Hô Chi Minh
Da Nang
Gulf of Thailand
South China Sea
Palawan
Panay
Iloilo
Negros
Leyte
Mindanao
Davao
Sulu Sea
Sulu Arch.
Celebes Sea
Talaud Is
Kota Kinabalu
SABAH
Bandar Seri Begawan
BRUNEI
SARAWAK
MALAYSIA
Ipoh
Medan
Kuala Lumpur
SINGAPORE
Kuching
Borneo
Balikpapan
Banjarmasin
Sumatera
Palembang
Java Sea
Jakarta
Bandung
Semarang
Surabaya
Java
Bali
Lombok
Sumbawa
Sumba
Flores Sea
Flores
Timor
EAST TIMOR
Sawu Sea
Kupang
Timor Sea
INDONESIA
Makassar Strait
Sulawesi
Palu
Parepare
Ujung Pandang
Manadao
Molucca Sea
Halmahera
Moluccas
Seram Sea
Seram
Banda Sea
Kepulauan Kai
Kepulauan Aru
Kepulauan Tanimbar
Arafura Sea
Biak
Jayapura
IRIAN JAYA
Puncak Jaya 5030
New Guinea
Dolak I.
PAPUA NEW GUINEA
G. of Papua
Port Moresby
Torres Strait
Bismarck Sea
Admiralty Is
New Ireland
New Britain
Solomon Sea
Coral Sea Islands Territory (Aust.)
Great Barrier Reef
Cairns
AUSTRALIA
Gulf of Carpentaria
C. Arnhem
Melville I.
Darwin
PALAU
Koror
Yap
Caroline Islands
FEDERATED STATES OF MICRONESIA
Gaferut
Pikelot
Hall Is
Chuuk
Nomoi Is
Pohnpei
Palikir
Northern Mariana Is (U.S.A.)
Pagan
Saipan
Tinian
Guam (U.S.A.)
Equator
Wake I. (U.S.A.)
Kure Atoll
Midway Is (U.S.A.)
Tropic of Cancer
NORTH PACIFIC OCEAN
RUSSIAN FEDERATION
MONGOLIA
CHINA
© Bartholomew
Km
Miles
1:35M

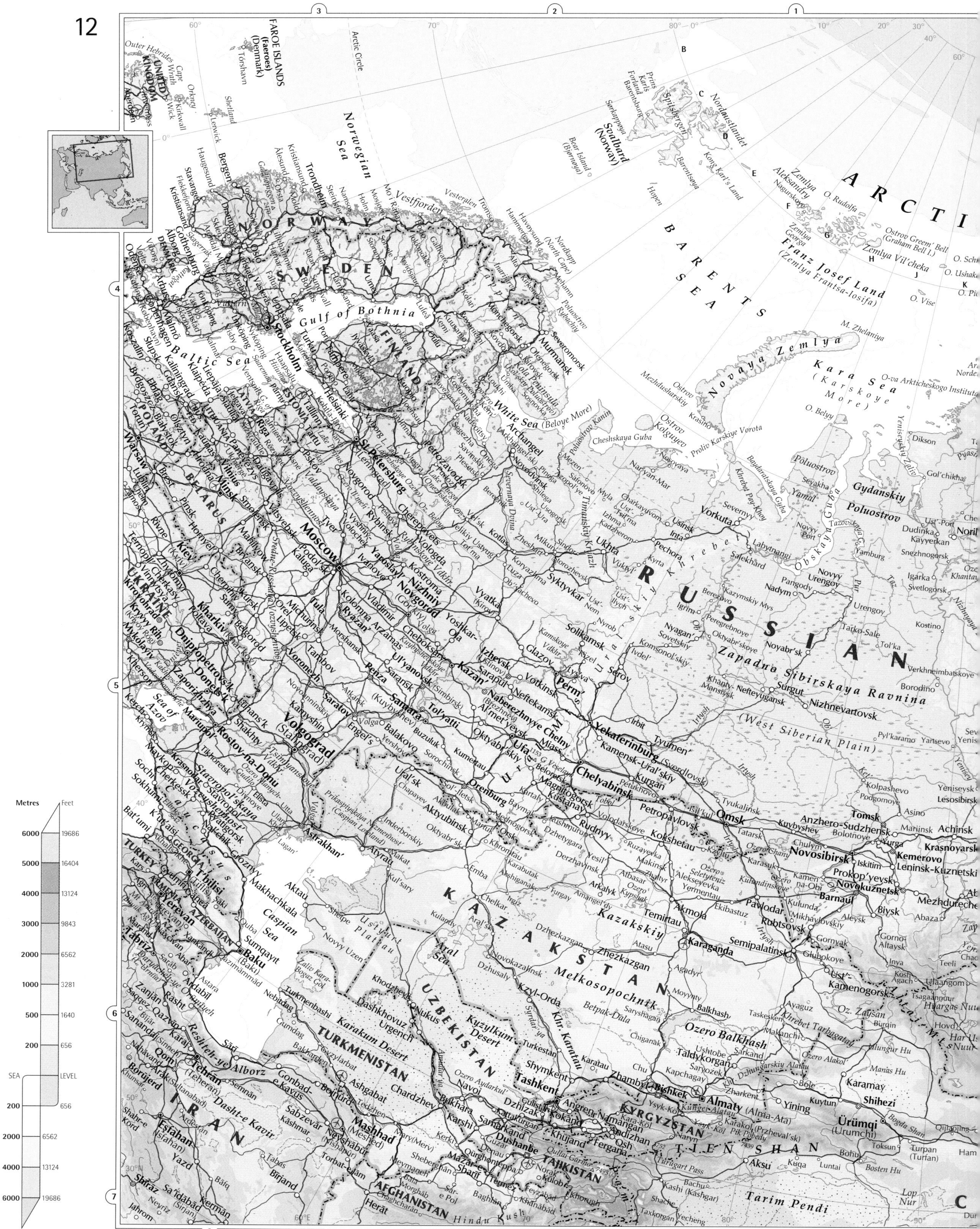
ARCTIC
Norwegian Sea
BARENTS SEA
Kara Sea (Karskoye More)
Svalbard (Norway)
Spitsbergen
Nordaustlandet
Franz Josef Land (Zemlya Frantsa-Iosifa)
Novaya Zemlya
FAROE ISLANDS (Faeroes) (Denmark)
Tórshavn
UNITED KINGDOM
Shetland
Orkney
Outer Hebrides
Arctic Circle
NORWAY
SWEDEN
FINLAND
Gulf of Bothnia
Baltic Sea
ESTONIA
LATVIA
LITHUANIA
POLAND
BELARUS
UKRAINE
RUSSIAN
Zapadno Sibirskaya Ravnina
(West Siberian Plain)
White Sea (Beloye More)
Ural'skiy Khrebet
Bergen
Trondheim
Stavanger
Oslo
Stockholm
Helsinki
Tallinn
Riga
Vilnius
Minsk
Warsaw
Kaliningrad
St Petersburg
Murmansk
Archangel
Petrozavodsk
Moscow
Kiev
Kharkiv
Dnipropetrovs'k
Donets'k
Odessa
Nizhniy Novgorod
Kazan'
Samara
Saratov
Volgograd (Stalingrad)
Rostov-na-Donu
Perm'
Yekaterinburg (Sverdlovsk)
Chelyabinsk
Ufa
Orenburg
Vorkuta
Syktyvkar
Surgut
Nizhnevartovsk
Omsk
Tomsk
Novosibirsk
Novokuznetsk
Barnaul
Kemerovo
Krasnoyarsk
Norilsk
Sea of Azov
Caspian Sea
GEORGIA
Tbilisi
ARMENIA
Yerevan
AZERBAIJAN
Baku
TURKEY
Tabriz
IRAN
Tehran
Mashhad
Esfahan
Shiraz
KAZAKHSTAN
Kazakhskiy Melkosopochnik
Karaganda
Akmola
Semipalatinsk
Aral Sea
Ozero Balkhash
Almaty (Alma-Ata)
Bishkek
KYRGYZSTAN
UZBEKISTAN
Tashkent
Samarkand
TURKMENISTAN
Karakum Desert
Kyzylkum Desert
Ashgabat
TAJIKISTAN
Dushanbe
AFGHANISTAN
Hindu Kush
TIEN SHAN
Ürümqi (Urumchi)
Tarim Pendi
Metres
Feet
6000 19686
5000 16404
4000 13124
3000 9843
2000 6562
1000 3281
500 1640
200 656
SEA LEVEL
200 656
2000 6562
4000 13124
6000 19686
Conic Equidistant Projection

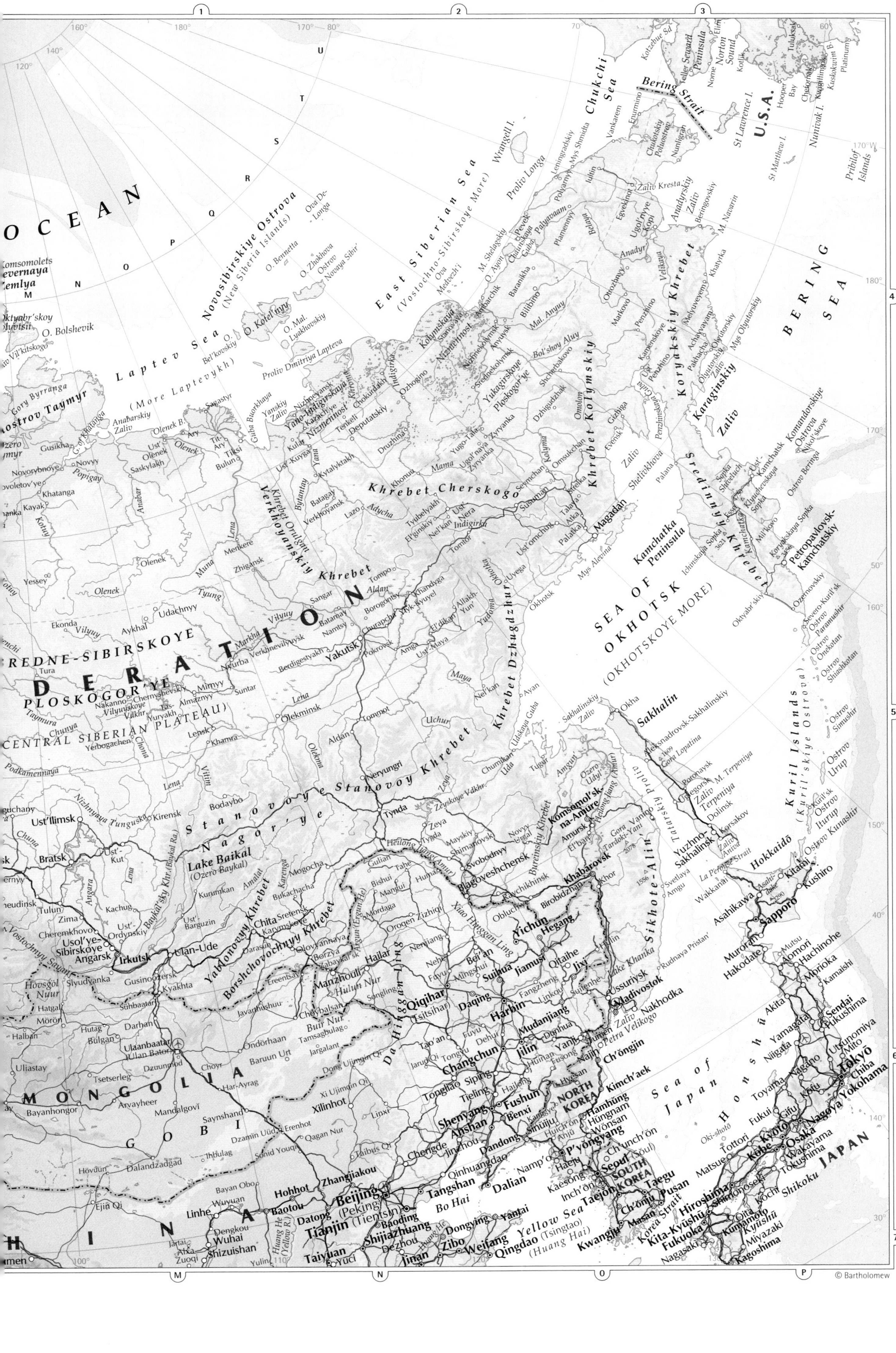

OCEAN
Chukchi Sea
Bering Strait
U.S.A.
East Siberian Sea
(Vostochno-Sibirskoye More)
Wrangell I.
Novosibirskiye Ostrova
(New Siberian Islands)
Laptev Sea
(More Laptevykh)
BERING SEA
Koryakskiy Khrebet
Karaginskiy Zaliv
Khrebet Cherskogo
Khrebet Kolymskiy
Verkhoyanskiy Khrebet
Kamchatka Peninsula
Sredinnyy Khrebet
Petropavlovsk-Kamchatskiy
SEA OF OKHOTSK
(OKHOTSKOYE MORE)
Magadan
Yakutsk
Khrebet Dzhugdzhur
Sakhalin
Kuril Islands
(Kuril'skiye Ostrova)
Stanovoy Khrebet
Stanovoye Nagor'ye
Lake Baikal
(Ozero Baykal)
Irkutsk
Ulan-Ude
Chita
Bratsk
Khabarovsk
Komsomol'sk-na-Amure
Vladivostok
Sikhote-Alin'
Hokkaidō
Sapporo
Sea of Japan
Honshū
JAPAN
Tokyo
Yokohama
Nagoya
Kyoto
Osaka
Kobe
Hiroshima
Fukuoka
Shikoku
Kyūshū
NORTH KOREA
P'yongyang
SOUTH KOREA
Seoul
Pusan
Yellow Sea
(Huang Hai)
Bo Hai
Beijing
(Peking)
Tianjin
Dalian
Shenyang
Harbin
Changchun
MONGOLIA
Ulaanbaatar
(Ulan Bator)
GOBI
CHINA
Da Hinggan Ling
Xiao Hinggan Ling
CENTRAL SIBERIAN PLATEAU
SREDNE-SIBIRSKOYE PLOSKOGOR'YE
FEDERATION
Km
Miles
1200
1000
800
600
400
200
0
600
450
300
150
0
1:21M
© Bartholomew

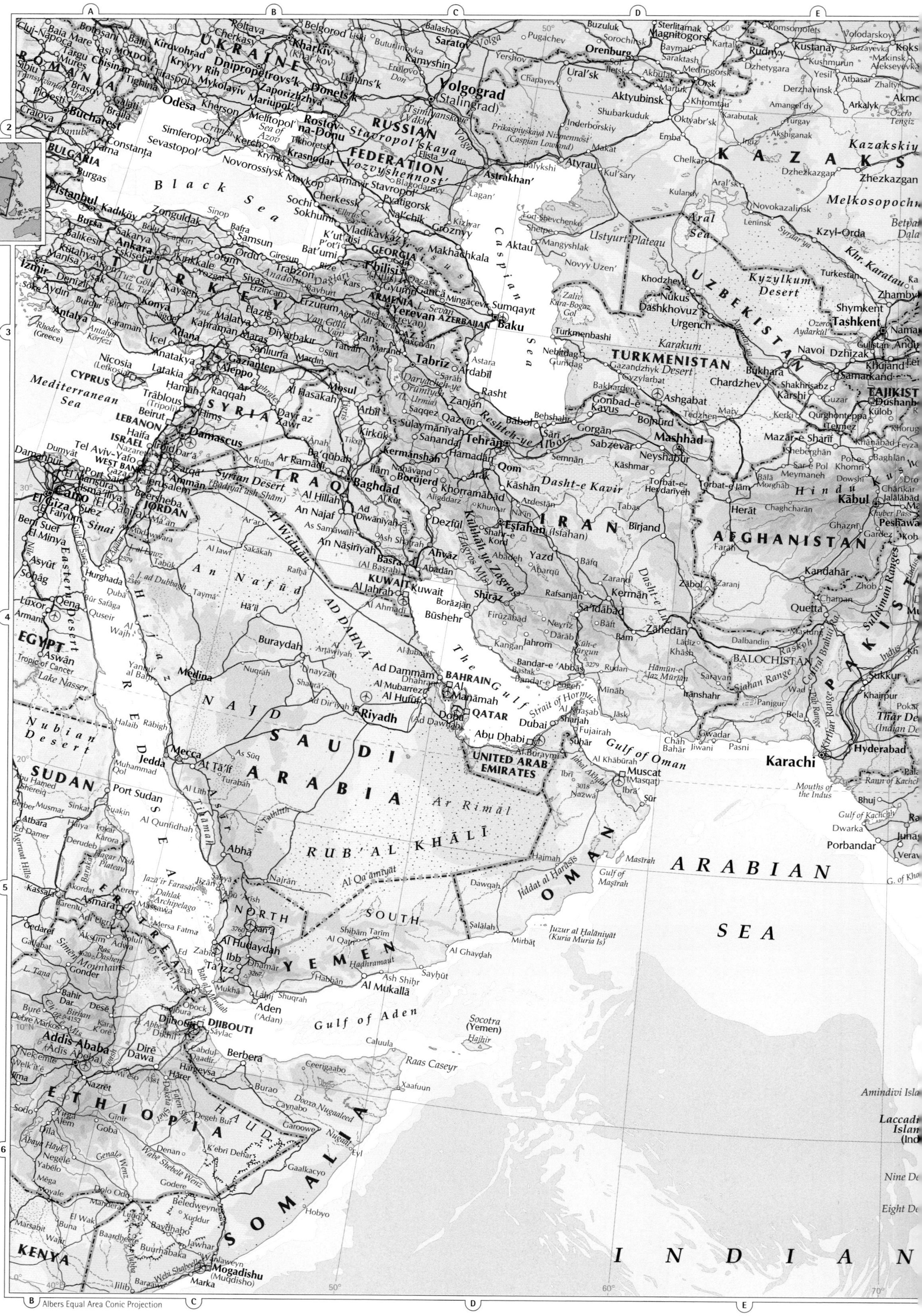

Black Sea
Caspian Sea
Mediterranean Sea
Red Sea
Gulf of Aden
Gulf of Oman
ARABIAN SEA
INDIAN
UKRAINE
ROMANIA
BULGARIA
TURKEY
RUSSIAN FEDERATION
GEORGIA
ARMENIA
AZERBAIJAN
KAZAKHSTAN
UZBEKISTAN
TURKMENISTAN
TAJIKISTAN
AFGHANISTAN
PAKISTAN
IRAN
IRAQ
SYRIA
CYPRUS
LEBANON
ISRAEL
WEST BANK
JORDAN
KUWAIT
BAHRAIN
QATAR
UNITED ARAB EMIRATES
OMAN
SAUDI ARABIA
NORTH YEMEN
SOUTH YEMEN
EGYPT
SUDAN
ERITREA
DJIBOUTI
ETHIOPIA
SOMALIA
KENYA
Volgograd (Stalingrad)
Odesa
Bucharest
İstanbul
Ankara
Tbilisi
Yerevan
Baku
Tehrān
Baghdād
Damascus
Beirut
Cairo
Riyadh
Mecca
Jedda
Medina
Muscat
Aden
Addis Ababa
Mogadishu
Kābul
Tashkent
Karachi
Mashhad
Eşfahān
Kuwait
Dubai
Abu Dhabi
Ar Rimāl
RUB' AL KHĀLĪ
NAJD
An Nafūd
Syrian Desert
Nubian Desert
Dasht-e Kavir
Karakum
Kyzylkum Desert
Ustyurt Plateau
Aral Sea
Socotra (Yemen)
Albers Equal Area Conic Projection

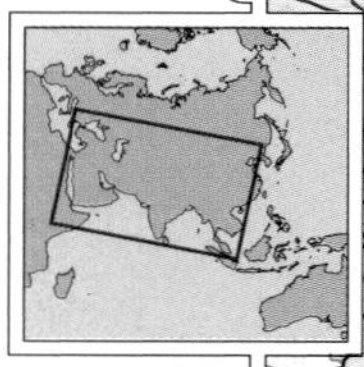

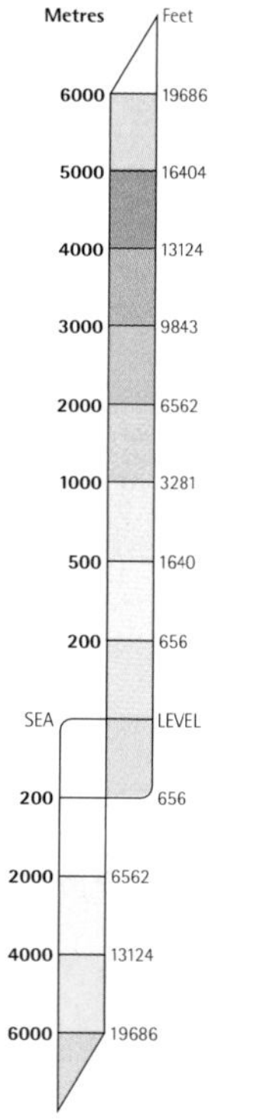

Metres
Feet
6000
19686
5000
16404
4000
13124
3000
9843
2000
6562
1000
3281
500
1640
200
656
SEA
LEVEL
200
656
2000
6562
4000
13124
6000
19686

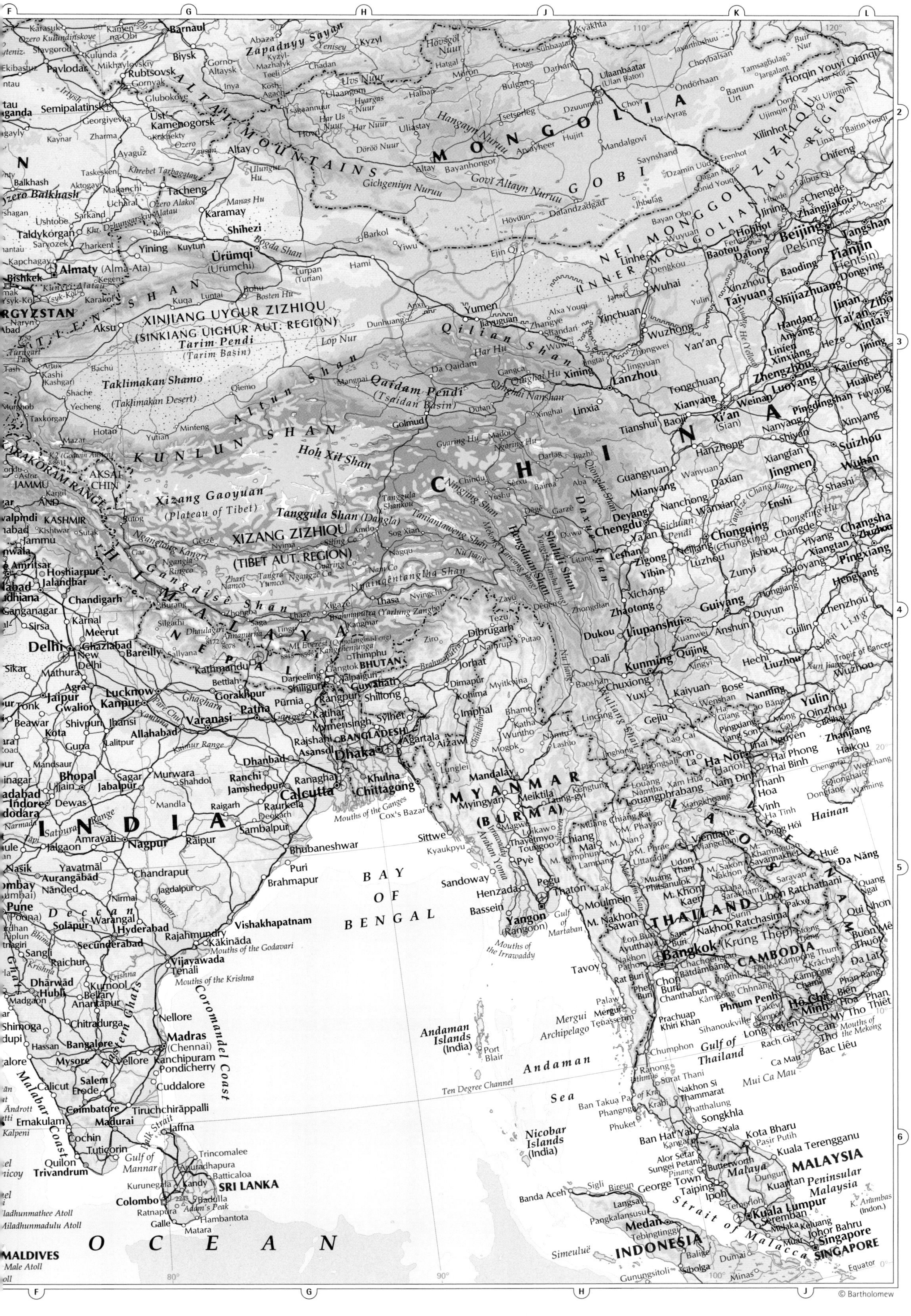
MONGOLIA
CHINA
INDIA
NEPAL
BHUTAN
BANGLADESH
MYANMAR
(BURMA)
LAOS
THAILAND
CAMBODIA
VIETNAM
MALAYSIA
SINGAPORE
INDONESIA
SRI LANKA
MALDIVES
XINJIANG UYGUR ZIZHIQU
(SINKIANG UIGHUR AUT. REGION)
XIZANG ZIZHIQU
(TIBET AUT. REGION)
NEI MONGGOL ZIZHIQU
(INNER MONGOLIAN AUT. REGION)
ALTAI MOUNTAINS
GOBI
TIEN SHAN
KUNLUN SHAN
HIMALAYA
Taklimakan Shamo
(Taklimakan Desert)
Xizang Gaoyuan
(Plateau of Tibet)
Qaidam Pendi
(Tsaidam Basin)
Tarim Pendi
(Tarim Basin)
Qilian Shan
Altun Shan
Tanggula Shan (Dangla)
Hengduan Shan
BAY OF BENGAL
Andaman Sea
Gulf of Thailand
OCEAN
Andaman Islands (India)
Nicobar Islands (India)
Strait of Malacca
Deccan
Coromandel Coast
Malabar Coast
Beijing
(Peking)
Tianjin
(Tientsin)
Ulaanbaatar
(Ulan Bator)
Ürümqi
(Urumchi)
Almaty (Alma-Ata)
Lhasa
Kathmandu
Thimphu
Dhaka
Delhi
New Delhi
Calcutta
Bombay
Madras
(Chennai)
Colombo
Yangon
(Rangoon)
Bangkok (Krung Thep)
Vientiane
Ha Noi
(Hanoi)
Phnum Penh
Ho Chi Minh
Kuala Lumpur
Chengdu
Chongqing
(Chungking)
Kunming
Xi'an
(Sian)
Lanzhou
Wuhan
Mt Everest
(Qomolangma Feng)
8848
K2 (Godwin Austen)
8611
Equator
Ten Degree Channel
© Bartholomew

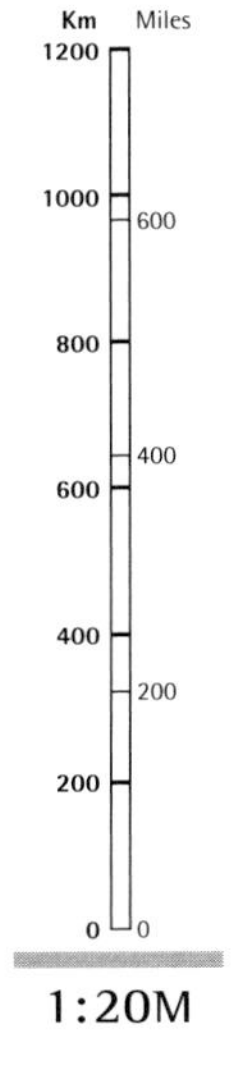
Km
Miles
1200
1000
800
600
400
200
0
600
400
200
0
1:20M

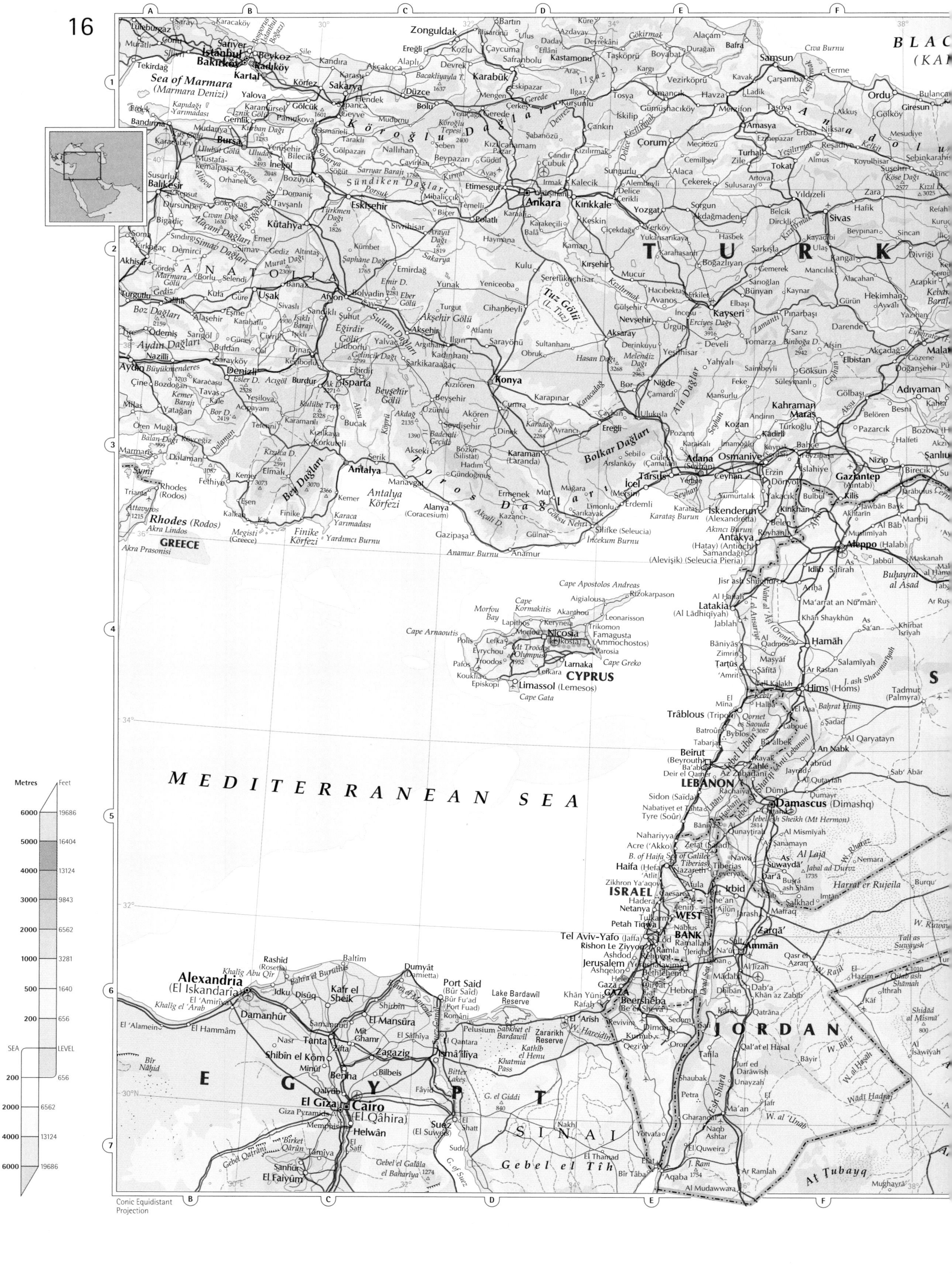

Metres
Feet
6000
19686
5000
16404
4000
13124
3000
9843
2000
6562
1000
3281
500
1640
200
656
SEA
LEVEL
200
656
2000
6562
4000
13124
6000
19686
BLAC
Sea of Marmara
(Marmara Denizi)
İstanbul
Bakırköy
Kadıköy
Kartal
Zonguldak
Karabük
Samsun
Ordu
Giresun
Bursa
Balıkesir
Eskişehir
Kütahya
Ankara
Kırıkkale
Çorum
Amasya
Tokat
Sivas
Yozgat
Kayseri
Nevşehir
Aksaray
Konya
Afyon
Isparta
Burdur
Denizli
Aydın
Muğla
Antalya
Alanya
Adana
Tarsus
Mersin
Osmaniye
Kahramanmaraş
Gaziantep
İskenderun
Antakya
Adıyaman
Malatya
ANATOLIA
TURK
Tuz Gölü
(L. Tuz)
Toros Dağları
Köroğlu Dağları
Bolkar Dağları
Antalya Körfezi
Rhodes (Rodos)
GREECE
Aleppo (Halab)
Idlib
Latakia
Hamāh
Hims (Homs)
Tadmur (Palmyra)
Trâblous (Tripoli)
Beirut
(Beyrouth)
LEBANON
Sidon (Saïda)
Tyre (Soûr)
Damascus (Dimashq)
Nicosia
Famagusta
(Ammochostos)
Larnaka
Limassol (Lemesos)
CYPRUS
Cape Apostolos Andreas
Cape Arnaoutis
Cape Greko
Cape Gata
MEDITERRANEAN SEA
Haifa
Acre ('Akko)
Nahariyya
ISRAEL
Netanya
Tel Aviv-Yafo (Jaffa)
Jerusalem
Ashdod
Ashqelon
WEST
BANK
GAZA
Beersheba
(Be'er Sheva)
Irbid
Zarqā'
'Ammān
JORDAN
Ma'ān
Aqaba
Al Mudawwara
At Tubayq
Alexandria
(El Iskandarîya)
Rashîd
(Rosetta)
Damanhûr
Dumyât
(Damietta)
Port Said
(Bûr Saîd)
El Mansûra
Tanta
Zagazig
Ismâ'iliya
Benha
El Gîza
Cairo
(El Qâhira)
Helwân
Suez
(El Suweis)
El Faiyûm
EGYPT
SINAI
Gebel el Tîh
El 'Arîsh
Lake Bardawil
Reserve
Conic Equidistant
Projection

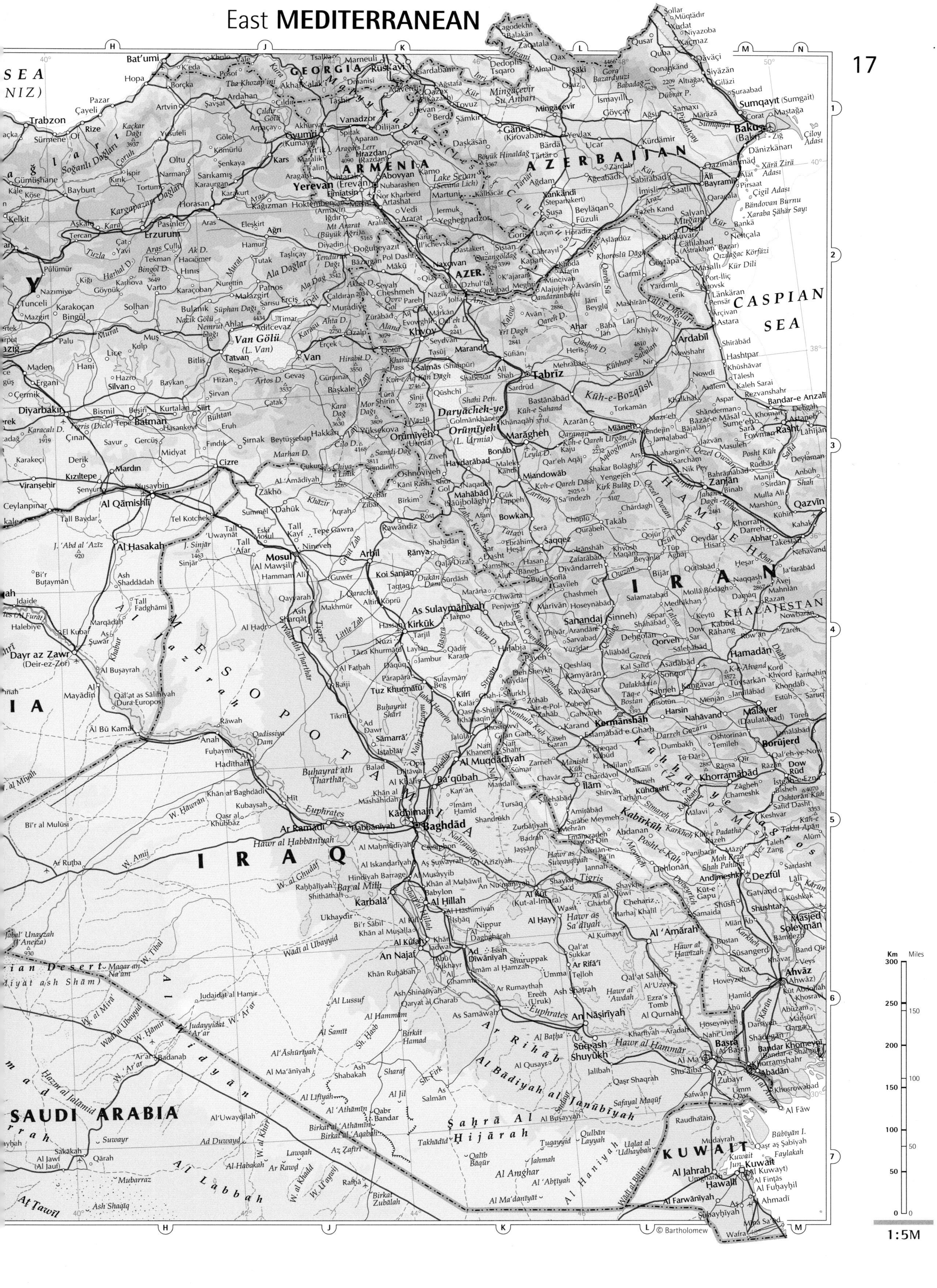
GEORGIA
ARMENIA
AZERBAIJAN
AZER.
IRAN
IRAQ
SAUDI ARABIA
KUWAIT
CASPIAN SEA
MESOPOTAMIA
KHAMSEH
KHALAJESTAN
Al Jazīrah
Van Gölü (L. Van)
Daryācheh-ye Orūmīyeh (L. Urmia)
Tbilisi
Yerevan (Erevan)
Baku (Bakı)
Sumqayıt (Sumgait)
Gäncä (Kirovabad)
Trabzon
Erzurum
Diyarbakır
Mardin
Batman
Mosul (Al Mawşil)
Arbīl
Kirkūk
As Sulaymānīyah
Baghdād
Karbalā'
An Najaf
Al Ḩillah
Al Kūt (Kut-al-Imara)
Al 'Amārah
An Nāşirīyah
Başra (Al Başra)
Ābādān
Bandar Khomeynī
Ahvāz (Ahwāz)
Dezfūl
Kermānshāh
Hamadān
Sanandaj (Sinneh)
Tabrīz
Orūmīyeh (Urmia)
Zanjān
Qazvīn
Rasht
Ardabīl
Kuwait (Al Kuwayt)
Al Jahrah
Ar Ramādī
Dayr az Zawr (Deir-ez-Zor)
Al Ḩasakah
Al Qāmishlī
Euphrates
Tigris
Hawr al Ḩammār
Buḩayrat ath Tharthār
Şaḩrā Al Ḩijārah
Al Bādiyah al Janūbīyah
Ar Rihāb
Km 300 250 200 150 100 50 0
Miles 150 100 50 0
1:5M
© Bartholomew

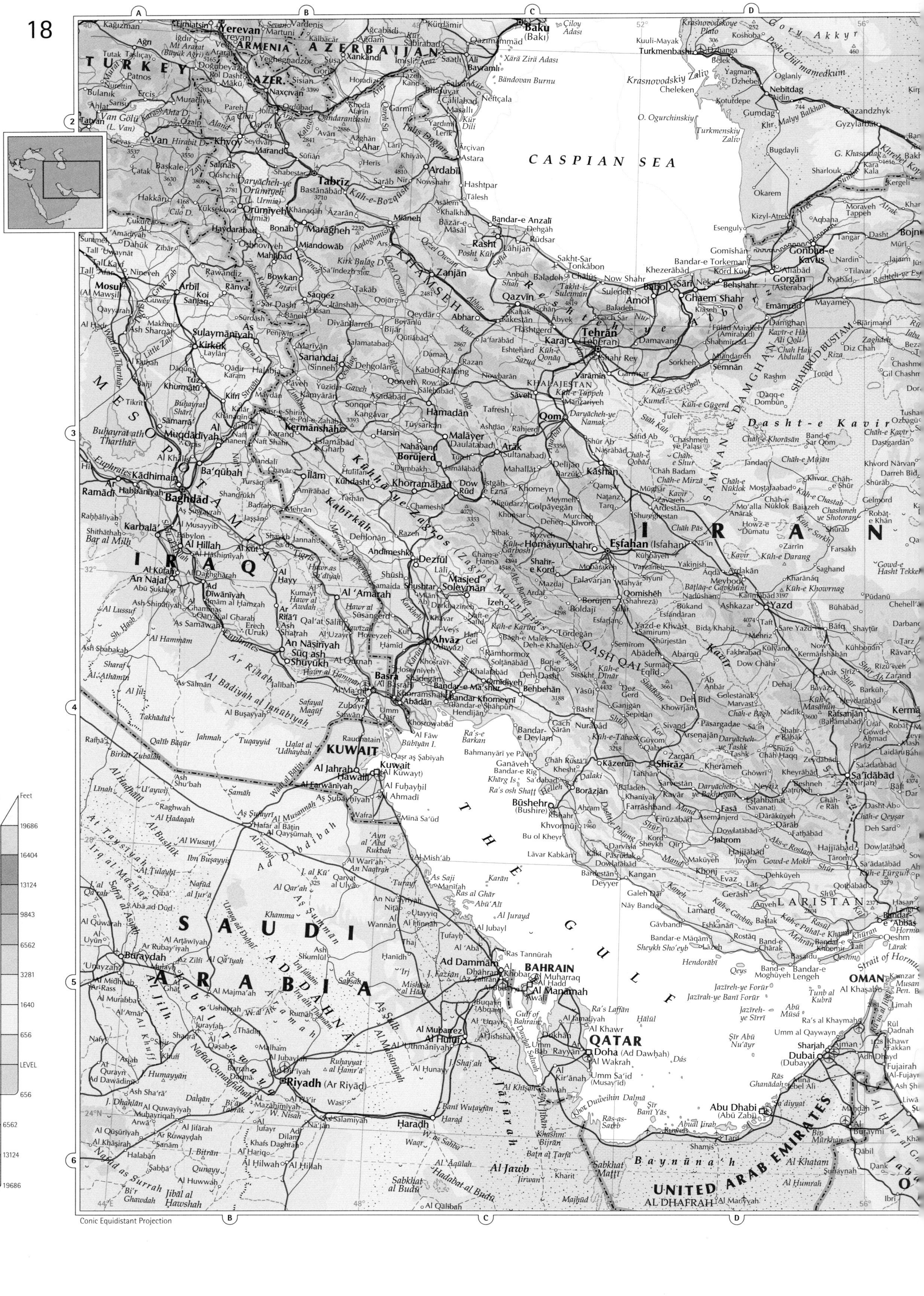

TURKEY
ARMENIA
AZERBAIJAN
AZER.
IRAQ
IRAN
KUWAIT
SAUDI ARABIA
BAHRAIN
QATAR
UNITED ARAB EMIRATES
OMAN
CASPIAN SEA
THE GULF
MESOPOTAMIA
KHAMSEH
Reshteh-ye Alborz
Kūhhā-ye Zāgros
Zagros Mountains
Dasht-e Kavir
LARISTAN
QASH QAI
AD DAHNĀ
Baku (Bakı)
Yerevan (Erevan)
Tehrān (Teheran)
Baghdād
Mosul (Al Mawşil)
Kirkūk
Arbīl
Basra (Al Başrah)
Kuwait (Al Kuwayt)
Riyadh (Ar Riyāḑ)
Doha (Ad Dawḩah)
Abu Dhabi (Abū Zabī)
Dubai (Dubayy)
Sharjah
Al Manamah
Ad Dammām
Eşfahān (Isfahan)
Shīrāz
Tabrīz
Hamadān
Kermānshāh
Ahvāz (Ahwaz)
Yazd
Qom
Rasht
Bandar-e 'Abbās
Bandar-e Anzalī
Turkmenbashi
Krasnovodskiy Zaliv
Strait of Hormuz
Gulf of Bahrain
Sabkhat Maţţī
Baynūnah
Conic Equidistant Projection

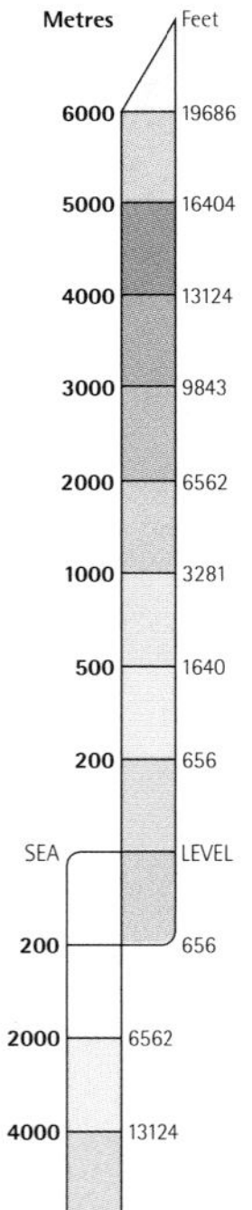

Metres
Feet
6000 19686
5000 16404
4000 13124
3000 9843
2000 6562
1000 3281
500 1640
200 656
SEA LEVEL
200 656
2000 6562
4000 13124
6000 19686

Conic Equidistant Projection

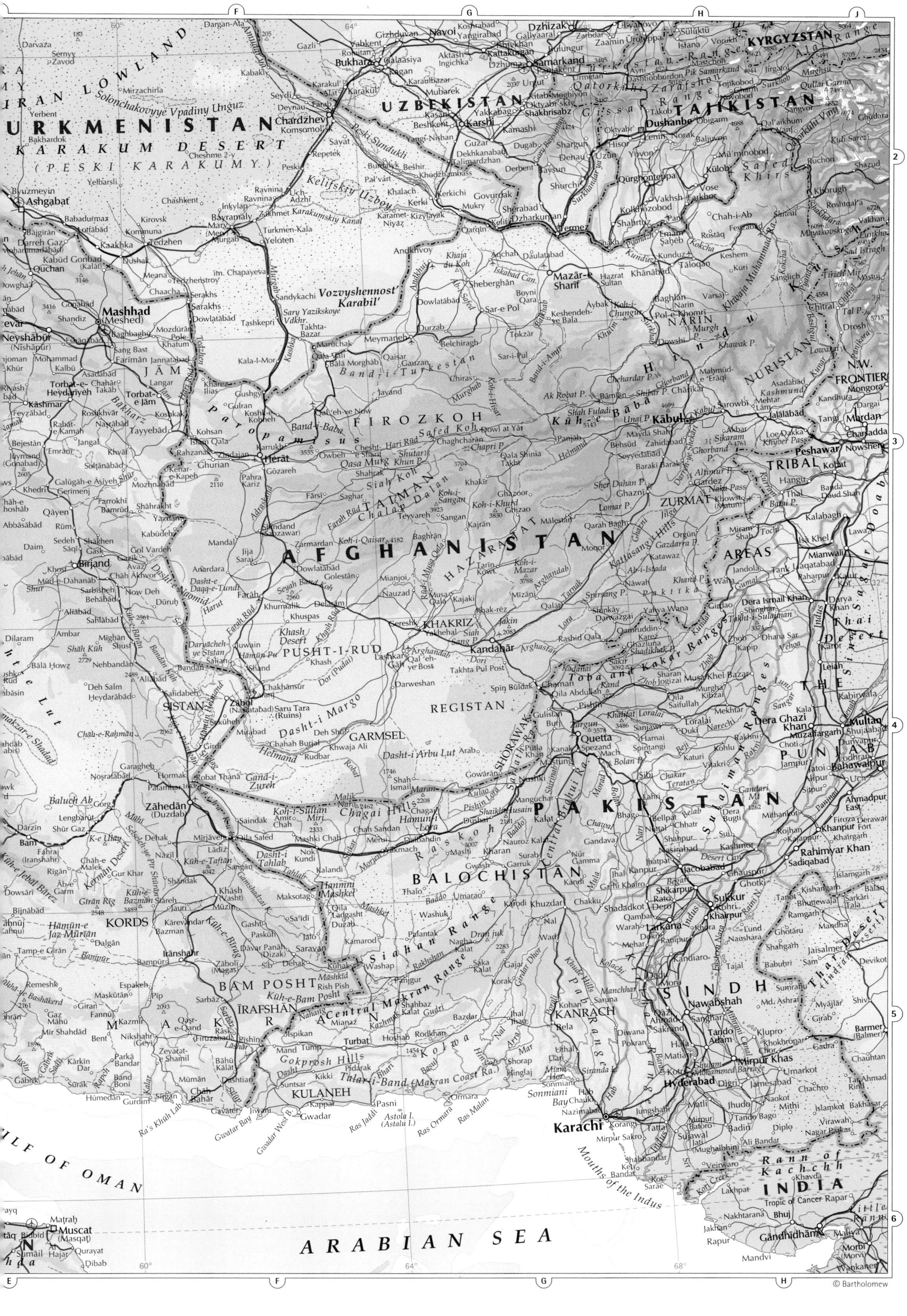

ARABIAN SEA

GULF OF OMAN

© Bartholomew

1:7M

Km	Miles
400	250
350	200
300	150
250	
200	100
150	
100	50
50	
0	0

ARABIAN PENINSULA

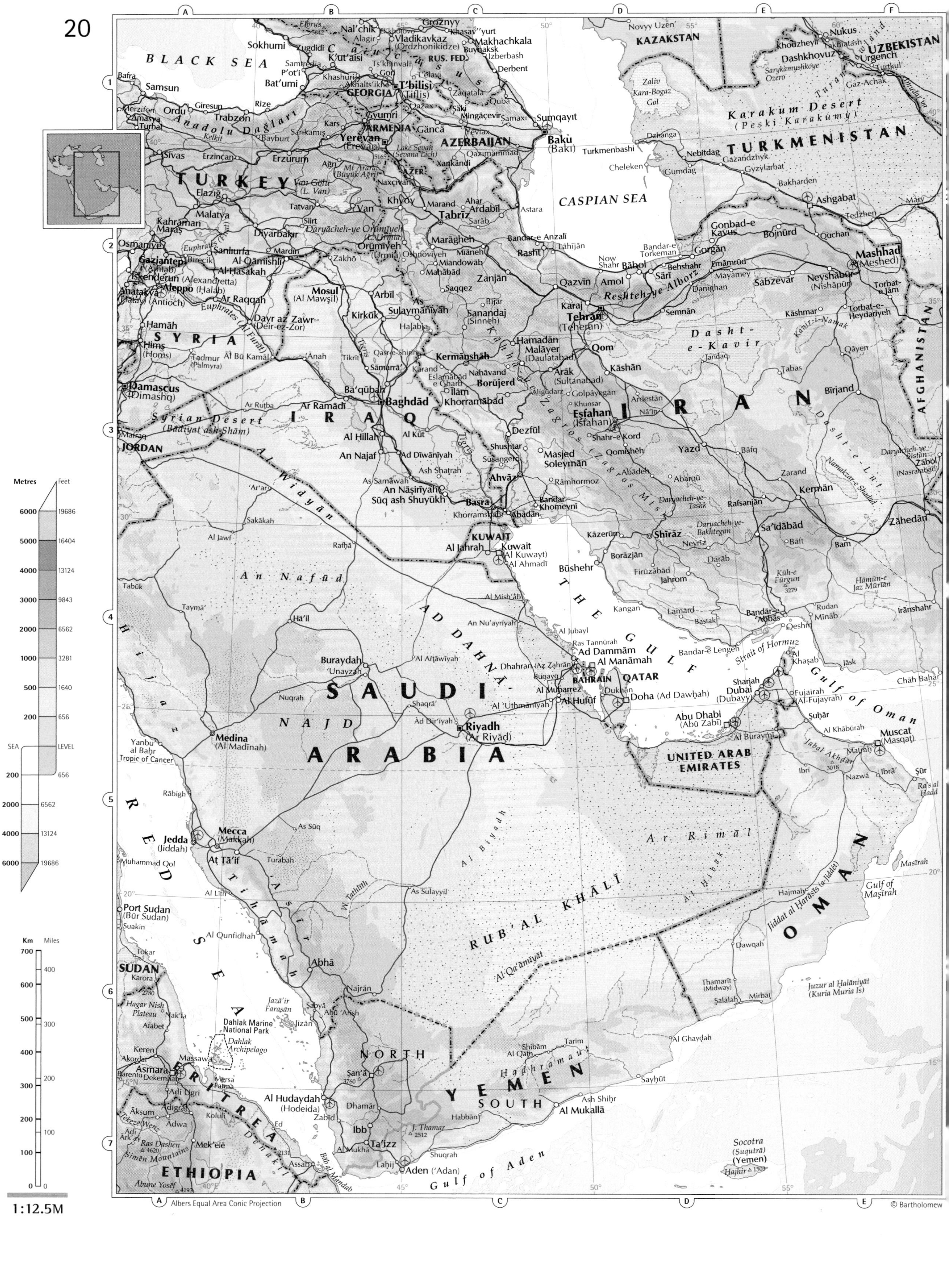

1:12.5M

Albers Equal Area Conic Projection

© Bartholomew

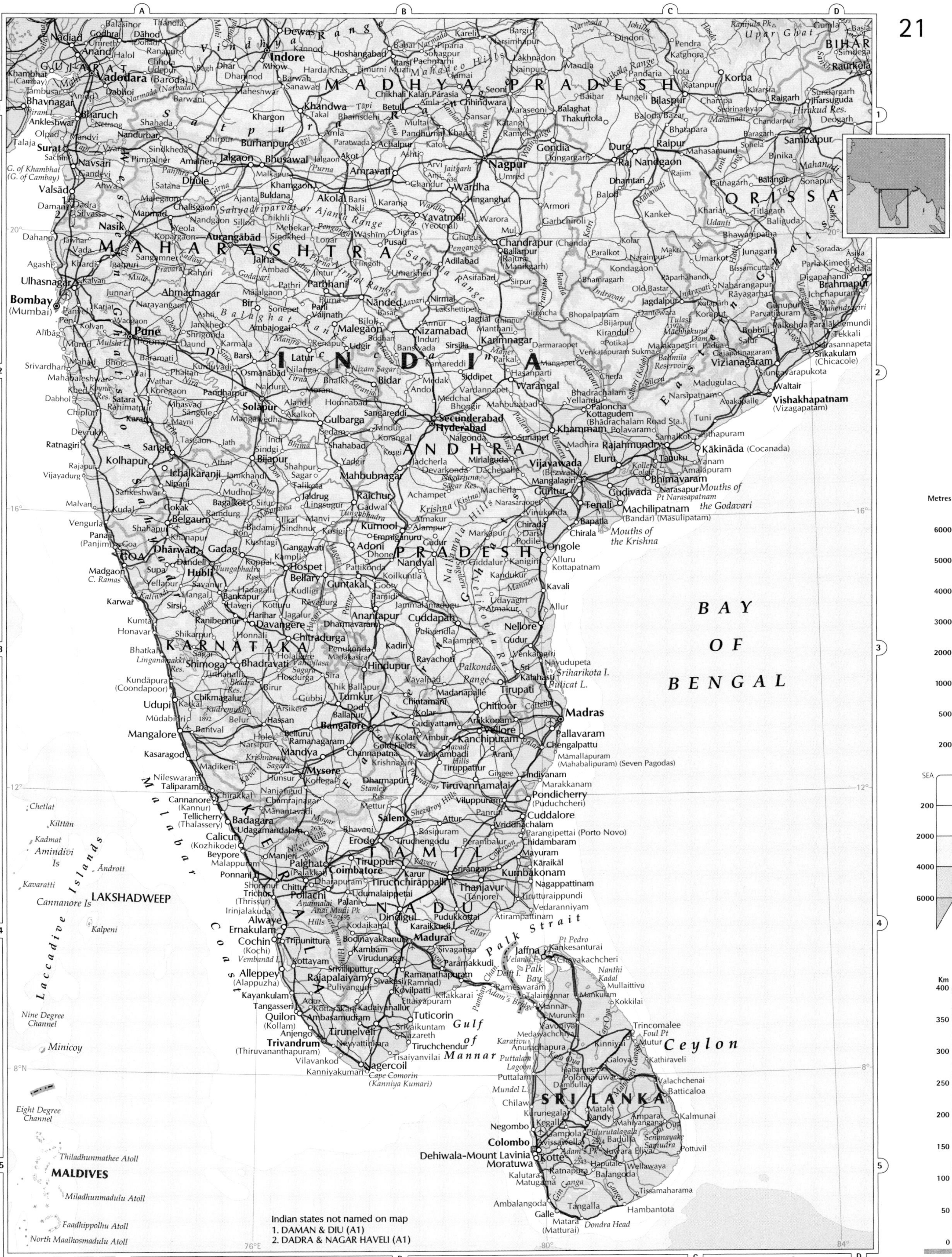

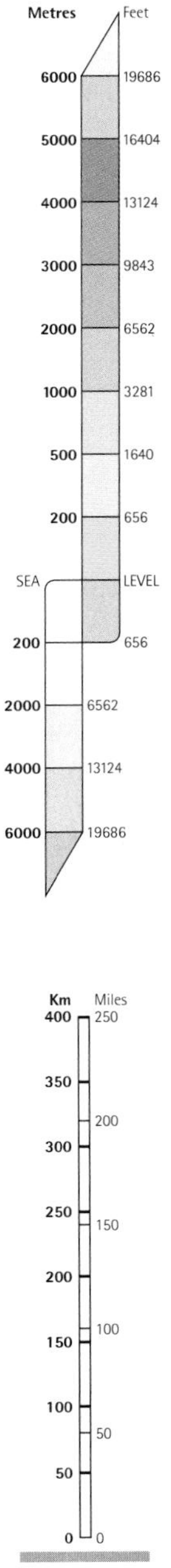

BAY

OF

BENGAL

© Bartholomew

Indian states not named on map
1. DAMAN & DIU (A1)
2. DADRA & NAGAR HAVELI (A1)

Metres	Feet
6000	19686
5000	16404
4000	13124
3000	9843
2000	6562
1000	3281
500	1640
200	656
SEA	LEVEL
200	656
2000	6562
4000	13124
6000	19686

Km	Miles
400	250
350	200
300	150
250	
200	100
150	
100	50
50	
0	0

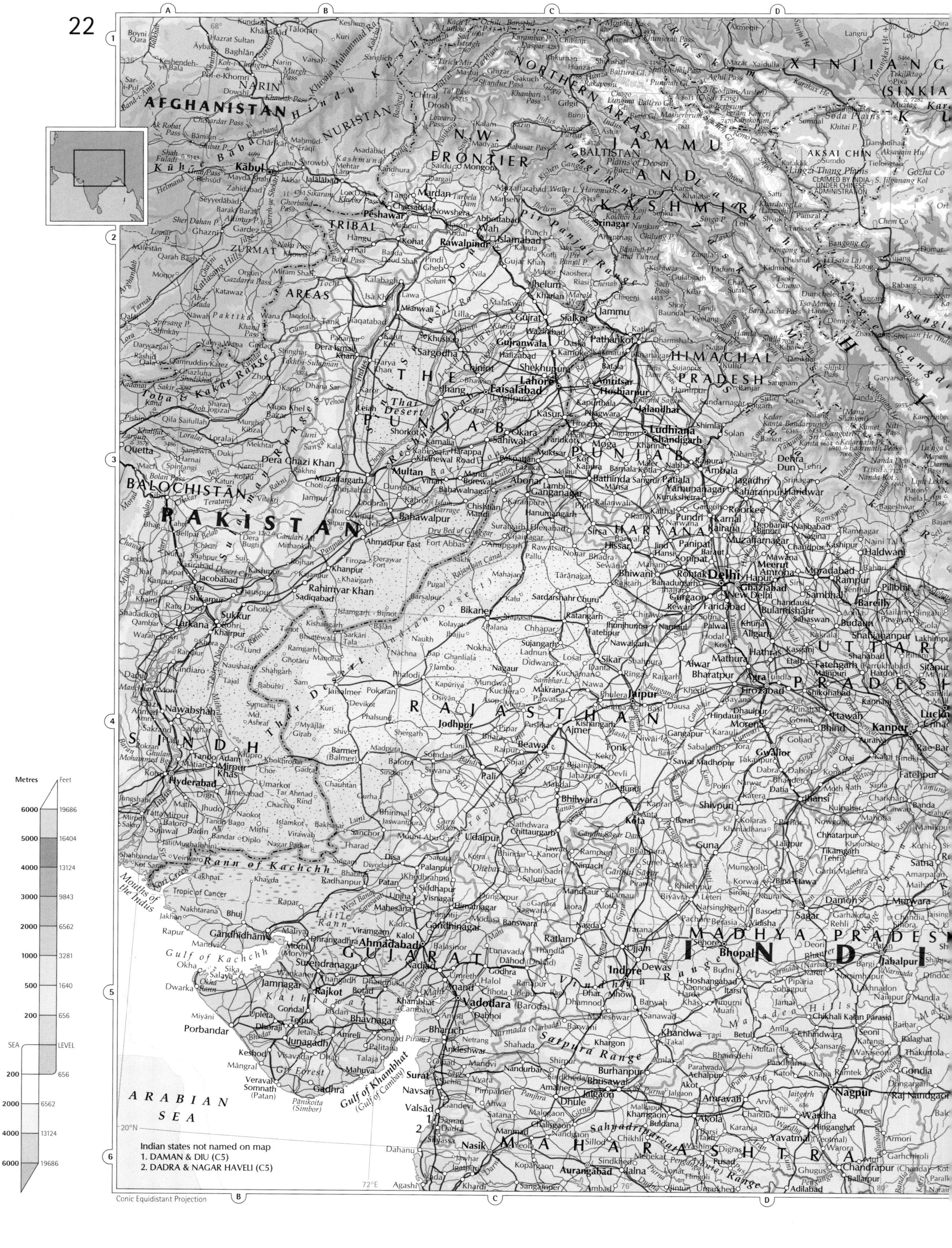
AFGHANISTAN
PAKISTAN
INDIA
XINJIANG
JAMMU AND KASHMIR
NORTHERN AREAS
NW FRONTIER
TRIBAL AREAS
BALOCHISTAN
SINDH
THE PUNJAB
PUNJAB
HIMACHAL PRADESH
HARYANA
RAJASTHAN
UTTAR PRADESH
MADHYA PRADESH
GUJARAT
MAHARASHTRA
ARABIAN SEA
Thar Desert
Rann of Kachchh
Gulf of Kachchh
Gulf of Khambhat (Gulf of Cambay)
Tropic of Cancer
Months of the Indus
Kabul
Islamabad
Lahore
Delhi
New Delhi
Karachi
Hyderabad
Ahmadabad
Jaipur
Indian states not named on map
1. DAMAN & DIU (C5)
2. DADRA & NAGAR HAVELI (C5)
Metres
Feet
6000
19686
5000
16404
4000
13124
3000
9843
2000
6562
1000
3281
500
1640
200
656
SEA
LEVEL
Conic Equidistant Projection

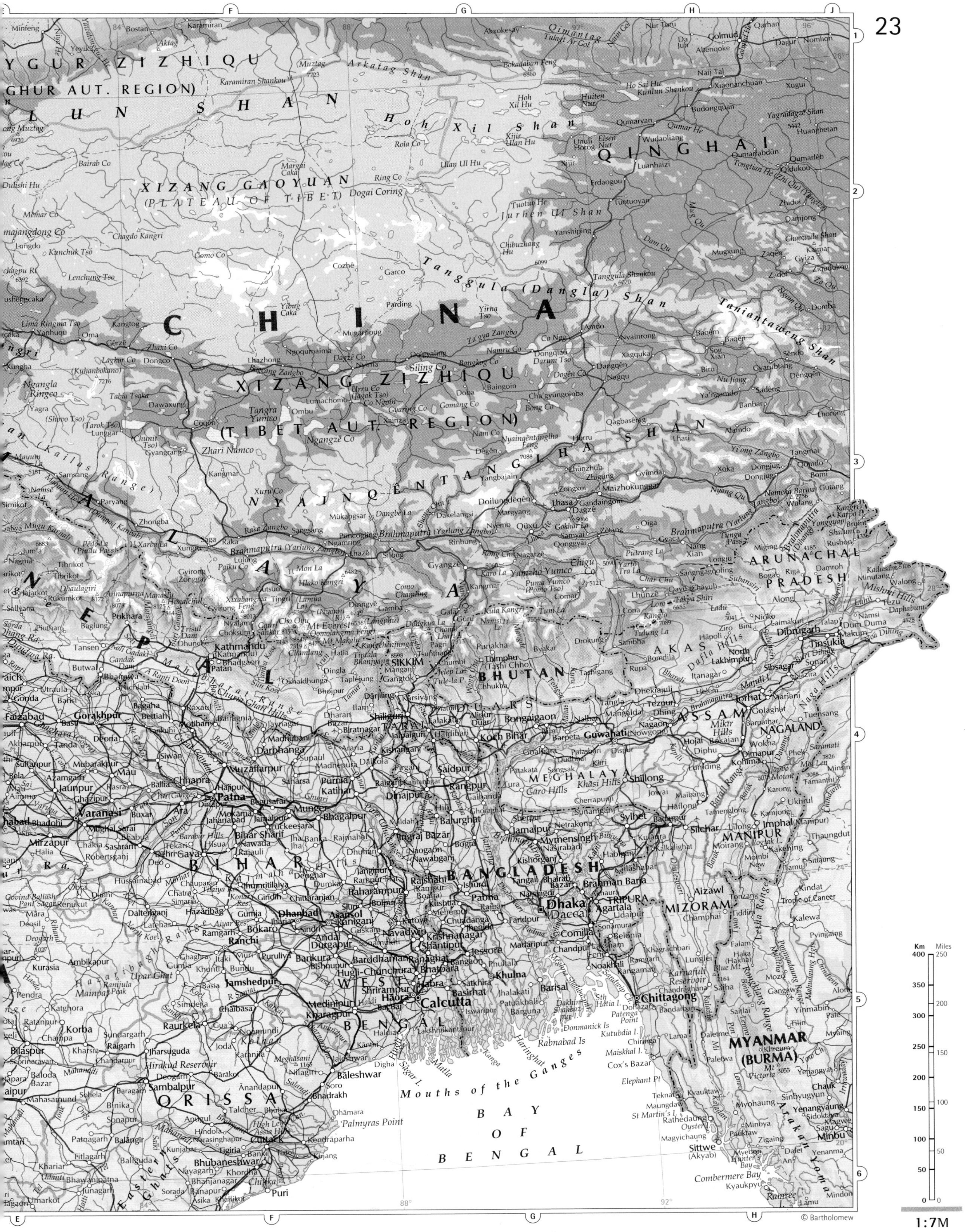

Km Miles
400 — 250
350 — 200
300 — 150
250 — 150
200 — 100
150 — 100
100 — 50
50 —
0 — 0

© Bartholomew

1:7M

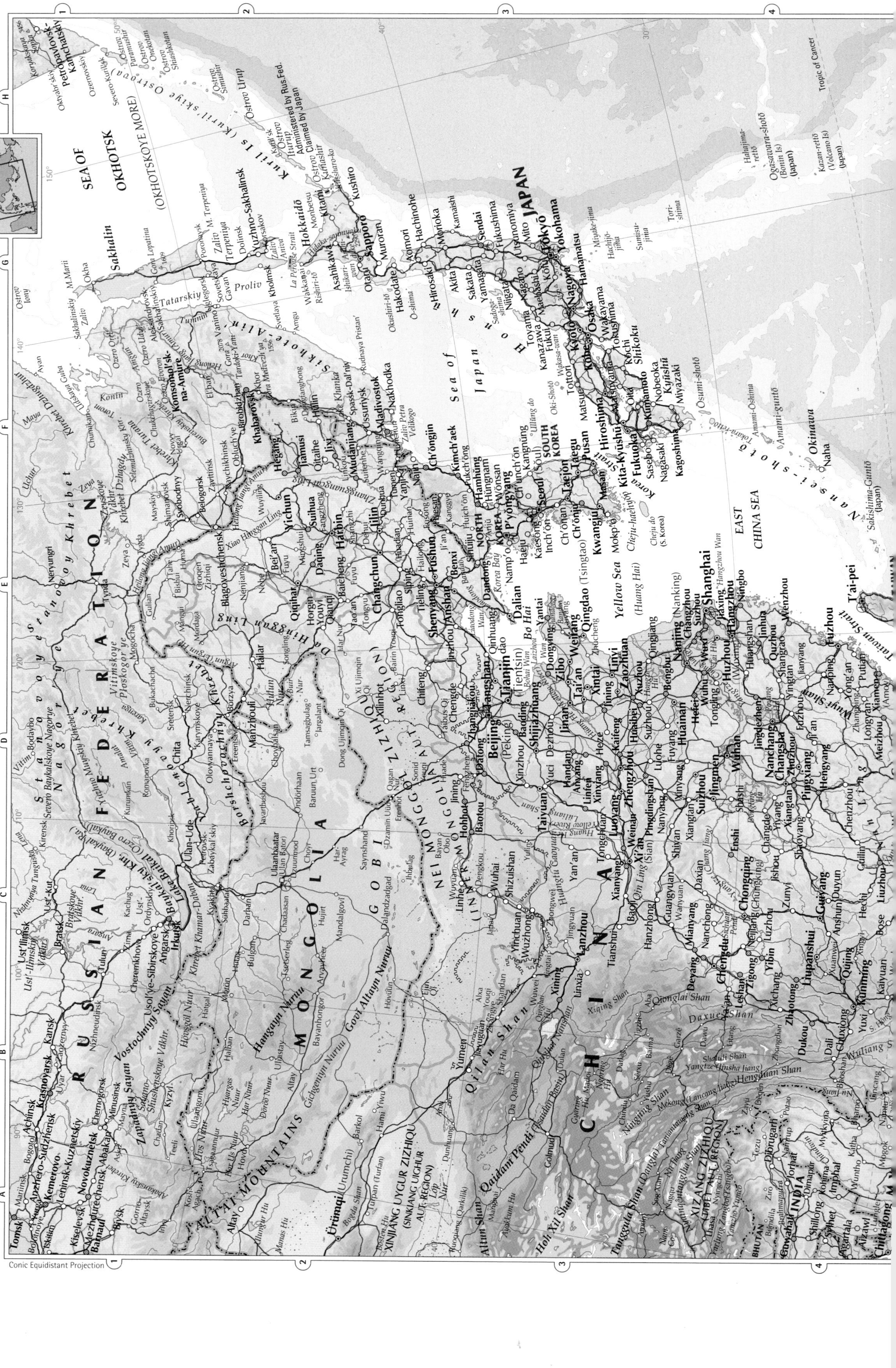

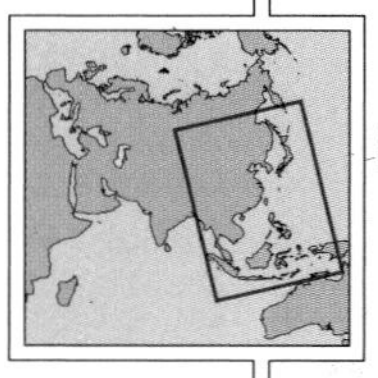

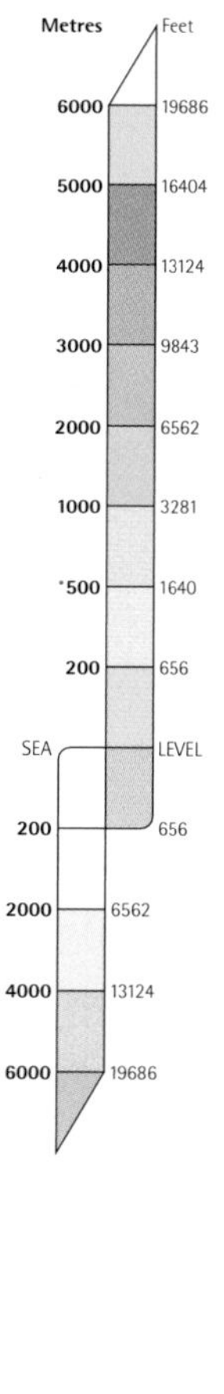

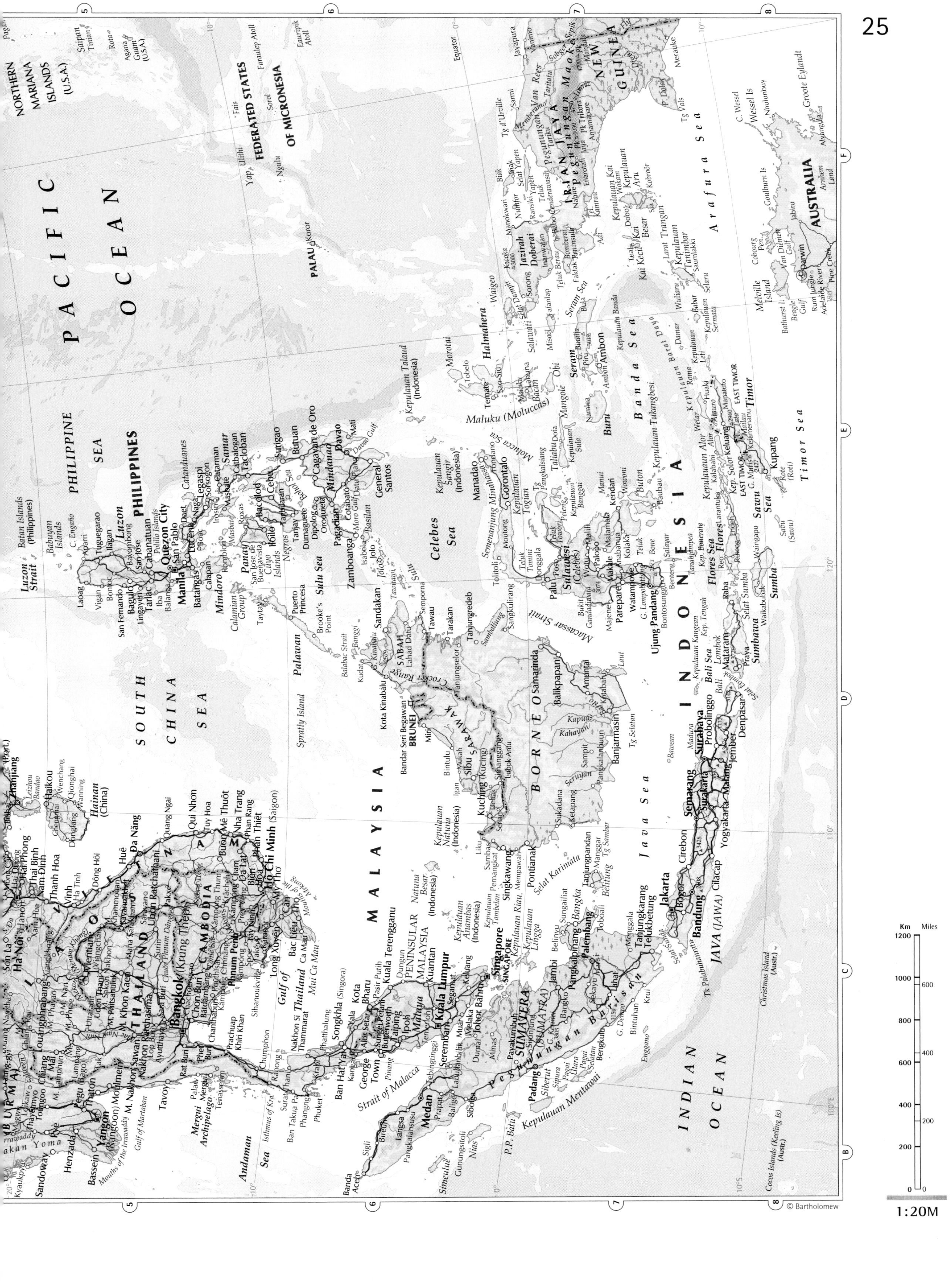
PACIFIC OCEAN
PHILIPPINE SEA
SOUTH CHINA SEA
PHILIPPINES
MALAYSIA
INDONESIA
BORNEO
CAMBODIA
THAILAND
Gulf of Thailand
Celebes Sea
Sulu Sea
Java Sea
Banda Sea
Flores Sea
Timor Sea
Arafura Sea
INDIAN OCEAN
AUSTRALIA
FEDERATED STATES OF MICRONESIA
NORTHERN MARIANA ISLANDS (U.S.A.)
PALAU
NEW GUINEA
Strait of Malacca
Macassar Strait
Andaman Sea
Manila
Bangkok (Krung Thep)
Singapore
Kuala Lumpur
Jakarta
Ho Chi Minh (Saigon)
Phnum Penh
Ha Noi (Hanoi)
Yangon (Rangoon)
Quezon City
Surabaya
Medan
Darwin
© Bartholomew
Km
Miles

1:20M

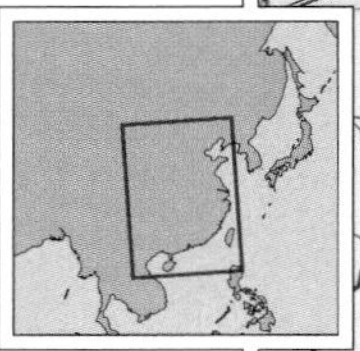

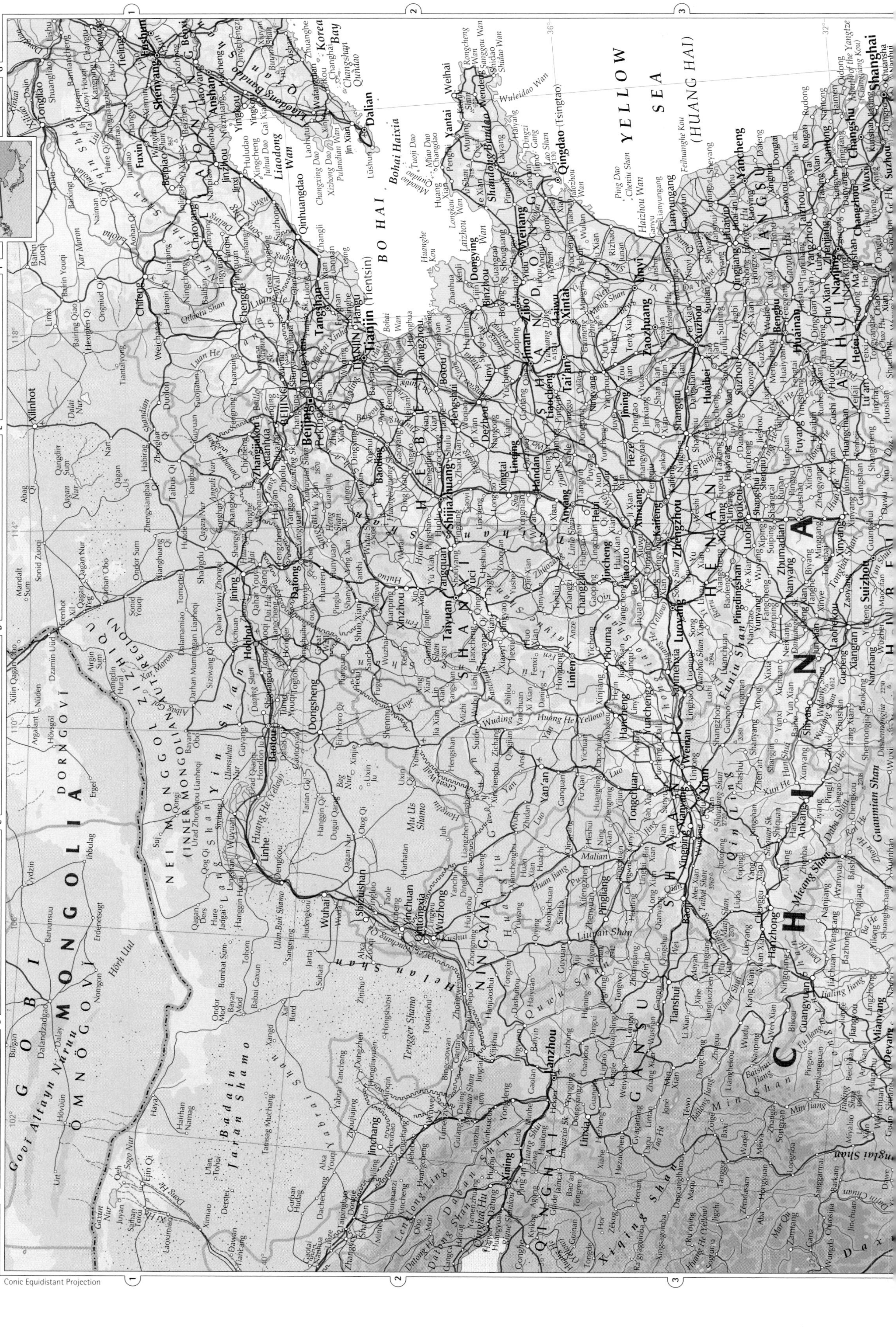

YELLOW SEA
(HUANG HAI)
BO HAI
Bohai Haixia
Liaodong Wan
Korea Bay
MONGOLIA
GOBI
DORNOGOVĬ
ÖMNÖGOVĬ
NEI MONGGOL ZIZHIQU
(INNER MONGOLIA AUTONOMOUS REGION)
CHINA
HEBEI
SHANXI
SHAANXI
HENAN
ANHUI
JIANGSU
SHANDONG
NINGXIA
GANSU
QINGHAI
LIAONING
Beijing
Tianjin
Shanghai
Dalian
Qingdao
Shenyang
Taiyuan
Shijiazhuang
Zhengzhou
Xi'an
Lanzhou
Xining
Yinchuan
Hohhot
Baotou
Jinan
Hefei
Nanjing
Huang He (Yellow)
Tengger Shamo
Badain Jaran Shamo
Mu Us Shamo
Qin Ling
Yin Shan
Helan Shan

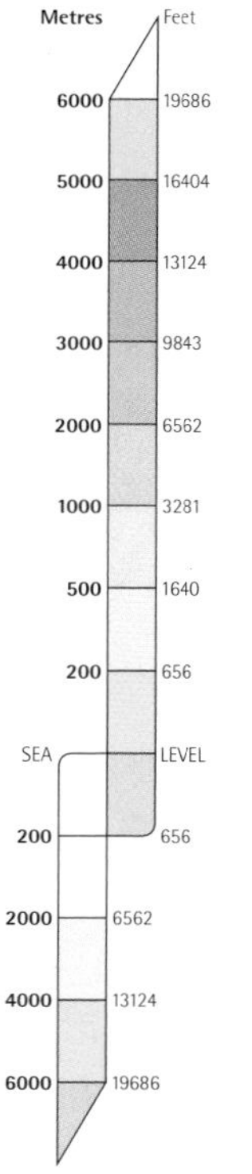

Metres
Feet
6000
19686
5000
16404
4000
13124
3000
9843
2000
6562
1000
3281
500
1640
200
656
SEA
LEVEL
200
656
2000
6562
4000
13124
6000
19686

Conic Equidistant Projection

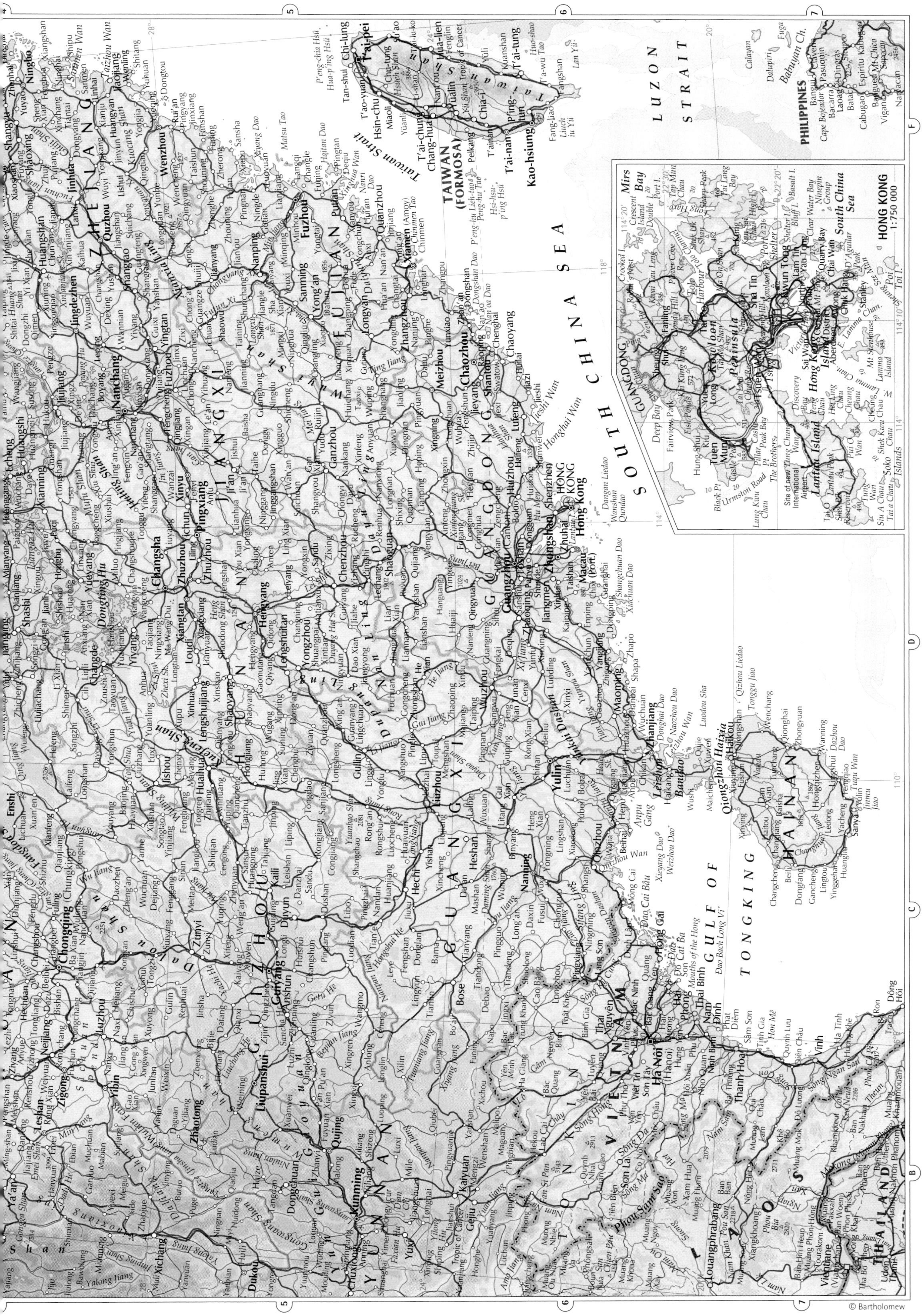
ZHEJIANG
FUJIAN
JIANGXI
HUNAN
GUIZHOU
YUNNAN
GUANGXI
GUANGDONG
HAINAN
VIETNAM
LAOS
THAILAND
TAIWAN (FORMOSA)
PHILIPPINES
SOUTH CHINA SEA
GULF OF TONGKING
LUZON STRAIT
Taiwan Strait
Changsha
Nanchang
Fuzhou
Kunming
Guiyang
Nanning
Guangzhou (Canton)
Hong Kong
Macau (Port.)
Chongqing (Chungking)
Hà Nôi (Hanoi)
T'ai-pei
Kao-hsiung
Xiamen (Amoy)
Haikou
HONG KONG
1:750 000
Km
Miles
© Bartholomew

1:7.5M

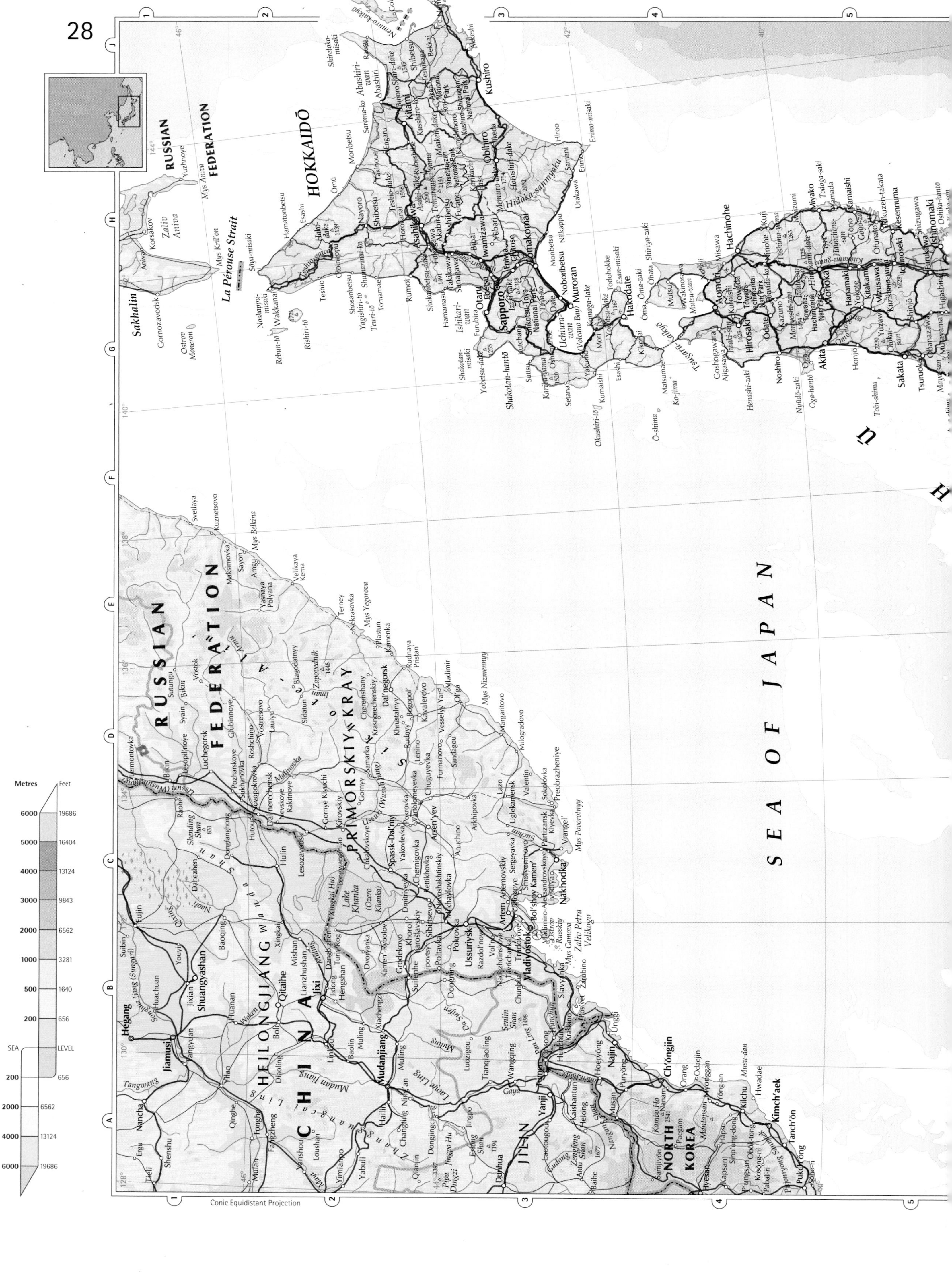

SEA OF JAPAN

RUSSIAN FEDERATION

HOKKAIDŌ

Sakhalin

La Pérouse Strait

PRIMORSKIY KRAY

HEILONGJIANG

CHINA

JILIN

NORTH KOREA

Metres / **Feet**

Metres	Feet
6000	19686
5000	16404
4000	13124
3000	9843
2000	6562
1000	3281
500	1640
200	656
SEA	LEVEL
200	656
2000	6562
4000	13124
6000	19686

Conic Equidistant Projection

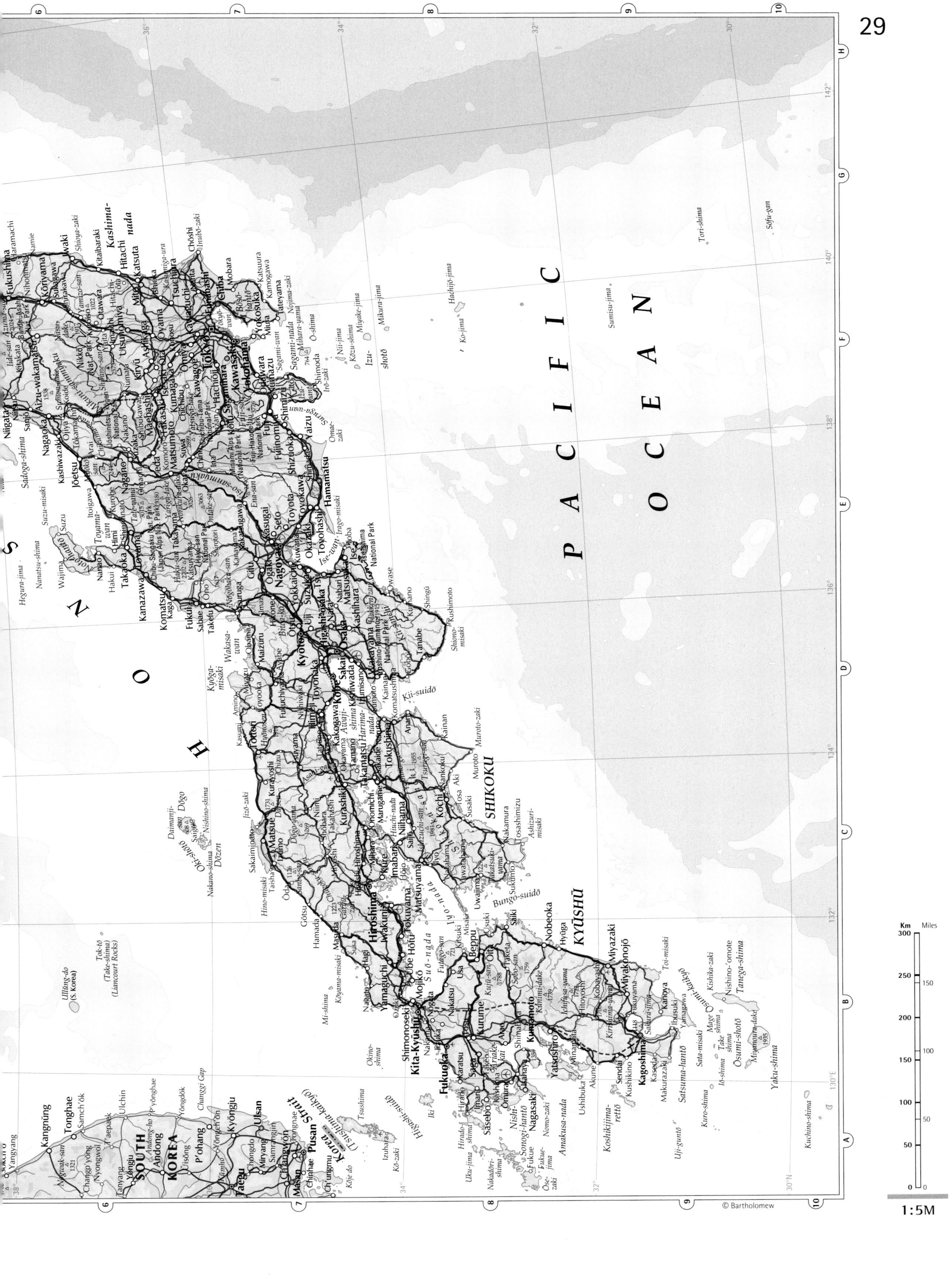

PACIFIC

OCEAN

© Bartholomew

1:5M

SHIKOKU
KYŪSHŪ
SOUTH KOREA
Korea Strait
Tōkyō
Yokohama
Kawasaki
Nagoya
Kyōto
Ōsaka
Kōbe
Hiroshima
Fukuoka
Kita-Kyūshū
Kagoshima
Nagasaki
Kumamoto
Miyazaki
Ōita
Matsuyama
Kōchi
Tokushima
Takamatsu
Okayama
Matsue
Tottori
Kanazawa
Toyama
Nagano
Niigata
Fukushima
Chiba
Shizuoka
Hamamatsu
Pusan
Taegu
Ulsan
Bungo-suidō
Kii-suidō
Tsushima
Yaku-shima
Tanega-shima
Hachijō-jima
Izu-shotō
Km
Miles
300
250
200
150
100
50
0

Northeast **CHINA, NORTH KOREA** and **SOUTH KOREA**

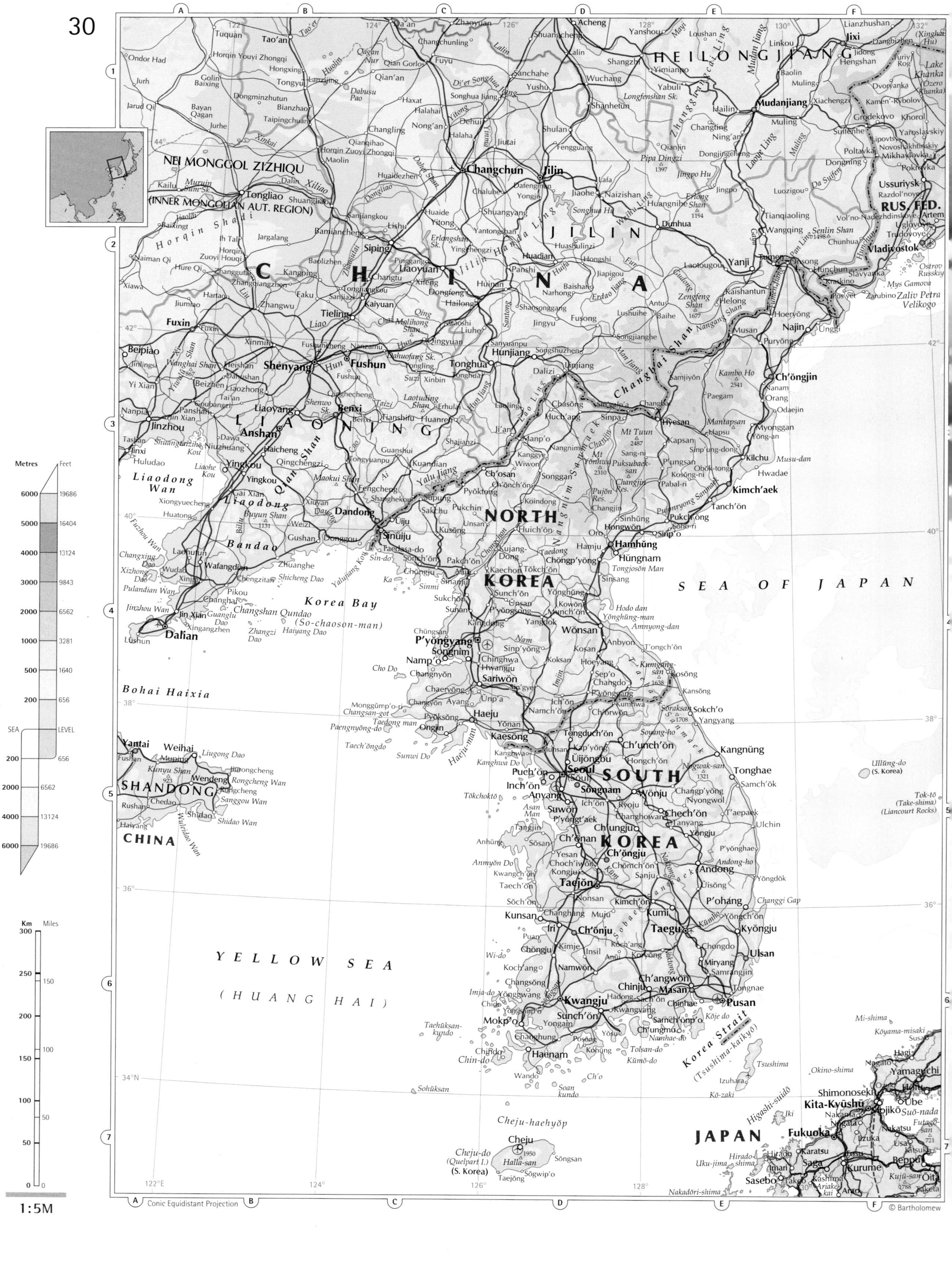

CHINA
NEI MONGGOL ZIZHIQU
(INNER MONGOLIAN AUT. REGION)
HEILONGJIANG
JILIN
LIAONING
SHANDONG
NORTH KOREA
SOUTH KOREA
JAPAN
RUS. FED.
SEA OF JAPAN
YELLOW SEA
(HUANG HAI)
Korea Bay
Liaodong Wan
Bohai Haixia
Korea Strait
(Tsushima-kaikyō)
Cheju-haehyŏp
Changchun
Jilin
Shenyang
Fushun
Anshan
Benxi
Liaoyang
Dalian
Dandong
Jixi
Mudanjiang
Vladivostok
Ussuriysk
Siping
Tonghua
P'yŏngyang
Namp'o
Sinŭiju
Hamhŭng
Hŭngnam
Wŏnsan
Ch'ŏngjin
Kimch'aek
Kaesŏng
Seoul
Inch'ŏn
Suwŏn
Taejŏn
Taegu
Pusan
Kwangju
Ulsan
Masan
Chinju
Mokp'o
Cheju
Halla-san
Tsushima
Kita-Kyūshū
Fukuoka
Shimonoseki
Ullŭng-do
(S. Korea)
Tok-tō
(Take-shima)
(Liancourt Rocks)
Metres
Feet
SEA
LEVEL
Km
Miles
1:5M
Conic Equidistant Projection
© Bartholomew

PHILIPPINES

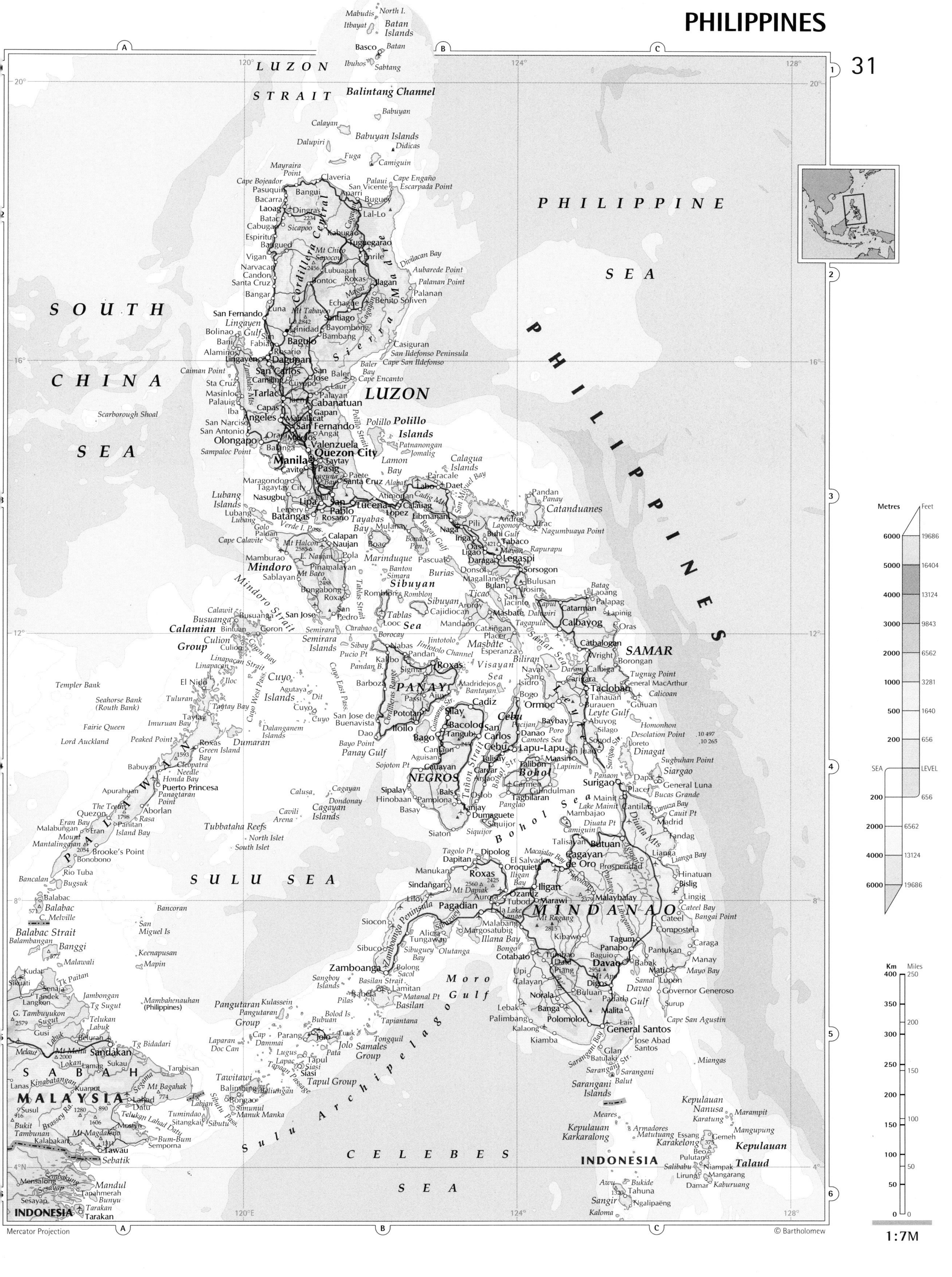
LUZON STRAIT
Balintang Channel
Batan Islands
Babuyan Islands
PHILIPPINE SEA
SOUTH CHINA SEA
PHILIPPINES
LUZON
Manila
Quezon City
Mindoro
Sibuyan Sea
Masbate
SAMAR
PANAY
NEGROS
Cebu
Bohol
Leyte
Bohol Sea
MINDANAO
SULU SEA
Moro Gulf
Sulu Archipelago
CELEBES SEA
Calamian Group
Cuyo Islands
PALAWAN
Puerto Princesa
Zamboanga
Davao
General Santos
SABAH
MALAYSIA
INDONESIA
Kepulauan Talaud
Metres
Feet
SEA LEVEL
Km
Miles
Mercator Projection
© Bartholomew
1:7M

THAILAND, CAMBODIA and Peninsular MALAYSIA

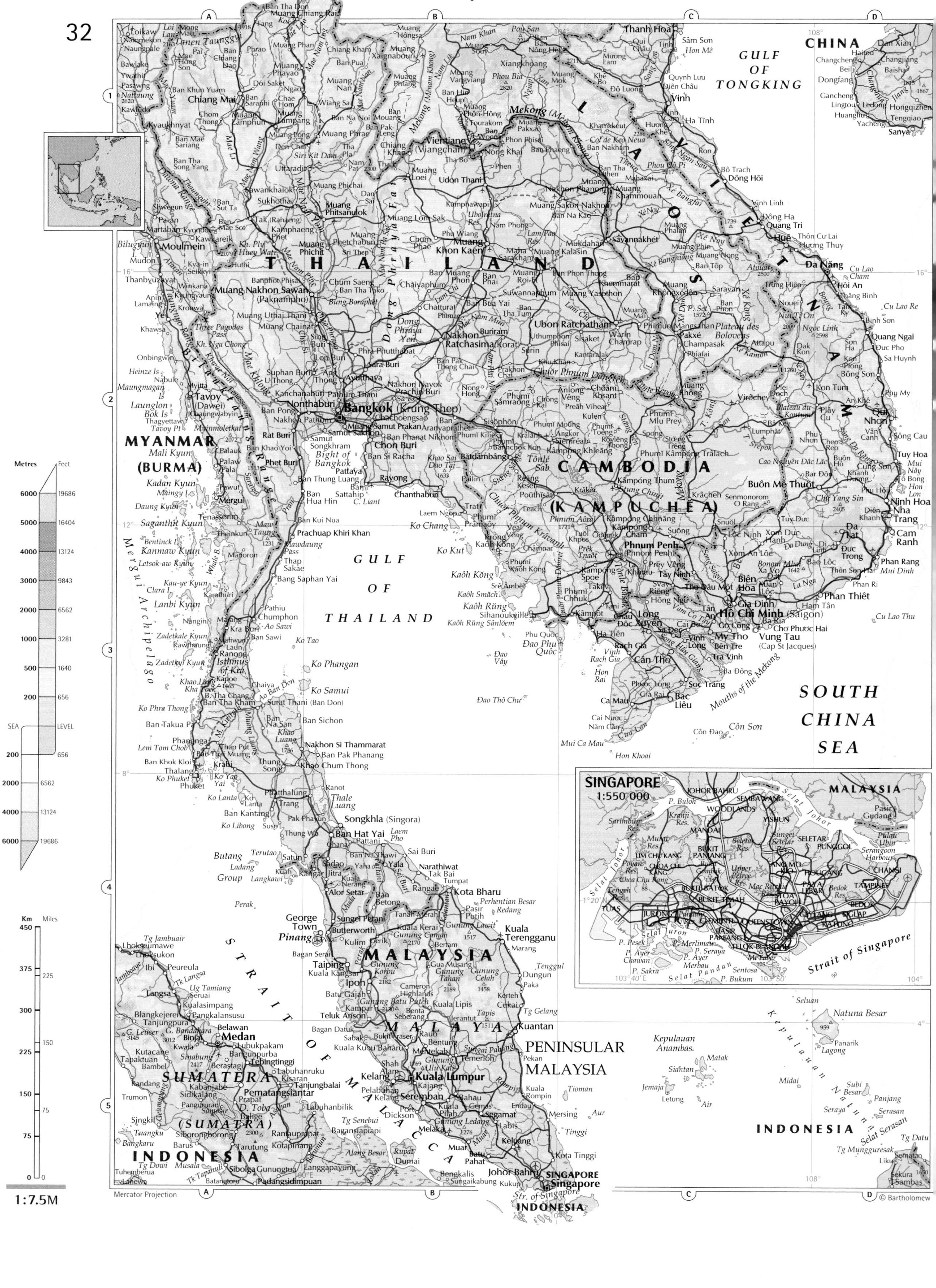

THAILAND
LAOS
VIETNAM
CAMBODIA
(KAMPUCHEA)
MYANMAR
(BURMA)
CHINA
MALAYSIA
MALAYA
PENINSULAR
MALAYSIA
SUMATERA
(SUMATRA)
INDONESIA
GULF OF TONGKING
GULF OF THAILAND
SOUTH CHINA SEA
STRAIT OF MALACCA
Mergui Archipelago
Bight of Bangkok
Bangkok (Krung Thep)
Vientiane (Viangchan)
Phnum Penh (Phnom Penh)
Hô Chi Minh (Saigon)
Kuala Lumpur
Singapore
Chiang Mai
Nakhon Ratchasima (Korat)
Ubon Ratchathani
Udon Thani
Khon Kaen
Hat Yai
Songkhla (Singora)
Pinang
Medan
Huê
Đa Nẵng
Mekong
Tônlé Sab
Mouths of the Mekong
SINGAPORE
1:550 000
JOHOR BAHRU
WOODLANDS
Strait of Singapore
Selat Johor
Metres
Feet
6000
5000
4000
3000
2000
1000
500
200
SEA
LEVEL
19686
16404
13124
9843
6562
3281
1640
656
Km
Miles
450
375
300
225
150
75
0
1:7.5M
Mercator Projection
© Bartholomew

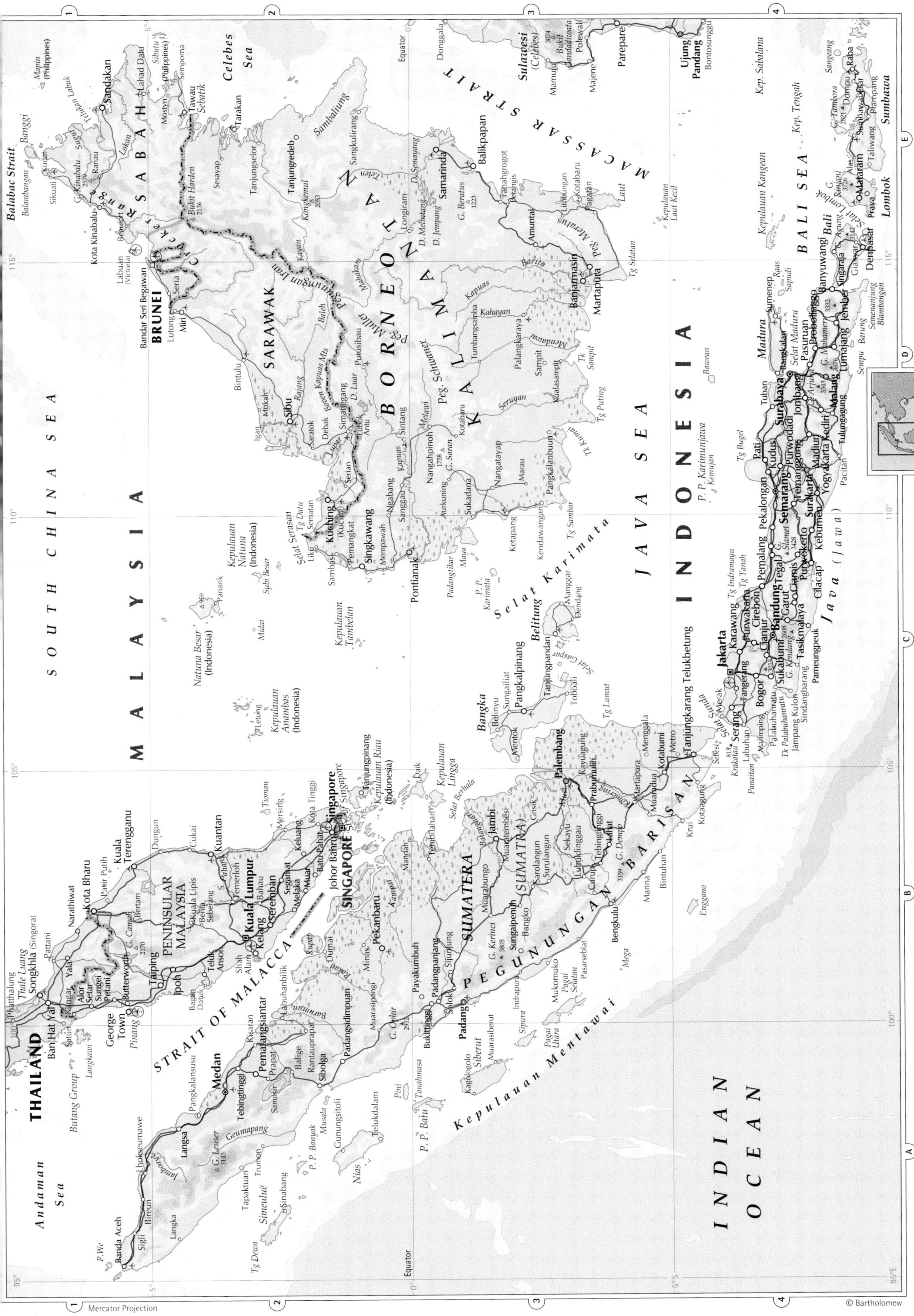
SOUTH CHINA SEA
MALAYSIA
INDONESIA
THAILAND
BRUNEI
SINGAPORE
SABAH
SARAWAK
BORNEO
KALIMANTAN
SUMATERA
(SUMATRA)
PENINSULAR MALAYSIA
JAVA SEA
INDIAN OCEAN
Andaman Sea
Celebes Sea
BALI SEA
MACASSAR STRAIT
STRAIT OF MALACCA
PEGUNUNGAN BARISAN
Kepulauan Mentawai
Selat Karimata
Java (Jawa)
Madura
Bali
Lombok
Sumbawa
Sulawesi (Celebes)
Bangka
Belitung
Kuala Lumpur
Jakarta
Medan
Palembang
Padang
Pekanbaru
Jambi
Bengkulu
Tanjungkarang Telukbetung
Bandung
Semarang
Surabaya
Yogyakarta
Malang
Pontianak
Kuching
Banjarmasin
Balikpapan
Samarinda
Kota Kinabalu
Sandakan
Bandar Seri Begawan
Johor Bahru
George Town
Kota Bharu
Kuala Terengganu
Kuantan
Ipoh
Banda Aceh
Ujung Pandang
Parepare
Denpasar
Mataram
Equator
Mercator Projection

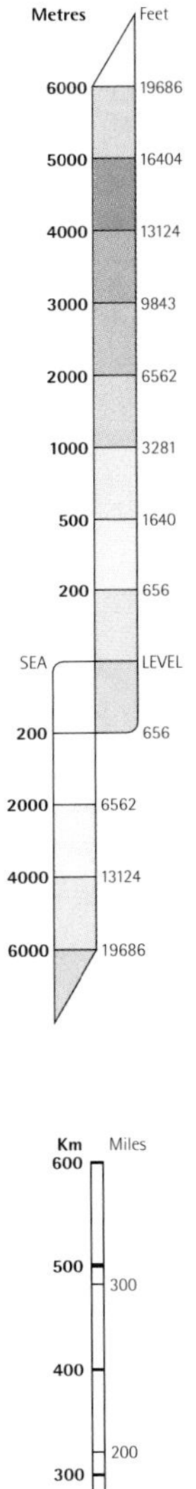
Metres
Feet
6000
19686
5000
16404
4000
13124
3000
9843
2000
6562
1000
3281
500
1640
200
656
SEA
LEVEL
200
656
2000
6562
4000
13124
6000
19686

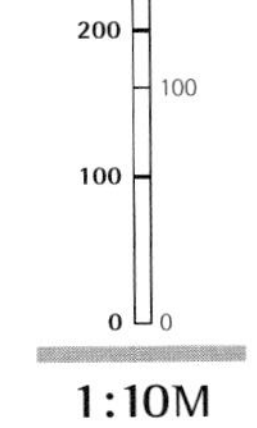
Km
Miles
600
500
300
400
200
300
200
100
100
0
0

1:10M

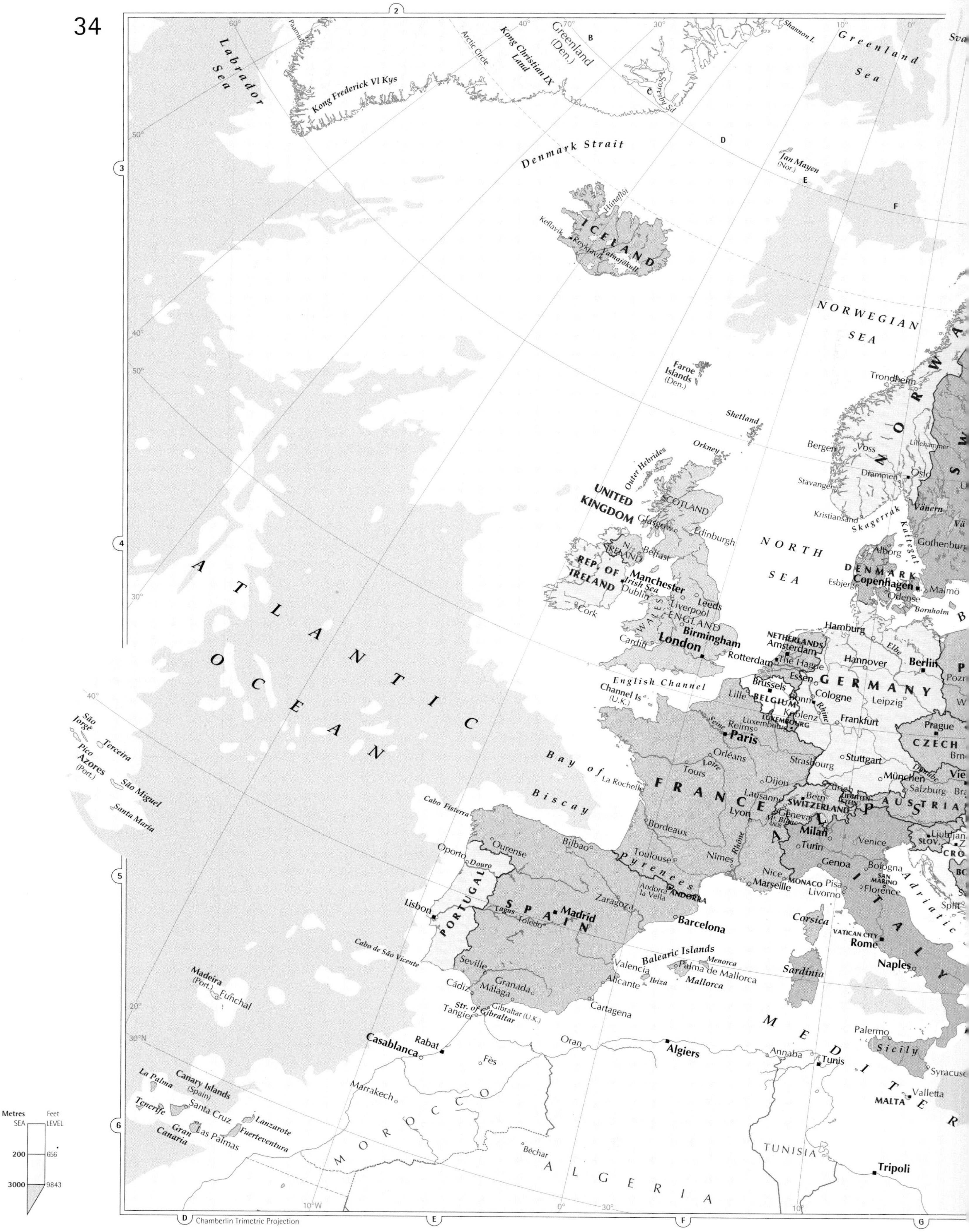

34

Labrador Sea

Paamiut

60°

Kong Frederick VI Kys

Greenland (Den.)

70°

40°

30°

Kong Christian IX Land

Arctic Circle

B

Shannon I.

10°

0°

Greenland Sea

50°

Scoresby Sd.

D

Denmark Strait

Jan Mayen (Nor.)

E

F

Keflavik Reykjavík *Vatnajökull*

Húnaflói

ICELAND

40°

NORWEGIAN SEA

Trondheim

N O R W A

50°

Faroe Islands (Den.)

Bergen Voss Lillehammer

S W E

Shetland

Stavanger

Oslo

Vä

Kristiansand Drammen

60°

Outer Hebrides Orkney

Vänern

Gothenburg

UNITED KINGDOM SCOTLAND

Glasgow Edinburgh

NORTH SEA

Ålborg

Kattegat

DENMARK Esbjerg **Copenhagen** Malmö

Bornholm

A T L A N T I C

IRELAND Belfast

REP OF IRELAND Irish Sea **Manchester** Leeds ENGLAND Liverpool

Dublin Cork

Hamburg

Odense

Pozn

Bremen

30°

Birmingham **London** **NETHERLANDS** Amsterdam Hannover **Berlin**

WALES Cardiff Rotterdam The Hague Elbe

English Channel Channel Is (U.K.) Brussels Essen **GERMANY**

Cologne Leipzig

BELGIUM Lille Bonn Frankfurt Prague

Seine **LUXEMBOURG** Koblenz **CZECH**

Reims Luxembourg Rhine

São Jorge

Terceira

Pico

Azores (Port.)

São Miguel

Santa Maria

O C E A N

Bay of Biscay

La Rochelle

Paris

Orléans

Loire

Tours

Dijon

Strasbourg

Stuttgart

München

Salzburg

Brn

Prague

Vie

A U S T R I A

Bra

40°

Cabo Fisterra

Oporto

Ourense

Douro

Bilbao

Toulouse

F R A N C E

Bordeaux

Nîmes

Lyon

Lausanne Bern

SWITZERLAND Geneva

Zürich Innsbruck

Mt Blanc 4808

Milan

Turin

Venice

SLOV.

Ljubljan.

Z

CRO

5

Lisbon

PORTUGAL

Tagus

SPAIN

Zaragoza

Andorra **ANDORRA** la Vella

Nice **MONACO** Marseille

Genoa

Livorno

Bologna

SAN MARINO

I T A L Y

Florence

Pisa

Adriatic

Split

BC

Toledo **Madrid**

Barcelona

Corsica

VATICAN CITY **Rome**

Sardinia

Naples

Cabo de São Vicente

Seville

Granada

Valencia

Balearic Islands

Menorca

Palma de Mallorca

Mallorca

20°

Madeira (Port.)

Funchal

Cádiz Málaga Alicante Ibiza

Cartagena

M E D I T E R

Palermo

Sicily

Str. of Gibraltar Gibraltar (U.K.)

Tangier

30°N

Casablanca Rabat

Oran

Algiers

Annaba Tunis

Syracuse

Fès

MALTA Valletta

La Palma **Canary Islands** (Spain)

Marrakech

M O R O C C O

R

6

Tenerife Santa Cruz Lanzarote

Gran Canaria Las Palmas Fuerteventura

Béchar

TUNISIA

A L G E R I A

Tripoli

10°W

0°

30°

10°

Metres Feet

SEA LEVEL

200 656

3000 9843

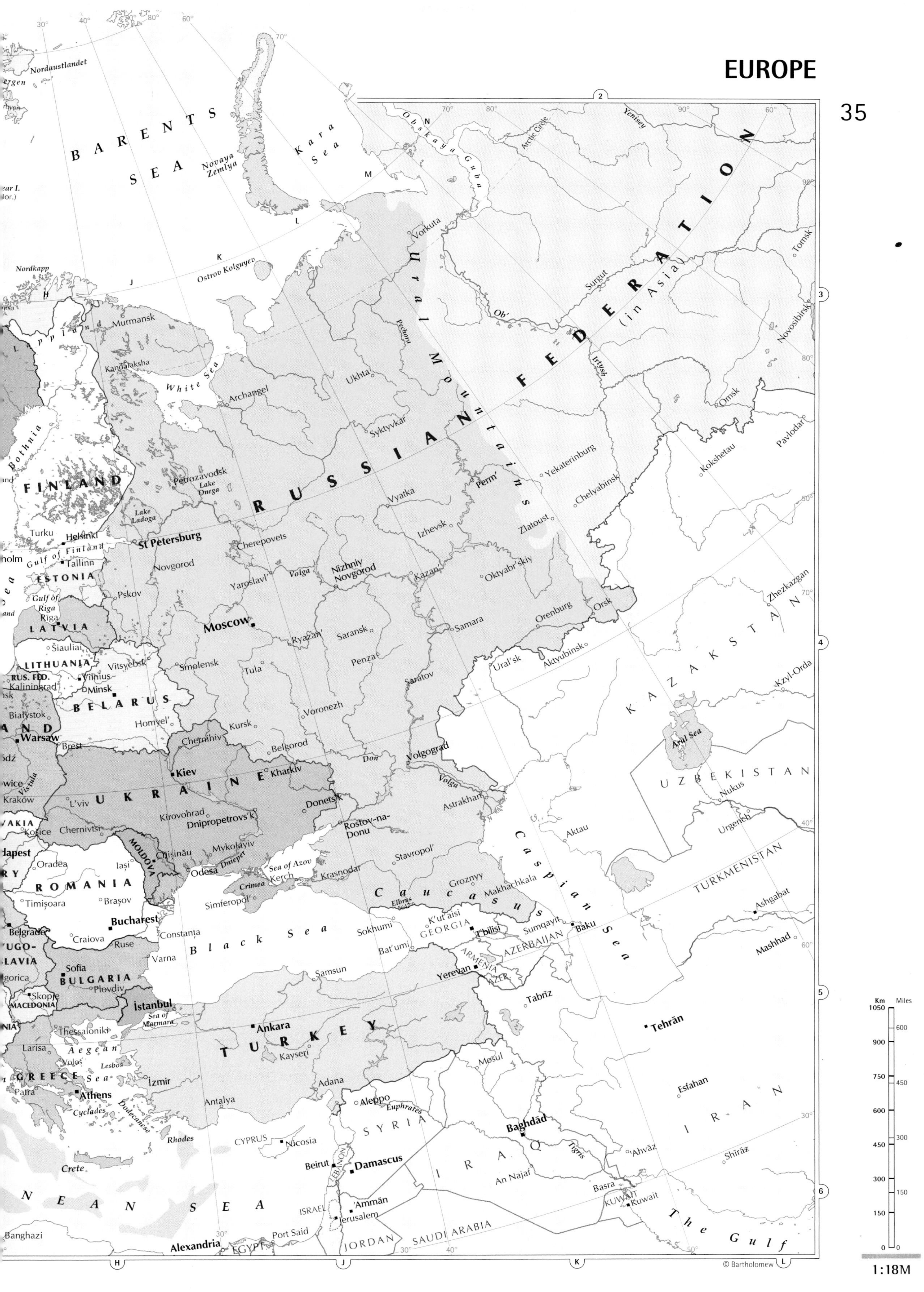

BARENTS SEA

Nordaustlandet

Kara Sea

Novaya Zemlya

Nordkapp

Ostrov Kolguyev

Vorkuta

Murmansk

Kandalaksha

White Sea

Archangel

Ukhta

RUSSIAN FEDERATION (in Asia)

Obskaya Guba

Arctic Circle

Yenisey

Surgut

Tomsk

Ob'

Irtysh

Novosibirsk

Petrozavodsk

Lake Onega

Syktyvkar

Yekaterinburg

Omsk

Pavlodar

FINLAND

Lake Ladoga

Vyatka

Perm'

Chelyabinsk

Kokshetau

Turku

Helsinki

St Petersburg

Cherepovets

Izhevsk

Zlatoust

Kzyl-Orda

Tallinn

ESTONIA

Novgorod

Yaroslavl'

Volga

Nizhniy Novgorod

Kazan

Oktyabr'skiy

Orenburg

Orsk

Zhezkazgan

Gulf of Finland

Pskov

Moscow

Ryazan'

Saransk

Samara

Aral Sea

K A Z A K S T A N

Gulf of Riga

Riga

LATVIA

Šiauliai

Smolensk

Tula

Penza

Saratov

Ural'sk

Aktyubinsk

LITHUANIA

Vilnius

Vitsyebsk

Voronezh

U Z B E K I S T A N

RUS. FED.

Kaliningrad

Minsk

BELARUS

Homyel'

Kursk

Belgorod

Don

Volgograd

Nukus

Warsaw

Białystok

Chernihiv

Volga

Astrakhan

Urgench

Brest

Kiev

Kharkiv

Łódź

Vistula

UKRAINE

Aktau

Kraków

L'viv

Kirovohrad

Dnipropetrovs'k

Donets'k

Rostov-na-Donu

C a s p i a n   S e a

TURKMENISTAN

VAKIA

Košice

Chernivtsi

MOLDOVA

Chişinău

Mykolayiv

Dnieper

Krasnodar

Stavropol'

Groznyy

Makhachkala

Ashgabat

dapest

Oradea

Iaşi

Odesa

Kerch

Crimea

C a u c a s u s

RY

ROMANIA

Braşov

Simferopol'

Elbrus

Mashhad

Timişoara

Bucharest

Sokhumi

K'ut'aisi

GEORGIA

Tbilisi

Sumqayıt

Baku

Belgrade

Craiova

Ruse

Constanţa

Bat'umi

ARMENIA

AZERBAIJAN

UGO-SLAVIA

Varna

B l a c k   S e a

Yerevan

AZER.

gorica

Sofia

BULGARIA

Plovdiv

Samsun

Tabrīz

Tehrān

Skopje

MACEDONIA

istanbul

Sea of Marmara

I R A N

NIA

Thessaloniki

Ankara

T U R K E Y

Larisa

Volos

Lesbos

Aegean

Kayseri

Mosul

Esfahan

GREECE

İzmir

Sea

Mus

Shirāz

Patra

Athens

Adana

Cyclades

Dodecanese

Antalya

Aleppo

Euphrates

Baghdād

Crete

Rhodes

SYRIA

I R A Q

Ahvāz

CYPRUS

Nicosia

Tigris

Banghazi

Beirut

Damascus

An Najaf

Basra

LEBANON

ISRAEL

'Ammān

JORDAN

SAUDI ARABIA

Kuwait

N E A N   S E A

Jerusalem

The Gulf

Alexandria

Port Said

EGYPT

Km   Miles

1050

900   600

750   450

600

450   300

300

150

150

0   0

1:18M

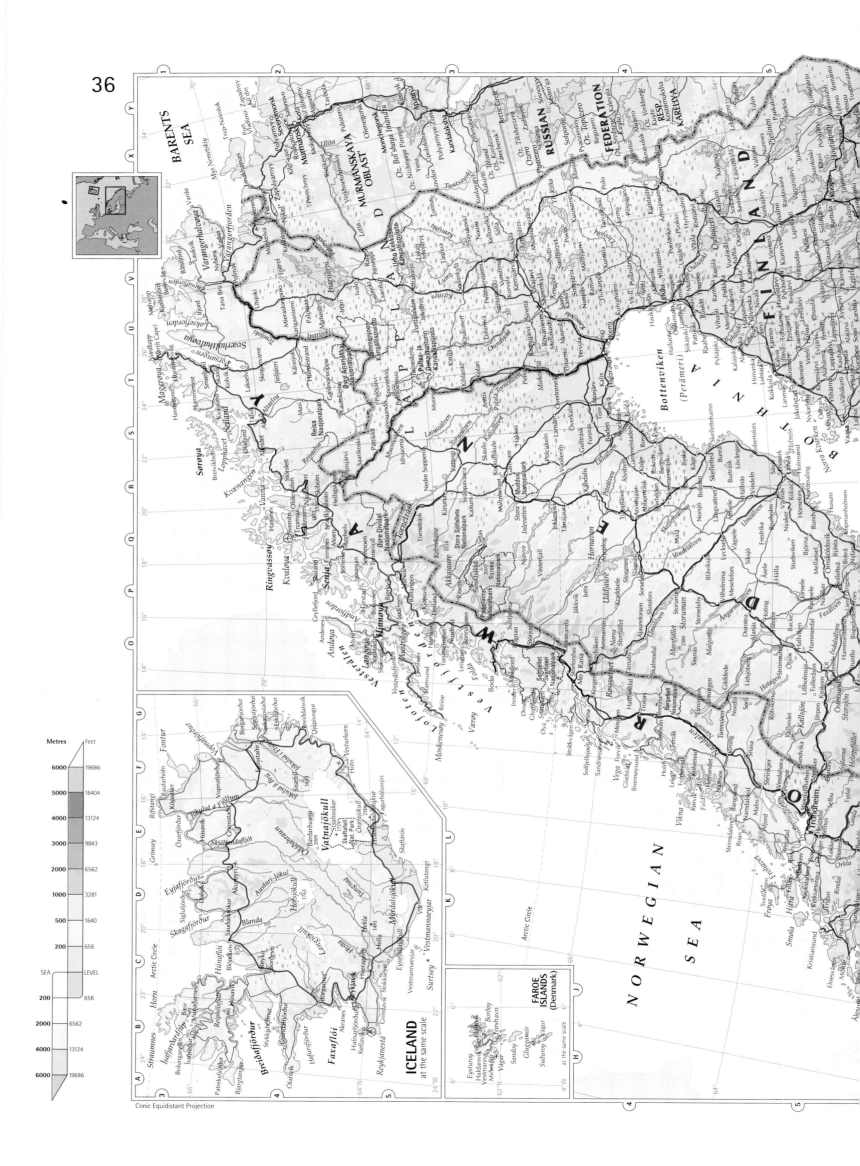

BARENTS SEA

MURMANSKAYA OBLAST

RUSSIAN FEDERATION

RESP. KARELYA

FINLAND

LAPPLAND

Bottenviken (Perämeri)

NORRBOTTEN

Soroya

Ringvassoy
Kvaloya
Senja
Andoya
Vesteralen
Lofoten

NORWEGIAN SEA

ICELAND
at the same scale

Vatnajökull

Faxaflói

Breiðafjörður

Arctic Circle

FAROE ISLANDS (Denmark)
at the same scale

Metres | Feet
6000 | 19686
5000 | 16404
4000 | 13124
3000 | 9843
2000 | 6562
1000 | 3281
500 | 1640
200 | 656
SEA | LEVEL
200 | 656
2000 | 6562
4000 | 13124
6000 | 19686

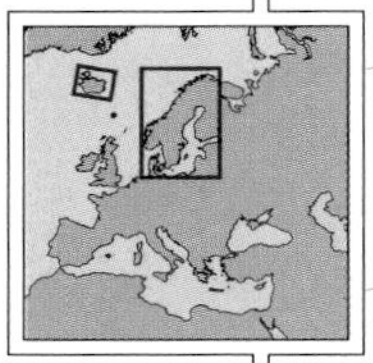

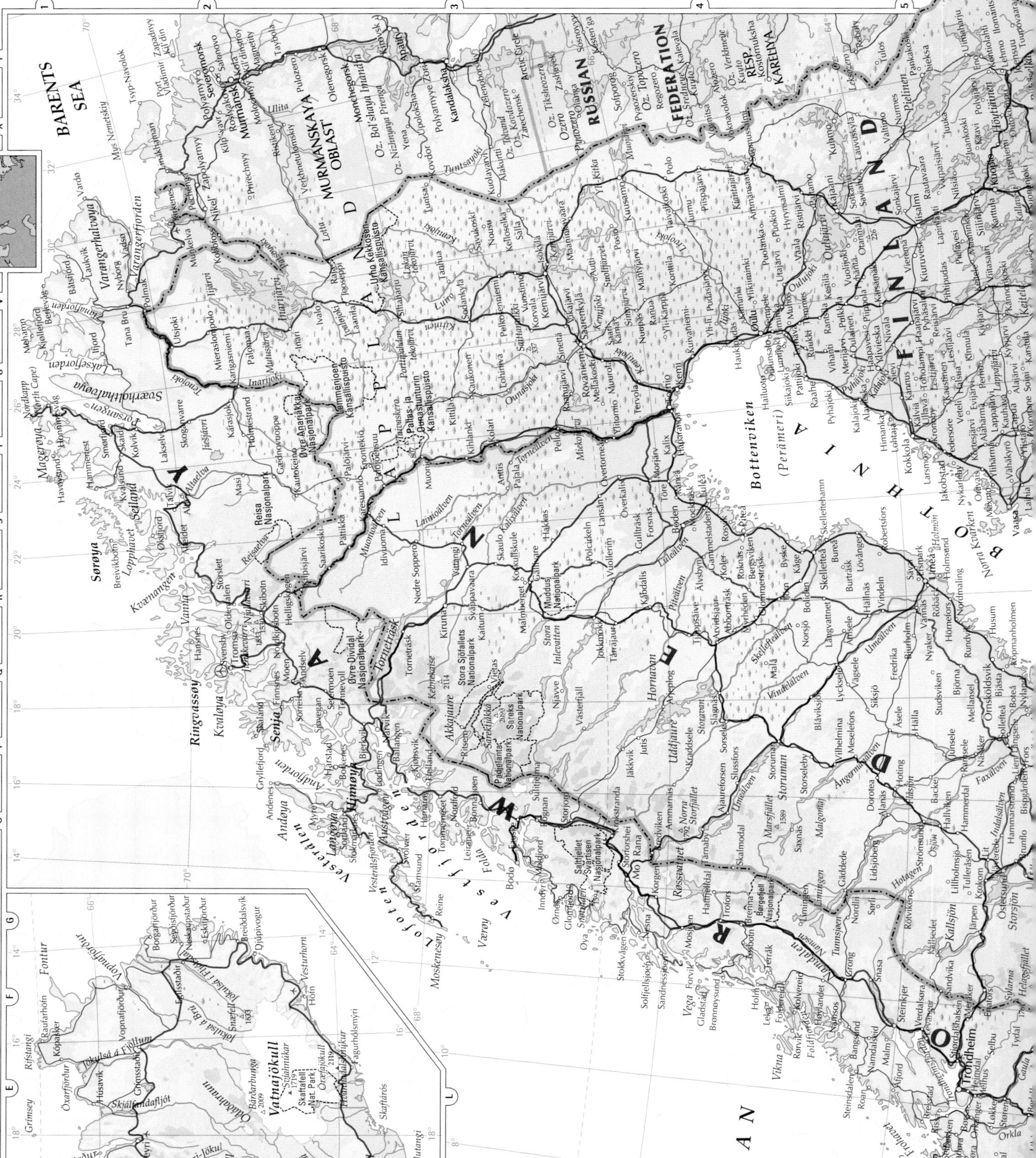

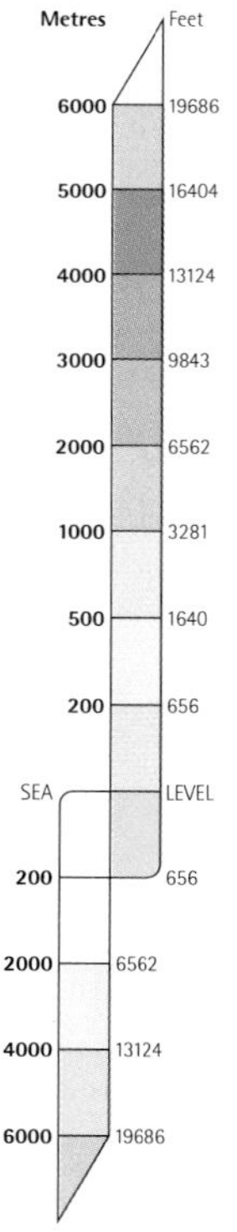

Conic Equidistant Projection

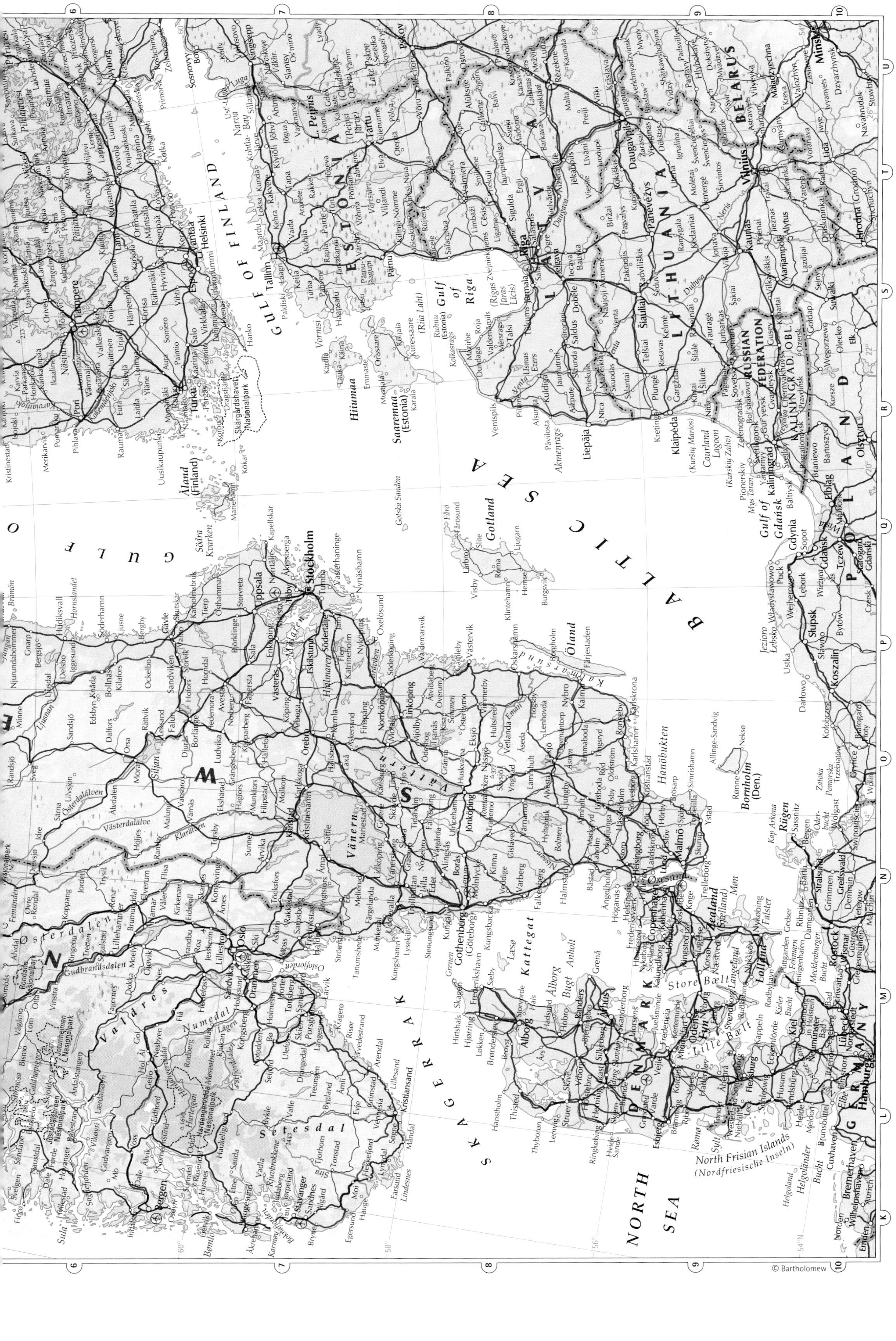

1:5M

© Bartholomew

NORTH SEA

IRISH SEA

Conic Equidistant Projection

Metres	Feet
6000	19686
5000	16404
4000	13124
3000	9843
2000	6562
1000	3281
500	1640
200	656
SEA	LEVEL
200	656
2000	6562
4000	13124
6000	19686

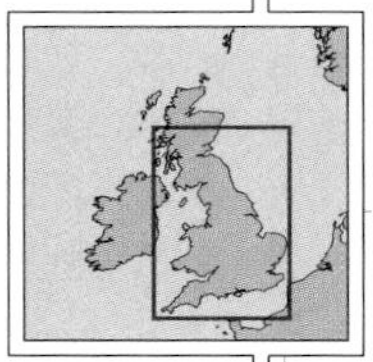

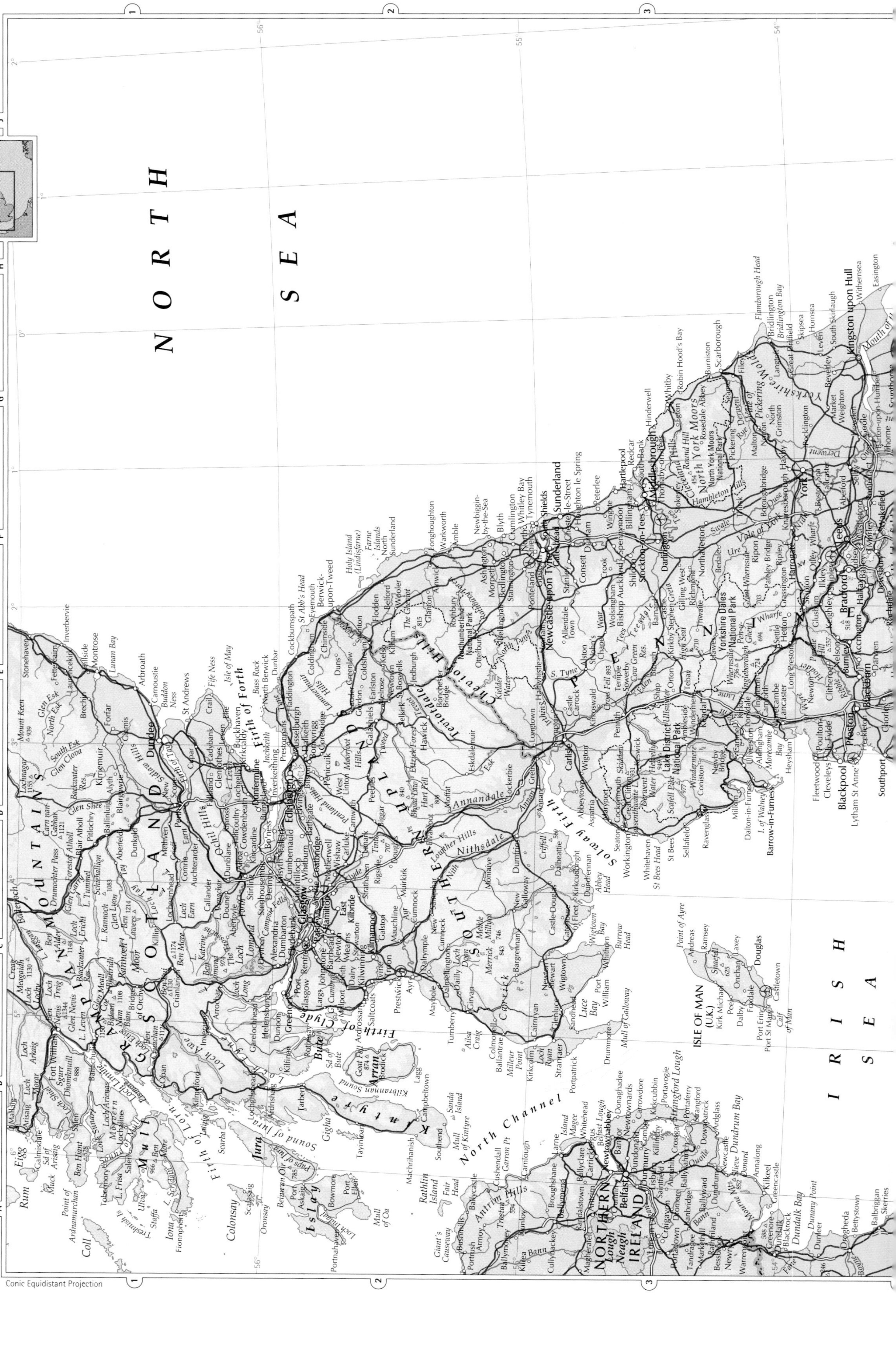

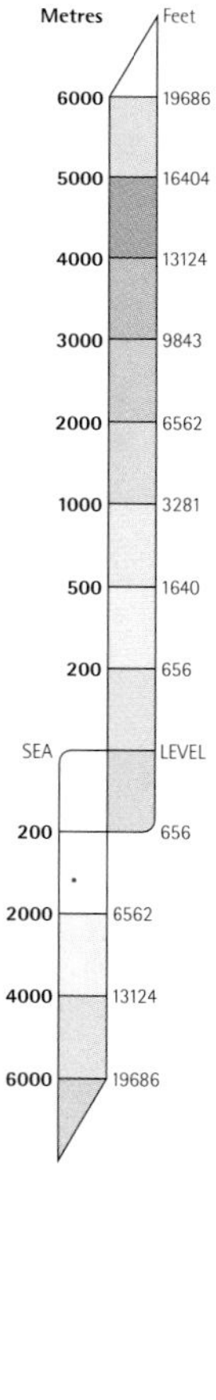

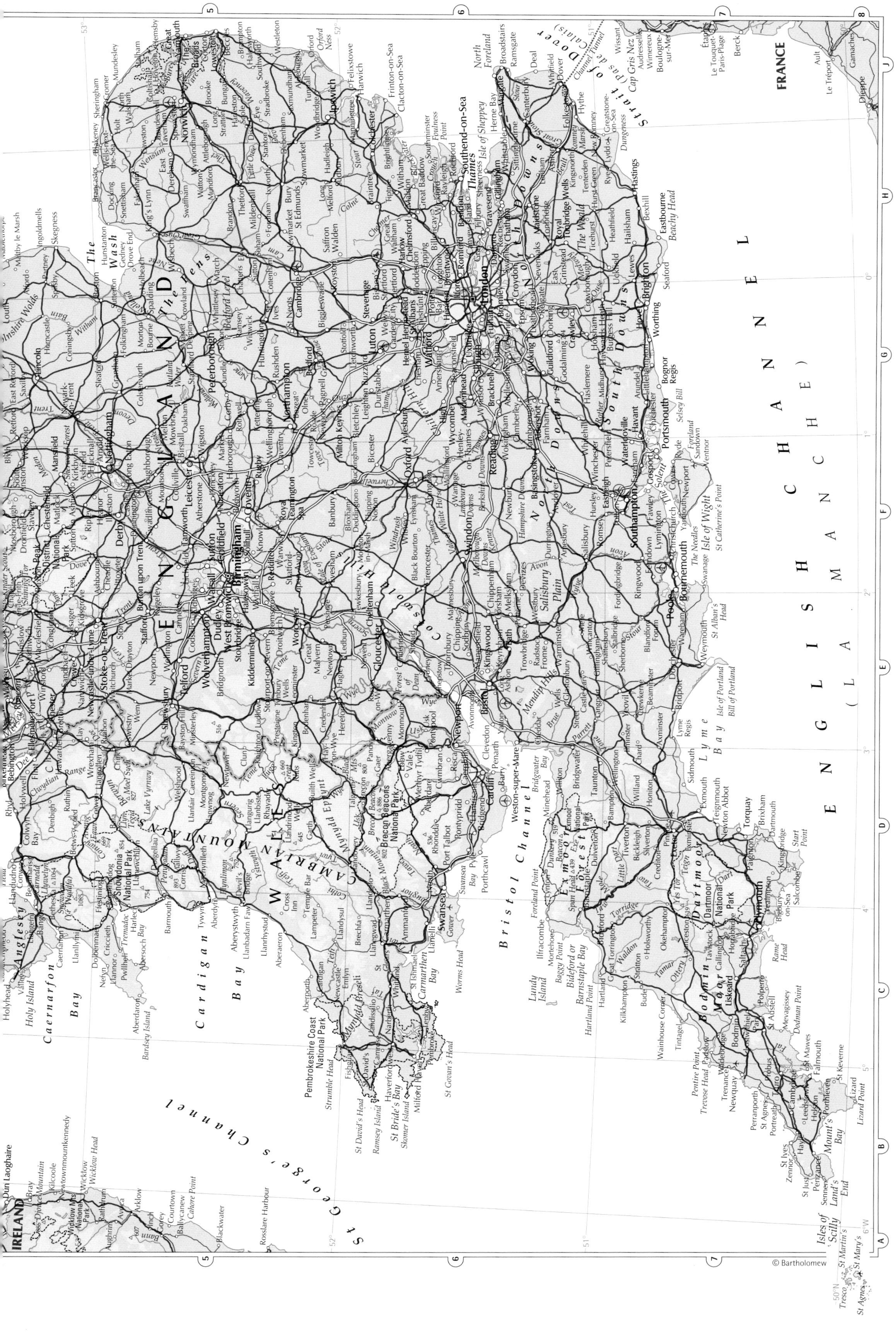

ENGLAND
WALES
IRELAND
FRANCE
ENGLISH CHANNEL
(LA MANCHE)
Bristol Channel
St George's Channel
Cardigan Bay
Caernarfon Bay
Lyme Bay
Strait of Dover (Pas de Calais)
CAMBRIAN MOUNTAINS
The Fens
The Wash
North Downs
South Downs
Cotswold Hills
Salisbury Plain
Exmoor Forest
Dartmoor National Park
Bodmin Moor
Brecon Beacons National Park
Snowdonia National Park
Pembrokeshire Coast National Park
Isle of Wight
Isles of Scilly
Anglesey
London
Birmingham
Bristol
Cardiff
Swansea
Southampton
Portsmouth
Brighton
Oxford
Cambridge
Norwich
Ipswich
Nottingham
Leicester
Coventry
Northampton
Peterborough
Gloucester
Plymouth
Exeter
Bournemouth
Reading
Southend-on-Sea
Stoke-on-Trent
Wolverhampton
© Bartholomew

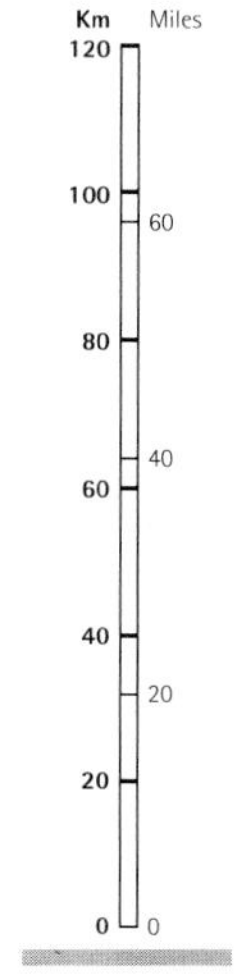

Km
Miles
120
100
80
60
40
20
0
60
40
20
0

1:2M

SCOTLAND

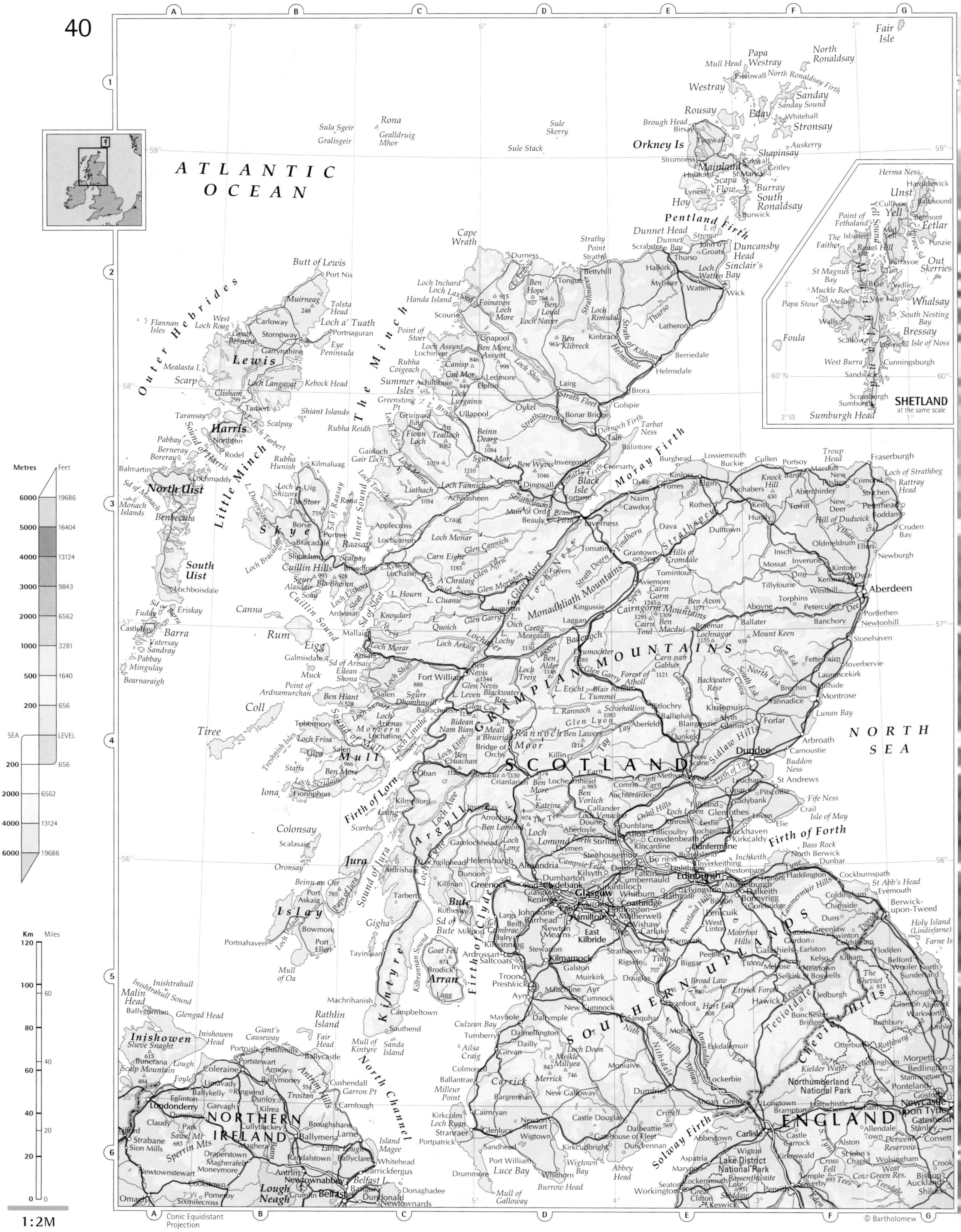
Metres
Feet
6000
19686
5000
16404
4000
13124
3000
9843
2000
6562
1000
3281
500
1640
200
656
SEA
LEVEL
200
656
2000
6562
4000
13124
6000
19686
Km
Miles
120
100
60
80
60
40
40
20
20
0
0
1:2M
Conic Equidistant Projection
© Bartholomew
ATLANTIC OCEAN
NORTH SEA
Fair Isle
North Ronaldsay
Papa Westray
Mull Head
Pierowall
North Ronaldsay Firth
Westray
Sanday
Sanday Sound
Rousay
Eday
Whitehall
Stronsay
Brough Head
Birsay
Orkney Is
Auskerry
Tingwall
Kirkwall
Shapinsay
Stromness
Mainland
Gritley
Houton
St Mary's
Scapa Flow
Burray
South Ronaldsay
Lyness
Hoy
Burwick
Pentland Firth
Dunnet Head
I. of Stroma
Dunnet Bay
John o' Groats
Duncansby Head
Scrabster
Thurso
Sinclair's Bay
Strathy Point
Strathy
Cape Wrath
Durness
Bettyhill
Tongue
Halkirk
Mybster
Watten
Loch Watten
Wick
Ben Hope
Ben Loyal
Loch Naver
Loch More
Foinaven
Loch Inchard
Loch Laxford
Handa Island
Scourie
Loch Rimsdal
Strathnaver
Kinbrace
Ben Klibreck
Strath of Kildonan
Helmsdale
Berriedale
Latheron
Sula Sgeir
Rona
Gralisgeir
Gealldruig Mhor
Sule Skerry
Sule Stack
Butt of Lewis
Port Nis
Tolsta Head
Muirneag
Flannan Isles
West Loch Roag
Carloway
Stornoway
Great Bernera
Garrynahine
Loch a' Tuath
Portnaguran
Eye Peninsula
Lewis
Outer Hebrides
Mealasta I.
Scarp
Loch Langavat
Kebock Head
Clisham
Tarbert
Harris
Taransay
Sound of Harris
Pabbay
Berneray
Boreray
Northton
Rodel
East Loch Tarbert
Scalpay
Shiant Islands
Rubha Reidh
Rubha Hunish
Kilmaluag
Balmartin
Lochmaddy
North Uist
Sd of Monach
Monach Islands
Benbecula
Little Minch
The Minch
Point of Stoer
Lochinver
Loch Assynt
Ben More Assynt
Canisp
Cul Mor
Ledmore
Achiltibuie
Elphin
Unapool
Loch Shin
Lairg
Rubha Coigeach
Summer Isles
Greenstone Pt
Gruinard Bay
Loch Broom
Ullapool
Loch Lurgainn
Oykel
Strath Fleet
Golspie
Brora
Bonar Bridge
Strathcarron
Dornoch Firth
Tain
Tarbat Ness
Balintore
Cromarty
Invergordon
Moray Firth
Fionn Loch
An Teallach
Beinn Dearg
Loch Ewe
Gairloch
Gair Loch
Loch Maree
Sgurr Mor
Ben Wyvis
Loch Fannich
Garve
Dingwall
Black Isle
Fortrose
Liathach
Achnasheen
Loch Torridon
Inner Sound
Strathconon
Muir of Ord
Beauly
Beauly Firth
Inverness
Uig
Loch Snizort
The Storr
Sd of Raasay
Rona
Raasay
Skye
Portree
Borve
Bracadale
Loch Bracadale
Sligachan
Cuillin Hills
Sgurr Alasdair
Soay
Bla Bheinn
Broadford
Scalpay
Kyle of Lochalsh
Applecross
Lochcarron
Craig
Loch Monar
Glen Cannich
Carn Eighe
Glen Affric
Glen Shiel
A'Chralaig
Glen Moriston
Glen More
Loch Ness
Foyers
Fort Augustus
L. Hourn
L. Cluanie
Knoydart
Loch Quoich
Glen Garry
L. Oich
L. Lochy
Creag Meagaidh
Loch Arkaig
Lochaber
Loch Morar
Loch Eishort
Sd of Sleat
Sleat
Ardvasar
Mallaig
Arisaig
Sd of Arisaig
Cuillin Sound
South Uist
Lochboisdale
Sd of Barra
Eriskay
Fuday
Castlebay
Barra
Vatersay
Sandray
Pabbay
Mingulay
Bearnaraigh
Canna
Rum
Eigg
Galmisdale
Muck
Eilean Shona
Point of Ardnamurchan
Loch Shiel
Salen
Ben Hiant
Fort William
Ben Nevis
Glen Nevis
Sgurr Dhomhnuill
L. Leven
Blackwater Res.
Loch Treig
Ballachulish
Glen Coe
Bidean Nam Bian
Meall a'Bhuiridh
Coll
Tiree
Tobermory
Loch Sunart
Morvern
Lochaline
Sound of Mull
Loch Linnhe
Lismore
Treshnish Isles
Loch Frisa
Salen
Ulva
Mull
Staffa
Ben More
Loch Scridain
Iona
Fionnphort
Oban
Loch Etive
Ben Cruachan
Bridge of Orchy
Rannoch Moor
Ben Lui
Crianlarich
Firth of Lorn
Kilmelford
Luing
Scarba
Colonsay
Scalasaig
Oronsay
Loch Awe
Argyll
Inveraray
Arrochar
Ben Lomond
Loch Lomond
Loch Long
Garelochhead
Lochgilphead
Helensburgh
Alexandria
Dumbarton
Jura
Sound of Jura
Paps of Jura
Beinn an Oir
Ardrishaig
Loch Fyne
Kilfinan
Dunoon
Greenock
Port Glasgow
Tarbert
Port Askaig
Islay
Loch Indaal
Bowmore
Port Ellen
Portnahaven
Gigha
Tayinloan
Mull of Oa
Kintyre
Kilbrannan Sound
Campbeltown
Southend
Machrihanish
Mull of Kintyre
Sanda Island
Bute
Rothesay
Sd of Bute
Millport
Great Cumbrae
Largs
Arran
Goat Fell
Brodick
Lagg
Firth of Clyde
Ardrossan
Saltcoats
Irvine
Troon
Prestwick
Ayr
Maybole
Culzean Bay
Turnberry
Ailsa Craig
Girvan
Colmonell
Ballantrae
Milleur Point
Cairnryan
Kirkcolm
Loch Ryan
Stranraer
Portpatrick
Glenluce
Sandhead
Port William
Luce Bay
Drummore
Mull of Galloway
Whithorn
Burrow Head
Wigtown
Wigtown Bay
Newton Stewart
Kirkcudbright
Gatehouse of Fleet
Castle Douglas
Dalbeattie
Abbey Head
Criffell
Dumfries
Solway Firth
Annan
Gretna
Lockerbie
Moffat
Eskdalemuir
Annandale
Nithsdale
Lowther Hills
Sanquhar
Carrick
Merrick
Loch Doon
Dalmellington
Dalrymple
Cumnock
New Cumnock
Mauchline
Kilmarnock
Galston
Muirkirk
Douglas
Tinto
Lanark
Carluke
Wishaw
Motherwell
Hamilton
East Kilbride
Strathaven
Newton Mearns
Barrhead
Paisley
Renfrew
Johnstone
Beith
Kilwinning
Stewarton
Glasgow
Clydebank
Coatbridge
Kirkintilloch
Cumbernauld
Kilsyth
Campsie Fells
Falkirk
Denny
Stenhousemuir
Stirling
Drymen
Aberfoyle
Doune
Dunblane
Callander
Loch Katrine
The Trossachs
Loch Venachar
Ben Vorlich
Ben More
Lochearnhead
Comrie
Crieff
Auchterarder
Loch Earn
Killin
Ben Lawers
Loch Tay
Aberfeldy
Glen Lyon
Schiehallion
L. Rannoch
L. Tummel
Blair Atholl
Pitlochry
Dunkeld
Blairgowrie
Forest of Atholl
Glen Garry
Drumochter Pass
Ben Alder
Loch Ericht
Loch Laggan
Laggan
Badenoch
Monadhliath Mountains
Kingussie
Aviemore
Cairngorm Mountains
Cairn Gorm
Cairn Toul
Ben Macdui
Ben Avon
Braemar
Lochnagar
Carn nan Gabhar
Glen Shee
Backwater Resr
Glen Clova
South Esk
North Esk
Glen Esk
Mount Keen
Ballater
Aboyne
Banchory
Peterculter
Dee
Don
Kemnay
Westhill
Torphins
Tillyfourie
Aberdeen
Portlethen
Newtonhill
Stonehaven
Fettercairn
Inverbervie
Laurencekirk
Edzell
Hillside
Brechin
Montrose
Kirriemuir
Alyth
Glamis
Forfar
Arbroath
Carnoustie
Lunan Bay
Dundee
Buddon Ness
Sidlaw Hills
Firth of Tay
New Scone
Perth
Methven
St Andrews
Leuchars
Cupar
Ladybank
Pitscottie
Fife Ness
Crail
Isle of May
Elie
Leven
Glenrothes
Falkland
Leslie
Kinross
Loch Leven
Ochil Hills
Tillicoultry
Alloa
Kincardine
Cowdenbeath
Dunfermline
Lochgelly
Buckhaven
Kirkcaldy
Burntisland
Inverkeithing
Firth of Forth
Bass Rock
North Berwick
Dunbar
Inchkeith
Prestonpans
Tranent
Haddington
Edinburgh
Musselburgh
Dalkeith
Bonnyrigg
Gorebridge
Penicuik
West Linton
Moorfoot Hills
Pentland Hills
Livingston
Bathgate
Linlithgow
Bo'ness
Whitburn
Peebles
Galashiels
Melrose
Selkirk
St Boswells
Kelso
Earlston
Gordon
Lauder
Greenlaw
Duns
Swinton
Coldstream
Chirnside
Coldingham
Eyemouth
St Abb's Head
Cockburnspath
Lammermuir Hills
Berwick-upon-Tweed
Holy Island (Lindisfarne)
Farne Is
Tweed
Biggar
Broad Law
Ettrick Forest
Hart Fell
Langholm
Hawick
Jedburgh
Teviotdale
Teviot
Newtown
Bonchester Bridge
Cheviot Hills
The Cheviot
Wooler
Belford
North Sunderland
Kilham
Flodden
Longhoughton
Glanton
Alnwick
Warkworth
Amble
Rothbury
Otterburn
Bellingham
Kielder Water
Northumberland National Park
Morpeth
Bedlington
Stannington
Ponteland
Gosforth
Newcastle upon Tyne
Gateshead
Stanley
Consett
Hexham
Haltwhistle
Longtown
Brampton
Carlisle
Wigton
Abbeytown
Aspatria
Maryport
Cockermouth
Bassenthwaite Lake
Lake District National Park
Keswick
Penrith
Castle Carrock
Kirkoswald
Alston
Allendale Town
Derwent Reservoir
Wolsingham
Cross Fell
Temple Sowerby
Cow Green Res.
Tees
Teesdale
Bishop Auckland
Crook
Shildon
ENGLAND
Seaton
Workington
Great Clifton
Skiddaw
Eden
SCOTLAND
GRAMPIAN MOUNTAINS
SOUTHERN UPLANDS
Burghead
Lossiemouth
Buckie
Cullen
Portsoy
Macduff
Troup Head
Fraserburgh
Loch of Strathbeg
Rattray Head
Crimond
Strichen
New Pitsligo
New Deer
Peterhead
Boddam
Cruden Bay
Hill of Dudwick
Ythan
Ellon
Newburgh
Oldmeldrum
Inverurie
Kintore
Dyce
Insch
Mossat
Turriff
Aberchirder
Knock Hill
Banff
Keith
Huntly
Rothes
Fochabers
Elgin
Lossie
Kinloss
Forres
Findhorn
Nairn
Cawdor
Dyke
Dava
Dufftown
Strathspey
Spey
Grantown-on-Spey
Hills of Cromdale
Tomintoul
Tomatin
Strath Dearn
Shetland
at the same scale
Herma Ness
Haroldswick
Unst
Baltasound
Cullivoe
Yell
Belmont
Point of Fethaland
Mid Yell
Fetlar
The Isbister
Yell Sound
Colgrave Sd
Funzie
The Faither
Ronas Hill
Burravoe
Out Skerries
St Magnus Bay
Muckle Roe
Brae
Vidlin
Toft
Papa Stour
Melby
Walls
Laxo
Whalsay
South Nesting Bay
Foula
Scalloway
Lerwick
Bressay
Isle of Noss
West Burra
Cunningsburgh
Sandwick
Scousburgh
Sumburgh
Sumburgh Head
Mainland
Inishtrahull
Inishtrahull Sound
Malin Head
Ballygorman
Glengad Head
Inishowen
Inishowen Head
Slieve Snaght
Buncrana
Lough Foyle
Scalp Mountain
Limavady
Coleraine
Portstewart
Portrush
Bushmills
Giant's Causeway
Ballycastle
Fair Head
Rathlin Island
Armoy
Ballymoney
Antrim Hills
Cushendall
Garron Pt
Trostan
Carnlough
North Channel
Ballykelly
Ringsend
Dunloy
Eglinton
Londonderry
Garvagh
Dungiven
Kilrea
Claudy
Park
Cullybackey
Strabane
Sion Mills
Sawel Mt
Sperrin Mts
NORTHERN IRELAND
Maghera
Broughshane
Ballymena
Larne
Larne Lough
Island Magee
Whitehead
Ballyclare
Carrickfergus
Randalstown
Antrim
Draperstown
Magherafelt
Moneymore
Newtownstewart
Cookstown
Omagh
Pomeroy
Sixmilecross
Lough Neagh
Crumlin
Newtownabbey
Belfast
Belfast L.
Bangor
Donaghadee
Dundonald
Newtownards

1:2M

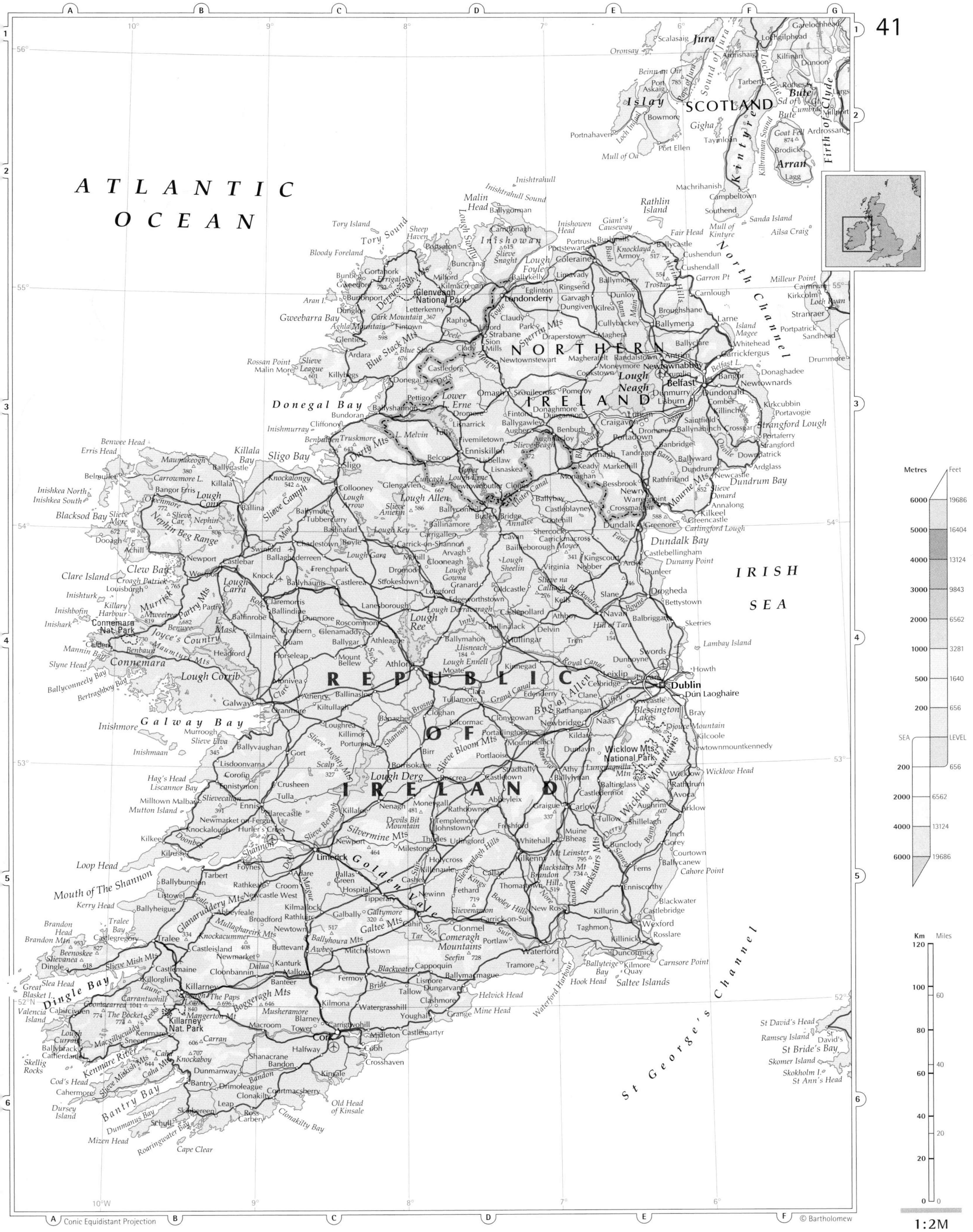

IRELAND

1:2M

© Bartholomew

Conic Equidistant Projection

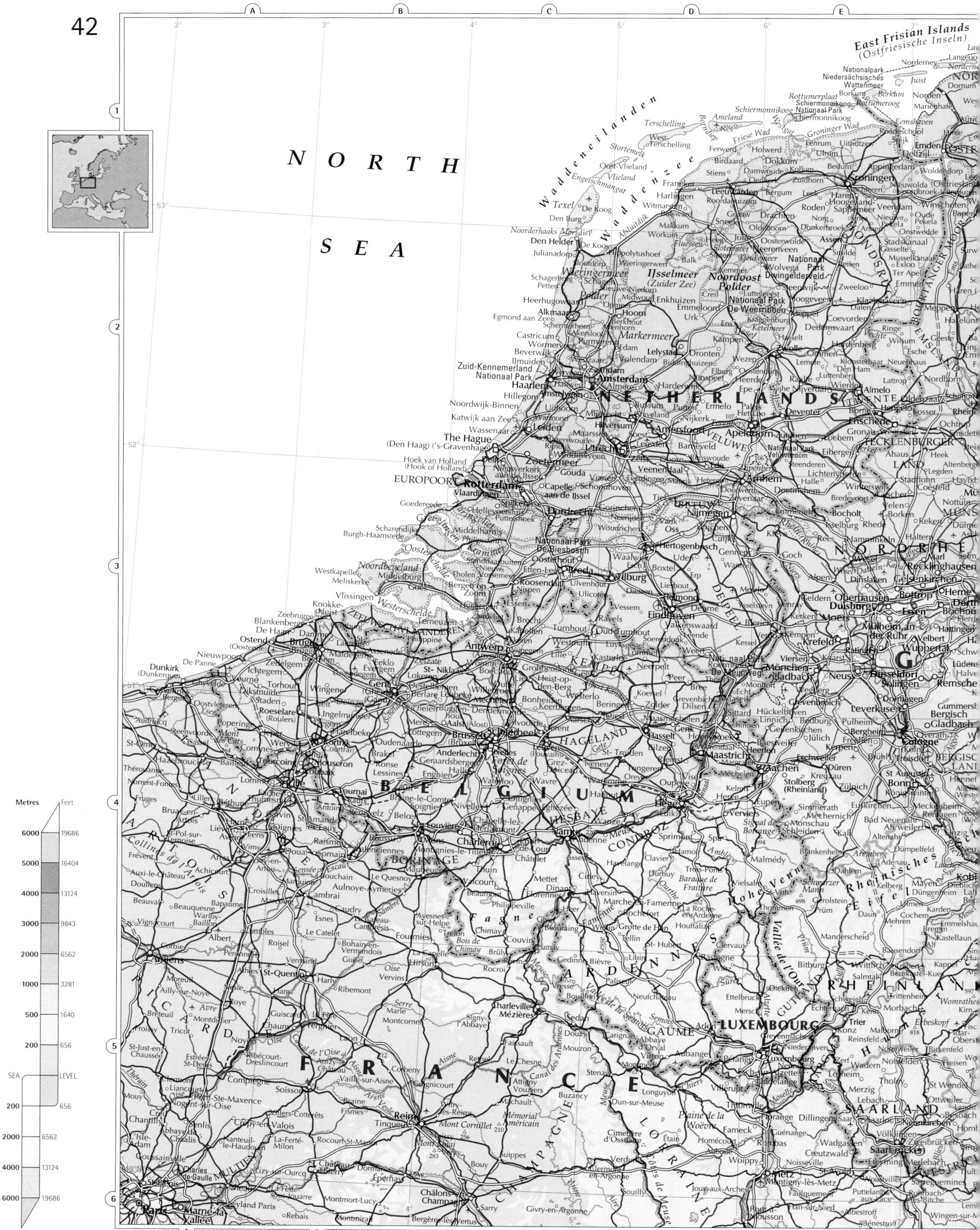
NORTH SEA
East Frisian Islands (Ostfriesische Inseln)
Waddeneilanden
Waddenzee
NETHERLANDS
BELGIUM
FRANCE
LUXEMBOURG
Amsterdam
The Hague (Den Haag) ('s-Gravenhage)
Rotterdam
EUROPOORT
Utrecht
Haarlem
Leiden
Groningen
Leeuwarden
Arnhem
Nijmegen
Eindhoven
Maastricht
Antwerp
Brussels (Bruxelles)
Gent
Brugge
Ostend (Oostende)
Liège
Namur
Charleroi
Mons
Lille
Dunkirk (Dunkerque)
Amiens
St-Quentin
Reims
Paris
Metz
Trier
Aachen
Cologne
Düsseldorf
Duisburg
Essen
Saarbrücken
IJsselmeer (Zuider Zee)
Markermeer
Noordoost Polder
Wieringermeer
VELUWE
BETUWE
KEMPEN
HESBAYE
CONDROZ
BORINAGE
HAGELAND
ARDENNES
GAUME
Fagne
Hohe Venn
Eifel
Rheinisches
SAARLAND
RHEINLAND
CHAMPAGNE
LORRAINE
PICARDIE
ARTOIS
FLANDRE
Metres
Feet
6000
19686
5000
16404
4000
13124
3000
9843
2000
6562
1000
3281
500
1640
200
656
SEA
LEVEL
200
656
2000
6562
4000
13124
6000
19686
A
B
C
D
E
1
2
3
4
5
6
2°
3°
4°
5°
6°
53°
52°
51°
Conic Equidistant Projection

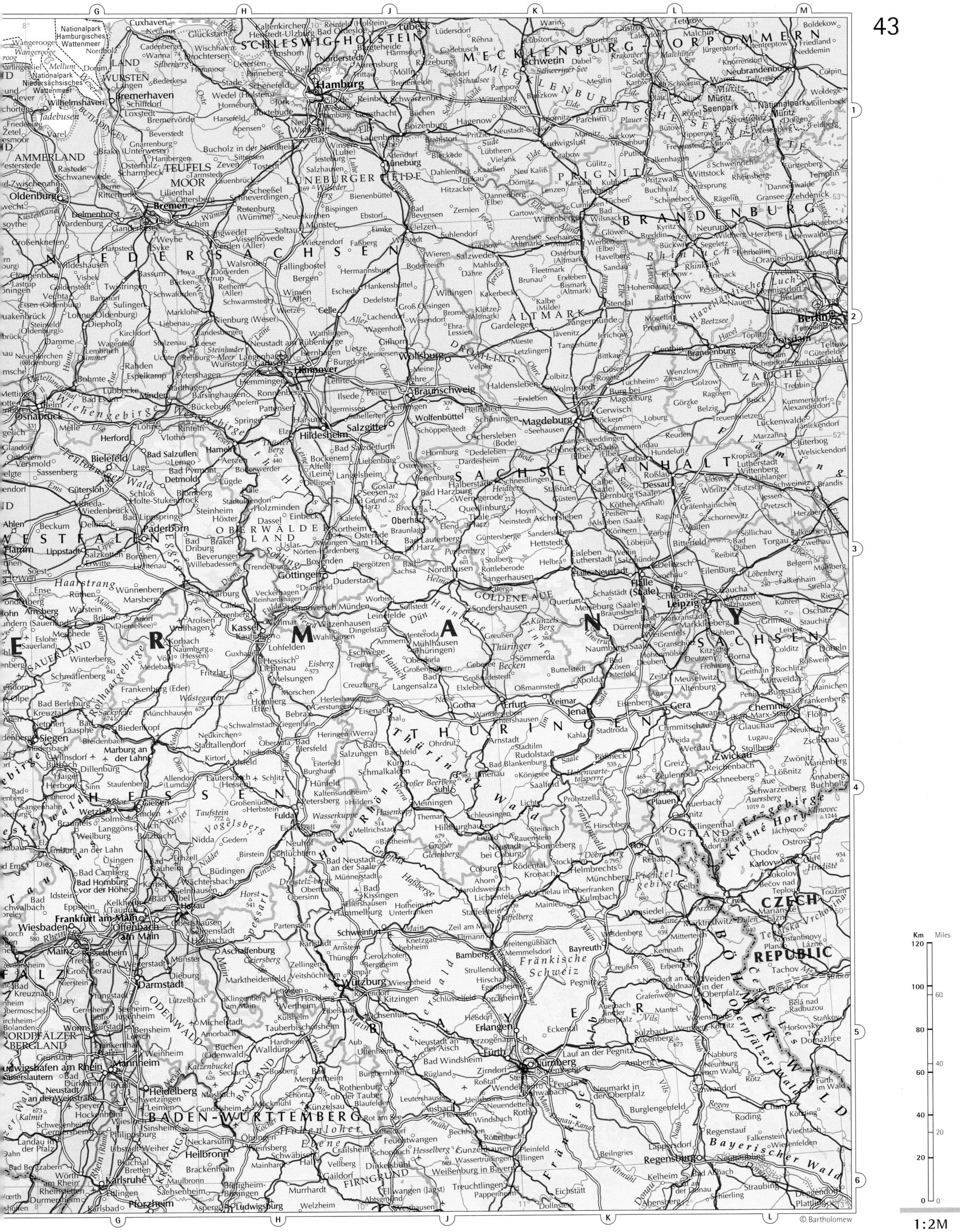
SCHLESWIG-HOLSTEIN
MECKLENBURG-VORPOMMERN
NIEDERSACHSEN
BRANDENBURG
SACHSEN-ANHALT
THÜRINGEN
SACHSEN
HESSEN
BADEN-WÜRTTEMBERG
BAYERN
GERMANY
CZECH REPUBLIC
LÜNEBURGER HEIDE
ALTMARK
PRIGNITZ
VOGTLAND
FIRNGRUND
Hamburg
Bremen
Bremerhaven
Hannover
Berlin
Potsdam
Magdeburg
Braunschweig
Leipzig
Halle (Saale)
Dresden
Erfurt
Kassel
Göttingen
Frankfurt am Main
Wiesbaden
Mainz
Darmstadt
Mannheim
Heidelberg
Heilbronn
Karlsruhe
Würzburg
Nürnberg
Regensburg
Bamberg
Bayreuth
Chemnitz
Zwickau
Plauen
Gera
Jena
Weimar
Schwerin
Lübeck
Osnabrück
Bielefeld
Paderborn
Siegen
Oldenburg
Fulda
Lüneburg
Wolfsburg
Dessau
Erlangen
Fürth
Km
Miles
120
100
80
60
40
20
0
60
40
20
0
1:2M
© Bartholomew

FRANCE

44

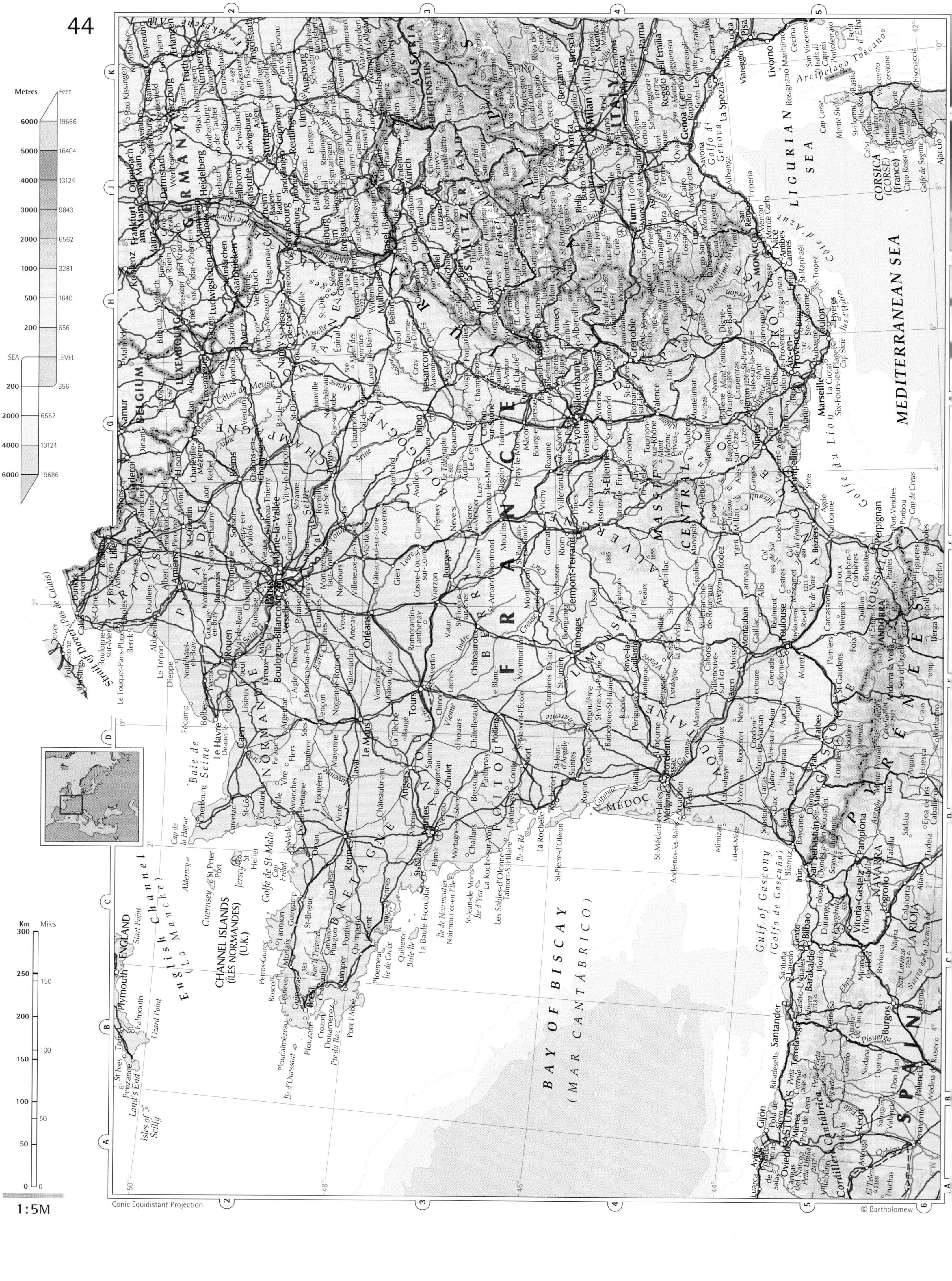

1:5M

Conic Equidistant Projection

© Bartholomew

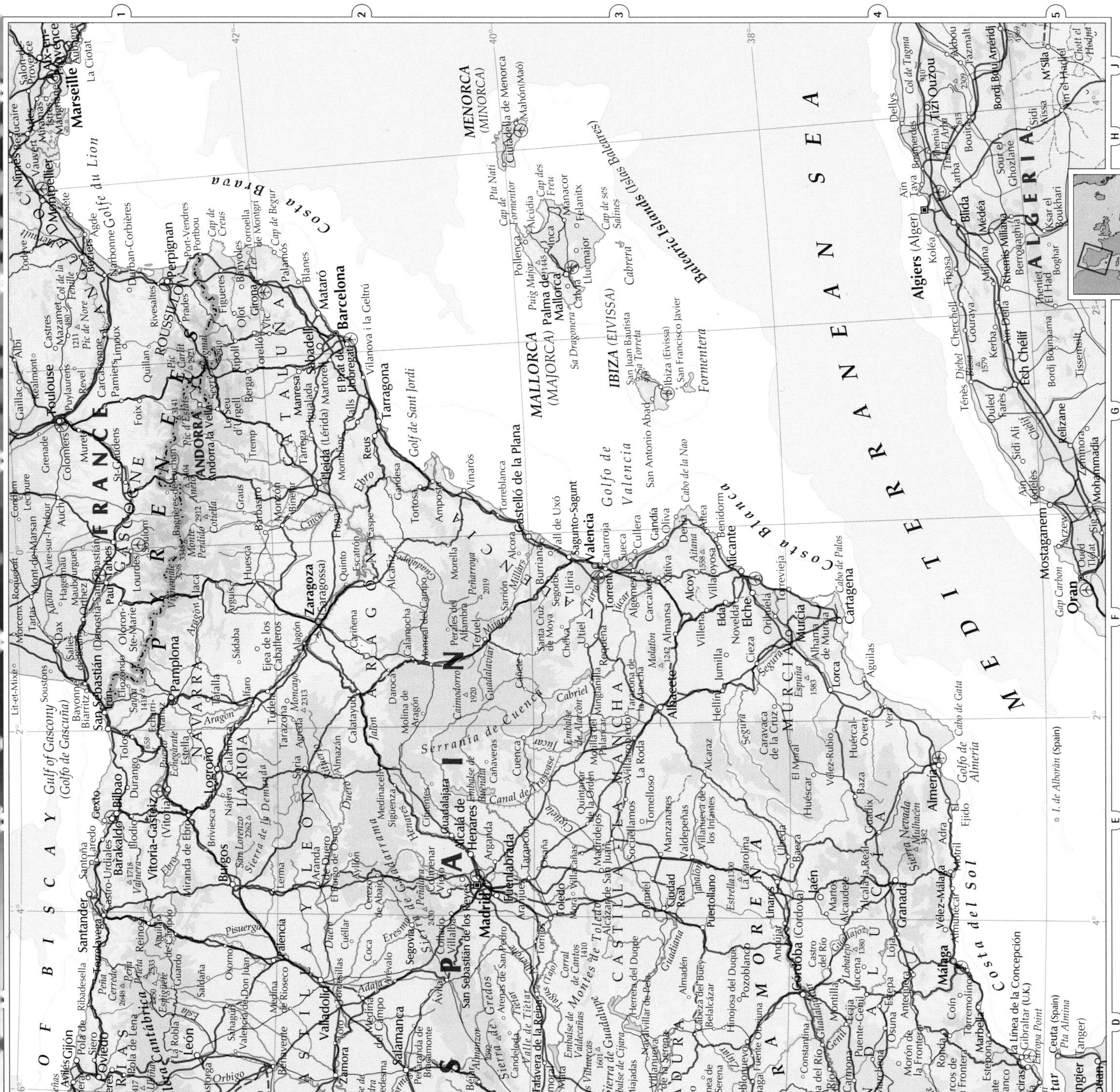

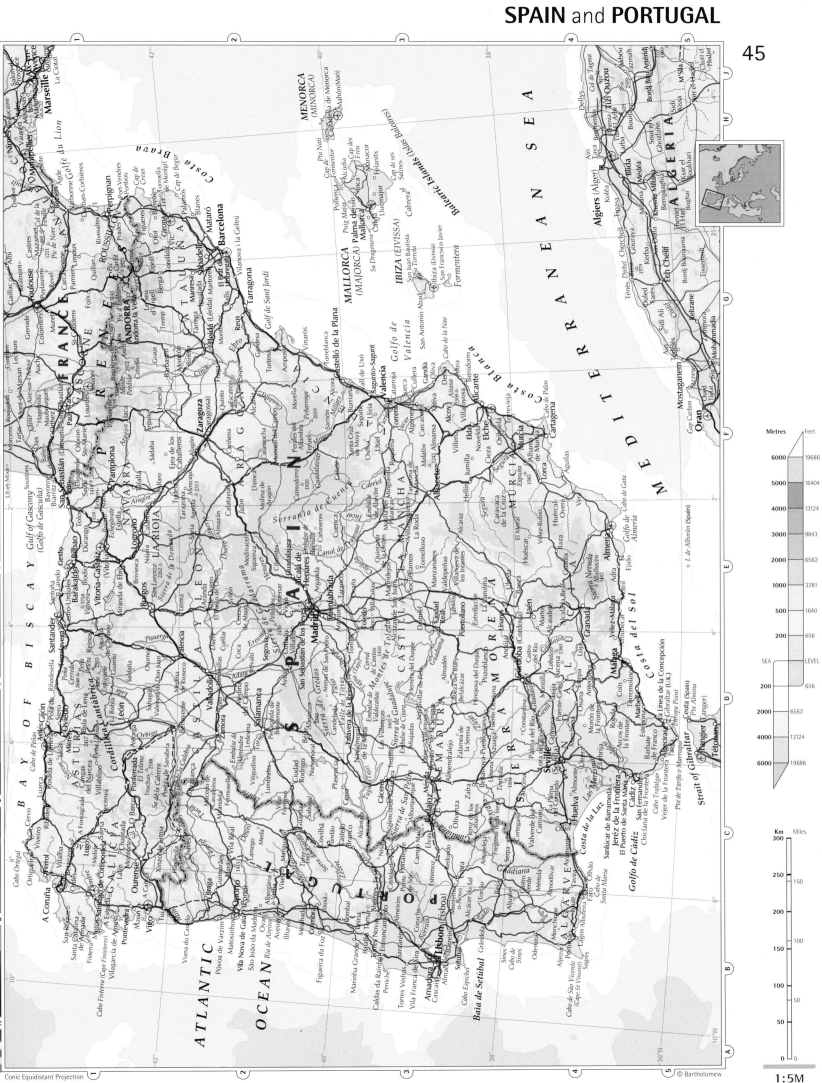

BAY OF BISCAY
Gulf of Gascony
(Golfo de Gascuña)
ATLANTIC
OCEAN
MEDITERRANEAN SEA
SPAIN
PORTUGAL
FRANCE
ALGERIA
ANDORRA
PYRENEES
Balearic Islands (Islas Baleares)
MENORCA
(MINORCA)
MALLORCA
(MAJORCA)
IBIZA (EIVISSA)
Formentera
Costa Brava
Costa Blanca
Costa del Sol
Costa de la Luz
Golfo de Valencia
Golfo de Cádiz
Golf de Sant Jordi
Golfe du Lion
Baía de Setúbal
Strait of Gibraltar
SIERRA MORENA
Sierra Nevada
Madrid
Lisbon (Lisboa)
Barcelona
Valencia
Zaragoza
(Saragossa)
Bilbao
Seville
(Sevilla)
Málaga
Córdoba (Cordova)
Granada
Murcia
Alicante
Oporto
(Porto)
Salamanca
Valladolid
Pamplona
Santander
Oviedo
Marseille
Toulouse
Perpignan
Algiers (Alger)
Oran
Mostaganem
Tangier
(Tanger)
Metres
Feet
6000
19686
5000
16404
4000
13124
3000
9843
2000
6562
1000
3281
500
1640
200
656
SEA
LEVEL
Km
Miles
300
250
200
150
100
50
0
1:5M
Conic Equidistant Projection
© Bartholomew

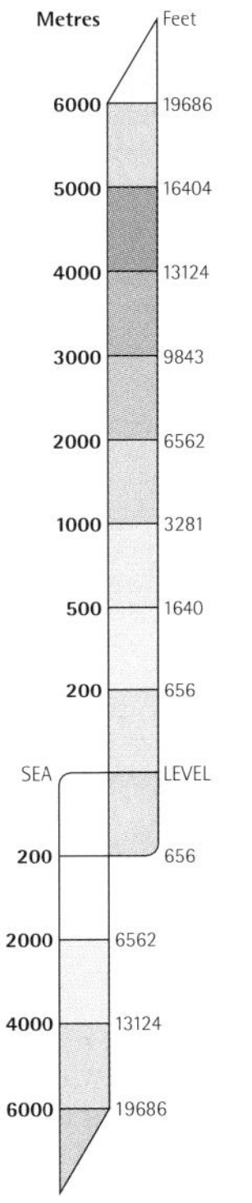

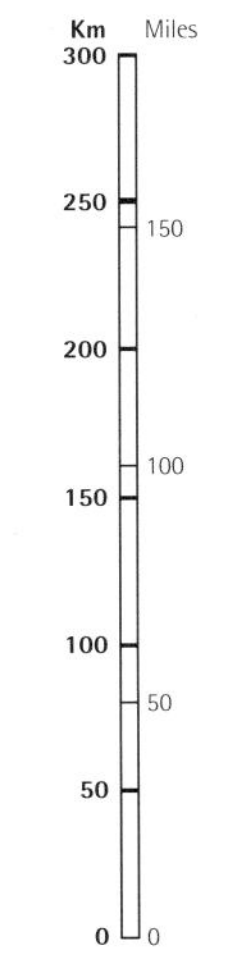

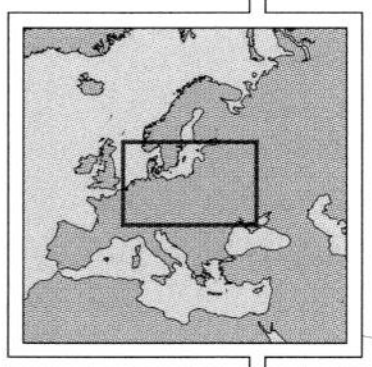

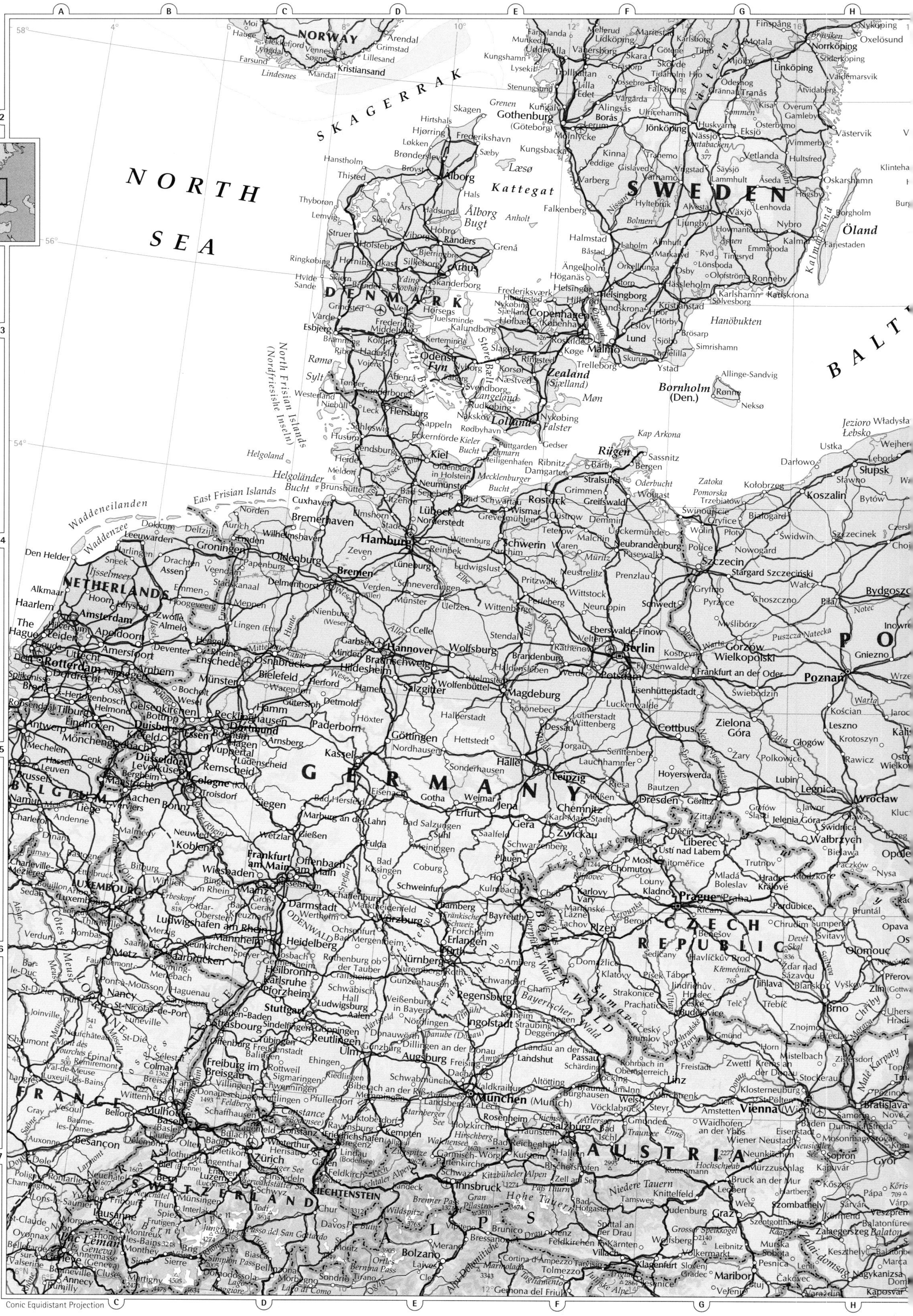
NORTH SEA
SKAGERRAK
Kattegat
SWEDEN
DENMARK
NORWAY
NETHERLANDS
BELGIUM
LUXEMBOURG
GERMANY
FRANCE
SWITZERLAND
LIECHTENSTEIN
AUSTRIA
CZECH REPUBLIC
ALPS
BALTI
PO
Hamburg
Berlin
Bremen
Hannover
Amsterdam
Rotterdam
Copenhagen (København)
Gothenburg (Göteborg)
Prague (Praha)
Vienna (Wien)
München (Munich)
Frankfurt am Main
Cologne (Köln)
Dresden
Leipzig
Stuttgart
Zürich
Szczecin
Poznań
Wrocław
Brussels
Luxembourg
Strasbourg
Bornholm (Den.)
Zealand (Sjælland)
Fyn
Lolland
Falster
Rügen
Öland
North Frisian Islands (Nordfriesische Inseln)
East Frisian Islands
Waddeneilanden
Conic Equidistant Projection

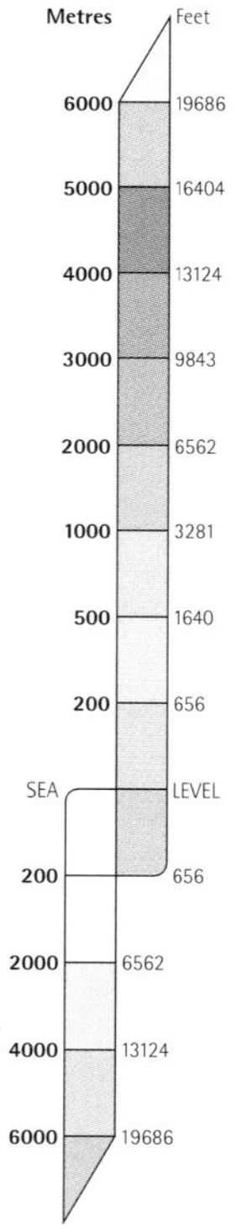
Metres
Feet
6000
19686
5000
16404
4000
13124
3000
9843
2000
6562
1000
3281
500
1640
200
656
SEA
LEVEL
200
656
2000
6562
4000
13124
6000
19686

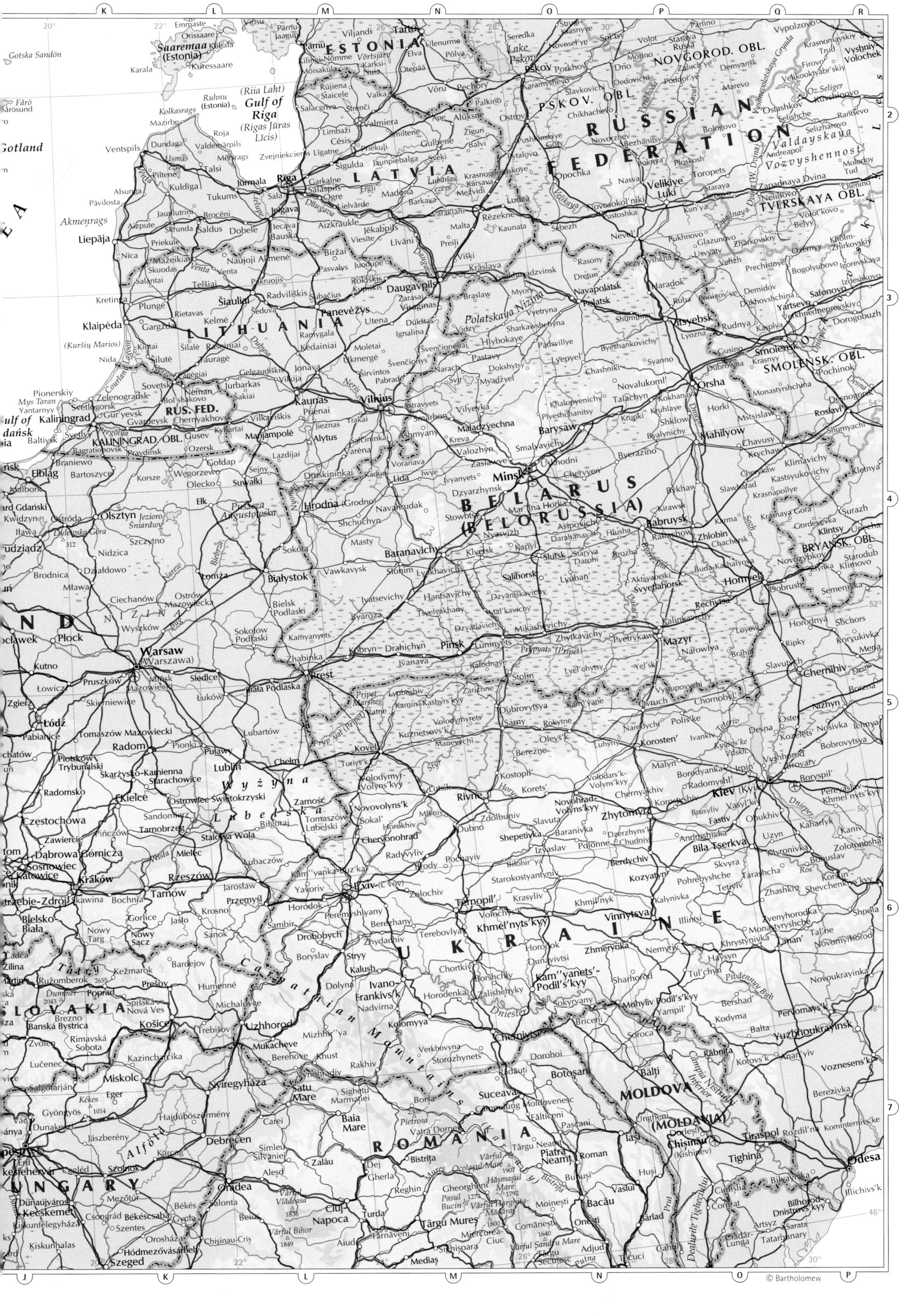
ESTONIA
LATVIA
LITHUANIA
RUS. FED.
KALININGRAD. OBL.
BELARUS (BELORUSSIA)
RUSSIAN FEDERATION
UKRAINE
MOLDOVA (MOLDAVIA)
ROMANIA
SLOVAKIA
UNGARY
PSKOV. OBL.
NOVGOROD. OBL.
TVERSKAYA OBL.
SMOLENSK. OBL.
BRYANSK. OBL.
Gulf of Riga (Rigas Jūras Līcis)
Saaremaa (Estonia)
Gotland
Riga
Vilnius
Minsk
Warsaw (Warszawa)
Kiev (Kyiv)
Chişinău (Kishinev)
Odesa
Kaliningrad
Kaunas
Tallinn
Tartu
Pskov
Daugavpils
Brest
Homyel'
Mahilyow
Vitsyebsk
Hrodna (Grodno)
L'viv (L'vov)
Kraków
Lublin
Białystok
Olsztyn
Debrecen
Cluj-Napoca
Iaşi
Carpathian Mountains
Polatskaya Nizina
Pripet Marshes
Wyżyna Lubelska
Valdayskaya Vozvyshennost'
Dnieper
Dniester
© Bartholomew

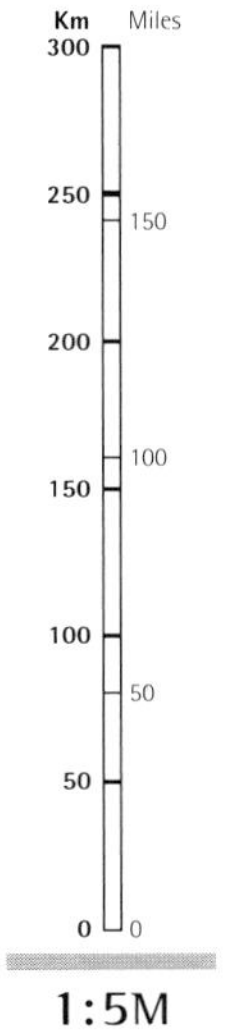
Km
Miles
300
250
200
150
100
50
0
150
100
50
0

1:5M

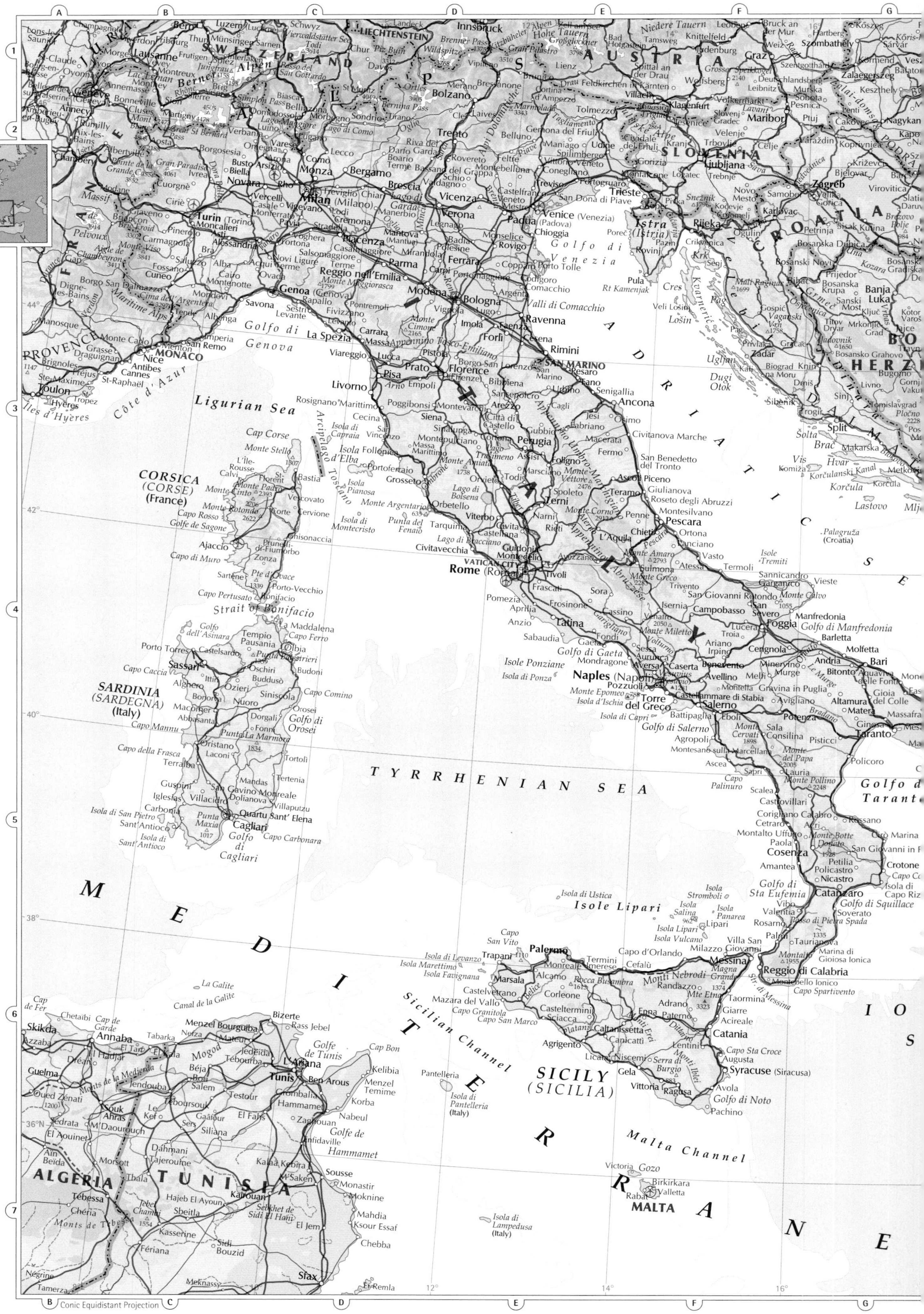

SWITZERLAND
LIECHTENSTEIN
AUSTRIA
SLOVENIA
CROATIA
FRANCE
ITALY
MONACO
SAN MARINO
VATICAN CITY
CORSICA (CORSE) (France)
SARDINIA (SARDEGNA) (Italy)
SICILY (SICILIA)
MALTA
TUNISIA
ALGERIA
ALPS
PROVENCE
ADRIATIC SEA
Ligurian Sea
TYRRHENIAN SEA
MEDITERRANEAN
Golfo di Genova
Golfo di Venezia
Strait of Bonifacio
Sicilian Channel
Malta Channel
Isole Lipari
Golfo di Taranto
Rome
Milan (Milano)
Turin (Torino)
Genoa (Genova)
Venice (Venezia)
Florence (Firenze)
Naples (Napoli)
Bologna
Palermo
Cagliari
Bari
Trieste
Ljubljana
Zagreb
Innsbruck
Lausanne
Bern
Nice
Tunis
Valletta
Conic Equidistant Projection

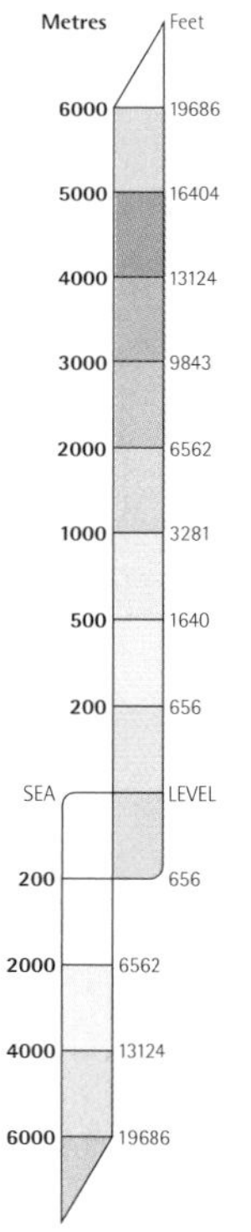

Metres
Feet
6000
19686
5000
16404
4000
13124
3000
9843
2000
6562
1000
3281
500
1640
200
656
SEA
LEVEL
200
656
2000
6562
4000
13124
6000
19686

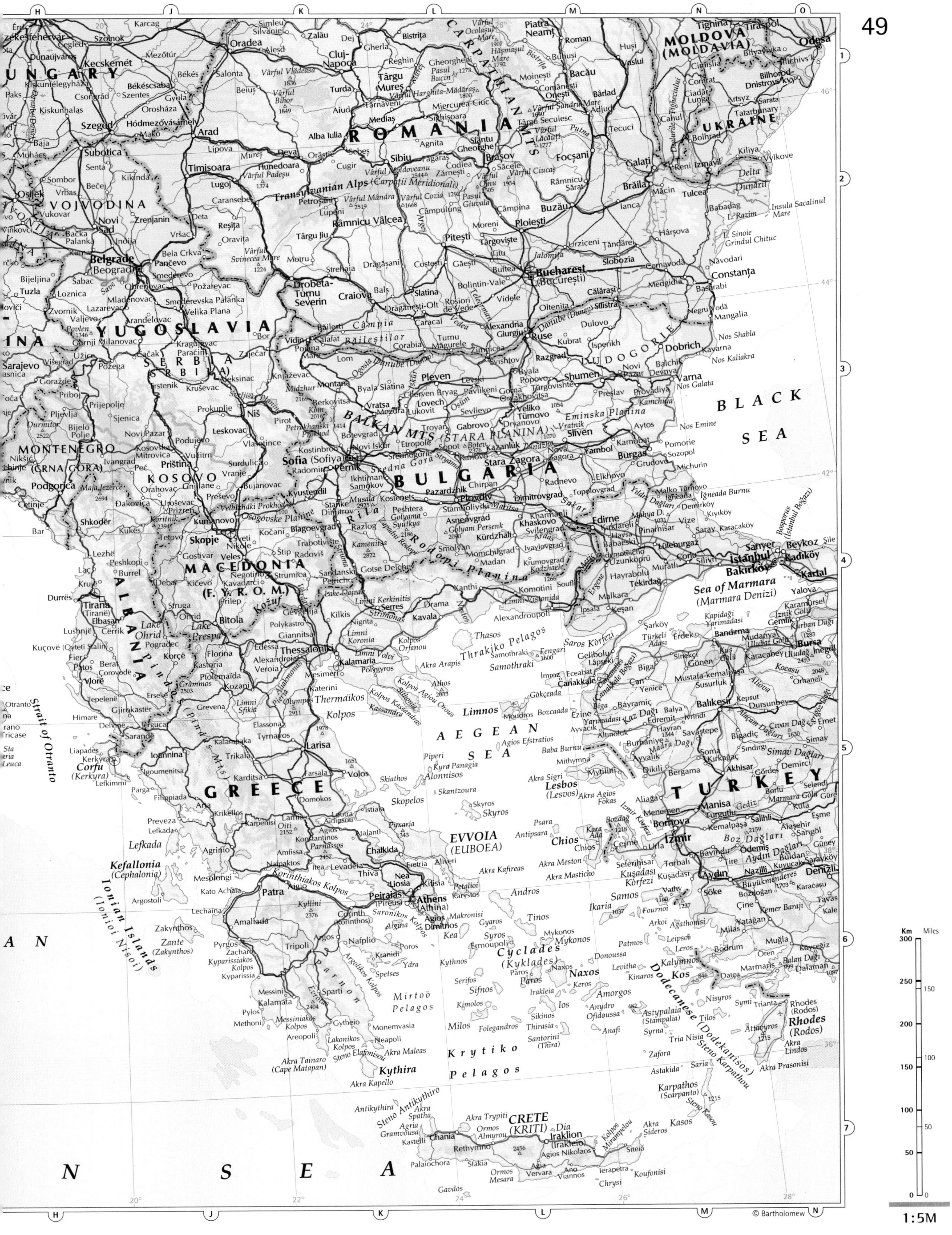

HUNGARY
ROMANIA
MOLDOVA (MOLDAVIA)
UKRAINE
YUGOSLAVIA
SERBIA (SRBIJA)
VOJVODINA
KOSOVO
MONTENEGRO (CRNA GORA)
BULGARIA
MACEDONIA (F.Y.R.O.M.)
ALBANIA
GREECE
TURKEY
CARPATHIAN MTS
Transylvanian Alps (Carpații Meridionali)
BALKAN MTS (STARA PLANINA)
Rodopi Planina
Rila
Pindus Mts
LUDOGORIE
Câmpia Băilestilor
Danube (Dunav)
Delta Dunării
BLACK SEA
Sea of Marmara (Marmara Denizi)
AEGEAN SEA
Thrakiko Pelagos
Thermaikos Kolpos
Mirtoö Pelagos
Krytiko Pelagos
Ionian Islands (Ionioi Nisoi)
Strait of Otranto
Bosporus (İstanbul Boğazı)
Cyclades (Kyklades)
Dodecanese (Dodekanisos)
CRETE (KRITI)
EVVOIA (EUBOEA)
Lesbos (Lesvos)
Chios
Samos
Rhodes (Rodos)
Karpathos (Scarpanto)
Kythira
Kefallonia (Cephalonia)
Corfu (Kerkyra)
Zakynthos
Zante (Zakynthos)
Lefkada
Limnos
Thasos
Samothraki
Naxos
Paros
Andros
Tinos
Mykonos
Kos
Bucharest (București)
Belgrade (Beograd)
Sofia (Sofiya)
Skopje
Tirana (Tiranë)
Athens (Athina)
Istanbul
Thessaloniki
Izmir
Constanța
Varna
Odesa
Cluj-Napoca
Timișoara
Craiova
Plovdiv
Burgas
Ploiești
Brașov
Galați
Brăila
Niš
Pristina
Podgorica
Sarajevo
Patra
Larisa
Iraklion (Iraklio)
Chania
Bursa
Edirne
Km 300 250 200 150 100 50 0
Miles 150 100 50 0
1:5M
© Bartholomew

Metres / Feet

6000 — 19686
5000 — 16404
4000 — 13124
3000 — 9843
2000 — 6562
1000 — 3281
500 — 1640
200 — 656
SEA — LEVEL
200 — 656
2000 — 6562
4000 — 13124
6000 — 19686

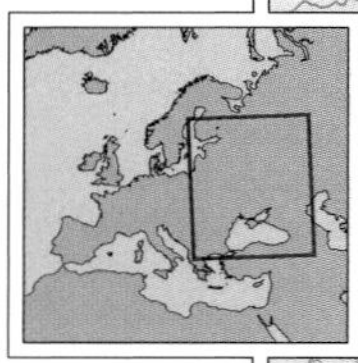

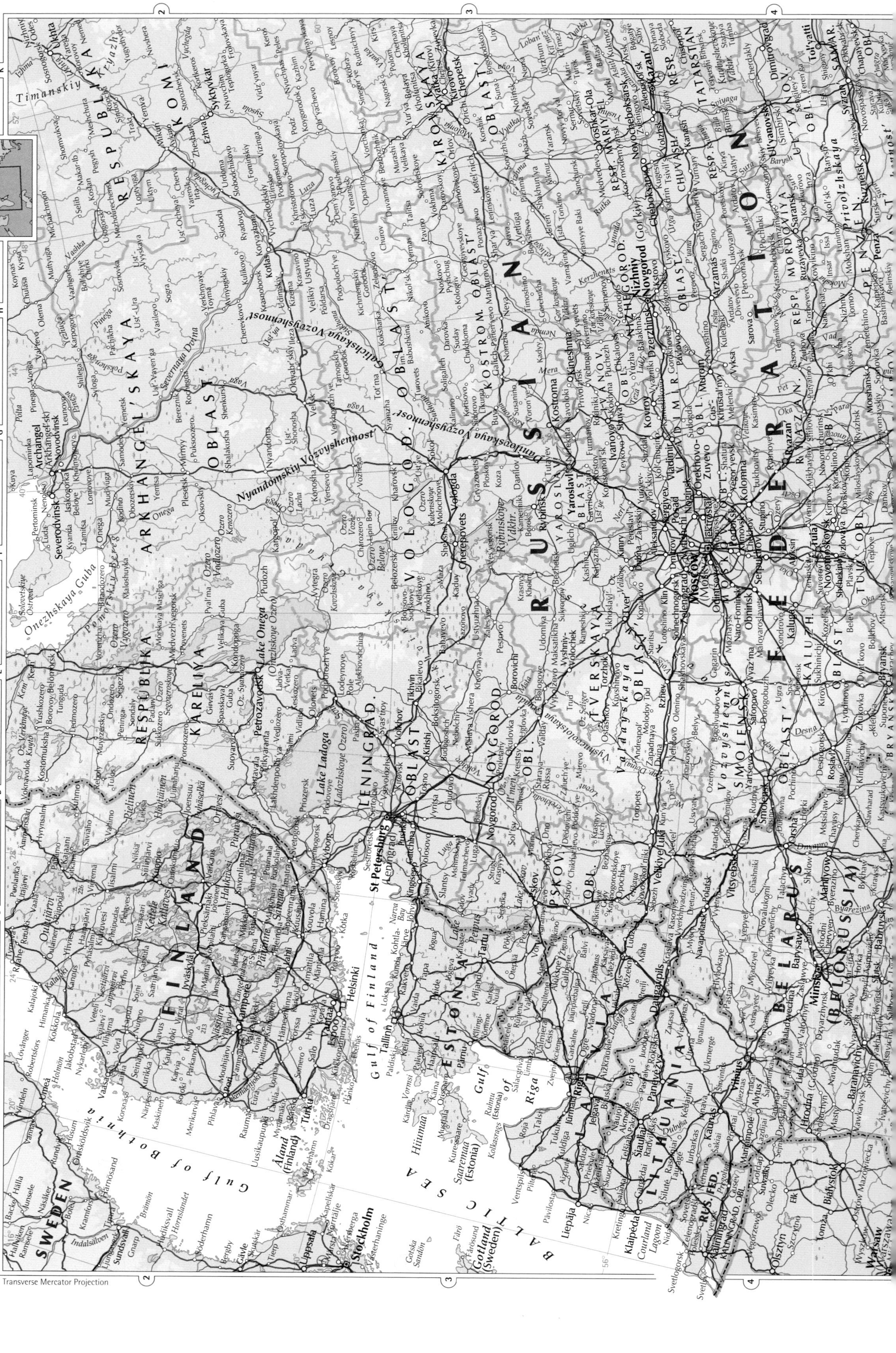

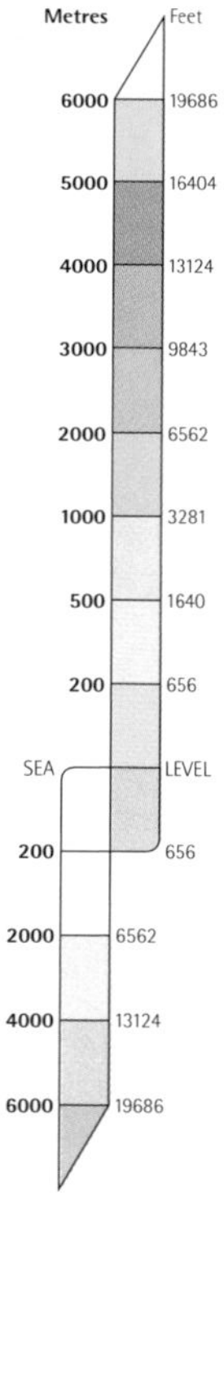

Transverse Mercator Projection

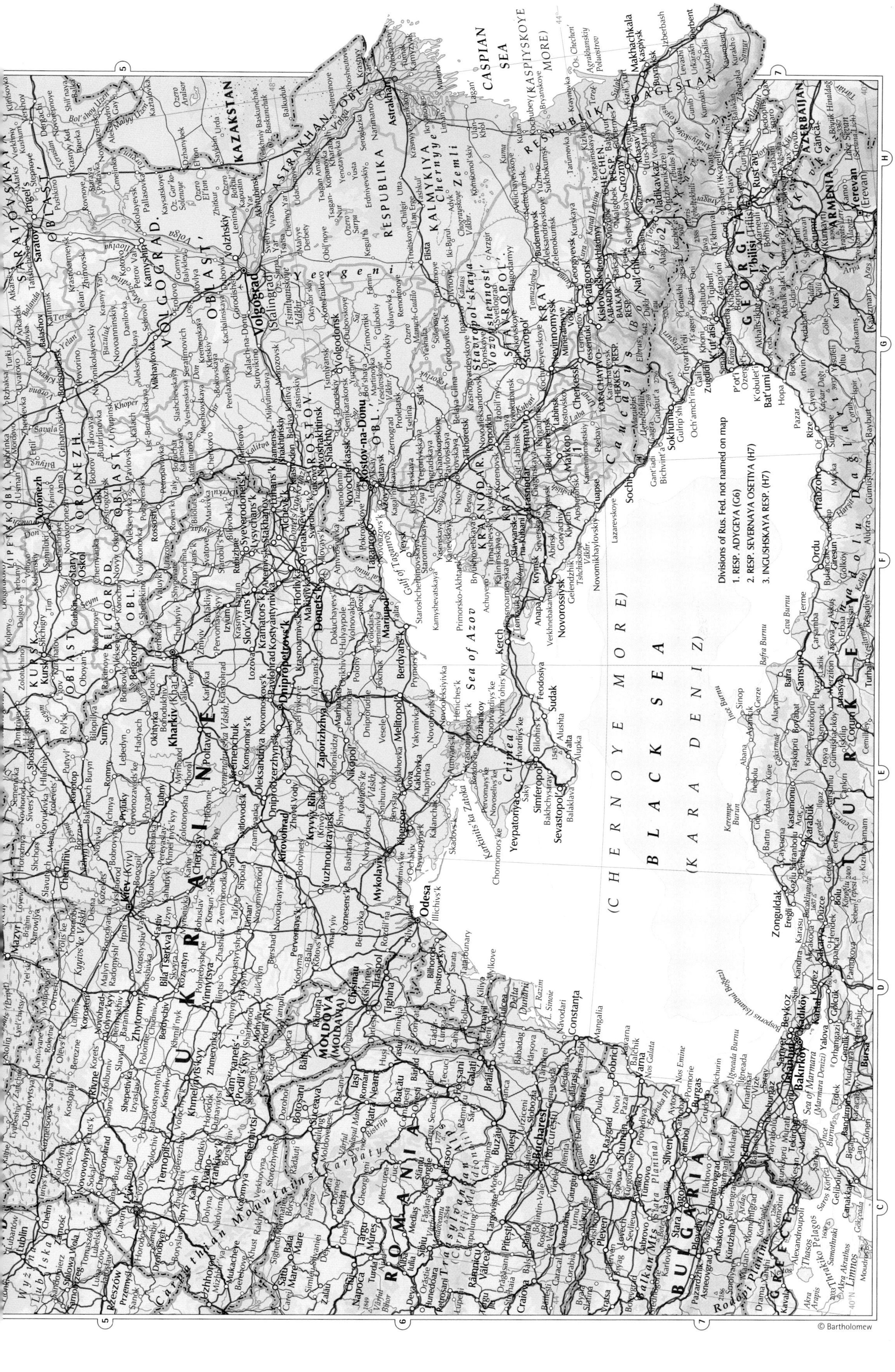

51

Divisions of Rus. Fed. not named on map
1. RESP. ADYGEYA (G6)
2. RESP. SEVERNAYA OSETIYA (H7)
3. INGUSHSKAYA RESP. (H7)

© Bartholomew

1:7M

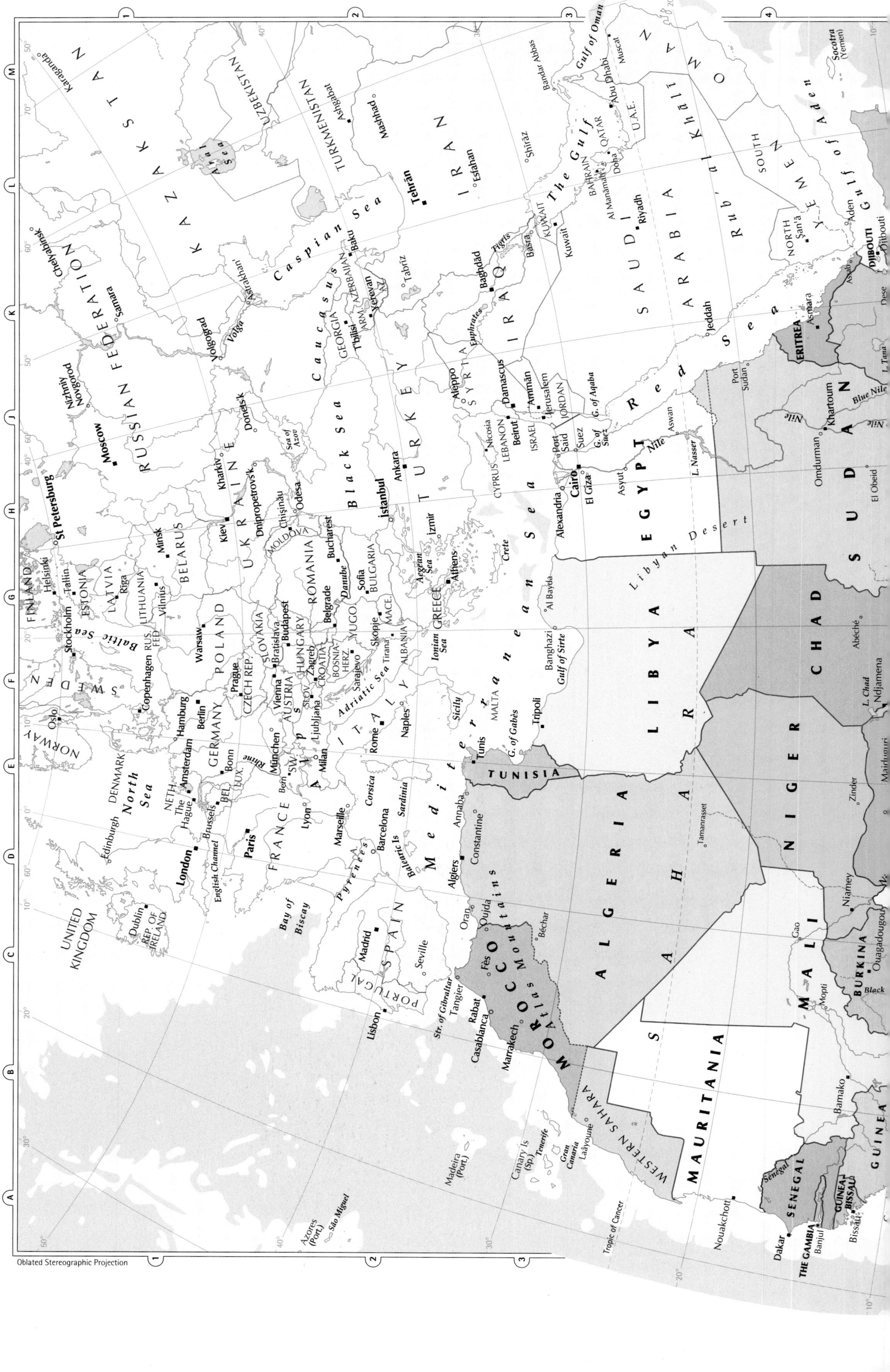

52

Metres | Feet
SEA | LEVEL
200 | 656
3000 | 9843

Oblated Stereographic Projection

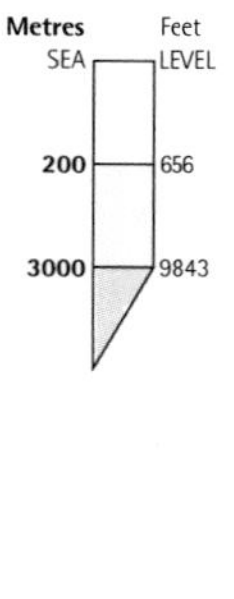

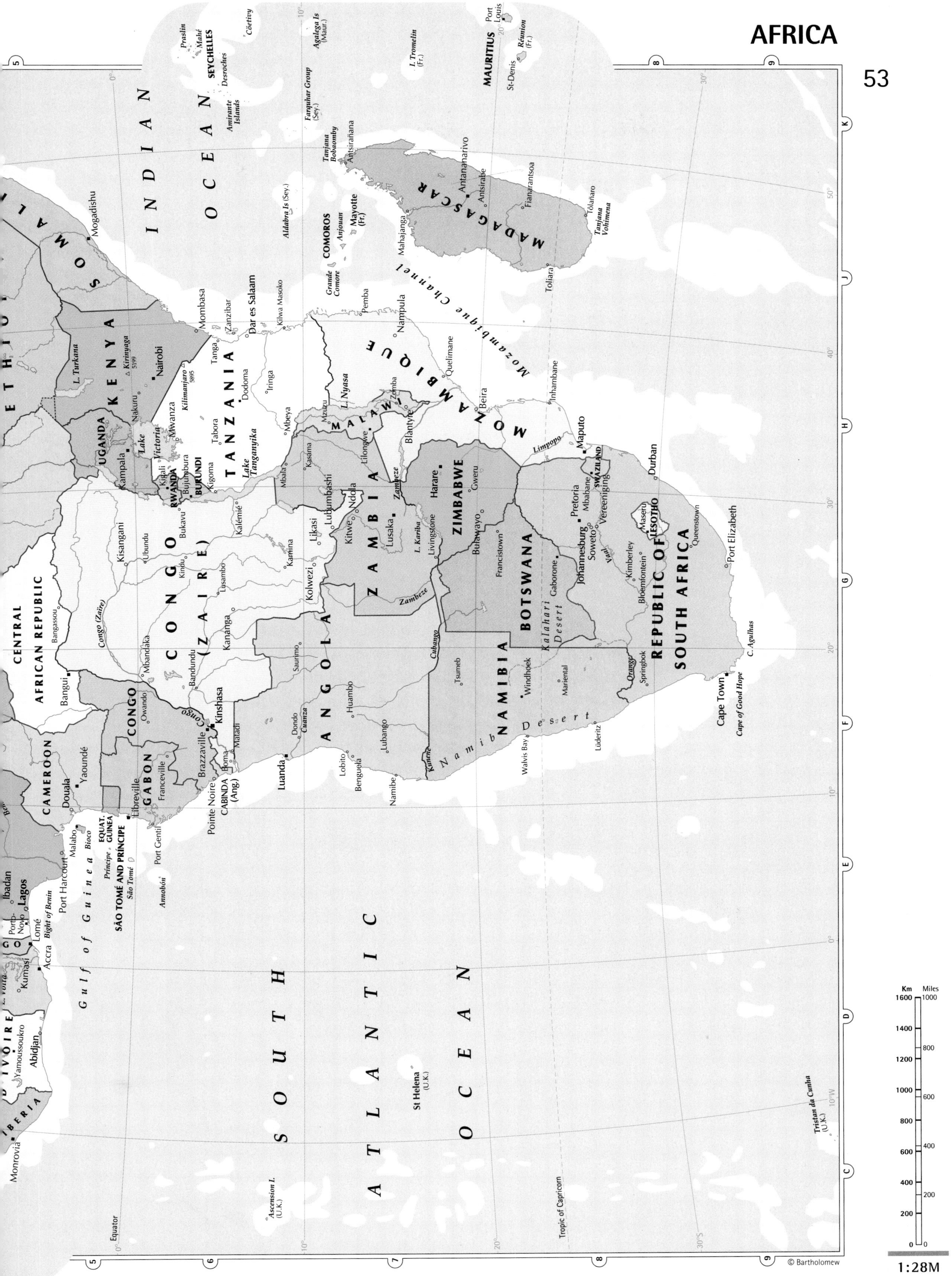

AFRICA

53

INDIAN OCEAN

Praslin
Malé
Coëtivy
SEYCHELLES
Desroches
Farquhar Group (Sey.)
Amirante Islands
Agalega Is (Maur.)
I. Tromelin (Fr.)
Réunion (Fr.)

MAURITIUS
Port Louis
St-Denis

Mogadishu

Aldabra Is (Sey.)
COMOROS
Grande Comore
Anjouan
Mayotte (Fr.)
Tanjona Bobaomby
Antsiranana
MADAGASCAR
Antananarivo
Antsirabe
Mahajanga
Fianarantsoa
Toamasina
Tôlañaro
Toliara
Tanjona Vohimena

SOMALIA

ETHIOPIA

KENYA
L. Turkana
Kirinyaga 5199
Nairobi
Nakuru
Kilimanjaro 5895
Mombasa
Zanzibar
Tanga
Dar es Salaam
Kilwa Masoko
Pemba

UGANDA
Kampala
Lake Victoria
Mwanza
RWANDA
Kigali
BURUNDI
Bujumbura
Kigoma

TANZANIA
Dodoma
Tabora
Iringa
Mbeya
Lake Tanganyika

CENTRAL AFRICAN REPUBLIC
Bangassou
Bangui

CONGO (ZAIRE)
Kisangani
Ubundu
Bukavu
Kindu
Kalemié
Lubumbashi
Kamina
Kananga
Lusambo
Kolwezi
Likasi
Mbuji-Mayi
Kabalo
Bandundu
Mbandaka
Ndola
Kitwe

CONGO
Owando
Brazzaville
Boma
Kinshasa
Matadi
Pointe Noire
CABINDA (Ang.)

CAMEROON
Yaoundé
Douala

GABON
Libreville
Franceville
Port Gentil

EQUAT. GUINEA
Malabo
Bioco
SÃO TOMÉ AND PRINCIPE
Príncipe
São Tomé
Annobón

Port Harcourt
Ibadan
Lagos
Porto-Novo
BENIN
Lomé
Accra
Kumasi
Abidjan
Yamoussoukro
CÔTE D'IVOIRE
LIBERIA
Monrovia

Gulf of Guinea
Bight of Benin

MALAWI
Mzuzu
L. Nyasa
Lilongwe
Blantyre

MOZAMBIQUE
Nampula
Quelimane
Beira
Inhambane
Maputo
Mozambique Channel

ZAMBIA
Kasama
Lusaka
L. Kariba
Livingstone
Zambeze

ZIMBABWE
Harare
Gweru
Bulawayo
Mutare
Limpopo

ANGOLA
Luanda
Dondo
Cuanza
Huambo
Lobito
Benguela
Lubango
Namibe
Cunene
Saurimo

NAMIBIA
Tsumeb
Windhoek
Walvis Bay
Lüderitz
Marienthal
Namib Desert

BOTSWANA
Francistown
Gaborone
Kalahari Desert
Orange

SWAZILAND
Mbabane
LESOTHO
Maseru

REPUBLIC OF SOUTH AFRICA
Pretoria
Johannesburg
Soweto
Vereeniging
Vaal
Kimberley
Bloemfontein
Springbok
Queenstown
Durban
Port Elizabeth
Cape Town
Cape of Good Hope
C. Agulhas

SOUTH ATLANTIC OCEAN

Ascension I. (U.K.)
St Helena (U.K.)
Tristan da Cunha (U.K.)

Equator
Tropic of Capricorn

© Bartholomew

1:28M

Km	Miles
1600	1000
1400	
1200	800
1000	600
800	
600	400
400	200
200	
0	0

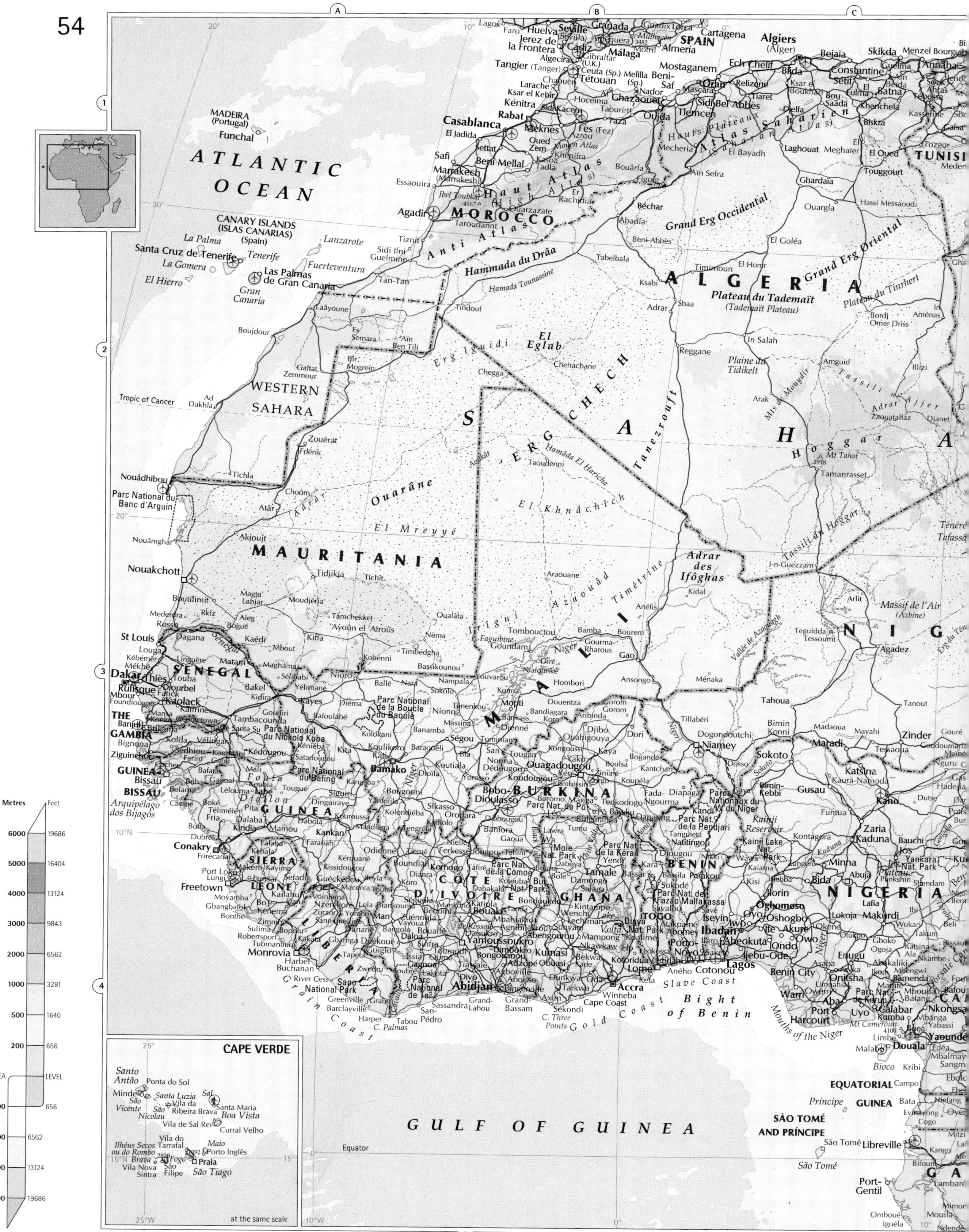

**ATLANTIC
OCEAN**

MADEIRA
(Portugal)
Funchal

CANARY ISLANDS
(ISLAS CANARIAS)
(Spain)

La Palma
Santa Cruz de Tenerife
La Gomera   Tenerife
El Hierro   Gran
Canaria
Las Palmas
de Gran Canaria
Lanzarote
Fuerteventura

Tropic of Cancer

**WESTERN
SAHARA**

Ad
Dakhla

Boujdour

Lagos Faro
Huelva Seville
(Sevilla) Granada Guadix Lorca Cartagena
Jerez de Cádiz Écija Antequera 3482   **SPAIN** Algiers
la Frontera Algeciras Gibraltar Málaga Almería (Alger)
Tangier Ceuta (Sp.) Melilla Mostaganem Bejaïa Skikda Menzel Bourguiba
Larache (Tanger) Chauen Tétouan (U.K.) Beni Saf Oran Relizane Blida Sétif Annaba
Ksar el Kebir Hoceima Sidi Kacem Taourirt Sidi Bel Abbès Tiaret Bou Saâda Constantine Aïn Tébessa
Casablanca Kénitra Fès (Fez) Taza Tlemcen Boukhmet Batna Khenchela
El Jadida **Rabat** Meknès Azrou Mecheria Aïn Sefra Laghouat Megrahef El Oued **TUNISIA**
Safi Settat Oued Moyen Atlas El Bayadh Touggourt
Beni Mellal Zem Khénifra Béchar Ghardaïa Hassi Messaoud
Essaouira Tadla Bouârfa Figuig Grand Erg Occidental Ouargla
Marrakech Haut Atlas (High Atlas) Ouarzazate Abadla El Goléa
(Marrakech) Ibel Toubkal Er Beni-Abbès Bordj
Agadir 4167 Rachidia Omer Driss
Taroudannt **MOROCCO** Tabelbala In Salah Aïn Illizi
Tiznit Anti Atlas Hamada du Drâa Hamada Tounassine Amguid
Sidi Ifni Guelmine Tabelbala Plateau du Tinrhert
Tan-Tan Hammada du Drâa Reggane Zaouatallaz Djanet
Laâyoune Ksabi Plateau du Tademaït Arak Tassili n' Ajjer
Es Aïn El Eglab Chenachane (Tademaït Plateau)
Semara Ben Tili Tindouf Adrar Sbaa In Salah Mts d'Mouydir
Bîr El Plaine du
Mogreïn Erg Iguidi Chegga Tidikelt

ALGERIA
Grand Erg Oriental
Hoggar
Mt Tahat
2918
Tamanrasset

SAHARA

Nouâdhibou

Parc National du
Banc d'Arguin

Nouâmghâr

Nouakchott

St Louis

Boutilimit
Medina Rkiz
Rosso
Dagana
Louga
Kébémèr
Mékhé

SENEGAL
Dakar Thiès
Rufisque Diourbel
Mbour Fatick
Foundiougne Kaolack

**THE
GAMBIA** Banjul
Bignona Brikama
Ziguinchor
Sédhiou
Kolda
GUINEA Farim
BISSAU Gabú
Arquipélago Bolama
dos Bijagós Boké

Akjoujt
Tidjikja Tichît
Moudjéria
Magta'
Lahjar Tâmchekket
Aleg Kiffa
Bôgué 'Ayoûn el 'Atroûs
Kaédi
Mbout
Matam Maghama
Sélibabi Kobénni
Yélimané Néma Timbedgha
Bakel Nioro Basikounou
Kayes Diéma Nara
Ba
Bafoulabé Parc National
Kéniéba de la Boucle
Satadougou du Baoulé
Kita Kolokani Niono Ké-Macina
Kangaba Banamba Ségou
Bamako Koulikoro Koutiala
Bougouni Dioïla San
Sikasso Orodara

MAURITANIA

Adrar

Choûm
Atâr

Ouarâne

El Mreyyé

Tombouctou
Bamba
Niger
Gao
Ansongo
Hombori
Gourma-
Rharous Ménaka
Douentza
Bandiagara Dori
Mopti Gorom Tillabéri
Barikass Gorom
Kaya Bogandé **Niamey**
Boulsa Dosso
Koupela
Fada-N'gourma
Diapaga

MALI

NIGER
Agadez
Arlit
Massif de l'Aïr
(Azbine)
Teguidda-n-
Tessoumt
Tahoua
Birnin
Konni Madaoua Mayahi Zinder
Tessaoua
Dogondoutchi Maradi Gouré
Sokoto Katsina Nguru
Kaura-Namoda Daura Hadejia

GUINEA
Conakry
Forécariah
Télimélé Pita Dabola
Fria Kindia Faranah
Kolenté Mamou
Kissidougou

**SIERRA
LEONE**
Freetown
Port Loko Makeni
Lungi Kabala
Moyamba Tonkolili
Gbangbama Bo Koidu
Bonthe Kenema
Sulima Bopolu
Robertsport Voinjama
Tubmanburg
Monrovia Gbarnga
Harbel
Buchanan
River Cess
LIBERIA
Zwedru
Sapo
National Park
Greenville Grabo
Barclayville
Harper
Tabou
C. Palmas

Parc National
du Niokolo Koba
Kédougou
Mali
Fouta
Djallon
Labé
Dinguiraye
Kankan
Kissidougou Kérouané Odienné
Macenta Beyla
Nzérékoré Man
Danané Séguéla
Tabou Tiassalé
Sassandra Grand-
San- Lahou
Pédro
C. Three
Points

Bobo-
Dioulasso
Banfora
Gaoua
Tumu

BURKINA
Ouagadougou
Koudougou Ziniaré
Réo Zorgo
Tenkodogo

Parc Nat. de Pô
Pô Nakambe

Parc National
de la Pendjari
Natitingou Kandi

BENIN
Parakou
Djougou
Savé
Abomey

TOGO
Sokodé
Kara
Atakpamé
Sotouboua

GHANA
Tamale
Bole
Wa
Kintampo
Sunyani
Kumasi Lake
Techiman Volta
Obuasi
Winneba
Accra
Cape Coast
Sekondi
Takoradi

Gulf of Guinea

**CÔTE
D'IVOIRE**
Bouaké
Yamoussoukro
Dimbokro Bondoukou
Daloa Divo Abengourou
Gagnoa Agboville
Abidjan
Aboisso
Grand-
Bassam

Parc
National Parc Nat.
de Taï de Comoé

Slave Coast

**Bight
of Benin**

NIGERIA
Abuja
Minna Jos Bauchi
Kaduna Zaria
Kano
Gusau
Ilorin Bida
Oyo Ogbomoso Oshogbo Ife Akure
Ibadan Abeokuta Ijebu-Ode Ondo Owo
Lagos Benin City
Porto- Cotonou Warri Onitsha
Novo Aba
Porto Port Enugu
Novo Harcourt Calabar
Uyo
Mt Cameroon
4100
Limbe
Douala
Malabo Bioco

**EQUATORIAL
GUINEA** Bata

**SÃO TOMÉ
AND PRÍNCIPE**
Príncipe

São Tomé Libreville

GULF OF GUINEA

Equator

São Tomé

Port-
Gentil

CAPE VERDE

25°

Santo
Antão Ponta do Sol
Mindelo Santa Luzia Sal
São Santa Maria
Vicente São Vila da Boa Vista
Nicolau Ribeira Brava
Vila de Sal Rei
Vila do
Ilhéus Secos Tarrafal Maio
ou do Rombo Curral Velho
Brava Fogo Porto Inglês
Vila Nova 2829 Praia
Sintra São São Tiago
Filipe

25°W

at the same scale

10°W

Metres feet

6000 19686
5000 16404
4000 13124
3000 9843
2000 6562
1000 3281
500 1640
200 656
SEA LEVEL
200 656
2000 6562
4000 13124
6000 19686

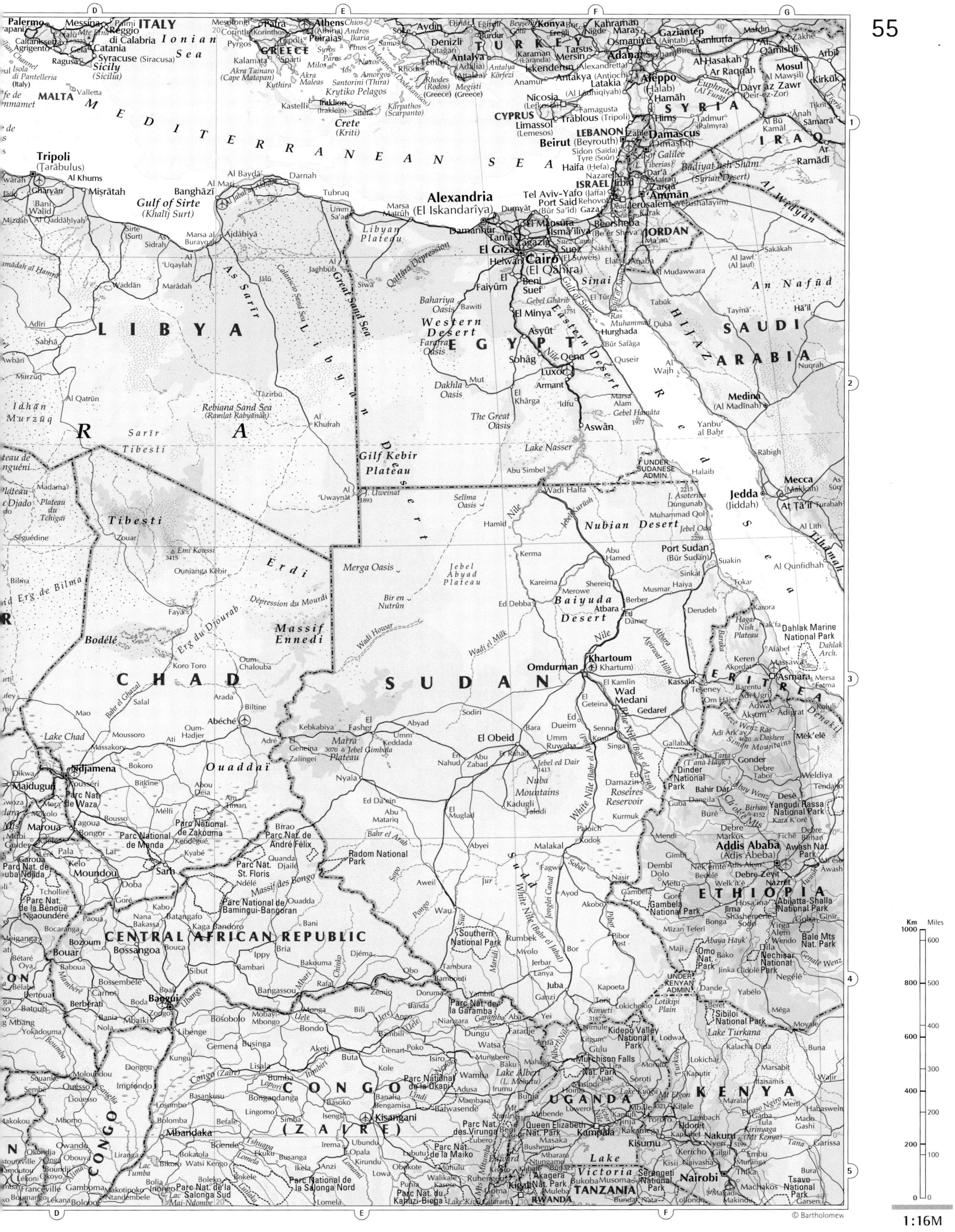

ITALY
Palermo
Messina
Reggio di Calabria
Catania
Syracuse (Siracusa)
Sicily (Sicilia)
MALTA
Valletta
Ionian Sea
GREECE
Athens (Athina)
Peiraias
Patra
Crete (Kriti)
Iraklion (Irakleio)
Kythira
Krytiko Pelagos
Rhodes (Rodos) (Greece)
TURKEY
Aydin
Denizli
Antalya
Konya
Mersin
Tarsus
Adana
Iskenderun (Alexandretta)
Antakya (Antioch)
Kahraman Maraş
Gaziantep (Aintab)
Şanlıurfa
Mardin
CYPRUS
Nicosia (Lefkosia)
Famagusta
Limassol (Lemesos)
SYRIA
Aleppo (Halab)
Latakia (Al Lādhiqīyah)
Hamāh
Hims
Tadmur (Palmyra)
Damascus (Dimashq)
Dayr az Zawr (Deir-ez-Zor)
Euphrates (Al Furat)
Al Hasakah
Ar Raqqah
Mosul (Al Mawşil)
IRAQ
Ar Ramādī
LEBANON
Beirut (Beyrouth)
Trāblous (Tripoli)
Sidon (Saïda)
Tyre (Soûr)
Haifa (Hefa)
ISRAEL
Tel Aviv-Yafo (Jaffa)
Jerusalem (Yerushalayim)
Gaza
Beersheba (Be'er Sheva)
Sea of Galilee
Dead Sea
JORDAN
'Ammān
Irbid
Zarqa
Bādiyat ash Shām (Syrian Desert)
Wādī al Wiryān
MEDITERRANEAN SEA
Tripoli (Ţarābulus)
Al Khums
Mişrātah
Gulf of Sirte (Khalīj Surt)
Sirte (Surt)
Banghāzī
Darnah
Ajdābiyā
Tubruq
LIBYA
Sabhā
Al Qatrūn
Rebiana Sand Sea (Ramlat Rabyānah)
Al Khufrah
Sarīr Tibesti
SAHARA
Great Sand Sea
Libyan Desert
Alexandria (El Iskandarîya)
Marsa Matrûh
Port Said (Bûr Sa'îd)
El Mansûra
Tanta
Zagazig
Ismâ'ilîya
Suez (El Suweis)
Suez Canal
El Giza
Cairo (El Qâhira)
Helwan
Faiyûm
Beni Suef
El Minya
Asyût
Sohâg
Qena
Luxor
Armant
Idfu
Aswân
Hurghada
Bûr Safâga
Quseir
Sinai
Gulf of Suez
Eastern Desert
Siwa
Qattâra Depression
Bahariya Oasis
Farafra Oasis
Dakhla Oasis
Kharga Oasis
The Great Oasis
Western Desert
EGYPT
Lake Nasser
Abu Simbel
Gilf Kebir Plateau
J. Uweinat 1893
Selîma Oasis
Wadi Halfa
UNDER SUDANESE ADMIN.
Halaib
Nubian Desert
Port Sudan (Bûr Sudân)
Suakin
Tokar
Dungunab
Kerma
Abu Hamed
Merowe
Baiyuda Desert
Atbara
Berber
Ed Damer
Khartoum (El Khartûm)
Omdurman
Kassala
Wad Medani
Gedaref
Sennar
El Obeid
Nuba Mountains
Kadugli
Malakal
Sudd
Jonglei Canal
White Nile (Bahr el Jebel)
Blue Nile (Bahr el Azraq)
Roseires Reservoir
Juba
Wau
Aweil
Southern National Park
Radom National Park
Merga Oasis
Jebel Abyad Plateau
Bir en Natrûn
Wadi Howar
Wadi el Milk
Jebel Marra 3070
El Fasher
Nyala
Geneina
SUDAN
Red Sea
Jedda (Jiddah)
Mecca (Makkah)
At Tā'if
Medina (Al Madīnah)
Yanbu' al Bahr
Rābigh
Al Wajh
Tabūk
Hā'il
An Nafūd
Al Jawf (Al Jauf)
HIJAZ
SAUDI ARABIA
Tihāmah
Al Qunfidhah
Al Līth
Tibesti
Emi Koussi 3415
Erdi
Ennedi
Massif Ennedi
Dépression du Mourdi
Erg du Djourab
Bodélé
Faya
Erg de Bilma
Bilma
Plateau du Djado
Ounianga Kébir
CHAD
Abéché
Ouaddaï
Lake Chad
Ndjamena
Maiduguri
Parc Nat. de Waza
Maroua
Moundou
Sarh
Parc National de Zakouma
Parc Nat. de André Félix
Parc Nat. St. Floris
Massif des Bongo
Parc National de Bamingui-Bangoran
CENTRAL AFRICAN REPUBLIC
Bossangoa
Bouar
Berbérati
Bangui
Bambari
Obo
Parc Nat. de la Garamba
Kisangani
Mbandaka
CONGO (ZAIRE)
Congo (Zaïre)
Ubangi
Lake Albert (L. Mobutu)
Murchison Falls Nat. Park
Kidepo Valley National Park
UGANDA
Kampala
Jinja
Lake Victoria
Kisumu
Nakuru
Nairobi
KENYA
Lake Turkana
Sibiloi National Park
Marsabit
Mt Elgon 4321
Mt Kenya (Kirinyaga) 5199
Parc Nat. des Virunga
Queen Elizabeth Nat. Park
RWANDA
Kigali
TANZANIA
Serengeti National Park
Tsavo National Park
ERITREA
Asmara
Massawa
Keren
Dahlak Marine National Park
Dahlak Arch.
ETHIOPIA
Addis Ababa (Adis Abeba)
Gonder
Lake Tana (T'ana Hayk')
Bahir Dar
Simēn Mountains
Ras Dashen 4620
Dessē
Awash Nat. Park
Bale Mts Nat. Park
Omo Nat. Park
Gambela National Park
Abijatta-Shalla National Park
UNDER KENYAN ADMIN.
Lotikipi Plain
Lake Turkana
Km
Miles
1:16M
© Bartholomew

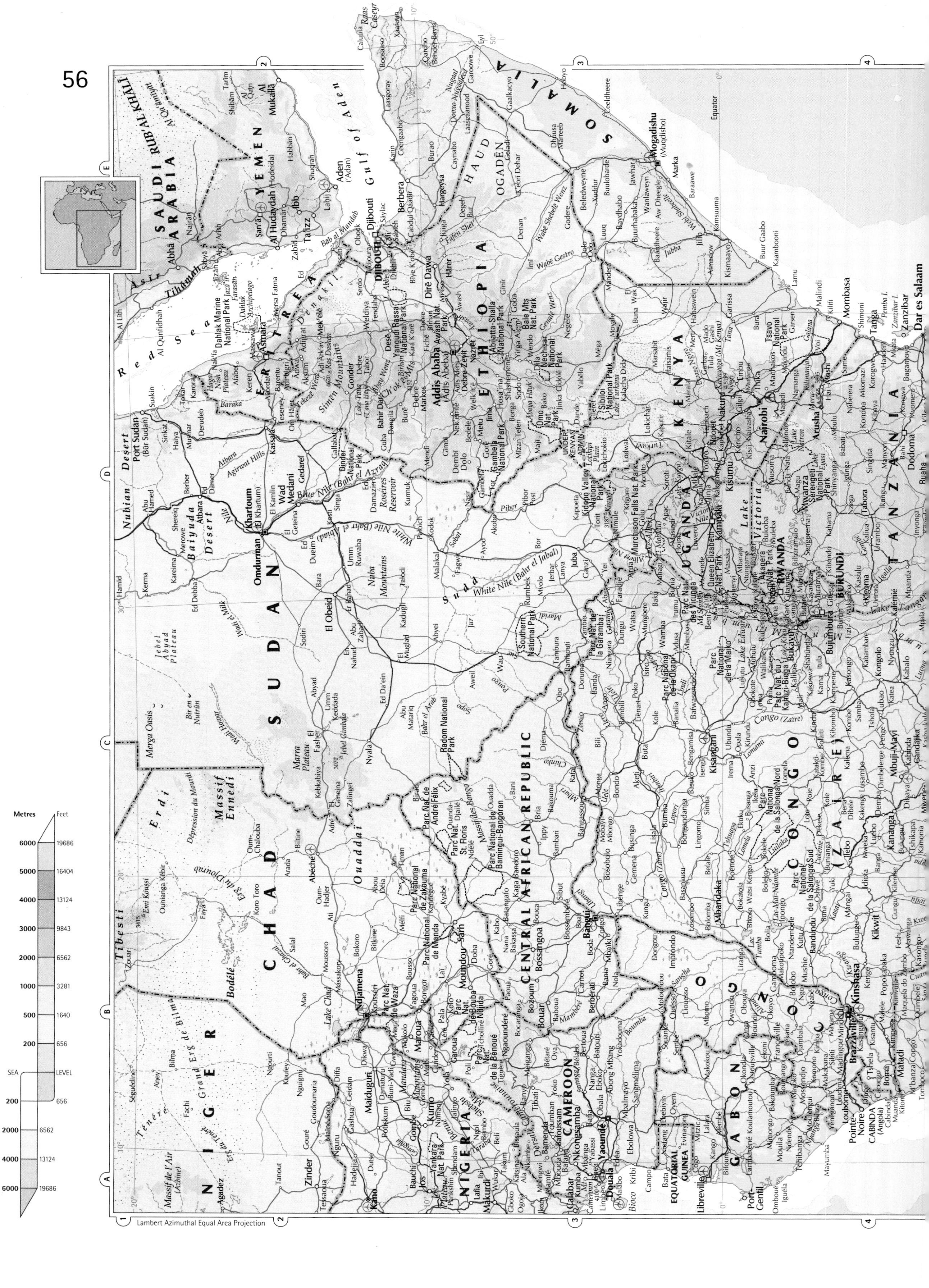
Metres
Feet
6000
19686
5000
16404
4000
13124
3000
9843
2000
6562
1000
3281
500
1640
200
656
SEA
LEVEL
200
656
2000
6562
4000
13124
6000
19686
SAUDI ARABIA
YEMEN
ERITREA
ETHIOPIA
SOMALIA
DJIBOUTI
SUDAN
CHAD
NIGER
NIGERIA
CAMEROON
CENTRAL AFRICAN REPUBLIC
KENYA
UGANDA
RWANDA
BURUNDI
TANZANIA
CONGO (ZAIRE)
CONGO
GABON
EQUATORIAL GUINEA
CABINDA (Angola)
Red Sea
Gulf of Aden
Khartoum
Addis Ababa
Mogadishu
Nairobi
Kampala
Ndjamena
Bangui
Yaoundé
Libreville
Kinshasa
Brazzaville
Dar es Salaam
Lake Victoria
Lake Chad
White Nile (Bahr el Abiad)
Blue Nile (Bahr el Azraq)
Lambert Azimuthal Equal Area Projection

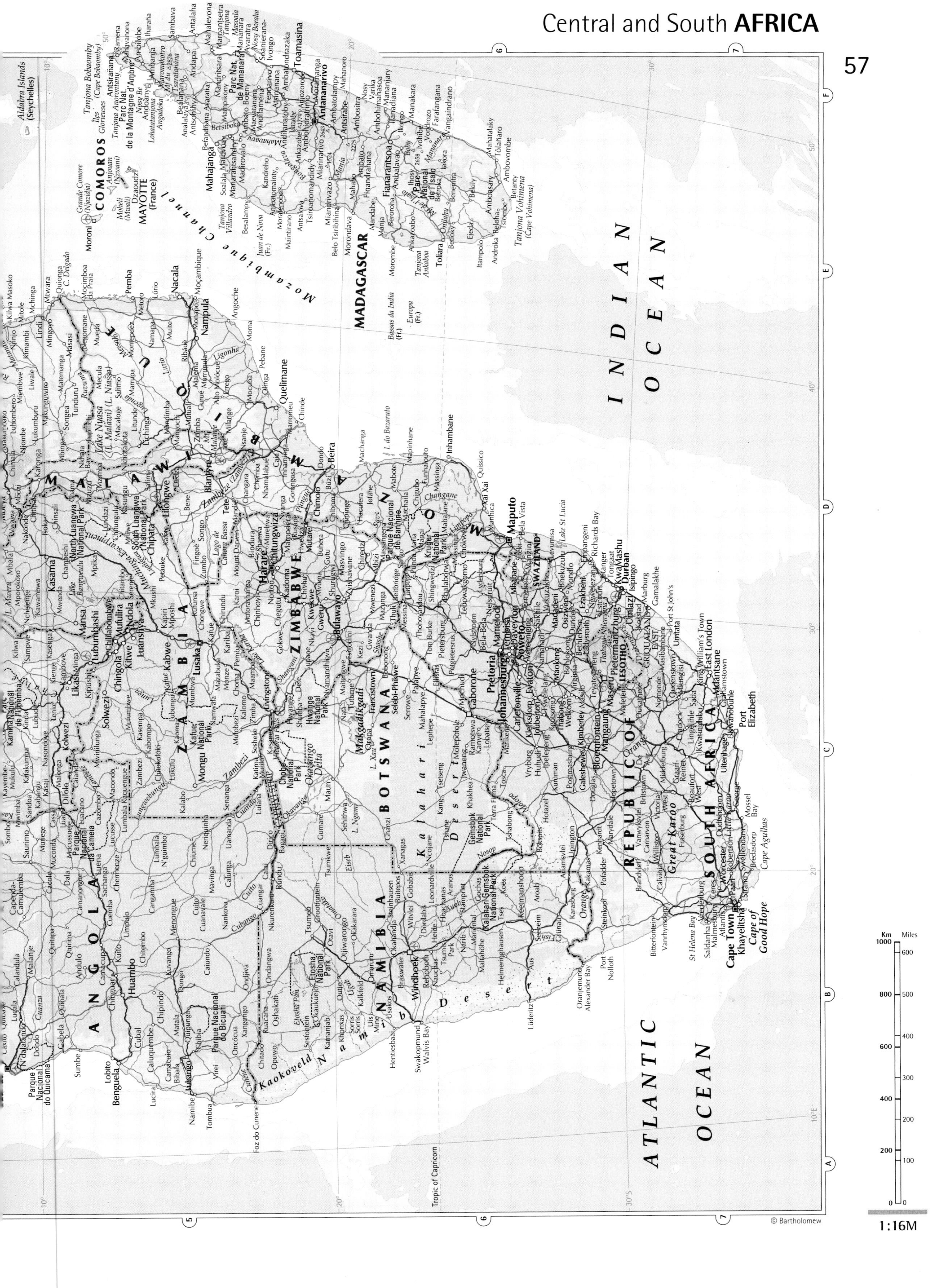
ANGOLA
ZAMBIA
MALAWI
MOZAMBIQUE
ZIMBABWE
BOTSWANA
NAMIBIA
REPUBLIC OF SOUTH AFRICA
LESOTHO
SWAZILAND
MADAGASCAR
COMOROS
MAYOTTE (France)
INDIAN OCEAN
ATLANTIC OCEAN
Mozambique Channel
Kalahari Desert
Namib Desert
Tropic of Capricorn
Cape of Good Hope
Cape Agulhas
Cape Town
Johannesburg
Pretoria
Maputo
Harare
Lusaka
Lilongwe
Gaborone
Windhoek
Antananarivo
Moroni
Durban
Port Elizabeth
East London
Bloemfontein
Maseru
Mbabane
Bulawayo
Luanda
Huambo
Benguela
Lobito
Beira
Quelimane
Nampula
Blantyre
Ndola
Kitwe
Toamasina
Mahajanga
Toliara
Fianarantsoa
Km
Miles
1000
800
600
400
200
0
600
500
400
300
200
100
0

© Bartholomew

1:16M

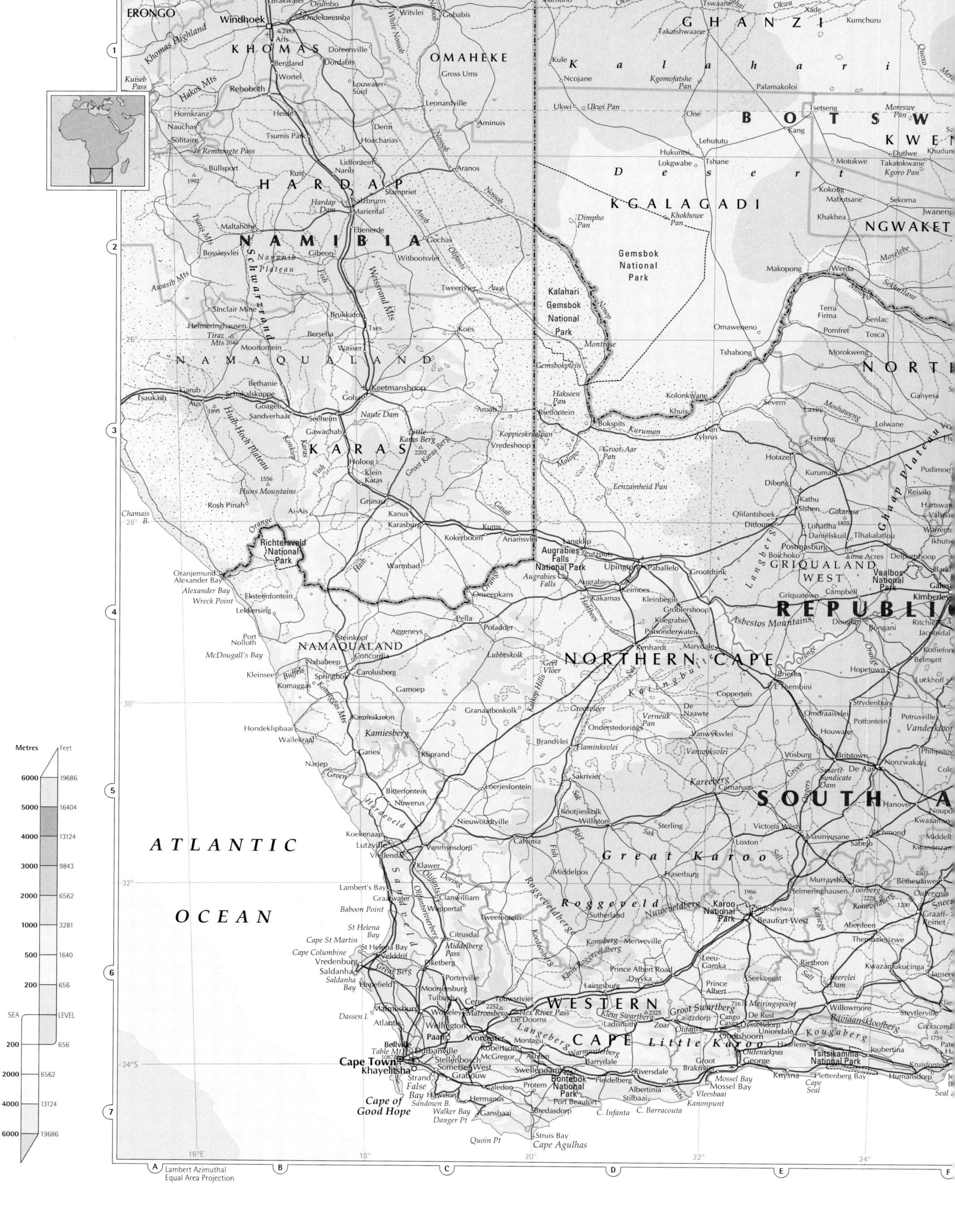

ERONGO
Windhoek
KHOMAS
Khomas Highland
OMAHEKE
Gobabis
Rehoboth
Kuiseb Pass
Hakos Mts
HARDAP
Mariental
Hardap Dam
NAMIBIA
Maltahöhe
Naukluft Plateau
Schwarzrand
Weissrand Mts
Tsaris Mts
Awasib Mts
NAMAQUALAND
Keetmanshoop
Bethanie
Lüderitz
Tsaukaib
Aus
Huib-Hoch Plateau
KARAS
Karasburg
Huns Mountains
Rosh Pinah
Richtersveld National Park
Oranjemund
Alexander Bay
Wreck Point
Port Nolloth
McDougall's Bay
Kleinsee
Springbok
Kamiesberg
Hondeklipbaai
GHANZI
Kalahari Desert
BOTSWANA
KWENENG
KGALAGADI
NGWAKETSE
Gemsbok National Park
Kalahari Gemsbok National Park
NORTH
Augrabies Falls National Park
Upington
Kuruman
Kathu
Sishen
GRIQUALAND WEST
Vaalbos National Park
Kimberley
REPUBLIC
Asbestos Mountains
NORTHERN CAPE
Kenhardt
Calvinia
Carnarvon
SOUTH A
Great Karoo
Roggeveld
Sutherland
Karoo National Park
Beaufort West
WESTERN CAPE
Little Karoo
Oudtshoorn
George
Knysna
Tsitsikamma National Park
Plettenberg Bay
Worcester
Paarl
Stellenbosch
Cape Town
Khayelitsha
Table Mt 1087
False Bay
Cape of Good Hope
Hermanus
Bontebok National Park
Mossel Bay
Cape Agulhas
Struis Bay
Saldanha
Vredenburg
St Helena Bay
Clanwilliam
Cedarberg
ATLANTIC
OCEAN
Lambert Azimuthal Equal Area Projection
Metres
Feet
6000 19686
5000 16404
4000 13124
3000 9843
2000 6562
1000 3281
500 1640
200 656
SEA LEVEL
200 656
2000 6562
4000 13124
6000 19686

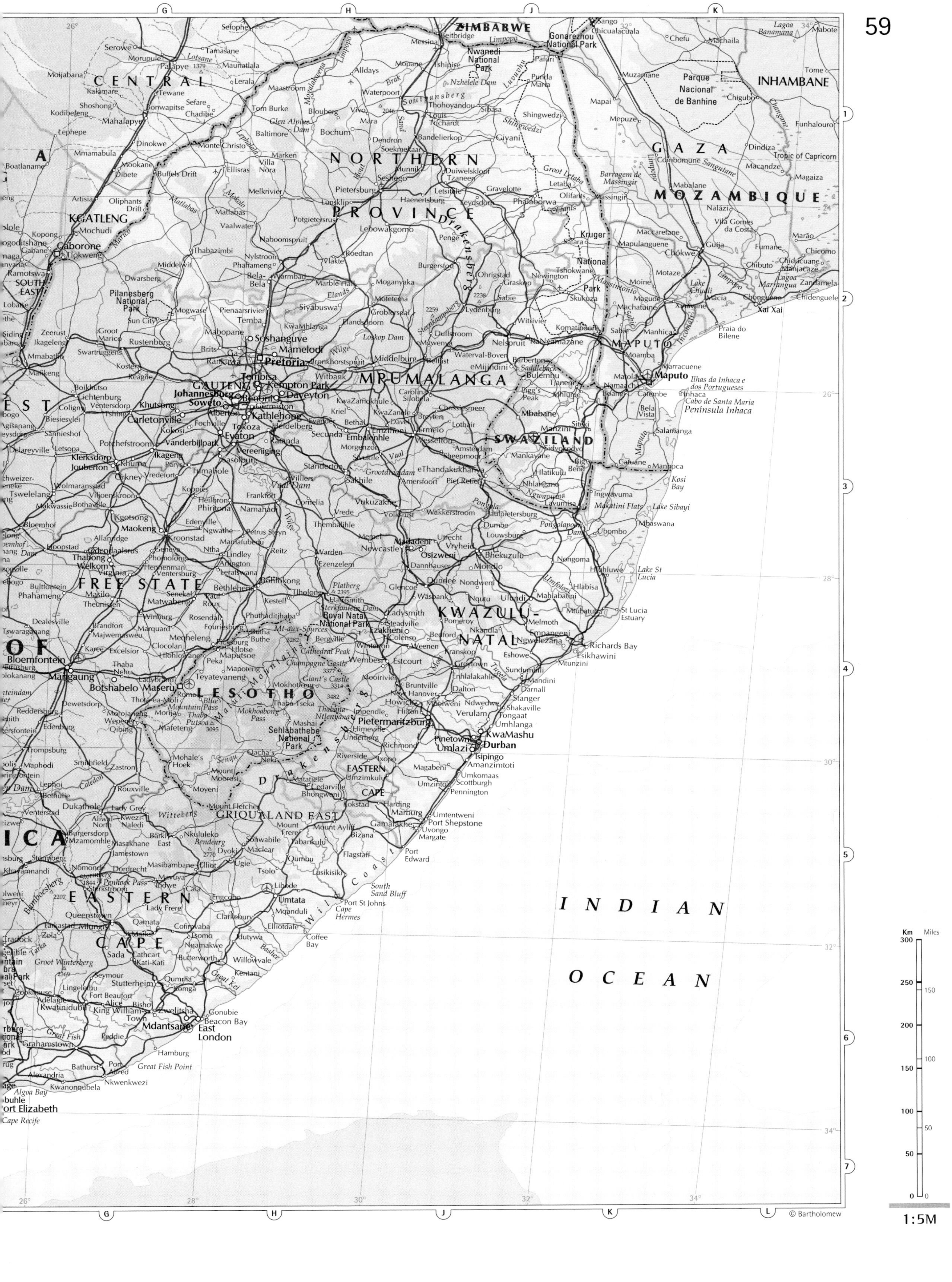
ZIMBABWE
Gonarezhou National Park
Nwanedi National Park
CENTRAL
KGATLENG
SOUTH EAST
NORTHERN PROVINCE
Parque Nacional de Banhine
INHAMBANE
GAZA
MOZAMBIQUE
Tropic of Capricorn
Kruger National Park
Pilanesberg National Park
MAPUTO
Maputo
Pretoria
GAUTENG
Johannesburg
Soweto
MPUMALANGA
SWAZILAND
Mbabane
Manzini
Ilhas da Inhaca e dos Portugueses
Península Inhaca
FREE STATE
Bloemfontein
Mangaung
KWAZULU-NATAL
LESOTHO
Maseru
Royal Natal National Park
Sehlabathebe National Park
Pietermaritzburg
Durban
KwaMashu
Umlazi
Richards Bay
Lake St Lucia
Kosi Bay
GRIQUALAND EAST
EASTERN CAPE
Umtata
East London
Mdantsane
Port Elizabeth
Grahamstown
Great Fish Point
Algoa Bay
Cape Recife
Coffee Bay
Port St Johns
Port Shepstone
Port Edward
Wild Coast
Drakensberg
INDIAN OCEAN
Km
Miles
300
250
200
150
100
50
0
© Bartholomew
1:5M

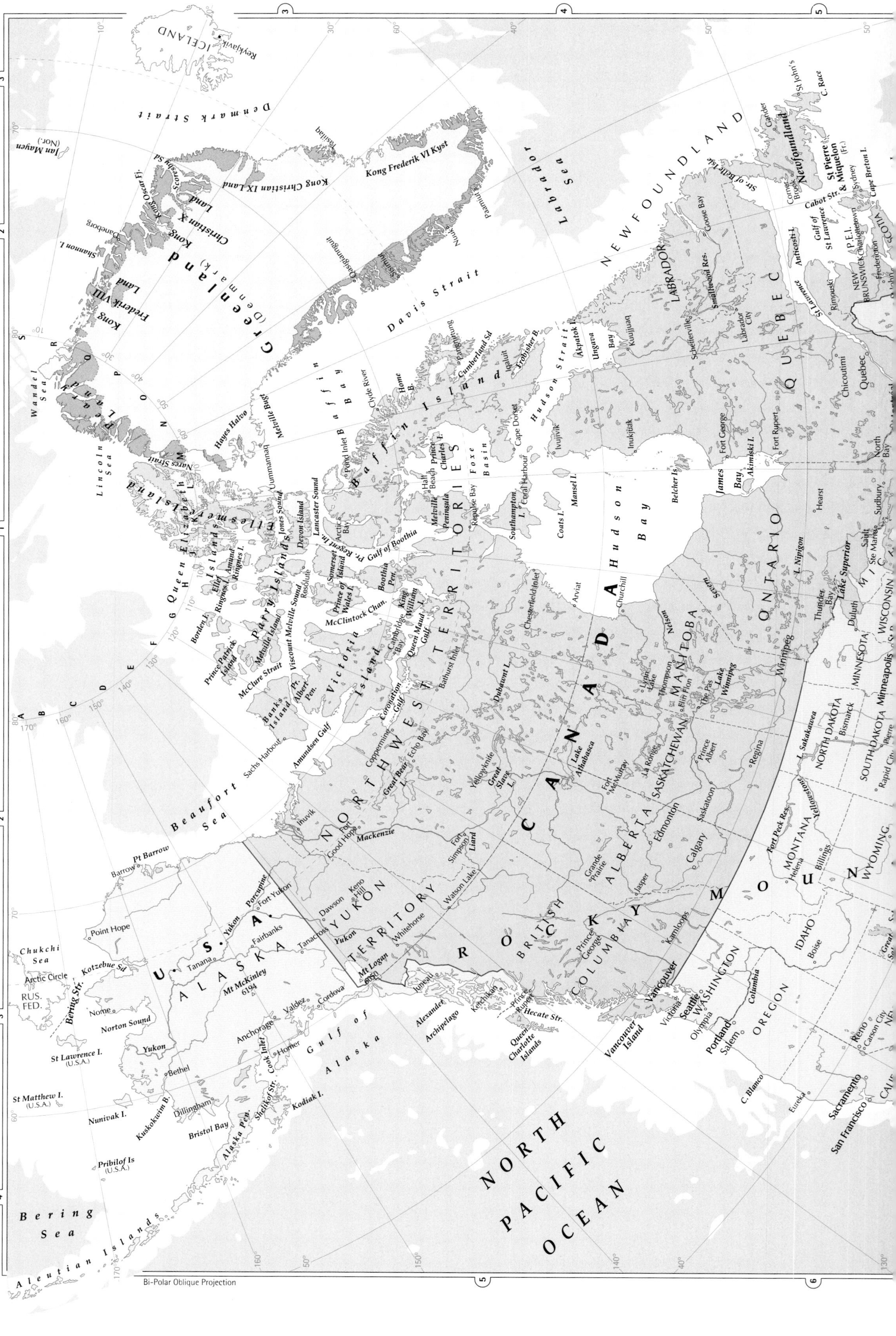

60

ICELAND
Reykjavik

Jan Mayen (Nor.)

Denmark Strait

Wandel Sea

Greenland (Denmark)

Kong Christian IX Land
Kong Christian X Land
Kong Frederik VI Kyst
Kong Frederik VIII Land

Scoresby Sd
Kong Oscar Fj
Danmarkshavn
Shannon I.

Peary Land

Lincoln Sea
Nares Strait
Hall Land
Hayes Halvø

Qaanaaq
Melville Bugt

Baffin Bay
Clyde River
Home B.
Pond Inlet
Arctic Inlet

Davis Strait

Labrador Sea

LABRADOR
Ungava Bay
Akpatok I.
Kuujjuaq
Schefferville
Smallwood Res.
Goose Bay
Labrador City

NEWFOUNDLAND

Str. of Belle Isle
Corner Brook
Gander
St John's
C. Race

St Pierre & Miquelon (Fr.)
Cape Breton I.
Sydney
P.E.I.
Charlottetown
Gulf of St Lawrence
Anticosti I.
NEW BRUNSWICK
Fredericton
Rimouski

QUEBEC
Chicoutimi
Quebec

Ellesmere Island
Queen Elizabeth Islands
Axel Heiberg Island
Jones Sound
Devon Island
Lancaster Sound
Eureka
Borden I.
Ellef Ringnes I.
Amund Ringnes I.
Somerset Island
Prince of Wales I.
Boothia Pen.
Resolute

Parry Islands
Bathurst Island
Melville Island
Prince Patrick Island
McClure Strait
Viscount Melville Sound
McClintock Chan.

Cumberland Sd
Iqaluit
Frobisher B.
Cape Dorset

Foxe Basin
Hall Beach
Prince Charles I.
Melville Peninsula

Repulse Bay
Coats I.
Mansel I.
Southampton I.
Coral Harbour
Belcher Is

Ivujivik
Inukjuak

Hudson Strait

Hudson Bay

Fort George
Fort Rupert
James Bay
Akimiski I.
North

ONTARIO
Hearst
Sudbury
L. Nipigon
Thunder Bay
Sault Ste Marie
Lake Superior

Banks Island
Victoria Island
Albert Pen.
Prince of Wales
King William I.
Cambridge Bay
Queen Maud Gulf
Coronation Gulf
Coppermine
Echo Bay
Great Bear Lake

NORTHWEST TERRITORIES

CANADA

Hudson Bay

Chesterfield Inlet
Arviat
Churchill

MANITOBA
Thompson
Flin Flon
The Pas
Lake Winnipeg
Nelson
Lynn Lake
Winnipeg

SASKATCHEWAN
Prince Albert
Saskatoon
Regina

Beaufort Sea

Sachs Harbour
Amundsen Gulf
Inuvik
Fort Good Hope
Mackenzie

Great Slave L.
Yellowknife

Dubawnt L.
L. Athabasca
Fort McMurray
La Ronge

ALBERTA
Grande Prairie
Edmonton
Jasper
Calgary

Pt Barrow
Barrow

Fort Yukon
Porcupine
Yukon

YUKON TERRITORY
Dawson
Keno Hill
Watson Lake
Whitehorse

Fort Simpson
Fort Liard

BRITISH COLUMBIA

ROCKY MOUNTAINS

Fort Peck Res.
MONTANA
Helena
Billings

Red Deer

NORTH DAKOTA
Bismarck

SOUTH DAKOTA
Pierre
Rapid City

U.S.A.

ALASKA
Tanana
Fairbanks
Tanana
Tanacross
Mt McKinley 6194
Mt Logan 6050

Chukchi Sea
Point Hope
Arctic Circle
RUS. FED.
Kotzebue Sd
Nome
Norton Sound
St Lawrence I. (U.S.A.)
St Matthew I. (U.S.A.)
Nunivak I.
Bethel
Yukon
Kuskokwim B.
Dillingham
Bristol Bay
Alaska Pen.
Pribilof Is (U.S.A.)

Bering Str.
Bering Sea

Anchorage
Valdez
Cordova
Cook Inlet
Homer
Kodiak I.
Shelikof Str.
Juneau
Alexander Archipelago
Ketchikan
Prince Rupert
Queen Charlotte Islands
Hecate Str.

Gulf of Alaska

Prince George
Kamloops
Vancouver
Vancouver Island
Victoria
Seattle
Olympia
WASHINGTON
Portland
Salem
OREGON
Columbia
C. Blanco
Eureka

IDAHO
Boise

WYOMING
Yellowstone

NEBRASKA
North Platte

MINNESOTA
Duluth
Minneapolis
St Paul
WISCONSIN

Reno
Carson City
Sacramento
San Francisco

Aleutian Islands

NORTH PACIFIC OCEAN

Bi-Polar Oblique Projection

Metres
SEA LEVEL
200
3000

Feet
SEA LEVEL
656
9843

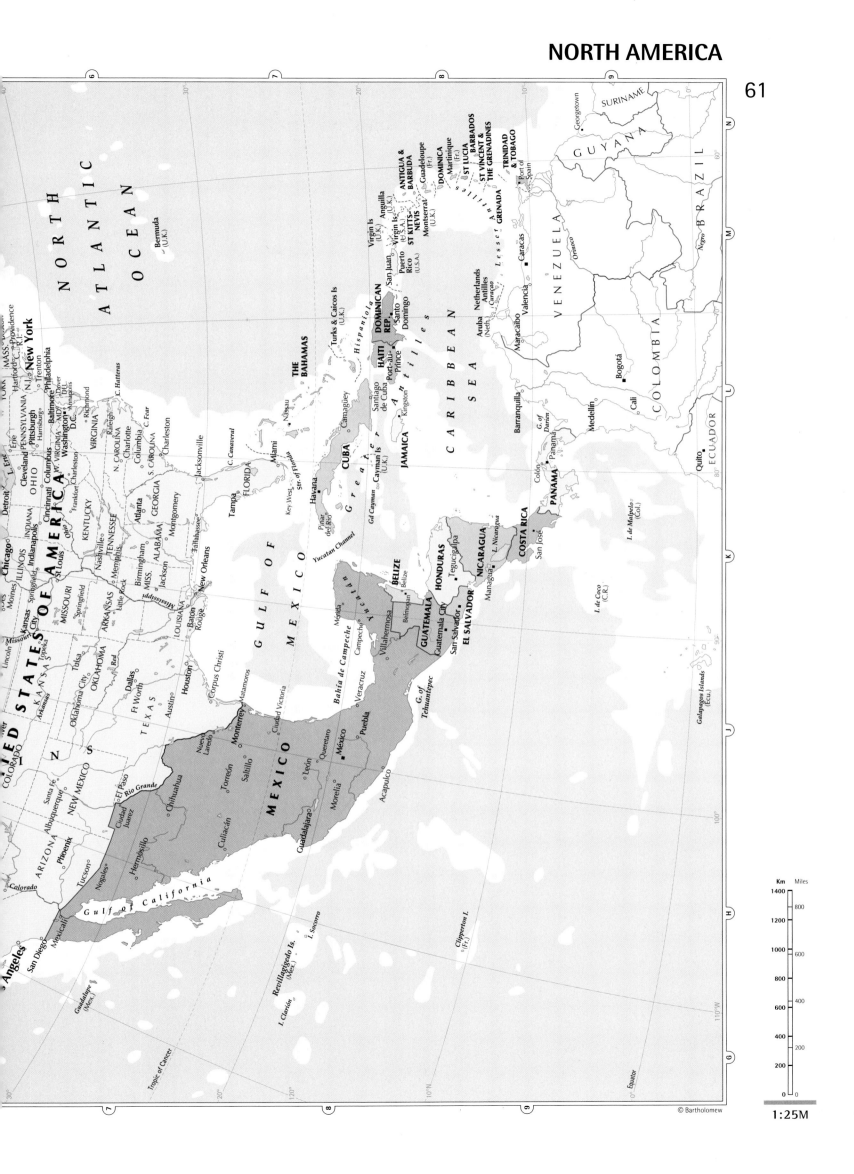

N O R T H   A T L A N T I C   O C E A N

Bermuda (U.K.)

GUYANA

SURINAME

Georgetown

BRAZIL

Negro

VENEZUELA

COLOMBIA

Orinoco

Caracas

Valencia

Maracaibo

Barranquilla

Medellín

Bogotá

Cali

ECUADOR

Quito

ANTIGUA & BARBUDA

Guadeloupe (Fr.)

DOMINICA

Martinique (Fr.)

ST LUCIA

BARBADOS

ST VINCENT & THE GRENADINES

GRENADA

TRINIDAD & TOBAGO

Port of Spain

ST KITTS-NEVIS

Montserrat (U.K.)

Virgin Is (U.K.)

Virgin Is (U.S.A.)

Anguilla (U.K.)

San Juan

Puerto Rico (U.S.A.)

Netherlands Antilles

Aruba (Neth.)

Curaçao

Lesser Antilles

CARIBBEAN SEA

Santo Domingo

DOMINICAN REP.

HAITI

Port-au-Prince

Hispaniola

Turks & Caicos Is (U.K.)

THE BAHAMAS

Nassau

CUBA

Camagüey

Santiago de Cuba

Greater Antilles

JAMAICA

Kingston

Cayman Is (U.K.)

Gd Cayman

Pinar del Río

Havana

Key West

Str. of Florida

UNITED STATES OF AMERICA

New York

MASS.
R.I.
CONN.
N.J.
DEL.
MD.

Providence
Hartford
Trenton
Philadelphia
Baltimore
Washington D.C.
Dover
Annapolis
Richmond
Harrisburg

YORK

Erie
L. Erie
Detroit
Cleveland
Pittsburgh
PENNSYLVANIA

OHIO
Columbus
Cincinnati
Frankfort
Columbia
Raleigh
Charlotte
N. CAROLINA
S. CAROLINA
Charleston
C. Hatteras
C. Fear

VIRGINIA
W. VIRGINIA

KENTUCKY

Chicago
ILLINOIS
INDIANA
Indianapolis
Springfield
St Louis
MISSOURI
Jefferson City

Des Moines

Lincoln

Kansas City

Topeka
KANSAS

OKLAHOMA
Oklahoma City

Tulsa

Little Rock
ARKANSAS

TENNESSEE
Nashville
Memphis
Birmingham
ALABAMA
MISS.
Jackson
Montgomery
GEORGIA
Atlanta
Tallahassee
Jacksonville
FLORIDA
Tampa
C. Canaveral
Miami
Orlando

Nashville

LOUISIANA
Baton Rouge
New Orleans
Mississippi

Jackson

NEW MEXICO
Santa Fe
Albuquerque
ARIZONA
Phoenix
Tucson
Nogales
Colorado
Rio Grande
El Paso

COLORADO

Red

S

PLAINS

TEXAS
Dallas
Ft Worth
Austin
Houston
Corpus Christi
San Antonio

Lincoln

Missouri

Los Angeles
San Diego
Mexicali

MEXICO

Ciudad Juárez
Chihuahua
Hermosillo
Culiacán
Torreón
Saltillo
Monterrey
Nuevo Laredo
Matamoros
Ciudad Victoria
Tampico
Guadalajara
León
Querétaro
México
Morelia
Puebla
Acapulco
Veracruz
Villahermosa
Mérida
Campeche
Bahía de Campeche
G. of Tehuantepec

Gulf of California

Tropic of Cancer

Revillagigedo Is. (Mex.)

I. Clarión

I. Socorro

Guadalupe (Mex.)

GULF OF MEXICO

Yucatán Channel

Yucatán

BELIZE
Belize
Belmopan

GUATEMALA
Guatemala City

EL SALVADOR
San Salvador

HONDURAS
Tegucigalpa

NICARAGUA
Managua
L. Nicaragua

COSTA RICA
San José

PANAMA
Panamá
Colón
G. of Darién

I. de Malpelo (Col.)

I. de Coco (C.R.)

Clipperton I. (Fr.)

Galápagos Islands (Ecu.)

Equator

Tropic of Cancer

© Bartholomew

Km	Miles
1400	
1200	800
1000	600
800	
600	400
400	200
200	
0	0

1:25M

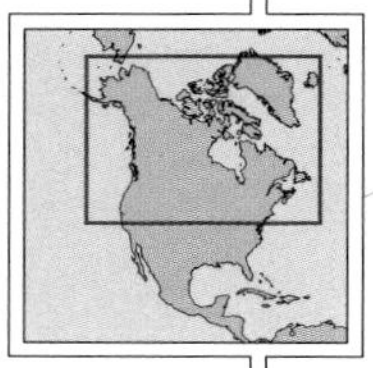

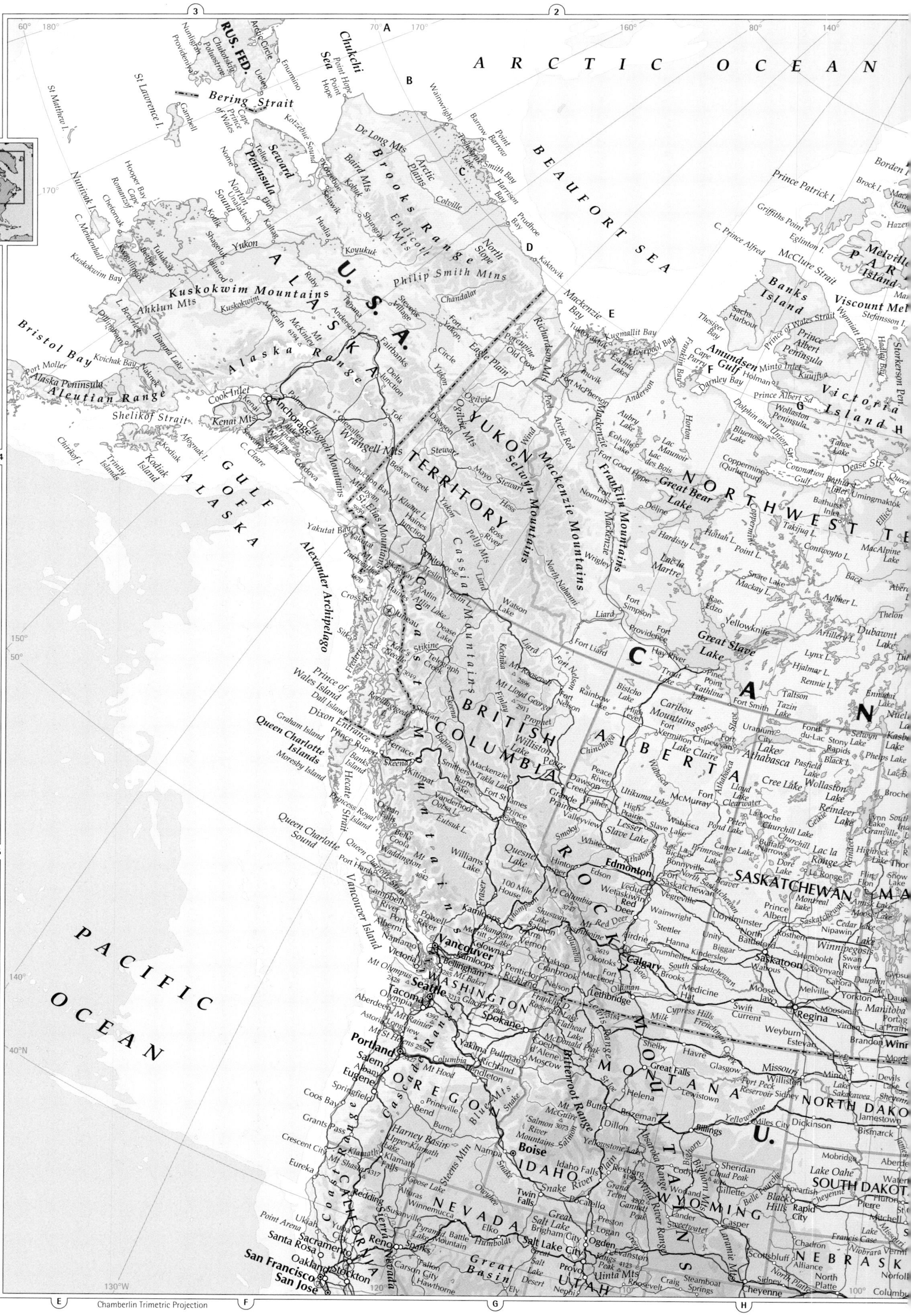

ARCTIC OCEAN
BEAUFORT SEA
PACIFIC OCEAN
GULF OF ALASKA
Bering Strait
Chukchi Sea
Bristol Bay
RUS. FED.
U.S.A.
ALASKA
Brooks Range
Alaska Range
Kuskokwim Mountains
Aleutian Range
Seward Peninsula
Kenai Mts
Chugach Mountains
Wrangell Mts
Philip Smith Mtns
Anchorage
Fairbanks
Juneau
Kodiak Island
Alexander Archipelago
Prince of Wales Island
Queen Charlotte Islands
Vancouver Island
YUKON TERRITORY
Mackenzie Mountains
Selwyn Mountains
Cassiar Mountains
Coast Mountains
BRITISH COLUMBIA
ALBERTA
SASKATCHEWAN
NORTHWEST TERRITORIES
CANADA
ROCKY MOUNTAINS
Great Bear Lake
Great Slave Lake
Lake Athabasca
Banks Island
Victoria Island
Melville Island
Prince Patrick I.
Amundsen Gulf
Whitehorse
Yellowknife
Edmonton
Calgary
Vancouver
Victoria
Kamloops
Prince George
Regina
Saskatoon
WASHINGTON
OREGON
IDAHO
MONTANA
WYOMING
NEVADA
UTAH
CALIFORNIA
NORTH DAKOTA
SOUTH DAKOTA
NEBRASKA
Seattle
Tacoma
Spokane
Portland
Salem
Eugene
Boise
Great Falls
Helena
Billings
Salt Lake City
Ogden
Provo
Reno
Sacramento
Oakland
San Francisco
San Jose
Stockton
Cheyenne
Great Basin
Cascade Range
Bitterroot Range
Blue Mts
Snake River Plain
Great Salt Lake
Yellowstone
Lake Sakakawea
Lake Oahe

Chamberlin Trimetric Projection

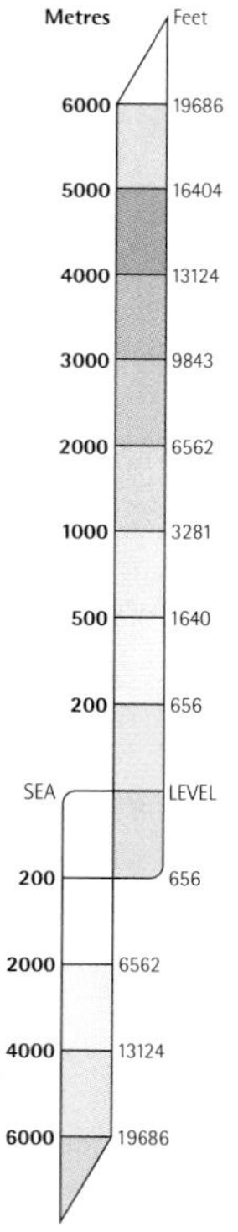

Metres
Feet
6000
19686
5000
16404
4000
13124
3000
9843
2000
6562
1000
3281
500
1640
200
656
SEA
LEVEL
200
656
2000
6562
4000
13124
6000
19686

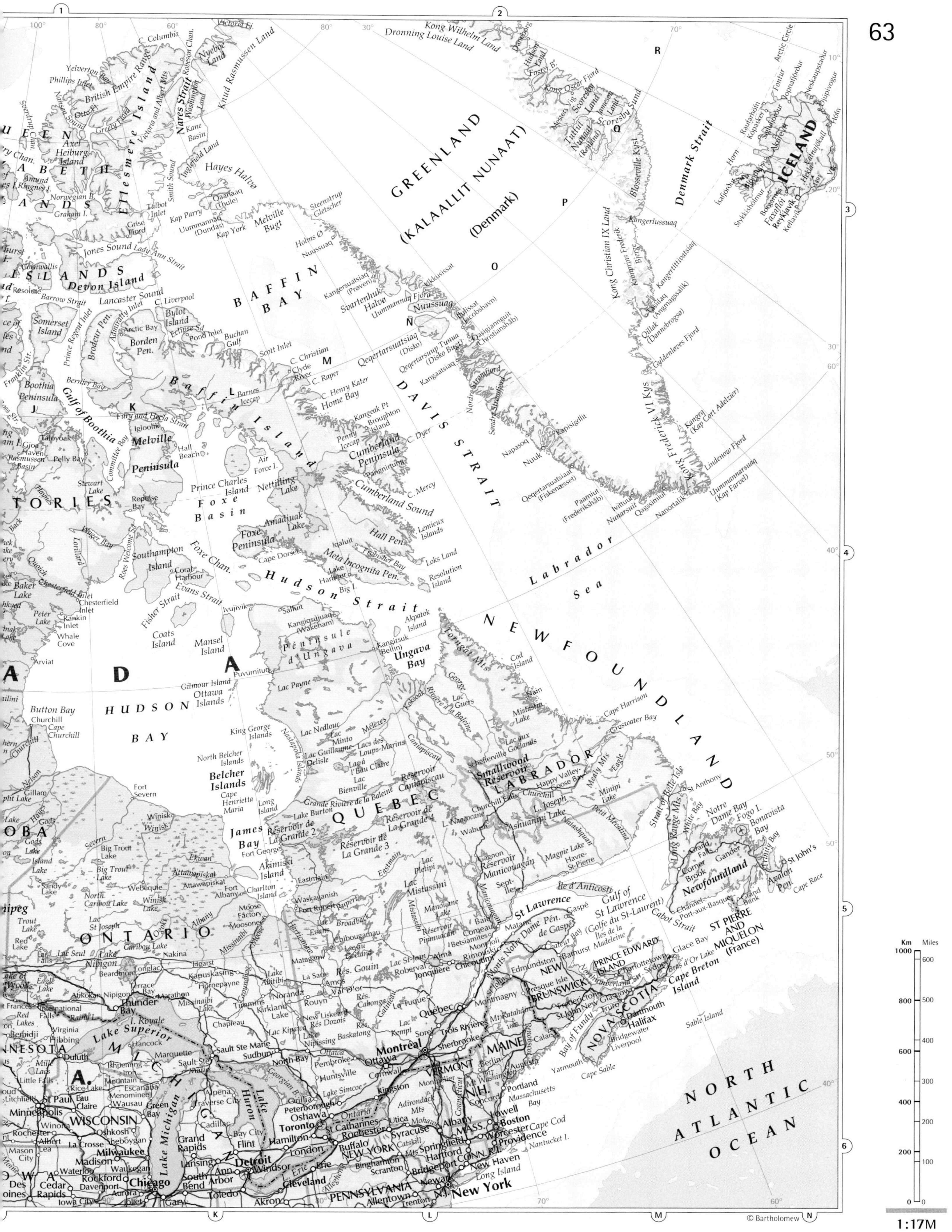

GREENLAND
(KALAALLIT NUNAAT)
(Denmark)
ICELAND
Reykjavík
Denmark Strait
Scoresby Sund
Kong Christian IX Land
Kong Frederick VI Kyst
Blosseville Kyst
Kangerlussuaq
Kong Wilhelm Land
Dronning Louise Land
Knud Rasmussen Land
Victoria Fj.
C. Columbia
Ellesmere Island
Nares Strait
Kane Basin
Smith Sound
Hayes Halvø
Qaanaaq (Thule)
Melville Bugt
Axel Heiburg Island
Devon Island
Jones Sound
Lancaster Sound
Barrow Strait
Somerset Island
Bylot Island
Borden Pen.
Brodeur Pen.
Boothia Peninsula
Gulf of Boothia
Melville Peninsula
BAFFIN BAY
Baffin Island
DAVIS STRAIT
Cumberland Peninsula
Cumberland Sound
Hall Pen.
Meta Incognita Pen.
Iqaluit
Nettilling Lake
Amadjuak Lake
Foxe Basin
Foxe Peninsula
Foxe Chan.
Southampton Island
Coats Island
Mansel Island
Hudson Strait
Ungava Bay
Péninsule d'Ungava
Labrador Sea
NEWFOUNDLAND
LABRADOR
Smallwood Reservoir
Cape Harrison
Groswater Bay
Strait of Belle Isle
Newfoundland
St John's
Cape Race
Avalon Pen.
Cabot Strait
ST PIERRE AND MIQUELON (France)
Gulf of St Lawrence
Île d'Anticosti
PRINCE EDWARD ISLAND
Charlottetown
NOVA SCOTIA
Halifax
Cape Breton Island
Sable Island
Bay of Fundy
NEW BRUNSWICK
Fredericton
St John
Cape Sable
Yarmouth
QUEBEC
Réservoir Caniapiscau
Réservoir de La Grande 2
Réservoir de La Grande 3
Réservoir de La Grande 4
Réservoir Manicouagan
Lac Mistassini
Québec
Montréal
Ottawa
Trois Rivières
Sherbrooke
HUDSON BAY
James Bay
Belcher Islands
Akimiski Island
Churchill
ONTARIO
Toronto
Hamilton
London
Windsor
Kingston
Sudbury
Sault Ste Marie
Thunder Bay
Lake Superior
Lake Huron
Lake Michigan
Lake Nipigon
Lake Nipissing
Lake Simcoe
Lake Erie
Ontario
TORIES
MAINE
Augusta
Portland
VERMONT
N.H.
Concord
MASS.
Boston
Worcester
Springfield
Providence
R.I.
CONN.
Hartford
New Haven
Bridgeport
Long Island
Cape Cod
Nantucket I.
NEW YORK
New York
Albany
Syracuse
Rochester
Buffalo
Utica
Binghamton
PENNSYLVANIA
Erie
Cleveland
Toledo
Akron
Detroit
Flint
Lansing
Grand Rapids
MICHIGAN
WISCONSIN
Milwaukee
Madison
Chicago
Gary
MINNESOTA
Minneapolis
St Paul
Duluth
IOWA
Cedar Rapids
Des Moines
NORTH ATLANTIC OCEAN
© Bartholomew
Km
Miles
1:17M

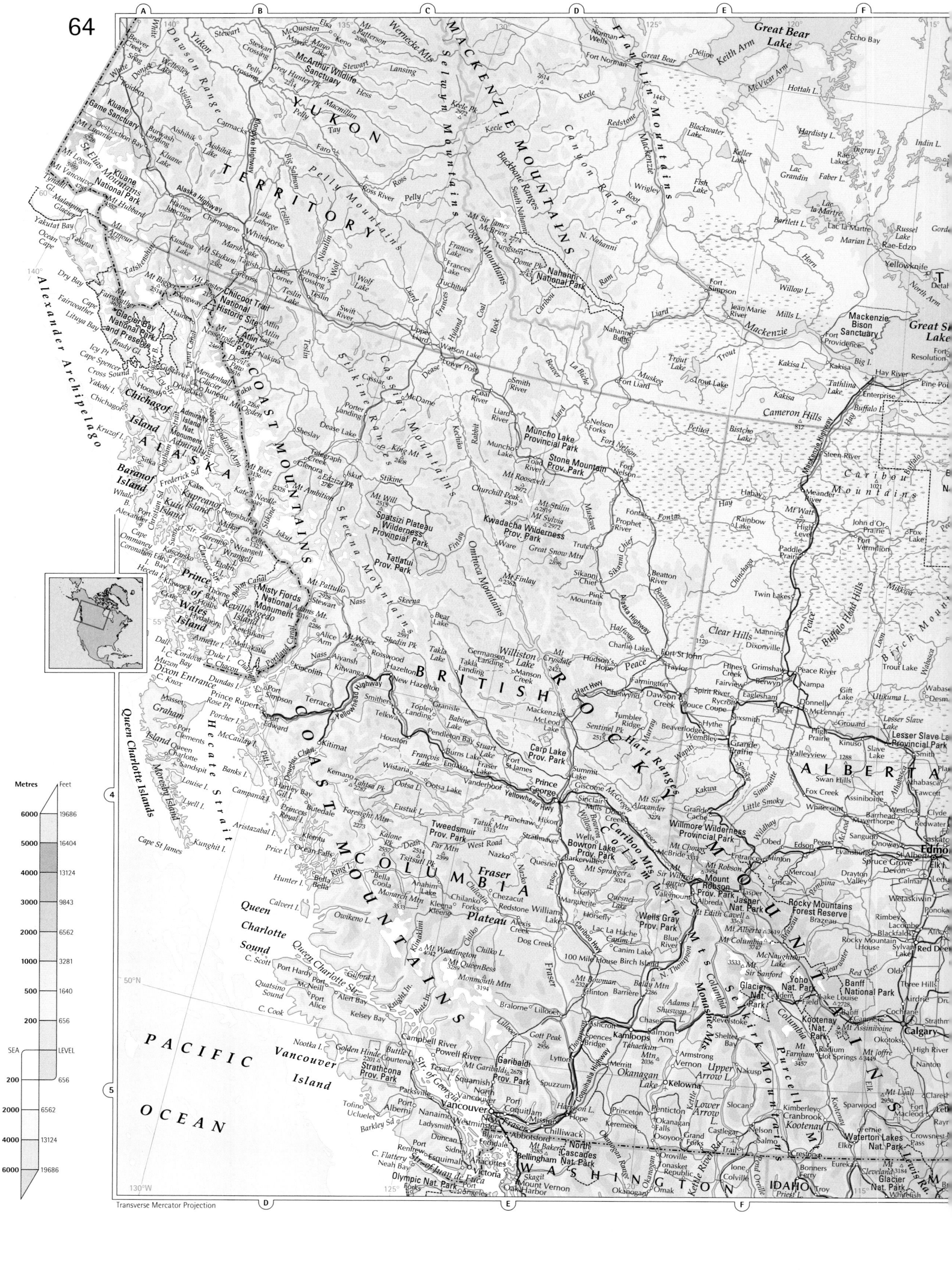
Great Bear Lake
MACKENZIE MOUNTAINS
Franklin Mountains
YUKON TERRITORY
Selwyn Mountains
Pelly Mountains
Dawson Range
St Elias Mountains
Kluane National Park
Alaska Highway
Whitehorse
Canyon Ranges
Backbone Ranges
Logan Mountains
Nahanni National Park
Alexander Archipelago
COAST MOUNTAINS
ALASKA
Chichagof Island
Baranof Island
Prince of Wales Island
Cassiar Mountains
Stikine Ranges
Skeena Mountains
Omineca Mountains
Muncho Lake Provincial Park
Stone Mountain Prov. Park
Kwadacha Wilderness Prov. Park
Spatsizi Plateau Wilderness Provincial Park
Tatlatui Prov. Park
Misty Fjords National Monument
Caribou Mountains
Cameron Hills
Clear Hills
Buffalo Head Hills
Birch Mountains
BRITISH COLUMBIA
ROCKY MOUNTAINS
Hart Ranges
ALBERTA
Queen Charlotte Islands
Graham Island
Moresby Island
Hecate Strait
Dixon Entrance
Queen Charlotte Sound
Tweedsmuir Prov. Park
Fraser Plateau
Cariboo Mts
Wells Gray Prov. Park
Mount Robson Prov. Park
Jasper Nat. Park
Willmore Wilderness Provincial Park
Banff National Park
Yoho Nat. Park
Kootenay Nat. Park
Selkirk Mountains
Purcell Mountains
Monashee Mts
PACIFIC OCEAN
Vancouver Island
Strathcona Prov. Park
Garibaldi Prov. Park
Vancouver
Victoria
Prince George
Prince Rupert
Kamloops
Kelowna
Calgary
Edmonton
WASHINGTON
IDAHO
North Cascades Nat. Park
Olympic Nat. Park
Waterton Lakes Nat. Park
Glacier Nat. Park
Metres
Feet
6000
19686
5000
16404
4000
13124
3000
9843
2000
6562
1000
3281
500
1640
200
656
SEA
LEVEL
200
656
2000
6562
4000
13124
6000
19686

Transverse Mercator Projection

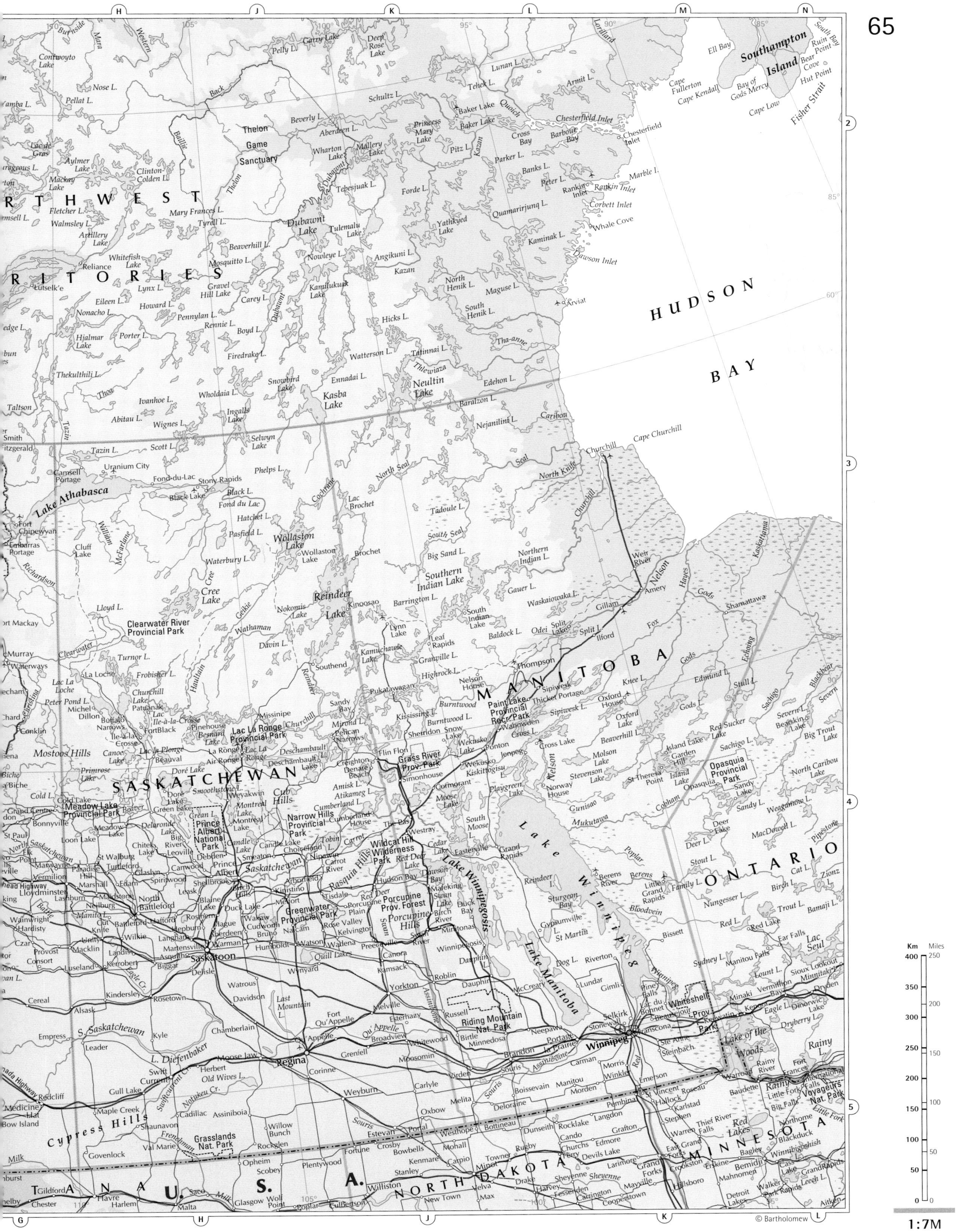
HUDSON BAY
Southampton Island
Fisher Strait
Cape Low
Bay of Gods Mercy
Cape Kendall
Cape Fullerton
Ell Bay
Chesterfield Inlet
Rankin Inlet
Corbett Inlet
Whale Cove
Dawson Inlet
Arviat
Cape Churchill
Churchill
Thelon Game Sanctuary
Baker Lake
Dubawnt Lake
Kasba Lake
Nueltin Lake
Lake Athabasca
Uranium City
Fort Chipewyan
Wollaston Lake
Reindeer Lake
Southern Indian Lake
Cree Lake
Clearwater River Provincial Park
Fort Mackay
Fort McMurray
Waterways
Lac La Ronge Provincial Park
Meadow Lake Provincial Park
Prince Albert National Park
Narrow Hills Provincial Park
Wildcat Hill Wilderness Park
Porcupine Prov. Forest
Greenwater Provincial Park
Grass River Prov. Park
Paint Lake Provincial Recr. Park
Opasquia Provincial Park
Riding Mountain Nat. Park
Whiteshell Prov. Park
Voyageurs Nat. Park
Grasslands Nat. Park
Cypress Hills
SASKATCHEWAN
MANITOBA
ONTARIO
NORTHWEST TERRITORIES
MINNESOTA
NORTH DAKOTA
U. S. A.
CANADA
Lake Winnipeg
Lake Winnipegosis
Lake Manitoba
Lake of the Woods
Thompson
Flin Flon
The Pas
Gillam
Nelson House
Norway House
Saskatoon
Regina
Winnipeg
Moose Jaw
Prince Albert
North Battleford
Lloydminster
Brandon
Yorkton
Melfort
Swift Current
Estevan
Weyburn
Minot
Grand Forks
Kenora
Fort Frances
Dryden
Sioux Lookout
Red Lake
Swan River
Dauphin
Selkirk
Steinbach
Portage la Prairie
Medicine Hat
Lake Diefenbaker
© Bartholomew
Km
Miles
400
350
300
250
200
150
100
50
0

1:7M

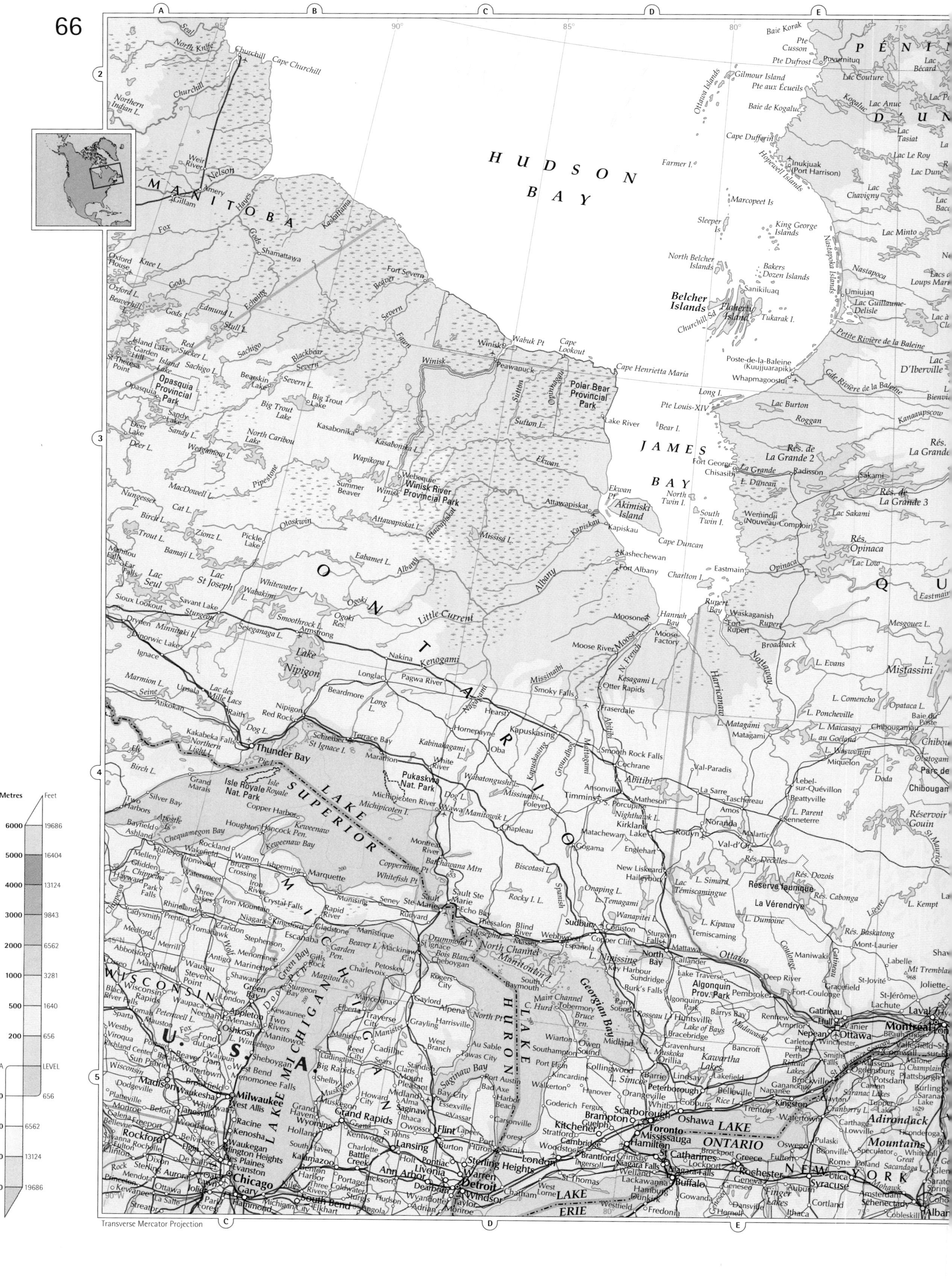
A
B
C
D
E
2
3
4
5
90°
85°
80°
75°
HUDSON BAY
JAMES BAY
MANITOBA
ONTARIO
LAKE SUPERIOR
LAKE MICHIGAN
LAKE HURON
LAKE ONTARIO
LAKE ERIE
MICHIGAN
WISCONSIN
U.S.A.
NEW YORK
Belcher Islands
Akimiski Island
Polar Bear Provincial Park
Opasquia Provincial Park
Winisk River Provincial Park
Pukaskwa Nat. Park
Isle Royale Nat. Park
Algonquin Prov. Park
Lake Nipigon
Lac Seul
Georgian Bay
North Channel
Adirondack Mountains
Churchill
Cape Churchill
Gillam
Shamattawa
Fort Severn
Winisk
Peawanuck
Cape Henrietta Maria
Attawapiskat
Kashechewan
Fort Albany
Moosonee
Moose Factory
Chisasibi
Radisson
Eastmain
Waskaganish
Inukjuak (Port Harrison)
Umiujaq
Sanikiluaq
Poste-de-la-Baleine (Kuujjuarapik)
Whapmagoostui
Puvirnituq
Sioux Lookout
Dryden
Thunder Bay
Nipigon
Marathon
Wawa
Hearst
Kapuskasing
Cochrane
Timmins
Kirkland Lake
Rouyn
Noranda
Val-d'Or
Amos
Chibougamau
Sault Ste Marie
Sudbury
North Bay
Gatineau
Hull
Ottawa
Montréal
Kingston
Peterborough
Oshawa
Toronto
Mississauga
Hamilton
Brampton
Scarborough
Kitchener
Guelph
London
Windsor
Detroit
Sterling Heights
Warren
Ann Arbor
Lansing
Flint
Saginaw
Grand Rapids
Milwaukee
Madison
Green Bay
Appleton
Oshkosh
Chicago
Gary
Rockford
Kenosha
Racine
Waukegan
Evanston
South Bend
St Catharines
Niagara Falls
Buffalo
Rochester
Syracuse
Schenectady
Transverse Mercator Projection
Metres
Feet
6000
5000
4000
3000
2000
1000
500
200
SEA LEVEL
19686
16404
13124
9843
6562
3281
1640
656

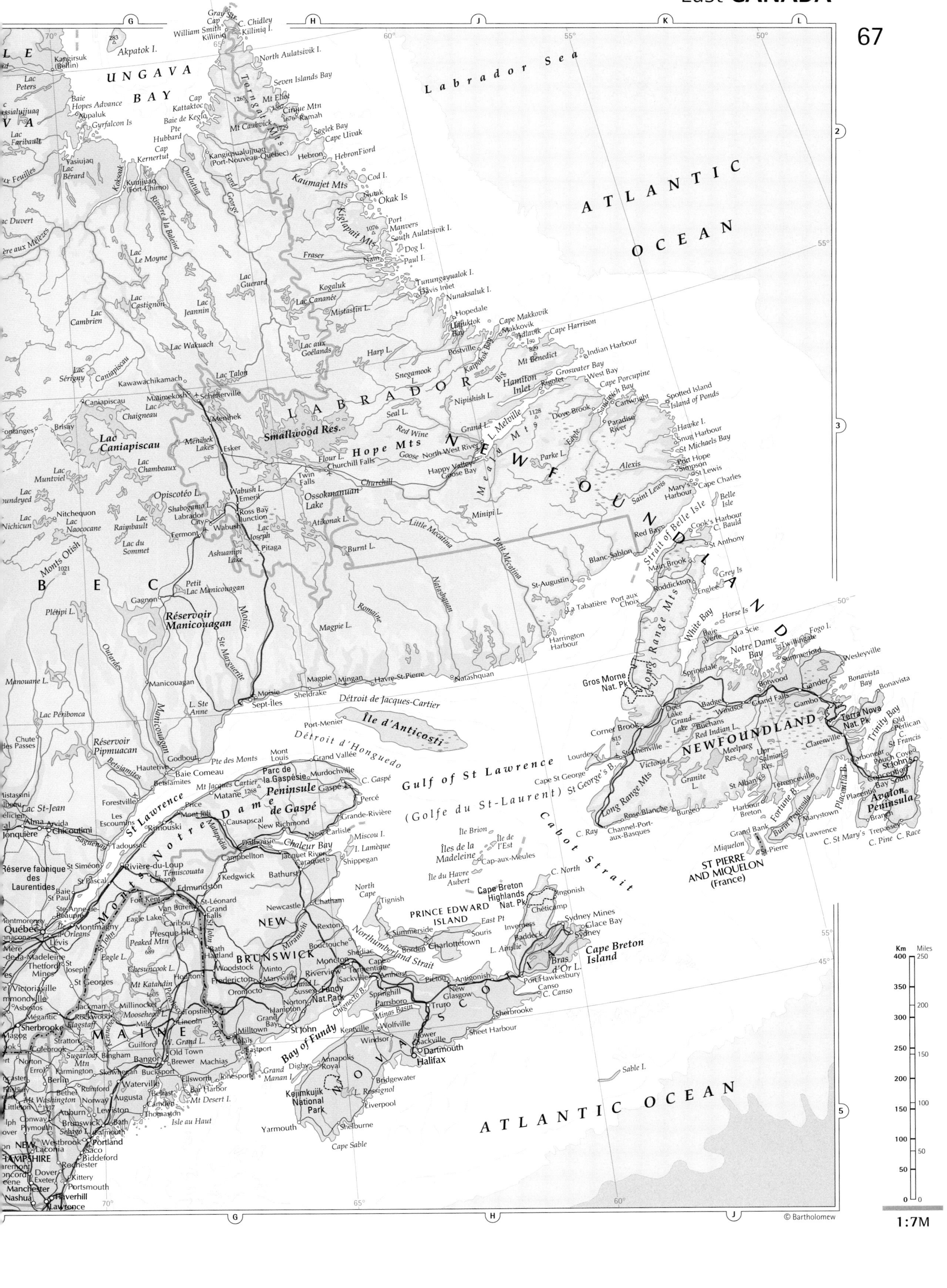

1:7M

Km Miles
400 — 250
350 — 200
300 —
250 — 150
200 — 100
150 —
100 — 50
50 —
0 — 0

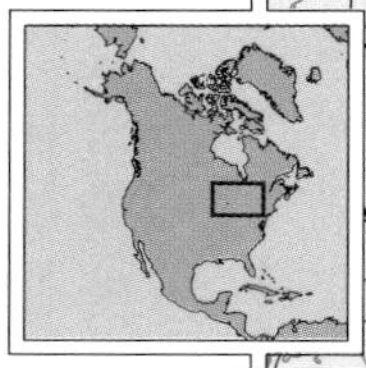

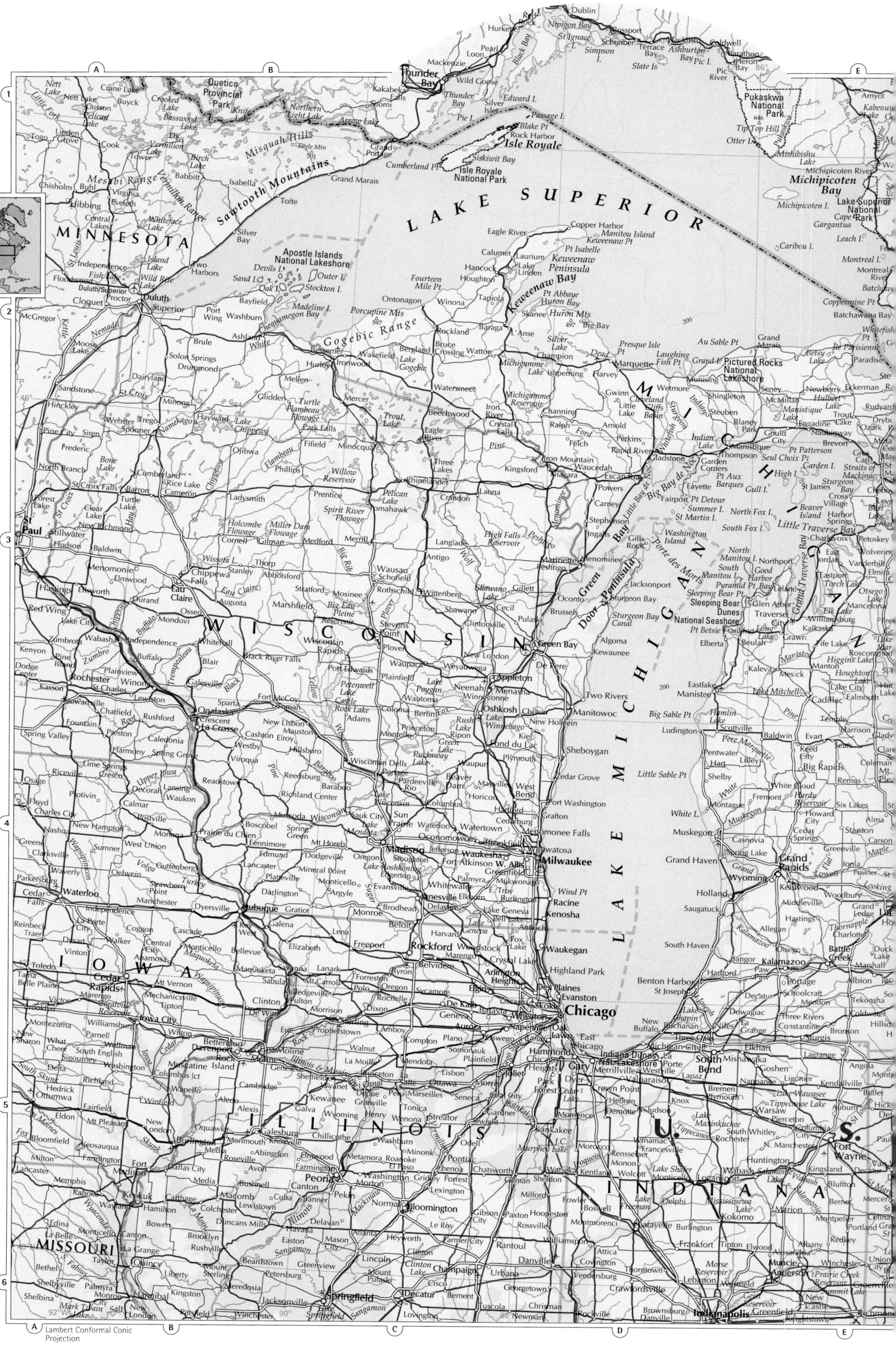
MINNESOTA
WISCONSIN
IOWA
ILLINOIS
INDIANA
MISSOURI
MICHIGAN
U. S.
LAKE SUPERIOR
LAKE MICHIGAN
Isle Royale
Isle Royale National Park
Apostle Islands National Lakeshore
Pictured Rocks National Lakeshore
Sleeping Bear Dunes National Seashore
Pukaskwa National Park
Lake Superior National Park
Quetico Provincial Park
Indiana Dunes Nat. Lakeshore
Thunder Bay
Duluth
St Paul
Green Bay
Milwaukee
Madison
Chicago
Rockford
Peoria
Springfield
Grand Rapids
Indianapolis
Fort Wayne
South Bend
Keweenaw Peninsula
Door Peninsula
Mesabi Range
Gogebic Range
Sawtooth Mountains
Michipicoten Bay
Lambert Conformal Conic Projection

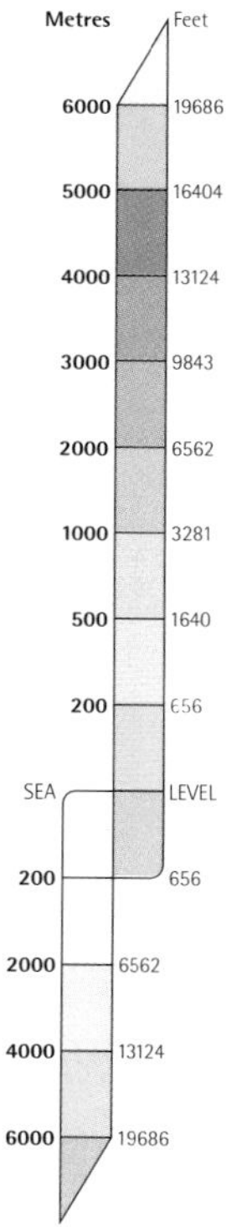
Metres
Feet
6000
19686
5000
16404
4000
13124
3000
9843
2000
6562
1000
3281
500
1640
200
656
SEA
LEVEL
200
656
2000
6562
4000
13124
6000
19686

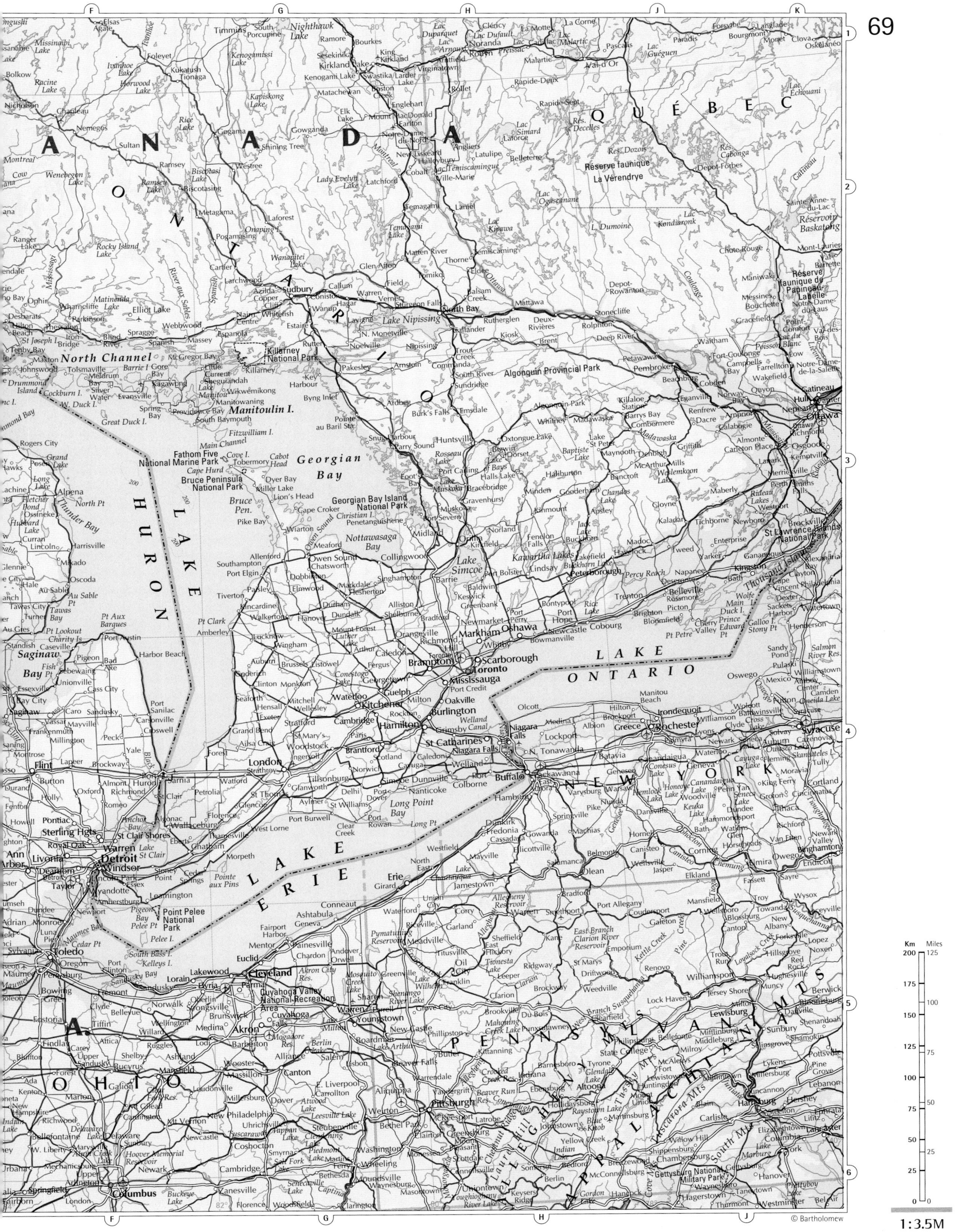

CANADA
ONTARIO
QUÉBEC
U.S.A.
OHIO
PENNSYLVANIA
NEW YORK
LAKE HURON
LAKE ERIE
LAKE ONTARIO
Georgian Bay
North Channel
Manitoulin I.
Lake Nipissing
Lake Simcoe
Saginaw Bay
Long Point Bay
Algonquin Provincial Park
Réserve faunique La Vérendrye
Bruce Peninsula National Park
Fathom Five National Marine Park
Georgian Bay Island National Park
Point Pelee National Park
St Lawrence Islands National Park
Cuyahoga Valley National Recreation Area
Gettysburg National Military Park
Killarney National Park
ALLEGHENY MTS
APPALACHIAN MTS
Toronto
Ottawa
Detroit
Cleveland
Buffalo
Pittsburgh
Rochester
Syracuse
Hamilton
London
Windsor
Toledo
Sudbury
North Bay
Kingston
Flint
Akron
Columbus
Harrisburg
Erie
Km
Miles

1:3.5M

© Bartholomew

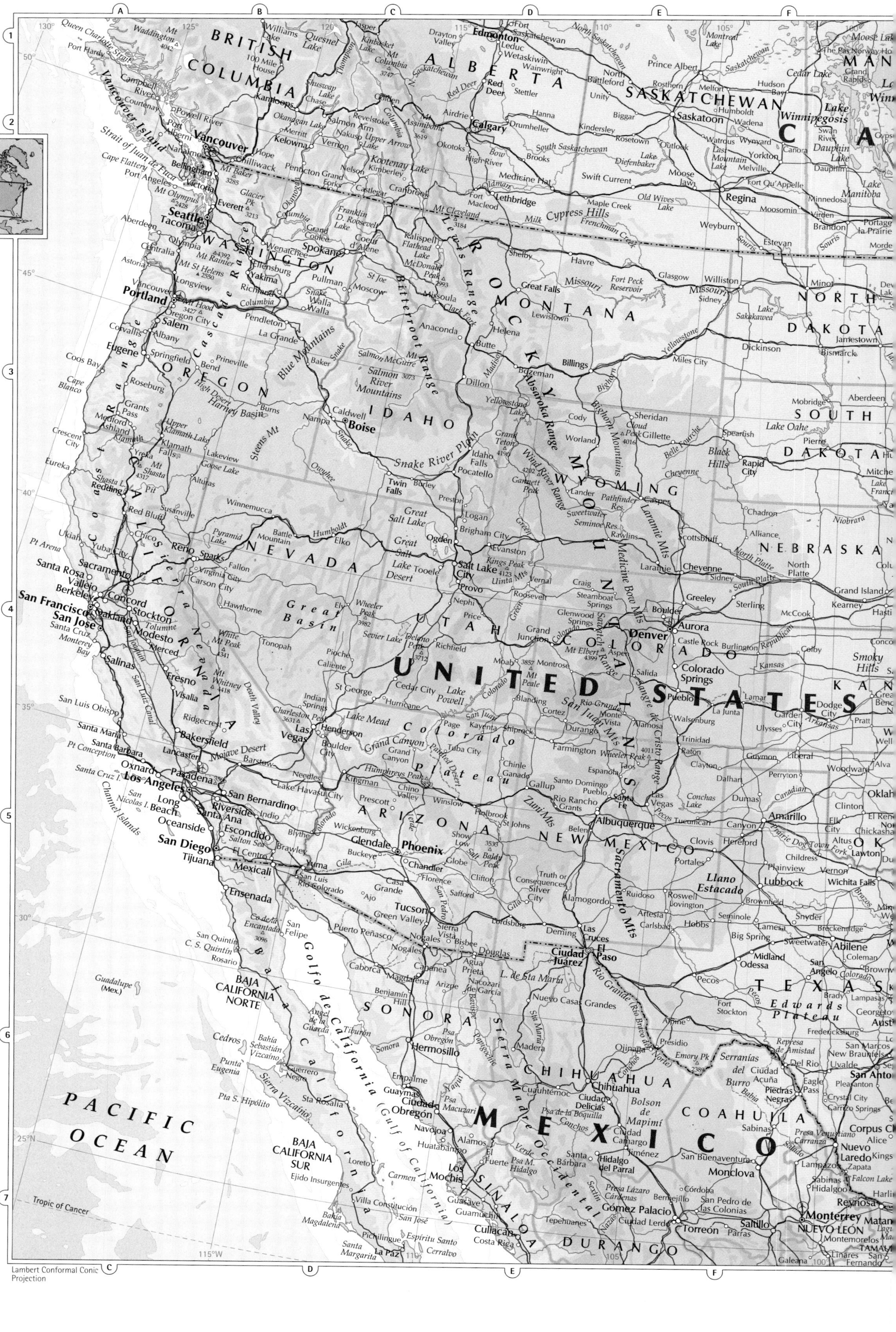

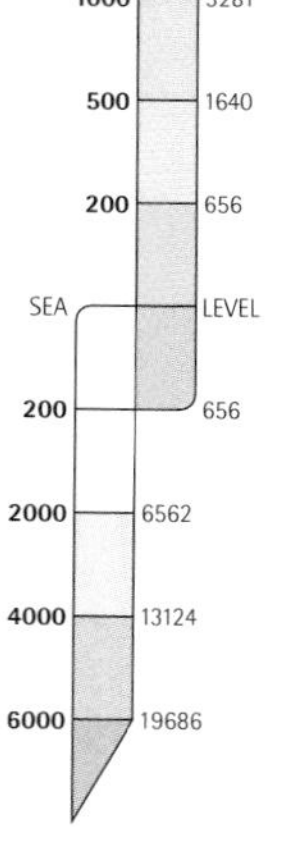

Metres
Feet
6000
19686
5000
16404
4000
13124
3000
9843
2000
6562
1000
3281
500
1640
200
656
SEA
LEVEL
200
656
2000
6562
4000
13124
6000
19686

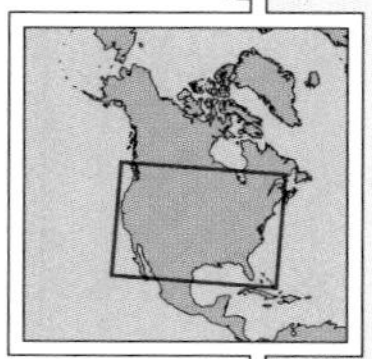

BRITISH COLUMBIA
ALBERTA
SASKATCHEWAN
WASHINGTON
OREGON
IDAHO
MONTANA
NORTH DAKOTA
SOUTH DAKOTA
WYOMING
NEBRASKA
NEVADA
UTAH
COLORADO
CALIFORNIA
ARIZONA
NEW MEXICO
TEXAS
UNITED STATES
MEXICO
SONORA
CHIHUAHUA
COAHUILA
SINALOA
DURANGO
NUEVO LEÓN
BAJA CALIFORNIA NORTE
BAJA CALIFORNIA SUR
PACIFIC OCEAN
Golfo de California (Gulf of California)
ROCKY MOUNTAINS
Vancouver Island
Edmonton
Calgary
Regina
Saskatoon
Vancouver
Victoria
Seattle
Tacoma
Spokane
Portland
Salem
Eugene
Boise
Great Falls
Billings
Helena
Salt Lake City
Great Salt Lake
Great Basin
Reno
Sacramento
San Francisco
Oakland
San Jose
Fresno
Bakersfield
Los Angeles
San Diego
Tijuana
Las Vegas
Phoenix
Tucson
Albuquerque
Santa Fe
Denver
Aurora
Cheyenne
Colorado Springs
El Paso
Ciudad Juárez
Chihuahua
Hermosillo
Culiacán
Monterrey
Torreón
Lubbock
Amarillo
Abilene
Colorado Plateau
Grand Canyon
Sierra Nevada
Cascade Range
Coast Ranges
Sierra Madre Occidental
Llano Estacado
Edwards Plateau
Tropic of Cancer
A
B
C
D
E
F
1
2
3
4
5
6
7

Lambert Conformal Conic Projection

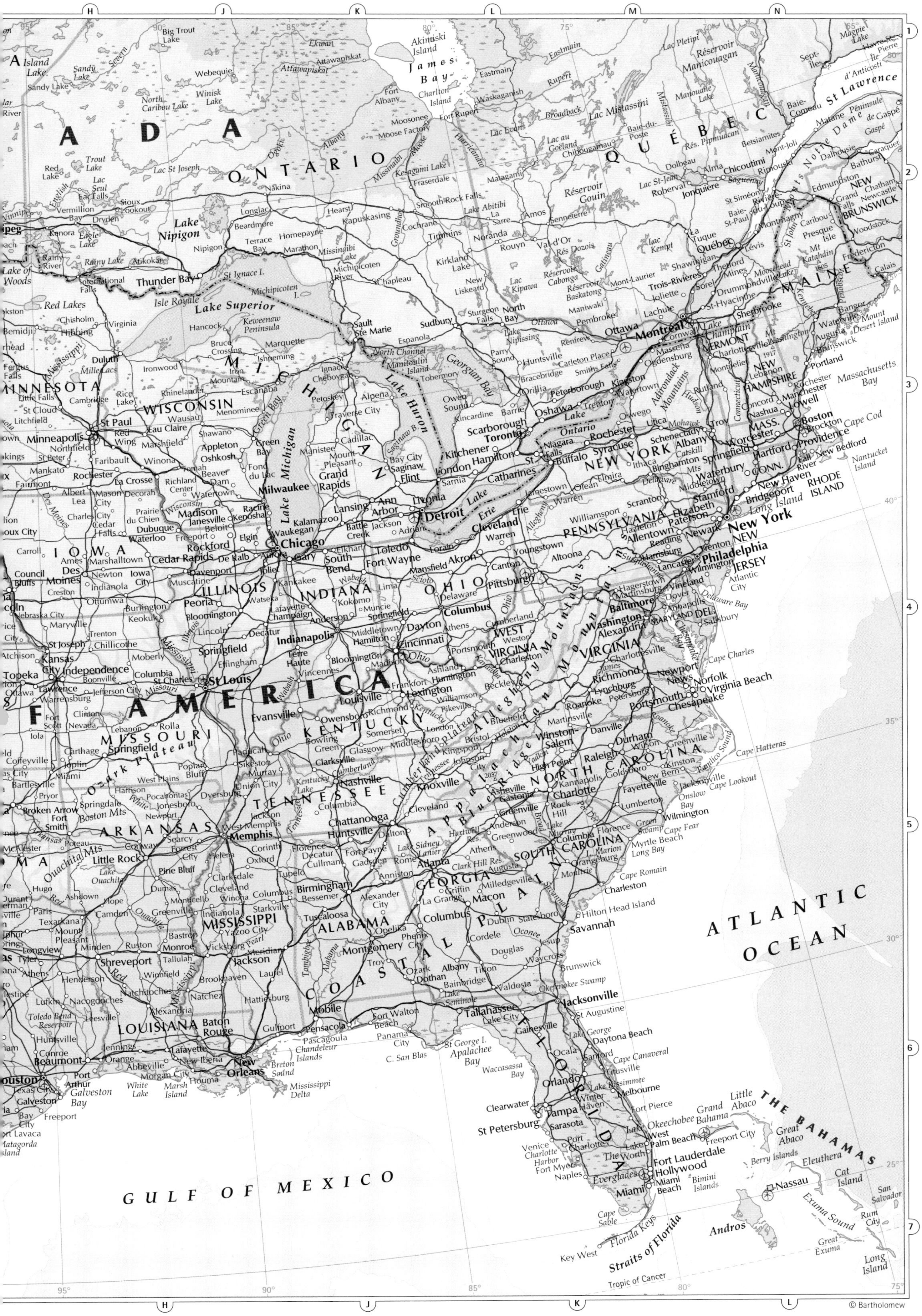
CANADA
ONTARIO
QUÉBEC
NEW BRUNSWICK
MAINE
VERMONT
NEW HAMPSHIRE
MASS.
CONN.
RHODE ISLAND
NEW YORK
PENNSYLVANIA
NEW JERSEY
MARYLAND
DEL.
VIRGINIA
WEST VIRGINIA
NORTH CAROLINA
SOUTH CAROLINA
GEORGIA
FLORIDA
ALABAMA
MISSISSIPPI
LOUISIANA
ARKANSAS
TENNESSEE
KENTUCKY
OHIO
INDIANA
ILLINOIS
MICHIGAN
WISCONSIN
MINNESOTA
IOWA
MISSOURI
AMERICA
Lake Superior
Lake Michigan
Lake Huron
Lake Erie
Lake Ontario
Georgian Bay
James Bay
Lake Nipigon
Appalachian Mountains
Allegheny Mountains
Blue Ridge
Cumberland Plateau
Ozark Plateau
COASTAL PLAIN
ATLANTIC OCEAN
GULF OF MEXICO
THE BAHAMAS
Straits of Florida
Florida Keys
Tropic of Cancer
New York
Philadelphia
Boston
Washington
Baltimore
Chicago
Detroit
Toronto
Montréal
Ottawa
Québec
Atlanta
Memphis
Nashville
St Louis
Indianapolis
Columbus
Cleveland
Pittsburgh
Cincinnati
Louisville
Jacksonville
Miami
Tampa
Orlando
New Orleans
Houston
Milwaukee
Minneapolis
St Paul
Kansas City
Nassau
© Bartholomew

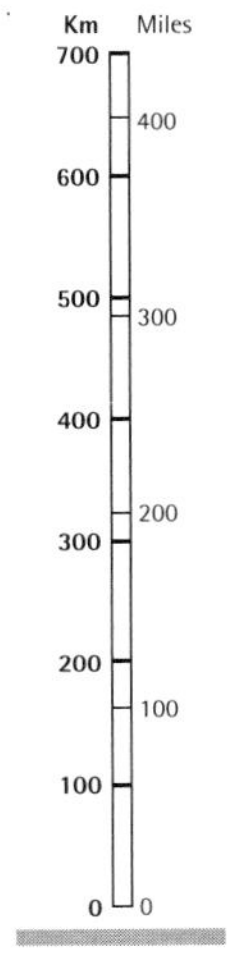
Km
Miles
700
600
500
400
300
200
100
0
400
300
200
100
0

1:12M

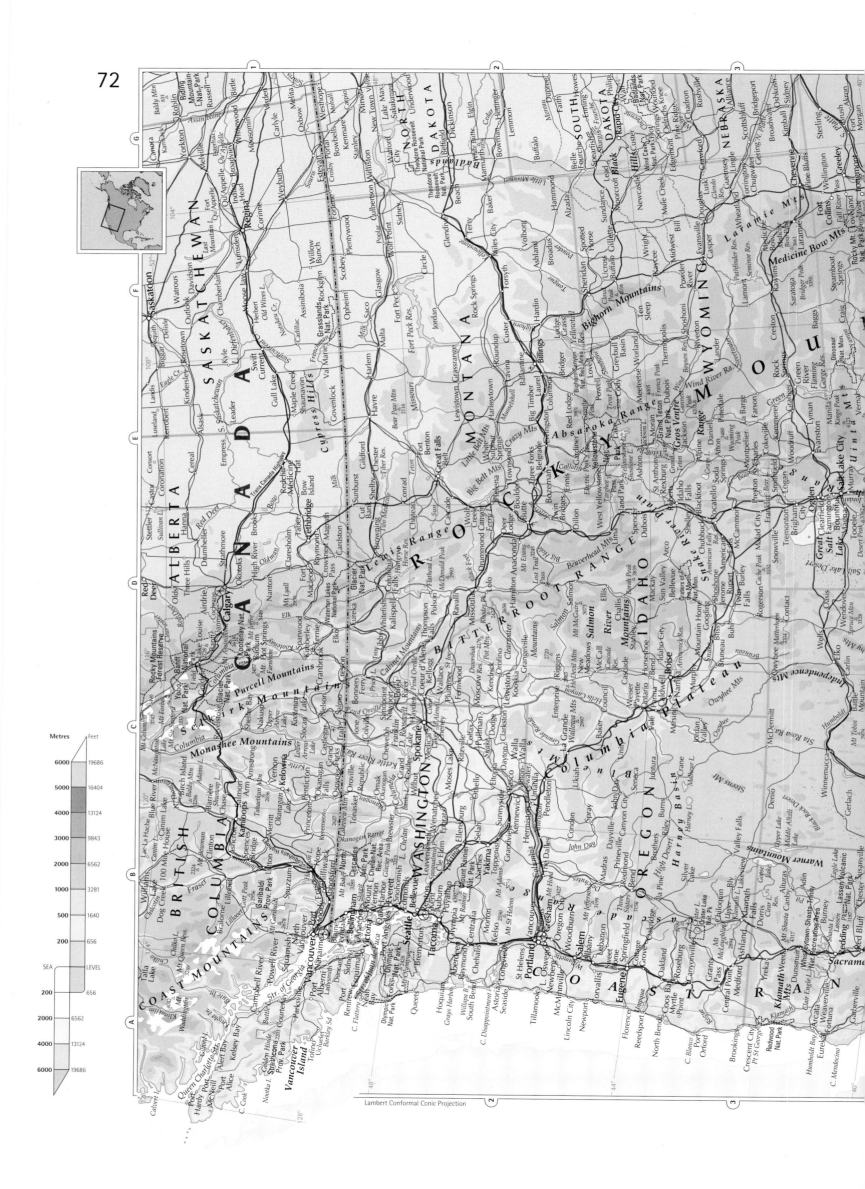
Metres
Feet
6000
19686
5000
16404
4000
13124
3000
9843
2000
6562
1000
3281
500
1640
200
656
SEA
LEVEL
200
656
2000
6562
4000
13124
6000
19686
BRITISH COLUMBIA
ALBERTA
SASKATCHEWAN
CANADA
WASHINGTON
OREGON
IDAHO
MONTANA
WYOMING
NORTH DAKOTA
SOUTH DAKOTA
NEBRASKA
ROCKY MOUNTAINS
COAST MOUNTAINS
COAST RANGES
BITTERROOT RANGE
Blue Mts
Columbia Plateau
Snake River Plain
Bighorn Mountains
Absaroka Range
Wind River Ra.
Laramie Mts
Medicine Bow Mts
Cascades
Monashee Mountains
Selkirk Mountains
Purcell Mountains
Cypress Hills
Black Hills
Harney Basin
Klamath Mts
Salmon River Mountains
Vancouver Island
Vancouver
Victoria
Seattle
Tacoma
Portland
Salem
Eugene
Spokane
Boise
Calgary
Regina
Saskatoon
Great Falls
Billings
Casper
Cheyenne
Salt Lake City
Great Salt Lake
Lambert Conformal Conic Projection

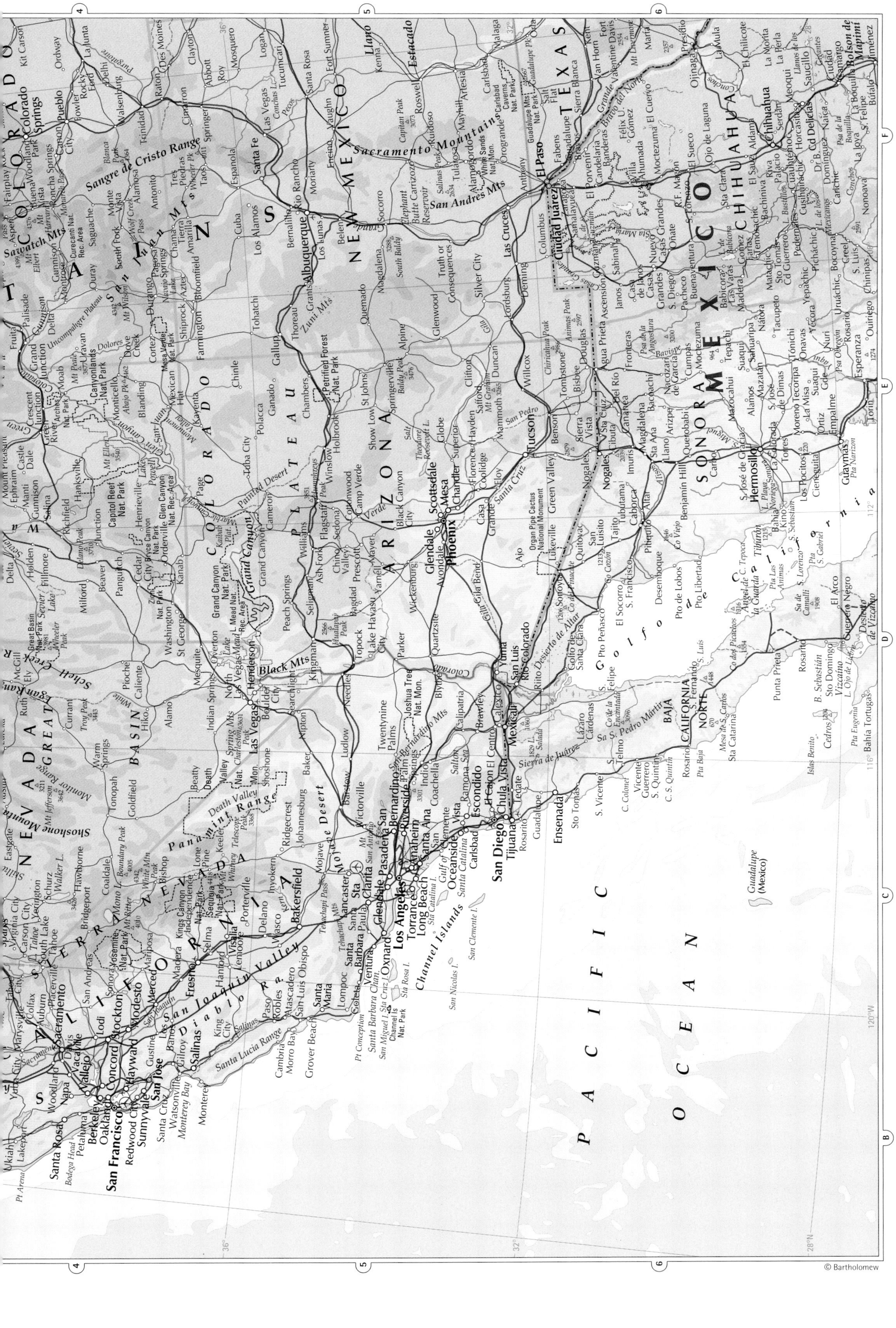
NEVADA
CALIFORNIA
UTAH
COLORADO
ARIZONA
NEW MEXICO
TEXAS
MEXICO
SONORA
CHIHUAHUA
BAJA CALIFORNIA NORTE
GREAT BASIN
COLORADO PLATEAU
PACIFIC OCEAN
Golfo de California
Sierra Nevada
San Joaquin Valley
Mojave Desert
Channel Islands
Los Angeles
San Diego
San Francisco
Sacramento
Las Vegas
Phoenix
Tucson
Albuquerque
El Paso
Ciudad Juárez
Chihuahua
Hermosillo
Tijuana
© Bartholomew

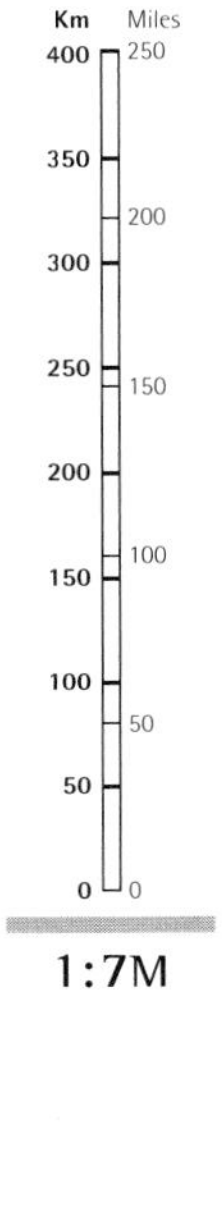
Km
Miles
400
350
300
250
200
150
100
50
0
250
200
150
100
50
0

1:7M

PACIFIC
OCEAN

SIERRA   NEVADA

CALIFORNIA

NEVADA

Mojave   Desert

Death Valley

OAHU
(Hawaii)
1:1.5M

Sunset Beach
Waialee   Kahuku Pt
Kahuku
Waimea   Mokuauia I.
Kaena Pt   Laie   Laie Pt
Haleiwa   Hauula
Waialua   Schofield   Kahana
Barracks
Wahiawa   Waikane
Makaha   Kaala   Kaneohe
Lahilahi Pt   Waianae   Mokapu Pen.
Waipahu   Pearl   Kailua
Nanakuli   City   Kaneohe
Ewa   Pearl Harbor   Waimanalo
Beach   Manana
Barbers Pt   Honolulu   Makapuu
Hd
Waikiki Beach   Koko Hd
Diamond Head   Maunalua B.

HAWAIIAN ISLANDS
(Main group)
(U.S.A.)
1:6M

PACIFIC

OCEAN

Hanalei   Kilauea
Kauai   Kekaha   Kapaa
Niihau   Lihue
Kaula
Kauai Channel
Oahu   Kahuku
Waialua   Wahiawa
Waianae   Kaneohe
Honolulu   Molokai
Kalaupapa
Kaunakakai   Halawa
Lanai   Wailuku   Maui
Lanai City   Lahaina   Kahului
Keokea   Hana
Kahoolawe
Hawi   Kapaau
Kawaihae   Honokaa
Waimea   Hakalau
Mauna Kea   Hilo   Hawaii
Kailua Kona   Mauna Loa   Pahoa
Captain Cook   Kilauea   Hawaii
Kealakekua Bay   Pahala   Volcanoes
National Park
Naalehu
Ka Lae (South Cape)

Metres   Feet

6000   19686
5000   16404
4000   13124
3000   9843
2000   6562
1000   3281
500   1640
200   656
SEA   LEVEL
200   656
2000   6562
4000   13124
6000   19686

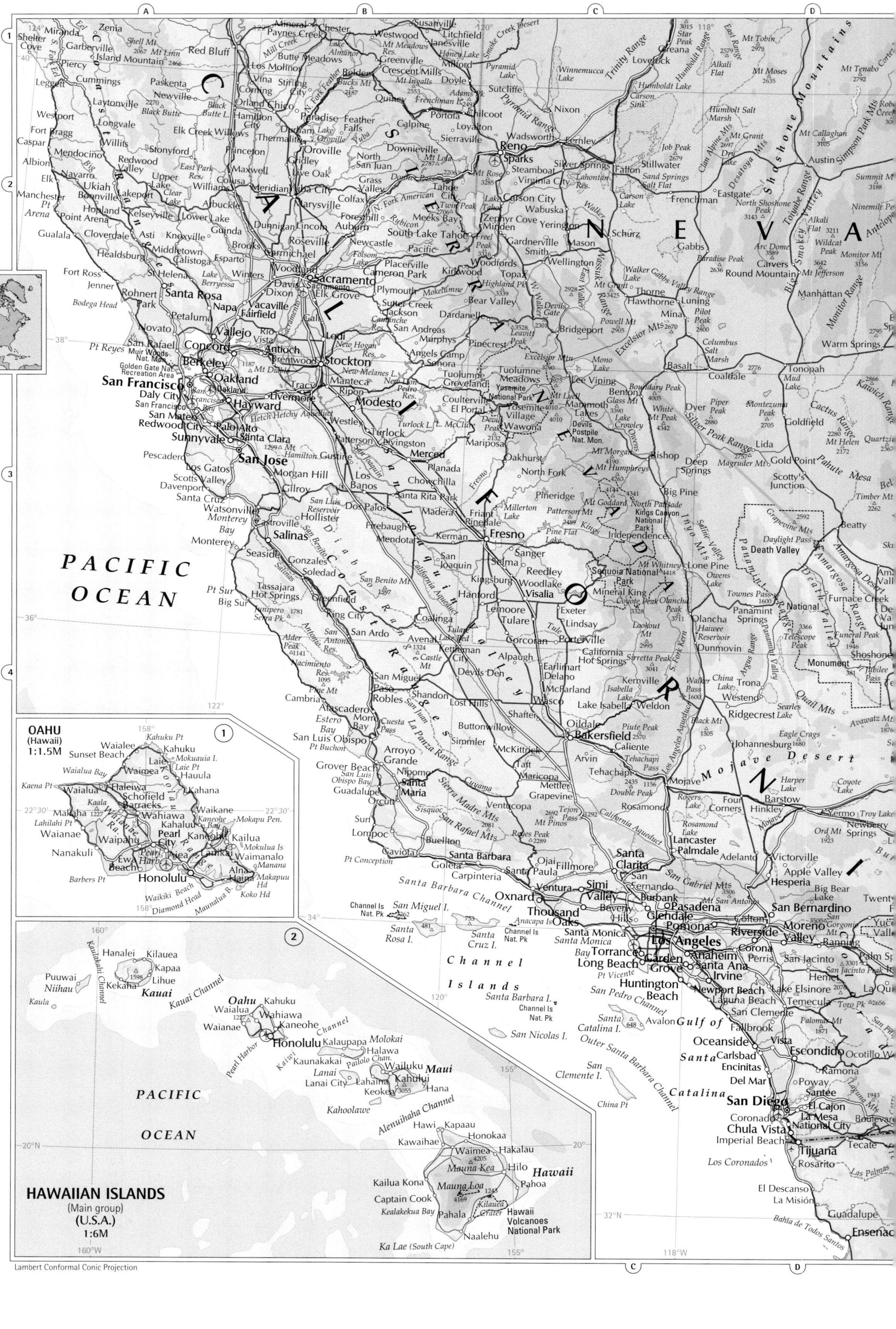

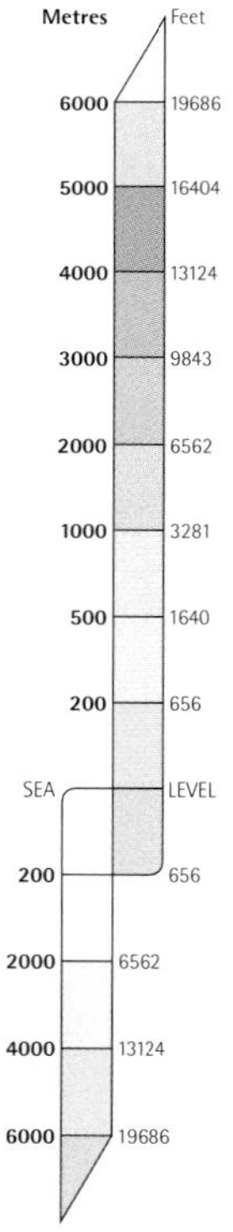

Lambert Conformal Conic Projection

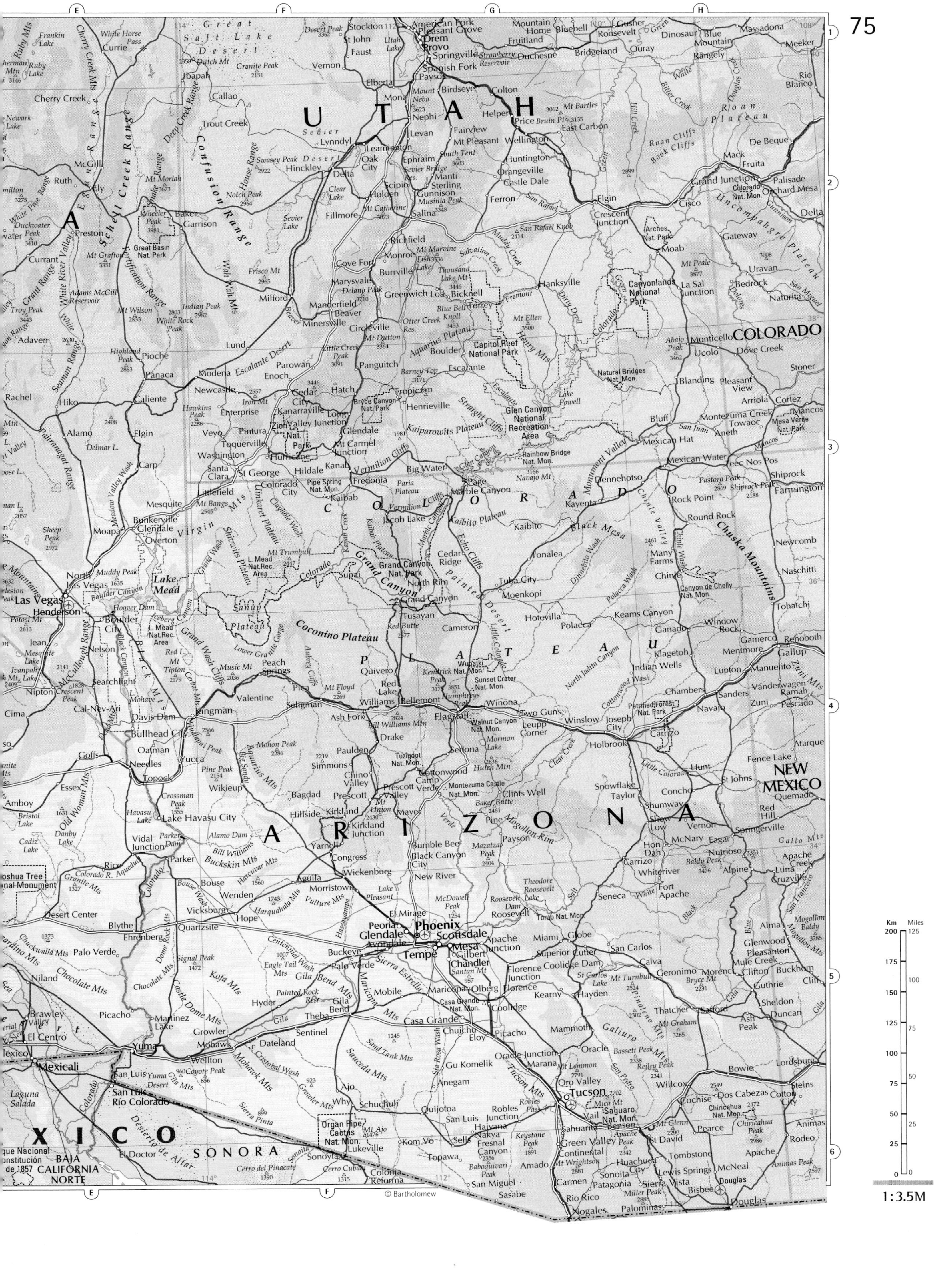
UTAH
ARIZONA
COLORADO
NEW MEXICO
MEXICO
SONORA
BAJA CALIFORNIA NORTE
COLORADO PLATEAU
Great Salt Lake Desert
Sevier Desert
Escalante Desert
Confusion Range
Grand Canyon
Grand Canyon Nat. Park
Lake Mead
Lake Powell
Coconino Plateau
Kaibab Plateau
Painted Desert
Black Mesa
Chuska Mountains
Mogollon Rim
Great Basin Nat. Park
Zion Nat. Park
Bryce Canyon Nat. Park
Capitol Reef National Park
Canyonlands National Park
Arches Nat. Park
Glen Canyon National Recreation Area
Petrified Forest Nat. Park
Organ Pipe Cactus Nat. Mon.
Colorado
Salt Lake City
Provo
Orem
Spanish Fork
Payson
Nephi
Price
Richfield
Cedar City
St George
Moab
Grand Junction
Las Vegas
Henderson
Boulder City
Kingman
Flagstaff
Williams
Sedona
Prescott
Phoenix
Glendale
Scottsdale
Tempe
Mesa
Chandler
Casa Grande
Tucson
Yuma
El Centro
Mexicali
Nogales
Douglas
Bisbee
Sierra Vista
Winslow
Holbrook
Gallup
Farmington
Shiprock
Cortez
Durango
Page
Tuba City
Lake Havasu City
Needles
Bullhead City
Blythe
Show Low
Safford
Lordsburg
© Bartholomew
Km
Miles
1:3.5M

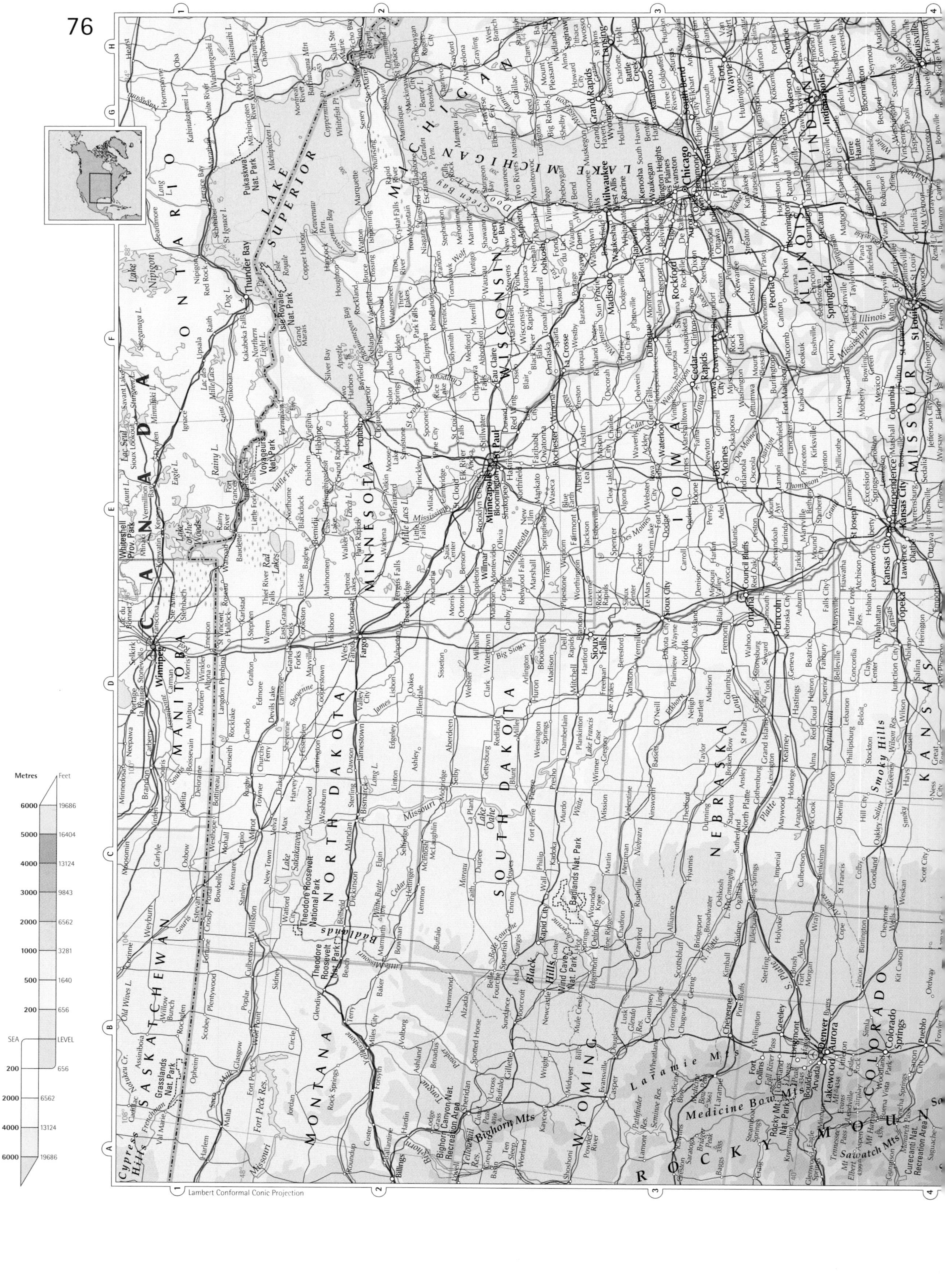
Metres
Feet
6000
19686
5000
16404
4000
13124
3000
9843
2000
6562
1000
3281
500
1640
200
656
SEA
LEVEL
200
656
2000
6562
4000
13124
6000
19686
C A N A D A
O N T A R I O
MANITOBA
SASKATCHEWAN
LAKE SUPERIOR
LAKE MICHIGAN
MICHIGAN
WISCONSIN
MINNESOTA
IOWA
ILLINOIS
INDIANA
MISSOURI
NORTH DAKOTA
SOUTH DAKOTA
NEBRASKA
KANSAS
MONTANA
WYOMING
COLORADO
ROCKY MOUNTAINS
Winnipeg
Minneapolis
St Paul
Chicago
Milwaukee
Des Moines
Omaha
Kansas City
St Louis
Denver
Indianapolis
Lambert Conformal Conic Projection

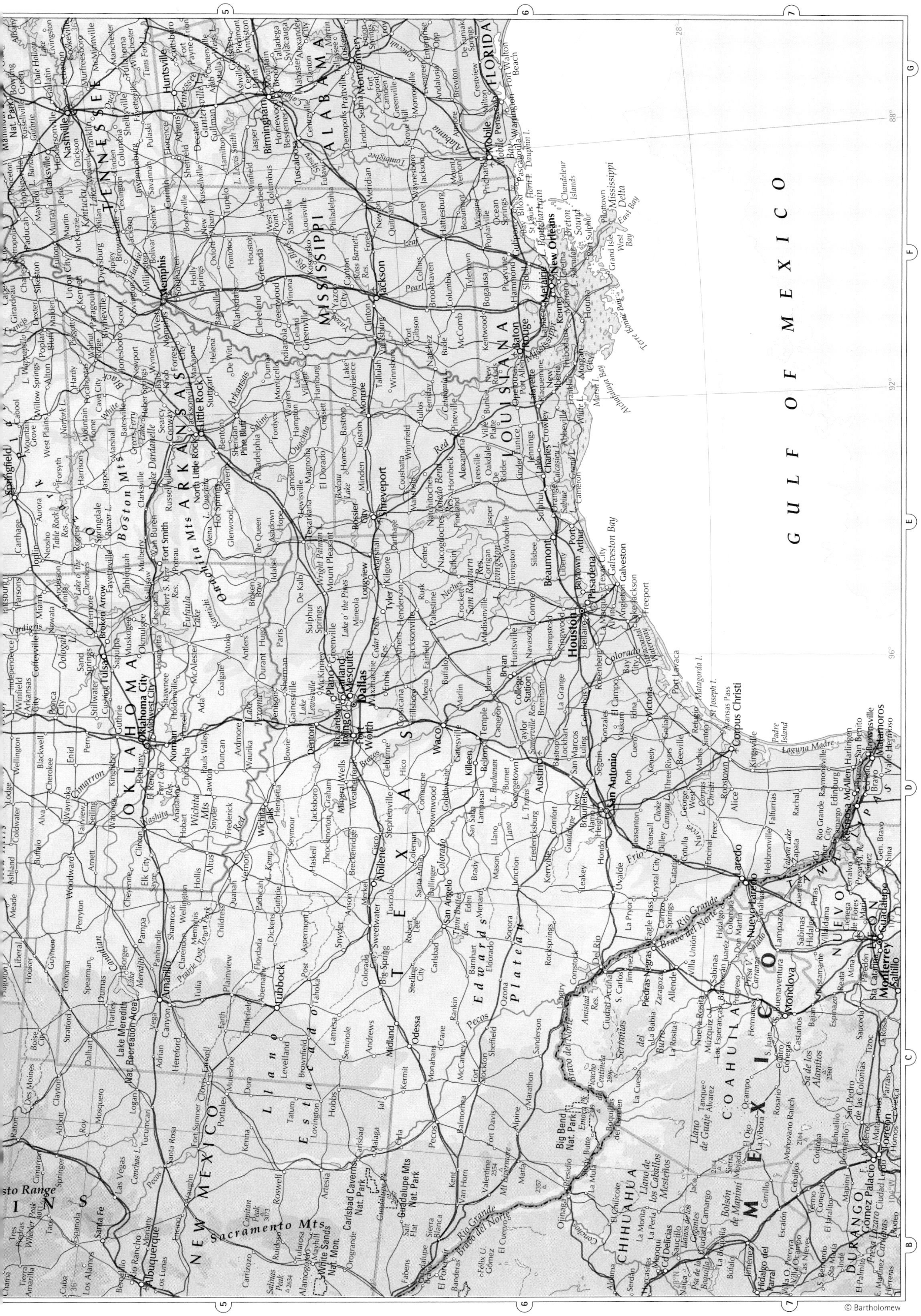

G U L F   O F   M E X I C O

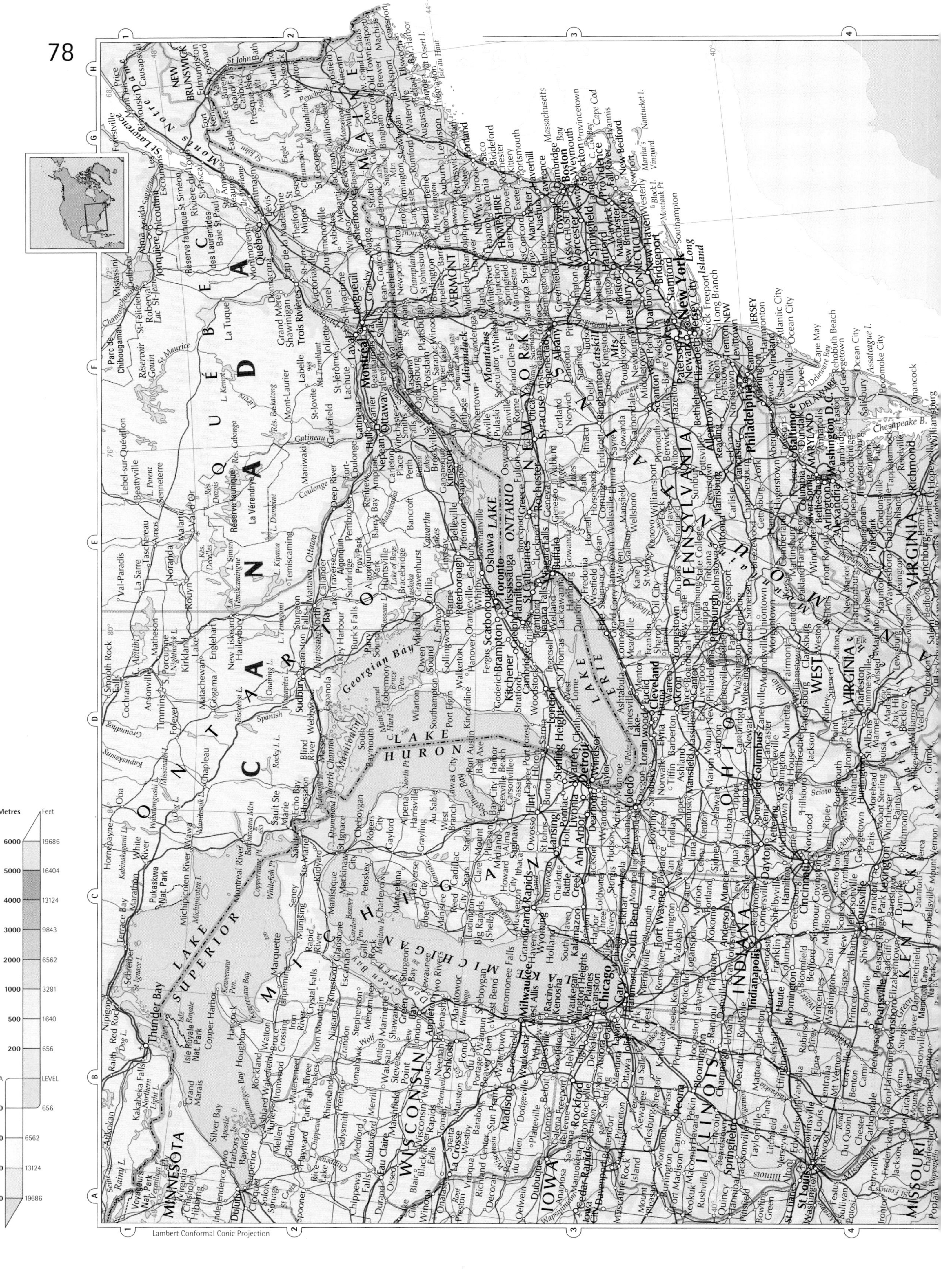
CANADA
ONTARIO
QUÉBEC
MAINE
NEW YORK
PENNSYLVANIA
OHIO
INDIANA
ILLINOIS
MICHIGAN
WISCONSIN
MINNESOTA
IOWA
MISSOURI
KENTUCKY
WEST VIRGINIA
VIRGINIA
LAKE SUPERIOR
LAKE MICHIGAN
LAKE HURON
LAKE ERIE
LAKE ONTARIO
Georgian Bay
Chesapeake B.
Metres
Feet
6000 19686
5000 16404
4000 13124
3000 9843
2000 6562
1000 3281
500 1640
200 656
SEA LEVEL
200 656
2000 6562
4000 13124
6000 19686

Lambert Conformal Conic Projection

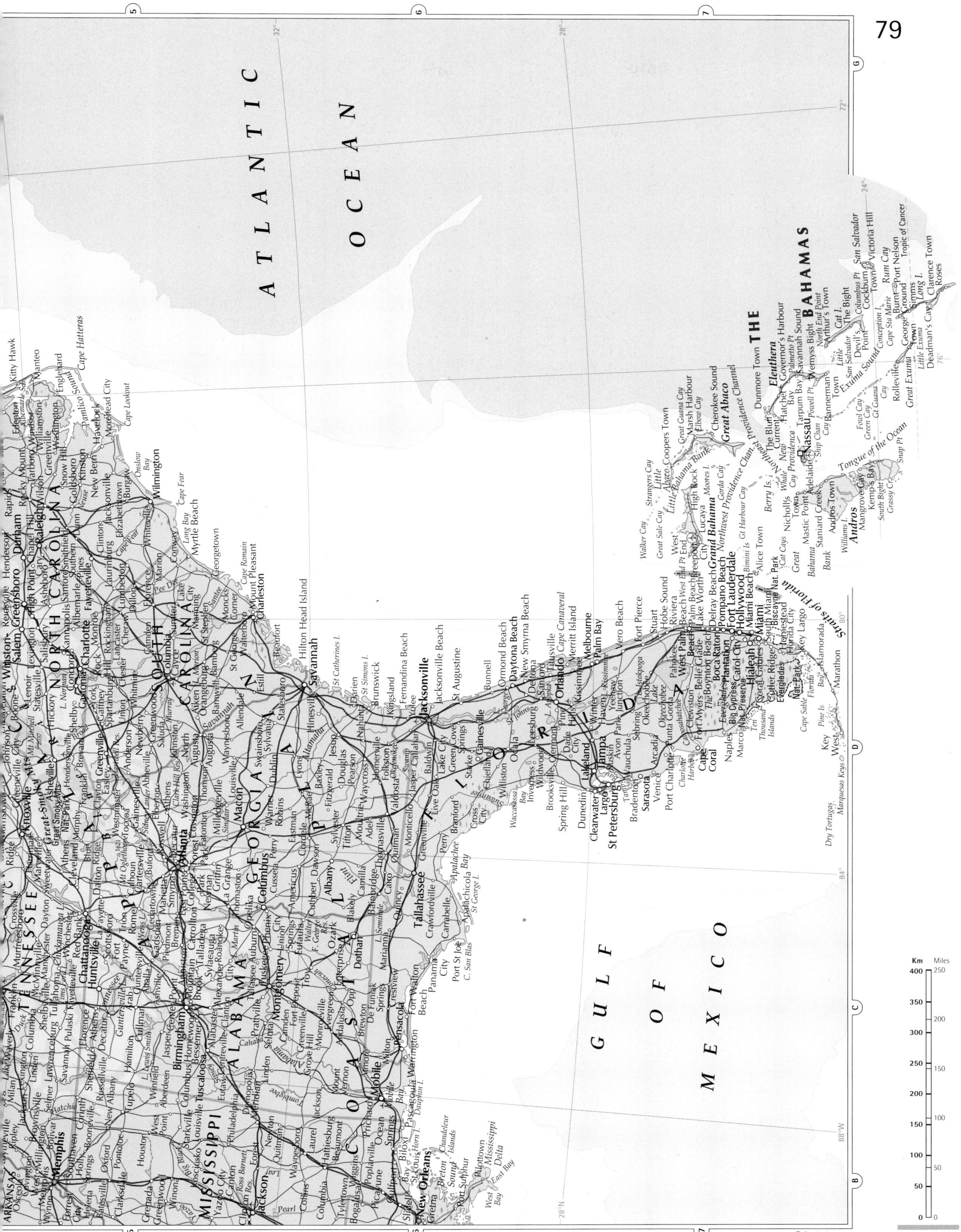

A T L A N T I C

O C E A N

G U L F

O F

M E X I C O

Km Miles
400 250
350 200
300
250 150
200 100
150
100 50
50
0 0

1:7M

© Bartholomew

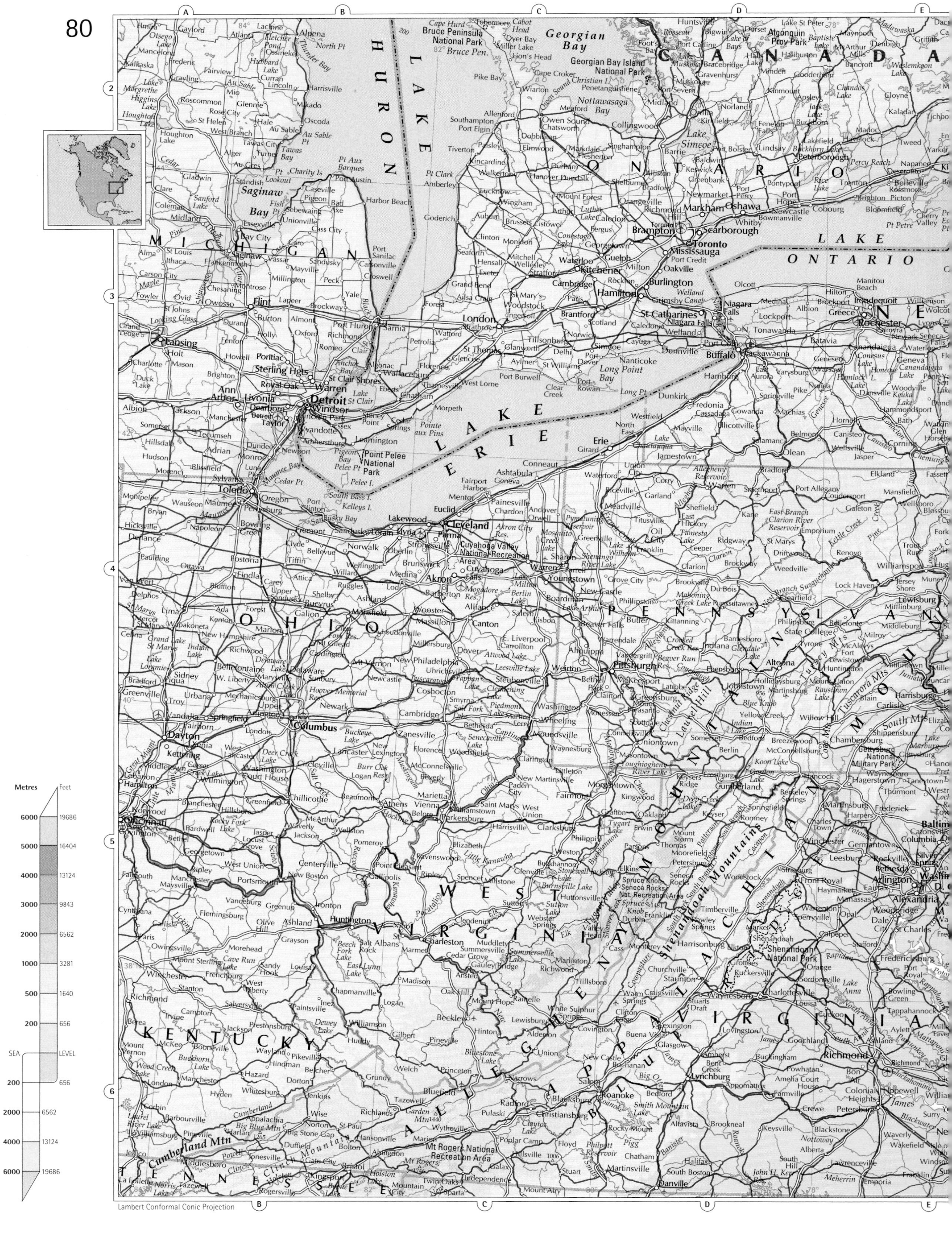

A
B
C
D
E
2
3
4
5
6
CANADA
ONTARIO
MICHIGAN
OHIO
PENNSYLVANIA
WEST VIRGINIA
VIRGINIA
KENTUCKY
TENNESSEE
LAKE HURON
LAKE ONTARIO
LAKE ERIE
Georgian Bay
Saginaw Bay
Lake Simcoe
Bruce Peninsula National Park
Georgian Bay Island National Park
Point Pelee National Park
Cuyahoga Valley National Recreation Area
Shenandoah National Park
Mt Rogers National Recreation Area
ALLEGHENY MOUNTAINS
APPALACHIAN MOUNTAINS
Blue Ridge
Cumberland Mtn
Toronto
Detroit
Cleveland
Columbus
Pittsburgh
Buffalo
Hamilton
Rochester
Richmond
Alexandria
Metres
Feet
6000
19686
5000
16404
4000
13124
3000
9843
2000
6562
1000
3281
500
1640
200
656
SEA
LEVEL
200
656
2000
6562
4000
13124
6000
19686

Lambert Conformal Conic Projection

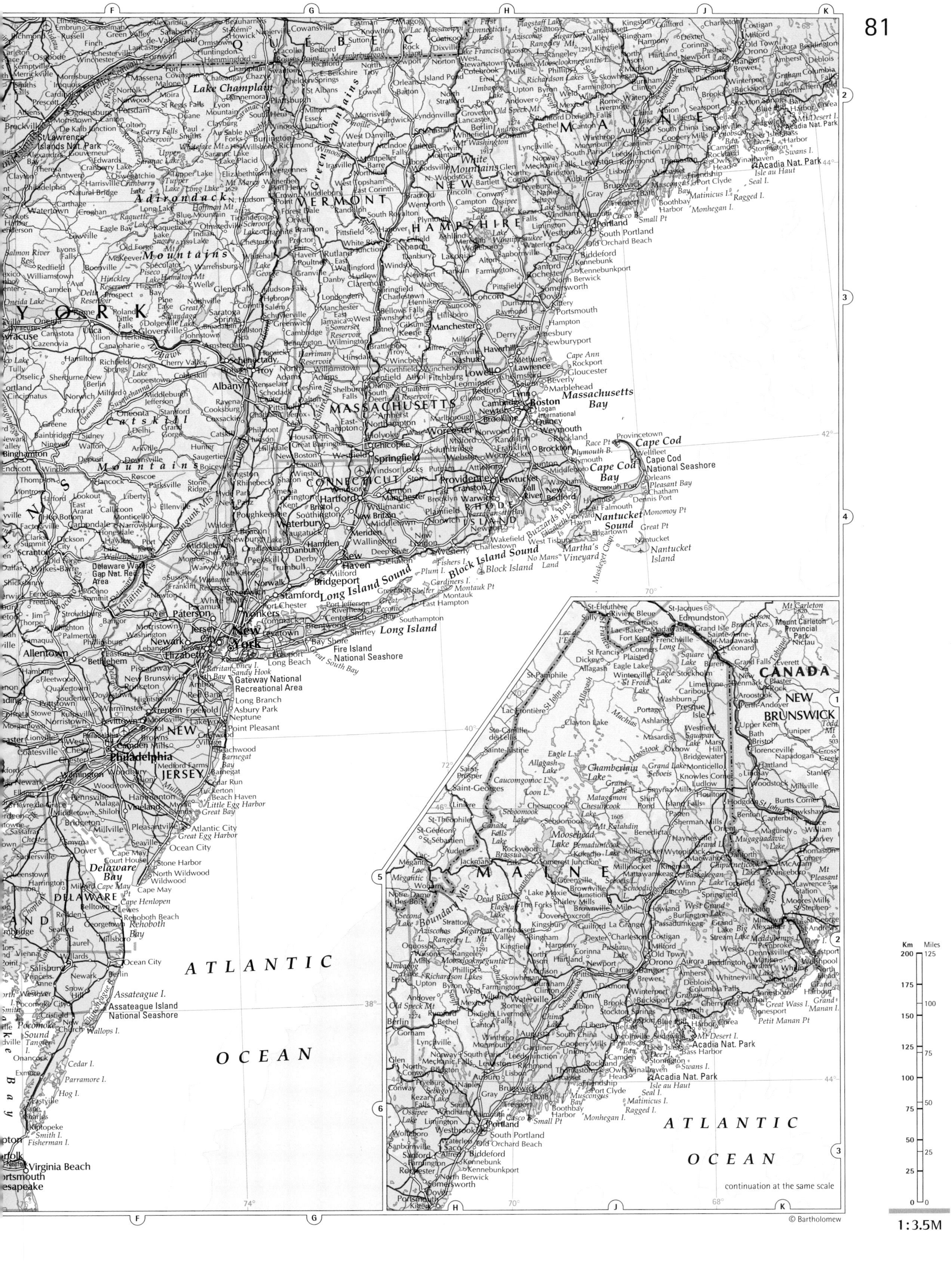
QUÉBEC
VERMONT
NEW HAMPSHIRE
MAINE
MASSACHUSETTS
CONNECTICUT
RHODE ISLAND
YORK
NEW JERSEY
DELAWARE
CANADA
NEW BRUNSWICK
Adirondack Mountains
Catskill Mountains
Green Mountains
White Mountains
Lake Champlain
Long Island Sound
Block Island Sound
Long Island
Cape Cod
Cape Cod Bay
Massachusetts Bay
Nantucket Sound
Nantucket Island
Martha's Vineyard
Delaware Bay
Boston
New York
Philadelphia
Albany
Providence
Hartford
Portland
Bangor
Augusta
Concord
Manchester
Springfield
Worcester
New Haven
Atlantic City
Virginia Beach
Acadia Nat. Park
Cape Cod National Seashore
Fire Island National Seashore
Gateway National Recreational Area
Assateague Island National Seashore
Delaware Water Gap Nat. Rec. Area
ATLANTIC OCEAN
continuation at the same scale
Km
Miles
© Bartholomew

1:3.5M

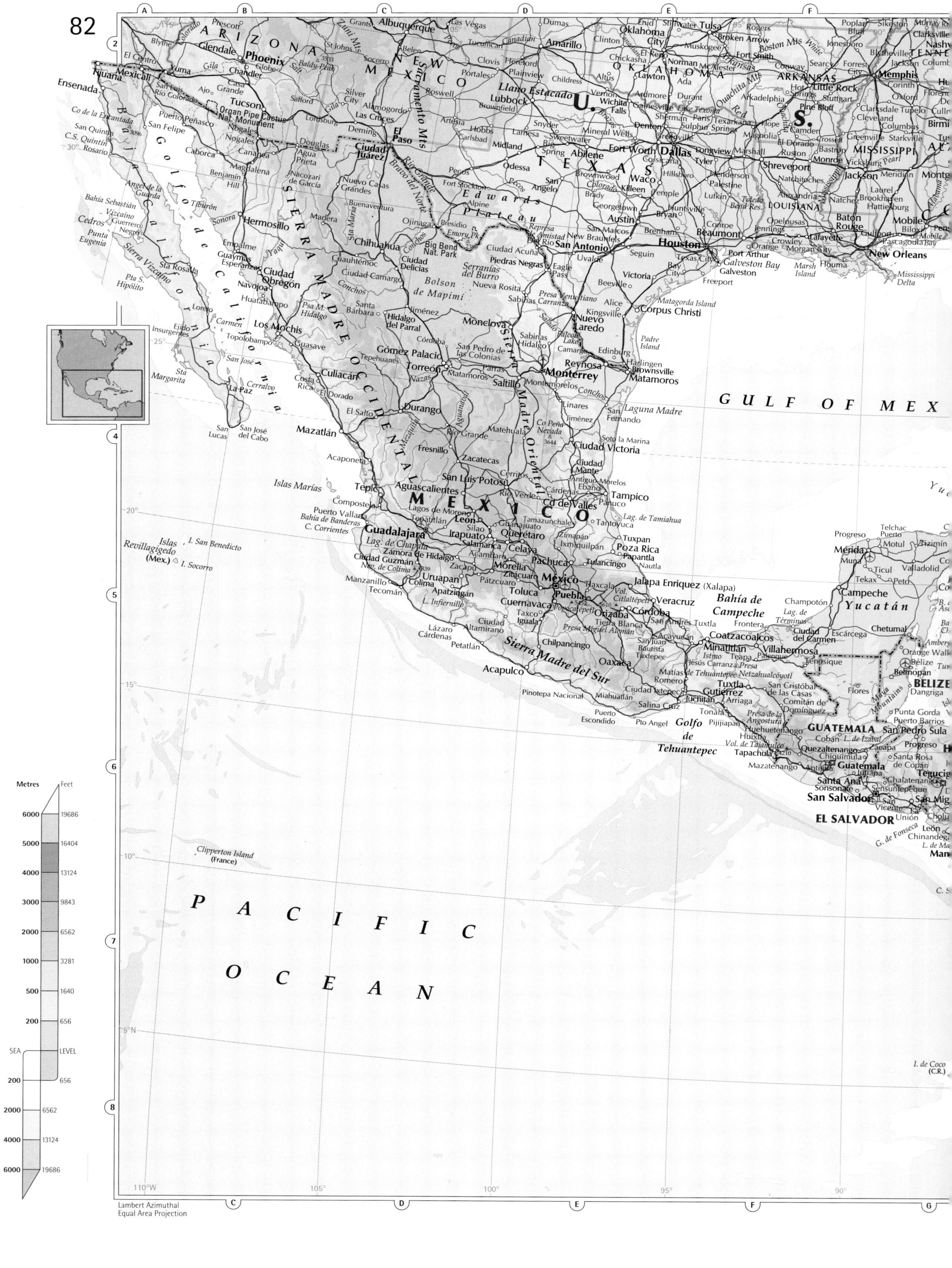

PACIFIC

OCEAN

GULF OF MEX

Lambert Azimuthal
Equal Area Projection

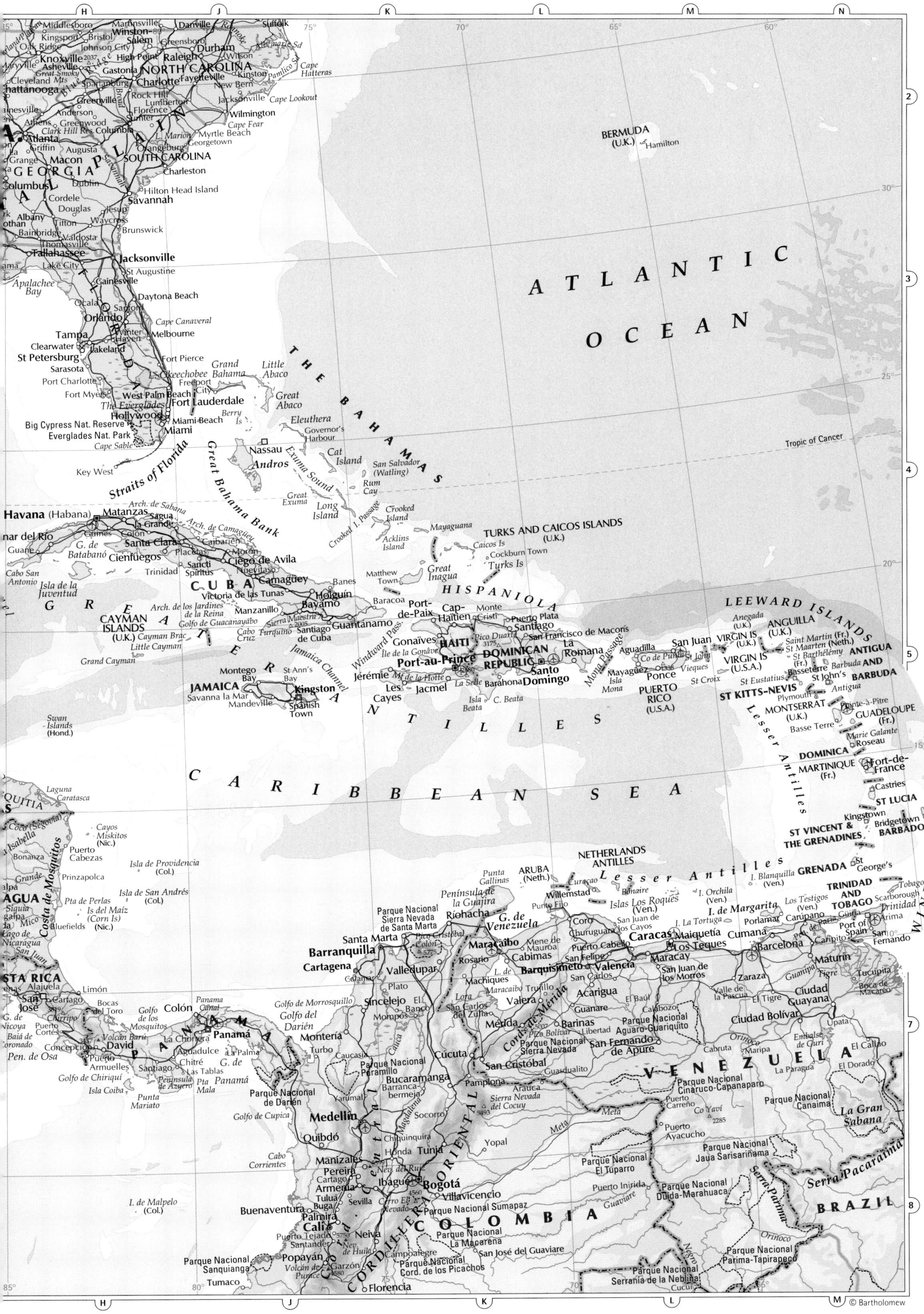

ATLANTIC OCEAN

BERMUDA (U.K.) Hamilton

Tropic of Cancer

THE BAHAMAS

Nassau
Andros
Cat Island
San Salvador (Watling)
Rum Cay
Long Island
Crooked Island
Acklins Island
Mayaguana
TURKS AND CAICOS ISLANDS (U.K.)
Caicos Is
Cockburn Town
Turks Is
Great Inagua

HISPANIOLA

LEEWARD ISLANDS

Anegada (U.K.)
ANGUILLA (U.K.)
Saint Martin (Fr.)
St Maarten (Neth.)
St Barthélémy (Fr.)
Basseterre Barbuda
ANTIGUA AND BARBUDA
St John's Antigua
ST KITTS-NEVIS
MONTSERRAT (U.K.)
GUADELOUPE (Fr.)
Basse Terre
Pointe-à-Pitre
Marie Galante
Roseau
DOMINICA
MARTINIQUE (Fr.)
Fort-de-France
St Croix
ST LUCIA
Castries
Kingstown
Bridgetown
ST VINCENT & THE GRENADINES
BARBADOS
GRENADA
St George's

Havana (Habana)
Matanzas
Sagua la Grande
Santa Clara
Cienfuegos
Placetas
Trinidad
Sancti Spiritus
Ciego de Avila
Camagüey
Victoria de las Tunas
Holguín
Bayamo
Manzanillo
Santiago de Cuba
Guantánamo
CUBA

Pinar del Rio
Guane
Cabo San Antonio
Isla de la Juventud

CAYMAN ISLANDS (U.K.)
Cayman Brac
Little Cayman
Grand Cayman

JAMAICA
Montego Bay
St Ann's Bay
Kingston
Spanish Town
Mandeville
Savanna la Mar

Port-de-Paix
Cap-Haïtien
Gonaïves
HAITI
Port-au-Prince
Jérémie
Les Cayes
Jacmel
Monte Cristi
Santiago
Puerto Plata
San Francisco de Macorís
DOMINICAN REPUBLIC
La Romana
Santo Domingo
Barahona

Aguadilla
San Juan
Mayagüez
Ponce
PUERTO RICO (U.S.A.)

VIRGIN IS (U.K.)
VIRGIN IS (U.S.A.)

GREATER ANTILLES

CARIBBEAN SEA

Lesser Antilles

WINDWARD ISLANDS

Swan Islands (Hond.)

Cayos Miskitos (Nic.)
Puerto Cabezas
Prinzapolca
Isla de Providencia (Col.)
Isla de San Andrés (Col.)
Islas del Maíz (Corn Is)
Bluefields

NETHERLANDS ANTILLES
ARUBA (Neth.)
Curaçao (Ven.)
Bonaire
Willemstad
Punta Fijo
GRENADA
TRINIDAD AND TOBAGO
Port of Spain
Scarborough
I. de Margarita (Ven.)
Porlamar
Los Testigos (Ven.)
I. Blanquilla (Ven.)
I. Orchila (Ven.)
Islas Los Roques (Ven.)
I. La Tortuga

Punta Gallinas
Península de la Guajira
Riohacha
Santa Marta
Barranquilla
Cartagena
Maracaibo
Cabimas
Coro
Puerto Cabello
Caracas
Maiquetía
Los Teques
Cumaná
Barcelona
Carúpano
Maturín

VENEZUELA

COLOMBIA

PANAMA
Colón
Panamá
David

COSTA RICA

Medellín
Bogotá
Cali
Pereira
Manizales
Armenia
Ibagué
Neiva
Popayán

Km 800 / Miles 500
700 / 400
600 / 300
500
400 / 200
300
200 / 100
100
0 / 0

© Bartholomew

1:14M

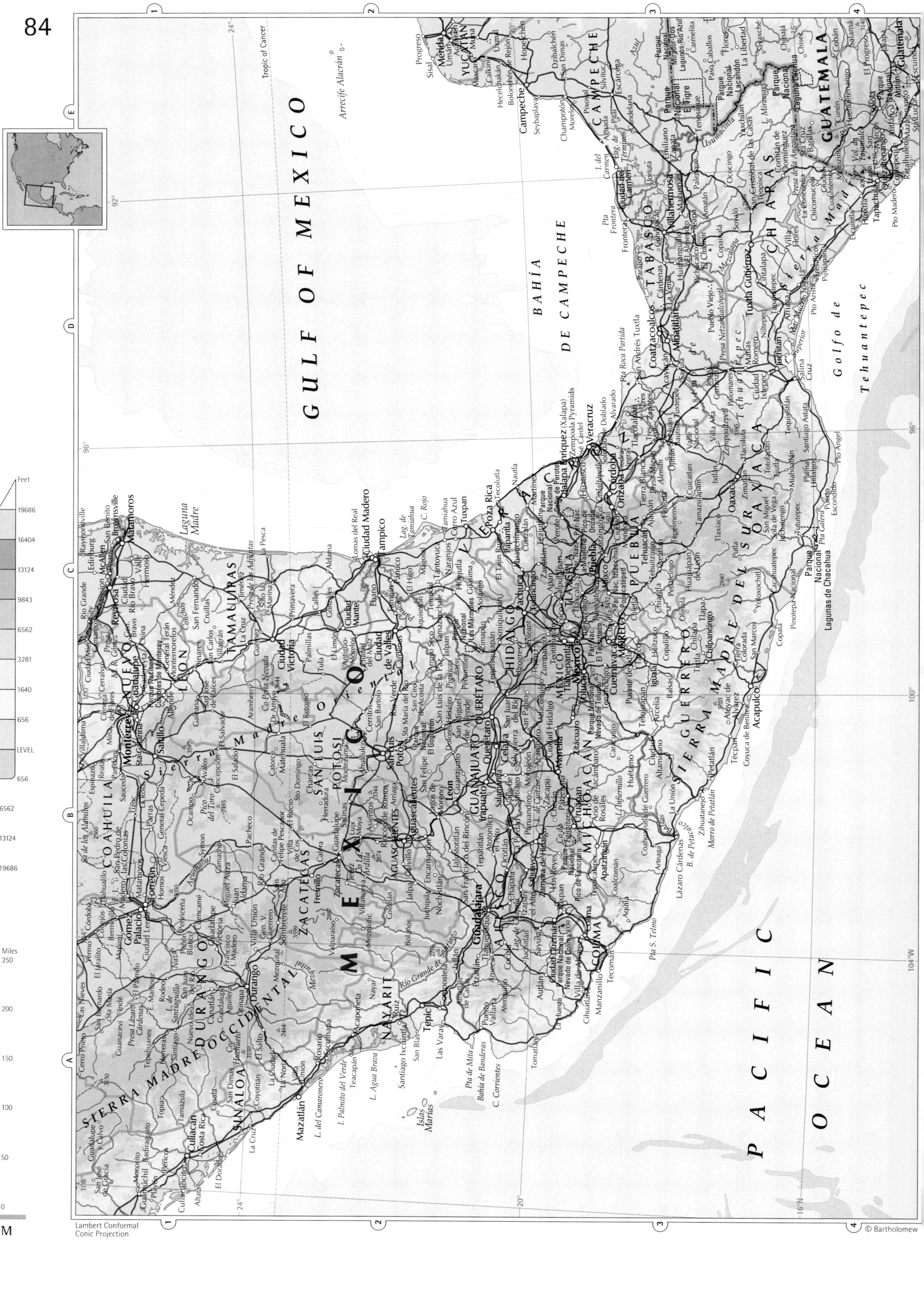

1:7M

Lambert Conformal
Conic Projection

© Bartholomew

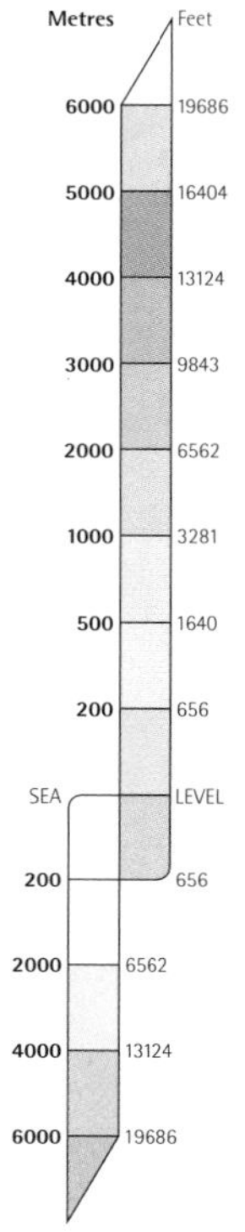

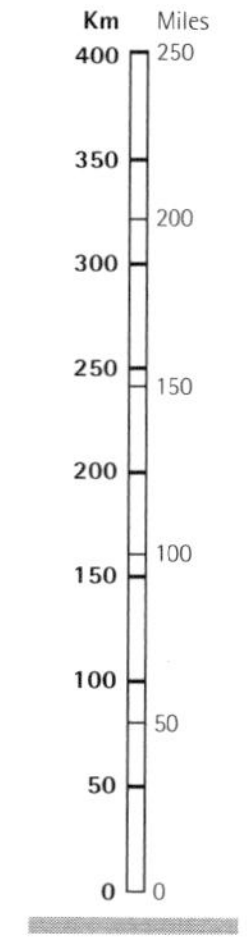

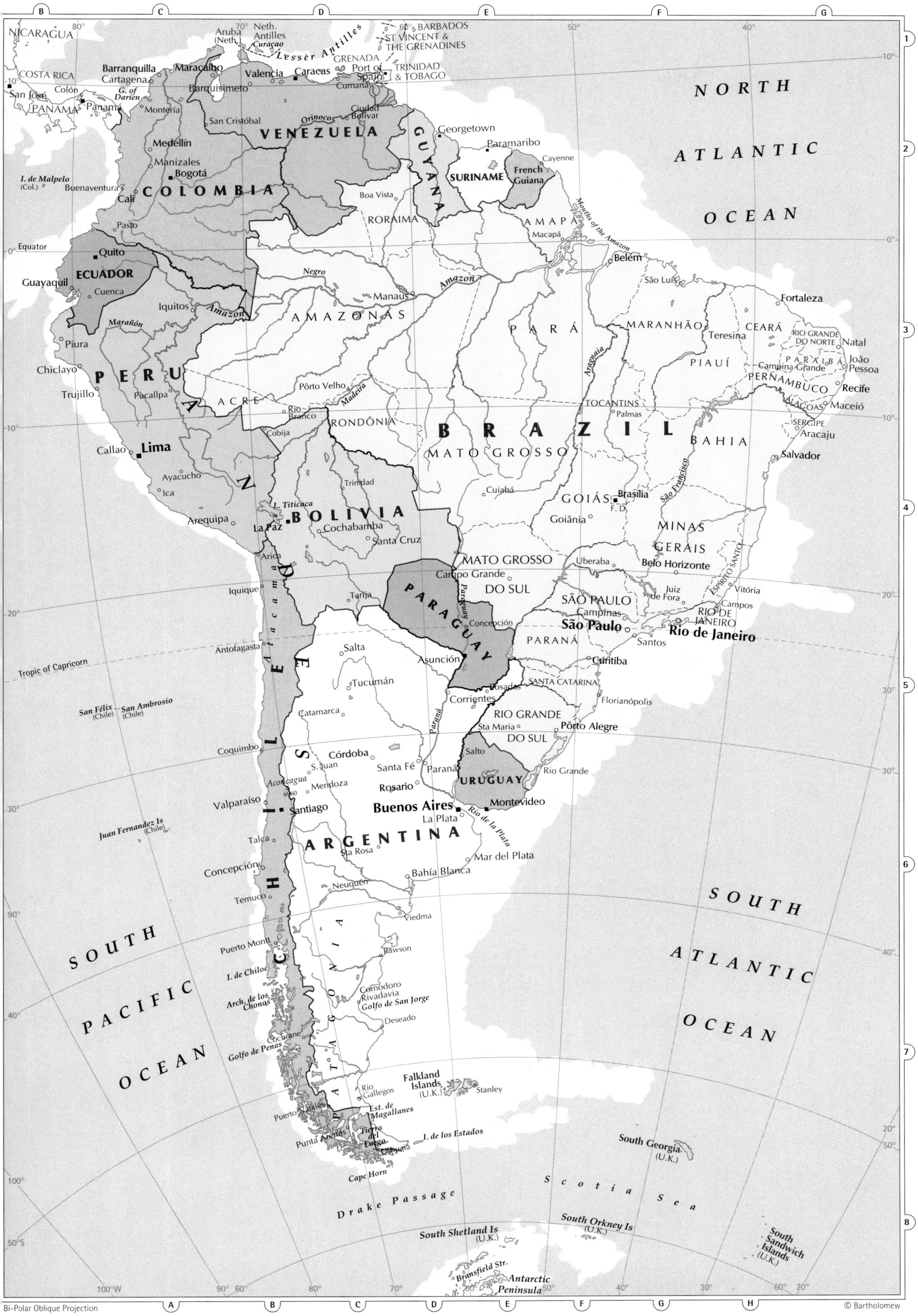

Grid References (top)

B | C | D | E | F | G

Map Labels

NORTH ATLANTIC OCEAN

SOUTH ATLANTIC OCEAN

SOUTH PACIFIC OCEAN

NICARAGUA
COSTA RICA
San José
PANAMA
Panamá
Colón
G. of Darién

Barranquilla
Cartagena
Monteria
Aruba (Neth.)
Neth. Antilles
Curaçao
Lesser Antilles
BARBADOS
ST VINCENT & THE GRENADINES
GRENADA
Port of Spain
TRINIDAD & TOBAGO
Cumaná
Maracaibo
Valencia
Caracas
Barquisimeto
San Cristóbal
VENEZUELA
Ciudad Bolívar
Orinoco
GUYANA
Georgetown
Paramaribo
SURINAME
Cayenne
French Guiana

Medellín
Manizales
Bogotá
Cali
Pasto
COLOMBIA
Buenaventura
I. de Malpelo (Col.)

Boa Vista
RORAIMA
AMAPÁ
Macapá
Mouths of the Amazon

ECUADOR
Quito
Cuenca
Guayaquil
Equator

Iquitos
Piura
Chiclayo
Trujillo
Marañón
Amazon
PERU
Pacallpa
Pôrto Velho
Rio Branco
Cobija
ACRE
RONDÔNIA
Madeira
Negro
Manaus
AMAZONAS

BRAZIL
Belém
São Luis
Fortaleza
MARANHÃO
Teresina
PIAUÍ
CEARÁ
Natal
RIO GRANDE DO NORTE
PARAÍBA
João Pessoa
Campina Grande
PERNAMBUCO
Recife
ALAGOAS
Maceió
SERGIPE
Aracaju
Salvador
BAHIA
TOCANTINS
Palmas
Araguaia
PARÁ

Callao
Lima
Ayacucho
Ica
Arequipa
L. Titicaca
La Paz
BOLIVIA
Cochabamba
Trinidad
Santa Cruz
Arica
Iquique
Antofagasta
Tropic of Capricorn
San Félix (Chile)
San Ambrosio (Chile)

MATO GROSSO
Cuiabá
GOIÁS
Goiânia
Brasília F.D.
São Francisco
Uberaba
MINAS GERAIS
Belo Horizonte
Juiz de Fora
ESPÍRITO SANTO
Vitória
Campos
RIO DE JANEIRO
Rio de Janeiro
Santos
São Paulo
SÃO PAULO
Campinas

MATO GROSSO DO SUL
Campo Grande
PARAGUAY
Paraguay
Concepción
Asunción
Tarija
Salta
Tucumán
Catamarca
PARANÁ
Curitiba
SANTA CATARINA
Florianópolis
Posadas
Corrientes
Paraná
RIO GRANDE DO SUL
Sta Maria
Pôrto Alegre
Salto
Rio Grande
URUGUAY
Montevideo

Coquimbo
Córdoba
S. Juan
Santa Fé
Paraná
Rosario
Mendoza
Aconcagua 6960
Valparaíso
Santiago
Talca
San Juan Fernandez Is (Chile)
ARGENTINA
Sta Rosa
Buenos Aires
La Plata
Río de la Plata
Mar del Plata
Concepción
Neuquén
Temuco
Bahía Blanca
Viedma
Puerto Montt
I. de Chiloé
Arch. de los Chonos
Golfo de Penas
Rawson
Comodoro Rivadavia
Golfo de San Jorge
Deseado
PATAGONIA
Río Gallegos
Est. de Magallanes
Punta Arenas
Puerto Natales
Tierra del Fuego
Ushuaia
I. de los Estados
Cape Horn
Drake Passage

Falkland Islands (U.K.)
Stanley
South Georgia (U.K.)
Scotia Sea
South Orkney Is (U.K.)
South Shetland Is (U.K.)
Bransfield Str.
Antarctic Peninsula
South Sandwich Islands (U.K.)

Scale

Metres SEA	Feet LEVEL
200	656
3000	9843

Km	Miles
1750	1000
1500	
1250	750
1000	500
750	
500	250
250	
0	0

Bi-Polar Oblique Projection

© Bartholomew

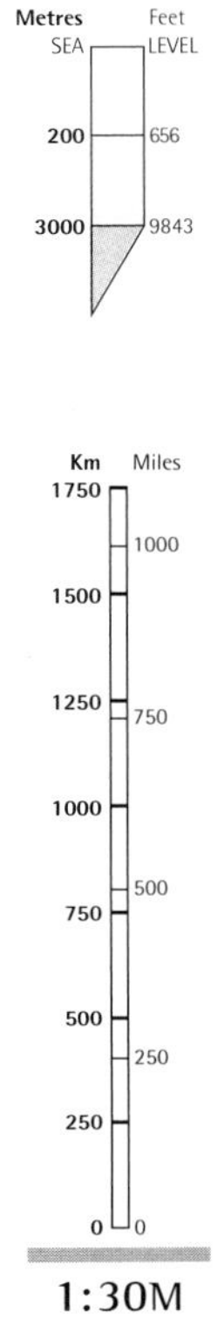

1:30M

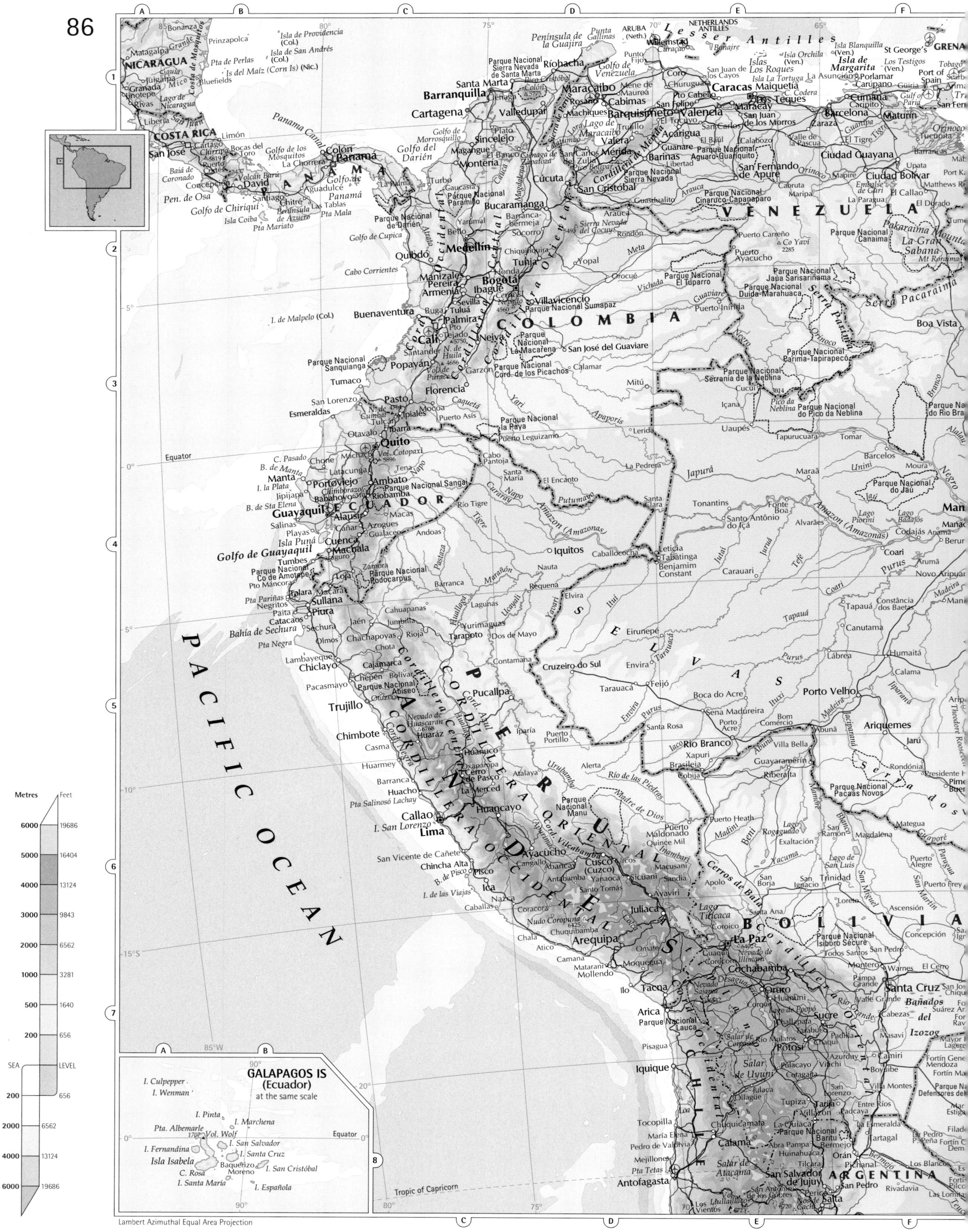
PACIFIC OCEAN
COLOMBIA
VENEZUELA
ECUADOR
PERU
BOLIVIA
ARGENTINA
CHILE
PANAMA
COSTA RICA
NICARAGUA
Lesser Antilles
NETHERLANDS ANTILLES
ARUBA (Neth.)
CORDILLERA OCCIDENTAL
CORDILLERA ORIENTAL
CORDILLERA CENTRAL
ANDES
SELVAS
GALAPAGOS IS (Ecuador) at the same scale
Equator
Tropic of Capricorn
Bogotá
Caracas
Quito
Lima
La Paz
Medellín
Cali
Barranquilla
Cartagena
Maracaibo
Guayaquil
Cusco (Cuzco)
Arequipa
Iquitos
Manaus
Panamá
San José
Santa Cruz
Cochabamba
Sucre
Potosí
Antofagasta
Salta
Amazon (Amazonas)
Lago Titicaca
Golfo de Guayaquil
Gulf of Paria
Metres
Feet
6000
19686
5000
16404
4000
13124
3000
9843
2000
6562
1000
3281
500
1640
200
656
SEA
LEVEL
Lambert Azimuthal Equal Area Projection

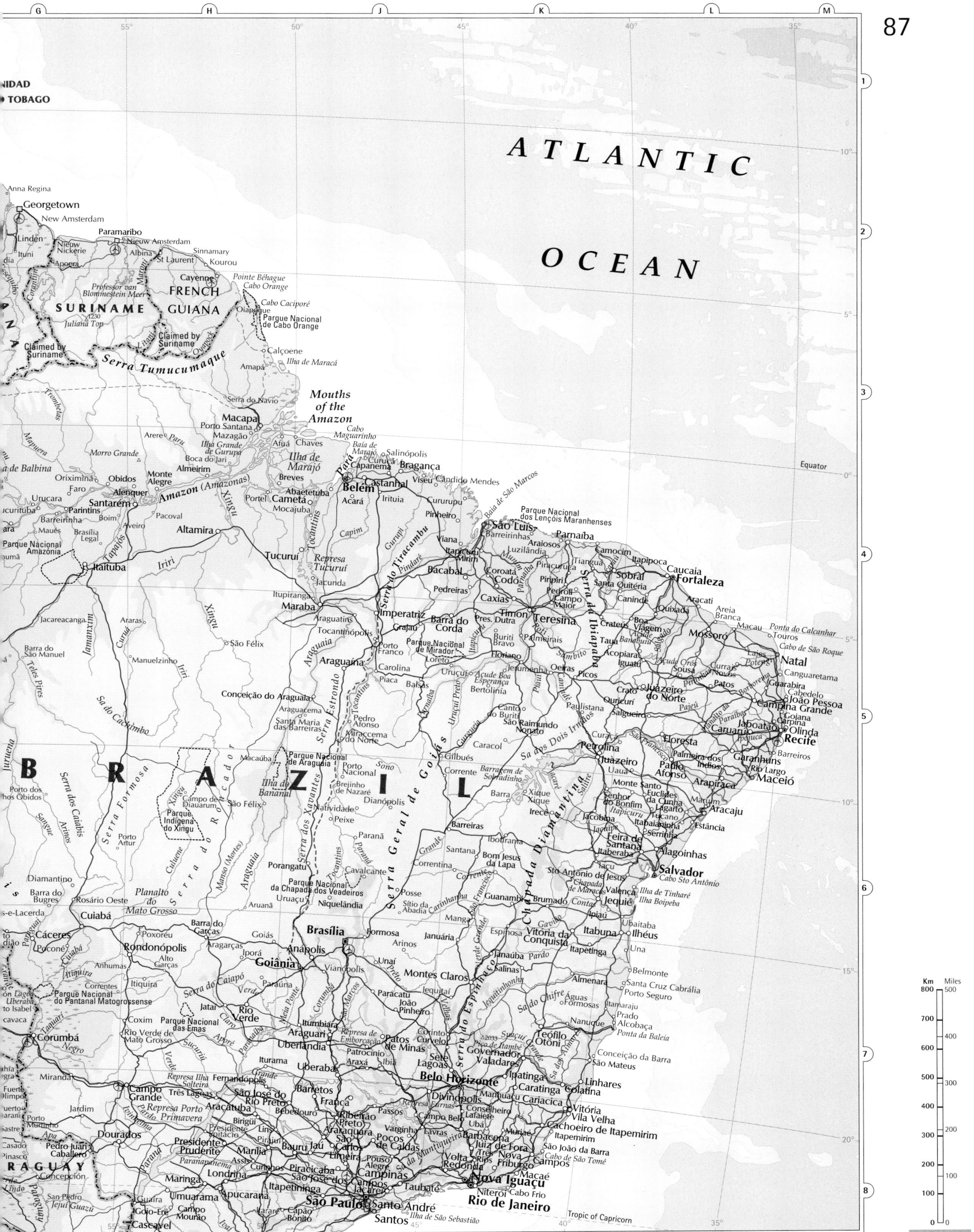

ATLANTIC

OCEAN

G H J K L M

TRINIDAD
TOBAGO

Anna Regina
Georgetown
New Amsterdam
Linden
Nieuw Nickerie
Albina
St Laurent
Ituni
Apoera
Sinnamary
Kourou
Professor van
Blommestein Meer
Cayenne
FRENCH
SURINAME GUIANA
Claimed by
Suriname
Juliana Top
Claimed by
Suriname
Pointe Béhague
Cabo Orange
Oiapoque
Parque Nacional
de Cabo Orange
Serra Tumucumaque
Calçoene
Ilha de Maracá
Amapá

Serra do Navio
Mouths
of the
Amazon
Macapá
Cabo
Maguarinho
Baía de
Marajó
Porto Santana
Mazagão
Salinópolis
Ilha Grande
de Gurupá
Afuá
Chaves
Curuçá
Capanema
Bragança
Morro Grande
Boca do Jari
Breves
Ilha de
Marajó
Viseu
Candido Mendes
Oriximiná
Óbidos
Monte
Alegre
Almeirim
Portel
Cametá
Abaetetuba
Acará
Irituia
Belém
Castanhal
São Luís
Barreirinhas
Parque Nacional
dos Lençóis Maranhenses
Parnaíba
Urucará
Faro
Alenquer
Mocajuba
Capim
Pinheiro
Baía de São Marcos
Araioses
Camocim
Itapipoca
Santarém
Boim
Pacoval
Aveiro
Viana
Itapicuru
Mirim
Luzilândia
Piracuruca
Tianguá
Sobral
Caucaia
Fortaleza
Maués
Brasília
Legal
Maraú
Cururupu
Coroatá
Parnaíba
Piripiri
Santa Quitéria
Canindé
Parque Nacional
Amazônia
Itaituba
Altamira
Tucuruí
Represa
Tucuruí
Jacunda
Bacabal
Codó
Pedreiras
Caxias
Timon
Pres. Dutra
Teresina
Crateús
Boa
Viagem
Quixadá
Aracati
Areia
Branca
Macau
Ponta do Calcanhar
Touros
Marabá
Imperatriz
Grajaú
Barra do
Corda
Buriti
Bravo
Floriano
Tauá
Acopiara
Iguatu
Açude Orós
Sousa
Lajes
Patos
Cabo de São Roque
Natal
Canguaretama
Jacareacanga
Araras
Itupiranga
Araguatins
Tocantinópolis
Porto
Franco
Parque Nacional
de Mirador
Loreto
Uruçuí
Bertolínia
Jerumenha
Oeiras
Picos
Crato
Juazeiro
do Norte
Quixirú
Currais
Novos
Potengi
Canguaretama
Cabedelo
Guarabira
João Pessoa
São Félix
Carolina
Piaçá
Balsas
Açude Boa
Esperança
Canto
do Buriti
São Raimundo
Nonato
Paulistana
Salgueiro
Campina Grande
Gojana
Jaboatão
Olinda
Recife
Conceição do Araguaia
Araguacema
Santa Maria
das Barreiras
Pedro
Afonso
Miracema
do Norte
Gilbués
Corrente
Caracol
Barragem de
Sobradinho
Xique
Xique
Petrolina
Juazeiro
Floresta
Palmeira dos
Índios
Curaçá
Garanhuns
Barreiros
Maceió
BRAZIL
Porto dos
Gaúchos
Macaúba
Ilha do
Bananal
Porto Nacional
Brejinho
de Nazaré
Natividade
Dianópolis
Barra
Xique
Xique
Senhor
do Bonfim
Euclides
da Cunha
Tucano
Matuipe
Aracaju
Serra dos Caiabis
Serra Formosa
São Félix
Peixe
Paranã
Barreiras
Ibotirama
Bom Jesus
da Lapa
Irecê
Jacobina
Feira de
Santana
Itaberaba
Estância
Alagoinhas
Arinos
Porto
Artur
Parque
Indígena
do Xingu
Porangatu
Cavalcante
Santana
Correntina
Correntes
Sto Antônio de Jesus
Guanambi
Brumado
Contas
Ipiaú
Salvador
Cabo Sto Antônio
Valença
Ilha de Tinharé
Ilha Boipeba
Diamantino
Barra do
Bugres
Rosário Oeste
Planalto
do
Mato Grosso
Parque Nacional
da Chapada dos Veadeiros
Uruaçu
Niquelândia
Posse
Sítio da
Abadia
Aruanã
Januária
Espinosa
Vitória da
Conquista
Itabuna
Ilhéus
Ubaitaba
Cáceres
Cuiabá
Barra do
Garças
Goiás
Anápolis
Brasília
Formosa
Montes Claros
Taiaúba
Pardo
Itapetinga
Una
Belmonte
Santa Cruz Cabrália
Porto Seguro
Rondonópolis
Alto
Garças
Iporá
Goiânia
Vianópolis
Unaí
Paracatu
João
Pinheiro
Salinas
Itamaraju
Prado
Alcobaça
Ponta da Baleia
Parque Nacional
do Pantanal Matogrossense
Coxim
Parque Nacional
das Emas
Jataí
Rio
Verde
Itumbiara
Corinto
Curvelo
Nanuque
Teófilo
Otoni
Conceição da Barra
São Mateus
Corumbá
Rio Verde de
Mato Grosso
Araguari
Represa de
Emborcação
Patos
de Minas
Patrocínio
Ibiá
Sete
Lagoas
Governador
Valadares
Linhares
Miranda
Campo
Grande
Represa Ilha
Solteira
Fernandópolis
Uberlândia
Uberaba
Araxá
Belo Horizonte
Ipatinga
Caratinga
Cariacica
Vitória
Vila Velha
Dourados
Jardim
Três Lagoas
São José
do Rio Preto
Barretos
Franca
Divinópolis
Conselheiro
Lafaiete
Manhuaçu
Itabira de Itapemirim
Itapemirim
Presidente
Prudente
Marília
Bauru
Jaú
Ribeirão
Preto
Araraquara
São
Carlos
Pocos
de Caldas
Campo Belo
Lavras
Pouso
Alegre
Barbacena
Juiz de Fora
Muriaé
Três
Rios
Nova
Friburgo
Nova
Iguaçu
Campos
São João da Barra
Ponta de São Tomé
Maringá
Londrina
Umuarama
Apucarana
Campo
Mourão
Itapetininga
Piracicaba
Limeira
Campinas
Jundiaí
Taubaté
Macaé
Cabo Frio
Niterói
Rio de Janeiro
Cascavel
Guaíra
Gojo-Erê
São Paulo
Santo André
Santos
Ilha de São Sebastião
Tropic of Capricorn

Km Miles
800 500
700
400
600
500 300
400
300 200
200
100 100
0 0

© Bartholomew

1:15M

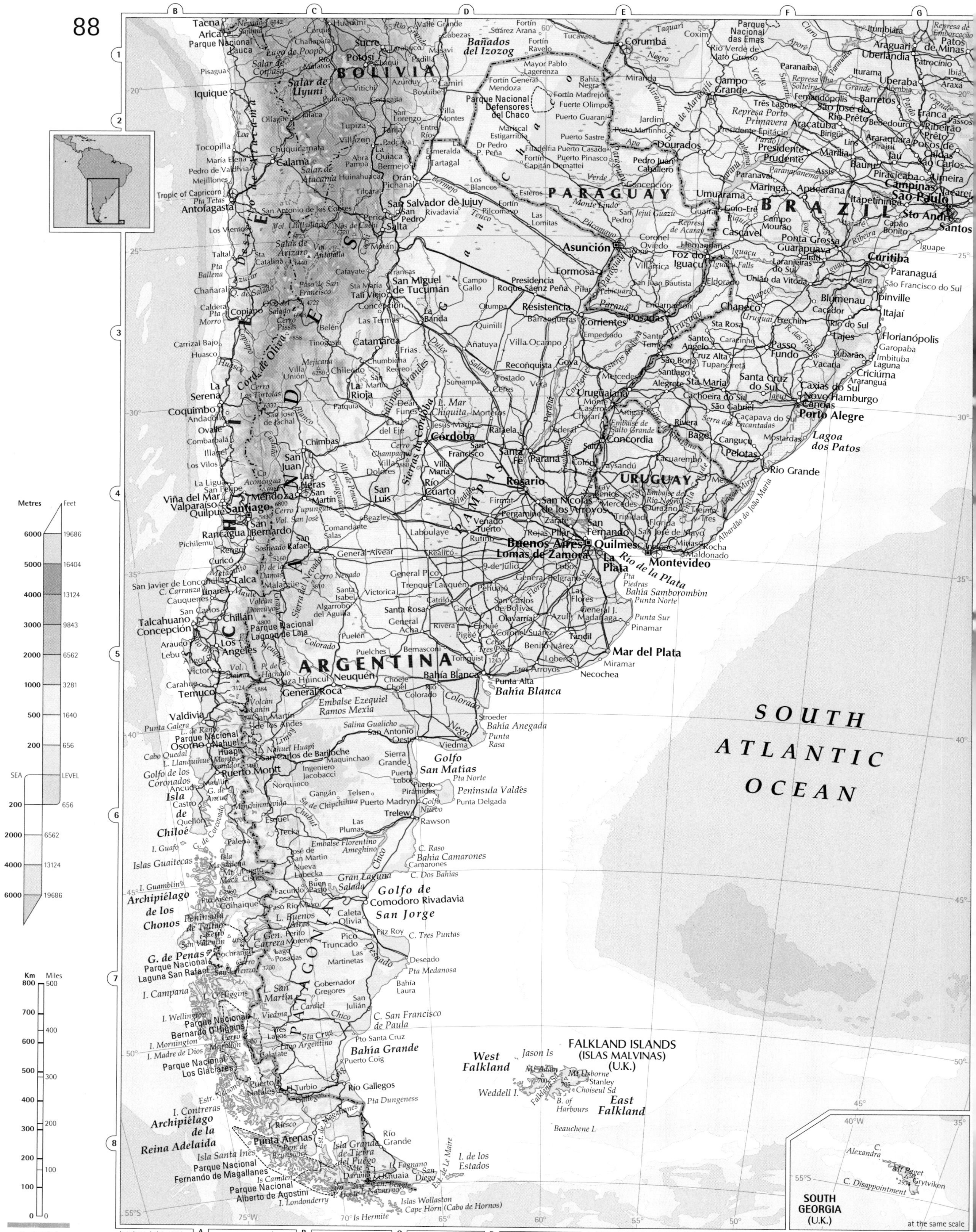

1:15M

Lambert Azimuthal
Equal Area Projection

© Bartholomew

VENEZUELA and COLOMBIA

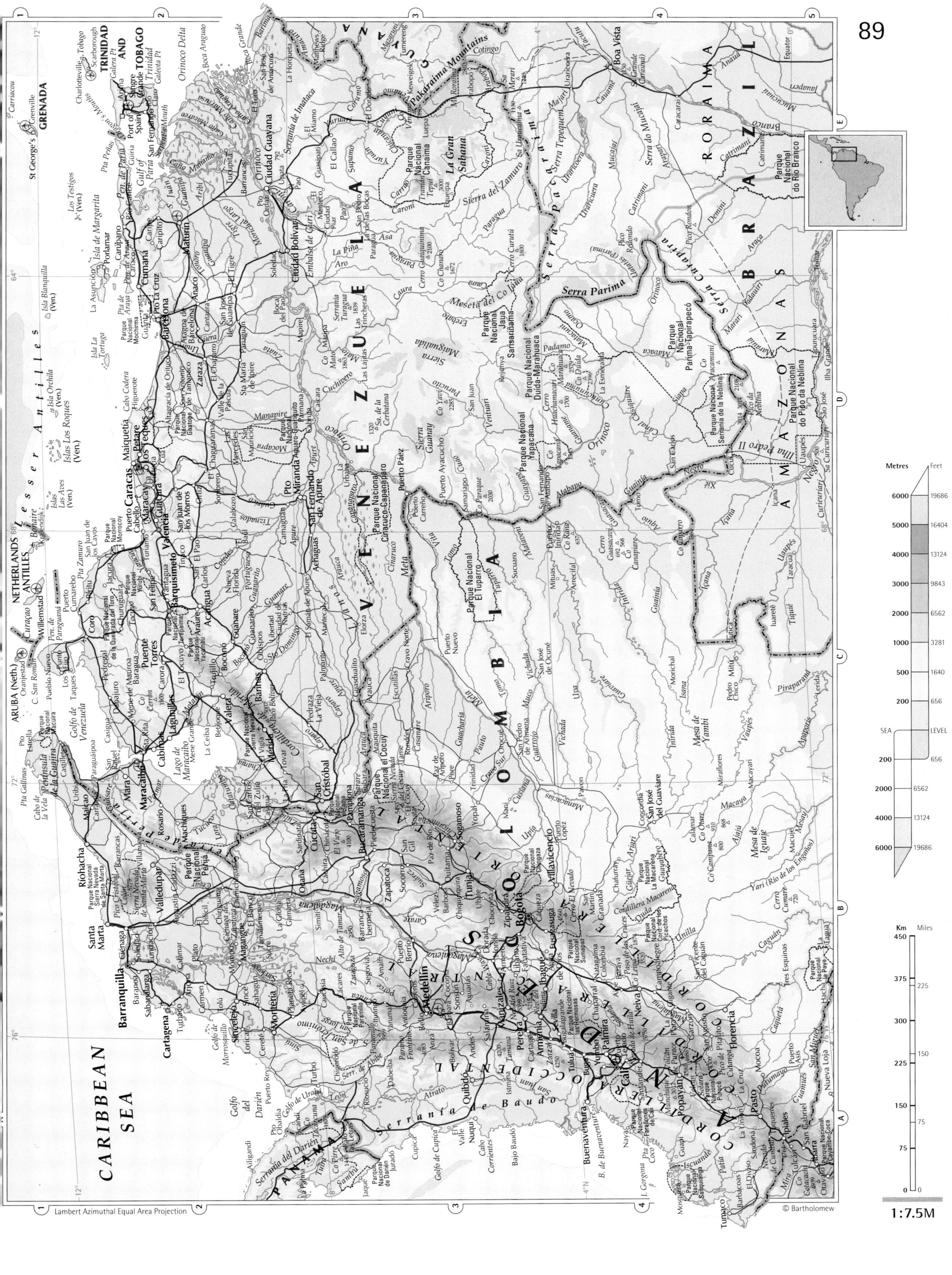

VENEZUELA
COLOMBIA
CARIBBEAN SEA
Lesser Antilles
NETHERLANDS ANTILLES
ARUBA (Neth.)
Curaçao
Bonaire
TRINIDAD AND TOBAGO
GRENADA
PANAMA
BRAZIL
AMAZONAS
RORAIMA
Caracas
Bogotá
Maracaibo
Barranquilla
Cartagena
Medellín
Cali
Valencia
Barquisimeto
Ciudad Guayana
Ciudad Bolívar
Cúcuta
Bucaramanga
Villavicencio
Boa Vista
Port of Spain
Serra Parima
Pakaraima Mountains
Lago de Maracaibo
Llanos
Orinoco
Meta
Magdalena
Lambert Azimuthal Equal Area Projection
© Bartholomew
Metres
Feet
SEA LEVEL
Km
Miles
1:7.5M

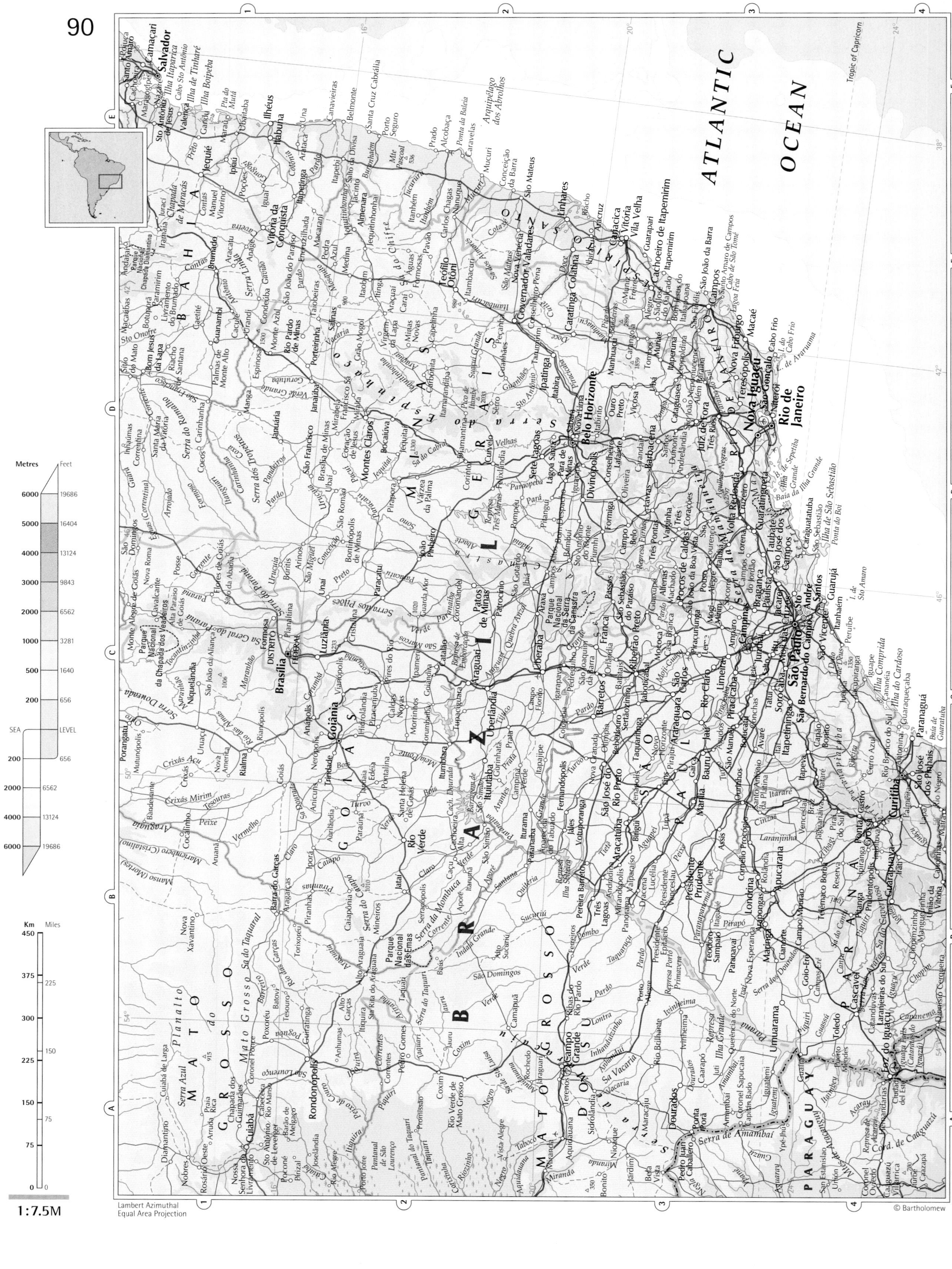

Metres / Feet

6000 — 19686
5000 — 16404
4000 — 13124
3000 — 9843
2000 — 6562
1000 — 3281
500 — 1640
200 — 656
SEA — LEVEL
200 — 656
2000 — 6562
4000 — 13124
6000 — 19686

Km / Miles

450 —
375 — 225
300 —
225 — 150
150 —
75 — 75
0 — 0

ATLANTIC

OCEAN

1 : 7.5M

Lambert Azimuthal
Equal Area Projection

© Bartholomew

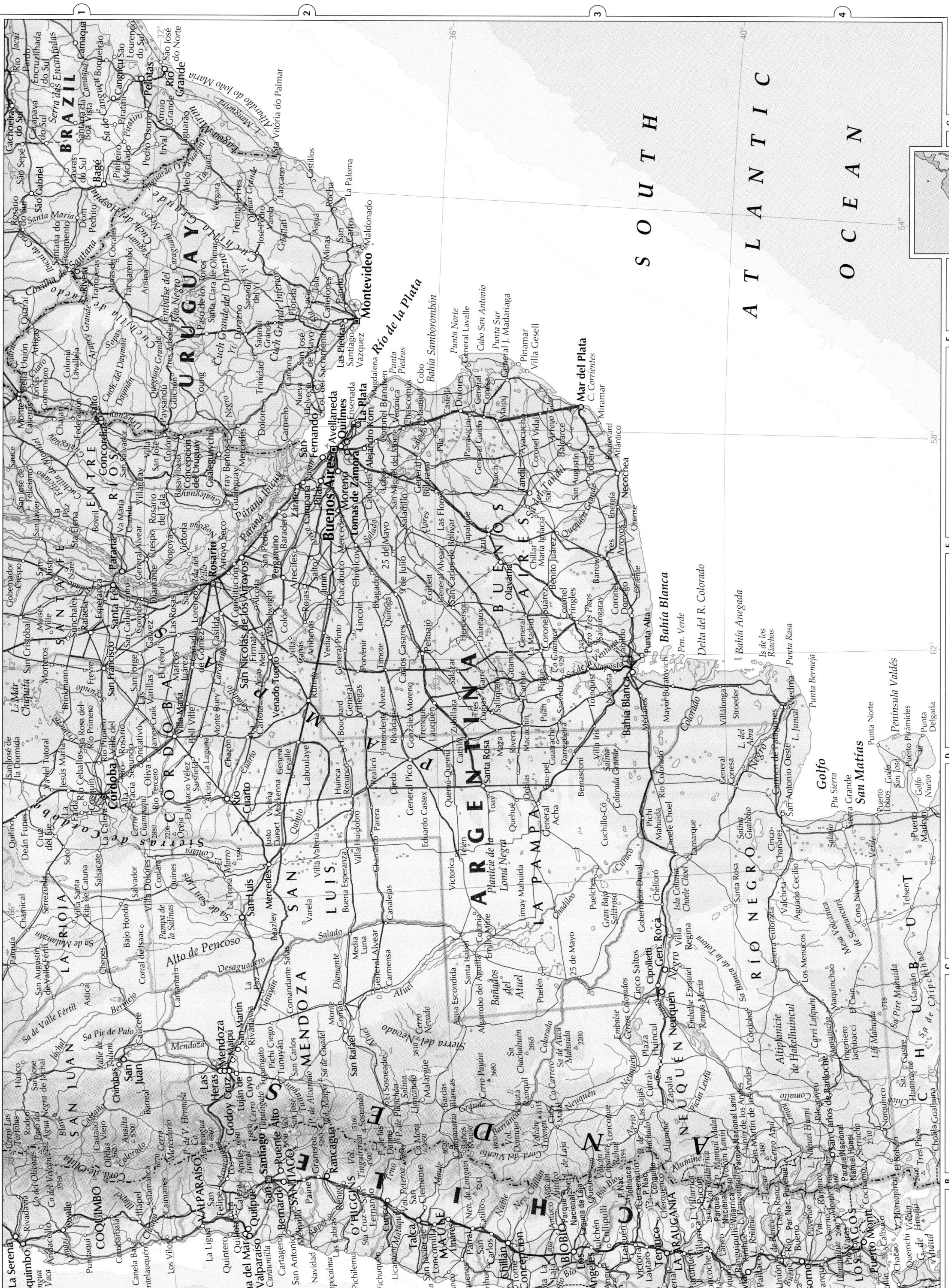

© Bartholomew

1:7.5M

ANTARCTICA

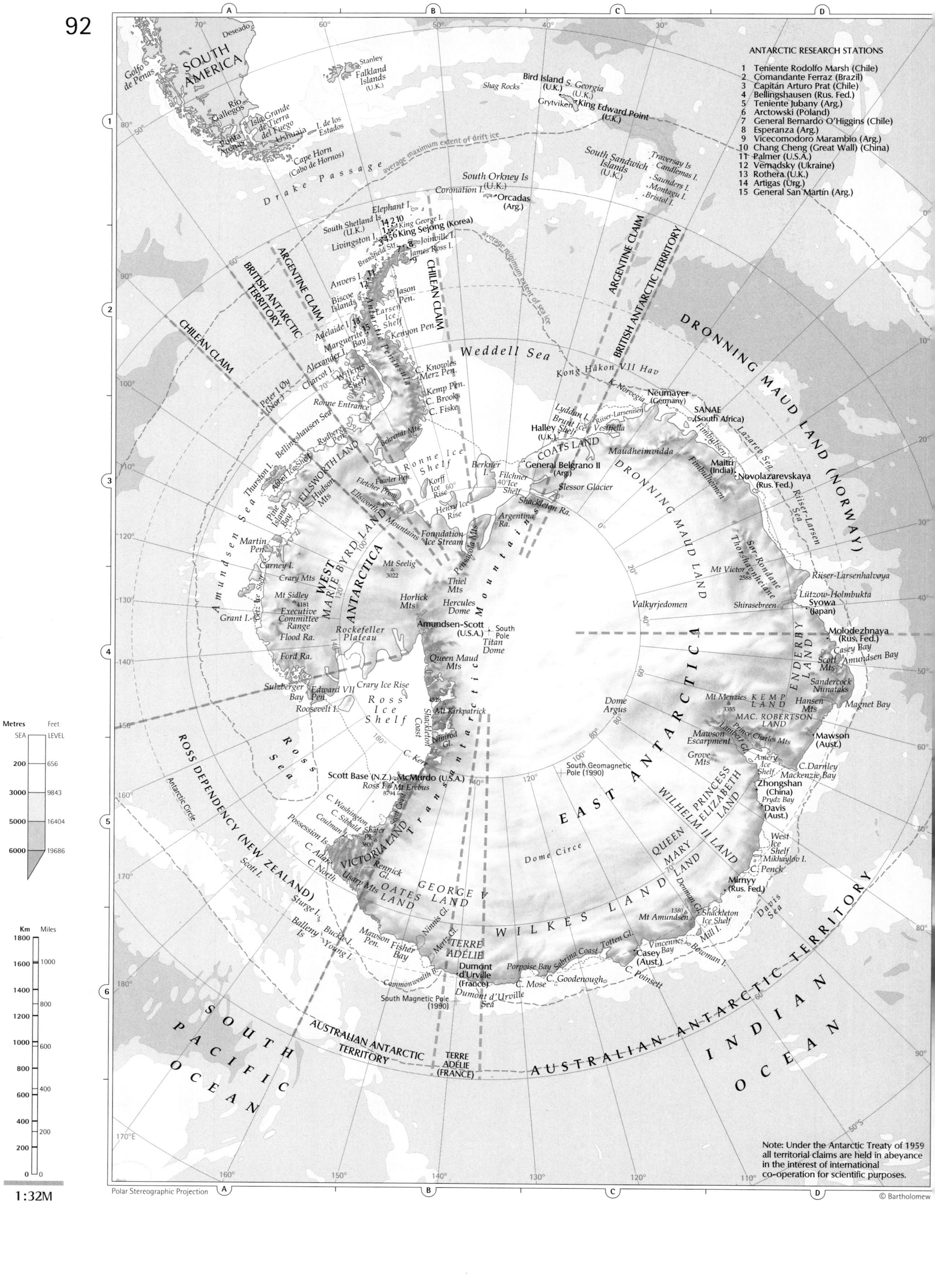

ANTARCTIC RESEARCH STATIONS

1 Teniente Rodolfo Marsh (Chile)
2 Comandante Ferraz (Brazil)
3 Capitán Arturo Prat (Chile)
4 Bellingshausen (Rus. Fed.)
5 Teniente Jubany (Arg.)
6 Arctowski (Poland)
7 General Bernardo O'Higgins (Chile)
8 Esperanza (Arg.)
9 Vicecomodoro Marambio (Arg.)
10 Chang Cheng (Great Wall) (China)
11 Palmer (U.S.A.)
12 Vernadsky (Ukraine)
13 Rothera (U.K.)
14 Artigas (Urg.)
15 General San Martín (Arg.)

Note: Under the Antarctic Treaty of 1959
all territorial claims are held in abeyance
in the interest of international
co-operation for scientific purposes.

Metres	Feet
SEA	LEVEL
200	656
3000	9843
5000	16404
6000	19686

Km	Miles
1800	
1600	1000
1400	800
1200	
1000	600
800	
600	400
400	
200	200
0	0

1:32M

Polar Stereographic Projection

© Bartholomew

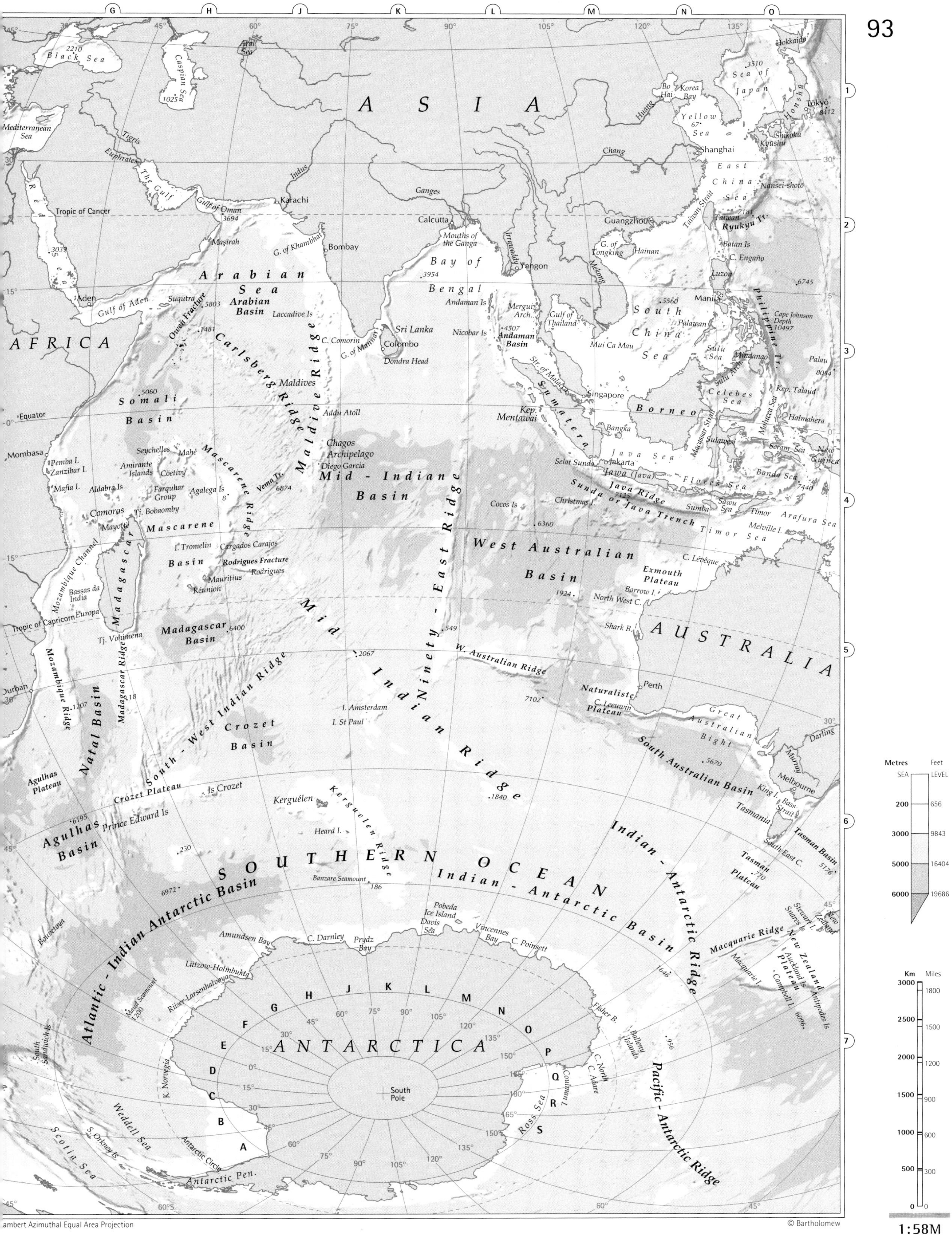

ASIA

AFRICA

AUSTRALIA

ANTARCTICA

South Pole

SOUTHERN OCEAN

Black Sea
Caspian Sea
Aral Sea
Mediterranean Sea
Red Sea
Tigris
Euphrates
The Gulf
Gulf of Oman
Tropic of Cancer
Aden
Gulf of Aden
Suqutra
Arabian Sea
Arabian Basin
Karachi
Mastrah
G. of Khambhat
Bombay
Indus
Ganges
Calcutta
Mouths of the Ganga
Bay of Bengal
Yangon
Irrawaddy
Chang
Huang
Shanghai
Guangzhou
East China Sea
Nansei-shoto
Taiwan Strait
Taiwan
Ryukyu Is.
Sea of Japan
Hokkaido
Honshu
Tokyo
Shikoku
Kyushu
Korea Bay
Bo Hai
Yellow Sea
Hainan
G. of Tongking
Mekong
South China Sea
Manila
Luzon
Cape Engaño
Batan Is
Palawan
Mindanao
Philippine Tr.
Cape Johnson Depth
Palau
Kep. Talaud
Celebes Sea
Sulu Sea
Sulu Arch.
Halmahera
Makassar Str.
Sulawesi
Seram Sea
Banda Sea
Ceram Sea
New Guinea
Timor
Arafura Sea
Timor Sea
Melville I.
C. Lévêque
Exmouth Plateau
Barrow I.
North West C.
Shark B.
Laccadive Is
Sri Lanka
Colombo
Dondra Head
C. Comorin
G. of Mannar
Maldives
Maldive Ridge
Carlsberg Ridge
Owen Fracture
Somali Basin
Equator
Mombasa
Pemba I.
Zanzibar I.
Mafia I.
Comoros
Mayotte
Aldabra Is
Seychelles
Mahé
Amirante Islands
Côetivy
Farquhar Group
Agalega Is
Mascarene Basin
I. Tromelin
Cargados Carajos
Rodrigues Fracture
Rodrigues
Mauritius
Réunion
Madagascar
Mascarene
Bassas da India
Europa
Tj. Bobaomby
Mozambique Channel
Mozambique Ridge
Natal Basin
Durban
Tropic of Capricorn
Agulhas Plateau
Agulhas Basin
Madagascar Ridge
Madagascar Basin
Tj. Vohimena
Chagos Archipelago
Diego Garcia
Addu Atoll
Mid - Indian Basin
Cocos Is
Christmas I.
Andaman Is
Nicobar Is
Andaman Basin
Mergui Arch.
Gulf of Thailand
Mui Ca Mau
Str. of Malacca
Sumatera
Singapore
Kep. Mentawai
Bangka
Borneo
Java Sea
Jakarta
Jawa (Java)
Selat Sunda
Sunda or Java Trench
Java Ridge
Flores Sea
Sumba
Sawu Sea
Bali
West Australian Basin
Ninety - East Ridge
Vema Tr.
Mid Indian Ridge
I. Amsterdam
I. St Paul
W. Australian Ridge
Naturaliste Plateau
C. Leeuwin
Perth
Great Australian Bight
South Australian Basin
Darling
Murray
Melbourne
Tasmania
Bass Str.
King I.
Tasman Basin
Tasman Plateau
Indian - Antarctic Basin
Indian - Antarctic Ridge
Macquarie Ridge
Macquarie I.
New Zealand
Auckland Is Plateau
Antipodes Is
Campbell I.
Stewart Is
Snares Is
Bounty Islands
Pacific - Antarctic Ridge
Kerguélen
Kerguelen Ridge
Heard I.
Crozet Basin
Crozet Plateau
Is Crozet
South - West Indian Ridge
Prince Edward Is
Banzare Seamount
Atlantic - Indian Antarctic Basin
Maud Seamount
South Sandwich Is
Scotia Sea
Waddell Sea
S. Orkney Is
K. Norvegia
Bouvetøya
Antarctic Circle
Antarctic Pen.
Lützow-Holmbukta
Riiser-Larsenhalvøya
Amundsen Bay
C. Darnley
Prydz Bay
Davis Sea
Pobeda Ice Island
Vincennes Bay
C. Poinsett
Ross Sea
C. Adare
C. North
Coulman I.
Balleny Islands
Fisher B.

Lambert Azimuthal Equal Area Projection

© Bartholomew

1:58M

Metres	Feet
SEA	LEVEL
200	656
3000	9843
5000	16404
6000	19686

Km	Miles
3000	1800
2500	1500
2000	1200
1500	900
1000	600
500	300
0	0

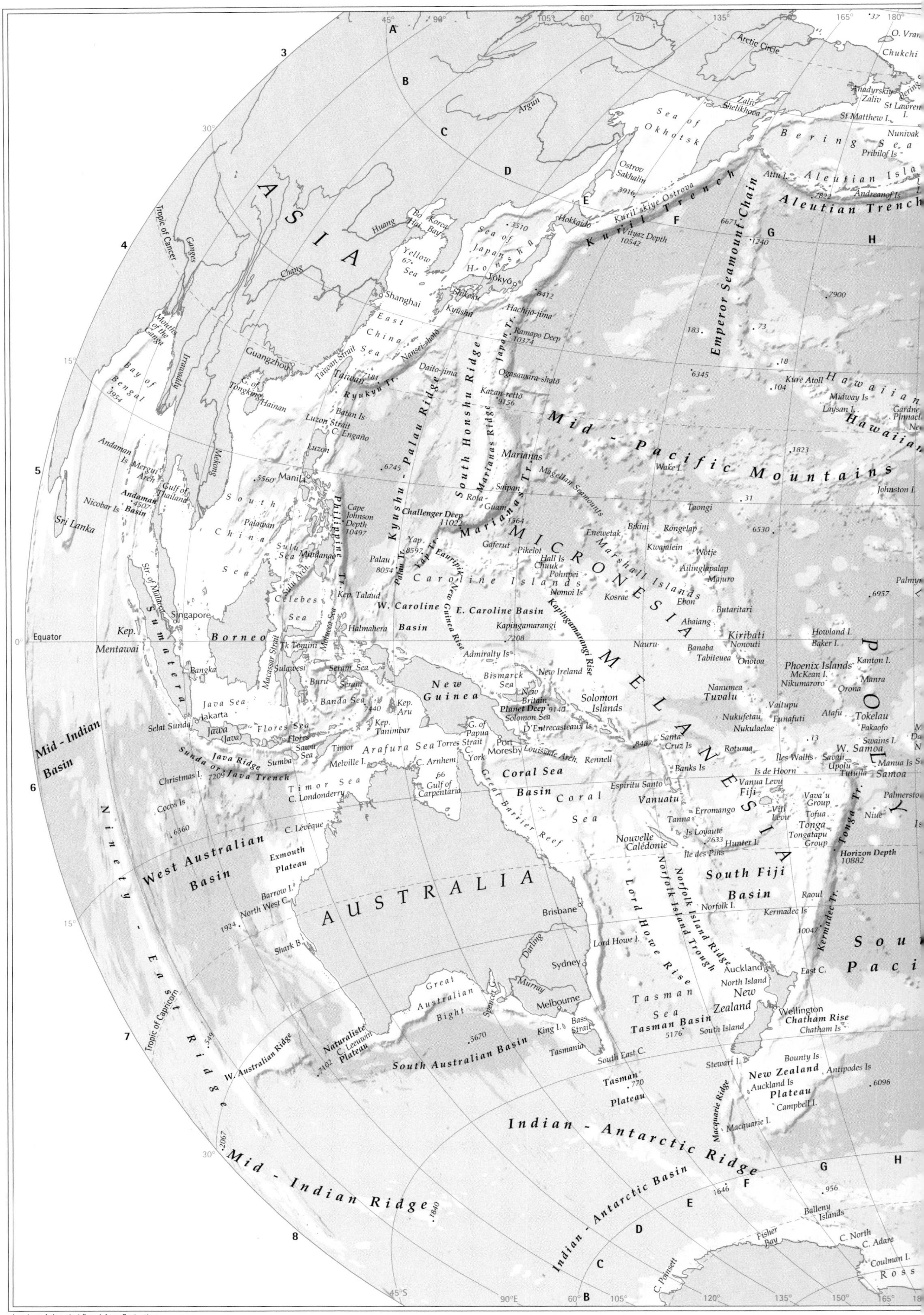

3

A
90°

B

C

30°

D

E

ASIA

Tropic of Cancer

4

Ganges

Argun

Sea of
Okhotsk

Ostrov
Sakhalin
3916

Hokkaido

Kuril'skiye Ostrova

Kuril'sk Trench

Vityaz Depth
10542

Emperor Seamount Chain

Aleutian Trench

Aleutian Islands

Arctic Circle

O. Vran

Chukchi

Zaliv
Shelikhova

Zaliv

Anadyrskiy
Zaliv

St Matthew I.

St Lawren

Bering

Nunivak I.
Pribilof Is

Attul.

Andreanof Is

.7022

667

.1240

G

.7900

H

Huang

Bo
Hai

Korea
Bay

Sea of
Japan

H
o
n
s
h
u

Tōkyō

6412

183.

.73

.18

Chang

Yellow
Sea
67.

Shikoku

Hachijō-jima

Ramapo Deep
10374

Japan Tr.

Kure Atoll

.104

Hawaiian

Shanghai

Kyūshū

.3510

.6345

Midway Is

Laysan Is

Hawaiian

15°

Guangzhou

East
China
Sea

Nansei-shotō

Daito-jima

Ogasawara-shotō

Mid - Pacific Mountains

Gardne
Pinnacle

G. of
Tōngkīng

Taiwan Strait

Taitung

101

Ryukyu Tr.

Kazan-rettō
9156

.1823

Hainan

Bay
of
Bengal
3954

Batan Is

Luzon Strait

Marianas

Wake I.

Saipan

Magellan Seamounts

Johnston I.

C. Engaño

5

Andaman
Is Mergui
Arch.

Luzon

.6745

Kyūshū - Palau Ridge

South Honshu Ridge

Marianas Ridge

Rota

Guam

Saipan

Taongi

.31

Andaman
Is Basin
.4507

.5560

Manila

Challenger Deep
11022

Mariana Tr.

.1564

MICRONESIA

Enewetak

Bikini

Rongelap

6530

Nicobar Is

Cape
Johnson
Depth
10497

Palawan

Philippine Tr.

Yap Tr.

Yap.
.8597

Gaferut

Pikelot

Hall Is

Kwajalein

Wotje

Sri Lanka

South
China
Sea

Palau
8054

Eauripik
New Guinea Rise

Caroline Islands

Chuuk

Pohnpei

Nomoi Is

Ailinglapalap

Majuro

Marshall Islands

.6957

Palmy

Mindanao

Sulu
Sea

Mindanao
Trench

W. Caroline
Basin

E. Caroline Basin

Kosrae

Ebon

Butaritari

Equator

Mentawai

Kep.

Borneo

Celebes
Sea

Halmahera

Kapingamarangi Rise

Kapingamarangi
7208

Abaiang

Nauru

Banaba

Tabiteuea

Kiribati

Onotoa

Howland I.

Baker I.

Kanton I.

Manra

POLY

Singapore

Tk Tomini

Molucca Sea

Admiralty Is

Bismarck
Sea

New Ireland

MELANESIA

Nanumea

Tuvalu

Phoenix Islands

McKean I.

Nikumaroro

Orona

Mentawai

Bangka

Sulawesi

Buru

Seram

Seram Sea

New
Guinea

New
Britain

Planet Deep 9140

Solomon
Islands

Nukufetau

Vaitupu

Funafuti

Atafu

Tokelau

Fakaofo

Macassar Strait

Banda Sea
7440

Kep.
Aru

New Britain

Solomon Sea

D'Entrecasteaux Is

.848

Santa
Cruz Is

Nukulaelae

Rotuma

Iles Wallis

Swains I.

Manua Is

W. Samoa

Mid - Indian

Basin

Java Sea

Jakarta

Jawa
(Java)

Flores Sea

Flores

Kep.
Tanimbar

Sawu

Timor

Torres Strait

G. of
Papua

Port
Moresby

Louisiade Arch.

Rennell

Banks Is

Is de Hoorn

Tutuila

Upolu

Samoa

6

Selat Sunda

Sunda or Java Trench

Java Ridge

Christmas I.

.7209

Sumba

Flores

Melville I.

Arafura Sea

C. Arnhem
C. York

Coral Sea
Basin

Espiritu Santo

Vanua Levu

Vava'u
Group

Niue

Ninety

Cocos Is

Timor Sea

Gulf of
Carpentaria

Great Barrier Reef

Coral

Sea

Vanuatu

Erromango

Tanna

Iles Loyauté

Viti
Levu

Fiji

Tofua

Tonga

Tongatapu
Group

Palmersto

.6360

C. Léveque

Nouvelle
Calédonie

.7633

Hunter I.

Horizon Depth
10882

15°

West Australian
Basin

Exmouth
Plateau

Barrow I.

North West C.

.1924

Shark B.

AUSTRALIA

Brisbane

Lord Howe Rise

Norfolk Island Ridge

Ile des Pins

Norfolk I.

Kermadec Is

South Fiji
Basin

Raoul

10442

Kermadec Tr.

Sou

Paci

East

7

Tropic of Capricorn

East
Indian
Ridge

Naturaliste
Plateau

C. Leeuwin

W. Australian Ridge

.7102

Darling

Sydney

Great
Australian
Bight

Melbourne

Murray

Bass
Strait

King I.

Lord Howe I.

Auckland

North Island

Tasman
Sea

New
Zealand

Wellington

South Island

New

Chatham Rise

Chatham Is

.5670

South Australian Basin

Tasmania

South East C.

Tasman Basin
5176

Stewart I.

Macquarie Ridge

Bounty Is

New Zealand
Plateau

Auckland Is

Antipodes Is

.6096

Tasman
.770
Plateau

Campbell I.

Macquarie I.

Indian - Antarctic Ridge

30°

Mid - Indian Ridge

.1840

Indian - Antarctic Basin

.2607

.1646

.956

F

Ballerny
Islands

E

D

C

Fisher
Bay

C. North

C. Adare

Coulman I.

C. Poinsett

Ross

8

45°S

90°E

60°

B

105°

120°

135°

150°

165°

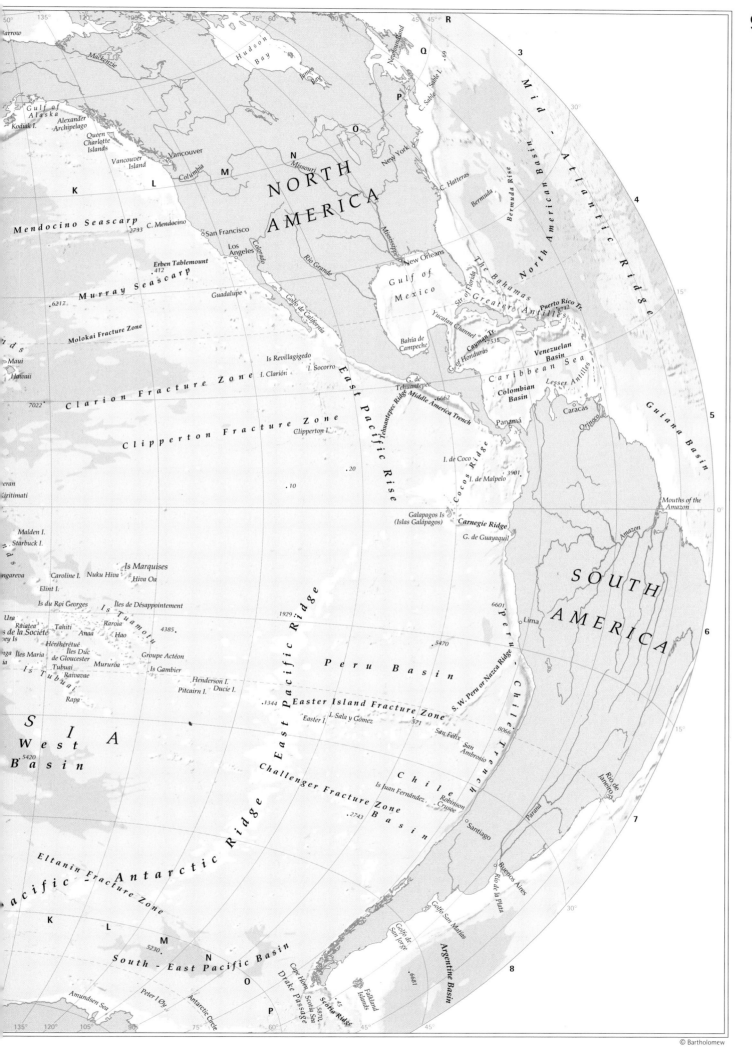

R
Q
P
O
3

Mid - Atlantic Ridge

Barrow
Mackenzie
Hudson Bay
James Bay
Newfoundland
C. Sable
Sable I.

Gulf of Alaska
Kodiak I.
Alexander Archipelago
Queen Charlotte Islands
Vancouver Island
Vancouver
Columbia
New York
C. Hatteras
Bermuda
Bermuda Rise
North American Basin
4

K
L
M
N
NORTH AMERICA
Missouri

Mendocino Seascarp
C. Mendocino
2733
San Francisco
Los Angeles
Colorado
Rio Grande
Mississippi
New Orleans
Gulf of Mexico
Str. of Florida
The Bahamas
Greater Antilles
Puerto Rico Tr.
8742

Erben Tablemount
412
Murray Seascarp
Guadalupe
Golfo de California
Bahía de Campeche
Gulf of Honduras
Cayman Tr.
7535
Venezuelan Basin
Caribbean Sea
Lesser Antilles
15°

6217
Molokai Fracture Zone

Maui
Hawaii
Is Revillagigedo
I. Clarión
I. Socorro
East Pacific Rise
Clarion Fracture Zone
G. de Tehuantepec
Tehuantepec Ridge
Middle America Trench
6662
Colombian Basin
Panamá
Caracas
Orinoco
Guiana Basin
5

7022
Clipperton Fracture Zone
Clipperton I.
I. de Coco
Cocos Ridge
I. de Malpelo
3901
Mouths of the Amazon
0°

.20
Galapagos Is (Islas Galápagos)
Carnegie Ridge
G. de Guayaquil
Amazon

.10
SOUTH AMERICA

eran
Kiritimati
Malden I.
Starbuck I.
Is Marquises
Caroline I.
Nuku Hiva
Hiva Oa
Lima
6601
Perú or Chile Trench
6

ngareva
Elint I.
Is du Roi Georges
Iles de Désappointement
Is Tuamotu
1929
East Pacific Ridge

Ura
Râiatea
s de la Société
Tahiti
Anaa
Raroia
Hao
4385.
.5470
S.W. Peru or Nazca Ridge
ey Is
Héréhérétué
Iles Duc de Gloucester
Groupe Actéon

ga
Iles Maria
Tubuai
Mururoa
Is Gambier
Peru Basin

Is Tubuai
Raivavae
Henderson I.
Ducie I.
8066
15°
Rapa
Pitcairn I.
.1344
Easter Island Fracture Zone

S
I
A
Easter I.
I. Sala y Gómez
571
San Felix
San Ambrosio
Chile

West
Challenger Fracture Zone
Chile
Robinson Crusoe
Is Juan Fernández
Basin
5420

Basin
.2743
Santiago
Rio de Janeiro

Pacific - Antarctic Ridge
Paraná

Eltanin Fracture Zone
Buenos Aires
Rio de la Plata
30°

K
L
M
Golfo de San Jorge
Argentine Basin

5230.
South - East Pacific Basin
N
O
P
Cape Horn
Scotia Sea
Drake Passage
Scotia Ridge
Falkland Islands
8

Amundsen Sea
Peter I Oy
Antarctic Circle
6681

© Bartholomew

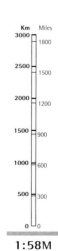

Km   Miles
3000   1800
2500   1500
2000   1200
1500   900
1000   600
500   300
0   0

ATLANTIC OCEAN

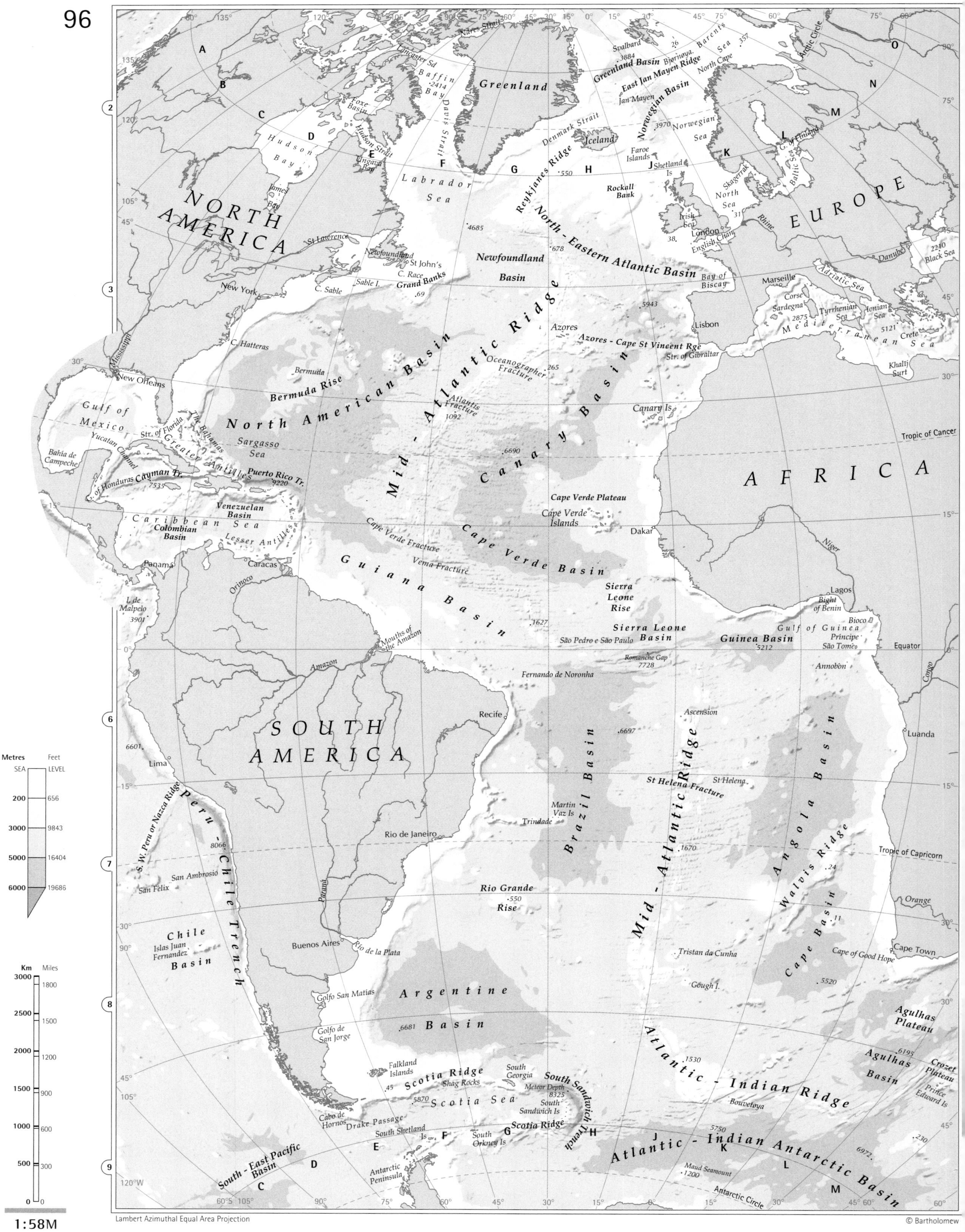

NORTH AMERICA

SOUTH AMERICA

EUROPE

AFRICA

Greenland

Baffin Bay

Hudson Bay

Labrador Sea

Newfoundland Basin

North - Eastern Atlantic Basin

Greenland Basin

Norwegian Basin

Norwegian Sea

East Jan Mayen Ridge

Bjørnøya

Barents Sea

Spitsbergen

North Cape

Iceland

Denmark Strait

Reykjanes Ridge

Faroe Islands

Rockall Bank

Shetland Is

North Sea

Baltic Sea

Gulf of Finland

Skagerrak

London

English Chan.

Irish Sea

Rhine

Danube

Black Sea

Bay of Biscay

Marseille

Lisbon

Corse

Sardegna

Tyrrhenian Sea

Adriatic Sea

Ionian Sea

Mediterranean Sea

Crete

Str. of Gibraltar

Azores

Azores - Cape St Vincent Rge

Oceanographer Fracture

Atlantis Fracture

Mid - Atlantic Ridge

North American Basin

Bermuda Rise

Bermuda

Sargasso Sea

New York

C. Hatteras

New Orleans

Gulf of Mexico

Bahia de Campeche

Yucatan Channel

Str. of Florida

The Bahamas

Greater Antilles

Cayman Tr.

Puerto Rico Tr.

G. of Honduras

Venezuelan Basin

Colombian Basin

Caribbean Sea

Lesser Antilles

Panama

Caracas

Orinoco

Guiana Basin

Mouths of the Amazon

Amazon

Canary Basin

Canary Is

Tropic of Cancer

Dakar

Cape Verde Plateau

Cape Verde Islands

Cape Verde Basin

Cape Verde Fracture

Vema Fracture

Sierra Leone Rise

Sierra Leone Basin

São Pedro e São Paulo

Romanche Gap

Gulf of Guinea

Guinea Basin

Príncipe

São Tomé

Annobón

Equator

Congo

Niger

Lagos

Bight of Benin

Bioco

Fernando de Noronha

Recife

Brazil Basin

Ascension

Mid - Atlantic Ridge

St Helena Fracture

St Helena

Angola Basin

Luanda

Lima

Rio de Janeiro

Martin Vaz Is

Trindade

Rio Grande Rise

Walvis Ridge

Tropic of Capricorn

Orange

Cape Basin

Buenos Aires

Rio de la Plata

Paraná

Tristan da Cunha

Gough I.

Cape Town

Cape of Good Hope

Argentine Basin

Golfo San Matias

Golfo de San Jorge

Agulhas Plateau

Agulhas Basin

Crozet Plateau

Prince Edward Is

Falkland Islands

Shag Rocks

Scotia Ridge

South Georgia

South Sandwich Is

South Sandwich Trench

South Orkney Is

Scotia Sea

Scotia Ridge

Meteor Depth

Atlantic - Indian Ridge

Bouvetøya

Maud Seamount

Atlantic - Indian Antarctic Basin

Antarctic Circle

Cabo de Hornos

Drake Passage

South Shetland Is

Antarctic Peninsula

South - East Pacific Basin

Chile Basin

Islas Juan Fernandez

San Ambrosio

San Felix

S.W. Peru or Nazca Ridge

Peru - Chile Trench

St Lawrence

St John's

Newfoundland

C. Race

Grand Banks

Sable I.

C. Sable

I. de Malpelo

L. de Malpelo

Metres / Feet

Metres	Feet
SEA	LEVEL
200	656
3000	9843
5000	16404
6000	19686

Km / Miles

Km	Miles
3000	1800
2500	1500
2000	1200
1500	900
1000	600
500	300
0	0

1:58M

Lambert Azimuthal Equal Area Projection

© Bartholomew

THE INDEX includes the names on the maps in the main map section of the ATLAS. The names are generally indexed to the largest scale map on which they appear, and can be located using the grid reference letters and numbers around the map frame. Names on insets have a symbol: □, followed by the inset number where more than one inset appears on the page.

Abbreviations used to describe features in the index are explained below.

Afgh. Afghanistan
AK Alaska
AL Alabama
Alg. Algeria
Alta Alberta
Ant. Antarctica
AR Arkansas
arch. archipelago
Arg. Argentina
Atl. Atlantic
Austr. Australia
AZ Arizona
Azer. Azerbaijan

b. bay
Bangl. Bangladesh
B.C. British Columbia
Bol. Bolivia
Bos.-Herz. Bosnia Herzegovina
Bulg. Bulgaria

c. cape
CA California
Can. Canada
C.A.R. Central African Republic
chan. channel
Co. County
CO Colorado
Col. Colombia
CT Connecticut

DC District of Colombia
DE Delaware
des. desert
div. division
Dom. Rep. Dominican Republic

Eng. England
escarp. escarpment
est. estuary
Eth. Ethiopia

Fin. Finland
FL Florida
Fr. Guiana French Guiana

g. gulf
GA Georgia
gl. glacier
Ger. Germany

h. hill, hills
hd headland
HI Hawaii

i. island
IA Iowa
ID Idaho
IL Illinois
in. inlet
IN Indiana
Indon. Indonesia
is islands
Isr. Israel
isth. isthmus

Kazak. Kazakstan
KS Kansas
KY Kentucky
Kyrg. Kyrgyzstan

l. lake, lakes
LA Louisiana
lag. lagoon
Lith. Lithuania
Lux. Luxembourg

MA Massachusetts
Madag. Madagascar
Man. Manitoba
Maur. Mauritania
MD Maryland
ME Maine
Mex. Mexico
MI Michigan
MN Minnesota
MO Missouri
Moz. Mozambique
MS Mississippi
mt mountain
MT Montana
mts mountains

N. North, Northern
nat. national
N.B. New Brunswick
NC North Carolina
ND North Dakota
NE Nebraska
Neth. Netherlands
Neth. Ant. Netherlands Antilles
Nfld Newfoundland
NH New Hampshire
Nic. Nicaragua
NJ New Jersey
NM New Mexico
N.S. Nova Scotia
N.S.W. New South Wales
NV Nevada
N.W.T. Northwest Territories
NY New York
N.Z. New Zealand

OH Ohio
OK Oklahoma
Ont. Ontario
OR Oregon

PA Pennsylvania
Pac. Pacific
Pak. Pakistan
Para. Paraguay
P.E.I. Prince Edward Island
pen. peninsula
Phil. Philippines
plat. plateau
P.N.G. Papua New Guinea
Pol. Poland
Port. Portugal
pt point

Qld. Queensland
Que. Quebec

r. river
reg. region
Rep. Republic
res. reserve
resr reservoir
rf reef
RI Rhode Island
Rus. Fed. Russian Federation

S. South
S.A. South Australia
Sask. Saskatchewan
S. Arabia Saudi Arabia
SC South Carolina
Scot. Scotland
SD South Dakota
Sing. Singapore
str. strait
Switz. Switzerland

Tajik. Tajikistan
Tanz. Tanzania
terr. territory
Thai. Thailand
TN Tennessee
Turk. Turkmenistan
TX Texas

U.A.E. United Arab Emirates
U.K. United Kingdom
Ukr. Ukraine
Uru. Uruguay
U.S.A. United States of America
UT Utah
Uzbek. Uzbekistan

v. valley
VA Virginia
Venez. Venezuela
Vic. Victoria
volc. volcano
VT Vermont

WA Washington
WV West Virginia
WY Wyoming

Y.T. Yukon Territory
Yugo. Yugoslavia

A

42 E4 Aachen Ger.
46 E6 Aalen Ger.
42 C4 Aalst Belgium
42 C4 Aarschot Belgium
26 A3 Aba China
56 D3 Aba Congo(Zaire)
54 C4 Aba Nigeria
18 B5 Abā ad Dūd S. Arabia
18 C4 Ābādān Iran
18 D4 Ābādeh Iran
54 B1 Abadla Alg.
90 D2 Abaeté r. Brazil
87 J4 Abaetetuba Brazil
26 E1 Abag Qi China
95 G5 Abaiang i. Pac. Oc.
73 E4 Abajo Pk summit U.S.A.
54 C4 Abakaliki Nigeria
24 B1 Abakan Rus. Fed.
24 A1 Abakanskiy Khrebet mts Rus. Fed.
51 E7 Abana Turkey
18 D4 Āb Anbār Iran
86 D6 Abancay Peru
18 D4 Abarqū Iran
28 J2 Abashiri Japan
28 J2 Abashiri-wan b. Japan
6 E3 Abau P.N.G.
56 D3 Ābaya Hāyk' l. Eth.
Ābay Wenz r. see Blue Nile
12 L4 Abaza Rus. Fed.
19 E3 Abbāsābād Iran
48 C4 Abbasanta Sardinia Italy
68 C2 Abbaye, Pt pt U.S.A.
56 E2 Abbe, L. l. Eth.
44 E1 Abbeville France
77 E6 Abbeville LA U.S.A.
79 D5 Abbeville SC U.S.A.
41 B5 Abbeyfeale Rep. of Ireland
40 E6 Abbey Head hd U.K.
41 D5 Abbeyleix Rep. of Ireland
38 D3 Abbeytown U.K.
36 Q4 Abborrträsk Sweden
92 A3 Abbot Ice Shelf ice feature Ant.
64 E5 Abbotsford Can.
68 B3 Abbotsford U.S.A.
73 F4 Abbott U.S.A.
22 C2 Abbottabad Pak.
17 H3 'Abd al 'Azīz, J. h. Syria
17 L5 Abdanan Iran
55 E3 Abéché Chad
19 E4 Āb-e Garm Iran
9 D4 Abel Tasman National Park N.Z.
54 B4 Abengourou Côte d'Ivoire
37 L9 Åbenrå Denmark
43 K6 Abensberg Ger.
54 C4 Abeokuta Nigeria
39 C5 Aberaeron U.K.
40 F3 Aberchirder U.K.
8 G2 Abercrombie r. Austr.
39 D6 Aberdare U.K.
39 C5 Aberdaron U.K.
8 H2 Aberdeen Austr.
65 H4 Aberdeen Can.
27 □ Aberdeen H.K. China
58 F6 Aberdeen S. Africa
40 F3 Aberdeen U.K.
81 E5 Aberdeen MD U.S.A.
77 F5 Aberdeen MS U.S.A.
76 D2 Aberdeen SD U.S.A.
72 B2 Aberdeen WA U.S.A.
65 J2 Aberdeen Lake l. Can.
39 C5 Aberdyfi U.K.
40 E4 Aberfeldy U.K.
38 F4 Aberford U.K.
40 D4 Aberfoyle U.K.
39 D6 Abergavenny U.K.
77 C5 Abernathy U.S.A.
39 C5 Aberporth U.K.
39 C5 Abersoch U.K.
39 C5 Aberystwyth U.K.
20 B6 Abhā S. Arabia
18 C2 Abhar Iran
18 C2 Abhar r. Iran
Abiad, Bahr el r. see White Nile
18 C3 Ab-i Bazuft r. Iran
89 A2 Abibe, Serranía de mts Col.
54 B4 Abidjan Côte d'Ivoire
19 H3 Ab-i-Istada l. Afgh.
56 D3 Abijatta-Shalla National Park Eth.
18 E3 Ab-i-Kavir salt flat Iran
76 D4 Abilene KS U.S.A.
77 D5 Abilene TX U.S.A.
39 F6 Abingdon U.K.
68 B5 Abingdon IL U.S.A.
80 C6 Abingdon VA U.S.A.
51 F6 Abinsk Rus. Fed.
19 G2 Ab-i-Safed r. Afgh.
86 C5 Abiseo, Parque Nacional nat. park Peru
65 H2 Abitau Lake l. Can.
66 D4 Abitibi r. Can.
66 E4 Abitibi, Lake l. Can.
54 B4 Aboisso Côte d'Ivoire
54 C4 Abomey Benin
22 C3 Abonar India
55 D4 Abong Mbang Cameroon
31 A4 Aborlan Phil.
55 D3 Abou Déia Chad
17 K1 Abovyan Armenia
40 F3 Aboyne U.K.
91 D4 Abra, L. del l. Arg.
45 B3 Abrantes Port.
88 C2 Abra Pampa Arg.
90 E2 Abrolhos, Arquipélago dos is Brazil
72 E2 Absaroka Range mts U.S.A.
43 H6 Abtsgmünd Ger.
18 C5 Abū'Alī i. S. Arabia
18 D5 Abual Jirab i. U.A.E.
20 B6 Abū 'Arīsh S. Arabia
20 D5 Abu Dhabi U.A.E.
55 F3 Abu Hamed Sudan
54 C4 Abuja Nigeria
55 E3 Abu Matariq Sudan
18 D5 Abū Mūsá i. U.A.E.
86 E5 Abunã Brazil
86 E6 Abunã r. Bol.
20 A7 Ābune Yosēf mt Eth.
16 C6 Abu Qîr, Khalîg b. Egypt
15 F4 Abu Road India
55 F2 Abu Simbel Egypt
17 K6 Abū Şukhayr Iraq
9 C5 Abut Head hd N.Z.
31 C4 Abuyog Phil.
55 E3 Abu Zabad Sudan
Abū Zabī see Abu Dhabi
17 M6 Abūzam Iran
55 E3 Abyad Sudan
55 E4 Abyei Sudan
18 C2 Ābyek Iran
81 J2 Acadia Nat. Park U.S.A.
84 B2 Acambaro Mex.
84 E2 Acancéh Mex.
89 A2 Acandí Col.
45 B1 A Cañiza Spain
84 A2 Acaponeta Mex.
84 C3 Acapulco Mex.
87 J4 Acará Brazil
87 K4 Acaraú r. Brazil
90 A4 Acaray r. Para.
88 E3 Acaray, Represa de resr Para.
89 C2 Acarigua Venez.
84 C3 Acatlan Mex.
84 C3 Acatzingo Mex.
84 D3 Acayucán Mex.
54 B4 Accra Ghana
38 E4 Accrington U.K.
89 C3 Achaguas Venez.
22 D5 Achalpur India
21 B2 Achampet India
13 T3 Achayvayam Rus. Fed.
30 D1 Acheng China
42 A4 Achicourt France
41 B4 Achill Rep. of Ireland
41 A4 Achill Island i. Rep. of Ireland
40 C2 Achiltibuie U.K.
43 H1 Achim Ger.
24 B1 Achinsk Rus. Fed.
40 C3 Achnasheen U.K.
40 C3 A'Chralaig mt U.K.
51 F6 Achuyevo Rus. Fed.
16 B3 Acıgöl l. Turkey
16 B3 Acıpayam Turkey
48 F6 Acireale Sicily Italy
76 E3 Ackley U.S.A.
83 K4 Acklins Island i. Bahamas
39 J5 Acle U.K.
91 B2 Aconcagua r. Chile
87 L5 Acopiara Brazil
45 B1 A Coruña Spain
48 C2 Acqui Terme Italy
16 E5 Acre Israel
48 G5 Acri Italy
46 J7 Ács Hungary
5 O7 Actéon, Groupe is Pac. Oc.
80 B4 Ada OH U.S.A.
77 D5 Ada OK U.S.A.
45 D2 Adaja r. Spain
8 G4 Adaminaby Austr.
88 E8 Adam, Mt h. Falkland Is
81 G3 Adams MA U.S.A.
68 C4 Adams WV U.S.A.
21 B4 Adam's Bridge rf India/Sri Lanka
64 F4 Adams L. l. Can.
75 E2 Adams McGill Reservoir U.S.A.
64 C3 Adams Mt. mt U.S.A.
72 B2 Adams, Mt mt U.S.A.
74 B2 Adams Peak mt U.S.A.
21 C5 Adam's Pk Sri Lanka
'Adan see Aden
16 E3 Adana Turkey
41 C5 Adare Rep. of Ireland
92 A5 Adare, C. c. Ant.
75 E2 Adaven U.S.A.
20 C5 Ad Dahnā' des. S. Arabia
54 A2 Ad Dakhla Western Sahara
20 D4 Ad Dammām S. Arabia
18 B5 Ad Dawādimī S. Arabia
Ad Dawḩah see Doha
17 J4 Ad Dawr Iraq
18 B5 Ad Dibdibah plain S. Arabia
18 B6 Ad Dilam S. Arabia
20 C5 Ad Dir'īyah S. Arabia
56 D3 Addis Ababa Eth.
81 K2 Addison U.S.A.
17 K6 Ad Dīwānīyah Iraq
39 G6 Addlestone U.K.
10 J10 Addu Atoll atoll Maldives
17 J6 Ad Duwayd well S. Arabia
79 D6 Adel GA U.S.A.
76 E3 Adel IA U.S.A.
8 B3 Adelaide Austr.
79 E7 Adelaide Bahamas
59 G6 Adelaide S. Africa
92 B2 Adelaide I i. Ant.
6 D3 Adelaide River Austr.
74 D4 Adelanto U.S.A.
8 G3 Adelong Austr.
20 C7 Aden Yemen
42 E4 Adenau Ger.
43 J1 Adendorf Ger.
20 C7 Aden, Gulf of g. Somalia/Yemen
18 D5 Adh Dhayd U.A.E.
25 F7 Adi i. Indon.
56 D2 Ādī Ārk'ay Eth.
56 D2 Ādīgrat Eth.
22 D6 Adilabad India
17 J2 Adilcevaz Turkey
72 B3 Adin U.S.A.
55 D2 Adīrī Libya
81 F2 Adirondack Mountains U.S.A.
Ādīs Ābeba see Addis Ababa
56 D3 Ādīs Alem Eth.
56 D2 Adi Ugri Eritrea
16 G3 Adıyaman Turkey
47 N7 Adjud Romania
84 C2 Adjuntas, Presa de las resr Mex.
67 J3 Adlavik Islands is Can.
6 C3 Admiralty Gulf b. Austr.
63 K2 Admiralty Inlet in. Can.
64 C3 Admiralty Island i. U.S.A.
64 C3 Admiralty Island Nat. Monument res. U.S.A.
6 E2 Admiralty Islands is P.N.G.
21 B3 Adoni India
43 L4 Adorf Ger.
43 G3 Adorf (Diemelsee) Ger.
44 D5 Adour r. France
45 E4 Adra Spain
48 F6 Adrano Sicily Italy
54 B2 Adrar Alg.
54 A2 Adrar mts Alg.
54 C3 Adrar des Ifôghas reg. Mali
54 A2 Adrar Maur
19 F3 Adraskand r. Afgh.
55 E3 Adré Chad
69 E5 Adrian MI U.S.A.
77 C5 Adrian TX U.S.A.
48 E2 Adriatic Sea sea Europe
21 B4 Adur India
56 C3 Adusa Congo(Zaire)
56 D2 Ādwa Eth.
13 P3 Adycha r. Rus. Fed.
51 F6 Adygeya, Respublika div. Rus. Fed.
51 F6 Adygeysk Rus. Fed.
51 H6 Adyk Rus. Fed.
54 B4 Adzopé Côte d'Ivoire
49 L5 Aegean Sea sea Greece/Turkey
43 H2 Aerzen Ger.
45 B1 A Estrada Spain
56 D2 Afabet Eritrea
17 K3 Afan Iran
10 H6 Afghanistan country Asia
36 M5 Åfjord Norway
56 E3 Afmadow Somalia
62 C4 Afognak I. i. U.S.A.
45 C1 A Fonsagrada Spain
16 F3 'Afrīn r. Syria/Turkey
16 F2 Afşin Turkey
42 D2 Afsluitdijk barrage Neth.
72 E3 Afton U.S.A.
87 H4 Afuá Brazil
16 E5 'Afula Israel
16 C2 Afyon Turkey
43 L4 Aga Ger.
54 C3 Agadez Niger
54 B1 Agadir Morocco
15 F2 Agadyr' Kazak.
53 K7 Agalega Islands is Mauritius
23 G5 Agartala India
22 C6 Agashi India
69 F2 Agate Can.
49 M6 Agathonisi i. Greece
54 B4 Agboville Côte d'Ivoire
17 L1 Ağcabädi Azer.
17 L2 Ağdam Azer.
44 F5 Agde France
44 E4 Agen France
58 C4 Aggeneys S. Africa
42 F4 Agger r. Ger.
22 D1 Aghil Pass China
41 C3 Aghla Mountain h. Rep. of Ireland
49 L7 Agia Vervara Greece
16 G2 Ağın Turkey
49 K6 Agios Dimitrios Greece
49 L5 Agios Efstratios i. Greece
49 M5 Agios Fokas, Akra pt Greece
49 K5 Agios Konstantinos Greece
49 L7 Agios Nikolaos Greece
49 K4 Agiou Orous, Kolpos b. Greece
55 F3 Agirwat Hills h. Sudan
59 F3 Agisanang S. Africa
54 B4 Agnibilékrou Côte d'Ivoire
49 L2 Agnita Romania
26 A2 Agong China
22 D4 Agra India
51 H7 Agrakhanskiy Poluostrov pen. Rus. Fed.
45 F2 Agreda Spain
17 J2 Ağrı Turkey
49 K7 Agria Gramvousa i. Greece
48 E6 Agrigento Sicily Italy
49 J5 Agrinio Greece
91 B3 Agrio r. Arg.
48 F4 Agropoli Italy
17 K1 Ağstafa Azer.
17 M1 Ağsu Azer.
84 A2 Agua Brava, L. lag. Mex.
84 E3 Aguada Mex.
89 B3 Aguadas Col.
89 B3 Agua de Dios Col.
83 L5 Aguadilla Puerto Rico
91 D4 Aguado Cecilio Arg.
83 H7 Aguadulce Panama
91 C3 Agua Escondida Arg.
84 B1 Aguanaval r. Mex.
91 C1 Agua Negra, Paso del pass Arg./Chile
90 B3 Aguapeí r. Brazil
82 C2 Agua Prieta Mex.
90 A3 Aguaray Guazú r. Para.
89 D2 Aguaro-Guariquito, Parque Nacional nat. park Venez.
84 B2 Aguascalientes Mex.
84 B2 Aguascalientes div. Mex.
90 E2 Águas Formosas Brazil
90 C3 Agudos Brazil
75 F5 Aguila U.S.A.
45 D1 Aguilar de Campóo Spain
45 F4 Águilas Spain
31 B4 Aguisan Phil.
93 F7 Agulhas Basin sea feature Ind. Ocean
58 D7 Agulhas, Cape c. S. Africa
90 D3 Agulhas Negras mt Brazil
93 F6 Agulhas Plateau sea feature Ind. Ocean
33 E4 Agung, G. volc. Indon.
31 C4 Agusan r. Phil.
31 B4 Agutaya Phil.
18 B2 Ahar Iran
9 C5 Ahaura N.Z.
42 F2 Ahaus Ger.
9 F3 Ahimanawa Ra. mts N.Z.
9 D1 Ahipara N.Z.
9 D1 Ahipara Bay b. N.Z.
62 B4 Ahklun Mts mts U.S.A.
17 J2 Ahlat Turkey
43 F3 Ahlen Ger.
22 C5 Ahmadabad India
18 E4 Ahmadī Iran
21 A2 Ahmadnagar India
22 B3 Ahmadpur East Pak.
43 J4 Ahorn Ger.
18 C4 Ahram Iran
43 J1 Ahrensburg Ger.
17 J2 Ahta D. mt Turkey
36 T5 Ähtäri Fin.
37 U7 Ahtme Estonia
17 M6 Āhū Iran
84 B2 Ahualulco Mex.
44 F3 Ahun France
9 B6 Ahuriri r. N.Z.
18 C4 Ahvāz Iran
22 C5 Ahwa India
Ahwāz see Ahvāz
30 C3 Ai r. China
58 B3 Ai-Ais Namibia
26 D1 Aibag Gol r. China
18 D2 Aidin Turkm.
74 □1 Aiea U.S.A.
16 E4 Aigialousa Cyprus
49 K6 Aigina i. Greece
49 K5 Aigio Greece
44 H4 Aigle de Chambeyron mt France
91 F2 Aiguá Uru.
29 F5 Aikawa Japan
79 D5 Aiken U.S.A.
89 A2 Ailigandi Panama
95 G5 Ailinglapalap i. Pac. Oc.
42 A5 Ailly-sur-Noye France
69 G4 Ailsa Craig Can.
40 C5 Ailsa Craig i. U.K.
90 E2 Aimorés, Sa dos h. Brazil
54 C1 Aïn Beïda Alg.
54 B2 'Aïn Ben Tili Maur.
45 H4 Aïn Defla Alg.
45 H5 Aïn el Hadjel Alg.
54 B1 Aïn Sefra Alg.
67 H4 Ainslie, Lake l. Can.
76 D3 Ainsworth U.S.A.
Aintab see Gaziantep
45 H4 Aïn Taya Alg.
45 G5 Aïn Tédélès Alg.
89 B4 Aipe Col.
32 C5 Air i. Indon.
64 G4 Airdrie Can.
40 E5 Airdrie U.K.
42 D6 Aire r. France
44 D5 Aire-sur-l'Adour France
63 L3 Air Force I. i. Can.
26 D1 Airgin Sum China
54 C3 Aïr, Massif de l' mts Niger
65 H3 Air Ronge Can.
88 B7 Aisén, Pto Chile
26 F2 Ai Shan h. China
64 B2 Aishihik Can.
64 B2 Aishihik Lake l. Can.
44 G2 Aisne r. France
45 F3 Aitana mt Spain
6 E2 Aitape P.N.G.
76 E2 Aitken U.S.A.
5 L6 Aitutaki i. Pac. Oc.
47 L7 Aiud Romania
44 G5 Aix-en-Provence France
44 G4 Aix-les-Bains France
64 D3 Aiyansh Can.
23 F5 Aiyar Res. resr India
23 H5 Aizawl India
37 T8 Aizkraukle Latvia
37 R8 Aizpute Latvia
29 F6 Aizu-wakamatsu Japan
48 C4 Ajaccio Corsica France
89 B4 Ajajú r. Col.
84 C3 Ajalpán Mex.
21 A1 Ajanta India
Ajanta Range h. see Sahyadriparvat Range
36 O4 Ajaureforsen Sweden
9 D5 Ajax, Mt mt N.Z.
55 E1 Ajdābiyā Libya
a-Jiddét gravel area see Jiddat al Ḩarāsīs
28 G4 Ajigasawa Japan
16 E5 'Ajlūn Jordan
18 D5 Ajman U.A.E.
22 C4 Ajmer India
75 F5 Ajo U.S.A.
75 F5 Ajo, Mt mt U.S.A.
31 B4 Ajuy Phil.
28 H3 Akabira Japan
56 D4 Akagera National Park Rwanda
21 B2 Akalkot India
28 J3 Akan National Park Japan
16 D4 Akanthou Cyprus
9 D5 Akaroa N.Z.
9 D5 Akaroa Har in. N.Z.
23 H4 Akas reg. India
19 H3 Akbar Afgh.
23 E4 Akbarpur India
45 J4 Akbou Alg.
12 G4 Akbulak Rus. Fed.
16 F2 Akçadağ Turkey
17 G3 Akçakale Turkey
16 C1 Akçakoca Turkey
16 D3 Akçali D. mt Turkey
16 C3 Ak D. mt Turkey
17 H2 Ak D. mts Turkey
16 C3 Akdağ mt Turkey
16 E2 Akdağmadeni Turkey
37 Q7 Åkersberga Sweden
42 C2 Akersloot Neth.
56 C3 Aketi Congo(Zaire)
17 J1 Akhalk'alak'i Georgia
51 G7 Akhalts'ikhe Georgia
23 G5 Akhaura Bangl.
20 E5 Akhḑar, Jabal mts Oman
16 A2 Akhisar Turkey
16 F3 Akhtarīn Syria
51 H5 Akhtubinsk Rus. Fed.
17 J1 Akhuryan Armenia
29 C8 Aki Japan
66 D3 Akimiski Island i. Can.
16 E3 Akıncı Burun pt Turkey
16 G1 Akıncılar Turkey
28 G5 Akita Japan
54 A3 Akjoujt Maur.
36 P3 Akkajaure l. Sweden
28 J3 Akkeshi Japan
'Akko see Acre
16 F1 Akkuş Turkey
18 D1 Akkyr, Gory h. Turkm.
22 D4 Aklera India
37 R8 Akmeņrags pt Latvia
22 D1 Akmeqit China
14 F1 Akmola Kazak.
29 D7 Akō Japan
55 F4 Akobo Sudan
22 D5 Akola India
56 D2 Akordat Eritrea
16 D3 Akören Turkey
22 D5 Akot India
63 M3 Akpatok Island i. Que. Can.
67 G1 Akpatok Island i. Can.
36 B4 Akranes Iceland
51 C7 Akrathos, Akra pt Greece
37 J7 Åkrehamne Norway
19 G3 Ak Robat Pass Afgh.
72 G3 Akron CO U.S.A.
80 C4 Akron OH U.S.A.
80 C4 Akron City Reservoir U.S.A.
22 D2 Aksai Chin terr. China/India
16 E2 Aksaray Turkey
51 F6 Aksay Rus. Fed.
22 D2 Aksayqin Hu l. China/Jammu and Kashmir
16 C2 Akşehir Turkey
16 C2 Akşehir Gölü l. Turkey
16 C3 Akseki Turkey
18 D4 Aks-e Rostam r. Iran
14 E2 Akshiganak Kazak.
15 G2 Aksu China
16 C3 Aksu r. Turkey
56 D2 Āksum Eth.
23 F1 Aktag mt China
17 K2 Aktas D. mt Turkey
19 G2 Aktash Uzbek.
14 D2 Aktau Kazak.
15 F2 Aktogay Kazak.
47 O4 Aktsyabrski Belarus
14 D1 Aktyubinsk Kazak.
29 B8 Akune Japan
54 C4 Akure Nigeria
36 D4 Akureyri Iceland
23 G1 Akxokesay China
Akyab see Sittwe
16 G3 Akziyaret Turkey
37 L6 Ål Norway
18 C5 Al 'Abā S. Arabia
79 C5 Alabama div. U.S.A.
79 C6 Alabama r. U.S.A.
79 C5 Alabaster U.S.A.
31 B3 Alabat i. Phil.
17 K7 Al 'Abţīyah well Iraq
16 E1 Alaca Turkey
16 F2 Alacahan Turkey
16 E1 Alaçam Turkey
16 B2 Alaçam Dağları mts Turkey
84 E2 Alacrán, Arrecife atoll Mex.
17 J2 Ala Dag mt Turkey
17 J2 Ala Dağlar mts Turkey
16 E3 Ala Dağlar mts Turkey
51 H7 Alagir Rus. Fed.
87 L6 Alagoinhas Brazil
45 F2 Alagón Spain
31 C5 Alah r. Phil.
36 S5 Alahärmä Fin.
17 L7 Al Ahmadī Kuwait
19 H2 Alai Range mts Asia
36 S5 Alajärvi Fin.
83 H6 Alajuela Costa Rica
17 L2 Alajujeh Iran
22 D3 Alaknanda r. India
15 G2 Alakol', Ozero l. Kazak.
36 W3 Alakurtti Rus. Fed.
86 F4 Alalaú r. Brazil
17 J3 Al 'Amādīyah Iraq
18 B5 Al'Amār S. Arabia
17 L6 Al 'Amārah Iraq
23 H3 Alamdo China
17 K7 Al Amghar waterhole Iraq
31 A2 Alaminos Phil.
84 B1 Alamítos, Sa de los mt Mex.
75 E3 Alamo U.S.A.
75 F4 Alamo Dam dam U.S.A.
73 F5 Alamogordo U.S.A.
77 D6 Alamo Heights U.S.A.
73 E6 Alamos Mex.
70 E6 Alamos Mex.
73 F4 Alamosa U.S.A.
21 B3 Alampur India
36 O4 Alanäs Sweden
21 B2 Aland India
37 Q6 Åland is Fin.
43 K1 Aland r. Ger.
18 B2 Aland r. Iran
32 B5 Alang Besar i. Indon.
68 E3 Alanson U.S.A.
16 D3 Alanya Turkey
16 C1 Alaplı Turkey
Alappuzha see Alleppey
18 C6 Al 'Āqūlah well S. Arabia
45 E3 Alarcón, Embalse de resr Spain
20 C4 Al Arţāwīyah S. Arabia
33 E4 Alas Indon.
16 B2 Alaşehir Turkey
17 J6 Al 'Āshūrīyah well Iraq
62 D3 Alaska div. U.S.A.
62 D4 Alaska, Gulf of g. U.S.A.
64 E3 Alaska Highway Can./U.S.A.
62 B4 Alaska Peninsula U.S.A.
62 D3 Alaska Range mts U.S.A.
17 M2 Älät Azer.
19 F2 Alat Uzbek.
17 J6 Al 'Athāmīn h. Iraq
50 H4 Alatyr' Rus. Fed.
50 H4 Alatyr' r. Rus. Fed.
86 C4 Alausí Ecuador
17 K1 Alaverdi Armenia
36 T4 Alavieska Fin.
36 S5 Alavus Fin.
8 C3 Alawoona Austr.
17 L1 Alazani r. Azer./Georgia
17 K5 Al 'Azīzīyah Iraq
48 C2 Alba Italy
16 F3 Al Bāb Syria
45 F3 Albacete Spain

8 C3 Albacutya, L. l. Austr.
17 K6 Al Bādiyah al Janūbīyah h. Iraq
49 K1 Alba Iulia Romania
66 F3 Albanel, L. l. Can.
35 G4 Albania country Europe
6 B5 Albany Austr.
79 C6 Albany GA U.S.A.
68 E5 Albany IN U.S.A.
78 C4 Albany KY U.S.A.
81 G3 Albany NY U.S.A.
72 B2 Albany OR U.S.A.
66 C3 Albany r. Can.
91 G2 Albardão do João Maria coastal area Brazil
18 B5 Al Barrah S. Arabia
Al Başrah see Basra
17 K6 Al Baţḩa' marsh Iraq
17 L7 Al Bāţin, Wādī watercourse Asia
6 E3 Albatross Bay b. Austr.
55 E1 Al Bayḑā' Libya
86 □ Albemarle, Pta pt Galapagos Is Ecuador
79 E5 Albemarle Sd chan. U.S.A.
48 C2 Albenga Italy
45 D3 Alberche r. Spain
6 D4 Alberga watercourse Austr.
45 B2 Albergaria-a-Velha Port.
8 F2 Albert Austr.
44 F2 Albert France
80 E6 Alberta U.S.A.
64 F4 Alberta div. Can.
64 F4 Alberta, Mt mt Can.
58 D7 Albertinia S. Africa
42 D4 Albert Kanaal canal Belgium
8 B3 Albert, Lake l. Austr.
56 D3 Albert, Lake l. Congo(Zaire)/Uganda
76 E3 Albert Lea U.S.A.
56 D3 Albert Nile r. Sudan/Uganda
88 B8 Alberto de Agostini, Parque Nacional nat. park Chile
59 H3 Alberton S. Africa
44 H4 Albertville France
42 E6 Albestroff France
44 F5 Albi France
87 H2 Albina Suriname
74 A2 Albion CA U.S.A.
81 J2 Albion ME U.S.A.
68 E4 Albion MI U.S.A.
80 D3 Albion NY U.S.A.
45 E5 Alborán, Isla de i. Spain
37 L8 Ålborg Denmark
37 M8 Ålborg Bugt b. Denmark
64 F4 Albreda Can.
18 C5 Al Budayyi Bahrain
18 C6 Al Budū', Sabkhat salt pan S. Arabia
45 B4 Albufeira Port.
17 H4 Āl Bū Kamāl Syria
73 F5 Albuquerque U.S.A.
20 E5 Al Buraymī Oman
45 C3 Alburquerque Spain
8 F4 Albury Austr.
17 H4 Al Buşayrah Syria
16 G7 Al Busayţā' plain S. Arabia
17 L6 Al Buşayyah Iraq
18 B4 Al Bushūk well S. Arabia
45 B3 Alcácer do Sal Port.
45 E2 Alcalá de Henares Spain
45 E4 Alcalá la Real Spain
48 E6 Alcamo Sicily Italy
45 F2 Alcañiz Spain
45 C3 Alcántara Spain
45 E3 Alcaraz Spain
45 D4 Alcaudete Spain
45 E3 Alcázar de San Juan Spain
51 F5 Alchevs'k Ukr.
91 D2 Alcira Arg.
90 E2 Alcobaça Brazil
45 F2 Alcora Spain
91 E2 Alcorta Arg.
45 F3 Alcoy Spain
45 H3 Alcúdia Spain
57 E4 Aldabra Islands is Seychelles
17 K5 Al Daghghārah Iraq
84 C2 Aldama Mex.
13 O4 Aldan Rus. Fed.
13 P3 Aldan r. Rus. Fed.
39 J5 Aldeburgh U.K.
9 F2 Aldermen Is, The is N.Z.
44 D2 Alderney i. Channel Is U.K.
74 B4 Alder Peak summit U.S.A.
39 G6 Aldershot U.K.
80 C6 Alderson U.S.A.
18 D6 Al Dhafrah reg. U.A.E.
38 D3 Aldingham U.K.
39 F5 Aldridge U.K.
68 B5 Aledo U.S.A.
54 A3 Aleg Maur.
90 E3 Alegre Brazil
88 E3 Alegrete Brazil
91 E2 Alejandro Korn Arg.
50 E2 Alekhovshchina Rus. Fed.
50 F3 Aleksandrov Rus. Fed.
51 J5 Aleksandrov Gay Rus. Fed.
51 H6 Aleksandrovskoye Rus. Fed.
13 Q4 Aleksandrovsk-Sakhalinskiy Rus. Fed.
14 F1 Alekseyevka Kazak.
51 F5 Alekseyevka Belgorod. Obl. Rus. Fed.
51 F5 Alekseyevka Belgorod. Obl. Rus. Fed.
51 G5 Alekseyevskaya Rus. Fed.
50 F4 Aleksin Rus. Fed.
49 J3 Aleksinac Yugo.
84 C3 Alemán, Presa Miguel resr Mex.
56 B4 Alèmbé Gabon
16 E1 Alembeyli Turkey
90 D3 Além Paraíba Brazil
36 M5 Ålen Norway
44 E2 Alençon France
87 H4 Alenquer Brazil
74 □2 Alenuihaha Channel U.S.A.
16 F3 Aleppo Syria
86 D6 Alerta Peru
64 D4 Alert Bay Can.
44 G4 Alès France
47 L7 Aleşd Romania
48 C2 Alessandria Italy
36 K5 Ålesund Norway
60 A4 Aleutian Islands is U.S.A.
62 C4 Aleutian Range mts U.S.A.
95 H2 Aleutian Trench sea feature Pac. Oc.
13 R4 Alevina, Mys c. Rus. Fed.
Alevişik see Samandağı
81 K2 Alexander U.S.A.
64 B3 Alexander Archipelago is U.S.A.
58 B4 Alexander Bay S. Africa
58 B4 Alexander Bay b. Namibia/S. Africa
79 C5 Alexander City U.S.A.
92 A2 Alexander I. i. Ant.
8 E4 Alexandra Austr.
9 B6 Alexandra N.Z.
88 □ Alexandra, C. c. Atl. Ocean
49 K4 Alexandreia Greece
Alexandretta see İskenderun
81 F2 Alexandria Can.
55 E1 Alexandria Egypt
49 L3 Alexandria Romania
59 G6 Alexandria S. Africa
40 D5 Alexandria U.K.
68 E5 Alexandria IN U.S.A.
77 E6 Alexandria LA U.S.A.
76 E2 Alexandria MN U.S.A.
80 E5 Alexandria VA U.S.A.
81 F2 Alexandria Bay U.S.A.
8 B3 Alexandrina, L. l. Austr.
49 L4 Alexandroupoli Greece
68 B5 Alexis U.S.A.
67 J3 Alexis r. Can.
64 E4 Alexis Creek Can.
12 K4 Aleysk Rus. Fed.
42 F4 Alf Ger.
45 F1 Alfaro Spain
17 L7 Al Farwānīyah Kuwait
17 J4 Al Fatḩah Iraq
17 M7 Al Fāw Iraq
43 H3 Alfeld (Leine) Ger.
90 D3 Alfenas Brazil
17 M7 Al Fintās Kuwait
47 K7 Alföld plain Hungary
39 H4 Alford U.K.
81 F2 Alfred Can.
81 H3 Alfred U.S.A.
17 M7 Al Fuḩayḩil Kuwait
Al-Fujayrah see Fujairah
18 B4 Al Fulayi watercourse S. Arabia
Al Furāt r. see Euphrates
37 J7 Algård Norway
91 C3 Algarrobo del Aguilla Arg.
45 B4 Algarve reg. Port.
50 G4 Algasovo Rus. Fed.
45 D4 Algeciras Spain
45 F3 Algemesí Spain
Alger see Algiers
69 E3 Alger U.S.A.
52 D3 Algeria country Africa
43 H2 Algermissen Ger.
17 K6 Al Ghammas Iraq
18 B5 Al Ghāţ S. Arabia
20 D6 Al Ghayḑah Yemen
48 C4 Alghero Sardinia Italy
54 C1 Algiers Alg.
59 F6 Algoa Bay b. S. Africa
68 D3 Algoma U.S.A.
76 E3 Algona U.S.A.
69 F4 Algonac U.S.A.
69 H3 Algonquin Park Can.
69 H3 Algonquin Provincial Park res. Can.
17 J7 Al Habakah well S. Arabia
18 B4 Al Ḩadaqah well S. Arabia
18 C5 Al Ḩadd Bahrain
18 A4 Al Hadhālīl plat. S. Arabia
17 J4 Al Hadīthah Iraq
17 J4 Al Ḩaḑr Iraq
16 F4 Al Ḩaffah Syria
18 B5 Al Ḩā'ir S. Arabia
19 E6 Al Hajar Oman
18 E5 Al Ḩajar al Gharbī mts Oman
17 G6 Al Hamad reg. Jordan/S. Arabia
55 D2 Al Ḩamādah al Ḩamrā' plat. Libya
45 F4 Alhama de Murcia Spain
17 J6 Al Hammām well Iraq
17 K7 Al Haniyah esc. Iraq
18 B6 Al Hariq S. Arabia
17 G6 Al Ḩarrah reg. S. Arabia
17 H3 Al Ḩasakah Syria
17 K5 Al Hāshimīyah Iraq
17 L5 Al Ḩayy Iraq
17 K5 Al Ḩillah Iraq
18 B6 Al Ḩillah S. Arabia
18 B6 Al Ḩilwah S. Arabia
18 C5 Al Ḩinnāh S. Arabia
54 B1 Al Hoceima Morocco
20 B7 Al Hudaydah Yemen
20 C4 Al Hufūf S. Arabia
18 D6 Al Ḩumrah reg. U.A.E.
18 C5 Al Ḩunayy S. Arabia
18 B6 Al Huwwah S. Arabia
18 D2 'Alīābād Iran
17 L4 'Alīābād Iran
19 E3 'Alīābād Iran
19 F4 'Alīābād Iran
49 M5 Aliağa Turkey
49 K4 Aliakmonas r. Greece
17 L5 'Alī al Gharbī Iraq
21 A2 Alībāg India
22 B4 Ali Bandar Pak.
17 M2 Äli Bayramlı Azer.
45 F3 Alicante Spain
59 G6 Alice S. Africa
77 D7 Alice U.S.A.
64 D3 Alice Arm Can.
6 D4 Alice Springs Austr.
79 E7 Alice Town Bahamas
31 B5 Alicia Phil.
22 D4 Aligarh India
18 C3 Alīgūdarz Iran
56 B4 Alima r. Congo
37 N8 Alingsås Sweden
16 B2 Aliova r. Turkey
22 B3 Alipur Pak.
23 G4 Alipur Duar India
80 C4 Aliquippa U.S.A.
56 E2 Ali Sabieh Djibouti
16 F6 'Al 'Īsāwīyah S. Arabia
17 K2 Alī Shah Iran
17 K5 Al Iskandarīyah Iraq
73 E6 Alisos r. Mex.
49 L5 Aliveri Greece
59 G5 Aliwal North S. Africa
64 G4 Alix Can.
55 E1 Al Jabal al Akhḑar mts Libya
18 C5 Al Jāfūrah des. S. Arabia
55 E2 Al Jaghbūb Libya
17 L7 Al Jahrah Kuwait
18 C5 Al Jamalīyah Qatar
18 C6 Al Jawb reg. S. Arabia
20 A4 Al Jawf S. Arabia
55 D1 Al Jawsh Libya
17 G3 Al Jazīrah reg. Iraq/Syria
45 B4 Aljezur Port.
18 C5 Al Jībān reg. S. Arabia
18 B6 Al Jifārah S. Arabia
17 J6 Al Jil well Iraq
18 B5 Al Jilh esc. S. Arabia
18 C5 Al Jishshah S. Arabia
16 E6 Al Jīzah Jordan
20 C4 Al Jubayl S. Arabia
18 B5 Al Jubaylah S. Arabia
18 B5 Al Jufayr S. Arabia
18 C5 Al Jurayd i. S. Arabia
18 B5 Al Jurayfah S. Arabia
45 B4 Aljustrel Port.
20 E5 Al Khābūrah Oman
17 K5 Al Khālis Iraq
20 E4 Al Khaşab Oman
18 A6 Al Khāşirah S. Arabia
18 D6 Al Khatam reg. U.A.E.
18 C5 Al Khawr Qatar
18 C5 Al Khīşah well S. Arabia
18 C5 Al Khobar S. Arabia
18 B5 Al Khuff reg. S. Arabia
55 E2 Al Khufrah Libya
55 D1 Al Khums Libya
17 K5 Al Kifl Iraq
18 C5 Al Kir'ānah Qatar
42 C2 Alkmaar Neth.
17 K5 Al Kūfah Iraq
17 L5 Al Kumayt Iraq
17 K5 Al Kūt Iraq
Al Kuwayt see Kuwait
17 H7 Al Labbah plain S. Arabia
Al Lādhiqīyah see Latakia
81 J1 Allagash ME U.S.A.
81 J1 Allagash r. ME U.S.A.
81 J1 Allagash Lake l. U.S.A.
23 E4 Allahabad India
16 F5 Al Lajā lava Syria
13 P3 Allakh-Yun' Rus. Fed.
59 G3 Allanridge S. Africa
59 H1 Alldays S. Africa
68 E4 Allegan U.S.A.
80 D4 Allegheny r. U.S.A.
80 C6 Allegheny Mountains U.S.A.
80 D4 Allegheny Reservoir U.S.A.
79 D5 Allendale U.S.A.
38 E3 Allendale Town U.K.
84 B1 Allende Mex.
43 G4 Allendorf (Lumda) Ger.
69 G3 Allenford Can.
41 C3 Allen, Lough l. Rep. of Ireland
81 F4 Allentown U.S.A.
21 B4 Alleppey India
43 J2 Aller r. Ger.
76 C3 Alliance NE U.S.A.
80 C4 Alliance OH U.S.A.
17 J6 Al Līfīyah well Iraq
37 O9 Allinge-Sandvig Denmark
69 H3 Alliston Can.
20 B5 Al Līth S. Arabia
40 E4 Alloa U.K.
21 C3 Allur India
21 C3 Alluru Kottapatnam India
17 J6 Al Lussuf well Iraq
67 F4 Alma Can.
68 E4 Alma MI U.S.A.
76 D3 Alma NE U.S.A.
75 H5 Alma NM U.S.A.
17 J6 Al Ma'ānīyah Iraq
45 B3 Almada Port.
17 K7 Al Ma'danīyāt well Iraq
45 D3 Almadén Spain
Al Madīnah see Medina
17 K5 Al Maḩmūdiyah Iraq
18 B5 Al Majma'ah S. Arabia
17 L1 Almalı Azer.
18 C5 Al Malsūnīyah reg. S. Arabia
18 C5 Al Manāmah Bahrain
74 B1 Almanor, Lake l. U.S.A.
45 F3 Almansa Spain
45 D2 Almanzor mt Spain
17 L6 Al Ma'qil Iraq
18 D6 Al Mariyyah U.A.E.
55 E1 Al Marj Libya
90 C1 Almas, Rio das r. Brazil
15 F2 Almaty Kazak.
Al Mawşil see Mosul
17 H4 Al Mayādīn Syria
18 B5 Al Mazāḩimīyah S. Arabia
45 E2 Almazán Spain
13 N3 Almaznyy Rus. Fed.
87 H4 Almeirim Brazil
45 B3 Almeirim Port.
42 E2 Almelo Neth.
90 E2 Almenara Brazil
45 C2 Almendra, Embalse de resr Spain
45 C3 Almendralejo Spain
42 D2 Almere Neth.
45 E4 Almería Spain
45 E4 Almería, Golfo de b. Spain
12 G4 Al'met'yevsk Rus. Fed.
37 O8 Älmhult Sweden
18 B5 Al Midhnab S. Arabia
45 D5 Almina, Pta pt Morocco
20 C4 Al Mish'āb S. Arabia
16 F5 Al Mismīyah Syria
45 B4 Almodôvar Port.
69 F4 Almont U.S.A.
69 J3 Almonte Can.
45 C4 Almonte Spain
20 C4 Al Mubarrez S. Arabia
16 E7 Al Mudawwara Jordan
18 C5 Al Muharraq Bahrain
20 C7 Al Mukallā Yemen
20 B7 Al Mukhā Yemen
45 E4 Almuñécar Spain
17 K5 Al Muqdādīyah Iraq
18 B5 Al Murabba S. Arabia
16 F1 Almus Turkey
18 B4 Al Musannāh ridge S. Arabia
17 K5 Al Musayyib Iraq
49 L7 Almyrou, Ormos b. Greece
74 □1 Alna Haina U.S.A.
38 F2 Alnwick U.K.
23 H5 Alon Myanmar
23 H3 Along India
49 K5 Alonnisos i. Greece
25 E7 Alor i. Indon.
25 E7 Alor, Kepulauan is Indon.
33 B1 Alor Setar Malaysia
Alost see Aalst
22 C5 Alot India
36 W4 Alozero Rus. Fed.
74 C4 Alpaugh U.S.A.
42 E3 Alpen Ger.
69 F3 Alpena U.S.A.
48 D1 Alpi Dolomitiche mts Italy
75 H5 Alpine AZ U.S.A.
77 C6 Alpine TX U.S.A.
72 E3 Alpine WY U.S.A.
34 F4 Alps mts Europe
20 C6 Al Qa'āmīyāt reg. S. Arabia
55 D1 Al Qaddāḩīyah Libya
16 F4 Al Qadmūs Syria
18 B5 Al Qā'īyah well S. Arabia
18 C6 Al Qalībah S. Arabia
17 H3 Al Qāmishlī Syria
18 B5 Al Qar'ah well S. Arabia
16 F4 Al Qaryatayn Syria
18 B5 Al Qaşab S. Arabia
20 C6 Al Qaţn Yemen
55 D2 Al Qatrūn Libya
18 B4 Al Qayşūmah S. Arabia
16 E5 Al Qunayţirah Syria
20 B6 Al Qunfidhah S. Arabia
18 A5 Al Qurayn S. Arabia
17 L6 Al Qurnah Iraq
17 K6 Al Qusayr Iraq
18 B6 Al Qūşūrīyah S. Arabia
16 F5 Al Quţayfah Syria
18 A5 Al Quwārah S. Arabia
18 B5 Al Quwayīyah S. Arabia
44 H2 Alsace reg. France
39 E4 Alsager U.K.
17 J6 Al Samīt well Iraq
65 H4 Alsask Can.
43 H4 Alsfeld Ger.
43 K3 Alsleben (Saale) Ger.
38 E3 Alston U.K.
37 R8 Alsunga Latvia
36 S2 Alta Norway
36 S2 Altaelva r. Norway
91 D1 Alta Gracia Arg.
89 D2 Altagracía de Orituco Venez.
10 K5 Altai Mountains China/Mongolia
79 D6 Altamaha r. U.S.A.
87 H4 Altamira Brazil
9 B6 Alta, Mt mt N.Z.
48 G4 Altamura Italy
90 C1 Alta Paraiso de Goiás Brazil
84 A1 Altata Mex.
80 D6 Altavista U.S.A.
15 G2 Altay China
24 B2 Altay Mongolia
45 F3 Altea Spain
36 S1 Alteidet Norway
42 E4 Altenahr Ger.
42 F2 Altenberge Ger.
43 L4 Altenburg Ger.
42 F4 Altenkirchen (Westerwald) Ger.
23 H1 Altenqoke China
43 M1 Altentreptow Ger.
17 M1 Altıağaç Azer.
19 H3 Altimur Pass Afgh.
17 K4 Altin Köprü Iraq
49 M5 Altınoluk Turkey
16 C2 Altıntaş Turkey
86 E7 Altiplano plain Bol.
43 K2 Altmark reg. Ger.
43 J5 Altmühl r. Ger.
90 B2 Alto Araguaia Brazil
91 C2 Alto de Pencoso h. Arg.
89 B3 Alto de Tamar mt Col.
90 B2 Alto Garças Brazil
57 D5 Alto Molócuè Moz.
78 B4 Alton IL U.S.A.
77 F4 Alton MO U.S.A.
81 H3 Alton NH U.S.A.
76 D1 Altona Can.
80 D4 Altoona U.S.A.
90 B2 Alto Sucuriú Brazil
46 F6 Altötting Ger.
39 E4 Altrincham U.K.
43 L1 Alt Schwerin Ger.
24 A3 Altun Shan mts China
72 B3 Alturas U.S.A.
77 D5 Altus U.S.A.
16 G1 Alucra Turkey
37 U8 Alūksne Latvia
17 M5 Alūm Iran
80 B4 Alum Creek Lake l. U.S.A.
91 B3 Aluminé r. Arg.
91 B3 Aluminé, L. l. Arg.
51 E6 Alupka Ukr.
55 D1 Al 'Uqaylah Libya
18 C5 Al 'Uqayr S. Arabia
51 E6 Alushta Ukr.
17 K4 'Alut Iran
20 C4 Al 'Uthmānīyah S. Arabia
55 E2 Al 'Uwaynāt Libya
17 J6 Al 'Uwayqīlah S. Arabia
18 A5 Al 'Uyūn S. Arabia
17 L6 Al 'Uzayr Iraq
77 D4 Alva U.S.A.
84 D3 Alvarado Mex.
91 C2 Alvarado, P. de pass Chile
86 F4 Alvarães Brazil
37 M5 Alvdal Norway
37 O6 Älvdalen Sweden
37 O8 Alvesta Sweden
37 K6 Ålvik Norway
77 E6 Alvin U.S.A.
36 R4 Älvsbyn Sweden
14 B4 Al Wajh S. Arabia
18 C5 Al Wakrah Qatar
18 C5 Al Wannān S. Arabia
22 D4 Alwar India
18 B5 Al Warī'ah S. Arabia
21 B4 Alwaye India
17 H5 Al Widyān plat. Iraq/S. Arabia
18 B4 'Al Wusayţ well S. Arabia
26 A2 Alxa Youqi China
26 B2 Alxa Zuoqi China
6 D3 Alyangula Austr.
40 E4 Alyth U.K.
37 T9 Alytus Lith.
72 F2 Alzada U.S.A.
42 E5 Alzette r. Lux.
43 G5 Alzey Ger.
89 E3 Amacuro r. Guyana/Venez.
6 D4 Amadeus, Lake salt flat Austr.
63 L3 Amadjuak Lake l. Can.
75 G6 Amado U.S.A.
45 B3 Amadora Port.
29 A8 Amakusa-nada b. Japan
37 N7 Åmal Sweden
21 C2 Amalapuram India
24 D1 Amalat r. Rus. Fed.
89 B3 Amalfi Col.
58 F3 Amalia S. Africa
49 J6 Amaliada Greece
22 C5 Amalner India
25 F7 Amamapare Indon.
90 A3 Amambaí Brazil
90 A3 Amambaí r. Brazil
90 A3 Amambaí, Serra de h. Brazil/Para.
24 E4 Amami-guntō is Japan
24 E4 Amami-Ōshima i. Japan
14 E1 Amangel'dy Kazak.
48 G5 Amantea Italy
59 J5 Amanzimtoti S. Africa
87 H3 Amapá Brazil
45 C3 Amareleja Port.
74 D3 Amargosa Desert des. U.S.A.
74 D3 Amargosa Range mts U.S.A.
74 D3 Amargosa Valley U.S.A.
77 C5 Amarillo U.S.A.
48 F3 Amaro, Monte mt Italy
22 E4 Amarpatan India
16 E1 Amasya Turkey
84 D3 Amatán Mex.
84 A2 Amatlán de Cañas Mex.
42 D4 Amay Belgium
87 H4 Amazon r. S. America
89 D4 Amazonas div. Brazil
Amazonas r. see Amazon
87 G4 Amazónia, Parque Nacional nat. park Brazil
87 J3 Amazon, Mouths of the est. Brazil
22 C6 Ambad India
21 B2 Ambajogai India
22 D3 Ambala India
21 C5 Ambalangoda Sri Lanka
57 E6 Ambalavao Madag.
57 E5 Ambanja Madag.
19 E4 Ambar Iran
13 S3 Ambarchik Rus. Fed.
21 B4 Ambasamudram India
86 C4 Ambato Ecuador
57 E5 Ambato Boeny Madag.
57 E6 Ambato Finandrahana Madag.
57 E5 Ambatolampy Madag.
57 E5 Ambatomainty Madag.
57 E5 Ambatondrazaka Madag.
43 K5 Amberg Ger.
82 G5 Ambergris Cay i. Belize
44 G4 Ambérieu-en-Bugey France
69 G3 Amberley Can.
23 E5 Ambikapur India
57 E5 Ambilobe Madag.
64 C3 Ambition, Mt mt Can.
38 F2 Amble U.K.
38 E3 Ambleside U.K.
42 D4 Amblève r. Belgium
57 E6 Amboasary Madag.
57 E5 Ambohidratrimo Madag.
57 E6 Ambohimahasoa Madag.
25 E7 Ambon Indon.
25 E7 Ambon i. Indon.
57 E6 Ambositra Madag.
57 E6 Ambovombe Madag.
75 E4 Amboy CA U.S.A.
68 C5 Amboy IL U.S.A.
81 F3 Amboy Center U.S.A.
57 B4 Ambriz Angola
7 G3 Ambrym i. Vanuatu
21 B3 Ambur India
23 G2 Amdo China
84 A2 Ameca Mex.
42 D1 Ameland i. Neth.
80 E6 Amelia Court House U.S.A.
81 G4 Amenia U.S.A.
72 D3 American Falls U.S.A.
72 D3 American Falls Res. resr U.S.A.
75 G1 American Fork U.S.A.
5 K6 American Samoa terr. Pac. Oc.
79 C5 Americus U.S.A.
42 D2 Amersfoort Neth.
59 H3 Amersfoort S. Africa
39 G6 Amersham U.K.
65 L3 Amery Can.
92 D5 Amery Ice Shelf ice feature Ant.
76 E3 Ames U.S.A.
39 F6 Amesbury U.K.
81 H3 Amesbury U.S.A.
23 E4 Amethi India
49 K5 Amfissa Greece
13 P3 Amga Rus. Fed.
24 F2 Amgu Rus. Fed.
54 C2 Amguid Alg.
24 F1 Amgun' r. Rus. Fed.
67 H4 Amherst Can.
81 G3 Amherst MA U.S.A.
81 J2 Amherst ME U.S.A.
80 D6 Amherst VA U.S.A.
69 F4 Amherstburg Can.
48 D3 Amiata, Monte mt Italy
44 F2 Amiens France
17 H5 Amij, Wādī watercourse Iraq
21 A4 Amindivi Islands is India
29 D7 Amino Japan
58 C1 Aminuis Namibia
18 B3 Amīrābād Iran
Amirabad see Fūlād Maīalleh
53 K6 Amirante Islands is Seychelles
19 F4 Amir Chah Pak.
65 J4 Amisk L. l. Can.
77 C6 Amistad Res. resr Mex./U.S.A.
22 D5 Amla Madhya Pradesh India
37 L7 Åmli Norway
39 C4 Amlwch U.K.
16 E6 'Ammān Jordan
39 D6 Ammanford U.K.
36 V4 Ämmänsaari Fin.
36 P4 Ammarnäs Sweden
43 F1 Ammerland reg. Ger.
43 J3 Ammern Ger.
46 E7 Ammersee l. Ger.
Ammochostos see Famagusta
30 D4 Amnyong-dan hd N. Korea
22 C5 Amod India
27 B6 Amo Jiang r. China
18 D2 Amol Iran
43 H5 Amorbach Ger.
49 L6 Amorgos i. Greece
66 E4 Amos Can.
Amoy see Xiamen
21 C5 Amparai India
90 C3 Amparo Brazil
46 E6 Amper r. Ger.
45 G2 Amposta Spain
22 D5 Amravati India
22 B5 Amreli India
22 B4 Amri Pak.
16 E4 'Amrit Syria
22 C3 Amritsar India
22 D3 Amroha India
36 Q4 Åmsele Sweden
42 C2 Amstelveen Neth.
42 C2 Amsterdam Neth.
59 J3 Amsterdam S. Africa
81 F3 Amsterdam U.S.A.
93 K6 Amsterdam, Île i. Ind. Ocean
46 G6 Amstetten Austria
55 E3 Am Timan Chad
19 F1 Amudar'ya r. Turkm./Uzbek.
63 J2 Amund Ringnes I. Can.
92 D4 Amundsen Bay b. Ant.
92 B4 Amundsen Gl. gl. Ant.
62 F2 Amundsen Gulf g. Can.
92 C5 Amundsen, Mt mt Ant.
92 B4 Amundsen-Scott U.S.A. Base Ant.
92 A3 Amundsen Sea sea Ant.
33 E3 Amuntai Indon.
Amur r. see Heilong Jiang
13 P4 Amursk Rus. Fed.
51 F6 Amvrosiyivka Ukr.
68 E1 Amyot Can.
23 H6 An Myanmar
25 E7 Anabanua Indon.
13 N2 Anabar r. Rus. Fed.
13 N2 Anabarskiy Zaliv b. Rus. Fed.
8 C2 Ana Branch r. Austr.
74 C4 Anacapa Is is U.S.A.
89 D2 Anaco Venez.
72 D2 Anaconda U.S.A.
72 B1 Anacortes U.S.A.
77 D5 Anadarko U.S.A.
16 F1 Anadolu Dağları mts Turkey
13 T3 Anadyr' r. Rus. Fed.
13 U3 Anadyrskiy Zaliv b. Rus. Fed.
49 L6 Anafi i. Greece
90 E1 Anagé Brazil
17 H4 'Ānah Iraq
74 D5 Anaheim U.S.A.
64 D4 Anahim Lake Can.
77 C7 Anáhuac Mex.
21 B4 Anaimalai Hills mts India
21 B4 Anai Mudi Pk mt India
21 C2 Anakapalle India
57 E5 Analalava Madag.
86 F4 Anamã Brazil
33 C2 Anambas, Kepulauan is Indon.
68 B4 Anamosa U.S.A.
16 D3 Anamur Turkey
16 D3 Anamur Burnu pt Turkey
29 D8 Anan Japan
22 C5 Anand India
23 F5 Ānandapur India
23 F5 Anandpur r. India
21 B3 Anantapur India
22 C2 Anantnag Jammu and Kashmir
51 D6 Anan'yiv Ukr.
51 F6 Anapa Rus. Fed.
90 C2 Anápolis Brazil
18 D4 Anār Iran
18 D3 Anārak Iran
18 C3 Anarbar r. Iran
19 F3 Anardara Afgh.
16 D2 Anatolia reg. Turkey
7 G4 Anatom i. Vanuatu
88 D3 Añatuya Arg.
89 E4 Anauá r. Brazil
18 C2 Anbūh Iran
30 D4 Anbyon N. Korea
44 D3 Ancenis France
62 D3 Anchorage U.S.A.
69 F4 Anchor Bay b. U.S.A.
48 E3 Ancona Italy
88 B6 Ancud Chile
91 B4 Ancud, Golfo de g. Chile
91 B1 Andacollo Chile
23 F5 Andal India
36 K5 Åndalsnes Norway
45 D4 Andalucía div. Spain
77 G6 Andalusia U.S.A.
15 H6 Andaman and Nicobar Islands div. India
93 L3 Andaman Basin sea feature Ind. Ocean
15 H5 Andaman Islands Andaman and Nicobar Is
33 A1 Andaman Sea sea Asia
57 E5 Andapa Madag.
90 E1 Andaraí Brazil
36 P2 Andenes Norway
42 D4 Andenne Belgium
42 C4 Anderlecht Belgium
44 D4 Andernos-les-Bains France
62 D3 Anderson AK U.S.A.
68 E5 Anderson IN U.S.A.
77 E4 Anderson MO U.S.A.
79 D5 Anderson SC U.S.A.
62 F3 Anderson r. N.W.T. Can.
85 C3 Andes mts S. America
76 D3 Andes, Lake U.S.A.
36 P2 Andfjorden chan. Norway
21 B2 Andhra Pradesh div. India
57 E5 Andilamena Madag.
57 E5 Andilanatoby Madag.
18 C3 Andīmeshk Iran
16 F3 Andırın Turkey
51 H7 Andiyskoye Koysu r. Rus. Fed.
14 F2 Andizhan Uzbek.
19 G2 Andkhui r. Afgh.
19 G2 Andkhvoy Afgh.
57 E5 Andoany Madag.
86 C4 Andoas Peru
21 B2 Andol India
30 E5 Andong S. Korea
30 E5 Andong-ho l. S. Korea
34 F4 Andorra country Europe
45 G1 Andorra la Vella Andorra
39 F6 Andover U.K.
81 H2 Andover ME U.S.A.
80 C4 Andover OH U.S.A.
36 O2 Andøya i. Norway
90 B3 Andradina Brazil
50 E3 Andreapol' Rus. Fed.
38 C3 Andreas U.K.
56 C3 André Félix, Parc National de nat. park C.A.R.
90 D3 Andrelândia Brazil
77 C5 Andrews U.S.A.
48 G4 Andria Italy
57 E6 Androka Madag.
79 E7 Andros i. Bahamas
49 L6 Andros i. Greece
81 H2 Androscoggin r. U.S.A.
79 E7 Andros Town Bahamas
21 A4 Āndrott i. India
51 D5 Andrushivka Ukr.
36 Q2 Andselv Norway
45 D3 Andújar Spain
57 B5 Andulo Angola
54 C3 Anéfis Mali
83 M5 Anegada i. Virgin Is
91 D4 Anegada, Bahía b. Arg.
75 F5 Anegam U.S.A.
54 C4 Aného Togo
'Aneiza, Jabal h. see 'Unayzah, Jabal
75 H3 Aneth U.S.A.
45 G1 Aneto mt Spain
55 D3 Aney Niger
27 E5 Anfu China
57 E5 Angadoka, Lohatanjona hd Madag.
24 B1 Angara r. Rus. Fed.
24 C1 Angarsk Rus. Fed.
31 B3 Angat Phil.
37 O5 Ånge Sweden
82 B3 Angel de la Guarda i. Mex.
31 B3 Angeles Phil.
37 N8 Ängelholm Sweden
74 B2 Angels Camp U.S.A.
36 P4 Ångermanälven r. Sweden
44 D3 Angers France
65 K2 Angikuni Lake l. Can.
32 B2 Angkor Cambodia
39 C4 Anglesey i. U.K.
77 E6 Angleton U.S.A.
69 H2 Angliers Can.
Angmagssalik see Tasiilaq
32 □ Ang Mo Kio Sing.
56 C3 Ango Congo(Zaire)
57 D5 Angoche Moz.
19 E5 Angohrān Iran
91 B3 Angol Chile
68 E5 Angola U.S.A.
53 F7 Angola country Africa
96 K7 Angola Basin sea feature Atl. Ocean
84 D3 Angostura, Presa de la resr Mex.
44 E4 Angoulême France
12 J5 Angren Uzbek.
32 B2 Ang Thong Thai.
61 M8 Anguilla terr. Caribbean Sea
26 E1 Anguli Nur l. China
26 E2 Anguo China
90 A3 Anhanduí r. Brazil
37 M8 Anholt i. Denmark
27 D4 Anhua China
26 E3 Anhui div. China
90 A2 Anhumas Brazil
30 D5 Anhŭng S. Korea
90 C2 Anicuns Brazil
50 G3 Anikovo Rus. Fed.
75 H6 Animas U.S.A.
75 H6 Animas Peak summit U.S.A.
32 A2 Anin Myanmar
28 H1 Aniva Rus. Fed.
28 H1 Aniva, Mys c. Rus. Fed.
24 G2 Aniva, Zaliv b. Rus. Fed.
7 G3 Aniwa i. Vanuatu
42 B5 Anizy-le-Château France
37 U6 Anjalankoski Fin.
21 B4 Anjengo India
27 F4 Anji China
22 D5 Anji India
19 E3 Anjoman Iran
44 D3 Anjou reg. France
57 E5 Anjouan i. Comoros
57 E5 Anjozorobe Madag.
30 C4 Anjŭ N. Korea
57 E6 Ankaboa, Tanjona pt Madag.
26 C3 Ankang China
16 D2 Ankara Turkey
57 E6 Ankazoabo Madag.
57 E5 Ankazobe Madag.
32 D2 An Khê Vietnam
22 C5 Ankleshwar India
27 B5 Anlong China
32 C2 Ânlong Vêng Cambodia
26 D4 Anlu China
30 D5 Anmyŏn Do i. S. Korea
51 G5 Anna Rus. Fed.
54 C1 Annaba Alg.
43 M4 Annaberg-Buchholtz Ger.
16 F4 An Nabk Syria
20 B4 An Nafūd des. S. Arabia
38 A3 Annahilt U.K.
17 K6 An Najaf Iraq
80 E5 Anna, Lake l. U.S.A.
41 D3 Annalee r. Rep. of Ireland
41 F3 Annalong U.K.
40 E6 Annan Scot. U.K.
40 E6 Annan r. U.K.
40 E5 Annandale v. U.K.
80 E5 Annapolis U.S.A.
67 G5 Annapolis Royal Can.
23 E3 Annapurna mt Nepal
18 C5 An Naqīrah well S. Arabia
69 F4 Ann Arbor U.S.A.
87 G2 Anna Regina Guyana
17 L6 An Nāşirīyah Iraq
81 H3 Ann, Cape hd U.S.A.
44 H4 Annecy France
44 H3 Annemasse France
42 E1 Annen Neth.
64 C4 Annette I. i. U.S.A.
27 B5 Anning China
79 C5 Anniston U.S.A.
53 E6 Annobón i. Equatorial Guinea
44 G4 Annonay France
20 C4 An Nu'ayrīyah S. Arabia
17 K5 An Nu'mānīyah Iraq
76 E2 Anoka U.S.A.
57 E5 Anorontany, Tanjona hd Madag.
49 L7 Ano Viannos Greece
27 D6 Anpu China
27 C6 Anpu Gang b. China
27 E4 Anqing China
26 F2 Anqiu China
27 D5 Anren China
42 D4 Ans Belgium
26 C2 Ansai China
16 F4 Ansariye, J. el mts Syria
43 J5 Ansbach Ger.
30 B3 Anshan China
27 B5 Anshun China
91 C1 Ansilta mt Arg.
91 F1 Ansina Uru.
76 D3 Ansley U.S.A.
77 D5 Anson U.S.A.
54 C3 Ansongo Mali
66 D4 Ansonville Can.
80 C5 Ansted U.S.A.
22 D4 Anta India
86 D6 Antabamba Peru
16 F3 Antakya Turkey
57 F5 Antalaha Madag.
16 C3 Antalya Turkey
16 C3 Antalya Körfezi g. Turkey
57 E5 Antananarivo Madag.
92 B2 Antarctic Peninsula Ant.
40 C3 An Teallach mt U.K.
74 D2 Antelope Range mts U.S.A.
45 D4 Antequera Spain
73 F5 Anthony U.S.A.
54 B2 Anti Atlas mts Morocco
44 H5 Antibes France
67 H4 Anticosti, Île d' i. Can.
68 C3 Antigo U.S.A.
67 H4 Antigonish Can.
82 F6 Antigua Guatemala
83 M5 Antigua i. Antigua
61 M8 Antigua and Barbuda country Caribbean Sea
84 C2 Antiguo-Morelos Mex.
49 K7 Antikythira i. Greece
49 K7 Antikythiro, Steno chan. Greece
Anti Lebanon mts see Sharqi, Jebel esh
Antioch see Antakya
74 B3 Antioch CA U.S.A.
68 C4 Antioch IL U.S.A.
89 B3 Antioquia Col.
4 J9 Antipodes Islands is N.Z.
49 L5 Antipsara i. Greece
77 E5 Antlers U.S.A.
88 B2 Antofagasta Chile
88 C3 Antofalla, Vol. volc. Arg.
42 B4 Antoing Belgium
90 C4 Antonina Brazil
90 E1 Antônio r. Brazil
74 B3 Antonio r. U.S.A.
73 F4 Antonito U.S.A.
41 E3 Antrim U.K.
41 E2 Antrim Hills h. U.K.
57 E5 Antsalova Madag.
57 E5 Antsirabe Madag.
57 E5 Antsirañana Madag.
57 E5 Antsohihy Madag.
36 S3 Anttis Sweden
37 U6 Anttola Fin.
30 E2 Antu China
91 B3 Antuco Chile
91 B3 Antuco, Volcán volc. Chile
81 F2 Antwerp U.S.A.

99

49 N2 Basarabi Romania
91 E2 Basavilbaso Arg.
31 B4 Basay Phil.
31 B1 Basco Phil.
46 C7 Basel Switz.
68 B1 Basewood Lake l. U.S.A.
19 E5 Bashākerd, Kūhhā-ye mts Iran
64 G4 Bashaw Can.
59 H6 Bashee r. S. Africa
19 H3 Bashgul r. Afgh.
50 G4 Bashmakovo Rus. Fed.
18 C4 Bāsht Iran
51 E6 Bashtanka Ukr.
22 D4 Basi India
23 F5 Basia India
31 B5 Basilan i. Phil.
31 B5 Basilan Strait chan. Phil.
39 H6 Basildon U.K.
72 E2 Basin U.S.A.
39 F6 Basingstoke U.K.
17 K4 Bāsīra r. Iraq
23 G5 Basirhat India
81 K2 Baskahegan Lake l. U.S.A.
17 K2 Başkale Turkey
69 K2 Baskatong, Réservoir resr Can.
51 H5 Baskunchak, Ozero l. Rus. Fed.
Basle see Basel
22 D5 Basoda India
56 C3 Basoko Congo(Zaire)
17 L6 Basra Iraq
48 D2 Bassano del Grappa Italy
54 C4 Bassar Togo
57 D6 Bassas da India i. Ind. Ocean
25 B5 Bassein Myanmar
38 D3 Bassenthwaite Lake l. U.K.
54 A3 Basse Santa Su The Gambia
83 M5 Basse Terre Guadeloupe
83 M5 Basseterre St Kitts-Nevis
76 D3 Bassett U.S.A.
75 G5 Bassett Peak summit U.S.A.
81 J2 Bass Harbor U.S.A.
54 B3 Bassikounou Maur.
54 C4 Bassila Benin
40 F4 Bass Rock i. U.K.
6 E5 Bass Strait str. Austr.
43 G2 Bassum Ger.
37 N8 Båstad Sweden
18 D5 Bastak Iran
18 B2 Bastānābād Iran
43 J4 Bastheim Ger.
23 E4 Basti India
48 C3 Bastia Corsica France
42 D4 Bastogne Belgium
77 F5 Bastrop LA U.S.A.
77 D6 Bastrop TX U.S.A.
19 G5 Basul r. Pak.
54 C4 Bata Equatorial Guinea
83 H4 Batabanó, Golfo de b. Cuba
31 B2 Batac Phil.
31 C3 Batag i. Phil.
13 P3 Batagay Rus. Fed.
22 B2 Batai Pass Pak.
22 C3 Batala India
45 B3 Batalha Port.
32 C5 Batam i. Indon.
13 O3 Batamay Rus. Fed.
31 B1 Batan i. Phil.
56 B3 Batangafo C.A.R.
31 B3 Batangas Phil.
33 B3 Batanghari r. Indon.
32 A5 Batangtoru Indon.
31 B1 Batan Islands is Phil.
90 C3 Batatais Brazil
68 C5 Batavia IL U.S.A.
80 D3 Batavia NY U.S.A.
51 F6 Bataysk Rus. Fed.
69 E2 Batchawana r. Can.
68 E2 Batchawana Bay Can.
66 D4 Batchawana Mtn h. Can.
6 D3 Batchelor Austr.
69 E2 Batchewana Can.
32 B2 Bătdâmbâng Cambodia
8 H3 Batemans B. b. Austr.
8 H3 Batemans Bay Austr.
77 F5 Batesville AR U.S.A.
77 F5 Batesville MS U.S.A.
50 D3 Batetskiy Rus. Fed.
67 G4 Bath N.B. Can.
69 J3 Bath Ont. Can.
39 E6 Bath U.K.
81 J3 Bath ME U.S.A.
80 E3 Bath NY U.S.A.
40 E5 Bathgate U.K.
22 C3 Bathinda India
8 G2 Bathurst Austr.
67 G4 Bathurst Can.
59 G6 Bathurst S. Africa
63 J2 Bathurst I. i. Can.
62 H3 Bathurst Inlet N.W.T. Can.
6 D3 Bathurst Island i. Austr.
8 G3 Bathurst, L. l. Austr.
18 D3 Bāṭlāq-e Gavkhūnī marsh Iran
38 F4 Batley U.K.
8 G3 Batlow Austr.
17 H3 Batman Turkey
54 C1 Batna Alg.
18 C6 Baṭn aṭ Ṭarfā' depression S. Arabia
77 F6 Baton Rouge U.S.A.
55 D4 Batouri Cameroon
90 B1 Batovi Brazil
16 E4 Batroûn Lebanon
36 V1 Båtsfjord Norway
21 C5 Batticaloa Sri Lanka
48 F4 Battipaglia Italy
65 G4 Battle r. Can.
68 E4 Battle Creek U.S.A.
65 H4 Battleford Can.
72 C3 Battle Mountain U.S.A.
22 C1 Battura Glacier gl. Jammu and Kashmir
32 B4 Batu Gajah Malaysia
31 C5 Batulaki Phil.
17 H1 Bat'umi Georgia
33 B2 Batu Pahat Malaysia
33 A3 Batu, Pulau Pulau is Indon.
32 B4 Batu Puteh, Gunung mt Malaysia
25 E7 Baubau Indon.
54 C3 Bauchi Nigeria
76 E1 Baudette U.S.A.
89 A3 Baudo, Serranía de mts Col.
44 D3 Baugé France
43 H5 Bauland reg. Ger.
67 K3 Bauld, C. hd Can.
44 H3 Baume-les-Dames France
22 C2 Baundal India
90 C3 Bauru Brazil
90 B2 Baús Brazil
42 E4 Bausendorf Ger.
37 T8 Bauska Latvia
46 G5 Bautzen Ger.
58 E6 Baviaanskloofberg mts S. Africa
70 E6 Bavispe r. Mex.
39 J5 Bawdeswell U.K.
33 D4 Bawean i. Indon.
42 F2 Bawinkel Ger.
55 E2 Bawiti Egypt
54 B3 Bawku Ghana
32 A1 Bawlake Myanmar
27 A4 Bawolung China
26 B3 Baxi China
26 E2 Ba Xian Hebei China
27 C4 Ba Xian Sichuan China
79 D6 Baxley U.S.A.
83 J4 Bayamo Cuba
22 D4 Bayana India
24 B3 Bayan Har Shan mts China
24 C2 Bayanhongor Mongolia
26 B1 Bayan Mod China
26 C1 Bayan Obo China
30 A1 Bayan Qagan China
18 D4 Bayāẓ Iran
31 C4 Baybay Phil.
17 H1 Bayburt Turkey
69 F4 Bay City MI U.S.A.
77 D6 Bay City TX U.S.A.
12 H3 Baydaratskaya Guba b. Rus. Fed.
56 E3 Baydhabo Somalia
43 L5 Bayerischer Wald mts Ger.
43 J5 Bayern div. Ger.
68 B2 Bayfield U.S.A.
49 M5 Bayındır Turkey
16 F6 Bāyir Jordan
Baykal, Ozero l. see Baikal, Lake
Baykal Range mts see Baykal'sky Khrebet
24 C1 Baykal'sky Khrebet mts Rus. Fed.
17 H2 Baykan Turkey
31 B3 Bay, Laguna de lag. Phil.
12 G4 Baymak Rus. Fed.
18 D6 Baynūna'h reg. U.A.E.
31 B2 Bayombong Phil.
44 D5 Bayonne France
31 B4 Bayo Point pt Phil.
19 F2 Bayramaly Turkm.
49 M5 Bayramiç Turkey
43 K5 Bayreuth Ger.
77 F6 Bay St Louis U.S.A.
81 G4 Bay Shore U.S.A.
39 E5 Bayston Hill U.K.
19 G2 Baysun Uzbek.
19 G2 Baysuntau, Gory mts Uzbek.
77 E6 Baytown U.S.A.
9 F3 Bay View N.Z.
45 E4 Baza Spain
17 L1 Bazardyuzi, Gora mt Azer./Rus. Fed.
18 C2 Bāzār-e Māsāl Iran
17 K2 Bāzargān Iran
51 H4 Bazarnyy Karabulak Rus. Fed.
57 D6 Bazaruto, Ilha do i. Moz.
19 G5 Bazdar Pak.
26 C4 Bazhong China
19 F5 Bazman Iran
19 F4 Bazmān, Kūh-e mt Iran
32 C3 Be r. Vietnam
76 C2 Beach U.S.A.
69 J3 Beachburg Can.
81 F5 Beach Haven U.S.A.
8 C4 Beachport Austr.
81 F5 Beachwood U.S.A.
39 H7 Beachy Head hd U.K.
80 E4 Beacon U.S.A.
59 G6 Beacon Bay S. Africa
27 □ Beacon Hill h. H.K. China
39 G6 Beaconsfield U.K.
88 C8 Beagle, Canal chan. Arg.
6 C3 Beagle Gulf b. Austr.
57 E5 Bealanana Madag.
39 E7 Beaminster U.K.
72 E3 Bear r. U.S.A.
65 N2 Bear Cove b. Can.
66 C4 Beardmore Can.
92 B4 Beardmore Gl. gl. Ant.
68 B5 Beardstown U.S.A.
66 D3 Bear Island i. Can.
12 C2 Bear Island i. Svalbard
72 E3 Bear L. l. U.S.A.
64 D3 Bear Lake Can.
22 D4 Bearma r. India
40 A4 Bearnaraigh i. U.K.
72 E1 Bear Paw Mtn mt U.S.A.
92 A3 Bear Pen. pen. Ant.
66 B3 Bearskin Lake Can.
74 B2 Bear Valley U.S.A.
22 C3 Beas r. India
22 C3 Beas Dam dam India
83 K5 Beata, Cabo c. Dom. Rep.
83 K5 Beata, I. i. Dom. Rep.
76 D3 Beatrice U.S.A.
64 E3 Beatton r. Can.
64 E3 Beatton River Can.
74 D3 Beatty U.S.A.
66 E4 Beattyville Can.
44 G5 Beaucaire France
88 E8 Beauchene I. i. Falkland Is
8 D4 Beaufort Austr.
33 E1 Beaufort Malaysia
79 D5 Beaufort U.S.A.
62 D2 Beaufort Sea Can./U.S.A.
58 E6 Beaufort West S. Africa
66 F4 Beauharnois Can.
40 D3 Beauly U.K.
40 D3 Beauly Firth est. U.K.
39 C4 Beaumaris U.K.
42 C4 Beaumont Belgium
9 B6 Beaumont N.Z.
77 F6 Beaumont MS U.S.A.
80 B5 Beaumont OH U.S.A.
77 E6 Beaumont TX U.S.A.
44 G3 Beaune France
44 D3 Beaupréau France
42 A4 Beauquesne France
42 C4 Beauraing Belgium
65 K4 Beausejour Can.
44 F2 Beauvais France
65 H3 Beauval Can.
42 A4 Beauval France
75 F2 Beaver U.S.A.
62 H4 Beaver r. Alta. Can.
64 D2 Beaver r. B.C./Y.T. Can.
66 C2 Beaver r. Ont. Can.
75 F2 Beaver r. U.S.A.
64 A2 Beaver Creek Can.
78 C4 Beaver Dam KY U.S.A.
68 C4 Beaver Dam WV U.S.A.
80 C4 Beaver Falls U.S.A.
72 D2 Beaverhead Mts mts U.S.A.
65 K4 Beaverhill L. l. Man. Can.
65 J2 Beaverhill L. l. N.W.T. Can.
68 E3 Beaver Island i. U.S.A.
77 E4 Beaver L. resr U.S.A.
64 F3 Beaverlodge Can.
80 D4 Beaver Run Reservoir U.S.A.
22 C4 Beawar India
91 C2 Beazley Arg.
90 C3 Bebedouro Brazil
39 D4 Bebington U.K.
43 H4 Bebra Ger.
66 F1 Bécard, Lac l. Can.
39 J5 Beccles U.K.
49 J2 Bečej Yugo.
45 C1 Becerreá Spain
54 B1 Béchar Alg.
43 J5 Bechhofen Ger.
80 C6 Beckley U.S.A.
43 G3 Beckum Ger.
43 L4 Bečov nad Teplou Czech Rep.
38 F3 Bedale U.K.
42 E4 Bedburg Ger.
81 J2 Beddington U.S.A.
56 D3 Bedelē Eth.
43 G1 Bederkesa Ger.
81 G2 Bedford Can.
59 J4 Bedford S. Africa
39 G5 Bedford U.K.
78 C4 Bedford IN U.S.A.
81 H3 Bedford MA U.S.A.
80 D4 Bedford PA U.S.A.
80 D6 Bedford VA U.S.A.
39 G5 Bedford Level lowland U.K.
8 F2 Bedgerebong Austr.
38 F2 Bedlington U.K.
32 □ Bedok Sing.
32 □ Bedok Res. resr Sing.
75 H2 Bedrock U.S.A.
42 E1 Bedum Neth.
39 F5 Bedworth U.K.
80 B5 Beech Fork Lake l. U.S.A.
68 C2 Beechwood U.S.A.
8 F4 Beechworth Austr.
8 H3 Beecroft Pen. pen. Austr.
43 L2 Beelitz Ger.
7 F4 Beenleigh Austr.
41 A5 Beenoskee h. Rep. of Ireland
42 B3 Beernem Belgium
16 E6 Beersheba Israel
Be'ér Sheva' see Beersheba
58 E6 Beervlei Dam dam S. Africa
43 L2 Beetzsee l. Ger.
77 D6 Beeville U.S.A.
56 C3 Befale Congo(Zaire)
57 E5 Befandriana Avaratra Madag.
8 G4 Bega Austr.
22 B3 Begari r. Pak.
45 H2 Begur, Cap de pt Spain
23 F4 Begusarai India
19 E3 Behābād Iran
87 H3 Béhague, Pointe pt Fr. Guiana
18 C4 Behbehān Iran
64 C3 Behm Canal in. U.S.A.
92 B3 Behrendt Mts mts Ant.
18 D2 Behshahr Iran
19 G3 Behsūd Afgh.
24 E2 Bei'an China
27 C4 Beibei China
26 B4 Beichuan China
27 C6 Beihai China
27 D6 Bei Jiang r. China
26 E2 Beijing China
26 E1 Beijing div. China
42 E2 Beilen Neth.
27 C7 Beili China
27 D6 Beiliu China
43 K5 Beilngries Ger.
40 C5 Beinn an Oir h. U.K.
40 D3 Beinn Dearg mt U.K.
30 A3 Beipiao China
57 D5 Beira Moz.
26 E3 Beiru r. China
16 E5 Beirut Lebanon
57 C6 Beitbridge Zimbabwe
40 D5 Beith U.K.
47 L7 Beiuş Romania
30 A3 Beizhen China
45 C3 Beja Port.
54 C1 Béja Tunisia
54 C1 Bejaïa Alg.
45 D2 Béjar Spain
19 E3 Bejestān Iran
22 B3 Beji r. Pak.
47 K7 Békés Hungary
47 K7 Békéscsaba Hungary
57 E6 Bekily Madag.
28 J3 Bekkai Japan
54 B4 Bekwai Ghana
23 E4 Bela India
19 G5 Bela Pak.
22 B3 Belab r. Pak.
59 H2 Bela-Bela S. Africa
55 D4 Bélabo Cameroon
49 J2 Bela Crkva Yugo.
81 E5 Bel Air U.S.A.
45 D3 Belalcázar Spain
43 L5 Bělá nad Radbuzou Czech Rep.
8 E2 Belaraboon Austr.
35 H3 Belarus country Europe
90 A3 Bela Vista Brazil
57 D6 Bela Vista Moz.
32 A5 Belawan Indon.
13 T3 Belaya r. Rus. Fed.
51 G6 Belaya Glina Rus. Fed.
51 G5 Belaya Kalitva Rus. Fed.
50 J3 Belaya Kholunitsa Rus. Fed.
47 J5 Bełchatów Pol.
80 B6 Belcher U.S.A.
63 K4 Belcher Islands is Can.
19 G3 Belchiragh Afgh.
16 F2 Belcik Turkey
41 D3 Belcoo U.K.
69 J1 Belcourt Can.
74 B1 Belden U.S.A.
56 E3 Beledweyne Somalia
18 D2 Belek Turkm.
87 J4 Belém Brazil
88 C3 Belén Arg.
16 F3 Belen Turkey
73 F5 Belen U.S.A.
7 G3 Bélep, Îles is New Caledonia
50 F4 Belev Rus. Fed.
9 D5 Belfast N.Z.
59 J2 Belfast S. Africa
41 F3 Belfast U.K.
81 J2 Belfast U.S.A.
41 F3 Belfast Lough in. U.K.
76 C2 Belfield U.S.A.
38 F2 Belford U.K.
44 H3 Belfort France
21 A3 Belgaum India
43 M3 Belgern Ger.
34 F3 Belgium country Europe
51 F5 Belgorod Rus. Fed.
51 F5 Belgorodskaya Oblast' div. Rus. Fed.
72 E2 Belgrade U.S.A.
49 J2 Belgrade Yugo.
54 D4 Beli Nigeria
48 E6 Belice r. Sicily Italy
50 G4 Belinskiy Rus. Fed.
33 C3 Belinyu Indon.
33 C3 Belitung i. Indon.
82 G5 Belize Belize
61 K8 Belize country Central America
28 E2 Belkina, Mys pt Rus. Fed.
13 P2 Bel'kovskiy, O. i. Rus. Fed.
8 G2 Bell r. Austr.
64 D4 Bella Bella Can.
44 E3 Bellac France
64 D4 Bella Coola Can.
77 E6 Bellaire U.S.A.
21 B3 Bellary India
91 F1 Bella Unión Uru.
80 B4 Bellefontaine U.S.A.
80 E4 Bellefonte U.S.A.
76 C2 Belle Fourche U.S.A.
76 C2 Belle Fourche r. U.S.A.
44 G3 Bellegarde-sur-Valserine France
79 D7 Belle Glade U.S.A.
44 C3 Belle-Île i. France
67 K3 Belle Isle i. Can.
63 N4 Belle Isle, Strait of Nfld Can.
67 J3 Belle Isle, Strait of str. Can.
75 G4 Bellemont U.S.A.
68 A5 Belle Plaine U.S.A.
69 H2 Belleterre Can.
69 J3 Belleville Can.
76 D4 Belleville U.S.A.
68 B4 Bellevue IA U.S.A.
72 D3 Bellevue ID U.S.A.
80 B4 Bellevue OH U.S.A.
72 B2 Bellevue WA U.S.A.
Bellin see Kangirsuk
38 E2 Bellingham U.K.
72 B1 Bellingham U.S.A.
92 B2 Bellingshausen Rus. Fed. Base Ant.
92 A3 Bellingshausen Sea sea Ant.
46 D7 Bellinzona Switz.
89 B3 Bello Col.
81 G3 Bellows Falls U.S.A.
22 B3 Bellpat Pak.
81 F5 Belltown U.S.A.
48 E1 Belluno Italy
21 B3 Belluru India
91 D2 Bell Ville Arg.
58 C6 Bellville S. Africa
43 G2 Belm Ger.
58 F4 Belmont S. Africa
40 □ Belmont U.K.
80 D3 Belmont U.S.A.
90 E1 Belmonte Brazil
82 G5 Belmopan Belize
41 B3 Belmullet Rep. of Ireland
42 B4 Belœil Belgium
81 G2 Beloeil Can.
24 E1 Belogorsk Rus. Fed.
57 E6 Beloha Madag.
90 D2 Belo Horizonte Brazil
76 D4 Beloit KS U.S.A.
68 C4 Beloit WV U.S.A.
50 E1 Belomorsk Rus. Fed.
23 G5 Belonia India
51 F6 Belorechensk Rus. Fed.
16 F3 Belören Turkey
12 G4 Beloretsk Rus. Fed.
Belorussia country see Belarus
57 E5 Belo Tsiribihina Madag.
50 F1 Beloye Rus. Fed.
Beloye More g. see White Sea
50 F2 Beloye, Ozero l. Rus. Fed.
50 F2 Belozersk Rus. Fed.
80 C5 Belpre U.S.A.
72 E2 Belt U.S.A.
74 D3 Belted Range mts U.S.A.
77 D6 Belton U.S.A.
21 A3 Belur India
31 A5 Beluran Malaysia
68 C4 Belvidere U.S.A.
50 H3 Belyshevo Rus. Fed.
50 E4 Belyy Rus. Fed.
12 J2 Belyy, O. i. Rus. Fed.
43 L2 Belzig Ger.
68 C6 Bement U.S.A.
76 E2 Bemidji U.S.A.
56 C4 Bena Dibele Congo(Zaire)
40 D4 Ben Alder mt U.K.
8 E4 Benalla Austr.
48 D6 Ben Arous Tunisia
45 D1 Benavente Spain
40 E3 Ben Avon mt U.K.
41 B4 Benbaun h. Rep. of Ireland
40 A3 Benbecula i. U.K.
41 C3 Benbulben h. Rep. of Ireland
41 E3 Benburb U.K.
40 C4 Ben Cruachan mt U.K.
72 B2 Bend U.S.A.
59 G5 Bendearg mt S. Africa
8 H1 Bendemeer Austr.
56 E3 Bender-Bayla Somalia
8 E4 Bendigo Austr.
8 G4 Bendoc Austr.
57 D5 Bene Moz.
81 J2 Benedicta U.S.A.
67 J3 Benedict, Mount h. Can.
57 E6 Benenitra Madag.
46 G6 Benešov Czech Rep.
42 E6 Bénestroff France
48 F4 Benevento Italy
26 F3 Beng r. China
10 K8 Bengal, Bay of sea Asia
56 C3 Bengamisa Congo(Zaire)
26 E3 Bengbu China
32 B5 Bengkalis Indon.
33 B3 Bengkulu Indon.
37 N7 Bengtsfors Sweden
57 B5 Benguela Angola
16 C6 Benha Egypt
40 B4 Ben Hiant h. U.K.
40 D2 Ben Hope mt U.K.
56 C3 Beni Congo(Zaire)
86 E6 Beni r. Bol.
54 B1 Beni-Abbès Alg.
45 F3 Benidorm Spain
54 B1 Beni Mellal Morocco
53 E5 Benin country Africa
54 C4 Benin, Bight of g. Africa
54 C4 Benin City Nigeria
54 B1 Beni-Saf Alg.
55 F2 Beni Suef Egypt
91 E3 Benito Juárez Arg.
31 B2 Benito Soliven Phil.
86 E4 Benjamim Constant Brazil
82 B2 Benjamín Hill Mex.
6 D2 Benjina Indon.
76 C3 Benkelman U.S.A.
40 D2 Ben Klibreck mt U.K.
40 D4 Ben Lawers mt U.K.
40 D4 Ben Lomond mt U.K.
40 D2 Ben Loyal h. U.K.
40 D4 Ben Lui mt U.K.
40 E3 Ben Macdui mt U.K.
40 D4 Ben More mt Scot. U.K.
40 B4 Ben More mt Scot. U.K.
40 D2 Ben More Assynt mt U.K.
9 C6 Benmore, L. l. N.Z.
13 Q2 Bennetta, O. i. Rus. Fed.
40 C4 Ben Nevis mt U.K.
81 G3 Bennington U.S.A.
59 H3 Benoni S. Africa
55 D4 Bénoué, Parc National de la nat. park Cameroon
43 G5 Bensheim Ger.
75 G6 Benson AZ U.S.A.
76 E2 Benson MN U.S.A.
19 E5 Bent Iran
33 B2 Benta Seberang Malaysia
80 D6 Bent Creek U.S.A.
25 E7 Benteng Indon.
6 D3 Bentinck I. i. Austr.
32 A3 Bentinck I. i. Myanmar
38 F4 Bentley U.K.
81 K2 Benton Can.
77 E5 Benton AR U.S.A.
74 C3 Benton CA U.S.A.
78 B4 Benton IL U.S.A.
68 D4 Benton Harbor U.S.A.
32 C3 Bên Tre Vietnam
32 B5 Bentung Malaysia
54 D4 Benue r. Nigeria
40 D4 Ben Vorlich mt U.K.
41 B4 Benwee h. Rep. of Ireland
41 B3 Benwee Head hd Rep. of Ireland
40 D3 Ben Wyvis mt U.K.
30 C3 Benxi Liaoning China
30 B3 Benxi Liaoning China
31 C5 Beo Indon.
Beograd see Belgrade
22 E5 Beohari India
54 B4 Béoumi Côte d'Ivoire
27 C5 Bepian Jiang r. China
29 B8 Beppu Japan
7 H3 Beqa i. Fiji
22 C4 Berach r. India
67 G2 Bérard, Lac l. Can.
22 D5 Berasia India
32 A5 Berastagi Indon.
49 H4 Berat Albania
33 E3 Beratus, Gunung mt Indon.
25 F7 Berau, Teluk b. Indon.
55 F3 Berber Sudan
56 E2 Berbera Somalia
56 B3 Berbérati C.A.R.
44 E1 Berck France
17 K1 Berd Armenia
13 O3 Berdigestyakh Rus. Fed.
24 A1 Berdsk Rus. Fed.
51 F6 Berdyans'k Ukr.
51 D5 Berdychiv Ukr.
80 A6 Berea U.S.A.
51 B5 Berehove Ukr.
6 E2 Bereina P.N.G.
65 K4 Berens r. Can.
65 K4 Berens River Can.
76 D3 Beresford U.S.A.
51 C5 Berezhany Ukr.
51 D6 Berezivka Ukr.
51 C5 Berezne Ukr.
50 G2 Bereznik Rus. Fed.
12 H3 Berezovo Rus. Fed.
43 K3 Berga Ger.
45 G1 Berga Spain
49 M5 Bergama Turkey
48 C2 Bergamo Italy
37 P6 Bergby Sweden
46 F3 Bergen Ger.
43 H2 Bergen Ger.
37 J6 Bergen Norway
42 C3 Bergen op Zoom Neth.
44 E4 Bergerac France
42 C6 Bergères-lès-Vertus France
42 E4 Bergheim Ger.
42 F4 Bergisches Land reg. Ger.
42 F4 Bergisch Gladbach Ger.
58 B1 Bergland Namibia
68 C2 Bergland U.S.A.
37 P6 Bergsjö Sweden
36 R4 Bergsviken Sweden
43 J5 Bergtheim Ger.
42 A4 Bergues France
42 E1 Bergum Neth.
59 H4 Bergville S. Africa
33 B3 Berhala, Selat chan. Indon.
13 S4 Beringa, O. i. Rus. Fed.
42 D3 Beringen Belgium
13 T3 Beringovskiy Rus. Fed.
13 T4 Bering Sea sea Pac. Oc.
62 B3 Bering Strait str. Rus. Fed./U.S.A.
18 E5 Berīzak Iran
36 M5 Berkåk Norway
42 E2 Berkel r. Neth.
74 A3 Berkeley U.S.A.
80 D5 Berkeley Springs U.S.A.
42 D2 Berkhout Neth.
92 B3 Berkner I. i. Ant.
49 K3 Berkovitsa Bulg.
39 F6 Berkshire Downs h. U.K.
42 C3 Berlare Belgium
36 V1 Berlevåg Norway
43 M2 Berlin Ger.
81 F5 Berlin MD U.S.A.
81 H2 Berlin NH U.S.A.
80 D5 Berlin PA U.S.A.
68 C4 Berlin WV U.S.A.
63 K2 Berlinguet Inlet in. Can.
80 C4 Berlin Lake l. U.S.A.
8 H4 Bermagui Austr.
91 D4 Bermeja, Pta pt Arg.
84 B1 Bermejillo Mex.
86 F8 Bermejo Bol.
91 C1 Bermejo r. San Juan Arg.
88 D2 Bermejo r. Chaco/Formosa Arg./Bol.
61 M6 Bermuda terr. Atl. Ocean
96 E3 Bermuda Rise sea feature Atl. Ocean
46 C7 Bern Switz.
73 F5 Bernalillo U.S.A.
88 A7 Bernardo O'Higgins, Parque Nacional nat. park Chile
91 D3 Bernasconi Arg.
43 K3 Bernburg (Saale) Ger.
43 G1 Berne Ger.
68 E5 Berne U.S.A.
46 C7 Berner Alpen mts Switz.
40 A3 Berneray i. U.K.
63 K2 Bernier Bay b. Can.
6 B4 Bernier I. i. Austr.
46 E7 Bernina Pass Switz.
42 F5 Bernkastel-Kues Ger.
57 E6 Beroroha Madag.
46 G6 Beroun Czech Rep.
46 F5 Berounka r. Czech Rep.
8 C3 Berri Austr.
40 E2 Berriedale U.K.
8 E3 Berrigan Austr.
8 H3 Berrima Austr.
45 H4 Berrouaghia Alg.
8 H3 Berry Austr.
44 E3 Berry reg. France
74 A2 Berryessa, Lake l. U.S.A.
79 E7 Berry Islands is Bahamas
58 B3 Berseba Namibia
43 F2 Bersenbrück Ger.
51 D5 Bershad' Ukr.
33 B1 Bertam Malaysia
87 K5 Bertolínia Brazil
55 D4 Bertoua Cameroon
41 B4 Bertraghboy Bay b. Rep. of Ireland
7 H2 Beru i. Kiribati
86 F4 Beruri Brazil
8 E5 Berwick Austr.
81 E4 Berwick U.S.A.
38 E2 Berwick-upon-Tweed U.K.
64 F3 Berwyn Can.
39 D5 Berwyn h. U.K.
51 E6 Beryslav Ukr.
57 E5 Besalampy Madag.
44 H3 Besançon France
19 G2 Beshir Turkm.
19 G2 Beshkent Uzbek.
18 D4 Beshneh Iran
17 H3 Beşiri Turkey
51 H7 Beslan Rus. Fed.
65 H3 Besnard Lake l. Can.
16 F3 Besni Turkey
41 E3 Bessbrook U.K.
79 C5 Bessemer AL U.S.A.
68 B2 Bessemer MI U.S.A.
57 E6 Betanty Madag.
45 B1 Betanzos Spain
55 D4 Bétaré Oya Cameroon
59 H3 Bethal S. Africa
58 B3 Bethanie Namibia
76 E3 Bethany MO U.S.A.
77 D5 Bethany OK U.S.A.
62 B3 Bethel AK U.S.A.
81 H2 Bethel ME U.S.A.
68 A6 Bethel MO U.S.A.
80 A5 Bethel OH U.S.A.
80 D4 Bethel Park U.S.A.
39 C4 Bethesda U.K.
80 E5 Bethesda MD U.S.A.
80 C4 Bethesda OH U.S.A.
58 F5 Bethesdaweg S. Africa
59 H4 Bethlehem S. Africa
81 F4 Bethlehem U.S.A.
16 E6 Bethlehem West Bank
59 F5 Bethulie S. Africa
42 A4 Béthune France
89 C2 Betijoque Venez.
57 E6 Betioky Madag.
14 F2 Betpak-Dala plain Kazak.
57 E6 Betroka Madag.
16 E5 Bet She'an Israel
67 G4 Betsiamites Can.
67 G4 Betsiamites r. Can.
57 E5 Betsiboka r. Madag.
68 D3 Betsie, Pt pt U.S.A.
68 E2 Betsy Lake l. U.S.A.
68 B5 Bettendorf U.S.A.
23 F4 Bettiah India
40 D2 Bettyhill U.K.
41 E4 Bettystown Rep. of Ireland
22 D5 Betul India
42 D3 Betuwe reg. Neth.
22 D4 Betwa r. India
39 D4 Betws-y-coed U.K.
43 F4 Betzdorf Ger.
8 D3 Beulah Austr.
68 D3 Beulah U.S.A.
39 H6 Beult r. U.K.
38 G4 Beverley U.K.
62 C4 Beverley, L. l. U.S.A.
81 H3 Beverly MA U.S.A.
80 C5 Beverly OH U.S.A.
74 C4 Beverly Hills U.S.A.
65 J2 Beverly Lake l. Can.
43 G1 Beverstedt Ger.
43 H3 Beverungen Ger.
42 C2 Beverwijk Neth.
42 F5 Bexbach Ger.
39 H7 Bexhill U.K.
18 B3 Beyānlū Iran
16 C3 Bey Dağları mts Turkey
16 B1 Beykoz Turkey
54 B4 Beyla Guinea
17 L2 Beyläqan Azer.
16 C1 Beypazarı Turkey
16 F2 Beypınarı Turkey
21 A4 Beypore India
Beyrouth see Beirut
16 C3 Beyşehir Turkey
16 C3 Beyşehir Gölü l. Turkey
51 F6 Beysug r. Rus. Fed.
17 J3 Beytüşşebap Turkey
18 E3 Bezameh Iran
50 J3 Bezbozhnik Rus. Fed.
50 D3 Bezhanitsy Rus. Fed.
50 F3 Bezhetsk Rus. Fed.
44 F5 Béziers France
Bezwada see Vijayawada
22 B4 Bhabhar India
23 E4 Bhabua India
22 B5 Bhadar r. India
23 F4 Bhadgaon Nepal
23 E4 Bhadohi India
22 C3 Bhadra India
21 C2 Bhadrachalam India
Bhadrachalam Road Sta. see Kottagudem
23 F5 Bhadrakh India
21 A3 Bhadra Reservoir India
21 A3 Bhadravati India
22 A3 Bhag Pak.
22 D2 Bhaga r. India
23 F4 Bhagalpur India
23 G5 Bhagirathi r. India
23 D5 Bhainsdehi India
23 G4 Bhairab Bazar Bangl.
23 E4 Bhairawa Nepal
21 B2 Bhalki India
24 B4 Bhamo Myanmar
21 C2 Bhamragarh India
22 D4 Bhander India
23 F6 Bhanjanagar India
22 C4 Bhanpura India
22 D5 Bhanrer Range h. India
22 D4 Bharatpur India
23 H4 Bhareli r. India
19 F5 Bhari r. Pak.
22 C5 Bharuch India
23 E5 Bhatapara India
21 A3 Bhatkal India
23 G5 Bhatpara India
21 B4 Bhavani India
21 B4 Bhavani r. India
22 C5 Bhavnagar India
22 C3 Bhawana Pak.
23 E6 Bhawanipatna India
59 J3 Bhekuzulu S. Africa
23 E3 Bheri r. Nepal
22 C4 Bhilwara India
21 B2 Bhima r. India
21 C2 Bhimavaram India
22 D4 Bhind India
22 C4 Bhindar India
23 E4 Bhinga India
22 C4 Bhinmal India
22 D3 Bhiwani India
23 F4 Bhojpur Nepal
21 B2 Bhongir India
59 H5 Bhongweni S. Africa
22 D5 Bhopal India
21 C2 Bhopalpatnam India
21 A2 Bhor India
23 F5 Bhuban India
23 F5 Bhubaneshwar India
22 B5 Bhuj India
22 C5 Bhusawal India
10 K7 Bhutan country Asia
22 B4 Bhuttewala India
18 E5 Biābān mts Iran
22 C2 Biafo Gl. gl. Pak.
25 F7 Biak Indon.
25 F7 Biak i. Indon.
47 L4 Biała Podlaska Pol.
46 G4 Białogard Pol.
47 L4 Białystok Pol.
54 B4 Biankouma Côte d'Ivoire
30 B1 Bianzhao China
18 D2 Biārjmand Iran
44 D5 Biarritz France
18 B5 Bi'ār Tabrāk well S. Arabia
46 D7 Biasca Switz.
28 G3 Bibai Japan
57 B5 Bibala Angola
8 G4 Bibbenluke Austr.
48 D3 Bibbiena Italy
46 D6 Biberach an der Riß Ger.
23 G4 Bibiyana r. Bangl.
43 G5 Biblis Ger.
16 C2 Biçer Turkey
39 F6 Bicester U.K.
65 G4 Biche, Lac la l. Can.
51 G7 Bichvint'a Georgia
6 D3 Bickerton I. i. Austr.
39 D7 Bickleigh U.K.
75 G2 Bicknell U.S.A.
57 B5 Bicuari, Parque Nacional do nat. park Angola
54 C4 Bida Nigeria
31 A5 Bidadari, Tg pt Malaysia
18 D4 Bida Khabit Iran
21 B2 Bidar India
19 E6 Bidbid Oman
81 H3 Biddeford U.S.A.
42 D2 Biddinghuizen Neth.
40 C4 Bidean Nam Bian mt U.K.
39 C6 Bideford U.K.
39 C6 Bideford Bay b. U.K.
47 L4 Biebrza r. Pol.
43 G4 Biedenkopf Ger.
46 C7 Biel Switz.
46 H5 Bielawa Pol.
43 G2 Bielefeld Ger.
48 C2 Biella Italy
47 J6 Bielsko-Biała Pol.
47 L4 Bielsk Podlaski Pol.
43 J1 Bienenbüttel Ger.
32 C3 Biên Hoa Vietnam
Bienne see Biel
66 F2 Bienville, Lac l. Can.
42 C3 Biesbosch, Nationaal Park de nat. park Neth.
59 F3 Biesiesvlei S. Africa
43 H6 Bietigheim-Bissingen Ger.
42 D5 Bièvre Belgium
56 B4 Bifoun Gabon
67 J3 Big r. Can.
74 A2 Big r. U.S.A.
51 C7 Biga Turkey
16 B2 Bigadiç Turkey
49 M5 Biga Yarımadası pen. Turkey
68 D2 Big Bay U.S.A.
68 D3 Big Bay de Noc b. U.S.A.
74 D4 Big Bear Lake U.S.A.
72 E2 Big Belt Mts mts U.S.A.
59 J3 Big Bend Swaziland
77 C6 Big Bend Nat. Park U.S.A.
77 F5 Big Black r. U.S.A.
39 D7 Bigbury-on-Sea U.K.
79 D7 Big Cypress Nat. Preserve res. U.S.A.
68 C3 Big Eau Pleine Reservoir U.S.A.
65 L5 Big Falls U.S.A.
65 H4 Biggar Can.
40 E5 Biggar U.K.
64 B3 Bigger, Mt mt Can.
39 G5 Biggleswade U.K.
72 D2 Big Hole r. U.S.A.
72 F2 Bighorn r. U.S.A.
72 E2 Bighorn Canyon Nat. Recreation Area res. U.S.A.
72 F2 Bighorn Mountains U.S.A.
79 F7 Bight, The Bahamas
63 L3 Big Island i. N.W.T. Can.
64 F2 Big Island i. Can.
81 K2 Big Lake l. U.S.A.
54 A3 Bignona Senegal
80 D6 Big Otter r. U.S.A.
74 C3 Big Pine U.S.A.
68 E4 Big Rapids U.S.A.
68 C3 Big Rib r. U.S.A.
65 H4 Big River Can.
68 D3 Big Sable Pt pt U.S.A.
64 C2 Big Salmon r. Can.
65 K3 Big Sand Lake l. Can.
75 F4 Big Sandy r. U.S.A.
76 D2 Big Sioux r. U.S.A.
74 D2 Big Smokey Valley v. U.S.A.
77 C5 Big Spring U.S.A.
76 C3 Big Springs U.S.A.
80 B6 Big Stone Gap U.S.A.
74 B3 Big Sur U.S.A.
72 E2 Big Timber U.S.A.
66 C3 Big Trout Lake Can.
66 C3 Big Trout Lake l. Can.
75 G3 Big Water U.S.A.
69 H3 Bigwin Can.
48 F2 Bihać Bos.-Herz.
23 F4 Bihar div. India
23 F4 Bihar Sharif India
28 J3 Bihoro Japan
47 L7 Bihor, Vârful mt Romania
54 A3 Bijagós, Arquipélago dos is Guinea-Bissau
22 C4 Bijainagar India
21 A2 Bijapur India
18 B3 Bījār Iran
21 C2 Bijārpur India
49 H2 Bijeljina Bos.-Herz.
49 H3 Bijelo Polje Yugo.
27 B5 Bijie China
19 E5 Bijnābād Iran
23 G4 Bijni India
22 D3 Bijnor India
22 B3 Bijnot Pak.
22 C3 Bikaner India
24 F2 Bikin Rus. Fed.
28 D1 Bikin r. Rus. Fed.
4 H4 Bikini i. Marshall Is
56 B4 Bikoro Congo(Zaire)
26 B3 Bikou China
22 C4 Bilara India

85 E4 Brazil country S. America
96 H7 Brazil Basin sea feature Atl. Ocean
77 D5 Brazos r. U.S.A.
56 B4 Brazzaville Congo
49 H2 Brčko Bos.-Herz.
9 A6 Breaksea Sd in. N.Z.
9 E1 Bream Bay b. N.Z.
9 E1 Bream Head hd N.Z.
39 C6 Brechfa U.K.
40 F4 Brechin U.K.
42 C3 Brecht Belgium
76 D2 Breckenridge MN U.S.A.
77 D5 Breckenridge TX U.S.A.
46 H6 Břeclav Czech Rep.
39 D6 Brecon U.K.
39 D6 Brecon Beacons h. U.K.
39 D6 Brecon Beacons National Park U.K.
42 C3 Breda Neth.
58 D7 Bredasdorp S. Africa
8 G3 Bredbo Austr.
43 L2 Breddin Ger.
42 E3 Bredevoort Neth.
36 O3 Bredviken Norway
42 D3 Bree Belgium
80 D5 Breezewood U.S.A.
46 D7 Bregenz Austria
36 B4 Breiðafjörður b. Iceland
36 F4 Breiðdalsvík Iceland
43 G4 Breidenbach Ger.
46 C6 Breisach am Rhein Ger.
43 J1 Breitenfelde Ger.
43 J5 Breitengüßbach Ger.
36 S1 Breivikbotn Norway
87 J6 Brejinho de Nazaré Brazil
36 L5 Brekstad Norway
43 G1 Bremen Ger.
79 C5 Bremen GA U.S.A.
68 D5 Bremen IN U.S.A.
43 G1 Bremerhaven Ger.
72 B2 Bremerton U.S.A.
43 H1 Bremervörde Ger.
42 F4 Bremm Ger.
77 D6 Brenham U.S.A.
36 N4 Brenna Norway
46 E7 Brenner Pass Austria/Italy
69 H2 Brent Can.
48 D2 Brenta r. Italy
39 H6 Brentwood U.K.
74 B3 Brentwood CA U.S.A.
81 G4 Brentwood NY U.S.A.
48 D2 Brescia Italy
48 D1 Bressanone Italy
40 □ Bressay i. U.K.
44 D3 Bressuire France
51 B4 Brest Belarus
44 B2 Brest France
44 C2 Bretagne reg. France
42 A5 Breteuil France
77 F6 Breton Sound b. U.S.A.
9 E1 Brett, Cape c. N.Z.
43 G5 Bretten Ger.
39 E4 Bretton U.K.
79 D5 Brevard U.S.A.
87 H4 Breves Brazil
68 E2 Brevort U.S.A.
6 E4 Brewarrina Austr.
81 J2 Brewer U.S.A.
72 C1 Brewster U.S.A.
77 G6 Brewton U.S.A.
59 H3 Breyten S. Africa
Brezhnev see Naberezhnyye Chelny
47 J6 Brezno Slovakia
48 G2 Brezovo Polje h. Croatia
56 C3 Bria C.A.R.
44 H4 Briançon France
8 F3 Bribbaree Austr.
51 C5 Briceni Moldova
44 H4 Bric Froid mt France/Italy
41 C5 Bride r. Rep. of Ireland
75 G1 Bridgeland U.S.A.
39 D6 Bridgend U.K.
40 D4 Bridge of Orchy U.K.
74 C2 Bridgeport CA U.S.A.
81 G4 Bridgeport CT U.S.A.
76 C3 Bridgeport NE U.S.A.
72 E2 Bridger U.S.A.
72 F3 Bridger Peak summit U.S.A.
81 F5 Bridgeton U.S.A.
83 N6 Bridgetown Barbados
67 H5 Bridgewater Can.
81 K1 Bridgewater U.S.A.
8 C5 Bridgewater, C. hd Austr.
39 E5 Bridgnorth U.K.
81 H2 Bridgton U.S.A.
39 D6 Bridgwater U.K.
39 D6 Bridgwater Bay b. U.K.
38 G3 Bridlington U.K.
38 G3 Bridlington Bay b. U.K.
39 E7 Bridport U.K.
46 C7 Brig Switz.
38 G4 Brigg U.K.
72 D3 Brigham City U.S.A.
8 F4 Bright Austr.
39 J6 Brightlingsea U.K.
69 J3 Brighton Can.
9 C6 Brighton N.Z.
39 G7 Brighton U.K.
69 F4 Brighton U.S.A.
44 H5 Brignoles France
54 A3 Brikama The Gambia
43 G3 Brilon Ger.
48 G4 Brindisi Italy
91 D1 Brinkmann Arg.
8 B2 Brinkworth Austr.
67 H4 Brion, Île i. Can.
44 F4 Brioude France
67 F3 Brisay Can.
7 F4 Brisbane Austr.
81 K1 Bristol Can.
39 E6 Bristol U.K.
81 G4 Bristol CT U.S.A.
81 F4 Bristol PA U.S.A.
80 B6 Bristol TN U.S.A.
62 B4 Bristol Bay b. U.S.A.
39 C6 Bristol Channel est. U.K.
92 C1 Bristol I. i. Atl. Ocean
75 E4 Bristol Lake l. U.S.A.
75 E4 Bristol Mts mts U.S.A.
92 A2 British Antarctic Territory reg. Ant.
64 D3 British Columbia div. Can.
63 K1 British Empire Range mts Can.
10 J10 British Ind. Ocean Territory terr. Ind. Ocean
59 G2 Brits S. Africa
58 E5 Britstown S. Africa
Brittany reg. see Bretagne
44 E4 Brive-la-Gaillarde France
45 E1 Briviesca Spain
39 D7 Brixham U.K.
46 H6 Brno Czech Rep.
79 D5 Broad r. U.S.A.
81 F3 Broadalbin U.S.A.
66 E3 Broadback r. Can.
8 E4 Broadford Austr.
41 C5 Broadford Rep. of Ireland
40 C3 Broadford U.K.
40 E5 Broad Law h. U.K.
39 J6 Broadstairs U.K.
72 F2 Broadus U.S.A.
65 J4 Broadview Can.
76 C3 Broadwater U.S.A.
9 D1 Broadwood N.Z.
37 S8 Broceni Latvia
65 J3 Brochet Can.
65 J3 Brochet, Lac l. Can.
43 J3 Brocken mt Ger.
62 G2 Brock I. i. Can.
80 E3 Brockport U.S.A.
81 H3 Brockton U.S.A.
69 K3 Brockville Can.
69 F4 Brockway MI U.S.A.
80 D4 Brockway PA U.S.A.
63 K2 Brodeur Peninsula pen. Can.
68 C4 Brodhead U.S.A.
40 C5 Brodick U.K.
47 J4 Brodnica Pol.
51 C5 Brody Ukr.
77 E4 Broken Arrow U.S.A.
8 H2 Broken B. b. Austr.
76 D3 Broken Bow NE U.S.A.
77 E5 Broken Bow OK U.S.A.
8 C1 Broken Hill Austr.
43 J2 Brome Ger.
39 G6 Bromley U.K.
39 E5 Bromsgrove U.K.
37 L8 Brønderslev Denmark
59 H2 Bronkhorstspruit S. Africa
36 N4 Brønnøysund Norway
68 E5 Bronson U.S.A.
39 J5 Brooke U.K.
31 A4 Brooke's Point Phil.
68 C4 Brookfield U.S.A.
77 F6 Brookhaven U.S.A.
72 A3 Brookings OR U.S.A.
76 D2 Brookings SD U.S.A.
81 H3 Brookline U.S.A.
68 A5 Brooklyn IA U.S.A.
68 B5 Brooklyn IL U.S.A.
76 E2 Brooklyn Center U.S.A.
80 D6 Brookneal U.S.A.
65 G4 Brooks Can.
74 A2 Brooks CA U.S.A.
81 J2 Brooks ME U.S.A.
92 B3 Brooks, C. c. Ant.
62 D3 Brooks Range mts U.S.A.
79 D6 Brooksville U.S.A.
80 D4 Brookville U.S.A.
6 C3 Broome Austr.
40 C3 Broom, Loch in. U.K.
40 E2 Brora U.K.
37 O9 Brösarp Sweden
41 D4 Brosna r. Rep. of Ireland
72 B3 Brothers U.S.A.
27 □ Brothers, The is H.K. China
38 E3 Brough U.K.
40 E1 Brough Head hd U.K.
41 E3 Broughshane U.K.
8 B2 Broughton r. Austr.
63 M3 Broughton Island Can.
47 P5 Brovary Ukr.
37 L8 Brovst Denmark
77 C5 Brownfield U.S.A.
72 D1 Browning U.S.A.
8 B2 Brown, Mt mt Austr.
68 D6 Brownsburg U.S.A.
81 F5 Browns Mills U.S.A.
79 B5 Brownsville TN U.S.A.
77 D7 Brownsville TX U.S.A.
81 J2 Brownville U.S.A.
81 J2 Brownville Junction U.S.A.
77 D6 Brownwood U.S.A.
47 O4 Brozha Belarus
44 F1 Bruay-en-Artois France
68 C2 Bruce Crossing U.S.A.
66 D4 Bruce Pen. pen. Can.
69 G3 Bruce Peninsula National Park Can.
43 G5 Bruchsal Ger.
43 L2 Brück Ger.
46 G7 Bruck an der Mur Austria
39 E6 Brue r. U.K.
42 B3 Bruges Belgium
Brugge see Bruges
43 G5 Brühl Baden-Württemberg Ger.
42 E4 Brühl Nordrhein-Westfalen Ger.
75 G2 Bruin Pt summit U.S.A.
23 J3 Bruint India
58 C2 Brukkaros Namibia
68 B2 Brule U.S.A.
42 C5 Brûly Belgium
90 E1 Brumado Brazil
37 M6 Brumunddal Norway
43 K2 Brunau Ger.
72 D3 Bruneau U.S.A.
72 D3 Bruneau r. U.S.A.
11 N9 Brunei country Asia
36 O5 Brunflo Sweden
48 D1 Brunico Italy
9 C5 Brunner, L. l. N.Z.
65 H4 Bruno Can.
46 D4 Brunsbüttel Ger.
79 D6 Brunswick GA U.S.A.
81 J3 Brunswick ME U.S.A.
80 C4 Brunswick OH U.S.A.
88 B8 Brunswick, Peninsula de pen. Chile
46 H6 Bruntál Czech Rep.
92 C3 Brunt Ice Shelf ice feature Ant.
59 J4 Bruntville S. Africa
6 E6 Bruny I. i. Austr.
72 G3 Brush U.S.A.
42 C4 Brussels Belgium
69 G4 Brussels Can.
68 D3 Brussels U.S.A.
47 O5 Brusyliv Ukr.
8 F4 Bruthen Austr.
Bruxelles see Brussels
80 A4 Bryan OH U.S.A.
77 D6 Bryan TX U.S.A.
92 A3 Bryan Coast coastal area Ant.
8 B2 Bryan, Mt h. Austr.
50 E4 Bryansk Rus. Fed.
50 E4 Bryanskaya Oblast' div. Rus. Fed.
51 H6 Bryanskoye Rus. Fed.
75 F3 Bryce Canyon Nat. Park U.S.A.
75 H5 Bryce Mt mt U.S.A.
37 J7 Bryne Norway
51 F6 Bryukhovetskaya Rus. Fed.
46 H5 Brzeg Pol.
7 F2 Buala Solomon Is
54 A3 Buba Guinea-Bissau
17 M7 Būbīyān I. i. Kuwait
31 B5 Bubuan i. Phil.
16 C3 Bucak Turkey
89 B3 Bucaramanga Col.
31 C4 Bucas Grande i. Phil.
8 G4 Buchan Austr.
54 A4 Buchanan Liberia
68 D5 Buchanan MI U.S.A.
80 D6 Buchanan VA U.S.A.
77 D6 Buchanan, L. l. U.S.A.
63 L2 Buchan Gulf b. Can.
67 J4 Buchans Can.
49 M2 Bucharest Romania
43 J1 Büchen Ger.
43 H5 Buchen (Odenwald) Ger.
43 L1 Buchholz Ger.
43 H1 Bucholz in der Nordheide Ger.
74 B4 Buchon, Point pt U.S.A.
47 M7 Bucin, Pasul pass Romania
8 E1 Buckambool Mt h. Austr.
43 H2 Bückeburg Ger.
43 H2 Bücken Ger.
75 F5 Buckeye U.S.A.
80 B5 Buckeye Lake l. U.S.A.
80 C5 Buckhannon U.S.A.
80 C5 Buckhannon r. U.S.A.
40 E4 Buckhaven U.K.
69 H3 Buckhorn Can.
75 H5 Buckhorn U.S.A.
69 H3 Buckhorn Lake l. Can.
80 B6 Buckhorn Lake l. U.S.A.
40 F3 Buckie U.K.
69 K3 Buckingham Can.
39 G5 Buckingham U.K.
80 D6 Buckingham U.S.A.
6 D3 Buckingham Bay b. Austr.
6 E4 Buckland Tableland reg. Austr.
92 A6 Buckle I. i. Ant.
75 F4 Buckskin Mts mts U.S.A.
74 B2 Bucks Mt mt U.S.A.
81 J2 Bucksport U.S.A.
43 L2 Bückwitz Ger.
București see Bucharest
80 B4 Bucyrus U.S.A.
47 P4 Buda-Kashalyova Belarus
47 J7 Budapest Hungary
22 D3 Budaun India
8 E1 Budda Austr.
92 C6 Budd Coast coastal area Ant.
40 F4 Buddon Ness pt U.K.
48 C4 Buddusò Sardinia Italy
39 C7 Bude U.K.
77 F6 Bude U.S.A.
51 H6 Budennovsk Rus. Fed.
43 H4 Büdingen Ger.
22 D5 Budni India
50 E3 Budogoshch' Rus. Fed.
23 H2 Budongquan China
48 C4 Budoni Sardinia Italy
54 C4 Buea Cameroon
74 B4 Buellton U.S.A.
91 D2 Buena Esperanza Arg.
89 A4 Buenaventura Col.
82 C3 Buenaventura Mex.
89 A4 Buenaventura, B. de b. Col.
73 F4 Buena Vista CO U.S.A.
80 D6 Buena Vista VA U.S.A.
45 E2 Buendia, Embalse de resr Spain
91 B4 Bueno r. Chile
91 E2 Buenos Aires Arg.
91 E3 Buenos Aires div. Arg.
88 B7 Buenos Aires, L. l. Arg./Chile
88 C7 Buen Pasto Arg.
80 D3 Buffalo NY U.S.A.
77 D4 Buffalo OK U.S.A.
76 C2 Buffalo SD U.S.A.
77 D6 Buffalo TX U.S.A.
68 B3 Buffalo WV U.S.A.
72 F2 Buffalo WY U.S.A.
64 G3 Buffalo r. Can.
68 B3 Buffalo r. U.S.A.
64 F3 Buffalo Head Hills h. Can.
64 F2 Buffalo Lake l. Can.
8 F4 Buffalo, Mt mt Austr.
65 H3 Buffalo Narrows Can.
58 B4 Buffels watercourse S. Africa
59 G1 Buffels Drift S. Africa
79 D5 Buford U.S.A.
49 L2 Buftea Romania
47 K4 Bug r. Pol.
89 A4 Buga Col.
89 A3 Bugalagrande Col.
8 G1 Bugaldie Austr.
18 D2 Bugdayli Turkm.
33 D4 Bugel, Tanjung pt Indon.
42 C3 Buggenhout Belgium
48 G2 Bugojno Bos.-Herz.
31 A4 Bugsuk i. Phil.
31 B2 Buguey Phil.
18 D4 Būhābād Iran
17 J5 Buḥayrat ath Tharthār l. Iraq
17 K4 Buḥayrat Shārī l. Iraq
57 D5 Buhera Zimbabwe
31 B3 Buhi Phil.
72 D3 Buhl ID U.S.A.
68 A2 Buhl MN U.S.A.
17 J3 Bühtan r. Turkey
47 N7 Buhuşi Romania
39 D5 Builth Wells U.K.
54 B4 Bui National Park Ghana
50 J4 Buinsk Rus. Fed.
17 L4 Bu'in Soflā Iran
24 D2 Buir Nur l. Mongolia
57 B6 Buitepos Namibia
49 J3 Bujanovac Yugo.
56 C4 Bujumbura Burundi
24 D1 Bukachacha Rus. Fed.
7 F2 Buka I. i. P.N.G.
18 D4 Būkand Iran
56 C4 Bukavu Congo(Zaire)
19 G2 Bukhara Uzbek.
31 C6 Bukide i. Indon.
32 □ Bukit Batok Sing.
32 B5 Bukit Fraser Malaysia
32 □ Bukit Panjang Sing.
32 □ Bukit Timah Sing.
33 B3 Bukittinggi Indon.
56 D4 Bukoba Tanz.
32 □ Bukum, P. i. Sing.
25 F7 Bula Indon.
50 J4 Bula r. Rus. Fed.
46 D7 Bülach Switz.
8 J2 Bulahdelah Austr.
31 B3 Bulan Phil.
16 G1 Bulancak Turkey
22 D3 Bulandshahr India
17 J2 Bulanık Turkey
57 C6 Bulawayo Zimbabwe
16 F3 Bulbul Syria
16 B2 Buldan Turkey
22 D5 Buldana India
59 J2 Bulembu Swaziland
26 B1 Bulgan Mongolia
24 C2 Bulgan Mongolia
35 H4 Bulgaria country Europe
9 D4 Buller r. N.Z.
8 F4 Buller, Mt mt Austr.
75 E4 Bullhead City U.S.A.
74 D4 Bullion Mts mts U.S.A.
58 B2 Büllsport Namibia
32 □ Buloh, P. i. Sing.
8 D4 Buloke, Lake l. Austr.
59 G4 Bultfontein S. Africa
31 C5 Buluan Phil.
6 C2 Bulukumba Indon.
13 O2 Bulun Rus. Fed.
56 B4 Bulungu Bandundu Congo(Zaire)
56 C4 Bulungu Kasai-Occidental Congo(Zaire)
19 G2 Bulungur Uzbek.
31 C3 Bulusan Phil.
56 C3 Bumba Congo(Zaire)
26 B1 Bumbat Sum China
75 F4 Bumble Bee U.S.A.
31 A5 Bum-Bum i. Malaysia
56 B4 Buna Congo(Zaire)
56 D3 Buna Kenya
56 D4 Bunazi Tanz.
41 C2 Bunbeg Rep. of Ireland
6 B5 Bunbury Austr.
41 E5 Bunclody Rep. of Ireland
41 D2 Buncrana Rep. of Ireland
56 D4 Bunda Tanz.
6 F4 Bundaberg Austr.
22 C4 Bundi India
41 C3 Bundoran Rep. of Ireland
23 F5 Bundu India
39 J5 Bungay U.K.
32 B2 Bung Boraphet l. Thai.
8 G3 Bungendore Austr.
92 C6 Bunger Hills h. Ant.
29 C8 Bungo-suidō chan. Japan
56 D3 Bunia Congo(Zaire)
56 C4 Bunianga Congo(Zaire)
8 D4 Buninyong Austr.
54 D3 Buni-Yadi Nigeria
22 C2 Bunji Jammu and Kashmir
75 E3 Bunkerville U.S.A.
77 E6 Bunkie U.S.A.
79 D6 Bunnell U.S.A.
16 E2 Bünyan Turkey
31 A6 Bunyu i. Indon.
18 C4 Bu ol Kheyr Iran
32 D2 Buôn Hô Vietnam
32 D2 Buôn Mê Thuôt Vietnam
13 P2 Buorkhaya, Guba b. Rus. Fed.
20 C4 Buqayq S. Arabia
56 D4 Bura Kenya
22 E3 Burang China
90 E2 Buranhaém r. Brazil
56 E3 Burao Somalia
31 C4 Burauen Phil.
20 B4 Buraydah S. Arabia
43 G4 Burbach Ger.
74 C4 Burbank U.S.A.
8 F2 Burcher Austr.
19 G2 Burdalyk Turkm.
16 C3 Burdur Turkey
56 D2 Burē Eth.
39 J5 Bure r. U.K.
36 R4 Bureå Sweden
24 F1 Bureinskiy Khrebet mts Rus. Fed.
16 D6 Būr Fu'ad Egypt
49 M3 Burgas Bulg.
79 E5 Burgaw U.S.A.
43 K2 Burg bei Magdeburg Ger.
43 J5 Burgbernheim Ger.
43 J2 Burgdorf Ger.
67 J4 Burgeo Can.
59 G5 Burgersdorp S. Africa
59 J2 Burgersfort S. Africa
39 G7 Burgess Hill U.K.
43 H4 Burghaun Ger.
46 F6 Burghausen Ger.
40 E3 Burghead U.K.
42 B3 Burgh-Haamstede Neth.
48 F6 Burgio, Serra di h. Sicily Italy
43 L5 Burglengenfeld Ger.
45 E1 Burgos Spain
43 L4 Burgstädt Ger.
37 Q8 Burgsvik Sweden
Burgundy reg. see Bourgogne
24 B3 Burhan Budai Shan mts China
49 M5 Burhaniye Turkey
22 D5 Burhanpur India
23 E5 Burhar-Dhanpuri India
23 F4 Burhi Gandak r. India
31 B3 Burias i. Phil.
23 H4 Buri Dihing r. India
23 E4 Buri Gandak r. Nepal
67 J4 Burin Peninsula pen. Can.
32 B2 Buriram Thai.
87 K5 Buritis Bravo Brazil
90 C1 Buritis Brazil
19 G4 Burj Pak.
92 A3 Burke I. i. Ant.
9 C6 Burke Pass N.Z.
6 D3 Burketown Austr.
52 D4 Burkina country Africa
69 H3 Burk's Falls Can.
72 D3 Burley U.S.A.
69 H4 Burlington Can.
76 C4 Burlington CO U.S.A.
68 B5 Burlington IA U.S.A.
68 D5 Burlington IN U.S.A.
81 J2 Burlington ME U.S.A.
81 G2 Burlington VT U.S.A.
68 C4 Burlington WV U.S.A.
Burma country see Myanmar
77 D6 Burnet U.S.A.
72 B3 Burney U.S.A.
81 J2 Burnham U.S.A.
6 E6 Burnie Austr.
38 G3 Burniston U.K.
38 E4 Burnley U.K.
72 C3 Burns U.S.A.
65 H1 Burnside r. Can.
62 F4 Burns Lake Can.
80 C5 Burnsville Lake l. U.S.A.
79 F7 Burnt Ground Bahamas
40 E4 Burntisland U.K.
67 H3 Burnt Lake l. Can.
65 K3 Burntwood r. Can.
65 J3 Burnt Wood Lake l. Can.
8 D3 Buronga Austr.
12 K5 Burqin China
16 G5 Burqu' Jordan
8 B2 Burra Austr.
40 □ Burravoe U.K.
40 F2 Burray i. U.K.
49 J4 Burrel Albania
8 G2 Burrendong Reservoir Austr.
8 H3 Burrewarra Pt pt Austr.
45 F3 Burriana Spain
8 G3 Burrinjuck Austr.
8 G3 Burrinjuck Reservoir Austr.
80 B5 Burr Oak ReservoirU.S.A.
82 D3 Burro, Serranías del mts Mex.
40 D6 Burrow Head hd U.K.
75 G2 Burrville U.S.A.
16 B1 Bursa Turkey
55 F2 Bûr Safâga Egypt
Bûr Sa'îd see Port Said
43 G5 Bürstadt Ger.
Bûr Sudan see Port Sudan
8 C2 Burta Austr.
68 E3 Burt Lake l. U.S.A.
69 F4 Burton U.S.A.
66 E3 Burton, Lac l. Can.
41 C3 Burtonport Rep. of Ireland
39 F5 Burton upon Trent U.K.
36 R4 Burträsk Sweden
81 K1 Burtts Corner Can.
8 D2 Burtundy Austr.
25 E7 Buru i. Indon.
16 C6 Burullus, Bahra el lag. Egypt
53 G6 Burundi country Africa
56 C4 Bururi Burundi
64 B2 Burwash Landing Can.
40 F2 Burwick U.K.
51 E5 Buryn' Ukr.
39 H5 Bury St Edmunds U.K.
22 C2 Burzil Pass Jammu and Kashmir
56 C4 Basanga Congo(Zaire)
41 E2 Bush r. U.K.
18 C4 Būshehr Iran
23 E2 Bushêngcaka China
56 D4 Bushenyi Uganda
Bushire see Būshehr
41 E2 Bushmills U.K.
68 B5 Bushnell U.S.A.
56 C3 Businga Congo(Zaire)
32 □ Busing, P. i. Sing.
16 F5 Buṣrá ash Shām Syria
6 B5 Busselton Austr.
42 D2 Bussum Neth.
77 C7 Bustamante Mex.
48 C2 Busto Arsizio Italy
31 A3 Busuanga Phil.
31 A3 Busuanga i. Phil.
56 C3 Buta Congo(Zaire)
32 A4 Butang Group is Thai.
91 C3 Buta Ranquil Arg.
56 C4 Butare Rwanda
95 G5 Butaritari i. Pac. Oc.
8 A2 Bute Austr.
40 C5 Bute i. U.K.
64 D4 Butedale Can.
64 D4 Bute In. in. Can.
40 C5 Bute, Sound of chan. U.K.
59 H4 Butha Buthe Lesotho
43 G1 Butjadingen reg. Ger.
68 E5 Butler IN U.S.A.
80 D4 Butler PA U.S.A.
41 D3 Butlers Bridge Rep. of Ireland
25 E7 Buton i. Indon.
43 L1 Bützow Ger.
72 D2 Butte U.S.A.
43 K3 Buttelstedt Ger.
74 B1 Butte Meadows U.S.A.
33 B1 Butterworth Malaysia
59 H6 Butterworth S. Africa
41 C5 Buttevant Rep. of Ireland
64 D5 Buttle L. l. Can.
40 B2 Butt of Lewis hd U.K.
63 J4 Button Bay b. Can.
74 C4 Buttonwillow U.S.A.
31 C4 Butuan Phil.
27 B5 Butuo China
51 G5 Buturlinovka Rus. Fed.
23 E4 Butwal Nepal
43 G4 Butzbach Ger.
56 E3 Buulobarde Somalia
56 E4 Buur Gaabo Somalia
56 E3 Buurhabaka Somalia
23 F4 Buxar India
43 H1 Buxtehude Ger.
39 F4 Buxton U.K.
50 G3 Buy Rus. Fed.
68 A1 Buyck U.S.A.
51 H7 Buynaksk Rus. Fed.
Büyük Ağri mt see Ararat, Mt
16 A3 Büyükmenderes r. Turkey
30 B3 Buyun Shan mt China
42 C5 Buzancy France
49 M2 Buzău Romania
57 D5 Búzi Moz.
12 G4 Buzuluk Rus. Fed.
51 G5 Buzuluk r. Rus. Fed.
81 H4 Buzzards Bay b. U.S.A.
23 G4 Byakar Bhutan
49 L3 Byala Bulg.
49 K3 Byala Slatina Bulg.
47 O4 Byalynichy Belarus
62 H2 Byam Martin I. i. Can.
50 D4 Byarezina r. Belarus
50 C4 Byaroza Belarus
16 E4 Byblos Lebanon
46 J4 Bydgoszcz Pol.
50 D4 Byerazino Belarus
72 F4 Byers U.S.A.
47 O3 Byeshankovichy Belarus
37 K7 Bygland Norway
50 D4 Bykhaw Belarus
37 K7 Bykle Norway
63 L2 Bylot Island i. Can.
69 G3 Byng Inlet Can.
92 B5 Byrd Gl. gl. Ant.
37 K6 Byrkjelo Norway
68 C4 Byron IL U.S.A.
81 H2 Byron ME U.S.A.
7 F4 Byron Bay Austr.
13 M2 Byrranga, Gory mts Rus. Fed.
36 R4 Byske Sweden
13 P3 Bytantay r. Rus. Fed.
47 J5 Bytom Pol.
46 H3 Bytów Pol.
19 E2 Byuzmeyin Turkm.

C

88 E3 Caacupé Para.
90 A4 Caaguazú, Cordillera de h. Para.
90 A4 Caaguazú Para.
90 A3 Caarapó Brazil
90 A4 Caazapá Para.
86 C6 Caballas Peru
86 D4 Caballococha Peru
31 B3 Cabanatuan Phil.
67 G4 Cabano Can.
56 E2 Cabdul Qaadir Somalia
90 A1 Cabeceira Rio Manso Brazil
87 M5 Cabedelo Brazil
45 D3 Cabeza del Buey Spain
86 F7 Cabezas Bol.
91 E3 Cabildo Arg.
89 C2 Cabimas Venez.
56 B4 Cabinda Angola
56 B4 Cabinda div. Angola
72 C1 Cabinet Mts mts U.S.A.
89 B3 Cable Way pass Col.
90 D3 Cabo Frio Brazil
90 E3 Cabo Frio, Ilha do i. Brazil
66 E4 Cabonga, Réservoir resr Can.
77 E4 Cabool U.S.A.
7 F4 Caboolture Austr.
87 H3 Cabo Orange, Parque Nacional de nat. park Brazil
86 C4 Cabo Pantoja Peru
82 B2 Caborca Mex.
69 G3 Cabot Head pt Can.
67 J4 Cabot Strait str. Can.
90 D2 Cabral, Serra do mts Brazil
17 L2 Cäbrayıl Azer.
45 H3 Cabrera i. Spain
45 C1 Cabrera, Sierra de la mts Spain
45 F3 Cabriel r. Spain
89 D3 Cabruta Venez.
31 B2 Cabugao Phil.
88 F3 Caçador Brazil
84 C3 Cacahuatepec Mex.
49 J3 Čačak Yugo.
91 G1 Caçapava do Sul Brazil
80 D5 Cacapon r. U.S.A.
89 B3 Cácares Col.
48 C4 Caccia, Capo pt Sardinia Italy
87 G7 Cáceres Brazil
45 C3 Cáceres Spain
72 D3 Cache Peak summit U.S.A.
54 A3 Cacheu Guinea-Bissau
88 C3 Cachi r. Arg.
87 H5 Cachimbo, Serra do h. Brazil
89 B3 Cáchira Col.
90 E1 Cachoeira Brazil
90 B2 Cachoeira Alta Brazil
91 G1 Cachoeira do Sul Brazil
90 E3 Cachoeiro de Itapemirim Brazil
54 A3 Cacine Guinea-Bissau
87 H3 Caciporé, Cabo pt Brazil
57 B5 Cacolo Angola
56 B4 Cacongo Angola
74 D3 Cactus Range mts U.S.A.
90 B2 Caçu Brazil
90 D1 Caculé Brazil
47 J6 Čadca Slovakia
43 H1 Cadenberge Ger.
84 B1 Cadereyta Mex.
31 B3 Cadig Mountains Phil.
69 H1 Cadillac Que. Can.
65 H5 Cadillac Sask. Can.
68 E3 Cadillac U.S.A.
31 B4 Cadiz Phil.
45 C4 Cádiz Spain
45 C4 Cádiz, Golfo de g. Spain
75 E4 Cadiz Lake l. U.S.A.
44 D2 Caen France
39 C4 Caernarfon U.K.
39 C4 Caernarfon Bay b. U.K.
39 D6 Caerphilly U.K.
80 B5 Caesar Creek Lake l. U.S.A.
16 E5 Caesarea Israel
90 D1 Caetité Brazil
88 C3 Cafayate Arg.
31 B4 Cagayan i. Phil.
31 B2 Cagayan r. Phil.
31 C4 Cagayan de Oro Phil.
31 B4 Cagayan Islands is Phil.
48 E3 Cagli Italy
48 C5 Cagliari Sardinia Italy
48 C5 Cagliari, Golfo di b. Sardinia Italy
89 B4 Caguán r. Col.
41 B6 Caha h. Rep. of Ireland
79 C5 Cahaba r. U.S.A.
41 B6 Caha Mts h. Rep. of Ireland
41 A6 Cahermore Rep. of Ireland
41 D5 Cahir Rep. of Ireland
41 A6 Cahirciveen Rep. of Ireland
57 D5 Cahora Bassa, Lago de resr Moz.
41 E5 Cahore Point pt Rep. of Ireland
44 E4 Cahors France
86 C5 Cahuapanas Peru
51 D6 Cahul Moldova
57 D5 Caia Moz.
87 G6 Caiabis, Serra dos h. Brazil
57 C5 Caianda Angola
90 B2 Caiapó r. Brazil
90 B2 Caiapônia Brazil
90 B2 Caiapó, Serra do mts Brazil
83 J4 Caibarién Cuba
32 C3 Cai Be Vietnam
89 D3 Caicara Venez.
83 K4 Caicos Is is Turks and Caicos Is
91 B1 Caimanes Chile
31 A3 Caiman Point pt Phil.
45 F2 Caimodorro mt Spain
32 C3 Cai Nước Vietnam
40 E3 Cairn Gorm mt U.K.
40 E3 Cairngorm Mountains U.K.
40 C6 Cairnryan U.K.
6 E3 Cairns Austr.
40 E3 Cairn Toul mt U.K.
55 F1 Cairo Egypt
79 C6 Cairo U.S.A.
48 C2 Cairo Montenotte Italy
57 B5 Caiundo Angola
86 C5 Cajamarca Peru
31 B3 Cajidiocan Phil.
48 G1 Čakovec Croatia
16 B2 Çal Turkey
59 G5 Cala S. Africa
54 C4 Calabar Nigeria
69 J3 Calabogie Can.
89 D2 Calabozo Venez.
49 K3 Calafat Romania
88 B8 Calafate Arg.
31 B3 Calagua Islands is Phil.
45 F1 Calahorra Spain
57 B5 Calai Angola
44 E1 Calais France
81 K2 Calais U.S.A.
86 F5 Calama Brazil
88 C2 Calama Chile
89 B2 Calamar Bolívar Col.
89 B4 Calamar Guaviare Col.
31 A4 Calamian Group is Phil.
45 F2 Calamocha Spain
57 B4 Calandula Angola
55 E2 Calanscio Sand Sea des. Libya
31 B3 Calapan Phil.
49 M2 Călăraşi Romania
45 F2 Calatayud Spain
31 B3 Calauag Phil.
31 B3 Calavite, Cape pt Phil.
31 A3 Calawit i. Phil.
31 B2 Calayan i. Phil.
31 C3 Calbayog Phil.
43 K3 Calbe (Saale) Ger.
31 C4 Calbiga Phil.
91 B4 Calbuco Chile
87 L5 Calcanhar, Ponta do pt Brazil
77 E6 Calcasieu L. l. U.S.A.
87 H3 Calçoene Brazil
23 G5 Calcutta India
45 B3 Caldas da Rainha Port.
90 C2 Caldas Novas Brazil
43 H3 Calden Ger.
88 B3 Caldera Chile
17 J2 Çaldıran Turkey
72 C3 Caldwell U.S.A.
80 D3 Caledon Can.
58 C7 Caledon S. Africa
59 G5 Caledon r. Lesotho/S. Africa
69 H4 Caledonia Can.
68 B4 Caledonia U.S.A.
84 B2 Calera Mex.
88 C7 Caleta Olivia Arg.
75 E5 Calexico U.S.A.
38 C3 Calf of Man i. U.K.
64 G4 Calgary Can.
79 C5 Calhoun U.S.A.
89 A4 Cali Col.
31 C4 Calicoan i. Phil.
21 A4 Calicut India
74 C4 Caliente CA U.S.A.
75 E3 Caliente NV U.S.A.
74 B3 California div. U.S.A.
74 B3 California Aqueduct canal U.S.A.
82 B2 California, Golfo de g. Mex.
74 C4 California Hot Springs U.S.A.
17 M2 Cälilabad Azer.
73 D5 Calipatria U.S.A.
74 A2 Calistoga U.S.A.
58 D6 Calitzdorp S. Africa
84 E2 Calkiní Mex.
74 D2 Callaghan, Mt mt U.S.A.
79 D6 Callahan U.S.A.
41 D5 Callan Rep. of Ireland
69 H2 Callander Can.
40 D4 Callander U.K.
86 C6 Callao Peru
75 F2 Callao U.S.A.
84 C2 Calles Mex.
81 F4 Callicoon U.S.A.
39 C7 Callington U.K.
69 G2 Callum Can.
64 G4 Calmar Can.
68 B4 Calmar U.S.A.
75 E4 Cal-Nev-Ari U.S.A.
79 D7 Caloosahatchee r. U.S.A.
74 B2 Calpine U.S.A.
84 C3 Calpulálpan Mex.
48 F6 Caltanissetta Sicily Italy
68 C2 Calumet U.S.A.
57 B5 Calunga Angola
57 B5 Caluquembe Angola
31 B4 Calusa i. Phil.
56 F2 Caluula Somalia
75 G5 Calva U.S.A.
64 D4 Calvert I. i. Can.
48 C3 Calvi Corsica France
45 H3 Calvià Spain
84 B2 Calvillo Mex.
58 C5 Calvinia S. Africa
48 F4 Calvo, Monte mt Italy
39 H5 Cam r. U.K.
90 E1 Camaçari Brazil
74 B2 Camache Reservoir U.S.A.
84 B1 Camacho Mex.
57 B5 Camacuio Angola
57 B5 Camacupa Angola
89 D2 Camaguán Venez.
83 J4 Camagüey Cuba
83 J4 Camagüey, Arch. de is Cuba
33 B1 Camah, Gunung mt Malaysia
Çamalan see Gülek
86 D7 Camana Peru
57 C5 Camanongue Angola
90 B2 Camapuã Brazil
91 G1 Camaquã Brazil
91 G1 Camaquã r. Brazil
16 E3 Çamardı Turkey
84 C1 Camargo Mex.
84 A2 Camaronero, L. del lag. Mex.
88 C6 Camarones Arg.
88 C6 Camarones, Bahía b. Arg.
72 B2 Camas U.S.A.
32 C3 Ca Mau Vietnam
Cambay see Khambhat
Cambay, Gulf of g. see Khambhat, Gulf of
39 G6 Camberley U.K.
11 M8 Cambodia country Asia
39 B7 Camborne U.K.
44 F1 Cambrai France
74 B4 Cambria U.S.A.
39 D5 Cambrian Mountains reg. U.K.
69 G4 Cambridge Can.
9 E2 Cambridge N.Z.
39 H5 Cambridge U.K.
68 B5 Cambridge IL U.S.A.
81 H3 Cambridge MA U.S.A.
81 E5 Cambridge MD U.S.A.
76 E2 Cambridge MN U.S.A.
81 G3 Cambridge NY U.S.A.
80 C4 Cambridge OH U.S.A.
67 G2 Cambrien, Lac l. Can.
8 H3 Camden Austr.
79 C5 Camden AL U.S.A.
77 E5 Camden AR U.S.A.
81 J2 Camden ME U.S.A.
81 F5 Camden NJ U.S.A.
81 F3 Camden NY U.S.A.
79 D5 Camden SC U.S.A.
88 B8 Camden, Isla i. Chile
57 C5 Cameia, Parque Nacional da nat. park Angola
75 G4 Cameron AZ U.S.A.
77 E6 Cameron LA U.S.A.
76 E4 Cameron MO U.S.A.
77 D6 Cameron TX U.S.A.
68 B3 Cameron WV U.S.A.
32 B4 Cameron Highlands Malaysia
64 F3 Cameron Hills h. Can.
74 B2 Cameron Park U.S.A.
53 F5 Cameroon country Africa
54 C4 Cameroun, Mt mt Cameroon
87 J4 Cametá Brazil
31 B2 Camiguin i. Phil.
31 C4 Camiguin i. Phil.
31 B3 Camiling Phil.
79 C6 Camilla U.S.A.
86 F8 Camiri Bol.
87 K4 Camocim Brazil
6 D3 Camooweal Austr.
31 C4 Camotes Sea g. Phil.
91 E2 Campana Arg.
89 B4 Campana, Co h. Col.
88 A7 Campana, I. i. Chile
91 B2 Campanario mt Arg./Chile
64 D4 Campania I. i. Can.
58 E4 Campbell S. Africa

9 E4 Campbell, Cape c. N.Z.
4 H10 Campbell Island i. N.Z.
64 D4 Campbell River Can.
69 J3 Campbells Bay Can.
78 C4 Campbellsville U.S.A.
67 G4 Campbellton Can.
40 C5 Campbeltown U.K.
84 E3 Campeche Mex.
84 E3 Campeche div. Mex.
84 D3 Campeche, Bahía de g. Mex.
8 D5 Camperdown Austr.
49 L2 Câmpina Romania
87 L5 Campina Grande Brazil
90 C3 Campinas Brazil
90 C2 Campina Verde Brazil
54 C4 Campo Cameroon
89 B4 Campoalegre Col.
48 F4 Campobasso Italy
90 D3 Campo Belo Brazil
87 H6 Campo de Diauarum Brazil
90 C2 Campo Florido Brazil
88 D3 Campo Gallo Arg.
90 A3 Campo Grande Brazil
87 K4 Campo Maior Brazil
45 C3 Campo Maior Port.
90 B4 Campo Mourão Brazil
90 E3 Campos Brazil
90 C2 Campos Altos Brazil
90 D3 Campos do Jordão Brazil
90 B4 Campos Eré reg. Brazil
40 D4 Campsie Fells h. U.K.
80 B6 Campton KY U.S.A.
81 H3 Campton NH U.S.A.
49 L2 Câmpulung Romania
47 M7 Câmpulung Moldovenesc Romania
75 G4 Camp Verde U.S.A.
32 D3 Cam Ranh Vietnam
64 G4 Camrose Can.
39 B6 Camrose U.K.
65 G2 Camsell Lake l. Can.
65 H3 Camsell Portage Can.
51 C7 Çan Turkey
81 G3 Canaan U.S.A.
60 G4 Canada country N. America
91 E2 Cañada de Gómez Arg.
81 H2 Canada Falls Lake l. U.S.A.
77 C5 Canadian r. U.S.A.
89 E3 Canaima, Parque Nacional nat. park Venez.
81 F3 Canajoharie U.S.A.
51 C7 Çanakkale Turkey
Çanakkale Boğazı str. see Dardanelles
91 C2 Canalejas Arg.
80 E3 Canandaigua U.S.A.
80 E3 Canandaigua Lake l. U.S.A.
82 B2 Cananea Mex.
67 H2 Cananée, Lac l. Can.
90 C4 Cananéia Brazil
89 C4 Canapiare, Co h. Col.
86 C4 Cañar Ecuador
Canarias, Islas is see Canary Islands
96 G4 Canary Basin sea feature Atl. Ocean
34 D6 Canary Islands div. Spain
81 F3 Canastota U.S.A.
90 C2 Canastra, Serra da mts Brazil
84 A1 Canatlán Mex.
79 D6 Canaveral, Cape c. U.S.A.
45 E2 Cañaveras Spain
90 E1 Canavieiras Brazil
8 F1 Canbelego Austr.
8 G3 Canberra Austr.
72 B3 Canby CA U.S.A.
76 D2 Canby MN U.S.A.
82 G4 Cancún Mex.
73 F6 Candelaria Chihuahua Mex.
84 E3 Candelaria Mex.
45 D2 Candeleda Spain
8 G4 Candelo Austr.
87 J4 Cândido Mendes Brazil
16 D1 Çandır Turkey
65 H4 Candle Lake Can.
65 H4 Candle Lake l. Can.
92 C1 Candlemas I. i. Atl. Ocean
81 G4 Candlewood, Lake l. U.S.A.
76 D1 Cando U.S.A.
31 B2 Candon Phil.
91 B1 Canela Baja Chile
91 F2 Canelones Uru.
91 B3 Cañete Chile
45 F2 Cañete Spain
86 D6 Cangallo Peru
57 B5 Cangamba Angola
45 C1 Cangas del Narcea Spain
58 E6 Cango Caves caves S. Africa
87 L5 Canguaretama Brazil
91 G1 Canguçu Brazil
91 G1 Canguçu, Sa do h. Brazil
27 D6 Cangwu China
26 E2 Cangzhou China
67 G3 Caniapiscau Can.
67 G2 Caniapiscau r. Can.
63 L4 Caniapiscau, Lac l. Can.
67 G3 Caniapiscau, Rés. resr Can.
48 E6 Canicattì Sicily Italy
64 E4 Canim Lake Can.
64 E4 Canim Lake l. Can.
87 L4 Canindé Brazil
87 K5 Canindé r. Brazil
40 C2 Canisp h. U.K.
80 E3 Canisteo U.S.A.
80 E3 Canisteo r. U.S.A.
84 B2 Cañitas de Felipe Pescador Mex.
16 D1 Çankırı Turkey
31 B4 Canlaon Phil.
64 F4 Canmore Can.
40 B3 Canna i. U.K.
21 A4 Cannanore India
21 A4 Cannanore Islands is India
44 H5 Cannes France
39 E5 Cannock U.K.
8 G4 Cann River Austr.
89 E2 Caño Araguao r. Venez.
88 F3 Canõas Brazil
65 H3 Canoe L. l. Can.
90 B4 Canoinhas Brazil
89 E2 Caño Macareo r. Venez.
89 E2 Caño Manamo r. Venez.
89 E2 Caño Mariusa r. Venez.
73 F4 Canon City U.S.A.
8 C2 Canopus Austr.
65 J4 Canora Can.
8 G2 Canowindra Austr.
67 H4 Canso, C. hd Can.
45 D1 Cantábrica, Cordillera mts Spain
91 C2 Cantantal Arg.
89 D2 Cantaura Venez.
81 K2 Canterbury Can.
39 J6 Canterbury U.K.
9 C6 Canterbury Bight b. N.Z.
9 C5 Canterbury Plains plain N.Z.
32 C3 Cân Thơ Vietnam
31 C4 Cantilan Phil.
87 K5 Canto do Buriti Brazil
Canton see Guangzhou
68 B5 Canton IL U.S.A.
81 H2 Canton ME U.S.A.
68 B5 Canton MO U.S.A.
77 F5 Canton MS U.S.A.
81 F2 Canton NY U.S.A.
80 C4 Canton OH U.S.A.
80 E4 Canton PA U.S.A.
90 B4 Cantu r. Brazil
90 B4 Cantu, Serra do h. Brazil
91 E2 Cañuelas Arg.
87 G4 Canumã Brazil
86 F5 Canutama Brazil
9 D4 Canvastown N.Z.
39 H6 Canvey Island U.K.
77 C5 Canyon U.S.A.
72 C2 Canyon City U.S.A.
75 H3 Canyon de Chelly National Monument res. U.S.A.
72 D2 Canyon Ferry L. l. U.S.A.
75 H2 Canyonlands National Park U.S.A.
64 D2 Canyon Ranges mts Can.
72 B3 Canyonville U.S.A.
30 C3 Cao r. China
27 C6 Cao Băng Vietnam
32 D2 Cao Nguyên Đắc Lăc plat. Vietnam
30 C2 Caoshi China
26 E3 Cao Xian China
31 B5 Cap i. Phil.
89 D3 Capanaparo r. Venez.
87 J4 Capanema Brazil
90 B4 Capanema r. Brazil
90 C4 Capão Bonito Brazil
89 C3 Caparo r. Venez.
89 C4 Caparro, Co h. Brazil
31 B3 Capas Phil.
67 H4 Cap-aux-Meules Can.
67 F4 Cap-de-la-Madeleine Can.
6 E6 Cape Barren Island i. Austr.
96 K8 Cape Basin sea feature Atl. Ocean
67 H4 Cape Breton Highlands Nat. Park Can.
67 H4 Cape Breton Island i. Can.
67 J3 Cape Charles Can.
81 E6 Cape Charles U.S.A.
54 B4 Cape Coast Ghana
81 H4 Cape Cod Bay b. U.S.A.
81 J4 Cape Cod National Seashore res. U.S.A.
79 D7 Cape Coral U.S.A.
69 G3 Cape Croker Can.
63 L3 Cape Dorset Can.
79 E5 Cape Fear r. U.S.A.
77 F4 Cape Girardeau U.S.A.
94 D5 Cape Johnson Depth depth Pac. Oc.
90 D2 Capelinha Brazil
42 C3 Capelle aan de IJssel Neth.
81 F5 Cape May U.S.A.
81 F5 Cape May Court House U.S.A.
81 F5 Cape May Pt pt U.S.A.
57 B4 Capenda-Camulemba Angola
63 M5 Cape Sable c. Can.
67 J4 Cape St George Can.
67 H4 Cape Tormentine Can.
58 C6 Cape Town S. Africa
96 G5 Cape Verde Basin sea feature Atl. Ocean
96 F5 Cape Verde Fracture sea feature Atl. Ocean
96 H4 Cape Verde Plateau sea feature Atl. Ocean
81 E2 Cape Vincent U.S.A.
6 E3 Cape York Peninsula Austr.
83 K5 Cap-Haïtien Haiti
87 J4 Capim r. Brazil
92 B2 Capitán Arturo Prat Chile Base Ant.
90 A3 Capitán Bado Para.
73 F5 Capitan Peak mt U.S.A.
75 G2 Capitol Reef National Park U.S.A.
48 G3 Čapljina Bos.-Herz.
48 F5 Capo d'Orlando Sicily Italy
41 D5 Cappoquin Rep. of Ireland
48 C3 Capraia, Isola di i. Italy
6 F4 Capricorn Channel chan. Austr.
48 F4 Capri, Isola di i. Italy
57 C5 Caprivi Strip reg. Namibia
Cap St Jacques see Vung Tau
74 □2 Captain Cook U.S.A.
8 G3 Captain's Flat Austr.
80 C5 Captina r. U.S.A.
31 C3 Capul i. Phil.
86 C3 Caquetá r. Col.
89 B3 Cáqueza Col.
31 B3 Carabao i. Phil.
49 L2 Caracal Romania
89 E4 Caracarai Brazil
89 D2 Caracas Venez.
87 K5 Caracol Brazil
84 B3 Carácuaro Mex.
31 C5 Caraga Phil.
91 F2 Caraguatá r. Uru.
90 D3 Caraguatatuba Brazil
91 B3 Carahue Chile
90 E2 Caraí Brazil
90 D3 Carandaí Brazil
90 D3 Carangola Brazil
49 K2 Caransebeş Romania
67 H4 Caraquet Can.
89 B3 Carare r. Col.
83 H5 Caratasca, Laguna lag. Honduras
90 D2 Caratinga Brazil
86 E4 Carauari Brazil
Carauná mt see Grande, Serra
45 F3 Caravaca de la Cruz Spain
90 E2 Caravelas Brazil
88 F3 Carazinho Brazil
76 D1 Carberry Can.
48 C5 Carbonara, Capo pt Sardinia Italy
78 B4 Carbondale IL U.S.A.
81 F4 Carbondale PA U.S.A.
67 K4 Carbonear Can.
48 C5 Carbonia Sardinia Italy
90 D2 Carbonita Brazil
45 F3 Carcaixent Spain
31 B4 Carcar Phil.
91 E2 Carcaraña r. Arg.
44 F5 Carcassonne France
64 C2 Carcross Can.
6 B4 Cardabia Austr.
21 B4 Cardamon Hills mts India
84 C2 Cárdenas San Luis Potosí Mex.
84 D3 Cárdenas Tabasco Mex.
88 B7 Cardiel, L. l. Arg.
39 D6 Cardiff U.K.
39 C5 Cardigan U.K.
39 C5 Cardigan Bay b. U.K.
81 F2 Cardinal Can.
80 B4 Cardington U.S.A.
91 F2 Cardona Uru.
90 C4 Cardoso, Ilha do i. Brazil
9 B6 Cardrona N.Z.
64 G5 Cardston Can.
47 L7 Carei Romania
44 D2 Carentan France
80 B4 Carey U.S.A.
6 C4 Carey, L. salt flat Austr.
65 J2 Carey Lake l. Can.
93 J5 Cargados Carajos is Mauritius
44 C2 Carhaix-Plouguer France
91 D3 Carhué Arg.
90 E3 Cariacica Brazil
89 E2 Cariaco Venez.
61 L8 Caribbean Sea sea Atl. Ocean
64 E4 Cariboo Mts mts Can.
81 K1 Caribou U.S.A.
65 K3 Caribou r. Man. Can.
64 D2 Caribou r. N.W.T. Can.
68 E2 Caribou I. i. Can.
63 K4 Caribou Lake l. Can.
64 F3 Caribou Mountains Can.
31 C4 Carigara Phil.
42 D5 Carignan France
45 F2 Cariñena Spain
90 D1 Carinhanha Brazil
90 D1 Carinhanha r. Brazil
89 E2 Caripe Venez.
89 E2 Caripito Venez.
41 D3 Cark Mountain h. Rep. of Ireland
69 J3 Carleton Place Can.
59 G3 Carletonville S. Africa
72 C3 Carlin U.S.A.
41 E3 Carlingford Lough in. Rep. of Ireland/U.K.
38 E3 Carlisle U.K.
80 A5 Carlisle KY U.S.A.
80 E4 Carlisle PA U.S.A.
44 E5 Carlit, Pic mt France
91 E2 Carlos Casares Arg.
90 E2 Carlos Chagas Brazil
41 E5 Carlow Rep. of Ireland
40 B2 Carloway U.K.
74 D5 Carlsbad CA U.S.A.
73 F5 Carlsbad NM U.S.A.
77 C6 Carlsbad TX U.S.A.
73 F5 Carlsbad Caverns Nat. Park U.S.A.
93 J3 Carlsberg Ridge sea feature Ind. Ocean
92 B3 Carlson In. in Ant.
40 E5 Carluke U.K.
65 J5 Carlyle Can.
64 B2 Carmacks Can.
48 B2 Carmagnola Italy
65 K5 Carman Can.
39 C6 Carmarthen U.K.
39 C6 Carmarthen Bay b. U.K.
44 F4 Carmaux France
81 J2 Carmel U.S.A.
39 C4 Carmel Head hd U.K.
84 E3 Carmelita Guatemala
91 E2 Carmelo Uru.
89 B2 Carmen Col.
31 C4 Carmen Phil.
75 G6 Carmen U.S.A.
82 B3 Carmen i. Mex.
91 D4 Carmen de Patagones Arg.
84 E3 Carmen, Isla del i. Mex.
91 C2 Carmensa Arg.
78 B4 Carmi U.S.A.
74 B2 Carmichael U.S.A.
45 D4 Carmona Spain
44 C3 Carnac France
58 E5 Carnarvon S. Africa
41 D2 Carndonagh Rep. of Ireland
39 D4 Carnedd Llywelyn mt U.K.
6 C4 Carnegie, L. salt flat Austr.
95 O6 Carnegie Ridge sea feature Pac. Oc.
40 C3 Carn Eighe mt U.K.
68 D3 Carney U.S.A.
92 A3 Carney I. i. Ant.
38 E3 Carnforth U.K.
41 F3 Carnlough U.K.
40 E4 Carn nan Gabhar mt U.K.
56 B3 Carnot C.A.R.
6 D5 Carnot, C. hd Austr.
40 F4 Carnoustie U.K.
41 E5 Carnsore Point pt Rep. of Ireland
40 E5 Carnwath U.K.
65 H4 Carnwood Can.
69 F4 Caro U.S.A.
79 D7 Carol City U.S.A.
87 J5 Carolina Brazil
59 J3 Carolina S. Africa
5 M5 Caroline I. i. Kiribati
4 F4 Caroline Islands is Pac. Oc.
9 A6 Caroline Pk summit N.Z.
58 B4 Carolusberg S. Africa
89 E2 Caroní r. Venez.
89 C2 Carora Venez.
75 E3 Carp U.S.A.
47 L6 Carpathian Mountains Romania/Ukraine
6 D3 Carpentaria, Gulf of g. Austr.
44 G4 Carpentras France
48 D2 Carpi Italy
87 L5 Carpina Brazil
74 C4 Carpinteria U.S.A.
65 J5 Carpio U.S.A.
64 E4 Carp Lake Prov. Park res. Can.
81 H2 Carrabassett Valley U.S.A.
79 C6 Carrabelle U.S.A.
89 B2 Carraipía Col.
41 B4 Carra, Lough l. Rep. of Ireland
41 B6 Carran h. Rep. of Ireland
41 B6 Carrantuohill mt Rep. of Ireland
91 B2 Carranza, C. pt Chile
82 D3 Carranza, Presa V. l. Mex.
89 E3 Carrao r. Venez.
48 D2 Carrara Italy
8 E3 Carrathool Austr.
91 C3 Carrero, Co mt Arg.
89 E1 Carriacou i. Grenada
40 D5 Carrick reg. U.K.
41 F3 Carrickfergus U.K.
41 E4 Carrickmacross Rep. of Ireland
41 C4 Carrick-on-Shannon Rep. of Ireland
41 D5 Carrick-on-Suir Rep. of Ireland
8 B2 Carrieton Austr.
41 D4 Carrigallen Rep. of Ireland
41 C6 Carrigtwohill Rep. of Ireland
91 C4 Carri Lafquén, L. l. Arg.
76 D2 Carrington U.S.A.
88 B3 Carrizal Bajo Chile
75 H4 Carrizo AZ U.S.A.
75 G4 Carrizo AZ U.S.A.
74 D5 Carrizo Cr. r. U.S.A.
77 D6 Carrizo Springs U.S.A.
73 F5 Carrizozo U.S.A.
76 E3 Carroll U.S.A.
79 C5 Carrollton GA U.S.A.
78 C4 Carrollton KY U.S.A.
76 E4 Carrollton MO U.S.A.
80 C4 Carrollton OH U.S.A.
65 J4 Carrot r. Can.
65 J4 Carrot River Can.
38 B3 Carrowdore U.K.
41 B3 Carrowmore Lake l. Rep. of Ireland
81 F2 Carry Falls Reservoir U.S.A.
16 F1 Çarşamba Turkey
68 E4 Carson City MI U.S.A.
74 C2 Carson City NV U.S.A.
74 C2 Carson Lake l. U.S.A.
74 C2 Carson Sink l. U.S.A.
69 F4 Carsonville U.S.A.
91 B2 Cartagena Chile
89 B2 Cartagena Col.
45 F4 Cartagena Spain
89 B3 Cartago Col.
83 H7 Cartago Costa Rica
79 C5 Cartersville U.S.A.
68 B5 Carthage IL U.S.A.
77 E4 Carthage MO U.S.A.
81 F2 Carthage NY U.S.A.
77 E5 Carthage TX U.S.A.
69 G2 Cartier Can.
38 E3 Cartmel U.K.
67 J3 Cartwright Can.
87 L5 Caruarú Brazil
89 E2 Carúpano Venez.
74 D2 Carvers U.S.A.
42 A4 Carvin France
79 E5 Cary U.S.A.
54 B1 Casablanca Morocco
90 C3 Casa Branca Brazil
73 E6 Casa de Janos Mex.
75 G5 Casa Grande U.S.A.
75 G5 Casa Grande National Monument res. U.S.A.
48 C2 Casale Monferrato Italy
48 D2 Casalmaggiore Italy
89 C3 Casanare r. Col.
49 H4 Casarano Italy
68 B4 Cascade IA U.S.A.
72 C2 Cascade ID U.S.A.
72 E2 Cascade MT U.S.A.
9 B6 Cascade r. N.Z.
9 B6 Cascade Pt pt N.Z.
72 B3 Cascade Range mts U.S.A.
72 D2 Cascade Res. resr U.S.A.
45 B3 Cascais Port.
90 B4 Cascavel Brazil
81 J3 Casco Bay b. U.S.A.
48 F4 Caserta Italy
69 F4 Caseville U.S.A.
92 C6 Casey Austr. Base Ant.
92 D4 Casey Bay b. Ant.
41 D5 Cashel Rep. of Ireland
68 B4 Cashton U.S.A.
89 C2 Casigua Falcón Venez.
89 B2 Casigua Zulia Venez.
31 B2 Casiguran Phil.
91 E2 Casilda Arg.
7 F4 Casino Austr.
89 D4 Casiquiare, Canal r. Venez.
86 C5 Casma Peru
68 E4 Casnovia U.S.A.
74 A2 Caspar U.S.A.
45 F2 Caspe Spain
72 F3 Casper U.S.A.
Caspian Lowland lowland see Prikaspiyskaya Nizmennost'
10 F5 Caspian Sea sea Asia/Europe
80 D5 Cass U.S.A.
69 F4 Cass r. U.S.A.
80 D3 Cassadaga U.S.A.
57 C5 Cassai Angola
69 F4 Cass City U.S.A.
42 A4 Cassel France
81 F2 Casselman Can.
64 D3 Cassiar Can.
64 C3 Cassiar Mountains Can.
8 G2 Cassilis Austr.
48 E4 Cassino Italy
76 E2 Cass Lake U.S.A.
87 J4 Castanhal Brazil
91 C1 Castaño r. Arg.
77 C7 Castaños Mex.
91 C1 Castaño Viejo Arg.
48 D2 Castelfranco Veneto Italy
44 E4 Casteljaloux France
48 F4 Castellammare di Stabia Italy
91 F3 Castelli Arg.
45 F3 Castelló de la Plana Spain
45 C3 Castelo Branco Port.
45 C3 Castelo de Vide Port.
48 C4 Castelsardo Sardinia Italy
48 E6 Casteltermini Sicily Italy
48 E6 Castelvetrano Sicily Italy
8 C4 Casterton Austr.
67 G2 Castignon, Lac l. Can.
45 E3 Castilla - La Mancha div. Spain
45 D2 Castilla y León div. Spain
89 C2 Castilletes Col.
91 G2 Castillos Uru.
41 B4 Castlebar Rep. of Ireland
40 A4 Castlebay U.K.
41 E4 Castlebellingham Rep. of Ireland
41 E3 Castleblayney Rep. of Ireland
41 E5 Castlebridge Rep. of Ireland
38 E3 Castle Carrock U.K.
39 E6 Castle Cary U.K.
75 G2 Castle Dale U.S.A.
41 D3 Castlederg U.K.
41 E5 Castledermot Rep. of Ireland
75 E5 Castle Dome Mts mts U.S.A.
39 F5 Castle Donnington U.K.
40 E6 Castle Douglas U.K.
38 F4 Castleford U.K.
64 F5 Castlegar Can.
41 A5 Castlegregory Rep. of Ireland
41 B5 Castleisland Rep. of Ireland
8 E4 Castlemaine Austr.
41 B5 Castlemaine Rep. of Ireland
41 C6 Castlemartyr Rep. of Ireland
74 B4 Castle Mt mt U.S.A.
27 □ Castle Peak h. H.K. China
27 □ Castle Peak Bay b. H.K. China
9 F4 Castlepoint N.Z.
41 D4 Castlepollard Rep. of Ireland
41 C4 Castlerea Rep. of Ireland
8 G1 Castlereagh r. Austr.
73 F4 Castle Rock U.S.A.
68 B4 Castle Rock Lake l. U.S.A.
38 C3 Castletown Isle of Man
41 D5 Castletown Rep. of Ireland
65 G4 Castor Can.
44 F5 Castres France
42 C2 Castricum Neth.
83 M6 Castries St Lucia
90 C4 Castro Brazil
88 B6 Castro Chile
45 D4 Castro del Río Spain
45 E1 Castro-Urdiales Spain
45 B4 Castro Verde Port.
48 G5 Castrovillari Italy
74 B3 Castroville U.S.A.
9 A6 Caswell Sd in. N.Z.
17 H2 Çat Turkey
86 B5 Catacaos Peru
90 D3 Cataguases Brazil
77 E6 Catahoula L. l. U.S.A.
31 B3 Cataiñgan Phil.
17 J3 Çatak Turkey
90 C2 Catalão Brazil
45 G2 Cataluña div. Spain
88 C3 Catamarca Arg.
31 C3 Catanduanes i. Phil.
90 B4 Catanduvas Brazil
48 F6 Catania Sicily Italy
48 G5 Catanzaro Italy
77 D6 Catarina U.S.A.
31 C3 Catarman Phil.
45 F3 Catarroja Spain
89 B2 Catatumbo r. Venez.
31 C4 Catbalogan Phil.
79 E7 Cat Cays is Bahamas
31 C5 Cateel Phil.
31 C5 Cateel Bay b. Phil.
59 K3 Catembe Moz.
8 G4 Cathcart Austr.
59 G6 Cathcart S. Africa
59 H4 Cathedral Peak mt S. Africa
41 A6 Catherdaniel Rep. of Ireland
75 F2 Catherine, Mt mt U.S.A.
91 B3 Catillo Chile
79 E7 Cat Island i. Bahamas
66 B3 Cat L. l. Can.
82 G4 Catoche, C. c. Mex.
80 E5 Catonsville U.S.A.
84 B2 Catorce Mex.
91 D3 Catriló Arg.
89 E4 Catrimani Brazil
89 E4 Catrimani r. Brazil
81 G3 Catskill U.S.A.
81 F4 Catskill Mts mts U.S.A.
42 A4 Cats, Mont des h. France
59 K3 Catuane Moz.
89 E4 Cauamé r. Brazil
31 B4 Cauayan Phil.
67 H2 Caubvick, Mount mt Can.
89 B3 Cauca r. Col.
87 L4 Caucaia Brazil
89 B3 Caucasia Col.
35 K4 Caucasus mts Asia/Europe
91 C1 Caucete Arg.
81 J1 Caucomgomoc Lake l. U.S.A.
42 B4 Caudry France
31 C4 Cauit Point pt Phil.
91 B2 Cauquenes Chile
89 D3 Caura r. Venez.
67 G4 Causapscal Can.
44 G5 Cavaillon France
90 C1 Cavalcante Brazil
54 B4 Cavally r. Côte d'Ivoire
41 D4 Cavan Rep. of Ireland
77 F4 Cave City U.S.A.
90 E1 Caveira r. Brazil
8 D4 Cavendish Austr.
90 B4 Cavernoso, Serra do mts Brazil
80 B5 Cave Run Lake l. U.S.A.
31 B4 Cavili rf Phil.
31 B3 Cavite Phil.
40 E3 Cawdor U.K.
8 C2 Cawndilla Lake l. Austr.
39 J5 Cawston U.K.
87 K4 Caxias Brazil
88 F3 Caxias do Sul Brazil
57 B4 Caxito Angola
16 C2 Çay Turkey
79 D5 Cayce U.S.A.
16 D1 Çaycuma Turkey
17 H1 Çayeli Turkey
87 H3 Cayenne Fr. Guiana
16 E3 Çayhan Turkey
16 C1 Çayırhan Turkey
83 J5 Cayman Brac i. Cayman Is
61 K8 Cayman Islands terr. Caribbean Sea
96 D4 Cayman Trench sea feature Atl. Ocean
56 E3 Caynabo Somalia
69 H4 Cayuga Can.
80 E3 Cayuga Lake l. U.S.A.
81 F3 Cazenovia U.S.A.
57 C5 Cazombo Angola
91 F2 Cebollatí r. Uru.
31 B4 Cebu Phil.
31 B4 Cebu i. Phil.
68 C3 Cecil U.S.A.
48 D3 Cecina Italy
68 A4 Cedar r. IA U.S.A.
76 C2 Cedar r. ND U.S.A.
68 D4 Cedarburg U.S.A.
75 F3 Cedar City U.S.A.
77 D5 Cedar Creek Res. resr U.S.A.
68 A4 Cedar Falls U.S.A.
68 D4 Cedar Grove WV U.S.A.
80 C5 Cedar Grove WV U.S.A.
81 F6 Cedar I. i. U.S.A.
65 J4 Cedar L. l. Can.
68 D5 Cedar Lake l. U.S.A.
80 B4 Cedar Pt pt U.S.A.
68 B5 Cedar Rapids U.S.A.
75 G3 Cedar Ridge U.S.A.
81 F5 Cedar Run U.S.A.
69 F4 Cedar Springs Can.
68 E4 Cedar Springs U.S.A.
79 C5 Cedartown U.S.A.
59 H5 Cedarville S. Africa
68 E3 Cedarville U.S.A.
82 A3 Cedros i. Mex.
6 D5 Ceduna Austr.
56 E3 Ceeldheere Somalia
56 E2 Ceerigaabo Somalia
48 F5 Cefalù Sicily Italy
47 J7 Cegléd Hungary
27 B5 Ceheng China
16 E1 Çekerek Turkey
32 B4 Celah, Gunung mt Malaysia
84 B2 Celaya Mex.
41 E4 Celbridge Rep. of Ireland
Celebes i. see Sulawesi
33 E2 Celebes Sea sea Indon./Phil.
80 A4 Celina U.S.A.
48 F1 Celje Slovenia
43 J2 Celle Ger.
16 E1 Cemilbey Turkey
16 G2 Çemişgezek Turkey
25 F7 Cenderawasih, Teluk b. Indon.
27 C5 Cengong China
75 F5 Centennial Wash r. U.S.A.
77 E6 Center U.S.A.
81 G4 Centereach U.S.A.
79 C5 Center Point U.S.A.
80 B5 Centerville U.S.A.
59 G1 Central div. Botswana
53 F5 Central African Republic country Africa
19 G4 Central Brahui Range mts Pak.
68 B4 Central City IA U.S.A.
76 D3 Central City NE U.S.A.
89 A4 Central, Cordillera mts Col.
86 C5 Central, Cordillera mts Peru
31 B2 Central, Cordillera mts Phil.
27 □ Central District H.K. China
78 B4 Centralia IL U.S.A.
72 B2 Centralia WA U.S.A.
68 A2 Central Lakes U.S.A.
19 G5 Central Makran Range mts Pak.
72 B3 Central Point U.S.A.
6 E2 Central Ra. mts P.N.G.
79 C5 Centreville U.S.A.
27 D6 Cenxi China
Cephalonia i. see Kefallonia
89 D3 Cerbatana, Sa de la mt Venez.
75 E4 Cerbat Mts mts U.S.A.
65 G4 Cereal Can.
88 D3 Ceres Arg.
58 C6 Ceres S. Africa
89 B2 Cereté Col.
45 E2 Cerezo de Abajo Spain
48 F4 Cerignola Italy
16 D2 Çerikli Turkey
16 D1 Çerkeş Turkey
16 G3 Çermelik r. Syria
17 G2 Çermik Turkey
49 N2 Cernavodă Romania
84 C1 Cerralvo Mex.
82 C4 Cerralvo i. Mex.
49 H4 Cërrik Albania
84 B2 Cerritos Mex.
90 C4 Cerro Azul Brazil
84 C2 Cerro Azul Mex.
86 B4 Cerro de Amotape, Parque Nacional nat. park Peru
86 C6 Cerro de Pasco Peru
89 D3 Cerro Jáua, Meseta del plat. Venez.
89 C2 Cerrón, Co mt Venez.
84 A1 Cerro Prieto Mex.
91 C3 Cerros Colorados, Embalse resr Arg.
48 F4 Cervati, Monte mt Italy
48 C3 Cervione Corsica France
45 C1 Cervo Spain
89 B2 César r. Col.
48 E2 Cesena Italy
37 T8 Cēsis Latvia
46 G6 České Budějovice Czech Rep.
46 G6 Český Krumlov Czech Rep.
43 L5 Český Les mts Czech Rep./Ger.
49 M5 Çeşme Turkey
8 H2 Cessnock Austr.
49 H3 Cetinje Yugo.
48 F5 Cetraro Italy
45 D5 Ceuta Spain
44 F4 Cévennes mts France
16 E3 Ceyhan Turkey
16 E3 Ceyhan r. Turkey
17 H3 Ceylanpınar Turkey
19 F2 Chaacha Turkm.
42 A5 Chaalis, Abbaye de France
91 E2 Chacabuco Arg.
91 B4 Chacao Chile
91 C3 Chachahuén, Sa mt Arg.
86 C5 Chachapoyas Peru
50 D4 Chachersk Belarus
32 B2 Chachoengsao Thai.
22 B4 Chachro Pak.
64 C4 Chacon, C. c. U.S.A.
52 F4 Chad country Africa
15 H1 Chadan Rus. Fed.
59 G1 Chadibe Botswana
91 C3 Chadileo r. Arg.
55 D3 Chad, Lake l. Africa
76 C3 Chadron U.S.A.
32 A1 Chae Hom Thai.
30 C4 Chaeryŏng N. Korea
89 B4 Chafurray Col.
19 G4 Chagai Pak.
19 F4 Chagai Hills mts Afgh./Pak.
23 F2 Chagdo Kangri reg. China
19 G3 Chaghcharān Afgh.
44 G3 Chagny France
10 J10 Chagos Archipelago is British Ind. Ocean Terr.
50 J4 Chagra r. Rus. Fed.
89 D2 Chaguaramas Venez.
23 G3 Cha'gyüngoinba China
19 F4 Chahah Burjal Afgh.
19 E3 Chāh Ākhvor Iran
19 E3 Chahār Takāb Iran
18 D3 Chāh Badam Iran
19 F5 Chāh Bahār Iran
18 D4 Chāh-e Bāgh well Iran
18 E3 Chāh-e Kavīr well Iran
18 D3 Chāh-e Khorāsān well Iran
19 E3 Chāh-e Khoshāb Iran
19 E4 Chāh-e Malek Iran
18 D3 Chāh-e Mirzā well Iran
18 D3 Chāh-e Mūjān well Iran
18 D3 Chāh-e Nūklok Iran
18 D3 Chāh-e Nūklok well Iran
18 D4 Chāh-e Qeyşar well Iran
18 D3 Chāh-e Qobād well Iran
18 D4 Chāh-e Rāh Iran
19 E4 Chāh-e-Raḩmān well Iran
18 D3 Chāh-e Shūr Iran
18 D3 Chāh-e Shur well Iran
18 D3 Chah Haji Abdulla well Iran
18 D4 Chāh Ḩaqq Iran
19 H2 Chah-i-Ab Afgh.
17 K4 Chah-i-Shurkh Iraq
18 D3 Chāh Pās well Iran
18 C4 Chāh Rūstā'ī Iran
19 F4 Chah Sandan Pak.
30 C2 Chai r. China
23 F5 Chāībāsa India
67 G3 Chaigneau, Lac l. Can.
32 B2 Chai Si r. Thai.
27 □ Chai Wan H.K. China
32 A3 Chaiya Thai.
32 B2 Chaiyaphum Thai.
91 F1 Chajarí Arg.
22 B3 Chakar r. Pak.
23 H5 Chakaria Bangl.
19 F4 Chakhānsūr Afgh.
23 E4 Chakia India
19 G5 Chakku Pak.
86 D7 Chala Peru
19 G3 Chalap Dalan mts Afgh.
82 G6 Chalatenango El Salvador
67 G4 Chaleur Bay in. Can.
27 D5 Chaling China
22 C5 Chalisgaon India
49 K5 Chalkida Greece
9 A7 Chalky Inlet in. N.Z.
44 D3 Challans France
86 E7 Challapata Bol.
94 E5 Challenger Deep depth Pac. Oc.
95 M8 Challenger Fracture Zone sea feature Pac. Oc.
72 D2 Challis U.S.A.
44 G2 Châlons-en-Champagne France
44 G3 Chalon-sur-Saône France
30 C2 Chaluhe China
18 C2 Chālūs Iran
43 L5 Cham Ger.
73 F4 Chama U.S.A.
57 D5 Chama Zambia
89 C2 Chama r. Venez.
91 D2 Chamaico Arg.
58 A3 Chamais Bay b. Namibia
19 G4 Chaman Pak.
22 D4 Chambal r. India
67 G3 Chambeaux, Lac l. Can.
65 H4 Chamberlain Can.
76 D3 Chamberlain U.S.A.
81 J1 Chamberlain Lake l. U.S.A.
75 H4 Chambers U.S.A.
80 E5 Chambersburg U.S.A.
44 G4 Chambéry France
57 D5 Chambeshi Zambia
48 C7 Chambi, Jebel mt Tunisia
44 G4 Chamechaude mt France
18 C3 Cham-e Ḩannā Iran
18 C3 Chameshk Iran
91 C1 Chamical Arg.
23 F4 Chamlang mt Nepal
32 B3 Châmnar Cambodia
66 F4 Chamouchouane r. Can.
23 E5 Champa India
64 B2 Champagne Can.
44 G2 Champagne reg. France
59 H4 Champagne Castle mt S. Africa
44 G3 Champagnole France
68 C5 Champaign U.S.A.
91 D1 Champaqui, Cerro mt Arg.
32 C2 Champasak Laos
23 H5 Champhai India
68 D2 Champion U.S.A.
81 G2 Champlain U.S.A.
81 G2 Champlain, L. l. Can./U.S.A.
84 E3 Champotón Mex.
21 B4 Chamrajnagar India
50 H4 Chamzinka Rus. Fed.
32 B4 Chana Thai.
88 B3 Chañaral Chile
89 E3 Chanaro, Co mt Venez.
91 B2 Chanco Chile
Chanda see Chandrapur
62 D3 Chandalar r. U.S.A.
23 E5 Chandarpur India
22 D3 Chandausi India
77 F6 Chandeleur Islands is U.S.A.
22 E5 Chandia India
22 D3 Chandigarh India
75 G5 Chandler U.S.A.
69 J3 Chandos Lake l. Can.
23 G5 Chandpur Bangl.
22 D3 Chandpur India
23 H5 Chandraghona Bangl.
22 D6 Chandrapur India
22 D5 Chandur India
57 D6 Changane r. Moz.
57 D5 Changara Moz.
30 E3 Changbai China
30 D3 Changbai Shan mts China/N. Korea
27 C7 Changcheng China
92 B1 Chang Cheng (Great Wall) China Base Ant.
30 C2 Changchun China
30 C1 Changchunling China
26 F2 Changdao China
27 D4 Changde China
30 D4 Changdo N. Korea
26 E3 Changfeng China
30 E5 Changgi Gap pt S. Korea
30 B4 Changhai China
30 D6 Changhang S. Korea
30 D5 Changhowan S. Korea
27 F5 Chang-hua Taiwan
32 D1 Changhua Jiang r. China
30 D6 Changhung S. Korea
32 □ Changi Sing.
27 C7 Changjiang China
Chang Jiang r. see Yangtze
Changjiang Kou est. see Yangtze, Mouth of the
30 D3 Changjin N. Korea
30 D3 Changjin Reservoir N. Korea
27 F5 Changle China
26 F2 Changli China
30 B1 Changling China
27 D5 Changning China
30 C4 Changnyŏn N. Korea
26 E1 Changping China
30 E5 Changp'yŏng S. Korea
30 C4 Changsan-got pt N. Korea
27 D4 Changsha China
27 F4 Changshan China
30 B4 Changshan Qundao is China
27 C4 Changshou China
27 D4 Changshoujie China
26 F4 Changshu China
27 C5 Changshun China
30 D6 Changsŏng S. Korea
27 E5 Changtai China
27 E5 Changting Fujian China
30 E1 Changting Heilongjiang China
30 C2 Changtu China
30 E6 Ch'angwŏn S. Korea
26 C3 Changwu China
30 A4 Changxing Dao i. China
27 D4 Changyang China
26 F2 Changyi China
30 C4 Changyŏn N. Korea
26 E3 Changyuan China
26 D2 Changzhi China
26 F4 Changzhou China
49 L7 Chania Greece
30 D3 Chanjin r. N. Korea
26 B3 Chankou China
21 B3 Channapatna India
74 C5 Channel Islands is U.S.A.
34 E4 Channel Islands terr. English Channel
74 B5 Channel Is Nat. Park U.S.A.
67 J4 Channel-Port-aux-Basques Can.
39 J6 Channel Tunnel tunnel France/U.K.
68 C2 Channing U.S.A.
45 C1 Chantada Spain

32 B2 Chanthaburi Thai.
44 F2 Chantilly France
77 E4 Chanute U.S.A.
12 J4 Chany, Ozero salt l. Rus. Fed.
26 E2 Chaobai Xinhe r. China
26 E4 Chao Hu l. China
32 B2 Chao Phraya r. Thai.
54 B1 Chaouèn Morocco
23 H2 Chaowula Shan mts China
26 E4 Chao Xian China
27 E6 Chaoyang Guangdong China
26 F1 Chaoyang Liaoning China
27 E6 Chaozhou China
90 E1 Chapada Diamantina, Parque Nacional nat. park Brazil
90 A1 Chapada dos Guimarães Brazil
90 C1 Chapada dos Veadeiros, Parque Nacional da nat. park Brazil
84 B2 Chapala Mex.
84 B2 Chapala, L. de l. Mex.
89 B4 Chaparral Col.
14 D1 Chapayev Kazak.
50 J4 Chapayevsk Rus. Fed.
88 F3 Chapecó Brazil
88 F3 Chapecó r. Brazil
39 F4 Chapel-en-le-Frith U.K.
79 E5 Chapel Hill U.S.A.
42 C4 Chapelle-lez-Herlaimont Belgium
39 F4 Chapeltown U.K.
68 D5 Chapin, Lake l. U.S.A.
69 F2 Chapleau Can.
50 F4 Chaplygin Rus. Fed.
51 E6 Chaplynka Ukr.
80 B6 Chapmanville U.S.A.
19 G3 Chapri Pass pass Afgh.
86 E7 Chaqui Bol.
22 D2 Char Jammu and Kashmir
84 B2 Charcas Mex.
23 H3 Char Chu r. China
92 A2 Charcot I. i. Ant.
65 G3 Chard Can.
39 E7 Chard U.K.
17 L3 Chārdagh Iran
17 L5 Chardāvol Iran
80 C4 Chardon U.S.A.
19 F2 Chardzhev Turkm.
44 E3 Charente r. France
19 H3 Chārīkār Afgh.
76 E3 Chariton r. U.S.A.
69 F3 Charity Is i. U.S.A.
12 G3 Charkayuvom Rus. Fed.
22 D4 Charkhari India
42 C4 Charleroi Belgium
71 L4 Charles, Cape pt VA U.S.A.
68 A4 Charles City U.S.A.
42 A5 Charles de Gaulle airport France
77 E6 Charles, Lake U.S.A.
9 C4 Charleston N.Z.
78 B4 Charleston IL U.S.A.
81 J2 Charleston ME U.S.A.
77 F4 Charleston MO U.S.A.
79 E5 Charleston SC U.S.A.
80 C5 Charleston WV U.S.A.
75 E3 Charleston Peak summit U.S.A.
41 C4 Charlestown Rep. of Ireland
81 G3 Charlestown NH U.S.A.
81 H4 Charlestown RI U.S.A.
80 E5 Charles Town U.S.A.
6 E4 Charleville Austr.
44 G2 Charleville-Mézières France
68 E3 Charlevoix U.S.A.
64 E3 Charlie Lake Can.
68 E4 Charlotte MI U.S.A.
79 D5 Charlotte NC U.S.A.
79 D7 Charlotte Harbor b. U.S.A.
80 D5 Charlottesville U.S.A.
67 H4 Charlottetown Can.
89 E2 Charlotteville Trinidad and Tobago
8 D4 Charlton Austr.
66 E3 Charlton I. i. Can.
50 F2 Charozero Rus. Fed.
82 B2 Charsadda Pak.
6 E4 Charters Towers Austr.
44 E2 Chartres France
91 E2 Chascomús Arg.
64 F4 Chase Can.
19 F2 Chashkent Turkm.
17 L4 Chashmeh Iran
18 E3 Chashmeh Nūrī Iran
18 D3 Chashmeh ye Palasi Iran
18 D3 Chashmeh ye Shotoran well Iran
50 D4 Chashniki Belarus
9 B7 Chaslands Mistake c. N.Z.
30 D3 Chasŏng N. Korea
18 D3 Chastab, Kūh-e mts Iran
44 D3 Châteaubriant France
44 E3 Château-du-Loir France
44 E3 Châteaudun France
81 F2 Chateaugay U.S.A.
81 G2 Châteauguay Can.
44 B2 Châteaulin France
44 F3 Châteauneuf-sur-Loire France
44 E3 Châteauroux France
42 E6 Château-Salins France
44 F2 Château-Thierry France
42 C4 Châtelet Belgium
44 E3 Châtellerault France
68 A4 Chatfield U.S.A.
67 G4 Chatham N.B. Can.
69 F4 Chatham Ont. Can.
39 H6 Chatham U.K.
81 H4 Chatham MA U.S.A.
81 G3 Chatham NY U.S.A.
80 D6 Chatham VA U.S.A.
7 J6 Chatham Islands is N.Z.
94 G8 Chatham Rise sea feature Pac. Oc.
64 C4 Chatham Sd chan. Can.
64 C3 Chatham Strait chan. U.S.A.
23 F4 Chatra India
69 G3 Chatsworth Can.
68 C5 Chatsworth U.S.A.
79 C5 Chattanooga U.S.A.
39 H5 Chatteris U.K.
32 B2 Chatturat Thai.
32 C3 Châu Đôc Vietnam
22 B4 Chauhtan India
23 H5 Chauk Myanmar
22 E4 Chauka r. India
44 G2 Chaumont France
32 A2 Chaungwabyin Myanmar
13 S3 Chaunskaya Guba b. Rus. Fed.
44 F2 Chauny France
23 F4 Chauparan India
80 D3 Chautauqua, Lake l. U.S.A.
21 C4 Chavakachcheri Sri Lanka
18 B3 Chavār Iran
87 J4 Chaves Brazil
45 C2 Chaves Port.
66 E2 Chavigny, Lac l. Can.
50 D4 Chavusy Belarus
22 A3 Chawal r. Pak.
27 B6 Chây r. Vietnam
Châyul see Qayü
91 D2 Chazón Arg.
81 G2 Chazy U.S.A.
39 F5 Cheadle U.K.
80 D5 Cheat r. U.S.A.
46 F5 Cheb Czech Rep.
48 D7 Chebba Tunisia
50 H3 Cheboksary Rus. Fed.
68 E3 Cheboygan U.S.A.
51 H7 Chechen', Ostrov i. Rus. Fed.
51 H7 Chechenskaya Respublika div. Rus. Fed.
30 E5 Chech'ŏn S. Korea
77 E5 Checotah U.S.A.
30 A5 Chedao China
39 E6 Cheddar U.K.
65 G3 Cheecham Can.
92 B5 Cheetham, C. c. Ant.
62 B3 Chefornak AK U.S.A.
59 K1 Chefu Moz.
54 B2 Chegga Maur.
57 D5 Chegutu Zimbabwe
72 B2 Chehalis U.S.A.
19 H3 Chehardar Pass Afgh.
17 L5 Chehariz Iraq
18 E4 Chehell'āyeh Iran
30 D7 Cheju S. Korea
30 D7 Cheju-do i. S. Korea
30 D7 Cheju-haehyŏp chan. S. Korea
50 F4 Chekhov Rus. Fed.
72 B2 Chelan, L. l. U.S.A.
18 D2 Cheleken Turkm.
91 C3 Chelforó Arg.
45 G4 Chélif r. Alg.
14 D2 Chelkar Kazak.
47 L5 Chełm Pol.
39 H6 Chelmer r. U.K.
47 J4 Chełmno Pol.
39 H6 Chelmsford U.K.
81 H3 Chelmsford U.S.A.
39 E6 Cheltenham U.K.
45 F3 Chelva Spain
12 H4 Chelyabinsk Rus. Fed.
57 D5 Chemba Moz.
22 D2 Chem Co l. China
43 L4 Chemnitz Ger.
80 E3 Chemung r. U.S.A.
22 B3 Chenab r. Pak.
54 B2 Chenachane Alg.
81 F3 Chenango r. U.S.A.
72 C2 Cheney U.S.A.
77 D4 Cheney Res. resr U.S.A.
21 C3 Chengalpattu India
26 E2 Cheng'an China
27 D5 Chengbu China
26 E1 Chengde China
27 B4 Chengdu China
26 C3 Chenggu China
27 E6 Chenghai China
26 C4 Chengkou China
25 D5 Chengmai China
30 B4 Chengzitan China
26 F3 Cheniu Shan i. China
68 C5 Chenoa U.S.A.
27 D5 Chenxi China
27 E5 Chenzhou China
32 D2 Cheo Reo Vietnam
86 C5 Chepén Peru
91 C1 Chepes Arg.
39 E6 Chepstow U.K.
50 J3 Cheptsa r. Rus. Fed.
17 L5 Cheqad Kabūd Iran
68 B2 Chequamegon Bay b. U.S.A.
44 F3 Cher r. France
84 B3 Cherán Mex.
79 E5 Cheraw U.S.A.
44 D2 Cherbourg France
45 H4 Cherchell Alg.
50 J4 Cherdakly Rus. Fed.
24 C1 Cheremkhovo Rus. Fed.
28 D2 Cheremshany Rus. Fed.
50 F3 Cherepovets Rus. Fed.
50 H2 Cherevkovo Rus. Fed.
48 B7 Chéria Alg.
51 E5 Cherkasy Ukr.
51 G6 Cherkessk Rus. Fed.
21 C2 Cherla India
57 C5 Chermenze Angola
12 K2 Chernaya Rus. Fed.
50 J3 Chernaya Kholunitsa Rus. Fed.
28 C2 Chernigovka Rus. Fed.
51 D5 Chernihiv Ukr.
51 F6 Cherninivka Ukr.
51 C5 Chernivtsi Ukr.
24 B1 Chernogorsk Rus. Fed.
50 H3 Chernovskoye Rus. Fed.
51 D5 Chernyakhiv Ukr.
47 K3 Chernyakhovsk Rus. Fed.
51 F5 Chernyanka Rus. Fed.
13 N3 Chernyshevskiy Rus. Fed.
51 H6 Chernyye Zemli reg. Rus. Fed.
51 H5 Chernyy Yar Rus. Fed.
76 E3 Cherokee IA U.S.A.
77 D4 Cherokee OK U.S.A.
77 E4 Cherokees, Lake o' the l. U.S.A.
79 E7 Cherokee Sound Bahamas
91 B3 Cherquenco Chile
23 G4 Cherrapunji India
75 E2 Cherry Creek U.S.A.
75 E1 Cherry Creek Mts mts U.S.A.
81 K2 Cherryfield U.S.A.
7 G3 Cherry Island i. Solomon Is
69 J4 Cherry Valley Can.
81 F3 Cherry Valley U.S.A.
13 Q3 Cherskogo, Khrebet mts Rus. Fed.
51 G5 Chertkovo Rus. Fed.
50 J2 Cherva Rus. Fed.
49 L3 Cherven Bryag Bulg.
51 C5 Chervonohrad Ukr.
51 E5 Chervonozavods'ke Ukr.
50 D4 Chervyen' Belarus
39 F6 Cherwell r. U.K.
50 D4 Cherykaw Belarus
69 E4 Chesaning U.S.A.
81 E6 Chesapeake U.S.A.
81 E5 Chesapeake Bay b. U.S.A.
39 G6 Chesham U.K.
81 G3 Cheshire U.S.A.
39 E4 Cheshire Plain lowland U.K.
19 F2 Cheshme 2-y Turkm.
12 F3 Cheshskaya Guba b. Rus. Fed.
19 F3 Chesht-e Sharīf Afgh.
39 G6 Cheshunt U.K.
39 E4 Chester U.K.
74 B1 Chester CA U.S.A.
78 B4 Chester IL U.S.A.
72 E1 Chester MT U.S.A.
81 F5 Chester PA U.S.A.
79 D5 Chester SC U.S.A.
81 E5 Chester r. U.S.A.
39 F4 Chesterfield U.K.
7 F3 Chesterfield, Îles is New Caledonia
63 J3 Chesterfield Inlet N.W.T. Can.
65 L2 Chesterfield Inlet Can.
65 L2 Chesterfield Inlet in. Can.
38 F3 Chester-le-Street U.K.
81 E5 Chestertown MD U.S.A.
81 G3 Chestertown NY U.S.A.
81 F2 Chesterville Can.
80 D4 Chestnut Ridge ridge U.S.A.
81 J1 Chesuncook U.S.A.
81 J1 Chesuncook Lake l. U.S.A.
48 B6 Chetaïbi Alg.
67 H4 Chéticamp Can.
21 A4 Chetlat i. India
82 G5 Chetumal Mex.
64 E3 Chetwynd Can.
27 □ Cheung Chau H.K. China
27 □ Cheung Chau i. H.K. China
9 D5 Cheviot N.Z.
38 E2 Cheviot Hills h. U.K.
38 E2 Cheviot, The h. U.K.
72 C1 Chewelah U.S.A.
77 D5 Cheyenne OK U.S.A.
72 F3 Cheyenne WY U.S.A.
76 C3 Cheyenne r. U.S.A.
76 C4 Cheyenne Wells U.S.A.
64 E4 Chezacut Can.
22 C4 Chhapar India
23 F4 Chhapra India
22 D4 Chhatarpur India
22 B3 Chhatr Pak.
22 D5 Chhindwara India
22 C5 Chhota Udepur India
22 C4 Chhoti Sadri India
23 G4 Chhukha Bhutan
27 F6 Chia-i Taiwan
32 B1 Chiang Kham Thai.
32 B1 Chiang Khan Thai.
32 A1 Chiang Mai Thai.
84 D3 Chiapas div. Mex.
48 C2 Chiari Italy
84 C3 Chiautla Mex.
29 G7 Chiba Japan
57 B5 Chibia Angola
57 D6 Chiboma Moz.
66 F4 Chibougamau Can.
66 F4 Chibougamau L. l. Can.
66 F4 Chibougamau, Parc de res. Can.
29 E6 Chibu-Sangaku Nat. Park Japan
59 K2 Chibuto Moz.
23 G2 Chibuzhang Hu l. China
Chicacole see Srikakulam
68 D5 Chicago U.S.A.
68 D5 Chicago Heights U.S.A.
68 C5 Chicago Ship Canal canal U.S.A.
89 B3 Chicamocha r. Col.
89 E3 Chicanán r. Venez.
64 B3 Chichagof U.S.A.
64 B3 Chichagof Island i. U.S.A.
26 E1 Chicheng China
39 G7 Chichester U.K.
6 B4 Chichester Range mts Austr.
29 F7 Chichibu Japan
29 F7 Chichibu-Tama National Park Japan
80 E6 Chickahominy r. U.S.A.
79 C5 Chickamauga L. l. U.S.A.
77 D5 Chickasha U.S.A.
45 C4 Chiclana de la Frontera Spain
86 C5 Chiclayo Peru
74 B2 Chico U.S.A.
88 C6 Chico r. Chubut Arg.
91 B4 Chico r. Chubut/Rio Negro Arg.
88 C7 Chico r. Santa Cruz Arg.
59 L2 Chicomo Moz.
84 D4 Chicomucelo Mex.
81 G3 Chicopee U.S.A.
31 B2 Chico Sapocoy, Mt mt Phil.
67 F4 Chicoutimi Can.
59 J1 Chicualacuala Moz.
21 B4 Chidambaram India
59 L2 Chidenguele Moz.
67 H1 Chidley, C. c. Can.
30 D6 Chido S. Korea
59 L2 Chiducuane Moz.
79 D6 Chiefland U.S.A.
46 F7 Chiemsee l. Ger.
42 D5 Chiers r. France
48 F3 Chieti Italy
84 C3 Chietla Mex.
26 F1 Chifeng China
90 E2 Chifre, Serra do mts Brazil
12 J5 Chiganak Kazak.
67 G4 Chignecto B. b. Can.
89 A3 Chigorodó Col.
57 D6 Chigubo Moz.
23 G3 Chigu Co l. China
82 C3 Chihuahua Mex.
27 D6 Chikan China
21 B3 Chik Ballapur India
50 D3 Chikhachevo Rus. Fed.
22 D5 Chikhali Kalan Parasia India
22 D5 Chikhli India
21 A3 Chikmagalur India
29 F6 Chikuma-gawa r. Japan
64 E4 Chilanko Forks Can.
84 C3 Chilapa Mex.
15 F3 Chilas Jammu and Kashmir
21 B5 Chilaw Sri Lanka
74 B2 Chilcoot U.S.A.
64 E4 Chilcotin r. Can.
77 C5 Childress U.S.A.
85 C7 Chile country S. America
95 O8 Chile Basin sea feature Pac. Oc.
88 C3 Chilecito Arg.
51 H6 Chilgir Rus. Fed.
23 F6 Chilika Lake l. India
57 C5 Chililabombwe Zambia
64 E4 Chilko r. Can.
64 E4 Chilko L. l. Can.
91 B3 Chillán Chile
91 B3 Chillán, Nevado mts Chile
91 E3 Chillar Arg.
76 E4 Chillicothe MO U.S.A.
80 B5 Chillicothe OH U.S.A.
68 C5 Chillicothe U.S.A.
22 C1 Chillinji Pak.
64 E5 Chilliwack Can.
18 D1 Chil'mamedkum, Peski des. Turkm.
88 B6 Chiloé, Isla de i. Chile
72 B3 Chiloquin U.S.A.
84 C3 Chilpancingo Mex.
8 F4 Chiltern Austr.
39 G6 Chiltern Hills h. U.K.
68 C3 Chilton U.S.A.
27 F5 Chi-lung Taiwan
22 D2 Chilung Pass pass India
57 D4 Chimala Tanz.
42 C4 Chimay Belgium
91 C1 Chimbas Arg.
86 C4 Chimborazo mt Ecuador
86 C5 Chimbote Peru
89 B2 Chimichaguá Col.
57 D5 Chimoio Moz.
84 C1 China Mex.
10 L6 China country Asia
89 B3 Chinácota Col.
84 E3 Chinajá Guatemala
74 D4 China Lake l. CA U.S.A.
81 J2 China Lake l. ME U.S.A.
82 G6 Chinandega Nic.
74 C5 China Pt pt U.S.A.
86 C6 Chincha Alta Peru
64 F3 Chinchaga r. Can.
81 F6 Chincoteague B. b. U.S.A.
57 D5 Chinde Moz.
30 D6 Chindo S. Korea
30 D6 Chin-do i. S. Korea
24 B3 Chindu China
23 H5 Chindwin r. Myanmar
22 C2 Chineni Jammu and Kashmir
89 B3 Chingaza, Parque Nacional nat. park Col.
30 C4 Chinghwa N. Korea
57 C5 Chingola Zambia
57 B5 Chinguar Angola
30 E6 Chinhae S. Korea
57 D5 Chinhoyi Zimbabwe
22 C3 Chiniot Pak.
30 E6 Chinju S. Korea
56 C3 Chinko r. C.A.R.
75 H3 Chinle U.S.A.
75 H3 Chinle Valley v. U.S.A.
75 H3 Chinle Wash r. U.S.A.
27 F5 Chinmen Taiwan
27 F5 Chinmen Tao i. Taiwan
21 B2 Chinnur India
29 F7 Chino Japan
44 E3 Chinon France
75 F4 Chino Valley U.S.A.
57 D5 Chinsali Zambia
21 B3 Chintamani India
48 E2 Chioggia Italy
49 M5 Chios Greece
49 L5 Chios i. Greece
57 D5 Chipata Zambia
91 C4 Chipchihua, Sa de mts Arg.
57 B5 Chipindo Angola
57 D6 Chipinge Zimbabwe
21 A2 Chiplun India
39 E6 Chippenham U.K.
68 B3 Chippewa r. U.S.A.
68 B3 Chippewa Falls U.S.A.
68 B2 Chippewa, Lake l. U.S.A.
39 F6 Chipping Norton U.K.
39 E6 Chipping Sodbury U.K.
81 K2 Chiputneticook Lakes l. U.S.A.
82 G6 Chiquimula Guatemala
89 B3 Chiquinquira Col.
51 G5 Chir r. Rus. Fed.
21 C3 Chirada India
21 A4 Chirakkal India
21 C3 Chirala India
19 G3 Chiras Afgh.
22 C3 Chirāwa India
57 D6 Chiredzi Zimbabwe
75 H5 Chiricahua National Monument res. U.S.A.
75 H6 Chiricahua Peak summit U.S.A.
89 B2 Chiriguaná Col.
62 C4 Chirikof I. i. U.S.A.
83 H7 Chiriquí, Golfo de b. Panama
39 D5 Chirk U.K.
40 F5 Chirnside U.K.
49 L3 Chirpan Bulg.
83 H7 Chirripo mt Costa Rica
57 C5 Chirundu Zambia
66 E3 Chisasibi Can.
84 E4 Chisec Guatemala
68 A2 Chisholm U.S.A.
22 C3 Chishtian Mandi Pak.
27 B4 Chishui China
51 D6 Chişinău Moldova
47 K7 Chişineu-Criş Romania
50 J4 Chistopol' Rus. Fed.
24 D1 Chita Rus. Fed.
57 B5 Chitado Angola
57 D5 Chitambo Zambia
56 C4 Chitato Angola
65 H4 Chitek Lake Can.
57 B5 Chitembo Angola
57 D4 Chitipa Malawi
57 C5 Chitokoloki Zambia
28 G3 Chitose Japan
21 B3 Chitradurga India
22 B2 Chitral Pak.
22 B2 Chitral r. Pak.
83 H7 Chitré Panama
23 G5 Chittagong Bangl.
23 F5 Chittaranjan India
22 C4 Chittaurgarh India
21 B3 Chittoor India
21 B4 Chittur India
57 D5 Chitungulu Zambia
57 D5 Chitungwiza Zimbabwe
57 C5 Chiume Angola
57 D5 Chivhu Zimbabwe
91 E2 Chivilcoy Arg.
27 D6 Chixi China
17 J3 Chiya-e Linik h. Iraq
29 D7 Chizu Japan
50 G3 Chkalovsk Rus. Fed.
28 C2 Chkalovskoye Rus. Fed.
30 D6 Ch'o i. S. Korea
32 □ Choa Chu Kang Sing.
32 □ Choa Chu Kang h. Sing.
32 C2 Choâm Khsant Cambodia
91 B1 Choapa r. Chile
57 C5 Chobe National Park Botswana
30 D5 Choch'iwŏn S. Korea
75 E5 Chocolate Mts mts U.S.A.
89 B3 Chocontá Col.
30 C4 Cho Do i. N. Korea
43 L4 Chodov Czech Rep.
91 D3 Choele Choel Arg.
22 C2 Chogo Lungma Gl. gl. Pak.
51 H6 Chograyskoye Vdkhr. resr Rus. Fed.
65 J4 Choiceland Can.
7 F2 Choiseul i. Solomon Is
88 E8 Choiseul Sound chan. Falkland Is
46 H4 Chojnice Pol.
28 G5 Chōkai-san volc. Japan
77 D6 Choke Canyon L. l. U.S.A.
56 D2 Ch'ok'ē Mts mts Eth.
23 F3 Choksum China
13 Q2 Chokurdakh Rus. Fed.
57 D6 Chókwé Moz.
44 D3 Cholet France
91 B4 Cholila Arg.
82 G6 Choluteca Honduras
57 C5 Choma Zambia
30 E5 Chŏmch'ŏn S. Korea
23 G4 Chomo Lhari mt Bhutan
32 A1 Chom Thong Thai.
46 F5 Chomutov Czech Rep.
13 M3 Chona r. Rus. Fed.
30 D5 Ch'ŏnan S. Korea
32 B2 Chon Buri Thai.
30 D3 Ch'ŏnch'ŏn N. Korea
86 B4 Chone Ecuador
27 F5 Chong'an China
30 C4 Chongchon r. N. Korea
30 E6 Chongdo S. Korea
30 E3 Ch'ŏngjin N. Korea
30 C4 Chŏngju N. Korea
30 D6 Chŏngju S. Korea
30 D5 Ch'ŏngju S. Korea
32 B2 Chŏng Kal Cambodia
30 D4 Chŏngp'yŏng N. Korea
27 C4 Chongqing China
27 E5 Chongren China
59 K2 Chonguene Moz.
57 C5 Chongwe Zambia
27 D4 Chongyang China
27 F5 Chongyang Xi r. China
27 E5 Chongyi China
27 C6 Chongzuo China
30 D6 Chŏnju S. Korea
23 F3 Cho Oyu mt China
32 C3 Chơ Phươc Hai Vietnam
90 B4 Chopim r. Brazil
90 B4 Chopimzinho Brazil
81 F5 Choptank r. U.S.A.
22 B4 Chor Pak.
38 E4 Chorley U.K.
51 D5 Chornobyl' Ukr.
51 E6 Chornomors'ke Ukr.
51 C5 Chortkiv Ukr.
30 D4 Ch'ŏrwŏn S. Korea
30 C3 Ch'osan N. Korea
29 G7 Chōshi Japan
91 B3 Chos Malal Arg.
46 G4 Choszczno Pol.
86 C5 Chota Peru
72 D2 Choteau U.S.A.
22 B3 Choti Pak.
54 A2 Choûm Maur.
74 B3 Chowchilla U.S.A.
64 F4 Chown, Mt mt Can.
24 D2 Choybalsan Mongolia
24 C2 Choyr Mongolia
46 H6 Chřiby h. Czech Rep.
68 D6 Chrisman U.S.A.
59 J3 Chrissiesmeer S. Africa
9 D5 Christchurch N.Z.
39 F7 Christchurch U.K.
59 F3 Christiana S. Africa
63 M2 Christian, C. pt Can.
69 G3 Christian I. i. Can.
Christianshåb see Qasigiannguit
80 C6 Christiansburg U.S.A.
64 C3 Christian Sound chan. U.S.A.
65 G3 Christina r. Can.
7 G6 Christina, Mt mt N.Z.
Christmas Island i. see Kiritimati
25 C8 Christmas Island terr. Ind. Ocean
46 G6 Chrudim Czech Rep.
49 L7 Chrysi i. Greece
15 F2 Chu Kazak.
12 H5 Chu r. Kazak.
23 G5 Chuadanga Bangl.
59 K2 Chuali, L. l. Moz.
26 F4 Chuansha China
72 D3 Chubbuck U.S.A.
91 C4 Chubut div. Arg.
88 C6 Chubut r. Arg.
75 E5 Chuckwalla Mts mts U.S.A.
51 D5 Chudniv Ukr.
50 D3 Chudovo Rus. Fed.
Chudskoye Ozero l. see Peipus, Lake
62 C4 Chugach Mountains mts U.S.A.
29 C7 Chūgoku-sanchi mts Japan
28 C2 Chuguyevka Rus. Fed.
72 F3 Chugwater U.S.A.
51 F5 Chuhuyiv Ukr.
75 G5 Chuichu U.S.A.
24 F1 Chukchagirskoye, Ozero l. Rus. Fed.
13 V3 Chukchi Sea sea Rus. Fed./U.S.A.
50 G3 Chukhloma Rus. Fed.
13 U3 Chukotskiy Poluostrov pen. Rus. Fed.
50 H1 Chulasa Rus. Fed.
74 D5 Chula Vista U.S.A.
12 K4 Chulym Rus. Fed.
23 G4 Chumbi China
88 C3 Chumbicha Arg.
24 F1 Chumikan Rus. Fed.
32 B1 Chum Phae Thai.
32 A3 Chumphon Thai.
32 B2 Chum Saeng Thai.
13 L4 Chuna r. Rus. Fed.
27 F4 Chun'an China
30 D5 Ch'unch'ŏn S. Korea
30 E5 Ch'ungju S. Korea
Chungking see Chongqing
30 E6 Ch'ungmu S. Korea
30 C4 Chŭngsan N. Korea
19 H3 Chungur, Koh-i- h. Afgh.
30 F2 Chunhua China
23 F3 Chunit Tso salt l. China
13 M3 Chunya r. Rus. Fed.
32 C3 Chuŏr Phnum Dâmrei mts Cambodia
32 C2 Chuŏr Phnum Dângrêk mts Cambodia/Thai.
32 B2 Chuŏr Phnum Krâvanh mts Cambodia
26 A4 Chuosijia China
17 L3 Chūplū Iran
86 D7 Chuquibamba Peru
88 C2 Chuquicamata Chile
46 D7 Chur Switz.
13 P3 Churapcha Rus. Fed.
65 L3 Churchill Can.
65 K3 Churchill r. Man./Sask. Can.
67 H3 Churchill r. Nfld Can.
63 J4 Churchill r. Sask. Can.
65 L3 Churchill, Cape c. Can.
67 H3 Churchill Falls Can.
65 H3 Churchill Lake l. Can.
64 D3 Churchill Peak summit Can.
66 E2 Churchill Sound chan. Can.
76 D1 Churchs Ferry U.S.A.
80 D5 Churchville U.S.A.
23 F4 Churia Ghati Hills mts Nepal
50 H3 Churov Rus. Fed.
22 C3 Churu India
89 C2 Churuguara Venez.
22 D2 Chushul Jammu and Kashmir
75 H3 Chuska Mountains mts U.S.A.
67 F4 Chute-des-Passes Can.
69 J2 Chute-Rouge Can.
69 K2 Chute-St-Philippe Can.
27 F5 Chu-tung Taiwan
4 G4 Chuuk i. Micronesia
50 H4 Chuvashskaya Respublika div. Rus. Fed.
26 F3 Chu Xian China
27 A5 Chuxiong China
32 D2 Chư Yang Sin mt Vietnam
17 K4 Chwārtā Iraq
51 D6 Ciadâr-Lunga Moldova
33 C4 Ciamis Indon.
33 C4 Cianjur Indon.
90 B3 Cianorte Brazil
73 E6 Cibuta Mex.
48 F2 Čičarija mts Croatia
16 E2 Çiçekdağı Turkey
51 E7 Cide Turkey
47 K4 Ciechanów Pol.
83 J4 Ciego de Avila Cuba
89 B2 Ciénaga Col.
89 B2 Ciénaga de Zapatoza l. Col.
84 B1 Ciénega de Flores Mex.
73 E6 Cieneguita Mex.
83 H4 Cienfuegos Cuba
45 F3 Cieza Spain
45 E2 Cifuentes Spain
17 M2 Çigil Adası i. Azer.
45 E3 Cigüela r. Spain
16 D2 Cihanbeyli Turkey
84 A3 Cihuatlán Mex.
45 D3 Cijara, Embalse de resr Spain
33 C4 Cilacap Indon.
17 J1 Çıldır Turkey
17 J1 Çıldır Gölü l. Turkey
27 D4 Cili China
17 K3 Cilo D. mt Turkey
17 N1 Çiloy Adası i. Azer.
75 E4 Cima U.S.A.
73 F4 Cimarron U.S.A.
77 D4 Cimarron r. U.S.A.
42 D5 Cimetière d'Ossuaire France
51 D6 Cimişlia Moldova
48 D2 Cimone, Monte mt Italy
17 H3 Çınar Turkey
89 C3 Cinaruco r. Venez.
89 D3 Cinaruco-Capanaparo, Parque Nacional nat. park Venez.
45 G2 Cinca r. Spain
80 A5 Cincinnati U.S.A.
81 F3 Cincinnatus U.S.A.
91 D4 Cinco Chañares Arg.
91 C3 Cinco Saltos Arg.
39 E6 Cinderford U.K.
16 B3 Çine Turkey
42 D4 Ciney Belgium
84 D3 Cintalapa Mex.
44 J5 Cinto, Monte mt France
90 B3 Cinzas r. Brazil
91 C3 Cipolletti Arg.
62 D3 Circle AK U.S.A.
72 F2 Circle U.S.A.
80 B5 Circleville OH U.S.A.
75 F2 Circleville UT U.S.A.
33 C4 Cirebon Indon.
39 F6 Cirencester U.K.
48 B2 Ciriè Italy
48 G5 Cirò Marina Italy
67 H2 Cirque Mtn mt Can.
68 C6 Cisco IL U.S.A.
77 D5 Cisco TX U.S.A.
75 H2 Cisco UT U.S.A.
89 B3 Cisneros Col.
84 C3 Citlaltépetl, Vol. volc. Mex.
48 G3 Čitluk Bos.-Herz.
58 C6 Citrusdal S. Africa
48 E3 Città di Castello Italy
49 L2 Ciucaş, Vârful mt Romania
82 D3 Ciudad Acuña Mex.
84 B3 Ciudad Altamirano Mex.
89 E3 Ciudad Bolívar Venez.
82 C3 Ciudad Camargo Mex.
84 E4 Ciudad Cuauhtémoc Mex.
84 E3 Ciudad del Carmen Mex.
90 A4 Ciudad del Este Para.
82 C3 Ciudad Delicias Mex.
84 C2 Ciudad del Maíz Mex.
89 C2 Ciudad de Nutrias Venez.
84 C2 Ciudad de Valles Mex.
89 E2 Ciudad Guayana Venez.
84 B3 Ciudad Guzmán Mex.
84 B3 Ciudad Hidalgo Mex.
84 D3 Ciudad Ixtepec Mex.
82 C2 Ciudad Juárez Mex.
84 B1 Ciudad Lerdo Mex.
84 C2 Ciudad Madero Mex.
84 C2 Ciudad Mante Mex.
84 C3 Ciudad Mendoza Mex.
84 C1 Ciudad Mier Mex.
82 C3 Ciudad Obregón Mex.
89 E3 Ciudad Piar Venez.
45 E3 Ciudad Real Spain
84 C1 Ciudad Río Bravo Mex.
45 C2 Ciudad Rodrigo Spain
84 C2 Ciudad Victoria Mex.
45 H2 Ciutadella de Menorca Spain
16 F1 Civa Burnu pt Turkey
16 B2 Civan Dağ mt Turkey
48 E1 Cividale del Friuli Italy
48 E3 Civita Castellana Italy
48 E3 Civitanova Marche Italy
48 D3 Civitavecchia Italy
16 B2 Çivril Turkey
27 F4 Cixi China
26 E2 Ci Xian China
17 J3 Cizre Turkey
39 J6 Clacton-on-Sea U.K.
41 D3 Clady U.K.
65 G3 Claire, Lake l. Can.
72 B3 Clair Engle L. resr U.S.A.
80 D4 Clairton U.S.A.
44 F3 Clamecy France
74 D2 Clan Alpine Mts mts U.S.A.
41 E4 Clane Rep. of Ireland
79 C5 Clanton U.S.A.
58 C6 Clanwilliam S. Africa
41 D4 Clara Rep. of Ireland
32 A3 Clara I. i. Myanmar
8 D2 Clare N.S.W. Austr.
8 B2 Clare S.A. Austr.
68 E4 Clare U.S.A.
41 C4 Clare r. Rep. of Ireland
41 C5 Clarecastle Rep. of Ireland
41 A4 Clare Island i. Rep. of Ireland
81 G3 Claremont U.S.A.
77 E4 Claremore U.S.A.
41 C4 Claremorris Rep. of Ireland
9 D5 Clarence N.Z.
92 B1 Clarence I. i. Ant.
64 C3 Clarence Str. chan. U.S.A.
79 F7 Clarence Town Bahamas
77 C5 Clarendon U.S.A.
67 K4 Clarenville Can.
64 G5 Claresholm Can.
76 E3 Clarinda U.S.A.
80 C5 Clarington U.S.A.
80 D4 Clarion U.S.A.
80 D4 Clarion r. U.S.A.
95 L4 Clarion Fracture Zone sea feature Pac. Oc.
61 G8 Clarión, Isla i. Mex.
76 D2 Clark U.S.A.
59 H5 Clarkebury S. Africa
6 E6 Clarke I. i. Austr.
70 D2 Clark Fork r. MT U.S.A.
79 D5 Clark Hill Res. resr U.S.A.
75 E4 Clark Mt mt U.S.A.
69 G3 Clark, Pt pt Can.
80 C5 Clarksburg U.S.A.
77 F5 Clarksdale U.S.A.
81 F4 Clarks Summit U.S.A.
72 C2 Clarkston U.S.A.
77 E5 Clarksville AR U.S.A.
68 A4 Clarksville IA U.S.A.
79 C4 Clarksville TN U.S.A.
90 B1 Claro r. Goiás Brazil
90 B2 Claro r. Goiás Brazil
41 D5 Clashmore Rep. of Ireland
41 D3 Claudy U.K.
31 B2 Claveria Phil.
42 D4 Clavier Belgium
81 G2 Clayburg U.S.A.
76 D4 Clay Center U.S.A.
75 F3 Clayhole Wash r. U.S.A.
79 D5 Clayton GA U.S.A.
73 G4 Clayton NM U.S.A.
81 E2 Clayton NY U.S.A.
81 J1 Clayton Lake U.S.A.
80 C6 Claytor Lake l. U.S.A.
41 B6 Clear, Cape c. Rep. of Ireland
69 G4 Clear Creek Can.
75 G4 Clear Creek r. U.S.A.
62 D4 Cleare, C. c. U.S.A.
80 D4 Clearfield PA U.S.A.
72 E3 Clearfield UT U.S.A.
80 B4 Clear Fork Reservoir U.S.A.
64 F3 Clear Hills mts Can.
76 E3 Clear Lake IA U.S.A.
68 A3 Clear Lake WI U.S.A.
74 A2 Clear Lake l. CA U.S.A.
75 F2 Clear Lake l. UT U.S.A.
72 B3 Clear L. Res. resr U.S.A.
79 D7 Clearwater U.S.A.
64 F4 Clearwater r. Alta. Can.
65 H3 Clearwater r. Sask. Can.
27 □ Clear Water Bay b. H.K. China
72 D2 Clearwater Mountains U.S.A.
65 H3 Clearwater River Provincial Park res. Can.
77 D5 Cleburne U.S.A.
72 B2 Cle Elum U.S.A.
38 G4 Cleethorpes U.K.
32 □ Clementi Sing.
80 C5 Clendenin U.S.A.
80 C4 Clendening Lake l. U.S.A.
31 A4 Cleopatra Needle mt Phil.
69 H1 Cléricy Can.
6 E4 Clermont Austr.
42 A5 Clermont France
79 D6 Clermont U.S.A.
42 D5 Clermont-en-Argonne France
44 F4 Clermont-Ferrand France
42 E4 Clervaux Lux.
48 D1 Cles Italy
39 E6 Clevedon U.K.
77 F5 Cleveland MS U.S.A.
80 C4 Cleveland OH U.S.A.
79 C5 Cleveland TN U.S.A.
68 D2 Cleveland Cliffs Basin l. U.S.A.
38 F3 Cleveland Hills h. U.K.
64 G5 Cleveland, Mt mt U.S.A.
38 D4 Cleveleys U.K.
41 B4 Clew Bay b. Rep. of Ireland
79 D7 Clewiston U.S.A.
41 A4 Clifden Rep. of Ireland
75 H5 Cliff U.S.A.
41 C3 Cliffony Rep. of Ireland
9 E4 Clifford Bay b. N.Z.
75 H5 Clifton U.S.A.
80 D6 Clifton Forge U.S.A.
80 B6 Clinch r. U.S.A.
80 B6 Clinch Mountain U.S.A.
64 E4 Clinton B.C. Can.
69 G4 Clinton Ont. Can.
81 G4 Clinton CT U.S.A.
68 B5 Clinton IA U.S.A.
68 C5 Clinton IL U.S.A.
81 H3 Clinton MA U.S.A.
81 J2 Clinton ME U.S.A.
76 E4 Clinton MO U.S.A.
77 F5 Clinton MS U.S.A.
79 E5 Clinton NC U.S.A.
77 D5 Clinton OK U.S.A.
65 H2 Clinton-Colden Lake l. Can.
68 C5 Clinton Lake l. U.S.A.
68 C3 Clintonville U.S.A.
75 G4 Clints Well U.S.A.
95 L5 Clipperton Fracture Zone sea feature Pac. Oc.
82 C6 Clipperton Island terr. Pac. Oc.
40 B3 Clisham h. U.K.
38 E4 Clitheroe U.K.
59 G4 Clocolan S. Africa
41 D4 Cloghan Rep. of Ireland
41 C6 Clonakilty Rep. of Ireland
41 C6 Clonakilty Bay b. Rep. of Ireland
41 C4 Clonbern Rep. of Ireland
6 E4 Cloncurry Austr.
41 D3 Clones Rep. of Ireland
41 D5 Clonmel Rep. of Ireland
41 D4 Clonygowan Rep. of Ireland
41 B5 Cloonbannin Rep. of Ireland
41 D4 Clooneagh Rep. of Ireland
43 G2 Cloppenburg Ger.
68 A2 Cloquet U.S.A.
72 F2 Cloud Peak summit U.S.A.
9 E4 Cloudy Bay b. N.Z.
27 □ Cloudy Hill h. H.K. China
69 K1 Clova Can.
74 A2 Cloverdale U.S.A.
77 C5 Clovis U.S.A.
69 J3 Cloyne Can.
40 C3 Cluanie, Loch l. U.K.
65 H3 Cluff Lake Can.
47 L7 Cluj-Napoca Romania
39 D5 Clun U.K.
8 D4 Clunes Austr.
44 H3 Cluses France
39 D4 Clwydian Range h. U.K.
64 G4 Clyde Can.
80 E3 Clyde NY U.S.A.
80 B4 Clyde OH U.S.A.
40 D5 Clyde r. U.K.
40 D5 Clydebank U.K.
40 D5 Clyde, Firth of est. U.K.

63 M2 **Clyde River** Can.
73 C5 **Coachella** U.S.A.
91 B2 **Co Aconcagua** *mt* Arg.
84 B3 **Coahuayutla de Guerrero** Mex.
84 B1 **Coahuila** *div.* Mex.
64 D2 **Coal** *r.* Can.
68 C5 **Coal City** U.S.A.
84 B3 **Coalcomán** Mex.
74 D3 **Coaldale** U.S.A.
77 D5 **Coalgate** U.S.A.
74 B3 **Coalinga** U.S.A.
64 D3 **Coal River** Can.
39 F5 **Coalville** U.K.
86 F4 **Coari** Brazil
86 F5 **Coari** *r.* Brazil
79 C6 **Coastal Plain** *plain* U.S.A.
64 D4 **Coast Mountains** *mts* Can.
72 B2 **Coast Range** *mts* U.S.A.
74 B3 **Coast Ranges** *mts* U.S.A.
40 E5 **Coatbridge** U.K.
84 E4 **Coatepeque** Guatemala
81 F5 **Coatesville** U.S.A.
67 F4 **Coaticook** Can.
63 K3 **Coats Island** *i.* Can.
92 C3 **Coats Land** *coastal area* Ant.
84 D3 **Coatzacoalcos** Mex.
69 H2 **Cobalt** Can.
82 F5 **Cobán** Guatemala
8 E1 **Cobar** Austr.
8 G4 **Cobargo** Austr.
8 G4 **Cobberas, Mt** *mt* Austr.
8 D5 **Cobden** Austr.
69 J3 **Cobden** Can.
41 C6 **Cóbh** Rep. of Ireland
65 K4 **Cobham** *r.* Can.
86 E6 **Cobija** Bol.
81 F3 **Cobleskill** U.S.A.
69 H4 **Cobourg** Can.
6 D3 **Cobourg Penina** *pen.* Austr.
8 E3 **Cobram** Austr.
43 J4 **Coburg** Ger.
45 D2 **Coca** Spain
90 B1 **Cocalinho** Brazil
Cocanada *see* **Kākināda**
86 E7 **Cochabamba** Bol.
91 B4 **Cochamó** Chile
42 F4 **Cochem** Ger.
21 B4 **Cochin** India
75 H5 **Cochise** U.S.A.
64 G4 **Cochrane** *Alta.* Can.
66 D4 **Cochrane** *Ont.* Can.
88 B7 **Cochrane** Chile
65 J3 **Cochrane** *r.* Can.
8 C2 **Cockburn** Austr.
69 F3 **Cockburn I.** *i.* Can.
40 F5 **Cockburnspath** U.K.
79 F7 **Cockburn Town** Bahamas
83 K4 **Cockburn Town** Turks and Caicos Is
38 D3 **Cockermouth** U.K.
58 F6 **Cockscomb** *summit* S. Africa
83 H6 **Coco** *r.* Honduras/Nic.
82 G7 **Coco, Isla de** *i.* Col.
75 F4 **Coconino Plateau** U.S.A.
8 F2 **Cocoparra Range** *h.* Austr.
89 A4 **Coco, Pta** *pt* Col.
89 B3 **Cocorná** Col.
90 D1 **Cocos** Brazil
93 L4 **Cocos Is** *is* Ind. Ocean
95 O5 **Cocos Ridge** *sea feature* Pac. Oc.
84 B2 **Cocula** Mex.
89 B3 **Cocuy, Parque Nacional el** *nat. park* Col.
89 B3 **Cocuy, Sierra Nevada del** *mt* Col.
86 F4 **Codajás** Brazil
81 H4 **Cod, Cape** *c.* U.S.A.
89 D2 **Codera, C.** *pt* Venez.
9 A7 **Codfish I.** *i.* N.Z.
48 E2 **Codigoro** Italy
67 H2 **Cod Island** *i.* Can.
49 L2 **Codlea** Romania
87 K4 **Codó** Brazil
39 E5 **Codsall** U.K.
41 A6 **Cod's Head** *hd* Rep. of Ireland
72 E2 **Cody** U.S.A.
6 E3 **Coen** Austr.
42 F3 **Coesfeld** Ger.
53 K6 **Coëtivy** *i.* Seychelles
72 C2 **Coeur d'Alene** U.S.A.
72 C2 **Coeur d'Alene L.** *l.* U.S.A.
42 E2 **Coevorden** Neth.
59 H5 **Coffee Bay** S. Africa
77 E4 **Coffeyville** U.S.A.
7 F5 **Coffs Harbour** Austr.
59 G6 **Cofimvaba** S. Africa
84 C3 **Cofre de Perote, Parque Nacional** *nat. park* Mex.
68 B4 **Coggon** U.S.A.
44 D4 **Cognac** France
54 C4 **Cogo** Equatorial Guinea
80 E3 **Cohocton** *r.* U.S.A.
81 G3 **Cohoes** U.S.A.
8 E3 **Cohuna** Austr.
83 H7 **Coiba, Isla** *i.* Panama
88 C8 **Coig** *r.* Arg.
88 B7 **Coihaique** Chile
21 B4 **Coimbatore** India
45 B2 **Coimbra** Port.
45 D4 **Coín** Spain
86 E7 **Coipasa, Salar de** *salt flat* Bol.
89 C2 **Cojedes** *r.* Venez.
72 E3 **Cokeville** U.S.A.
8 D5 **Colac** Austr.
Colair L. *l.* *see* **Kolleru L.**
90 E2 **Colatina** Brazil
43 K2 **Colbitz** Ger.
76 C4 **Colby** U.S.A.
86 D7 **Colca** *r.* Peru
39 H6 **Colchester** U.K.
68 B5 **Colchester** U.S.A.
40 F5 **Coldingham** U.K.
43 L3 **Colditz** Ger.
65 G4 **Cold L.** *l.* Can.
65 G4 **Cold Lake** Can.
40 F5 **Coldstream** U.K.
77 D4 **Coldwater** *KS* U.S.A.
68 E5 **Coldwater** *MI* U.S.A.
68 D1 **Coldwell** Can.
81 H2 **Colebrook** U.S.A.
68 E4 **Coleman** *MI* U.S.A.
77 D6 **Coleman** *TX* U.S.A.
59 H4 **Colenso** S. Africa
8 C4 **Coleraine** Austr.
41 E2 **Coleraine** U.K.
9 C5 **Coleridge, L.** *l.* N.Z.
21 B4 **Coleroon** *r.* India
58 F5 **Colesberg** S. Africa
74 B2 **Colfax** *CA* U.S.A.
72 C2 **Colfax** *WA* U.S.A.
40 □ **Colgrave Sound** *chan.* U.K.
59 G3 **Coligny** S. Africa
84 B3 **Colima** Mex.
84 B3 **Colima** *div.* Mex.
40 B4 **Coll** *i.* U.K.
45 E2 **Collado Villalba** Spain
79 C5 **College Park** U.S.A.
77 D6 **College Station** U.S.A.
8 G1 **Collie** Austr.
6 C3 **Collier Bay** *b.* Austr.
69 G3 **Collingwood** Can.
9 D4 **Collingwood** N.Z.
77 F6 **Collins** U.S.A.
78 B4 **Collinsville** U.S.A.
91 B3 **Collipulli** Chile
41 C3 **Collooney** Rep. of Ireland
44 H2 **Colmar** France
45 E2 **Colmenar Viejo** Spain
40 D5 **Colmonell** U.K.
39 H6 **Colne** *r.* U.K.
8 H2 **Colo** *r.* Austr.
42 F4 **Cologne** Ger.
68 C3 **Coloma** U.S.A.
90 C3 **Colômbia** Brazil
77 D7 **Colombia** Mex.
85 C2 **Colombia** *country* S. America
96 D5 **Colombian Basin** *sea feature* Atl. Ocean
21 B5 **Colombo** Sri Lanka
44 E5 **Colomiers** France
91 E2 **Colón** *Buenos Aires* Arg.
91 E2 **Colón** *Entre Ríos* Arg.
83 H4 **Colón** Cuba
83 J7 **Colón** Panama
73 C6 **Colonet, C.** *c.* Mex.
90 E1 **Colônia** *r.* Brazil
91 D3 **Colonia Choele Choel, Isla** *i.* Arg.
91 F2 **Colonia del Sacramento** Uru.
91 C3 **Colonia Emilio Mitre** Arg.
91 F1 **Colonia Lavalleja** Uru.
80 E6 **Colonial Heights** U.S.A.
75 F6 **Colonia Reforma** Mex.
48 G5 **Colonna, Capo** *pt* Italy
40 B4 **Colonsay** *i.* U.K.
91 D3 **Colorada Grande, Salina** *l.* Arg.
73 F4 **Colorado** *div.* U.S.A.
91 D3 **Colorado** *r.* *La Pampa/Río Negro* Arg.
91 C1 **Colorado** *r.* *San Juan* Arg.
75 E5 **Colorado** *r.* Mex./U.S.A.
77 D6 **Colorado** *r.* U.S.A.
75 F3 **Colorado City** *AZ* U.S.A.
77 C5 **Colorado City** *TX* U.S.A.
91 D3 **Colorado, Delta del Río** *delta* Arg.
74 D5 **Colorado Desert** U.S.A.
75 H2 **Colorado National Monument** *res.* U.S.A.
75 G3 **Colorado Plateau** U.S.A.
75 E4 **Colorado River Aqueduct** *canal* U.S.A.
73 F4 **Colorado Springs** U.S.A.
84 B2 **Colotlán** Mex.
43 M1 **Cölpin** Ger.
39 G5 **Colsterworth** U.K.
39 J5 **Coltishall** U.K.
74 D4 **Colton** *CA* U.S.A.
81 F2 **Colton** *NY* U.S.A.
75 G2 **Colton** *UT* U.S.A.
81 E5 **Columbia** *MD* U.S.A.
76 E4 **Columbia** *MO* U.S.A.
77 F6 **Columbia** *MS* U.S.A.
80 E4 **Columbia** *PA* U.S.A.
79 D5 **Columbia** *SC* U.S.A.
79 C5 **Columbia** *TN* U.S.A.
72 B2 **Columbia** *r.* Can./U.S.A.
63 L1 **Columbia, C.** *c.* Can.
68 E5 **Columbia City** U.S.A.
80 E5 **Columbia, District of** *div.* U.S.A.
81 K2 **Columbia Falls** *ME* U.S.A.
72 D1 **Columbia Falls** *MT* U.S.A.
64 F4 **Columbia Mountains** Can.
64 F4 **Columbia, Mt** *mt* Can.
72 C2 **Columbia Plateau** *plat.* U.S.A.
58 B6 **Columbine, Cape** *pt* S. Africa
79 C5 **Columbus** *GA* U.S.A.
78 C4 **Columbus** *IN* U.S.A.
77 F5 **Columbus** *MS* U.S.A.
72 E2 **Columbus** *MT* U.S.A.
76 D3 **Columbus** *NE* U.S.A.
73 F6 **Columbus** *NM* U.S.A.
80 B5 **Columbus** *OH* U.S.A.
77 D6 **Columbus** *TX* U.S.A.
68 C4 **Columbus** *WI* U.S.A.
68 B5 **Columbus Jct** U.S.A.
79 F7 **Columbus Pt** *pt* Bahamas
74 D2 **Columbus Salt Marsh** *salt marsh* U.S.A.
74 A2 **Colusa** U.S.A.
9 E2 **Colville** N.Z.
72 C1 **Colville** U.S.A.
62 C3 **Colville** *r.* *AK* U.S.A.
9 E2 **Colville Channel** *chan.* N.Z.
62 F3 **Colville Lake** Can.
39 D4 **Colwyn Bay** U.K.
48 E2 **Comacchio** Italy
48 E2 **Comacchio, Valli di** *lag.* Italy
23 G3 **Comai** China
91 B4 **Comallo** *r.* Arg.
77 D6 **Comanche** U.S.A.
92 B1 **Comandante Ferraz** *Brazil Base* Ant.
91 C2 **Comandante Salas** Arg.
47 N7 **Comănești** Romania
91 B1 **Combarbalá** Chile
41 F3 **Comber** U.K.
69 J3 **Combermere** Can.
23 H6 **Combermere Bay** *b.* Myanmar
42 A4 **Combles** France
59 K1 **Combomune** Moz.
66 E3 **Comencho, L.** *l.* Can.
41 D5 **Comeragh Mountains** *h.* Rep. of Ireland
77 D6 **Comfort** U.S.A.
23 G5 **Comilla** Bangl.
42 A4 **Comines** Belgium
48 C4 **Comino, Capo** *pt* *Sardinia* Italy
84 D3 **Comitán de Domínguez** Mex.
81 G4 **Commack** U.S.A.
69 H3 **Commanda** Can.
63 K3 **Committee Bay** *b.* Can.
92 B6 **Commonwealth B.** *b.* Ant.
48 C2 **Como** Italy
23 G3 **Como Chamling** *l.* China
88 C7 **Comodoro Rivadavia** Arg.
54 B4 **Comoé, Parc National de la** *nat. park* Côte d'Ivoire
48 C2 **Como, Lago di** *l.* Italy
21 B4 **Comorin, Cape** *c.* India
53 J7 **Comoros** *country* Africa
44 F2 **Compiègne** France
84 A2 **Compostela** Mex.
31 C5 **Compostela** Phil.
90 C4 **Comprida, Ilha** *i.* Brazil
68 C5 **Compton** U.S.A.
51 D6 **Comrat** Moldova
40 E4 **Comrie** U.K.
77 C6 **Comstock** U.S.A.
23 H4 **Cona** China
54 A4 **Conakry** Guinea
91 C4 **Cona Niyeo** Arg.
90 C2 **Conceição** *r.* Brazil
90 E2 **Conceição da Barra** Brazil
87 J5 **Conceição do Araguaia** Brazil
88 C3 **Concepción** Arg.
86 F7 **Concepción** Bol.
91 B3 **Concepción** Chile
84 B1 **Concepción** Mex.
83 H7 **Concepción** Panama
88 E2 **Concepción** Para.
91 E2 **Concepción del Uruguay** Arg.
67 K4 **Conception Bay South** Can.
79 F7 **Conception I.** *i.* Bahamas
74 B4 **Conception, Pt** *pt* U.S.A.
90 C3 **Conchas** Brazil
73 F5 **Conchas L.** *l.* U.S.A.
75 H4 **Concho** U.S.A.
82 D3 **Conchos** *r.* *Chihuahua* Mex.
84 C1 **Conchos** *r.* *Tamaulipas* Mex.
74 A3 **Concord** *CA* U.S.A.
79 D5 **Concord** *NC* U.S.A.
81 H3 **Concord** *NH* U.S.A.
91 F1 **Concordia** Arg.
89 B4 **Concordia** Col.
58 B4 **Concordia** S. Africa
76 D4 **Concordia** U.S.A.
32 C3 **Côn Đao** Vietnam
90 E1 **Condeúba** Brazil
8 F2 **Condobolin** Austr.
44 E5 **Condom** France
72 B2 **Condon** U.S.A.
42 D4 **Condroz** *reg.* Belgium
79 C6 **Conecuh** *r.* U.S.A.
48 E2 **Conegliano** Italy
84 B1 **Conejos** Mex.
80 D4 **Conemaugh** *r.* U.S.A.
69 G4 **Conestogo Lake** *l.* Can.
80 E3 **Conesus Lake** *l.* U.S.A.
81 G4 **Coney I.** *i.* U.S.A.
6 F3 **Conflict Group** *is* P.N.G.
44 E3 **Confolens** France
75 F2 **Confusion Range** *mts* U.S.A.
27 D6 **Conghua** China
27 C5 **Congjiang** China
39 E4 **Congleton** U.K.
53 F5 **Congo** *country* Africa
53 G6 **Congo** *country* Africa
56 B4 **Congo** *r.* Africa
75 F4 **Congress** U.S.A.
91 B3 **Conguillo, Parque Nacional** *nat. park* Chile
39 G4 **Coningsby** U.K.
66 D4 **Coniston** Can.
38 D3 **Coniston** U.K.
65 G3 **Conklin** Can.
91 D2 **Conlara** Arg.
91 D2 **Conlara** *r.* Arg.
80 C4 **Conneaut** U.S.A.
81 G4 **Connecticut** *div.* U.S.A.
78 F3 **Connecticut** *r.* U.S.A.
80 D4 **Connellsville** U.S.A.
41 B4 **Connemara** *reg.* Rep. of Ireland
81 J1 **Conners** Can.
78 C4 **Connersville** U.S.A.
41 B3 **Conn, Lough** *l.* Rep. of Ireland
8 E2 **Conoble** Austr.
27 B6 **Co Nôi** Vietnam
81 E5 **Conowingo** U.S.A.
72 E1 **Conrad** U.S.A.
77 E6 **Conroe** U.S.A.
90 D3 **Conselheiro Lafaiete** Brazil
90 E2 **Conselheiro Pena** Brazil
38 F3 **Consett** U.K.
32 C3 **Côn Sơn** *i.* Vietnam
65 G4 **Consort** Can.
46 D7 **Constance, Lake** *l.* Ger./Switz.
86 F5 **Constância dos Baetas** Brazil
49 N2 **Constanța** Romania
45 D4 **Constantina** Spain
54 C1 **Constantine** Alg.
68 E5 **Constantine** U.S.A.
75 E6 **Constitución de 1857, Parque Nacional** *nat. park* Mex.
72 D3 **Contact** U.S.A.
86 C5 **Contamana** Peru
90 E1 **Contas** *r.* Brazil
75 G6 **Continental** U.S.A.
81 H3 **Contoocook** *r.* U.S.A.
88 B8 **Contreras, I.** *i.* Chile
65 G1 **Contwoyto Lake** *l.* Can.
77 E5 **Conway** *AR* U.S.A.
81 H3 **Conway** *NH* U.S.A.
79 E5 **Conway** *SC* U.S.A.
7 H4 **Conway Reef** *rf* Fiji
39 D4 **Conwy** U.K.
39 D4 **Conwy** *r.* U.K.
6 D4 **Coober Pedy** Austr.
68 A2 **Cook** U.S.A.
64 D4 **Cook, C.** *c.* Can.
79 C4 **Cookeville** U.S.A.
59 F6 **Cookhouse** S. Africa
62 C3 **Cook Inlet** *chan.* U.S.A.
5 L6 **Cook Islands** *terr.* Pac. Oc.
9 C5 **Cook, Mt** *mt* N.Z.
81 F3 **Cooksburg** U.S.A.
67 J3 **Cook's Harbour** Can.
41 E3 **Cookstown** U.K.
9 E4 **Cook Strait** *str.* N.Z.
6 E3 **Cooktown** Austr.
8 F1 **Coolabah** Austr.
8 G1 **Coolah** Austr.
8 F3 **Coolamon** Austr.
6 C5 **Coolgardie** Austr.
75 G5 **Coolidge** U.S.A.
75 G5 **Coolidge Dam** U.S.A.
8 G4 **Cooma** Austr.
41 A6 **Coomacarrea** *h.* Rep. of Ireland
8 C2 **Coombah** Austr.
8 B3 **Coonalpyn** Austr.
8 G1 **Coonamble** Austr.
8 C4 **Coonawarra** Austr.
8 G1 **Coonabarabran** Austr.
Coondapoor *see* **Kundāpura**
6 D4 **Cooper Creek** *watercourse* Austr.
81 J2 **Coopers Mills** U.S.A.
79 E7 **Coopers Town** Bahamas
76 D2 **Cooperstown** *ND* U.S.A.
81 F3 **Cooperstown** *NY* U.S.A.
8 B3 **Coorong, The** *in.* Austr.
72 A3 **Coos Bay** U.S.A.
8 G3 **Cootamundra** Austr.
41 D3 **Cootehill** Rep. of Ireland
91 B3 **Copahue, Volcán** *mt* Chile
84 D3 **Copainalá** Mex.
84 C3 **Copala** Mex.
84 C3 **Copalillo** Mex.
72 G4 **Cope** U.S.A.
37 N9 **Copenhagen** Denmark
88 B3 **Copiapo** Chile
88 B3 **Copiapo** *r.* Chile
48 D2 **Copparo** Italy
69 G2 **Copper Cliff** Can.
68 D2 **Copper Harbor** U.S.A.
62 G3 **Coppermine** *N.W.T.* Can.
62 G3 **Coppermine** *r.* *N.W.T.* Can.
68 E2 **Coppermine Pt** *pt* Can.
58 E4 **Copperton** S. Africa
23 F3 **Coqên** China
91 B1 **Coquimbo** Chile
91 B1 **Coquimbo** *div.* Chile
49 L3 **Corabia** Romania
90 D2 **Coração de Jesus** Brazil
Coracesium *see* **Alanya**
86 D7 **Coracora** Peru
79 D7 **Coral Gables** U.S.A.
63 K3 **Coral Harbour** Can.
7 F3 **Coral Sea** *sea* Coral Sea Is Terr.
94 E6 **Coral Sea Basin** *sea feature* Pac. Oc.
4 F6 **Coral Sea Islands Territory** *terr.* Pac. Oc.
68 B5 **Coralville Reservoir** U.S.A.
8 D5 **Corangamite, L.** *l.* Austr.
87 G3 **Corantijn** *r.* Suriname
17 M1 **Corat** Azer.
42 B5 **Corbeny** France
91 E2 **Corbett** Arg.
65 L2 **Corbett Inlet** *in.* Can.
42 A5 **Corbie** France
80 A6 **Corbin** U.S.A.
39 G5 **Corby** U.K.
74 C3 **Corcoran** U.S.A.
88 B6 **Corcovado, G. de** *b.* Chile
79 D6 **Cordele** U.S.A.
89 B4 **Cordillera de los Picachos, Parque Nacional** *nat. park* Col.
31 B4 **Cordilleras Range** *mts* Phil.
91 C4 **Córdoba** *Río Negro* Arg.
91 D1 **Córdoba** Arg.
84 B1 **Córdoba** *Durango* Mex.
84 C3 **Córdoba** *Veracruz* Mex.
45 D4 **Córdoba** Spain
91 D2 **Córdoba** *div.* Arg.
91 D2 **Córdoba, Sierras de** *mts* Arg.
Cordova *see* **Córdoba**
62 D3 **Cordova** *AK* U.S.A.
64 C4 **Cordova Bay** *b.* U.S.A.
81 K2 **Corea** U.S.A.
49 H5 **Corfu** *i.* Greece
45 C3 **Coria** Spain
8 H2 **Coricudgy** *mt* Austr.
48 G5 **Corigliano Calabro** Italy
81 J2 **Corinna** U.S.A.
65 J4 **Corinne** Can.
77 F5 **Corinth** *MS* U.S.A.
81 G3 **Corinth** *NY* U.S.A.
90 D2 **Corinto** Brazil
87 G7 **Corixa Grande** *r.* Bol./Brazil
90 A2 **Corixinha** *r.* Brazil
41 C6 **Cork** Rep. of Ireland
48 E6 **Corleone** *Sicily* Italy
16 A1 **Çorlu** Turkey
65 J4 **Cormorant** Can.
59 H3 **Cornelia** S. Africa
90 B3 **Cornélio Procópio** Brazil
68 B3 **Cornell** U.S.A.
67 J4 **Corner Brook** Can.
8 F5 **Corner Inlet** *b.* Austr.
42 C5 **Cornillet, Mont** *h.* France
74 A2 **Corning** *CA* U.S.A.
80 E3 **Corning** *NY* U.S.A.
Corn Islands *is see* **Maíz, Islas del**
48 E3 **Corno, Monte** *mt* Italy
66 F4 **Cornwall** Can.
63 J2 **Cornwallis I.** *i.* Can.
89 C2 **Coro** Venez.
87 K4 **Coroatá** Brazil
86 E7 **Corocoro** Bol.
41 B5 **Corofin** Rep. of Ireland
86 E7 **Coroico** Bol.
90 C2 **Coromandel** Brazil
9 E2 **Coromandel Peninsula** N.Z.
9 E2 **Coromandel Range** *h.* N.Z.
31 B3 **Coron** Phil.
8 C1 **Corona** Austr.
74 D5 **Corona** U.S.A.
74 D5 **Coronado** U.S.A.
83 H7 **Coronado, Baiá de** *b.* Costa Rica
91 B4 **Coronados, Golfo de los** *b.* Chile
65 G4 **Coronation** Can.
62 G3 **Coronation Gulf** Can.
92 B1 **Coronation I.** *i.* Atl. Ocean
64 C3 **Coronation Island** *i.* U.S.A.
31 B4 **Coron Bay** *b.* Phil.
91 E1 **Coronda** Arg.
91 E2 **Coronel Brandsen** Arg.
91 E3 **Coronel Dorrego** Arg.
88 E3 **Coronel Oviedo** Para.
90 A1 **Coronel Ponce** Brazil
91 E3 **Coronel Pringles** Arg.
90 A3 **Coronel Sapucaia** Brazil
91 E3 **Coronel Suárez** Arg.
91 F3 **Coronel Vidal** Arg.
49 J4 **Çorovodë** Albania
8 F3 **Corowa** Austr.
77 D7 **Corpus Christi** U.S.A.
77 D6 **Corpus Christi, L.** *l.* U.S.A.
86 E7 **Corque** Bol.
45 D3 **Corral de Cantos** *mt* Spain
91 C1 **Corral de Isaac** Arg.
87 J6 **Corrente** Brazil
90 D1 **Corrente** *r.* *Bahia* Brazil
90 B2 **Corrente** *r.* *Goiás* Brazil
90 C1 **Corrente** *r.* Brazil
90 A2 **Correntes** Brazil
90 A2 **Correntes** *r.* Brazil
90 D1 **Correntina** Brazil
Correntina *r.* *see* **Éguas**
41 B4 **Corrib, Lough** *l.* Rep. of Ireland
88 E3 **Corrientes** Arg.
88 E3 **Corrientes** *r.* Arg.
84 A2 **Corrientes, C.** *c.* Mex.
91 F3 **Corrientes, C.** *hd* Arg.
89 A3 **Corrientes, Cabo** *hd* Col.
77 E6 **Corrigan** U.S.A.
39 D5 **Corris** U.K.
80 D4 **Corry** U.S.A.
8 F4 **Corryong** Austr.
Corse *i.* *see* **Corsica**
48 C3 **Corse, Cap** *hd* *Corsica* France
39 E6 **Corsham** U.K.
44 J5 **Corsica** *i.* France
77 D5 **Corsicana** U.S.A.
Cort Adelzier, Kap *hd see* **Kangeq**
48 C3 **Corte** *Corsica* France
45 C4 **Cortegana** Spain
75 H3 **Cortez** U.S.A.
74 D1 **Cortez Mts** *mts* U.S.A.
48 E1 **Cortina d'Ampezzo** Italy
81 E3 **Cortland** U.S.A.
39 J5 **Corton** U.K.
48 D3 **Cortona** Italy
45 B3 **Coruche** Port.
17 H1 **Çoruh** *r.* Turkey
16 E1 **Çorum** Turkey
87 G7 **Corumbá** Brazil
90 C2 **Corumbá** *r.* Brazil
90 C2 **Corumbaíba** Brazil
89 E3 **Corumo** *r.* Venez.
72 B2 **Corvallis** U.S.A.
39 D5 **Corwen** U.K.
84 A1 **Cosalá** Mex.
48 G5 **Cosenza** Italy
80 C4 **Coshocton** U.S.A.
44 F3 **Cosne-Cours-sur-Loire** France
91 D1 **Cosquín** Arg.
45 F3 **Costa Blanca** *coastal area* Spain
45 H2 **Costa Brava** *coastal area* France/Spain
45 C4 **Costa de la Luz** *coastal area* Spain
45 D4 **Costa del Sol** *coastal area* Spain
83 H6 **Costa de Mosquitos** *coastal area* Nic.
84 A1 **Costa Rica** Mex.
61 K8 **Costa Rica** *country* Central America
49 L2 **Costești** Romania
81 J2 **Costigan** U.S.A.
43 L3 **Coswig** Ger.
31 C5 **Cotabato** Phil.
89 A4 **Cotacachi, Co** *mt* Ecuador
86 E8 **Cotagaita** Bol.
90 E2 **Cotaxé** *r.* Brazil
44 H5 **Côte d'Azur** *coastal area* France
53 D5 **Côte d'Ivoire** *country* Africa
64 C3 **Cote, Mt** *mt* U.S.A.
44 G2 **Côtes de Meuse** *ridge* France
39 D5 **Cothi** *r.* U.K.
45 G1 **Cotiella** *mt* Spain
89 E3 **Cotingo** *r.* Brazil
54 C4 **Cotonou** Benin
86 C4 **Cotopaxi, Volcán** *volc.* Ecuador
39 E6 **Cotswold Hills** *h.* U.K.
72 B3 **Cottage Grove** U.S.A.
46 G5 **Cottbus** Ger.
21 B3 **Cotteliar** *r.* India
39 H5 **Cottenham** U.K.
75 H5 **Cotton City** U.S.A.
75 F4 **Cottonwood** U.S.A.
75 G4 **Cottonwood Wash** *r.* U.S.A.
77 D6 **Cotulla** U.S.A.
80 D4 **Coudersport** U.S.A.
92 B5 **Coulman I.** *i.* Ant.
44 F2 **Coulommiers** France
69 J2 **Coulonge** *r.* Can.
74 B3 **Coulterville** U.S.A.
72 C2 **Council** U.S.A.
76 E3 **Council Bluffs** U.S.A.
65 G2 **Courageous Lake** *l.* Can.
37 R9 **Courland Lagoon** *lag.* Lith./Rus. Fed.
64 E5 **Courtenay** Can.
41 C6 **Courtmacsherry** Rep. of Ireland
41 E5 **Courtown** Rep. of Ireland
Courtrai *see* **Kortrijk**
77 E5 **Coushatta** U.S.A.
44 D2 **Coutances** France
66 E2 **Couture, Lac** *l.* Can.
42 C4 **Couvin** Belgium
75 F2 **Cove Fort** U.S.A.
69 G3 **Cove I.** *i.* Can.
80 E5 **Cove Mts** *h.* U.S.A.
39 F5 **Coventry** U.K.
81 E5 **Cove Point** U.S.A.
45 C2 **Covilhã** Port.
79 D5 **Covington** *GA* U.S.A.
68 D5 **Covington** *IN* U.S.A.
80 A5 **Covington** *KY* U.S.A.
79 B5 **Covington** *TN* U.S.A.
80 D6 **Covington** *VA* U.S.A.
69 F2 **Cow** *r.* Can.
8 F2 **Cowal, L.** *l.* Austr.
6 C5 **Cowan, L.** *salt flat* Austr.
81 G2 **Cowansville** Can.
40 E4 **Cowdenbeath** U.K.
8 E5 **Cowes** Austr.
39 F7 **Cowes** U.K.
38 E3 **Cow Green Reservoir** U.K.
80 D5 **Cowpasture** *r.* U.S.A.
8 G2 **Cowra** Austr.
90 D1 **Coxá** *r.* Brazil
91 F1 **Coxilha de Santana** *h.* Brazil/Uru.
90 A2 **Coxim** Brazil
90 A2 **Coxim** *r.* Brazil
81 G3 **Coxsackie** U.S.A.
23 H5 **Cox's Bazar** Bangl.
74 D4 **Coyote Lake** *l.* U.S.A.
75 E5 **Coyote Peak** *summit AZ* U.S.A.
74 C3 **Coyote Peak** *summit CA* U.S.A.
84 A2 **Coyotitán** Mex.
84 B3 **Coyuca de Benitez** Mex.
23 F2 **Cozhê** China
49 L2 **Cozia, Vârful** *mt* Romania
73 D6 **Cozón, Co** *mt* Mex.
82 G4 **Cozumel** Mex.
82 G4 **Cozumel, I. de** *i.* Mex.
8 G2 **Craboon** Austr.
8 B1 **Cradock** Austr.
59 F6 **Cradock** S. Africa
40 C3 **Craig** U.K.
64 C3 **Craig** *AK* U.S.A.
72 F3 **Craig** *CO* U.S.A.
41 E3 **Craigavon** U.K.
8 E4 **Craigieburn** Austr.
80 D5 **Craigsville** U.S.A.
40 F4 **Crail** U.K.
43 J5 **Crailsheim** Ger.
49 K2 **Craiova** Romania
38 F2 **Cramlington** U.K.
81 F2 **Cranberry L.** *l.* U.S.A.
81 F2 **Cranberry Lake** U.S.A.
8 E5 **Cranbourne** Austr.
64 F5 **Cranbrook** Can.
68 C3 **Crandon** U.S.A.
72 C3 **Crane** *OR* U.S.A.
77 C6 **Crane** *TX* U.S.A.
68 A1 **Crane Lake** U.S.A.
81 H4 **Cranston** U.S.A.
92 B4 **Crary Ice Rise** *ice feature* Ant.
92 A4 **Crary Mts** *mts* Ant.
72 B3 **Crater L.** *l.* U.S.A.
72 B3 **Crater Lake Nat. Pk** U.S.A.
72 D3 **Craters of the Moon Nat. Mon.** *res.* U.S.A.
87 K5 **Crateús** Brazil
87 L5 **Crato** Brazil
89 C3 **Cravo Norte** Col.
89 C3 **Cravo Sur** *r.* Col.
76 C3 **Crawford** U.S.A.
68 D5 **Crawfordsville** U.S.A.
79 C6 **Crawfordville** U.S.A.
39 G6 **Crawley** U.K.
72 E2 **Crazy Mts** *mts* U.S.A.
40 D4 **Creag Meagaidh** *mt* U.K.
65 H4 **Crean L.** *l.* Can.
39 E5 **Credenhill** U.K.
39 D7 **Crediton** U.K.
65 H3 **Cree** *r.* Can.
65 H3 **Cree Lake** *l.* Can.
65 J4 **Creighton** Can.
42 A5 **Creil** France
42 D2 **Creil** Neth.
43 J2 **Cremlingen** Ger.
48 D2 **Cremona** Italy
44 F2 **Crépy-en-Valois** France
48 F2 **Cres** *i.* Croatia
72 A3 **Crescent City** U.S.A.
27 □ **Crescent I.** *i.* *H.K.* China
75 H2 **Crescent Junction** U.S.A.
74 B1 **Crescent Mills** U.S.A.
75 E4 **Crescent Peak** *summit* U.S.A.
68 A4 **Cresco** U.S.A.
91 E2 **Crespo** Arg.
8 D5 **Cressy** Austr.
64 F5 **Creston** Can.
76 E3 **Creston** *IA* U.S.A.
72 F3 **Creston** *WY* U.S.A.
79 C6 **Crestview** U.S.A.
81 F5 **Crestwood Village** U.S.A.
8 D4 **Creswick** Austr.
49 L7 **Crete** *i.* Greece
45 H1 **Creus, Cap de** *pt* Spain
44 E3 **Creuse** *r.* France
43 K5 **Creußen** Ger.
42 E5 **Creutzwald** France
43 J3 **Creuzburg** Ger.
39 E4 **Crewe** U.K.
80 D6 **Crewe** U.S.A.
39 E7 **Crewkerne** U.K.
40 D4 **Crianlarich** U.K.
39 C5 **Criccieth** U.K.
88 G3 **Criciúma** Brazil
40 E4 **Crieff** U.K.
40 E6 **Criffell** *h.* U.K.
48 F2 **Crikvenica** Croatia
51 E6 **Crimea** *pen.* Ukr.
43 L4 **Crimmitschau** Ger.
40 G3 **Crimond** U.K.
81 F6 **Crisfield** U.S.A.
90 C2 **Cristalina** Brazil
Cristalino *r.* *see* **Mariembero**
89 B2 **Cristóbal Colón, Pico** *mt* Col.
90 C1 **Crixás** Brazil
90 C1 **Crixás Açu** *r.* Brazil
90 B1 **Crixás Mirim** *r.* Brazil
Crna Gora *div. see* **Montenegro**
48 F2 **Črnomelj** Slovenia
41 B4 **Croagh Patrick** *h.* Rep. of Ireland
8 G4 **Croajingolong Nat. Park** Austr.
34 G4 **Croatia** *country* Europe
33 E2 **Crocker Range** *mts* Malaysia
77 E6 **Crockett** U.S.A.
81 F3 **Croghan** U.S.A.
42 A4 **Croisilles** France
6 D3 **Croker I.** *i.* Austr.
40 D3 **Cromarty** U.K.
40 D3 **Cromarty Firth** *est.* U.K.
40 E3 **Cromdale, Hills of** *h.* U.K.
39 J5 **Cromer** U.K.
9 B6 **Cromwell** N.Z.
38 F3 **Crook** U.K.
80 D4 **Crooked Creek Reservoir** U.S.A.
27 □ **Crooked I.** *i.* *H.K.* China
83 K4 **Crooked I. Passage** *chan.* Bahamas
83 K4 **Crooked Island** *i.* Bahamas
68 B1 **Crooked Lake** *l.* Can./U.S.A.
76 D2 **Crookston** U.S.A.
8 G3 **Crookwell** Austr.
41 C5 **Croom** Rep. of Ireland
38 D4 **Crosby** U.K.
65 J5 **Crosby** U.S.A.
65 L2 **Cross Bay** *b.* Can.
79 D6 **Cross City** U.S.A.
81 K1 **Cross Creek** Can.
77 E5 **Crossett** U.S.A.
38 E3 **Cross Fell** *h.* U.K.
41 F3 **Crossgar** U.K.
41 C6 **Crosshaven** Rep. of Ireland
39 C5 **Cross Inn** U.K.
65 K4 **Cross Lake** Can.
65 K4 **Cross Lake** *l.* Can.
80 E3 **Cross Lake** *l.* U.S.A.
9 D5 **Crossley, Mt** *mt* N.Z.
41 E3 **Crossmaglen** U.K.
75 E4 **Crossman Peak** *summit* U.S.A.
64 B3 **Cross Sound** *chan.* U.S.A.
68 E3 **Cross Village** U.S.A.
79 C5 **Crossville** U.S.A.
69 F4 **Croswell** U.S.A.
48 G5 **Crotone** Italy
39 H6 **Crouch** *r.* U.K.
8 F1 **Crowal** *r.* Austr.
39 H6 **Crowborough** U.K.
8 E2 **Crowl** *r.* Austr.
39 G5 **Crowland** U.K.
77 E6 **Crowley** U.S.A.
74 C3 **Crowley, Lake** *l.* U.S.A.
68 D5 **Crown Point** *IN* U.S.A.
81 G3 **Crown Point** *NY* U.S.A.
92 C3 **Crown Princess Martha Coast** *coastal area* Ant.
64 G5 **Crowsnest Pass** Can.
39 G6 **Croydon** U.K.
93 H6 **Crozet Basin** *sea feature* Ind. Ocean
93 H7 **Crozet, Îles** *is* Ind. Ocean
93 G6 **Crozet Plateau** *sea feature* Ind. Ocean
62 G2 **Crozier Chan.** *chan.* Can.
44 B2 **Crozon** France
40 G3 **Cruden Bay** U.K.
84 C1 **Cruillas** Mex.
41 E3 **Crumlin** U.K.
41 C5 **Crusheen** Rep. of Ireland
88 F3 **Cruz Alta** Brazil
83 J5 **Cruz, Cabo** *c.* Cuba
91 D1 **Cruz del Eje** Arg.
90 D3 **Cruzeiro** Brazil
86 D5 **Cruzeiro do Sul** Brazil
75 H5 **Cruzville** U.S.A.
64 E3 **Crysdale, Mt** *mt* Can.
8 B2 **Crystal Brook** Austr.
77 D6 **Crystal City** U.S.A.
68 C2 **Crystal Falls** U.S.A.
68 C4 **Crystal Lake** U.S.A.
47 K7 **Csongrád** Hungary
17 K5 **Ctesiphon** Iraq
89 D2 **Cúa** Venez.
32 C3 **Cửa Lớn** *r.* Vietnam
57 C5 **Cuando** *r.* Angola/Zambia
57 B5 **Cuangar** Angola
56 B4 **Cuango** *r.* Angola/Congo(Zaire)
57 B4 **Cuanza** *r.* Angola
89 D3 **Cuao** *r.* Venez.
91 F1 **Cuaró** *r.* Uru.
91 D2 **Cuarto** *r.* Arg.
82 C3 **Cuauhtémoc** Mex.
84 C3 **Cuautla** Mex.
68 B5 **Cuba** *IL* U.S.A.
73 F4 **Cuba** *NM* U.S.A.
61 K7 **Cuba** *country* Caribbean Sea
75 F6 **Cubabi, Cerro** *summit* Mex.
57 B5 **Cubal** Angola
57 B5 **Cubango** *r.* Angola/Namibia
89 B3 **Cubara** Col.
65 J4 **Cub Hills** *h.* Can.
16 D1 **Çubuk** Turkey
91 F1 **Cuchilla Grande Inferior** *h.* Uru.
91 D3 **Cuchillo-Có** Arg.
89 D3 **Cuchivero** *r.* Venez.
80 E6 **Cuckoo** U.S.A.
89 D4 **Cucuí** Brazil
89 B3 **Cúcuta** Col.
21 B4 **Cuddalore** India
21 B3 **Cuddapah** India
65 H4 **Cudworth** Can.
45 D2 **Cuéllar** Spain
57 B5 **Cuemba** Angola
86 C4 **Cuenca** Ecuador
45 E2 **Cuenca** Spain
84 B1 **Cuencamé** Mex.
45 E2 **Cuenca, Serranía de** *mts* Spain
84 C3 **Cuernavaca** Mex.
77 D6 **Cuero** U.S.A.
74 B4 **Cuesta Pass** *pass* U.S.A.
84 C2 **Cuetzalán** Mex.
49 K2 **Cugir** Romania
87 G5 **Cuiabá** *Amazonas* Brazil
90 A1 **Cuiabá** *Mato Grosso* Brazil
90 A2 **Cuiabá** *r.* Brazil
90 A1 **Cuiabá de Larga** Brazil
84 C3 **Cuicatlan** Mex.
42 D3 **Cuijk** Neth.
40 B3 **Cuillin Hills** *mts* U.K.
40 B3 **Cuillin Sound** *chan.* U.K.
57 B4 **Cuilo** Angola
90 E2 **Cuité** *r.* Brazil
57 B5 **Cuito** *r.* Angola
57 B5 **Cuito Cuanavale** Angola
84 B3 **Cuitzeo, L. de** *l.* Mex.
33 B2 **Cukai** Malaysia
17 J3 **Çukurca** Turkey
32 D2 **Cu Lao Cham** *i.* Vietnam
32 D2 **Cu Lao Re** *i.* Vietnam
32 D3 **Cu Lao Thu** *i.* Vietnam
72 F1 **Culbertson** *MT* U.S.A.
76 C3 **Culbertson** *NE* U.S.A.
8 F3 **Culcairn** Austr.
45 C2 **Culebra, Sierra de la** *mts* Spain
17 K2 **Culfa** Azer.
84 A1 **Culiacán** Mex.
84 A1 **Culiacancito** Mex.
31 A4 **Culion** Phil.
31 A4 **Culion** *i.* Phil.
40 F3 **Cullen** U.K.
45 F3 **Cullera** Spain
40 □ **Cullivoe** U.K.
79 C5 **Cullman** U.S.A.
17 H2 **Çullu** Turkey
41 E3 **Cullybackey** U.K.
40 C2 **Cul Mor** *h.* U.K.
80 D5 **Culpeper** U.S.A.
86 □ **Culpepper, Isla** *i.* *Galapagos Is* Ecuador
87 H6 **Culuene** *r.* Brazil
9 D5 **Culverden** N.Z.
40 D5 **Culzean Bay** *b.* U.K.
89 D2 **Cumaná** Venez.
89 B4 **Cumare, Cerro** *h.* Col.
89 A4 **Cumbal, Nevado de** *mt* Col.
80 D5 **Cumberland** *MD* U.S.A.
68 A3 **Cumberland** *WI* U.S.A.
78 C4 **Cumberland** *r.* U.S.A.
65 J4 **Cumberland House** Can.
65 J4 **Cumberland Lake** *l.* Can.
80 B6 **Cumberland Mtn** *mts* U.S.A.
63 M3 **Cumberland Peninsula** Can.
78 C4 **Cumberland Plateau** *plat.* U.S.A.
68 C2 **Cumberland Pt** *pt* U.S.A.
63 M3 **Cumberland Sound** *chan.* Can.
40 E5 **Cumbernauld** U.K.
84 B1 **Cumbres de Monterey, Parque Nacional** *nat. park* Mex.
43 K1 **Cumlosen** Ger.
74 A2 **Cummings** U.S.A.
8 G2 **Cumnock** Austr.
40 D5 **Cumnock** U.K.
16 D3 **Çumra** Turkey
41 D3 **Cuncagh** *h.* Rep. of Ireland/U.K.
84 D3 **Cunduacán** Mex.
84 E4 **Cunén** Guatemala
57 B5 **Cunene** *r.* Angola
48 B2 **Cuneo** Italy
32 D2 **Cung Sơn** Vietnam
17 G2 **Çüngüş** Turkey
6 E4 **Cunnamulla** Austr.
40 □ **Cunningsburgh** U.K.
89 D4 **Cunucunuma** *r.* Venez.
48 B2 **Cuorgnè** Italy
40 E4 **Cupar** U.K.
89 A3 **Cupica** Col.
89 A3 **Cupica, Golfo de** *b.* Col.
87 L5 **Curaçá** Brazil
83 L6 **Curaçao** *i.* Neth. Ant.
91 B3 **Curacautín** Chile
91 D3 **Curacó** *r.* Arg.
91 B3 **Curanilahue** Chile
89 D4 **Curapira, Serra** *mts* Brazil/Venez.
86 D4 **Curaray** *r.* Ecuador
91 B2 **Curaumilla, Punta** *pt* Chile
73 F4 **Curecanti Nat. Rec. Area** *res.* U.S.A.
91 B2 **Curicó** Chile
89 D5 **Curicuriari, Sa.** *h.* Brazil
89 D5 **Curieuriari** *r.* Brazil
90 C4 **Curitiba** Brazil
8 B1 **Curnamona** Austr.
8 H1 **Currabubula** Austr.
87 L5 **Currais Novos** Brazil
54 □ **Curral Velho** Cape Verde
69 F3 **Curran** U.S.A.
41 A6 **Currane, Lough** *l.* Rep. of Ireland

75 E2 Currant U.S.A.
8 E1 Curranyalpa Austr.
79 E7 Current Bahamas
6 E5 Currie Austr.
75 E1 Currie U.S.A.
8 H3 Currockbilly, Mt Austr.
6 F4 Curtis I. i. Austr.
87 H5 Curuá r. Brazil
87 J4 Curuçá Brazil
33 B3 Curup Indon.
87 K4 Cururupu Brazil
89 E3 Curutú, Cerro mt Venez.
90 D2 Curvelo Brazil
86 D6 Cusco Peru
41 E2 Cushendall U.K.
41 E2 Cushendun U.K.
77 D4 Cushing U.S.A.
89 C3 Cusiana r. Col.
79 C5 Cusseta U.S.A.
68 A1 Cusson U.S.A.
66 E1 Cusson, Pte pt Can.
72 F2 Custer MT U.S.A.
76 C3 Custer SD U.S.A.
89 A4 Cutanga, Pico de mt Col.
72 D1 Cut Bank U.S.A.
79 C6 Cuthbert U.S.A.
65 H4 Cut Knife Can.
81 K2 Cutler U.S.A.
79 D7 Cutler Ridge U.S.A.
91 C3 Cutral-Co Arg.
23 F5 Cuttack India
75 G5 Cutter U.S.A.
43 G1 Cuxhaven Ger.
80 C4 Cuyahoga Falls U.S.A.
80 C4 Cuyahoga Valley National Recreation Area res. U.S.A.
74 C4 Cuyama r. U.S.A.
31 B3 Cuyapo Phil.
31 B4 Cuyo Phil.
31 B4 Cuyo i. Phil.
31 B4 Cuyo East Pass. chan. Phil.
31 B4 Cuyo Islands is Phil.
31 B4 Cuyo West Pass. chan. Phil.
89 E3 Cuyuni r. Guyana
Cuzco see Cusco
39 D6 Cwmbran U.K.
56 C4 Cyangugu Rwanda
49 L6 Cyclades is Greece
80 A5 Cynthiana U.S.A.
65 G5 Cypress Hills mts Can.
10 E6 Cyprus country Asia
65 G4 Czar Can.
34 G4 Czech Republic country Europe
46 H4 Czersk Pol.
47 J5 Częstochowa Pol.

D

30 C1 Da'an China
16 F6 Dab'a Jordan
89 C2 Dabajuro Venez.
54 B4 Dabakala Côte d'Ivoire
26 A2 Daban Shan mts China
26 C3 Daba Shan mts China
89 A3 Dabeiba Col.
43 K1 Dabel Ger.
22 C5 Dabhoi India
21 A2 Dabhol India
26 E4 Dabie Shan mts China
22 D4 Daboh India
54 A3 Dabola Guinea
54 B4 Daboya Ghana
22 D4 Dabra India
47 J5 Dąbrowa Górnicza Pol.
27 E5 Dabu China
30 B1 Dabusu Pao l. China
Dacca see Dhaka
46 E6 Dachau Ger.
26 A2 Dachechang China
21 B2 Dachepalle India
69 J3 Dacre Can.
16 D1 Daday Turkey
79 D6 Dade City U.S.A.
22 C5 Dadra India
22 C5 Dadra and Nagar Haveli div. India
22 A4 Dadu Pak.
27 B4 Dadu He r. China
32 C3 Đa Dung r. Vietnam
31 B3 Daet Phil.
27 B5 Dafang China
26 F3 Dafeng China
30 D2 Dafengman China
23 H4 Dafla Hills mts India
54 A3 Dagana Senegal
26 B3 Dagcanglhamo China
51 H7 Dagestan, Respublika div. Rus. Fed.
26 F2 Dagu r. China
27 B5 Daguan China
27 □ D'Aguilar Peak h. H.K. China
31 B2 Dagupan Phil.
23 H1 Dagur China
23 G3 Dagzê China
23 F3 Dagzê Co salt l. China
22 C6 Dahanu India
26 D1 Dahei r. China
30 C2 Dahei Shan mts China
28 C1 Dahezhen China
24 D2 Da Hinggan Ling mts China
56 E2 Dahlak Archipelago is Eritrea
56 E2 Dahlak Marine National Park Eritrea
42 E4 Dahlem Ger.
43 J1 Dahlenburg Ger.
48 C7 Dahmani Tunisia
43 F5 Dahn Ger.
22 C5 Dāhod India
22 D2 Dahongliutan China/Jammu and Kashmir
43 J2 Dähre Ger.
17 J3 Dahūk Iraq
30 C3 Dahuofang Shuiku resr China
30 B3 Dahushan China
26 D1 Dai Hai l. China
33 B3 Daik Indon.
40 D5 Dailly U.K.
19 E3 Daim Iran
29 C6 Daimanji-san h. Japan
45 E3 Daimiel Spain
91 E3 Daireaux Arg.
68 A2 Dairyland U.S.A.
29 C7 Daisen volc. Japan
27 G4 Daishan China
27 F5 Daiyun Shan mts China
6 D4 Dajarra Austr.
26 A4 Dajin Chuan r. China
26 B2 Dajing China
23 H1 Da Juh China
54 A3 Dakar Senegal
23 G3 Dakelangsi China
23 G5 Dakhin Shahbaz-pur I. i. Bangl.
55 E2 Dakhla Oasis oasis Egypt
32 C2 Dak Kon Vietnam
50 D4 Dakol'ka r. Belarus
76 D3 Dakota City U.S.A.
49 J3 Đakovica Yugo.
49 H2 Đakovo Croatia
57 C5 Dala Angola
54 A3 Dalaba Guinea
26 D1 Dalad Qi China
26 E1 Dalai Nur l. China
18 C4 Dalaki, Rud-e r. Iran
26 D1 Dalamamiao China
16 B3 Dalaman Turkey
16 B3 Dalaman r. Turkey
24 C2 Dalandzadgad Mongolia
31 B4 Dalanganem Islands is Phil.
4 J4 Dalap-Uliga-Darrit Marshall Is
32 D3 Đa Lat Vietnam
26 B1 Dalay Mongolia
19 G4 Dalbandin Pak.
40 E6 Dalbeattie U.K.
6 F4 Dalby Austr.
38 C3 Dalby U.K.
37 J6 Dale Hordaland Norway
37 J6 Dale Sogn og Fjordane Norway
80 E5 Dale City U.S.A.
77 G4 Dale Hollow Lake l. U.S.A.
42 E2 Dalen Neth.
23 H6 Dalet Myanmar
23 H5 Daletme Myanmar
37 O6 Dalfors Sweden
19 E5 Dalgān Iran
8 G4 Dalgety Austr.
77 C4 Dalhart U.S.A.
67 G4 Dalhousie Can.
26 D3 Dali Shaanxi China
24 C4 Dali Yunnan China
30 A4 Dalian China
27 B4 Daliang Shan mts China
30 B2 Dalin China
26 F1 Daling r. China
30 D3 Dalizi China
40 E5 Dalkeith U.K.
23 F4 Dālkola India
81 F4 Dallas PA U.S.A.
77 D5 Dallas TX U.S.A.
68 B5 Dallas City U.S.A.
72 B2 Dalles, The U.S.A.
64 C4 Dall I. i. U.S.A.
18 D5 Dalmā i. U.A.E.
91 D2 Dalmacio Vélez Sarsfield Arg.
22 E4 Dalman India
48 G3 Dalmatia reg. Croatia
40 D5 Dalmellington U.K.
28 D2 Dal'negorsk Rus. Fed.
28 C2 Dal'nerechensk Rus. Fed.
54 B4 Daloa Côte d'Ivoire
27 C5 Dalou Shan mts China
18 B5 Dalqān well S. Arabia
40 D5 Dalry U.K.
40 D5 Dalrymple U.K.
6 E4 Dalrymple, L. l. Austr.
6 E4 Dalrymple, Mt mt Austr.
23 F4 Daltenganj India
69 E1 Dalton Can.
59 J4 Dalton S. Africa
79 C5 Dalton GA U.S.A.
81 G3 Dalton MA U.S.A.
38 D3 Dalton-in-Furness U.K.
69 E1 Dalton Mills Can.
41 C5 Dalua r. Rep. of Ireland
31 B2 Dalupiri i. Phil.
31 C3 Dalupiri i. Phil.
36 D4 Dalvík Iceland
6 D3 Daly r. Austr.
74 A3 Daly City U.S.A.
6 D3 Daly Waters Austr.
22 C5 Daman India
22 C5 Daman and Diu div. India
55 F1 Damanhûr Egypt
18 C3 Damaq Iran
26 E1 Damaqun Shan mts China
31 C6 Damar Indon.
25 E7 Damar i. Indon.
16 F5 Damascus Syria
91 B2 Damas, P. de las pass Arg./Chile
54 D3 Damaturu Nigeria
18 D3 Damavand Iran
21 C5 Dambulla Sri Lanka
18 D2 Damghan Iran
26 E2 Daming China
27 C6 Daming Shan mt China
23 H2 Damjong China
31 B5 Dammai i. Phil.
42 B3 Damme Belgium
43 G2 Damme Ger.
22 D5 Damoh India
54 B4 Damongo Ghana
6 E2 Dampier Strait chan. P.N.G.
25 F7 Dampir, Selat chan. Indon.
Damqoq Kanbab r. see Maquan He
23 H2 Dam Qu r. China
23 H3 Damroh India
42 E1 Damwoude Neth.
54 B4 Danané Côte d'Ivoire
32 D1 Đa Năng Vietnam
31 C4 Danao Phil.
26 A4 Danba China
81 G4 Danbury CT U.S.A.
81 H3 Danbury NH U.S.A.
81 G3 Danby U.S.A.
75 E4 Danby Lake l. U.S.A.
26 E3 Dancheng China
56 D3 Dande Eth.
21 A3 Dandeli India
8 E4 Dandenong Austr.
30 C3 Dandong China
39 E4 Dane r. U.K.
63 Q2 Daneborg Greenland
81 K2 Danforth U.S.A.
27 E6 Dangan Liedao is China
23 G3 Dangbe La pass China
28 B2 Dangbizhen Rus. Fed.
26 B3 Dangchang China
5 P5 Danger Islands is Pac. Oc.
58 C7 Danger Pt pt S. Africa
56 D2 Dangila Eth.
Dangla mts see Tanggula Shan
23 G3 Dangqên China
82 G5 Dangriga Belize
26 E3 Dangshan China
26 F4 Dangtu China
27 D4 Dangyang China
72 E3 Daniel U.S.A.
58 E4 Daniëlskuil S. Africa
50 G3 Danilov Rus. Fed.
51 H5 Danilovka Rus. Fed.
50 G3 Danilovskaya Vozvyshennost' reg. Rus. Fed.
26 D2 Daning China
17 M1 Dänizkänarı Azer.
26 D3 Danjiangkou Sk. resr China
18 E6 Dank Oman
22 D2 Dankhar India
50 F4 Dankov Rus. Fed.
27 B4 Danleng China
82 G6 Danlí Honduras
Dannebrogsø i. see Qillak
81 G2 Dannemora U.S.A.
43 K1 Dannenberg (Elbe) Ger.
43 M1 Dannenwalde Ger.
9 F4 Dannevirke N.Z.
59 J4 Dannhauser S. Africa
32 B1 Dan Sai Thai.
80 E3 Dansville U.S.A.
22 C4 Danta India
21 C2 Dantewara India
49 M3 Danube r. Europe
68 D5 Danville IL U.S.A.
68 D6 Danville IN U.S.A.
78 C4 Danville KY U.S.A.
69 J5 Danville PA U.S.A.
80 D6 Danville VA U.S.A.
27 C7 Dan Xian China
26 F4 Danyang China
27 C5 Danzhai China
31 B4 Dao Phil.
27 C6 Đao Bach Long Vi i. Vietnam
27 C6 Đao Cai Bâu i. Vietnam
27 C6 Đao Cat Ba i. Vietnam
32 B3 Đao Phu Quôc i. Vietnam
32 B3 Đao Thô Chư i. Vietnam
54 B4 Daoukro Côte d'Ivoire
32 B3 Đao Vây i. Vietnam
27 D5 Dao Xian China
27 D5 Daozhen China
31 C4 Dapa Phil.
54 C3 Dapaong Togo
23 J4 Daphabum mt India
31 B4 Dapiak, Mt mt Phil.
31 B4 Dapitan Phil.
15 H3 Da Qaidam China
24 E2 Daqing China
18 D3 Daqq-e Dombūn Iran
19 F3 Daqq-e-Tundi, Dasht-e l. Afgh.
26 D1 Daquing Shan mts China
17 K4 Dāqūq Iraq
27 G4 Daqu Shan i. China
16 F5 Dar'ā Syria
18 D4 Dārāb Iran
31 B3 Daraga Phil.
47 O4 Darahanava Belarus
54 D1 Daraj Libya
18 D4 Dārākūyeh Iran
31 C4 Daram i. Phil.
18 D3 Darang, Kūh-e h. Iran
13 N4 Darasun Rus. Fed.
18 E4 Darband Iran
23 F4 Darbhanga India
74 C2 Dardanelle U.S.A.
77 E5 Dardanelle, Lake l. U.S.A.
49 M4 Dardanelles str. Turkey
43 J3 Dardesheim Ger.
16 F2 Darende Turkey
56 D4 Dar es Salaam Tanz.
48 D2 Darfo Boario Terme Italy
22 B2 Dargai Pak.
19 F1 Dargan-Ata Turkm.
9 D1 Dargaville N.Z.
8 F4 Dargo Austr.
24 C2 Darhan Mongolia
26 D1 Darhan Muminggan Lianheqi China
79 D6 Darien U.S.A.
89 A2 Darién, Golfo del g. Col.
83 J7 Darién, Parque Nacional de nat. park Panama
89 A2 Darién, Serranía del mts Panama
23 G4 Dārjiling India
18 C4 Darkhazīneh Iran
24 B3 Darlag China
8 D2 Darling r. Austr.
6 E4 Darling Downs reg. Austr.
6 B5 Darling Range h. Austr.
38 F3 Darlington U.K.
68 B4 Darlington U.S.A.
8 F3 Darlington Point Austr.
46 H3 Darłowo Pol.
18 B5 Darmā S. Arabia
22 E3 Darma Pass China/India
21 B2 Darmaraopet India
18 E4 Dar Mazār Iran
43 G5 Darmstadt Ger.
22 C5 Darna r. India
55 E1 Darnah Libya
59 J4 Darnall S. Africa
8 D2 Darnick Austr.
62 F3 Darnley Bay b. Can.
92 D5 Darnley, C. c. Ant.
45 F2 Daroca Spain
50 G3 Darovka Rus. Fed.
50 H3 Darovskoy Rus. Fed.
91 D3 Darregueira Arg.
18 D3 Darreh Bīd Iran
18 E3 Darreh Gaz Iran
17 L4 Darreh Gozaru r. Iran
19 H3 Darreh-ye Shekārī r. Afgh.
21 B3 Darsi India
17 M6 Darsīyeh Iran
39 D7 Dart r. U.K.
39 H6 Dartford U.K.
8 C4 Dartmoor Austr.
39 C7 Dartmoor reg. U.K.
39 D7 Dartmoor National Park U.K.
67 H5 Dartmouth Can.
39 D7 Dartmouth U.K.
38 F4 Darton U.K.
41 C3 Darty Mts h. Rep. of Ireland
6 E2 Daru P.N.G.
54 A4 Daru Sierra Leone
23 G3 Darum Tso l. China
48 G2 Daruvar Croatia
19 E1 Darvaza Turkm.
18 C4 Darvīsla Iran
19 G4 Darwazgai Afgh.
8 E2 Darwen U.K.
19 G4 Darweshan Afgh.
6 D3 Darwin Austr.
88 C8 Darwin, Mte mt Chile
22 B3 Darya Khan Pak.
19 E4 Dārzīn Iran
18 D5 Dās i. U.A.E.
26 D4 Dashennongjia mt China
20 E1 Dashkhovuz Turkm.
18 E2 Dasht Iran
19 F5 Dasht r. Pak.
18 E4 Dasht Āb Iran
18 C4 Dasht-e Palang r. Iran
19 F5 Dashtiari Iran
19 H2 Dashtiobburdon Tajik.
26 C2 Dashuikeng China
26 B2 Dashuitou China
22 C2 Daska Pak.
17 L1 Daşkäsän Azer.
22 C1 Daspar mt Pak.
43 H3 Dassel Ger.
58 C6 Dassen Island i. S. Africa
17 L2 Dastakert Armenia
18 E3 Dastgardān Iran
30 F2 Da Suifen r. China
49 M6 Datça Turkey
28 G3 Date Japan
75 F5 Dateland U.S.A.
22 D4 Datia India
27 E5 Datian China
26 A2 Datong Qinghai China
26 D1 Datong Shanxi China
26 B2 Datong He r. China
26 A2 Datong Shan mts China
31 C5 Datu Piang Phil.
33 C2 Datu, Tanjung c. Indon./Malaysia
50 C3 Daugava r. Belarus/Latvia
37 U9 Daugavpils Latvia
19 G2 Daulatabad Afgh.
22 C6 Daulatabad India
Daulatabad see Malāyer
42 E4 Daun Ger.
21 A2 Daund India
32 A2 Daung Kyun i. Myanmar
65 J4 Dauphin Can.
44 G4 Dauphiné reg. France
77 F6 Dauphin I. i. U.S.A.
65 K4 Dauphin L. l. Can.
22 D4 Dausa India
40 E3 Dava U.K.
17 M1 Däväçi Azer.
21 A3 Davangere India
31 C5 Davao Phil.
31 C5 Davao Gulf b. Phil.
19 F5 Dāvar Panāh Iran
59 H3 Davel S. Africa
74 A3 Davenport CA U.S.A.
68 B5 Davenport IA U.S.A.
39 F5 Daventry U.K.
59 H3 Daveyton S. Africa
83 H7 David Panama
65 H4 Davidson Can.
65 J3 Davin Lake l. Can.
74 B2 Davis U.S.A.
92 D5 Davis Austr. Base Ant.
75 E4 Davis Dam U.S.A.
67 H2 Davis Inlet Can.
92 D5 Davis Sea sea Ant.
63 N3 Davis Strait str. Can./Greenland
46 D7 Davos Switz.
30 B3 Dawa China
26 A1 Dawan China
23 F3 Dawaxung China
26 B4 Dawe China
Dawei see Tavoy
26 E3 Dawen r. China
18 C5 Dawhat Salwah b. Qatar/S. Arabia
32 A1 Dawna Range mts Myanmar/Thai.
20 D6 Dawqah Oman
62 E3 Dawson Y.T. Can.
79 C6 Dawson GA U.S.A.
76 D2 Dawson ND U.S.A.
65 J4 Dawson Bay b. Can.
64 E3 Dawson Creek Can.
65 L2 Dawson Inlet in. Can.
64 B2 Dawson Range mts Can.
26 E4 Dawu Hubei China
24 C3 Dawu Sichuan China
44 D5 Dax France
26 C4 Daxian China
27 C6 Daxin China
26 E2 Daxing China
27 A4 Daxue Shan mts China
30 B4 Dayang r. China
23 H4 Dayang r. India
27 D6 Dayao Shan mts China
27 E4 Daye China
27 B4 Dayi China
8 E4 Daylesford Austr.
74 D3 Daylight Pass U.S.A.
91 F1 Daymán r. Uru.
91 F1 Daymán, Cuchilla del h. Uru.
27 D4 Dayong China
17 H4 Dayr az Zawr Syria
80 A5 Dayton OH U.S.A.
79 C5 Dayton TN U.S.A.
72 C2 Dayton WA U.S.A.
79 D6 Daytona Beach U.S.A.
27 E5 Dayu China
27 D5 Dayu Ling mts China
26 F3 Da Yunhe r. China
72 C2 Dayville U.S.A.
27 D7 Dazhou Dao i. China
27 C4 Dazhu China
27 B4 Dazu China
58 F5 De Aar S. Africa
68 D2 Dead r. U.S.A.
79 F7 Deadman's Cay Bahamas
75 E4 Dead Mts mts U.S.A.
81 H2 Dead River r. U.S.A.
16 E6 Dead Sea salt l. Asia
39 J6 Deal U.K.
59 F4 Dealesville S. Africa
27 E4 De'an China
64 D4 Dean r. Can.
39 E6 Dean, Forest of forest U.K.
91 D1 Deán Funes Arg.
69 F4 Dearborn U.S.A.
64 D3 Dease r. Can.
64 C3 Dease Lake Can.
62 H3 Dease Strait chan. Can.
74 D3 Death Valley v. U.S.A.
74 D3 Death Valley Junction U.S.A.
74 D3 Death Valley National Monument res. U.S.A.
44 E2 Deauville France
33 D2 Debak Malaysia
27 C6 Debao China
49 J4 Debar Macedonia
65 H4 Debden Can.
39 J5 Debenham U.K.
75 H2 De Beque U.S.A.
81 J2 Deblois U.S.A.
56 D3 Debre Birhan Eth.
47 K7 Debrecen Hungary
56 D2 Debre Markos Eth.
56 D2 Debre Tabor Eth.
56 D3 Debre Zeyit Eth.
79 C5 Decatur AL U.S.A.
79 C5 Decatur GA U.S.A.
68 C6 Decatur IL U.S.A.
68 E5 Decatur IN U.S.A.
68 E4 Decatur MI U.S.A.
21 B2 Deccan plat. India
69 H2 Decelles, Réservoir resr Can.
46 G5 Děčín Czech Rep.
68 B4 Decorah U.S.A.
39 F6 Deddington U.K.
43 J2 Dedeleben Ger.
43 J2 Dedelstorf Ger.
42 E2 Dedemsvaart Neth.
90 C4 Dedo de Deus mt Brazil
58 C6 De Doorns S. Africa
17 L1 Dedoplis Tsqaro Georgia
54 B3 Dédougou Burkina
50 D3 Dedovichi Rus. Fed.
57 D5 Dedza Malawi
39 D4 Dee est. Wales U.K.
39 E4 Dee r. Eng./Wales U.K.
40 F3 Dee r. Scot. U.K.
41 C5 Deel r. Rep. of Ireland
41 E4 Deele r. Rep. of Ireland
27 □ Deep Bay b. H.K. China
80 D5 Deep Creek Lake l. U.S.A.
75 F2 Deep Creek Range mts U.S.A.
69 J2 Deep River Can.
81 G4 Deep River U.S.A.
65 K1 Deep Rose Lake l. Can.
74 D3 Deep Springs U.S.A.
80 B5 Deer Creek Lake l. U.S.A.
81 K2 Deer I. i. Can.
81 J2 Deer I. i. U.S.A.
81 J2 Deer Isle U.S.A.
66 B3 Deer L. l. Can.
67 J4 Deer Lake Nfld Can.
66 B3 Deer Lake Ont. Can.
72 D2 Deer Lodge U.S.A.
88 D2 Defensores del Chaco, Parque Nacional nat. park Para.
80 A4 Defiance U.S.A.
79 C6 De Funiak Springs U.S.A.
24 B3 Dêgê China
56 E3 Degeh Bur Eth.
23 G3 Dêgên China
43 L6 Deggendorf Ger.
22 C3 Degh r. Pak.
42 B3 De Haan Belgium
18 D4 Dehaj Iran
19 F4 Dehak Iran
19 F5 Dehak Iran
18 D4 Deh Bīd Iran
18 C4 Deh-Dasht Iran
18 C4 Deh-e Khalīfeh Iran
18 C3 Deheq Iran
18 C2 Dehgāh Iran
18 B3 Dehgolān Iran
21 B5 Dehiwala-Mount Lavinia Sri Lanka
18 D5 Dehkūyeh Iran
18 B3 Dehlonān Iran
22 D3 Dehra Dun India
23 F4 Dehri India
19 E4 Deh Salm Iran
18 E4 Deh Sard Iran
17 K4 Deh Sheykh Iran
19 F4 Deh Shū Afgh.
27 F5 Dehua China
30 C1 Dehui China
42 B4 Deinze Belgium
16 E5 Deir el Qamer Lebanon
Deir-ez-Zor see Dayr az Zawr
47 L7 Dej Romania
27 C4 Dejiang China
68 C5 De Kalb IL U.S.A.
77 E5 De Kalb TX U.S.A.
81 F2 De Kalb Junction U.S.A.
20 A6 Dekemhare Eritrea
56 C4 Dekese Congo(Zaire)
19 G2 Dekhkanabad Uzbek.
42 C1 De Koog Neth.
42 C2 De Kooy Neth.
74 C4 Delano U.S.A.
75 F2 Delano Peak summit U.S.A.
19 F3 Delārām Afgh.
59 F3 Delareyville S. Africa
65 H4 Delaronde Lake l. Can.
68 C5 Delavan IL U.S.A.
68 C4 Delavan WV U.S.A.
80 B4 Delaware U.S.A.
81 F5 Delaware div. U.S.A.
81 F4 Delaware r. U.S.A.
81 F5 Delaware Bay b. U.S.A.
80 B4 Delaware Lake l. U.S.A.
81 F4 Delaware Water Gap National Recreational Area res. U.S.A.
43 G3 Delbrück Ger.
8 G4 Delegate Austr.
46 C7 Delémont Switz.
42 C2 Delft Neth.
21 B4 Delft I. i. Sri Lanka
42 E1 Delfzijl Neth.
57 E5 Delgado, Cabo pt Moz.
69 G4 Delhi Can.
22 D3 Delhi India
73 F4 Delhi CO U.S.A.
81 F3 Delhi NY U.S.A.
17 J2 Deli r. Turkey
16 E2 Delice Turkey
16 E1 Delice r. Turkey
18 C3 Delījān Iran
64 E1 Déljne Can.
24 B3 Delingha China
65 H4 Delisle Can.
43 L3 Delitzsch Ger.
43 H3 Delligsen Ger.
76 D3 Dell Rapids U.S.A.
45 H4 Dellys Alg.
74 D5 Del Mar U.S.A.
75 E3 Delmar L. l. U.S.A.
43 G1 Delmenhorst Ger.
13 R2 De-Longa, O-va is Rus. Fed.
62 B3 De Long Mts mts U.S.A.
65 J5 Deloraine Can.
68 D5 Delphi U.S.A.
80 A4 Delphos U.S.A.
58 F4 Delportshoop S. Africa
79 D7 Delray Beach U.S.A.
73 E6 Del Río Mex.
77 C6 Del Rio U.S.A.
37 P6 Delsbo Sweden
75 H2 Delta CO U.S.A.
68 A5 Delta IA U.S.A.
75 F2 Delta UT U.S.A.
62 D3 Delta Junction U.S.A.
81 F3 Delta Reservoir resr U.S.A.
79 D6 Deltona U.S.A.
41 D4 Delvin Rep. of Ireland
49 J5 Delvinë Albania
45 E1 Demanda, Sierra de la mts Spain
56 C4 Demba Congo(Zaire)
56 D3 Dembī Dolo Eth.
50 D4 Demidov Rus. Fed.
73 F5 Deming U.S.A.
89 E4 Demini r. Brazil
16 B2 Demirci Turkey
49 M4 Demirköy Turkey
46 F4 Demmin Ger.
79 C5 Demopolis U.S.A.
68 D5 Demotte U.S.A.
33 B3 Dempo, G. volc. Indon.
22 D2 Dêmqog China/India
50 H2 Dem'yanovo Rus. Fed.
47 Q2 Demyansk Rus. Fed.
58 D5 De Naawte S. Africa
56 E2 Denakil reg. Eritrea
56 E3 Denan Eth.
65 J4 Denare Beach Can.
19 G2 Denau Uzbek.
69 J3 Denbigh Can.
39 D4 Denbigh U.K.
42 C1 Den Burg Neth.
32 B1 Den Chai Thai.
33 C3 Dendang Indon.
42 C3 Dendermonde Belgium
59 H1 Dendron S. Africa
26 C1 Dengkou China
23 H3 Dêngqên China
26 D3 Deng Xian China
Den Haag see The Hague
6 B4 Denham Austr.
42 E2 Den Ham Neth.
42 C2 Den Helder Neth.
45 G3 Denia Spain
8 E3 Deniliquin Austr.
72 C3 Denio U.S.A.
76 E3 Denison IA U.S.A.
77 D5 Denison TX U.S.A.
16 B3 Denizli Turkey
8 H2 Denman Austr.
92 C5 Denman Glacier gl. Ant.
6 B5 Denmark Austr.
34 F3 Denmark country Europe
34 C2 Denmark Strait str. Greenland/Iceland
75 H3 Dennehotso U.S.A.
81 H4 Dennis Port U.S.A.
40 E4 Denny U.K.
81 K2 Dennysville U.S.A.
33 E4 Denpasar Indon.
81 F5 Denton MD U.S.A.
77 D5 Denton TX U.S.A.
6 F2 D'Entrecasteaux Islands is P.N.G.
6 B5 d'Entrecasteaux, Pt pt Austr.
7 G3 d'Entrecasteaux, Récifs rf New Caledonia
72 F4 Denver U.S.A.
23 F4 Deo India
22 D3 Deoband India
23 F5 Deogarh India
23 E5 Deogarh mt India
23 F4 Deoghar India
22 D5 Deori India
23 E4 Deoria India
22 C2 Deosai, Plains of plain Pak.
23 E5 Deosil India
42 A3 De Panne Belgium
42 D3 De Peel reg. Neth.
68 C3 De Pere U.S.A.
81 F3 Deposit U.S.A.
69 J2 Depot-Forbes Can.
69 J2 Depot-Rowanton Can.
68 C5 Depue U.S.A.
13 P3 Deputatskiy Rus. Fed.
24 B4 Dêqên China
27 D6 Deqing Guangdong China
27 F4 Deqing Zhejiang China
27 F5 Deqiu China
77 E5 De Queen U.S.A.
22 B3 Dera Bugti Pak.
22 B3 Dera Ghazi Khan Pak.
22 B3 Dera Ismail Khan Pak.
22 B3 Derawar Fort Pak.
51 J7 Derbent Rus. Fed.
19 G2 Derbent Uzbek.
6 C3 Derby Austr.
39 F5 Derby U.K.
81 G4 Derby CT U.S.A.
77 D4 Derby KS U.S.A.
41 D3 Derg r. Rep. of Ireland/U.K.
51 J5 Dergachi Rus. Fed.
41 C5 Derg, Lough l. Rep. of Ireland
51 F5 Derhachi Ukr.
77 E6 De Ridder U.S.A.
17 H3 Derik Turkey
16 E2 Derinkuyu Turkey
51 F5 Derkul r. Rus. Fed./Ukr.
58 C1 Derm Namibia
41 D4 Derravaragh, Lough l. Rep. of Ireland
81 H3 Derry U.S.A.
41 E5 Derry r. Rep. of Ireland
41 C3 Derryveagh Mts h. Rep. of Ireland
26 A1 Derstei China
55 F3 Derudeb Sudan
58 E6 De Rust S. Africa
48 G2 Derventa Bos.-Herz.
6 E6 Derwent r. Austr.
38 G4 Derwent r. U.K.
40 G6 Derwent Reservoir resr U.K.
38 D3 Derwent Water l. U.K.
14 E1 Derzhavinsk Kazak.
91 C2 Desaguadero r. Arg.
86 E7 Desaguadero r. Bol.
5 N6 Désappointement, Îles du is Pac. Oc.
74 D2 Desatoya Mts mts U.S.A.
69 F2 Desbarats Can.
62 F3 Des Bois, Lac l. Can.
65 J3 Deschambault L. l. Can.
65 J4 Deschambault Lake Can.
72 B2 Deschutes r. U.S.A.
56 D2 Desē Eth.
88 C7 Deseado Arg.
88 C7 Deseado r. Arg.
69 J3 Deseronto Can.
22 B3 Desert Canal canal Pak.
75 E5 Desert Center U.S.A.
75 F1 Desert Peak summit U.S.A.
64 G3 Desmarais Can.
76 E3 Des Moines IA U.S.A.
73 G4 Des Moines NM U.S.A.
68 A5 Des Moines r. IA U.S.A.
51 D5 Desna Ukr.
50 E5 Desna r. Rus. Fed.
50 E4 Desnogorsk Rus. Fed.
31 C4 Desolation Point pt Phil.
68 D4 Des Plaines U.S.A.
53 K6 Desroches i. Seychelles
43 L3 Dessau Ger.
42 B3 Destelbergen Belgium
69 H1 Destor Can.
64 B2 Destruction Bay Can.
49 J2 Deta Romania
64 G2 Detah Can.
57 C5 Dete Zimbabwe
43 G3 Detmold Ger.
68 D3 Detour, Pt pt U.S.A.
69 F3 De Tour Village U.S.A.
69 F4 Detroit U.S.A.
76 E2 Detroit Lakes U.S.A.
8 G3 Deua Nat. Park Austr.
43 L3 Deuben Ger.
42 D3 Deurne Neth.
48 F1 Deutschlandsberg Austria
43 L3 Deutzen Ger.
69 H2 Deux-Rivières Can.
49 K2 Deva Romania
21 B2 Devarkonda India
16 E2 Develi Turkey
42 E2 Deventer Neth.
46 H6 Devét Skal h. Czech Rep.
22 B4 Devikot India
41 D5 Devils Bit Mountain h. Rep. of Ireland
39 D5 Devil's Bridge U.K.
74 C4 Devils Den U.S.A.
74 C2 Devils Gate pass U.S.A.
68 B2 Devils I. i. U.S.A.
76 D1 Devils Lake U.S.A.
74 C3 Devils Peak summit U.S.A.
74 C3 Devils Postpile National Monument res. U.S.A.
79 F7 Devil's Pt Bahamas
39 F6 Devizes U.K.
22 C4 Devli India
49 M3 Devnya Bulg.
64 G4 Devon Can.
39 G5 Devon r. U.K.
63 J2 Devon Island i. Can.
6 E6 Devonport Austr.
16 C1 Devrek Turkey
16 D1 Devrekâni Turkey
16 E1 Devrez r. Turkey
21 A2 Devrukh India
22 D5 Dewas India
33 A2 Dewa, Tanjung pt Indon.
59 G4 Dewetsdorp S. Africa
80 B6 Dewey Lake l. U.S.A.
77 F5 De Witt AR U.S.A.
68 B5 De Witt IA U.S.A.
38 F4 Dewsbury U.K.
27 E4 Dexing China
81 J2 Dexter ME U.S.A.
77 F4 Dexter MO U.S.A.
81 E2 Dexter NY U.S.A.
26 B4 Deyang China
18 E3 Deyhuk Iran
17 M3 Deylaman Iran
19 F2 Deynau Turkm.
6 D2 Deyong, Tg pt Indon.
18 C5 Deyyer Iran
17 M6 Dez r. Iran
18 C3 Dezfūl Iran
18 C4 Dez Gerd Iran
26 E2 Dezhou China
18 B5 Dhahlān, J. h. S. Arabia
20 D4 Dhahran S. Arabia
23 G5 Dhaka Bangl.
23 G5 Dhaleswari r. Bangl.
23 H4 Dhaleswari r. India
20 B7 Dhamār Yemen
23 F5 Dhāmara India
22 C5 Dhamnod India
23 E5 Dhamtari India
22 B3 Dhana Sar Pak.
23 F5 Dhanbad India
22 C5 Dhandhuka India
23 E3 Dhang Ra. mts Nepal
22 C5 Dhar India
23 F4 Dharan Bazar Nepal
21 B4 Dharapuram India
22 B5 Dhari India
21 B3 Dharmapuri India
21 B3 Dharmavaram India
22 D2 Dharmshala India
21 A3 Dhārwād India
22 D4 Dhasan r. India
23 E3 Dhaulagiri mt Nepal
22 D4 Dhaulpur India
22 C4 Dhebar L. l. India
23 H4 Dhekiajuli India
16 E6 Dhībān Jordan
23 H4 Dhing India
21 B3 Dhone India
22 B5 Dhoraji India
22 B5 Dhrangadhra India
22 C5 Dhule India
23 F4 Dhulian India
23 F4 Dhunche Nepal
22 D4 Dhund r. India
56 E3 Dhuusa Marreeb Somalia
49 L7 Dia i. Greece
74 B3 Diablo, Mt mt U.S.A.
74 B3 Diablo Range mts U.S.A.
91 E2 Diamante Arg.
91 C2 Diamante r. Arg.
90 D2 Diamantina Brazil
6 D4 Diamantina watercourse Austr.
87 K6 Diamantina, Chapada plat. Brazil
90 A1 Diamantino Brazil
74 □1 Diamond Head hd U.S.A.
75 E2 Diamond Peak summit U.S.A.
27 D6 Dianbai China
27 B5 Dian Chi l. China
27 C4 Dianjiang China
87 J6 Dianópolis Brazil
54 B4 Dianra Côte d'Ivoire
28 B2 Diaoling China
54 C3 Diapaga Burkina
19 E6 Dibab Oman
23 H4 Dibang r. India
56 C4 Dibaya Congo(Zaire)
58 E3 Dibeng S. Africa
66 F2 D'Iberville, Lac l. Can.
59 G1 Dibete Botswana
23 H4 Dibrugarh India
77 C5 Dickens U.S.A.
81 J1 Dickey U.S.A.
76 C2 Dickinson U.S.A.
79 C4 Dickson U.S.A.
81 F4 Dickson City U.S.A.
Dicle r. see Tigris
31 B2 Didicas i. Phil.
22 C4 Didwana India
49 M4 Didymoteicho Greece
44 G4 Die France
42 F4 Dieblich Ger.
54 B3 Diébougou Burkina
43 G5 Dieburg Ger.
65 H4 Diefenbaker, L. l. Can.
93 J4 Diego Garcia i. British Ind. Ocean Terr.
42 E5 Diekirch Lux.
54 B3 Diéma Mali
43 H3 Diemel r. Ger.
27 B6 Điện Biên Vietnam
32 C1 Điện Châu Vietnam
32 D2 Điện Khanh Vietnam
43 G2 Diepholz Ger.
44 E2 Dieppe France
26 C2 Di'er Nonchang Qu r. China
30 C1 Di'er Songhua Jiang r. China
42 D3 Diessen Neth.
42 D4 Diest Belgium
46 D7 Dietikon Switz.
43 G4 Diez Ger.
55 D3 Diffa Niger
21 D2 Digapahandi India
67 G5 Digby Can.
23 F5 Digha India
44 H4 Digne-les-Bains France
44 F3 Digoin France
31 C5 Digos Phil.
22 D5 Digras India
22 B4 Digri Pak.
25 F7 Digul r. Indon.

E

46 D3 Eckernförde Ger.
63 L2 Eclipse Sound *chan.* Can.
85 C3 Ecuador *country* S. America
66 E2 Écueils, Pte aux *pt* Can.
56 E2 Ed Eritrea
37 M7 Ed Sweden
65 H4 Edam Can.
42 D2 Edam Neth.
40 F1 Eday *i.* U.K.
55 E3 Ed Da'ein Sudan
55 F3 Ed Damazin Sudan
55 F3 Ed Damer Sudan
55 F3 Ed Debba Sudan
55 F3 Ed Dueim Sudan
6 E6 Eddystone Pt *pt* Austr.
42 D2 Ede Neth.
54 D4 Edéa Cameroon
65 K2 Edehon Lake *l.* Can.
90 C2 Edéia Brazil
8 G4 Eden Austr.
77 D6 Eden *TX* U.S.A.
38 E3 Eden *r.* U.K.
59 F4 Edenburg S. Africa
9 B7 Edendale N.Z.
41 D4 Edenderry Rep. of Ireland
8 C4 Edenhope Austr.
79 E4 Edenton U.S.A.
59 G3 Edenville S. Africa
49 K4 Edessa Greece
43 F1 Edewecht Ger.
81 H4 Edgartown U.S.A.
76 D2 Edgeley U.S.A.
76 C3 Edgemont U.S.A.
68 C4 Edgerton U.S.A.
41 D4 Edgeworthstown
Rep. of Ireland
68 A5 Edina U.S.A.
77 D7 Edinburg U.S.A.
40 E5 Edinburgh U.K.
51 C7 Edirne Turkey
64 F4 Edith Cavell, Mt *mt* Can.
72 B2 Edmonds U.S.A.
64 G4 Edmonton Can.
65 K5 Edmore U.S.A.
68 B4 Edmund U.S.A.
65 L4 Edmund L. *l.* Can.
67 G4 Edmundston Can.
77 D6 Edna U.S.A.
64 C3 Edna Bay U.S.A.
49 M5 Edremit Turkey
37 O6 Edsbyn Sweden
64 F4 Edson Can.
91 D2 Eduardo Castex Arg.
8 E3 Edward *r.* Austr.
68 C1 Edward I. *i.* Can.
56 C4 Edward, Lake *l.*
Congo(Zaire)/Uganda
81 F2 Edwards U.S.A.
77 C6 Edwards Plateau *plat.* U.S.A.
78 B4 Edwardsville U.S.A.
92 D4 Edward VIII Ice Shelf
ice feature Ant.
92 A4 Edward VII Pen. *pen.* Ant.
64 C3 Edziza Pk *mt* Can.
42 B3 Eeklo Belgium
74 A1 Eel *r.* U.S.A.
42 E1 Eemshaven *pt* Neth.
42 E1 Eenrum Neth.
58 D3 Eenzamheid Pan *salt pan*
S. Africa
7 G3 Éfaté *i.* Vanuatu
78 B4 Effingham U.S.A.
16 D1 Eflâni Turkey
75 E2 Egan Range *mts* U.S.A.
69 J3 Eganville Can.
47 K7 Eger Hungary
37 K7 Egersund Norway
43 G3 Eggegebirge *h.* Ger.
43 K5 Eggolsheim Ger.
42 C4 Eghezée Belgium
36 F4 Egilsstaðir Iceland
16 C3 Eğirdir Turkey
16 C3 Eğirdir Gölü *l.* Turkey
44 F4 Égletons France
41 D2 Eglinton U.K.
62 F2 Eglinton I. *i.* Can.
42 C2 Egmond aan Zee Neth.
9 D3 Egmont, Cape *c.* N.Z.
9 E3 Egmont, Mt *volc.* N.Z.
9 E3 Egmont National Park N.Z.
16 B2 Eğrigöz Dağı *mts* Turkey
38 G3 Egton U.K.
90 D1 Éguas *r.* Brazil
13 V3 Egvekinot Rus. Fed.
52 G3 Egypt *country* Africa
46 D6 Ehingen (Donau) Ger.
43 J2 Ehra-Lessien Ger.
75 E5 Ehrenberg U.S.A.
43 J5 Eibelstadt Ger.
42 E2 Eibergen Neth.
43 H4 Eichenzell Ger.
43 K6 Eichstätt Ger.
37 K6 Eidfjord Norway
37 M6 Eidsvoll Norway
42 E4 Eifel *reg.* Ger.
40 B4 Eigg *i.* U.K.
21 A4 Eight Degree Chan.
India/Maldives
92 A3 Eights Coast *coastal area*
Ant.
6 C3 Eighty Mile Beach *beach*
Austr.
8 E4 Eildon Austr.
8 F4 Eildon, Lake *l.* Austr.
40 C4 Eilean Shona *i.* U.K.
65 H2 Eileen Lake *l.* Can.
43 L3 Eilenburg Ger.
43 J2 Eimke Ger.
43 H3 Einbeck Ger.
42 D3 Eindhoven Neth.
46 D7 Einsiedeln Switz.
86 E5 Eirunepé Brazil
43 H3 Eisberg *h.* Ger.
57 C5 Eiseb *watercourse* Namibia
43 J4 Eisenach Ger.
43 K4 Eisenberg Ger.
46 G4 Eisenhüttenstadt Ger.
46 H7 Eisenstadt Austria
43 J4 Eisfeld Ger.
40 C3 Eishort, Loch *in.* U.K.
43 K3 Eisleben Lutherstadt Ger.
43 H4 Eiterfeld Ger.
Eivissa *see* Ibiza
Eivissa *i. see* Ibiza
45 F1 Ejea de los Caballeros Spain
57 E6 Ejeda Madag.
82 B3 Ejido Insurgentes Mex.
26 C2 Ejin Horo Qi China
26 A1 Ejin Qi China
17 K1 Ejmiatsin Armenia
84 C3 Ejutla Mex.
37 S7 Ekenäs Fin.
42 C3 Ekeren Belgium
9 E4 Eketahuna N.Z.
15 F1 Ekibastuz Kazak.
13 M3 Ekonda Rus. Fed.
37 N6 Ekshärad Sweden
37 O8 Eksjö Sweden
58 B4 Eksteenfontein S. Africa
56 C4 Ekuku Congo(Zaire)
66 D3 Ekwan *r.* Can.
66 D3 Ekwan Point *pt* Can.
49 K6 Elafonisou, Steno *chan.*
Greece
16 B6 El 'Alamein Egypt
84 D3 El Almendro Mex.
16 B6 El 'Amirîya Egypt
59 H2 Elands *r.* S. Africa
59 H2 Elandsdoorn S. Africa
48 B7 El Aouinet Alg.
16 B6 El 'Arab, Khalîg *b.* Egypt
16 D6 El 'Arîsh Egypt
49 K5 Elassona Greece
16 E7 Elat Israel
17 G2 Elazığ Turkey
48 D3 Elba, Isola d' *i.* Italy
24 F1 El'ban Rus. Fed.
89 B2 El Banco Col.
16 D6 El Bardawîl, Sabkhet *lag.*
Egypt
49 J4 Elbasan Albania
16 E2 Elbaşı Turkey
89 C2 El Baúl Venez.
54 C1 El Bayadh Alg.
43 J1 Elbe *r.* Ger.
68 D3 Elberta *MI* U.S.A.
75 G2 Elberta *UT* U.S.A.
73 F4 Elbert, Mount *mt* U.S.A.
79 D5 Elberton U.S.A.
44 E2 Elbeuf France
16 F2 Elbistan Turkey
47 J3 Elbląg Pol.
91 B4 El Bolsón Arg.
79 E7 Elbow Cay *i.* Bahamas
51 G7 Elbrus *mt* Rus. Fed.
42 D2 Elburg Neth.
45 E2 El Burgo de Osma Spain
91 C4 El Cain Arg.
74 D5 El Cajon U.S.A.
89 E3 El Callao Venez.
77 D6 El Campo U.S.A.
75 E5 El Centro U.S.A.
86 F7 El Cerro Bol.
89 D2 El Chaparro Venez.
45 F3 Elche Spain
84 D3 El Chichón *volc.* Mex.
6 D3 Elcho I. *i.* Austr.
89 B3 El Cocuy Col.
45 F3 Elda Spain
43 K1 Elde *r.* Ger.
69 H2 Eldee Can.
74 D5 El Descanso Mex.
89 B2 El Difícil Col.
13 P3 El'dikan Rus. Fed.
89 A4 El Diviso Col.
75 E6 El Doctor Mex.
68 A5 Eldon *IA* U.S.A.
76 E4 Eldon *MO* U.S.A.
88 F3 Eldorado Arg.
84 A1 El Dorado Mex.
77 E5 El Dorado *AR* U.S.A.
77 D4 El Dorado *KS* U.S.A.
77 C6 Eldorado U.S.A.
89 E3 El Dorado Venez.
56 D3 Eldoret Kenya
72 E2 Electric Peak *summit* U.S.A.
54 B2 El Eglab *plat.* Alg.
45 E4 El Ejido Spain
50 F4 Elektrostal' Rus. Fed.
86 D4 El Encanto Col.
43 J3 Elend Ger.
73 F5 Elephant Butte Res. *resr*
U.S.A.
92 B1 Elephant I. *i.* Ant.
23 H5 Elephant Point *pt* Bangl.
17 J2 Eleşkirt Turkey
54 C1 El Eulma Alg.
79 E7 Eleuthera *i.* Bahamas
48 C6 El Fahs Tunisia
55 F2 El Faiyûm Egypt
55 E3 El Fasher Sudan
43 H4 Elfershausen Ger.
70 E6 El Fuerte Mex.
55 E3 El Geneina Sudan
55 F3 El Geteina Sudan
40 E3 Elgin U.K.
68 C4 Elgin *IL* U.S.A.
76 C2 Elgin *ND* U.S.A.
75 E3 Elgin *NV* U.S.A.
75 G2 Elgin *UT* U.S.A.
13 Q3 El'ginskiy Rus. Fed.
55 F2 El Gîza Egypt
84 B2 El Gogorrón, Parque
Nacional *nat. park* Mex.
54 C1 El Goléa Alg.
55 F4 Elgon, Mount *mt* Uganda
48 B6 El Hadjar Alg.
16 B6 El Hammâm Egypt
16 F6 El Hazim Jordan
54 A2 El Hierro *i.* Canary Is
84 C2 El Higo Mex.
54 C2 El Homr Alg.
40 F4 Elie U.K.
9 C5 Elie de Beaumont *mt* N.Z.
62 B3 Elim *AK* U.S.A.
67 H2 Eliot, Mount *mt* Can.
45 F1 Eliozondo Spain
El Iskandarîya *see*
Alexandria
51 H6 Elista Rus. Fed.
68 B4 Elizabeth *IL* U.S.A.
81 F4 Elizabeth *NJ* U.S.A.
80 C5 Elizabeth *WV* U.S.A.
79 E4 Elizabeth City U.S.A.
81 H4 Elizabeth Is *is* U.S.A.
79 D4 Elizabethton U.S.A.
78 C4 Elizabethtown *KY* U.S.A.
79 E5 Elizabethtown *NC* U.S.A.
81 G2 Elizabethtown *NY* U.S.A.
80 E4 Elizabethtown *PA* U.S.A.
54 B1 El Jadida Morocco
16 F6 El Jafr Jordan
84 A1 El Jaralito Mex.
48 D7 El Jem Tunisia
47 L4 Ełk Pol.
74 A2 Elk *r.* U.S.A.
64 G4 Elk *r.* Can.
80 C5 Elk *r.* U.S.A.
16 F4 El Kaa Lebanon
48 C6 El Kala Alg.
55 F3 El Kamlin Sudan
77 D5 Elk City U.S.A.
74 A2 Elk Creek U.S.A.
74 B2 Elk Grove U.S.A.
55 F2 El Khârga Egypt
68 E5 Elkhart U.S.A.
El Khartum *see* Khartoum
54 B2 El Khnâchîch *esc.* Mali
68 C4 Elkhorn U.S.A.
76 D3 Elkhorn *r.* U.S.A.
49 M3 Elkhovo Bulg.
80 D5 Elkins U.S.A.
64 G4 Elk Island Nat. Park Can.
69 G2 Elk Lake Can.
68 E3 Elk Lake *l.* U.S.A.
80 E4 Elkland U.S.A.
64 F5 Elko Can.
72 D3 Elko U.S.A.
65 G4 Elk Point Can.
76 E2 Elk River U.S.A.
81 F5 Elkton *MD* U.S.A.
80 D5 Elkton *VA* U.S.A.
17 G4 El Kubar Syria
65 M2 Ell Bay *b.* Can.
63 H2 Ellef Ringnes I. *i.* Can.
22 C3 Ellenabad India
76 D2 Ellendale U.S.A.
75 G2 Ellen, Mt *mt* U.S.A.
72 B2 Ellensburg U.S.A.
81 F4 Ellenville U.S.A.
8 G4 Ellery, Mt *mt* Austr.
63 K2 Ellesmere Island *i.* Can.
9 D5 Ellesmere, Lake *l.* N.Z.
39 E4 Ellesmere Port U.K.
62 H3 Ellice *r.* Can.
80 D3 Ellicottville U.S.A.
84 C2 El Limón Mex.
43 J5 Ellingen Ger.
59 G5 Elliot S. Africa
59 H5 Elliotdale S. Africa
69 F2 Elliot Lake Can.
72 D2 Ellis U.S.A.
59 G1 Ellisras S. Africa
40 F3 Ellon U.K.
81 J2 Ellsworth *ME* U.S.A.
68 A3 Ellsworth *WV* U.S.A.
92 A3 Ellsworth Land *reg.* Ant.
92 B3 Ellsworth Mountains Ant.
43 J6 Ellwangen (Jagst) Ger.
16 B3 Elmalı Turkey
74 D6 El Maneadero Mex.
55 F1 El Mansûra Egypt
89 E3 El Manteco Venez.
54 C1 El Meghaïer Alg.
89 E3 El Miamo Venez.
16 E4 El Mîna Lebanon
55 F2 El Minya Egypt
68 E3 Elmira *MI* U.S.A.
80 E3 Elmira *NY* U.S.A.
75 F5 El Mirage U.S.A.
45 E4 El Moral Spain
8 E4 Elmore Austr.
91 D2 El Morro *mt* Arg.
54 B2 El Mreyyé *reg.* Maur.
43 H1 Elmshorn Ger.
55 E3 El Muglad Sudan
69 G3 Elmwood Can.
68 C5 Elmwood *IL* U.S.A.
68 A3 Elmwood *WV* U.S.A.
36 K5 Elnesvågen Norway
89 B3 El Nevado, Cerro *mt* Col.
31 A4 El Nido Phil.
55 F3 El Obeid Sudan
89 C3 Elorza Venez.
54 C1 El Oued Alg.
75 G5 Eloy U.S.A.
84 A1 El Palmito Mex.
89 E2 El Pao *Bolívar* Venez.
89 C2 El Pao *Cojedes* Venez.
68 C5 El Paso *IL* U.S.A.
73 F6 El Paso *TX* U.S.A.
40 C2 Elphin U.K.
74 C3 El Portal U.S.A.
45 H2 El Prat de Llobregat Spain
84 E4 El Progreso Guatemala
45 C4 El Puerto de Santa María
Spain
El Qâhira *see* Cairo
16 D6 El Qantara Egypt
16 E7 El Quweira Jordan
77 D5 El Reno U.S.A.
84 B2 El Retorno Mex.
68 B4 Elroy U.S.A.
84 B2 El Rucio Mex.
64 B2 Elsa Can.
16 C7 El Saff Egypt
84 B1 El Salado Mex.
16 D6 El Sâlhîya Egypt
84 A2 El Salto Mex.
84 B1 El Salvador Mex.
31 C4 El Salvador Phil.
61 K8 El Salvador *country*
Central America
89 C3 El Samán de Apure Venez.
69 F1 Elsas Can.
43 G2 Else *r.* Ger.
23 H2 Elsen Nur *l.* China
16 D7 El Shatt Egypt
89 D2 El Sombrero Venez.
91 C2 El Sosneado Arg.
El Suweis *see* Suez
84 C2 El Tajin Ruins Mex.
95 L9 Eltanin Fracture Zone
sea feature Pac. Oc.
48 C6 El Tarf Alg.
45 C1 El Teleno *mt* Spain
84 C3 El Tepozteco, Parque
Nacional *nat. park* Mex.
16 E7 El Thamad Egypt
89 D2 El Tigre Venez.
84 E3 El Tigre, Parque Nacional
nat. park Guatemala
43 J5 Eltmann Ger.
89 C2 El Tocuyo Venez.
51 H5 El'ton Rus. Fed.
51 H5 El'ton, Ozero *l.* Rus. Fed.
72 C2 Eltopia U.S.A.
89 E2 El Toro Venez.
91 C2 El Trébol Arg.
89 C3 El Tuparro, Parque Nacional
nat. park Col.
55 F2 El Tur Egypt
88 B8 El Turbio Chile
21 C2 Eluru India
37 U7 Elva Estonia
89 A3 El Valle Col.
40 E5 Elvanfoot U.K.
45 C3 Elvas Port.
37 M6 Elverum Norway
89 B3 El Viejo *mt* Col.
89 C2 El Vigía Venez.
86 D5 Elvira Brazil
56 E3 El Wak Kenya
68 E5 Elwood U.S.A.
43 J3 Elxleben Ger.
39 H5 Ely U.K.
68 B2 Ely *MN* U.S.A.
75 E2 Ely *NV* U.S.A.
80 B4 Elyria U.S.A.
43 G4 Elz Ger.
43 H2 Elze Ger.
7 G3 Émaé *i.* Vanuatu
18 D2 Emāmrūd Iran
19 H2 Emām Şaḩēb Afgh.
17 L5 Emāmzadeh Naşrod Dīn Iran
37 O8 Emån *r.* Sweden
90 B2 Emas, Parque Nacional das
nat. park Brazil
14 D2 Emba Kazak.
59 H3 Embalenhle S. Africa
65 G3 Embarras Portage Can.
90 C2 Emborcação, Represa de
resr Brazil
81 F2 Embrun Can.
56 D4 Embu Kenya
42 F1 Emden Ger.
27 B4 Emei China
27 B4 Emei Shan *mt* China
8 E4 Emerald *Vic.* Austr.
6 E4 Emerald Austr.
67 G3 Emeril Can.
65 K5 Emerson Can.
16 B2 Emet Turkey
59 J2 Emgwenya S. Africa
75 E3 Emigrant Valley *v.* U.S.A.
59 J2 Emijindini S. Africa
55 D3 Emi Koussi *mt* Chad
84 E3 Emiliano Zapata Mex.
49 M3 Eminska Planina *h.* Bulg.
16 C2 Emir D. *mt* Turkey
16 C2 Emirdağ Turkey
37 O8 Emmaboda Sweden
37 S7 Emmaste Estonia
42 D2 Emmeloord Neth.
42 F4 Emmelshausen Ger.
42 E2 Emmen Neth.
46 D7 Emmen Switz.
42 E3 Emmerich Ger.
21 B3 Emmiganuru India
77 C6 Emory Pk *summit* U.S.A.
82 B3 Empalme Mex.
59 J4 Empangeni S. Africa
88 E3 Empedrado Arg.
94 G3 Emperor Seamount Chain
sea feature Pac. Oc.
48 D3 Empoli Italy
76 D4 Emporia *KS* U.S.A.
80 E6 Emporia *VA* U.S.A.
80 D4 Emporium U.S.A.
65 G4 Empress Can.
19 E3 'Emrānī Iran
42 F2 Ems *r.* Ger.
69 H3 Emsdale Can.
42 F2 Emsdetten Ger.
42 F1 Ems-Jade-Kanal *canal* Ger.
42 F2 Emsland *reg.* Ger.
59 H3 Emzinoni S. Africa
36 N5 Enafors Sweden
25 F7 Enarotali Indon.
29 E7 Ena-san *mt* Japan
82 A2 Encantada, Co de la *mt*
Mex.
91 G1 Encantadas, Serra das *h.*
Brazil
31 B3 Encanto, Cape *pt* Phil.
84 B2 Encarnación Mex.
88 E3 Encarnación Para.
77 D6 Encinal U.S.A.
74 D5 Encinitas U.S.A.
73 F5 Encino U.S.A.
8 B3 Encounter Bay *b.* Austr.
90 E1 Encruzilhada Brazil
91 G1 Encruzilhada do Sul Brazil
64 D4 Endako Can.
32 B5 Endau Malaysia
6 E3 Endeavour Strait *chan.*
Austr.
25 E7 Endeh Indon.
92 D4 Enderby Land *reg.* Ant.
81 E3 Endicott U.S.A.
64 C3 Endicott Arm *in.* U.S.A.
62 C3 Endicott Mts *mts* U.S.A.
91 E3 Energía Arg.
51 E6 Enerhodar Ukr.
94 F5 Enewetak *i.* Pac. Oc.
48 D6 Enfidaville Tunisia
79 E4 Enfield U.S.A.
68 E2 Engadine U.S.A.
36 L5 Engan Norway
31 B2 Engaño, Cape *c.* Phil.
Engaños, Río de los *r. see*
Yari
28 H2 Engaru Japan
59 G5 Engcobo S. Africa
51 H5 Engel's Rus. Fed.
42 C1 Engelschmangat *chan.* Neth.
33 B4 Enggano *i.* Indon.
42 C4 Enghien Belgium
34 E3 England *div.* U.K.
67 J3 Englee Can.
79 F5 Englehard U.S.A.
69 H2 Englehart Can.
39 D7 English Channel *str.*
France/U.K.
51 G7 Enguri *r.* Georgia
59 J4 Enhlalakahle S. Africa
77 D4 Enid U.S.A.
28 G3 Eniwa Japan
42 D2 Enkhuizen Neth.
37 P7 Enköping Sweden
48 F6 Enna *Sicily* Italy
65 J2 Ennadai Lake *l.* Can.
55 E3 En Nahud Sudan
55 E3 Ennedi, Massif *mts* Chad
41 D4 Ennell, Lough *l.*
Rep. of Ireland
76 C2 Enning U.S.A.
41 C5 Ennis Rep. of Ireland
72 E2 Ennis *MT* U.S.A.
77 D5 Ennis *TX* U.S.A.
41 E5 Enniscorthy Rep. of Ireland
41 D3 Enniskillen U.K.
41 B5 Ennistymon Rep. of Ireland
46 G7 Enns *r.* Austria
36 W5 Eno Fin.
75 F3 Enoch U.S.A.
36 S2 Enontekiö Fin.
27 D6 Enping China
31 B2 Enrile Phil.
42 D2 Ens Neth.
8 F4 Ensay Austr.
42 E2 Enschede Neth.
43 G3 Ense Ger.
82 A2 Ensenada Mex.
91 F2 Ensenada Arg.
27 C4 Enshi China
64 F2 Enterprise *N.W.T.* Can.
69 J3 Enterprise *Ont.* Can.
79 C6 Enterprise *AL* U.S.A.
72 C2 Enterprise *OR* U.S.A.
75 F3 Enterprise *UT* U.S.A.
64 F4 Entrance Can.
86 F8 Entre Ríos Bol.
91 E2 Entre Ríos *div.* Arg.
45 B3 Entroncamento Port.
54 C4 Enugu Nigeria
13 V3 Enurmino Rus. Fed.
86 D5 Envira Brazil
86 D5 Envira *r.* Brazil
9 C5 Enys, Mt *mt* N.Z.
29 F7 Enzan Japan
42 D2 Epe Neth.
42 B5 Épernay France
75 G2 Ephraim U.S.A.
81 E4 Ephrata *PA* U.S.A.
72 C2 Ephrata *WA* U.S.A.
7 G3 Épi *i.* Vanuatu
44 H2 Épinal France
16 D4 Episkopi Cyprus
48 E4 Epomeo, Monte *h.* Italy
39 H6 Epping U.K.
43 G4 Eppstein Ger.
39 G6 Epsom U.K.
91 D3 Epu-pel Arg.
18 D4 Eqlīd Iran
53 E5 Equatorial Guinea *country*
Africa
89 E3 Equeipa Venez.
31 A4 Eran Phil.
31 A4 Eran Bay *b.* Phil.
16 F1 Eratak Turkey
43 L5 Erbendorf Ger.
95 L3 Erben Tablemount *depth*
Pac. Oc.
42 F5 Erbeskopf *h.* Ger.
17 J2 Erçek Turkey
17 J2 Erciş Turkey
16 E2 Erciyes Dağı *mt* Turkey
47 J7 Érd Hungary
23 H2 Erdaogou China
30 D2 Erdao Jiang *r.* China
16 A1 Erdek Turkey
16 E3 Erdemli Turkey
26 C1 Erdenetsogt Mongolia
55 E3 Erdi *reg.* Chad
51 H6 Erdniyevskiy Rus. Fed.
89 D3 Erebato *r.* Venez.
92 B5 Erebus, Mt *mt* Ant.
17 K6 Erech Iraq
88 F3 Erechim Brazil
24 D2 Ereentsav Mongolia
16 E3 Ereğli *Konya* Turkey
16 C1 Ereğli *Zonguldak* Turkey
48 F6 Erei, Monti *mts Sicily* Italy
26 D1 Erenhot China
18 E3 Eresk Iran
45 D2 Eresma *r.* Spain
49 K5 Eretria Greece
Erevan *see* Yerevan
43 K4 Erfurt Ger.
17 G2 Ergani Turkey
54 B2 'Erg Chech *sand dunes*
Alg./Mali
55 D3 Erg du Djourab *sand dunes*
Chad
54 D3 Erg du Ténéré *des.* Niger
26 C1 Ergel Mongolia
49 M4 Ergene *r.* Turkey
54 B2 Erg Iguidi *sand dunes*
Alg./Maur.
37 T8 Ērgļi Latvia
28 A1 Ergu China
Ergun He *r. see* Argun'
30 C3 Erhulai China
40 D2 Eriboll, Loch *in.* U.K.
40 D4 Ericht, Loch *l.* U.K.
68 B5 Erie *IL* U.S.A.
77 E4 Erie *KS* U.S.A.
80 C3 Erie *PA* U.S.A.
69 G4 Erie, Lake *l.* Can./U.S.A.
28 H3 Erimo Japan
28 H4 Erimo-misaki *c.* Japan
40 A3 Eriskay *i.* U.K.
52 H4 Eritrea *country* Africa
16 E2 Erkilet Turkey
43 K5 Erlangen Ger.
6 D4 Erldunda Austr.
30 E2 Erlong Shan *mt* China
30 C2 Erlongshan Sk. *resr* China
42 D2 Ermelo Neth.
59 H3 Ermelo S. Africa
16 D3 Ermenek Turkey
49 L6 Ermoupoli Greece
21 B4 Ernakulam India
21 B4 Erode India
58 A1 Erongo *div.* Namibia
42 D3 Erp Neth.
54 B1 Er Rachidia Morocco
55 F3 Er Rahad Sudan
57 D5 Errego Moz.
48 D7 Er Remla Tunisia
41 C2 Errigal *h.* Rep. of Ireland
41 A3 Erris Head *hd* Rep. of Ireland
81 H2 Errol U.S.A.
7 G3 Erromango *i.* Vanuatu
49 J4 Ersekë Albania
76 D2 Erskine U.S.A.
36 R5 Ersmark Sweden
51 G5 Ertil' Rus. Fed.
8 B1 Erudina Austr.
17 J3 Eruh Turkey
91 G2 Erval Brazil
80 D5 Erwin U.S.A.
43 G3 Erwitte Ger.
43 K2 Erxleben *Sachsen-Anhalt*
Ger.
43 K2 Erxleben *Sachsen-Anhalt*
Ger.
43 L4 Erzgebirge *mts*
Czech Rep./Ger.
16 F3 Erzin Turkey
17 G2 Erzincan Turkey
17 H2 Erzurum Turkey
28 G4 Esan-misaki *pt* Japan
28 G4 Esashi Japan
28 H2 Esashi Japan
37 L9 Esbjerg Denmark
75 G3 Escalante U.S.A.
75 G3 Escalante *r.* U.S.A.
75 F3 Escalante Desert *des.* U.S.A.
68 D3 Escanaba U.S.A.
84 E3 Escárcega Mex.
31 B2 Escarpada Point *pt* Phil.
45 F2 Escatrón Spain
42 B4 Escaut *r.* Belgium
42 D3 Esch Neth.
42 E2 Esche Ger.
43 J2 Eschede Ger.
42 D5 Esch-sur-Alzette Lux.
43 J3 Eschwege Ger.
42 E4 Eschweiler Ger.
74 D5 Escondido U.S.A.
84 A2 Escuinapa Mex.
84 E4 Escuintla Guatemala
84 D4 Escuintla Mex.
89 C3 Escutillas Col.
16 B3 Eşen Turkey
18 D2 Esenguly Turkm.
42 F1 Esens Ger.
18 C3 Eşfahan Iran
18 D4 Esfandāran Iran
18 C4 Esfarjan Iran
19 E3 Eshāqābād Iran
18 D5 Eshkanān Iran
59 J4 Eshowe S. Africa
16 E6 Esh Sharā *mts* Jordan
18 C3 Eshtehārd Iran
57 C6 Esigodini Zimbabwe
59 K4 Esikhawini S. Africa
38 D2 Esk *r.* U.K.
40 E5 Eskdalemuir U.K.
67 G3 Esker Can.
36 F4 Eskifjörður Iceland
37 P7 Eskilstuna Sweden
62 E3 Eskimo Lakes *l.* Can.
17 J3 Eski Mosul Iraq
16 D1 Eskipazar Turkey
16 C2 Eskişehir Turkey
45 D1 Esla *r.* Spain
18 B3 Eslamābād e Gharb Iran
16 B3 Esler D. *mt* Turkey
43 G3 Eslohe (Sauerland) Ger.
37 N9 Eslöv Sweden
16 B2 Eşme Turkey
86 C3 Esmeraldas Ecuador
68 E1 Esnagi Lake *l.* Can.
42 B4 Esnes France
19 F5 Espakeh Iran
44 F4 Espalion France
69 G2 Espanola Can.
73 F4 Espanola U.S.A.
86 □ Española, Isla *i. Galapagos Is*
Ecuador
74 A2 Esparto U.S.A.
43 G2 Espelkamp Ger.
6 C5 Esperance Austr.
91 E1 Esperanza Arg.
82 C3 Esperanza Mex.
31 C4 Esperanza Phil.
92 B2 Esperanza *Arg. Base* Ant.
45 B3 Espichel, Cabo *hd* Port.
45 D1 Espigüete *mt* Spain
84 B1 Espinazo Mex.
90 D2 Espinhaço, Serra do *mts*
Brazil
90 D1 Espinosa Brazil
90 E2 Espírito Santo *div.* Brazil
31 B2 Espiritu Phil.
70 D7 Espíritu Santo *i.* Mex.
7 G3 Espiritu Santo *i.* Vanuatu
37 T6 Espoo Fin.
45 F4 Espuña *mt* Spain
88 B6 Esquel Arg.
64 E5 Esquimalt Can.
31 C5 Essang Indon.
54 B1 Essaouira Morocco
54 A2 Es Semara Western Sahara
42 C3 Essen Belgium
42 F3 Essen Ger.
43 F2 Essen (Oldenburg) Ger.
87 G3 Essequibo *r.* Guyana
69 F4 Essex Can.
75 E4 Essex U.S.A.
81 G2 Essex Junction U.S.A.
69 F4 Essexville U.S.A.
13 R4 Esso Rus. Fed.
88 D8 Estados, I. de los *i.* Arg.
18 D4 Eşţahbānāt Iran
69 G2 Estaire Can.
87 L6 Estância Brazil
45 G1 Estats, Pic d' *mt*
France/Spain
59 H4 Estcourt S. Africa
43 H1 Este *r.* Ger.
45 E1 Estella Spain
45 D4 Estepa Spain
45 D4 Estepona Spain
65 J4 Esterhazy Can.
74 B4 Estero Bay *b.* U.S.A.
88 D2 Esteros Para.
88 E3 Esteros del Iberá *marsh* Arg.
65 J5 Estevan Can.
76 E3 Estherville U.S.A.
67 H4 Est, Île de l' *i.* Can.
79 D5 Estill U.S.A.
81 J1 Est, Lac de l' *l.* Can.
35 H3 Estonia *country* Europe
42 A5 Estrées-St-Denis France
45 C2 Estrela, Serra da *mts* Port.
45 E3 Estrella *mt* Spain
45 C3 Estremoz Port.
87 J5 Estrondo, Serra *h.* Brazil
17 M4 Estūh Iran
22 D4 Etah India
42 D5 Étain France
44 F2 Étampes France
44 E1 Étaples France
22 D4 Etawah India
59 J3 eThandakukhanya S. Africa
58 E4 E'Thembini S. Africa
53 H5 Ethiopia *country* Africa
16 D2 Etimesğut Turkey
40 C4 Etive, Loch *in.* U.K.
48 F6 Etna, Monte *volc. Sicily*
Italy
37 J7 Etne Norway
64 C3 Etolin I. *i.* U.S.A.
57 B5 Etosha National Park
Namibia
57 B5 Etosha Pan *salt pan*
Namibia
49 L3 Etropole Bulg.
21 B4 Ettaiyapuram India
42 E5 Ettelbruck Lux.
42 C3 Etten-Leur Neth.
43 G6 Ettlingen Ger.
40 E5 Ettrick Forest *reg.* U.K.
84 A2 Etzatlán Mex.
8 F2 Euabalong Austr.
Euboea *i. see* Evvoia
6 C5 Eucla Austr.
80 C4 Euclid U.S.A.
87 L6 Euclides da Cunha Brazil
8 G4 Eucumbene, L. *l.* Austr.
8 B3 Eudunda Austr.
79 C6 Eufaula U.S.A.
77 E5 Eufaula Lake *resr* U.S.A.
72 B2 Eugene U.S.A.
82 A3 Eugenia, Pta *c.* Mex.
8 G2 Eugowra Austr.
8 G1 Eumungerie Austr.
77 E6 Eunice U.S.A.
42 E4 Eupen Belgium
17 K6 Euphrates *r.* Asia
37 S6 Eura Fin.
44 E2 Eure *r.* France
72 A3 Eureka *CA* U.S.A.
72 D1 Eureka *MT* U.S.A.
75 E2 Eureka *NV* U.S.A.
8 C1 Eurinilla *r.* Austr.
8 C1 Euriowie Austr.
8 E4 Euroa Austr.
57 E6 Europa, Île *i.* Ind. Ocean
45 D4 Europa Point *pt* Gibraltar
42 C3 Europoort *reg.* Neth.
42 E4 Euskirchen Ger.
8 D3 Euston Austr.
64 D4 Eustuk Lake *l.* Can.
79 C5 Eutaw U.S.A.
43 L3 Eutzsch Ger.
59 H3 Evander S. Africa
64 F4 Evansburg Can.
92 B3 Evans Ice Stream *ice feature*
Ant.
66 E3 Evans, L. *l.* Can.
73 F4 Evans, Mt *mt CO* U.S.A.
72 D2 Evans, Mt *mt MT* U.S.A.
63 K3 Evans Strait Can.
68 D4 Evanston *IL* U.S.A.
72 E3 Evanston *WY* U.S.A.
69 F3 Evansville Can.
78 C4 Evansville *IN* U.S.A.
68 C4 Evansville *WI* U.S.A.
72 F3 Evansville *WY* U.S.A.
68 E4 Evart U.S.A.
59 G3 Evaton S. Africa
18 D5 Evaz Iran
68 A2 Eveleth U.S.A.
13 R3 Evensk Rus. Fed.
6 D4 Everard Range *h.* Austr.
42 D3 Everdingen Neth.
23 F4 Everest, Mt *mt* China
81 K1 Everett Can.
72 B1 Everett U.S.A.
42 B3 Evergem Belgium
79 D7 Everglades Nat. Park U.S.A.
79 D7 Everglades, The *swamp*
U.S.A.
77 G6 Evergreen U.S.A.
39 F5 Evesham U.K.
39 F5 Evesham, Vale of *reg.* U.K.
36 S5 Evijärvi Fin.
54 D4 Evinayong Equatorial Guinea
37 K7 Evje Norway
45 C3 Évora Port.
24 F1 Evoron, Ozero *l.* Rus. Fed.
17 K2 Evowghlī Iran
44 E2 Évreux France
49 K6 Evrotas *r.* Greece
16 D4 Evrychou Cyprus
49 L5 Evvoia *i.* Greece
74 □1 Ewa Beach U.S.A.
56 D3 Ewaso Ngiro *r.* Kenya
40 C3 Ewe, Loch *in.* U.K.
92 B2 Ewing I. *i.* Ant.
86 E6 Exaltación Bol.
59 G4 Excelsior S. Africa
74 C2 Excelsior Mtn *mt* U.S.A.
74 C2 Excelsior Mts *mts* U.S.A.
76 E4 Excelsior Springs U.S.A.
39 D6 Exe *r.* U.K.
92 A4 Executive Committee Range
mts Ant.
8 H3 Exeter Austr.
69 G4 Exeter Can.
39 D7 Exeter U.K.
74 C3 Exeter *CA* U.S.A.
81 H3 Exeter *NH* U.S.A.
42 E2 Exloo Neth.
39 D7 Exminster U.K.
39 D6 Exmoor Forest *reg.* U.K.
39 D6 Exmoor National Park U.K.
81 F6 Exmore U.S.A.
39 D7 Exmouth U.K.
6 B4 Exmouth Gulf *b.* Austr.
8 G1 Exmouth, Mt *mt* Austr.
93 M5 Exmouth Plateau
sea feature Ind. Ocean
45 D3 Extremadura *div.* Spain
79 E7 Exuma Sound *chan.*
Bahamas
56 D4 Eyasi, Lake *salt l.* Tanz.
39 J5 Eye U.K.
40 F5 Eyemouth U.K.
40 B2 Eye Peninsula *pen.* U.K.
36 D5 Eyjafjallajökull *ice cap*
Iceland
36 D3 Eyjafjörður *in.* Iceland
56 E3 Eyl Somalia
39 F6 Eynsham U.K.
6 D4 Eyre, Lake (North) *salt flat*
Austr.
6 D4 Eyre, Lake (South) *salt flat*
Austr.
9 B6 Eyre Mountains *mts* N.Z.
6 D5 Eyre Peninsula *pen.* Austr.
43 H2 Eystrup Ger.
36 □ Eysturoy *i.* Faroe Is
59 J4 Ezakheni S. Africa
59 H3 Ezenzeleni S. Africa
91 C3 Ezequiel Ramos Mexía,
Embalse *resr* Arg.
50 J2 Ezhva Rus. Fed.
49 M5 Ezine Turkey
16 F1 Ezinepazar Turkey
17 L6 Ezra's Tomb Iraq

F

21 A5 Faadhippolhu Atoll
Maldives
77 B6 Fabens U.S.A.
64 F2 Faber Lake *l.* Can.
32 □ Faber, Mt *h.* Sing.
37 M9 Fåborg Denmark
48 E3 Fabriano Italy
89 B3 Facatativá Col.
42 B4 Faches-Thumesnil France
54 D3 Fachi Niger
81 F4 Factoryville U.S.A.
88 B7 Facundo Arg.
54 C3 Fada-Ngourma Burkina
48 D2 Faenza Italy
Faeroes *terr. see* Faroe
Islands
25 F7 Fafanlap Indon.
56 E3 Fafen Shet' *watercourse*
Eth.
49 L2 Făgăraş Romania
37 L6 Fagernes Norway
37 O7 Fagersta Sweden
88 C8 Fagnano, L. *l.* Arg./Chile
42 C4 Fagne *reg.* Belgium
54 B3 Faguibine, Lac *l.* Mali
36 E5 Fagurhólsmýri Iceland
55 F4 Fagwir Sudan
19 E4 Fahraj Iran
62 D3 Fairbanks U.S.A.
80 B5 Fairborn U.S.A.
76 D3 Fairbury U.S.A.
80 E5 Fairfax U.S.A.
74 A2 Fairfield *CA* U.S.A.
68 B5 Fairfield *IA* U.S.A.
78 C4 Fairfield *OH* U.S.A.
77 D6 Fairfield *TX* U.S.A.
81 G3 Fair Haven U.S.A.
41 E2 Fair Head *hd* U.K.
31 A4 Fairie Queen *sand bank*
Phil.
40 G1 Fair Isle *i.* U.K.
76 E3 Fairmont *MN* U.S.A.
80 C5 Fairmont *WV* U.S.A.
73 F4 Fairplay U.S.A.
68 D3 Fairport U.S.A.
80 C4 Fairport Harbor U.S.A.
64 F3 Fairview Can.
69 E3 Fairview *MI* U.S.A.
77 D4 Fairview *OK* U.S.A.
75 G2 Fairview *UT* U.S.A.
27 □ Fairview Park *H.K.* China
64 B3 Fairweather, Cape *c.* U.S.A.
64 B3 Fairweather, Mt *mt*
Can./U.S.A.
25 G6 Fais *i.* Micronesia
22 C3 Faisalabad Pak.
42 C5 Faissault France
76 C2 Faith U.S.A.
40 □ Faither, The *pt* U.K.
23 E4 Faizabad India
7 J2 Fakaofo *i.* Tokelau
39 H5 Fakenham U.K.
36 O5 Fåker Sweden
25 F7 Fakfak Indon.

79 D6 Gainesville *FL* U.S.A.
79 D5 Gainesville *GA* U.S.A.
77 D5 Gainesville *TX* U.S.A.
39 G4 Gainsborough U.K.
6 D5 Gairdner, Lake *salt flat* Austr.
40 C3 Gairloch U.K.
40 C3 Gair Loch *in.* U.K.
30 B3 Gai Xian China
21 C2 Gajapatinagaram India
19 G5 Gajar Pak.
58 E3 Gakarosa *mt* S. Africa
22 C1 Gakuch Jammu and Kashmir
23 G3 Gala China
19 G2 Galaasiya Uzbek.
16 C7 Galâla el Baharîya, G. el *plat.* Egypt
56 D4 Galana *r.* Kenya
40 F5 Galashiels U.K.
49 N2 Galaţi Romania
49 H4 Galatina Italy
80 C6 Galax U.S.A.
41 C5 Galbally Rep. of Ireland
37 L6 Galdhøpiggen *summit* Norway
84 B1 Galeana Mex.
18 D5 Galeh Dār Iran
68 B4 Galena U.S.A.
89 E2 Galeota Pt *pt* Trinidad and Tobago
89 E2 Galera Pt *pt* Trinidad and Tobago
84 C4 Galera, Pta *pt* Mex.
91 B4 Galera, Punta *pt* Chile
68 B5 Galesburg U.S.A.
58 F4 Galeshewe S. Africa
68 B3 Galesville U.S.A.
80 E4 Galeton U.S.A.
51 G7 Gali Georgia
50 G3 Galich Rus. Fed.
50 G2 Galichskaya Vozvyshennost' *reg.* Rus. Fed.
45 C1 Galicia *div.* Spain
16 E5 Galilee, Sea of *l.* Israel
80 B4 Galion U.S.A.
48 C6 Galite, Canal de la *chan.* Tunisia
75 G5 Galiuro Mts *mts* U.S.A.
55 F3 Gallabat Sudan
79 C4 Gallatin U.S.A.
72 E2 Gallatin *r.* U.S.A.
21 C5 Galle Sri Lanka
88 B8 Gallegos *r.* Arg.
89 C1 Gallinas, Pta *pt* Col.
48 H4 Gallipoli Italy
80 B5 Gallipolis U.S.A.
36 R3 Gällivare Sweden
36 O5 Gällö Sweden
81 E3 Gallo I. *i.* U.S.A.
75 H4 Gallo Mts *mts* U.S.A.
40 D6 Galloway, Mull of *c.* U.K.
75 H4 Gallup U.S.A.
19 G1 Gallyaaral Uzbek.
40 B4 Galmisdale U.K.
8 G3 Galong Austr.
21 C4 Galoya Sri Lanka
21 C5 Gal Oya *r.* Sri Lanka
40 D5 Galston U.K.
74 B2 Galt U.S.A.
54 A2 Galtat Zemmour Western Sahara
41 C5 Galtee Mountains *h.* Rep. of Ireland
41 C5 Galtymore *h.* Rep. of Ireland
19 E3 Galūgāh-e Āsīyeh Iran
68 B5 Galva U.S.A.
77 E6 Galveston U.S.A.
77 E6 Galveston Bay *b.* U.S.A.
91 E2 Galvez Arg.
23 E3 Galwa Nepal
41 B4 Galway Rep. of Ireland
41 B4 Galway Bay *g.* Rep. of Ireland
27 B6 Gâm *r.* Vietnam
39 J8 Gamaches France
59 J5 Gamalakhe S. Africa
89 B2 Gamarra Col.
23 G3 Gamba China
56 D3 Gambēla Eth.
56 D3 Gambela National Park Eth.
62 A3 Gambell U.S.A.
22 D4 Gambhir *r.* India
52 C4 Gambia, The *country* Africa
5 O7 Gambier, Îles *is* Pac. Oc.
67 K4 Gambo Can.
56 B4 Gamboma Congo
75 H4 Gamerco U.S.A.
37 P8 Gamleby Sweden
36 S4 Gammelstaden Sweden
58 C4 Gamoep S. Africa
28 B3 Gamova, Mys *pt* Rus. Fed.
21 C5 Gampola Sri Lanka
19 F4 Gamshadzai K. *mts* Iran
10 J10 Gan Maldives
26 A3 Gana China
75 H4 Ganado U.S.A.
69 J3 Gananoque Can.
18 C4 Ganāveh Iran
17 L1 Gäncä Azer.
27 C7 Gancheng China
Gand *see* Gent
33 E3 Gandadiwata, Bukit *mt* Indon.
23 G3 Gandaingoin China
56 C4 Gandajika Congo(Zaire)
23 E4 Gandak Dam *dam* Nepal
22 B3 Gandari Mountain *mt* Pak.
22 A3 Gandava Pak.
67 K4 Gander Can.
43 G1 Ganderkesee Ger.
45 G2 Gandesa Spain
22 C5 Gandevi India
22 B5 Gāndhīdhām India
22 C5 Gandhinagar India
22 C4 Gāndhi Sāgar *resr* India
22 C4 Gāndhi Sāgar Dam *dam* India
45 F3 Gandía Spain
19 F4 Gand-i-Zureh *plain* Afgh.
90 E1 Gandu Brazil
21 C5 Ganga *r.* Sri Lanka
91 C4 Gangán Arg.
22 C3 Ganganagar India
22 D4 Gangapur India
23 H5 Gangaw Myanmar
21 B3 Gangawati India
26 A2 Gangca China
22 E3 Gangdisê Shan *mts* China
44 F5 Ganges France
23 G5 Ganges, Mouths of the *est.* Bangl./India
22 D3 Gangoh India
22 D3 Gangotri *mt* India
23 G4 Gangtok India
26 B3 Gangu China
21 D2 Ganjam India
18 C4 Ganjgān Iran
27 E4 Gan Jiang *r.* China
27 B4 Ganluo China
8 F3 Ganmain Austr.
44 F3 Gannat France
72 E3 Gannett Peak *summit* U.S.A.
22 C5 Ganora India
26 C2 Ganquan China
58 C7 Gansbaai S. Africa
26 B3 Gansu *div.* China
26 B2 Gantang China
51 G7 Gant'iadi Georgia
27 E5 Gan Xian China
58 F3 Ganyesa S. Africa
26 F3 Ganyu China
27 E5 Ganzhou China
55 F4 Ganzi Sudan
54 B3 Gao Mali
27 E4 Gao'an China
26 E2 Gaocheng China
26 F4 Gaochun China
27 E4 Gaohebu China
26 B2 Gaolan China
26 F2 Gaomi China
27 D5 Gaomutang China
26 D3 Gaoping China
26 A2 Gaotai China
26 E2 Gaotang China
26 C2 Gaotouyao China
54 B3 Gaoua Burkina
54 A3 Gaoual Guinea
27 B4 Gao Xian China
26 E2 Gaoyang China
26 E2 Gaoyi China
26 F3 Gaoyou China
26 F3 Gaoyou Hu *l.* China
27 D6 Gaozhou China
44 H4 Gap France
31 B3 Gapan Phil.
45 F5 Gap Carbon *hd* Alg.
22 E2 Gar China
19 F4 Garagheh Iran
41 C4 Gara, Lough *l.* Rep. of Ireland
56 C3 Garamba *r.* Congo(Zaire)
56 C3 Garamba, Park National de la *nat. park* Congo(Zaire)
87 L5 Garanhuns Brazil
59 G2 Ga-Rankuwa S. Africa
56 D3 Garba Tula Kenya
74 A1 Garberville U.S.A.
18 C3 Garbosh, Kūh-e *mt* Iran
43 H2 Garbsen Ger.
90 C3 Garça Brazil
90 B1 Garças, Rio das *r.* Brazil
23 G2 Garco China
17 K1 Gardabani Georgia
48 D2 Garda, Lago di *l.* Italy
48 B6 Garde, Cap de *hd* Alg.
43 K2 Gardelegen Ger.
76 C4 Garden City U.S.A.
68 D3 Garden Corners U.S.A.
74 C5 Garden Grove U.S.A.
65 L4 Garden Hill Can.
68 E3 Garden I. *i.* U.S.A.
78 C2 Garden Pen. *pen.* U.S.A.
19 H3 Gardez Afgh.
81 J2 Gardiner *ME* U.S.A.
72 E2 Gardiner *MT* U.S.A.
81 G4 Gardiners I. *i.* U.S.A.
68 C5 Gardner U.S.A.
81 K2 Gardner Lake *l.* U.S.A.
5 L2 Gardner Pinnacles *is HI* U.S.A.
74 C2 Gardnerville U.S.A.
40 D4 Garelochhead U.K.
68 E2 Gargantua, Cape *c.* Can.
17 M6 Gargar Iran
37 R9 Gargždai Lith.
22 D5 Garhakota India
22 E5 Garhchiroli India
22 A3 Garhi Khairo Pak.
22 D4 Garhi Malehra India
64 E5 Garibaldi, Mt *mt* Can.
64 E5 Garibaldi Prov. Park *nat. park* Can.
59 F5 Gariep Dam *resr* S. Africa
58 B5 Garies S. Africa
48 E4 Garigliano *r.* Italy
56 D4 Garissa Kenya
37 T8 Garkalne Latvia
80 D4 Garland *PA* U.S.A.
77 D5 Garland *TX* U.S.A.
18 C2 Garmī Iran
46 E7 Garmisch-Partenkirchen Ger.
18 D3 Garmsar Iran
19 F4 Garmsel *reg.* Afgh.
76 E4 Garnett U.S.A.
8 D2 Garnpung Lake *l.* Austr.
23 G4 Gāro Hills *h.* India
44 D4 Garonne *r.* France
56 E3 Garoowe Somalia
88 G3 Garopaba Brazil
54 D4 Garoua Cameroon
91 D3 Garré Arg.
75 E2 Garrison U.S.A.
41 F2 Garron Point *pt* U.K.
19 G4 Garruk Pak.
65 J1 Garry Lake *l.* Can.
40 D4 Garry, Loch *l.* U.K.
40 B2 Garrynahine U.K.
56 E4 Garsen Kenya
39 D5 Garth U.K.
43 K1 Gartow Ger.
58 B3 Garub Namibia
33 C4 Garut Indon.
41 E3 Garvagh U.K.
40 D3 Garve U.K.
68 D5 Gary U.S.A.
22 E3 Garyarsa China
29 C7 Garyū-zan *mt* Japan
22 D2 Gar Zangbo *r.* China
24 B3 Garzê China
89 B4 Garzón Col.
44 D5 Gascogne *reg.* France
76 E4 Gasconade *r.* U.S.A.
44 C5 Gascony, Gulf of *g.* France/Spain
6 B4 Gascoyne *r.* Austr.
Gascuña, Golfo de *g. see* Gascony, Gulf of
22 D2 Gasherbrum *mt* China/Jammu and Kashmir
19 F5 Gasht Iran
54 D3 Gashua Nigeria
19 E3 Gask Iran
33 C3 Gaspar, Selat *chan.* Indon.
67 H4 Gaspé Can.
67 H4 Gaspé, C. *c.* Can.
67 G4 Gaspé, Péninsule de *pen.* Can.
67 G4 Gaspésie, Parc de la *nat. park* Can.
42 E2 Gasselte Neth.
79 D5 Gastonia U.S.A.
91 C4 Gastre Arg.
45 E4 Gata, Cabo de *c.* Spain
16 D4 Gata, Cape *c.* Cyprus
50 D3 Gatchina Rus. Fed.
80 B6 Gate City U.S.A.
40 D6 Gatehouse of Fleet U.K.
38 F3 Gateshead U.K.
77 D6 Gatesville U.S.A.
75 H2 Gateway U.S.A.
81 F4 Gateway National Recreational Area *res.* U.S.A.
69 K3 Gatineau Can.
69 K2 Gatineau *r.* Can.
18 D4 Gaţrūyeh Iran
17 M5 Gatvand Iran
7 H3 Gau *i.* Fiji
65 K3 Gauer Lake *l.* Can.
36 M5 Gaula *r.* Norway
80 C5 Gauley Bridge U.S.A.
42 D5 Gaume *reg.* Belgium
23 F4 Gauri Sankar *mt* China
59 G3 Gauteng *div.* S. Africa
19 G3 Gauzan Afgh.
19 F5 Gavāter Iran
18 D5 Gāvbandī Iran
18 D5 Gāvbūs, Kūh-e *mts* Iran
49 L7 Gavdos *i.* Greece
18 B3 Gaveh *r.* Iran
90 E1 Gavião *r.* Brazil
17 L4 Gavīleh Iran
74 B4 Gaviota U.S.A.
18 E4 Gāv Koshī Iran
37 P6 Gävle Sweden
57 F3 Gavrilov-Yam Rus. Fed.
58 B3 Gawachab Namibia
8 B3 Gawler Austr.
26 A1 Gaxun Nur *salt l.* China
23 F4 Gaya India
54 C3 Gaya Niger
30 E2 Gaya *r.* China
68 E3 Gaylord U.S.A.
16 E6 Gaza Gaza
59 K1 Gaza *div.* Moz.
16 E6 Gaza *terr.* Asia
20 F1 Gaz-Achak Turkm.
18 D2 Gazandzhyk Turkm.
19 H3 Gazdarra Pass Afgh.
16 F3 Gaziantep Turkey
19 F3 Gazik Iran
16 D3 Gazipaşa Turkey
19 F1 Gazli Uzbek.
19 E5 Gaz Māhū Iran
19 E4 Gaz Şāleḩ Iran
54 A4 Gbangbatok Sierra Leone
54 B4 Gbarnga Liberia
54 C4 Gboko Nigeria
47 J3 Gdańsk Pol.
47 J3 Gdańsk, Gulf of *g.* Pol./Rus. Fed.
50 C3 Gdov Rus. Fed.
47 J3 Gdynia Pol.
40 C1 Gealldruig Mhor *i.* U.K.
43 J3 Gebesee Ger.
55 F3 Gedaref Sudan
43 H4 Gedern Ger.
42 C5 Gedinne Belgium
16 B2 Gediz Turkey
16 A2 Gediz *r.* Turkey
39 H5 Gedney Drove End U.K.
37 M9 Gedser Denmark
42 D3 Geel Belgium
8 E5 Geelong Austr.
58 D4 Geel Vloer *salt pan* S. Africa
42 F2 Geeste Ger.
43 J1 Geesthacht Ger.
26 F4 Ge Hu *l.* China
54 D3 Geidam Nigeria
43 H5 Geiersberg *h.* Ger.
65 J3 Geikie *r.* Can.
42 E4 Geilenkirchen Ger.
37 L6 Geilo Norway
37 K5 Geiranger Norway
68 E6 Geist Reservoir U.S.A.
43 L3 Geithain Ger.
27 B6 Gejiu China
48 F6 Gela *Sicily* Italy
56 E3 Geladī Eth.
32 B4 Gelang, Tanjung *pt* Malaysia
42 E3 Geldern Ger.
51 F6 Gelendzhik Rus. Fed.
47 L3 Gelgaudiškis Lith.
51 C7 Gelibolu Turkey
16 C2 Gelincik Dağı *mt* Turkey
18 E3 Gelmord Iran
43 H4 Gelnhausen Ger.
42 F3 Gelsenkirchen Ger.
32 B5 Gemas Malaysia
31 C5 Gemeh Indon.
56 B3 Gemena Congo(Zaire)
16 F2 Gemerek Turkey
16 B1 Gemlik Turkey
48 E1 Gemona del Friuli Italy
57 C6 Gemsbok National Park Botswana
58 D3 Gemsbokplein *well* S. Africa
56 E3 Genalē Wenz *r.* Eth.
42 C4 Genappe Belgium
91 D3 General Acha Arg.
91 E3 General Alvear *Buenos Aires* Arg.
91 E1 General Alvear *Entre Rios* Arg.
91 C2 General Alvear *Mendoza* Arg.
91 E2 General Belgrano Arg.
92 B3 General Belgrano II *Arg. Base* Ant.
92 B2 General Bernardo O'Higgins *Chile Base* Ant.
84 C1 General Bravo Mex.
88 B7 General Carrera, L. *l.* Chile
84 B1 General Cepeda Mex.
91 F3 General Conesa *Buenos Aires* Arg.
91 D4 General Conesa *Rio Negro* Arg.
91 F3 General Guido Arg.
91 F3 General J. Madariaga Arg.
91 E3 General La Madrid Arg.
91 F3 General Lavalle Arg.
91 D2 General Levalle Arg.
31 C4 General Luna Phil.
31 C4 General MacArthur Phil.
91 D2 General Pico Arg.
91 E2 General Pinto Arg.
91 C3 General Roca Arg.
92 B2 General San Martin *Arg. Base* Ant.
31 C5 General Santos Phil.
84 C1 General Terán Mex.
84 B2 General Vicente Guerrero Mex.
91 D2 General Villegas Arg.
80 D3 Genesee *r.* U.S.A.
68 B5 Geneseo *IL* U.S.A.
80 E3 Geneseo *NY* U.S.A.
59 G3 Geneva S. Africa
Geneva *see* Genève
68 C5 Geneva *IL* U.S.A.
76 D3 Geneva *NE* U.S.A.
80 E3 Geneva *NY* U.S.A.
80 C4 Geneva *OH* U.S.A.
Geneva, Lake *l. see* Léman, Lac
68 C4 Geneva, Lake *l.* U.S.A.
46 C7 Genève Switz.
45 D4 Genil *r.* Spain
42 D4 Genk Belgium
42 D3 Gennep Neth.
8 G4 Genoa Austr.
48 C2 Genoa Italy
Genova *see* Genoa
48 C2 Genova, Golfo di *g.* Italy
42 B3 Gent Belgium
43 L2 Genthin Ger.
6 B5 Geographe Bay *b.* Austr.
58 E6 George S. Africa
67 G2 George *r.* Can.
8 G3 George, L. *l. N.S.W.* Austr.
8 B4 George, L. *l. S.A.* Austr.
79 D6 George, L. *l.* U.S.A.
81 G3 George, Lake *l.* U.S.A.
9 A6 George Sd *in.* N.Z.
8 B2 Georgetown *S.A.* Austr.
79 F7 George Town Bahamas
69 H4 Georgetown Can.
87 G2 Georgetown Guyana
33 B1 George Town Malaysia
54 A3 Georgetown The Gambia
81 F5 Georgetown *DE* U.S.A.
68 D6 Georgetown *IL* U.S.A.
78 C4 Georgetown *KY* U.S.A.
80 B5 Georgetown *OH* U.S.A.
79 E5 Georgetown *SC* U.S.A.
77 D6 Georgetown *TX* U.S.A.
92 B2 George VI Sd *chan.* Ant.
92 B5 George V Land *reg.* Ant.
77 D6 George West U.S.A.
10 F5 Georgia *country* Asia
79 D5 Georgia *div.* U.S.A.
69 G3 Georgian Bay *l.* Can.
69 H3 Georgian Bay Island National Park Can.
64 E5 Georgia, Strait of *chan.* Can.
6 D4 Georgina *watercourse* Austr.
15 G2 Georgiyevka Kazak.
51 G6 Georgiyevsk Rus. Fed.
50 H3 Georgiyevskoye Rus. Fed.
43 L4 Gera Ger.
42 B4 Geraardsbergen Belgium
87 J6 Geral de Goiás, Serra *h.* Brazil
9 C6 Geraldine N.Z.
90 B4 Geral do Paraná, Serra *h.* Brazil
6 B4 Geraldton Austr.
18 D5 Gerāsh Iran
17 H3 Gercüş Turkey
16 D1 Gerede Turkey
16 D1 Gerede *r.* Turkey
19 G4 Gereshk Afgh.
32 B4 Gerik Malaysia
19 E3 Gerimenj Iran
76 C3 Gering U.S.A.
72 C3 Gerlach U.S.A.
64 E3 Germansen Landing Can.
80 E5 Germantown U.S.A.
34 F3 Germany *country* Europe
43 G5 Germersheim Ger.
59 H3 Germiston S. Africa
43 G5 Gernsheim Ger.
42 E4 Gerolstein Ger.
43 J5 Gerolzhofen Ger.
75 G5 Geronimo U.S.A.
8 H3 Gerringong Austr.
43 H4 Gersfeld Ger.
43 J4 Gerstungen Ger.
43 K2 Gerwisch Ger.
23 F2 Gêrzê China
51 E7 Gerze Turkey
42 F3 Gescher Ger.
18 D3 Getcheh, Kūh-e *h.* Iran
42 D4 Gete *r.* Belgium
80 E5 Gettysburg *PA* U.S.A.
76 D2 Gettysburg *SD* U.S.A.
80 E5 Gettysburg National Military Park *res.* U.S.A.
27 C5 Getu He *r.* China
92 A4 Getz Ice Shelf *ice feature* Ant.
33 A2 Geumapang *r.* Indon.
8 G2 Geurie Austr.
17 J2 Gevaş Turkey
49 K4 Gevgelija Macedonia
45 E1 Gexto Spain
Gey *see* Nikshahr
32 ▫ Geylang Sing.
59 F3 Geysdorp S. Africa
16 C1 Geyve Turkey
58 F2 Ghaap Plateau S. Africa
54 C1 Ghadāmis Libya
18 D2 Ghaem Shahr Iran
22 C3 Ghaggar, Dry Bed of *watercourse* Pak.
22 E4 Ghaghara *r.* India
23 F5 Ghaghra India
53 D5 Ghana *country* Africa
18 D5 Ghanādah, Rās *pt* U.A.E.
22 C4 Ghanliala India
57 C6 Ghanzi Botswana
58 E1 Ghanzi *div.* Botswana
16 E6 Gharandal Jordan
54 C1 Ghardaïa Alg.
19 H2 Gharm Tajik.
18 C5 Ghār, Ras al *pt* S. Arabia
55 D1 Gharyān Libya
54 D2 Ghāt Libya
22 B3 Ghauspur Pak.
55 D3 Ghazal, Bahr el *watercourse* Chad
54 B1 Ghazaouet Alg.
22 D3 Ghaziabad India
23 E4 Ghazipur India
22 A3 Ghazluna Pak.
19 H3 Ghaznī Afgh.
19 H3 Ghazni *r.* Afgh.
19 G3 Ghazoor Afgh.
Ghent *see* Gent
47 M7 Gheorgheni Romania
47 L7 Gherla Romania
48 C3 Ghisonaccia *Corsica* France
19 G3 Ghizao Afgh.
22 C1 Ghizar Pak.
21 A2 Ghod *r.* India
23 G4 Ghoraghat Bangl.
19 H3 Ghorband *r.* Afgh.
19 H3 Ghorband Pass Afgh.
22 B4 Ghotāru India
22 B4 Ghotki Pak.
18 D4 Ghōwrī Iran
23 F4 Ghuari *r.* India
17 J5 Ghudāf, Wādī al *watercourse* Iraq
19 J2 Ghŭdara Tajik.
22 D6 Ghugus India
22 B4 Ghulam Mohammed Barrage *barrage* Pak.
19 F3 Ghurian Afgh.
42 A3 Ghyvelde France
32 C3 Gia Đinh Vietnam
51 G6 Giaginskaya Rus. Fed.
49 K4 Giannitsa Greece
59 H4 Giant's Castle *mt* S. Africa
41 E2 Giant's Causeway U.K.
33 E4 Gianyar Indon.
32 C3 Gia Rai Vietnam
48 F6 Giarre *Sicily* Italy
48 B2 Giaveno Italy
58 B2 Gibeon Namibia
34 E5 Gibraltar *terr.* Europe
45 C5 Gibraltar, Strait of *str.* Morocco/Spain
68 C5 Gibson City U.S.A.
6 C4 Gibson Desert Austr.
24 B2 Gichgeniyn Nuruu *mts* Mongolia
21 B3 Giddalur India
16 D6 Giddi, G. el *h.* Egypt
56 D3 Gīdolē Eth.
44 F3 Gien France
43 G4 Gießen Ger.
43 J2 Gifhorn Ger.
64 F3 Gift Lake Can.
29 E7 Gifu Japan
89 B4 Gigante Col.
77 B7 Gigantes, Llanos de los *plain* Mex.
40 C5 Gigha *i.* U.K.
45 D1 Gijón Spain
75 F5 Gila *r.* U.S.A.
75 F5 Gila Bend U.S.A.
75 F5 Gila Bend Mts *mts* U.S.A.
75 E5 Gila Mts *mts* U.S.A.
17 K4 Gīlān Garb Iran
17 M1 Gilāzi Azer.
75 G5 Gilbert *AZ* U.S.A.
80 C6 Gilbert *WV* U.S.A.
6 E3 Gilbert *r.* Austr.
7 H2 Gilbert Islands *is* Kiribati
87 J5 Gilbués Brazil
18 E3 Gil Chashmeh Iran
72 E1 Gildford U.S.A.
55 E2 Gilf Kebir Plateau *plat.* Egypt
64 D4 Gilford I. *i.* Can.
8 G1 Gilgandra Austr.
56 D4 Gilgil Kenya
22 C2 Gilgit Jammu and Kashmir
22 C2 Gilgit *r.* Jammu and Kashmir
8 F2 Gilgunnia Austr.
64 D4 Gil Island *i.* Can.
65 L3 Gillam Can.
68 C3 Gillett U.S.A.
72 F2 Gillette U.S.A.
39 H6 Gillingham *Eng.* U.K.
39 E6 Gillingham *Eng.* U.K.
38 F3 Gilling West U.K.
92 D5 Gillock I. *i.* Ant.
68 D3 Gills Rock U.S.A.
68 D5 Gilman *IL* U.S.A.
68 B3 Gilman *WV* U.S.A.
66 E2 Gilmour Island *i.* Can.
74 B3 Gilroy U.S.A.
81 G3 Gilsum U.S.A.
55 E3 Gimbala, Jebel *mt* Sudan
56 D3 Gīmbī Eth.
65 K4 Gimli Can.
21 C5 Gin Ganga *r.* Sri Lanka
21 B3 Gingee India
56 E3 Gīnīr Eth.
48 G4 Ginosa Italy
48 G4 Gioia del Colle Italy
8 E5 Gippsland *reg.* Austr.
22 B4 Girab India
19 E5 Giran Iran
19 E4 Gīrān Rīg *mt* Iran
80 C3 Girard U.S.A.
22 B3 Girdao Pak.
19 G5 Girdar Dhor *r.* Pak.
19 F4 Girdi Iran
16 G1 Giresun Turkey
22 B5 Gir Forest *forest* India
23 F4 Girīdīh India
8 F1 Girilambone Austr.
22 C5 Girna *r.* India
45 H2 Girona Spain
44 D4 Gironde *est.* France
8 F2 Girral Austr.
40 D5 Girvan U.K.
50 E2 Girvas Rus. Fed.
22 E4 Girwan India
9 G3 Gisborne N.Z.
64 E4 Giscome Can.
37 N8 Gislaved Sweden
19 G2 Gissar Range *mts* Tajik./Uzbek.
56 C4 Gitarama Rwanda
56 C4 Gitega Burundi
48 E3 Giulianova Italy
49 L3 Giurgiu Romania
49 L2 Giuvala, Pasul *pass* Romania
42 C4 Givet France
44 G4 Givors France
42 C6 Givry-en-Argonne France
59 J1 Giyani S. Africa
16 C7 Giza Pyramids Egypt
19 G1 Gizhduvan Uzbek.
13 S3 Gizhiga Rus. Fed.
49 J4 Gjirokastër Albania
63 J3 Gjoa Haven Can.
36 L5 Gjøra Norway
37 M6 Gjøvik Norway
67 J4 Glace Bay Can.
64 C3 Glacier B. *b.* U.S.A.
64 B3 Glacier Bay National Park and Preserve U.S.A.
64 F4 Glacier Nat. Park Can.
72 D1 Glacier Nat. Park U.S.A.
72 B1 Glacier Peak *volc.* U.S.A.
36 M4 Gladstad Norway
8 B2 Gladstone *S.A.* Austr.
6 F4 Gladstone Austr.
68 D3 Gladstone U.S.A.
68 E4 Gladwin U.S.A.
40 E4 Glamis U.K.
31 C5 Glan Phil.
42 F5 Glan *r.* Ger.
41 B5 Glanaruddery Mts *h.* Rep. of Ireland
43 G2 Glandorf Ger.
38 F2 Glanton U.K.
69 G4 Glanworth Can.
40 D5 Glasgow U.K.
78 C4 Glasgow *KY* U.S.A.
72 F1 Glasgow *MT* U.S.A.
80 D6 Glasgow *VA* U.S.A.
65 H4 Glaslyn Can.
74 C3 Glass Mt *mt* U.S.A.
39 E6 Glastonbury U.K.
43 L4 Glauchau Ger.
12 G4 Glazov Rus. Fed.
51 F4 Glazunovka Rus. Fed.
47 P3 Glazunovo Rus. Fed.
81 H2 Glen U.S.A.
40 C3 Glen Affric *v.* U.K.
69 G2 Glen Afton Can.
9 E2 Glen Afton N.Z.
62 D3 Glenallen U.S.A.
59 H1 Glen Alpine Dam *dam* S. Africa
41 C4 Glenamaddy Rep. of Ireland
68 E3 Glen Arbor U.S.A.
9 C6 Glenavy N.Z.
40 C3 Glen Cannich *v.* U.K.
73 E4 Glen Canyon *gorge* U.S.A.
75 G3 Glen Canyon National Recreation Area *res.* U.S.A.
40 E4 Glen Clova *v.* U.K.
8 C4 Glencoe Austr.
69 G4 Glencoe Can.
59 J4 Glencoe S. Africa
40 C4 Glen Coe *v.* U.K.
69 E2 Glendale Can.
75 F5 Glendale *AZ* U.S.A.
74 C4 Glendale *CA* U.S.A.
75 E3 Glendale *NV* U.S.A.
75 F3 Glendale *UT* U.S.A.
80 D4 Glendale Lake *l.* U.S.A.
8 H2 Glen Davis Austr.
72 F2 Glendive U.S.A.
65 G4 Glendon Can.
72 F3 Glendo Res. *l.* U.S.A.
8 C4 Glenelg *r.* Austr.
40 F4 Glen Esk *v.* U.K.
40 A5 Glengad Head *hd* Rep. of Ireland
40 C3 Glen Garry *v. Scot.* U.K.
40 D4 Glen Garry *v. Scot.* U.K.
41 D3 Glengavlen Rep. of Ireland
6 F4 Glen Innes Austr.
40 D6 Glenluce U.K.
40 D4 Glen Lyon *v.* U.K.
40 D3 Glen More *v.* U.K.
40 D3 Glen Moriston *v.* U.K.
40 C4 Glen Nevis *v.* U.K.
69 F3 Glennie U.S.A.
75 G6 Glenn, Mt *mt* U.S.A.
80 E6 Glenns U.S.A.
64 C3 Glenora Can.
81 F2 Glen Robertson Can.
40 E4 Glenrothes U.K.
81 G3 Glens Falls U.S.A.
40 E4 Glen Shee *v.* U.K.
40 C3 Glen Shiel *v.* U.K.
41 C3 Glenties Rep. of Ireland
41 D2 Glenveagh National Park Rep. of Ireland
80 C5 Glenville U.S.A.
77 E5 Glenwood *AR* U.S.A.
75 H5 Glenwood *NM* U.S.A.
73 F4 Glenwood Springs U.S.A.
68 B2 Glidden U.S.A.
43 J1 Glinde Ger.
47 J5 Gliwice Pol.
75 G5 Globe U.S.A.
46 H5 Głogów Pol.
36 N3 Glomfjord Norway
37 M5 Glomma *r.* Norway
57 E5 Glorieuses, Îles *is* Ind. Ocean
8 H1 Gloucester Austr.
39 E6 Gloucester U.K.
81 H3 Gloucester *MA* U.S.A.
80 E6 Gloucester *VA* U.S.A.
81 F3 Gloversville U.S.A.
43 L2 Glöwen Ger.
28 D1 Glubinnoye Rus. Fed.
51 G6 Glubokiy Rus. Fed.
15 G1 Glubokoye Kazak.
43 H1 Glückstadt Ger.
36 ▫ Gluggarnir *h.* Faroe Is
38 F4 Glusburn U.K.
51 H5 Gmelinka Rus. Fed.
46 G6 Gmünd Austria
46 F7 Gmunden Austria
37 P5 Gnarp Sweden
43 H1 Gnarrenburg Ger.
46 H4 Gniezno Pol.
49 J3 Gnjilane Yugo.
21 A3 Goa India
21 A3 Goa *div.* India
58 B3 Goageb Namibia
8 H4 Goalen Head *hd* Austr.
23 G4 Goalpara India
40 C5 Goat Fell *h.* U.K.
56 E3 Goba Eth.
57 B6 Gobabis Namibia
58 C3 Gobas Namibia
91 E1 Gobernador Crespo Arg.
91 C3 Gobernador Duval Arg.
88 B7 Gobernador Gregores Arg.
11 M5 Gobi *des.* Mongolia
29 D8 Gobō Japan
42 E3 Goch Ger.
57 B6 Gochas Namibia
32 C3 Go Công Vietnam
39 G6 Godalming U.K.
21 C2 Godavari *r.* India
21 C2 Godavari, Mouths of the *river mouth* India
67 G4 Godbout Can.
74 C3 Goddard, Mt *mt* U.S.A.
56 E3 Godere Eth.
69 G4 Goderich Can.
22 C5 Godhra India
91 C2 Godoy Cruz Arg.
65 L3 Gods *r.* Can.
65 L4 Gods Lake *l.* Can.
65 M2 Gods Mercy, Bay of *b.* Can.
Godwin Austen *mt see* K2
42 B3 Goedereede Neth.
66 E4 Goéland, Lac au *l.* Can.
67 H2 Goélands, Lac aux *l.* Can.
42 B3 Goes Neth.
69 E2 Goetzville U.S.A.
75 E4 Goffs U.S.A.
69 G2 Gogama Can.
68 C2 Gogebic, Lake *l.* U.S.A.
68 C2 Gogebic Range *h.* U.S.A.
Gogra *r. see* Ghaghara
22 D4 Gohad India
87 M5 Goiana Brazil
90 C2 Goiandira Brazil
90 C2 Goiânia Brazil
90 B1 Goiás Brazil
90 B2 Goiás *div.* Brazil
90 B4 Goio-Erê Brazil
22 C3 Gojra Pak.
21 A2 Gokak India
51 C7 Gökçeada *i.* Turkey
16 B2 Gökçedağ Turkey
23 G3 Gokhar La *pass* China
16 E1 Gökirmak *r.* Turkey
19 F5 Gokprosh Hills *mts* Pak.
16 F2 Göksun Turkey
16 E3 Göksu Nehri *r.* Turkey
57 C5 Gokwe Zimbabwe
37 L6 Gol Norway
22 E3 Gola India
23 H4 Golaghat India
16 F3 Gölbaşı Turkey
12 K2 Gol'chikha Rus. Fed.
16 B1 Gölcük Turkey
47 L3 Gołdap Pol.
43 L1 Goldberg Ger.
7 F4 Gold Coast Austr.
54 B4 Gold Coast *coastal area* Ghana
64 F4 Golden Can.
9 D4 Golden Bay *b.* N.Z.
43 J3 Goldene Aue *reg.* Ger.
74 A3 Golden Gate National Recreation Area *res.* U.S.A.
64 D5 Golden Hinde *mt* Can.
43 G2 Goldenstedt Ger.
41 C5 Golden Vale *lowland* Rep. of Ireland
74 D3 Goldfield U.S.A.
74 D3 Gold Point U.S.A.
79 E5 Goldsboro U.S.A.
77 D6 Goldthwaite U.S.A.
17 J1 Göle Turkey
19 F3 Golestān Afgh.
18 D4 Golestānak Iran
74 C4 Goleta U.S.A.
77 D6 Goliad U.S.A.
30 A1 Golin Baixing China
16 F1 Gölköy Turkey
43 L2 Golm Ger.
17 K3 Golmānkhānen Iran
24 B3 Golmud China
23 H1 Golmud He *r.* China
31 B3 Golo *i.* Phil.
28 J3 Golovnino Rus. Fed.
18 C3 Golpāyegān Iran
16 C1 Gölpazarı Turkey
40 E3 Golspie U.K.
19 F3 Gol Vardeh Iran
49 L4 Golyama Syutkya *mt* Bulg.
49 L4 Golyam Persenk *mt* Bulg.
43 L2 Golzow Ger.
56 C4 Goma Congo(Zaire)
23 G3 Gomang Co *salt l.* China
22 E4 Gomati *r.* India
32 ▫ Gombak, Bukit *h.* Sing.
54 D3 Gombe Nigeria
56 D4 Gombe *r.* Tanz.
55 D3 Gombi Nigeria
54 A2 Gomera, La *i.* Canary Is
84 B1 Gómez Palacio Mex.
84 C1 Gómez, Presa M. R. *resr* Mex.
18 D2 Gomīshān Iran
43 K2 Gommern Ger.
23 F2 Gomo Co *salt l.* China
19 E2 Gonābād Iran
Gonabad *see* Jūymand
83 K5 Gonaïves Haiti
59 J1 Gonarezhou National Park Zimbabwe
83 K5 Gonâve, Île de la *i.* Haiti
18 D2 Gonbad-e Kavus Iran
23 E4 Gonda India
22 B5 Gondal India
56 D2 Gonder Eth.
22 E5 Gondia India
16 A1 Gönen Turkey
27 D4 Gong'an China
27 D5 Gongcheng China
27 A4 Gongga Shan *mt* China
26 A2 Gonghe China
26 E1 Gonghui China
90 E1 Gongogi *r.* Brazil
54 D3 Gongola *r.* Nigeria
27 B5 Gongwang Shan *mts* China
26 D3 Gong Xian *Henan* China
27 B4 Gong Xian *Sichuan* China
59 H6 Gonubie S. Africa
84 C2 Gonzáles Mex.
74 B3 Gonzales *CA* U.S.A.
77 D6 Gonzales *TX* U.S.A.
91 D2 González Moreno Arg.
80 E6 Goochland U.S.A.
92 C6 Goodenough, C. *c.* Ant.
6 F2 Goodenough I. *i.* P.N.G.
69 H3 Gooderham Can.
68 E3 Good Harbor Bay *b.* U.S.A.
58 C7 Good Hope, Cape of *c.* S. Africa
72 D3 Gooding U.S.A.
76 C4 Goodland U.S.A.
38 G4 Goole U.K.
8 E3 Goolgowi Austr.
8 G2 Goolma Austr.
8 G2 Gooloogong Austr.
8 B3 Goolwa Austr.
6 F4 Goondiwindi Austr.
67 H3 Goose *r.* Can.
72 B3 Goose L. *l.* U.S.A.
21 B3 Gooty India
46 D6 Göppingen Ger.
23 E4 Gorakhpur India
49 H3 Goražde Bos.-Herz.
50 G3 Gorchukha Rus. Fed.
79 E7 Gorda Cay *i.* Bahamas
16 B2 Gördes Turkey
47 P4 Gordeyevka Rus. Fed.
40 F5 Gordon U.K.
6 E6 Gordon, L. *l.* Austr.
64 G2 Gordon Lake *l.* Can.
80 D5 Gordon Lake *l.* U.S.A.
80 D5 Gordonsville U.S.A.
55 D4 Goré Chad
56 D3 Gorē Eth.
9 B7 Gore N.Z.
69 F3 Gore Bay Can.
40 E5 Gorebridge U.K.
41 E5 Gorey Rep. of Ireland
19 E4 Gorg Iran
18 D2 Gorgān Iran
89 A4 Gorgona, I. *i.* Col.
81 H2 Gorham U.S.A.
51 H7 Gori Georgia
42 C3 Gorinchem Neth.
17 L2 Goris Armenia
48 E2 Gorizia Italy
Gor'kiy *see* Nizhniy Novgorod
51 H5 Gor'ko-Solenoye, Ozero *l.* Rus. Fed.
50 G3 Gor'kovskoye Vdkhr. *resr* Rus. Fed.
47 K6 Gorlice Pol.
46 G5 Görlitz Ger.
22 D4 Gormi India
49 L3 Gorna Oryakhovitsa Bulg.
49 J2 Gornji Milanovac Yugo.
48 G3 Gornji Vakuf Bos.-Herz.
24 A1 Gorno-Altaysk Rus. Fed.
28 G1 Gornozavodsk Rus. Fed.
12 K4 Gornyak Rus. Fed.
28 C2 Gornye Klyuchi Rus. Fed.
28 C2 Gornyy *Primorskiy Kray* Rus. Fed.
51 J5 Gornyy *Saratov. Obl.* Rus. Fed.
51 H5 Gornyy Balykley Rus. Fed.
50 G3 Gorodets Rus. Fed.
51 H5 Gorodishche Rus. Fed.
51 G6 Gorodovikovsk Rus. Fed.
6 E2 Goroka P.N.G.
8 C4 Goroke Austr.
50 G3 Gorokhovets Rus. Fed.
54 B3 Gorom Gorom Burkina
57 D5 Gorongosa Moz.

25 E6 Gorontalo Indon.
51 F5 Gorshechnoye Rus. Fed.
41 C4 Gort Rep. of Ireland
41 C2 Gortahork Rep. of Ireland
90 D1 Gorutuba r. Brazil
51 F6 Goryachiy Klyuch Rus. Fed.
43 L2 Görzke Ger.
46 G4 Gorzów Wielkopolski Pol.
8 H2 Gosford Austr.
38 F2 Gosforth U.K.
68 E5 Goshen IN U.S.A.
81 F4 Goshen NY U.S.A.
28 G4 Goshogawara Japan
43 J3 Goslar Ger.
48 F2 Gospić Croatia
39 F7 Gosport U.K.
49 J4 Gostivar Macedonia
Göteborg see Gothenburg
37 N7 Götene Sweden
43 J4 Gotha Ger.
37 M8 Gothenburg Sweden
76 C3 Gothenburg U.S.A.
37 Q8 Gotland i. Sweden
49 K4 Gotse Delchev Bulg.
37 Q7 Gotska Sandön i. Sweden
29 C7 Gōtsu Japan
43 H3 Göttingen Ger.
64 E4 Gott Peak summit Can.
Gottwaldow see Zlín
30 A3 Goubangzi China
42 C2 Gouda Neth.
54 A3 Goudiri Senegal
54 D3 Goudoumaria Niger
68 E1 Goudreau Can.
96 J8 Gough Island i. Atl. Ocean
66 F4 Gouin, Réservoir resr Can.
68 E2 Goulais River Can.
8 G3 Goulburn Austr.
8 H2 Goulburn r. N.S.W. Austr.
8 E4 Goulburn r. Vic. Austr.
6 D3 Goulburn Is is Austr.
68 F2 Gould City U.S.A.
92 B4 Gould Coast coastal area Ant.
54 B3 Goundam Mali
45 G4 Gouraya Alg.
54 D3 Gouré Niger
58 D7 Gourits r. S. Africa
54 B3 Gourma-Rharous Mali
44 E2 Gournay-en-Bray France
8 G4 Gourock Range mts Austr.
42 A5 Goussainville France
81 F2 Gouverneur U.S.A.
65 H5 Govenlock Can.
90 E2 Governador Valadares Brazil
31 C5 Governor Generoso Phil.
79 E7 Governor's Harbour Bahamas
24 B2 Govĭ Altayn Nuruu mts Mongolia
23 E4 Govind Ballash Pant Sāgar resr India
22 D3 Govind Sagar resr India
19 G2 Govurdak Turkm.
80 D3 Gowanda U.S.A.
19 G4 Gowārān Afgh.
18 D4 Gowd-e Aḥmad Iran
18 E3 Gowd-e Hasht Tekkeh waterhole Iran
18 D4 Gowd-e Mokh l. Iran
39 C6 Gower pen. U.K.
69 G2 Gowganda Can.
19 E4 Gowk Iran
41 D4 Gowna, Lough l. Rep. of Ireland
88 E3 Goya Arg.
17 L1 Göyçay Azer.
17 H2 Göynük Turkey
28 G5 Goyō-zan mt Japan
17 M2 Göytäpä Azer.
19 F3 Gōzareh Afgh.
16 G2 Gözene Turkey
22 E2 Gozha Co salt l. China
48 F6 Gozo i. Malta
58 F6 Graaff-Reinet S. Africa
58 C6 Graafwater S. Africa
43 J4 Grabfeld plain Ger.
54 B4 Grabo Côte d'Ivoire
58 C7 Grabouw S. Africa
43 K1 Grabow Ger.
48 F2 Gračac Croatia
69 J2 Gracefield Can.
43 L3 Gräfenhainichen Ger.
43 K5 Grafenwöhr Ger.
7 F4 Grafton Austr.
76 D1 Grafton ND U.S.A.
68 D4 Grafton WV U.S.A.
80 C5 Grafton WV U.S.A.
75 E2 Grafton, Mt mt U.S.A.
77 D5 Graham U.S.A.
Graham Bell Island i. see Greem-Bell, Ostrov
63 J2 Graham I. i. Can.
64 C4 Graham Island i. Can.
81 J2 Graham Lake l. U.S.A.
92 B2 Graham Land reg. Ant.
75 H5 Graham, Mt mt U.S.A.
59 G6 Grahamstown S. Africa
41 E5 Graigue Rep. of Ireland
54 A4 Grain Coast coastal area Liberia
87 J5 Grajaú Brazil
40 B1 Gralisgeir i. U.K.
49 J4 Grámmos mt Greece
40 D4 Grampian Mountains U.K.
8 D4 Grampians mts Austr.
58 C5 Granaatboskolk S. Africa
89 B4 Granada Col.
83 G6 Granada Nic.
45 E4 Granada Spain
76 C4 Granada U.S.A.
41 D4 Granard Rep. of Ireland
91 C3 Gran Bajo Salitroso salt flat Arg.
66 F4 Granby Can.
54 A2 Gran Canaria i. Canary Is
88 D3 Gran Chaco reg. Arg./Para.
78 C3 Grand r. MI U.S.A.
76 E3 Grand r. MO U.S.A.
79 E7 Grand Bahama i. Bahamas
67 J4 Grand Bank Can.
96 F2 Grand Banks sea feature Atl. Ocean
54 B4 Grand-Bassam Côte d'Ivoire
67 G4 Grand Bay Can.
69 G4 Grand Bend Can.
41 D4 Grand Canal canal Rep. of Ireland
75 F3 Grand Canyon U.S.A.
75 F3 Grand Canyon gorge U.S.A.
75 F3 Grand Canyon Nat. Park U.S.A.
83 H5 Grand Cayman i. Cayman Is
65 G4 Grand Centre Can.
72 C2 Grand Coulee U.S.A.
91 C3 Grande r. Arg.
87 J6 Grande r. Bahia Brazil
90 B2 Grande r. São Paulo Brazil
88 C8 Grande, Bahía b. Arg.
64 F4 Grande Cache Can.
44 H4 Grande Casse, Pointe de la mt France
57 E5 Grande Comore i. Comoros
91 F1 Grande, Cuchilla h. Uru.
90 D3 Grande, Ilha i. Brazil
64 F3 Grande Prairie Can.
55 D3 Grand Erg de Bilma sand dunes Niger
54 B1 Grand Erg Occidental des. Alg.
54 C2 Grand Erg Oriental des. Alg.
67 H4 Grande-Rivière Can.
66 F3 Grande Rivière de la Baleine r. Can.
72 C2 Grande Ronde r. U.S.A.
89 E4 Grande, Serra mt Brazil
67 G4 Grand Falls N.B. Can.
67 J4 Grand Falls Nfld Can.
64 F5 Grand Forks Can.
76 D2 Grand Forks U.S.A.
81 F3 Grand Gorge U.S.A.
81 K2 Grand Harbour Can.
68 D4 Grand Haven U.S.A.
64 F2 Grandin, Lac l. Can.
76 D3 Grand Island U.S.A.
68 D2 Grand Island i. U.S.A.
77 F6 Grand Isle LA U.S.A.
81 J1 Grand Isle ME U.S.A.
75 H2 Grand Junction U.S.A.
54 B4 Grand-Lahou Côte d'Ivoire
67 G4 Grand Lake l. N.B. Can.
67 J4 Grand Lake l. Nfld Can.
67 H3 Grand Lake l. Nfld Can.
77 E6 Grand Lake l. LA U.S.A.
81 K2 Grand Lake l. ME U.S.A.
69 F3 Grand Lake l. MI U.S.A.
81 J1 Grand Lake Matagamon l. U.S.A.
80 A4 Grand Lake St Marys l. U.S.A.
81 J1 Grand Lake Seboeis l. U.S.A.
81 K2 Grand Lake Stream U.S.A.
68 E4 Grand Ledge U.S.A.
67 G5 Grand Manan I. i. Can.
68 E2 Grand Marais MI U.S.A.
68 B2 Grand Marais MN U.S.A.
67 F4 Grand-Mère Can.
45 B3 Grândola Port.
7 G3 Grand Passage chan. New Caledonia
68 C2 Grand Portage U.S.A.
65 K4 Grand Rapids Can.
68 E4 Grand Rapids MI U.S.A.
76 E2 Grand Rapids MN U.S.A.
7 G3 Grand Récif de Cook rf New Caledonia
7 G4 Grand Récif du Sud rf New Caledonia
72 E3 Grand Teton mt U.S.A.
72 E3 Grand Teton Nat. Park U.S.A.
68 E3 Grand Traverse Bay b. U.S.A.
67 G4 Grand Vallée Can.
72 C2 Grandview U.S.A.
75 F3 Grand Wash r. U.S.A.
75 E4 Grand Wash Cliffs cliff U.S.A.
91 B2 Graneros Chile
41 D6 Grange Rep. of Ireland
72 E3 Granger U.S.A.
37 O6 Grängesberg Sweden
72 C2 Grangeville U.S.A.
64 D3 Granisle Can.
76 E2 Granite Falls U.S.A.
67 J4 Granite Lake l. Can.
75 E4 Granite Mts mts U.S.A.
72 E2 Granite Peak summit MT U.S.A.
75 F1 Granite Peak summit UT U.S.A.
48 E6 Granitola, Capo c. Sicily Italy
88 C6 Gran Laguna Salada l. Arg.
37 O7 Gränna Sweden
48 B2 Gran Paradiso mt Italy
46 E7 Gran Pilastro mt Austria/Italy
43 L3 Granschütz Ger.
43 M1 Gransee Ger.
39 G5 Grantham U.K.
92 A4 Grant I. i. Ant.
74 D2 Grant, Mt mt NV U.S.A.
74 C2 Grant, Mt mt NV U.S.A.
40 E3 Grantown-on-Spey U.K.
75 E2 Grant Range mts U.S.A.
73 F5 Grants U.S.A.
72 B3 Grants Pass U.S.A.
44 D2 Granville France
68 C5 Granville IL U.S.A.
81 G3 Granville NY U.S.A.
65 J3 Granville Lake l. Can.
90 D2 Grão Mogol Brazil
74 C4 Grapevine U.S.A.
74 D3 Grapevine Mts mts U.S.A.
81 G3 Graphite U.S.A.
59 J2 Graskop S. Africa
65 G2 Gras, Lac de l. Can.
81 F2 Grass r. U.S.A.
44 H5 Grasse France
38 F3 Grassington U.K.
65 H5 Grasslands Nat. Park Can.
72 E2 Grassrange U.S.A.
65 J4 Grass River Prov. Park res. Can.
74 B2 Grass Valley U.S.A.
79 E7 Grassy Cr. r. Bahamas
37 N7 Grästorp Sweden
68 B4 Gratiot U.S.A.
45 G1 Graus Spain
65 J2 Gravel Hill Lake l. Can.
42 A4 Gravelines France
59 J1 Gravelotte S. Africa
69 H3 Gravenhurst Can.
39 H6 Gravesend U.K.
48 G4 Gravina in Puglia Italy
68 E3 Grawn U.S.A.
44 G3 Gray France
81 H3 Gray U.S.A.
68 E3 Grayling U.S.A.
39 H6 Grays U.K.
72 A2 Grays Harbor in. U.S.A.
72 E3 Grays L. l. U.S.A.
80 B5 Grayson U.S.A.
67 H1 Gray Strait chan. Can.
78 B4 Grayville U.S.A.
46 G7 Graz Austria
79 E7 Great Abaco i. Bahamas
6 C5 Great Australian Bight g. Austr.
39 H6 Great Baddow U.K.
83 J3 Great Bahama Bank sea feature Bahamas
9 E2 Great Barrier Island i. N.Z.
6 E3 Great Barrier Reef rf Austr.
81 G3 Great Barrington U.S.A.
73 C4 Great Basin basin U.S.A.
75 E2 Great Basin Nat. Park U.S.A.
81 F5 Great Bay b. U.S.A.
64 E1 Great Bear r. Can.
64 E1 Great Bear Lake l. Can.
76 D4 Great Bend U.S.A.
58 C6 Great Berg r. S. Africa
40 B2 Great Bernera i. U.K.
41 A5 Great Blasket I. i. Rep. of Ireland
38 D3 Great Clifton U.K.
40 D5 Great Cumbrae i. U.K.
8 F4 Great Dividing Range mts Austr.
38 G3 Great Driffield U.K.
69 F3 Great Duck I. i. Can.
81 F5 Great Egg Harbor in. U.S.A.
83 H4 Greater Antilles is Caribbean Sea
83 J4 Great Exuma i. Bahamas
72 E2 Great Falls U.S.A.
59 G6 Great Fish r. S. Africa
59 G6 Great Fish Point pt S. Africa
23 F4 Great Gandak r. India
79 E7 Great Guana Cay i. Bahamas
79 E7 Great Harbour Cay i. Bahamas
83 K4 Great Inagua i. Bahamas
58 D5 Great Karoo plat. S. Africa
59 H6 Great Kei r. S. Africa
6 E6 Great Lake l. Austr.
39 E5 Great Malvern U.K.
80 A5 Great Miami r. U.S.A.
55 F2 Great Oasis, The oasis Egypt
39 D4 Great Ormes Head hd U.K.
39 H5 Great Ouse r. U.K.
81 G4 Great Peconic Bay b. U.S.A.
81 H4 Great Pt pt U.S.A.
39 D5 Great Rhos h. U.K.
56 D4 Great Ruaha r. Tanz.
81 F3 Great Sacandaga L. l. U.S.A.
48 B2 Great St Bernard Pass Italy/Switz.
79 E7 Great Sale Cay i. Bahamas
72 D3 Great Salt Lake l. U.S.A.
72 D3 Great Salt Lake Desert U.S.A.
55 E2 Great Sand Sea des. Egypt/Libya
6 C4 Great Sandy Desert Austr.
7 H3 Great Sea Reef rf Fiji
62 G3 Great Slave Lake N.W.T. Can.
64 G2 Great Slave Lake l. Can.
79 D5 Great Smoky Mts mts U.S.A.
79 D5 Great Smoky Mts Nat. Park U.S.A.
64 E3 Great Snow Mtn mt Can.
81 G4 Great South Bay b. U.S.A.
39 H7 Greatstone-on-Sea U.K.
39 J6 Great Stour r. U.K.
39 C7 Great Torrington U.K.
6 C4 Great Victoria Desert Austr.
26 F1 Great Wall China
39 H6 Great Waltham U.K.
81 G4 Great Wass I. i. U.S.A.
38 F3 Great Whernside h. U.K.
39 J5 Great Yarmouth U.K.
17 J3 Great Zab r. Iraq
48 E4 Greco, Monte mt Italy
45 D2 Gredos, Sa de mts Spain
35 H5 Greece country Europe
72 F3 Greeley U.S.A.
63 K1 Greely Fiord in. Can.
12 H1 Greem-Bell, Ostrov i. Rus. Fed.
78 C4 Green r. KY U.S.A.
75 H2 Green r. UT/WY U.S.A.
69 H3 Greenbank Can.
68 C3 Green Bay U.S.A.
68 D3 Green Bay b. U.S.A.
8 H4 Green C. hd Austr.
41 E3 Greencastle U.K.
78 C4 Greencastle U.S.A.
79 E7 Green Cay i. Bahamas
79 D6 Green Cove Springs U.S.A.
68 A4 Greene IA U.S.A.
81 F3 Greene NY U.S.A.
79 D4 Greeneville U.S.A.
74 B3 Greenfield CA U.S.A.
68 E6 Greenfield IN U.S.A.
81 G3 Greenfield MA U.S.A.
80 B5 Greenfield OH U.S.A.
68 C4 Greenfield WI U.S.A.
31 A4 Green Island Bay b. Phil.
65 H4 Green Lake Can.
68 C4 Green Lake l. U.S.A.
60 N2 Greenland terr. Arctic Ocean
96 J1 Greenland Basin sea feature Arctic Ocean
34 E1 Greenland Sea sea Arctic Ocean
40 F5 Greenlaw U.K.
81 G2 Green Mountains U.S.A.
40 D5 Greenock U.K.
41 E3 Greenore Rep. of Ireland
81 G4 Greenport U.S.A.
73 E4 Green River UT U.S.A.
72 E3 Green River WY U.S.A.
79 E4 Greensboro U.S.A.
78 C4 Greensburg IN U.S.A.
77 D4 Greensburg KS U.S.A.
80 D4 Greensburg PA U.S.A.
40 C3 Greenstone Point pt U.K.
71 L5 Green Swamp swamp NC U.S.A.
80 B5 Greenup U.S.A.
81 F2 Green Valley Can.
75 G6 Green Valley U.S.A.
58 C6 Greenview U.S.A.
54 B4 Greenville Liberia
79 C6 Greenville AL U.S.A.
74 B1 Greenville CA U.S.A.
79 D6 Greenville FL U.S.A.
81 J2 Greenville ME U.S.A.
68 E4 Greenville MI U.S.A.
77 F5 Greenville MS U.S.A.
79 E5 Greenville NC U.S.A.
81 H3 Greenville NH U.S.A.
80 A4 Greenville OH U.S.A.
80 C4 Greenville PA U.S.A.
79 D5 Greenville SC U.S.A.
77 D5 Greenville TX U.S.A.
65 J4 Greenwater Provincial Park res. Can.
8 H3 Greenwell Point Austr.
81 G4 Greenwich CT U.S.A.
81 G3 Greenwich NY U.S.A.
75 G2 Greenwich UT U.S.A.
77 F5 Greenwood MS U.S.A.
79 D5 Greenwood SC U.S.A.
77 E5 Greers Ferry Lake l. U.S.A.
76 D3 Gregory U.S.A.
6 C4 Gregory Lake salt flat Austr.
6 E3 Gregory Range h. Austr.
46 F3 Greifswald Ger.
43 L4 Greiz Ger.
16 E4 Greko, Cape c. Cyprus
37 M8 Grenå Denmark
77 F5 Grenada U.S.A.
61 M8 Grenada country Caribbean Sea
44 E5 Grenade France
37 M8 Grenen spit Denmark
8 G2 Grenfell Austr.
65 J4 Grenfell Can.
44 G4 Grenoble France
89 E1 Grenville Grenada
6 E3 Grenville, C. hd Austr.
72 B2 Gresham U.S.A.
38 F3 Greta r. U.K.
40 E6 Gretna U.K.
77 F6 Gretna U.S.A.
43 J3 Greußen Ger.
42 B3 Grevelingen chan. Neth.
42 F2 Greven Ger.
49 J4 Grevena Greece
42 D3 Grevenbicht Neth.
42 E3 Grevenbroich Ger.
42 E5 Grevenmacher Lux.
46 E4 Grevesmühlen Ger.
9 C5 Grey r. N.Z.
72 E2 Greybull U.S.A.
64 B2 Grey Hunter Pk summit Can.
67 J3 Grey Is is Can.
9 C5 Greymouth N.Z.
6 E4 Grey Range h. Austr.
59 J4 Greytown S. Africa
42 C4 Grez-Doiceau Belgium
51 G5 Gribanovskiy Rus. Fed.
74 B2 Gridley CA U.S.A.
68 C5 Gridley IL U.S.A.
79 C5 Griffin U.S.A.
8 F3 Griffith Austr.
69 J3 Griffith Can.
62 F2 Griffiths Point pt Can.
43 L3 Grimma Ger.
46 F3 Grimmen Ger.
69 H4 Grimsby Can.
38 G4 Grimsby U.K.
36 E3 Grímsey i. Iceland
64 F3 Grimshaw Can.
36 E4 Grímsstaðir Iceland
37 L7 Grimstad Norway
36 B5 Grindavík Iceland
37 L9 Grindsted Denmark
49 N2 Grindul Chituc spit Romania
76 E3 Grinnell U.S.A.
59 H5 Griqualand East reg. S. Africa
58 E4 Griqualand West reg. S. Africa
58 E4 Griquatown S. Africa
63 K2 Grise Fiord Can.
33 B3 Grisik Indon.
39 J7 Gris Nez, Cap pt France
40 F2 Gritley U.K.
48 G2 Grmeč mts Bos.-Herz.
42 C3 Grobbendonk Belgium
59 H2 Groblersdal S. Africa
58 E4 Grobleshoop S. Africa
28 B2 Grodekovo Rus. Fed.
Grodno see Hrodna
58 B5 Groen watercourse Northern Cape S. Africa
58 E5 Groen watercourse Northern Cape S. Africa
44 C3 Groix, Île de i. France
48 D6 Grombalia Tunisia
42 F2 Gronau (Westfalen) Ger.
36 N4 Grong Norway
42 E1 Groningen Neth.
42 E1 Groninger Wad tidal flats Neth.
75 E3 Groom L. l. U.S.A.
58 D3 Groot-Aar Pan salt pan S. Africa
58 E7 Groot Brakrivier S. Africa
59 H3 Grootdraaidam dam S. Africa
58 D4 Grootdrink S. Africa
6 D3 Groote Eylandt i. Austr.
57 B5 Grootfontein Namibia
58 C3 Groot Karas Berg plat. Namibia
59 J1 Groot Letaba r. S. Africa
59 G2 Groot Marico S. Africa
58 D6 Groot Swartberg mts S. Africa
58 D5 Grootvloer salt pan S. Africa
59 G6 Groot Winterberg mt S. Africa
68 E3 Gros Cap U.S.A.
67 J4 Gros Morne Nat. Pk Can.
43 J3 Großengottern Ger.
43 G2 Großenkneten Ger.
43 H4 Großenlüder Ger.
43 J4 Großer Beerberg h. Ger.
43 J4 Großer Gleichberg h. Ger.
46 G7 Grosser Speikkogel mt Austria
48 D3 Grosseto Italy
43 G5 Groß-Gerau Ger.
48 E1 Großglockner mt Austria
43 J2 Groß Oesingen Ger.
43 K3 Großrudestedt Ger.
43 M2 Groß Schönebeck Ger.
58 C1 Gross Ums Namibia
72 E3 Gros Ventre Range mts U.S.A.
67 J3 Groswater Bay b. Can.
81 E3 Groton U.S.A.
80 D5 Grottoes U.S.A.
64 F3 Grouard Can.
66 D4 Groundhog r. Can.
42 D1 Grouw Neth.
80 C4 Grove City U.S.A.
79 C6 Grove Hill U.S.A.
74 B3 Groveland U.S.A.
92 D5 Grove Mts mts Ant.
74 B4 Grover Beach U.S.A.
81 H2 Groveton U.S.A.
75 F5 Growler U.S.A.
75 F5 Growler Mts mts U.S.A.
51 H7 Groznyy Rus. Fed.
49 M3 Grudovo Bulg.
47 J4 Grudziądz Pol.
40 C3 Gruinard Bay b. U.K.
57 B6 Grünau Namibia
36 B4 Grundarfjörður Iceland
80 B6 Grundy U.S.A.
43 G5 Grünstadt Ger.
51 F4 Gryazi Rus. Fed.
50 G3 Gryazovets Rus. Fed.
46 G4 Gryfice Pol.
46 G4 Gryfino Pol.
46 G5 Gryfów Śląski Pol.
36 P2 Gryllefjord Norway
88 □ Grytviken Atl. Ocean
23 F5 Gua India
83 J4 Guacanayabo, Golfo de b. Cuba
89 D2 Guacara Venez.
89 C3 Guacharía r. Col.
45 D4 Guadajoz r. Spain
84 B2 Guadalajara Mex.
45 E2 Guadalajara Spain
45 F2 Guadalaviar r. Spain
7 G2 Guadalcanal i. Solomon Is
45 C4 Guadalete r. Spain
45 F2 Guadalope r. Spain
45 D4 Guadalquivir r. Spain
84 B1 Guadalupe Nuevo León Mex.
84 B2 Guadalupe Zacatecas Mex.
74 B4 Guadalupe U.S.A.
70 C6 Guadalupe i. Mex.
77 D6 Guadalupe r. U.S.A.
84 A1 Guadalupe Aguilera Mex.
77 B6 Guadalupe Mts Nat. Park U.S.A.
77 B6 Guadalupe Pk mt U.S.A.
45 D3 Guadalupe, Sierra de mts Spain
84 A1 Guadalupe Victoria Mex.
84 A1 Guadalupe y Calvo Mex.
45 D2 Guadarrama, Sierra de mts Spain
61 M8 Guadeloupe terr. Caribbean Sea
91 C2 Guadel, Sa de mts Arg.
45 C4 Guadiana r. Port./Spain
45 E4 Guadix Spain
88 B6 Guafo, I. i. Chile
89 D4 Guainía r. Col./Venez.
89 E3 Guaiquinima, Cerro mt Venez.
90 A4 Guaíra Brazil
88 B6 Guaitecas, Islas is Chile
89 C1 Guajira, Península de pen. Col.
86 C4 Gualaceo Ecuador
74 A2 Gualala U.S.A.
91 E2 Gualeguay Arg.
91 E2 Gualeguay r. Arg.
91 E2 Gualeguaychu Arg.
91 B4 Gualjaina Arg.
4 F3 Guam terr. Pac. Oc.
88 A6 Guamblin, I. i. Chile
91 D3 Guaminí Arg.
84 A1 Guamúchil Mex.
89 A4 Guamués r. Col.
32 B4 Gua Musang Malaysia
84 A1 Guanacevi Mex.
91 D3 Guanaco, Co h. Arg.
84 B2 Guanajuato Mex.
84 B2 Guanajuato div. Mex.
90 D1 Guanambi Brazil
89 D4 Guaname r. Venez.
89 C2 Guanare Venez.
89 C2 Guanare r. Venez.
89 C2 Guanarito Venez.
89 C2 Guanarito r. Venez.
89 D3 Guanay, Sierra mts Venez.
26 D2 Guandi Shan mt China
83 H4 Guane Cuba
27 C4 Guang'an China
27 D6 Guangdong div. China
27 F4 Guangfeng China
27 D6 Guanghai China
26 B4 Guanghan China
27 E5 Guanghang China
26 B3 Guanghe China
27 E4 Guangji China
26 E2 Guangling China
30 B4 Guanglu Dao i. China
27 B5 Guangnan China
27 D6 Guangning China
26 F2 Guangrao China
26 E4 Guangshan China
26 D4 Guangshui China
27 C6 Guangxi div. China
26 B3 Guangyuan China
27 E5 Guangze China
27 D6 Guangzhou China
90 D2 Guanhães Brazil
90 D2 Guanhães r. Brazil
89 E2 Guanipa r. Venez.
27 B5 Guanling China
26 C4 Guanmian Shan mts China
26 D3 Guanpo China
30 C3 Guanshui China
89 D2 Guanta Venez.
83 J4 Guantánamo Cuba
26 E1 Guanting Sk. resr China
26 B4 Guan Xian China
27 D5 Guanyang China
26 F3 Guanyun China
89 A4 Guapí Col.
86 F6 Guaporé r. Bol./Brazil
86 E7 Guaqui Bol.
90 D1 Guará r. Brazil
87 L5 Guarabira Brazil
90 E3 Guarapari Brazil
90 B4 Guarapuava Brazil
90 C4 Guaraqueçaba Brazil
90 D3 Guaratinguetá Brazil
90 C4 Guaratuba, Baía de b. Brazil
45 C2 Guarda Port.
90 C2 Guarda Mor Brazil
45 D1 Guardo Spain
89 D2 Guárico r. Venez.
89 C3 Guarrojo r. Col.
90 C4 Guarujá Brazil
89 D4 Guasacavi r. Col.
89 C4 Guasacavi, Cerro h. Col.
89 B2 Guasare r. Venez.
82 C3 Guasave Mex.
89 C3 Guasdualito Venez.
84 C2 Guasima Mex.
89 E3 Guasipati Venez.
90 B4 Guassú r. Brazil
82 F6 Guatemala Guatemala
61 J8 Guatemala country Central America
89 D2 Guatope, Parque Nacional nat. park Venez.
91 D3 Guatrache Arg.
89 C4 Guaviare r. Col.
90 C3 Guaxupé Brazil
89 B4 Guayabero r. Col.
89 D3 Guayapo r. Venez.
86 C4 Guayaquil Ecuador
86 B4 Guayaquil, Golfo de g. Ecuador
86 E6 Guayaramerín Bol.
82 B3 Guaymas Mex.
56 D2 Guba Eth.
21 B3 Gubbi India
48 E3 Gubbio Italy
51 F5 Gubkin Rus. Fed.
26 D3 Gucheng China
51 G7 Gudaut'a Georgia
37 M6 Gudbrandsdalen v. Norway
51 H7 Gudermes Rus. Fed.
21 C2 Gudivada India
21 B3 Gudiyattam India
30 E2 Gudong r. China
19 G5 Gudri r. Pak.
16 D1 Güdül Turkey
21 B3 Gudur Andhra Pradesh India
37 K6 Gudvangen Norway
54 A4 Guéckédou Guinea
69 J1 Guéguen, Lac l. Can.
89 B4 Güejar r. Col.
54 C1 Guelma Alg.
54 A2 Guelmine Morocco
69 G4 Guelph Can.
84 C2 Guémez Mex.
42 E5 Guénange France
89 D2 Güera r. Venez.
67 G2 Guérard, Lac l. Can.
44 E3 Guéret France
72 F3 Guernsey U.S.A.
44 C2 Guernsey i. Channel Is U.K.
84 B3 Guerrero div. Mex.
82 B3 Guerrero Negro Mex.
63 M4 Guers, Lac l. Can.
18 D3 Gūgerd, Kūh-e mts Iran
96 F5 Guiana Basin sea feature Atl. Ocean
8 B4 Guichen B. b. Austr.
27 E4 Guichi China
91 F2 Guichón Uru.
26 A3 Guide China
55 D4 Guider Cameroon
27 C5 Guiding China
48 E4 Guidonia-Montecelio Italy
54 B4 Guiglo Côte d'Ivoire
42 B5 Guignicourt France
59 K2 Guija Moz.
27 D6 Gui Jiang r. China
27 F4 Guiji Shan mts China
39 G6 Guildford U.K.
81 J2 Guilford U.S.A.
27 D5 Guilin China
66 E2 Guillaume-Delisle, Lac l. Can.
45 B2 Guimarães Port.
31 B4 Guimaras Str. chan. Phil.
26 E3 Guimeng Ding mt China
26 A3 Guinan China
74 A2 Guinda U.S.A.
31 C4 Guindulman Phil.
52 C4 Guinea country Africa
96 J5 Guinea Basin sea feature Atl. Ocean
52 C4 Guinea-Bissau country Africa
53 D5 Guinea, Gulf of g. Africa
83 H4 Güines Cuba
44 C2 Guingamp France
44 B2 Guipavas France
27 D6 Guiping China
90 B2 Guiratinga Brazil
89 E2 Güiria Venez.
42 B5 Guiscard France
42 B5 Guise France
31 C4 Guiuan Phil.
27 E4 Guixi China
27 C6 Gui Xian China
27 C5 Guiyang Guizhou China
27 D5 Guiyang Hunan China
27 C5 Guizhou div. China
22 B5 Gujarat div. India
22 C2 Gujar Khan Pak.
22 C2 Gujranwala Pak.
22 C2 Gujrat Pak.
75 G5 Gu Komelik U.S.A.
51 F5 Gukovo Rus. Fed.
17 K3 Gūk Tappeh Iran
22 D2 Gulabgarh Jammu and Kashmir
26 B2 Gulang China
8 G1 Gulargambone Austr.
21 B2 Gulbarga India
37 U8 Gulbene Latvia
16 E3 Gülek Turkey
77 F6 Gulfport U.S.A.
18 C4 Gulf, The g. Asia
8 G2 Gulgong Austr.
24 E1 Gulian China
27 B5 Gulin China
19 G4 Gulistan Pak.
14 E2 Gulistan Uzbek.
43 K1 Gülitz Ger.
68 E3 Gull I. i. U.S.A.
65 H4 Gull Lake Can.
36 R3 Gullträsk Sweden
16 D3 Gülnar Turkey
19 F3 Gulran Afgh.
51 G7 Gulrip'shi Georgia
16 E2 Gülşehir Turkey
56 D3 Gulu Uganda
22 B3 Gumal r. Pak.
57 C5 Gumare Botswana
18 D2 Gumdag Turkm.
23 F5 Gumia India
23 F5 Gumla India
42 F3 Gummersbach Ger.
16 E1 Gümüşhacıköy Turkey
17 G1 Gümüşhane Turkey
22 D4 Guna India
8 E3 Gunbar Austr.
8 G3 Gundagai Austr.
43 H5 Gundelsheim Ger.
16 D3 Gündoğmuş Turkey
16 B2 Güney Turkey
56 B4 Gungu Congo(Zaire)
51 H7 Gunib Rus. Fed.
65 K4 Gunisao r. Can.
8 H1 Gunnedah Austr.
92 D3 Gunnerus Ridge sea feature Ant.
8 G3 Gunning Austr.
73 F4 Gunnison CO U.S.A.
75 G2 Gunnison UT U.S.A.
73 E4 Gunnison r. U.S.A.
21 B3 Guntakal India
43 J3 Güntersberge Ger.
79 C5 Guntersville U.S.A.
79 C5 Guntersville L. l. U.S.A.
21 C2 Guntur India
33 A2 Gunungsitoli Indon.
32 A5 Gunungtua Indon.
21 C2 Gunupur India
46 E6 Günzburg Ger.
43 J5 Gunzenhausen Ger.
26 E1 Guojiatun China
26 E3 Guoyang China
26 A2 Gurban Hudag China
26 D1 Gurban Obo China
19 F5 Gurdim Iran
16 B2 Güre Turkey
22 D3 Gurgaon India
87 K5 Gurgueia r. Brazil
22 B4 Gurha India
89 E3 Guri, Embalse de resr Venez.
90 C2 Gurinhatã Brazil
51 H7 Gurjaani Georgia
19 E4 Gur Khar Iran
17 J2 Gürpınar Turkey
23 G3 Guru China
57 D5 Guruè Moz.
16 F2 Gürün Turkey
87 J4 Gurupi r. Brazil
22 C4 Guru Sikhar mt India
50 B4 Gur'yevsk Rus. Fed.
54 C3 Gusau Nigeria
43 K2 Güsen Ger.
50 B4 Gusev Rus. Fed.
30 B4 Gushan China
75 H1 Gusher U.S.A.
19 F3 Gushgy Turkm.
26 E3 Gushi China
31 A5 Gusi Malaysia
13 M2 Gusikha Rus. Fed.
50 D4 Gusino Rus. Fed.
13 M4 Gusinoozersk Rus. Fed.
23 F5 Guskara India
50 G4 Gus'-Khrustal'nyy Rus. Fed.
48 C5 Guspini Sardinia Italy
64 B3 Gustavus U.S.A.
43 K3 Güsten Ger.
74 B3 Gustine U.S.A.
43 L1 Güstrow Ger.
23 H3 Gutang China
43 M2 Güterfelde Ger.
43 G3 Gütersloh Ger.
75 H5 Guthrie AZ U.S.A.
78 C4 Guthrie KY U.S.A.
77 D5 Guthrie OK U.S.A.
77 C5 Guthrie TX U.S.A.
27 E5 Gutian Fujian China
27 F5 Gutian Fujian China
42 E5 Gutland reg. Ger./Lux.
23 F3 Gutsuo China
68 B4 Guttenberg U.S.A.
57 D5 Gutu Zimbabwe
23 G4 Guwahati India
17 J3 Guwēr Iraq
43 H3 Guxhagen Ger.
85 E2 Guyana country S. America
26 D1 Guyang China
77 C4 Guymon U.S.A.
18 D4 Gūyom Iran
8 H1 Guyra Austr.
26 E1 Guyuan Hebei China
26 C3 Guyuan Ningxia China
19 G2 Guzar Uzbek.
27 C4 Guzhang China
26 E3 Guzhen China
47 K3 Gvardeysk Rus. Fed.
8 G1 Gwabegar Austr.
19 F5 Gwadar Pak.
19 F5 Gwadar West Bay b. Pak.
22 D4 Gwalior India
57 C6 Gwanda Zimbabwe
19 G4 Gwash Pak.
19 F5 Gwatar Bay b. Pak.
41 C3 Gweebarra Bay b. Rep. of Ireland
41 C2 Gweedore Rep. of Ireland
57 C5 Gweru Zimbabwe
68 D2 Gwinn U.S.A.
55 D3 Gwoza Nigeria
8 H1 Gwydir r. Austr.
23 H3 Gyaca China
26 B3 Gyagartang China
23 F3 Gyangrang China
23 G3 Gyangzê China
23 G3 Gyaring Co l. China
24 B3 Gyaring Hu l. China
49 L6 Gyaros i. Greece
23 H3 Gyarubtang China
12 J2 Gydanskiy Poluostrov pen. Rus. Fed.
23 H3 Gyimda China
23 F3 Gyirong Xizang China
23 F3 Gyirong Xizang China
23 H2 Gyiza China
63 O3 Gyldenløves Fjord in. Greenland
7 F4 Gympie Austr.
47 J7 Gyöngyös Hungary
46 H7 Győr Hungary
65 K4 Gypsumville Can.
67 G2 Gyrfalcon Is i. Can.
49 K6 Gytheio Greece
47 K7 Gyula Hungary
17 J1 Gyumri Armenia
18 E2 Gyzylarbat Turkm.

H

36 T5 Haapajärvi Fin.
36 T4 Haapavesi Fin.
37 S7 Haapsalu Estonia
42 C2 Haarlem Neth.
58 E6 Haarlem S. Africa
43 G3 Haarstrang ridge Ger.
9 B5 Haast N.Z.
19 G5 Hab r. Pak.
Habana see Havana
21 C4 Habarane Sri Lanka
56 D3 Habaswein Kenya
64 F3 Habay Can.
20 C7 Habbān Yemen
17 J5 Habbānīyah Iraq
17 J5 Ḥabbānīyah, Hawr al l. Iraq
19 G5 Hab Chauki Pak.
23 G4 Habiganj Bangl.
26 E1 Habirag China
23 G5 Habra India
89 B5 Hacha Col.
91 B3 Hachado, P. de pass Arg./Chile
29 F8 Hachijō-jima i. Japan
28 G4 Hachinohe Japan
29 F7 Hachiōji Japan
16 E2 Hacıbektaş Turkey
17 H2 Hacıömer Turkey
57 D6 Hacufera Moz.
18 C6 Hadabat al Budū plain S. Arabia
21 A3 Hadagalli India
40 F5 Haddington U.K.
54 D3 Hadejia Nigeria
16 E5 Hadera Israel
37 L9 Haderslev Denmark
20 C6 Ḥadhramaut reg. Yemen
16 D3 Hadım Turkey
39 H5 Hadleigh U.K.
62 H2 Hadley Bay b. Can.
30 D6 Hadong S. Korea
16 F6 Ḥadraj, Wādī watercourse S. Arabia
37 M8 Hadsund Denmark
51 E5 Hadyach Ukr.
91 F1 Haedo, Cuchilla de h. Uru.
30 C4 Haeju N. Korea
30 C5 Haeju-man b. N. Korea
30 D6 Haenam S. Korea
59 H1 Haenertsburg S. Africa
18 B4 Hafar al Bāṭin S. Arabia
65 H4 Hafford Can.
16 F2 Hafik Turkey
22 C2 Hafizabad Pak.
23 H4 Hāflong India
36 C4 Hafnarfjörður Iceland
18 C4 Haft Gel Iran
36 B4 Hafursfjörður b. Iceland
69 G2 Hagar Can.
21 B3 Hagari r. India
56 D2 Hagar Nish Plateau plat. Eritrea
42 C4 Hageland reg. Belgium
42 F3 Hagen Ger.
6 E2 Hagen, Mount mt P.N.G.
43 K1 Hagenow Ger.
80 E5 Hagerstown U.S.A.
44 D5 Hagetmau France

37 N6 Hagfors Sweden
29 B7 Hagi Japan
27 B6 Ha Giang Vietnam
39 E5 Hagley U.K.
41 B5 Hag's Head hd Rep. of Ireland
65 H4 Hague Can.
44 D2 Hague, Cap de la pt France
44 H2 Haguenau France
24 G4 Hahajima-rettō is Japan
56 D4 Hai Tanz.
26 E2 Hai r. China
26 F3 Hai'an China
58 B4 Haib watercourse Namibia
30 B3 Haicheng China
43 K5 Haidenaab r. Ger.
27 C6 Hai Dương Vietnam
16 E5 Haifa Israel
16 E5 Haifa, Bay of b. Israel
27 E6 Haifeng China
43 G4 Haiger Ger.
27 D6 Haikang China
27 D6 Haikou China
20 B4 Hā'il S. Arabia
24 D2 Hailar China
69 H2 Haileybury Can.
30 E1 Hailin China
30 C2 Hailong China
39 H7 Hailsham U.K.
36 T4 Hailuoto Fin.
26 F4 Haimen China
27 C7 Hainan div. China
27 D7 Hainan i. China
64 B3 Haines U.S.A.
64 B2 Haines Junction Can.
43 J3 Hainich ridge Ger.
43 M4 Hainichen Ger.
43 J3 Hainleite ridge Ger.
27 C6 Hai Phong Vietnam
26 A2 Hairag China
26 B1 Hairhan Namag China
27 F5 Haitan Dao i. China
61 L8 Haiti country Caribbean Sea
27 C7 Haitou China
75 G5 Haivana Nakya U.S.A.
74 D3 Haiwee Reservoir U.S.A.
26 E2 Haixing China
55 F3 Haiya Sudan
26 A2 Haiyan Qinghai China
27 F4 Haiyan Zhejiang China
30 A5 Haiyang China
30 B4 Haiyang Dao i. China
26 B2 Haiyuan China
26 F3 Haizhou Wan b. China
47 K7 Hajdúböszörmény Hungary
48 C7 Hajeb El Ayoun Tunisia
20 D7 Ḥajhir mt Yemen
28 F5 Hajiki-zaki pt Japan
23 F4 Hajipur India
18 D4 Ḥajjīābād Iran
18 D4 Ḥajjīābād Iran
20 E6 Ḥajmah Oman
23 H5 Haka Myanmar
74 □2 Hakalau U.S.A.
91 C4 Hakelhuincul, Altiplanicie de plat. Arg.
Hakha see Haka
17 J3 Hakkâri Turkey
36 R3 Hakkas Sweden
29 D7 Hakken-zan mt Japan
28 H2 Hako-dake mt Japan
28 G4 Hakodate Japan
58 B1 Hakos Mts mts Namibia
58 D3 Hakseen Pan salt pan S. Africa
29 E6 Hakui Japan
29 E6 Haku-san volc. Japan
29 E6 Haku-san National Park Japan
22 B4 Hala Pak.
Ḥalab see Aleppo
18 B6 Halabān S. Arabia
17 K4 Ḥalabja Iraq
30 C1 Halaha China
30 C1 Halahai China
55 F2 Halaib Sudan
20 E6 Ḥalāniyāt, Juzur al is Oman
74 □2 Halawa U.S.A.
16 F4 Halba Lebanon
24 B2 Halban Mongolia
43 K3 Halberstadt Ger.
31 B3 Halcon, Mt mt Phil.
36 □ Haldarsvík Faroe Is
37 M7 Halden Norway
43 K2 Haldensleben Ger.
23 G5 Haldi r. India
23 G5 Haldia India
23 G4 Haldibari India
22 D3 Haldwani India
69 F3 Hale U.S.A.
17 G4 Halebiye Syria
74 □1 Haleiwa U.S.A.
39 E5 Halesowen U.K.
39 J5 Halesworth U.K.
16 F3 Halfeti Turkey
9 B7 Halfmoon Bay N.Z.
41 C6 Halfway Rep. of Ireland
64 E3 Halfway r. Can.
42 C2 Halfweg Neth.
23 E4 Halia India
69 H3 Haliburton Can.
67 H5 Halifax Can.
38 F4 Halifax U.K.
80 D6 Halifax U.S.A.
40 E2 Halkirk U.K.
36 P5 Hälla Sweden
30 D7 Halla-san mt S. Korea
63 K3 Hall Beach Can.
42 C4 Halle Belgium
42 E3 Halle Neth.
37 O7 Hällefors Sweden
46 F7 Hallein Austria
43 K3 Halle-Neustadt Ger.
43 K3 Halle (Saale) Ger.
92 A5 Hallett, C. c. Ant.
92 C3 Halley U.K. Base Ant.
4 G4 Hall Islands is Micronesia
36 Q4 Hällnäs Sweden
76 D1 Hallock U.S.A.
63 M3 Hall Peninsula pen. Can.
37 O7 Hallsberg Sweden
6 C3 Halls Creek Austr.
69 H3 Halls Lake Can.
42 B4 Halluin France
36 O5 Hallviken Sweden
25 E6 Halmahera i. Indon.
37 N8 Halmstad Sweden
22 C5 Halol India
37 M8 Hals Denmark
36 T5 Halsua Fin.
42 F3 Haltern Ger.
38 E3 Haltwhistle U.K.
18 D5 Ḥālūl i. Qatar
42 F3 Halver Ger.
42 B5 Ham France
29 C7 Hamada Japan
54 B2 Hamâda El Ḥaricha des. Mali
18 C3 Hamadān Iran
54 B2 Hamada Tounassine des. Alg.
16 F4 Ḥamāh Syria
28 G3 Hamamasu Japan
29 E7 Hamamatsu Japan
37 M6 Hamar Norway
36 O2 Hamarøy Norway
28 H2 Hamatonbetsu Japan
21 C5 Hambantota Sri Lanka
43 G1 Hambergen Ger.
38 F3 Hambleton Hills h. U.K.
43 H1 Hamburg Ger.
59 G6 Hamburg S. Africa
77 F5 Hamburg AR U.S.A.
80 D3 Hamburg NY U.S.A.
81 F4 Hamburg PA U.S.A.
43 G1 Hamburgisches Wattenmeer, Nationalpark nat. park Ger.
81 G4 Hamden U.S.A.
37 T6 Hämeenlinna Fin.
43 H2 Hameln Ger.
6 B4 Hamersley Range mts Austr.
30 D4 Hamhŭng N. Korea
24 B2 Hami China
18 C4 Ḥamīd Iran
55 F2 Hamid Sudan
8 D4 Hamilton Austr.
83 M2 Hamilton Bermuda
69 H4 Hamilton Can.
9 E2 Hamilton N.Z.
40 D5 Hamilton U.K.
79 C5 Hamilton AL U.S.A.
68 B5 Hamilton IL U.S.A.
72 D2 Hamilton MT U.S.A.
81 F3 Hamilton NY U.S.A.
80 A5 Hamilton OH U.S.A.
74 A2 Hamilton City U.S.A.
74 B3 Hamilton, Mt mt CA U.S.A.
75 E2 Hamilton, Mt mt NV U.S.A.
37 U6 Hamina Fin.
22 D3 Hamirpur India
17 H6 Ḥāmir, W. watercourse S. Arabia
67 J3 Hamiton Inlet in. Can.
30 D4 Hamju N. Korea
8 B3 Hamley Bridge Austr.
68 D3 Hamlin Lake l. U.S.A.
43 F3 Hamm Ger.
54 B2 Hammada du Drâa plat. Alg.
17 J3 Hammam Ali Iraq
48 D6 Hammamet Tunisia
55 D1 Hammamet, Golfe de b. Tunisia
17 L6 Ḥammār, Hawr al l. Iraq
36 P5 Hammarstrand Sweden
43 H4 Hammelburg Ger.
36 O5 Hammerdal Sweden
36 S1 Hammerfest Norway
42 E3 Hamminkeln Ger.
8 B2 Hammond Austr.
68 D5 Hammond IN U.S.A.
77 F6 Hammond LA U.S.A.
72 F2 Hammond MT U.S.A.
69 E3 Hammond Bay b. U.S.A.
80 E3 Hammondsport U.S.A.
81 F5 Hammonton U.S.A.
42 D4 Hamoir Belgium
9 C6 Hampden N.Z.
39 F6 Hampshire Downs h. U.K.
67 G4 Hampton Can.
77 E5 Hampton AR U.S.A.
81 H3 Hampton NH U.S.A.
81 E6 Hampton VA U.S.A.
17 K4 Ḥamrīn, Jabal h. Iraq
32 C3 Ham Tân Vietnam
22 D2 Hamta Pass pass India
19 E5 Hāmūn-e Jaz Mūrīān salt marsh Iran
19 F4 Hāmūn Helmand salt flat Afgh./Iran
19 G4 Hamun-i-Lora l. Pak.
19 F4 Hāmūn Pu marsh Afgh.
17 J2 Hamur Turkey
74 □2 Hana U.S.A.
58 E1 Hanahai watercourse Botswana/Namibia
74 □2 Hanalei U.S.A.
28 G5 Hanamaki Japan
43 G4 Hanau Ger.
26 D3 Hancheng China
80 D5 Hancock MD U.S.A.
68 C2 Hancock MI U.S.A.
81 F4 Hancock NY U.S.A.
40 C2 Handa Island i. U.K.
26 E2 Handan China
56 D4 Handeni Tanz.
74 C3 Hanford U.S.A.
21 A3 Hangal India
24 B2 Hangayn Nuruu mts Mongolia
26 C1 Hanggin Houqi China
26 C2 Hanggin Qi China
42 D4 Han, Grotte de Belgium
26 E2 Hangu China
22 B2 Hangu Pak.
27 D5 Hanguang China
27 F4 Hangzhou China
27 F4 Hangzhou Wan b. China
17 H2 Hani Turkey
18 C5 Ḥanīdh S. Arabia
26 B2 Hanjiaoshui China
43 J2 Hankensbüttel Ger.
58 F6 Hankey S. Africa
37 S7 Hanko Fin.
75 G2 Hanksville U.S.A.
22 D2 Hanle Jammu and Kashmir
9 D5 Hanmer Springs N.Z.
19 F4 Hanmi Mashkel salt flat Pak.
65 G4 Hanna Can.
66 D3 Hannah Bay b. Can.
68 B6 Hannibal U.S.A.
43 H2 Hannover Ger.
43 H3 Hannoversch Münden Ger.
42 D4 Hannut Belgium
37 O9 Hanöbukten b. Sweden
27 B6 Ha Nôi Vietnam
Hanoi see Ha Nôi
69 G3 Hanover Can.
58 F5 Hanover S. Africa
81 G3 Hanover NH U.S.A.
80 E5 Hanover PA U.S.A.
92 D4 Hansen Mts mts Ant.
27 D4 Hanshou China
26 E4 Han Shui r. China
22 D3 Hansi India
36 Q2 Hansnes Norway
68 B5 Hansonville U.S.A.
37 L8 Hanstholm Denmark
42 E6 Han-sur-Nied France
50 C4 Hantsavichy Belarus
22 C3 Hanumangarh India
8 F3 Hanwood Austr.
27 E4 Hanyang China
26 C3 Hanyin China
27 B4 Hanyuan China
26 C3 Hanzhong China
5 N6 Hao i. Pac. Oc.
23 G5 Hāora India
36 T4 Haparanda Sweden
23 H4 Hāpoli India
67 H3 Happy Valley-Goose Bay Can.
30 E3 Hapsu N. Korea
22 D3 Hapur India
21 C5 Haputale Sri Lanka
18 C5 Ḥaraḍ well S. Arabia
18 C5 Ḥaraḍh S. Arabia
50 D4 Haradok Belarus
29 G6 Haramachi Japan
22 C2 Haramukh mt India
22 C3 Harappa Road Pak.
57 D5 Harare Zimbabwe
24 C2 Har-Ayrag Mongolia
54 A4 Harbel Liberia
24 E2 Harbin China
69 F4 Harbor Beach U.S.A.
68 E3 Harbor Springs U.S.A.
67 J4 Harbour Breton Can.
88 E8 Harbours, B. of b. Falkland Is
75 F5 Harcuvar Mts mts U.S.A.
22 D5 Harda Khās India
37 K6 Hardangervidda plat. Norway
37 K6 Hardangervidda Nasjonalpark nat. park Norway
58 B2 Hardap div. Namibia
58 B2 Hardap Dam dam Namibia
42 E2 Hardenberg Neth.
33 E2 Harden, Bukit mt Indon.
42 D2 Harderwijk Neth.
58 C5 Hardeveld mts S. Africa
43 H5 Hardheim Ger.
72 F2 Hardin U.S.A.
59 H5 Harding S. Africa
65 G4 Hardisty Can.
64 F2 Hardisty Lake l. Can.
22 E4 Hardoi India
81 G2 Hardwick U.S.A.
77 F4 Hardy U.S.A.
68 E4 Hardy Reservoir resr U.S.A.
16 D6 Hareidīn, W. watercourse Egypt
42 B4 Harelbeke Belgium
42 E1 Haren Neth.
42 F2 Haren (Ems) Ger.
56 E3 Hārer Eth.
81 F4 Harford U.S.A.
56 E3 Hargeysa Somalia
47 M7 Harghita-Mădăraș, Vârful mt Romania
17 H2 Harhal D. mts Turkey
26 C2 Harhatan China
24 B3 Har Hu l. China
22 D3 Haridwar India
21 A3 Harihar India
9 C5 Harihari N.Z.
29 D7 Harima-nada b. Japan
23 G5 Haringhat r. Bangl.
42 C3 Haringvliet est. Neth.
19 G3 Hari Rūd r. Afgh./Iran
37 S6 Harjavalta Fin.
76 E3 Harlan IA U.S.A.
80 B6 Harlan KY U.S.A.
39 C5 Harlech U.K.
72 E1 Harlem U.S.A.
39 J5 Harleston U.K.
42 D1 Harlingen Neth.
77 D7 Harlingen U.S.A.
39 H6 Harlow U.K.
72 E2 Harlowtown U.S.A.
42 B5 Harly France
81 J2 Harmony ME U.S.A.
68 A4 Harmony MN U.S.A.
43 J1 Harmsdorf Ger.
22 A3 Harnai Pak.
42 A4 Harnes France
72 B3 Harney Basin basin U.S.A.
72 C3 Harney L. l. U.S.A.
37 P5 Härnösand Sweden
24 E2 Har Nur China
24 B2 Har Nuur l. Mongolia
40 □ Haroldswick U.K.
54 B4 Harper Liberia
74 D4 Harper Lake l. U.S.A.
80 E5 Harpers Ferry U.S.A.
67 H2 Harp Lake l. Can.
43 G2 Harpstedt Ger.
17 G2 Harput Turkey
26 F1 Harqin China
26 F1 Harqin Qi China
75 F5 Harquahala Mts mts U.S.A.
17 G3 Harran Turkey
16 F5 Harrat er Rujeila lava Jordan
66 E3 Harricanaw r. Can.
79 C5 Harriman U.S.A.
81 G3 Harriman Reservoir U.S.A.
81 F5 Harrington U.S.A.
67 J3 Harrington Harbour Can.
40 B3 Harris U.K.
78 B4 Harrisburg IL U.S.A.
80 E4 Harrisburg PA U.S.A.
59 H4 Harrismith S. Africa
77 E4 Harrison AR U.S.A.
68 E3 Harrison MI U.S.A.
62 C2 Harrison Bay b. U.S.A.
80 D5 Harrisonburg U.S.A.
67 J3 Harrison, Cape c. Can.
64 E5 Harrison L. l. Can.
76 E4 Harrisonville U.S.A.
40 A3 Harris, Sound of chan. U.K.
69 F3 Harrisville MI U.S.A.
81 F2 Harrisville NY U.S.A.
80 C5 Harrisville WV U.S.A.
38 F4 Harrogate U.K.
43 H1 Harsefeld Ger.
18 B3 Harsin Iran
16 G1 Harşit r. Turkey
49 M2 Hârșova Romania
36 P2 Harstad Norway
43 H2 Harsum Ger.
68 D4 Hart U.S.A.
30 B2 Hartao China
58 D4 Hartbees watercourse S. Africa
46 G7 Hartberg Austria
37 K6 Harteigan mt Norway
40 E5 Hart Fell h. U.K.
81 G4 Hartford CT U.S.A.
68 D4 Hartford MI U.S.A.
76 D3 Hartford SD U.S.A.
68 C4 Hartford WI U.S.A.
64 E3 Hart Highway Can.
67 G4 Hartland Can.
39 C7 Hartland U.K.
81 J2 Hartland U.S.A.
39 C6 Hartland Point pt U.K.
38 F3 Hartlepool U.K.
77 C5 Hartley U.S.A.
64 D4 Hartley Bay Can.
37 U6 Hartola Fin.
64 E4 Hart Ranges mts Can.
46 E6 Härtsfeld h. Ger.
58 F3 Hartswater S. Africa
79 D5 Hartwell Res. resr U.S.A.
24 B2 Har Us Nuur l. Mongolia
19 F3 Harut watercourse Afgh.
68 C4 Harvard U.S.A.
73 F4 Harvard, Mt mt U.S.A.
81 K2 Harvey Can.
68 D2 Harvey MI U.S.A.
76 C2 Harvey ND U.S.A.
39 J6 Harwich U.K.
22 C3 Haryana div. India
16 F6 Ḥaṣāh, Wādī al watercourse Jordan
18 B2 Hasan Iran
22 C2 Hasan Abdal Pak.
16 E2 Hasan Dağı mts Turkey
17 H3 Hasankeyf Turkey
18 E5 Ḥasan Langī Iran
21 B2 Hasanparti India
16 E5 Hasbani r. Lebanon
16 E2 Hasbek Turkey
17 K6 Ḥasb, Sha'īb watercourse Iraq
23 E5 Hasdo r. India
43 F2 Hase r. Ger.
42 F2 Haselünne Ger.
43 J4 Hasenkopf h. Ger.
18 C3 Hashtgerd Iran
18 C2 Hashtpar Iran
77 D5 Haskell U.S.A.
39 G6 Haslemere U.K.
47 M7 Hășmașul Mare mt Romania
21 B3 Hassan India
17 K4 Hassan Iraq
75 F5 Hassayampa r. U.S.A.
43 J4 Haßberge reg. Ger.
42 D4 Hasselt Belgium
42 E2 Hasselt Neth.
54 C1 Hassi Messaoud Alg.
37 N8 Hässleholm Sweden
8 E5 Hastings Austr.
9 F3 Hastings N.Z.
39 H7 Hastings U.K.
68 E4 Hastings MI U.S.A.
68 A3 Hastings MN U.S.A.
76 D3 Hastings NE U.S.A.
Hatay see Antakya
75 F3 Hatch U.S.A.
79 E7 Hatchet Bay Bahamas
65 J3 Hatchet Lake l. Can.
79 B5 Hatchie r. U.S.A.
8 D2 Hatfield Austr.
38 G4 Hatfield U.K.
24 C1 Hatgal Mongolia
22 D4 Hathras India
23 F4 Hatia Nepal
32 C3 Ha Tiên Vietnam
32 C1 Ha Tĩnh Vietnam
8 D3 Hattah Austr.
79 F5 Hatteras, Cape c. U.S.A.
36 N4 Hattfjelldal Norway
23 E6 Hatti r. India
79 B6 Hattiesburg U.S.A.
42 F3 Hattingen Ger.
56 E3 Haud reg. Eth.
37 K7 Hauge Norway
37 J7 Haugesund Norway
9 E3 Hauhungaroa mt N.Z.
37 K7 Haukeligrend Norway
36 T4 Haukipudas Fin.
37 V5 Haukivesi l. Fin.
65 H3 Haultain r. Can.
9 E2 Hauraki Gulf g. N.Z.
9 A7 Hauroko, L. l. N.Z.
54 B1 Haut Atlas mts Morocco
67 G4 Hauterive Can.
81 J3 Haut, Isle au i. U.S.A.
54 B1 Hauts Plateaux plat. Alg.
74 □1 Hauula U.S.A.
83 H4 Havana Cuba
68 B5 Havana U.S.A.
39 G7 Havant U.K.
75 E4 Havasu Lake l. U.S.A.
43 L2 Havel r. Ger.
42 D4 Havelange Belgium
43 L2 Havelberg Ger.
43 L2 Havelländisches Luch marsh Ger.
69 J3 Havelock Can.
79 E5 Havelock U.S.A.
9 F3 Havelock North N.Z.
39 C6 Haverfordwest U.K.
81 H3 Haverhill U.S.A.
21 A3 Haveri India
42 D4 Haversin Belgium
42 F3 Havixbeck Ger.
46 G6 Havlíčkův Brod Czech Rep.
36 T1 Havøysund Norway
49 M5 Havran Turkey
72 E1 Havre U.S.A.
67 H4 Havre Aubert, Île du i. Can.
81 E5 Havre de Grace U.S.A.
67 H3 Havre-St-Pierre Can.
49 M4 Havsa Turkey
16 E1 Havza Turkey
74 □2 Hawaii i. U.S.A.
5 K2 Hawaiian Islands is Pac. Oc.
94 H4 Hawaiian Ridge sea feature Pac. Oc.
74 □2 Hawaii Volcanoes National Park U.S.A.
17 L7 Ḥawallī Kuwait
39 D4 Hawarden U.K.
9 B6 Hawea, L. l. N.Z.
9 E3 Hawera N.Z.
38 E3 Hawes U.K.
74 □2 Hawi U.S.A.
40 F5 Hawick U.K.
17 L6 Ḥawīzah, Hawr al l. Iraq
9 B6 Hawkdun Range mts N.Z.
9 F3 Hawke Bay b. N.Z.
67 J3 Hawke Island i. Can.
8 B1 Hawker Austr.
81 F2 Hawkesbury Can.
75 F3 Hawkins Peak summit U.S.A.
69 F3 Hawks U.S.A.
81 K2 Hawkshaw Can.
81 F4 Hawley U.S.A.
17 J5 Ḥawrān, Wādī watercourse Iraq
58 C7 Hawston S. Africa
74 C2 Hawthorne U.S.A.
30 C1 Haxat China
38 F3 Haxby U.K.
8 E3 Hay Austr.
64 F2 Hay r. Can.
68 B3 Hay r. U.S.A.
26 B1 Haya China
28 G5 Hayachine-san mt Japan
18 B2 Haydarābad Iran
75 G5 Hayden AZ U.S.A.
72 C2 Hayden ID U.S.A.
65 L3 Hayes r. Can.
63 M2 Hayes Halvø pen. Greenland
39 B7 Hayle U.K.
16 D2 Haymana Turkey
80 E5 Haymarket U.S.A.
63 J3 Haynes r. Can.
81 J2 Haynesville U.S.A.
39 D5 Hay-on-Wye U.K.
51 C7 Hayrabolu Turkey
64 F2 Hay River Can.
76 D4 Hays U.S.A.
51 D5 Haysyn Ukr.
74 A3 Hayward CA U.S.A.
68 B2 Hayward WI U.S.A.
39 G7 Haywards Heath U.K.
19 G3 Hazarajat reg. Afgh.
80 B6 Hazard U.S.A.
23 F5 Hazāribāg India
23 E5 Hazaribagh Range mts India
42 A4 Hazebrouck France
64 D3 Hazelton Can.
81 F4 Hazelton U.S.A.
62 G2 Hazen Strait chan. Can.
42 C2 Hazerswoude-Rijndijk Neth.
17 G6 Ḥazm al Jalāmid ridge S. Arabia
19 G2 Hazrat Sultan Afgh.
17 H2 Hazro Turkey
41 B4 Headford Rep. of Ireland
74 A2 Healdsburg U.S.A.
8 E4 Healesville Austr.
39 F4 Heanor U.K.
93 J7 Heard Island i. Ind. Ocean
77 D6 Hearne U.S.A.
66 D4 Hearst Can.
92 B2 Hearst I. i. Ant.
39 H7 Heathfield U.K.
81 E6 Heathsville U.S.A.
77 D7 Hebbronville U.S.A.
26 E2 Hebei div. China
77 E5 Heber Springs U.S.A.
26 E3 Hebi China
67 H2 Hebron Can.
68 D5 Hebron IN U.S.A.
76 D3 Hebron NE U.S.A.
81 G3 Hebron NY U.S.A.
16 E6 Hebron West Bank
67 H2 Hebron Fiord in. Can.
62 E4 Hecate Strait B.C. Can.
64 C4 Hecate Strait chan. Can.
84 E2 Hecelchakán Mex.
64 C3 Heceta I. i. U.S.A.
27 C5 Hechi China
27 C4 Hechuan China
37 N5 Hede Sweden
37 O6 Hedemora Sweden
27 D6 Hede Sk. resr China
72 C2 He Devil Mt. mt U.S.A.
68 A5 Hedrick U.S.A.
42 D2 Heeg Neth.
42 F2 Heek Ger.
42 C4 Heer Belgium
42 E2 Heerde Neth.
42 D2 Heerenveen Neth.
42 C2 Heerhugowaard Neth.
42 D4 Heerlen Neth.
Ḥefa see Haifa
26 E4 Hefei China
27 D4 Hefeng China
24 E2 Hegang China
29 E6 Hegura-jima i. Japan
43 K3 Heidberg h. Ger.
46 D3 Heide Ger.
57 B6 Heide Namibia
43 G5 Heidelberg Ger.
59 H3 Heidelberg Gauteng S. Africa
58 D7 Heidelberg Western Cape S. Africa
59 G3 Heilbron S. Africa
43 H5 Heilbronn Ger.
46 E3 Heiligenhafen Ger.
27 □ Hei Ling Chau i. H.K. China
30 E1 Heilongjiang div. China
24 E2 Heilong Jiang r. China/Rus. Fed.
43 J5 Heilsbronn Ger.
36 M5 Heimdal Norway
37 U6 Heinola Fin.
32 A2 Heinze Is is Myanmar
30 B3 Heishan China
42 C3 Heist-op-den-Berg Belgium
26 E2 Hejian China
27 B4 Hejiang China
27 D6 He Jiang r. China
26 D3 Hejin China
16 F2 Hekimhan Turkey
36 D5 Hekla volc. Iceland
26 B2 Hekou Gansu China
27 B6 Hekou Yunnan China
36 N5 Helagsfjället mt Sweden
26 B2 Helan Shan mts China
43 K3 Helbra Ger.
23 H4 Helem India
77 F5 Helena AR U.S.A.
72 E2 Helena MT U.S.A.
74 D3 Helen, Mt mt U.S.A.
40 D4 Helensburgh U.K.
16 E6 Ḥelez Israel
46 C3 Helgoland i. Ger.
46 D3 Helgoländer Bucht b. Ger.
36 C5 Hella Iceland
36 M5 Helland Norway
18 C4 Helleh r. Iran
42 C3 Hellevoetsluis Neth.
36 R2 Helligskogen Norway
45 F3 Hellín Spain
72 C2 Hells Canyon gorge U.S.A.
19 F4 Helmand r. Afgh.
43 K4 Helmbrechts Ger.
43 J3 Helme r. Ger.
57 B6 Helmeringhausen Namibia
58 E6 Helmeringhausen S. Africa
42 D3 Helmond Neth.
40 E2 Helmsdale U.K.
40 E2 Helmsdale r. U.K.
43 K2 Helmstedt Ger.
30 E2 Helong China
75 G2 Helper U.S.A.
37 N8 Helsingborg Sweden
37 N8 Helsingør Denmark
37 T6 Helsinki Fin.
39 B7 Helston U.K.
38 D3 Helvellyn mt U.K.
41 D5 Helvick Head hd Rep. of Ireland
55 F2 Helwān Egypt
39 G6 Hemel Hempstead U.K.
74 D5 Hemet U.S.A.
80 E3 Hemlock Lake l. U.S.A.
43 H2 Hemmingen Ger.
81 G2 Hemmingford Can.
43 H1 Hemmoor Ger.
77 D6 Hempstead U.S.A.
39 J5 Hemsby U.K.
37 Q8 Hemse Sweden
26 A3 Henan Qinghai China
26 D3 Henan div. China
45 E2 Henares r. Spain
28 F4 Henashi-zaki pt Japan
16 C1 Hendek Turkey
91 E3 Henderson Arg.
78 C4 Henderson KY U.S.A.
79 E4 Henderson NC U.S.A.
75 E3 Henderson NV U.S.A.
81 E3 Henderson NY U.S.A.
77 E5 Henderson TX U.S.A.
5 P7 Henderson Island i. Pac. Oc.
79 D5 Hendersonville NC U.S.A.
79 C4 Hendersonville TN U.S.A.
18 C4 Hendījān Iran
39 G6 Hendon U.K.
18 D5 Hendorābī i. Iran
24 B4 Hengduan Shan mts China
42 E2 Hengelo Neth.
27 D5 Hengshan Hunan China
26 C2 Hengshan Shaanxi China
30 F1 Hengshan China
27 D5 Heng Shan mt Hunan China
26 D2 Heng Shan mt China
26 E2 Hengshui China
27 C6 Heng Xian China
27 D5 Hengyang Hunan China
51 E6 Heniches'k Ukr.
9 C6 Henley N.Z.
39 G6 Henley-on-Thames U.K.
81 F5 Henlopen, Cape pt U.S.A.
42 F4 Hennef (Sieg) Ger.
59 G3 Hennenman S. Africa
43 M2 Hennigsdorf Berlin Ger.
81 H3 Henniker U.S.A.
77 D5 Henrietta U.S.A.
66 D2 Henrietta Maria, Cape c. Can.
75 G3 Henrieville U.S.A.
68 C5 Henry U.S.A.
92 B3 Henry Ice Rise ice feature Ant.
63 M3 Henry Kater, C. hd Can.
75 G2 Henry Mts mts U.S.A.
69 G4 Hensall Can.
43 H1 Henstedt-Ulzburg Ger.
57 B6 Hentiesbaai Namibia
8 F3 Henty Austr.
25 B5 Henzada Myanmar
65 H4 Hepburn Can.
27 E5 Heping China
27 C6 Hepu China
26 D2 Hequ China
19 F3 Herāt Afgh.
44 F5 Hérault r. France
65 H4 Herbert Can.
43 G4 Herborn Ger.
43 H4 Herbstein Ger.
92 B4 Hercules Dome ice feature Ant.
42 F3 Herdecke Ger.
43 F4 Herdorf Ger.
39 E5 Hereford U.K.
77 C5 Hereford U.S.A.
5 N6 Héréhérétué i. Pac. Oc.
42 C4 Herent Belgium
43 G2 Herford Ger.
43 J4 Heringen (Werra) Ger.
76 D4 Herington U.S.A.
18 B2 Herīs Iran
46 D7 Herisau Switz.
92 B3 Heritage Ra. mts Ant.
81 F3 Herkimer U.S.A.
43 J3 Herleshausen Ger.
40 □ Herma Ness hd U.K.
43 J2 Hermannsburg Ger.
58 C7 Hermanus S. Africa
59 H5 Hermes, Cape pt S. Africa
8 F1 Hermidale Austr.
72 C2 Hermiston U.S.A.
88 C9 Hermite, Is i. Chile
6 E2 Hermit Is is P.N.G.
Hermon, Mount mt see Sheikh, Jebel esh
91 B2 Hermosa, P. de V. pass Chile
89 B4 Hermosas, Parque Nacional las nat. park Col.
82 B3 Hermosillo Mex.
88 F3 Hernandarias Para.
42 F3 Herne Ger.
39 J6 Herne Bay U.K.
37 L8 Herning Denmark
68 D1 Heron Bay Can.
84 B2 Herradura Mex.
45 D3 Herrera del Duque Spain
84 A1 Herreras Mex.
43 J5 Herrieden Ger.
80 E4 Hershey U.S.A.
39 G6 Hertford U.K.
59 F4 Hertzogville S. Africa
42 D4 Herve Belgium
7 F4 Hervey Bay b. Austr.
5 M6 Hervey Islands is Pac. Oc.
43 L2 Herzberg Brandenburg Ger.
43 M3 Herzberg Brandenburg Ger.
42 F2 Herzlake Ger.
43 J5 Herzogenaurach Ger.
43 L1 Herzsprung Ger.
17 M4 Ḥeşar Iran
42 C4 Hesbaye reg. Belgium
42 F1 Hesel Ger.
27 C6 Heshan China
26 C3 Heshui China
26 D2 Heshun China
74 D4 Hesperia U.S.A.
64 C2 Hess r. Can.
43 J5 Heßdorf Ger.
43 J5 Hesselberg h. Ger.
43 H4 Hessen div. Ger.
43 H3 Hessisch Lichtenau Ger.
27 B6 Het r. Laos
74 B3 Hetch Hetchy Aqueduct canal U.S.A.
42 D3 Heteren Neth.
76 C2 Hettinger U.S.A.
38 E3 Hetton U.K.
43 K3 Hettstedt Ger.
38 E3 Hexham U.K.
26 F4 He Xian Anhui China
27 D5 He Xian Guangxi China
26 B2 Hexibao China
26 E1 Hexigten Qi China
58 C6 Hex River Pass S. Africa
26 D3 Heyang China
18 D4 Ḥeydarābād Iran
19 F4 Ḥeydarābād Iran
38 E3 Heysham U.K.
27 E6 Heyuan China
8 C5 Heywood Austr.
38 E4 Heywood U.K.
68 C5 Heyworth U.S.A.
26 E3 Heze China
27 B5 Hezhang China
26 B3 Hezheng China
26 B3 Hezuozhen China
79 D7 Hialeah U.S.A.
76 E4 Hiawatha U.S.A.
68 A2 Hibbing U.S.A.
79 D5 Hickory U.S.A.
9 G2 Hicks Bay N.Z.
65 K2 Hicks L. l. Can.
80 A4 Hicksville U.S.A.
77 D5 Hico U.S.A.
28 H3 Hidaka-sanmyaku mts Japan
84 C2 Hidalgo div. Mex.
82 C3 Hidalgo del Parral Mex.
82 C3 Hidalgo, Psa M. resr Mex.
90 C2 Hidrolândia Brazil
29 C7 Higashi-Hiroshima Japan
28 G5 Higashine Japan
29 D7 Higashi-ōsaka Japan
29 A8 Higashi-suidō chan. Japan
81 F3 Higgins Bay U.S.A.
68 E3 Higgins Lake l. U.S.A.
High Atlas mts see Haut Atlas
72 B3 High Desert U.S.A.
68 C3 High Falls Reservoir U.S.A.
68 E3 High I. i. U.S.A.
27 □ High Island Res. H.K. China
68 D4 Highland Park U.S.A.
74 C2 Highland Peak summit CA U.S.A.
75 E3 Highland Peak summit NV U.S.A.
64 F3 High Level Can.
23 F5 High Level Canal canal India
79 E5 High Point U.S.A.
64 F3 High Prairie Can.
64 G4 High River Can.
79 E7 High Rock Bahamas
65 J3 Highrock Lake l. Can.
38 E3 High Seat h. U.K.
81 F4 Hightstown U.S.A.
39 G6 High Wycombe U.K.
89 D2 Higuerote Venez.
37 S7 Hiiumaa i. Estonia
20 A4 Hijaz reg. S. Arabia
75 E3 Hiko U.S.A.
29 E7 Hikone Japan
9 G2 Hikurangi mt N.Z.
75 F3 Hildale U.S.A.
43 J4 Hildburghausen Ger.
43 J4 Hilders Ger.
43 H2 Hildesheim Ger.
23 G4 Hili Bangl.
92 B5 Hillary Coast coastal area Ant.
76 D4 Hill City U.S.A.
75 H2 Hill Creek r. U.S.A.
42 C2 Hillegom Neth.
37 N9 Hillerød Denmark
76 D2 Hillsboro ND U.S.A.
81 H3 Hillsboro NH U.S.A.
80 B5 Hillsboro OH U.S.A.
77 D5 Hillsboro TX U.S.A.
68 B4 Hillsboro WI U.S.A.
80 C5 Hillsboro WV U.S.A.
68 E5 Hillsdale MI U.S.A.
81 G3 Hillsdale NY U.S.A.
80 E4 Hillsgrove U.S.A.
40 F4 Hillside U.K.
75 F4 Hillside U.S.A.
8 E2 Hillston Austr.
80 C6 Hillsville U.S.A.
8 H3 Hilltop Austr.
74 □2 Hilo U.S.A.
59 J4 Hilton S. Africa
80 E3 Hilton U.S.A.
69 F2 Hilton Beach Can.
79 D5 Hilton Head Island U.S.A.
17 G3 Hilvan Turkey
42 D2 Hilversum Neth.
22 D3 Himachal Pradesh div. India
10 J6 Himalaya mts Asia
23 F3 Himalchul mt Nepal
36 S4 Himanka Fin.
49 H4 Himarë Albania
22 C5 Himatnagar India
29 D7 Himeji Japan
28 G5 Himekami-dake mt Japan
59 H4 Himeville S. Africa
29 E6 Himi Japan
16 F4 Ḥimṣ Syria
16 F4 Ḥimṣ, Baḥrat resr Syria
31 C4 Hinatuan Phil.
6 E3 Hinchinbrook I. i. Austr.
39 F5 Hinckley U.K.
68 A2 Hinckley MN U.S.A.
75 F2 Hinckley UT U.S.A.
81 F3 Hinckley Reservoir U.S.A.
22 D3 Hindan r. India
22 D4 Hindaun India
38 G3 Hinderwell U.K.
17 K5 Hindīyah Barrage Iraq
38 E4 Hindley U.K.
80 B6 Hindman U.S.A.
8 C4 Hindmarsh, L. l. Austr.
23 F5 Hindola India
19 G3 Hindu Kush mts Afgh./Pak.
21 B3 Hindupur India
64 F3 Hines Creek Can.
79 D6 Hinesville U.S.A.
22 D5 Hinganghat India
19 G5 Hinglaj Pak.
19 G5 Hingol r. Pak.
22 D6 Hingoli India
17 H2 Hınıs Turkey
74 D4 Hinkley U.S.A.
36 O2 Hinnøya i. Norway
31 B4 Hinobaan Phil.
45 D3 Hinojosa del Duque Spain
29 C7 Hino-misaki pt Japan
81 G3 Hinsdale U.S.A.
42 F1 Hinte Ger.
64 F4 Hinton Can.
80 C6 Hinton U.S.A.
42 C2 Hippolytushoef Neth.
17 K2 Hirabit Dağ mt Turkey
29 A8 Hirado Japan
29 A8 Hirado-shima i. Japan
23 E5 Hirakud Reservoir India
28 H3 Hiroo Japan
28 G4 Hirosaki Japan
29 C7 Hiroshima Japan
43 K5 Hirschaid Ger.
43 K4 Hirschberg Ger.
46 E7 Hirschberg mt Ger.
44 G2 Hirson France
37 L8 Hirtshals Denmark
17 M3 Hisar Iran
19 G3 Hisar, Koh-i- mts Afgh.
16 D1 Hisarönü Turkey
16 E6 Hisban Jordan
19 H2 Hisor Tajik.
83 K4 Hispaniola i. Caribbean Sea
22 C3 Hissar India
23 F4 Hisua India
17 J5 Hīt Iraq
29 G6 Hitachi Japan
29 G6 Hitachi-ōta Japan
29 B8 Hitoyoshi Japan
36 L5 Hitra i. Norway
43 K1 Hitzacker Ger.
29 C7 Hiuchi-nada b. Japan
5 O5 Hiva Oa i. Pac. Oc.
64 E4 Hixon Can.
17 J2 Hizan Turkey
37 O7 Hjälmaren l. Sweden
65 H2 Hjalmar Lake l. Can.
37 L5 Hjerkinn Norway
37 O7 Hjo Sweden
37 M8 Hjørring Denmark
59 J4 Hlabisa S. Africa
23 F3 Hlako Kangri mt China

59 J3 **Hlatikulu** Swaziland
51 E5 **Hlobyne** Ukr.
59 G4 **Hlohlowane** S. Africa
59 H4 **Hlotse** Lesotho
59 K4 **Hluhluwe** S. Africa
51 E5 **Hlukhiv** Ukr.
47 O4 **Hlusha** Belarus
50 C4 **Hlybokaye** Belarus
54 C4 **Ho** Ghana
57 B6 **Hoachanas** Namibia
6 E6 **Hobart** Austr.
77 D5 **Hobart** U.S.A.
77 C5 **Hobbs** U.S.A.
92 A4 **Hobbs Coast** *coastal area* Ant.
79 D7 **Hobe Sound** U.S.A.
37 L8 **Hobro** Denmark
56 E3 **Hobyo** Somalia
43 H5 **Höchberg** Ger.
32 C3 **Hô Chi Minh** Vietnam
46 G7 **Hochschwab** *mt* Austria
43 G5 **Hockenheim** Ger.
80 B5 **Hocking** *r.* U.S.A.
22 D4 **Hodal** India
38 E4 **Hodder** *r.* U.K.
39 G6 **Hoddesdon** U.K.
Hodeida *see* **Al Hudaydah**
81 K1 **Hodgdon** U.S.A.
47 K7 **Hódmezővásárhely** Hungary
45 J5 **Hodna, Chott el** *salt l.* Alg.
30 D4 **Hodo dan** *pt* N. Korea
42 C3 **Hoek van Holland** Neth.
42 D4 **Hoensbroek** Neth.
30 E2 **Hoeryŏng** N. Korea
30 D4 **Hoeyang** N. Korea
43 K4 **Hof** Ger.
43 J4 **Hofheim in Unterfranken** Ger.
59 F5 **Hofmeyr** S. Africa
36 F4 **Höfn** Iceland
37 P6 **Hofors** Sweden
36 D4 **Hofsjökull** *ice cap* Iceland
29 B7 **Hōfu** Japan
37 N8 **Höganäs** Sweden
54 C2 **Hoggar** *plat.* Alg.
81 F6 **Hog I.** *i.* U.S.A.
37 P8 **Högsby** Sweden
43 H5 **Hohenloher Ebene** *plain* Ger.
43 L3 **Hohenmölsen** Ger.
43 L2 **Hohennauen** Ger.
43 K4 **Hohenwarte-talsperre** *resr* Ger.
43 H4 **Hohe Rhön** *mts* Ger.
46 F7 **Hohe Tauern** *mts* Austria
42 E4 **Hohe Venn** *moorland* Belgium
26 D1 **Hohhot** China
23 G2 **Hoh Xil Hu** *salt l.* China
23 G2 **Hoh Xil Shan** *mts* China
32 D2 **Hôi An** Vietnam
56 D3 **Hoima** Uganda
27 B6 **Hôi Xuân** Vietnam
23 H4 **Hojai** India
29 C8 **Hōjo** Japan
9 D1 **Hokianga Harbour** *in.* N.Z.
9 C5 **Hokitika** N.Z.
28 H3 **Hokkaidō** *i.* Japan
37 L7 **Hokksund** Norway
17 K1 **Hoktemberyan** Armenia
37 L6 **Hol** Norway
21 B3 **Holalkere** India
37 M9 **Holbæk** Denmark
39 H5 **Holbeach** U.K.
75 G4 **Holbrook** U.S.A.
68 B3 **Holcombe Flowage** *resr* U.S.A.
65 G4 **Holden** Can.
75 F2 **Holden** U.S.A.
77 D5 **Holdenville** U.S.A.
76 D3 **Holdrege** U.S.A.
21 B3 **Hole Narsipur** India
83 J4 **Holguín** Cuba
37 N6 **Höljes** Sweden
68 D4 **Holland** U.S.A.
80 D4 **Hollidaysburg** U.S.A.
64 C3 **Hollis** *AK* U.S.A.
77 D5 **Hollis** *OK* U.S.A.
74 B3 **Hollister** U.S.A.
69 F4 **Holly** U.S.A.
77 F5 **Holly Springs** U.S.A.
79 D7 **Hollywood** U.S.A.
36 N4 **Holm** Norway
62 G2 **Holman** Can.
36 T2 **Holmestrand** *Finnmark* Norway
37 M7 **Holmestrand** *Vestfold* Norway
36 R5 **Holmön** *i.* Sweden
63 M2 **Holms Ø** *i.* Greenland
36 R5 **Holmsund** Sweden
58 B3 **Holoog** Namibia
37 L8 **Holstebro** Denmark
79 D4 **Holston** *r.* U.S.A.
80 C6 **Holston Lake** *l.* U.S.A.
39 C7 **Holsworthy** U.K.
39 J5 **Holt** U.K.
68 E4 **Holt** U.S.A.
76 E4 **Holton** U.S.A.
42 D1 **Holwerd** Neth.
41 D5 **Holycross** Rep. of Ireland
39 C4 **Holyhead** U.K.
39 C4 **Holyhead Bay** *b.* U.K.
38 F2 **Holy Island** *i. Eng.* U.K.
39 C4 **Holy Island** *i. Wales* U.K.
81 G3 **Holyoke** U.S.A.
39 D4 **Holywell** U.K.
43 L3 **Holzhausen** Ger.
46 E7 **Holzkirchen** Ger.
43 H3 **Holzminden** Ger.
18 C3 **Homâyunshahr** Iran
43 H3 **Homberg (Efze)** Ger.
54 B3 **Hombori** Mali
42 F5 **Homburg** Ger.
63 M3 **Home Bay** *b.* Can.
42 D5 **Homécourt** France
77 E5 **Homer** U.S.A.
79 D6 **Homerville** U.S.A.
79 D7 **Homestead** U.S.A.
79 C5 **Homewood** U.S.A.
21 B2 **Homnabad** India
31 C4 **Homonhon** *pt* Phil.
Homs *see* **Ḥimṣ**
51 D4 **Homyel'** Belarus
21 A3 **Honavar** India
89 B3 **Honda** Col.
31 A4 **Honda Bay** *b.* Phil.
75 H4 **Hon Dah** U.S.A.
58 B5 **Hondeklipbaai** S. Africa
26 C1 **Hondlon Ju** China
77 D6 **Hondo** U.S.A.
42 E1 **Hondsrug** *reg.* Neth.
61 K8 **Honduras** *country* Central America
37 M6 **Hønefoss** Norway
81 F4 **Honesdale** U.S.A.
74 B1 **Honey Lake** *l.* U.S.A.
81 E3 **Honeyoye Lake** *l.* U.S.A.
44 E2 **Honfleur** France
26 E4 **Hong'an** China
30 D5 **Hongch'ŏn** S. Korea
27 C6 **Hông Gai** Vietnam
27 E6 **Honghai Wan** *b.* China
27 B6 **Honghe** China
26 E3 **Hong He** *r.* China
27 D4 **Honghu** China
27 C5 **Hongjiang** China
27 E6 **Hong Kong** China
27 E6 **Hong Kong** *div.* China
27 □ **Hong Kong Island** *i. H.K.* China
26 C2 **Hongliu** *r.* China
26 B2 **Hongliuyuan** China
32 C3 **Hông Ngư** Vietnam
27 C6 **Hong or Red River, Mouths of the** *est.* Vietnam
27 C7 **Hongqizhen** China
26 B2 **Hongshansi** China
30 D2 **Hongshi** China
27 D6 **Hongshui He** *r.* China
27 C6 **Hông, Sông** *r.* Vietnam
26 D2 **Hongtong** China
67 G4 **Honguedo, Détroit d'** *chan.* Can.
30 D3 **Hongwŏn** N. Korea
30 B1 **Hongxing** China
26 B3 **Hongyuan** China
26 F3 **Hongze** China
26 F3 **Hongze Hu** *l.* China
7 F2 **Honiara** Solomon Is
39 D7 **Honiton** U.K.
28 G5 **Honjō** Japan
37 S6 **Honkajoki** Fin.
32 C3 **Hon Khoai** *i.* Vietnam
32 D2 **Hon Lơn** *i.* Vietnam
32 C1 **Hon Mê** *i.* Vietnam
21 A3 **Honnali** India
36 T1 **Honningsvåg** Norway
74 □2 **Honokaa** U.S.A.
74 □1 **Honolulu** U.S.A.
32 C3 **Hon Rai** *i.* Vietnam
29 C7 **Honshū** *i.* Japan
72 B2 **Hood, Mt** *volc.* U.S.A.
6 B5 **Hood Pt** *pt* Austr.
42 E2 **Hoogeveen** Neth.
42 E1 **Hoogezand-Sappemeer** Neth.
77 C4 **Hooker** U.S.A.
41 E5 **Hook Head** *hd* Rep. of Ireland
Hook of Holland *see* **Hoek van Holland**
64 B3 **Hoonah** U.S.A.
62 B3 **Hooper Bay** *AK* U.S.A.
81 E5 **Hooper I.** *i.* U.S.A.
68 D5 **Hoopeston** U.S.A.
59 F3 **Hoopstad** S. Africa
37 N9 **Höör** Sweden
42 D2 **Hoorn** Neth.
81 G3 **Hoosick** U.S.A.
75 E3 **Hoover Dam** *dam* U.S.A.
80 B4 **Hoover Memorial Reservoir** U.S.A.
17 H1 **Hopa** Turkey
81 F4 **Hop Bottom** U.S.A.
64 E5 **Hope** *B.C.* Can.
77 E5 **Hope** *AR* U.S.A.
75 F5 **Hope** *AZ* U.S.A.
9 D5 **Hope** *r.* N.Z.
67 J2 **Hopedale** Can.
58 C6 **Hopefield** S. Africa
84 E3 **Hopelchén** Mex.
67 H3 **Hope Mountains** Can.
12 D2 **Hopen** *i.* Svalbard
62 B3 **Hope, Point** *c.* U.S.A.
9 D4 **Hope Saddle** *pass* N.Z.
67 G2 **Hopes Advance, Baie** *b.* Can.
8 D3 **Hopetoun** Austr.
58 F4 **Hopetown** S. Africa
80 E6 **Hopewell** U.S.A.
66 E2 **Hopewell Islands** *is* Can.
6 C4 **Hopkins, L.** *salt flat* Austr.
78 C4 **Hopkinsville** U.S.A.
74 A2 **Hopland** U.S.A.
72 B2 **Hoquiam** U.S.A.
26 A3 **Hor** China
17 L2 **Horadiz** Azer.
17 J1 **Horasan** Turkey
37 N9 **Hörby** Sweden
68 C4 **Horeb, Mount** U.S.A.
26 B1 **Hörh Uul** *mts* Mongolia
68 C4 **Horicon** U.S.A.
26 D1 **Horinger** China
94 H6 **Horizon Depth** *depth* Pac. Oc.
50 D4 **Horki** Belarus
92 B4 **Horlick Mts** *mts* Ant.
51 F5 **Horlivka** Ukr.
19 F4 **Hormak** Iran
18 E5 **Hormoz** *i.* Iran
18 E5 **Hormuz, Strait of** *str.* Iran/Oman
46 G6 **Horn** Austria
36 B3 **Horn** *c.* Iceland
64 F2 **Horn** *r.* Can.
36 P3 **Hornavan** *l.* Sweden
77 E6 **Hornbeck** U.S.A.
43 J2 **Hornburg** Ger.
88 C9 **Horn, Cape** *c.* Chile
39 G4 **Horncastle** U.K.
37 P6 **Horndal** Sweden
43 H1 **Horneburg** Ger.
36 Q5 **Hörnefors** Sweden
80 E3 **Hornell** U.S.A.
66 D4 **Hornepayne** Can.
79 B6 **Horn I.** *i.* U.S.A.
46 D6 **Hornisgrinde** *mt* Ger.
7 J3 **Horn, Îsles de** *is* Wallis and Futuna Is
58 B1 **Hornkranz** Namibia
91 B4 **Hornopiren, V.** *volc.* Chile
84 B1 **Hornos** Mex.
Hornos, Cabo de *c. see* **Horn, Cape**
8 H2 **Hornsby** Austr.
38 G4 **Hornsea** U.K.
37 P6 **Hornslandet** *pen.* Sweden
47 M6 **Horodenka** Ukr.
51 D5 **Horodnya** Ukr.
51 C5 **Horodok** *Khmel'nyts'kyy* Ukr.
51 B5 **Horodok** *L'viv* Ukr.
28 H2 **Horokanai** Japan
47 M5 **Horokhiv** Ukr.
28 H3 **Horoshiri-dake** *mt* Japan
30 A2 **Horqin Shadi** *reg.* China
24 E2 **Horqin Youyi Qianqi** China
30 A1 **Horqin Youyi Zhongqi** China
30 B2 **Horqin Zuoyi Houqi** China
30 B1 **Horqin Zuoyi Zhongqi** China
39 C7 **Horrabridge** U.K.
23 G3 **Horru** China
64 E4 **Horsefly** Can.
80 E3 **Horseheads** U.S.A.
67 J3 **Horse Is** *is* Can.
41 C4 **Horseleap** Rep. of Ireland
37 L9 **Horsens** Denmark
72 C3 **Horseshoe Bend** U.S.A.
8 D4 **Horsham** Austr.
39 G6 **Horsham** U.K.
43 L5 **Horšovský Týn** Czech Rep.
43 H4 **Horst** *h.* Ger.
42 F2 **Hörstel** Ger.
37 M7 **Horten** Norway
62 F3 **Horton** *r.* Can.
69 F1 **Horwood Lake** *l.* Can.
47 N5 **Horyn'** *r.* Ukr.
23 H2 **Ho Sai Hu** *l.* China
56 D3 **Hosa'ina** Eth.
43 H4 **Hösbach** Ger.
21 B3 **Hosdurga** India
17 L4 **Hoseynābād** Iran
18 C4 **Ḥoseynīyeh** Iran
19 F5 **Hoshab** Pak.
22 D5 **Hoshangabad** India
22 C3 **Hoshiarpur** India
21 B3 **Hospet** India
41 C5 **Hospital** Rep. of Ireland
91 F1 **Hospital, Cuchilla del** *h.* Uru.
88 C9 **Hoste, I.** *i.* Chile
36 O5 **Hotagen** *l.* Sweden
15 G3 **Hotan** China
58 E3 **Hotazel** S. Africa
75 G4 **Hotevilla** U.S.A.
8 F4 **Hotham, Mt** *mt* Austr.
36 P4 **Hoting** Sweden
77 E5 **Hot Springs** *AR* U.S.A.
76 C3 **Hot Springs** *SD* U.S.A.
64 F1 **Hottah Lake** *l.* Can.
83 K5 **Hotte, Massif de la** *mts* Haiti
42 D4 **Houffalize** Belgium
32 □ **Hougang** Sing.
68 C2 **Houghton** U.S.A.
68 E3 **Houghton Lake** U.S.A.
68 E3 **Houghton Lake** *l.* U.S.A.
38 F3 **Houghton le Spring** U.K.
81 K1 **Houlton** U.S.A.
26 D3 **Houma** China
77 F6 **Houma** U.S.A.
40 C3 **Hourn, Loch** *in.* U.K.
81 G3 **Housatonic** U.S.A.
75 F2 **House Range** *mts* U.S.A.
64 D4 **Houston** Can.
77 F4 **Houston** *MO* U.S.A.
77 F5 **Houston** *MS* U.S.A.
77 E6 **Houston** *TX* U.S.A.
59 H1 **Hout** *r.* S. Africa
6 B4 **Houtman Abrolhos** *is* Austr.
40 E2 **Houton** U.K.
58 E5 **Houwater** S. Africa
24 B2 **Hovd** Mongolia
39 G7 **Hove** U.K.
39 J5 **Hoveton** U.K.
18 C4 **Hoveyzeh** Iran
37 O8 **Hovmantorp** Sweden
26 C1 **Hövsgöl** Mongolia
24 C1 **Hövsgöl Nuur** *l.* Mongolia
24 C2 **Hövüün** Mongolia
68 E4 **Howard City** U.S.A.
65 H2 **Howard Lake** *l.* Can.
38 G4 **Howden** U.K.
8 G4 **Howe, C.** *hd* Austr.
69 F4 **Howell** U.S.A.
76 C2 **Howes** U.S.A.
81 G2 **Howick** Can.
59 J4 **Howick** S. Africa
8 F4 **Howitt, Mt** *mt* Austr.
81 J2 **Howland** U.S.A.
7 J1 **Howland Island** *i.* Pac. Oc.
8 F3 **Howlong** Austr.
41 E4 **Howth** Rep. of Ireland
18 D3 **Ḥowz-e Dūmatu** Iran
18 E4 **Ḥowz-e Panj** Iran
43 H3 **Höxter** Ger.
40 E2 **Hoy** *i.* U.K.
43 H2 **Hoya** Ger.
37 K6 **Hoyanger** Norway
46 G5 **Hoyerswerda** Ger.
36 N4 **Høylandet** Norway
43 K3 **Hoym** Ger.
36 V5 **Höytiäinen** *l.* Fin.
17 G2 **Hozat** Turkey
46 G5 **Hradec Králové** Czech Rep.
43 M4 **Hradiště** *h.* Czech Rep.
49 H3 **Hrasnica** Bos.-Herz.
17 K1 **Hrazdan** Armenia
51 E5 **Hrebinka** Ukr.
50 B4 **Hrodna** Belarus
27 F6 **Hsi-hsu-p'ing Hsü** *i.* Taiwan
27 F5 **Hsin-chu** Taiwan
27 F5 **Hsueh Shan** *mt* Taiwan
27 E5 **Hua'an** China
89 D4 **Huachamacari, Cerro** *mt* Venez.
26 C2 **Huachi** China
86 C6 **Huacho** Peru
28 B1 **Huachuan** China
75 G6 **Huachuca City** U.S.A.
91 C1 **Huaco** Arg.
26 D1 **Huade** China
30 D2 **Huadian** China
26 E1 **Huai'an** *Hebei* China
26 F3 **Huai'an** *Jiangsu* China
26 E3 **Huaibei** China
26 E3 **Huaibin** China
30 C2 **Huaide** China
30 C2 **Huaidezhen** China
26 F3 **Huai He** *r.* China
27 C5 **Huaihua** China
27 D6 **Huaiji** China
26 E1 **Huailai** China
27 B7 **Huai Luang** *r.* Thai.
26 E3 **Huainan** China
27 E4 **Huaining** China
26 D2 **Huairen** China
26 E3 **Huaiyang** China
26 F3 **Huaiyin** China
26 E3 **Huaiyuan** *Anhui* China
27 C5 **Huaiyuan** *Guangxi* China
26 B3 **Huajialing** China
84 C3 **Huajuápan de León** Mex.
25 E7 **Huaki** Indon.
75 F4 **Hualapai Peak** *summit* U.S.A.
27 F5 **Hua-lien** Taiwan
86 C5 **Huallaga** *r.* Peru
26 B2 **Hualong** China
57 B5 **Huambo** Angola
28 B1 **Huanan** China
91 C4 **Huancache, Sa** *mts* Arg.
86 C6 **Huancayo** Peru
26 E2 **Huangbizhuang Sk.** *resr* China
26 A2 **Huangcheng** China
26 E3 **Huangchuan** China
27 E4 **Huanggang** China
Huang Hai *sea see* **Yellow Sea**
26 E2 **Huang He** *r.* China
26 F2 **Huanghe Kou** *est.* China
23 H2 **Huanghetan** China
26 E2 **Huanghua** China
26 C3 **Huangling** China
27 C7 **Huangliu** China
27 E4 **Huangmei** China
30 D2 **Huangnihe** China
27 E4 **Huangpi** China
27 C5 **Huangping** China
26 D1 **Huangqi Hai** *l.* China
27 F4 **Huangshan** China
27 F4 **Huang Shan** *mt* China
27 E4 **Huangshi** China
26 B2 **Huang Shui** *r.* China
26 C2 **Huangtu Gaoyuan** *plat.* China
26 F2 **Huang Xian** China
27 F4 **Huangyan** China
26 A2 **Huangyuan** China
27 C5 **Huanjiang** China
26 C2 **Huan Jiang** *r.* China
30 C3 **Huanren** China
26 F2 **Huantai** China
86 C5 **Huanuco** Peru
86 E7 **Huanuni** Bol.
26 C2 **Huan Xian** China
27 G5 **Hua-p'ing Hsü** *i.* Taiwan
86 C5 **Huaráz** Peru
86 C6 **Huarmey** Peru
27 D4 **Huarong** China
86 C5 **Huascaran, Nevado de** *mt* Peru
88 B3 **Huasco** Chile
88 B3 **Huasco** *r.* Chile
30 D2 **Huashulinzi** China
82 C3 **Huatabampo** Mex.
26 C3 **Huating** China
30 A3 **Huatong** China
84 C3 **Huatusco** Mex.
84 C2 **Huauchinango** Mex.
84 C3 **Huautla** Mex.
27 D6 **Hua Xian** *Guangdong* China
26 E3 **Hua Xian** *Henan* China
26 D4 **Huayuan** *Hubei* China
27 C4 **Huayuan** *Hunan* China
27 C4 **Huayun** China
27 D6 **Huazhou** China
69 F3 **Hubbard Lake** *l.* U.S.A.
64 B2 **Hubbard, Mt** *mt* Can./U.S.A.
67 G2 **Hubbard, Pointe** *hd* Can.
26 D4 **Hubei** *div.* China
21 A3 **Hubli** India
30 D3 **Huch'ang** N. Korea
42 E3 **Hückelhoven** Ger.
39 F4 **Hucknall** U.K.
38 F4 **Huddersfield** U.K.
80 B6 **Huddy** U.S.A.
37 P6 **Hudiksvall** Sweden
68 E5 **Hudson** *MI* U.S.A.
81 G3 **Hudson** *NY* U.S.A.
68 A3 **Hudson** *WV* U.S.A.
78 F3 **Hudson** *r.* U.S.A.
65 J4 **Hudson Bay** *Sask.* Can.
63 K4 **Hudson Bay** *b.* Can.
81 G3 **Hudson Falls** U.S.A.
63 Q2 **Hudson Land** *reg.* Greenland
92 A3 **Hudson Mts** *mts* Ant.
64 E3 **Hudson's Hope** Can.
63 L3 **Hudson Strait** *str.* Can.
32 C1 **Huê** Vietnam
91 A4 **Huechucuicui, Pta** *pt* Chile
82 F5 **Huehuetenango** Guatemala
84 A1 **Huehueto, Cerro** *mt* Mex.
84 C3 **Huejotzingo** Mex.
84 C2 **Huejutla** Mex.
45 C4 **Huelva** Spain
91 B1 **Huentelauquén** Chile
91 B4 **Huequi, Volcán** *volc.* Chile
45 F4 **Huércal-Overa** Spain
45 F1 **Huesca** Spain
45 E4 **Huéscar** Spain
84 B3 **Huétamo** Mex.
80 E4 **Hughesville** U.S.A.
23 F5 **Hugli** *est.* India
23 G5 **Hugli-Chunchura** India
77 E5 **Hugo** U.S.A.
77 C4 **Hugoton** U.S.A.
26 D2 **Huguan** China
58 F3 **Huhudi** S. Africa
27 F5 **Hui'an** China
26 C2 **Hui'anbu** China
9 F3 **Huiarau Range** *mts* N.Z.
58 B3 **Huib-Hoch Plateau** *plat.* Namibia
27 E5 **Huichang** China
30 D3 **Huich'ŏn** N. Korea
27 E6 **Huidong** *Guangdong* China
27 B5 **Huidong** *Sichuan* China
30 D2 **Huifa** *r.* China
42 C3 **Huijbergen** Neth.
26 E3 **Huiji** *r.* China
27 E6 **Huilai** China
89 B4 **Huila, Nevado de** *mt* Col.
27 B5 **Huili** China
84 D3 **Huimanguillo** Mex.
26 E2 **Huimin** China
88 C2 **Huinahuaca** Arg.
30 D2 **Huinan** China
91 D2 **Huinca Renancó** Arg.
26 B3 **Huining** China
27 C5 **Huishui** China
23 G2 **Huiten Nur** *l.* China
27 C5 **Huitong** China
37 S6 **Huittinen** Fin.
84 C3 **Huitzuco** Mex.
26 C3 **Hui Xian** *Gansu* China
26 D3 **Hui Xian** *Henan* China
84 D4 **Huixtla** Mex.
27 B5 **Huize** China
27 E6 **Huizhou** China
24 C2 **Hujirt** Mongolia
27 E4 **Hukou** China
58 D1 **Hukuntsi** Botswana
68 E2 **Hulbert Lake** *l.* U.S.A.
18 B3 **Hulilan** Iran
28 C2 **Hulin** China
69 K3 **Hull** Can.
37 O8 **Hultsfred** Sweden
30 A3 **Huludao** China
24 D2 **Hulun Nur** *l.* China
51 F6 **Hulyaypole** Ukr.
24 E1 **Huma** China
86 F5 **Humaitá** Brazil
58 F7 **Humansdorp** S. Africa
18 B5 **Humayyān, J.** *h.* S. Arabia
38 H4 **Humber, Mouth of the** *est.* U.K.
65 H4 **Humboldt** Can.
72 C3 **Humboldt** *r.* U.S.A.
72 A3 **Humboldt Bay** *b.* U.S.A.
74 C1 **Humboldt Lake** *l.* U.S.A.
74 C1 **Humboldt Range** *mts* U.S.A.
74 D2 **Humbolt Salt Marsh** *marsh* U.S.A.
19 E5 **Hūmedān** Iran
27 D6 **Hu Men** *chan.* China
47 K6 **Humenné** Slovakia
8 F3 **Hume Reservoir** *resr* Austr.
74 C3 **Humphreys, Mt** *mt* U.S.A.
75 G4 **Humphreys Peak** *summit* U.S.A.
30 B3 **Hun** *r.* China
36 C4 **Húnaflói** *b.* Iceland
27 D5 **Hunan** *div.* China
30 F2 **Hunchun** China
30 F2 **Hunchun** *r.* China
43 L3 **Hundeluft** Ger.
37 M9 **Hundested** Denmark
49 K2 **Hunedoara** Romania
43 H4 **Hünfeld** Ger.
34 G4 **Hungary** *country* Europe
6 E4 **Hungerford** Austr.
30 D4 **Hŭngnam** N. Korea
72 D1 **Hungry Horse Res.** *resr* U.S.A.
27 □ **Hung Shui Kiu** *H.K.* China
27 C6 **Hưng Yên** Vietnam
30 D3 **Hunjiang** China
30 C3 **Hun Jiang** *r.* China
58 B3 **Huns Mountains** Namibia
42 F5 **Hunsrück** *reg.* Ger.
39 H5 **Hunstanton** U.K.
21 B3 **Hunsur** India
75 H4 **Hunt** U.S.A.
43 G2 **Hunte** *r.* Ger.
81 F3 **Hunter** U.S.A.
8 H2 **Hunter** *r.* Austr.
64 D4 **Hunter I.** *i.* Can.
7 H4 **Hunter I.** *i.* New Caledonia
6 E6 **Hunter Is** *is* Austr.
23 H6 **Hunter's Bay** *b.* Myanmar
9 C6 **Hunters Hills, The** *h.* N.Z.
81 F2 **Huntingdon** Can.
39 G5 **Huntingdon** U.K.
80 E4 **Huntingdon** U.S.A.
68 E5 **Huntington** *IN* U.S.A.
75 G2 **Huntington** *UT* U.S.A.
80 B5 **Huntington** *WV* U.S.A.
74 D5 **Huntington Beach** U.S.A.
9 E2 **Huntly** N.Z.
40 F3 **Huntly** U.K.
69 H3 **Huntsville** Can.
79 C5 **Huntsville** *AL* U.S.A.
77 E6 **Huntsville** *TX* U.S.A.
26 D2 **Hunyuan** China
22 C1 **Hunza** Pak.
22 C2 **Hunza** *r.* Pak.
30 B1 **Huolin** *r.* China
26 E2 **Huolu** China
32 C1 **Hương Khê** Vietnam
32 C1 **Hương Thuy** Vietnam
6 E2 **Huon Peninsula** *pen.* P.N.G.
26 E3 **Huoqiu** China
26 E4 **Huoshan** China
26 E4 **Huo Shan** *mt* China
27 F6 **Huo-shao Tao** *i.* Taiwan
26 D2 **Huo Xian** China
18 E4 **Ḥūr** Iran
69 G3 **Hurd, Cape** *hd* Can.
26 C1 **Hure Jadgai** China
30 A2 **Hure Qi** China
55 F2 **Hurghada** Egypt
68 C1 **Hurkett** Can.
41 C5 **Hurler's Cross** Rep. of Ireland
68 B2 **Hurley** U.S.A.
76 D2 **Huron** U.S.A.
68 C2 **Huron Bay** *b.* U.S.A.
69 F3 **Huron, Lake** *l.* Can./U.S.A.
68 D2 **Huron Mts** *h.* U.S.A.
75 F3 **Hurricane** U.S.A.
39 F6 **Hursley** U.K.
39 H6 **Hurst Green** U.K.
9 D5 **Hurunui** *r.* N.Z.
36 E3 **Húsavík** *Norðurland eystra* Iceland
36 C4 **Húsavík** *Vestfirðir* Iceland
47 O7 **Huși** Romania
37 O8 **Huskvarna** Sweden
62 C3 **Huslia** U.S.A.
37 J7 **Husnes** Norway
23 F4 **Hussainabad** India
46 D3 **Husum** Ger.
36 Q5 **Husum** Sweden
24 C2 **Hutag** Mongolia
76 D4 **Hutchinson** U.S.A.
75 G4 **Hutch Mtn** *mt* U.S.A.
32 A1 **Huthi** Myanmar
28 C2 **Hutou** China
65 N2 **Hut Point** *pt* Can.
80 D5 **Huttonsville** U.S.A.
26 D2 **Hutuo** *r.* China
16 G3 **Hüvek** Turkey
26 C3 **Hu Xian** China
26 F4 **Huzhou** China
26 A2 **Huzhu** China
36 E4 **Hvannadalshnúkur** *mt* Iceland
48 G3 **Hvar** *i.* Croatia
51 E6 **Hvardiys'ke** Ukr.
36 C4 **Hveragerði** Iceland
37 L8 **Hvide Sande** Denmark
36 C4 **Hvíta** *r.* Iceland
30 E3 **Hwadae** N. Korea
57 C5 **Hwange** Zimbabwe
57 C5 **Hwange National Park** Zimbabwe
30 C4 **Hwangju** N. Korea
57 D5 **Hwedza** Zimbabwe
81 H4 **Hyannis** *MA* U.S.A.
76 C3 **Hyannis** *NE* U.S.A.
24 B2 **Hyargas Nuur** *l.* Mongolia
64 C3 **Hydaburg** U.S.A.
9 C6 **Hyde** N.Z.
6 B5 **Hyden** Austr.
80 B6 **Hyden** U.S.A.
81 G4 **Hyde Park** U.S.A.
75 F5 **Hyder** U.S.A.
21 B2 **Hyderabad** India
22 B4 **Hyderabad** Pak.
44 H5 **Hyères** France
44 H5 **Hyères, Îles d'** *is* France
30 E3 **Hyesan** N. Korea
64 D2 **Hyland** *r.* Can.
37 J6 **Hyllestad** Norway
37 N8 **Hyltebruk** Sweden
8 C4 **Hynam** Austr.
29 D7 **Hyōnosen** *mt* Japan
36 V4 **Hyrynsalmi** Fin.
64 F3 **Hythe** Can.
39 J6 **Hythe** U.K.
29 B8 **Hyūga** Japan
37 T6 **Hyvinkää** Fin.

I

86 E6 **Iaco** *r.* Brazil
87 K6 **Iaçu** Brazil
57 E6 **Iakora** Madag.
49 M2 **Ialomița** *r.* Romania
49 M2 **Ianca** Romania
47 N7 **Iași** Romania
31 A3 **Iba** Phil.
54 C4 **Ibadan** Nigeria
89 B3 **Ibagué** Col.
75 F1 **Ibapah** U.S.A.
86 C3 **Ibarra** Ecuador
20 B7 **Ibb** Yemen
43 F2 **Ibbenbüren** Ger.
32 A4 **Ibi** Indon.
54 C4 **Ibi** Nigeria
90 C2 **Ibiá** Brazil
87 K4 **Ibiapaba, Serra da** *h.* Brazil
91 F1 **Ibicuí da Cruz** *r.* Brazil
90 E2 **Ibiraçu** Brazil
45 G3 **Ibiza** Spain
45 G3 **Ibiza** *i. Balearic Is* Spain
48 F6 **Iblei, Monti** *mts Sicily* Italy
18 B5 **Ibn Buşayyiş** *well* S. Arabia
87 K6 **Ibotirama** Brazil
20 E5 **Ibrā'** Oman
20 E5 **Ibrī** Oman
31 B1 **Ibuhos** *i.* Phil.
29 B9 **Ibusuki** Japan
86 C6 **Ica** Peru
89 D4 **Içana** Brazil
89 D4 **Içana** *r.* Brazil
75 E3 **Iceberg Canyon** U.S.A.
16 E3 **İçel** Turkey
34 C2 **Iceland** *country* Europe
21 A2 **Ichalkaranji** India
21 D2 **Ichchapuram** India
29 B8 **Ichifusa-yama** *mt* Japan
28 G5 **Ichinoseki** Japan
13 R4 **Ichinskaya Sopka** *mt* Rus. Fed.
51 E5 **Ichnya** Ukr.
30 D4 **Ich'ŏn** N. Korea
30 D5 **Ich'ŏn** S. Korea
42 B3 **Ichtegem** Belgium
43 J4 **Ichtershausen** Ger.
64 B3 **Icy Pt** *pt* U.S.A.
64 B3 **Icy Strait** *chan.* U.S.A.
77 E5 **Idabel** U.S.A.
72 D2 **Idaho** *div.* U.S.A.
72 D3 **Idaho City** U.S.A.
72 D3 **Idaho Falls** U.S.A.
42 F5 **Idar-Oberstein** Ger.
55 F2 **Idfu** Egypt
54 D2 **Idhān Awbārī** *des.* Libya
55 D2 **Idhān Murzūq** *des.* Libya
56 B4 **Idiofa** Congo(Zaire)
62 C3 **Iditarod** U.S.A.
36 S2 **Idivuoma** Sweden
16 C6 **Idku** Egypt
16 F4 **Idlib** Syria
37 N6 **Idre** Sweden
43 G4 **Idstein** Ger.
59 H6 **Idutywa** S. Africa
37 T8 **Iecava** Latvia
90 B3 **Iepê** Brazil
42 A4 **Ieper** Belgium
49 L7 **Ierapetra** Greece
57 D4 **Ifakara** Tanz.
57 E6 **Ifanadiana** Madag.
54 C4 **Ife** Nigeria
36 U1 **Ifjord** Norway
33 D2 **Igan** Malaysia
90 C3 **Igarapava** Brazil
12 K3 **Igarka** Rus. Fed.
22 C6 **Igatpuri** India
17 K2 **Iğdır** Turkey
37 P6 **Iggesund** Sweden
48 C5 **Iglesias** *Sardinia* Italy
63 K3 **Igloolik** Can.
66 B4 **Ignace** Can.
37 U9 **Ignalina** Lith.
51 C7 **İğneada** Turkey
49 N4 **İğneada Burnu** *pt* Turkey
47 Q3 **Igorevskaya** Rus. Fed.
49 J5 **Igoumenitsa** Greece
12 H3 **Igrim** Rus. Fed.
90 B4 **Iguaçu** *r.* Brazil
90 A4 **Iguaçu Falls** *waterfall* Arg./Brazil
90 E1 **Iguaí** Brazil
89 B4 **Iguaje, Mesa de** *h.* Col.
84 C3 **Iguala** Mex.
45 G2 **Igualada** Spain
90 C4 **Iguape** Brazil
90 D3 **Iguarapé** Brazil
90 A3 **Iguatemi** Brazil
90 A3 **Iguatemi** *r.* Brazil
87 L5 **Iguatu** Brazil
Iguazú, Cataratas do *waterfall see* **Iguaçu Falls**
56 A4 **Iguéla** Gabon
56 D4 **Igunga** Tanz.
57 E5 **Iharaña** Madag.
24 C2 **Ihbulag** Mongolia
57 E6 **Ihosy** Madag.
30 B2 **Ih Tal** China
29 F6 **Iide-san** *mt* Japan
36 U2 **Iijärvi** *l.* Fin.
36 T4 **Iijoki** *r.* Fin.
36 U5 **Iisalmi** Fin.
29 B8 **Iizuka** Japan
54 C4 **Ijebu-Ode** Nigeria
17 K1 **Ijevan** Armenia
42 C2 **IJmuiden** Neth.
42 D2 **IJssel** *r.* Neth.
42 D2 **IJsselmeer** *l.* Neth.
37 S6 **Ikaalinen** Fin.
59 G2 **Ikageleng** S. Africa
59 G3 **Ikageng** S. Africa
49 M6 **Ikaria** *i.* Greece
37 L8 **Ikast** Denmark
28 H3 **Ikeda** Japan
56 C4 **Ikela** Congo(Zaire)
49 K3 **Ikhtiman** Bulg.
58 F4 **Ikhutseng** S. Africa
29 A8 **Iki** *i.* Japan
51 H6 **Iki-Burul** Rus. Fed.
54 C4 **Ikom** Nigeria
57 E6 **Ikongo** Madag.
51 H6 **Ikryanoye** Rus. Fed.
56 D4 **Ikungu** Tanz.
31 B2 **Ilagan** Phil.
56 D3 **Ilaisamis** Kenya
18 B3 **Īlām** Iran
23 F4 **Ilam** Nepal
54 C4 **Ilaro** Nigeria
47 J4 **Iława** Pol.
65 H3 **Île-à-la-Crosse** Can.
65 H3 **Île-à-la-Crosse, Lac** *l.* Can.
56 C4 **Ilebo** Congo(Zaire)
56 D3 **Ileret** Kenya
50 G2 **Ileza** Rus. Fed.
65 K3 **Ilford** Can.
39 H6 **Ilford** U.K.
39 C6 **Ilfracombe** U.K.
16 D1 **Ilgaz** Turkey
16 D1 **Ilgaz D.** *mts* Turkey
16 C2 **Ilgın** Turkey
89 D5 **Ilha Grande** Brazil
90 D3 **Ilha Grande, Baía da** *b.* Brazil
90 B3 **Ilha Grande, Represa** *resr* Brazil
90 B3 **Ilha Solteíra, Represa** *resr* Brazil
45 B2 **Ílhavo** Port.
90 E1 **Ilhéus** Brazil
54 □ **Ilhéus Secos ou do Rombo** *i.* Cape Verde
62 C4 **Iliamna Lake** *l.* U.S.A.
16 G2 **İliç** Turkey
31 C4 **Iligan** Phil.
31 C4 **Iligan Bay** *b.* Phil.
50 H2 **Il'insko-Podomskoye** Rus. Fed.
81 F3 **Ilion** U.S.A.
21 B3 **Ilkal** India
39 F5 **Ilkeston** U.K.
38 F4 **Ilkley** U.K.
31 B5 **Illana Bay** *b.* Phil.
91 B1 **Illapel** Chile
91 B1 **Illapel** *r.* Chile
46 E7 **Iller** *r.* Ger.
51 D6 **Illichivs'k** Ukr.
86 E7 **Illimani, Nevado de** *mt* Bol.
68 C5 **Illinois** *div.* U.S.A.
68 C5 **Illinois** *r.* U.S.A.
68 B5 **Illinois and Mississippi Canal** *canal* U.S.A.
51 D5 **Illintsi** Ukr.
54 C2 **Illizi** Alg.
43 K4 **Ilm** *r.* Ger.
36 S5 **Ilmajoki** Fin.
43 J4 **Ilmenau** Ger.
43 J1 **Ilmenau** *r.* Ger.
50 D3 **Il'men', Ozero** *l.* Rus. Fed.
39 E7 **Ilminster** U.K.
86 D7 **Ilo** Peru
31 A4 **Iloc** *i.* Phil.
31 B4 **Iloilo** Phil.
36 W5 **Ilomantsi** Fin.
54 C4 **Ilorin** Nigeria
51 F6 **Ilovays'k** Ukr.
51 G5 **Ilovlya** Rus. Fed.
51 H5 **Ilovlya** *r.* Rus. Fed.
43 J2 **Ilsede** Ger.
63 N3 **Ilulissat** Greenland
29 C7 **Imabari** Japan
29 F6 **Imaichi** Japan
17 K6 **Imām al Ḥamzah** Iraq
16 E3 **İmamoğlu** Turkey
17 K5 **Imām Ḥamīd** Iraq
28 D2 **Iman** *r.* Rus. Fed.
29 A8 **Imari** Japan
89 E3 **Imataca, Serranía de** *mts* Venez.
37 V6 **Imatra** Fin.
29 E7 **Imazu** Japan
88 G3 **Imbituba** Brazil
90 B4 **Imbituva** Brazil
50 G3 **Imeni Babushkina** Rus. Fed.
19 F2 **Imeni Chapayeva** Turkm.
56 E3 **Īmī** Eth.
17 M2 **İmişli** Azer.
30 D6 **Imja-do** *i.* S. Korea
30 D4 **Imjin** *r.* N. Korea
48 D2 **Imola** Italy
59 H4 **Impendle** S. Africa
87 J5 **Imperatriz** Brazil
48 C3 **Imperia** Italy
76 C3 **Imperial** U.S.A.
74 D5 **Imperial Beach** U.S.A.
75 E5 **Imperial Valley** *v.* U.S.A.
56 B3 **Impfondo** Congo
23 H4 **Imphal** India
49 L4 **İmroz** Turkey
16 F5 **Imtān** Syria
31 A4 **Imuruan Bay** *b.* Phil.
29 E7 **Ina** Japan
86 E6 **Inambari** *r.* Peru
54 C2 **In Aménas** Alg.
9 C4 **Inangahua Junction** N.Z.
25 F7 **Inanwatan** Indon.
36 U2 **Inari** Fin.
36 U2 **Inarijärvi** *l.* Fin.
36 T2 **Inarijoki** *r.* Fin./Norway
45 H3 **Inca** Spain
51 C7 **İnce Burnu** *pt* Turkey
51 E7 **İnce Burnu** *pt* Turkey
16 D3 **İncekum Burnu** *pt* Turkey
16 E2 **İncesu** Turkey
41 E5 **Inch** Rep. of Ireland
40 C2 **Inchard, Loch** *b.* U.K.
40 E4 **Inchkeith** *i.* U.K.
30 D5 **Inch'ŏn** S. Korea
59 K2 **Incomati** *r.* Moz.
40 B5 **Indaal, Loch** *in.* U.K.
90 D2 **Indaiá** *r.* Brazil
90 B2 **Indaiá Grande** *r.* Brazil
36 P5 **Indalsälven** *r.* Sweden
37 J6 **Indalstø** Norway
84 A1 **Indé** Mex.
74 C3 **Independence** *CA* U.S.A.
68 B4 **Independence** *IA* U.S.A.
77 E4 **Independence** *KS* U.S.A.
68 A2 **Independence** *MN* U.S.A.
76 E4 **Independence** *MO* U.S.A.
80 C6 **Independence** *VA* U.S.A.
68 B3 **Independence** *WV* U.S.A.
72 C3 **Independence Mts** U.S.A.
14 D2 **Inderborskiy** Kazak.
21 B2 **Indi** India
10 J7 **India** *country* Asia
68 D2 **Indian** *r.* U.S.A.
80 D4 **Indiana** U.S.A.
68 D5 **Indiana** *div.* U.S.A.
68 D5 **Indiana Dunes National Lakeshore** *res.* U.S.A.
93 M7 **Indian-Antarctic Basin** *sea feature* Ind. Ocean
93 O7 **Indian-Antarctic Ridge** *sea feature* Pac. Oc.
68 D6 **Indianapolis** U.S.A.
Indian Desert *see* **Thar Desert**
67 J3 **Indian Harbour** Can.
81 F3 **Indian Lake** *NY* U.S.A.
68 D3 **Indian Lake** *l. MI* U.S.A.
80 B4 **Indian Lake** *l. OH* U.S.A.
80 D4 **Indian Lake** *l. PA* U.S.A.
76 E3 **Indianola** *IA* U.S.A.
77 F5 **Indianola** *MS* U.S.A.
75 F2 **Indian Peak** *summit* U.S.A.
68 E3 **Indian River** U.S.A.
75 E3 **Indian Springs** U.S.A.
75 G4 **Indian Wells** U.S.A.
13 Q2 **Indigirka** *r.* Rus. Fed.
49 J2 **Inđija** Yugo.
64 F2 **Indin Lake** *l.* Can.
74 D5 **Indio** U.S.A.
7 G3 **Indispensable Reefs** *rf* Solomon Is
11 N10 **Indonesia** *country* Asia
22 C5 **Indore** India
33 C4 **Indramayu, Tanjung** *pt* Indon.
33 B3 **Indrapura** Indon.
21 C2 **Indravati** *r.* India
44 E3 **Indre** *r.* France
Indur *see* **Nizamabad**
22 B4 **Indus** *r.* Pak.
22 A5 **Indus, Mouths of the** *est.* Pak.
59 G5 **Indwe** S. Africa
51 E7 **İnebolu** Turkey
16 B1 **İnegöl** Turkey
80 B6 **Inez** U.S.A.
58 D7 **Infanta, Cape** *hd* S. Africa
84 B3 **Infiernillo, L.** *l.* Mex.
68 D3 **Ingalls** U.S.A.
65 J2 **Ingalls Lake** *l.* Can.

56 C4 Kashyukulu Congo(Zaire)
50 G4 Kasimov Rus. Fed.
78 B4 Kaskaskia r. U.S.A.
65 L3 Kaskattama r. Can.
37 R5 Kaskinen Fin.
56 C4 Kasongo Congo(Zaire)
56 B4 Kasongo-Lunda Congo(Zaire)
49 M7 Kasos i. Greece
49 M7 Kasou, Steno chan. Greece
51 H7 Kaspi Georgia
51 H7 Kaspiysk Rus. Fed.
Kaspiyskoye More sea see Caspian Sea
47 P3 Kasplya Rus. Fed.
55 F3 Kassala Sudan
49 K4 Kassandra pen. Greece
49 K4 Kassandras, Kolpos b. Greece
43 H3 Kassel Ger.
54 C1 Kasserine Tunisia
68 A3 Kasson U.S.A.
16 D1 Kastamonu Turkey
42 F4 Kastellaun Ger.
49 K7 Kastelli Greece
42 C3 Kasterlee Belgium
49 J4 Kastoria Greece
50 E4 Kastsyukovichy Belarus
29 E7 Kasugai Japan
56 D4 Kasulu Tanz.
29 D7 Kasumi Japan
29 G6 Kasumiga-ura l. Japan
51 J7 Kasumkent Rus. Fed.
57 D5 Kasungu Malawi
22 C3 Kasur Pak.
81 J2 Katahdin, Mt mt U.S.A.
22 D2 Kataklik Jammu and Kashmir
56 C4 Katako-Kombe Congo(Zaire)
22 D5 Katangi India
6 B5 Katanning Austr.
19 H3 Katawaz Afgh.
56 C4 Katea Congo(Zaire)
49 K4 Katerini Greece
64 C3 Kate's Needle mt Can./U.S.A.
57 D5 Katete Zambia
23 E5 Katghora India
24 B4 Katha Myanmar
6 D3 Katherine r. Austr.
22 B5 Kathiawar pen. India
16 D6 Kathīb el Henu sand dunes Egypt
21 C4 Kathiraveli Sri Lanka
59 H3 Kathlehong S. Africa
23 F4 Kathmandu Nepal
58 E3 Kathu S. Africa
22 C2 Kathua Jammu and Kashmir
54 B3 Kati Mali
23 F4 Katihar India
9 E2 Katikati N.Z.
59 G6 Kati-Kati S. Africa
57 C5 Katima Mulilo Namibia
54 B4 Katiola Côte d'Ivoire
58 D4 Katkop Hills reg. S. Africa
Katmandu see Kathmandu
49 J5 Kato Achaïa Greece
22 D5 Katol India
32 □ Katong Sing.
8 H2 Katoomba Austr.
47 J5 Katowice Pol.
23 G5 Katoya India
37 P7 Katrineholm Sweden
40 D4 Katrine, Loch l. U.K.
54 C3 Katsina Nigeria
54 C4 Katsina-Ala Nigeria
29 G6 Katsuta Japan
29 G7 Katsuura Japan
29 E6 Katsuyama Japan
67 G2 Kattaktoc, Cap hd Can.
19 G2 Kattakurgan Uzbek.
19 G3 Kattasang Hills mts Afgh.
37 M8 Kattegat str. Denmark/Sweden
22 B3 Katuri Pak.
42 C2 Katwijk aan Zee Neth.
43 H5 Katzenbuckel h. Ger.
74 □2 Kauai i. U.S.A.
74 □2 Kauai Channel U.S.A.
43 F4 Kaub Ger.
43 H3 Kaufungen Ger.
37 S5 Kauhajoki Fin.
36 S5 Kauhava Fin.
36 T3 Kaukonen Fin.
74 □2 Kaula i. U.S.A.
74 □2 Kaulakahi Channel U.S.A.
67 H2 Kaumajet Mts mts Can.
74 □2 Kaunakakai U.S.A.
37 S9 Kaunas Lith.
37 U8 Kaunata Latvia
54 C3 Kaura-Namoda Nigeria
27 □ Kau Sai Chau i. H.K. China
36 S5 Kaustinen Fin.
36 S2 Kautokeino Norway
32 A3 Kau-ye Kyun i. Myanmar
49 K4 Kavadarci Macedonia
16 F1 Kavak Turkey
49 L4 Kavala Greece
28 D2 Kavalerovo Rus. Fed.
21 C3 Kavali India
18 D4 Kavār Iran
21 A4 Kavaratti i. India
49 N3 Kavarna Bulg.
21 B4 Kāveri r. India
18 D4 Kavīr des. Iran
18 D3 Kavir salt flat Iran
18 D3 Kavir salt flat Iran
18 D3 Kavir, Dasht-e des. Iran
18 D3 Kavīr-e Hāj Ali Qoli salt l. Iran
18 D3 Kavīr-i-Namak salt flat Iran
29 F7 Kawagoe Japan
29 F7 Kawaguchi Japan
74 □2 Kawaihae U.S.A.
9 E1 Kawakawa N.Z.
57 C4 Kawambwa Zambia
66 E5 Kawartha Lakes l. Can.
29 F7 Kawasaki Japan
9 E2 Kawau I. i. N.Z.
67 G2 Kawawachikamach Can.
9 F3 Kawerau N.Z.
9 E3 Kawhia N.Z.
9 E3 Kawhia Harbour in. N.Z.
74 D3 Kawich Range mts U.S.A.
32 A1 Kawkareik Myanmar
32 A1 Kawludo Myanmar
18 E6 Kawr, J. mt Oman
32 A3 Kawthaung Myanmar
54 B3 Kaya Burkina
16 F2 Kayadibi Turkey
13 M2 Kayak Rus. Fed.
33 E2 Kayan r. Indon.
56 C4 Kayanaza Burundi
21 B4 Kayankulam India
72 F3 Kaycee U.S.A.
57 C4 Kayembe-Mukulu Congo(Zaire)
75 G3 Kayenta U.S.A.
54 A3 Kayes Mali
54 A4 Kayima Sierra Leone
15 F2 Kaynar Kazak.
16 F2 Kaynar Turkey
16 F3 Kaypak Turkey
51 H5 Kaysatskoye Rus. Fed.
16 E2 Kayseri Turkey
33 B3 Kayuagung Indon.
12 K3 Kayyerkan Rus. Fed.
13 P2 Kazach'ye Rus. Fed.
Kazakh see Qazax
14 F1 Kazakskiy Melkosopochnik reg. Kazak.
10 G5 Kazakstan country Asia
50 J4 Kazan' Rus. Fed.
65 K2 Kazan r. Can.
16 D3 Kazancı Turkey
50 J4 Kazanka r. Rus. Fed.
49 L3 Kazanlŭk Bulg.
24 G4 Kazan-rettō is Japan
51 G5 Kazanskaya Rus. Fed.
51 H7 Kazbek mt Georgia/Rus. Fed.
49 M5 Kaz Dağı mts Turkey
18 C4 Kāzerūn Iran
50 J2 Kazhim Rus. Fed.
19 F5 Kazhmak r. Pak.
47 K6 Kazincbarcika Hungary
19 F5 Kazmīr Iran
51 H7 Kazret'i Georgia
51 J5 Kaztalovka Kazak.
28 G4 Kazuno Japan
12 H3 Kazymskiy Mys Rus. Fed.
49 L6 Kea i. Greece
41 E3 Keady U.K.
74 □2 Kealakekua Bay b. U.S.A.
17 M4 K-e-Alvand mt Iran
75 G4 Keams Canyon U.S.A.
76 D3 Kearney U.S.A.
75 G5 Kearny U.S.A.
16 G2 Keban Turkey
16 G2 Keban Barajı resr Turkey
54 A3 Kébémèr Senegal
16 F4 Kebīr r. Lebanon/Syria
55 E3 Kebkabiya Sudan
36 Q3 Kebnekaise mt Sweden
80 B2 Kebock Head hd U.K.
56 E3 K'ebrī Dehar Eth.
33 C4 Kebumen Indon.
64 D3 Kechika r. Can.
16 C3 Keçiborlu Turkey
47 J7 Kecskemét Hungary
17 H1 K'eda Georgia
37 S9 Kėdainiai Lith.
17 L4 K-e Dalakhānī h. Iraq
22 D3 Kedar Kanta mt India
22 D3 Kedarnath Peak mt India
67 G4 Kedgwick Can.
33 D4 Kediri Indon.
54 A3 Kédougou Senegal
64 D2 Keele r. Can.
64 C2 Keele Pk summit Can.
73 C4 Keeler U.S.A.
31 A5 Keenapusan i. Phil.
81 G3 Keene U.S.A.
40 F4 Keen, Mount mt U.K.
8 H1 Keepit Reservoir Austr.
42 C3 Keerbergen Belgium
57 B6 Keetmanshoop Namibia
65 L6 Keewatin Can.
65 L5 Keewatin U.S.A.
49 J5 Kefallonia i. Greece
25 E7 Kefamenanu Indon.
36 B4 Keflavík Iceland
21 C5 Kegalla Sri Lanka
15 F2 Kegen Kazak.
62 G2 Keglo, Baie de b. Can.
51 H6 Kegul'ta Rus. Fed.
37 T7 Kehra Estonia
38 F4 Keighley U.K.
37 T7 Keila Estonia
58 D4 Keimoes S. Africa
36 U5 Keitele Fin.
36 T5 Keitele l. Fin.
8 C4 Keith Austr.
40 F3 Keith U.K.
64 E1 Keith Arm b. Can.
67 G5 Kejimkujik National Park Can.
74 □2 Kekaha U.S.A.
47 K7 Kékes mt Hungary
22 C4 Kekri India
15 F6 Kelai i. Maldives
26 D2 Kelan China
33 B2 Kelang Malaysia
32 B4 Kelantan r. Malaysia
42 E4 Kelberg Ger.
43 K6 Kelheim Ger.
48 D6 Kelibia Tunisia
19 G2 Kelif Turkm.
19 F2 Kelifskiy Uzboy marsh Turkm.
43 G4 Kelkheim (Taunus) Ger.
17 G1 Kelkit Turkey
16 F1 Kelkit r. Turkey
64 E2 Keller Lake l. Can.
80 B4 Kelleys I. i. U.S.A.
72 C2 Kellogg U.S.A.
36 V3 Kelloselkä Fin.
41 E4 Kells Rep. of Ireland
37 S9 Kelmė Lith.
42 E4 Kelmis Belgium
55 D4 Kelo Chad
64 F5 Kelowna Can.
64 D4 Kelsey Bay Can.
74 A2 Kelseyville U.S.A.
40 F5 Kelso U.K.
75 E4 Kelso CA U.S.A.
72 B2 Kelso WA U.S.A.
33 B2 Keluang Malaysia
65 J4 Kelvington Can.
50 E1 Kem' Rus. Fed.
50 E1 Kem' r. Rus. Fed.
17 G2 Kemah Turkey
16 G2 Kemaliye Turkey
49 M5 Kemalpaşa Turkey
64 D4 Kemano Can.
16 C3 Kemer Antalya Turkey
16 B3 Kemer Muğla Turkey
16 B3 Kemer Barajı resr Turkey
24 A1 Kemerovo Rus. Fed.
36 T4 Kemi Fin.
36 U3 Kemijärvi Fin.
36 U3 Kemijärvi l. Fin.
36 T3 Kemijoki r. Fin.
72 E3 Kemmerer U.S.A.
43 K5 Kemnath Ger.
40 F3 Kemnay U.K.
36 T4 Kempele Fin.
42 E3 Kempen Ger.
42 C3 Kempen reg. Belgium
77 D5 Kemp, L. l. U.S.A.
92 D4 Kemp Land reg. Ant.
92 B2 Kemp Pen. pen. Ant.
79 E7 Kemp's Bay Bahamas
46 E7 Kempten (Allgäu) Ger.
66 F4 Kempt, L. l. Can.
59 H3 Kempton Park S. Africa
69 K3 Kemptville Can.
33 D4 Kemujan i. Indon.
22 E4 Ken r. India
62 C3 Kenai U.S.A.
62 C4 Kenai Mts mts U.S.A.
19 F3 Kenar-e-Kapeh Afgh.
38 E3 Kendal U.K.
65 M2 Kendall, Cape hd Can.
68 E5 Kendallville U.S.A.
33 C4 Kendang, Gunung volc. Indon.
25 E7 Kendari Indon.
33 D3 Kendawangan Indon.
55 D3 Kendégué Chad
23 F5 Kendrāparha India
72 C2 Kendrick U.S.A.
75 G4 Kendrick Peak summit U.S.A.
8 G1 Kenebri Austr.
77 D6 Kenedy U.S.A.
54 A4 Kenema Sierra Leone
56 B4 Kenge Congo(Zaire)
25 B4 Kengtung Myanmar
58 D4 Kenhardt S. Africa
54 B3 Kéniéba Mali
54 B1 Kénitra Morocco
26 F2 Kenli China
41 B6 Kenmare Rep. of Ireland
76 C1 Kenmare U.S.A.
41 A6 Kenmare River in. Rep. of Ireland
42 E5 Kenn Ger.
73 G5 Kenna U.S.A.
81 J2 Kennebec r. U.S.A.
81 H3 Kennebunk U.S.A.
81 H3 Kennebunkport U.S.A.
77 F6 Kenner U.S.A.
39 F6 Kennet r. U.K.
77 F4 Kennett U.S.A.
72 C2 Kennewick U.S.A.
69 G1 Kenogami Lake Can.
69 G1 Kenogamissi Lake l. Can.
64 B2 Keno Hill Can.
65 L5 Kenora Can.
68 D4 Kenosha U.S.A.
50 F2 Kenozero, Ozero l. Rus. Fed.
81 G4 Kent CT U.S.A.
77 B6 Kent TX U.S.A.
72 B2 Kent WA U.S.A.
38 E3 Kent r. U.K.
59 H6 Kentani S. Africa
68 D5 Kentland U.S.A.
80 B4 Kenton U.S.A.
80 A6 Kentucky div. U.S.A.
71 K4 Kentucky r. KY U.S.A.
79 B4 Kentucky Lake l. U.S.A.
67 H4 Kentville Can.
77 F6 Kentwood LA U.S.A.
68 E4 Kentwood MI U.S.A.
53 H5 Kenya country Africa
Kenya, Mount mt see Kirinyaga
68 A3 Kenyon U.S.A.
92 B2 Kenyon Pen. pen. Ant.
74 □2 Keokea U.S.A.
68 B5 Keokuk U.S.A.
32 C1 Keo Neua, Col de pass Laos/Vietnam
68 B5 Keosauqua U.S.A.
6 F4 Keppel Bay b. Austr.
32 □ Keppel Harbour chan. Sing.
16 B2 Kepsut Turkey
19 E4 Kerāh Iran
21 A4 Kerala div. India
8 D3 Kerang Austr.
54 C4 Kéran, Parc National de la nat. park Togo
37 T6 Kerava Fin.
45 G4 Kerba Alg.
51 F6 Kerch Ukr.
6 E2 Kerema P.N.G.
64 F5 Keremeos Can.
51 E7 Kerempe Burun pt Turkey
56 D2 Keren Eritrea
18 E2 Kergeli Turkm.
93 J7 Kerguélen i. Ind. Ocean
93 J7 Kerguelen Ridge sea feature Ind. Ocean
56 D4 Kericho Kenya
9 D1 Kerikeri N.Z.
37 V6 Kerimäki Fin.
33 B3 Kerinci, G. volc. Indon.
23 E2 Keriya Shankou pass China
42 E3 Kerken Ger.
19 G2 Kerki Turkm.
19 G2 Kerkichi Turkm.
49 K4 Kerkinitis, Limni l. Greece
49 H5 Kerkyra Greece
Kerkyra i. see Corfu
55 F3 Kerma Sudan
5 K8 Kermadec Islands is N.Z.
94 H8 Kermadec Tr. sea feature Pac. Oc.
18 E4 Kermān Iran
74 B3 Kerman U.S.A.
19 E4 Kermān Desert des. Iran
18 B3 Kermānshāh Iran
18 D4 Kermānshāhān Iran
77 C6 Kermit U.S.A.
73 C5 Kern r. U.S.A.
67 G2 Kernertut, Cap pt Can.
74 C4 Kernville U.S.A.
50 K2 Keros Rus. Fed.
49 L6 Keros i. Greece
54 B4 Kérouané Guinea
42 E4 Kerpen Ger.
92 B5 Kerr, C. c. Ant.
65 H4 Kerrobert Can.
77 D6 Kerrville U.S.A.
41 B5 Kerry Head hd Rep. of Ireland
32 B4 Kerteh Malaysia
37 M9 Kerteminde Denmark
16 D4 Keryneia Cyprus
50 H3 Kerzhenets r. Rus. Fed.
66 D3 Kesagami Lake l. Can.
37 V6 Kesälahti Fin.
51 C7 Keşan Turkey
16 G1 Keşap Turkey
28 G5 Kesennuma Japan
19 H2 Keshem Afgh.
19 G2 Keshendeh-ye Bala Afgh.
22 B5 Keshod India
17 M5 Keshvar Iran
16 D2 Keskin Turkey
50 E2 Keskozero Rus. Fed.
42 E3 Kessel Neth.
59 H4 Kestell S. Africa
36 W4 Kesten'ga Rus. Fed.
36 U4 Kestilä Fin.
69 H3 Keswick Can.
38 D3 Keswick U.K.
46 H7 Keszthely Hungary
12 K4 Ket' r. Rus. Fed.
54 C4 Keta Ghana
32 □ Ketam, P. i. Sing.
33 D3 Ketapang Indon.
64 C3 Ketchikan U.S.A.
42 D2 Ketelmeer l. Neth.
19 G5 Keti Bandar Pak.
39 G5 Kettering U.K.
80 A5 Kettering U.S.A.
64 F5 Kettle r. Can.
68 A2 Kettle r. U.S.A.
80 E4 Kettle Creek r. U.S.A.
74 C3 Kettleman City U.S.A.
72 C1 Kettle River Ra. mts U.S.A.
80 E3 Keuka Lake l. U.S.A.
37 T5 Keuruu Fin.
68 C5 Kewanee U.S.A.
68 D3 Kewaunee U.S.A.
68 C2 Keweenaw Bay b. U.S.A.
68 C2 Keweenaw Peninsula U.S.A.
68 D2 Keweenaw Pt pt U.S.A.
89 E3 Keweigek Guyana
66 F3 Keyano Can.
69 G3 Key Harbour Can.
79 D7 Key Largo U.S.A.
41 C3 Key, Lough l. Rep. of Ireland
39 E6 Keynsham U.K.
80 D5 Keyser U.S.A.
80 D5 Keysers Ridge U.S.A.
75 G6 Keystone Peak summit U.S.A.
80 D6 Keysville U.S.A.
9 A6 Key, The N.Z.
17 M4 Keytū Iran
79 D7 Key West FL U.S.A.
68 B4 Key West IA U.S.A.
81 H3 Kezar Falls U.S.A.
57 C6 Kezi Zimbabwe
47 K6 Kežmarok Slovakia
58 D2 Kgalagadi div. Botswana
59 G2 Kgatleng div. Botswana
58 D1 Kgomofatshe Pan salt pan Botswana
58 F2 Kgoro Pan salt pan Botswana
59 G3 Kgotsong S. Africa
24 F2 Khabarovsk Rus. Fed.
Khabis see Shahdāb
17 H4 Khabur r. Syria
17 J7 Khadd, W. al watercourse S. Arabia
18 B6 Khafs Daghrah S. Arabia
22 E4 Khaga India
23 G5 Khagrachari Bangl.
22 B3 Khairgarh Pak.
22 B4 Khairpur Pak.
19 G2 Khaja du Koh h. Afgh.
22 D4 Khajurāho India
57 C6 Khakhea Botswana
19 G3 Khakīr Afgh.
19 G4 Khak-rēz Afgh.
19 G4 Khakriz reg. Afgh.
19 G2 Khalach Turkm.
18 C4 Khalafabād Iran
18 C3 Khalajestan reg. Iran
22 D2 Khalatse Jammu and Kashmir
22 A3 Khalifat mt Pak.
19 E3 Khalilabad Iran
18 B2 Khalkhāl Iran
23 F6 Khallikot India
50 D4 Khalopyenichy Belarus
24 C1 Khamar-Daban, Khrebet mts Rus. Fed.
22 C5 Khambhat India
22 B5 Khambhat, Gulf of g. India
22 D5 Khamgaon India
32 C1 Khamkkeut Laos
18 B5 Khamma well S. Arabia
21 C2 Khammam India
13 N3 Khamra Rus. Fed.
18 C3 Khamseh reg. Iran
19 H2 Khānābād Afgh.
17 J5 Khān al Baghdādī Iraq
17 K5 Khān al Maḥāwīl Iraq
17 K5 Khān al Mashāhidah Iraq
17 K5 Khān al Muşalla Iraq
21 A3 Khanapur India
18 B2 Khānaqāh Iran
17 K4 Khānaqīn Iraq
17 K2 Khanasur Pass Iran/Turkey
16 F6 Khān az Zabīb Jordan
22 C2 Khanbari Pass pass Jammu and Kashmir
8 G4 Khancoban Austr.
22 B2 Khand Pass Afgh./Pak.
22 D5 Khandwa India
13 P3 Khandyga Rus. Fed.
22 B3 Khanewal Pak.
32 D2 Khanh Dương Vietnam
22 D4 Khaniadhana India
18 D4 Khanīyak Iran
17 K5 Khān Jadwal Iraq
28 C2 Khanka, Lake l. China/Rus. Fed.
Khanka, Ozero l. see Khanka, Lake
22 C2 Khanki Weir barrage Pak.
22 D3 Khanna India
22 B3 Khanpur Pak.
17 K6 Khān Ruḥābah Iraq
16 F4 Khān Shaykhūn Syria
15 F2 Khantau Kazak.
12 L3 Khantayskoye, Ozero l. Rus. Fed.
12 H3 Khanty-Mansiysk Rus. Fed.
16 E6 Khān Yūnis Gaza
32 A3 Khao Chum Thong Thai.
22 D5 Khapa India
18 C3 Khar r. Iran
51 H6 Kharabali Rus. Fed.
23 F5 Kharagpur India
18 E2 Kharakī Iran
19 G4 Kharan Pak.
18 E5 Khārān r. Iran
18 D3 Kharānaq Iran
22 B2 Kharbin Pass Afgh.
22 C6 Khardi India
22 D2 Khardung La pass India
19 F3 Kharez Ilias Afgh.
17 L6 Kharfiyah Iraq
18 C4 Khārg Islands is Iran
22 C5 Khargon India
22 C4 Khari r. Rajasthan India
22 C2 Kharian Pak.
23 E5 Khariar India
18 C6 Kharit S. Arabia
51 F5 Kharkiv Ukr.
Khar'kov see Kharkiv
49 L4 Kharmanli Bulg.
50 G3 Kharovsk Rus. Fed.
23 E5 Kharsia India
55 F3 Khartoum Sudan
18 E2 Khasardag, Gora mt Turkm.
51 H7 Khasav'yurt Rus. Fed.
19 F4 Khash Afgh.
19 F4 Khāsh Iran
19 F4 Khash Desert des. Afgh.
18 C5 Khashm Bijrān h. S. Arabia
19 F4 Khash Rūd r. Afgh.
51 G7 Khashuri Georgia
23 G4 Khāsi Hills h. India
49 L4 Khaskovo Bulg.
13 M2 Khatanga Rus. Fed.
13 M2 Khatanga, Gulf of b. Rus. Fed.
16 D6 Khatmia Pass Egypt
13 T3 Khatyrka Rus. Fed.
18 C4 Khāvar Iran
22 B5 Khavda India
19 H3 Khawak Pass Afgh.
18 E5 Khawr Fakkan U.A.E.
32 A2 Khawsa Myanmar
59 F5 Khayamnandi S. Africa
58 C7 Khayelitsha S. Africa
17 J3 Khāzir r. Iraq
32 C1 Khê Bo Vietnam
21 A2 Khed India
22 C4 Khedbrahma India
19 E3 Khedrī Iran
22 E3 Khela India
45 H4 Khemis Miliana Alg.
54 C1 Khenchela Alg.
54 B1 Khenifra Morocco
18 D4 Kherāmeh Iran
22 D4 Kherli India
18 C4 Khersan r. Iran
51 E6 Kherson Ukr.
18 C4 Khesht Iran
13 L2 Kheta r. Rus. Fed.
18 D4 Kheyrābād Iran
18 D2 Khezerābād Iran
22 D4 Khilchipur India
16 F4 Khirbat Isrīyah Syria
17 J6 Khirr, Wādī al watercourse S. Arabia
22 D2 Khitai P. pass China/Jammu and Kashmir
18 B2 Khīyāv Iran
37 V6 Khiytola Rus. Fed.
51 C5 Khmel'nyts'kyy Ukr.
51 C5 Khmil'nyk Ukr.
18 B2 Khodā Āfarīn Iran
19 G2 Khodzhambass Turkm.
14 D2 Khodzheyli Uzbek.
58 D2 Khokhowe Pan salt pan Botswana
22 B4 Khokhropar Pak.
50 G1 Kholmogory Rus. Fed.
24 G2 Kholmsk Rus. Fed.
47 Q3 Kholm-Zhirkovskiy Rus. Fed.
17 M3 Khoman Iran
58 B1 Khomas div. Namibia
58 A1 Khomas Highland reg. Namibia
18 C3 Khomeyn Iran
17 M4 Khondāb Iran
51 G7 Khoni Georgia
18 D5 Khonj Iran
13 Q3 Khonuu Rus. Fed.
51 G5 Khoper r. Rus. Fed.
24 F2 Khor Rus. Fed.
24 F2 Khor r. Rus. Fed.
22 B4 Khora Pak.
23 F5 Khordha India
18 C5 Khor Duweihin b. S. Arabia/U.A.E.
24 C1 Khorinsk Rus. Fed.
57 B6 Khorixas Namibia
28 C2 Khorol Rus. Fed.
51 E5 Khorol Ukr.
17 L2 Khoroslū Dāgh h. Iran
18 C3 Khorramābād Iran
17 M3 Khorram Darreh Iran
18 C4 Khorramshahr Iran
19 H2 Khorugh Tajik.
19 E3 Khosf Iran
51 H6 Khosheutovo Rus. Fed.
18 C4 Khosravī Iran
18 C4 Khosrowābād Iran
17 K4 Khosrowvī Iran
18 D4 Khowrjān Iran
18 D3 Khowrnag, Kūh-e mt Iran
19 H3 Khowst Afgh.
24 E1 Khrebet Dzhagdy mts Rus. Fed.
23 H5 Khreum Myanmar
23 G4 Khri r. India
50 H2 Khristoforovo Rus. Fed.
13 Q2 Khroma r. Rus. Fed.
14 D1 Khromtau Kazak.
28 D2 Khrustalnyy Rus. Fed.
47 O6 Khrystynivka Ukr.
19 G5 Khude Hills mts Pak.
58 F1 Khudumelapye Botswana
18 B5 Khuff S. Arabia
19 F5 Khūh Lab, Ra's pt Iran
58 D3 Khuis Botswana
14 E2 Khŭjand Tajik.
32 C2 Khu Khan Thai.
19 G3 Khulm r. Afgh.
23 G5 Khulna Bangl.
17 J1 Khulo Georgia
59 G3 Khuma S. Africa
22 C2 Khunjerab Pass China/Jammu and Kashmir
18 C3 Khunsar Iran
23 F5 Khunti India
18 C3 Khūr Iran
22 D4 Khurai India
18 D5 Khūran chan. Iran
19 G3 Khurd, Koh-i- mt Afgh.
22 D3 Khurja India
19 F3 Khurmalik Afgh.
22 C2 Khushab Pak.
17 M3 Khūshāvar Iran
19 E4 Khushk Rud Iran
19 F3 Khuspas Afgh.
51 B5 Khust Ukr.
59 G3 Khutsong S. Africa
19 G5 Khuzdar Pak.
19 F3 Khvāf Iran
50 J4 Khvalynsk Rus. Fed.
18 D3 Khvor Iran
18 E3 Khvord Nārvan Iran
18 C4 Khvormūj Iran
17 L3 Khvosh Maqām Iran
18 B2 Khvoy Iran
50 E3 Khvoynaya Rus. Fed.
32 A2 Khwae Noi r. Thai.
19 F4 Khwaja Ali Afgh.
19 H2 Khwaja Muhammad Range mts Afgh.
22 B2 Khyber Pass Afgh./Pak.
8 H3 Kiama Austr.
31 C5 Kiamba Phil.
56 C4 Kiambi Congo(Zaire)
77 E5 Kiamichi r. U.S.A.
36 V4 Kiantajärvi l. Fin.
18 D2 Kīāseh Iran
22 D2 Kibar India
31 C5 Kibawe Phil.
56 D4 Kibaya Tanz.
57 D4 Kibiti Tanz.
56 C4 Kibombo Congo(Zaire)
56 D4 Kibondo Tanz.
49 J4 Kičevo Macedonia
50 H3 Kichmengskiy Gorodok Rus. Fed.
54 C3 Kidal Mali
39 E5 Kidderminster U.K.
56 D3 Kidepo Valley National Park Uganda
54 A3 Kidira Senegal
22 D2 Kidmang Jammu and Kashmir
9 F3 Kidnappers, Cape c. N.Z.
39 E4 Kidsgrove U.K.
46 E3 Kiel Ger.
68 C4 Kiel U.S.A.
47 K5 Kielce Pol.
38 E2 Kielder Water resr U.K.
46 E3 Kieler Bucht b. Ger.
57 C5 Kienge Congo(Zaire)
42 F3 Kierspe Ger.
51 D5 Kiev Ukr.
54 A3 Kiffa Maur.
49 K5 Kifisia Greece
17 K4 Kifrī Iraq
56 D4 Kigali Rwanda
17 H2 Kiğı Turkey
67 H2 Kiglapait Mts mts Can.
56 C4 Kigoma Tanz.
36 S3 Kihlanki Fin.
37 S5 Kihniö Fin.
36 T4 Kiiminki Fin.
29 D8 Kii-sanchi mts Japan
29 D8 Kii-suidō chan. Japan
49 J2 Kikinda Yugo.
19 F5 Kikki Pak.
50 H3 Kiknur Rus. Fed.
28 G4 Kikonai Japan
57 C4 Kikondja Congo(Zaire)
6 E2 Kikori P.N.G.
6 E2 Kikori r. P.N.G.
56 B4 Kikwit Congo(Zaire)
37 P6 Kilafors Sweden
21 B4 Kilakkarai India
22 D2 Kilar India
74 □2 Kilauea U.S.A.
74 □2 Kilauea Crater crater U.S.A.
40 C5 Kilbrannan Sound chan. U.K.
30 E3 Kilchu N. Korea
41 E4 Kilcoole Rep. of Ireland
41 D4 Kilcormac Rep. of Ireland
41 E4 Kildare Rep. of Ireland
36 X2 Kil'dinstroy Rus. Fed.
56 B4 Kilembe Congo(Zaire)
40 C5 Kilfinan U.K.
77 E5 Kilgore U.S.A.
38 E2 Kilham U.K.
56 D4 Kilifi Kenya
56 D4 Kilimanjaro mt Tanz.
7 F2 Kilinailau Is is P.N.G.
57 D4 Kilindoni Tanz.
37 T7 Kilingi-Nõmme Estonia
16 F3 Kilis Turkey
51 D6 Kiliya Ukr.
41 B5 Kilkee Rep. of Ireland
41 F3 Kilkeel U.K.
41 D5 Kilkenny Rep. of Ireland
39 C7 Kilkhampton U.K.
49 K4 Kilkis Greece
41 B3 Killala Rep. of Ireland
41 B3 Killala Bay b. Rep. of Ireland
41 C5 Killaloe Rep. of Ireland
69 J3 Killaloe Station Can.
65 G4 Killam Can.
69 G3 Killarney Can.
41 B5 Killarney Rep. of Ireland
69 G2 Killarney National Park Can.
41 B6 Killarney National Park Rep. of Ireland
41 B4 Killary Harbour b. Rep. of Ireland
77 D6 Killeen U.S.A.
41 D5 Killenaule Rep. of Ireland
41 C4 Killimor Rep. of Ireland
40 D4 Killin U.K.
41 F3 Killinchy U.K.
41 E5 Killinick Rep. of Ireland
67 H1 Killiniq Can.
67 H1 Killiniq Island i. Can.
41 B5 Killorglin Rep. of Ireland
41 E5 Killurin Rep. of Ireland
41 C3 Killybegs Rep. of Ireland
41 D2 Kilmacrenan Rep. of Ireland
41 B4 Kilmaine Rep. of Ireland
41 C5 Kilmallock Rep. of Ireland
40 B3 Kilmaluag U.K.
40 D5 Kilmarnock U.K.
40 C4 Kilmelford U.K.
50 J3 Kil'mez' Rus. Fed.
50 J3 Kil'mez' r. Rus. Fed.
41 C6 Kilmona Rep. of Ireland
8 E4 Kilmore Austr.
41 E5 Kilmore Quay Rep. of Ireland
56 D4 Kilosa Tanz.
36 R2 Kilpisjärvi Fin.
36 X2 Kilp"yavr Rus. Fed.
41 E3 Kilrea U.K.
41 B5 Kilrush Rep. of Ireland
40 D5 Kilsyth U.K.
21 A4 Kiltān i. India
41 C4 Kiltullagh Rep. of Ireland
57 C4 Kilwa Congo(Zaire)
57 D4 Kilwa Masoko Tanz.
40 D5 Kilwinning U.K.
57 D4 Kimambi Tanz.
56 B4 Kimba Congo
76 C3 Kimball U.S.A.
6 F2 Kimbe P.N.G.
64 F5 Kimberley Can.
58 F4 Kimberley S. Africa
6 C3 Kimberley Plateau plat. Austr.
9 E4 Kimbolton N.Z.
30 E3 Kimch'aek N. Korea
30 E5 Kimch'ŏn S. Korea
37 S6 Kimito Fin.
30 D6 Kimje S. Korea
49 L6 Kimolos i. Greece
50 F4 Kimovsk Rus. Fed.
56 B4 Kimpese Congo(Zaire)
29 F5 Kimpoku-san mt Japan
50 F3 Kimry Rus. Fed.
56 B4 Kimvula Congo(Zaire)
33 E1 Kinabalu, Gunung mt Malaysia
31 A5 Kinabatangan r. Malaysia
49 M6 Kinaros i. Greece
40 E2 Kinbrace U.K.
69 G3 Kincardine Can.
40 E4 Kincardine U.K.
8 D2 Kinchega National Park Austr.
64 D3 Kincolith Can.
57 C4 Kinda Congo(Zaire)
23 H5 Kindat Myanmar
77 E6 Kinder U.S.A.
39 F4 Kinder Scout h. U.K.
65 H4 Kindersley Can.
54 A3 Kindia Guinea
56 C4 Kindu Congo(Zaire)
50 G3 Kineshma Rus. Fed.
6 F4 Kingaroy Austr.
74 B3 King City U.S.A.
92 C1 King Edward Point U.K. Base Ant.
80 E3 King Ferry U.S.A.
81 H2 Kingfield U.S.A.
77 D5 Kingfisher U.S.A.
92 B1 King George I. i. Ant.
66 E2 King George Islands is Can.
64 D4 King I. i. Can.
50 D3 Kingisepp Rus. Fed.
6 E5 King Island i. Austr.
69 H1 King Island Can.
92 D5 King Leopold and Queen Astrid Coast coastal area Ant.
6 C3 King Leopold Ranges h. Austr.
75 E4 Kingman AZ U.S.A.
77 D4 Kingman KS U.S.A.
81 J2 Kingman ME U.S.A.
64 D3 King Mtn mt Can.
92 A3 King Pen. pen. Ant.
41 D5 Kings r. Rep. of Ireland
74 C3 Kings r. U.S.A.
39 D7 Kingsbridge U.K.
74 C3 Kingsburg U.S.A.
81 J2 Kingsbury U.S.A.
74 C3 Kings Canyon National Park U.S.A.
8 A3 Kingscote Austr.
41 E4 Kingscourt Rep. of Ireland
92 B2 King Sejong Korea Base Ant.
68 C3 Kingsford U.S.A.
79 D6 Kingsland GA U.S.A.
68 E5 Kingsland IN U.S.A.
39 H5 King's Lynn U.K.
7 H2 Kingsmill Group is Kiribati
39 H6 Kingsnorth U.K.
6 C3 King Sound b. Austr.
72 E3 Kings Peak summit U.S.A.
80 B6 Kingsport U.S.A.
69 J3 Kingston Can.
83 J5 Kingston Jamaica
9 B6 Kingston N.Z.
68 B6 Kingston IL U.S.A.
81 F4 Kingston NY U.S.A.
75 E4 Kingston Peak summit U.S.A.
8 B4 Kingston South East Austr.
38 G4 Kingston upon Hull U.K.
83 M6 Kingstown St Vincent
77 D7 Kingsville U.S.A.
39 E6 Kingswood U.K.
39 D5 Kington U.K.
40 D3 Kingussie U.K.
63 J3 King William I. i. Can.
59 G6 King William's Town S. Africa
77 E6 Kingwood TX U.S.A.
80 D5 Kingwood WV U.S.A.
65 J4 Kinistino Can.
28 G5 Kinka-san i. Japan
9 B6 Kinloch N.Z.
40 E3 Kinloss U.K.
69 H3 Kinmount Can.
37 N8 Kinna Sweden
41 D4 Kinnegad Rep. of Ireland
21 C4 Kinniyai Sri Lanka
36 T5 Kinnula Fin.
65 J3 Kinoosao Can.
40 E4 Kinross U.K.
41 C6 Kinsale Rep. of Ireland
56 B4 Kinshasa Congo(Zaire)
76 D4 Kinsley U.S.A.
79 E5 Kinston U.S.A.
37 R9 Kintai Lith.
54 B4 Kintampo Ghana
40 F3 Kintore U.K.
40 C5 Kintyre pen. U.K.
40 C5 Kintyre, Mull of hd U.K.
64 F3 Kinuso Can.
55 F4 Kinyeti mt Sudan
43 H4 Kinzig r. Ger.
69 H2 Kiosk Can.
66 E4 Kipawa, Lac l. Can.
81 F6 Kiptopeke U.S.A.
57 C5 Kipushi Congo(Zaire)
7 G3 Kirakira Solomon Is
21 C2 Kirandul India
50 D4 Kirawsk Belarus
43 G2 Kirchdorf Ger.
43 G5 Kirchheim-Bolanden Ger.
24 C1 Kirensk Rus. Fed.
5 L5 Kiribati country Pac. Oc.
17 H1 Kırık Turkey
16 F3 Kırıkhan Turkey
16 D2 Kırıkkale Turkey
50 F3 Kirillov Rus. Fed.
56 D3 Kirinyaga mt Kenya
50 E3 Kirishi Rus. Fed.
29 B9 Kirishima-yama volc. Japan
5 M4 Kiritimati i. Kiribati
16 A2 Kırkağaç Turkey
18 B2 Kirk Bulāg D. mt Iran
39 E4 Kirkby U.K.
39 F4 Kirkby in Ashfield U.K.
38 E3 Kirkby Lonsdale U.K.
38 E3 Kirkby Stephen U.K.
40 E4 Kirkcaldy U.K.
40 C6 Kirkcolm U.K.
41 F3 Kirkcubbin U.K.
40 D6 Kirkcudbright U.K.
37 N6 Kirkenær Norway
36 W2 Kirkenes Norway
69 H3 Kirkfield Can.
40 D5 Kirkintilloch U.K.
37 T6 Kirkkonummi Fin.
75 F4 Kirkland U.S.A.
75 F4 Kirkland Junction U.S.A.
69 G1 Kirkland Lake Can.
51 C7 Kırklareli Turkey
38 C3 Kirk Michael U.K.
38 E3 Kirkoswald U.K.
76 E3 Kirksville U.S.A.
17 K4 Kirkūk Iraq
40 F2 Kirkwall U.K.
59 F6 Kirkwood S. Africa
74 B2 Kirkwood CA U.S.A.
76 F4 Kirkwood MO U.S.A.
16 C1 Kırmır r. Turkey
42 F5 Kirn Ger.
50 E4 Kirov Kaluzh. Obl. Rus. Fed.
Kirov see Vyatka
Kirovabad see Gäncä
50 J3 Kirovo-Chepetsk Rus. Fed.
51 E5 Kirovohrad Ukr.
17 M2 Kirovsk Azer.
50 D3 Kirovsk Leningrad. Rus. Fed.
36 X3 Kirovsk Murmansk. Rus. Fed.
19 F2 Kirovsk Turkm.
50 J3 Kirovskaya Oblast' div. Rus. Fed.
28 C2 Kirovskiy Rus. Fed.
92 B4 Kirpatrick, Mt mt Ant.
18 E2 Kirpili Turkm.
40 E4 Kirriemuir U.K.
50 K3 Kirs Rus. Fed.
50 G4 Kirsanov Rus. Fed.
16 E2 Kırşehir Turkey
19 G5 Kirthar Range mts Pak.
43 H4 Kirtorf Ger.
36 R3 Kiruna Sweden
56 C4 Kirundu Congo(Zaire)
50 H4 Kirya Rus. Fed.
29 F6 Kiryū Japan
37 O8 Kisa Sweden
56 C3 Kisangani Congo(Zaire)

29 B8 Kurume Japan
24 D1 Kurumkan Rus. Fed.
21 C5 Kurunegala Sri Lanka
55 F2 Kurūsh, Jebel reg. Sudan
49 M6 Kuşadası Turkey
49 M6 Kuşadası Körfezi b. Turkey
64 B2 Kusawa Lake l. Can.
42 F5 Kusel Ger.
16 A1 Kuş Gölü l. Turkey
51 F6 Kushchevskaya Rus. Fed.
29 B9 Kushikino Japan
29 D8 Kushimoto Japan
28 J3 Kushiro Japan
28 J3 Kushiro-Shitsugen National Park Japan
19 F3 Kushka r. Turkm.
17 M5 Kūshkak Iran
14 E1 Kushmurun Kazak.
21 B3 Kushtagi India
23 G5 Kushtia Bangl.
26 C2 Kushui r. China
62 C3 Kuskokwim r. U.S.A.
62 B4 Kuskokwim Bay b. U.S.A.
62 C3 Kuskokwim Mts U.S.A.
30 C4 Kusŏng N. Korea
28 J3 Kussharo-ko l. Japan
14 E1 Kustanay Kazak.
43 F1 Küstenkanal canal Ger.
18 C4 Kut Iran
17 M6 Küt Abdollāh Iran
32 A5 Kutacane Indon.
16 B2 Kütahya Turkey
51 G7 K'ut'aisi Georgia
Kut-al-Imara see Al Kūt
51 H6 Kutan Rus. Fed.
28 G3 Kutchan Japan
17 M5 Kūt-e Gapu Iran
48 G2 Kutina Croatia
48 G2 Kutjevo Croatia
47 J4 Kutno Pol.
56 B4 Kutu Congo(Zaire)
23 G5 Kutubdia I. i. Bangl.
62 G2 Kuujjua r. Can.
67 G2 Kuujjuaq Can.
Kuujjuarapik see Poste-de-la-Baleine
18 D1 Kuuli-Mayak Turkm.
36 V4 Kuusamo Fin.
37 U6 Kuusankoski Fin.
57 B5 Kuvango Angola
50 E3 Kuvshinovo Rus. Fed.
17 L7 Kuwait Kuwait
10 F7 Kuwait country Asia
17 L7 Kuwait Jun b. Kuwait
29 E7 Kuwana Japan
50 G1 Kuya Rus. Fed.
12 J4 Kuybyshev Novosibirsk Rus. Fed.
Kuybyshev see Samara
50 J4 Kuybyshevskoye Vdkhr. resr Rus. Fed.
26 D2 Kuye r. China
15 G2 Kuytun China
49 N6 Kuyucak Turkey
37 V6 Kuznechnoye Rus. Fed.
50 H4 Kuznetsk Rus. Fed.
28 F1 Kuznetsovo Rus. Fed.
51 C5 Kuznetsovs'k Ukr.
36 R1 Kvænangen chan. Norway
36 Q2 Kvaløya i. Norway
36 S1 Kvalsund Norway
Kvareli see Qvareli
48 F2 Kvarnerić chan. Croatia
62 C4 Kvichak Bay b. U.S.A.
64 D3 Kwadacha Wilderness Prov. Park res. Can.
27 □ Kwai Tau Leng h. H.K. China
95 G5 Kwajalein i. Pac. Oc.
32 A5 Kwala Indon.
59 J4 KwaMashu S. Africa
59 H2 KwaMhlanga S. Africa
30 D5 Kwangch'ŏn S. Korea
30 D6 Kwangju S. Korea
56 B4 Kwango r. Congo(Zaire)
56 D4 Kwangwazi Tanz.
30 D6 Kwangyang S. Korea
59 F6 Kwanobuhle S. Africa
59 F6 KwaNojoli S. Africa
59 G6 Kwanonqubela S. Africa
58 F5 Kwanonzame S. Africa
59 G6 Kwatinidubu S. Africa
59 H3 KwaZamokhule S. Africa
58 F6 Kwazamukucinga S. Africa
58 F5 Kwazamuxolo S. Africa
59 H3 KwaZanele S. Africa
59 J4 Kwazulu-Natal div. S. Africa
57 C5 Kwekwe Zimbabwe
58 F1 Kweneng div. Botswana
56 B4 Kwenge r. Congo(Zaire)
59 G5 Kwezi-Naledi S. Africa
47 J4 Kwidzyn Pol.
62 B4 Kwigillingok AK U.S.A.
6 E2 Kwikila P.N.G.
56 B4 Kwilu r. Angola/Congo(Zaire)
25 F7 Kwoka mt Indon.
27 □ Kwun Tong H.K. China
55 D4 Kyabé Chad
8 E4 Kyabram Austr.
32 A1 Kya-in Seikkyi Myanmar
24 C1 Kyakhta Rus. Fed.
8 D3 Kyalite Austr.
6 D5 Kyancutta Austr.
50 F1 Kyanda Rus. Fed.
32 A1 Kyaukhnyat Myanmar
23 H6 Kyaukpyu Myanmar
23 H5 Kyauktaw Myanmar
37 S9 Kybartai Lith.
8 C4 Kybybolite Austr.
22 D2 Kyelang India
26 A2 Kyikug China
Kyiv see Kiev
Kyklades is see Cyclades
65 H4 Kyle Can.
40 C3 Kyle of Lochalsh U.K.
42 E5 Kyll r. Ger.
49 K6 Kyllini mt Greece
8 E4 Kyneton Austr.
56 D3 Kyoga, Lake l. Uganda
29 D7 Kyōga-misaki pt Japan
32 A1 Kyondo Myanmar
30 E6 Kyŏngju S. Korea
29 D7 Kyōto Japan
49 J6 Kyparissia Greece
49 J6 Kyparissiakos Kolpos b. Greece
12 H4 Kypshak, Ozero salt l. Kazak.
49 L5 Kyra Panagia i. Greece
10 J5 Kyrgyzstan country Asia
43 L2 Kyritz Ger.
36 L5 Kyrksæterøra Norway
12 G3 Kyrta Rus. Fed.
50 H1 Kyssa Rus. Fed.
13 P3 Kytalyktakh Rus. Fed.
49 K6 Kythira i. Greece
49 L6 Kythnos i. Greece
32 A2 Kyungyaung Myanmar
29 B8 Kyūshū i. Japan
94 D5 Kyushu - Palau Ridge sea feature Pac. Oc.
49 K3 Kyustendil Bulg.
8 F3 Kywong Austr.
51 D5 Kyyivs'ke Vdskh. resr Ukr.
36 T5 Kyyjärvi Fin.
24 B1 Kyzyl Rus. Fed.
14 E2 Kyzylkum Desert Uzbek.
15 H1 Kyzyl-Mazhalyk Rus. Fed.
14 E2 Kzyl-Orda Kazak.
14 F1 Kzyltu Kazak.

L

42 F4 Laacher See l. Ger.
37 T7 Laagri Estonia
36 U2 Laanila Fin.
91 B3 La Araucania div. Chile
56 E3 Laascaanood Somalia
56 E2 Laasgoray Somalia
89 E2 La Asunción Venez.
54 A2 Laâyoune Western Sahara
51 G6 Laba r. Rus. Fed.
77 C6 La Babia Mex.
88 D3 La Banda Arg.
72 E3 La Barge U.S.A.
7 H3 Labasa Fiji
44 C3 La Baule-Escoublac France
54 A3 Labé Guinea
66 F4 Labelle Can.
68 B5 La Belle U.S.A.
64 B2 Laberge, Lake l. Can.
31 A5 Labian, Tg pt Malaysia
64 E2 La Biche r. Can.
51 G6 Labinsk Rus. Fed.
32 B5 Labis Malaysia
31 B3 Labo Phil.
16 F4 Laboué Lebanon
44 D4 Labouheyre France
91 D2 Laboulaye Arg.
67 H3 Labrador Can.
67 G3 Labrador City Can.
63 N3 Labrador Sea Can./Greenland
86 F5 Lábrea Brazil
33 E1 Labuan Malaysia
33 C4 Labuhan Indon.
33 B2 Labuhanbilik Indon.
32 A5 Labuhanruku Indon.
31 A5 Labuk r. Malaysia
33 E1 Labuk, Telukan b. Malaysia
25 E7 Labuna Indon.
12 H3 Labytnangi Rus. Fed.
49 H4 Laç Albania
91 D1 La Calera Arg.
91 B2 La Calera Chile
84 E3 Lacandón, Parque Nacional nat. park Guatemala
44 F2 La Capelle France
91 B4 Lacar, L. l. Arg.
91 D2 La Carlota Arg.
45 E3 La Carolina Spain
49 M2 Lăcăuţi, Vârful mt Romania
81 J1 Lac-Baker Can.
14 F5 Laccadive Islands India
65 K4 Lac du Bonnet Can.
82 G5 La Ceiba Honduras
89 C2 La Ceiba Venez.
8 B4 Lacepede B. b. Austr.
81 E4 Laceyville U.S.A.
81 H1 Lac Frontière Can.
50 F2 Lacha, Ozero l. Rus. Fed.
43 J2 Lachendorf Ger.
69 F3 Lachine U.S.A.
8 E3 Lachlan r. Austr.
83 J7 La Chorrera Panama
66 F4 Lachute Can.
17 L2 Laçın Azer.
44 G5 La Ciotat France
84 A2 La Ciudad Mex.
80 D3 Lackawanna U.S.A.
65 G4 Lac La Biche Can.
64 E4 Lac La Hache Can.
64 F2 Lac la Martre Can.
65 H3 Lac La Ronge Provincial Park res. Can.
67 F4 Lac Mégantic Can.
81 G2 Lacolle Can.
73 E6 La Colorada Mex.
64 G4 Lacombe Can.
84 D3 La Concordia Mex.
48 C5 Laconi Sardinia Italy
81 H3 Laconia U.S.A.
69 J1 La Corne Can.
68 B4 La Crescent U.S.A.
68 B4 La Crosse U.S.A.
89 A4 La Cruz Col.
84 A2 La Cruz Sinaloa Mex.
84 C1 La Cruz Tamaulipas Mex.
76 E4 La Cygne U.S.A.
22 D2 Ladakh Range mts India
32 A4 Ladang i. Thai.
16 E1 Lâdik Turkey
58 D6 Ladismith S. Africa
19 F4 Lādīz Iran
22 C4 Ladnun India
89 B3 La Dorada Col.
Ladozhskoye Ozero l. see Ladoga, Lake
23 H4 Ladu mt India
50 E2 Ladva Rus. Fed.
50 E2 Ladva-Vetka Rus. Fed.
63 K2 Lady Ann Strait chan. Can.
40 E4 Ladybank U.K.
59 G4 Ladybrand S. Africa
69 G2 Lady Evelyn Lake l. Can.
59 G5 Lady Frere S. Africa
59 G5 Lady Grey S. Africa
64 E5 Ladysmith Can.
59 H4 Ladysmith S. Africa
68 B3 Ladysmith U.S.A.
6 E2 Lae P.N.G.
32 B2 Laem Ngop Thai.
32 B4 Laem Pho pt Thai.
37 K6 Lærdalsøyri Norway
86 F8 La Esmeralda Bol.
89 D4 La Esmeralda Venez.
37 M8 Læsø i. Denmark
30 D2 Lafa China
91 D1 La Falda Arg.
72 F4 Lafayette CO U.S.A.
68 D5 Lafayette IN U.S.A.
77 E6 Lafayette LA U.S.A.
79 C5 La Fayette U.S.A.
42 B5 La Fère France
42 B5 La-Ferté-Milon France
42 B6 La Ferté-sous-Jouarre France
18 C5 Laffān, Ra's pt Qatar
54 C4 Lafia Nigeria
44 D3 La Flèche France
80 A6 La Follette U.S.A.
69 H2 Laforce Can.
69 G2 Laforest Can.
67 G3 Laforge Can.
89 B2 La Fría Venez.
18 D5 Laft Iran
48 C6 La Galite i. Tunisia
51 H6 Lagan' Rus. Fed.
41 E3 Lagan r. U.K.
87 L6 Lagarto Brazil
43 G3 Lage Ger.
37 L7 Lågen r. Norway
40 C5 Lagg U.K.
40 D3 Laggan U.K.
40 D4 Laggan, Loch l. U.K.
54 C1 Laghouat Alg.
23 F2 Lagkor Co salt l. China
89 B2 La Gloria Col.
90 D2 Lagoa Santa Brazil
50 D2 Lagoda, Lake l. Rus. Fed.
17 L1 Lagodekhi Georgia
32 D5 Lagong i. Indon.
31 B3 Lagonoy Gulf b. Phil.
88 B7 Lago Posadas Arg.
91 B4 Lago Ranco Chile
54 C4 Lagos Nigeria
45 B4 Lagos Port.
84 B2 Lagos de Moreno Mex.
72 C2 La Grande U.S.A.
66 E3 La Grande r. Can.
66 E3 La Grande 2, Réservoir de resr Can.
66 E3 La Grande 3, Réservoir de resr Can.
66 F3 La Grande 4, Réservoir de resr Can.
6 C3 Lagrange Austr.
79 C5 La Grange GA U.S.A.
81 J2 La Grange ME U.S.A.
68 D5 La Grange MI U.S.A.
68 B5 La Grange MO U.S.A.
77 D6 La Grange TX U.S.A.
68 E5 Lagrange U.S.A.
89 E3 La Gran Sabana plat. Venez.
88 G3 Laguna Brazil
74 D5 Laguna Beach U.S.A.
91 B3 Laguna de Laja, Parque Nacional nat. park Chile
84 E4 Laguna Lachua, Parque Nacional nat. park Guatemala
74 D5 Laguna Mts mts U.S.A.
86 C5 Lagunas Peru
88 A7 Laguna San Rafael, Parque Nacional nat. park Chile
84 C3 Lagunas de Chacahua, Parque Nacional nat. park Mex.
89 C2 Lagunillas Venez.
33 E1 Lahad Datu Malaysia
31 A5 Lahad Datu, Telukan b. Malaysia
74 □2 Lahaina U.S.A.
17 M3 Lahargin Iran
33 B3 Lahat Indon.
32 A5 Lahewa Indon.
20 B7 Laḥij Yemen
18 C2 Lāhījān Iran
74 □1 Lahilahi Pt pt U.S.A.
43 F4 Lahn r. Ger.
42 F4 Lahnstein Ger.
37 N8 Laholm Sweden
74 C2 Lahontan Res. resr U.S.A.
22 C3 Lahore Pak.
89 E3 La Horqueta Venez.
22 B3 Lahri Pak.
37 T6 Lahti Fin.
84 A3 La Huerta Mex.
55 D4 Laï Chad
26 F3 Lai'an China
27 C6 Laibin China
18 E4 Laidāru Iran
74 □1 Laie U.S.A.
74 □1 Laie Pt pt U.S.A.
27 C4 Laifeng China
44 E2 L'Aigle France
36 S5 Laihia Fin.
23 H4 Laimakuri India
58 D6 Laingsburg S. Africa
36 S3 Lainioälven r. Sweden
40 D2 Lairg U.K.
31 C5 Lais Phil.
37 R6 Laitila Fin.
48 D1 Laives Italy
26 E2 Laiwu China
26 F2 Laiyang China
26 E2 Laiyuan China
26 F2 Laizhou Wan b. China
91 B3 Laja r. Chile
91 B3 Laja, Lago de l. Chile
6 D3 Lajamanu Austr.
87 L5 Lajes Rio Grande do Norte Brazil
88 F3 Lajes Santa Catarina Brazil
73 G4 La Junta U.S.A.
72 E2 Lake U.S.A.
7 J3 Lakeba i. Fiji
16 D6 Lake Bardawîl Reserve Egypt
8 D4 Lake Bolac Austr.
8 G2 Lake Cargelligo Austr.
72 B1 Lake Chelan Nat. Recreation Area res. U.S.A.
79 D6 Lake City FL U.S.A.
68 E3 Lake City MI U.S.A.
68 A3 Lake City MN U.S.A.
79 E5 Lake City SC U.S.A.
38 D3 Lake District Nat. Park U.K.
74 D5 Lake Elsinore U.S.A.
69 H3 Lakefield Can.
68 C4 Lake Geneva U.S.A.
63 M3 Lake Harbour Can.
75 E4 Lake Havasu City U.S.A.
74 C4 Lake Isabella U.S.A.
79 D6 Lakeland U.S.A.
68 C2 Lake Linden U.S.A.
64 F4 Lake Louise Can.
75 E4 Lake Mead National Recreation Area res. U.S.A.
81 J2 Lake Moxie U.S.A.
72 B2 Lake Oswego U.S.A.
9 B5 Lake Paringa N.Z.
81 G2 Lake Placid U.S.A.
74 A2 Lakeport U.S.A.
9 C6 Lake Pukaki N.Z.
66 D3 Lake River Can.
69 H3 Lake St Peter Can.
8 G4 Lakes Entrance Austr.
68 E2 Lake Superior National Park Can.
8 H3 Lake Tabourie Austr.
9 C6 Lake Tekapo N.Z.
66 E4 Lake Traverse Can.
72 B3 Lakeview U.S.A.
73 F4 Lakewood CO U.S.A.
81 F4 Lakewood NJ U.S.A.
80 C4 Lakewood OH U.S.A.
79 D7 Lake Worth U.S.A.
50 D2 Lakhdenpokh'ya Rus. Fed.
22 E4 Lakhimpur India
22 D5 Lakhnadon India
22 B5 Lakhpat India
49 K6 Lakonikos Kolpos b. Greece
54 B4 Lakota Côte d'Ivoire
36 U1 Laksefjorden chan. Norway
36 T1 Lakselv Norway
14 F5 Lakshadweep div. India
23 G5 Laksham Bangl.
21 B2 Lakshettipet India
23 G5 Lakshmikantapur India
31 B5 Lala Phil.
91 D2 La Laguna Arg.
91 B3 La Laja Chile
56 B3 Lalara Gabon
43 L1 Lalendorf Ger.
18 C3 Lālī Iran
84 E3 La Libertad Guatemala
91 B2 La Ligua Chile
30 D1 Lalin China
45 B1 Lalín Spain
30 C1 Lalin r. China
45 D4 La Línea de la Concepción Spain
22 D4 Lalitpur India
31 B2 Lal-Lo Phil.
65 H3 La Loche Can.
65 H3 La Loche, Lac l. Can.
42 C4 La Louvière Belgium
50 H2 Lal'sk Rus. Fed.
23 H5 Lama Bangl.
48 C4 La Maddalena Sardinia Italy
31 A5 Lamag Malaysia
32 A2 Lamaing Myanmar
La Manche str. see English Channel
76 C4 Lamar CO U.S.A.
77 E4 Lamar MO U.S.A.
18 D5 Lamard Iran
48 C5 La Marmora, Punta mt Sardinia Italy
91 D3 Lamarque Arg.
77 E6 La Marque U.S.A.
64 F2 La Martre, Lac l. Can.
56 B4 Lambaréné Gabon
86 C5 Lambayeque Peru
41 F4 Lambay Island i. Rep. of Ireland
92 D4 Lambert Gl. gl. Ant.
58 C6 Lambert's Bay S. Africa
22 C3 Lambi India
39 F6 Lambourn Downs h. U.K.
32 C2 Lam Chi r. Thai.
45 C2 Lamego Port.
67 H4 Lamèque, I. i. Can.
86 C6 La Merced Peru
8 C3 Lameroo Austr.
77 C5 Lamesa U.S.A.
74 D5 La Mesa U.S.A.
49 K5 Lamia Greece
73 E6 Lá Misa Mex.
74 D5 La Misión Mex.
31 B5 Lamitan Phil.
27 □ Lamma I. i. H.K. China
9 B6 Lammerlaw Ra. mts N.Z.
40 F5 Lammermuir Hills h. U.K.
37 O8 Lammhult Sweden
37 T6 Lammi Fin.
68 C5 La Moille U.S.A.
81 G2 Lamoille r. U.S.A.
68 B5 La Moine r. U.S.A.
31 B3 Lamon Bay b. Phil.
76 E3 Lamoni U.S.A.
72 F3 Lamont U.S.A.
77 B6 La Morita Mex.
69 H1 La Motte Can.
32 B1 Lam Pao Res. resr Thai.
77 D6 Lampasas U.S.A.
70 F6 Lampazos Mex.
48 E7 Lampedusa, Isola di i. Sicily Italy
39 C5 Lampeter U.K.
32 B2 Lam Plai Mat r. Thai.
50 F4 Lamskoye Rus. Fed.
27 □ Lam Tin H.K. China
56 E4 Lamu Kenya
23 H6 Lamu Myanmar
74 □2 Lanai i. U.S.A.
74 □2 Lanai City U.S.A.
31 C5 Lanao, Lake l. Phil.
69 J3 Lanark Can.
40 E5 Lanark U.K.
68 C4 Lanark U.S.A.
31 A5 Lanas Malaysia
32 A3 Lanbi Kyun i. Myanmar
Lancang Jiang r. see Mekong
81 F2 Lancaster Can.
38 E3 Lancaster U.K.
74 C4 Lancaster CA U.S.A.
68 A5 Lancaster MO U.S.A.
81 H2 Lancaster NH U.S.A.
80 B5 Lancaster OH U.S.A.
81 E4 Lancaster PA U.S.A.
79 D5 Lancaster SC U.S.A.
68 B4 Lancaster WV U.S.A.
38 E4 Lancaster Canal canal U.K.
63 K2 Lancaster Sound str. Can.
48 F3 Lanciano Italy
91 B3 Lanco Chile
26 F2 Lancun China
46 F6 Landau an der Isar Ger.
43 G5 Landau in der Pfalz Ger.
46 E7 Landeck Austria
72 E3 Lander U.S.A.
43 H2 Landesbergen Ger.
65 H4 Landis Can.
46 E6 Landsberg am Lech Ger.
39 B7 Land's End pt U.K.
46 F6 Landshut Ger.
37 N9 Landskrona Sweden
42 F5 Landstuhl Ger.
43 G1 Land Wursten reg. Ger.
41 D4 Lanesborough Rep. of Ireland
32 C3 La Nga r. Vietnam
22 E3 La'nga Co l. China
26 C3 Langao China
19 F3 Langar Iran
40 B2 Langavat, Loch l. U.K.
58 E4 Langberg mts S. Africa
76 D1 Langdon U.S.A.
58 C6 Langeberg mts S. Africa
37 M9 Langeland i. Denmark
37 T6 Längelmäki Fin.
37 T6 Längelmävesi l. Fin.
43 J3 Langelsheim Ger.
43 G1 Langen Ger.
43 H2 Langenhagen Ger.
43 F4 Langenhahn Ger.
43 F5 Langenlonsheim Ger.
46 C7 Langenthal Switz.
43 K2 Langenweddingen Ger.
42 F1 Langeoog Ger.
42 F1 Langeoog i. Ger.
37 L7 Langesund Norway
32 B5 Langgapayung Indon.
43 G4 Langgöns Ger.
65 H4 Langham Can.
36 C4 Langjökull ice cap Iceland
33 A2 Langka Indon.
33 A1 Langkawi i. Malaysia
32 A3 Lang Kha Toek, Khao mt Thai.
58 D4 Langklip S. Africa
31 A5 Langkon Malaysia
69 K1 Langlade Can.
68 C3 Langlade U.S.A.
44 F4 Langogne France
36 O2 Langøya i. Norway
23 F3 Langphu mt China
39 E6 Langport U.K.
27 F5 Langqi China
44 G3 Langres France
22 D1 Langru China
33 A2 Langsa Indon.
32 A4 Langsa, Teluk b. Indon.
36 P5 Långsele Sweden
26 C1 Langshan China
26 C1 Lang Shan mts China
27 C6 Lang Sơn Vietnam
38 G3 Langtoft U.K.
77 C6 Langtry U.S.A.
44 F5 Languedoc reg. France
36 R4 Långvattnet Sweden
43 H2 Langwedel Ger.
26 F4 Langxi China
26 C4 Langzhong China
69 H2 Laniel Can.
65 H4 Lanigan Can.
74 □1 Lanikai U.S.A.
91 B3 Lanín, Parque Nacional nat. park Arg.
91 B3 Lanín, Volcán volc. Arg.
26 E3 Lankao China
17 M2 Länkäran Azer.
44 C2 Lannion France
84 A2 La Noria Mex.
36 S3 Lansån Sweden
68 C2 L'Anse U.S.A.
68 B4 Lansing IA U.S.A.
68 E4 Lansing MI U.S.A.
64 C2 Lansing r. Can.
27 D6 Lantau I. i. H.K. China
27 □ Lantau Island i. H.K. China
27 □ Lantau Peak h. H.K. China
31 C4 Lanuza Bay b. Phil.
27 F4 Lanxi China
55 F4 Lanya Sudan
27 F6 Lan Yü i. Taiwan
54 A2 Lanzarote i. Canary Is
26 B2 Lanzhou China
30 B1 Lanzijing China
31 B2 Laoag Phil.
31 C3 Laoang Phil.
27 B6 Lao Cai Vietnam
26 F1 Laoha r. China
26 D3 Laohekou China
30 A4 Laohutun China
30 D3 Laoling China
30 D3 Lao Ling mts China
44 F2 Laon France
68 C3 Laona U.S.A.
11 M7 Laos country Asia
26 F2 Lao Shan mt China
30 E2 Laotougou China
30 C3 Laotuding Shan h. China
Laowohi pass see Khardung La
26 A1 Laoximiao China
30 E2 Laoye Ling mts China
90 C4 Lapa Brazil
31 B5 Lapac i. Phil.
83 J7 La Palma Panama
45 C4 La Palma del Condado Spain
91 F2 La Paloma Uru.
91 D3 La Pampa div. Arg.
74 B4 La Panza Range mts U.S.A.
89 E3 La Paragua Venez.
31 A5 Laparan i. Phil.
91 E1 La Paz Entre Ríos Arg.
91 C2 La Paz Mendoza Arg.
86 E7 La Paz Bol.
82 B4 La Paz Mex.
68 D5 Lapaz U.S.A.
86 E4 La Pedrera Col.
69 F4 Lapeer U.S.A.
28 G2 La Pérouse Strait str. Japan/Rus. Fed.
84 C2 La Pesca Mex.
84 B2 La Piedad Mex.
89 E3 La Piña r. Venez.
72 B3 La Pine U.S.A.
31 C3 Lapinig Phil.
31 C4 Lapinin i. Phil.
36 U5 Lapinlahti Fin.
16 D4 Lapithos Cyprus
77 F6 Laplace U.S.A.
76 C2 La Plant U.S.A.
91 F2 La Plata Arg.
89 B4 La Plata Col.
50 G1 Lapominka Rus. Fed.
68 D5 La Porte U.S.A.
68 A4 La Porte City U.S.A.
36 S5 Lappajärvi Fin.
36 S5 Lappajärvi l. Fin.
37 V6 Lappeenranta Fin.
43 L5 Lappersdorf Ger.
36 S2 Lappland reg. Europe
81 G2 La Prairie Can.
77 D6 La Pryor U.S.A.
49 M4 Lâpseki Turkey
Laptevykh, More sea see Laptev Sea
13 N2 Laptev Sea sea Rus. Fed.
36 S5 Lapua Fin.
31 B4 Lapu-Lapu Phil.
88 C2 La Quiaca Arg.
48 E3 L'Aquila Italy
74 D5 La Quinta U.S.A.
18 D5 Lār Iran
54 B1 Larache Morocco
18 E5 Lārak i. Iran
72 F3 Laramie U.S.A.
72 F3 Laramie Mts mts U.S.A.
Laranda see Karaman
90 B4 Laranjeiras do Sul Brazil
90 B3 Laranjinha r. Brazil
25 E7 Larantuka Indon.
25 F7 Larat i. Indon.
45 H4 Larba Alg.
37 Q8 Lärbro Sweden
69 G2 Larchwood Can.
69 H1 Larder Lake Can.
45 E1 Laredo Spain
77 D7 Laredo U.S.A.
79 D7 Largo U.S.A.
40 D5 Largs U.K.
18 B2 Lārī Iran
48 D6 L'Ariana Tunisia
65 K5 Larimore U.S.A.
88 C3 La Rioja Arg.
91 C1 La Rioja div. Arg.
45 E1 La Rioja div. Spain
49 K5 Larisa Greece
18 E5 Laristan reg. Iran
22 B4 Larkana Pak.
46 C7 Larmont mt France/Switz.
16 D4 Larnaka Cyprus
41 F3 Larne U.K.
76 D4 Larned U.S.A.
40 C6 Larne Lough in U.K.
45 D1 La Robla Spain
42 D4 La Roche-en-Ardenne Belgium
44 D3 La Rochelle France
44 D3 La Roche-sur-Yon France
45 E3 La Roda Spain
83 L5 La Romana Dom. Rep.
65 H3 La Ronge Can.
84 B1 La Rosa Mex.
6 D3 Larrimah Austr.
92 B2 Larsen Ice Shelf ice feature Ant.
36 S5 Larsmo Fin.
37 M7 Larvik Norway
75 H2 La Sal Junction U.S.A.
81 G2 La Salle Can.
68 C5 La Salle U.S.A.
66 E4 La Sarre Can.
89 D2 Las Aves, Islas is Venez.
91 B2 Las Cabras Chile
67 J4 La Scie Can.
73 F5 Las Cruces U.S.A.
83 K5 La Selle mt Haiti
91 B1 La Serena Chile
77 C7 Las Esperanças Mex.
91 E3 Las Flores Arg.
19 F5 Lāshār r. Iran
65 H4 Lashburn Can.
91 C2 Las Heras Arg.
24 B4 Lashio Myanmar
19 G4 Lashkar Gāh Afgh.
91 B3 Las Lajas Arg.
89 D3 Las Lajitas Venez.
88 D2 Las Lomitas Arg.
45 C4 Las Marismas marsh Spain
88 C7 Las Martinetas Arg.
89 D2 Las Mercedes Venez.
84 A1 Las Nieves Mex.
74 D5 Las Palmas r. Mex.
54 A2 Las Palmas de Gran Canaria Canary Is
48 C2 La Spezia Italy
91 F2 Las Piedras Uru.
88 C6 Las Plumas Arg.
91 E2 Las Rosas Arg.
72 B3 Lassen Pk volc. U.S.A.
72 B3 Lassen Volcanic Nat. Park U.S.A.
92 B2 Lassiter Coast coastal area Ant.
83 H7 Las Tablas Panama
88 D3 Las Termas Arg.
65 H4 Last Mountain L. l. Can.
56 B4 Lastoursville Gabon
48 G3 Lastovo i. Croatia
89 D3 Las Trincheras Venez.
43 F2 Lastrup Ger.
73 F6 Las Varas Chihuahua Mex.
84 A2 Las Varas Mex.
91 D1 Las Varillas Arg.
73 F5 Las Vegas NM U.S.A.
75 E3 Las Vegas NV U.S.A.
45 D3 Las Villuercas mt Spain
67 J3 La Tabatière Can.
86 C4 Latacunga Ecuador
92 A2 Latady I. i. Ant.
89 B5 La Tagua Col.
16 E4 Latakia Syria
69 H2 Latchford Can.
23 F5 Latehar India
44 D4 La Teste France
42 F2 Lathen Ger.
40 E2 Latheron U.K.
48 E4 Latina Italy
91 D2 La Toma Arg.
89 D2 La Tortuga, Isla i. Venez.
80 D4 Latrobe U.S.A.
42 E2 Lattrop Neth.
69 H2 Latulipe Can.
66 F4 La Tuque Can.
21 B2 Latur India
35 H3 Latvia country Europe
88 C1 Lauca, Parque Nacional nat. park Chile
46 F5 Lauchhammer Ger.
40 F5 Lauder U.K.
43 H1 Lauenbrück Ger.
43 J1 Lauenburg (Elbe) Ger.
43 K5 Lauf an der Pegnitz Ger.
44 H3 Laufen Switz.
68 D2 Laughing Fish Pt pt U.S.A.
37 S7 Lauka Estonia
36 V1 Laukvik Norway
28 D2 Laulyu Rus. Fed.
32 A3 Laun Thai.
6 E6 Launceston Austr.
39 C7 Launceston U.K.
41 B5 Laune r. Rep. of Ireland
32 A2 Launglon Bok Is is Myanmar
91 B4 La Unión Chile
89 A4 La Unión Col.
82 G6 La Unión El Salvador
84 B3 La Unión Mex.
31 B3 Laur Phil.
8 B2 Laura S.A. Austr.
6 E3 Laura Austr.
89 D3 La Urbana Venez.
81 F5 Laurel DE U.S.A.
77 F6 Laurel MS U.S.A.
72 E2 Laurel MT U.S.A.
80 D4 Laurel Hill h. U.S.A.
80 A6 Laurel River Lake l. U.S.A.
40 F4 Laurencekirk U.K.
67 F4 Laurentides, Réserve faunique des res. Can.
48 F4 Lauria Italy
79 E5 Laurinburg U.S.A.
68 C2 Laurium U.S.A.
46 C7 Lausanne Switz.
33 E3 Laut i. Indon.
91 B3 Lautaro Chile
43 H4 Lautersbach (Hessen) Ger.
33 E3 Laut Kecil, Kepulauan is Indon.
7 H3 Lautoka Fiji
36 V5 Lauvuskylä Fin.
66 F4 Laval Can.
44 D2 Laval France
48 F1 Lavant r. Austria/Slovenia
88 B5 Lavapié, Pta pt Chile
18 C4 Lāvar Kabkān Iran
84 D3 La Venta Mex.
6 C4 Laverton Austr.
89 D2 La Victoria Venez.
69 G2 Lavigne Can.
72 E2 Lavina U.S.A.
90 D3 Lavras Brazil
91 G1 Lavras do Sul Brazil
59 J3 Lavumisa Swaziland
22 B2 Lawa Pak.
92 C6 Law Dome ice feature Ant.
32 B4 Lawit, Gunung mt Malaysia
17 J7 Lawqah waterhole S. Arabia
54 B3 Lawra Ghana
76 E4 Lawrence KS U.S.A.
81 H3 Lawrence MA U.S.A.
79 C5 Lawrenceburg U.S.A.
81 K2 Lawrence Station Can.
80 E6 Lawrenceville U.S.A.
77 D5 Lawton U.S.A.
14 B4 Lawz, J. al mt S. Arabia
37 O7 Laxå Sweden
58 E3 Laxey S. Africa
38 C3 Laxey U.K.
40 C2 Laxford, Loch in. U.K.
40 □ Laxo U.K.
8 D5 Layers Hill Austr.
17 K4 Laylān Iraq
5 K2 Laysan Island i. HI U.S.A.
74 A2 Laytonville U.S.A.
49 J2 Lazarevac Yugo.
92 D3 Lazarev Sea sea Ant.
51 F7 Lazarevskoye Rus. Fed.
73 D6 Lázaro Cárdenas Baja California Mex.
84 B3 Lázaro Cárdenas Mex.
84 A1 Lázaro Cárdenas, Presa resr Mex.
91 F2 Lazcano Uru.
37 S9 Lazdijai Lith.
18 D5 Lāzeh Iran
13 P3 Lazo Rus. Fed.
28 C3 Lazo Rus. Fed.
32 B2 Leach Cambodia
68 E2 Leach I. i. Can.
76 C2 Lead U.S.A.
65 H4 Leader Can.
8 G2 Leadville Austr.
73 F4 Leadville U.S.A.
77 F6 Leaf r. U.S.A.
65 J3 Leaf Rapids Can.
77 D6 Leakey U.S.A.
69 F4 Leamington Can.
75 F2 Leamington U.S.A.
39 F5 Leamington Spa, Royal U.K.
27 E5 Le'an China
41 B5 Leane, Lough l. Rep. of Ireland
41 B6 Leap Rep. of Ireland
65 H4 Leask Can.
39 G6 Leatherhead U.K.
76 E4 Leavenworth KS U.S.A.
72 B2 Leavenworth WA U.S.A.
74 C2 Leavitt Peak summit U.S.A.
42 E5 Lebach Ger.
31 C5 Lebak Phil.
68 D5 Lebanon IN U.S.A.
76 D4 Lebanon KS U.S.A.
77 E4 Lebanon MO U.S.A.
81 G3 Lebanon NH U.S.A.
81 F4 Lebanon NJ U.S.A.
80 A5 Lebanon OH U.S.A.
72 B2 Lebanon OR U.S.A.
81 E4 Lebanon PA U.S.A.
79 C4 Lebanon TN U.S.A.
10 E6 Lebanon country Asia
42 C3 Lebbeke Belgium
50 F4 Lebedyan' Rus. Fed.
51 E5 Lebedyn Ukr.
44 E3 Le Blanc France
46 H3 Lębork Pol.
59 H2 Lebowakgomo S. Africa
45 C4 Lebrija Spain
46 H3 Łebsko, Jezioro lag. Pol.
91 B3 Lebu Chile
42 B4 Le Cateau-Cambrésis France
42 B4 Le Catelet France
49 H4 Lecce Italy
48 C2 Lecco Italy
46 E7 Lech r. Austria/Ger.
49 J6 Lechaina Greece
27 D5 Lechang China
42 C5 Le Chesne France
46 E7 Lechtaler Alpen mts Austria
46 D3 Leck Ger.
44 G3 Le Creusot France
44 E5 Lectoure France
32 B5 Ledang, Gunung mt Malaysia
39 E5 Ledbury U.K.
45 D2 Ledesma Spain
40 D2 Ledmore U.K.
50 E1 Ledmozero Rus. Fed.
27 C7 Ledong China
26 B2 Ledu China
64 G4 Leduc Can.
81 G3 Lee U.S.A.
76 E2 Leech L. l. U.S.A.
38 F4 Leeds U.K.
81 H2 Leeds Junction U.S.A.
39 B7 Leedstown U.K.
42 E1 Leek Neth.
39 E4 Leek U.K.
42 D3 Leende Neth.
80 D4 Leeper U.S.A.
42 F1 Leer (Ostfriesland) Ger.
79 D6 Leesburg FL U.S.A.
80 E5 Leesburg VA U.S.A.
43 H2 Leese Ger.
77 E6 Leesville U.S.A.
80 C4 Leesville Lake l. U.S.A.
8 F3 Leeton Austr.
58 D6 Leeu-Gamka S. Africa
42 D1 Leeuwarden Neth.
6 B5 Leeuwin, C. c. Austr.
74 C3 Lee Vining U.S.A.
83 M5 Leeward Islands is Caribbean Sea
16 D4 Lefka Cyprus
49 J5 Lefkada Greece
49 J5 Lefkada i. Greece
16 D4 Lefkara Cyprus
49 J5 Lefkimmi Greece
Lefkosia see Nicosia
31 B3 Legaspi Phil.
42 F2 Legden Ger.
74 A2 Leggett U.S.A.
48 D2 Legnago Italy
46 H5 Legnica Pol.
22 D2 Leh Jammu and Kashmir
44 E2 Le Havre France
81 F4 Lehighton U.S.A.
36 V5 Lehmo Fin.
43 L2 Lehnin Ger.
43 J2 Lehre Ger.
43 H2 Lehrte Ger.
36 S5 Lehtimäki Fin.
58 D1 Lehututu Botswana
22 B3 Leiah Pak.
46 G7 Leibnitz Austria
39 F5 Leicester U.K.
6 D3 Leichhardt r. Austr.
42 C2 Leiden Neth.
9 E2 Leigh N.Z.
38 E4 Leigh U.K.
39 G6 Leighton Buzzard U.K.
43 G5 Leimen Ger.
43 H2 Leine r. Ger.
43 J3 Leinefelde Ger.
41 E5 Leinster, Mount h. Rep. of Ireland
49 M6 Leipsoi i. Greece
43 L3 Leipzig Ger.
36 O3 Leiranger Norway
45 B3 Leiria Port.

43 L4 Lößnitz Ger.
89 C2 Los Taques Venez.
89 D2 Los Teques Venez.
89 E2 Los Testigos is Venez.
74 C4 Lost Hills U.S.A.
72 D2 Lost Trail Pass pass U.S.A.
39 C7 Lostwithiel U.K.
88 C2 Los Vientos Chile
91 B1 Los Vilos Chile
91 B3 Lota Chile
19 E2 Lotfābād Iran
59 J3 Lothair S. Africa
56 D3 Lotikipi Plain plain Kenya
56 C4 Loto Congo(Zaire)
50 E3 Lotoshino Rus. Fed.
59 G1 Lotsane r. Botswana
36 V2 Lotta r. Fin./Rus. Fed.
43 F2 Lotte Ger.
25 C4 Louang Namtha Laos
25 C5 Louangphrabang Laos
56 B4 Loubomo Congo
44 C2 Loudéac France
27 D5 Loudi China
56 B4 Loudima Congo
80 B4 Loudonville U.S.A.
54 A3 Louga Senegal
39 F5 Loughborough U.K.
39 C6 Loughor r. U.K.
41 C4 Loughrea Rep. of Ireland
39 H6 Loughton U.K.
80 B5 Louisa KY U.S.A.
80 E5 Louisa VA U.S.A.
41 B4 Louisburgh Rep. of Ireland
64 C4 Louise I. i. Can.
7 F3 Louisiade Archipelago is P.N.G.
77 E6 Louisiana div. U.S.A.
59 H1 Louis Trichardt S. Africa
79 D5 Louisville GA U.S.A.
78 C4 Louisville KY U.S.A.
77 F5 Louisville MS U.S.A.
66 E3 Louis-XIV, Pointe c. Can.
12 E3 Loukhi Rus. Fed.
45 B4 Loulé Port.
65 L4 Lount L. l. Can.
46 F5 Louny Czech Rep.
76 D3 Loup r. U.S.A.
66 F2 Loups Marins, Lacs des l. Can.
67 J4 Lourdes Can.
44 D5 Lourdes France
45 B2 Lousã Port.
30 E1 Loushan China
39 G4 Louth U.K.
49 K5 Loutra Aidipsou Greece
Louvain see Leuven
58 B1 Louwater-Suid Namibia
59 J3 Louwsburg S. Africa
36 R4 Lövånger Sweden
50 D3 Lovat' r. Rus. Fed.
49 L3 Lovech Bulg.
72 F3 Loveland U.S.A.
72 E2 Lovell U.S.A.
74 C1 Lovelock U.S.A.
42 B3 Lovendegem Belgium
37 U6 Loviisa Fin.
80 D6 Lovingston U.S.A.
68 C6 Lovington IL U.S.A.
77 C5 Lovington NM U.S.A.
69 K3 Low Can.
56 C4 Lowa Congo(Zaire)
22 B2 Lowarai Pass pass Pak.
65 M2 Low, Cape c. Can.
81 H3 Lowell MA U.S.A.
68 E4 Lowell MI U.S.A.
81 G2 Lowell VT U.S.A.
64 F5 Lower Arrow L. l. Can.
75 F4 Lower Granite Gorge gorge U.S.A.
9 E4 Lower Hutt N.Z.
74 A2 Lower Lake U.S.A.
41 D3 Lower Lough Erne l. U.K.
32 □ Lower Peirce Res. resr Sing.
64 D3 Lower Post Can.
67 H5 Lower Sackville Can.
39 J5 Lowestoft U.K.
47 J4 Łowicz Pol.
66 E3 Low, Lac l. Can.
40 E5 Lowther Hills h. U.K.
81 F3 Lowville U.S.A.
43 G1 Loxstedt Ger.
8 C3 Loxton Austr.
58 E5 Loxton S. Africa
80 E4 Loyalsock Creek r. U.S.A.
74 B2 Loyalton U.S.A.
Loyalty Is is see Loyauté, Îs
7 G4 Loyauté, Îs is New Caledonia
51 D5 Loyew Belarus
49 H2 Loznica Yugo.
51 F5 Lozova Ukr.
57 C5 Luacano Angola
26 E4 Lu'an China
26 D3 Luanchuan China
57 B4 Luanda Angola
32 A3 Luang, Khao mt Thai.
57 D5 Luangwa r. Zambia
23 H2 Luanhaizi China
26 F1 Luan He r. China
26 F2 Luannan China
26 E1 Luanping China
57 C5 Luanshya Zambia
26 F2 Luan Xian China
57 C4 Luanza Congo(Zaire)
45 C1 Luarca Spain
33 D2 Luar, Danau l. Indon.
57 C5 Luau Angola
47 L5 Lubaczów Pol.
37 U8 Lubāna l. Latvia
31 B3 Lubang Phil.
31 B3 Lubang i. Phil.
31 A3 Lubang Islands is Phil.
57 B5 Lubango Angola
56 C4 Lubao Congo(Zaire)
47 L5 Lubartów Pol.
43 G2 Lübbecke Ger.
58 C4 Lubbeskolk salt pan S. Africa
77 C5 Lubbock U.S.A.
43 K2 Lübbow Ger.
43 J1 Lübeck Ger.
47 L5 Lubelska, Wyżyna reg. Pol.
56 C4 Lubero Congo(Zaire)
46 H5 Lubin Pol.
47 L5 Lublin Pol.
51 E5 Lubny Ukr.
33 D2 Lubok Antu Malaysia
43 K1 Lübstorf Ger.
43 K1 Lübtheen Ger.
31 B2 Lubuagan Phil.
57 C4 Lubudi Congo(Zaire)
33 B3 Lubuklinggau Indon.
32 A5 Lubukpakam Indon.
57 C5 Lubumbashi Congo(Zaire)
57 C5 Lubungu Zambia
56 C4 Lubutu Congo(Zaire)
43 L1 Lübz Ger.
57 B4 Lucala Angola
41 E4 Lucan Rep. of Ireland
64 A2 Lucania, Mt mt Can.
57 C4 Lucapa Angola
79 E7 Lucaya Bahamas
48 D3 Lucca Italy
40 D6 Luce Bay b. U.K.
90 B3 Lucélia Brazil
31 B3 Lucena Phil.
45 D4 Lucena Spain
47 J6 Lučenec Slovakia
48 F4 Lucera Italy
Lucerne see Luzern
28 D1 Luchegorsk Rus. Fed.
27 D6 Luchuan China
27 B6 Lüchun China
8 C4 Lucindale Austr.
57 B5 Lucira Angola
23 F4 Luckeesarai India
43 M2 Luckenwalde Ger.
58 F4 Luckhoff S. Africa
69 G4 Lucknow Can.
22 E4 Lucknow India
57 C5 Lucusse Angola
50 F1 Luda Rus. Fed.
42 F3 Lüdenscheid Ger.
57 B6 Lüderitz Namibia
43 J1 Lüdersdorf Ger.
22 C3 Ludhiana India
27 B5 Ludian China
68 D4 Ludington U.S.A.
39 E5 Ludlow U.K.
74 D4 Ludlow CA U.S.A.
81 J1 Ludlow ME U.S.A.
81 G3 Ludlow VT U.S.A.
49 M3 Ludogorie reg. Bulg.
37 O6 Ludvika Sweden
43 H6 Ludwigsburg Ger.
43 M2 Ludwigsfelde Ger.
43 G5 Ludwigshafen am Rhein Ger.
43 K1 Ludwigslust Ger.
37 U8 Ludza Latvia
56 C4 Luebo Congo(Zaire)
57 B5 Luena Angola
89 E3 Luepa Venez.
26 C3 Lüeyang China
27 E6 Lufeng China
77 E6 Lufkin U.S.A.
50 D3 Luga Rus. Fed.
50 D3 Luga r. Rus. Fed.
48 C1 Lugano Switz.
43 L4 Lugau Ger.
43 H3 Lügde Ger.
57 D5 Lugenda r. Moz.
39 D5 Lugg r. U.K.
48 D2 Lugo Italy
45 C1 Lugo Spain
49 J2 Lugoj Romania
31 B5 Lugus i. Phil.
51 F5 Luhans'k Ukr.
26 F3 Luhe China
43 J1 Luhe r. Ger.
23 H4 Luhit r. India
57 D4 Luhombero Tanz.
51 D5 Luhyny Ukr.
57 C5 Luiana Angola
Luik see Liège
56 C4 Luilaka r. Congo(Zaire)
40 C4 Luing i. U.K.
48 C2 Luino Italy
36 U3 Luiro r. Fin.
84 B2 Luis Moya Mex.
56 C4 Luiza Congo(Zaire)
91 E2 Luján r. Arg.
91 C2 Luján de Cuyo Arg.
26 E4 Lujiang China
49 H2 Lukavac Bos.-Herz.
56 C4 Lukenie r. Congo(Zaire)
75 F6 Lukeville U.S.A.
50 G3 Lukh r. Rus. Fed.
50 F4 Lukhovitsy Rus. Fed.
49 L3 Lukovit Bulg.
47 L5 Łuków Pol.
50 H4 Lukoyanov Rus. Fed.
57 C5 Lukulu Zambia
57 D4 Lukumburu Tanz.
36 S4 Luleå Sweden
36 R4 Luleälven r. Sweden
16 A1 Lüleburgaz Turkey
27 B5 Luliang China
26 D2 Lüliang Shan mts China
77 D6 Luling U.S.A.
26 F2 Lulong China
23 F3 Lülung China
23 F3 Lumachomo China
33 D4 Lumajang Indon.
23 E2 Lumajangdong Co salt l. China
57 C5 Lumbala Kaquengue Angola
57 C5 Lumbala N'guimbo Angola
79 E5 Lumberton U.S.A.
45 C2 Lumbrales Spain
23 H4 Lumding India
36 T4 Lumijoki Fin.
32 C2 Lumphăt Cambodia
9 B6 Lumsden N.Z.
33 C3 Lumut, Tanjung pt Indon.
31 B2 Luna Phil.
75 H5 Luna U.S.A.
40 F4 Lunan Bay b. U.K.
65 L2 Lunan Lake l. Can.
69 F5 Luna Pier U.S.A.
22 C5 Lunavada India
22 B4 Lund Pak.
37 N9 Lund Sweden
75 F2 Lund U.S.A.
65 K4 Lundar Can.
57 D5 Lundazi Zambia
39 C6 Lundy Island i. U.K.
38 E3 Lune r. U.K.
43 J1 Lüneburg Ger.
43 J1 Lüneburger Heide reg. Ger.
42 F3 Lünen Ger.
44 H2 Lunéville France
57 C5 Lunga r. Zambia
23 E2 Lungdo China
23 E3 Lunggar China
54 A4 Lungi Sierra Leone
27 □ Lung Kwu Chau h. H.K. China
23 H5 Lunglei India
41 E5 Lungnaquilla Mountain mt Rep. of Ireland
57 C5 Lungwebungu r. Zambia
22 C4 Luni India
22 C4 Luni r. India
22 B3 Luni r. Pak.
74 C2 Luning U.S.A.
50 H4 Lunino Rus. Fed.
51 C4 Luninyets Belarus
22 C1 Lunkho mt Afgh./Pak.
42 F2 Lünne Ger.
54 A4 Lunsar Sierra Leone
59 H2 Lunsklip S. Africa
15 G2 Luntai China
26 D3 Luo r. Henan China
26 C3 Luo r. Shaanxi China
27 C5 Luocheng China
26 C3 Luochuan China
27 C5 Luodian China
27 D6 Luoding China
27 D6 Luodou Sha i. China
26 E3 Luohe China
26 D3 Luoning China
27 B5 Luoping China
26 E4 Luoshan China
27 E4 Luotian China
26 D3 Luoyang China
27 F5 Luoyuan China
30 F2 Luozigou China
57 C5 Lupane Zimbabwe
33 D2 Lupar r. Malaysia
49 K2 Lupeni Romania
57 D5 Lupilichi Moz.
31 C5 Lupon Phil.
75 H4 Lupton U.S.A.
26 B3 Luqu China
27 B5 Luquan China
17 K3 Lūrā Shīrīn Iran
57 B4 Luremo Angola
40 C2 Lurgainn, Loch l. U.K.
41 E3 Lurgan U.K.
57 E5 Lúrio Moz.
57 D5 Lurio r. Moz.
57 C5 Lusaka Zambia
56 C4 Lusambo Congo(Zaire)
6 F2 Lusancay Islands and Reefs is P.N.G.
64 F4 Luscar Can.
65 H4 Luseland Can.
26 D3 Lushi China
49 H4 Lushnjë Albania
30 D2 Lushuihe China
30 A4 Lüshun China
59 H5 Lusikisiki S. Africa
72 F3 Lusk U.S.A.
19 E4 Lut, Dasht-e des. Iran
27 D6 Lutau Macau
69 G4 Luther Lake l. Can.
43 L3 Lutherstadt Wittenberg Ger.
39 G6 Luton U.K.
33 D2 Lutong Malaysia
65 G2 Łutselk'e Can.
51 C5 Luts'k Ukr.
42 D2 Luttelgeest Neth.
42 E2 Luttenberg Neth.
43 H5 Lützelbach Ger.
92 D4 Lützow-Holmbukta b. Ant.
58 D4 Lutzputs S. Africa
58 C5 Lutzville S. Africa
31 B5 Luuk Phil.
37 U6 Luumäki Fin.
56 E3 Luuq Somalia
76 D3 Luverne U.S.A.
56 C4 Luvua r. Congo(Zaire)
59 J1 Luvuvhu r. S. Africa
56 D3 Luwero Uganda
42 E5 Luxembourg Lux.
34 F4 Luxembourg country Europe
44 H3 Luxeuil-les-Bains France
27 D4 Luxi Hunan China
27 B5 Luxi Yunnan China
59 G5 Luxolweni S. Africa
55 F2 Luxor Egypt
26 E3 Luyi China
42 D3 Luyksgestel Neth.
50 H2 Luza Rus. Fed.
50 J2 Luza r. Rus. Fed.
46 D7 Luzern Switz.
27 C5 Luzhai China
27 B5 Luzhi China
27 B4 Luzhou China
90 C2 Luziânia Brazil
87 K4 Luzilândia Brazil
31 B3 Luzon i. Phil.
31 B1 Luzon Strait str. Phil.
44 F3 Luzy France
51 C5 L'viv Ukr.
L'vov see L'viv
50 D3 Lyady Rus. Fed.
50 C4 Lyakhavichy Belarus
65 H3 Lyall, Mt mt Can.
Lyallpur see Faisalabad
36 Q4 Lycksele Sweden
39 H7 Lydd U.K.
92 C3 Lyddan I. i. Ant.
59 J2 Lydenburg S. Africa
39 E6 Lydney U.K.
51 D5 Lyel'chytsy Belarus
64 C4 Lyell I. i. Can.
74 C3 Lyell, Mt mt U.S.A.
50 D4 Lyepyel' Belarus
80 E4 Lykens U.S.A.
72 E3 Lyman U.S.A.
39 E7 Lyme Bay b. U.K.
39 E7 Lyme Regis U.K.
39 F7 Lymington U.K.
80 D6 Lynchburg U.S.A.
81 H2 Lynchville U.S.A.
8 G2 Lyndhurst Austr.
81 G2 Lyndonville U.S.A.
40 E2 Lyness U.K.
37 K7 Lyngdal Norway
81 H3 Lynn U.S.A.
64 B3 Lynn Canal chan. U.S.A.
75 F2 Lynndyl U.S.A.
65 J3 Lynn Lake Can.
39 D6 Lynton U.K.
65 H2 Lynx Lake l. Can.
44 G4 Lyon France
81 G2 Lyon Mountain U.S.A.
79 D5 Lyons GA U.S.A.
80 E3 Lyons NY U.S.A.
81 F3 Lyons Falls U.S.A.
50 D4 Lyozna Belarus
7 F2 Lyra Reef rf P.N.G.
37 M7 Lysekil Sweden
50 H3 Lyskovo Rus. Fed.
12 G4 Lys'va Rus. Fed.
51 F5 Lysychans'k Ukr.
38 D4 Lytham St Anne's U.K.
64 E4 Lytton Can.
50 D4 Lyuban' Belarus
51 C5 Lyubeshiv Ukr.
50 E4 Lyudinovo Rus. Fed.
50 H3 Lyunda r. Rus. Fed.

M

57 C5 Maamba Zambia
16 E6 Ma'an Jordan
36 U5 Maaninka Fin.
36 V3 Maaninkavaara Fin.
26 F4 Ma'anshan China
37 T7 Maardu Estonia
16 F4 Ma'arrat an Nu'mān Syria
42 D2 Maarssen Neth.
42 E3 Maas r. Neth.
42 D3 Maaseik Belgium
31 C4 Maasin Phil.
42 D4 Maasmechelen Belgium
42 D4 Maastricht Neth.
59 H1 Maastroom S. Africa
31 B3 Mabalacat Phil.
57 D6 Mabalane Moz.
86 G2 Mabaruma Guyana
69 J3 Maberly Can.
27 B4 Mabian China
39 H4 Mablethorpe U.K.
59 H2 Mabopane S. Africa
57 D6 Mabote Moz.
31 B1 Mabudis i. Phil.
58 F2 Mabule Botswana
58 E2 Mabutsane Botswana
91 D3 Macachín Arg.
81 K2 MacAdam Can.
90 E3 Macaé Brazil
31 C4 Macajalar Bay b. Phil.
77 E5 McAlester U.S.A.
80 E4 McAlevys Fort U.S.A.
8 G3 McAlister mt Austr.
8 F4 Macalister r. Austr.
77 D7 McAllen U.S.A.
57 D5 Macaloge Moz.
62 H3 MacAlpine Lake l. Can.
88 B7 Macá, Mt mt Chile
59 K1 Macandze Moz.
87 H3 Macapá Brazil
86 C4 Macará Ecuador
90 E1 Macarani Brazil
89 B4 Macarena, Cordillera mts Col.
89 B4 Macarena, Parque Nacional La nat. park Col.
8 D5 Macarthur Austr.
80 B5 McArthur U.S.A.
69 J3 McArthur Mills Can.
64 B2 McArthur Wildlife Sanctuary res. Can.
86 C4 Macas Ecuador
33 E3 Macassar Strait str. Indon.
87 L5 Macau Brazil
27 D6 Macau Macau
87 H6 Macaúba Brazil
90 D1 Macaúbas Brazil
89 B4 Macaya r. Col.
89 B4 Macayari Col.
64 E4 McBride Can.
72 C2 McCall U.S.A.
77 C6 McCamey U.S.A.
72 D3 McCammon U.S.A.
59 K2 Maccaretane Moz.
64 C4 McCauley I. i. Can.
39 E4 Macclesfield U.K.
62 H2 McClintock Chan. Can.
74 B3 McClure, L. l. U.S.A.
62 F2 McClure Strait Can.
77 F6 McComb U.S.A.
76 C3 McConaughy, L. l. U.S.A.
80 E5 McConnellsburg U.S.A.
80 C5 McConnelsville U.S.A.
76 C3 McCook U.S.A.
65 K4 McCreary Can.
75 E4 McCullough Range mts U.S.A.
64 D3 McDame Can.
72 C3 McDermitt U.S.A.
6 C4 Macdonald, L. salt flat Austr.
72 D2 McDonald Peak summit U.S.A.
6 D4 Macdonnell Ranges mts Austr.
58 B4 McDougall's Bay b. S. Africa
66 B3 MacDowell L. l. Can.
75 G5 McDowell Peak summit U.S.A.
40 F3 Macduff U.K.
45 C2 Macedo de Cavaleiros Port.
8 E4 Macedon mt Austr.
35 H4 Macedonia country Europe
87 L5 Maceió Brazil
54 B4 Macenta Guinea
48 E3 Macerata Italy
74 C4 McFarland U.S.A.
65 H3 McFarlane r. Can.
6 D5 Macfarlane, L. salt flat Austr.
75 E2 McGill U.S.A.
41 B6 Macgillycuddy's Reeks mts Rep. of Ireland
62 C3 McGrath U.S.A.
58 C6 McGregor S. Africa
68 A2 McGregor U.S.A.
64 E4 McGregor r. Can.
69 G2 McGregor Bay Can.
72 D2 McGuire, Mt mt U.S.A.
22 A3 Mach Pak.
86 C4 Machachi Ecuador
90 D3 Machado Brazil
57 D6 Machaila Moz.
56 D4 Machakos Kenya
86 C4 Machala Ecuador
57 D6 Machanga Moz.
59 K2 Machatuine Moz.
42 C5 Machault France
26 E4 Macheng China
21 B2 Macherla India
21 C2 Māchhakund Dam dam India
81 K2 Machias ME U.S.A.
80 D3 Machias NY U.S.A.
81 J1 Machias r. U.S.A.
21 C2 Machilipatnam India
89 B2 Machiques Venez.
40 C5 Machrihanish U.K.
39 D5 Machynlleth U.K.
59 K2 Macia Moz.
49 N2 Măcin Romania
81 G2 McIndoe Falls U.S.A.
76 C2 McIntosh U.S.A.
75 H2 Mack U.S.A.
17 G1 Maçka Turkey
6 E4 Mackay Austr.
72 D2 Mackay U.S.A.
65 G2 Mackay Lake l. Can.
6 C4 Mackay, Lake salt flat Austr.
7 J2 McKean Island i. Kiribati
80 A6 McKee U.S.A.
80 D4 McKeesport U.S.A.
81 F3 McKeever U.S.A.
64 E3 Mackenzie B.C. Can.
68 C1 Mackenzie Ont. Can.
79 B4 McKenzie U.S.A.
62 E3 Mackenzie r. Can.
92 D5 Mackenzie Bay b. Ant.
62 E3 Mackenzie Bay b. Y.T. Can.
64 F2 Mackenzie Bison Sanctuary res. Can.
62 G2 Mackenzie King I. Can.
64 C2 Mackenzie Mountains mts Can.
62 E3 Mackenzie Mts Can.
68 E3 Mackinac I. i. U.S.A.
68 E3 Mackinac, Straits of chan. U.S.A.
68 C5 Mackinaw r. U.S.A.
68 E3 Mackinaw City U.S.A.
62 C3 McKinley, Mt U.S.A.
77 D5 McKinney U.S.A.
92 B2 Mackintosh, C. c. Ant.
74 C4 McKittrick U.S.A.
65 H4 Macklin Can.
7 F5 Macksville Austr.
76 C2 McLaughlin U.S.A.
59 H5 Maclear S. Africa
64 F3 McLennan Can.
64 F4 McLeod r. Can.
64 E3 McLeod Lake Can.
6 B4 Macleod, Lake l. Austr.
72 B3 McLoughlin, Mt mt U.S.A.
68 E2 McMillan U.S.A.
64 C2 Macmillan r. Can.
72 B2 McMinnville OR U.S.A.
79 C5 McMinnville TN U.S.A.
92 B5 McMurdo U.S.A. Base Ant.
75 H4 McNary U.S.A.
64 F4 McNaughton Lake l. Can.
75 H6 McNeal U.S.A.
68 B5 Macomb U.S.A.
48 C4 Macomer Sardinia Italy
44 G3 Mâcon France
79 D5 Macon GA U.S.A.
76 E4 Macon MO U.S.A.
57 C5 Macondo Angola
76 D4 McPherson U.S.A.
8 F1 Macquarie r. Austr.
6 E6 Macquarie Harbour in. Austr.
4 G10 Macquarie Island i. Austr.
8 H2 Macquarie, L. b. Austr.
8 F1 Macquarie Marshes marsh Austr.
8 G2 Macquarie Mt mt Austr.
94 F9 Macquarie Ridge sea feature Pac. Oc.
64 B2 McQuesten r. Can.
79 D5 McRae U.S.A.
32 □ MacRitchie Res. resr Sing.
92 D4 Mac. Robertson Land reg. Ant.
41 C6 Macroom Rep. of Ireland
89 C1 Macuira, Parque Nacional nat. park Col.
89 B4 Macuje Col.
6 D4 Macumba watercourse Austr.
86 D6 Macusani Peru
84 D3 Macuspana Mex.
70 E6 Macuzari, Presa resr Mex.
64 E1 McVicar Arm b. Can.
81 J2 Macwahoc U.S.A.
16 E6 Mādabā Jordan
59 J3 Madadeni S. Africa
53 J8 Madagascar country Africa
93 H5 Madagascar Basin sea feature Ind. Ocean
93 G6 Madagascar Ridge sea feature Ind. Ocean
21 B3 Madakasira India
55 D2 Madama Niger
49 L4 Madan Bulg.
21 B3 Madanapalle India
6 E2 Madang P.N.G.
54 C3 Madaoua Niger
23 G5 Madaripur Bangl.
69 J3 Madawaska Can.
81 J1 Madawaska U.S.A.
69 J3 Madawaska r. Can.
86 F5 Madeira r. Brazil
34 D5 Madeira terr. Port.
67 H4 Madeleine, Îles de la is Can.
68 B2 Madeline I. i. U.S.A.
17 G2 Maden Turkey
82 C3 Madera Mex.
74 B3 Madera U.S.A.
21 A3 Madgaon India
23 F4 Madhepura India
21 C2 Madhira India
23 F4 Madhubani India
22 D5 Madhya Pradesh div. India
59 F3 Madibogo S. Africa
21 A3 Madikeri India
56 B4 Madingou Congo
86 E6 Madini r. Bol.
57 E5 Madirovalo Madag.
78 C4 Madison IN U.S.A.
81 J2 Madison ME U.S.A.
76 D2 Madison MN U.S.A.
76 D3 Madison NE U.S.A.
76 D2 Madison SD U.S.A.
68 C4 Madison WI U.S.A.
80 C5 Madison WV U.S.A.
70 D2 Madison r. MT U.S.A.
78 C4 Madisonville KY U.S.A.
77 E6 Madisonville TX U.S.A.
33 D4 Madiun Indon.
69 J3 Madoc Can.
56 D3 Mado Gashi Kenya
24 B3 Madoi China
37 U8 Madona Latvia
22 B4 Madpura India
49 M5 Madra Dağı mts Turkey
21 C3 Madras India
72 B2 Madras U.S.A.
86 D6 Madre de Dios r. Peru
88 A8 Madre de Dios, I. i. Chile
84 B3 Madre del Sur, Sierra mts Mex.
84 C1 Madre, Laguna lag. Mex.
77 D7 Madre, Laguna lag. U.S.A.
84 A1 Madre Occidental, Sierra mts Mex.
84 B1 Madre Oriental, Sierra mts Mex.
31 B2 Madre, Sierra mt Phil.
84 D3 Madre, Sierra mts Mex.
31 C4 Madrid Phil.
45 E2 Madrid Spain
31 B4 Madridejos Phil.
45 E3 Madridejos Spain
21 C2 Madugula India
33 D4 Madura i. Indon.
21 B4 Madurai India
33 D4 Madura, Selat chan. Indon.
23 E4 Madwas India
22 C2 Madyan Pak.
51 H7 Madzhalis Rus. Fed.
29 F6 Maebashi Japan
32 A1 Mae Hong Son Thai.
32 B2 Mae Khlong r. Thai.
32 A1 Mae Lao r. Thai.
32 A1 Mae Li r. Thai.
32 B1 Mae Nam Ing r. Thai.
32 C2 Mae Nam Mun r. Thai.
32 B2 Mae Nam Nan r. Thai.
32 B2 Mae Nam Pa Sak r. Thai.
32 B2 Mae Nam Ping r. Thai.
32 A1 Mae Nam Wang r. Thai.
32 B2 Mae Nam Yom r. Thai.
83 J5 Maestra, Sierra mts Cuba
57 E5 Maevatanana Madag.
7 G3 Maéwo i. Vanuatu
32 A1 Mae Yuam r. Myanmar/Thai.
65 J4 Mafeking Can.
59 G4 Mafeteng Lesotho
8 F4 Maffra Austr.
57 D4 Mafia I. i. Tanz.
59 F2 Mafikeng S. Africa
57 D4 Mafinga Tanz.
90 C4 Mafra Brazil
16 F5 Mafraq Jordan
59 J5 Magabeni S. Africa
13 R4 Magadan Rus. Fed.
56 D4 Magadi Kenya
59 K1 Magaiza Moz.
31 B3 Magallanes Phil.
88 B8 Magallanes, Estrecho de chan. Chile
89 B2 Magangue Col.
16 D3 Mağara Turkey
Magas see Zābolī
31 B2 Magat r. Phil.
91 F2 Magdalena Arg.
86 F6 Magdalena Bol.
82 B2 Magdalena Mex.
73 F5 Magdalena U.S.A.
89 B3 Magdalena r. Col.
70 D7 Magdalena, Bahía b. Mex.
88 B6 Magdalena, Isla i. Chile
31 A5 Magdaleno, Mt mt Malaysia
43 K2 Magdeburg Ger.
94 F4 Magellan Seamounts sea feature Pac. Oc.
36 T1 Magerøya i. Norway
29 B9 Mage-shima i. Japan
48 C2 Maggiorasca, Monte mt Italy
48 C2 Maggiore, Lago l. Italy
54 A3 Maghama Maur.
41 E3 Maghera U.K.
41 E3 Magherafelt U.K.
38 E4 Maghull U.K.
72 D3 Magna U.S.A.
48 F6 Magna Grande mt Sicily Italy
92 D4 Magnet Bay b. Ant.
6 E3 Magnetic I. i. Austr.
36 X2 Magnetity Rus. Fed.
12 G4 Magnitogorsk Rus. Fed.
77 E5 Magnolia U.S.A.
67 F4 Magog Can.
84 C2 Magosal Mex.
67 H3 Magpie Can.
68 E1 Magpie r. Can.
67 H3 Magpie r. Can.
68 E1 Magpie Lake l. Can.
64 G5 Magrath Can.
74 D3 Magruder Mt mt U.S.A.
54 A3 Magta' Lahjar Maur.
56 D4 Magu Tanz.
27 B6 Maguan China
87 J4 Maguarinho, Cabo pt Brazil
59 K2 Magude Moz.
81 K2 Magundy Can.
65 K2 Maguse Lake l. Can.
23 H5 Magwe Myanmar
23 H5 Magyichaung Myanmar
18 B2 Mahābād Iran
21 A2 Mahabaleshwar India
Mahabalipuram see Māmallapuram
23 F4 Mahabharat Range mts Nepal
57 E6 Mahabo Madag.
21 A2 Mahad India
22 D5 Mahadeo Hills h. India
56 D3 Mahagi Congo(Zaire)
22 C3 Mahajan India
57 E5 Mahajanga Madag.
33 D2 Mahakam r. Indon.
57 C6 Mahalapye Botswana
57 E5 Mahalevona Madag.
18 C3 Mahallāt Iran
22 D3 Maham India
33 D4 Mahameru, Gunung volc. Indon.
18 E4 Mahān Iran
23 F5 Mahanadi r. India
57 E5 Mahanoro Madag.
22 C6 Maharashtra div. India
23 E5 Mahasamund India
32 B1 Maha Sarakham Thai.
57 E6 Mahatalaky Madag.
57 E5 Mahavavy r. Madag.
21 C5 Mahaweli Ganga r. Sri Lanka
32 C1 Mahaxai Laos
21 C2 Mahbubabad India
21 B2 Mahbubnagar India
18 D5 Maḩḑah Oman
87 G2 Mahdia Guyana
48 D7 Mahdia Tunisia
53 K6 Mahé i. Seychelles
21 D2 Mahendragiri mt India
22 C5 Mahesāna India
22 C5 Maheshwar India
22 C5 Mahi r. India
19 E4 Māhī watercourse Iran
9 F3 Mahia Peninsula pen. N.Z.
50 D4 Mahilyow Belarus
21 C5 Mahiyangana Sri Lanka
59 J4 Mahlabatini S. Africa
43 K2 Mahlsdorf Ger.
19 H3 Maḩmūd-e 'Erāqī Afgh.
17 M4 Mahnīān Iran
76 D2 Mahnomen U.S.A.
22 D4 Mahoba India
45 J3 Mahón Spain
80 D4 Mahoning Creek Lake l. U.S.A.
23 H5 Mahudaung Hgts mts Myanmar
22 B5 Mahuva India
49 M4 Mahya Dağı mt Turkey
18 C3 Mahyār Iran
23 H4 Maibang India
89 B2 Maicao Col.
66 E4 Maicasagi, Lac l. Can.
27 C6 Maichen China
39 G6 Maidenhead U.K.
65 H4 Maidstone Can.
39 H6 Maidstone U.K.
55 D3 Maiduguri Nigeria
89 D3 Maigualida, Sierra mts Venez.
41 C5 Maigue r. Rep. of Ireland
22 E4 Maihar India
26 C3 Maiji Shan mt China
22 E5 Maikala Range h. India
56 C4 Maiko, Parc National de la nat. park Congo(Zaire)
22 E3 Mailani India
43 H5 Main r. Ger.
41 E3 Main r. U.K.
67 J3 Main Brook Can.
69 F3 Main Channel Can.
56 B4 Mai-Ndombe, Lac l. Congo(Zaire)
43 K5 Main-Donau-Kanal canal Ger.
69 J4 Main Duck I. i. Can.
81 J2 Maine div. U.S.A.
54 D3 Maïné-Soroa Niger
32 A2 Maingy I. i. Myanmar
43 H5 Mainhardt Ger.
31 C4 Mainit Phil.
31 C4 Mainit, Lake l. Phil.
40 E1 Mainland i. Orkney U.K.
40 □ Mainland i. Shetland U.K.
43 K4 Mainleus Ger.
23 E5 Mainpat reg. India
22 D4 Mainpuri India
57 E5 Maintirano Madag.
43 G4 Mainz Ger.
54 □ Maio i. Cape Verde
91 C2 Maipó, Vol. volc. Chile
91 F3 Maipú Buenos Aires Arg.
91 C2 Maipú Mendoza Arg.
89 D2 Maiquetía Venez.
23 G5 Maiskhal I. i. Bangl.
57 C6 Maitengwe Botswana
8 H2 Maitland N.S.W. Austr.
8 A3 Maitland S.A. Austr.
92 D3 Maitri India Base Ant.
23 G3 Maizhokunggar China
83 H6 Maíz, Islas del is Nic.
29 D7 Maizuru Japan
49 H3 Maja Jezercë mt Albania
21 B2 Mājalgaon India
89 E4 Majari r. Brazil
33 E3 Majene Indon.
18 C6 Majhūd well S. Arabia
56 D3 Majī Eth.
26 E2 Majia r. China
27 D6 Majiang China
Majorca i. see Mallorca
23 H4 Majuli I. i. India
95 G5 Majuro i. Pac. Oc.
59 G4 Majwemasweu S. Africa
56 B4 Makabana Congo
74 □1 Makaha U.S.A.
25 D7 Makale Indon.
23 F4 Makalu, Mt mt China
56 C4 Makamba Burundi
15 G2 Makanchi Kazak.
74 □1 Makapuu Hd hd U.S.A.
50 J2 Makar-Ib Rus. Fed.
48 G3 Makarska Croatia
14 D2 Makat Kazak.
59 K3 Makatini Flats lowland S. Africa
54 A4 Makeni Sierra Leone
57 C6 Makgadikgadi salt pan Botswana
51 H7 Makhachkala Rus. Fed.
16 G4 Makhfar al Ḩammām Syria
17 J4 Makhmūr Iraq
56 D4 Makindu Kenya
14 F1 Makinsk Kazak.
51 F5 Makiyivka Ukr.
Makkah see Mecca
67 J2 Makkovik Can.
67 J2 Makkovik, Cape c. Can.
42 D1 Makkum Neth.
49 J1 Makó Hungary
56 B3 Makokou Gabon
57 D4 Makongolosi Tanz.
58 E2 Makopong Botswana
56 B4 Makotipoko Congo
19 F5 Makran reg. Iran/Pak.
22 C4 Makrana India
Makran Coast Range mts see Talar-i-Band
23 E6 Makri India
49 L6 Makronisi i. Greece
50 E3 Maksatikha Rus. Fed.
28 E1 Maksimovka Rus. Fed.
19 F4 Maksotag Iran
18 B2 Mākū Iran
23 H4 Makum India
57 D4 Makumbako Tanz.
57 D5 Makunguwiro Tanz.
29 B9 Makurazaki Japan
54 C4 Makurdi Nigeria
18 D4 Makūyeh Iran
59 F3 Makwassie S. Africa
36 Q4 Malå Sweden
31 C5 Malabang Phil.
21 A3 Malabar Coast coastal area India
54 C4 Malabo Equatorial Guinea
31 A4 Malabuñgan Phil.
33 A2 Malacca, Strait of str. Indon./Malaysia
72 D3 Malad City U.S.A.
50 C4 Maladzyechna Belarus
45 D4 Málaga Spain
81 F5 Malaga NJ U.S.A.
73 F5 Malaga NM U.S.A.
7 G2 Malaita i. Solomon Is
55 F4 Malakal Sudan
21 C2 Malakanagiri India
7 G3 Malakula i. Vanuatu
22 C2 Malakwal Pak.
25 E7 Malamala Indon.
33 D4 Malang Indon.
57 B4 Malanje Angola
19 G5 Malan, Ras pt Pak.
91 C1 Malanzán, Sa de mts Arg.
21 B4 Malappuram India
83 H7 Mala, Pta pt Panama
37 P7 Mälaren l. Sweden
91 C2 Malargüe Arg.
69 H1 Malartic Can.
69 H1 Malartic, Lac l. Can.
64 A3 Malaspina Glacier gl. U.S.A.
16 G2 Malatya Turkey
22 C3 Malaut India
17 L5 Malāvi Iran
31 A5 Malawali i. Malaysia
53 H6 Malawi country Africa
Malawi, Lake l. see Nyasa, Lake
50 E3 Malaya Vishera Rus. Fed.
31 C4 Malaybalay Phil.
18 C3 Malāyer Iran
11 M9 Malaysia country Asia
17 J2 Malazgirt Turkey
47 J3 Malbork Pol.
42 E5 Malborn Ger.
43 L1 Malchin Ger.
43 L1 Malchiner See l. Ger.
23 G4 Māldah India
42 B3 Maldegem Belgium
77 F4 Malden U.S.A.
5 M5 Malden I. i. Kiribati
93 J4 Maldive Ridge sea feature Ind. Ocean
10 J9 Maldives country Ind. Ocean
39 H6 Maldon U.K.
91 F2 Maldonado Uru.
10 J9 Male Maldives
49 K6 Maleas, Akra i. Greece
15 F6 Male Atoll Maldives
59 F4 Malebogo S. Africa
21 B2 Malegaon India
22 C5 Malegaon India
46 H6 Malé Karpaty h. Slovakia
17 L3 Malek Kandī Iran
56 B4 Malele Congo(Zaire)
57 D5 Malema Moz.
22 C3 Maler Kotla India
19 G3 Mālestān Afgh.
51 H7 Malgobek Rus. Fed.
36 P4 Malgomaj l. Sweden
18 B5 Malham S. Arabia
72 C3 Malheur L. l. U.S.A.

69 F4 Mayville MI U.S.A.
76 D2 Mayville ND U.S.A.
80 D3 Mayville NY U.S.A.
68 C4 Mayville WI U.S.A.
76 C3 Maywood U.S.A.
91 D3 Maza Arg.
50 F3 Maza Rus. Fed.
57 C5 Mazabuka Zambia
87 H4 Mazagão Brazil
44 F5 Mazamet France
22 D1 Mazar China
48 E6 Mazara del Vallo Sicily Italy
19 G2 Mazār-e Sharīf Afgh.
19 G3 Mazar, Koh-i- mt Afgh.
89 E3 Mazaruni r. Guyana
82 F6 Mazatenango Guatemala
84 A2 Mazatlán Mex.
75 G4 Mazatzal Peak summit U.S.A.
18 C3 Mazdaj Iran
37 S8 Mažeikiai Lith.
17 G2 Mazgirt Turkey
37 S8 Mazirbe Latvia
56 D4 Mazomora Tanz.
17 M3 Mazr'eh Iran
17 M5 Māzū Iran
57 C6 Mazunga Zimbabwe
51 D4 Mazyr Belarus
59 J3 Mbabane Swaziland
54 B4 Mbahiakro Côte d'Ivoire
56 B3 Mbaïki C.A.R.
57 D4 Mbala Zambia
56 D3 Mbale Uganda
54 D4 Mbalmayo Cameroon
56 B4 Mbandaka Congo(Zaire)
54 C4 Mbanga Cameroon
56 B4 M'banza Congo Angola
56 D4 Mbarara Uganda
56 C3 Mbari r. C.A.R.
59 K3 Mbaswana S. Africa
54 D4 Mbengwi Cameroon
57 D4 Mbeya Tanz.
57 D5 Mbinga Tanz.
57 D6 Mbizi Zimbabwe
56 B3 Mbomo Congo
54 D4 Mbouda Cameroon
54 A3 Mbour Senegal
54 A3 Mbout Maur.
57 D4 Mbozi Tanz.
56 C4 Mbuji-Mayi Congo(Zaire)
56 D4 Mbulu Tanz.
56 D4 Mbuyuni Tanz.
57 D4 Mchinga Tanz.
59 G6 Mdantsane S. Africa
48 B6 M'Daourouch Alg.
77 C4 Meade U.S.A.
75 E3 Mead, Lake l. U.S.A.
65 H4 Meadow Lake Can.
65 H4 Meadow Lake Provincial Park res. Can.
75 E3 Meadow Valley Wash r. U.S.A.
80 C4 Meadville U.S.A.
69 G3 Meaford Can.
28 J3 Meaken-dake volc. Japan
40 A2 Mealasta Island i. U.K.
45 B2 Mealhada Port.
40 D4 Meall a'Bhuiridh mt U.K.
67 J3 Mealy Mountains Can.
19 F2 Meana Turkm.
64 F3 Meander River Can.
31 C5 Meares i. Indon.
44 F2 Meaux France
56 B4 Mebridege r. Angola
20 A5 Mecca S. Arabia
81 H2 Mechanic Falls U.S.A.
80 B4 Mechanicsburg U.S.A.
68 B5 Mechanicsville U.S.A.
42 C3 Mechelen Belgium
42 D4 Mechelen Neth.
54 B1 Mecheria Alg.
42 E4 Mechernich Ger.
16 E1 Mecitözü Turkey
42 F4 Meckenheim Ger.
46 E3 Mecklenburger Bucht b. Ger.
43 K1 Mecklenburgische Seenplatte reg. Ger.
43 L1 Mecklenburg-Vorpommern div. Ger.
57 D5 Mecula Moz.
45 C2 Meda Port.
21 B2 Medak India
33 A2 Medan Indon.
91 D3 Médanos Arg.
88 C7 Medanosa, Pta pt Arg.
21 C4 Medawachchiya Sri Lanka
21 B2 Medchal India
81 K2 Meddybemps L. l. U.S.A.
45 H4 Médéa Alg.
43 G3 Medebach Ger.
89 B3 Medellín Col.
39 F4 Meden r. U.K.
54 D1 Medenine Tunisia
54 A3 Mederdra Maur.
72 B3 Medford OR U.S.A.
68 B3 Medford WI U.S.A.
81 F5 Medford Farms U.S.A.
49 N2 Medgidia Romania
17 L4 Medhīkhan Iran
68 B5 Media U.S.A.
91 C2 Media Luna Arg.
47 M7 Mediaş Romania
72 C2 Medical Lake U.S.A.
72 F3 Medicine Bow U.S.A.
72 F3 Medicine Bow Mts mts U.S.A.
72 F3 Medicine Bow Peak summit U.S.A.
65 G4 Medicine Hat Can.
77 D4 Medicine Lodge U.S.A.
90 E2 Medina Brazil
20 A5 Medina S. Arabia
80 D3 Medina NY U.S.A.
80 C4 Medina OH U.S.A.
45 E2 Medinaceli Spain
45 D2 Medina del Campo Spain
45 D2 Medina de Rioseco Spain
23 F5 Medinīpur India
34 F5 Mediterranean Sea sea Africa/Europe
48 B6 Medjerda, Monts de la mts Alg.
12 G4 Mednogorsk Rus. Fed.
94 G2 Mednyy, Ostrov i. Rus. Fed.
44 D4 Médoc reg. France
50 H3 Medvedevo Rus. Fed.
51 H5 Medveditsa r. Rus. Fed.
48 F2 Medvednica mts Croatia
13 S2 Medvezh'i, O-va is Rus. Fed.
24 F2 Medvezh'ya, Gora mt China/Rus. Fed.
50 E2 Medvezh'yegorsk Rus. Fed.
39 H6 Medway r. U.K.
6 B4 Meekatharra Austr.
75 H1 Meeker U.S.A.
74 B2 Meeks Bay U.S.A.
67 J4 Meelpaeg Res. resr Can.
43 L4 Meerane Ger.
42 E3 Meerlo Neth.
22 D3 Meerut India
72 E2 Meeteetse U.S.A.
56 D3 Mēga Eth.
33 B3 Mega i. Indon.
23 G4 Meghalaya div. India
23 F5 Meghāsani mt India
23 G5 Meghna r. Bangl.
17 L2 Meghri Armenia
16 B3 Megisti i. Greece
36 U1 Mehamn Norway
19 G5 Mehar Pak.
6 B4 Meharry, Mt mt Austr.
22 D5 Mehekar India
23 G5 Meherpur Bangl.
80 E6 Meherrin r. U.S.A.
5 N6 Méhétia i. Pac. Oc.
17 L2 Mehrābān Iran
17 L5 Mehrān Iraq
18 D5 Mehrān watercourse Iran
42 E4 Mehren Ger.
18 D4 Mehriz Iran
19 H3 Mehtar Lām Afgh.
90 C2 Meia Ponte r. Brazil
55 D4 Meiganga Cameroon
27 B4 Meigu China
27 E5 Mei Jiang r. China
42 D3 Meijnweg, Nationaal Park De nat. park Neth.
40 D5 Meikle Millyea h. U.K.
25 B4 Meiktila Myanmar
43 J2 Meine Ger.
43 J2 Meinersen Ger.
43 J4 Meiningen Ger.
58 E6 Meiringspoort pass S. Africa
27 B4 Meishan China
46 F5 Meißen Ger.
27 C5 Meitan China
26 C3 Mei Xian China
27 E5 Meizhou China
22 D4 Mej r. India
88 C3 Mejicana mt Arg.
88 B2 Mejillones Chile
56 D2 Mek'elē Eth.
54 A3 Mékhé Senegal
22 B3 Mekhtar Pak.
48 C7 Meknassy Tunisia
54 B1 Meknès Morocco
32 C2 Mekong r. Asia
24 B3 Mekong r. China
32 C3 Mekong, Mouths of the est. Vietnam
33 B2 Melaka Malaysia
94 G6 Melanesia is Pac. Oc.
31 A5 Melaut r. Malaysia
33 D3 Melawi r. Indon.
8 E4 Melbourne Austr.
79 D6 Melbourne U.S.A.
40 □ Melby U.K.
46 D3 Meldorf Ger.
69 F3 Meldrum Bay Can.
16 E2 Melendiz Dağı mt Turkey
50 G4 Melenki Rus. Fed.
67 F2 Mélèzes, Rivière aux r. Can.
55 D3 Mélfi Chad
48 F4 Melfi Italy
65 J4 Melfort Can.
36 M5 Melhus Norway
45 C1 Melide Spain
54 B1 Melilla Spain
91 E2 Melincué Arg.
33 E3 Melintang, Danau l. Indon.
91 B2 Melipilla Chile
42 B3 Meliskerke Neth.
65 J5 Melita Can.
51 E6 Melitopol' Ukr.
46 G6 Melk Austria
59 H1 Melkrivier S. Africa
39 E6 Melksham U.K.
36 T3 Mellakoski Fin.
36 O5 Mellansel Sweden
43 G2 Melle Ger.
68 B2 Mellen U.S.A.
37 N7 Mellerud Sweden
43 J4 Mellrichstadt Ger.
43 G1 Mellum i. Ger.
59 J4 Melmoth S. Africa
91 F2 Melo Uru.
8 B2 Melrose Austr.
40 F5 Melrose U.K.
43 H3 Melsungen Ger.
31 A5 Melta, Mt mt Malaysia
39 G5 Melton Mowbray U.K.
44 F2 Melun France
65 J4 Melville Can.
63 M2 Melville Bugt b. Greenland
6 E3 Melville, C. c. Austr.
31 A5 Melville, C. c. Phil.
6 D3 Melville Island i. Austr.
62 G2 Melville Island i. Can.
67 J3 Melville, Lake l. Can.
63 K3 Melville Peninsula Can.
41 C3 Melvin, Lough l. Rep. of Ireland/U.K.
13 T3 Melyuveyem Rus. Fed.
23 E2 Mêmar Co salt l. China
25 F7 Memberamo r. Indon.
59 H3 Memel S. Africa
43 J5 Memmelsdorf Ger.
46 E7 Memmingen Ger.
42 C5 Mémorial Américain h. France
33 C2 Mempawah Indon.
16 C7 Memphis Egypt
68 A5 Memphis MO U.S.A.
79 B5 Memphis TN U.S.A.
77 C5 Memphis TX U.S.A.
81 G2 Memphrémagog, Lac l. Can.
28 H3 Memuro-dake mt Japan
51 E5 Mena Ukr.
77 E5 Mena U.S.A.
54 C3 Ménaka Mali
Mènam Khong r. see Mekong
77 D6 Menard U.S.A.
68 C3 Menasha U.S.A.
33 D3 Mendawai r. Indon.
44 F4 Mende France
17 M3 Mendejīn Iran
62 B4 Mendenhall, C. pt U.S.A.
64 C3 Mendenhall Glacier gl. U.S.A.
84 C1 Méndez Mex.
56 D3 Mendī Eth.
6 E2 Mendi P.N.G.
39 E6 Mendip Hills h. U.K.
74 A2 Mendocino U.S.A.
72 A3 Mendocino, C. c. U.S.A.
95 K3 Mendocino Seascarp sea feature Pac. Oc.
68 E4 Mendon U.S.A.
8 G1 Mendooran Austr.
74 B3 Mendota CA U.S.A.
68 C5 Mendota IL U.S.A.
68 C4 Mendota, Lake l. U.S.A.
91 C2 Mendoza Arg.
91 C2 Mendoza div. Arg.
91 C2 Mendoza r. Arg.
89 C2 Mene de Mauroa Venez.
89 C2 Mene Grande Venez.
49 M5 Menemen Turkey
26 E3 Mengcheng China
33 C3 Menggala Indon.
27 D5 Mengshan China
26 F3 Meng Shan mts China
26 E3 Mengyin China
27 B6 Mengzi China
67 G3 Menihek Can.
67 G3 Menihek Lakes l. Can.
8 D2 Menindee Austr.
8 D2 Menindee Lake l. Austr.
8 B3 Meningie Austr.
17 M4 Menjān Iran
13 O3 Menkere Rus. Fed.
44 F2 Mennecy France
68 D3 Menominee U.S.A.
68 D3 Menominee r. U.S.A.
68 C4 Menomonee Falls U.S.A.
68 B3 Menomonie U.S.A.
57 B5 Menongue Angola
45 J2 Menorca i. Spain
31 A6 Mensalong Indon.
33 A3 Mentawai, Kepulauan is Indon.
32 B5 Mentekab Malaysia
43 J3 Menteroda Ger.
75 H4 Mentmore U.S.A.
33 C3 Mentok Indon.
44 H5 Menton France
80 C4 Mentor U.S.A.
54 C1 Menzel Bourguiba Tunisia
48 D6 Menzel Temime Tunisia
6 C4 Menzies Austr.
92 D4 Menzies, Mt mt Ant.
42 E2 Meppel Neth.
42 F2 Meppen Ger.
59 K1 Mepuze Moz.
59 G4 Meqheleng S. Africa
50 G3 Mera r. Rus. Fed.
33 C4 Merak Indon.
36 M5 Meråker Norway
76 F4 Meramec r. U.S.A.
48 D1 Merano Italy
89 E3 Merari, Sa. mt Brazil
58 F1 Meratswe r. Botswana
33 E3 Meratus, Pegunungan mts Indon.
25 G7 Merauke Indon.
8 D3 Merbein Austr.
74 B3 Merced U.S.A.
91 B1 Mercedario, Cerro mt Arg.
91 E2 Mercedes Buenos Aires Arg.
88 E3 Mercedes Corrientes Arg.
91 D2 Mercedes San Luis Arg.
91 F2 Mercedes Uru.
80 A4 Mercer OH U.S.A.
68 B2 Mercer WI U.S.A.
64 F4 Mercoal Can.
9 E2 Mercury Islands is N.Z.
63 M3 Mercy, C. hd Can.
42 B4 Mere Belgium
39 E6 Mere U.K.
81 H3 Meredith U.S.A.
77 C5 Meredith, Lake l. U.S.A.
77 C5 Meredith Nat. Recreation Area, Lake res. U.S.A.
68 B6 Meredosia U.S.A.
51 F5 Merefa Ukr.
55 E3 Merga Oasis oasis Sudan
32 A2 Mergui Myanmar
32 A3 Mergui Archipelago is Myanmar
8 C3 Meribah Austr.
49 M4 Meriç r. Greece/Turkey
84 E2 Mérida Mex.
45 C3 Mérida Spain
89 C2 Mérida Venez.
89 C2 Mérida, Cordillera de mts Venez.
81 G4 Meriden U.S.A.
74 B2 Meridian CA U.S.A.
77 F5 Meridian MS U.S.A.
44 D4 Mérignac France
36 T4 Merijärvi Fin.
37 R6 Merikarvia Fin.
8 G4 Merimbula Austr.
8 C3 Meringur Austr.
8 C4 Merino Austr.
77 C5 Merkel U.S.A.
32 □ Merlimau, P. i. Sing.
55 F3 Merowe Sudan
6 B5 Merredin Austr.
40 D5 Merrick h. U.K.
69 K3 Merrickville Can.
68 C3 Merrill U.S.A.
68 D5 Merrillville U.S.A.
76 C3 Merriman U.S.A.
64 E4 Merritt Can.
79 D6 Merritt Island U.S.A.
8 H2 Merriwa Austr.
8 G1 Merrygoen Austr.
56 E2 Mersa Fatma Eritrea
42 E5 Mersch Lux.
43 K3 Merseburg (Saale) Ger.
39 E4 Mersey est. U.K.
Mersin see İçel
33 B2 Mersing Malaysia
37 S8 Mērsrags Latvia
22 C4 Merta India
39 D6 Merthyr Tydfil U.K.
56 D3 Merti Kenya
45 C4 Mértola Port.
92 B6 Mertz Gl. gl. Ant.
56 D4 Meru volc. Tanz.
19 F4 Merui Pak.
Merv see Mary
58 D6 Merweville S. Africa
16 E1 Merzifon Turkey
42 E5 Merzig Ger.
92 B2 Merz Pen. pen. Ant.
75 G5 Mesa U.S.A.
68 A2 Mesabi Range h. U.S.A.
48 G4 Mesagne Italy
49 L7 Mesara, Ormos b. Greece
75 H3 Mesa Verde Nat. Park U.S.A.
89 B4 Mesay r. Col.
43 G3 Meschede Ger.
36 P4 Meselefors Sweden
66 F3 Mesgouez L. l. Can.
50 J2 Meshchura Rus. Fed.
Meshed see Mashhad
19 E2 Meshkān Iran
51 G5 Meshkovskaya Rus. Fed.
68 E3 Mesick U.S.A.
49 K4 Mesimeri Greece
49 J5 Mesolongi Greece
17 J4 Mesopotamia reg. Iraq
75 E3 Mesquite NV U.S.A.
77 D5 Mesquite TX U.S.A.
75 E4 Mesquite Lake l. U.S.A.
57 D5 Messalo r. Moz.
48 F5 Messina Sicily Italy
59 J1 Messina S. Africa
48 F5 Messina, Stretta di str. Italy
69 J2 Messines Can.
49 K6 Messini Greece
49 K6 Messiniakos Kolpos b. Greece
63 Q2 Mesters Vig Greenland
43 K1 Mestlin Ger.
49 L5 Meston, Akra pt Greece
48 E2 Mestre Italy
16 F1 Mesudiye Turkey
89 C3 Meta r. Col./Venez.
69 G2 Metagama Can.
63 L3 Meta Incognita Pen. Can.
77 F6 Metairie U.S.A.
68 C5 Metamora U.S.A.
88 C3 Metán Arg.
96 H9 Meteor Depth depth Atl. Ocean
49 J6 Methoni Greece
81 H3 Methuen U.S.A.
40 E4 Methven U.K.
48 G3 Metković Croatia
64 C3 Metlakatla U.S.A.
57 D5 Metoro Moz.
33 C4 Metro Indon.
78 B4 Metropolis U.S.A.
42 C4 Mettet Belgium
43 F2 Mettingen Ger.
74 C4 Mettler U.S.A.
21 B4 Mettur India
56 D3 Metu Eth.
44 H2 Metz France
42 D4 Meuse r. Belgium/France
43 L3 Meuselwitz Ger.
39 C7 Mevagissey U.K.
26 B3 Mêwa China
77 D6 Mexia U.S.A.
82 A2 Mexicali Mex.
75 H3 Mexican Hat U.S.A.
73 F6 Mexicanos, L. de los l. Mex.
75 H3 Mexican Water U.S.A.
84 C3 México Mex.
81 H2 Mexico ME U.S.A.
76 F4 Mexico MO U.S.A.
81 E3 Mexico NY U.S.A.
61 H7 Mexico country Central America
84 C3 México div. Mex.
61 J7 Mexico, Gulf of g. Mex./U.S.A.
18 D3 Meybod Iran
43 L1 Meyenburg Ger.
19 G3 Meymaneh Afgh.
18 C3 Meymeh Iran
18 B3 Meymeh r. Iran
84 D3 Mezcalapa r. Mex.
49 K3 Mezdra Bulg.
12 F3 Mezen' Rus. Fed.
44 G4 Mézenc, Mont mt France
50 J2 Mezhdurechensk Rus. Fed.
24 A1 Mezhdurechensk Rus. Fed.
12 G2 Mezhdusharskiy, O. i. Rus. Fed.
47 K7 Mezőtúr Hungary
84 A2 Mezquital Mex.
84 A2 Mezquital r. Mex.
84 B2 Mezquitic Mex.
37 U8 Mežvidi Latvia
57 D5 Mfuwe Zambia
21 A2 Mhasvad India
59 J3 Mhlume Swaziland
22 C5 Mhow India
23 H5 Mi r. Myanmar
84 C3 Miahuatlán Mex.
45 D3 Miajadas Spain
75 G5 Miami AZ U.S.A.
79 D7 Miami FL U.S.A.
77 E4 Miami OK U.S.A.
79 D7 Miami Beach U.S.A.
18 C4 Mīān Āb Iran
19 F5 Mianaz Pak.
18 D3 Mīāndarreh Iran
18 B2 Miandowāb Iran
57 E5 Miandrivazo Madag.
18 B2 Mīāneh Iran
31 C5 Miangas i. Phil.
19 G5 Miani Hor b. Pak.
19 G3 Mianjoi Afgh.
27 B4 Mianning China
22 B2 Mianwali Pak.
26 C3 Mian Xian China
27 D4 Mianyang Hubei China
26 B4 Mianyang Sichuan China
26 B4 Mianzhu China
26 F2 Miao Dao i. China
26 F2 Miaodao Qundao is China
27 F5 Miaoli Taiwan
57 E5 Miarinarivo Madag.
12 H4 Miass Rus. Fed.
75 G5 Mica Mt mt U.S.A.
26 C3 Micang Shan mts China
47 K6 Michalovce Slovakia
65 H3 Michel Can.
43 K4 Michelau in Oberfranken Ger.
43 H5 Michelstadt Ger.
43 M2 Michendorf Ger.
68 C2 Michigamme Lake l. U.S.A.
68 C2 Michigamme Reservoir U.S.A.
68 D2 Michigan div. U.S.A.
68 D5 Michigan City U.S.A.
68 D4 Michigan, Lake l. U.S.A.
68 E2 Michipicoten Bay b. Can.
68 E2 Michipicoten I. i. Can.
68 E1 Michipicoten River Can.
84 B3 Michoacán div. Mex.
49 M3 Michurin Bulg.
50 G4 Michurinsk Rus. Fed.
83 H6 Mico r. Nic.
94 E5 Micronesia is Pac. Oc.
4 F4 Micronesia, Federated States of country Pac. Oc.
33 C2 Midai i. Indon.
96 F4 Mid-Atlantic Ridge sea feature Atl. Ocean
58 C6 Middelberg Pass S. Africa
42 B3 Middelburg Neth.
58 F5 Middelburg Eastern Cape S. Africa
59 H2 Middelburg Mpumalanga S. Africa
37 L9 Middelfart Denmark
42 C3 Middelharnis Neth.
58 D5 Middelpos S. Africa
59 G2 Middelwit S. Africa
72 C3 Middle Alkali Lake l. U.S.A.
94 N5 Middle America Trench sea feature Pac. Oc.
81 H4 Middleboro U.S.A.
80 E4 Middleburg U.S.A.
81 F3 Middleburgh U.S.A.
81 G2 Middlebury U.S.A.
9 C6 Middlemarch N.Z.
80 B6 Middlesboro U.S.A.
38 F3 Middlesbrough U.K.
74 A2 Middletown CA U.S.A.
81 G4 Middletown CT U.S.A.
81 F5 Middletown DE U.S.A.
81 F4 Middletown NY U.S.A.
80 A5 Middletown OH U.S.A.
68 E4 Middleville U.S.A.
39 G7 Midhurst U.K.
93 K4 Mid-Indian Basin sea feature Ind. Ocean
93 K6 Mid-Indian Ridge sea feature Ind. Ocean
69 H3 Midland Can.
69 E4 Midland MI U.S.A.
77 C5 Midland TX U.S.A.
41 C6 Midleton Rep. of Ireland
94 F4 Mid-Pacific Mountains sea feature Pac. Oc.
36 □ Miðvágur Faroe Is
Midway see Thamarīt
5 K2 Midway Islands is HI U.S.A.
72 F3 Midwest U.S.A.
77 D5 Midwest City U.S.A.
42 D2 Midwoud Neth.
17 H3 Midyat Turkey
40 □ Mid Yell U.K.
49 K3 Midzhur mt Bulg./Yugo.
37 U6 Miehikkälä Fin.
36 T3 Miekojärvi l. Fin.
47 K5 Mielec Pol.
57 D4 Miembwe Tanz.
36 U2 Mieraslompolo Fin.
47 M7 Miercurea-Ciuc Romania
45 D1 Mieres Spain
56 E3 Mī'ēso Eth.
43 K2 Mieste Ger.
80 E4 Mifflinburg U.S.A.
80 E4 Mifflintown U.S.A.
26 C3 Migang Shan mt China
59 F3 Migdol S. Africa
19 E4 Mīghān Iran
23 H3 Miging India
84 B1 Miguel Auza Mex.
16 C2 Mihalıççık Turkey
29 C7 Mihara Japan
29 F7 Mihara-yama volc. Japan
45 F2 Mijares r. Spain
42 C2 Mijdrecht Neth.
69 F3 Mikado U.S.A.
47 N4 Mikashevichy Belarus
50 F4 Mikhaylov Rus. Fed.
92 D5 Mikhaylov I. i. Ant.
28 C3 Mikhaylovka Primorskiy Kray Rus. Fed.
51 G5 Mikhaylovka Volgograd. Rus. Fed.
12 J4 Mikhaylovskiy Rus. Fed.
23 H4 Mikir Hills mts India
37 U6 Mikkeli Fin.
37 U6 Mikkelin mlk Fin.
64 G3 Mikkwa r. Can.
56 D4 Mikumi Tanz.
50 J2 Mikun' Rus. Fed.
29 F6 Mikuni-sammyaku mts Japan
29 F8 Mikura-jima i. Japan
76 E2 Milaca U.S.A.
21 A5 Miladhunmadulu Atoll atoll Maldives
48 C2 Milan Italy
79 B5 Milan U.S.A.
8 B3 Milang Austr.
57 D5 Milange Moz.
Milano see Milan
16 A3 Milas Turkey
48 F5 Milazzo Sicily Italy
76 D2 Milbank U.S.A.
39 H5 Mildenhall U.K.
8 D3 Mildura Austr.
27 B5 Mile China
72 F2 Miles City U.S.A.
41 C5 Milestone Rep. of Ireland
48 F4 Miletto, Monte mt Italy
41 D2 Milford Rep. of Ireland
74 B1 Milford CA U.S.A.
81 G4 Milford CT U.S.A.
81 F5 Milford DE U.S.A.
68 D5 Milford IL U.S.A.
81 H3 Milford MA U.S.A.
81 J2 Milford ME U.S.A.
81 H3 Milford NH U.S.A.
81 F3 Milford NY U.S.A.
75 F2 Milford UT U.S.A.
39 B6 Milford Haven U.K.
9 A6 Milford Sound N.Z.
9 A6 Milford Sound in. N.Z.
45 H4 Miliana Alg.
62 G5 Milk r. Alta. Can.
72 F1 Milk r. Can./U.S.A.
13 R4 Mil'kovo Rus. Fed.
45 F2 Millárs r. Spain
44 F4 Millau France
74 B1 Mill Creek r. U.S.A.
79 D5 Milledgeville GA U.S.A.
68 C5 Milledgeville IL U.S.A.
76 E2 Mille Lacs L. l. U.S.A.
66 B4 Mille Lacs, Lac des l. Can.
76 D2 Miller U.S.A.
68 B3 Miller Dam Flowage resr U.S.A.
69 G3 Miller Lake Can.
51 G5 Millerovo Rus. Fed.
75 G6 Miller Peak summit U.S.A.
80 C4 Millersburg OH U.S.A.
80 E4 Millersburg PA U.S.A.
80 E6 Millers Tavern U.S.A.
74 C3 Millerton Lake l. U.S.A.
40 C5 Milleur Point pt U.K.
92 C6 Mill I. i. Ant.
8 C4 Millicent Austr.
69 F4 Millington MI U.S.A.
79 B5 Millington TN U.S.A.
81 J2 Millinocket U.S.A.
38 D3 Millom U.K.
40 D5 Millport U.K.
81 F5 Millsboro U.S.A.
64 F2 Mills Lake l. Can.
80 C5 Millstone U.S.A.
67 G4 Milltown Can.
41 B5 Milltown Malbay Rep. of Ireland
81 K1 Millville Can.
81 F5 Millville U.S.A.
81 J2 Milo U.S.A.
28 D3 Milogradovo Rus. Fed.
49 L6 Milos i. Greece
50 F4 Miloslavskoye Rus. Fed.
80 E4 Milroy U.S.A.
69 H4 Milton Can.
9 B7 Milton N.Z.
79 C6 Milton FL U.S.A.
68 A5 Milton IA U.S.A.
80 E4 Milton PA U.S.A.
81 G2 Milton VT U.S.A.
72 C2 Milton-Freewater U.S.A.
39 G5 Milton Keynes U.K.
80 C4 Milton, Lake l. U.S.A.
27 D4 Miluo China
68 D4 Milwaukee U.S.A.
51 G5 Milyutinskaya Rus. Fed.
44 D4 Mimizan France
56 B4 Mimongo Gabon
84 B1 Mina Mex.
74 C2 Mina U.S.A.
18 E5 Mīnāb Iran
25 E6 Minahassa, Semenanjung pen. Indon.
18 D5 Mina Jebel Ali U.A.E.
65 L4 Minaki Can.
29 B8 Minamata Japan
29 E7 Minami Alps National Park Japan
33 B2 Minas Indon.
91 F2 Minas Uru.
17 M7 Mīnā Sa'ūd Kuwait
67 H4 Minas Basin b. Can.
91 F1 Minas de Corrales Uru.
90 D2 Minas Gerais div. Brazil
90 D2 Minas Novas Brazil
84 D3 Minatitlán Mex.
23 H5 Minbu Myanmar
23 H5 Minbya Myanmar
88 B6 Minchinmávida volc. Chile
40 C2 Minch, The str. U.K.
48 D2 Mincio r. Italy
17 L2 Mincivan Azer.
31 C5 Mindanao i. Phil.
8 C3 Mindarie Austr.
54 □ Mindelo Cape Verde
69 H3 Minden Can.
43 G2 Minden Ger.
77 E5 Minden LA U.S.A.
74 C2 Minden NV U.S.A.
23 H6 Mindon Myanmar
8 D2 Mindona L. l. Austr.
31 B3 Mindoro i. Phil.
31 A3 Mindoro Strait str. Phil.
56 B4 Mindouli Congo
39 D6 Minehead U.K.
41 D6 Mine Head hd Rep. of Ireland
90 B2 Mineiros Brazil
77 E5 Mineola U.S.A.
74 B1 Mineral U.S.A.
74 C3 Mineral King U.S.A.
51 G6 Mineral'nyye Vody Rus. Fed.
68 B4 Mineral Point U.S.A.
77 D5 Mineral Wells U.S.A.
75 F2 Minersville U.S.A.
48 G4 Minervino Murge Italy
23 E1 Minfeng China
57 C5 Minga Congo(Zaire)
17 L1 Mingäçevir Azer.
17 L1 Mingäçevir Su Anbarı resr Azer.
67 H3 Mingan Can.
8 C2 Mingary Austr.
26 E3 Minggang China
45 F3 Minglanilla Spain
57 D5 Mingoyo Tanz.
27 B4 Ming-shan China
24 E2 Mingshui China
40 A4 Mingulay i. U.K.
27 E5 Mingxi China
26 B2 Minhe China
27 F5 Minhou China
21 A4 Minicoy i. India
6 B4 Minilya Austr.
67 H3 Minipi Lake l. Can.
65 J4 Minitonas Can.
27 F5 Min Jiang r. Fujian China
26 B4 Min Jiang r. Sichuan China
26 A2 Minle China
54 C4 Minna Nigeria
37 O5 Minne Sweden
76 E2 Minneapolis U.S.A.
65 K4 Minnedosa Can.
68 A2 Minnesota div. U.S.A.
71 G2 Minnesota r. MN U.S.A.
66 B4 Minnitaki L. l. Can.
45 B2 Miño r. Port./Spain
68 C3 Minocqua U.S.A.
68 B2 Minong U.S.A.
68 C5 Minonk U.S.A.
Minorca i. see Menorca
76 C1 Minot U.S.A.
26 B2 Minqin China
27 F5 Minqing China
26 B3 Min Shan mts China
23 H4 Minsin Myanmar
50 C4 Minsk Belarus
47 K4 Mińsk Mazowiecki Pol.
39 E5 Minsterley U.K.
22 C1 Mintaka Pass pass China/Jammu and Kashmir
67 G4 Minto Can.
62 G2 Minto Inlet in. Can.
66 F2 Minto, Lac l. Can.
73 F4 Minturn U.S.A.
16 C6 Minūf Egypt
24 B1 Minusinsk Rus. Fed.
23 J3 Minutang India
26 B3 Min Xian China
8 D4 Minyip Austr.
69 E3 Mio U.S.A.
66 E4 Miquelon Can.
67 J4 Miquelon i. N. America
89 A4 Mira r. Col.
19 F4 Mirabad Afgh.
81 F2 Mirabel Can.
90 D2 Mirabela Brazil
87 J5 Miracema do Norte Brazil
87 J5 Mirador, Parque Nacional de nat. park Brazil
89 B4 Miraflores Col.
90 D2 Miralta Brazil
91 F3 Miramar Arg.
84 E3 Miramar, L. l. Mex.
44 G5 Miramas France
67 G4 Miramichi r. Can.
49 L7 Mirampelou, Kolpos b. Greece
22 B2 Miram Shah Pak.
90 A3 Miranda Brazil
74 A1 Miranda U.S.A.
90 A3 Miranda r. Brazil
45 E1 Miranda de Ebro Spain
45 C2 Mirandela Port.
48 D2 Mirandola Italy
90 B3 Mirandópolis Brazil
17 H5 Mirā', Wādī al watercourse Iraq/S. Arabia
20 D6 Mirbāṭ Oman
44 E5 Mirepoix France
33 D2 Miri Malaysia
19 F4 Miri mt Pak.
21 B2 Mirialguda India
91 G2 Mirim, Lagoa l. Brazil
19 F4 Mīrjāveh Iran
50 G2 Mirnyy Rus. Fed.
13 N3 Mirnyy Rus. Fed.
92 D5 Mirnyy Rus. Fed. Base Ant.
65 J3 Mirond L. l. Can.
43 L1 Mirow Ger.
22 C2 Mirpur Pak.
22 B4 Mirpur Batoro Pak.
22 B4 Mirpur Khas Pak.
22 A4 Mirpur Sakro Pak.
64 G4 Mirror Can.
27 □ Mirs Bay b. H.K. China
19 E5 Mīr Shahdād Iran
49 K6 Mirtoö Pelagos sea Greece
30 E6 Miryang S. Korea
19 F2 Mirzachirla Turkm.
23 E4 Mirzapur India
29 C8 Misaki Japan
28 G4 Misawa Japan
67 H4 Miscou I. i. Can.
22 C1 Misgar Pak.
28 B2 Mishan China
18 C5 Mishāsh al Hādī well S. Arabia
68 D5 Mishawaka U.S.A.
68 E1 Mishibishu Lake l. Can.
29 B7 Mi-shima i. Japan
23 H3 Mishmi Hills mts India
6 F3 Misima I. i. P.N.G.
83 H6 Miskitos, Cayos atolls Nic.
47 K6 Miskolc Hungary
25 F7 Misoöl i. Indon.
68 B2 Misquah Hills h. U.S.A.
55 D1 Miṣrātah Libya
22 E4 Misrikh India
69 E1 Missanabie Can.
66 D3 Missinaibi r. Can.
69 F1 Missinaibi Lake l. Can.
65 J3 Missinipe Can.
76 C3 Mission SD U.S.A.
84 C1 Mission TX U.S.A.
64 E5 Mission City Can.
66 D3 Missisa L. l. Can.
69 F2 Missisagi r. Can.
69 H4 Mississauga Can.
68 E5 Mississinewa Lake l. U.S.A.
77 F5 Mississippi div. U.S.A.
69 J3 Mississippi r. Can.
77 F6 Mississippi r. U.S.A.
77 F6 Mississippi Delta delta U.S.A.
72 D2 Missoula U.S.A.
68 A6 Missouri div. U.S.A.
76 C2 Missouri r. U.S.A.
76 E3 Missouri Valley U.S.A.
63 L4 Mistassibi r. Can.
67 F4 Mistassini Can.
67 F4 Mistassini r. Can.
66 F3 Mistassini, L. l. Can.
67 H2 Mistastin Lake l. Can.
46 H6 Mistelbach Austria
64 C3 Misty Fjords National Monument res. U.S.A.
84 A2 Mita, Pta de hd Mex.
6 E4 Mitchell Austr.
69 G4 Mitchell Can.
76 D3 Mitchell U.S.A.
6 E3 Mitchell r. Qld. Austr.
8 F4 Mitchell r. Vic. Austr.
68 E3 Mitchell, Lake l. U.S.A.
79 D5 Mitchell, Mt mt U.S.A.
41 C5 Mitchelstown Rep. of Ireland
16 C6 Mīt Ghamr Egypt
22 B3 Mithankot Pak.
22 B4 Mithi Pak.
22 B4 Mithrani Canal canal Pak.
49 M5 Mithymna Greece
64 C3 Mitkof I. i. U.S.A.
29 G6 Mito Japan
57 D4 Mitole Tanz.
9 E4 Mitre mt N.Z.
7 H3 Mitre Island i. Solomon Is
8 H3 Mittagong Austr.
8 F4 Mitta Mitta Austr.
43 G2 Mittellandkanal canal Ger.
43 L5 Mitterteich Ger.
43 L4 Mittweida Ger.
89 C4 Mitú Col.
89 C4 Mituas Col.
57 C5 Mitumba, Chaîne des mts Congo(Zaire)
56 C4 Mitumba, Monts mts Congo(Zaire)
56 B3 Mitzic Gabon
29 F7 Miura Japan
17 G4 Miyah, Wādī el watercourse Syria
29 F7 Miyake-jima i. Japan
28 G5 Miyako Japan
29 B9 Miyakonojō Japan
26 B4 Miyaluo China
22 B5 Miyāni India
29 B9 Miyazaki Japan
29 D7 Miyazu Japan
27 B5 Miyi China
29 C7 Miyoshi Japan
26 E1 Miyun China
26 E1 Miyun Sk. resr China
19 G3 Mīzāni Afgh.
56 D3 Mīzan Teferī Eth.
55 D1 Mizdah Libya
41 B6 Mizen Head hd Rep. of Ireland
51 B5 Mizhhir"ya Ukr.
26 D2 Mizhi China
23 H5 Mizoram div. India
28 G5 Mizusawa Japan
37 O7 Mjölby Sweden
56 D4 Mkata Tanz.
56 D4 Mkomazi Tanz.
57 C5 Mkushi Zambia
46 G5 Mladá Boleslav Czech Rep.
49 J2 Mladenovac Yugo.
47 K4 Mława Pol.
48 G3 Mljet i. Croatia
59 G5 Mlungisi S. Africa
47 M5 Mlyniv Ukr.
59 F2 Mmabatho S. Africa
59 G1 Mmamabula Botswana
59 F2 Mmathethe Botswana
37 J6 Mo Norway
75 H2 Moab U.S.A.
6 E3 Moa I. i. Austr.
7 H3 Moala i. Fiji
18 D3 Mo'alla Iran
59 K2 Moamba Moz.
75 E3 Moapa U.S.A.
41 D4 Moate Rep. of Ireland
56 C4 Moba Congo(Zaire)
29 G7 Mobara Japan
18 C3 Mobārakeh Iran
56 C3 Mobayi-Mbongo Congo(Zaire)
76 E4 Moberly U.S.A.
79 B6 Mobile AL U.S.A.
75 F5 Mobile AZ U.S.A.
79 B6 Mobile Bay b. U.S.A.
76 C2 Mobridge U.S.A.
Mobutu, Lake l. see Albert, Lake
87 J4 Mocajuba Brazil
57 E5 Moçambique Moz.
89 D2 Mocapra r. Venez.
27 B6 Môc Châu Vietnam
89 D2 Mochirma, Parque Nacional nat. park Venez.
57 C6 Mochudi Botswana
57 E5 Mocimboa da Praia Moz.
43 K2 Möckern Ger.
43 H5 Möckmühl Ger.
36 R4 Mockträsk Sweden
89 A4 Mocoa Col.

90 C3 Mococa Brazil
84 A1 Mocorito Mex.
84 B2 Moctezuma Mex.
57 D5 Mocuba Moz.
44 H4 Modane France
22 C5 Modasa India
58 F4 Modder r. S. Africa
48 D2 Modena Italy
75 F3 Modena U.S.A.
74 B3 Modesto U.S.A.
8 F5 Moe Austr.
39 D5 Moel Sych h. U.K.
37 M6 Moely Norway
36 Q2 Moen Norway
75 G3 Moenkopi U.S.A.
9 C6 Moeraki Pt pt N.Z.
42 E3 Moers Ger.
40 E5 Moffat U.K.
22 C3 Moga India
Mogadishu see Muqdisho
80 C4 Mogadore Reservoir resr U.S.A.
59 H1 Mogalakwena r. S. Africa
59 H2 Moganyaka S. Africa
43 L2 Mögelin Ger.
19 G2 Moghiyon Tajik.
90 C3 Mogi-Mirim Brazil
24 D1 Mogocha Rus. Fed.
48 C6 Mogod mts Tunisia
59 F2 Mogoditshane Botswana
24 B4 Mogok Myanmar
75 H5 Mogollon Baldy mt U.S.A.
75 H5 Mogollon Mts mts U.S.A.
75 G4 Mogollon Rim plat. U.S.A.
59 G2 Mogwase S. Africa
49 H2 Mohács Hungary
9 F3 Mohaka r. N.Z.
59 G5 Mohale's Hoek Lesotho
65 J5 Mohall U.S.A.
19 E3 Mohammad Iran
Mohammadābād see Darreh Gaz
45 G5 Mohammadia Alg.
22 E3 Mohan r. India/Nepal
75 E4 Mohave, L. l. U.S.A.
75 F5 Mohawk U.S.A.
81 F3 Mohawk r. U.S.A.
75 F5 Mohawk Mts mts U.S.A.
57 E5 Moheli i. Comoros
41 D4 Mohill Rep. of Ireland
43 G3 Möhne r. Ger.
75 F4 Mohon Peak summit U.S.A.
57 D4 Mohoro Tanz.
77 C5 Mohovano Ranch Mex.
17 M5 Moh Reza Shah Pahlavi resr Iran
51 C5 Mohyliv Podil's'kyy Ukr.
37 K7 Moi Norway
59 G1 Moijabana Botswana
59 K2 Moine Moz.
47 N7 Moinești Romania
81 F2 Moira U.S.A.
36 O3 Mo i Rana Norway
23 H4 Moirang India
37 T7 Mõisaküla Estonia
91 E1 Moisés Ville Arg.
67 G3 Moisie Can.
67 G3 Moisie r. Can.
44 E4 Moissac France
74 C4 Mojave U.S.A.
74 D4 Mojave r. U.S.A.
74 D4 Mojave Desert des. U.S.A.
90 C3 Moji das Cruzes Brazil
90 C3 Moji-Guaçu r. Brazil
29 B8 Mojikō Japan
23 F4 Mokāma India
74 □1 Mokapu Pen. pen. U.S.A.
9 E3 Mokau N.Z.
9 E3 Mokau r. N.Z.
74 B2 Mokelumne r. U.S.A.
59 H4 Mokhoabong Pass Lesotho
59 H4 Mokhotlong Lesotho
48 D7 Moknine Tunisia
9 E1 Mokohinau Is is N.Z.
55 D3 Mokolo Cameroon
59 G2 Mokolo r. S. Africa
30 D6 Mokp'o S. Korea
50 G4 Moksha r. Rus. Fed.
50 H4 Mokshan Rus. Fed.
74 □1 Mokuauia I. i. U.S.A.
74 □1 Mokulua Is is U.S.A.
84 C2 Molango Mex.
45 F3 Molatón mt Spain
Moldavia country see Moldova
36 K5 Molde Norway
36 O3 Moldjord Norway
35 H4 Moldova country Europe
49 L2 Moldoveanu, Vârful mt Romania
39 D7 Mole r. U.K.
54 B4 Mole National Park Ghana
57 C6 Molepolole Botswana
37 T9 Molėtai Lith.
48 G4 Molfetta Italy
30 C2 Molihong Shan h. China
45 F2 Molina de Aragón Spain
68 B5 Moline U.S.A.
37 N7 Molkom Sweden
17 M4 Mollā Bodāgh Iran
23 H4 Mol Len mt India
43 M1 Möllenbeck Ger.
86 D7 Mollendo Peru
43 J1 Mölln Ger.
37 N8 Mölnlycke Sweden
50 F3 Molochnoye Rus. Fed.
36 X2 Molochnyy Rus. Fed.
92 D4 Molodezhnaya Rus. Fed. Base Ant.
50 E3 Molodoy Tud Rus. Fed.
74 □2 Molokai i. U.S.A.
95 K4 Molokai Fracture Zone sea feature Pac. Oc.
50 J3 Moloma r. Rus. Fed.
8 G2 Molong Austr.
58 F2 Molopo watercourse Botswana/S. Africa
55 D4 Moloundou Cameroon
65 K4 Molson L. l. Can.
Moluccas is see Maluku
25 E7 Molucca Sea g. Indon.
57 D5 Moma Moz.
8 D1 Momba Austr.
56 D4 Mombasa Kenya
23 H4 Mombi New India
90 B2 Mombuca, Serra da h. Brazil
51 C7 Momchilgrad Bulg.
68 D5 Momence U.S.A.
89 B2 Mompós Col.
37 N9 Møn i. Denmark
75 G2 Mona U.S.A.
40 A3 Monach Islands is U.K.
40 A3 Monach, Sound of chan. U.K.
34 F4 Monaco country Europe
40 D3 Monadhliath Mountains mts U.K.
41 E3 Monaghan Rep. of Ireland
77 C6 Monahans U.S.A.
83 L5 Mona, I. i. Puerto Rico
83 L5 Mona Passage chan. Dom. Rep./Puerto Rico
57 E5 Monapo Moz.
64 D4 Monarch Mt. mt Can.
73 F4 Monarch Pass U.S.A.
40 C3 Monar, Loch l. U.K.
64 F4 Monashee Mts mts Can.
48 D7 Monastir Tunisia
47 P3 Monastyrshchina Rus. Fed.
51 D5 Monastyrshche Ukr.
28 H2 Monbetsu Japan
28 H3 Monbetsu Japan
48 B2 Moncalieri Italy
45 F2 Moncayo mt Spain
36 X3 Monchegorsk Rus. Fed.
42 E3 Mönchengladbach Ger.
45 B4 Monchique Port.
79 E5 Moncks Corner U.S.A.
82 D3 Monclova Mex.
67 H4 Moncton Can.
45 C2 Mondego r. Port.
59 J3 Mondlo S. Africa
48 B2 Mondovi Italy
68 B3 Mondovi U.S.A.
48 E4 Mondragone Italy
49 K6 Monemvasia Greece
28 G1 Moneron, Ostrov i. Rus. Fed.
80 D4 Monessen U.S.A.
69 K1 Monet Can.
41 D5 Moneygall Rep. of Ireland
41 E3 Moneymore U.K.
48 E2 Monfalcone Italy
45 C1 Monforte Spain
56 C3 Monga Congo(Zaire)
27 C6 Mông Cai Vietnam
30 C4 Monggŭmp'o-ri N. Korea
32 A1 Mong Mau Myanmar
10 L5 Mongolia country Asia
22 C2 Mongora Pak.
57 C5 Mongu Zambia
81 J3 Monhegan I. i. U.S.A.
40 E5 Moniaive U.K.
74 D2 Monitor Mt mt U.S.A.
74 D2 Monitor Range mts U.S.A.
41 C4 Monivea Rep. of Ireland
69 G4 Monkton Can.
23 F3 Mon La pass China
39 E6 Monmouth U.K.
68 B5 Monmouth IL U.S.A.
81 H2 Monmouth ME U.S.A.
64 E4 Monmouth Mt. mt Can.
39 E6 Monnow r. U.K.
54 C3 Mono r. Togo
74 C3 Mono Lake l. U.S.A.
81 H4 Monomoy Pt pt U.S.A.
68 D5 Monon U.S.A.
68 B4 Monona U.S.A.
48 G4 Monopoli Italy
80 C5 Monongahela r. U.S.A.
45 F2 Monreal del Campo Spain
48 E5 Monreale Sicily Italy
77 E5 Monroe LA U.S.A.
69 F5 Monroe MI U.S.A.
79 D5 Monroe NC U.S.A.
81 F4 Monroe NY U.S.A.
75 F2 Monroe UT U.S.A.
68 C4 Monroe WV U.S.A.
68 B6 Monroe City U.S.A.
79 C6 Monroeville U.S.A.
54 A4 Monrovia Liberia
42 B4 Mons Belgium
42 E4 Monschau Ger.
48 D2 Monselice Italy
43 F4 Montabaur Ger.
57 E5 Montagne d'Ambre, Parc National de la nat. park Madag.
58 D6 Montagu S. Africa
68 D4 Montague U.S.A.
92 C1 Montagu I. i. Atl. Ocean
48 F5 Montalto mt Italy
48 G5 Montalto Uffugo Italy
49 K3 Montana Bulg.
72 E2 Montana div. U.S.A.
44 F3 Montargis France
44 E4 Montauban France
81 G4 Montauk U.S.A.
81 H4 Montauk Pt pt U.S.A.
44 G3 Montbard France
45 G2 Montblanc Spain
44 G4 Montbrison France
44 G3 Montceau-les-Mines France
42 C5 Montcornet France
44 D5 Mont-de-Marsan France
44 F2 Montdidier France
87 H4 Monte Alegre Brazil
90 C1 Monte Alegre de Goiás Brazil
90 D1 Monte Azul Brazil
66 E4 Montebello Can.
48 F6 Montebello Ionico Italy
48 E2 Montebelluna Italy
91 D2 Monte Buey Arg.
44 H5 Monte Carlo Monaco
91 F1 Monte Caseros Arg.
59 G1 Monte Christo S. Africa
91 C2 Monte Comán Arg.
83 K5 Monte Cristi Dom. Rep.
48 D3 Montecristo, Isola di i. Italy
83 J5 Montego Bay Jamaica
44 G4 Montélimar France
88 E2 Monte Lindo r. Para.
48 F4 Montella Italy
68 C4 Montello U.S.A.
84 C1 Montemorelos Mex.
45 B3 Montemor-o-Novo Port.
48 H3 Montenegro div. Yugo.
57 D5 Montepuez Moz.
48 D3 Montepulciano Italy
44 F2 Montereau-faut-Yonne France
74 B3 Monterey CA U.S.A.
80 D5 Monterey VA U.S.A.
74 B3 Monterey Bay b. U.S.A.
89 B2 Montería Col.
86 F7 Montero Bol.
84 B1 Monterrey Mex.
48 F4 Montesano sulla Marcellana Italy
87 L6 Monte Santo Brazil
90 D2 Montes Claros Brazil
48 F3 Montesilvano Italy
48 D3 Montevarchi Italy
91 F2 Montevideo Uru.
76 E2 Montevideo U.S.A.
73 F4 Monte Vista U.S.A.
68 A5 Montezuma U.S.A.
75 G4 Montezuma Castle National Monument res. U.S.A.
75 H3 Montezuma Creek U.S.A.
74 D3 Montezuma Peak summit U.S.A.
42 D3 Montfort Neth.
39 D5 Montgomery U.K.
79 C5 Montgomery U.S.A.
46 C7 Monthey Switz.
77 F5 Monticello AR U.S.A.
79 D6 Monticello FL U.S.A.
68 B4 Monticello IA U.S.A.
68 D5 Monticello IN U.S.A.
81 K1 Monticello ME U.S.A.
68 B5 Monticello MO U.S.A.
81 F4 Monticello NY U.S.A.
75 H3 Monticello UT U.S.A.
68 C4 Monticello WV U.S.A.
91 E1 Montiel, Cuchilla de h. Arg.
44 E4 Montignac France
42 C4 Montignies-le-Tilleul Belgium
42 E5 Montigny-lès-Metz France
45 D4 Montilla Spain
67 G4 Mont Joli Can.
69 K2 Mont-Laurier Can.
67 G4 Mont Louis Can.
44 F3 Montluçon France
67 F4 Montmagny Can.
42 D5 Montmédy France
42 B6 Montmirail France
68 D5 Montmorenci U.S.A.
67 F4 Montmorency Can.
44 E3 Montmorillon France
42 B6 Montmort-Lucy France
6 F4 Monto Austr.
72 E3 Montpelier ID U.S.A.
68 E5 Montpelier IN U.S.A.
80 A4 Montpelier OH U.S.A.
81 G2 Montpelier VT U.S.A.
44 F5 Montpellier France
66 F4 Montréal Can.
69 G2 Montreal r. Can.
69 F2 Montreal r. Can.
68 E2 Montreal I. i. Can.
65 H4 Montreal L. l. Can.
65 H4 Montreal Lake Can.
81 F2 Montréal-Mirabel Can.
68 E2 Montreal River Can.
46 C7 Montreux Switz.
40 F4 Montrose U.K.
73 F4 Montrose CO U.S.A.
69 F4 Montrose MI U.S.A.
81 F4 Montrose PA U.S.A.
58 D3 Montrose well S. Africa
61 M8 Montserrat terr. Caribbean Sea
67 G4 Monts, Pte des pt Can.
75 G3 Monument Valley reg. U.S.A.
24 B4 Monywa Myanmar
48 C2 Monza Italy
57 C5 Monze Zambia
45 G2 Monzón Spain
59 J4 Mooi r. S. Africa
58 B3 Mooifontein Namibia
59 J4 Mooirivier S. Africa
59 G1 Mookane Botswana
8 H1 Moonbi Ra. mts Austr.
8 A3 Moonta Austr.
72 F2 Moorcroft U.S.A.
80 D5 Moorefield U.S.A.
6 B4 Moore, Lake salt flat Austr.
79 E7 Moores I. i. Bahamas
81 K2 Moores Mills Can.
40 E5 Moorfoot Hills h. U.K.
76 D2 Moorhead U.S.A.
8 D2 Moornanyah Lake Austr.
8 C3 Moorook Austr.
8 E4 Mooroopna Austr.
58 C6 Moorreesburg S. Africa
66 D3 Moose r. Can.
66 D3 Moose Factory Can.
81 J2 Moosehead Lake l. U.S.A.
65 H4 Moose Jaw Can.
68 A2 Moose Lake U.S.A.
65 J4 Moose Lake l. Can.
81 H2 Mooselookmeguntic Lake l. U.S.A.
66 D3 Moose River Can.
65 J4 Moosomin Can.
66 D3 Moosonee Can.
8 D1 Mootwingee Austr.
59 H1 Mopane S. Africa
54 B3 Mopti Mali
19 G3 Moqor Afgh.
86 D7 Moquegua Peru
55 D3 Mora Cameroon
45 E3 Mora Spain
37 O6 Mora Sweden
91 B2 Mora, Cerro mt Arg./Chile
22 A3 Morad r. Pak.
22 D3 Moradabad India
57 E5 Morafenobe Madag.
21 B2 Moram India
57 E5 Moramanga Madag.
68 E3 Moran MI U.S.A.
72 E3 Moran WY U.S.A.
40 C4 Morar, Loch l. U.K.
21 B5 Moratuwa Sri Lanka
46 H6 Morava r. Austria/Slovakia
18 D2 Moraveh Tappeh Iran
81 E3 Moravia U.S.A.
40 E3 Moray Firth est. U.K.
42 F5 Morbach Ger.
48 C1 Morbegno Italy
22 B5 Morbi India
44 D4 Morcenx France
24 E1 Mordaga China
17 K3 Mor Dağı mt Turkey
65 K5 Morden Can.
8 E5 Mordialloc Austr.
50 H4 Mordoviya, Respublika div. Rus. Fed.
51 G4 Mordovo Rus. Fed.
76 C2 Moreau r. U.S.A.
38 E3 Morecambe U.K.
38 D3 Morecambe Bay b. U.K.
6 E4 Moree Austr.
6 E2 Morehead P.N.G.
80 B5 Morehead U.S.A.
79 E5 Morehead City U.S.A.
22 D4 Morel r. India
84 B3 Morelia Mex.
45 F2 Morella Spain
40 D2 More, Loch l. U.K.
84 E3 Morelos Mex.
84 C3 Morelos div. Mex.
22 D4 Morena India
45 D3 Morena, Sierra mts Spain
75 H5 Morenci AZ U.S.A.
69 E5 Morenci MI U.S.A.
49 L2 Moreni Romania
91 E2 Moreno Arg.
73 E6 Moreno Mex.
74 D5 Moreno Valley U.S.A.
64 C4 Moresby Island i. Can.
58 F1 Moreswe Pan salt pan Botswana
39 F6 Moreton-in-Marsh U.K.
42 A5 Moreuil France
16 D4 Morfou Cyprus
16 D4 Morfou Bay b. Cyprus
8 B3 Morgan Austr.
77 F6 Morgan City U.S.A.
74 B3 Morgan Hill U.S.A.
74 C3 Morgan, Mt mt U.S.A.
81 F4 Morgantown PA U.S.A.
80 D5 Morgantown WV U.S.A.
59 H3 Morgenzon S. Africa
46 C7 Morges Switz.
23 F4 Morhar r. India
28 G3 Mori Japan
75 E2 Moriah, Mt mt U.S.A.
73 F5 Moriarty U.S.A.
89 C4 Morichal Col.
89 E2 Morichal Largo r. Venez.
59 G4 Morija Lesotho
43 H3 Moringen Ger.
50 D3 Morino Rus. Fed.
28 G5 Morioka Japan
8 H2 Morisset Austr.
28 G5 Moriyoshi-zan volc. Japan
36 S3 Morjärv Sweden
19 F4 Morjen r. Pak.
50 J3 Morki Rus. Fed.
44 C2 Morlaix France
38 F4 Morley U.K.
75 G4 Mormon Lake l. U.S.A.
6 D3 Mornington, I. i. Austr.
88 A7 Mornington, I. i. Chile
22 A4 Moro Pak.
6 E2 Morobe P.N.G.
68 D5 Morocco U.S.A.
52 D3 Morocco country Africa
56 D4 Morogoro Tanz.
31 B5 Moro Gulf g. Phil.
59 G4 Morojaneng S. Africa
58 E3 Morokweng S. Africa
84 B2 Moroleón Mex.
57 E6 Morombe Madag.
83 J4 Morón Cuba
24 C2 Mörön Mongolia
57 E6 Morondava Madag.
45 D4 Morón de la Frontera Spain
57 E5 Moroni Comoros
25 E6 Morotai i. Indon.
56 D3 Moroto Uganda
51 G5 Morozovsk Rus. Fed.
69 G4 Morpeth Can.
38 F2 Morpeth U.K.
90 C2 Morrinhos Brazil
65 K5 Morris Can.
68 C5 Morris IL U.S.A.
76 E2 Morris MN U.S.A.
81 F2 Morrisburg Can.
68 C5 Morrison U.S.A.
75 F5 Morristown AZ U.S.A.
81 F4 Morristown NJ U.S.A.
81 F2 Morristown NY U.S.A.
79 D4 Morristown TN U.S.A.
81 F4 Morrisville PA U.S.A.
81 G2 Morrisville VT U.S.A.
74 B4 Morro Bay U.S.A.
89 C2 Morrocoy, Parque Nacional nat. park Venez.
87 H4 Morro Grande h. Brazil
88 B3 Morro, Pta pt Chile
89 B2 Morrosquillo, Golfo de b. Col.
43 H3 Morschen Ger.
68 D5 Morse Reservoir resr U.S.A.
50 G4 Morshansk Rus. Fed.
50 E2 Morskaya Masel'ga Rus. Fed.
48 C7 Morsott Alg.
44 E2 Mortagne-au-Perche France
44 D3 Mortagne-sur-Sèvre France
39 C6 Mortehoe U.K.
91 E1 Morteros Arg.
Mortes r. see Manso
8 D5 Mortlake Austr.
Mortlock Is is see Tauu
39 G5 Morton U.K.
68 C5 Morton IL U.S.A.
72 B2 Morton WA U.S.A.
8 H3 Morton Nat. Park Austr.
8 F3 Morundah Austr.
59 G1 Morupule Botswana
8 H3 Moruya Austr.
40 C4 Morvern reg. U.K.
Morvi see Morbi
8 F5 Morwell Austr.
43 H5 Mosbach Ger.
39 F4 Mosborough U.K.
50 F4 Moscow Rus. Fed.
72 C2 Moscow U.S.A.
92 C6 Moscow Univ. Ice Shelf ice feature Ant.
92 B6 Mose, C. c. Ant.
42 F4 Mosel r. Ger.
58 E2 Moselebe watercourse Botswana
44 H2 Moselle r. France
43 K2 Möser Ger.
72 C2 Moses Lake U.S.A.
74 D1 Moses, Mt mt U.S.A.
9 C6 Mosgiel N.Z.
58 E3 Moshaweng watercourse S. Africa
56 D4 Moshi Tanz.
68 C3 Mosinee U.S.A.
36 N4 Mosjøen Norway
36 N3 Moskenesøy i. Norway
50 F4 Moskovskaya Oblast' div. Rus. Fed.
Moskva see Moscow
46 H7 Mosonmagyaróvár Hungary
89 A4 Mosquera Col.
73 F5 Mosquero U.S.A.
83 H5 Mosquitia reg. Honduras
90 E1 Mosquito r. Brazil
80 C4 Mosquito Creek Lake l. U.S.A.
83 H7 Mosquitos, Golfo de los b. Panama
65 J2 Mosquito Lake l. Can.
37 M7 Moss Norway
40 F3 Mossat U.K.
9 B6 Mossburn N.Z.
58 E7 Mossel Bay S. Africa
58 E7 Mossel Bay b. S. Africa
56 B4 Mossendjo Congo
8 E2 Mossgiel Austr.
6 E3 Mossman Austr.
87 L5 Mossoró Brazil
8 H3 Moss Vale Austr.
46 F5 Most Czech Rep.
18 D3 Moştafaabad Iran
54 C1 Mostaganem Alg.
48 G3 Mostar Bos.-Herz.
88 F4 Mostardas Brazil
65 G3 Mostoos Hills h. Can.
51 G6 Mostovskoy Rus. Fed.
33 E2 Mostyn Malaysia
17 J3 Mosul Iraq
37 L7 Møsvatnet l. Norway
37 O7 Motala Sweden
89 C2 Motatán r. Venez.
59 K2 Motaze Moz.
59 H2 Motetema S. Africa
22 D4 Moth India
40 E5 Motherwell U.K.
23 F4 Motihari India
45 F3 Motilla del Palancar Spain
9 F2 Motiti I. i. N.Z.
30 B3 Motlan Ling h. China
58 E2 Motokwe Botswana
84 D4 Motozintla Mex.
45 E4 Motril Spain
49 K2 Motru Romania
82 G4 Motul Mex.
5 M6 Motu One i. Pac. Oc.
27 A5 Mouding China
54 A3 Moudjéria Maur.
49 L5 Moudros Greece
37 S6 Mouhijärvi Fin.
56 B4 Mouila Gabon
8 E3 Moulamein Austr.
56 B4 Moulèngui Binza Gabon
44 F3 Moulins France
32 A1 Moulmein Myanmar
79 D6 Moultrie U.S.A.
71 L5 Moultrie, L. l. SC U.S.A.
78 B4 Mound City IL U.S.A.
76 E3 Mound City MO U.S.A.
55 D4 Moundou Chad
80 C5 Moundsville U.S.A.
22 C4 Mount Abu India
79 C5 Mountain Brook U.S.A.
80 C6 Mountain City U.S.A.
77 E4 Mountain Grove U.S.A.
77 E4 Mountain Home AR U.S.A.
72 D3 Mountain Home ID U.S.A.
59 F6 Mountain Zebra National Park S. Africa
80 C6 Mount Airy U.S.A.
9 B6 Mount Aspiring National Park N.Z.
59 H5 Mount Ayliff S. Africa
76 E3 Mount Ayr U.S.A.
8 B3 Mount Barker Austr.
8 F4 Mount Beauty Austr.
41 C4 Mount Bellew Rep. of Ireland
8 F4 Mt Bogong Nat.Park Austr.
8 F4 Mount Buffalo National Park Austr.
81 K1 Mount Carleton Provincial Park res. Can.
75 F3 Mount Carmel Junction U.S.A.
68 C4 Mount Carroll U.S.A.
9 C5 Mount Cook N.Z.
9 C5 Mount Cook National Park N.Z.
57 D5 Mount Darwin Zimbabwe
81 J2 Mount Desert Island i. U.S.A.
59 H5 Mount Fletcher S. Africa
69 G4 Mount Forest Can.
59 H5 Mount Frere S. Africa
8 C4 Mount Gambier Austr.
80 B4 Mount Gilead U.S.A.
6 E2 Mount Hagen P.N.G.
8 E2 Mount Hope N.S.W. Austr.
80 C6 Mount Hope U.S.A.
6 D4 Mount Isa Austr.
81 G4 Mount Kisco U.S.A.
8 B3 Mount Lofty Range mts Austr.
69 G2 Mount MacDonald Can.
6 B4 Mount Magnet Austr.
8 D2 Mount Manara Austr.
74 B1 Mount Meadows Reservoir U.S.A.
41 D4 Mountmellick Rep. of Ireland
59 G5 Mount Moorosi Lesotho
8 D1 Mount Murchison Austr.
68 B5 Mount Pleasant IA U.S.A.
68 E4 Mount Pleasant MI U.S.A.
78 C3 Mount Pleasant MI U.S.A.
80 D4 Mount Pleasant PA U.S.A.
79 E5 Mount Pleasant SC U.S.A.
77 E5 Mount Pleasant TX U.S.A.
75 G2 Mount Pleasant UT U.S.A.
68 C5 Mount Pulaski U.S.A.
72 B2 Mount Rainier Nat. Park U.S.A.
64 F4 Mount Robson Prov. Park res. Can.
80 C6 Mount Rogers National Recreation Area res. U.S.A.
39 B7 Mount's Bay b. U.K.
39 F5 Mountsorrel U.K.
68 B6 Mount Sterling IL U.S.A.
80 B5 Mount Sterling KY U.S.A.
80 D5 Mount Storm U.S.A.
80 E4 Mount Union U.S.A.
79 B6 Mount Vernon AL U.S.A.
68 B5 Mount Vernon IA U.S.A.
78 B4 Mount Vernon IL U.S.A.
80 A6 Mount Vernon KY U.S.A.
80 B4 Mount Vernon OH U.S.A.
72 B1 Mount Vernon WA U.S.A.
92 C3 Mt. Victor mt Ant.
6 E4 Moura Austr.
86 F4 Moura Brazil
55 E3 Mourdi, Dépression du depression Chad
41 D3 Mourne r. U.K.
41 E3 Mourne Mountains h. U.K.
42 B4 Mouscron Belgium
55 D3 Moussoro Chad
25 E6 Moutong Indon.
42 A5 Mouy France
54 C2 Mouydir, Mts de plat. Alg.
42 D5 Mouzon France
41 C4 Moy r. Rep. of Ireland
56 D3 Moyale Eth.
54 A4 Moyamba Sierra Leone
21 B4 Moyar r. India
54 B1 Moyen Atlas mts Morocco
59 G5 Moyeni Lesotho
41 E4 Moyer h. Rep. of Ireland
67 G2 Moyne, Lac le l. Can.
15 F2 Moyynty Kazak.
53 H8 Mozambique country Africa
57 E5 Mozambique Channel str. Africa
93 G5 Mozambique Ridge sea feature Ind. Ocean
51 H7 Mozdok Rus. Fed.
19 F2 Mozdūrān Iran
50 F4 Mozhaysk Rus. Fed.
19 F3 Mozhnābād Iran
23 H5 Mozo Myanmar
56 C4 Mpala Congo(Zaire)
56 D4 Mpanda Tanz.
57 D5 Mpika Zambia
59 J4 Mpolweni S. Africa
57 D4 Mporokoso Zambia
59 H2 Mpumalanga div. S. Africa
59 H5 Mqanduli S. Africa
48 G2 Mrkonjić-Grad Bos.-Herz.
54 D1 M'Saken Tunisia
50 D3 Mshinskaya Rus. Fed.
45 J5 M'Sila Alg.
50 E3 Msta r. Rus. Fed.
50 D4 Mstsislaw Belarus
59 H4 Mt-aux-Sources mt Lesotho
50 F4 Mtsensk Rus. Fed.
59 K4 Mtubatuba S. Africa
59 J4 Mtunzini S. Africa
57 E5 Mtwara Tanz.
56 B4 Muanda Congo(Zaire)
32 B2 Muang Chainat Thai.
32 A1 Muang Chiang Rai Thai.
27 B6 Muang Hiam Laos
32 B1 Muang Hôngsa Laos
32 B1 Muang Kalasin Thai.
32 C1 Muang Khammouan Laos
32 C2 Muang Không Laos
32 C2 Muang Khôngxédôn Laos
32 B1 Muang Khon Kaen Thai.
27 B6 Muang Khoua Laos
32 A3 Muang Kirirath r. Thai.
32 A1 Muang Lampang Thai.
32 A1 Muang Lamphun Thai.
32 B1 Muang Loei Thai.
32 B1 Muang Lom Sak Thai.
32 A1 Muang Long Thai.
32 A3 Muang Luang r. Thai.
32 C2 Muang Mai Thai.
32 C1 Muang Mok Laos
32 C1 Muang Nakhon Phanom Thai.
32 B2 Muang Nakhon Sawan Thai.
32 B1 Muang Nan Thai.
27 B6 Muang Ngoy Laos
32 C1 Muang Nong Laos
27 A6 Muang Ou Nua Laos
32 B1 Muang Pakxan Laos
32 C1 Muang Phalan Laos
32 A1 Muang Phan Thai.
32 A1 Muang Phayao Thai.
32 B1 Muang Phetchabun Thai.
32 B1 Muang Phiang Laos
32 B1 Muang Phichai Thai.
32 B1 Muang Phichit Thai.
32 C1 Muang Phin Laos
32 B1 Muang Phitsanulok Thai.
32 B1 Muang Phôn-Hông Laos
32 B1 Muang Phrae Thai.
32 B1 Muang Roi Et Thai.
32 C1 Muang Sakon Nakhon Thai.
32 B2 Muang Samut Prakan Thai.
32 B1 Muang Souy Laos
32 B2 Muang Uthai Thani Thai.
27 B6 Muang Va Laos
32 B1 Muang Vangviang Laos
32 B1 Muang Xaignabouri Laos
27 B6 Muang Xay Laos
27 B6 Muang Xon Laos
32 C2 Muang Yasothon Thai.
33 B2 Muar Malaysia
32 B5 Muar r. Malaysia
33 B3 Muarabungo Indon.
33 B3 Muaradua Indon.
33 A3 Muarasiberut Indon.
33 A2 Muarasipongi Indon.
33 B3 Muaratembesi Indon.
23 E4 Mubarakpur India
19 G2 Mubarek Uzbek.
17 H7 Mubarraz well S. Arabia
56 D3 Mubende Uganda
55 D3 Mubi Nigeria
89 E4 Mucajaí r. Brazil
89 E4 Mucajaí, Serra do mts Brazil
42 F4 Much Ger.
57 D5 Muchinga Escarpment esc. Zambia
27 B4 Muchuan China
40 B4 Muck i. U.K.
40 □ Muckle Roe i. U.K.
89 C3 Muco r. Col.
57 C5 Muconda Angola
89 E4 Mucucuaú r. Brazil
16 E2 Mucur Turkey
90 E2 Mucuri Brazil
90 E2 Mucuri r. Brazil
57 C5 Mucussueje Angola
32 B4 Muda r. Malaysia
21 A3 Mūdabidri India
30 E1 Mudanjiang China
30 E1 Mudan Jiang r. China
16 B1 Mudanya Turkey
17 L7 Mudayrah Kuwait
80 C5 Muddlety U.S.A.
36 R3 Muddus Nationalpark nat. park Sweden
75 G2 Muddy Creek r. U.S.A.
75 E3 Muddy Peak summit U.S.A.
19 E3 Mūd-e-Dahanāb Iran
43 F4 Mudersbach Ger.
8 G2 Mudgee Austr.
21 A2 Mudhol India
22 C3 Mudki India
74 D3 Mud Lake l. U.S.A.
32 A1 Mudon Myanmar
16 C1 Mudurnu Turkey
50 F2 Mud'yuga Rus. Fed.
57 D5 Mueda Moz.
84 D3 Muerto, Mar l. Mex.
50 H1 Muftyuga Rus. Fed.
57 C5 Mufulira Zambia
57 C5 Mufumbwe Zambia
27 E4 Mufu Shan mts China
81 K2 Mugaguadavic Lake l. Can.
17 M2 Muğan Düzü lowland Azer.
23 F2 Mugarripug China
Mughalbhin see Jati
23 E4 Mughal Sarai India
18 D3 Mūghār Iran
16 F7 Mughayrā' S. Arabia
19 H2 Mughsu r. Tajik.
16 B3 Muğla Turkey
23 H2 Mug Qu r. China
23 E3 Mugu Karnali r. Nepal
23 H2 Mugxung China
55 F2 Muhammad Qol Sudan
18 B5 Muḩayriqah S. Arabia
43 L3 Mühlanger Ger.
43 M3 Mühlberg Ger.
43 J3 Mühlhausen (Thüringen) Ger.
36 T4 Muhos Fin.
56 C4 Muhulu Congo(Zaire)
32 C3 Mui Ca Mau c. Vietnam
32 D3 Mui Dinh hd Vietnam
32 D2 Mui Nây pt Vietnam
41 E5 Muine Bheag Rep. of Ireland
40 D5 Muirkirk U.K.
40 B2 Muirneag h. U.K.
40 D3 Muir of Ord U.K.
74 A3 Muir Woods National Monument res. U.S.A.
57 D5 Muite Moz.
30 D6 Muju S. Korea
51 B5 Mukacheve Ukr.
33 D2 Mukah Malaysia
23 F3 Mukangsar China
32 C1 Mukdahan Thai.
6 B5 Mukinbudin Austr.
33 B3 Mukomuko Indon.
19 G2 Mukry Turkm.
22 C3 Muktsar India
65 K4 Mukutawa r. Can.
68 C4 Mukwonago U.S.A.
22 D5 Mul India
21 A2 Mula r. India
22 A3 Mula r. Pak.
28 A2 Mulan China
31 B3 Mulanay Phil.
57 D5 Mulanje, Mt mt Malawi
18 B5 Mulayḩ S. Arabia
77 E5 Mulberry U.S.A.
91 B3 Mulchén Chile
43 L3 Mulde r. Ger.
56 D4 Muleba Tanz.
75 H5 Mule Creek NM U.S.A.
72 F3 Mule Creek WY U.S.A.
77 C5 Muleshoe U.S.A.
45 E4 Mulhacén mt Spain
42 E3 Mülheim an der Ruhr Ger.
44 H3 Mulhouse France
27 A5 Muli China
30 F1 Muling China
30 F1 Muling China
30 G1 Muling r. China
40 C4 Mull i. U.K.
17 M3 Mulla Ali Iran
41 B5 Mullaghareirk Mts h. Rep. of Ireland
21 C4 Mullaittivu Sri Lanka
8 G1 Mullaley Austr.
8 F1 Mullengudgery Austr.
33 D2 Muller, Pegunungan mts Indon.
68 E3 Mullett Lake l. U.S.A.
6 B4 Mullewa Austr.
40 F1 Mull Head hd U.K.
81 F5 Mullica r. U.S.A.
41 D4 Mullingar Rep. of Ireland
8 G2 Mullion Cr. Austr.
40 B4 Mull, Sound of chan. U.K.
57 C5 Mulobezi Zambia
21 A2 Mulshi L. l. India
22 D5 Multai India
22 B3 Multan Pak.
37 T5 Multia Fin.
42 A6 Multien reg. France
19 F5 Mūmān Iran
Mumbai see Bombay
8 G2 Mumbil Austr.
57 C5 Mumbwa Zambia
19 H2 Mū'minobod Tajik.
51 H6 Mumra Rus. Fed.
84 E2 Muna Mex.
13 N3 Muna r. Rus. Fed.
36 C3 Munaðarnes Iceland
43 K4 Münchberg Ger.
46 E6 München Ger.
43 G4 Münchhausen Ger.
89 A4 Munchique, Co mt Col.
64 D3 Muncho Lake Can.
64 D3 Muncho Lake Provincial Park res. Can.
30 D4 Munch'ŏn N. Korea
68 E5 Muncie U.S.A.
80 E4 Muncy U.S.A.
21 B5 Mundel L. l. Sri Lanka
39 J5 Mundesley U.K.
39 H5 Mundford U.K.
6 C5 Mundrabilla Austr.
22 C4 Mundwa India
21 C2 Muneru r. India
22 D4 Mungaoli India
56 C3 Mungbere Congo(Zaire)
23 E5 Mungeli India
23 F4 Munger India
32 D5 Munggresak, Tanjung pt Indon.
6 E4 Mungindi Austr.
Munich see München
87 K4 Munim r. Brazil
68 D2 Munising U.S.A.
90 E3 Muniz Freire Brazil
37 M7 Munkedal Sweden
36 V2 Munkelva Norway
37 N7 Munkfors Sweden
43 J4 Münnerstadt Ger.
59 H1 Munnik S. Africa
30 D5 Munsan S. Korea
46 C7 Münsingen Switz.
43 G5 Münster Hessen Ger.
43 J2 Münster Niedersachsen Ger.
42 F3 Münster Nordrhein-Westfalen Ger.
42 F3 Münsterland reg. Ger.
67 F3 Muntviel, Lac l. Can.
36 V4 Muojärvi l. Fin.
32 C1 Mương Lam Vietnam
27 B6 Mương Nhie Vietnam
36 S3 Muonio Fin.
36 S2 Muonioälven r. Fin./Sweden
30 A5 Muping China
56 E3 Muqdisho Somalia
17 M1 Müqtädir Azer.
17 J2 Muradiye Turkey
28 F5 Murakami Japan
88 B7 Murallón, Cerro mt Chile
56 C4 Muramvya Burundi
56 D4 Muranga Kenya
32 □ Mura Res. resr Sing.
50 J3 Murashi Rus. Fed.
17 H2 Murat r. Turkey
16 B2 Murat Dağı mts Turkey
16 A1 Muratlı Turkey
28 G5 Murayama Japan
18 C3 Murcheh Khvort Iran
8 E4 Murchison Austr.
6 B4 Murchison watercourse Austr.
56 D3 Murchison Falls National Park Uganda
45 F4 Murcia Spain
45 F4 Murcia div. Spain
76 C3 Murdo U.S.A.
67 G4 Murdochville Can.
57 D5 Murehwa Zimbabwe
47 M7 Mureș r. Romania
44 E5 Muret France
79 E4 Murfreesboro NC U.S.A.
79 C5 Murfreesboro TN U.S.A.
19 F2 Murgab Turkm.
19 F2 Murgab r. Turkm.
19 G3 Murghab r. Afgh.
22 B3 Murgha Kibzai Pak.
15 F3 Murghob Tajik.
19 H3 Murgh Pass Afgh.
26 A2 Muri China
23 F5 Muri India
18 E2 Mūrī Iran
90 D3 Muriaé Brazil
57 C4 Muriege Angola
43 L1 Müritz l. Ger.
43 M1 Müritz, Nationalpark nat. park Ger.
43 L1 Müritz Seenpark res. Ger.
36 X2 Murmansk Rus. Fed.
36 W2 Murmanskaya Oblast' div. Rus. Fed.
48 C4 Muro, Capo di pt Corsica France
50 G4 Murom Rus. Fed.
28 G3 Muroran Japan
45 B1 Muros Spain
29 D8 Muroto Japan
29 D8 Muroto-zaki pt Japan

68 D5 Murphey Lake, J. C. l. U.S.A.
72 C3 Murphy ID U.S.A.
79 D5 Murphy NC U.S.A.
74 B2 Murphys U.S.A.
78 B4 Murray KY U.S.A.
72 E3 Murray UT U.S.A.
8 C3 Murray r. Austr.
64 E3 Murray r. Can.
8 B3 Murray Bridge Austr.
79 D5 Murray, L. l. U.S.A.
6 E2 Murray, Lake l. P.N.G.
58 E5 Murraysburg S. Africa
95 L3 Murray Seascarp sea feature Pac. Oc.
8 C3 Murrayville Austr.
43 H6 Murrhardt Ger.
8 G3 Murringo Austr.
41 B4 Murrisk reg. Rep. of Ireland
41 B4 Murroogh Rep. of Ireland
8 G3 Murrumbateman Austr.
8 E3 Murrumbidgee r. Austr.
57 D5 Murrupula Moz.
8 H1 Murrurundi Austr.
48 G1 Murska Sobota Slovenia
8 D4 Murtoa Austr.
21 A2 Murud India
30 A2 Muruin Sum Sk. resr China
21 C4 Murunkan Sri Lanka
9 F3 Murupara N.Z.
5 O7 Mururoa i. Pac. Oc.
22 E5 Murwara India
55 D2 Murzūq Libya
46 G7 Mürzzuschlag Austria
17 H2 Muş Turkey
22 B3 Musa Khel Bazar Pak.
33 A2 Musala i. Indon.
49 K3 Musala mt Bulg.
30 E2 Musan N. Korea
18 E5 Musandam Peninsula Oman
19 G3 Musa Qala Afgh.
19 G3 Musa Qala, Rūd-i r. Afgh.
Musay'īd see Umm Sa'id
20 E5 Muscat Oman
68 B5 Muscatine U.S.A.
68 B4 Muscoda U.S.A.
81 J3 Muscongus Bay b. U.S.A.
6 D4 Musgrave Ranges mts Austr.
41 C5 Musheramore h. Rep. of Ireland
56 B4 Mushie Congo(Zaire)
21 B2 Musi r. India
33 B3 Musi r. Indon.
75 F4 Music Mt mt U.S.A.
75 G2 Musinia Peak summit U.S.A.
64 E2 Muskeg r. Can.
81 H4 Muskeget Channel chan. U.S.A.
68 D4 Muskegon U.S.A.
68 D4 Muskegon r. U.S.A.
80 C5 Muskingum r. U.S.A.
77 E5 Muskogee U.S.A.
69 H3 Muskoka Can.
69 H3 Muskoka, Lake l. Can.
64 E3 Muskwa r. Can.
16 F3 Muslimīyah Syria
55 F3 Musmar Sudan
56 D4 Musoma Tanz.
6 E2 Mussau I. i. P.N.G.
40 E5 Musselburgh U.K.
42 F2 Musselkanaal Neth.
72 E2 Musselshell r. U.S.A.
16 B1 Mustafakemalpaşa Turkey
37 S7 Mustjala Estonia
30 E3 Musu-dan pt N. Korea
8 H2 Muswellbrook Austr.
55 E2 Mut Egypt
16 D3 Mut Turkey
90 E1 Mutá, Pta do pt Brazil
57 D5 Mutare Zimbabwe
25 E7 Mutis, G. mt Indon.
8 C2 Mutooroo Austr.
57 D5 Mutorashanga Zimbabwe
28 G4 Mutsu Japan
28 G4 Mutsu-wan b. Japan
9 B7 Muttonbird Is is N.Z.
9 A7 Muttonbird Islands is N.Z.
41 B5 Mutton Island i. Rep. of Ireland
57 D5 Mutuali Moz.
90 C1 Mutunópolis Brazil
21 C4 Mutur Sri Lanka
36 U2 Mutusjärvi r. Fin.
36 T3 Muurola Fin.
26 C2 Mu Us Shamo des. China
57 B4 Muxaluando Angola
50 E2 Muyezerskiy Rus. Fed.
56 D4 Muyinga Burundi
56 C4 Muyumba Congo(Zaire)
26 D4 Muyuping China
22 C2 Muzaffarabad Pak.
22 B3 Muzaffargarh Pak.
22 D3 Muzaffarnagar India
23 F4 Muzaffarpur India
59 K1 Muzamane Moz.
19 F5 Mūzīn Iran
64 C4 Muzon, C. c. U.S.A.
22 E2 Muztag mt China
23 F1 Muztag mt China
55 E4 Mvolo Sudan
56 D4 Mvomero Tanz.
57 D5 Mvuma Zimbabwe
Mwali i. see Moheli
57 C4 Mwanza Congo(Zaire)
56 D4 Mwanza Tanz.
41 B4 Mweelrea h. Rep. of Ireland
56 C4 Mweka Congo(Zaire)
57 C5 Mwenda Zambia
56 C4 Mwene-Ditu Congo(Zaire)
57 D6 Mwenezi Zimbabwe
57 C4 Mweru, Lake l. Congo(Zaire)/Zambia
57 C4 Mwimba Congo(Zaire)
57 C5 Mwinilunga Zambia
50 C4 Myadzyel Belarus
23 H5 Myaing Myanmar
22 B4 Myājlār India
10 L7 Myanmar country Asia
29 B9 Myanoura-dake mt Japan
40 E2 Mybster U.K.
23 H5 Myebon Myanmar
25 B4 Myingyan Myanmar
32 A2 Myinmoletkat mt Myanmar
24 B4 Myitkyina Myanmar
32 A2 Myitta Myanmar
23 H5 Myittha r. Myanmar
51 E6 Mykolayiv Ukr.
49 L6 Mykonos Greece
49 L6 Mykonos i. Greece
12 G3 Myla Rus. Fed.
23 G4 Mymensingh Bangl.
37 S6 Mynämäki Fin.
39 D5 Mynydd Eppynt h. U.K.
39 C6 Mynydd Preseli h. U.K.
23 H5 Myohaung Myanmar
29 F6 Myōkō-san volc. Japan
30 E3 Myonggan N. Korea
50 C4 Myory Belarus
36 D5 Mýrdalsjökull ice cap Iceland
36 O2 Myre Norway
36 R4 Myrheden Sweden
51 E5 Myrhorod Ukr.
51 D5 Myronivka Ukr.
79 E5 Myrtle Beach U.S.A.
8 F4 Myrtleford Austr.
72 A3 Myrtle Point U.S.A.
46 G4 Myślibórz Pol.
21 B3 Mysore India
13 U3 Mys Shmidta Rus. Fed.
81 F5 Mystic Islands U.S.A.
32 C3 My Tho Vietnam
49 M5 Mytilini Greece
50 F4 Mytishchi Rus. Fed.
59 G5 Mzamomhle S. Africa
43 L5 Mže r. Czech Rep.
57 D5 Mzimba Malawi
57 D5 Mzuzu Malawi

N

43 K5 Naab r. Ger.
74 □2 Naalehu U.S.A.
37 S6 Naantali Fin.
41 E4 Naas Rep. of Ireland
58 B4 Nababeep S. Africa
21 C2 Nabarangapur India
29 E7 Nabari Japan
31 B4 Nabas Phil.
16 E5 Nabatiyet et Tahta Lebanon
43 L5 Nabburg Ger.
56 D4 Naberera Tanz.
12 G4 Naberezhnyye Chelny Rus. Fed.
55 D1 Nabeul Tunisia
22 D3 Nabha India
8 J2 Nabiac Austr.
19 E4 Nabīd Iran
25 F7 Nabire Indon.
16 E5 Nablus West Bank
59 H2 Naboomspruit S. Africa
32 A2 Nabule Myanmar
57 E5 Nacala Moz.
72 B2 Naches U.S.A.
22 B4 Nāchna India
74 B4 Nacimiento Reservoir U.S.A.
77 E6 Nacogdoches U.S.A.
82 C2 Nacozari de García Mex.
22 C5 Nadiad India
18 D4 Nadīk Iran
54 B1 Nador Morocco
18 D3 Nadūshan Iran
51 C5 Nadvirna Ukr.
12 E3 Nadvoitsy Rus. Fed.
12 J3 Nadym Rus. Fed.
37 M9 Næstved Denmark
49 J5 Nafpaktos Greece
49 K6 Nafplio Greece
17 K5 Naft r. Iraq
18 C4 Naft-e Safīd Iran
17 K5 Naft Khaneh Iraq
18 B3 Naft Shahr Iran
18 B5 Nafūd al Jur'ā sand dunes S. Arabia
18 A6 Nafūd as Surrah sand dunes S. Arabia
18 B5 Nafūd Qunayfidhah sand dunes S. Arabia
18 A5 Nafy S. Arabia
31 B3 Naga Phil.
66 D4 Nagagami r. Can.
29 C8 Nagahama Japan
23 H4 Naga Hills mts India
29 G5 Nagai Japan
23 H4 Nagaland div. India
8 E4 Nagambie Austr.
29 F6 Nagano Japan
29 F6 Nagaoka Japan
23 H4 Nagaon India
21 B4 Nagappattinam India
22 B2 Nagar India
21 B2 Nāgārjuna Sāgar Reservoir India
22 B4 Nagar Parkar Pak.
23 G3 Nagarzê China
29 A8 Nagasaki Japan
29 B7 Nagato Japan
22 C4 Nagaur India
21 C2 Nagavali r. India
23 G2 Nag, Co l. China
22 C5 Nagda India
21 B4 Nagercoil India
19 G5 Nagha Kalat Pak.
22 D3 Nagina India
23 E3 Nagma Nepal
50 J3 Nagorsk Rus. Fed.
29 E7 Nagoya Japan
22 D5 Nagpur India
23 H3 Nagqu China
31 C3 Nagumbuaya Point pt Phil.
12 F1 Nagurskoye Rus. Fed.
48 G1 Nagyatád Hungary
46 H7 Nagykanizsa Hungary
24 E4 Naha Japan
22 D3 Nahan India
19 F5 Nahang r. Iran/Pak.
64 E2 Nahanni Butte Can.
64 D2 Nahanni National Park Can.
16 E5 Nahariyya Israel
18 C3 Nahāvand Iran
43 F5 Nahe r. Ger.
17 K5 Nahrawān canal Iraq
17 L6 Nahr 'Umr Iraq
91 B3 Nahuelbuta, Parque Nacional nat. park Chile
91 B4 Nahuel Huapí, L. l. Arg.
91 B4 Nahuel Huapí, Parque Nacional nat. park Arg.
79 D6 Nahunta U.S.A.
23 H2 Naij Tal China
30 A2 Naiman Qi China
67 H2 Nain Can.
18 D3 Nā'īn Iran
22 D3 Naini Tal India
22 E5 Nainpur India
40 E3 Nairn U.K.
69 G2 Nairn Centre Can.
56 D4 Nairobi Kenya
56 D4 Naivasha Kenya
30 D2 Naizishan China
18 B5 Na'jān S. Arabia
20 B4 Najd reg. S. Arabia
45 E1 Nájera Spain
22 D3 Najibabad India
30 F2 Najin N. Korea
20 B6 Najrān S. Arabia
29 A8 Nakadōri-shima i. Japan
29 B8 Nakama Japan
29 C8 Nakamura Japan
13 M3 Nakanno Rus. Fed.
29 F6 Nakano Japan
29 C6 Nakano-shima i. Japan
19 H3 Naka Pass Afgh.
29 B8 Nakatsu Japan
29 E7 Nakatsugawa Japan
56 D2 Nak'fa Eritrea
55 F1 Nakhl Egypt
24 F2 Nakhodka Rus. Fed.
32 B2 Nakhon Nayok Thai.
32 B2 Nakhon Pathom Thai.
32 B2 Nakhon Ratchasima Thai.
32 A3 Nakhon Si Thammarat Thai.
22 B5 Nakhtarana India
64 C3 Nakina B.C. Can.
66 C3 Nakina Ont. Can.
62 C4 Naknek U.S.A.
57 D4 Nakonde Zambia
37 M9 Nakskov Denmark
30 E6 Naktong r. S. Korea
56 D4 Nakuru Kenya
64 F4 Nakusp Can.
19 G5 Nal Pak.
19 G5 Nal r. Pak.
59 K2 Nalázi Moz.
23 G4 Nalbari India
51 G7 Nal'chik Rus. Fed.
21 B2 Naldurg India
21 B2 Nalgonda India
21 B3 Nallamala Hills h. India
16 C1 Nallıhan Turkey
54 D1 Nālūt Libya
30 D4 Nam r. N. Korea
59 K2 Namaacha Moz.
59 H3 Namahadi S. Africa
18 C3 Namak, Daryācheh-ye salt flat Iran
19 E4 Namakzar-e Shadad salt flat Iran
56 D4 Namanga Kenya
14 F2 Namangan Uzbek.
57 D5 Namapa Moz.
58 B3 Namaqualand reg. Namibia
58 B4 Namaqualand reg. S. Africa
6 F2 Namatanai P.N.G.
7 F4 Nambour Austr.
32 C3 Năm Căn Vietnam
23 H3 Namcha Barwa mt China
30 D4 Namch'ŏn N. Korea
24 B3 Nam Co l. China
36 N4 Namdalen v. Norway
36 M4 Namdalseid Norway
27 C6 Nam Đinh Vietnam
68 B3 Namekagon r. U.S.A.
30 E6 Namhae-do i. S. Korea
57 B6 Namib Desert des. Namibia
57 B5 Namibe Angola
53 F8 Namibia country Africa
29 G6 Namie Japan
32 B1 Nam Khan r. Laos
25 E7 Namlea Indon.
32 B1 Nam Lik r. Laos
32 A1 Nammekon Myanmar
27 B6 Nam Na r. China/Vietnam
32 B1 Nam Ngum r. Laos
8 H1 Namoi r. Austr.
27 B6 Nam Ou r. Laos
64 F3 Nampa Can.
72 C3 Nampa U.S.A.
22 E3 Nampa mt Nepal
54 B3 Nampala Mali
32 B1 Nam Pat Thai.
32 B1 Nam Phong Thai.
30 C4 Namp'o N. Korea
57 D5 Nampula Moz.
23 G2 Namru Co l. China
15 H4 Namrup India
27 B7 Nam Sam r. Laos/Vietnam
23 E3 Namsê La pass Nepal
36 N4 Namsen r. Norway
17 K3 Namshir Iran
23 H4 Namsi India
23 G3 Namsi La pass Bhutan
36 M4 Namsos Norway
13 O3 Namtsy Rus. Fed.
24 B4 Namtu Myanmar
42 C4 Namur Belgium
57 C5 Namwala Zambia
30 D6 Namwŏn S. Korea
56 B3 Nana Bakassa C.A.R.
64 E5 Nanaimo Can.
74 □1 Nanakuli U.S.A.
30 E3 Nanam N. Korea
27 F5 Nan'an China
58 B2 Nananib Plateau plat. Namibia
27 E6 Nan'ao China
29 E6 Nanao Japan
29 E6 Nanatsu-shima i. Japan
26 C4 Nanbu China
28 A1 Nancha China
27 E4 Nanchang Jiangxi China
27 E5 Nancheng China
27 C4 Nanchong China
27 C4 Nanchuan China
44 H2 Nancy France
22 E3 Nanda Devi mt India
22 E3 Nanda Kot mt India
27 C5 Nandan China
21 B2 Nānded India
22 C5 Nandgaon India
27 D6 Nandu Jiang r. China
22 C5 Nandurbar India
21 B3 Nandyal India
27 D6 Nanfeng Guangdong China
27 E5 Nanfeng Jiangxi China
55 D4 Nanga Eboko Cameroon
33 D3 Nangahpinoh Indon.
30 E2 Nangang Shan mts China/N. Korea
22 C2 Nanga Parbat mt Jammu and Kashmir
33 D3 Nangatayap Indon.
32 A3 Nangin Myanmar
30 D3 Nangnim N. Korea
30 D3 Nangnim Sanmaek mts N. Korea
26 E2 Nangong China
57 D4 Nangulangwa Tanz.
23 H3 Nang Xian China
26 A2 Nanhua China
26 F4 Nanhui China
21 B3 Nanjangud India
26 C3 Nanjiang China
27 F5 Nanjing Fujian China
26 F3 Nanjing Jiangsu China
27 E5 Nankang China
Nanking see Nanjing
29 C8 Nankoku Japan
57 B5 Nankova Angola
26 E2 Nanle China
26 F4 Nanling China
27 D5 Nan Ling mts China
27 C6 Nanliu Jiang r. China
27 C6 Nanning China
27 E6 Nan'oa Dao i. China
63 O3 Nanortalik Greenland
27 C5 Nanpan Jiang r. China
30 A3 Nanpiao China
27 F5 Nanping Fujian China
26 B3 Nanping Sichuan China
27 F5 Nanri Dao i. China
24 E4 Nansei-shotō is Japan
63 J1 Nansen Sound chan. Can.
44 D3 Nantes France
42 A5 Nanteuil-le-Haudouin France
21 C4 Nanthi Kadal lag. Sri Lanka
69 G4 Nanticoke Can.
81 F5 Nanticoke r. U.S.A.
64 G4 Nanton Can.
26 F3 Nantong Jiangsu China
26 F4 Nantong Jiangsu China
27 F6 Nant'ou Taiwan
81 H4 Nantucket U.S.A.
81 H4 Nantucket I. i. U.S.A.
81 H4 Nantucket Sound g. U.S.A.
39 E4 Nantwich U.K.
7 H2 Nanumanga i. Tuvalu
7 H2 Nanumea i. Tuvalu
90 E2 Nanuque Brazil
31 C5 Nanusa, Kepulauan is Indon.
27 B4 Nanxi China
27 D4 Nan Xian China
27 E5 Nanxiong China
26 D3 Nanyang China
30 C3 Nanzamu China
26 D4 Nanzhang China
26 D3 Nanzhao China
45 G3 Nao, Cabo de la hd Spain
67 F3 Naococane, Lac l. Can.
23 G4 Naogaon Bangl.
22 B4 Naokot Pak.
28 C1 Naoli r. China
19 F3 Naomid, Dasht-e des. Afgh./Iran
22 C2 Naoshera Jammu and Kashmir
27 D6 Naozhou Dao i. China
74 A2 Napa U.S.A.
81 K1 Napadogan Can.
69 J3 Napanee Can.
22 C4 Napasar India
63 N3 Napasoq Greenland
68 C5 Naperville U.S.A.
9 F3 Napier N.Z.
92 D4 Napier Mts mts Ant.
81 G2 Napierville Can.
48 F4 Naples Italy
79 D7 Naples FL U.S.A.
81 H3 Naples ME U.S.A.
27 B6 Napo China
86 D4 Napo r. Ecuador/Peru
80 A4 Napoleon U.S.A.
Napoli see Naples
91 D3 Naposta Arg.
91 D3 Naposta r. Arg.
68 E5 Nappanee U.S.A.
17 K3 Naqadeh Iran
16 E6 Naqb Ashtar Jordan
17 M4 Naqqash Iran
29 D7 Nara Japan
54 B3 Nara Mali
47 N3 Narach Belarus
8 C4 Naracoorte Austr.
8 F2 Naradhan Austr.
22 C4 Naraina India
22 E6 Narainpur India
84 C2 Naranjos Mex.
21 D2 Narasannapeta India
21 C2 Narasapatnam, Pt pt India
21 C2 Narasapur India
21 C2 Narasaraopet India
23 F5 Narasinghapur India
32 B4 Narathiwat Thai.
21 A2 Narayangaon India
Narbada r. see Narmada
39 C6 Narberth U.K.
44 F5 Narbonne France
45 C1 Narcea r. Spain
18 D2 Nardin Iran
48 H4 Nardò Italy
91 E1 Nare Arg.
22 B3 Narechi r. Pak.
63 M1 Nares Strait str. Can./Greenland
47 K4 Narew r. Pol.
30 D2 Narhong China
22 A3 Nari r. Pak.
57 B6 Narib Namibia
58 B5 Nariep S. Africa
51 H6 Narimanov Rus. Fed.
19 H2 Narin Afgh.
19 H3 Narin reg. Afgh.
16 G3 Narince Turkey
23 H1 Narin Gol watercourse China
29 G7 Narita Japan
22 C5 Narmada r. India
17 H1 Narman Turkey
22 D3 Narnaul India
48 E3 Narni Italy
47 O5 Narodychi Ukr.
50 F4 Naro-Fominsk Rus. Fed.
8 H4 Narooma Austr.
50 G4 Narovchat Rus. Fed.
51 D5 Narowlya Belarus
37 R5 Närpes Fin.
81 H4 Narragansett Bay b. U.S.A.
8 F3 Narrandera Austr.
8 G2 Narromine Austr.
80 C6 Narrows U.S.A.
81 F4 Narrowsburg U.S.A.
22 D5 Narsimhapur India
23 G5 Narsingdi Bangl.
22 D5 Narsinghgarh India
21 C2 Narsipatnam India
26 E1 Nart China
29 D7 Naruto Japan
37 V7 Narva Estonia
37 U7 Narva Bay b. Estonia/Rus. Fed.
31 B2 Narvacan Phil.
36 P2 Narvik Norway
37 V7 Narvskoye Vdkhr. resr Estonia/Rus. Fed.
22 D3 Narwana India
22 D4 Narwar India
12 G3 Nar'yan-Mar Rus. Fed.
15 F2 Naryn Kyrg.
36 P5 Nåsåker Sweden
75 H3 Naschitti U.S.A.
9 C6 Naseby N.Z.
68 A4 Nashua IA U.S.A.
81 H3 Nashua NH U.S.A.
79 C4 Nashville U.S.A.
16 F5 Nasib Syria
37 S6 Näsijärvi l. Fin.
22 C5 Nasik India
55 F4 Nasir Sudan
Nasirabad see Mymensingh
22 B3 Nasirabad Pak.
57 C5 Nasondoye Congo(Zaire)
16 C6 Nasr Egypt
18 C3 Naşrābād Iran
19 E3 Naşrābād Iran
Nasratabad see Zābol
17 L5 Nasrīān-e-Pā'īn Iran
64 D3 Nass r. Can.
79 E7 Nassau Bahamas
5 L6 Nassau i. Cook Is Pac. Oc.
55 F2 Nasser, Lake resr Egypt
37 O8 Nässjö Sweden
66 E2 Nastapoca r. Can.
66 E2 Nastapoka Islands is Can.
29 F6 Nasu-dake volc. Japan
31 B3 Nasugbu Phil.
47 P2 Nasva Rus. Fed.
57 C6 Nata Botswana
56 D4 Nata Tanz.
89 B4 Natagaima Col.
87 L5 Natal Brazil
Natal div. see Kwazulu-Natal
93 G6 Natal Basin sea feature Ind. Ocean
18 C3 Naţanz Iran
67 H3 Natashquan Can.
67 H3 Natashquan r. Can.
77 F6 Natchez U.S.A.
77 E6 Natchitoches U.S.A.
8 E4 Nathalia Austr.
22 C4 Nathdwara India
8 C4 Natimuk Austr.
74 D5 National City U.S.A.
45 H2 Nati, Pta pt Spain
54 C3 Natitingou Benin
87 J6 Natividade Brazil
28 G5 Natori Japan
56 D4 Natron, Lake salt l. Tanz.
32 A1 Nattaung mt Myanmar
33 C2 Natuna Besar i. Indon.
33 C2 Natuna, Kepulauan is Indon.
81 F2 Natural Bridge U.S.A.
75 G3 Natural Bridges National Monument res. U.S.A.
93 M6 Naturaliste Plateau sea feature Ind. Ocean
75 H2 Naturita U.S.A.
68 E2 Naubinway U.S.A.
57 B6 Nauchas Namibia
43 L2 Nauen Ger.
81 G4 Naugatuck U.S.A.
31 B3 Naujan Phil.
31 B3 Naujan, L. l. Phil.
37 S8 Naujoji Akmenė Lith.
22 C4 Naukh India
43 H3 Naumburg (Hessen) Ger.
43 K3 Naumburg (Saale) Ger.
32 A1 Naungpale Myanmar
16 E6 Na'ūr Jordan
19 G4 Nauroz Kalat Pak.
4 H5 Nauru country Pac. Oc.
22 B4 Naushara Pak.
37 J6 Naustdal Norway
86 D4 Nauta Peru
58 C3 Naute Dam dam Namibia
84 C2 Nautla Mex.
19 G3 Nauzad Afgh.
23 G5 Navadwip India
50 C4 Navahrudak Belarus
75 H4 Navajo U.S.A.
73 F4 Navajo Lake l. U.S.A.
75 G3 Navajo Mt mt U.S.A.
31 C4 Naval Phil.
45 D3 Navalmoral de la Mata Spain
45 D3 Navalvillar de Pela Spain
41 E4 Navan Rep. of Ireland
50 D4 Navapolatsk Belarus
13 T3 Navarin, Mys c. Rus. Fed.
88 C9 Navarino, I. i. Chile
45 F1 Navarra div. Spain
8 D4 Navarre Austr.
74 A2 Navarro U.S.A.
50 G4 Navashino Rus. Fed.
77 D6 Navasota U.S.A.
36 O5 Näverede Sweden
40 D2 Naver, Loch l. U.K.
91 B2 Navidad Chile
87 H3 Navio, Serra do Brazil
50 E4 Navlya Rus. Fed.
49 N2 Năvodari Romania
19 G1 Navoi Uzbek.
82 C3 Navojoa Mex.
50 G3 Navoloki Rus. Fed.
22 C5 Navsari India
22 C4 Nawa India
16 F5 Nawá Syria
23 G4 Nawabganj Bangl.
22 B4 Nawabshah Pak.
23 F4 Nawada India
19 G3 Nāwah Afgh.
22 C4 Nawalgarh India
17 K2 Naxçıvan Azer.
27 B4 Naxi China
49 L6 Naxos Greece
49 L6 Naxos i. Greece
89 A4 Naya Col.
23 F5 Nayagarh India
84 A2 Nayar Mex.
84 A2 Nayarit div. Mex.
18 D5 Nāy Band Iran
28 H2 Nayoro Japan
21 B3 Nāyudupeta India
90 E1 Nazaré Brazil
21 B4 Nazareth India
16 E5 Nazareth Israel
77 B7 Nazas Mex.
84 A1 Nazas r. Mex.
86 D6 Nazca Peru
Nazca Ridge sea feature see South-West Peru Ridge
17 K2 Nāzīk Iran
17 J2 Nazik Gölü l. Turkey
19 F4 Nāzīl Iran
16 B3 Nazilli Turkey
19 G5 Nazimabad Pak.
17 G2 Nazımiye Turkey
23 H4 Nazira India
64 E4 Nazko Can.
64 E4 Nazko r. Can.
17 K3 Nāzlū r. Iran
51 H7 Nazran' Rus. Fed.
56 D3 Nazrēt Eth.
20 E5 Nazwá Oman
57 C4 Nchelenge Zambia
57 C6 Ncojane Botswana
57 B4 N'dalatando Angola
56 C3 Ndélé C.A.R.
56 B4 Ndendé Gabon
7 G3 Ndeni i. Solomon Is
55 D3 Ndjamena Chad
57 C5 Ndola Zambia
59 J4 Ndwedwe S. Africa
41 E3 Neagh, Lough l. U.K.
72 A1 Neah Bay U.S.A.
6 D4 Neale, L. salt flat Austr.
49 K5 Nea Liosia Greece
49 K6 Neapoli Greece
39 D6 Neath U.K.
39 D6 Neath r. U.K.
18 D2 Nebitdag Turkm.
50 E3 Nebolchi Rus. Fed.
75 G2 Nebo, Mount mt U.S.A.
76 C3 Nebraska div. U.S.A.
76 E3 Nebraska City U.S.A.
48 F6 Nebrodi, Monti mts Sicily Italy
77 E6 Neches r. U.S.A.
89 B3 Nechí r. Col.
56 D3 Nechisar National Park Eth.
43 G5 Neckar r. Ger.
43 H5 Neckarsulm Ger.
5 L2 Necker Island i. HI U.S.A.
91 E3 Necochea Arg.
43 M1 Neddemin Ger.
66 F2 Neddouc, Lac l. Can.
36 R2 Nedre Soppero Sweden
75 E4 Needles U.S.A.
39 F7 Needles, The stack U.K.
68 C3 Neenah U.S.A.
65 K4 Neepawa Can.
63 K2 Neergaard Lake l. Can.
42 D3 Neerijnen Neth.
42 D3 Neerpelt Belgium
17 M2 Neftçala Azer.
12 G4 Neftekamsk Rus. Fed.
51 H6 Neftekumsk Rus. Fed.
12 J3 Nefteyugansk Rus. Fed.
39 C5 Nefyn U.K.
48 C6 Nefza Tunisia
56 B4 Negage Angola
56 D3 Negēlē Eth.
90 A3 Negla r. Para.
57 D5 Negomane Moz.
21 B5 Negombo Sri Lanka
49 K4 Negotino Macedonia
86 C5 Negra, Cordillera mts Peru
86 B5 Negra, Pta pt Peru
48 B7 Nègrine Alg.
86 B4 Negritos Peru
91 D4 Negro r. Arg.
90 A2 Negro r. Mato Grosso do Sul Brazil
86 F4 Negro r. S. America
91 F2 Negro r. Uru.
31 B4 Negros i. Phil.
49 N3 Negru Vodă Romania
17 M4 Nehavand Iran
19 F4 Nehbandān Iran
24 E2 Nehe China
27 B4 Neijiang China
65 H4 Neilburg Can.
30 A2 Nei Monggol Zizhiqu div. China
43 K3 Neinstedt Ger.
46 G5 Neiß r. Ger./Pol.
89 B4 Neiva Col.
26 D3 Neixiang China
65 K3 Nejanilini Lake l. Can.
18 D2 Neka Iran
56 D3 Nek'emtē Eth.
28 E2 Nekrasovka Rus. Fed.
37 O9 Neksø Denmark
50 E3 Nelidovo Rus. Fed.
76 D3 Neligh U.S.A.
13 Q3 Nel'kan Rus. Fed.
24 F1 Nel'kan Rus. Fed.
21 B3 Nellore India
64 F5 Nelson Can.
9 D4 Nelson N.Z.
38 E4 Nelson U.K.
75 E4 Nelson U.S.A.
63 J4 Nelson r. Man. Can.
65 L3 Nelson r. Can.
8 J2 Nelson Bay Austr.
8 C5 Nelson, C. c. Austr.
88 B8 Nelson, Estrecho chan. Chile
64 E3 Nelson Forks Can.
65 K3 Nelson House Can.
59 J2 Nelspruit S. Africa
54 B3 Néma Maur.
50 J3 Nema Rus. Fed.
68 A2 Nemadji r. U.S.A.
50 B4 Neman Rus. Fed.
16 F5 Nemara Syria
50 G3 Nemda r. Rus. Fed.
50 K2 Nemed Rus. Fed.
69 F2 Nemegos Can.
36 W2 Nemetskiy, Mys c. Rus. Fed.
44 F2 Nemours France
17 J2 Nemrut Dağı h. Turkey
28 J3 Nemuro Japan
28 J3 Nemuro-kaikyō chan. Japan
51 D5 Nemyriv Ukr.
41 C5 Nenagh Rep. of Ireland
39 H5 Nene r. U.K.
24 E2 Nenjiang China
42 E5 Nennig Ger.
50 F1 Nenoksa Rus. Fed.
77 E4 Neosho U.S.A.
76 E4 Neosho r. U.S.A.
10 K7 Nepal country Asia
69 K3 Nepean Can.
75 G2 Nephi U.S.A.
41 B3 Nephin h. Rep. of Ireland
41 B3 Nephin Beg Range h. Rep. of Ireland
56 C3 Nepoko r. Congo(Zaire)
81 F4 Neptune U.S.A.
44 E4 Nérac France
24 D1 Nerchinsk Rus. Fed.
50 G3 Nerekhta Rus. Fed.
48 G3 Neretva r. Bos.-Herz./Croatia
57 C5 Neriquinha Angola
37 T9 Neris r. Lith.
50 F3 Nerl' r. Rus. Fed.
90 C2 Nerópolis Brazil
24 E1 Neryungri Rus. Fed.
42 D1 Nes Neth.
37 L6 Nes Norway
37 L6 Nesbyen Norway
36 G4 Neskaupstaður Iceland
42 A5 Nesle France
36 N3 Nesna Norway
76 D4 Ness City U.S.A.
43 J4 Nesse r. Ger.
64 C3 Nesselrode, Mt mt Can./U.S.A.
40 D3 Ness, Loch l. U.K.
49 L4 Nestos r. Greece
16 E5 Netanya Israel
65 N2 Netchek, Cape c. Can.
34 F3 Netherlands country Europe
61 M8 Netherlands Antilles terr. Caribbean Sea
43 G4 Netphen Ger.
23 G4 Netrakona Bangl.
22 C5 Netrang India
63 L3 Nettilling Lake l. Can.
68 A1 Nett Lake U.S.A.
68 A1 Nett Lake l. U.S.A.
84 D3 Netzahualcóyotl, Presa resr Mex.
43 M1 Neubrandenburg Ger.
46 C7 Neuchâtel Switz.
46 C7 Neuchâtel, Lac de l. Switz.
43 J5 Neuendettelsau Ger.
42 E2 Neuenhaus Ger.
43 H1 Neuenkirchen Ger.
43 G2 Neuenkirchen (Oldenburg) Ger.
42 D5 Neufchâteau Belgium
44 G2 Neufchâteau France
44 E2 Neufchâtel-en-Bray France
43 F1 Neuharlingersiel Ger.
43 H1 Neuhaus (Oste) Ger.
43 H4 Neuhof Ger.
43 K1 Neu Kaliß Ger.
43 H4 Neukirchen Hessen Ger.
43 L4 Neukirchen Sachsen Ger.
65 K2 Neultin Lake l. Can.
43 K5 Neumarkt in der Oberpfalz Ger.
92 C2 Neumayer Ger. Base Ant.
46 D3 Neumünster Ger.
43 L5 Neunburg vorm Wald Ger.
46 H7 Neunkirchen Austria
42 F5 Neunkirchen Ger.
91 C3 Neuquén Arg.
91 C3 Neuquén div. Arg.
91 C3 Neuquén r. Arg.
43 L2 Neuruppin Ger.
79 E5 Neuse r. U.S.A.
46 H7 Neusiedler See l. Austria/Hungary
42 E3 Neuss Ger.
43 H2 Neustadt am Rübenberge Ger.
43 J5 Neustadt an der Aisch Ger.
43 L5 Neustadt an der Waldnaab Ger.
43 G5 Neustadt an der Weinstraße Ger.
43 K4 Neustadt bei Coburg Ger.
43 K1 Neustadt-Glewe Ger.
42 F4 Neustadt (Wied) Ger.
43 M1 Neustrelitz Ger.
43 L6 Neutraubling Ger.
42 F4 Neuwied Ger.
43 H1 Neu Wulmstorf Ger.
77 E4 Nevada MO U.S.A.
74 D2 Nevada div. U.S.A.
45 E4 Nevada, Sierra mts Spain
91 C2 Nevado, Cerro mt Arg.
82 D5 Nevado de Colima volc. Mex.
84 B3 Nevado de Colima, Parque Nacional nat. park Mex.
84 C3 Nevado de Toluca, Parque Nacional nat. park Mex.
91 C3 Nevado, Sierra del mts Arg.
50 D3 Nevel' Rus. Fed.
44 F3 Nevers France
8 F1 Nevertire Austr.
49 H3 Nevesinje Bos.-Herz.
51 G6 Nevinnomyssk Rus. Fed.
40 C3 Nevis, Loch in. U.K.
16 E2 Nevşehir Turkey
28 C2 Nevskoye Rus. Fed.
75 E5 New r. CA U.S.A.
80 C6 New r. WV U.S.A.
78 C4 New Albany IN U.S.A.
77 F5 New Albany MS U.S.A.
81 E4 New Albany PA U.S.A.
87 G2 New Amsterdam Guyana
81 F5 Newark DE U.S.A.
81 E5 Newark MD U.S.A.
81 F4 Newark NJ U.S.A.
80 E3 Newark NY U.S.A.
80 B4 Newark OH U.S.A.
75 E2 Newark Lake l. U.S.A.
39 G4 Newark-on-Trent U.K.
81 E3 Newark Valley U.S.A.
81 H4 New Bedford U.S.A.
72 B2 Newberg U.S.A.
81 F3 New Berlin U.S.A.
79 E5 New Bern U.S.A.
68 E2 Newberry MI U.S.A.
79 D5 Newberry SC U.S.A.
74 D4 Newberry Springs U.S.A.
38 F2 Newbiggin-by-the-Sea U.K.
69 J3 Newboro Can.
81 G3 New Boston MA U.S.A.
80 B5 New Boston OH U.S.A.
77 D6 New Braunfels U.S.A.
41 E4 Newbridge Rep. of Ireland
81 G4 New Britain U.S.A.
6 E2 New Britain i. P.N.G.
81 F4 New Brunswick U.S.A.
67 G4 New Brunswick div. Can.
68 D5 New Buffalo U.S.A.
40 F3 Newburgh U.K.
81 F4 Newburgh U.S.A.
39 F6 Newbury U.K.
81 H3 Newburyport U.S.A.
38 E3 Newby Bridge U.K.
4 H7 New Caledonia terr. Pac. Oc.
67 G4 New Carlisle Can.
8 H2 Newcastle Austr.
67 G4 Newcastle N.B. Can.
69 H4 Newcastle Ont. Can.
41 E4 Newcastle Rep. of Ireland
59 H3 Newcastle S. Africa
41 F3 Newcastle N. Ireland U.K.
74 B2 Newcastle CA U.S.A.
68 E6 New Castle IN U.S.A.
80 B4 Newcastle OH U.S.A.
80 C4 New Castle PA U.S.A.
75 F3 Newcastle UT U.S.A.
80 C6 New Castle VA U.S.A.
72 F3 Newcastle WY U.S.A.
39 C5 Newcastle Emlyn U.K.
39 E4 Newcastle-under-Lyme U.K.
38 F3 Newcastle upon Tyne U.K.
41 B5 Newcastle West Rep. of Ireland
81 F6 New Church U.S.A.
75 H3 Newcomb U.S.A.
40 D5 New Cumnock U.K.
40 F3 New Deer U.K.
22 D3 New Delhi India
81 K1 New Denmark Can.
74 B3 New Don Pedro Reservoir U.S.A.
8 H1 New England Range mts Austr.
39 E6 Newent U.K.
67 J4 Newfoundland div. Can.
63 N5 Newfoundland i. Can.
96 G2 Newfoundland Basin sea feature Atl. Ocean
40 D5 New Galloway U.K.
7 F2 New Georgia i. Solomon Is
7 F2 New Georgia Islands is Solomon Is
67 H4 New Glasgow Can.
25 G7 New Guinea i. Asia
80 B4 New Hampshire OH U.S.A.
81 G3 New Hampshire div. U.S.A.
68 A4 New Hampton U.S.A.
59 J4 New Hanover S. Africa
6 F2 New Hanover i. P.N.G.
81 G4 New Haven U.S.A.
64 D3 New Hazelton Can.
74 B2 New Hogan Reservoir U.S.A.
68 C4 New Holstein U.S.A.
77 F6 New Iberia U.S.A.
59 J2 Newington S. Africa
41 D5 Newinn Rep. of Ireland
6 F2 New Ireland i. P.N.G.

81 F5 New Jersey div. U.S.A.
80 E6 New Kent U.S.A.
80 B5 New Lexington U.S.A.
68 B4 New Lisbon U.S.A.
69 H2 New Liskeard Can.
81 G4 New London CT U.S.A.
68 B5 New London IA U.S.A.
68 B6 New London MO U.S.A.
68 C3 New London WV U.S.A.
6 B4 Newman Austr.
68 D6 Newman U.S.A.
69 H3 Newmarket Can.
41 B5 Newmarket Rep. of Ireland
39 H5 Newmarket U.K.
80 D5 New Market U.S.A.
41 C5 Newmarket on-Fergus Rep. of Ireland
80 C5 New Martinsville U.S.A.
72 C2 New Meadows U.S.A.
74 B3 New Melanes L. l. U.S.A.
73 F5 New Mexico div. U.S.A.
79 C5 Newnan U.S.A.
77 F6 New Orleans U.S.A.
81 F4 New Paltz U.S.A.
80 C4 New Philadelphia U.S.A.
40 F3 New Pitsligo U.K.
9 E3 New Plymouth N.Z.
41 B4 Newport Mayo Rep. of Ireland
41 C5 Newport Tipperary Rep. of Ireland
39 E5 Newport Eng. U.K.
39 F7 Newport Eng. U.K.
39 D6 Newport Wales U.K.
77 F5 Newport AR U.S.A.
80 A5 Newport KY U.S.A.
81 J2 Newport ME U.S.A.
69 F5 Newport MI U.S.A.
81 G3 Newport NH U.S.A.
72 A2 Newport OR U.S.A.
81 H4 Newport RI U.S.A.
81 G2 Newport VT U.S.A.
72 C1 Newport WA U.S.A.
74 D5 Newport Beach U.S.A.
80 E6 Newport News U.S.A.
39 G5 Newport Pagnell U.K.
79 E7 New Providence i. Bahamas
39 B7 Newquay U.K.
67 G4 New Richmond Can.
68 A3 New Richmond U.S.A.
75 F5 New River U.S.A.
77 F6 New Roads U.S.A.
39 H7 New Romney U.K.
41 E5 New Ross Rep. of Ireland
41 E3 Newry U.K.
40 E4 New Scone U.K.
68 A5 New Sharon U.S.A.
New Siberia Islands is see Novosibirskiye Ostrova
79 D6 New Smyrna Beach U.S.A.
8 D2 New South Wales div. Austr.
27 New Territories reg. H.K. China
38 E4 Newton U.K.
76 E3 Newton IA U.S.A.
76 D4 Newton KS U.S.A.
81 H3 Newton MA U.S.A.
77 F5 Newton MS U.S.A.
81 F4 Newton NJ U.S.A.
39 D7 Newton Abbot U.K.
40 F3 Newtonhill U.K.
40 D5 Newton Mearns U.K.
40 D6 Newton Stewart U.K.
41 C5 Newtown Rep. of Ireland
39 E5 Newtown Eng. U.K.
39 D5 Newtown Wales U.K.
76 C1 New Town U.S.A.
41 F3 Newtownabbey U.K.
41 F3 Newtownards U.K.
41 D3 Newtownbutler U.K.
41 E4 Newtownmountkennedy Rep. of Ireland
40 F5 Newtown St Boswells U.K.
41 D3 Newtownstewart U.K.
76 E2 New Ulm U.S.A.
74 A2 Newville U.S.A.
64 E5 New Westminster Can.
81 G4 New York U.S.A.
81 E3 New York div. U.S.A.
81 G4 New York-John F. Kennedy airport U.S.A.
81 F4 New York-Newark airport U.S.A.
4 J9 New Zealand country Oceania
94 G9 New Zealand Plateau sea feature Pac. Oc.
50 G3 Neya Rus. Fed.
18 D4 Neyrīz Iran
19 E2 Neyshābūr Iran
21 B4 Neyyattinkara India
33 D2 Ngabang Indon.
56 B4 Ngabé Congo
32 A2 Nga Chong, Khao mt Myanmar/Thai.
31 C6 Ngalipaëng Indon.
57 C6 Ngami, Lake l. Botswana
23 F3 Ngamring China
23 E3 Ngangla Ringco salt l. China
22 E2 Nganglong Kangri mt China
22 E2 Nganglong Kangri mts Xizang China
23 F3 Ngangzê Co salt l. China
32 A1 Ngao Thai.
55 D4 Ngaoundéré Cameroon
9 E2 Ngaruawahia N.Z.
9 F3 Ngaruroro r. N.Z.
9 E3 Ngauruhoe, Mt volc. N.Z.
32 B1 Ngiap r. Laos
56 B4 Ngo Congo
32 C2 Ngoc Linh mt Vietnam
23 F3 Ngoin, Co salt l. China
54 D4 Ngol Bembo Nigeria
23 H2 Ngom Qu r. China
23 F2 Ngoqumaima China
24 B3 Ngoring Hu l. China
55 D3 Ngourti Niger
55 D3 Nguigmi Niger
25 F6 Ngulu i. Micronesia
54 D3 Nguru Nigeria
27 B6 Nguyên Binh Vietnam
58 E2 Ngwaketse div. Botswana
59 G3 Ngwathe S. Africa
59 J3 Ngwavuma r. Swaziland
59 J4 Ngwelezana S. Africa
57 D5 Nhamalabué Moz.
32 D2 Nha Trang Vietnam
8 C4 Nhill Austr.
59 J3 Nhlangano Swaziland
27 B6 Nho Quan Vietnam
6 D3 Nhulunbuy Austr.
65 J4 Niacam Can.
54 B3 Niafounké Mali
68 D3 Niagara U.S.A.
69 H4 Niagara Falls Can.
80 D3 Niagara Falls U.S.A.
69 H4 Niagara River r. Can./U.S.A.
54 C3 Niamey Niger
31 C5 Niampak Indon.
57 D4 Niangandu Tanz.
56 C3 Niangara Congo(Zaire)
33 A2 Nias i. Indon.
Niassa, Lago l. see Nyasa, Lake
37 R8 Nīca Latvia
61 K8 Nicaragua country Central America
83 G6 Nicaragua, Lago de l. Nic.
48 G5 Nicastro Italy
44 H5 Nice France
67 F3 Nichicun, Lac l. Can.
23 E4 Nichlaul India
79 E7 Nicholl's Town Bahamas
69 F2 Nicholson Can.
15 H6 Nicobar Islands is Andaman and Nicobar Is
16 D4 Nicosia Cyprus
83 H7 Nicoya, G. de b. Costa Rica
83 G7 Nicoya, Pen. de pen. Costa Rica
81 K1 Nictau Can.
37 R9 Nida Lith.
38 F4 Nidd r. U.K.
43 H4 Nidda Ger.
43 H4 Nidder r. Ger.
47 K4 Nidzica Pol.
46 D3 Niebüll Ger.
42 E5 Niederanven Lux.
43 H4 Niederaula Ger.
46 F7 Niedere Tauern mts Austria
43 G2 Niedersachsen div. Ger.
42 E1 Niedersächsisches Wattenmeer, Nationalpark nat. park Ger.
54 D4 Niefang Equatorial Guinea
54 B4 Niellé Côte d'Ivoire
43 H2 Nienburg (Weser) Ger.
42 E3 Niers r. Ger.
43 G5 Nierstein Ger.
87 G2 Nieuw Amsterdam Suriname
42 C2 Nieuwe-Niedorp Neth.
42 E1 Nieuwe Pekela Neth.
42 C3 Nieuwerkerk aan de IJssel Neth.
87 G2 Nieuw Nickerie Suriname
42 E1 Nieuwolda Neth.
58 C5 Nieuwoudtville S. Africa
42 A3 Nieuwpoort Belgium
42 C3 Nieuw-Vossemeer Neth.
16 E3 Niğde Turkey
52 E4 Niger country Africa
54 C4 Niger r. Africa
53 E5 Nigeria country Africa
54 C4 Niger, Mouths of the est. Nigeria
69 G1 Nighthawk Lake l. Can.
49 K4 Nigrita Greece
29 G6 Nihonmatsu Japan
29 F6 Niigata Japan
29 C8 Niihama Japan
74 2 Niihau i. U.S.A.
29 F7 Nii-jima i. Japan
28 H3 Niikappu Japan
29 C7 Niimi Japan
29 F6 Niitsu Japan
42 D2 Nijkerk Neth.
42 D3 Nijmegen Neth.
42 E2 Nijverdal Neth.
36 W2 Nikel' Rus. Fed.
54 C4 Nikki Benin
29 F6 Nikkō Nat. Park Japan
50 H4 Nikolayevka Rus. Fed.
51 H5 Nikolayevsk Rus. Fed.
50 H4 Nikol'sk Penzen. Rus. Fed.
50 H3 Nikol'sk Vologod. Rus. Fed.
13 S4 Nikol'skoye Rus. Fed.
51 E6 Nikopol' Ukr.
17 M3 Nik Pey Iran
16 F1 Niksar Turkey
19 F5 Nikshahr Iran
49 H3 Nikšić Yugo.
7 J2 Nikumaroro i. Kiribati
7 H2 Nikunau i. Kiribati
22 C2 Nila Pak.
23 F5 Nilagiri India
75 E5 Niland U.S.A.
22 D3 Nilang India
21 B2 Nilanga India
56 D2 Nile r. Africa
68 D5 Niles U.S.A.
21 A3 Nileswaram India
21 B4 Nilgiri Hills mts India
36 V5 Nilsiä Fin.
84 D3 Niltepec Mex.
22 C4 Nimach India
44 G5 Nîmes France
8 G4 Nimmitabel Austr.
92 B4 Nimrod Glacier gl. Ant.
55 F4 Nimule Sudan
21 A4 Nine Degree Chan. India
8 D1 Nine Mile Lake Austr.
74 D2 Ninemile Peak summit U.S.A.
27 Ninepin Group is H.K. China
93 K5 Ninety-East Ridge sea feature Ind. Ocean
8 F5 Ninety Mile Beach beach Austr.
9 D1 Ninety Mile Beach beach N.Z.
17 J3 Nineveh Iraq
81 F3 Nineveh U.S.A.
30 E1 Ning'an China
27 F4 Ningbo China
26 F1 Ningcheng China
27 F5 Ningde China
27 E5 Ningdu China
27 D5 Ninggang China
27 F4 Ningguo China
27 F4 Ninghai China
26 E2 Ninghe China
27 E5 Ninghua China
24 B3 Ningjing Shan mts China
26 E3 Ningling China
27 C6 Ningming China
27 B5 Ningnan China
26 C3 Ningqiang China
26 C3 Ningshan China
26 D2 Ningwu China
26 B2 Ningxia div. China
26 C3 Ning Xian China
27 D4 Ningxiang China
26 E3 Ningyang China
27 D5 Ningyuan China
27 C6 Ninh Binh Vietnam
32 D2 Ninh Hoa Vietnam
92 B6 Ninnis Gl. gl. Ant.
28 G4 Ninohe Japan
90 A3 Nioaque Brazil
76 C3 Niobrara r. U.S.A.
23 H4 Nioko India
54 C3 Niokolo Koba, Parc National du nat. park Senegal
54 B3 Niono Mali
54 B3 Nioro Mali
44 D3 Niort France
21 A2 Nipani India
65 J4 Nipawin Can.
65 J4 Nipawin Provincial Park res. Can.
66 C4 Nipigon Can.
68 C1 Nipigon Bay b. Can.
66 C4 Nipigon, Lake l. Can.
67 H3 Nipishish Lake l. Can.
69 H2 Nipissing Can.
69 G2 Nipissing, L. l. Can.
74 B4 Nipomo U.S.A.
17 K5 Nippur Iraq
75 E4 Nipton U.S.A.
90 C1 Niquelândia Brazil
18 B2 Nir Iran
21 A2 Nira r. India
21 B2 Nirmal India
21 B2 Nirmal Range h. India
49 J3 Niš Yugo.
45 C3 Nisa Port.
18 B5 Nisah, W. watercourse S. Arabia
48 F6 Niscemi Sicily Italy
Nishāpūr see Neyshābūr
29 B9 Nishino-'omote Japan
29 C6 Nishino-shima i. Japan
29 A8 Nishi-Sonogi-hantō pen. Japan
29 D7 Nishiwaki Japan
64 B2 Nisling r. Can.
42 C3 Nispen Neth.
37 N8 Nissan r. Sweden
47 O7 Nistrului Inferior, Câmpia lowland Moldova
64 C2 Nisutlin r. Can.
49 M6 Nisyros i. Greece
18 C5 Niţā S. Arabia
67 F3 Nitchequon Can.
90 D3 Niterói Brazil
40 E5 Nith r. U.K.
40 E5 Nithsdale v. U.K.
22 D3 Niti Pass pass China
46 J6 Nitra Slovakia
80 C5 Nitro U.S.A.
7 J3 Niuatoputopu i. Tonga
5 L6 Niue terr. Pac. Oc.
7 H3 Niulakita i. Tuvalu
27 B5 Niulan Jiang r. China
7 H2 Niutao i. Tuvalu
30 B3 Niuzhuang China
36 T5 Nivala Fin.
42 C4 Nivelles Belgium
50 K2 Nivshera Rus. Fed.
22 C4 Niwāi India
74 C2 Nixon U.S.A.
23 E1 Niya He r. China
17 M1 Niyazoba Azer.
21 B2 Nizamabad India
21 B2 Nizam Sagar l. India
50 H3 Nizhegorodskaya Oblast' div. Rus. Fed.
13 S3 Nizhnekolymsk Rus. Fed.
24 B1 Nizhneudinsk Rus. Fed.
12 J3 Nizhnevartovsk Rus. Fed.
13 P2 Nizhneyansk Rus. Fed.
50 G4 Nizhniy Lomov Rus. Fed.
50 G3 Nizhniy Novgorod Rus. Fed.
50 K2 Nizhniy Odes Rus. Fed.
50 H3 Nizhniy Yenangsk Rus. Fed.
51 D5 Nizhyn Ukr.
47 K4 Nizina reg. Pol.
16 F3 Nizip Turkey
28 D3 Nizmennyy, Mys pt Rus. Fed.
36 R2 Njallavarri mt Norway
36 Q3 Njavve Sweden
Njazidja i. see Grande Comore
57 D4 Njinjo Tanz.
57 D4 Njombe Tanz.
37 P5 Njurundabommen Sweden
54 D4 Nkambe Cameroon
59 J4 Nkandla S. Africa
54 B4 Nkawkaw Ghana
57 C5 Nkayi Zimbabwe
57 D5 Nkhata Bay Malawi
57 D5 Nkhotakota Malawi
54 C4 Nkongsamba Cameroon
59 G5 Nkululeko S. Africa
57 B5 Nkurenkuru Namibia
59 G6 Nkwenkwezi S. Africa
23 J4 Noa Dihing r. India
23 G5 Noakhali Bangl.
23 F5 Noamundi India
41 E4 Nobber Rep. of Ireland
29 B8 Nobeoka Japan
28 G3 Noboribetsu Japan
90 A1 Nobres Brazil
84 B2 Nochistlán Mex.
69 G2 Noelville Can.
82 B2 Nogales Mex.
70 D5 Nogales AZ U.S.A.
29 B8 Nōgata Japan
44 E2 Nogent-le-Rotrou France
42 A5 Nogent-sur-Oise France
50 F4 Noginsk Rus. Fed.
29 E7 Nōgōhaku-san mt Japan
91 E2 Nogoya Arg.
91 E2 Nogoya r. Arg.
30 E5 Nogwak-san mt S. Korea
22 C3 Nohar India
28 G4 Noheji Japan
42 F5 Nohfelden Ger.
44 C3 Noirmoutier-en-l'Île France
44 C3 Noirmoutier, Île de i. France
42 E5 Noisseville France
29 F7 Nojima-zaki c. Japan
22 C4 Nokha India
19 F4 Nok Kundi Pak.
65 J3 Nokomis Lake l. Can.
56 B3 Nola C.A.R.
50 J3 Nolinsk Rus. Fed.
81 H4 No Mans Land i. U.S.A.
62 B3 Nome AK U.S.A.
26 B1 Nomgon Mongolia
23 J1 Nomhon China
4 G4 Nomoi Islands is Micronesia
59 G5 Nomonde S. Africa
29 A8 Nomo-zaki pt Japan
50 G3 Nomzha Rus. Fed.
65 H2 Nonacho Lake l. Can.
59 J4 Nondweni S. Africa
30 C1 Nong'an China
32 C1 Nông Hèt Laos
32 B2 Nong Hong Thai.
32 B1 Nong Khai Thai.
59 J3 Nongoma S. Africa
42 E5 Nonnweiler Ger.
7 H2 Nonouti i. Kiribati
30 D5 Nonsan S. Korea
32 B2 Nonthaburi Thai.
58 F5 Nonzwakazi S. Africa
42 B3 Noordbeveland i. Neth.
42 E1 Noordbroek-Uiterburen Neth.
42 C2 Noorderhaaks i. Neth.
42 D2 Noordoost Polder reclaimed land Neth.
42 C2 Noordwijk-Binnen Neth.
64 D5 Nootka I. i. Can.
19 H2 Norak Tajik.
31 C5 Norala Phil.
69 H1 Noranda Can.
37 O6 Norberg Sweden
12 D2 Nordaustlandet i. Svalbard
42 F1 Norden Ger.
12 L2 Nordenshel'da, Arkhipelag is Rus. Fed.
42 F1 Norderland reg. Ger.
42 F1 Norderney Ger.
42 F1 Norderney i. Ger.
43 J1 Norderstedt Ger.
37 J6 Nordfjordeid Norway
36 O3 Nordfold Norway
Nordfriesische Inseln is see North Frisian Islands
43 J3 Nordhausen Ger.
43 G1 Nordholz Ger.
42 F2 Nordhorn Ger.
36 T1 Nordkapp c. Norway
36 Q2 Nordkjosbotn Norway
36 N4 Nordli Norway
46 E6 Nördlingen Ger.
36 Q5 Nordmaling Sweden
46 D3 Nord-Ostsee-Kanal canal Ger.
43 F5 Nordpfälzer Bergland reg. Ger.
63 N3 Nordre Strømfjord in. Greenland
42 F3 Nordrhein-Westfalen div. Ger.
41 D5 Nore r. Rep. of Ireland
44 F5 Nore, Pic de mt France
76 D3 Norfolk NE U.S.A.
81 F2 Norfolk NY U.S.A.
81 E6 Norfolk VA U.S.A.
7 G4 Norfolk Island terr. Pac. Oc.
94 G7 Norfolk Island Ridge sea feature Pac. Oc.
94 F7 Norfolk Island Trough sea feature Pac. Oc.
77 E4 Norfork L. l. U.S.A.
42 E1 Norg Neth.
37 K6 Norheimsund Norway
29 E6 Norikura-dake volc. Japan
12 K3 Noril'sk Rus. Fed.
17 K1 Nor Kharberd Armenia
69 H3 Norland Can.
68 C5 Normal U.S.A.
77 D5 Norman U.S.A.
6 F2 Normanby I. i. P.N.G.
Normandes, Îles terr. see Channel Islands
44 D2 Normandie reg. France
79 D5 Norman, L. l. U.S.A.
6 E3 Normanton Austr.
8 B3 Normanville Austr.
64 D1 Norman Wells Can.
91 B4 Ñorquinco Arg.
36 R5 Norra Kvarken str. Fin./Sweden
36 O4 Norra Storfjället mts Sweden
42 A4 Norrent-Fontes France
80 B6 Norris Lake l. U.S.A.
81 F4 Norristown U.S.A.
37 P7 Norrköping Sweden
37 Q7 Norrtälje Sweden
6 C5 Norseman Austr.
36 Q4 Norsjö Sweden
7 G3 Norsup Vanuatu
43 H3 Nörten-Hardenberg Ger.
91 F3 Norte, Pta pt Buenos Aires Arg.
88 D6 Norte, Pta pt Chubut Arg.
20 C6 North div. Yemen
81 G3 North Adams U.S.A.
38 F3 Northallerton U.K.
96 E4 North American Basin sea feature Atl. Ocean
6 B4 Northampton Austr.
39 G5 Northampton U.K.
81 G3 Northampton U.S.A.
80 E5 North Anna r. U.S.A.
81 J2 North Anson U.S.A.
64 G2 North Arm b. Can.
79 D5 North Augusta U.S.A.
67 H2 North Aulatsivik Island i. Can.
65 H4 North Battleford Can.
69 H2 North Bay Can.
66 E2 North Belcher Islands is Can.
72 A3 North Bend U.S.A.
40 F4 North Berwick U.K.
81 H3 North Berwick U.S.A.
68 A3 North Branch U.S.A.
92 A5 North, C. c. Ant.
67 H4 North, C. c. Can.
North Cape c. see Nordkapp
9 D1 North Cape c. N.Z.
67 H4 North Cape pt P.E.I. Can.
66 B3 North Caribou Lake l. Can.
79 D5 North Carolina div. U.S.A.
72 B1 North Cascades Nat. Park U.S.A.
69 F2 North Channel chan. Can.
41 E2 North Channel str. N. Ireland/Scot. U.K.
81 H2 North Conway U.S.A.
76 C2 North Dakota div. U.S.A.
39 H6 North Downs h. U.K.
80 D3 North East U.S.A.
96 H2 North-Eastern Atlantic Basin sea feature Atl. Ocean
79 E7 Northeast Providence Chan. chan. Bahamas
43 H3 Northeim Ger.
79 F7 North End Pt pt Bahamas
22 C1 Northern Areas div. Pak.
58 D4 Northern Cape div. S. Africa
65 K3 Northern Indian Lake l. Can.
34 E3 Northern Ireland div. U.K.
66 B4 Northern Light L. l. Can.
4 F3 Northern Mariana Islands terr. Pac. Oc.
59 H1 Northern Province div. S. Africa
6 D3 Northern Territory div. Austr.
40 F4 North Esk r. U.K.
81 G3 Northfield MA U.S.A.
76 E2 Northfield MN U.S.A.
81 G2 Northfield VT U.S.A.
39 J6 North Foreland c. U.K.
74 C3 North Fork U.S.A.
74 B2 North Fork American r. U.S.A.
74 B2 North Fork Feather r. U.S.A.
68 E3 North Fox I. i. U.S.A.
76 C3 North French r. Can.
46 C3 North Frisian Islands is Ger.
38 G3 North Grimston U.K.
81 K2 North Head Can.
9 E2 North Head hd N.Z.
65 K2 North Henik Lake l. Can.
81 G3 North Hudson U.S.A.
9 E3 North Island i. N.Z.
31 B1 North Island i. Phil.
31 B4 North Islet rf Phil.
75 G4 North Jadito Canyon U.S.A.
68 D5 North Judson U.S.A.
65 K3 North Knife r. Can.
23 E4 North Koel r. India
23 H4 North Lakhimpur India
75 E3 North Las Vegas U.S.A.
77 E5 North Little Rock U.S.A.
57 D5 North Luangwa National Park nat. park Zambia
68 E5 North Manchester U.S.A.
68 D3 North Manitou I. i. U.S.A.
64 D2 North Nahanni r. Can.
65 L5 Northome U.S.A.
74 C3 North Palisade summit U.S.A.
76 C3 North Platte U.S.A.
76 C3 North Platte r. U.S.A.
27 North Point H.K. China
78 D2 North Point pt U.S.A.
68 E3 Northport U.S.A.
75 F3 North Rim U.S.A.
40 F1 North Ronaldsay i. U.K.
40 F1 North Ronaldsay Firth chan. U.K.
74 B2 North San Juan U.S.A.
65 G4 North Saskatchewan r. Can.
34 F3 North Sea sea Europe
65 J3 North Seal r. Can.
38 F2 North Shields U.K.
74 D2 North Shoshone Peak summit U.S.A.
62 D3 North Slope plain U.S.A.
39 H4 North Somercotes U.K.
81 H2 North Stratford U.S.A.
38 F2 North Sunderland U.K.
9 E3 North Taranaki Bight b. N.Z.
64 F4 North Thompson r. Can.
40 A3 Northton U.K.
80 D3 North Tonawanda U.S.A.
22 D3 North Tons r. India
9 A7 North Trap rf N.Z.
81 G2 North Troy U.S.A.
66 D3 North Twin I. i. Can.
38 E2 North Tyne r. U.K.
40 A3 North Uist i. U.K.
38 E2 Northumberland National Park U.K.
67 H4 Northumberland Strait chan. Can.
64 E5 North Vancouver Can.
81 F3 Northville U.S.A.
39 J5 North Walsham U.K.
58 F3 North West div. S. Africa
6 B4 North West C. c. Austr.
22 C2 North West Frontier div. Pak.
79 E7 Northwest Providence Chan. chan. Bahamas
67 J3 North West River Can.
65 G2 Northwest Territories div. Can.
39 E4 Northwich U.K.
81 F5 North Wildwood U.S.A.
81 H2 North Woodstock U.S.A.
38 G3 North York Moors reg. U.K.
38 G3 North York Moors National Park U.K.
67 G4 Norton Can.
38 G3 Norton U.K.
76 D4 Norton KS U.S.A.
80 B6 Norton VA U.S.A.
81 G2 Norton VT U.S.A.
57 D5 Norton Zimbabwe
62 B3 Norton Sound b. AK U.S.A.
92 C2 Norvegia, C. c. Ant.
81 G4 Norwalk CT U.S.A.
80 B4 Norwalk OH U.S.A.
81 H2 Norway U.S.A.
34 F2 Norway country Europe
69 J3 Norway Bay Can.
65 K4 Norway House Can.
96 J1 Norwegian Basin sea feature Atl. Ocean
63 J2 Norwegian Bay b. Can.
34 F2 Norwegian Sea sea Atl. Ocean
69 G4 Norwich Can.
39 J5 Norwich U.K.
81 G4 Norwich CT U.S.A.
81 F3 Norwich NY U.S.A.
81 H3 Norwood MA U.S.A.
81 F2 Norwood NY U.S.A.
80 A5 Norwood OH U.S.A.
88 C2 Nos de Cachi mt Arg.
65 H1 Nose Lake l. Can.
49 M3 Nos Emine pt Bulg.
49 M3 Nos Galata pt Bulg.
28 G2 Noshappu-misaki hd Japan
28 G4 Noshiro Japan
51 D5 Nosivka Ukr.
49 N3 Nos Kaliakra pt Bulg.
50 H3 Noskovo Rus. Fed.
58 D2 Nosop r. Botswana/S. Africa
12 G3 Nosovaya Rus. Fed.
19 E4 Noşratābād Iran
90 A1 Nossa Senhora do Livramento Brazil
37 N7 Nossebro Sweden
49 N3 Nos Shabla pt Bulg.
40 Noss, Isle of i. U.K.
58 C2 Nossob r. Namibia
57 E5 Nosy Be i. Madag.
57 F5 Nosy Boraha i. Madag.
57 E6 Nosy Varika Madag.
75 F2 Notch Peak summit U.S.A.
46 H4 Noteć r. Pol.
37 L7 Notodden Norway
48 F6 Noto, Golfo di g. Sicily Italy
29 E6 Noto-hantō pen. Japan
67 K4 Notre Dame Bay b. Can.
69 K3 Notre-Dame-de-la-Salette Can.
81 H2 Notre-Dame-des-Bois Can.
69 K2 Notre-Dame-du-Laus Can.
69 H2 Notre-Dame-du-Nord Can.
67 G4 Notre Dame, Monts mts Can.
69 G3 Nottawasaga Bay b. Can.
66 E3 Nottaway r. Can.
39 F5 Nottingham U.K.
80 E6 Nottoway r. U.S.A.
42 F3 Nottuln Ger.
65 H5 Notukeu Cr. r. Can.
54 A2 Nouâdhibou Maur.
54 A3 Nouakchott Maur.
54 A3 Nouâmghâr Maur.
32 C2 Nouei Vietnam
7 G4 Nouméa New Caledonia
54 B3 Nouna Burkina
58 F5 Noupoort S. Africa
36 V3 Nousu Fin.
Nouveau-Comptoir see Wemindji
Nouvelle Calédonie is see New Caledonia
90 C1 Nova América Brazil
90 B3 Nova Esperança Brazil
90 D3 Nova Friburgo Brazil
48 G2 Nova Gradiška Croatia
90 C3 Nova Granada Brazil
90 D3 Nova Iguaçu Brazil
51 E6 Nova Kakhovka Ukr.
90 D2 Nova Lima Brazil
50 D4 Novalukoml' Belarus
51 D6 Nova Odesa Ukr.
48 C2 Novara Italy
90 C1 Nova Roma Brazil
67 H5 Nova Scotia div. Can.
74 A2 Novato U.S.A.
90 E2 Nova Venécia Brazil
90 B1 Nova Xavantino Brazil
13 R2 Novaya Sibir', Ostrov i. Rus. Fed.
12 G2 Novaya Zemlya is Rus. Fed.
49 M3 Nova Zagora Bulg.
45 F3 Novelda Spain
46 J7 Nové Zámky Slovakia
50 D3 Novgorod Rus. Fed.
50 E3 Novgorodskaya Oblast' div. Rus. Fed.
51 E5 Novhorod-Sivers'kyy Ukr.
49 K3 Novi Iskŭr Bulg.
48 C2 Novi Ligure Italy
49 M3 Novi Pazar Bulg.
49 J3 Novi Pazar Yugo.
49 H2 Novi Sad Yugo.
51 G6 Novoaleksandrovsk Rus. Fed.
51 G5 Novoanninskiy Rus. Fed.
86 F5 Novo Aripuanã Brazil
51 F6 Novoazovs'k Ukr.
19 H2 Novobod Tajik.
50 H3 Novocheboksarsk Rus. Fed.
51 G6 Novocherkassk Rus. Fed.
50 G1 Novodvinsk Rus. Fed.
88 F3 Novo Hamburgo Brazil
90 C3 Novo Horizonte Brazil
46 G6 Novohradské Hory mts Czech Rep.
51 C5 Novohrad-Volyns'kyy Ukr.
14 E2 Novokazalinsk Kazak.
51 G6 Novokubansk Rus. Fed.
24 A1 Novokuznetsk Rus. Fed.
92 D3 Novolazarevskaya Rus. Fed. Base Ant.
13 M2 Novoletov'ye Rus. Fed.
48 F2 Novo Mesto Slovenia
50 F4 Novomichurinsk Rus. Fed.
51 F6 Novomikhaylovskiy Rus. Fed.
50 F4 Novomoskovsk Rus. Fed.
51 E5 Novomoskovs'k Ukr.
51 D5 Novomyrhorod Ukr.
51 G5 Novonikolayevskiy Rus. Fed.
51 E6 Novooleksiyivka Ukr.
28 D2 Novopokrovka Rus. Fed.
51 G6 Novopokrovskaya Rus. Fed.
51 J5 Novorepnoye Rus. Fed.
51 F6 Novorossiysk Rus. Fed.
13 M2 Novorybnoye Rus. Fed.
47 O2 Novorzhev Rus. Fed.
51 E6 Novoselivs'ke Ukr.
47 O1 Novosel'ye Rus. Fed.
51 F6 Novoshakhtinsk Rus. Fed.
28 C2 Novoshakhtinskiy Rus. Fed.
12 K4 Novosibirsk Rus. Fed.
13 Q2 Novosibirskiye Ostrova is Rus. Fed.
50 D3 Novosokol'niki Rus. Fed.
50 H4 Novospasskoye Rus. Fed.
51 E6 Novotroyits'ke Ukr.
51 D5 Novoukrayinka Ukr.
51 J5 Novouzensk Rus. Fed.
51 C5 Novovolyns'k Ukr.
51 F5 Novovoronezh Rus. Fed.
51 D4 Novozybkov Rus. Fed.
46 H6 Nový Jičín Czech Rep.
13 M2 Novyy Rus. Fed.
51 F5 Novyy Oskol Rus. Fed.
12 J3 Novyy Port Rus. Fed.
50 J3 Novyy Tor'yal Rus. Fed.
12 J3 Novyy Urengoy Rus. Fed.
24 F1 Novyy Urgal Rus. Fed.
14 D2 Novyy Uzen' Kazak.
18 D4 Now Iran
77 E4 Nowata U.S.A.
18 C3 Nowbarān Iran
19 E3 Now Deh Iran
17 M3 Nowdī Iran
Nowgong see Nagaon
22 D4 Nowgong Madhya Pradesh India
65 J2 Nowleye Lake l. Can.
46 G4 Nowogard Pol.
8 H3 Nowra Austr.
18 C2 Now Shahr Iran
18 C2 Nowshahr Iran
22 C2 Nowshera Pak.
47 K6 Nowy Sącz Pol.
47 K6 Nowy Targ Pol.
81 E4 Noxen U.S.A.
12 J3 Noyabr'sk r. Rus. Fed.
64 C3 Noyes I. i. U.S.A.
44 F2 Noyon France
32 C1 Noy, Xé r. Laos
32 C1 Noy, Xé r. Laos
59 F5 Nozizwe S. Africa
59 G6 Nqamakwe S. Africa
59 J4 Nqutu S. Africa
57 D5 Nsanje Malawi
56 B4 Ntandembele Congo(Zaire)
59 G3 Ntha S. Africa
56 D4 Ntungamo Uganda
55 F3 Nuba Mountains mts Sudan
17 K1 Nubarashen Armenia
55 F2 Nubian Desert des. Sudan
91 B3 Nuble r. Chile
26 D1 Nüden Mongolia
86 D7 Nudo Coropuna mt Peru
77 D6 Nueces r. U.S.A.
89 C2 Nueva Florida Venez.
91 F2 Nueva Helvecia Uru.
91 B3 Nueva Imperial Chile
89 A4 Nueva Loja Ecuador
88 B6 Nueva Lubecka Arg.
82 D3 Nueva Rosita Mex.
83 J4 Nuevitas Cuba
82 C2 Nuevo Casas Grandes Mex.
91 D4 Nuevo, Golfo g. Arg.
84 A1 Nuevo Ideal Mex.
82 E3 Nuevo Laredo Mex.
84 C1 Nuevo León div. Mex.
56 E3 Nugaal watercourse Somalia
9 B7 Nugget Pt pt N.Z.
7 F2 Nuguria Is is P.N.G.
9 F3 Nuhaka N.Z.
7 H2 Nui i. Tuvalu
32 C2 Nui Ti On mt Vietnam
24 B3 Nu Jiang r. China
7 J4 Nuku'alofa Tonga
7 H2 Nukufetau i. Tuvalu
5 N5 Nuku Hiva i. Pac. Oc.
7 H2 Nukulaelae i. Tuvalu
7 F2 Nukumanu Is is P.N.G.
7 J2 Nukunono i. Pac. Oc.
14 D2 Nukus Uzbek.
6 C4 Nullagine Austr.
6 C5 Nullarbor Plain plain Austr.
26 F1 Nulu'erhu Shan mts China
54 D4 Numan Nigeria
29 F6 Numata Japan
29 F7 Numazu Japan
37 L6 Numedal v. Norway
25 F7 Numfor i. Indon.
8 E4 Numurkah Austr.
67 H2 Nunaksaluk Island i. Can.
63 O3 Nunarsuit i. Greenland
80 E3 Nunda U.S.A.
8 H1 Nundle Austr.
39 F5 Nuneaton U.K.
66 B3 Nungesser L. l. Can.
62 B4 Nunivak I. i. AK U.S.A.
22 D2 Nunkun mt India
13 U3 Nunligran Rus. Fed.
45 C2 Nuñomoral Spain
42 D2 Nunspeet Neth.
48 C4 Nuoro Sardinia Italy
7 G3 Nupani i. Solomon Is
20 B4 Nuqrah S. Arabia
89 A3 Nuquí Col.
22 E1 Nur China
18 D2 Nur r. Iran
18 C4 Nurābād Iran
Nuremberg see Nürnberg
17 J2 Nurettin Turkey
19 G4 Nūr Gamma Pak.
8 B3 Nuriootpa Austr.
19 H3 Nuristan reg. Afgh.
50 J4 Nurlaty Rus. Fed.
36 V5 Nurmes Fin.
36 S5 Nurmo Fin.
43 K5 Nürnberg Ger.
8 F1 Nurri, Mt h. Austr.
23 H1 Nur Turu China
17 H3 Nusaybin Turkey
19 G4 Nushki Pak.
67 H2 Nutak Can.
75 H5 Nutrioso U.S.A.
22 B3 Nuttal Pak.
36 U3 Nuupas Fin.
63 N2 Nuussuaq Greenland
63 N2 Nuussuaq pen. Greenland
21 C5 Nuwara Eliya Sri Lanka
58 C5 Nuwerus S. Africa
58 D6 Nuweveldberg mts S. Africa
17 K4 Nuzi Iraq
59 J1 Nwanedi National Park nat. park S. Africa
12 H3 Nyagan' Rus. Fed.
8 D3 Nyah West Austr.
23 G3 Nyainqêntanglha Feng mt China
23 G3 Nyainqêntanglha Shan mts China
23 H2 Nyainrong China
36 Q5 Nyaker Sweden
55 E3 Nyala Sudan
23 F3 Nyalam China
57 C5 Nyamandhlovu Zimbabwe
50 G2 Nyandoma Rus. Fed.
50 F2 Nyandomskiy Vozvyshennost' reg. Rus. Fed.
57 D5 Nyanga Zimbabwe
56 B4 Nyanga r. Gabon
23 H3 Nyang Qu r. Xizang China
23 G3 Nyang Qu r. Xizang China
57 D5 Nyasa, Lake l. Africa
50 C4 Nyasvizh Belarus
37 M9 Nyborg Denmark
36 V1 Nyborg Norway
37 O8 Nybro Sweden
63 N1 Nyeboe Land reg. Greenland
23 G3 Nyêmo China
56 D4 Nyeri Kenya
23 F3 Nyima China
24 B4 Nyingchi China
47 K7 Nyíregyháza Hungary
36 S5 Nykarleby Fin.
37 M9 Nykøbing Denmark
37 M9 Nykøbing Sjælland Denmark
37 P7 Nyköping Sweden
36 P5 Nyland Sweden
59 H2 Nylstroom S. Africa
8 F2 Nymagee Austr.
37 P7 Nynäshamn Sweden
8 F1 Nyngan Austr.
47 L4 Nyoman r. Belarus/Lith.
46 C7 Nyon Switz.
30 E5 Nyongwol S. Korea
23 F3 Nyonni Ri mt China
44 G4 Nyons France
12 G3 Nyrob Rus. Fed.
46 H5 Nysa Pol.
Nysa Łużycka r. see Neiße
50 J2 Nyuchpas Rus. Fed.
28 F5 Nyūdō-zaki pt Japan
56 C4 Nyunzu Congo(Zaire)
13 N3 Nyurba Rus. Fed.
50 J2 Nyuvchim Rus. Fed.
51 E6 Nyzhn'ohirs'kyy Ukr.
56 D4 Nzega Tanz.
54 B4 Nzérékoré Guinea
56 B4 N'zeto Angola
59 J1 Nzhelele Dam dam S. Africa
Nzwani i. see Anjouan

O

76 C2 Oahe, Lake l. U.S.A.
74 1 Oahu i. U.S.A.
8 C2 Oakbank Austr.
75 F2 Oak City U.S.A.
77 E6 Oakdale U.S.A.
76 D2 Oakes U.S.A.
39 G5 Oakham U.K.
72 B1 Oak Harbor U.S.A.
80 C6 Oak Hill U.S.A.
74 C3 Oakhurst U.S.A.
68 B2 Oak I. i. U.S.A.
74 A3 Oakland CA U.S.A.
80 D5 Oakland MD U.S.A.
76 D3 Oakland NE U.S.A.
72 B3 Oakland OR U.S.A.
8 F3 Oaklands Austr.
68 D5 Oak Lawn U.S.A.
76 C4 Oakley U.S.A.
6 C4 Oakover r. Austr.
79 C4 Oak Ridge U.S.A.
72 B3 Oakridge U.S.A.
8 C2 Oakvale Austr.
69 H4 Oakville Can.
9 C6 Oamaru N.Z.
40 B5 Oa, Mull of hd U.K.
9 D5 Oaro N.Z.
31 B3 Oas Phil.
72 D3 Oasis U.S.A.
92 B5 Oates Land reg. Ant.
75 E4 Oatman U.S.A.
84 C3 Oaxaca Mex.
84 C3 Oaxaca div. Mex.

12 H3 Ob' r. Rus. Fed.
54 D4 Obala Cameroon
29 D7 Obama Japan
40 C4 Oban U.K.
28 G5 Obanazawa Japan
45 C1 O Barco Spain
66 F4 Obatogama L. l. Can.
64 F4 Obed Can.
9 B6 Obelisk mt N.Z.
43 H4 Oberaula Ger.
43 J3 Oberdorla Ger.
43 J3 Oberharz nat. park Ger.
42 E3 Oberhausen Ger.
76 C4 Oberlin KS U.S.A.
80 B4 Oberlin OH U.S.A.
43 F5 Obermoschel Ger.
8 G2 Oberon Austr.
43 L5 Oberpfälzer Wald mts Ger.
43 H4 Obersinn Ger.
43 H4 Oberthulba Ger.
43 G4 Obertshausen Ger.
43 H3 Oberwälder Land reg. Ger.
25 E7 Obi i. Indon.
87 G4 Óbidos Brazil
19 H2 Obigarm Tajik.
28 H3 Obihiro Japan
51 H6 Obil'noye Rus. Fed.
89 C2 Obispos Venez.
24 F2 Obluch'ye Rus. Fed.
50 F4 Obninsk Rus. Fed.
56 C3 Obo C.A.R.
26 A2 Obo China
56 E2 Obock Djibouti
56 C4 Obokote Congo(Zaire)
30 E3 Obŏk-tong N. Korea
56 B4 Obouya Congo
51 F5 Oboyan' Rus. Fed.
50 G2 Obozerskiy Rus. Fed.
23 E4 Obra India
23 E4 Obra Dam dam India
70 E6 Obregón, Presa resr Mex.
49 J2 Obrenovac Yugo.
16 D2 Obruk Turkey
12 J2 Obskaya Guba chan. Rus. Fed.
54 B4 Obuasi Ghana
51 D5 Obukhiv Ukr.
50 J2 Ob''yachevo Rus. Fed.
79 D6 Ocala U.S.A.
89 D4 Ocamo r. Venez.
84 B1 Ocampo Mex.
89 B2 Ocaña Col.
45 E3 Ocaña Spain
86 E7 Occidental, Cordillera mts Chile
89 A4 Occidental, Cordillera mts Col.
86 C6 Occidental, Cordillera mts Peru
64 B3 Ocean Cape pt U.S.A.
81 F5 Ocean City MD U.S.A.
81 F5 Ocean City NJ U.S.A.
64 D4 Ocean Falls Can.
96 G3 Oceanographer Fracture sea feature Atl. Ocean
74 D5 Oceanside U.S.A.
77 F6 Ocean Springs U.S.A.
51 D6 Ochakiv Ukr.
51 G7 Och'amch'ire Georgia
40 E4 Ochil Hills h. U.K.
22 C1 Ochili Pass Afgh.
43 J5 Ochsenfurt Ger.
42 F2 Ochtrup Ger.
37 P6 Ockelbo Sweden
84 D3 Ococingo Mex.
47 M7 Ocolașul Mare, Vârful mt Romania
71 K5 Oconee r. GA U.S.A.
68 C4 Oconomowoc U.S.A.
68 D3 Oconto U.S.A.
74 D5 Ocotillo Wells U.S.A.
84 B2 Ocotlán Mex.
54 B4 Oda Ghana
29 C7 Ōda Japan
36 E4 Ódáðahraun lava Iceland
30 E3 Odaejin N. Korea
28 G4 Ōdate Japan
29 F7 Odawara Japan
37 K6 Odda Norway
65 K3 Odei r. Can.
68 C5 Odell U.S.A.
45 B4 Odemira Port.
16 A2 Ödemiş Turkey
59 G3 Odendaalsrus S. Africa
37 M9 Odense Denmark
43 G5 Odenwald reg. Ger.
43 J3 Oder r. Ger./Pol.
46 G3 Oderbucht b. Ger.
51 D6 Odesa Ukr.
37 O7 Ödeshog Sweden
77 C6 Odessa U.S.A.
45 C4 Odiel r. Spain
54 B4 Odienné Côte d'Ivoire
50 F4 Odintsovo Rus. Fed.
32 C3 Ôdôngk Cambodia
46 J6 Odra r. Ger./Pol.
87 K5 Oeiras Brazil
76 C3 Oelrichs U.S.A.
43 L4 Oelsnitz Ger.
68 B4 Oelwein U.S.A.
42 D1 Oenkerk Neth.
17 H1 Of Turkey
48 G4 Ofanto r. Italy
43 G4 Offenbach am Main Ger.
42 F6 Offenburg Ger.
49 M6 Ofidoussa i. Greece
28 G5 Ōfunato Japan
28 F5 Oga Japan
56 E3 Ogadēn reg. Eth.
28 F5 Oga-hantō pen. Japan
29 E7 Ōgaki Japan
76 C3 Ogallala U.S.A.
24 G4 Ogasawara-shotō is Japan
69 H2 Ogascanane, Lac l. Can.
54 C4 Ogbomoso Nigeria
76 E3 Ogden IA U.S.A.
72 E3 Ogden UT U.S.A.
64 C3 Ogden, Mt mt Can.
81 F2 Ogdensburg U.S.A.
62 E3 Ogilvie r. Can.
62 E3 Ogilvie Mts mts Can.
18 D2 Oglanly Turkm.
79 C5 Oglethorpe, Mt mt U.S.A.
48 D1 Oglio r. Italy
54 C4 Ogoja Nigeria
66 C3 Ogoki r. Can.
66 C3 Ogoki Res. resr Can.
49 K3 Ogosta r. Bulg.
37 T8 Ogre Latvia
48 F2 Ogulin Croatia
18 D2 Ogurchinskiy, Ostrov i. Turkm.
17 L1 Oğuz Azer.
9 A6 Ohai N.Z.
9 E3 Ohakune N.Z.
28 G4 Ōhata Japan
9 B6 Ohau, L. l. N.Z.
91 B2 O'Higgins div. Chile
88 B7 O'Higgins, L. l. Chile
80 B4 Ohio div. U.S.A.
78 C4 Ohio r. U.S.A.
43 G4 Ohm r. Ger.
43 J4 Ohrdruf Ger.
43 L4 Ohře r. Czech Rep.
43 K2 Ohre r. Ger.
49 J4 Ohrid Macedonia
49 J4 Ohrid, Lake l. Albania/Macedonia
59 J2 Ohrigstad S. Africa
43 H5 Öhringen Ger.
9 E3 Ohura N.Z.
87 H3 Oiapoque Brazil
40 D3 Oich, Loch l. U.K.
23 H3 Oiga China
42 A4 Oignies France
80 D4 Oil City U.S.A.
74 C4 Oildale U.S.A.
44 F2 Oise r. France
42 B5 Oise à l'Aisne, Canal de l' canal France
29 B8 Ōita Japan
49 K5 Oiti mt Greece
74 C4 Ojai U.S.A.
91 D2 Ojeda Arg.
68 B3 Ojibwa U.S.A.
82 D3 Ojinaga Mex.
84 C3 Ojitlán Mex.
29 F6 Ojiya Japan
88 C3 Ojos del Salado mt Arg.
50 G4 Oka r. Rus. Fed.
57 B6 Okahandja Namibia
9 E3 Okahukura N.Z.
57 B6 Okakarara Namibia
67 H2 Okak Islands is Can.
64 F5 Okanagan Falls Can.
64 F4 Okanagan Lake l. Can.
64 F5 Okanogan U.S.A.
72 C1 Okanogan r. Can./U.S.A.
72 B1 Okanogan Range mts U.S.A.
56 C3 Okapi, Parc National de la nat. park Congo(Zaire)
22 C3 Okara Pak.
18 D2 Okarem Turkm.
57 B5 Okaukuejo Namibia
57 C5 Okavango r. Botswana/Namibia
57 C5 Okavango Delta swamp Botswana
29 F6 Okaya Japan
29 C7 Okayama Japan
29 E7 Okazaki Japan
79 D7 Okeechobee U.S.A.
79 D7 Okeechobee, L. l. U.S.A.
79 D6 Okefenokee Swamp swamp U.S.A.
39 C7 Okehampton U.K.
54 C4 Okene Nigeria
43 J2 Oker r. Ger.
22 B5 Okha India
24 G1 Okha Rus. Fed.
23 F4 Okhaldhunga Nepal
22 B5 Okha Rann marsh India
13 Q3 Okhotka r. Rus. Fed.
13 Q4 Okhotsk Rus. Fed.
24 G2 Okhotsk, Sea of g. Rus. Fed.
51 E5 Okhtyrka Ukr.
24 E4 Okinawa i. Japan
29 B7 Okino-shima i. Japan
29 C6 Oki-shotō is Japan
77 D5 Oklahoma div. U.S.A.
77 D5 Oklahoma City U.S.A.
77 D5 Okmulgee U.S.A.
56 B4 Okondja Gabon
64 G4 Okotoks Can.
50 E4 Okovskiy Les forest Rus. Fed.
56 B4 Okoyo Congo
36 S1 Øksfjord Norway
50 F2 Oksovskiy Rus. Fed.
19 H2 Oktyabr' Tajik.
14 D2 Oktyabr'sk Kazak.
50 J4 Oktyabr'sk Rus. Fed.
50 G2 Oktyabr'skiy Archangel. Rus. Fed.
51 G6 Oktyabr'skiy Volgograd. Rus. Fed.
24 H1 Oktyabr'skiy Rus. Fed.
12 G4 Oktyabr'skiy Rus. Fed.
19 G2 Oktyabr'skiy Uzbek.
12 H3 Oktyabr'skoye Rus. Fed.
13 L2 Oktyabr'skoy Revolyutsii, Ostrov i. Rus. Fed.
50 E3 Okulovka Rus. Fed.
28 F3 Okushiri-tō i. Japan
58 E1 Okwa watercourse Botswana
36 B4 Ólafsvík Iceland
74 C3 Olancha U.S.A.
74 C3 Olancha Peak summit U.S.A.
37 P8 Öland i. Sweden
36 W3 Olanga Rus. Fed.
8 C2 Olary Austr.
8 C2 Olary r. Austr.
76 E4 Olathe U.S.A.
91 E3 Olavarría Arg.
46 H5 Oława Pol.
75 G5 Olberg U.S.A.
48 C4 Olbia Sardinia Italy
80 D3 Olcott U.S.A.
21 C2 Old Bastar India
41 D4 Oldcastle Rep. of Ireland
62 E3 Old Crow Can.
42 D1 Oldeboorn Neth.
43 G1 Oldenburg Ger.
46 E3 Oldenburg in Holstein Ger.
42 E2 Oldenzaal Neth.
36 R2 Olderdalen Norway
81 F3 Old Forge NY U.S.A.
81 F4 Old Forge PA U.S.A.
38 E4 Oldham U.K.
41 C6 Old Head of Kinsale hd Rep. of Ireland
64 G4 Oldman r. Can.
40 F3 Oldmeldrum U.K.
81 H3 Old Orchard Beach U.S.A.
67 K4 Old Perlican Can.
64 G4 Olds Can.
81 J2 Old Town U.S.A.
65 H4 Old Wives L. l. Can.
75 E4 Old Woman Mts mts U.S.A.
80 D3 Olean U.S.A.
47 L3 Olecko Pol.
13 O4 Olekma r. Rus. Fed.
13 O3 Olekminsk Rus. Fed.
51 E5 Oleksandriya Ukr.
50 H1 Olema Rus. Fed.
37 J7 Ølen Norway
36 X2 Olenegorsk Rus. Fed.
13 N3 Olenek Rus. Fed.
13 O2 Olenek r. Rus. Fed.
13 O2 Olenek B. b. Rus. Fed.
50 E3 Olenino Rus. Fed.
51 C5 Olevs'k Ukr.
28 D3 Ol'ga Rus. Fed.
45 C4 Olhão Port.
59 J1 Olifants S. Africa
58 C5 Olifants r. S. Africa
58 C2 Olifants watercourse Namibia
58 E3 Olifantshoek S. Africa
58 C6 Olifantsrivierberg mts S. Africa
91 F2 Olimar Grande r. Uru.
90 C3 Olímpia Brazil
84 C3 Olinalá Mex.
87 M5 Olinda Brazil
57 D5 Olinga Moz.
59 G2 Oliphants Drift Botswana
91 D2 Oliva Arg.
45 F3 Oliva Spain
88 C3 Oliva, Cordillera de mts Arg./Chile
91 C1 Olivares, Co del mt Chile
80 B5 Olive Hill U.S.A.
90 D3 Oliveira Brazil
45 C3 Olivenza Spain
76 E2 Olivia U.S.A.
50 G4 Ol'khi Rus. Fed.
88 C2 Ollagüe Chile
91 B1 Ollita, Cordillera de mts Arg./Chile
91 B1 Ollitas mt Arg.
86 C5 Olmos Peru
81 G3 Olmstedville U.S.A.
39 G5 Olney U.K.
78 C4 Olney U.S.A.
37 O8 Olofström Sweden
46 H6 Olomouc Czech Rep.
50 E2 Olonets Rus. Fed.
31 B3 Olongapo Phil.
44 D5 Oloron-Ste-Marie France
45 H1 Olot Spain
24 D1 Olovyannaya Rus. Fed.
22 C5 Olpad India
43 F3 Olpe Ger.
47 K4 Olsztyn Pol.
46 C7 Olten Switz.
49 M2 Oltenița Romania
17 H1 Oltu Turkey
31 B5 Olutanga i. Phil.
72 B2 Olympia U.S.A.
72 A2 Olympic Nat. Park WA U.S.A.
72 B2 Olympic Nat. Park WA U.S.A.
Olympus mt see Troödos, Mount
49 K4 Olympus mt Greece
72 B2 Olympus, Mt mt U.S.A.
13 S3 Olyutorskiy Rus. Fed.
13 T4 Olyutorskiy, Mys c. Rus. Fed.
13 S4 Olyutorskiy Zaliv b. Rus. Fed.
23 E2 Oma China
28 G4 Ōma Japan
29 E6 Ōmachi Japan
29 F7 Omae-zaki pt Japan
41 D3 Omagh U.K.
76 E3 Omaha U.S.A.
58 C1 Omaheke div. Namibia
72 C1 Omak U.S.A.
10 G8 Oman country Asia
19 E5 Oman, Gulf of g. Asia
9 B6 Omarama N.Z.
57 B6 Omaruru Namibia
57 B5 Omatako watercourse Namibia
86 D7 Omate Peru
58 E2 Omaweneno Botswana
28 G4 Ōma-zaki c. Japan
56 A4 Omboué Gabon
48 D3 Ombrone r. Italy
23 F3 Ombu China
58 E5 Omdraaisvlei S. Africa
55 F3 Omdurman Sudan
48 C2 Omegna Italy
8 F4 Omeo Austr.
56 D2 Om Hājer Eritrea
18 C4 Omīdiyeh Iran
64 D3 Omineca Mountains Can.
58 C1 Omitara Namibia
29 F7 Ōmiya Japan
64 C3 Ommaney, Cape hd U.S.A.
42 E2 Ommen Neth.
26 B1 Ömnögovĭ div. Mongolia
13 R3 Omolon r. Rus. Fed.
56 D3 Omo National Park Eth.
28 G5 Omono-gawa r. Japan
12 J4 Omsk Rus. Fed.
13 R3 Omsukchan Rus. Fed.
28 H2 Ōmū Japan
29 A8 Ōmura Japan
49 L2 Omu, Vârful mt Romania
68 B4 Onalaska U.S.A.
81 F6 Onancock U.S.A.
66 D4 Onaping Lake l. Can.
69 E3 Onaway U.S.A.
32 A2 Onbingwin Myanmar
91 D1 Oncativo Arg.
38 C3 Onchan U.K.
57 B5 Oncócua Angola
57 B5 Ondangwa Namibia
58 B1 Ondekaremba Namibia
58 D5 Onderstedorings S. Africa
57 B5 Ondjiva Angola
54 C4 Ondo Nigeria
24 D2 Öndörhaan Mongolia
30 A1 Ondor Had China
26 B1 Ondor Mod China
26 D1 Ondor Sum China
50 E2 Ondozero Rus. Fed.
58 D1 One Botswana
50 F2 Onega Rus. Fed.
50 F2 Onega r. Rus. Fed.
50 E2 Onega, Lake l. Rus. Fed.
64 E4 100 Mile House Can.
81 F3 Oneida U.S.A.
81 F3 Oneida Lake l. U.S.A.
76 D3 O'Neill U.S.A.
24 H2 Onekotan, O. i. Rus. Fed.
81 F3 Oneonta U.S.A.
9 E2 Oneroa N.Z.
47 N7 Onești Romania
50 E1 Onezhskaya Guba g. Rus. Fed.
Onezhskoye Ozero l. see Onega, Lake
23 E5 Ong r. India
56 B4 Onga Gabon
9 F3 Ongaonga N.Z.
58 E4 Ongers watercourse S. Africa
30 C5 Ongjin N. Korea
26 F1 Ongniud Qi China
21 C3 Ongole India
51 G7 Oni Georgia
57 E6 Onilahy r. Madag.
54 C4 Onitsha Nigeria
58 B1 Onjati Mountain mt Namibia
29 E7 Ōno Japan
7 J4 Ono-i-Lau i. Fiji
29 C7 Onomichi Japan
7 H2 Onotoa i. Kiribati
64 G4 Onoway Can.
58 C4 Onseepkans S. Africa
6 B4 Onslow Austr.
79 E5 Onslow Bay b. U.S.A.
30 F2 Onsong N. Korea
42 F1 Onstwedde Neth.
29 E7 Ontake-san volc. Japan
72 C2 Ontario U.S.A.
66 B3 Ontario div. Can.
69 H4 Ontario, Lake l. Can./U.S.A.
68 C2 Ontonagon U.S.A.
7 F2 Ontong Java Atoll atoll Solomon Is
6 D4 Oodnadatta Austr.
77 E4 Oologah L. resr U.S.A.
42 B3 Oostburg Neth.
Oostende see Ostend
42 D2 Oostendorp Neth.
42 C3 Oosterhout Neth.
42 B3 Oosterschelde est. Neth.
42 E2 Oosterwolde Neth.
42 A4 Oostvleteren Belgium
42 D1 Oost-Vlieland Neth.
64 D4 Ootsa Lake Can.
64 D4 Ootsa Lake l. Can.
80 E5 Opal U.S.A.
56 C4 Opala Congo(Zaire)
50 J3 Oparino Rus. Fed.
66 B3 Opasquia Can.
66 B3 Opasquia Provincial Park res. Can.
66 F3 Opataca L. l. Can.
46 H6 Opava Czech Rep.
79 C5 Opelika U.S.A.
77 E6 Opelousas U.S.A.
72 F1 Opheim U.S.A.
69 F2 Ophir Can.
33 B2 Ophir, Gunung volc. Indon.
9 C6 Opihi r. N.Z.
66 E3 Opinaca r. Can.
66 E3 Opinaca, Réservoir resr Can.
66 D3 Opinnagau r. Can.
17 K5 Opis Iraq
67 G3 Opiscotéo L. l. Can.
42 C2 Opmeer Neth.
50 D3 Opochka Rus. Fed.
46 H5 Opole Pol.
45 B2 Oporto Port.
9 F3 Opotiki N.Z.
79 C6 Opp U.S.A.
36 L5 Oppdal Norway
9 D3 Opunake N.Z.
57 B5 Opuwo Namibia
68 B5 Oquawka U.S.A.
81 H2 Oquossoc U.S.A.
75 G5 Oracle U.S.A.
75 G5 Oracle Junction U.S.A.
47 K7 Oradea Romania
36 E4 Öræfajökull gl. Iceland
49 J3 Orahovac Yugo.
22 D4 Orai India
54 B1 Oran Alg.
88 D2 Orán Arg.
32 C2 O Rang Cambodia
30 E3 Orang N. Korea
8 G2 Orange Austr.
44 G4 Orange France
81 G3 Orange MA U.S.A.
77 E6 Orange TX U.S.A.
80 D5 Orange VA U.S.A.
57 B6 Orange r. Namibia/S. Africa
79 D5 Orangeburg U.S.A.
87 H3 Orange, Cabo c. Brazil
Orange Free State div. see Free State
69 G3 Orangeville Can.
75 G2 Orangeville U.S.A.
82 G5 Orange Walk Belize
31 B3 Orani Phil.
43 M2 Oranienburg Ger.
57 B6 Oranjemund Namibia
89 C1 Oranjestad Aruba
41 C4 Oranmore Rep. of Ireland
57 C6 Orapa Botswana
31 C3 Oras Phil.
49 K2 Orăștie Romania
36 S5 Oravais Fin.
49 J2 Oravita Romania
22 E2 Orba Co l. China
48 D3 Orbetello Italy
45 D1 Orbigo r. Spain
8 G4 Orbost Austr.
92 B1 Orcadas Arg. Base Ant.
75 H2 Orchard Mesa U.S.A.
89 D2 Orchila, Isla i. Venez.
74 B4 Orcutt U.S.A.
6 C3 Ord r. Austr.
73 D4 Orderville U.S.A.
45 B1 Ordes Spain
6 C3 Ord, Mt h. Austr.
74 D4 Ord Mt mt U.S.A.
16 F1 Ordu Turkey
17 L2 Ordubad Azer.
73 G4 Ordway U.S.A.
Ordzhonikidze see Vladikavkaz
51 E6 Ordzhonikidze Ukr.
74 C1 Oreana U.S.A.
37 O7 Örebro Sweden
68 C4 Oregon IL U.S.A.
80 B4 Oregon OH U.S.A.
68 C4 Oregon WV U.S.A.
72 B3 Oregon div. U.S.A.
72 B2 Oregon City U.S.A.
50 F4 Orekhovo-Zuyevo Rus. Fed.
50 F4 Orel Rus. Fed.
24 F1 Orel', Ozero l. Rus. Fed.
75 G1 Orem U.S.A.
49 M6 Ören Turkey
16 A2 Ören Turkey
12 G4 Orenburg Rus. Fed.
91 E3 Orense Arg.
9 A7 Orepuki N.Z.
37 N9 Øresund str. Denmark
9 B7 Oreti r. N.Z.
9 E2 Orewa N.Z.
42 D4 Oreye Belgium
49 K4 Orfanou, Kolpos b. Greece
39 J5 Orford U.K.
39 J5 Orford Ness spit U.K.
75 F5 Organ Pipe Cactus National Monument res. U.S.A.
19 H3 Orgūn Afgh.
16 B2 Orhaneli Turkey
51 D7 Orhangazi Turkey
50 J3 Orichi Rus. Fed.
81 K2 Orient U.S.A.
86 E7 Oriental, Cordillera mts Bol.
89 B3 Oriental, Cordillera mts Col.
86 D6 Oriental, Cordillera mts Peru
91 E3 Oriente Arg.
45 F3 Orihuela Spain
51 E6 Orikhiv Ukr.
69 H3 Orillia Can.
37 T6 Orimattila Fin.
89 E2 Orinoco r. Col./Venez.
89 E2 Orinoco Delta delta Venez.
23 F5 Orissa div. India
37 S7 Orissaare Estonia
48 C5 Oristano Sardinia Italy
37 T6 Orivesi Fin.
36 V5 Orivesi l. Fin.
87 G4 Oriximiná Brazil
84 C3 Orizaba Mex.
36 L5 Orkanger Norway
37 N8 Örkelljunga Sweden
36 L5 Orkla r. Norway
59 G3 Orkney S. Africa
40 E1 Orkney Islands is U.K.
77 C6 Orla U.S.A.
74 A2 Orland U.S.A.
90 C3 Orlândia Brazil
79 D6 Orlando U.S.A.
44 E3 Orléans France
81 J4 Orleans MA U.S.A.
81 G2 Orleans VT U.S.A.
50 J3 Orlov Rus. Fed.
50 F4 Orlovskaya Oblast' div. Rus. Fed.
51 G6 Orlovskiy Rus. Fed.
19 G5 Ormara Pak.
19 G5 Ormara, Ras hd Pak.
31 C4 Ormoc Phil.
79 D6 Ormond Beach U.S.A.
38 E4 Ormskirk U.K.
81 G2 Ormstown Can.
44 D2 Orne r. France
36 N3 Ørnes Norway
36 Q5 Örnsköldsvik Sweden
30 D4 Oro N. Korea
89 C3 Orocué Col.
54 B3 Orodara Burkina
72 C2 Orofino U.S.A.
73 F5 Orogrande U.S.A.
67 G4 Oromocto Can.
16 E6 Oron Israel
7 J2 Orona i. Kiribati
81 J2 Orono U.S.A.
40 B4 Oronsay i. U.K.
Orontes r. see 'Āṣī, Nahr al
24 E1 Oroqen Zizhiqi China
31 B4 Oroquieta Phil.
87 L5 Orós, Açude resr Brazil
48 C4 Orosei Sardinia Italy
48 C4 Orosei, Golfo di b. Sardinia Italy
47 K7 Orosháza Hungary
75 G5 Oro Valley U.S.A.
74 B2 Oroville CA U.S.A.
72 C1 Oroville WA U.S.A.
74 B2 Oroville, Lake l. U.S.A.
8 B2 Orroroo Austr.
37 O6 Orsa Sweden
50 D4 Orsha Belarus
12 G4 Orsk Rus. Fed.
37 K5 Ørsta Norway
45 C1 Ortegal, Cabo c. Spain
44 D5 Orthez France
45 C1 Ortigueira Spain
89 D2 Ortíz Venez.
48 D1 Ortles mt Italy
38 E3 Orton U.K.
48 F3 Ortona Italy
76 D2 Ortonville U.S.A.
13 O3 Orulgan, Khrebet mts Rus. Fed.
58 B1 Orumbo Namibia
18 B2 Orūmīyeh Iran
18 B2 Orūmīyeh, Daryācheh-ye salt l. Iran
86 E7 Oruro Bol.
42 D5 Orval, Abbaye d' Belgium
48 E3 Orvieto Italy
92 B3 Orville Coast coastal area Ant.
80 C4 Orwell OH U.S.A.
81 G3 Orwell VT U.S.A.
37 M5 Os Norway
68 A4 Osage U.S.A.
76 E4 Osage r. U.S.A.
29 D7 Ōsaka Japan
83 H7 Osa, Pen. de pen. Costa Rica
37 N8 Osby Sweden
77 F5 Osceola AR U.S.A.
76 E3 Osceola IA U.S.A.
43 M3 Oschatz Ger.
43 K2 Oschersleben (Bode) Ger.
48 C4 Oschiri Sardinia Italy
69 F3 Oscoda U.S.A.
50 F4 Osetr r. Rus. Fed.
29 A8 Ōse-zaki pt Japan
69 K3 Osgoode Can.
15 F2 Osh Kyrg.
57 B5 Oshakati Namibia
28 G3 Oshamanbe Japan
69 H4 Oshawa Can.
28 G5 Oshika-hantō pen. Japan
28 F4 Ō-shima i. Japan
29 F7 Ō-shima i. Japan
76 C3 Oshkosh NE U.S.A.
68 C3 Oshkosh WV U.S.A.
18 B2 Oshnovīyeh Iran
54 C4 Oshogbo Nigeria
17 M5 Oshtorān Kūh mt Iran
17 M5 Oshtorīnān Iran
56 B4 Oshwe Congo(Zaire)
49 H2 Osijek Croatia
48 E3 Osimo Italy
22 C4 Osiyān India
59 J3 Osizweni S. Africa
48 G2 Osječenica mt Bos.-Herz.
36 O5 Ösjön l. Sweden
76 E3 Oskaloosa U.S.A.
37 P8 Oskarshamn Sweden
69 K1 Oskélanéo Can.
51 F5 Oskol r. Rus. Fed.
37 M7 Oslo Norway
31 B4 Oslob Phil.
37 M7 Oslofjorden chan. Norway
21 B2 Osmānābād India
16 E1 Osmancık Turkey
16 B1 Osmaneli Turkey
16 F3 Osmaniye Turkey
37 V7 Os'mino Rus. Fed.
43 G2 Osnabrück Ger.
49 K3 Osogovske Planine mts Bulg./Macedonia
91 B4 Osorno Chile
45 D1 Osorno Spain
91 B4 Osorno, Vol. volc. Chile
64 F5 Osoyoos Can.
37 J6 Osøyri Norway
6 E3 Osprey Reef rf Coral Sea Is Terr.
42 D3 Oss Neth.
6 E6 Ossa, Mt mt Austr.
68 B3 Osseo U.S.A.
69 F3 Ossineke U.S.A.
81 H3 Ossipee Lake l. U.S.A.
43 K3 Oßmannstedt Ger.
67 H3 Ossokmanuan Lake l. Can.
50 E3 Ostashkov Rus. Fed.
43 F2 Ostbevern Ger.
43 H1 Oste r. Ger.
42 A3 Ostend Belgium
47 P5 Oster Ukr.
43 K2 Osterburg (Altmark) Ger.
37 O8 Österbymo Sweden
37 N6 Österdalälven l. Sweden
37 M5 Østerdalen v. Norway
43 K3 Osterfeld Ger.
43 G1 Osterholz-Scharmbeck Ger.
43 J3 Osterode am Harz Ger.
36 O5 Östersund Sweden
43 J3 Osterwieck Ger.
Ostfriesische Inseln is see East Frisian Islands
42 F1 Ostfriesland reg. Ger.
37 Q6 Östhammar Sweden
46 J6 Ostrava Czech Rep.
47 J4 Ostróda Pol.
51 F5 Ostrogozhsk Rus. Fed.
43 L4 Ostrov Czech Rep.
50 D3 Ostrov Rus. Fed.
47 K5 Ostrowiec Świętokrzyski Pol.
47 K4 Ostrów Mazowiecka Pol.
46 H5 Ostrów Wielkopolski Pol.
49 L3 Osŭm r. Bulg.
29 B9 Ōsumi-Kaikyō chan. Japan
29 B9 Ōsumi-shotō is Japan
45 D4 Osuna Spain
81 F2 Oswegatchie U.S.A.
68 C5 Oswego IL U.S.A.
80 E3 Oswego NY U.S.A.
81 E3 Oswego r. U.S.A.
39 D5 Oswestry U.K.
29 F6 Ōta Japan
9 C6 Otago Peninsula pen. N.Z.
9 E4 Otaki N.Z.
36 U4 Otanmäki Fin.
89 B4 Otare, Co h. Col.
28 G3 Otaru Japan
9 B7 Otatara N.Z.
86 C3 Otavalo Ecuador
57 B5 Otavi Namibia
29 G6 Ōtawara Japan
9 C6 Otematata N.Z.
37 U7 Otepää Estonia
72 C2 Othello U.S.A.
84 A1 Otinapa Mex.
9 C5 Otira N.Z.
81 E3 Otisco Lake l. U.S.A.
67 F3 Otish, Monts mts Can.
57 B6 Otjiwarongo Namibia
38 F4 Otley U.K.
26 C2 Otog Qi China
28 H2 Otoineppu Japan
9 E3 Otorohanga N.Z.
66 C3 Otoskwin r. Can.
49 H4 Otranto Italy
49 H4 Otranto, Strait of str. Albania/Italy
13 T3 Otrozhnyy Rus. Fed.
68 E4 Otsego U.S.A.
68 E3 Otsego Lake l. MI U.S.A.
81 F3 Otsego Lake l. NY U.S.A.
81 F3 Otselic U.S.A.
29 D7 Ōtsu Japan
37 L6 Otta Norway
69 K3 Ottawa Can.
68 C5 Ottawa IL U.S.A.
76 E4 Ottawa KS U.S.A.
80 A4 Ottawa OH U.S.A.
69 H2 Ottawa r. Can.
66 D2 Ottawa Islands is Can.
38 E2 Otterburn U.K.
75 G2 Otter Creek Reservoir U.S.A.
68 D1 Otter I. i. Can.
66 D3 Otter Rapids Can.
43 H1 Ottersberg Ger.
39 C7 Ottery r. U.K.
42 C4 Ottignies Belgium
63 K1 Otto Fjord in. Can.
68 A5 Ottumwa U.S.A.
42 F5 Ottweiler Ger.
54 C4 Otukpo Nigeria
88 D3 Otumpa Arg.
86 C5 Otuzco Peru
8 D5 Otway, C. c. Austr.
77 E5 Ouachita r. U.S.A.
77 E5 Ouachita, L. l. U.S.A.
77 E5 Ouachita Mts mts U.S.A.
56 C3 Ouadda C.A.R.
55 E3 Ouaddaï reg. Chad
54 B3 Ouagadougou Burkina
54 B3 Ouahigouya Burkina
54 B3 Oualâta Maur.
56 C3 Ouanda-Djailé C.A.R.
54 B2 Ouarâne reg. Maur.
54 C1 Ouargla Alg.
54 B1 Ouarzazate Morocco
58 F6 Oubergpas pass S. Africa
42 B4 Oudenaarde Belgium
42 F1 Oude Pekela Neth.
58 E6 Oudtshoorn S. Africa
42 C3 Oud-Turnhout Belgium
45 F5 Oued Tlélat Alg.
54 B1 Oued Zem Morocco
48 B6 Oued Zénati Alg.
44 B2 Ouessant, Île d' i. France
56 B3 Ouésso Congo
54 C4 Ouidah Benin
54 B1 Oujda Morocco
36 T4 Oulainen Fin.
45 G4 Ouled Farès Alg.
36 T4 Oulu Fin.
36 U4 Oulujärvi l. Fin.
36 U4 Oulujoki r. Fin.
36 T4 Oulunsalo Fin.
44 H4 Oulx Italy
55 E3 Oum-Chalouba Chad
54 B4 Oumé Côte d'Ivoire
55 D3 Oum-Hadjer Chad
36 T3 Ounasjoki r. Fin.
39 G5 Oundle U.K.
55 E3 Ounianga Kébir Chad
42 D4 Oupeye Belgium
42 E5 Our r. Lux.
73 F4 Ouray CO U.S.A.
75 H1 Ouray UT U.S.A.
45 C1 Ourense Spain
87 K5 Ouricurí Brazil
90 C3 Ourinhos Brazil
90 C1 Ouro r. Brazil
90 D3 Ouro Preto Brazil
42 D4 Ourthe r. Belgium
42 E5 Our, Vallée de l' v. Ger./Lux.
38 G4 Ouse r. Eng. U.K.
39 H7 Ouse r. Eng. U.K.
67 G3 Outardes r. Can.
58 E6 Outeniekpas pass S. Africa
40 A2 Outer Hebrides is U.K.
68 B2 Outer I. i. U.S.A.
74 C5 Outer Santa Barbara Channel chan. U.S.A.
57 B6 Outjo Namibia
62 H4 Outlook Can.
36 V5 Outokumpu Fin.
40 [illegible] Out Skerries is U.K.
7 G4 Ouvéa i. New Caledonia
27 D5 Ouyang Hai Sk. resr China
8 D3 Ouyen Austr.
39 G5 Ouzel r. U.K.
48 C4 Ovace, Pte d' mt Corsica France
17 G2 Ovacık Turkey
48 C2 Ovada Italy
7 H3 Ovalau i. Fiji
91 B1 Ovalle Chile
45 B2 Ovar Port.
91 D2 Oveja mt Arg.
8 F4 Ovens r. Austr.
42 F4 Overath Ger.
36 S3 Överkalix Sweden
75 E3 Overton U.S.A.
36 S3 Övertorneå Sweden
37 P8 Överum Sweden
42 C2 Overveen Neth.
68 E4 Ovid U.S.A.
45 D1 Oviedo Spain
36 T2 Øvre Anarjåkka Nasjonalpark nat. park Norway
36 Q2 Øvre Dividal Nasjonalpark nat. park Norway
37 M6 Øvre Rendal Norway
51 D5 Ovruch Ukr.
9 B7 Owaka N.Z.
56 B4 Owando Congo
29 E7 Owase Japan
76 E2 Owatonna U.S.A.
19 F3 Owbeh Afgh.
81 E3 Owego U.S.A.
93 H3 Owen Fracture sea feature Ind. Ocean
41 B3 Owenmore r. Rep. of Ireland
9 D4 Owen River N.Z.
74 C3 Owens r. U.S.A.
78 C4 Owensboro U.S.A.
74 D3 Owens Lake l. U.S.A.
69 G3 Owen Sound Can.
69 G3 Owen Sound in. Can.
6 E2 Owen Stanley Range mts P.N.G.
54 C4 Owerri Nigeria
64 D4 Owikeno L. l. Can.
80 B5 Owingsville U.S.A.
81 J2 Owls Head U.S.A.
54 C4 Owo Nigeria
69 E4 Owosso U.S.A.
17 L4 Owrāmān, Kūh-e mts Iran/Iraq
72 C3 Owyhee U.S.A.
72 C3 Owyhee r. U.S.A.
72 C3 Owyhee Mts mts U.S.A.
86 C6 Oxapampa Peru
36 E3 Öxarfjörður b. Iceland
65 J5 Oxbow Can.
81 J1 Oxbow U.S.A.
37 P7 Oxelösund Sweden
9 D5 Oxford N.Z.
39 F6 Oxford U.K.
69 F4 Oxford MI U.S.A.
77 F5 Oxford MS U.S.A.
81 F3 Oxford NY U.S.A.
81 F5 Oxford PA U.S.A.
65 K4 Oxford House Can.
65 K4 Oxford L. l. Can.
8 E3 Oxley Austr.
8 H1 Oxleys Pk mt Austr.
74 C4 Oxnard U.S.A.
69 H3 Oxtongue Lake Can.
36 N3 Øya Norway
29 F6 Oyama Japan
87 H3 Oyapock r. Brazil/Fr. Guiana
56 B3 Oyem Gabon
40 D3 Oykel r. U.K.
54 C4 Oyo Nigeria
44 G3 Oyonnax France
23 H5 Oyster I. i. Myanmar
43 H1 Oyten Ger.
17 J2 Özalp Turkey
31 B4 Ozamiz Phil.
79 C6 Ozark AL U.S.A.
68 E2 Ozark MI U.S.A.
77 E4 Ozark Plateau plat. U.S.A.
76 E4 Ozarks, Lake of the l. U.S.A.
18 E3 Ozbagū Iran
51 G7 Ozerget'i Georgia
24 H1 Ozernovskiy Rus. Fed.
50 E4 Ozernyy Rus. Fed.
47 L3 Ozersk Rus. Fed.
50 F4 Ozery Rus. Fed.
13 Q3 Ozhogino Rus. Fed.
48 C4 Ozieri Sardinia Italy
77 C6 Ozona U.S.A.
29 B7 Ozuki Japan

P

63 O3 Paamiut Greenland
32 A1 Pa-an Myanmar
58 C6 Paarl S. Africa
58 D4 Paballelo S. Africa
30 E3 Pabal-ri N. Korea
40 A3 Pabbay i. Scot. U.K.
40 A4 Pabbay i. Scot. U.K.
47 J5 Pabianice Pol.
23 G4 Pabna Bangl.
37 T9 Pabradė Lith.
19 G5 Pab Range mts Pak.
86 F6 Pacaás Novos, Parque Nacional nat. park Brazil
89 E4 Pacaraima, Serra mts Brazil
86 C5 Pacasmayo Peru
73 E6 Pacheco Chihuahua Mex.
84 B1 Pacheco Mex.
50 H2 Pachikha Rus. Fed.
48 F6 Pachino Sicily Italy
21 B1 Pachmarhi India
22 D5 Pachore India
84 C2 Pachuca Mex.
74 B2 Pacific U.S.A.
95 L9 Pacific-Antarctic Ridge sea feature Pac. Oc.
29 F8 Pacific Ocean ocean
31 C4 Pacijan i. Phil.
33 D4 Pacitan Indon.
87 H4 Pacoval Brazil
90 D2 Pacuí r. Brazil
46 H5 Paczków Pol.
31 C5 Padada Phil.
89 D4 Padamo r. Venez.
33 B3 Padang Indon.
33 B3 Padangpanjang Indon.
33 A2 Padangsidimpuan Indon.
33 C3 Padangtikar i. Indon.
50 E2 Padany Rus. Fed.
17 M5 Padatha, Kūh-e mt Iran
89 D4 Padauiri r. Brazil
86 F8 Padcaya Bol.
64 F3 Paddle Prairie Can.
80 C5 Paden City U.S.A.
43 G3 Paderborn Ger.
49 K2 Padeșu, Vârful mt Romania
86 F7 Padilla Bol.
36 P3 Padjelanta Nationalpark nat. park Sweden
23 G5 Padma r. Bangl.
Padova see Padua
77 D7 Padre Island i. U.S.A.
48 C3 Padro, Monte mt Corsica France
39 C7 Padstow U.K.

47 N3 Padsvillye Belarus
8 C4 Padthaway Austr.
21 C2 Pādua India
48 D2 Padua Italy
78 B4 Paducah KY U.S.A.
77 C5 Paducah TX U.S.A.
22 D2 Padum Jammu and Kashmir
30 E3 Paegam N. Korea
30 C5 Paengnyŏng-do i. N. Korea
9 E2 Paeroa N.Z.
31 B3 Paete Phil.
16 D4 Pafos Cyprus
59 J1 Pafúri Moz.
48 F2 Pag Croatia
48 F2 Pag i. Croatia
31 B5 Pagadian Phil.
33 B3 Pagai Selatan i. Indon.
33 B3 Pagai Utara i. Indon.
25 G5 Pagan i. N. Mariana Is
33 E3 Pagatan Indon.
75 G3 Page U.S.A.
37 R9 Pagėgiai Lith.
88 □ Paget, Mt mt Atl. Ocean
73 F4 Pagosa Springs U.S.A.
23 G4 Pagri China
66 C3 Pagwa River Can.
74 □2 Pahala U.S.A.
22 B2 Paharpur Pak.
9 A7 Pahia Pt pt N.Z.
74 □2 Pahoa U.S.A.
79 D7 Pahokee U.S.A.
19 F3 Pahra Kariz Afgh.
75 E3 Pahranagat Range mts U.S.A.
22 D4 Pahuj r. India
74 D3 Pahute Mesa plat. U.S.A.
32 A1 Pai Thai.
37 T7 Paide Estonia
39 D7 Paignton U.K.
37 T6 Päijänne l. Fin.
23 F3 Paiku Co l. China
32 B2 Pailin Cambodia
91 B4 Paillaco Chile
74 □2 Pailolo Chan. chan. U.S.A.
37 S6 Paimio Fin.
91 B2 Paine Chile
80 C4 Painesville U.S.A.
75 G3 Painted Desert des. U.S.A.
75 F5 Painted Rock Reservoir U.S.A.
65 K3 Paint Lake Provincial Recr. Park res. Can.
80 B6 Paintsville U.S.A.
69 G3 Paisley Can.
40 D5 Paisley U.K.
86 B5 Paita Peru
31 A5 Paitan, Teluk b. Malaysia
27 D4 Paizhou China
36 S3 Pajala Sweden
87 L5 Pajeú r. Brazil
32 B4 Paka Malaysia
86 F2 Pakaraima Mountains Guyana
30 C4 Pakch'ŏn N. Korea
69 G3 Pakesley Can.
13 S3 Pakhacha Rus. Fed.
10 H7 Pakistan country Asia
Paknampho see Muang Nakhon Sawan
9 D1 Pakotai N.Z.
22 C3 Pakpattan Pak.
32 B4 Pak Phayun Thai.
37 S9 Pakruojis Lith.
47 J7 Paks Hungary
19 H3 Paktīkā reg. Afgh.
32 C2 Pakxé Laos
55 D4 Pala Chad
32 A2 Pala Myanmar
33 C4 Palabuhanratu Indon.
33 C4 Palabuhanratu, Teluk b. Indon.
48 G3 Palagruža i. Croatia
49 K7 Palaiochora Greece
44 F2 Palaiseau France
Palakkat see Palghat
21 D1 Pāla Laharha India
58 E1 Palamakoloi Botswana
45 H2 Palamós Spain
22 C4 Palana India
13 R4 Palana Rus. Fed.
31 B2 Palanan Phil.
31 B2 Palanan Point pt Phil.
19 F4 Palangān, Kūh-e mts Iran
33 D3 Palangkaraya Indon.
21 B4 Palani India
22 C4 Palanpur India
19 G5 Palantak Pak.
31 C3 Palapag Phil.
57 C6 Palapye Botswana
21 B3 Palar r. India
23 G4 Palasbari India
13 R3 Palatka Rus. Fed.
11 P9 Palau country Pac. Oc.
31 B2 Palaui i. Phil.
31 A3 Palauig Phil.
32 A2 Palauk Myanmar
94 E5 Palau Tr. sea feature Pac. Oc.
32 A2 Palaw Myanmar
31 A4 Palawan i. Phil.
31 B3 Palayan Phil.
37 T7 Paldiski Estonia
23 H5 Pale Myanmar
42 D2 Paleis Het Loo Neth.
33 B3 Palembang Indon.
88 B6 Palena Chile
45 D1 Palencia Spain
84 E3 Palenque Mex.
48 E5 Palermo Sicily Italy
77 E6 Palestine U.S.A.
23 H5 Paletwa Myanmar
21 B4 Palghat India
22 C4 Pali India
4 G4 Palikir Micronesia
31 C5 Palimbang Phil.
48 F4 Palinuro, Capo c. Italy
75 H2 Palisade U.S.A.
42 D5 Paliseul Belgium
22 B5 Palitana India
37 S7 Palivere Estonia
21 B4 Palk Bay b. Sri Lanka
50 D3 Palkino Rus. Fed.
21 C2 Pālkohda India
21 B3 Palkonda Range mts India
15 F6 Palk Strait str. India/Sri Lanka
41 C5 Pallas Green Rep. of Ireland
36 S2 Pallas-ja Ounastunturin Kansallispuisto nat. park Fin.
51 H5 Pallasovka Rus. Fed.
21 C3 Pallavaram India
21 B2 Palleru r. India
9 E4 Palliser Bay b. N.Z.
9 E4 Palliser, Cape c. N.Z.
22 C3 Pallu India
45 D4 Palma del Río Spain
45 H3 Palma de Mallorca Spain
54 A2 Palma, La i. Canary Is
89 B2 Palmar r. Venez.
89 C3 Palmarito Venez.
54 B4 Palmas, Cape c. Liberia
90 D1 Palmas de Monte Alto Brazil
79 D7 Palm Bay U.S.A.
79 D7 Palm Beach U.S.A.
74 C4 Palmdale U.S.A.
90 B4 Palmeira Brazil
87 L5 Palmeira dos Índios Brazil
87 K5 Palmeirais Brazil
62 D3 Palmer AK U.S.A.
92 B2 Palmer U.S.A. Base Ant.
92 B2 Palmer Land reg. Ant.
9 C6 Palmerston N.Z.
5 L6 Palmerston Island i. Pac. Oc.
9 E4 Palmerston North N.Z.
81 F4 Palmerton U.S.A.
79 E7 Palmetto Pt pt Bahamas
48 F5 Palmi Italy
84 C2 Palmillas Mex.
89 A4 Palmira Col.
84 A2 Palmito del Verde, Isla i. Mex.
74 D5 Palm Springs U.S.A.
Palmyra see Tadmur
68 B6 Palmyra MO U.S.A.
80 E3 Palmyra NY U.S.A.
68 C4 Palmyra WV U.S.A.
5 L4 Palmyra I. i. Pac. Oc.
23 F5 Palmyras Point pt India
74 A3 Palo Alto U.S.A.
89 A3 Palo de las Letras Col.
55 F3 Paloich Sudan
36 S2 Palojärvi Fin.
36 U2 Palomaa Fin.
84 D3 Palomares Mex.
74 D5 Palomar Mt mt U.S.A.
75 G6 Palominas U.S.A.
21 C2 Paloncha India
25 E7 Palopo Indon.
45 F4 Palos, Cabo de c. Spain
75 F5 Palo Verde AZ U.S.A.
75 E5 Palo Verde CA U.S.A.
36 U4 Paltamo Fin.
25 D7 Palu Indon.
17 G2 Palu Turkey
31 B3 Paluan Phil.
19 G2 Pal'vart Turkm.
22 D3 Palwal India
13 T3 Palyavaam r. Rus. Fed.
21 B4 Pamban Channel India
8 G4 Pambula Austr.
33 C4 Pameungpeuk Indon.
21 B3 Pamidi India
44 E5 Pamiers France
15 F3 Pamir mts Asia
79 E5 Pamlico Sound chan. U.S.A.
77 C5 Pampa U.S.A.
91 C2 Pampa de la Salinas salt pan Arg.
86 F7 Pampa Grande Bol.
91 D2 Pampas reg. Arg.
89 B3 Pamplona Col.
31 B4 Pamplona Phil.
45 F1 Pamplona Spain
43 K1 Pampow Ger.
16 C1 Pamukova Turkey
80 E6 Pamunkey r. U.S.A.
22 D2 Pamzal Jammu and Kashmir
78 B4 Pana U.S.A.
31 C5 Panabo Phil.
75 E3 Panaca U.S.A.
31 A4 Panagtaran Point pt Phil.
33 C4 Panaitan i. Indon.
21 A3 Panaji India
83 J7 Panamá Panama
61 K9 Panama country Central America
83 J7 Panama Canal canal Panama
79 C6 Panama City U.S.A.
83 J7 Panamá, Golfo de b. Panama
74 D3 Panamint Range mts U.S.A.
74 D3 Panamint Springs U.S.A.
74 D3 Panamint Valley U.S.A.
31 C4 Panaon i. Phil.
23 G4 Panar r. India
48 F5 Panarea, Isola i. Italy
33 C2 Panarik Indon.
31 C3 Panay i. Phil.
31 B4 Panay i. Phil.
31 B4 Panay Gulf b. Phil.
75 E2 Pancake Range mts U.S.A.
49 J2 Pančevo Yugo.
31 C3 Pandan Phil.
31 B4 Pandan Phil.
31 B4 Pandan B. b. Phil.
32 □ Pandan Res. resr Sing.
22 E5 Pandaria India
90 D1 Pandeiros r. Brazil
21 A2 Pandharpur India
22 D5 Pandhurna India
91 F2 Pando Uru.
39 E6 Pandy U.K.
37 T9 Panevėžys Lith.
22 C2 Pangi Range mts Pak.
33 D3 Pangkalanbuun Indon.
33 A2 Pangkalansusu Indon.
33 C3 Pangkalpinang Indon.
25 E7 Pangkalsiang, Tanjung pt Indon.
31 B4 Panglao i. Phil.
63 M3 Pangnirtung Can.
12 J3 Pangody Rus. Fed.
22 D2 Pangong Tso l. India
91 B3 Panguipulli Chile
91 B3 Panguipulli, L. l. Chile
75 F3 Panguitch U.S.A.
32 A5 Pangururan Indon.
31 B5 Pangutaran i. Phil.
31 B5 Pangutaran Group is Phil.
77 C5 Panhandle U.S.A.
56 C4 Pania-Mwanga Congo(Zaire)
22 B5 Pānikoita i. India
51 G5 Panino Rus. Fed.
22 D3 Panipat India
31 A4 Panitan Phil.
19 H2 Panj Tajik.
19 G3 Panjāb Afgh.
19 G2 Panjakent Tajik.
32 D5 Panjang i. Indon.
17 L5 Panjbarār Iran
19 G5 Panjgur Pak.
22 C5 Panjhra r. India
Panjim see Panaji
22 B2 Panjkora r. Pak.
22 B3 Panjnad r. Pak.
36 W5 Pankakoski Fin.
54 C4 Pankshin Nigeria
30 F2 Pan Ling mts China
22 D4 Panna reg. India
6 B4 Pannawonica Austr.
90 B3 Panorama Brazil
21 B4 Panruti India
30 B3 Panshan China
30 D2 Panshi China
90 A2 Pantanal de São Lourenço marsh Brazil
90 A2 Pantanal do Taquari marsh Brazil
87 G7 Pantanal Matogrossense, Parque Nacional do nat. park Brazil
48 D6 Pantelleria Sicily Italy
48 E6 Pantelleria, Isola di i. Sicily Italy
31 C5 Pantukan Phil.
84 C2 Pánuco Mex.
84 C2 Pánuco r. Mex.
21 A2 Panvel India
27 B5 Pan Xian China
27 D6 Panyu China
58 B4 Panzi Congo(Zaire)
89 E3 Pao r. Venez.
48 G5 Paola Italy
78 C4 Paoli U.S.A.
56 B3 Paoua C.A.R.
46 H7 Pápa Hungary
9 E2 Papakura N.Z.
48 D3 Papa, Monte del mt Italy
84 C2 Papantla Mex.
21 C2 Pāparhāhandi India
9 C5 Paparoa Range mts N.Z.
40 □ Papa Stour i. U.K.
9 E2 Papatoetoe N.Z.
9 B7 Papatowai N.Z.
40 F1 Papa Westray i. U.K.
42 F1 Papenburg Ger.
70 E6 Papigochic r. Mex.
69 K2 Papineau-Labelle, Réserve faunique de res. Can.
75 E3 Papoose L. l. U.S.A.
43 J6 Pappenheim Ger.
40 B5 Paps of Jura h. U.K.
41 B5 Paps, The h. Rep. of Ireland
6 E2 Papua, Gulf of g. P.N.G.
4 F5 Papua New Guinea country Oceania
32 A1 Papun Myanmar
39 C7 Par U.K.
87 J4 Pará r. Brazil
90 D2 Pará r. Brazil
50 G4 Para r. Rus. Fed.
6 B4 Paraburdoo Austr.
31 B3 Paracale Phil.
90 C2 Paracatu Minas Gerais Brazil
90 D2 Paracatu r. Brazil
8 B1 Parachilna Austr.
49 J3 Paraćin Yugo.
90 D2 Pará de Minas Brazil
69 J1 Paradis Can.
74 B2 Paradise CA U.S.A.
68 E2 Paradise MI U.S.A.
65 H4 Paradise Hill Can.
74 D2 Paradise Peak summit U.S.A.
67 J3 Paradise River Can.
77 F4 Paragould U.S.A.
86 F6 Paragua r. Bol.
89 E3 Paragua r. Venez.
87 G7 Paraguai r. Brazil
89 C2 Paraguáipoa Venez.
89 C1 Paraguaná, Pen. de pen. Venez.
85 D5 Paraguay country S. America
88 E3 Paraguay r. Arg./Para.
87 L5 Paraíba r. Brazil
90 D3 Paraíba do Sul r. Brazil
84 D3 Paraíso Mex.
54 C4 Parakou Benin
21 D2 Parālkhemundi India
22 E6 Paralkot India
21 B4 Paramakkudi India
87 G2 Paramaribo Suriname
89 B3 Paramillo mt Col.
89 A3 Paramillo, Parque Nacional nat. park Col.
90 D1 Paramirim Brazil
89 A3 Páramo Frontino mt Col.
81 F4 Paramus U.S.A.
24 H1 Paramushir, O. i. Rus. Fed.
91 E1 Paraná Arg.
87 J6 Paranã Brazil
90 B4 Paraná div. Brazil
90 C1 Paranã r. Brazil
91 E2 Paraná r. S. America
90 C4 Paranaguá Brazil
90 B2 Paranaíba Brazil
90 B2 Paranaíba r. Brazil
91 E2 Paraná Ibicuy r. Arg.
90 B3 Paranapanema r. Brazil
90 C4 Paranapiacaba, Serra mts Brazil
90 C1 Paranã, Sa do h. Brazil
90 B3 Paranavaí Brazil
31 B5 Parang Phil.
21 B4 Parangipettai India
49 K2 Parângul Mare, Vârful mt Romania
22 C5 Parantij India
90 D2 Paraopeba r. Brazil
17 K4 Pārapāra Iraq
9 E4 Paraparaumu N.Z.
89 D3 Paraque, Co mt Venez.
77 D7 Paras Mex.
22 D5 Paratwada India
90 B2 Paraúna Brazil
44 G3 Paray-le-Monial France
22 D4 Parbati r. India
21 B2 Parbhani India
43 K1 Parchim Ger.
68 C4 Pardeeville U.S.A.
23 G2 Parding China
90 E1 Pardo r. Bahia/Minas Gerais Brazil
90 B3 Pardo r. Mato Grosso do Sul Brazil
90 D1 Pardo r. Minas Gerais Brazil
90 C3 Pardo r. São Paulo Brazil
46 G5 Pardubice Czech Rep.
22 D2 Pare Chu r. China
23 G4 Pare Chu r. China
86 F6 Parecis, Serra dos h. Brazil
84 B1 Paredón Mex.
18 B2 Pareh Iran
9 D1 Parengarenga Harbour in. N.Z.
66 E4 Parent, Lac l. Can.
9 C6 Pareora N.Z.
33 E3 Parepare Indon.
91 D2 Parera Arg.
50 G3 Parfen'yevo Rus. Fed.
47 P2 Parfino Rus. Fed.
49 J5 Parga Greece
37 S6 Pargas Fin.
89 D2 Pariaguán Venez.
89 E2 Paria, Gulf of g. Trinidad/Venez.
89 E2 Paria, Península de pen. Venez.
75 F3 Paria Plateau plat. U.S.A.
37 V6 Parikkala Fin.
Parima r. see Uatatás
89 D4 Parima, Serra mts Brazil
89 D4 Parima-Tapirapecó, Parque Nacional nat. park Venez.
86 B4 Pariñas, Pta pt Peru
8 C3 Paringa Austr.
87 G4 Parintins Brazil
69 G4 Paris Can.
44 F2 Paris France
80 A5 Paris KY U.S.A.
79 B4 Paris TN U.S.A.
77 E5 Paris TX U.S.A.
68 E2 Parisienne, Île i. Can.
18 D4 Pārīz Iran
41 D3 Park U.K.
19 E5 Parkā Bandar Iran
21 B2 Parkal India
37 S5 Parkano Fin.
67 J3 Parke Lake l. Can.
75 F4 Parker U.S.A.
75 E4 Parker Dam dam U.S.A.
65 K2 Parker Lake l. Can.
27 □ Parker, Mt h. H.K. China
68 A4 Parkersburg IA U.S.A.
80 C5 Parkersburg WV U.S.A.
8 G2 Parkes Austr.
68 B3 Park Falls U.S.A.
68 D5 Park Forest U.S.A.
69 F2 Parkinson Can.
76 E2 Park Rapids U.S.A.
64 E5 Parksville Can.
81 F4 Parksville U.S.A.
21 D2 Parla Kimedi India
21 B2 Parli Vaijnath India
48 D2 Parma Italy
72 C3 Parma ID U.S.A.
80 C4 Parma OH U.S.A.
89 D3 Parmana Venez.
87 K4 Parnaíba Brazil
87 K4 Parnaíba r. Brazil
49 K5 Parnassos mt Greece
9 D5 Parnassus N.Z.
68 A5 Parnell U.S.A.
49 K6 Parnon mts Greece
37 T7 Pärnu Estonia
37 T7 Pärnu-Jaagupi Estonia
19 F3 Paropamisus mts Afgh.
49 L6 Paros Greece
49 L6 Paros i. Greece
75 F3 Parowan U.S.A.
91 B3 Parral Chile
81 F6 Parramore I. i. U.S.A.
84 B1 Parras Mex.
91 F3 Parravicini Arg.
39 E6 Parrett r. U.K.
67 H4 Parrsboro Can.
62 F2 Parry, Cape pt Can.
62 G2 Parry Islands is Can.
63 L2 Parry, Kap c. Greenland
69 G3 Parry Sound Can.
77 E4 Parsons KS U.S.A.
80 D5 Parsons WV U.S.A.
43 H4 Partenstein Ger.
44 D3 Parthenay France
28 C3 Partizansk Rus. Fed.
39 H4 Partney U.K.
41 B4 Partry Rep. of Ireland
41 B4 Partry Mts h. Rep. of Ireland
87 H4 Paru r. Brazil
89 D3 Parucito r. Venez.
21 C2 Parvatipuram India
22 C4 Parvatsar India
22 D4 Parwan r. India
23 E3 Paryang China
59 G3 Parys S. Africa
74 C4 Pasadena CA U.S.A.
77 E6 Pasadena TX U.S.A.
86 B4 Pasado, C. pt Ecuador
18 D4 Pasargadae Iran
33 B3 Pasarseblat Indon.
32 A1 Pasawng Myanmar
77 F6 Pascagoula U.S.A.
69 J1 Pascalis Can.
47 N7 Paşcani Romania
72 C2 Pasco U.S.A.
90 E2 Pascoal, Monte h. Brazil
31 B3 Pascual Phil.
Pas de Calais str. see Dover, Strait of
46 G4 Pasewalk Ger.
65 H3 Pasfield Lake l. Can.
50 E2 Pasha Rus. Fed.
31 B3 Pasig Phil.
17 H2 Pasinler Turkey
32 □ Pasir Gudang Malaysia
32 □ Pasir Panjang Sing.
33 B1 Pasir Putih Malaysia
74 A2 Paskenta U.S.A.
19 E5 Paskūh Iran
19 F5 Pasni Pak.
84 E3 Paso Caballos Guatemala
89 B4 Paso de las Cruces mt Col.
91 F2 Paso de los Toros Uru.
88 B7 Paso Río Mayo Arg.
74 B4 Paso Robles U.S.A.
65 J4 Pasquia Hills h. Can.
18 D4 Pasrūdak Iran
81 J2 Passadumkeag U.S.A.
68 C1 Passage I. i. U.S.A.
46 F6 Passau Ger.
31 B4 Passi Phil.
88 F3 Passo Fundo Brazil
90 C3 Passos Brazil
50 C4 Pastavy Belarus
86 C4 Pastaza r. Peru
65 J4 Pas, The Can.
89 A4 Pasto Col.
75 H3 Pastora Peak summit U.S.A.
31 B2 Pasuquin Phil.
33 D4 Pasuruan Indon.
37 T8 Pasvalys Lith.
31 B5 Pata i. Phil.
75 G6 Patagonia U.S.A.
85 C8 Patagonia reg. Arg.
23 G4 Patakata India
19 F4 Patambar Iran
22 C5 Patan Gujarat India
22 D5 Patan Madhya Pradesh India
Patan see Somnath
23 F4 Patan Nepal
8 D3 Patchewollock Austr.
9 E3 Patea N.Z.
9 E3 Patea r. N.Z.
38 F3 Pateley Bridge U.K.
23 G5 Patenga Point pt Bangl.
58 F6 Patensie S. Africa
48 F6 Paternò Sicily Italy
8 H2 Paterson Austr.
81 F4 Paterson U.S.A.
22 C2 Pathankot India
72 F3 Pathfinder Res. resr U.S.A.
32 A3 Pathiu Thai.
21 B2 Pathri India
32 B2 Pathum Thani Thai.
33 D4 Pati Indon.
89 A4 Patía r. Col.
22 D3 Patiala India
49 M6 Patmos i. Greece
23 F4 Patna India
23 E5 Patnagarh India
31 B3 Patnanongan i. Phil.
17 J2 Patnos Turkey
22 E3 Paton India
49 H4 Patos Albania
87 L5 Patos Brazil
90 C2 Patos de Minas Brazil
88 F4 Patos, Lagoa dos l. Brazil
91 C1 Patquia Arg.
49 J5 Patra Greece
36 B4 Patreksfjörður Iceland
90 C2 Patrocínio Brazil
36 V2 Patsoyoki r. Europe
32 B4 Pattani Thai.
32 B4 Pattani r. Thai.
32 B2 Pattaya Thai.
81 J2 Patten U.S.A.
43 H2 Pattensen Ger.
74 B3 Patterson U.S.A.
80 D5 Patterson r. U.S.A.
64 C2 Patterson, Mt mt Can.
74 C3 Patterson Mt mt U.S.A.
68 E3 Patterson, Pt pt U.S.A.
36 T4 Pattijoki Fin.
36 R2 Pättikkä Fin.
21 B3 Pattikonda India
64 D3 Pattullo, Mt mt Can.
23 G5 Patuakhali Bangl.
65 H3 Patuanak Can.
80 E5 Patuxent r. U.S.A.
92 B3 Patuxent Ra. mts Ant.
84 B3 Pátzcuaro Mex.
44 D5 Pau France
44 D4 Pauillac France
23 H5 Pauktaw Myanmar
75 F4 Paulden U.S.A.
80 A4 Paulding U.S.A.
67 H2 Paul Island i. Can.
87 K5 Paulistana Brazil
87 L5 Paulo Afonso Brazil
59 J3 Paulpietersburg S. Africa
59 G4 Paul Roux S. Africa
81 F2 Paul Smiths U.S.A.
77 D5 Pauls Valley U.S.A.
89 C3 Pauto r. Col.
90 E2 Pavão Brazil
18 B3 Pāveh Iran
48 C2 Pavia Italy
37 R8 Pāvilosta Latvia
50 H3 Pavino Rus. Fed.
49 L3 Pavlikeni Bulg.
15 F1 Pavlodar Kazak.
51 E5 Pavlohrad Ukr.
50 H4 Pavlovka Rus. Fed.
50 G4 Pavlovo Rus. Fed.
51 G5 Pavlovsk Rus. Fed.
51 F6 Pavlovskaya Rus. Fed.
89 B4 Pavon Col.
22 E3 Pawayan India
68 E4 Paw Paw U.S.A.
81 H4 Pawtucket U.S.A.
32 A2 Pawut Myanmar
68 C5 Paxton U.S.A.
33 B3 Payakumbuh Indon.
32 □ Paya Lebar Sing.
89 B4 Paya, Parque Nacional la nat. park Col.
72 C2 Payette U.S.A.
12 H3 Pay-Khoy, Khrebet h. Rus. Fed.
66 F2 Payne, Lac l. Can.
74 B1 Paynes Creek U.S.A.
91 E2 Paysandú Uru.
75 G4 Payson AZ U.S.A.
75 G1 Payson UT U.S.A.
91 C3 Payún, Cerro volc. Arg.
16 D1 Pazar Turkey
17 H1 Pazar Turkey
16 F3 Pazarcık Turkey
49 L3 Pazardzhik Bulg.
89 C3 Paz de Ariporo Col.
89 B3 Paz de Rio Col.
48 E2 Pazin Croatia
64 G3 Peace r. Can.
62 G4 Peace r. Can.
64 F3 Peace River Can.
75 F4 Peach Springs U.S.A.
39 F4 Peak District National Park U.K.
67 G4 Peaked Mt. h. U.S.A.
31 A4 Peaked Point pt Phil.
8 G2 Peak Hill Austr.
75 H2 Peale, Mt mt U.S.A.
75 H6 Pearce U.S.A.
68 C1 Pearl Can.
77 F6 Pearl r. U.S.A.
74 □1 Pearl City U.S.A.
74 □1 Pearl Harbor in. U.S.A.
77 D6 Pearsall U.S.A.
79 D6 Pearson U.S.A.
63 H2 Peary Channel Can.
66 C2 Peawanuck Can.
57 D5 Pebane Moz.
49 J3 Peć Yugo.
90 D2 Peçanha Brazil
36 W2 Pechenga Rus. Fed.
12 G3 Pechora Rus. Fed.
50 C3 Pechory Rus. Fed.
69 F4 Peck U.S.A.
77 C6 Pecos U.S.A.
77 C6 Pecos r. U.S.A.
49 H1 Pécs Hungary
59 G6 Peddie S. Africa
36 S5 Pedersöre Fin.
23 E3 Pêdo La pass China
90 E1 Pedra Azul Brazil
89 C3 Pedraza La Vieja Venez.
89 C2 Pedregal Venez.
90 C3 Pedregulho Brazil
87 K4 Pedreiras Brazil
84 B1 Pedriceña Mex.
87 J5 Pedro Afonso Brazil
89 C4 Pedro Chico Col.
88 C2 Pedro de Valdivia Chile
90 A2 Pedro Gomes Brazil
89 D4 Pedro II, Ilha i. Brazil
88 E2 Pedro Juan Caballero Para.
87 K4 Pedroll Brazil
91 G1 Pedro Osório Brazil
21 C4 Pedro, Pt pt Sri Lanka
40 E5 Peebles U.K.
79 E5 Pee Dee r. U.S.A.
81 G4 Peekskill U.S.A.
38 C3 Peel U.K.
8 H1 Peel r. Austr.
62 E3 Peel r. N.W.T. Can.
42 D3 Peer Belgium
64 F4 Peers Can.
9 D5 Pegasus Bay b. N.Z.
43 K5 Pegnitz Ger.
43 K5 Pegnitz r. Ger.
25 B5 Pegu Myanmar
50 J2 Pegysh Rus. Fed.
91 E2 Pehuajó Arg.
27 F6 Peikang Taiwan
43 J2 Peine Ger.
Peipsi Järve l. see Peipus, Lake
37 U7 Peipus, Lake l. Estonia/Rus. Fed.
49 K6 Peiraias Greece
43 K3 Peißen Ger.
26 E3 Peitun China
87 J6 Peixe Brazil
90 B1 Peixe r. Goiás Brazil
90 B3 Peixe r. São Paulo Brazil
26 E3 Pei Xian Jiangsu China
26 F3 Pei Xian Jiangsu China
90 A2 Peixo de Couro r. Brazil
59 G4 Peka Lesotho
33 C4 Pekalongan Indon.
32 B5 Pekan Malaysia
33 B2 Pekanbaru Indon.
68 C5 Pekin U.S.A.
32 B5 Pelabuhan Kelang Malaysia
69 F5 Pelee I. i. Can.
69 F5 Pelee Pt pt Can.
25 E7 Peleng i. Indon.
50 J2 Peles Rus. Fed.
68 A1 Pelican Lake l. MN U.S.A.
68 C3 Pelican Lake l. WV U.S.A.
65 J3 Pelican Narrows Can.
36 U3 Pelkosenniemi Fin.
58 C4 Pella S. Africa
65 H1 Pellat Lake l. Can.
6 E2 Pelleluhu Is is P.N.G.
68 C4 Pell Lake U.S.A.
36 S3 Pello Fin.
64 B2 Pelly r. Can.
63 K3 Pelly Bay Can.
64 B2 Pelly Crossing Can.
65 J1 Pelly Lake l. Can.
64 C2 Pelly Mountains mts Can.
91 G1 Pelotas Brazil
88 F3 Pelotas, R. das r. Brazil
16 D6 Pelusium Egypt
44 H4 Pelvoux, Massif du mts France
81 J2 Pemadumcook Lake l. U.S.A.
33 C4 Pemalang Indon.
33 C2 Pemangkat Indon.
33 A2 Pematangsiantar Indon.
57 E5 Pemba Moz.
57 C5 Pemba Zambia
56 D4 Pemba I. i. Tanz.
76 D1 Pembina U.S.A.
64 F4 Pembina r. Can.
69 J3 Pembroke Can.
39 C6 Pembroke U.K.
81 K2 Pembroke U.S.A.
39 B5 Pembrokeshire Coast National Park U.K.
21 A2 Pen India
23 H5 Pen r. Myanmar
45 D1 Peña Cerredo mt Spain
45 E2 Peñalara mt Spain
84 C2 Peñamiller Mex.
84 C2 Peña Nevada, Cerro mt Mex.
90 B3 Penápolis Brazil
45 D1 Peña Prieta mt Spain
45 D2 Peñaranda de Bracamonte Spain
8 D3 Penarie Austr.
45 F2 Peñarroya mt Spain
45 D3 Peñarroya-Pueblonuevo Spain
39 D6 Penarth U.K.
45 D1 Peñas, Cabo de c. Spain
82 B2 Peñasco, Pto Mex.
88 A7 Penas, Golfo de b. Chile
89 E2 Peñas, Pta pt Venez.
45 D1 Peña Ubiña mt Spain
22 D5 Pench r. India
92 D5 Penck, C. c. Ant.
54 C3 Pendjari, Parc National de la nat. park Benin
38 E4 Pendle Hill h. U.K.
72 C2 Pendleton U.S.A.
64 D4 Pendleton Bay Can.
72 C1 Pend Oreille r. U.S.A.
72 C2 Pend Oreille L. l. U.S.A.
23 E5 Pendra India
69 H3 Penetanguishene Can.
26 C4 Peng'an China
21 B2 Penganga r. India
22 D6 Penganga r. India
27 □ Peng Chau i. H.K. China
27 G5 P'eng-chia Hsü i. Taiwan
56 C4 Penge Congo(Zaire)
59 J2 Penge S. Africa
27 F6 P'eng-hu Lieh-tao is Taiwan
27 F6 Peng-hu Tao i. Taiwan
32 □ Peng Kang h. Sing.
26 F2 Penglai China
27 B4 Pengshan China
27 C4 Pengshui China
27 B4 Pengxi China
27 E4 Pengze China
59 G5 Penhoek Pass S. Africa
45 B3 Peniche Port.
40 E5 Penicuik U.K.
43 L4 Penig Ger.
50 E2 Peninga Rus. Fed.
33 B2 Peninsular Malaysia pen. Malaysia
17 K4 Penjwin Iraq
48 E3 Penne Italy
92 A5 Pennell Coast coastal area Ant.
21 B3 Penner r. India
8 A3 Penneshaw Austr.
38 E3 Pennines h. U.K.
59 J5 Pennington S. Africa
81 F5 Pennsville U.S.A.
80 D4 Pennsylvania div. U.S.A.
80 E3 Penn Yan U.S.A.
63 M3 Penny Icecap ice cap Can.
65 H2 Pennylan Lake l. Can.
92 B4 Penny Pt pt Ant.
81 J2 Penobscot r. U.S.A.
81 J2 Penobscot Bay b. U.S.A.
8 C4 Penola Austr.
84 A1 Peñón Blanco Mex.
6 D5 Penong Austr.
38 E3 Penrith U.K.
79 C6 Pensacola U.S.A.
92 B3 Pensacola Mts mts Ant.
17 M2 Pensär Azer.
8 D4 Penshurst Austr.
7 G3 Pentecost I. i. Vanuatu
64 F5 Penticton Can.
39 B7 Pentire Point pt U.K.
40 E2 Pentland Firth chan. U.K.
40 E5 Pentland Hills h. U.K.
68 D4 Pentwater U.S.A.
21 B3 Penukonda India
39 D5 Penygadair h. U.K.
38 E3 Pen-y-Ghent h. U.K.
50 H4 Penza Rus. Fed.
39 B7 Penzance U.K.
50 H4 Penzenskaya Oblast' div. Rus. Fed.
13 S3 Penzhino Rus. Fed.
13 S3 Penzhinskaya Guba b. Rus. Fed.
75 F5 Peoria AZ U.S.A.
68 C5 Peoria IL U.S.A.
32 B4 Perai Malaysia
32 A4 Perak i. Malaysia
32 B4 Perak r. Malaysia
45 F2 Perales del Alfambra Spain
21 B4 Perambalur India
Perämeri g. see Bottenviken
67 H4 Percé Can.
81 H2 Percy U.S.A.
6 F4 Percy Is is Austr.
69 J3 Percy Reach l. Can.
45 G1 Perdido, Monte mt Spain
12 H3 Peregrebnoye Rus. Fed.
89 B3 Pereira Col.
90 B3 Pereira Barreto Brazil
50 D3 Perekhoda r. Rus. Fed.
51 G5 Perelazovskiy Rus. Fed.
68 D4 Pere Marquette r. U.S.A.
92 C6 Peremennyy, C. c. Ant.
47 M6 Peremyshlyany Ukr.
50 F3 Pereslavl'-Zalesskiy Rus. Fed.
50 H4 Perevoz Rus. Fed.
51 D5 Pereyaslav-Khmel'nyts'kyy Ukr.
91 E2 Pergamino Arg.
32 B4 Perhentian Besar i. Malaysia
36 T5 Perho Fin.
67 F3 Péribonca, Lac l. Can.
88 C2 Perico Arg.
84 A1 Pericos Mex.
44 E4 Périgueux France
89 B2 Perijá, Parque Nacional nat. park Venez.
89 B2 Perijá, Sierra de mts Venez.
88 B7 Perito Moreno Arg.
68 D3 Perkins U.S.A.
83 H6 Perlas, Pta de pt Nic.
43 K1 Perleberg Ger.
12 G4 Perm' Rus. Fed.
50 H3 Permas Rus. Fed.
49 K3 Pernik Bulg.
44 F2 Péronne France
84 C3 Perote Mex.
44 F5 Perpignan France
39 B7 Perranporth U.K.
74 D5 Perris U.S.A.
44 C2 Perros-Guirec France
79 D6 Perry FL U.S.A.
79 D5 Perry GA U.S.A.
76 E3 Perry IA U.S.A.
77 D4 Perry OK U.S.A.
80 B4 Perrysburg U.S.A.
77 C4 Perryton U.S.A.
77 F4 Perryville U.S.A.
39 E5 Pershore U.K.
17 G2 Pertek Turkey
6 B5 Perth Austr.
69 J3 Perth Can.
40 E4 Perth U.K.
81 F4 Perth Amboy U.S.A.
81 K1 Perth-Andover Can.
50 F1 Pertominsk Rus. Fed.
44 G5 Pertuis France
37 U6 Pertunmaa Fin.
48 C4 Pertusato, Capo pt Corsica France
68 C5 Peru U.S.A.
85 C3 Peru country S. America
95 N7 Peru Basin sea feature Pac. Oc.
95 P7 Peru-Chile Trench sea feature Pac. Oc.
48 E3 Perugia Italy
90 C4 Peruíbe Brazil
42 B4 Péruwelz Belgium
50 G4 Pervomaysk Rus. Fed.
51 D5 Pervomays'k Ukr.
50 K2 Pervomayskaya Rus. Fed.
51 E6 Pervomays'ke Ukr.
50 G4 Pervomayskiy Rus. Fed.
51 F5 Pervomays'kyy Ukr.
48 E3 Pesaro Italy
74 A3 Pescadero U.S.A.
75 H4 Pescado U.S.A.
48 F3 Pescara Italy
48 F3 Pescara r. Italy
51 G6 Peschanokopskoye Rus. Fed.
32 □ Pesek, P. i. Sing.
22 B2 Peshawar Pak.
49 J4 Peshkopi Albania
49 L3 Peshtera Bulg.
68 D3 Peshtigo U.S.A.
68 C3 Peshtigo r. U.S.A.
19 F2 Peski Turkm.
48 F1 Pesnica Slovenia
44 D4 Pessac France
43 L2 Pessin Ger.
50 E3 Pestovo Rus. Fed.
50 G4 Pet r. Rus. Fed.
84 B3 Petacalco, Bahía de b. Mex.
16 E5 Petah Tiqwa Israel
49 L5 Petalioi i. Greece
74 A2 Petaluma U.S.A.
42 D5 Pétange Lux.
33 E3 Petangis Indon.
89 D2 Petare Venez.
84 B3 Petatlán Mex.
84 B3 Petatlán, Morro de hd Mex.
57 D5 Petauke Zambia
69 J3 Petawawa Can.
68 C3 Petenwell Lake l. U.S.A.
92 A3 Peter I Øy i. Ant.
8 B2 Peterborough S.A. Austr.
8 D5 Peterborough Vic. Austr.
69 H3 Peterborough Can.
39 G5 Peterborough U.K.
40 F3 Peterculter U.K.
40 G3 Peterhead U.K.
65 L2 Peter Lake l. Can.
38 F3 Peterlee U.K.
6 C4 Petermann Ranges mts Austr.
91 B2 Peteroa, Vol. volc. Chile
65 H3 Peter Pond L. l. Can.
43 H4 Petersberg Ger.
64 C3 Petersburg AK U.S.A.
68 C6 Petersburg IL U.S.A.
80 E6 Petersburg VA U.S.A.
80 D5 Petersburg WV U.S.A.
39 G6 Petersfield U.K.
43 G2 Petershagen Ger.
67 F2 Peters, Lac l. Can.
48 G5 Petilia Policastro Italy
66 E2 Petite Rivière de la Baleine r. Can.
67 G3 Petit Lac Manicouagan l. Can.
81 K2 Petit Manan Pt pt U.S.A.
67 J3 Petit Mécatina r. Can.
64 E3 Petitot r. Can.
84 C3 Petlalcingo Mex.
82 G4 Peto Mex.
68 E3 Petoskey U.S.A.
16 E6 Petra Jordan
24 F2 Petra Velikogo, Zaliv b. Rus. Fed.
69 J4 Petre, Pt pt Can.
49 K4 Petrich Bulg.
75 H4 Petrified Forest Nat. Park U.S.A.
48 G2 Petrinja Croatia

49 K3 Petrokhanski Prokhod pass Bulg.
69 F4 Petrolia Can.
87 K5 Petrolina Brazil
51 G5 Petropavlovka Rus. Fed.
12 H4 Petropavlovsk Kazak.
24 H1 Petropavlovsk-Kamchatskiy Rus. Fed.
49 K2 Petroşani Romania
51 H4 Petrovsk Rus. Fed.
24 C1 Petrovsk-Zabaykal'skiy Rus. Fed.
51 H5 Petrov Val Rus. Fed.
50 E2 Petrozavodsk Rus. Fed.
59 F4 Petrusburg S. Africa
59 H3 Petrus Steyn S. Africa
58 F5 Petrusville S. Africa
42 C2 Petten Neth.
41 D3 Pettigo U.K.
12 H4 Petukhovo Rus. Fed.
32 A4 Peureula Indon.
13 T3 Pevek Rus. Fed.
46 H6 Pezinok Slovakia
43 F5 Pfälzer Wald forest Ger.
43 G6 Pforzheim Ger.
46 D7 Pfullendorf Ger.
43 G5 Pfungstadt Ger.
22 C3 Phagwara India
59 G4 Phahameng Free State S. Africa
59 H2 Phahameng Northern Province S. Africa
59 J1 Phalaborwa S. Africa
22 C4 Phalodi India
22 B4 Phalsund India
21 A2 Phaltan India
32 A3 Phangnga Thai.
32 D3 Phan Rang Vietnam
32 D3 Phan Ri Vietnam
32 D3 Phan Thiêt Vietnam
77 D7 Pharr U.S.A.
27 C6 Phat Diêm Vietnam
32 B4 Phatthalung Thai.
23 H4 Phek India
65 J3 Phelps Lake l. Can.
32 B1 Phen Thai.
79 C5 Phenix City U.S.A.
32 A2 Phet Buri Thai.
32 C2 Phiafai Laos
77 F5 Philadelphia MS U.S.A.
81 F2 Philadelphia NY U.S.A.
81 F5 Philadelphia PA U.S.A.
76 C2 Philip U.S.A.
42 C4 Philippeville Belgium
80 C5 Philippi U.S.A.
42 B3 Philippine Neth.
11 O8 Philippines country Asia
31 C2 Philippine Sea sea Phil.
94 D5 Philippine Trench sea feature Pac. Oc.
59 F5 Philippolis S. Africa
43 G5 Philippsburg Ger.
80 D4 Philipsburg U.S.A.
42 C3 Philipsdam barrage Neth.
62 D3 Philip Smith Mts U.S.A.
58 F5 Philipstown S. Africa
8 E5 Phillip I. i. Austr.
81 H2 Phillips ME U.S.A.
68 B3 Phillips WV U.S.A.
76 D4 Phillipsburg KS U.S.A.
81 F4 Phillipsburg NJ U.S.A.
63 J1 Phillips Inlet in. Can.
80 D4 Phillipston U.S.A.
81 G3 Philmont U.S.A.
65 G3 Philomena Can.
80 C6 Philpott Reservoir resr U.S.A.
32 B2 Phimae Thai.
32 C2 Phimun Mangsahan Thai.
59 G3 Phiritona S. Africa
Phnom Penh see Phnum Penh
32 C2 Phnum Aôral mt Cambodia
32 C3 Phnum Penh Cambodia
75 F5 Phoenix U.S.A.
7 J2 Phoenix Islands is Pac. Oc.
59 G3 Phomolong S. Africa
25 C4 Phôngsali Laos
27 B6 Phong Thô Vietnam
32 B1 Phon Phisai Thai.
32 B1 Phou Bia mt Laos
32 C1 Phou Cô Pi mt Laos/Vietnam
27 B6 Phou Sam Sao mts Laos/Vietnam
32 A1 Phrao Thai.
32 B2 Phra Phutthabat Thai.
27 B6 Phuc Yên Vietnam
32 D2 Phu Hôi Vietnam
32 A4 Phuket Thai.
22 C4 Phulera India
23 G5 Phultala Bangl.
27 B6 Phu Ly Vietnam
32 B2 Phumĭ Bânhchok Kon Cambodia
32 C3 Phumĭ Chhuk Cambodia
32 C2 Phumĭ Kâmpóng Trâlach Cambodia
32 B3 Phumĭ Kaôh Kŏng Cambodia
32 B2 Phumĭ Kiliĕk Cambodia
32 C2 Phumĭ Mlu Prey Cambodia
32 B2 Phumĭ Moŭng Cambodia
32 B2 Phumĭ Prâmaôy Cambodia
32 B2 Phumĭ Sâmraŏng Cambodia
32 C2 Phumĭ Toêng Cambodia
32 D2 Phu My Vietnam
32 D2 Phu Nhơn Vietnam
32 C3 Phươc Long Vietnam
32 C3 Phu Quôc Vietnam
59 H4 Phuthaditjhaba S. Africa
27 B6 Phư Tho Vietnam
32 B1 Phu Wiang Thai.
87 J5 Piaca Brazil
48 C2 Piacenza Italy
26 D2 Pianguan China
48 D3 Pianosa, Isola i. Italy
47 N7 Piatra Neamţ Romania
87 K5 Piauí r. Brazil
48 E1 Piave r. Italy
55 F4 Pibor r. Sudan
55 F4 Pibor Post Sudan
68 D1 Pic r. Can.
75 F4 Pica U.S.A.
75 G5 Picacho AZ U.S.A.
75 E5 Picacho CA U.S.A.
44 F2 Picardie reg. France
79 B6 Picayune U.S.A.
88 D2 Pichanal Arg.
91 C2 Pichi Ciego Arg.
91 B2 Pichilemu Chile
70 D7 Pichilingue Mex.
91 D3 Pichi Mahuida Arg.
22 D4 Pichor India
84 D3 Pichucalco Mex.
68 D1 Pic, I. i. Can.
38 G3 Pickering U.K.
38 G3 Pickering, Vale of v. U.K.
68 E2 Pickford U.S.A.
66 B3 Pickle Lake Can.
34 C5 Pico i. Port.
89 C2 Pico Bolívar mt Venez.
89 D4 Pico da Neblina mt Brazil
89 D4 Pico da Neblina, Parque Nacional do nat. park Brazil
84 C3 Pico de Orizaba, Parque Nacional nat. park Mex.
84 B3 Pico de Tancitaro, Parque Nacional nat. park Mex.
83 K5 Pico Duarte mt Dom. Rep.
89 E4 Pico Redondo summit Brazil
89 E4 Pico Rondon summit Brazil
87 K5 Picos Brazil
88 C7 Pico Truncado Arg.
68 D1 Pic River Can.
8 H3 Picton Austr.
69 J4 Picton Can.
67 H4 Pictou Can.
68 D2 Pictured Rocks National Lakeshore res. U.S.A.
91 C3 Picún Leufú r. Arg.
19 F5 Pidarak Pak.
21 C5 Pidurutalagala mt Sri Lanka
89 B3 Piedecuesta Col.
91 C1 Pie de Palo, Sa mts Arg.
79 C5 Piedmont U.S.A.
80 C4 Piedmont Lake l. U.S.A.
82 D3 Piedras Negras Coahuila Mex.
84 C3 Piedras Negras Veracruz Mex.
91 F2 Piedras, Punta pt Arg.
86 D6 Piedras, Río de las r. Peru
68 C1 Pie Island i. Can.
36 U5 Pieksämäki Fin.
36 U5 Pielavesi Fin.
36 V5 Pielinen l. Fin.
59 H2 Pienaarsrivier S. Africa
68 E5 Pierceton U.S.A.
74 A2 Piercy U.S.A.
49 K4 Pieria mts Greece
40 F1 Pierowall U.K.
76 C2 Pierre U.S.A.
44 G4 Pierrelatte France
59 J4 Pietermaritzburg S. Africa
59 H1 Pietersburg S. Africa
48 G5 Pietra Spada, Passo di pass Italy
59 J3 Piet Retief S. Africa
47 M7 Pietrosa mt Romania
69 F4 Pigeon U.S.A.
69 F5 Pigeon Bay b. Can.
80 D6 Pigg r. U.S.A.
77 F4 Piggott U.S.A.
59 J2 Pigg's Peak Swaziland
91 D3 Pigüé Arg.
84 C2 Piguicas mt Mex.
22 E4 Pihani India
26 E3 Pi He r. China
37 V6 Pihlajavesi l. Fin.
37 R6 Pihlava Fin.
36 T5 Pihtipudas Fin.
36 T4 Piippola Fin.
36 V4 Piispajärvi Fin.
84 D4 Pijijiapan Mex.
50 E3 Pikalevo Rus. Fed.
80 D3 Pike U.S.A.
69 G3 Pike Bay Can.
4 G4 Pikelot i. Micronesia
58 C6 Piketberg S. Africa
80 B6 Pikeville U.S.A.
30 B4 Pikou China
91 E3 Pila Arg.
46 H4 Piła Pol.
59 G2 Pilanesberg National Park S. Africa
91 E2 Pilar Arg.
88 E3 Pilar Para.
31 B5 Pilas i. Phil.
91 B3 Pilcaniyeu Arg.
88 E2 Pilcomayo r. Bol./Para.
31 B3 Pili Phil.
22 D3 Pilibhit India
27 □ Pillar Pt pt H.K. China
91 E2 Pillo, Isla del i. Arg.
90 C2 Pilões, Serra dos mts Brazil
74 D2 Pilot Peak summit U.S.A.
8 G4 Pilot, The mt Austr.
77 F6 Pilottown U.S.A.
37 R8 Piltene Latvia
86 F6 Pimenta Bueno Brazil
22 C5 Pimpalner India
22 D2 Pin r. India
75 F6 Pinacate, Cerro del summit Mex.
22 D4 Pinahat India
75 G5 Pinaleno Mts mts U.S.A.
31 B3 Pinamalayan Phil.
91 F3 Pinamar Arg.
33 B1 Pinang i. Malaysia
16 F2 Pınarbaşı Turkey
83 H4 Pinar del Río Cuba
51 C7 Pinarhisar Turkey
47 K5 Pińczów Pol.
22 D3 Pindar r. India
87 J4 Pindaré r. Brazil
22 C2 Pindi Gheb Pak.
49 J5 Pindos mts Greece
Pindu Pass see Pêdo La
Pindus Mts mts see Pindos
75 G4 Pine AZ U.S.A.
68 E4 Pine r. MI U.S.A.
68 E3 Pine r. MI U.S.A.
68 C3 Pine r. WI U.S.A.
77 E5 Pine Bluff U.S.A.
72 F3 Pine Bluffs U.S.A.
67 K4 Pine, C. c. Can.
68 A3 Pine City U.S.A.
6 D3 Pine Creek Austr.
80 E4 Pine Creek r. U.S.A.
74 B2 Pinecrest U.S.A.
74 C3 Pinedale CA U.S.A.
72 E3 Pinedale WY U.S.A.
65 K4 Pine Falls Can.
74 C3 Pine Flat Lake l. U.S.A.
50 G1 Pinega Rus. Fed.
50 G1 Pinega r. Rus. Fed.
81 E4 Pine Grove U.S.A.
79 D6 Pine Hills U.S.A.
65 H3 Pinehouse Can.
68 A3 Pine Island U.S.A.
92 A3 Pine Island Bay b. Ant.
81 F3 Pine Lake U.S.A.
77 E6 Pineland U.S.A.
74 B4 Pine Mt mt U.S.A.
75 F4 Pine Peak summit U.S.A.
64 G2 Pine Point Can.
76 C3 Pine Ridge U.S.A.
74 C3 Pineridge U.S.A.
48 B2 Pinerolo Italy
77 E5 Pines, Lake O' the l. U.S.A.
59 J4 Pinetown S. Africa
80 B6 Pineville KY U.S.A.
77 E6 Pineville LA U.S.A.
80 C6 Pineville WV U.S.A.
26 B2 Ping'an China
27 B6 Pingbian China
26 F3 Ping Dao i. China
26 D2 Pingding China
26 D3 Pingdingshan China
26 F2 Pingdu China
30 C2 Pinggang China
27 C6 Pingguo China
27 E5 Pinghe China
27 D4 Pingjiang China
27 D5 Pingle China
26 C3 Pingli China
26 C3 Pingliang China
26 D2 Pinglu China
26 C2 Pingluo China
27 F5 Pingnan Fujian China
27 D6 Pingnan Guangxi China
26 F1 Pingquan China
26 E2 Pingshan China
27 D5 Pingshi China
27 F5 Pingtan China
27 C5 Pingtang China
27 F6 P'ing-tung Taiwan
26 B3 Pingwu China
27 C6 Pingxiang Guangxi China
27 D5 Pingxiang Jiangxi China
27 F5 Pingyang China
26 D2 Pingyao China
26 E3 Pingyi China
26 E2 Pingyin China
26 E3 Pingyu China
27 E5 Pingyuan China
27 B6 Pingyuanjie China
27 □ Ping Yuen Ho r. H.K. China
27 C5 Pingzhai China
87 J4 Pinheiro Brazil
91 G1 Pinheiro Machado Brazil
39 D7 Pinhoe U.K.
33 A2 Pini i. Indon.
64 E3 Pink Mountain Can.
9 D4 Pinnacle mt N.Z.
8 C3 Pinnaroo Austr.
43 H1 Pinneberg Ger.
74 C4 Pinos, Mt mt U.S.A.
84 C3 Pinotepa Nacional Mex.
7 G4 Pins, Î. des i. New Caledonia
51 C4 Pinsk Belarus
69 G4 Pins, Pointe aux pt Can.
86 □ Pinta, Isla i. Galapagos Is Ecuador
75 F5 Pinta, Sierra summit U.S.A.
75 F3 Pintura U.S.A.
75 E3 Pioche U.S.A.
57 C4 Piodi Congo(Zaire)
12 K1 Pioner, O. i. Rus. Fed.
47 K3 Pionerskiy Rus. Fed.
47 K5 Pionki Pol.
9 E3 Piopio N.Z.
86 F4 Piorini, Lago l. Brazil
47 J5 Piotrków Trybunalski Pol.
19 F5 Pip Iran
30 E2 Pipa Dingzi mt China
22 C4 Pipar India
22 D5 Piparia India
49 L5 Piperi i. Greece
74 D3 Piper Peak summit U.S.A.
75 F3 Pipe Spring Nat. Mon. nat. park U.S.A.
76 D3 Pipestone U.S.A.
66 B3 Pipestone r. Can.
9 E3 Pipiriki N.Z.
22 C3 Pipli India
67 F4 Pipmuacan, Réservoir resr Can.
23 E4 Pipra Dam dam India
80 A4 Piqua U.S.A.
90 A2 Piquiri r. Mato Grosso do Sul Brazil
90 B4 Piquiri r. Paraná Brazil
90 C2 Piracanjuba Brazil
90 C3 Piracicaba Brazil
90 D2 Piracicaba r. Minas Gerais Brazil
90 C3 Piracicaba r. São Paulo Brazil
90 C3 Piraçununga Brazil
87 K4 Piracuruca Brazil
Piraeus see Peiraias
90 C4 Piraí do Sul Brazil
90 C3 Pirajuí Brazil
22 C5 Piram I. i. India
90 B2 Piranhas Brazil
90 B2 Piranhas r. Goiás Brazil
87 L5 Piranhas r. Paraíba/Rio Grande do Norte Brazil
89 C4 Piraparaná r. Col.
90 B3 Pirapó r. Brazil
90 D2 Pirapora Brazil
91 G1 Piratini Brazil
91 G1 Piratini r. Brazil
22 D4 Pirawa India
91 C4 Pire Mahuida, Sa mts Arg.
90 C2 Pires do Rio Brazil
23 G4 Pirganj Bangl.
87 K4 Piripiri Brazil
89 C2 Piritu Venez.
90 A2 Pirizal Brazil
42 F5 Pirmasens Ger.
49 K3 Pirot Yugo.
22 C2 Pir Panjal Pass India
22 C2 Pir Panjal Range mts India/Pak.
89 A3 Pirre, Co mt Panama
17 M2 Pirsaat Azer.
17 M1 Pirsaatçay r. Azer.
25 F7 Piru Indon.
48 D3 Pisa Italy
88 B1 Pisagua Chile
9 B6 Pisa, Mt mt N.Z.
81 F4 Piscataway U.S.A.
86 C6 Pisco Peru
86 C6 Pisco, B. de b. Peru
81 F3 Piseco Lake l. U.S.A.
46 G6 Písek Czech Rep.
19 F5 Pishin Iran
22 A3 Pishin Pak.
19 G4 Pishin Lora r. Pak.
88 C3 Pissis, Cerro mt Arg.
48 G4 Pisticci Italy
48 D3 Pistoia Italy
45 D1 Pisuerga r. Spain
72 B3 Pit r. U.S.A.
54 A3 Pita Guinea
67 G3 Pitaga Can.
84 E3 Pital Mex.
89 A4 Pitalito Col.
90 B4 Pitanga Brazil
90 D2 Pitangui Brazil
8 D3 Pitarpunga, L. l. Austr.
5 P7 Pitcairn Islands i. Pitcairn Is Pac. Oc.
5 P7 Pitcairn Islands terr. Pac. Oc.
36 R4 Piteå Sweden
36 R4 Piteälven r. Sweden
51 H5 Piterka Rus. Fed.
49 L2 Piteşti Romania
21 C2 Pithapuram India
73 D6 Pitiquito Mex.
50 D2 Pitkyaranta Rus. Fed.
40 E4 Pitlochry U.K.
91 B3 Pitrufquén Chile
59 F2 Pitsane Siding Botswana
40 F4 Pitscottie U.K.
64 D4 Pitt I. i. Can.
7 J6 Pitt Island i. Pac. Oc.
77 E4 Pittsburg U.S.A.
80 D4 Pittsburgh U.S.A.
68 B6 Pittsfield IL U.S.A.
81 G3 Pittsfield MA U.S.A.
81 J2 Pittsfield ME U.S.A.
81 H3 Pittsfield NH U.S.A.
81 G3 Pittsfield VT U.S.A.
65 K2 Pitz Lake l. Can.
90 D3 Piumhí Brazil
86 B5 Piura Peru
74 C4 Piute Peak summit U.S.A.
23 E3 Piuthan Nepal
47 O6 Pivdennyy Buh r. Ukr.
48 F2 Pivka Slovenia
22 D1 Pixa China
84 E3 Pixoyal Mex.
46 E7 Piz Buin mt Austria/Switz.
50 H3 Pizhma Rus. Fed.
50 H3 Pizhma r. Rus. Fed.
67 K4 Placentia Can.
67 K4 Placentia B. b. Can.
31 B4 Placer Phil.
31 C4 Placer Phil.
74 B2 Placerville U.S.A.
83 J4 Placetas Cuba
81 H4 Plainfield CT U.S.A.
68 C5 Plainfield IL U.S.A.
68 C3 Plainfield WI U.S.A.
68 A3 Plainview MN U.S.A.
76 D3 Plainview NE U.S.A.
77 C5 Plainview TX U.S.A.
81 J1 Plaisted U.S.A.
13 T3 Plamennyy Rus. Fed.
64 G4 Plamondon Can.
33 E4 Plampang Indon.
43 L5 Planá Czech Rep.
74 B3 Planada U.S.A.
90 C1 Planaltina Brazil
91 B2 Planchón, P. de pass Arg.
89 B2 Planeta Rica Col.
94 F6 Planet Deep depth Pac. Oc.
76 D3 Plankinton U.S.A.
68 C5 Plano IL U.S.A.
77 D5 Plano TX U.S.A.
79 D7 Plantation U.S.A.
77 F6 Plaquemine U.S.A.
45 C2 Plasencia Spain
81 K1 Plaster Rock Can.
28 E2 Plastun Rus. Fed.
86 B4 Plata, I. la i. Ecuador
48 E6 Platani r. Sicily Italy
91 F2 Plata, Río de la chan. Arg./Uru.
59 H4 Platberg mt S. Africa
13 V4 Platinum U.S.A.
89 B2 Plato Col.
76 C3 Platte r. U.S.A.
68 B4 Platteville U.S.A.
43 L6 Plattling Ger.
81 G2 Plattsburgh U.S.A.
76 E3 Plattsmouth U.S.A.
43 L1 Plau Ger.
43 L4 Plauen Ger.
43 L1 Plauer See l. Ger.
50 F4 Plavsk Rus. Fed.
73 E6 Playa Noriega, L. l. Mex.
86 B4 Playas Ecuador
32 D2 Plây Cu Vietnam
65 K4 Playgreen L. l. Can.
81 A4 Playón Mex.
91 C3 Plaza Huincul Arg.
81 J4 Pleasant Bay b. U.S.A.
75 G1 Pleasant Grove U.S.A.
75 F5 Pleasant, Lake l. U.S.A.
75 H5 Pleasanton NM U.S.A.
77 D6 Pleasanton TX U.S.A.
9 C6 Pleasant Point N.Z.
75 H3 Pleasant View U.S.A.
81 F5 Pleasantville U.S.A.
78 C4 Pleasure Ridge Park U.S.A.
44 F4 Pleaux France
32 C2 Plei Doch Vietnam
43 J5 Pleinfeld Ger.
9 F2 Plenty, Bay of b. N.Z.
72 F1 Plentywood U.S.A.
50 G2 Plesetsk Rus. Fed.
67 F3 Plétipi L. l. Can.
43 F3 Plettenberg Ger.
58 E7 Plettenberg Bay S. Africa
49 L3 Pleven Bulg.
49 H3 Pljevlja Yugo.
47 J4 Płock Pol.
48 G3 Pločno mt Bos.-Herz.
50 D2 Plodovoye Rus. Fed.
44 C2 Ploemeur France
49 M2 Ploieşti Romania
65 H3 Plonge, Lac la l. Can.
47 P2 Ploskosh' Rus. Fed.
50 G3 Ploskoye Rus. Fed.
46 G4 Płoty Pol.
44 B2 Ploudalmézeau France
44 B2 Plouzané France
49 L3 Plovdiv Bulg.
68 C3 Plover U.S.A.
68 C3 Plover r. U.S.A.
27 □ Plover Cove Res. resr H.K. China
84 C4 Pluma Hidalgo Mex.
81 G4 Plum I. i. U.S.A.
72 C2 Plummer U.S.A.
37 R9 Plungė Lith.
47 N3 Plyeshchanitsy Belarus
32 A1 Ply Huey Wati, Khao mt Myanmar/Thai.
83 M5 Plymouth Montserrat
39 C7 Plymouth U.K.
74 B2 Plymouth CA U.S.A.
68 D5 Plymouth IN U.S.A.
81 H4 Plymouth MA U.S.A.
81 H3 Plymouth NH U.S.A.
78 F3 Plymouth PA U.S.A.
68 D4 Plymouth WI U.S.A.
81 H4 Plymouth Bay b. U.S.A.
39 D5 Plynlimon h. U.K.
46 F6 Plzeň Czech Rep.
54 B3 Pô Burkina
93 L8 Pobeda Ice Island ice feature Ant.
12 K5 Pobedy, Pik mt China/Kyrg.
77 F4 Pocahontas U.S.A.
80 C5 Pocatalico r. U.S.A.
72 D3 Pocatello U.S.A.
51 C5 Pochayiv Ukr.
50 E4 Pochep Rus. Fed.
50 H4 Pochinki Rus. Fed.
50 E4 Pochinok Rus. Fed.
41 B6 Pocket, The h. Rep. of Ireland
46 F6 Pocking Ger.
38 G4 Pocklington U.K.
90 E1 Poções Brazil
81 F5 Pocomoke City U.S.A.
81 F6 Pocomoke Sound b. U.S.A.
90 A2 Poconé Brazil
81 F4 Pocono Mountains h. U.S.A.
81 F4 Pocono Summit U.S.A.
90 C3 Poços de Caldas Brazil
50 D3 Poddor'ye Rus. Fed.
51 F5 Podgorenskiy Rus. Fed.
49 H3 Podgorica Yugo.
12 K4 Podgornoye Rus. Fed.
21 B3 Podile India
13 L3 Podkamennaya r. Rus. Fed.
86 C4 Podocarpus, Parque Nacional nat. park Ecuador
50 F4 Podol'sk Rus. Fed.
50 E2 Podporozh'ye Rus. Fed.
48 G1 Podravina reg. Hungary
49 J3 Podujevo Yugo.
50 H2 Podvoloch'ye Rus. Fed.
50 J2 Podz' Rus. Fed.
58 C4 Pofadder S. Africa
69 G2 Pogamasing Can.
51 E4 Pogar Rus. Fed.
48 D3 Poggibonsi Italy
49 J4 Pogradec Albania
90 A2 Poguba r. Brazil
30 E5 P'ohang S. Korea
4 G4 Pohnpei i. Micronesia
51 D5 Pohrebyshche Ukr.
22 D4 Pohri India
49 K3 Poiana Mare Romania
56 C4 Poie Congo(Zaire)
92 C6 Poinsett, C. c. Ant.
74 A2 Point Arena U.S.A.
69 K2 Point-Comfort Can.
83 M5 Pointe-à-Pitre Guadeloupe
69 G3 Pointe au Baril Sta. Can.
56 B4 Pointe-Noire Congo
62 B3 Point Hope U.S.A.
64 G1 Point Lake l. Can.
69 F5 Point Pelee National Park Can.
81 F4 Point Pleasant NJ U.S.A.
80 B5 Point Pleasant WV U.S.A.
69 K3 Poisson Blanc, Lac du l. Can.
44 E3 Poitiers France
27 □ Poi Toi I. i. H.K. China
44 D3 Poitou reg. France
90 E1 Pojuca Brazil
22 B4 Pokaran India
23 E3 Pokhara Nepal
56 C3 Poko Congo(Zaire)
22 A4 Pokran Pak.
28 C2 Pokrovka Rus. Fed.
28 B3 Pokrovka Rus. Fed.
13 O3 Pokrovsk Rus. Fed.
51 F6 Pokrovskoye Rus. Fed.
50 H2 Pokshen'ga r. Rus. Fed.
31 B3 Pola Phil.
75 G4 Polacca U.S.A.
75 G4 Polacca Wash r. U.S.A.
45 D1 Pola de Lena Spain
45 D1 Pola de Siero Spain
81 F3 Poland U.S.A.
34 G3 Poland country Europe
66 D3 Polar Bear Provincial Park res. Can.
16 D2 Polatlı Turkey
50 D4 Polatsk Belarus
47 N3 Polatskaya Nizina lowland Belarus
21 C2 Polavaram India
36 R3 Polcirkeln Sweden
50 H2 Poldarsa Rus. Fed.
18 B2 Pol Dasht Iran
19 F2 Pole-Khatum Iran
19 H3 Pol-e-Khomrī Afgh.
50 B4 Polessk Rus. Fed.
33 E3 Polewali Indon.
55 D4 Poli Cameroon
46 G4 Police Pol.
48 G4 Policoro Italy
44 G3 Poligny France
31 B3 Polillo i. Phil.
31 B3 Polillo Islands is Phil.
31 B3 Polillo Strait chan. Phil.
16 D4 Polis Cyprus
51 D5 Polis'ke Ukr.
46 H5 Polkowice Pol.
21 B4 Pollachi India
43 H3 Polle Ger.
45 H3 Pollença Spain
48 G5 Pollino, Monte mt Italy
36 U1 Polmak Norway
36 V4 Polo Fin.
68 C5 Polo U.S.A.
51 F6 Polohy Ukr.
50 J3 Polom Rus. Fed.
31 C5 Polomoloc Phil.
21 C5 Polonnaruwa Sri Lanka
51 C5 Polonne Ukr.
39 C7 Polperro U.K.
72 D2 Polson U.S.A.
50 G1 Polta r. Rus. Fed.
51 E5 Poltava Ukr.
28 B2 Poltavka Rus. Fed.
37 T7 Põltsamaa Estonia
37 U7 Põlva Estonia
36 V5 Polvijärvi Fin.
36 X2 Polyarnyy Rus. Fed.
13 T3 Polyarnyy Rus. Fed.
36 X3 Polyarnyye Zori Rus. Fed.
49 K4 Polygyros Greece
49 K4 Polykastro Greece
94 H6 Polynesia is Pac. Oc.
37 S6 Pomarkku Fin.
90 D3 Pomba r. Brazil
45 B3 Pombal Port.
90 B3 Pombo r. Brazil
59 J4 Pomeroy S. Africa
41 E3 Pomeroy U.K.
80 B5 Pomeroy U.S.A.
48 E4 Pomezia Italy
58 E2 Pomfret S. Africa
6 F2 Pomio P.N.G.
74 D4 Pomona U.S.A.
49 M3 Pomorie Bulg.
46 G3 Pomorska, Zatoka b. Pol.
50 E1 Pomorskiy Bereg coastal area Rus. Fed.
Pomo Tso l. see Puma Yumco
79 D7 Pompano Beach U.S.A.
90 D2 Pompéu Brazil
50 H3 Ponazyrevo Rus. Fed.
77 D4 Ponca City U.S.A.
83 L5 Ponce Puerto Rico
73 F4 Poncha Springs U.S.A.
66 E3 Poncheville, Lac l. Can.
21 B4 Pondicherry India
63 L2 Pond Inlet Can.
67 J3 Ponds, Island of i. Can.
45 C1 Ponferrada Spain
9 F4 Pongaroa N.Z.
55 E4 Pongo watercourse Sudan
59 J3 Pongola r. S. Africa
59 J3 Pongolapoort Dam resr S. Africa
47 P3 Ponizov'ye Rus. Fed.
21 B3 Ponnaiyar r. India
21 A4 Ponnani India
23 H5 Ponnyadaung Range mts Myanmar
64 G4 Ponoka Can.
54 □ Ponta do Sol Cape Verde
90 B4 Ponta Grossa Brazil
90 C2 Pontalina Brazil
44 H2 Pont-à-Mousson France
90 A3 Ponta Porã Brazil
44 H3 Pontarlier France
77 F6 Pontchartrain, L. l. U.S.A.
42 C4 Pont-de-Loup Belgium
45 B3 Ponte de Sôr Port.
38 F4 Pontefract U.K.
38 F2 Ponteland U.K.
87 G7 Pontes-e-Lacerda Brazil
45 B1 Pontevedra Spain
68 C5 Pontiac IL U.S.A.
69 F4 Pontiac MI U.S.A.
33 C3 Pontianak Indon.
44 C2 Pontivy France
44 B3 Pont-l'Abbé France
44 F2 Pontoise France
65 K4 Ponton Can.
77 F5 Pontotoc U.S.A.
48 C2 Pontremoli Italy
42 A5 Pont-Ste-Maxence France
69 H3 Pontypool Can.
39 D6 Pontypool U.K.
39 D6 Pontypridd U.K.
48 E4 Ponza, Isola di i. Italy
48 E4 Ponziane, Isole is Italy
39 F7 Poole U.K.
Poona see Pune
8 D2 Pooncarie Austr.
8 E1 Poopelloe, L. l. Austr.
86 E7 Poopó, Lago de l. Bol.
9 E1 Poor Knights Is is N.Z.
54 B3 Pô, Parc National de nat. park Burkina
89 A4 Popayán Col.
42 A4 Poperinge Belgium
13 M2 Popigay r. Rus. Fed.
8 C2 Popiltah Austr.
8 C2 Popilta L. l. Austr.
72 F1 Poplar U.S.A.
65 K4 Poplar r. Can.
77 F4 Poplar Bluff U.S.A.
80 C6 Poplar Camp U.S.A.
77 F6 Poplarville U.S.A.
84 C3 Popocatépetl volc. Mex.
56 B4 Popokabaka Congo(Zaire)
49 M3 Popovo Bulg.
43 J3 Poppenberg h. Ger.
47 K6 Poprad Slovakia
19 G5 Porali r. Pak.
9 F4 Porangahau N.Z.
90 C1 Porangatu Brazil
22 B5 Porbandar India
89 B3 Porce r. Col.
64 C4 Porcher I. i. Can.
62 E3 Porcupine r. Can./U.S.A.
67 J3 Porcupine, Cape c. Can.
65 J4 Porcupine Hills h. Can.
68 C2 Porcupine Mts mts U.S.A.
65 J4 Porcupine Plain Can.
65 J4 Porcupine Prov. Forest res. Can.
89 C3 Pore Col.
48 E2 Poreč Croatia
50 H4 Poretskoye Rus. Fed.
37 R6 Pori Fin.
9 E4 Porirua N.Z.
50 D3 Porkhov Rus. Fed.
89 E2 Porlamar Venez.
44 C3 Pornic France
31 C4 Poro i. Phil.
24 G2 Poronaysk Rus. Fed.
49 K6 Poros Greece
50 E2 Porosozero Rus. Fed.
92 C6 Porpoise Bay b. Ant.
36 T1 Porsangen chan. Norway
37 L7 Porsgrunn Norway
16 C2 Porsuk r. Turkey
8 B3 Port Adelaide Austr.
41 E3 Portadown U.K.
41 F3 Portaferry U.K.
81 J1 Portage ME U.S.A.
68 E4 Portage MI U.S.A.
68 C4 Portage WI U.S.A.
65 K5 Portage la Prairie Can.
76 C1 Portal U.S.A.
64 E5 Port Alberni Can.
8 F5 Port Albert Austr.
45 C3 Portalegre Port.
77 C5 Portales U.S.A.
64 C3 Port Alexander U.S.A.
59 G6 Port Alfred S. Africa
64 D4 Port Alice Can.
80 D4 Port Allegany U.S.A.
77 F6 Port Allen U.S.A.
72 B1 Port Angeles U.S.A.
41 D4 Portarlington Rep. of Ireland
6 E6 Port Arthur Austr.
77 E6 Port Arthur U.S.A.
40 B5 Port Askaig U.K.
8 A2 Port Augusta Austr.
83 K5 Port-au-Prince Haiti
69 F3 Port Austin U.S.A.
67 J3 Port aux Choix Can.
41 F3 Portavogie U.K.
58 D7 Port Beaufort S. Africa
15 H5 Port Blair Andaman and Nicobar Is
69 H3 Port Bolster Can.
45 H1 Portbou Spain
69 G4 Port Burwell Can.
8 D5 Port Campbell Austr.
69 H3 Port Carling Can.
9 C6 Port Chalmers N.Z.
79 D7 Port Charlotte U.S.A.
81 G4 Port Chester U.S.A.
64 C4 Port Clements Can.
80 B4 Port Clinton U.S.A.
81 J3 Port Clyde U.S.A.
69 H4 Port Colborne Can.
64 E5 Port Coquitlam Can.
69 H4 Port Credit Can.
83 K5 Port-de-Paix Haiti
32 B5 Port Dickson Malaysia
80 C3 Port Dover Can.
68 D3 Porte des Morts chan. U.S.A.
64 C4 Port Edward Can.
59 J5 Port Edward S. Africa
68 C3 Port Edwards U.S.A.
90 D1 Porteirinha Brazil
87 H4 Portel Brazil
69 G3 Port Elgin Can.
59 F6 Port Elizabeth S. Africa
40 B5 Port Ellen U.K.
8 B3 Port Elliot Austr.
38 C3 Port Erin U.K.
65 H2 Porter Lake l. Can.
64 C3 Porter Landing Can.
58 C6 Porterville S. Africa
74 C3 Porterville U.S.A.
8 D5 Port Fairy Austr.
9 E2 Port Fitzroy N.Z.
Port Fuad see Bûr Fu'ad
56 A4 Port-Gentil Gabon
8 B2 Port Germein Austr.
77 F6 Port Gibson U.S.A.
40 D5 Port Glasgow U.K.
54 C4 Port Harcourt Nigeria
64 D4 Port Hardy Can.
Port Harrison see Inukjuak
67 H4 Port Hawkesbury Can.
39 D6 Porthcawl U.K.
6 B4 Port Hedland Austr.
81 G2 Port Henry U.S.A.
39 B7 Porthleven U.K.
39 C5 Porthmadog U.K.
69 H4 Port Hope Can.
67 J3 Port Hope Simpson Can.
69 F4 Port Huron U.S.A.
17 M2 Port-İliç Azer.
45 B4 Portimão Port.
27 □ Port Island i. H.K. China
8 H2 Port Jackson in. Austr.
81 G4 Port Jefferson U.S.A.
81 F4 Port Jervis U.S.A.
86 G2 Port Kaituma Guyana
8 H3 Port Kembla Austr.
8 G2 Portland N.S.W. Austr.
8 C5 Portland Vic. Austr.
68 E5 Portland IN U.S.A.
81 H3 Portland ME U.S.A.
72 B2 Portland OR U.S.A.
64 C3 Portland Canal in. Can.
9 F3 Portland I. i. N.Z.
39 E7 Portland, Isle of pen. U.K.
41 D4 Portlaoise Rep. of Ireland
77 D6 Port Lavaca U.S.A.
41 D5 Portlaw Rep. of Ireland
40 F3 Portlethen U.K.
6 D5 Port Lincoln Austr.
54 A4 Port Loko Sierra Leone
8 C5 Port MacDonnell Austr.
64 D4 Port McNeill Can.
7 F5 Port Macquarie Austr.
67 H2 Port Manvers in. Can.
67 H4 Port-Menier Can.
62 B4 Port Moller b. U.S.A.
72 B1 Port Moody Can.
6 E2 Port Moresby P.N.G.
40 B2 Portnaguran U.K.
40 B5 Portnahaven U.K.
79 F7 Port Nelson Bahamas
40 B2 Port Nis U.K.
58 B4 Port Nolloth S. Africa
Port-Nouveau-Québec see Kangiqsualujjuaq
Porto see Oporto
86 E5 Porto Acre Brazil
90 B3 Porto Alegre Mato Grosso do Sul Brazil
88 F4 Porto Alegre Rio Grande do Sul Brazil
87 G6 Porto Artur Brazil
87 G6 Porto dos Gaúchos Óbidos Brazil
87 G7 Porto Esperidião Brazil
48 D3 Portoferraio Italy
87 J5 Porto Franco Brazil
89 E2 Port of Spain Trinidad and Tobago
48 E2 Portogruaro Italy
54 □ Porto Inglês Cape Verde
90 A2 Porto Jofre Brazil
74 B2 Portola U.S.A.
48 D2 Portomaggiore Italy
87 G8 Porto Murtinho Brazil
87 J6 Porto Nacional Brazil
54 C4 Porto-Novo Benin
Porto Novo see Parangipettai
90 B3 Porto Primavera, Represa resr Brazil
72 A3 Port Orford U.S.A.
87 H4 Porto Santana Brazil
90 E2 Porto Seguro Brazil
48 E2 Porto Tolle Italy
48 C4 Porto Torres Sardinia Italy
48 C4 Porto-Vecchio Corsica France
86 F5 Porto Velho Brazil
86 B4 Portoviejo Ecuador
40 C6 Portpatrick U.K.
69 H3 Port Perry Can.
8 E5 Port Phillip Bay b. Austr.
8 B2 Port Pirie Austr.
39 B7 Portreath U.K.
40 B3 Portree U.K.
64 E5 Port Renfrew Can.
69 G4 Port Rowan Can.
80 E5 Port Royal U.S.A.
41 E2 Portrush U.K.
55 F1 Port Said Egypt
79 C6 Port St Joe U.S.A.
59 H5 Port St Johns S. Africa
38 C3 Port St Mary U.K.
41 D2 Portsalon Rep. of Ireland
69 F4 Port Sanilac U.S.A.
69 H3 Port Severn Can.
27 □ Port Shelter b. H.K. China
59 J5 Port Shepstone S. Africa
64 C4 Port Simpson Can.
39 F7 Portsmouth U.K.
81 H3 Portsmouth NH U.S.A.
80 B5 Portsmouth OH U.S.A.
81 E6 Portsmouth VA U.S.A.
40 F3 Portsoy U.K.
41 E2 Portstewart U.K.
55 F3 Port Sudan Sudan
79 B6 Port Sulphur U.S.A.
39 D6 Port Talbot U.K.
36 U2 Porttipahdan tekojärvi l. Fin.
34 E5 Portugal country Europe
89 C2 Portuguesa r. Venez.
41 C4 Portumna Rep. of Ireland
44 F5 Port-Vendres France
7 G3 Port Vila Vanuatu
36 X2 Port Vladimir Rus. Fed.
9 E2 Port Waikato N.Z.
8 B3 Port Wakefield Austr.
68 D4 Port Washington U.S.A.
40 D6 Port William U.K.
68 B2 Port Wing U.S.A.
91 D2 Porvenir Arg.
37 T6 Porvoo Fin.
45 D1 Posada de Llanera Spain
88 E3 Posadas Arg.
49 H2 Posavina reg. Bos.-Herz./Croatia
69 F3 Posen U.S.A.
17 L5 Posht-é-Kūh mts Iran
18 C2 Posht Kūh h. Iran
36 V3 Posio Fin.
25 E7 Poso Indon.
17 J1 Posof Turkey
30 D6 Posŏng S. Korea
90 C1 Posse Brazil
92 A5 Possession Is is Ant.
43 K4 Pößneck Ger.
77 C5 Post U.S.A.
66 E2 Poste-de-la-Baleine Can.

58 E4 Postmasburg S. Africa
67 J3 Postville Can.
68 B4 Postville U.S.A.
48 G3 Posušje Bos.-Herz.
28 B3 Pos'yet Rus. Fed.
59 G3 Potchefstroom S. Africa
77 E5 Poteau U.S.A.
87 L5 Potengi *r.* Brazil
48 F4 Potenza Italy
9 A7 Poteriteri, L. *l.* N.Z.
58 F5 Potfontein S. Africa
59 H2 Potgietersrus S. Africa
77 D6 Poth U.S.A.
66 F2 Potherie, Lac La *l.* Can.
51 G7 P'ot'i Georgia
87 K5 Poti *r.* Brazil
21 C2 Potikal India
54 D3 Potiskum Nigeria
72 D2 Pot Mt. *mt* U.S.A.
80 E5 Potomac *r.* U.S.A.
80 D5 Potomac South Branch *r.* U.S.A.
86 E7 Potosí Bol.
76 F4 Potosi U.S.A.
75 E4 Potosi Mt *mt* U.S.A.
31 B4 Pototan Phil.
43 M2 Potsdam Ger.
81 F2 Potsdam U.S.A.
39 E6 Potterne U.K.
39 G6 Potters Bar U.K.
81 F4 Pottstown U.S.A.
81 E4 Pottsville U.S.A.
21 C5 Pottuvil Sri Lanka
64 E3 Pouce Coupe Can.
67 K4 Pouch Cove Can.
81 G4 Poughkeepsie U.S.A.
81 G3 Poultney U.S.A.
38 E4 Poulton-le-Fylde U.K.
32 B1 Pou San *mt* Laos
90 D3 Pouso Alegre Brazil
32 B2 Poŭthĭsăt Cambodia
47 J6 Považská Bystrica Slovakia
50 E2 Povenets Rus. Fed.
9 F3 Poverty Bay *b.* N.Z.
49 H2 Povlen *mt* Yugo.
45 B2 Póvoa de Varzim Port.
51 G5 Povorino Rus. Fed.
28 C3 Povorotnyy, Mys *hd* Rus. Fed.
74 D5 Poway U.S.A.
72 F2 Powder *r.* U.S.A.
72 F3 Powder River U.S.A.
72 E2 Powell U.S.A.
80 B6 Powell *r.* U.S.A.
75 G3 Powell, Lake *resr* U.S.A.
74 C2 Powell Mt *mt* U.S.A.
79 E7 Powell Pt *pt* Bahamas
64 E5 Powell River Can.
68 D3 Powers U.S.A.
80 E6 Powhatan U.S.A.
90 A1 Poxoréu Brazil
27 E4 Poyang Hu *l.* China
32 □ Poyan Res. *resr* Sing.
68 C3 Poygan, Lake *l.* U.S.A.
16 E3 Pozantı Turkey
49 J2 Požarevac Yugo.
84 C2 Poza Rica Mex.
48 G2 Požega Croatia
49 J3 Požega Yugo.
28 D1 Pozharskoye Rus. Fed.
46 H4 Poznań Pol.
45 D3 Pozoblanco Spain
48 F4 Pozzuoli Italy
33 B3 Prabumulih Indon.
46 G6 Prachatice Czech Rep.
23 F6 Prachi *r.* India
32 B2 Prachin Buri Thai.
32 A3 Prachuap Khiri Khan Thai.
44 F5 Prades France
90 E2 Prado Brazil
46 G5 Prague Czech Rep.
Praha *see* Prague
54 □ Praia Cape Verde
59 K2 Praia do Bilene Moz.
90 A1 Praia Rica Brazil
68 E5 Prairie Creek Reservoir U.S.A.
77 C5 Prairie Dog Town Fork *r.* U.S.A.
68 B4 Prairie du Chien U.S.A.
32 B2 Prakhon Chai Thai.
32 B2 Pran *r.* Thai.
21 B2 Pranhita *r.* India
33 A2 Prapat Indon.
53 K6 Praslin *i.* Seychelles
49 M7 Prasonisi, Akra *pt* Greece
90 C2 Prata Brazil
90 C2 Prata *r.* Brazil
48 D3 Prato Italy
77 D4 Pratt U.S.A.
77 G5 Prattville U.S.A.
21 A2 Pravara *r.* India
47 K3 Pravdinsk Rus. Fed.
33 E4 Praya Indon.
32 C2 Preăh Vihear Cambodia
47 Q3 Prechistoye Rus. Fed.
65 J4 Preeceville Can.
50 B4 Pregolya *r.* Rus. Fed.
37 U8 Preiļi Latvia
69 H1 Preissac, Lac *l.* Can.
32 C3 Prêk Tnaôt *l.* Cambodia
8 G1 Premer Austr.
44 F3 Prémery France
43 L2 Premnitz Ger.
68 B3 Prentice U.S.A.
46 F4 Prenzlau Ger.
28 C3 Preobrazheniye Rus. Fed.
46 H6 Přerov Czech Rep.
81 F2 Prescott Can.
75 F4 Prescott U.S.A.
75 F4 Prescott Valley U.S.A.
49 J3 Preševo Yugo.
76 C3 Presho U.S.A.
88 D3 Presidencia Roque Sáenz Peña Arg.
87 K5 Presidente Dutra Brazil
90 B3 Presidente Epitácio Brazil
86 F6 Presidente Hermes Brazil
90 B3 Presidente Prudente Brazil
90 B3 Presidente Venceslau Brazil
77 B6 Presidio U.S.A.
49 M3 Preslav Bulg.
47 K6 Prešov Slovakia
49 J4 Prespa, Lake *l.* Europe
81 K1 Presque Isle U.S.A.
68 D2 Presque Isle Pt *pt* U.S.A.
39 D5 Presteigne U.K.
38 E4 Preston U.K.
72 E3 Preston *ID* U.S.A.
68 A4 Preston *MN* U.S.A.
77 E4 Preston *MO* U.S.A.
75 E2 Preston *NV* U.S.A.
40 F5 Prestonpans U.K.
80 B6 Prestonsburg U.S.A.
40 D5 Prestwick U.K.
90 E1 Preto *r.* *Bahia* Brazil
90 C2 Preto *r.* *Minas Gerais* Brazil
59 H2 Pretoria S. Africa
80 E5 Prettyboy Lake *l.* U.S.A.
43 L3 Pretzsch Ger.
49 J5 Preveza Greece
32 C3 Prey Vêng Cambodia
13 V4 Pribilof Islands *is* U.S.A.
49 H3 Priboj Yugo.
67 G4 Price Can.
75 G2 Price U.S.A.
64 D4 Price I. *i.* Can.
79 B6 Prichard U.S.A.
37 R8 Priekule Latvia
37 T8 Priekuļi Latvia
37 S9 Prienai Lith.
58 E4 Prieska S. Africa
72 C1 Priest L. *l.* U.S.A.
72 C1 Priest River U.S.A.
47 J6 Prievidza Slovakia
43 L1 Prignitz *reg.* Ger.
48 G2 Prijedor Bos.-Herz.
49 H3 Prijepolje Yugo.
12 F5 Prikaspiyskaya Nizmennost' *lowland* Kazak./Rus. Fed.
49 J4 Prilep Macedonia
84 C2 Primavera Mex.
43 L5 Přimda Czech Rep.
91 D1 Primero *r.* Arg.
37 V6 Primorsk Rus. Fed.
28 C2 Primorskiy Kray *div.* Rus. Fed.
51 F6 Primorsko-Akhtarsk Rus. Fed.
65 H4 Primrose Lake *l.* Can.
65 H4 Prince Albert Can.
58 E6 Prince Albert S. Africa
92 B5 Prince Albert Mts *mts* Ant.
65 H4 Prince Albert National Park Can.
62 G2 Prince Albert Peninsula Can.
58 D6 Prince Albert Road S. Africa
62 G2 Prince Albert Sound *chan.* Can.
62 F2 Prince Alfred, C. *c.* Can.
63 L3 Prince Charles I. Can.
92 D4 Prince Charles Mts *mts* Ant.
67 H4 Prince Edward Island *div.* Can.
93 G7 Prince Edward Islands *is* Ind. Ocean
69 J4 Prince Edward Pt *pt* Can.
80 E5 Prince Frederick U.S.A.
64 E4 Prince George Can.
62 B3 Prince of Wales, Cape *c.* U.S.A.
63 J2 Prince of Wales I. *N.W.T.* Can.
6 E3 Prince of Wales I. *i.* Austr.
64 C3 Prince of Wales Island *i.* U.S.A.
62 G2 Prince of Wales Strait *chan.* Can.
62 F2 Prince Patrick I. *i.* Can.
63 J2 Prince Regent Inlet *chan.* Can.
64 C4 Prince Rupert Can.
65 K2 Princes Mary Lake *l.* Can.
81 F5 Princess Anne U.S.A.
92 D3 Princess Astrid Coast *coastal area* Ant.
6 E3 Princess Charlotte Bay *b.* Austr.
92 D5 Princess Elizabeth Land *reg.* Ant.
92 D3 Princess Ragnhild Coast *coastal area* Ant.
64 D4 Princess Royal I. *i.* Can.
64 E5 Princeton Can.
74 A2 Princeton *CA* U.S.A.
68 C5 Princeton *IL* U.S.A.
78 C4 Princeton *IN* U.S.A.
78 C4 Princeton *KY* U.S.A.
81 K2 Princeton *ME* U.S.A.
76 E3 Princeton *MO* U.S.A.
81 F4 Princeton *NJ* U.S.A.
68 C4 Princeton *WV* U.S.A.
80 C6 Princeton *WV* U.S.A.
81 K2 Prince William Can.
62 D3 Prince William Sound *b.* U.S.A.
54 C4 Príncipe *i.* Sao Tome and Principe
72 B2 Prineville U.S.A.
12 C2 Prins Karls Forland *i.* Svalbard
83 H6 Prinzapolca Nic.
50 D2 Priozersk Rus. Fed.
Pripet *r.* *see* Pryp"yat
36 W2 Prirechnyy Rus. Fed.
49 J3 Priština Yugo.
43 K1 Pritzier Ger.
43 L1 Pritzwalk Ger.
44 G4 Privas France
48 F2 Privlaka Croatia
50 G3 Privolzhsk Rus. Fed.
50 H4 Privolzhskaya Vozvyshennost' *reg.* Rus. Fed.
51 G6 Priyutnoye Rus. Fed.
49 J3 Prizren Yugo.
33 D4 Probolinggo Indon.
43 K4 Probstzella Ger.
39 C7 Probus U.K.
68 A2 Proctor *MN* U.S.A.
81 G3 Proctor *VT* U.S.A.
87 G3 Professor van Blommestein Meer *resr* Suriname
82 G5 Progreso Honduras
77 C7 Progreso *Coahuila* Mex.
84 C2 Progreso *Hidalgo* Mex.
84 E2 Progreso *Yucatán* Mex.
51 H7 Prokhladnyy Rus. Fed.
12 K4 Prokop'yevsk Rus. Fed.
49 J3 Prokuplje Yugo.
50 D3 Proletariy Rus. Fed.
51 G6 Proletarsk Rus. Fed.
90 A2 Promissão Brazil
62 F4 Prophet *r.* Can.
64 E3 Prophet River Can.
68 C5 Prophetstown U.S.A.
6 E4 Proserpine Austr.
81 F3 Prospect U.S.A.
31 C4 Prosperidad Phil.
58 D7 Protem S. Africa
68 A4 Protivin U.S.A.
49 M3 Provadiya Bulg.
Prøven *see* Kangersuatsiaq
44 H5 Provence *reg.* France
81 H4 Providence U.S.A.
69 F3 Providence Bay Can.
9 A7 Providence, Cape *c.* N.Z.
77 F5 Providence, Lake U.S.A.
86 B1 Providencia, Isla de *i.* Col.
62 A3 Provideniya Rus. Fed.
81 H3 Provincetown U.S.A.
75 G1 Provo U.S.A.
65 G4 Provost Can.
90 B4 Prudentópolis Brazil
62 D2 Prudhoe Bay U.S.A.
42 E4 Prüm Ger.
42 E4 Prüm *r.* Ger.
48 C3 Prunelli-di-Fiumorbo *Corsica* France
47 K4 Pruszków Pol.
51 D6 Prut *r.* Moldova/Romania
92 D5 Prydz Bay *b.* Ant.
51 E5 Pryluky Ukr.
51 F6 Prymors'k Ukr.
71 G4 Pryor *OK* U.S.A.
47 M5 Pryp"yat *r.* Ukr.
47 N4 Prypyats' *r.* Belarus
47 L6 Przemyśl Pol.
49 L5 Psara *i.* Greece
51 G6 Psebay Rus. Fed.
51 F6 Pshish *r.* Rus. Fed.
50 D3 Pskov Rus. Fed.
37 U7 Pskov, Lake *l.* Estonia/Rus. Fed.
50 D3 Pskovskaya Oblast' *div.* Rus. Fed.
49 J4 Ptolemaïda Greece
48 F1 Ptuj Slovenia
26 C3 Pu *r.* China
91 D3 Puán Arg.
27 B5 Pu'an China
30 D6 Puan S. Korea
27 C6 Pubei China
86 D5 Pucallpa Peru
27 F5 Pucheng *Fujian* China
26 C3 Pucheng *Shaanxi* China
50 G3 Puchezh Rus. Fed.
30 D5 Puch'ŏn S. Korea
31 B4 Pucio Pt *pt* Phil.
46 J3 Puck Pol.
68 C4 Puckaway Lake *l.* U.S.A.
91 B3 Pucón Chile
Pudai *watercourse see* Dor
18 D3 Pūdanū Iran
36 U4 Pudasjärvi Fin.
58 F3 Pudimoe S. Africa
50 F2 Pudozh Rus. Fed.
38 F4 Pudsey U.K.
Puduchcheri *see* Pondicherry
21 B4 Pudukkottai India
84 C3 Puebla Mex.
84 C3 Puebla *div.* Mex.
45 C1 Puebla de Sanabria Spain
73 F4 Pueblo U.S.A.
89 C2 Pueblo Nuevo Venez.
84 D3 Pueblo Viejo Mex.
91 D3 Puelches Arg.
91 C3 Puelén Arg.
91 B2 Puente Alto Chile
84 C3 Puente de Ixtla Mex.
45 D4 Puente-Genil Spain
89 C2 Puente Torres Venez.
86 F6 Puerto Alegre Bol.
84 C4 Puerto Angel Mex.
84 D4 Puerto Arista Mex.
83 H7 Puerto Armuelles Panama
89 A4 Puerto Asís Col.
89 D3 Puerto Ayacucho Venez.
82 G5 Puerto Barrios Guatemala
89 B3 Puerto Berrío Col.
89 C2 Puerto Cabello Venez.
83 H6 Puerto Cabezas Nic.
89 D3 Puerto Carreño Col.
88 E2 Puerto Casado Para.
88 B6 Puerto Cisnes Chile
88 C8 Puerto Coig Arg.
83 H7 Puerto Cortés Costa Rica
89 C2 Puerto Cumarebo Venez.
84 C4 Puerto Escondido Mex.
89 C1 Puerto Estrella Col.
86 F6 Puerto Frey Bol.
88 E2 Puerto Guarani Para.
86 E6 Puerto Heath Bol.
89 D4 Puerto Inírida Col.
87 G7 Puerto Isabel Bol.
89 D2 Puerto La Cruz Venez.
86 D4 Puerto Leguizamo Col.
45 D3 Puertollano Spain
91 D4 Puerto Lobos Arg.
89 B3 Puerto Lopéz Col.
84 D4 Puerto Madero Mex.
91 D4 Puerto Madryn Arg.
86 E6 Puerto Maldonado Peru
86 B4 Puerto Máncora Peru
90 A4 Puerto Mendes Para.
89 D3 Puerto Miranda Venez.
91 B4 Puerto Montt Chile
88 B8 Puerto Natáles Chile
89 C3 Puerto Nuevo Col.
89 A2 Puerto Obaldia Panama
89 E2 Puerto Ordaz Venez.
89 D3 Puerto Páez Venez.
88 E2 Puerto Pinasco Para.
91 D4 Puerto Pirámides Arg.
83 K5 Puerto Plata Dom. Rep.
86 D5 Puerto Portillo Peru
31 A4 Puerto Princesa Phil.
89 A2 Puerto Rey Col.
61 M8 Puerto Rico *terr.* Caribbean Sea
92 E4 Puerto Rico Trench *sea feature* Atl. Ocean
88 E2 Puerto Sastre Para.
89 A4 Puerto Tejado Col.
84 A2 Puerto Vallarta Mex.
91 B4 Puerto Varas Chile
51 J4 Pugachev Rus. Fed.
22 C3 Pugal India
27 B5 Puge China
18 D5 Pūhāl-e Khamīr, Kūh-e *mts* Iran
45 H3 Puig Major *mt* Spain
45 H1 Puigmal *mt* France/Spain
27 □ Pui O Wan *b.* *H.K.* China
27 F4 Pujiang China
30 D3 Pujŏn Reservoir *resr* N. Korea
30 E3 Pujonryong Sanmaek *mts* N. Korea
9 C6 Pukaki, Lake *l.* N.Z.
68 E1 Pukaskwa *r.* Can.
68 E1 Pukaskwa National Park Can.
65 J3 Pukatawagan Can.
30 C3 Pukchin N. Korea
30 E3 Pukch'ŏng N. Korea
9 E2 Pukekohe N.Z.
9 D5 Puketeraki Ra. *mts* N.Z.
9 F4 Puketoi Range *h.* N.Z.
9 C6 Pukeuri Junction N.Z.
47 P3 Pukhnovo Rus. Fed.
50 G2 Puksoozero Rus. Fed.
30 D3 Puksubaek-san *mt* N. Korea
48 E2 Pula Croatia
86 E8 Pulacayo Bol.
30 A4 Pulandian Wan *b.* China
31 C5 Pulangi *r.* Phil.
81 E3 Pulaski *NY* U.S.A.
79 C5 Pulaski *TN* U.S.A.
80 C6 Pulaski *VA* U.S.A.
68 C3 Pulaski *WV* U.S.A.
47 K5 Puławy Pol.
42 E3 Pulheim Ger.
21 C3 Pulicat L. *b.* India
21 B3 Pulivendla India
21 B4 Puliyangudi India
36 T4 Pulkkila Fin.
72 C2 Pullman U.S.A.
36 X2 Pulozero Rus. Fed.
22 E1 Pulu China
17 G2 Pülümür Turkey
31 C5 Pulutan Indon.
23 G3 Puma Yumco *l.* China
86 B4 Puná, Isla *i.* Ecuador
23 G4 Punakha Bhutan
22 C2 Punch Jammu and Kashmir
64 E4 Punchaw Can.
23 G3 Püncogling China
59 J1 Punda Maria S. Africa
22 D3 Pundri India
21 A2 Pune India
32 □ Punggol Sing.
30 E3 P'ungsan N. Korea
57 D5 Púnguè *r.* Moz.
56 C4 Punia Congo(Zaire)
91 B1 Punitaqui Chile
22 C3 Punjab *div.* India
22 B3 Punjab *div.* Pak.
22 D2 Punmah Gl. *gl.* China/Jammu and Kashmir
23 F4 Punpun *r.* India
91 D3 Punta Alta Arg.
88 B8 Punta Arenas Chile
48 C4 Punta Balestrieri *mt* Italy
83 L5 Punta, Cerro de *mt* Puerto Rico
91 D4 Punta Delgada Arg.
82 G5 Punta Gorda Belize
79 D7 Punta Gorda U.S.A.
91 D4 Punta Norte Arg.
83 H6 Puntarenas Costa Rica
89 C2 Punto Fijo Venez.
80 D4 Punxsutawney U.S.A.
36 U4 Puokio Fin.
36 U4 Puolanka Fin.
27 D4 Puqi China
18 E5 Pūr Iran
12 J3 Pur *r.* Rus. Fed.
89 A4 Puracé, Parque Nacional *nat. park* Col.
89 A4 Purace, Volcán de *volc.* Col.
77 D5 Purcell U.S.A.
64 F4 Purcell Mts *mts* Can.
91 B3 Purén Chile
73 G4 Purgatoire *r.* U.S.A.
23 F6 Puri India
42 C2 Purmerend Neth.
21 B2 Purna India
22 D5 Purna *r.* *Maharashtra* India
22 D6 Purna *r.* *Maharashtra* India
21 B1 Purna *r.* India
23 G4 Purnabhaba *r.* India
23 F4 Pūrnia India
91 B4 Purranque Chile
84 B2 Puruandíro Mex.
23 F5 Puruliya India
86 F4 Purus *r.* Brazil
37 V6 Puruvesi *l.* Fin.
33 C4 Purwakarta Indon.
33 D4 Purwodadi Indon.
33 C4 Purwokerto Indon.
30 E2 Puryŏng N. Korea
22 D6 Pus *r.* India
22 D6 Pusad India
30 E6 Pusan S. Korea
81 J2 Pushaw Lake *l.* U.S.A.
50 H2 Pushemskiy Rus. Fed.
22 C4 Pushkar India
50 D3 Pushkin Rus. Fed.
51 H5 Pushkino Rus. Fed.
50 D3 Pushkinskiye Gory Rus. Fed.
19 F4 Pusht-i-Rud *reg.* Afgh.
47 O2 Pustoshka Rus. Fed.
47 L4 Puszcza Augustowska *forest* Pol.
46 G4 Puszcza Natecka *forest* Pol.
24 B4 Putao Myanmar
27 F5 Putian China
33 D3 Puting, Tanjung *pt* Indon.
84 C3 Putla Mex.
19 G4 Putla Khan Afgh.
43 L1 Putlitz Ger.
49 M2 Putna *r.* Romania
81 H4 Putnam U.S.A.
81 G3 Putney U.S.A.
23 H3 Putrang La *pass* China
58 D4 Putsonderwater S. Africa
21 B4 Puttalam Sri Lanka
21 B4 Puttalam Lagoon *lag.* Sri Lanka
42 E5 Puttelange-aux-Lacs France
42 D2 Putten Neth.
42 C3 Puttershoek Neth.
46 E3 Puttgarden Ger.
86 D4 Putumayo *r.* Col.
16 G2 Pütürge Turkey
33 D2 Putusibau Indon.
50 G4 Putyatino Rus. Fed.
51 E5 Putyvl' Ukr.
37 V6 Puumala Fin.
74 □2 Puuwai U.S.A.
66 E1 Puvurnituq Can.
72 B2 Puyallup U.S.A.
26 E3 Puyang China
91 B4 Puyehue Chile
91 B4 Puyehue, Parque Nacional *nat. park* Chile
44 F5 Puylaurens France
9 A7 Puysegur Pt *pt* N.Z.
57 C4 Pweto Congo(Zaire)
39 C5 Pwllheli U.K.
50 E2 Pyal'ma Rus. Fed.
50 H4 P'yana *r.* Rus. Fed.
22 B1 Pyandzh *r.* Afgh./Tajik.
36 W3 Pyaozero, Ozero *l.* Rus. Fed.
36 W4 Pyaozerskiy Rus. Fed.
12 K2 Pyasina *r.* Rus. Fed.
51 G6 Pyatigorsk Rus. Fed.
51 E5 P"yatykhatky Ukr.
25 B5 Pyè Myanmar
9 B7 Pye, Mt *h.* N.Z.
51 D4 Pyetrykaw Belarus
36 T4 Pyhäjoki Fin.
36 T4 Pyhäjoki *r.* Fin.
36 U4 Pyhäntä Fin.
36 T5 Pyhäsalmi Fin.
36 V5 Pyhäselkä *l.* Fin.
23 H5 Pyingaing Myanmar
39 D6 Pyle U.K.
12 K3 Pyl'karamo Rus. Fed.
49 J6 Pylos Greece
80 C4 Pymatuning Reservoir U.S.A.
30 C5 Pyŏksŏng N. Korea
30 C3 Pyŏktong N. Korea
30 D4 P'yŏnggang N. Korea
30 E5 P'yŏnghae S. Korea
30 C4 P'yŏngsong N. Korea
30 D5 P'yŏngt'aek S. Korea
30 C4 P'yŏngyang N. Korea
8 E4 Pyramid Hill Austr.
74 C1 Pyramid Lake *l.* U.S.A.
68 E3 Pyramid Pt *pt* U.S.A.
74 C2 Pyramid Range *mts* U.S.A.
34 E4 Pyrenees *mts* France/Spain
49 J6 Pyrgos Greece
51 E5 Pyryatyn Ukr.
46 G4 Pyrzyce Pol.
50 H3 Pyshchug Rus. Fed.
47 N2 Pytalovo Rus. Fed.
49 K5 Pyxaria *mt* Greece

Q

63 M2 Qaanaaq Greenland
18 D6 Qābil Oman
17 J6 Qabr Bandar Iraq
59 H5 Qacha's Nek Lesotho
17 K4 Qādir Karam Iraq
17 J4 Qadissiya Dam *dam* Iraq
26 C1 Qagan Ders China
26 C2 Qagan Nur China
26 D1 Qagan Nur China
30 C1 Qagan Nur *l.* *Jilin* China
26 E1 Qagan Nur *l.* *Nei Monggol* China
26 E1 Qagan Nur *resr* China
26 D1 Qagan Teg China
26 E1 Qagan Us China
23 H3 Qagbasêrag China
23 E2 Qagcaka China
63 O3 Qagssimiut Greenland
26 D1 Qahar Youyi Qianqi China
26 D1 Qahar Youyi Zhongqi China
24 B3 Qaidam Pendi *basin* China
19 G3 Qaisar Afgh.
19 G3 Qaisar, Koh-i- *mt* Afgh.
17 K3 Qalā Diza Iraq
19 H2 Qal'aikhum Tajik.
19 G3 Qala Shinia Takht Afgh.
19 G3 Qalāt Afgh.
18 D4 Qalat Iran
17 H4 Qal'at as Sālihīyah Syria
16 E6 Qal'at el Hasal Jordan
17 L6 Qal'at Sālih Iraq
17 L6 Qal'at Sukkar Iraq
19 F3 Qala Vali Afgh.
18 B2 Qal'eh D. *mt* Iran
19 F3 Qal 'eh-ve Now Afgh.
19 G4 Qal 'eh-ye Bost Afgh.
17 M5 Qal'eh-ye-Now Iran
17 K7 Qalīb Bāqūr *well* Iraq
16 C6 Qalyûb Egypt
59 G5 Qamata S. Africa
22 B4 Qambar Pak.
22 B3 Qamruddin Karez Pak.
18 C3 Qamşar Iran
18 B2 Qandaranbashi *mt* Iran
26 E1 Qangdin Sum China
17 M2 Qaraçala Azer.
17 J4 Qarachōq, J. *mts* Iraq
17 K4 Qara D. *r.* Iraq
17 H7 Qārah S. Arabia
19 H3 Qarah Bāgh Afgh.
18 A5 Qa'rah, J. al *h.* S. Arabia
17 L3 Qaranqu *r.* Iran
56 E3 Qardho Somalia
17 L3 Qar'eh Aqāj Iran
17 L2 Qareh D. *mts* Iran
17 L3 Qareh Dāsh, Kūh-e *mt* Iran
18 B2 Qareh Sū *r.* Iran
17 L3 Qareh Urgān, Kūh-e *mt* Iran
23 H1 Qarhan China
19 G2 Qarqīn Afgh.
17 K6 Qaryat al Gharab Iraq
18 B5 Qaryat al Ulyā S. Arabia
18 E3 Qasamī Iran
19 F3 Qasa Murg *mts* Afgh.
18 C4 Qash Qai *reg.* Iran
63 N3 Qasigiannguit Greenland
17 J5 Qasr al Khubbāz Iraq
17 M7 Qaşr aş Şabīyah Kuwait
16 F6 Qasr el Azraq Jordan
19 F5 Qaşr-e-Qand Iran
18 B3 Qasr-e-Shirin Iran
17 L6 Qaşr Shaqrah Iraq
16 F5 Qaţanā Syria
10 G7 Qatar *country* Asia
16 F6 Qatrāna Jordan
16 C7 Qaţrâni, Gebel *esc.* Egypt
55 E2 Qattâra Depression *depression* Egypt
17 L1 Qax Azer.
19 E3 Qāyen Iran
23 H3 Qayü China
17 J4 Qayyarah Iraq
17 L2 Qazangöldağ *mt* Azer.
17 K1 Qazax Azer.
22 B4 Qazi Ahmad Pak.
17 M1 Qazımämmäd Azer.
18 C2 Qazvīn Iran
26 A1 Qeh China
55 F2 Qena Egypt
63 N3 Qeqertarsuatsiaat Greenland
63 N3 Qeqertarsuatsiaq *i.* Greenland
63 N3 Qeqertarsuup Tunua *b.* Greenland
18 B3 Qeshlag *r.* Iran
17 L4 Qeshlaq Iran
18 E5 Qeshm Iran
18 C2 Qeydār Iran
18 D5 Qeys *i.* Iran
18 C2 Qezel Owzan *r.* Iran
16 E6 Qezi'ot Israel
26 C3 Qian *r.* China
26 F2 Qian'an China
30 C1 Qian'an China
27 C5 Qiancheng China
26 F3 Qiang *r.* China
30 C1 Qian Gorlos China
27 D4 Qianjiang *Hubei* China
27 C4 Qianjiang *Sichuan* China
30 E1 Qianjin China
26 A4 Qianning China
30 B1 Qianqihao China
30 B3 Qian Shan *mts* China
27 C5 Qianxi China
26 C3 Qian Xian China
27 D5 Qianyang *Hunan* China
26 C3 Qianyang *Shaanxi* China
27 F4 Qianyang *Zhejiang* China
26 D2 Qiaocun China
27 B5 Qiaojia China
17 K2 Qīās Iran
18 B5 Qibā' S. Arabia
59 G4 Qibing S. Africa
27 D5 Qidong *Hunan* China
26 F4 Qidong *Jiangsu* China
23 H2 Qidukou China
15 G3 Qiemo China
26 E2 Qihe China
27 C4 Qijiang China
12 L5 Qijiaojing China
19 G4 Qila Abdullah Pak.
19 F5 Qila Ladgasht Pak.
26 E1 Qilaotu Shan *mts* China
19 F4 Qila Safed Pak.
22 B3 Qila Saifullah Pak.
24 B3 Qilian Shan *mts* China
63 P3 Qillak *i.* Greenland
23 G1 Qimantag *mts* China
27 E4 Qimen China
26 D3 Qin *r.* China
26 B3 Qin'an China
30 C2 Qing *r.* China
30 B3 Qingchengzi China
26 F2 Qingdao China
26 A2 Qinghai *div.* China
26 A2 Qinghai Hu *salt l.* China
24 B3 Qinghai Nanshan *mts* China
28 A1 Qinghe China
30 C3 Qinghecheng China
26 D2 Qingjian China
26 F3 Qingjiang *Jiangsu* China
27 E4 Qingjiang *Jiangxi* China
27 D4 Qing Jiang *r.* China
27 E5 Qingliu China
27 B5 Qinglong *Guizhou* China
26 F1 Qinglong *Hebei* China
26 F2 Qinglong *r.* China
27 C6 Qingping China
26 F4 Qingpu China
26 C3 Qingshui China
26 D2 Qingshuihe China
27 F4 Qingtian China
26 E2 Qing Xian China
26 D2 Qingxu China
27 E4 Qingyang *Anhui* China
26 C2 Qingyang *Gansu* China
27 D6 Qingyuan *Guangdong* China
27 F5 Qingyuan *Zhejiang* China
30 C2 Qingyuan China
27 C5 Qingzhen China
26 F2 Qinhuangdao China
26 C3 Qin Ling *mts* China
26 C2 Qintongxia China
26 D2 Qin Xian China
26 D3 Qinyang China
26 D2 Qinyuan China
27 C6 Qinzhou China
27 C6 Qinzhou Wan *b.* China
27 D7 Qionghai China
27 B4 Qionglai China
26 B4 Qionglai Shan *mts* China
27 D7 Qiongshan China
27 C6 Qiongzhou Haixia *str.* China
24 E2 Qiqihar China
17 M5 Qīr Iran
18 D4 Qīr Iran
22 E1 Qira China
16 E6 Qiryat Gat Israel
16 F6 Qitab ash Shāmah *crater* S. Arabia
28 B2 Qitaihe China
27 B5 Qiubei China
26 F2 Qixia China
26 E3 Qi Xian *Henan* China
26 D2 Qi Xian *Shanxi* China
28 C1 Qixing *r.* China
27 D5 Qiyang China
26 C2 Qiying China
27 D7 Qizhou Liedao *i.* China
17 M2 Qızılağac Körfäzi *b.* Azer.
Qogir Feng *mt see* K2
26 C1 Qog Qi China
18 B2 Qojūr Iran
18 C3 Qom Iran
23 H3 Qomdo China
18 C3 Qomishēh Iran
Qomolangma Feng *mt see* Everest, Mt
17 M1 Qonaqkänd Azer.
18 C3 Qonāq, Kūh-e *h.* Iran
23 G3 Qonggyai China
26 C1 Qongi China
16 F4 Qornet es Saouda *mt* Lebanon
18 B3 Qorveh Iran
18 E5 Qoţbābād Iran
17 K2 Qoţūr Iran
81 G3 Quabbin Reservoir U.S.A.
74 D4 Quail Mts *mts* U.S.A.
43 F2 Quakenbrück Ger.
81 F4 Quakertown U.S.A.
65 K2 Quamarirjunq Lake *l.* Can.
8 D3 Quambatook Austr.
8 F1 Quambone Austr.
77 D5 Quanah U.S.A.
26 D3 Quanbao Shan *mt* China
32 D2 Quang Ngai Vietnam
32 C1 Quang Tri Vietnam
27 C6 Quang Yen Vietnam
27 E5 Quannan China
27 F5 Quanzhou *Fujian* China
27 D5 Quanzhou *Guangxi* China
65 J4 Qu'Appelle Can.
65 J4 Qu'Appelle *r.* Can.
91 F1 Quaraí Brazil
91 F1 Quaraí *r.* Brazil
27 □ Quarry Bay *H.K.* China
48 C5 Quartu Sant'Elena *Sardinia* Italy
74 D3 Quartzite Mt *mt* U.S.A.
75 E5 Quartzsite U.S.A.
64 D4 Quatsino Sound *in.* Can.
17 M1 Quba Azer.
19 E2 Quchan Iran
8 G3 Queanbeyan Austr.
67 F4 Québec Can.
63 L4 Quebec *div.* Can.
90 C2 Quebra Anzol *r.* Brazil
89 C2 Quebrada del Toro, Parque Nacional de la *nat. park* Venez.
91 B4 Quedal, C. *hd* Chile
43 K3 Quedlinburg Ger.
64 E4 Queen Bess, Mt *mt* Can.
64 C4 Queen Charlotte Can.
64 C4 Queen Charlotte Islands *is* Can.
64 D4 Queen Charlotte Sound *chan.* Can.
64 D4 Queen Charlotte Str. *chan.* Can.
63 H1 Queen Elizabeth Islands Can.
56 D3 Queen Elizabeth National Park *nat. park* Uganda
92 C5 Queen Mary Land *reg.* Ant.
62 H3 Queen Maud Gulf *b.* Can.
Queen Maud Land *reg. see* Dronning Maud Land
92 B4 Queen Maud Mts *mts* Ant.
6 E4 Queensland *div.* Austr.
6 E6 Queenstown Austr.
9 B6 Queenstown N.Z.
59 G5 Queenstown S. Africa
32 □ Queenstown Sing.
81 E5 Queenstown U.S.A.
72 A2 Queets U.S.A.
91 F2 Queguay Grande *r.* Uru.
91 D3 Quehué Arg.
87 H4 Queimada ou Serraria, Ilha *i.* Brazil
57 D5 Quelimane Moz.
88 B6 Quellón Chile
Quelpart Island *i. see* Cheju-do
75 H4 Quemado U.S.A.
91 B4 Quemchi Chile
91 D3 Quemú-Quemú Arg.
91 E3 Quequén Grande *r.* Arg.
90 B3 Querência do Norte Brazil
84 B2 Querétaro Mex.
84 C2 Querétaro *div.* Mex.
43 K3 Querfurt Ger.
26 E3 Queshan China
64 E4 Quesnel Can.
64 E4 Quesnel *r.* Can.
64 E4 Quesnel L. *l.* Can.
68 B1 Quetico Provincial Park *res.* Can.
22 A3 Quetta Pak.
91 B3 Queuco Chile
91 B3 Queule Chile
82 F6 Quezaltenango Guatemala
31 A4 Quezon Phil.
31 B3 Quezon City Phil.
26 E3 Qufu China
57 B5 Quibala Angola
57 B4 Quibaxe Angola
89 A3 Quibdó Col.
44 C3 Quiberon France
57 B4 Quicama, Parque Nacional do *nat. park* Angola
32 C1 Qui Châu Vietnam
75 F5 Quijotoa U.S.A.
91 D1 Quilino Arg.
44 F5 Quillan France
65 J4 Quill Lakes *l.* Can.
91 B2 Quillota Chile
91 E2 Quilmes Arg.
21 B4 Quilon India
6 E4 Quilpie Austr.
91 B2 Quilpué Chile
56 B4 Quimbele Angola
88 D3 Quimilí Arg.
44 B3 Quimper France
44 C3 Quimperlé France
86 D6 Quince Mil Peru
74 B2 Quincy *CA* U.S.A.
79 C6 Quincy *FL* U.S.A.
68 B6 Quincy *IL* U.S.A.
81 H3 Quincy *MA* U.S.A.
91 D2 Quines Arg.
32 D2 Qui Nhơn Vietnam
75 E3 Quinn Canyon Range *mts* U.S.A.
45 E3 Quintanar de la Orden Spain
91 B2 Quintero Chile
45 F2 Quinto Spain
91 D2 Quinto *r.* Arg.
57 E5 Quionga Moz.
57 B5 Quipungo Angola
91 B3 Quirihue Chile
57 B5 Quirima Angola
8 H1 Quirindi Austr.
91 E2 Quiroga Arg.
57 D6 Quissico Moz.
57 B5 Quitapa Angola
90 B2 Quitéria *r.* Brazil
79 D6 Quitman *GA* U.S.A.
79 B5 Quitman *MS* U.S.A.
86 C4 Quito Ecuador
73 D6 Quitovac Mex.
75 F4 Quivero U.S.A.
87 L4 Quixadá Brazil
27 D5 Qujiang China
27 C4 Qu Jiang *r.* China
27 D6 Qujie China
27 B5 Qujing China
17 L7 Qulbān Layyah *well* Iraq
19 H2 Qullai Garmo *mt* Tajik.
23 H2 Qumar He *r.* China
23 H2 Qumarlêb China
23 H2 Qumarrabdün China
23 H2 Qumaryan China
59 H5 Qumbu S. Africa
59 G6 Qumrha S. Africa
18 B6 Qunayy *well* S. Arabia
65 L2 Quoich *r.* Can.
40 C3 Quoich, Loch *l.* U.K.
41 F3 Quoile *r.* U.K.
58 C7 Quoin Pt *pt* S. Africa
23 E2 Quong Muztag *mt* China
58 F1 Quoxo *r.* Botswana
17 L3 Qurābeh Iran
19 E6 Qurayat Oman
19 H2 Qŭrghonteppa Tajik.
Qurlurtuuq *see* Coppermine
67 G2 Qurlutu *r.* Can.
17 K2 Qūrū Gol *pass* Iran
17 M1 Qusar Azer.
55 F2 Quseir Egypt
18 B2 Qūshchī Iran
17 L2 Qūsheh D. *mts* Iran
18 C3 Qūtīābād Iran
26 B2 Quwu Shan *mts* China
26 C4 Qu Xian China
23 G3 Qüxü China
32 C1 Quynh Lưu Vietnam
27 B6 Quynh Nhai Vietnam
69 J3 Quyon Can.
26 E2 Quzhou *Hebei* China
27 F4 Quzhou *Zhejiang* China
51 H7 Qvareli Georgia
Qyteti Stalin *see* Kuçovë

R

46 H7 Raab *r.* Austria
36 T4 Raahe Fin.
36 V5 Rääkkylä Fin.
42 E2 Raalte Neth.
36 T3 Raanujärvi Fin.
33 D4 Raas *i.* Indon.
40 B3 Raasay *i.* U.K.
40 B3 Raasay, Sound of *chan.* U.K.
56 F2 Raas Caseyr *c.* Somalia
33 E4 Raba Indon.
22 E2 Rabang China
48 F7 Rabat Malta
54 B1 Rabat Morocco
19 E3 Rabāt-e Kamah Iran
6 F2 Rabaul P.N.G.
64 D3 Rabbit *r.* Can.
20 A5 Rābigh S. Arabia
23 G5 Rabnabad Islands *is* Bangl.
51 D6 Râbniţa Moldova
18 E4 Rābor Iran
80 B5 Raccoon Creek *r.* U.S.A.
67 K4 Race, C. *c.* Can.
81 H3 Race Pt *pt* U.S.A.
16 E5 Rachaïya Lebanon
77 D7 Rachal U.S.A.
75 E3 Rachel U.S.A.
32 C3 Rach Gia Vietnam
46 J5 Racibórz Pol.
68 D4 Racine U.S.A.
69 F1 Racine Lake *l.* Can.
68 E2 Raco U.S.A.

47 M7 Rădăuţi Romania
78 C4 Radcliff U.S.A.
80 C6 Radford U.S.A.
22 B5 Radhanpur India
66 E3 Radisson Can.
64 F4 Radium Hot Springs Can.
49 L3 Radnevo Bulg.
47 K5 Radom Pol.
49 K3 Radomir Bulg.
55 E4 Radom National Park Sudan
47 J5 Radomsko Pol.
51 D5 Radomyshl' Ukr.
49 K4 Radoviš Macedonia
39 E6 Radstock U.K.
50 C4 Radun' Belarus
37 S9 Radviliškis Lith.
47 M5 Radyvyliv Ukr.
22 E4 Rae Bareli India
64 F2 Rae-Edzo Can.
64 F2 Rae Lakes Can.
9 E3 Raetihi N.Z.
91 E1 Rafaela Arg.
16 E6 Rafah Gaza
56 C3 Rafaï C.A.R.
20 B4 Rafhā S. Arabia
18 E4 Rafsanjān Iran
31 C5 Ragang, Mt *volc.* Phil.
31 B3 Ragay Gulf *b.* Phil.
43 L1 Rägelin Ger.
81 J3 Ragged I. *i.* U.S.A.
18 B4 Raghwah S. Arabia
43 L2 Ragösen Ger.
43 L3 Raguhn Ger.
48 F6 Ragusa *Sicily* Italy
26 A3 Ra'gyagoinba China
6 C2 Raha Indon.
50 D4 Rahachow Belarus
Rahaeng *see* Tak
43 G2 Rahden Ger.
17 J5 Rahhālīyah Iraq
21 A2 Rahimatpur India
22 B3 Rahimyar Khan Pak.
18 C3 Rāhjerd Iran
91 B3 Rahue *mt* Chile
21 A2 Rahuri India
19 F3 Rahzanak Afgh.
21 B2 Raichur India
23 G4 Raiganj India
23 E5 Raigarh India
75 E2 Railroad Valley *v.* U.S.A.
67 G3 Raimbault, Lac *l.* Can.
8 D3 Rainbow Austr.
75 G3 Rainbow Bridge Nat. Mon. *res.* U.S.A.
64 F3 Rainbow Lake Can.
80 C6 Rainelle U.S.A.
72 B2 Rainier, Mt *volc.* U.S.A.
22 B3 Raini N. *r.* Pak.
66 B4 Rainy *r.* U.S.A.
63 J5 Rainy Lake *l.* Can.
65 L5 Rainy River Can.
23 E5 Raipur *Madhya Pradesh* India
22 C4 Raipur *Rajasthan* India
37 S6 Raisio Fin.
42 B4 Raismes France
21 C2 Rajahmundry India
36 V2 Raja-Jooseppi Fin.
21 B3 Rajampet India
33 D2 Rajang *r.* Malaysia
21 B4 Rajapalaiyam India
21 A2 Rajapur India
22 C4 Rajasthan *div.* India
22 C3 Rajasthan Canal *canal* India
23 F4 Rajauli India
23 G5 Rajbari Bangl.
22 C3 Rajgarh *Rajasthan* India
22 D4 Rajgarh *Rajasthan* India
16 F6 Rajil, W. *watercourse* Jordan
23 E5 Rajim India
22 B5 Rajkot India
23 F4 Rajmahal India
23 F4 Rajmahal Hills *h.* India
22 E5 Raj Nandgaon India
22 D3 Rajpura India
23 G4 Rajshahi Bangl.
21 B2 Rajura India
23 F3 Raka China
5 L5 Rakahanga *i.* Pac. Oc.
9 C5 Rakaia *r.* N.Z.
22 C1 Rakaposhi *mt* Pak.
23 F3 Raka Zangbo *r.* China
51 C5 Rakhiv Ukr.
22 B3 Rakhni Pak.
19 G5 Rakhshan *r.* Pak.
51 E5 Rakitnoye *Belgorod. Obl.* Rus. Fed.
28 D2 Rakitnoye *Primorskiy Kray* Rus. Fed.
37 U7 Rakke Estonia
37 M7 Rakkestad Norway
22 B3 Rakni *r.* Pak.
37 U7 Rakvere Estonia
79 E5 Raleigh U.S.A.
4 H4 Ralik Chain *is* Marshall Is
68 D2 Ralph U.S.A.
64 E2 Ram *r.* Can.
67 H2 Ramah Can.
75 H4 Ramah U.S.A.
90 D1 Ramalho, Serra do *h.* Brazil
16 E6 Ramallah West Bank
21 B3 Ramanagaram India
21 B4 Ramanathapuram India
94 E3 Ramapo Deep *depth* Pac. Oc.
21 A3 Ramas, C. *c.* India
59 F2 Ramatlabama S. Africa
6 E2 Rambutyo I. *i.* P.N.G.
21 A3 Ramdurg India
39 C7 Rame Head *hd* U.K.
57 E5 Ramena Madag.
50 F3 Rameshki Rus. Fed.
21 B4 Rameswaram India
22 D4 Ramganga *r.* India
23 G5 Ramgarh Bangl.
23 F5 Ramgarh *Bihar* India
22 B4 Ramgarh *Rajasthan* India
18 C4 Rāmhormoz Iran
16 E7 Ram, Jebel *mt* Jordan
16 E6 Ramla Israel
Ramlat Rabyānah *des. see* Rebiana Sand Sea
Ramnad *see* Ramanathapuram
22 D3 Ramnagar India
49 M2 Râmnicu Sărat Romania
49 L2 Râmnicu Vâlcea Romania
74 D5 Ramona U.S.A.
69 G1 Ramore Can.
57 C6 Ramotswa Botswana
22 D3 Rampur India
22 C4 Rampura India
Rampur Boalia *see* Rajshahi
23 F4 Rampur Hat India
23 H6 Ramree I. *i.* Myanmar
36 P5 Ramsele Sweden
69 F2 Ramsey Can.
38 C3 Ramsey Isle of Man
39 G5 Ramsey *Eng.* U.K.
39 B6 Ramsey Island *i.* U.K.
69 F2 Ramsey Lake *l.* Can.
39 J6 Ramsgate U.K.
22 D5 Ramtek India
37 T9 Ramygala Lith.
89 C4 Rana, Co *h.* Col.
23 G5 Ranaghat India
22 C5 Ranapur India
33 E1 Ranau Malaysia
91 B2 Rancagua Chile
23 F5 Ranchi India
91 B4 Ranco, L. de *l.* Chile
8 F3 Rand Austr.
41 E3 Randalstown U.K.
48 F6 Randazzo *Sicily* Italy
37 M8 Randers Denmark
81 H3 Randolph *MA* U.S.A.
81 G3 Randolph *VT* U.S.A.
37 N5 Randsjö Sweden
36 S4 Råneå Sweden
9 C6 Ranfurly N.Z.
32 B4 Rangae Thai.
23 H5 Rangamati Bangl.
9 D1 Rangaunu Bay *b.* N.Z.
81 H2 Rangeley U.S.A.
81 H2 Rangeley Lake *l.* U.S.A.
75 H1 Rangely U.S.A.
69 F2 Ranger Lake Can.
9 D5 Rangiora N.Z.
5 N6 Rangiroa *i.* Pac. Oc.
9 F3 Rangitaiki *r.* N.Z.
9 C5 Rangitata *r.* N.Z.
9 E4 Rangitikei *r.* N.Z.
Rangoon *see* Yangon
23 G4 Rangpur Bangl.
21 A3 Ranibennur India
23 F5 Raniganj India
23 E5 Ranijula Peak *mt* India
22 B4 Ranipur Pak.
37 C6 Rankin U.S.A.
65 L2 Rankin Inlet Can.
65 L2 Rankin Inlet *in.* Can.
8 F2 Rankin's Springs Austr.
37 U7 Ranna Estonia
40 D4 Rannoch, L. *l.* U.K.
40 D4 Rannoch Moor *moorland* U.K.
22 B4 Rann of Kachchh *marsh* India
32 A3 Ranong Thai.
32 B4 Ranot Thai.
50 G4 Ranova *r.* Rus. Fed.
17 M5 Rānsa Iran
37 N6 Ransby Sweden
25 F7 Ransiki Indon.
37 V5 Rantasalmi Fin.
33 A2 Rantauprapat Indon.
68 C5 Rantoul U.S.A.
47 R2 Rantsevo Rus. Fed.
36 T4 Rantsila Fin.
36 U4 Ranua Fin.
17 K3 Rānya Iraq
28 C1 Raohe China
27 E6 Raoping China
5 K7 Raoul *i.* N.Z.
5 N7 Rapa *i.* Pac. Oc.
48 C2 Rapallo Italy
22 B5 Rapar India
19 E5 Rapch *watercourse* Iran
91 B2 Rapel *r.* Chile
63 M3 Raper, C. *pt* Can.
41 D3 Raphoe Rep. of Ireland
80 E5 Rapidan *r.* U.S.A.
8 B3 Rapid Bay Austr.
76 C2 Rapid City U.S.A.
69 H2 Rapide-Deux Can.
69 H2 Rapide-Sept Can.
68 D3 Rapid River U.S.A.
37 T7 Rapla Estonia
80 E5 Rappahannock *r.* U.S.A.
23 E4 Rapti *r.* India
22 B5 Rapur India
31 C3 Rapurapu *i.* Phil.
81 F2 Raquette *r.* U.S.A.
81 F3 Raquette Lake U.S.A.
81 F3 Raquette Lake *l.* U.S.A.
81 F4 Raritan Bay *b.* U.S.A.
5 M7 Rarotonga *i.* Pac. Oc.
31 A4 Rasa *i.* Phil.
20 E5 Ra's al Ḥadd *pt* Oman
18 D5 Ra's al Khaymah U.A.E.
91 D4 Rasa, Pta *pt* Arg.
56 D2 Ras Dashen *mt* Eth.
37 S9 Raseiniai Lith.
16 C6 Rashid Egypt
19 G4 Rashid Qala Afgh.
18 D3 Rashm Iran
18 C2 Rasht Iran
21 B4 Rasipuram India
19 F5 Rāsk Iran
22 C1 Raskam *mts* China
19 G4 Raskoh *mts* Pak.
55 F2 Ras Muhammad *c.* Egypt
63 J3 Rasmussen Basin *b.* Can.
88 C6 Raso, C. *pt* Arg.
50 D4 Rasony Belarus
23 E4 Rasra India
48 D6 Rass Jebel Tunisia
50 G4 Rasskazovo Rus. Fed.
20 D4 Ras Tannūrah S. Arabia
43 G1 Rastede Ger.
43 K1 Rastow Ger.
18 D5 Rasūl *watercourse* Iran
4 J3 Ratak Chain *is* Marshall Is
37 O5 Rätan Sweden
59 H3 Ratanda S. Africa
22 C3 Ratangarh India
22 C5 Ratanpur India
37 O5 Rätansbyn Sweden
32 A2 Rat Buri Thai.
22 D4 Rath India
41 E4 Rathangan Rep. of Ireland
41 D5 Rathdowney Rep. of Ireland
41 E5 Rathdrum Rep. of Ireland
23 H5 Rathedaung Myanmar
43 L2 Rathenow Ger.
41 E3 Rathfriland U.K.
41 C5 Rathkeale Rep. of Ireland
41 E2 Rathlin Island *i.* U.K.
41 C5 Rathluirc Rep. of Ireland
42 E3 Ratingen Ger.
22 C3 Ratiya India
22 C5 Ratlam India
21 A2 Ratnagiri India
21 C5 Ratnapura Sri Lanka
51 C5 Ratne Ukr.
22 B4 Rato Dero Pak.
73 F4 Raton U.S.A.
40 G3 Rattray Head *hd* U.K.
37 O6 Rättvik Sweden
43 J1 Ratzeburg Ger.
64 C3 Ratz, Mt *mt* Can.
32 B5 Raub Malaysia
91 E3 Rauch Arg.
17 L7 Raudhatain Kuwait
43 K4 Rauenstein Ger.
36 F3 Raufarhöfn Iceland
9 G2 Raukumara *mt* N.Z.
9 F3 Raukumara Range *mts* N.Z.
37 R6 Rauma Fin.
23 F5 Raurkela India
28 J2 Rausu Japan
36 V5 Rautavaara Fin.
37 V6 Rautjärvi Fin.
72 D2 Ravalli U.S.A.
17 L4 Ravānsar Iran
18 E4 Rāvar Iran
42 C3 Ravels Belgium
81 G3 Ravena U.S.A.
38 D3 Ravenglass U.K.
48 E2 Ravenna Italy
46 D7 Ravensburg Ger.
80 C5 Ravenswood U.S.A.
22 C3 Ravi *r.* Pak.
19 F2 Ravnina Turkm.
19 F2 Ravnina Turkm.
17 H4 Rāwah Iraq
5 K5 Rawaki *i.* Kiribati
22 C2 Rawalpindi Pak.
17 K3 Rawāndiz Iraq
22 C3 Rawatsar India
46 H5 Rawicz Pol.
80 D5 Rawley Springs U.S.A.
72 F3 Rawlins U.S.A.
88 C6 Rawson Arg.
23 F4 Raxaul India
21 B3 Rayachoti India
21 B3 Rāyadurg India
21 C2 Rāyagarha India
16 F5 Rayak Lebanon
67 J4 Ray, C. *hd* Can.
24 E2 Raychikhinsk Rus. Fed.
39 H6 Rayleigh U.K.
64 G5 Raymond Can.
81 H3 Raymond *NH* U.S.A.
72 B2 Raymond *WA* U.S.A.
8 H2 Raymond Terrace Austr.
77 D7 Raymondville U.S.A.
32 B2 Rayong Thai.
80 D4 Raystown Lake *l.* U.S.A.
18 C3 Razan Iran
17 M5 Rāzān Iran
Razdan *see* Hrazdan
28 B3 Razdol'noye Rus. Fed.
18 C3 Razeh Iran
49 M3 Razgrad Bulg.
49 N2 Razim, Lacul *lag.* Romania
49 K4 Razlog Bulg.
44 B2 Raz, Pte du *pt* France
39 G6 Reading U.K.
81 F4 Reading U.S.A.
68 B4 Readstown U.S.A.
59 G2 Reagile S. Africa
91 D2 Realicó Arg.
44 F5 Réalmont France
32 B2 Reăng Kesei Cambodia
84 B1 Reata Mex.
42 B6 Rebais France
55 E2 Rebiana Sand Sea *des.* Libya
50 D2 Reboly Rus. Fed.
28 G2 Rebun-tō *i.* Japan
6 C5 Recherche, Archipelago of the *is* Austr.
22 C3 Rechna Doab *lowland* Pak.
51 D4 Rechytsa Belarus
87 M5 Recife Brazil
59 F7 Recife, Cape *c.* S. Africa
42 F3 Recklinghausen Ger.
88 E3 Reconquista Arg.
88 C3 Recreo Arg.
65 K5 Red *r.* Can./U.S.A.
77 E6 Red *r.* U.S.A.
32 B4 Redang *i.* Malaysia
81 F4 Red Bank *NJ* U.S.A.
79 C5 Red Bank *TN* U.S.A.
67 J3 Red Bay Can.
74 A1 Red Bluff U.S.A.
75 F4 Red Butte *summit* U.S.A.
38 F3 Redcar U.K.
65 G4 Redcliff Can.
8 D3 Red Cliffs Austr.
76 D3 Red Cloud U.S.A.
64 G4 Red Deer *Alta.* Can.
65 G4 Red Deer *r. Alta.* Can.
65 J4 Red Deer *r. Sask.* Can.
65 J4 Red Deer L. *l.* Can.
81 F5 Redden U.S.A.
59 G4 Reddersburg S. Africa
72 B3 Redding U.S.A.
39 F5 Redditch U.K.
81 F3 Redfield *NY* U.S.A.
76 D2 Redfield *SD* U.S.A.
8 B2 Redhill Austr.
75 H4 Red Hill U.S.A.
77 D4 Red Hills *h.* U.S.A.
67 J4 Red Indian L. *l.* Can.
68 E5 Redkey U.S.A.
75 E4 Red L. *l.* U.S.A.
65 L4 Red L. *l.* Can.
65 L4 Red Lake Can.
76 E1 Red Lakes *l.* U.S.A.
72 E2 Red Lodge U.S.A.
72 B2 Redmond U.S.A.
76 E3 Red Oak U.S.A.
45 C3 Redondo Port.
68 C1 Red Rock Can.
81 E4 Red Rock U.S.A.
52 H3 Red Sea *sea* Africa/Asia
64 E4 Redstone Can.
64 D2 Redstone *r.* Can.
65 L4 Red Sucker L. *l.* Can.
64 G4 Redwater Can.
67 H3 Red Wine *r.* Can.
68 A3 Red Wing U.S.A.
74 A3 Redwood City U.S.A.
76 E2 Redwood Falls U.S.A.
72 B3 Redwood Nat. Park U.S.A.
72 A2 Redwood Valley U.S.A.
68 E4 Reed City U.S.A.
74 C3 Reedley U.S.A.
68 C4 Reedsburg U.S.A.
72 A3 Reedsport U.S.A.
81 E6 Reedville U.S.A.
92 B4 Reedy Gl. *gl.* Ant.
9 C5 Reefton N.Z.
41 D4 Ree, Lough *l.* Rep. of Ireland
42 E3 Rees Ger.
16 G2 Refahiye Turkey
77 D6 Refugio U.S.A.
46 F6 Regen Ger.
43 L5 Regen *r.* Ger.
43 L5 Regensburg Ger.
43 L5 Regenstauf Ger.
54 C2 Reggane Alg.
48 F5 Reggio di Calabria Italy
48 D2 Reggio nell'Emilia Italy
47 M7 Reghin Romania
65 J4 Regina Can.
19 G4 Registan *reg.* Afgh.
36 W4 Regozero Rus. Fed.
43 L4 Rehau Ger.
43 H2 Rehburg Ger.
22 D5 Rehli India
43 K1 Rehna Ger.
57 B6 Rehoboth Namibia
75 H4 Rehoboth U.S.A.
81 F5 Rehoboth Bay *b.* U.S.A.
81 F5 Rehoboth Beach U.S.A.
16 E6 Rehovot Israel
43 L3 Reibitz Ger.
43 L4 Reichenbach Ger.
43 F6 Reichshoffen France
79 E4 Reidsville U.S.A.
39 G6 Reigate U.K.
44 D3 Ré, Île de *i.* France
75 G5 Reiley Peak *summit* U.S.A.
44 G2 Reims France
88 B8 Reina Adelaida, Archipiélago de la *is* Chile
68 A4 Reinbeck U.S.A.
43 J1 Reinbek Ger.
65 J3 Reindeer *r.* Can.
65 K4 Reindeer I. *i.* Can.
65 J3 Reindeer Lake *l.* Can.
36 N3 Reine Norway
43 J1 Reinfeld (Holstein) Ger.
9 D1 Reinga, Cape *c.* N.Z.
45 D1 Reinosa Spain
42 E5 Reinsfeld Ger.
36 B4 Reipholsfjöll *mt* Iceland
36 R2 Reisaelva *r.* Norway
36 S2 Reisa Nasjonalpark *nat. park* Norway
36 T5 Reisjärvi Fin.
59 H3 Reitz S. Africa
58 F3 Reivilo S. Africa
42 F3 Reken Ger.
65 H2 Reliance Can.
54 C1 Relizane Alg.
43 H1 Rellingen Ger.
42 F4 Remagen Ger.
8 B2 Remarkable, Mt Austr.
19 E5 Remeshk Iran
58 B1 Remhoogte Pass Namibia
46 C6 Remiremont France
22 D2 Remo Gl. *gl.* India
51 G6 Remontnoye Rus. Fed.
42 F3 Remscheid Ger.
68 E4 Remus U.S.A.
37 M6 Rena Norway
21 B2 Renapur India
78 B4 Rend L. *l.* U.S.A.
7 F2 Rendova *i.* Solomon Is
46 D3 Rendsburg Ger.
69 J3 Renfrew Can.
40 D5 Renfrew U.K.
91 B2 Rengo Chile
26 C3 Ren He *r.* China
26 E4 Renheji China
27 D5 Renhua China
27 C5 Renhuai China
51 D6 Reni Ukr.
Renland *reg. see* Tuttut Nunaat
8 C3 Renmark Austr.
7 G3 Rennell *i.* Solomon Is
43 G4 Rennerod Ger.
44 D2 Rennes France
92 B5 Rennick Gl. *gl.* Ant.
65 H2 Rennie Lake *l.* Can.
74 C2 Reno U.S.A.
48 D2 Reno *r.* Italy
80 E4 Renovo U.S.A.
26 E2 Renqiu China
27 B4 Renshou China
68 D5 Rensselaer *IN* U.S.A.
81 G3 Rensselaer *NY* U.S.A.
42 D2 Renswoude Neth.
72 B2 Renton U.S.A.
23 E4 Renukut India
9 D4 Renwick N.Z.
54 B3 Réo Burkina
25 E7 Reo Indon.
19 F2 Repetek Turkm.
72 C1 Republic U.S.A.
76 D3 Republican *r.* U.S.A.
63 K3 Repulse Bay Can.
86 D5 Requena Peru
45 F3 Requena Spain
16 F1 Reşadiye Turkey
17 J2 Reşadiye Turkey
90 B4 Reserva Brazil
18 C2 Reshteh-ye Alborz *mts* Iran
18 E2 Reshteh-ye Esfarayen *mts* Iran
88 E3 Resistencia Arg.
49 J2 Reşiţa Romania
63 J2 Resolute Can.
63 M3 Resolution Island *i. N.W.T.* Can.
9 A6 Resolution Island *i.* N.Z.
84 E4 Retalhuleu Guatemala
32 Retan Laut, P. *i.* Sing.
39 G4 Retford U.K.
44 G2 Rethel France
43 H2 Rethem (Aller) Ger.
49 L7 Rethymno Greece
28 C2 Rettikhovka Rus. Fed.
43 L2 Reuden Ger.
53 K8 Réunion *terr.* Ind. Ocean
45 G2 Reus Spain
43 L1 Reuterstadt Stavenhagen Ger.
46 D6 Reutlingen Ger.
74 D3 Reveille Peak *summit* U.S.A.
44 F5 Revel France
64 F4 Revelstoke Can.
64 C3 Revillagigedo I. *i.* U.S.A.
82 B5 Revillagigedo, Islas *is* Mex.
42 C5 Revin France
16 E6 Revivim Israel
22 E4 Rewa India
22 D3 Rewari India
72 E3 Rexburg U.S.A.
67 H4 Rexton Can.
74 C4 Reyes Peak *summit* U.S.A.
74 A2 Reyes, Point *pt* U.S.A.
16 F3 Reyhanlı Turkey
36 C4 Reykir Iceland
96 G2 Reykjanes Ridge *sea feature* Atl. Ocean
36 B5 Reykjanestá *pt* Iceland
36 C4 Reykjavík Iceland
84 C1 Reynosa Mex.
37 U8 Rēzekne Latvia
17 M3 Rezvanshahr Iran
16 F5 Rharaz, W. *watercourse* Syria
39 D5 Rhayader U.K.
43 G3 Rheda-Wiedenbrück Ger.
42 E3 Rhede Ger.
Rhein *r.* Ger./Switz. *see* Rhine
42 F2 Rheine Ger.
42 E4 Rheinisches Schiefergebirge *h.* Ger.
42 F5 Rheinland-Pfalz *div.* Ger.
43 L1 Rheinsberg Ger.
43 G6 Rheinstetten Ger.
Rhin *r.* France *see* Rhine
46 C5 Rhine *r.* Europe
81 G4 Rhinebeck U.S.A.
68 C3 Rhinelander U.S.A.
43 L2 Rhinkanal *canal* Ger.
43 L2 Rhinluch *marsh* Ger.
43 L2 Rhinow Ger.
48 C2 Rho Italy
81 H4 Rhode Island *div.* U.S.A.
49 N6 Rhodes Greece
49 N6 Rhodes *i.* Greece
72 D2 Rhodes Pk *summit* U.S.A.
39 D6 Rhondda U.K.
44 G4 Rhône *r.* France/Switz.
39 D4 Rhyl U.K.
90 E2 Riacho Brazil
90 D1 Riacho de Santana Brazil
91 D4 Riachos, Is de los *i.* Arg.
90 C1 Rialma Brazil
90 C1 Rianópolis Brazil
22 C2 Riasi Jammu and Kashmir
33 B2 Riau, Kepulauan *is* Indon.
45 C1 Ribadeo Spain
45 D1 Ribadesella Spain
90 B3 Ribas do Rio Pardo Brazil
57 D5 Ribáuè Moz.
38 E4 Ribble *r.* U.K.
37 L9 Ribe Denmark
42 A5 Ribécourt-Dreslincourt France
90 C4 Ribeira *r.* Brazil
90 C3 Ribeirão Preto Brazil
42 B5 Ribemont France
44 E4 Ribérac France
86 E6 Riberalta Bol.
46 F3 Ribnitz-Damgarten Ger.
46 G6 Říčany Czech Rep.
75 E4 Rice U.S.A.
68 B3 Rice Lake U.S.A.
69 F2 Rice Lake *l.* Can.
68 A4 Riceville *IA* U.S.A.
80 D4 Riceville *PA* U.S.A.
59 K4 Richards Bay S. Africa
77 D5 Richardson U.S.A.
65 G3 Richardson *r.* Can.
81 H2 Richardson Lakes *l.* U.S.A.
62 E3 Richardson Mts *N.W.T.* Can.
9 B6 Richardson Mts *mts* N.Z.
75 F2 Richfield U.S.A.
81 F3 Richfield Springs U.S.A.
81 E3 Richford *NY* U.S.A.
81 G2 Richford *VT* U.S.A.
70 C2 Richland *WA* U.S.A.
68 B5 Richland U.S.A.
68 B4 Richland Center U.S.A.
80 C6 Richlands U.S.A.
8 H2 Richmond *N.S.W.* Austr.
6 E4 Richmond Austr.
69 K3 Richmond Can.
9 D4 Richmond N.Z.
59 J4 Richmond *Kwazulu-Natal* S. Africa
58 E5 Richmond *Northern Cape* S. Africa
38 F3 Richmond U.K.
68 E6 Richmond *IN* U.S.A.
80 A6 Richmond *KY* U.S.A.
81 J2 Richmond *ME* U.S.A.
69 F4 Richmond *MI* U.S.A.
80 E6 Richmond *VA* U.S.A.
81 G2 Richmond *VT* U.S.A.
69 H4 Richmond Hill Can.
9 D4 Richmond, Mt *mt* N.Z.
58 B4 Richtersveld National Park S. Africa
80 B4 Richwood *OH* U.S.A.
80 C5 Richwood *WV* U.S.A.
69 K3 Rideau *r.* Can.
69 J3 Rideau Lakes *l.* Can.
74 D4 Ridgecrest U.S.A.
80 D4 Ridgway U.S.A.
65 J4 Riding Mountain Nat. Park Can.
46 D6 Riedlingen Ger.
42 D4 Riemst Belgium
43 M3 Riesa Ger.
88 B8 Riesco, Isla *i.* Chile
58 D5 Riet *r.* S. Africa
37 R9 Rietavas Lith.
58 E6 Rietbron S. Africa
58 D3 Rietfontein S. Africa
48 E3 Rieti Italy
73 F4 Rifle U.S.A.
36 E3 Rifstangi *pt* Iceland
23 H3 Riga India
37 T8 Rīga Latvia
37 S8 Riga, Gulf of *g.* Estonia/Latvia
19 E4 Rīgān Iran
Rīgas Jūras Līcis *g. see* Riga, Gulf of
81 F2 Rigaud Can.
72 C2 Riggins U.S.A.
67 J3 Rigolet Can.
40 E5 Rigside U.K.
18 E3 Rīgū Iran
23 E4 Rihand *r.* India
23 E4 Rihand Dam *dam* India
Riia Laht *g. see* Riga, Gulf of
37 T6 Riihimäki Fin.
92 D4 Riiser-Larsenhalvøya *pen.* Ant.
92 C3 Riiser-Larsenisen *ice feature* Ant.
92 D3 Riiser-Larsen Sea *sea* Ant.
73 D5 Riito Mex.
48 F2 Rijeka Croatia
Rijn *r.* Neth. *see* Rhine
28 G5 Rikuzen-takata Japan
49 K3 Rila *mts* Bulg.
72 C3 Riley U.S.A.
44 G4 Rillieux-la-Pape France
47 K6 Rimavská Sobota Slovakia
64 G4 Rimbey Can.
48 E2 Rimini Italy
67 G4 Rimouski Can.
43 H5 Rimpar Ger.
40 D2 Rimsdale, Loch *l.* U.K.
23 G3 Rinbung China
84 B2 Rincón de Romos Mex.
22 E4 Rind *r.* India
36 L5 Rindal Norway
22 C4 Ringas India
23 G2 Ring Co *salt l.* China
42 E2 Ringe Ger.
37 M6 Ringebu Norway
37 L8 Ringkøbing Denmark
41 E2 Ringsend U.K.
37 M9 Ringsted Denmark
36 Q2 Ringvassøy *i.* Norway
39 F7 Ringwood U.K.
91 B3 Riñihue Chile
91 B3 Riñihue, L. *l.* Chile
33 E4 Rinjani, G. *volc.* Indon.
43 H2 Rinteln Ger.
68 C4 Rio U.S.A.
90 A2 Rio Alegre Brazil
86 C4 Riobamba Ecuador
75 H2 Rio Blanco U.S.A.
86 E6 Rio Branco Brazil
90 C4 Rio Branco do Sul Brazil
89 E4 Rio Branco, Parque Nacional do *nat. park* Brazil
90 A3 Rio Brilhante Brazil
91 B4 Rio Bueno Chile
89 E2 Río Caribe Venez.
91 D1 Río Ceballos Arg.
90 C3 Rio Claro Brazil
89 E2 Rio Claro Trinidad and Tobago
91 D3 Río Colorado Arg.
91 D2 Río Cuarto Arg.
90 D3 Rio de Janeiro Brazil
90 D3 Rio de Janeiro *div.* Brazil
88 G3 Rio do Sul Brazil
88 C8 Río Gallegos Arg.
88 C8 Río Grande Arg.
91 G2 Rio Grande Brazil
84 B2 Río Grande Mex.
86 F7 Río Grande *r.* Bol.
82 C2 Rio Grande *r.* Mex./U.S.A.
77 D7 Rio Grande City U.S.A.
96 G7 Rio Grande Rise *sea feature* Atl. Ocean
89 B2 Ríohacha Col.
86 C5 Rioja Peru
87 L5 Rio Largo Brazil
44 F4 Riom France
86 E7 Río Mulatos Bol.
90 C4 Rio Negro Brazil
91 C4 Río Negro *div.* Arg.
91 F2 Río Negro, Embalse del *resr* Uru.
51 G7 Rioni *r.* Georgia
91 G1 Rio Pardo Brazil
90 D1 Rio Pardo de Minas Brazil
91 D1 Río Primero Arg.
73 F5 Rio Rancho U.S.A.
75 G6 Rio Rico U.S.A.
91 D1 Río Segundo Arg.
89 A3 Ríosucio Col.
91 D2 Río Tercero Arg.
86 C4 Río Tigre Ecuador
31 A4 Rio Tuba Phil.
90 B2 Rio Verde Brazil
84 C2 Río Verde Mex.
90 A2 Rio Verde de Mato Grosso Brazil
74 B2 Rio Vista U.S.A.
90 A2 Riozinho *r.* Brazil
47 P5 Ripky Ukr.
38 F3 Ripley *Eng.* U.K.
39 F4 Ripley *Eng.* U.K.
80 B5 Ripley *OH* U.S.A.
79 B5 Ripley *TN* U.S.A.
80 C5 Ripley *WV* U.S.A.
45 H1 Ripoll Spain
38 F3 Ripon U.K.
74 B3 Ripon *CA* U.S.A.
68 C4 Ripon *WV* U.S.A.
39 D6 Risca U.K.
18 C4 Rīshahr Iran
28 G2 Rishiri-tō *i.* Japan
16 E6 Rishon Le Ziyyon Israel
19 F5 Rish Pish Iran
37 L7 Risør Norway
36 L5 Rissa Norway
37 U6 Ristiina Fin.
36 V4 Ristijärvi Fin.
36 W2 Ristikent Rus. Fed.
58 F4 Ritchie S. Africa
36 P3 Ritsem Sweden
43 G1 Ritterhude Ger.
73 C4 Ritter, Mt *mt* U.S.A.
45 E2 Rituerto *r.* Spain
72 C2 Ritzville U.S.A.
91 C2 Rivadavia *Mendoza* Arg.
91 D2 Rivadavia *Pampas* Arg.
88 D2 Rivadavia *Salta* Arg.
91 B1 Rivadavia Chile
48 D2 Riva del Garda Italy
83 G6 Rivas Nic.
19 E3 Rīvash Iran
91 D3 Rivera Arg.
91 F1 Rivera Uru.
54 B4 River Cess Liberia
81 G4 Riverhead U.S.A.
8 E3 Riverina *reg.* Austr.
58 D7 Riversdale S. Africa
59 H5 Riverside S. Africa
74 D5 Riverside U.S.A.
8 B3 Riverton Austr.
65 K4 Riverton Can.
9 B7 Riverton N.Z.
72 E3 Riverton U.S.A.
67 H4 Riverview Can.
44 F5 Rivesaltes France
79 D7 Riviera Beach U.S.A.
81 J1 Rivière Bleue Can.
67 G4 Rivière-du-Loup Can.
51 C5 Rivne Ukr.
9 D4 Riwaka N.Z.
20 C5 Riyadh S. Arabia
26 A2 Riyue Shankou *pass* China
18 D3 Riza *well* Iran
17 H1 Rize Turkey
26 F3 Rizhao China
16 E4 Rizokarpason Cyprus
18 E4 Rīzū'īyeh Iran
37 L7 Rjukan Norway
37 K7 Rjuvbrokkene *mt* Norway
54 A3 Rkîz Maur.
22 D3 Rnyar *r.* India
37 M6 Roa Norway
39 G5 Roade U.K.
36 M4 Roan Norway
75 H2 Roan Cliffs *cliff* U.S.A.
44 G3 Roanne France
79 C5 Roanoke *AL* U.S.A.
68 C5 Roanoke *IL* U.S.A.
80 D6 Roanoke *VA* U.S.A.
78 E4 Roanoke *r. VA* U.S.A.
79 E4 Roanoke Rapids U.S.A.
75 H2 Roan Plateau *plat.* U.S.A.
41 B6 Roaringwater Bay *b.* Rep. of Ireland
36 R5 Röbäck Sweden
18 E4 Robāţ Iran
19 F4 Robat *r.* Afgh.
18 E3 Robāţ-e Khān Iran
19 F4 Robat Thana Pak.
6 E6 Robbins I. *i.* Austr.
8 B4 Robe Austr.
41 B4 Robe *r.* Rep. of Ireland
43 L1 Röbel Ger.
8 C1 Robe, Mt *h.* Austr.
77 C6 Robert Lee U.S.A.
72 D3 Roberts U.S.A.
74 D2 Roberts Creek Mt *mt* U.S.A.
36 R4 Robertsfors Sweden
23 E4 Robertsganj India
77 E5 Robert S. Kerr Res. *resr* U.S.A.
58 C6 Robertson S. Africa
92 B2 Robertson I. *i.* Ant.
54 A4 Robertsport Liberia
8 B2 Robertstown Austr.
67 F4 Roberval Can.
63 M1 Robeson Channel *chan.* Can./Greenland
38 G3 Robin Hood's Bay U.K.
27 Robin's Nest *h. H.K.* China
78 C4 Robinson U.S.A.
95 O8 Robinson Crusoe *i.* Pac. Oc.
6 B4 Robinson Ranges *h.* Austr.
8 D3 Robinvale Austr.
75 G5 Robles Junction U.S.A.
75 G5 Robles Pass U.S.A.
65 J4 Roblin Can.
64 F4 Robson, Mt *mt* Can.
77 D7 Robstown U.S.A.
84 D3 Roca Partida, Pta *hd* Mex.
48 E6 Rocca Busambra *mt Sicily* Italy
91 F2 Rocha Uru.
38 E4 Rochdale U.K.
90 A2 Rochedo Brazil
42 D4 Rochefort Belgium
44 D4 Rochefort France
66 F2 Rochefort, Lac *l.* Can.
50 G2 Rochegda Rus. Fed.
68 C5 Rochelle U.S.A.
8 E4 Rochester Austr.
39 H6 Rochester U.K.
68 D5 Rochester *IN* U.S.A.
68 A3 Rochester *MN* U.S.A.
81 H3 Rochester *NH* U.S.A.
80 E3 Rochester *NY* U.S.A.
39 H6 Rochford U.K.
43 L3 Rochlitz Ger.
44 C2 Roc'h Trévezel *h.* France
64 D2 Rock *r.* Can.
68 B5 Rock *r.* U.S.A.
96 H2 Rockall Bank *sea feature* Atl. Ocean
92 B4 Rockefeller Plateau *plat.* Ant.
68 C4 Rockford U.S.A.
65 H5 Rockglen Can.
6 F4 Rockhampton Austr.
68 C1 Rock Harbor U.S.A.
79 D5 Rock Hill U.S.A.
6 B5 Rockingham Austr.
79 E5 Rockingham U.S.A.
81 G2 Rock Island Can.
68 B5 Rock Island U.S.A.
76 D1 Rocklake U.S.A.
81 F2 Rockland Can.
81 H3 Rockland *MA* U.S.A.
81 J2 Rockland *ME* U.S.A.
68 C2 Rockland *MI* U.S.A.
8 D4 Rocklands Reservoir Austr.
75 H3 Rock Point U.S.A.
81 H3 Rockport U.S.A.
76 D3 Rock Rapids U.S.A.
72 F2 Rock Springs *MT* U.S.A.
72 E3 Rock Springs *WY* U.S.A.
77 C6 Rocksprings U.S.A.
8 F3 Rock, The Austr.
80 D3 Rockton Can.
68 D6 Rockville *IN* U.S.A.
80 E5 Rockville *MD* U.S.A.
81 J2 Rockwood U.S.A.
73 G4 Rocky Ford U.S.A.
80 B5 Rocky Fork Lake *l.* U.S.A.
69 F2 Rocky Island Lake *l.* Can.
79 E5 Rocky Mount *NC* U.S.A.
80 D6 Rocky Mount *VA* U.S.A.
64 G4 Rocky Mountain House Can.
72 F3 Rocky Mountain Nat. Park U.S.A.
60 E4 Rocky Mountains Can./U.S.A.
64 F4 Rocky Mountains Forest Reserve *res.* Can.
42 B5 Rocourt-St-Martin France
42 C5 Rocroi France
37 L6 Rodberg Norway
37 M9 Rødbyhavn Denmark
67 J3 Roddickton Can.
40 B3 Rodel U.K.
42 E1 Roden Neth.
43 K4 Rödental Ger.
91 C1 Rodeo Arg.
84 A1 Rodeo Mex.
75 H6 Rodeo U.S.A.
44 F4 Rodez France
43 L5 Roding Ger.
19 G5 Rodkhan Pak.
50 G3 Rodniki Rus. Fed.
49 L4 Rodopi Planina *mts* Bulg./Greece
Rodos *see* Rhodes
Rodos *i. see* Rhodes
93 J5 Rodrigues *i.* Ind. Ocean
93 J5 Rodrigues Fracture *sea feature* Ind. Ocean
6 B4 Roebourne Austr.
6 C3 Roebuck Bay *b.* Austr.
59 H2 Roedtan S. Africa
42 D3 Roermond Neth.
42 B4 Roeselare Belgium
63 K3 Roes Welcome Sound *chan.* Can.
86 E6 Rogaguado, Lago *l.* Bol.
43 K2 Rogätz Ger.
77 E4 Rogers U.S.A.
69 F3 Rogers City U.S.A.
74 D4 Rogers Lake *l.* U.S.A.
72 D3 Rogerson U.S.A.
80 B6 Rogersville U.S.A.
66 E3 Roggan *r.* Can.
58 D6 Roggeveld *plat.* S. Africa
58 D6 Roggeveldberge *esc.* S. Africa
36 O3 Rognan Norway
72 A3 Rogue *r.* U.S.A.
74 A2 Rohnert Park U.S.A.
46 F6 Rohrbach in Oberösterreich Austria
42 F5 Rohrbach-lès-Bitche France
22 B4 Rohri Pak.
22 D3 Rohtak India
5 N6 Roi Georges, Îles du *is* Pac. Oc.
42 B5 Roisel France
37 S8 Roja Latvia
91 E2 Rojas Arg.
22 B3 Rojhan Pak.
84 C2 Rojo, C. *c.* Mex.
33 B2 Rokan *r.* Indon.
37 T9 Rokiškis Lith.
36 R4 Roknäs Sweden
51 C5 Rokytne Ukr.
23 G2 Rola Co *salt l.* China
90 B3 Rolândia Brazil
76 F4 Rolla U.S.A.
37 L6 Rollag Norway
9 D5 Rolleston N.Z.
69 H2 Rollet Can.
79 F7 Rolleville Bahamas
69 J2 Rolphton Can.
6 E4 Roma Austr.
Roma *see* Rome
59 G4 Roma Lesotho
37 Q8 Roma Sweden
25 E7 Roma *i.* Indon.
79 E5 Romain, Cape *c.* U.S.A.
67 H3 Romaine *r.* Can.
47 N7 Roman Romania

57 D5 **Salimo** Moz.
76 D4 **Salina** *KS* U.S.A.
75 G2 **Salina** *UT* U.S.A.
84 D3 **Salina Cruz** Mex.
91 D4 **Salina Gualicho** *salt flat* Arg.
48 F5 **Salina, Isola** *i.* Italy
91 C2 **Salina Llancanelo** *salt flat* Arg.
90 D2 **Salinas** Brazil
86 B4 **Salinas** Ecuador
84 B2 **Salinas** Mex.
74 B3 **Salinas** *CA* U.S.A.
74 B3 **Salinas** *r. CA* U.S.A.
88 C4 **Salinas Grandes** *salt flat* Arg.
73 F5 **Salinas Peak** *summit* U.S.A.
77 E5 **Saline** *r. AR* U.S.A.
76 C4 **Saline** *r. KS* U.S.A.
45 H3 **Salines, Cap de ses** *pt* Spain
74 D3 **Saline Valley** *v.* U.S.A.
87 J4 **Salinópolis** Brazil
86 C6 **Salinosó Lachay, Pta** *pt* Peru
39 F6 **Salisbury** U.K.
81 F5 **Salisbury** *MD* U.S.A.
79 D5 **Salisbury** *NC* U.S.A.
39 E6 **Salisbury Plain** *plain* U.K.
87 K6 **Salitre** *r.* Brazil
16 F5 **Şalkhad** Syria
23 F5 **Salki** *r.* India
36 V3 **Salla** Fin.
91 D3 **Salliqueló** Arg.
77 E5 **Sallisaw** U.S.A.
63 L3 **Salluit** Can.
23 E3 **Sallyana** Nepal
18 B2 **Salmās** Iran
50 D2 **Salmi** Rus. Fed.
64 F5 **Salmo** Can.
72 D2 **Salmon** U.S.A.
72 D2 **Salmon** *r.* U.S.A.
64 F4 **Salmon Arm** Can.
81 F3 **Salmon Reservoir** *resr* U.S.A.
72 D2 **Salmon River Mountains** U.S.A.
42 E5 **Salmtal** Ger.
37 S6 **Salo** Fin.
23 E4 **Salon** India
44 G5 **Salon-de-Provence** France
56 C4 **Salonga Nord, Parc National de la** *nat. park* Congo(Zaire)
56 C4 **Salonga Sud, Parc National de la** *nat. park* Congo(Zaire)
47 K7 **Salonta** Romania
91 D1 **Salsacate** Arg.
51 G6 **Sal'sk** Rus. Fed.
48 C2 **Salsomaggiore Terme** Italy
16 E5 **Salt** Jordan
75 G5 **Salt** *r. AZ* U.S.A.
68 B6 **Salt** *r. MO* U.S.A.
58 E5 **Salt** *watercourse* S. Africa
88 C2 **Salta** Arg.
39 C7 **Saltash** U.K.
40 D5 **Saltcoats** U.K.
80 B5 **Salt Creek** *r.* U.S.A.
41 E5 **Saltee Islands** *is* Rep. of Ireland
36 O3 **Saltfjellet Svartisen Nasjonalpark** *nat. park* Norway
77 B6 **Salt Flat** U.S.A.
80 C4 **Salt Fork Lake** *l.* U.S.A.
84 B1 **Saltillo** Mex.
72 E3 **Salt Lake City** U.S.A.
91 E2 **Salto** Arg.
90 C3 **Salto** Brazil
91 F1 **Salto** Uru.
90 E2 **Salto da Divisa** Brazil
88 E4 **Salto Grande, Embalse de** *resr* Uru.
75 E5 **Salton Sea** *salt l.* U.S.A.
22 C2 **Salt Ra.** *h.* Pak.
65 G2 **Salt River** Can.
80 B5 **Salt Rock** U.S.A.
79 D5 **Saluda** *SC* U.S.A.
80 E6 **Saluda** *VA* U.S.A.
22 C4 **Salumbar** India
21 C2 **Salur** India
48 B2 **Saluzzo** Italy
91 D1 **Salvador** Arg.
90 E1 **Salvador** Brazil
77 F6 **Salvador, L.** *l.* U.S.A.
84 B2 **Salvatierra** Mex.
75 G2 **Salvation Creek** *r.* U.S.A.
18 C5 **Salwah** Qatar
25 B5 **Salween** *r.* Myanmar
17 M2 **Salyan** Azer.
80 B6 **Salyersville** U.S.A.
58 B2 **Salzbrunn** Namibia
46 F7 **Salzburg** Austria
43 J2 **Salzgitter** Ger.
43 J1 **Salzhausen** Ger.
43 G3 **Salzkotten** Ger.
43 K3 **Salzmünde** Ger.
43 K2 **Salzwedel** Ger.
22 B4 **Sam** India
18 B4 **Samāh** *well* S. Arabia
18 B3 **Samaida** Iran
31 C5 **Samal** *i.* Phil.
31 B5 **Samales Group** *is* Phil.
21 C2 **Samalkot** India
16 E3 **Samandağı** Turkey
28 H3 **Samani** Japan
16 C6 **Samannûd** Egypt
31 C4 **Samar** *i.* Phil.
12 G4 **Samara** Rus. Fed.
89 D3 **Samariapo** Venez.
33 E3 **Samarinda** Indon.
28 D2 **Samarka** Rus. Fed.
19 G2 **Samarkand** Uzbek.
19 H2 **Samarkand, Pik** *mt* Tajik.
17 J4 **Sāmarrā'** Iraq
31 C4 **Samar Sea** *g.* Phil.
50 J4 **Samarskaya Oblast'** *div.* Rus. Fed.
17 M1 **Şamaxı** Azer.
56 C4 **Samba** Congo(Zaire)
33 E2 **Sambaliung** *mts* Indon.
23 F5 **Sambalpur** India
33 D3 **Sambar, Tanjung** *pt* Indon.
33 C2 **Sambas** Indon.
57 F5 **Sambava** Madag.
23 G4 **Sambha** India
22 D3 **Sambhal** India
22 C4 **Sambhar L.** *l.* India
51 B5 **Sambir** Ukr.
87 K5 **Sambito** *r.* Brazil
91 F2 **Samborombón, Bahía** *b.* Arg.
42 B4 **Sambre** *r.* Belgium/France
89 A3 **Sambú** *r.* Panama
30 E5 **Samch'ŏk** S. Korea
30 E6 **Samch'ŏnp'o** S. Korea
17 K3 **Samdi Dag** *mt* Turkey
56 D4 **Same** Tanz.
Samirum *see* **Yazd-e Khvāst**
30 E3 **Samjiyŏn** N. Korea
17 L1 **Şämkir** Azer.
18 D3 **Samnan va Damghan** *reg.* Iran
48 F2 **Samobor** Croatia
50 G2 **Samoded** Rus. Fed.
49 K3 **Samokov** Bulg.
46 H6 **Šamorín** Slovakia
49 M6 **Samos** *i.* Greece
33 A2 **Samosir** *i.* Indon.
49 L4 **Samothraki** Greece
49 L4 **Samothraki** *i.* Greece
31 B3 **Sampaloc Point** *pt* Phil.
33 D3 **Sampit** Indon.
33 D3 **Sampit, Teluk** *b.* Indon.
57 C4 **Sampwe** Congo(Zaire)
30 E6 **Samrangjin** S. Korea
77 E6 **Sam Rayburn Res.** *resr* U.S.A.
23 E3 **Samsang** China
32 C1 **Sâm Sơn** Vietnam
16 F1 **Samsun** Turkey
51 G7 **Samtredia** Georgia
51 J7 **Samur** *r.* Azer./Rus. Fed.
32 B2 **Samut Sakhon** Thai.
32 B2 **Samut Songkhram** Thai.
23 G3 **Samyai** China
54 B3 **San** Mali
20 B6 **Şan'ā** Yemen
92 C3 **Sanae** *S. Africa Base* Ant.
55 D4 **Sanaga** *r.* Cameroon
89 A4 **San Agustín** Col.
31 C5 **San Agustin, Cape** *c.* Phil.
18 B6 **Sanām** S. Arabia
85 C5 **San Ambrosio** *i.* Chile
18 B3 **Sanandaj** Iran
74 B2 **San Andreas** U.S.A.
31 C3 **San Andres** Phil.
86 B1 **San Andrés, Isla de** *i.* Col.
73 F5 **San Andres Mts** *mts* U.S.A.
84 D3 **San Andrés Tuxtla** Mex.
77 C6 **San Angelo** U.S.A.
91 B2 **San Antonio** Chile
31 B3 **San Antonio** Phil.
77 D6 **San Antonio** U.S.A.
45 G3 **San Antonio Abad** Spain
83 H4 **San Antonio, C.** *pt* Cuba
91 F3 **San Antonio, Cabo** *pt* Arg.
88 C2 **San Antonio de los Cobres** Arg.
89 D2 **San Antonio de Tamanaco** Venez.
74 D4 **San Antonio, Mt** *mt* U.S.A.
91 D4 **San Antonio Oeste** Arg.
74 B4 **San Antonio Reservoir** U.S.A.
74 B3 **San Ardo** U.S.A.
91 E3 **San Augustín** Arg.
91 C1 **San Augustín de Valle Fértil** Arg.
22 D5 **Sanawad** India
84 B2 **San Bartolo** Mex.
48 E3 **San Benedetto del Tronto** Italy
82 B5 **San Benedicto, I.** *i.* Mex.
77 D7 **San Benito** U.S.A.
74 B3 **San Benito** *r.* U.S.A.
74 B3 **San Benito Mt** *mt* U.S.A.
74 D4 **San Bernardino** U.S.A.
73 C5 **San Bernardino Mts** *mts* U.S.A.
91 B2 **San Bernardo** Chile
84 A1 **San Bernardo** Mex.
29 C7 **Sanbe-san** *volc.* Japan
84 A2 **San Blas** Mex.
79 C6 **San Blas, C.** *c.* U.S.A.
86 E6 **San Borja** Bol.
81 H3 **Sanbornville** U.S.A.
70 F6 **San Buenaventura** Mex.
91 C2 **San Carlos** Arg.
91 B3 **San Carlos** Chile
77 C6 **San Carlos** *Coahuila* Mex.
84 C1 **San Carlos** *Tamaulipas* Mex.
31 B3 **San Carlos** *Luzon* Phil.
31 B4 **San Carlos** *Negros* Phil.
91 F2 **San Carlos** Uru.
75 G5 **San Carlos** U.S.A.
89 D4 **San Carlos** *Amazonas* Venez.
89 C2 **San Carlos** *Cojedes* Venez.
91 E1 **San Carlos Centro** Arg.
91 B4 **San Carlos de Bariloche** Arg.
91 E3 **San Carlos de Bolívar** Arg.
89 C2 **San Carlos del Zulia** Venez.
73 D6 **San Carlos, Mesa de** *h.* Mex.
26 C2 **Sancha** *Gansu* China
26 D2 **Sancha** *Shanxi* China
30 D1 **Sanchahe** China
27 C5 **Sancha He** *r.* China
27 B6 **San Chien Pau** *mt* Laos
22 B4 **Sanchor** India
26 D2 **Sanchuan** *r.* China
50 H3 **Sanchursk** Rus. Fed.
84 C2 **San Ciro de Acosta** Mex.
91 B2 **San Clemente** Chile
74 D5 **San Clemente** U.S.A.
74 C5 **San Clemente I.** *i.* U.S.A.
44 F3 **Sancoins** France
91 E1 **San Cristóbal** Arg.
89 B3 **San Cristóbal** Venez.
7 G3 **San Cristobal** *i.* Solomon Is
84 D3 **San Cristóbal de las Casas** Mex.
86 □ **San Cristóbal, Isla** *i.* *Galapagos Is* Ecuador
75 F5 **San Cristobal Wash** *r.* U.S.A.
83 J4 **Sancti Spíritus** Cuba
59 H1 **Sand** *r.* S. Africa
28 D3 **Sandagou** Rus. Fed.
40 C5 **Sanda Island** *i.* U.K.
33 E1 **Sandakan** Malaysia
37 K6 **Sandane** Norway
49 K4 **Sandanski** Bulg.
43 L2 **Sandau** Ger.
40 F1 **Sanday** *i.* U.K.
40 F1 **Sanday Sound** *chan.* U.K.
39 E4 **Sandbach** U.K.
37 M7 **Sandefjord** Norway
92 D4 **Sandercock Nunataks** *nunatak* Ant.
75 H4 **Sanders** U.S.A.
43 K3 **Sandersleben** Ger.
77 C6 **Sanderson** U.S.A.
40 D6 **Sandhead** U.K.
68 B2 **Sand I.** *i.* U.S.A.
86 E6 **Sandia** Peru
74 D5 **San Diego** U.S.A.
88 C8 **San Diego, C.** *c.* Arg.
16 C2 **Sandıklı** Turkey
22 E4 **Sandila** India
84 E3 **San Dimas** *Campeche* Mex.
84 A1 **San Dimas** *Durango* Mex.
68 E2 **Sand Lake** Can.
37 J7 **Sandnes** Norway
36 N3 **Sandnessjøen** Norway
57 C4 **Sandoa** Congo(Zaire)
47 K5 **Sandomierz** Pol.
89 A4 **Sandoná** Col.
48 E2 **San Donà di Piave** Italy
25 B5 **Sandoway** Myanmar
39 F7 **Sandown** U.K.
58 C7 **Sandown Bay** *b.* S. Africa
36 □ **Sandoy** *i.* Faroe Is
72 C1 **Sandpoint** U.S.A.
40 A4 **Sandray** *i.* U.K.
47 N7 **Şandrul Mare, Vârful** *mt* Romania
37 O6 **Sandsjö** Sweden
64 C4 **Sandspit** Can.
77 D4 **Sand Springs** U.S.A.
74 C2 **Sand Springs Salt Flat** *salt flat* U.S.A.
68 A2 **Sandstone** U.S.A.
75 F5 **Sand Tank Mts** *mts* U.S.A.
27 C5 **Sandu** *Guizhou* China
27 D5 **Sandu** *Hunan* China
69 F4 **Sandusky** *MI* U.S.A.
80 B4 **Sandusky** *OH* U.S.A.
80 B4 **Sandusky Bay** *b.* U.S.A.
58 C5 **Sandveld** *mts* S. Africa
58 B3 **Sandverhaar** Namibia
37 M7 **Sandvika** Norway
36 N5 **Sandvika** Sweden
37 P6 **Sandviken** Sweden
67 J3 **Sandwich Bay** *b.* Can.
40 □ **Sandwick** U.K.
23 G5 **Sandwip Ch.** *chan.* Bangl.
81 H2 **Sandy** *r.* U.S.A.
65 J3 **Sandy Bay** Can.
7 F4 **Sandy Cape** *c.* Austr.
80 B5 **Sandy Hook** U.S.A.
81 F4 **Sandy Hook** *pt* U.S.A.
19 F2 **Sandykachi** Turkm.
66 B3 **Sandy L.** *l.* Can.
66 B3 **Sandy Lake** Can.
81 E3 **Sandy Pond** U.S.A.
90 A4 **San Estanislao** Para.
31 B2 **San Fabian** Phil.
91 B2 **San Felipe** Chile
82 B2 **San Felipe** *Baja California Norte* Mex.
84 B2 **San Felipe** *Guanajuato* Mex.
89 C2 **San Felipe** Venez.
85 B5 **San Félix** *i.* Chile
91 E2 **San Fernando** Arg.
91 B2 **San Fernando** Chile
84 C1 **San Fernando** Mex.
31 B2 **San Fernando** *Luzon* Phil.
31 B3 **San Fernando** *Luzon* Phil.
45 C4 **San Fernando** Spain
89 E2 **San Fernando** Trinidad and Tobago
74 C4 **San Fernando** U.S.A.
89 D3 **San Fernando de Apure** Venez.
89 D3 **San Fernando de Atabapo** Venez.
74 D5 **San Filipe Creek** *r.* U.S.A.
79 D6 **Sanford** *FL* U.S.A.
81 H3 **Sanford** *ME* U.S.A.
79 E5 **Sanford** *NC* U.S.A.
68 E4 **Sanford Lake** *l.* U.S.A.
91 D1 **San Francisco** Arg.
74 A3 **San Francisco** *CA* U.S.A.
75 H5 **San Francisco** *r. NM* U.S.A.
74 A3 **San Francisco Bay** *in.* U.S.A.
84 B2 **San Francisco del Rincón** Mex.
83 K5 **San Francisco de Macorís** Dom. Rep.
88 C7 **San Francisco de Paula, C.** *pt* Arg.
45 G3 **San Francisco Javier** Spain
88 C3 **San Francisco, Paso de** *pass* Arg.
89 A4 **San Gabriel** Ecuador
74 C4 **San Gabriel Mts** *mts* U.S.A.
86 C4 **Sangai, Parque Nacional** *nat. park* Ecuador
22 C6 **Sangamner** India
68 C6 **Sangamon** *r.* U.S.A.
19 G3 **Sangan** Afgh.
19 F4 **Sangān** Iran
19 G3 **Sangan, Koh-i-** *mt* Afgh.
13 O3 **Sangar** Rus. Fed.
22 B3 **Sangar** *r.* Pak.
21 B2 **Sangāreddi** India
48 C5 **San Gavino Monreale** *Sardinia* Italy
19 E3 **Sang Bast** Iran
31 B5 **Sangboy Islands** *is* Phil.
33 E4 **Sangeang** *i.* Indon.
26 B1 **Sangejing** China
74 C3 **Sanger** U.S.A.
43 K3 **Sangerhausen** Ger.
26 E1 **Sanggan** *r.* China
26 B3 **Sanggarmai** China
33 D2 **Sanggau** Indon.
30 B5 **Sanggou Wan** *b.* China
56 B3 **Sangha** *r.* Congo
22 B4 **Sanghar** Pak.
89 B3 **San Gil** Col.
48 G5 **San Giovanni in Fiore** Italy
48 F4 **San Giovanni Rotondo** Italy
31 C6 **Sangir** *i.* Indon.
25 E6 **Sangir, Kepulauan** *is* Indon.
33 E2 **Sangkulirang** Indon.
21 A2 **Sangli** India
19 H2 **Sanglich** Afgh.
54 D4 **Sangmélima** Cameroon
22 D3 **Sangnam** India
23 H3 **Sangngagqoling** China
30 E3 **Sang-ni** N. Korea
57 D6 **Sango** Zimbabwe
21 A2 **Sāngole** India
74 D4 **San Gorgonio Mt** *mt* U.S.A.
46 D7 **San Gottardo, Passo del** *pass* Switz.
73 F4 **Sangre de Cristo Range** *mts* U.S.A.
89 E2 **Sangre Grande** Trinidad and Tobago
22 C3 **Sangrur** India
23 F3 **Sangsang** China
64 G4 **Sangudo** Can.
87 G6 **Sangue** *r.* Brazil
59 K1 **Sangutane** *r.* Moz.
19 H2 **Sangvor** Tajik.
27 D4 **Sangzhi** China
82 B3 **San Hipólito, Pta** *pt* Mex.
16 C7 **Sanhûr** Egypt
86 E6 **San Ignacio** *Beni* Bol.
86 F7 **San Ignacio** *Santa Cruz* Bol.
66 E2 **Sanikiluaq** Can.
31 B2 **San Ildefonso, Cape** *c.* Phil.
31 B2 **San Ildefonso Peninsula** Phil.
31 C4 **San Isidro** Phil.
31 B3 **San Jacinto** Phil.
74 D5 **San Jacinto** U.S.A.
74 D5 **San Jacinto Peak** *summit* U.S.A.
23 F5 **Sanjai, R** *r.* India
91 E1 **San Javier** Arg.
91 B2 **San Javier de Loncomilla** Chile
22 B3 **Sanjawi** Pak.
57 D4 **Sanje** Tanz.
89 A3 **San Jerónimo, Serranía de** *mts* Col.
27 C5 **Sanjiang** China
30 B2 **Sanjiangkou** China
30 B2 **Sanjiazi** China
29 F6 **Sanjō** Japan
74 B3 **San Joaquin** *CA* U.S.A.
74 B3 **San Joaquin** *r. CA* U.S.A.
74 B3 **San Joaquin Valley** *v.* U.S.A.
91 E1 **San Jorge** Arg.
89 B2 **San Jorge** *r.* Col.
88 C7 **San Jorge, Golfo de** *g.* Arg.
83 H7 **San José** Costa Rica
31 B3 **San Jose** Phil.
74 B3 **San Jose** U.S.A.
82 B4 **San José** *i.* Mex.
89 E2 **San José de Amacuro** Venez.
31 B4 **San Jose de Buenavista** Phil.
86 F7 **San José de Chiquitos** Bol.
91 E1 **San José de Feliciano** Arg.
84 A1 **San José de Gracia** Mex.
89 D2 **San José de Guanipa** Venez.
91 C1 **San Jose de Jáchal** Arg.
91 D1 **San José de la Dormida** Arg.
91 B3 **San José de la Mariquina** Chile
82 C4 **San José del Cabo** Mex.
89 B4 **San José del Guaviare** Col.
91 F2 **San José de Mayo** Uru.
89 C3 **San José de Ocuné** Col.
84 B1 **San José de Raíces** Mex.
91 D4 **San José, Golfo** *g.* Arg.
91 C2 **San José, Vol.** *volc.* Chile
30 E5 **Sanju** S. Korea
91 C1 **San Juan** Arg.
77 C7 **San Juan** Mex.
31 C4 **San Juan** Phil.
83 L5 **San Juan** Puerto Rico
89 D3 **San Juan** Venez.
91 C1 **San Juan** *div.* Arg.
89 A3 **San Juan** *r.* Col.
83 H6 **San Juan** *r.* Costa Rica/Nic.
74 B4 **San Juan** *r. CA* U.S.A.
75 H3 **San Juan** *r. UT* U.S.A.
88 E3 **San Juan Bautista** Para.
45 G3 **San Juan Bautista** Spain
84 C3 **San Juan Bautista Tuxtepec** Mex.
91 B4 **San Juan dela Costa** Chile
89 C2 **San Juan de los Cayos** Venez.
89 D2 **San Juan de los Morros** Venez.
84 A1 **San Juan del Río** *Durango* Mex.
84 C2 **San Juan del Río** *Querétaro* Mex.
75 F4 **San Juan Mts** *mts* U.S.A.
22 D1 **Sanju He** *watercourse* China
88 C7 **San Julián** Arg.
91 E1 **San Justo** Arg.
21 A2 **Sankeshwar** India
23 F5 **Sankh** *r.* India
Sankt-Peterburg *see* **St Petersburg**
16 G3 **Şanlıurfa** Turkey
91 E2 **San Lorenzo** Arg.
86 F8 **San Lorenzo** Bol.
86 C3 **San Lorenzo** Ecuador
73 F6 **San Lorenzo** Mex.
45 E1 **San Lorenzo** *mt* Spain
88 B7 **San Lorenzo, Cerro** *mt* Arg./Chile
86 C6 **San Lorenzo, I.** *i.* Peru
45 C4 **Sanlúcar de Barrameda** Spain
82 C4 **San Lucas** Mex.
91 C2 **San Luis** Arg.
75 E5 **San Luis** *AZ* U.S.A.
75 G5 **San Luis** *AZ* U.S.A.
91 C2 **San Luis** *div.* Arg.
84 B2 **San Luis de la Paz** Mex.
86 F6 **San Luis, Lago de** *l.* Bol.
74 B4 **San Luis Obispo** U.S.A.
74 B4 **San Luis Obispo Bay** *b.* U.S.A.
84 B2 **San Luis Potosí** Mex.
84 B2 **San Luis Potosí** *div.* Mex.
74 B3 **San Luis Reservoir** U.S.A.
82 B2 **San Luis Río Colorado** Mex.
91 C2 **San Luis, Sa de** *mts* Arg.
48 E6 **San Marco, Capo** *c. Sicily* Italy
84 E4 **San Marcos** Guatemala
84 C3 **San Marcos** Mex.
77 D6 **San Marcos** U.S.A.
48 E3 **San Marino** San Marino
34 G4 **San Marino** *country* Europe
88 C3 **San Martín** *Catamarca* Arg.
91 C2 **San Martín** *Mendoza* Arg.
89 B4 **San Martín** Col.
86 F6 **San Martín** *r.* Bol.
91 B4 **San Martín de los Andes** Arg.
88 B7 **San Martín, L.** *l.* Arg./Chile
74 A3 **San Mateo** U.S.A.
91 D4 **San Matías, Golfo** *g.* Arg.
89 D2 **San Mauricio** Venez.
27 F4 **Sanmen** China
27 F4 **Sanmen Wan** *b.* China
26 D3 **Sanmenxia** China
82 G6 **San Miguel** El Salvador
75 G6 **San Miguel** *AZ* U.S.A.
74 B4 **San Miguel** *CA* U.S.A.
86 F6 **San Miguel** *r.* Bol.
89 B4 **San Miguel** *r.* Col.
75 H2 **San Miguel** *r.* U.S.A.
31 B3 **San Miguel Bay** *b.* Phil.
84 B2 **San Miguel de Allende** Mex.
91 E2 **San Miguel del Monte** Arg.
88 C3 **San Miguel de Tucumán** Arg.
74 B4 **San Miguel I.** *i.* U.S.A.
31 A5 **San Miguel Islands** *is* Phil.
84 C3 **San Miguel Sola de Vega** Mex.
27 E5 **Sanming** China
31 B3 **San Narciso** Phil.
48 F4 **Sannicandro Garganico** Italy
91 E2 **San Nicolás de los Arroyos** Arg.
74 C5 **San Nicolas I.** *i.* U.S.A.
59 F3 **Sannieshof** S. Africa
54 B4 **Sanniquellie** Liberia
47 L6 **Sanok** Pol.
84 C2 **San Pablo** Mex.
31 B3 **San Pablo** Phil.
91 E2 **San Pedro** *Buenos Aires* Arg.
88 D2 **San Pedro** *Jujuy* Arg.
86 F7 **San Pedro** Bol.
54 B4 **San-Pédro** Côte d'Ivoire
88 E2 **San Pedro** Para.
31 B3 **San Pedro** Phil.
75 G5 **San Pedro** *r.* U.S.A.
74 C5 **San Pedro Channel** U.S.A.
89 C3 **San Pedro de Arimena** Col.
89 E3 **San Pedro de las Bocas** Venez.
84 B1 **San Pedro de las Colonias** Mex.
45 C3 **San Pedro, Sierra de** *mts* Spain
82 G5 **San Pedro Sula** Honduras
48 C5 **San Pietro, Isola di** *i.* *Sardinia* Italy
40 E5 **Sanquhar** U.K.
86 C3 **Sanquianga, Parque Nacional** *nat. park* Col.
82 A2 **San Quintín** Mex.
91 C2 **San Rafael** Arg.
74 A3 **San Rafael** U.S.A.
89 C2 **San Rafael** Venez.
75 G2 **San Rafael** *r.* U.S.A.
75 G2 **San Rafael Knob** *summit* U.S.A.
74 C4 **San Rafael Mts** *mts* U.S.A.
86 F6 **San Ramón** Bol.
48 B3 **San Remo** Italy
89 C1 **San Román, C.** *pt* Venez.
45 B1 **San Roque** Spain
77 D6 **San Saba** U.S.A.
91 E1 **San Salvador** Arg.
82 G6 **San Salvador** El Salvador
83 K4 **San Salvador** *i.* Bahamas
88 C2 **San Salvador de Jujuy** Arg.
86 □ **San Salvador, Isla** *i.* *Galapagos Is* Ecuador
22 D5 **Sansar** India
45 F1 **San Sebastián** Spain
45 E2 **San Sebastián de los Reyes** Spain
48 E3 **Sansepolcro** Italy
48 F4 **San Severo** Italy
27 F5 **Sansha** China
27 D6 **Sanshui** China
48 G2 **Sanski Most** Bos.-Herz.
27 C5 **Sansui** China
32 C2 **San, T.** *r.* Cambodia
86 E7 **Santa Ana** Bol.
82 G6 **Santa Ana** El Salvador
74 D5 **Santa Ana** U.S.A.
7 G3 **Santa Ana** *i.* Solomon Is
77 D6 **Santa Anna** U.S.A.
89 B3 **Sta Bárbara** Col.
82 C3 **Santa Bárbara** Mex.
74 C4 **Santa Barbara** U.S.A.
74 B4 **Santa Barbara Channel** U.S.A.
74 C5 **Santa Barbara I.** *i.* U.S.A.
88 C3 **Sta Catalina** Chile
45 B1 **Santa Catalina de Armada** Spain
74 D5 **Santa Catalina, Gulf of** *b.* U.S.A.
74 C5 **Santa Catalina I.** *i.* U.S.A.
84 B1 **Sta Catarina** Mex.
86 E4 **Santa Clara** Col.
83 J4 **Santa Clara** Cuba
74 B3 **Santa Clara** *CA* U.S.A.
75 F3 **Santa Clara** *UT* U.S.A.
91 F2 **Santa Clara de Olimar** Uru.
74 C4 **Santa Clarita** U.S.A.
48 F6 **Sta Croce, Capo** *c. Sicily* Italy
86 F7 **Santa Cruz** Bol.
91 B2 **Sta Cruz** Chile
31 B3 **Santa Cruz** *Luzon* Phil.
31 B2 **Santa Cruz** *Luzon* Phil.
31 A3 **Sta Cruz** Phil.
74 A3 **Santa Cruz** U.S.A.
88 C8 **Santa Cruz** *r.* Arg.
73 E5 **Santa Cruz** *r.* U.S.A.
84 E4 **Sta Cruz Barillas** Guatemala
90 E2 **Santa Cruz Cabrália** Brazil
45 F3 **Santa Cruz de Moya** Spain
54 A2 **Santa Cruz de Tenerife** Canary Is
88 F3 **Santa Cruz do Sul** Brazil
74 C4 **Santa Cruz I.** *i.* U.S.A.
86 □ **Santa Cruz, Isla** *i.* *Galapagos Is* Ecuador
7 G3 **Santa Cruz Islands** *is* Solomon Is
88 C8 **Santa Cruz, Pto** Arg.
91 E1 **Sta Elena** Arg.
86 B4 **Sta Elena, B. de** *b.* Ecuador
82 G6 **Sta Elena, C.** *hd* Costa Rica
48 G5 **Sta Eufemia, Golfo di** *g.* Italy
91 E1 **Santa Fé** Arg.
73 F5 **Santa Fe** U.S.A.
91 E1 **Santa Fé** *div.* Arg.
90 B2 **Santa Helena de Goiás** Brazil
26 B4 **Santai** China
88 B8 **Santa Inés, Isla** *i.* Chile
91 C3 **Santa Isabel** Arg.
7 F2 **Santa Isabel** *i.* Solomon Is
84 E4 **Sta Lucia** Guatemala
91 F2 **Sta Lucia** *r.* Uru.
73 B4 **Santa Lucia Range** *mts* U.S.A.
90 A2 **Santa Luisa, Serra de** *h.* Brazil
54 □ **Santa Luzia** *i.* Cape Verde
82 B4 **Sta Margarita** *i.* Mex.
88 C3 **Sta María** Arg.
87 G4 **Santa Maria** *Amazonas* Brazil
88 F3 **Santa Maria** *Rio Grande do Sul* Brazil
54 □ **Santa Maria** Cape Verde
84 A1 **Sta María** Mex.
86 D4 **Santa María** Peru
74 B4 **Santa Maria** U.S.A.
34 C5 **Santa Maria** *i. Azores* Port.
91 F1 **Santa Maria** *r.* Brazil
73 F6 **Sta María** *r.* Mex.
82 C2 **Sta Maria** *r.* Mex.
45 C4 **Santa Maria, Cabo de** *c.* Port.
59 K3 **Santa Maria, Cabo de** *pt* Moz.
87 J5 **Santa Maria das Barreiras** Brazil
90 D1 **Santa Maria da Vitória** Brazil
89 D2 **Sta María de Ipire** Venez.
84 B2 **Sta María del Río** Mex.
49 H5 **Sta Maria di Leuca, Capo** *c.* Italy
91 B3 **Santa María, I.** *i.* Chile
7 G3 **Santa Maria I.** *i.* Vanuatu
86 □ **Santa María, Isla** *i.* *Galapagos Is* Ecuador
70 E5 **Sta María, L. de** *l.* Mex.
79 F7 **Sta Marie, Cape** *c.* Bahamas
89 B2 **Santa Marta** Col.
89 B2 **Santa Marta, Sierra Nevada de** *mts* Col.
74 C4 **Santa Monica** U.S.A.
74 C5 **Santa Monica Bay** *b.* U.S.A.
87 K6 **Santana** Brazil
90 B2 **Santana** *r.* Brazil
91 G1 **Santana da Boa Vista** Brazil
91 F1 **Santana do Livramento** Brazil
89 A4 **Santander** Col.
45 E1 **Santander** Spain
75 G5 **Santan Mt** *mt* U.S.A.
48 C5 **Sant'Antioco** *Sardinia* Italy
48 C5 **Sant'Antioco, Isola di** *i.* *Sardinia* Italy
74 C4 **Santa Paula** U.S.A.
87 K4 **Santa Quitéria** Brazil
87 H4 **Santarém** Brazil
45 B3 **Santarém** Port.
89 C2 **Sta Rita** Venez.
90 B2 **Sta Rita do Araguaia** Brazil
74 B3 **Santa Rita Park** U.S.A.
91 D3 **Santa Rosa** *La Pampa* Arg.
91 C4 **Santa Rosa** *Rio Negro* Arg.
86 D5 **Santa Rosa** *Acre* Brazil
88 F3 **Sta Rosa** Brazil
74 A2 **Santa Rosa** *CA* U.S.A.
73 F5 **Santa Rosa** *NM* U.S.A.
82 G6 **Santa Rosa de Copán** Honduras
91 D1 **Sta Rosa del Río Primero** Arg.
74 B5 **Santa Rosa I.** *i.* U.S.A.
82 B3 **Sta Rosalía** Mex.
72 C3 **Sta Rosa Ra.** *mts* U.S.A.
75 G5 **Santa Rosa Wash** *r.* U.S.A.
91 G2 **Sta Vitória do Palmar** Brazil
74 D5 **Santee** U.S.A.
79 E5 **Santee** *r.* U.S.A.
84 B3 **San Telmo, Pta** *pt* Mex.
88 F3 **Santiago** Brazil
91 B2 **Santiago** Chile
83 K5 **Santiago** Dom. Rep.
84 A1 **Santiago** Mex.
83 H7 **Santiago** Panama
31 B2 **Santiago** Phil.
91 B2 **Santiago** *div.* Chile
84 D3 **Santiago Astata** Mex.
45 B1 **Santiago de Compostela** Spain
83 J4 **Santiago de Cuba** Cuba
84 A2 **Santiago Ixcuintla** Mex.
84 A2 **Santiago, Río Grande de** *r.* Mex.
91 F2 **Santiago Vazquez** Uru.
84 A1 **Santiaguillo, L. de** *l.* Mex.
65 N2 **Santianna Point** *pt* Can.
45 G2 **Sant Jordi, Golf de** *g.* Spain
90 E1 **Santo Amaro** Brazil
90 E3 **Santo Amaro de Campos** Brazil
90 C4 **Sto Amaro, I. de** *i.* Brazil
90 C3 **Santo André** Brazil
88 F3 **Santo Angelo** Brazil
54 □ **Santo Antão** *i.* Cape Verde
90 D2 **Sto Antônio** *r.* Brazil
90 E1 **Sto Antônio, Cabo** *c.* Brazil
90 B3 **Santo Antônio da Platina** Brazil
90 E1 **Sto Antônio de Jesus** Brazil
90 A1 **Sto Antônio de Leverger** Brazil
86 E4 **Santo Antônio do Içá** Brazil
90 D3 **Santo Antônio do Monte** Brazil
87 G7 **Santo Corazón** Bol.
83 L5 **Santo Domingo** Dom. Rep.
84 B2 **Sto Domingo** Mex.
89 C2 **Sto Domingo** *r.* Venez.
70 E4 **Santo Domingo Pueblo** *NM* U.S.A.
45 E1 **Santoña** Spain
30 D2 **Santong** *r.* China
90 D1 **Sto Onofre** *r.* Brazil
49 L6 **Santorini** *i.* Greece
90 C3 **Santos** Brazil
90 D3 **Santos Dumont** Brazil
86 D6 **Santo Tomás** Peru
88 E3 **Santo Tomé** Arg.
75 F3 **Sanup Plateau** *plat.* U.S.A.
88 B7 **San Valentín, Cerro** *mt* Chile
82 G6 **San Vicente** El Salvador
31 B2 **San Vicente** Phil.
86 C6 **San Vicente de Cañete** Peru
89 B4 **San Vicente del Caguán** Col.
48 D3 **San Vincenzo** Italy
48 E5 **San Vito, Capo** *c. Sicily* Italy
27 C7 **Sanya** China
26 C3 **Sanyuan** China
30 C2 **Sanyuanpu** China
56 B4 **Sanza Pombo** Angola
90 C3 **São Bernardo do Campo** Brazil
88 E3 **São Borja** Brazil
90 C3 **São Carlos** Brazil
90 C1 **São Domingos** Brazil
90 B2 **São Domingos** *r.* Brazil
87 H6 **São Félix** *Mato Grosso* Brazil
87 H5 **São Félix** *Pará* Brazil
90 E3 **São Fidélis** Brazil
54 □ **São Filipe** Cape Verde
90 D1 **São Francisco** Brazil
87 L5 **São Francisco** *r.* Brazil
88 G3 **São Francisco do Sul** Brazil
91 F1 **São Gabriel** Brazil
90 D3 **São Gonçalo** Brazil
90 D2 **São Gotardo** Brazil
90 C1 **São João da Aliança** Brazil
90 E3 **São João da Barra** Brazil
90 C3 **São João da Boa Vista** Brazil
45 B2 **São João da Madeira** Port.
90 D1 **São João do Paraíso** Brazil
90 D3 **São João Nepomuceno** Brazil
90 C3 **São Joaquim da Barra** Brazil
34 C5 **São Jorge** *i.* Port.
89 D5 **São José** Brazil
90 E3 **São José do Calçado** Brazil
91 G2 **São José do Norte** Brazil
90 C3 **São José do Rio Preto** Brazil
90 D3 **São José dos Campos** Brazil
90 C4 **São José dos Pinhais** Brazil
90 D3 **São Lourenço** Brazil
90 A2 **São Lourenço** *r.* Brazil
91 G1 **São Lourenço do Sul** Brazil
87 K4 **São Luís** Brazil
90 C3 **São Manuel** Brazil
90 C2 **São Marcos** *r.* Brazil
87 K4 **São Marcos, Baía de** *b.* Brazil
90 E2 **São Mateus** Brazil
90 E2 **São Mateus** *r.* Brazil
34 C5 **São Miguel** *i. Azores* Port.
90 C2 **São Miguel** *r.* Brazil
44 G3 **Saône** *r.* France
54 □ **São Nicolau** *i.* Cape Verde
90 C3 **São Paulo** Brazil
90 C3 **São Paulo** *div.* Brazil
96 H5 **São Pedro e São Paulo** *is* Atl. Ocean
87 K5 **São Raimundo Nonato** Brazil
90 D2 **São Romão** Brazil
87 L5 **São Roque, Cabo de** *pt* Brazil
90 D3 **São Sebastião** Brazil
90 C3 **São Sebastião do Paraíso** Brazil
90 D3 **São Sebastião, Ilha de** *i.* Brazil
91 G1 **São Sepé** Brazil
90 B2 **São Simão** Brazil
90 B2 **São Simão, Barragem de** *resr* Brazil
25 E6 **Sao-Siu** Indon.
54 □ **São Tiago** *i.* Cape Verde
54 C4 **São Tomé** *i.* Sao Tome and Principe
53 E5 **São Tomé and Príncipe** *country* Africa
90 E3 **São Tomé, Cabo de** *c.* Brazil
90 C3 **São Vicente** Brazil
54 □ **São Vicente** *i.* Cape Verde
45 B4 **São Vicente, Cabo de** *c.* Port.
16 C1 **Sapanca** Turkey
6 C2 **Saparua** Indon.
16 C2 **Şaphane Dağı** *mt* Turkey
54 B4 **Sapo National Park** *nat. park* Liberia
28 G3 **Sapporo** Japan
48 F4 **Sapri** Italy
33 D4 **Sapudi** *i.* Indon.
77 D4 **Sapulpa** U.S.A.
19 E3 **Sāqī** Iran
18 B2 **Saqqez** Iran
18 B2 **Sarāb** Iran
17 L5 **Sarābe Meymeh** Iran
32 B2 **Sara Buri** Thai.
Saragossa *see* **Zaragoza**
86 C4 **Saraguro** Ecuador
49 H3 **Sarajevo** Bos.-Herz.
19 F2 **Sarakhs** Iran
14 D1 **Saraktash** Rus. Fed.
23 H4 **Saramati** *mt* India
81 G2 **Saranac** *r.* U.S.A.
81 F2 **Saranac Lake** U.S.A.
66 E5 **Saranac Lakes** *l.* U.S.A.
49 J5 **Sarandë** Albania
91 F2 **Sarandí del Yí** Uru.
91 F2 **Sarandí Grande** Uru.
31 C5 **Sarangani** *i.* Phil.
31 C5 **Sarangani Bay** *b.* Phil.
31 C5 **Sarangani Islands** *is* Phil.
31 C5 **Sarangani Str.** *chan.* Phil.
33 D3 **Saran, Gunung** *mt* Indon.
50 H4 **Saransk** Rus. Fed.
12 G4 **Sarapul** Rus. Fed.
89 C3 **Sarare** *r.* Venez.
79 D7 **Sarasota** U.S.A.
22 B5 **Saraswati** *r.* India
51 D6 **Sarata** Ukr.
72 F3 **Saratoga** U.S.A.
81 G3 **Saratoga Springs** U.S.A.
33 D2 **Saratok** Malaysia
51 H5 **Saratov** Rus. Fed.
51 H5 **Saratovskaya Oblast'** *div.* Rus. Fed.
50 J4 **Saratovskoye Vdkhr.** *resr* Rus. Fed.
19 F5 **Saravan** Iran
32 C2 **Saravan** Laos
32 A2 **Sarawa** *r.* Myanmar
33 D2 **Sarawak** *div.* Malaysia
16 A1 **Saray** Turkey
16 B3 **Sarayköy** Turkey
16 D2 **Sarayönü** Turkey
19 F5 **Sarbāz** Iran
19 F5 **Sarbāz** *r.* Iran
19 E3 **Sarbīsheh** Iran
48 D2 **Sarca** *r.* Italy
17 M3 **Sarcham** Iran
22 E3 **Sarda** *r.* India/Nepal
23 E3 **Sarda** *r.* Nepal
22 C3 **Sardarshahr** India
18 B2 **Sar Dasht** Iran
17 M5 **Sardasht** Iran
Sardegna *i. see* **Sardinia**
89 B2 **Sardinata** Col.
48 C4 **Sardinia** *i. Sardinia* Italy
17 L3 **Sardrūd** Iran
18 C5 **Sareb, Rās-as** *pt* U.A.E.
36 P3 **Sareks Nationalpark** *nat. park* Sweden
36 P3 **Sarektjåkkå** *mt* Sweden
19 G2 **Sar-e Pol** Afgh.
18 B3 **Sar-e-Pol-e-Zahāb** Iran
18 D4 **Sare Yazd** Iran
96 E4 **Sargasso Sea** *sea* Atl. Ocean
22 C2 **Sargodha** Pak.
55 D4 **Sarh** Chad
18 D2 **Sārī** Iran
49 M7 **Saria** *i.* Greece
16 B2 **Sarıgöl** Turkey
17 J1 **Sarıkamış** Turkey
16 D3 **Sarıkavak** Turkey
22 D4 **Sarila** India
32 □ **Sarimbun Res.** *resr* Sing.
6 E4 **Sarina** Austr.
16 E2 **Sarıoğlan** Turkey
19 G3 **Sar-i-Pul** Afgh.
55 D2 **Sarīr Tibesti** *des.* Libya
17 J2 **Sarısu** Turkey
30 C4 **Sariwŏn** N. Korea
16 C2 **Sarıyar Barajı** *resr* Turkey
16 B1 **Sarıyer** Turkey
16 F2 **Sarız** Turkey
22 E4 **Sarju** *r.* India
15 F2 **Sarkand** Kazak.
22 B4 **Sarkāri Tala** India
16 C2 **Şarkikaraağaç** Turkey
16 F2 **Şarkişla** Turkey
51 C7 **Şarköy** Turkey
19 G4 **Sarlath Range** *mts* Afgh./Pak.
44 E4 **Sarlat-la-Canéda** France
25 F7 **Sarmi** Indon.
37 N6 **Särna** Sweden
17 L5 **Sarneh** Iran
48 C1 **Sarnen** Switz.
69 F4 **Sarnia** Can.
51 C5 **Sarny** Ukr.
33 B3 **Sarolangun** Indon.
28 H2 **Saroma-ko** *l.* Japan
49 K6 **Saronikos Kolpos** *g.* Greece
51 C7 **Saros Körfezi** *b.* Turkey
22 C4 **Sarotra** India
50 G4 **Sarova** Rus. Fed.
19 H3 **Sarowbī** Afgh.
51 H6 **Sarpa, Ozero** *l. Kalmykiya* Rus. Fed.
51 H5 **Sarpa, Ozero** *l. Volgograd.* Rus. Fed.
37 M7 **Sarpsborg** Norway
44 H2 **Sarrebourg** France
42 F5 **Sarreguemines** France
45 C1 **Sarria** Spain
45 F2 **Sarrión** Spain
42 C6 **Sarry** France
48 C4 **Sartène** *Corsica* France
18 C3 **Sarud** *r.* Iran
19 G5 **Saruna** Pak.
17 M4 **Saruq** Iran
17 K2 **Şärur** Azer.
19 F4 **Saru Tara** Afgh.
17 L4 **Sarvabad** Iran
46 H7 **Sárvár** Hungary
18 D4 **Sarvestān** Iran
20 E1 **Sarykamyshkoye Ozero** *salt l.* Turkm.

9 G1 Shillington Can.
3 G4 Shillong India
1 J5 Shil'naya Balka Kazak.
1 F5 Shiloh U.S.A.
6 D2 Shilou China
0 G4 Shilovo Rus. Fed.
9 B8 Shimabara Japan
9 F7 Shimada Japan
4 E1 Shimanovsk Rus. Fed.
7 D4 Shimen China
7 B4 Shimian China
9 F7 Shimizu Japan
3 D3 Shimla India
9 F7 Shimoda Japan
1 A3 Shimoga India
6 D4 Shimoni Kenya
9 B8 Shimonoseki Japan
22 C1 Shimshal Jammu and Kashmir
50 D3 Shimsk Rus. Fed.
27 C6 Shinan China
19 F3 Shīndand Afgh.
22 B3 Shinghar Pak.
22 C1 Shinghshal Pass Pak.
68 D2 Shingleton U.S.A.
27 □ Shing Mun Res. resr H.K. China
29 E8 Shingū Japan
59 J1 Shingwedzi S. Africa
59 J1 Shingwedzi r. S. Africa
39 E4 Shining Tor h. U.K.
69 G2 Shining Tree Can.
28 G5 Shinjō Japan
19 G4 Shīnkāy Afgh.
40 D2 Shin, Loch l. U.K.
29 E6 Shinminato Japan
81 J1 Shin Pond U.S.A.
56 D4 Shinyanga Tanz.
28 G5 Shiogama Japan
29 D8 Shiono-misaki c. Japan
29 G6 Shioya-zaki pt Japan
79 F7 Ship Chan Cay i. Bahamas
27 B6 Shiping China
22 D3 Shipki Pass China/India
38 F4 Shipley U.K.
67 H4 Shippegan Can.
80 E4 Shippensburg U.S.A.
75 H3 Shiprock U.S.A.
75 H3 Shiprock Peak summit U.S.A.
27 F4 Shipu China
27 C5 Shiqian China
26 C3 Shiquan China
22 E2 Shiquan He r. China
26 C3 Shiquan Sk. resr China
17 M2 Shīrābād Iran
29 G6 Shirakawa Japan
24 F3 Shirane-san mt Japan
29 F6 Shirane-san volc. Japan
92 D4 Shirasebreen ice feature Ant.
92 A4 Shirase Coast coastal area Ant.
18 D4 Shīrāz Iran
16 C6 Shirbīn Egypt
28 J2 Shiretoko-misaki c. Japan
19 G4 Shirinab r. Pak.
28 G4 Shiriya-zaki c. Japan
81 G4 Shirley U.S.A.
81 J2 Shirley Mills U.S.A.
29 E7 Shirotori Japan
22 C5 Shirpur India
19 E2 Shīrvān Iran
17 L5 Shīrvān Iran
27 D4 Shishou China
27 E4 Shitai China
27 F4 Shitang China
17 J5 Shithāthah Iraq
22 B4 Shiv India
78 C4 Shively U.S.A.
22 D4 Shivpuri India
75 F3 Shivwits Plateau plat. U.S.A.
19 H2 Shiwal l. Afgh.
27 C6 Shiwan Dashan mts China
27 E5 Shixing China
26 D3 Shiyan China
27 C4 Shizhu China
27 B5 Shizong China
28 G5 Shizugawa Japan
26 C2 Shizuishan China
29 F7 Shizuoka Japan
50 D4 Shklow Belarus
49 H3 Shkodër Albania
12 K1 Shmidta, Ostrov i. Rus. Fed.
29 C7 Shōbara Japan
28 G3 Shokanbetsu-dake mt Japan
50 J2 Shomvukva Rus. Fed.
22 D2 Shor India
21 B4 Shoranur India
19 G5 Shorap Pak.
19 G4 Shorawak reg. Afgh.
17 K3 Shor Gol Iran
22 C3 Shorkot Pak.
28 G2 Shosanbetsu Japan
74 D4 Shoshone CA U.S.A.
72 D3 Shoshone ID U.S.A.
72 E2 Shoshone r. U.S.A.
72 E2 Shoshone L. l. U.S.A.
73 C4 Shoshone Mts mts U.S.A.
59 G1 Shoshong Botswana
72 E3 Shoshoni U.S.A.
51 E5 Shostka Ukr.
26 F2 Shouguang China
27 F5 Shouning China
26 E3 Shou Xian China
26 D2 Shouyang China
26 C3 Shouyang Shan mt China
23 E3 Shovo Tso salt l. China
75 G4 Show Low U.S.A.
51 G6 Shpakovskoye Rus. Fed.
51 D5 Shpola Ukr.
77 E5 Shreveport U.S.A.
39 E5 Shrewsbury U.K.
21 A2 Shrigonda India
23 G5 Shrirampur India
26 F3 Shu r. China
17 L6 Shu'aiba Iraq
27 A5 Shuangbai China
30 D1 Shuangcheng China
26 C4 Shuanghechang China
30 B2 Shuangliao China
27 D5 Shuangpai China
30 A3 Shuangtaizihe Kou b. China
30 C2 Shuangyang China
28 B1 Shuangyashan China
14 D2 Shubarkuduk Kazak.
26 E4 Shucheng China
27 F5 Shuiji China
26 A2 Shuiquanzi China
22 B3 Shujaabad Pak.
18 C4 Shūl watercourse Iran
30 D1 Shulan China
26 E2 Shulu China
28 H2 Shumarinai-ko l. Japan
57 C5 Shumba Zimbabwe
49 M3 Shumen Bulg.
50 H4 Shumerlya Rus. Fed.
47 O3 Shumilina Belarus
75 G4 Shumway U.S.A.
50 E4 Shumyachi Rus. Fed.
27 E5 Shunchang China
27 D6 Shunde China
62 C3 Shungnak U.S.A.
26 E1 Shunyi China
27 C6 Shuolong China
26 D2 Shuo Xian China
20 C7 Shuqrah Yemen
19 F3 Shūr r. Iran
18 D4 Shūr r. Iran
18 D4 Shūr r. Iran
19 E3 Shūr watercourse Iran
18 D4 Shūr watercourse Iran
18 D5 Shūr watercourse Iran
18 E3 Shūrāb Iran
18 D3 Shūrāb Iran
18 C3 Shūr Āb Iran
18 E4 Shūr Āb watercourse Iran
19 G2 Shurchi Uzbek.
18 D3 Shūreghestan Iran
19 E4 Shūr Gaz Iran
18 D4 Shūrjestān Iran
57 D5 Shurugwi Zimbabwe
17 K6 Shuruppak Iraq
19 F4 Shusf Iran
18 C3 Shūsh Iran
18 C3 Shushtar Iran
64 F4 Shuswap L. l. Can.
19 G3 Shutar Khun Pass Afgh.
50 G3 Shuya Rus. Fed.
26 F3 Shuyang China
18 D4 Shūzū Iran
32 A1 Shwegun Myanmar
14 E2 Shymkent Kazak.
22 D2 Shyok Jammu and Kashmir
22 D2 Shyok r. India
51 F5 Shypuvate Ukr.
51 E6 Shyroke Ukr.
25 F7 Sia Indon.
22 D2 Siachen Gl. gl. India
19 F5 Siahan Range mts Pak.
19 G3 Siah Koh mts Afgh.
18 D3 Siāh Kūh mts Iran
19 G4 Siah Sang Pas Afgh.
22 C2 Sialkot Pak.
32 C5 Siantan i. Indon.
89 D4 Siapa r. Venez.
19 F4 Siāreh Iran
31 C4 Siargao i. Phil.
31 B5 Siasi Phil.
31 B5 Siasi i. Phil.
31 B4 Siaton Phil.
37 S9 Šiauliai Lith.
19 F5 Sib Iran
18 C3 Sībak Iran
59 J1 Sibasa S. Africa
31 B4 Sibay i. Phil.
59 K3 Sibayi, Lake l. S. Africa
92 B5 Sibbald, C. c. Ant.
48 F3 Šibenik Croatia
33 A3 Siberut i. Indon.
22 A3 Sibi Pak.
56 D3 Sibiloi National Park Kenya
28 C2 Sibirtsevo Rus. Fed.
56 B4 Sibiti Congo
49 L2 Sibiu Romania
33 A2 Sibolga Indon.
32 A5 Siborongborong Indon.
23 H4 Sibsagar India
33 D2 Sibu Malaysia
31 B5 Sibuco Phil.
31 B5 Sibuguey r. Phil.
31 B5 Sibuguey Bay b. Phil.
56 B3 Sibut C.A.R.
31 A5 Sibutu i. Phil.
31 A5 Sibutu Passage chan. Phil.
31 B3 Sibuyan i. Phil.
31 B3 Sibuyan Sea sea Phil.
31 B2 Sicapoo mt Phil.
27 B4 Sichuan div. China
27 B4 Sichuan Pendi basin China
44 G5 Sicié, Cap c. France
Sicilia i. see Sicily
48 E6 Sicilian Channel Italy/Tunisia
48 E6 Sicily i. Italy
86 D6 Sicuani Peru
28 D2 Sidatun Rus. Fed.
22 C5 Siddhapur India
21 B2 Siddipet India
49 M7 Sideros, Akra pt Greece
58 E6 Sidesaviwa S. Africa
45 H5 Sidi Aïssa Alg.
45 G4 Sidi Ali Alg.
54 B1 Sidi Bel Abbès Alg.
48 C7 Sidi Bouzid Tunisia
48 D7 Sidi El Hani, Sebkhet de salt pan Tunisia
54 A2 Sidi Ifni Morocco
54 B1 Sidi Kacem Morocco
32 A5 Sidikalang Indon.
40 E4 Sidlaw Hills h. U.K.
92 A4 Sidley, Mt mt Ant.
39 D7 Sidmouth U.K.
64 E5 Sidney Can.
72 F2 Sidney MT U.S.A.
76 C3 Sidney NE U.S.A.
81 F3 Sidney NY U.S.A.
80 A4 Sidney OH U.S.A.
79 D5 Sidney Lanier, L. l. U.S.A.
23 H5 Sidoktaya Myanmar
16 E5 Sidon Lebanon
50 G3 Sidorovo Rus. Fed.
90 A3 Sidrolândia Brazil
59 J3 Sidvokodvo Swaziland
44 F5 Sié, Col de pass France
47 L4 Siedlce Pol.
43 G4 Sieg r. Ger.
32 B2 Siĕmréab Cambodia
48 D3 Siena Italy
47 J5 Sieradz Pol.
77 B6 Sierra Blanca U.S.A.
91 C4 Sierra Colorada Arg.
75 F5 Sierra Estrella mts U.S.A.
91 D4 Sierra Grande Arg.
52 C5 Sierra Leone country Africa
96 H5 Sierra Leone Basin sea feature Atl. Ocean
96 H5 Sierra Leone Rise sea feature Atl. Ocean
74 C4 Sierra Madre Mts mts U.S.A.
74 B1 Sierra Nevada mts U.S.A.
89 B2 Sierra Nevada de Santa Marta, Parque Nacional nat. park Col.
89 C2 Sierra Nevada, Parque Nacional nat. park Venez.
91 D4 Sierra, Punta pt Arg.
74 B2 Sierraville U.S.A.
75 G6 Sierra Vista U.S.A.
46 C7 Sierre Switz.
36 T5 Sievi Fin.
27 C6 Sifang Ling mts China
49 L6 Sifnos i. Greece
45 F5 Sig Alg.
47 L7 Sighetu Marmației Romania
47 M7 Sighișoara Romania
32 □ Siglap Sing.
33 A1 Sigli Indon.
36 D3 Siglufjörður Iceland
31 B4 Sigma Phil.
46 D6 Sigmaringen Ger.
42 E4 Signal de Botrange h. Belgium
75 E5 Signal Peak summit U.S.A.
92 B1 Signy U.K. Base Ant.
42 C5 Signy-l'Abbaye France
68 A5 Sigourney U.S.A.
49 L5 Sigri, Akra pt Greece
45 E2 Sigüenza Spain
54 B3 Siguiri Guinea
37 T8 Sigulda Latvia
32 B3 Sihanoukville Cambodia
26 F3 Sihong China
22 E5 Sihora India
27 D6 Sihui China
36 T4 Siikajoki Fin.
36 U5 Siilinjärvi Fin.
17 H3 Siirt Turkey
33 B3 Sijunjung Indon.
22 B5 Sika India
64 E3 Sikanni Chief Can.
64 E3 Sikanni Chief r. Can.
22 C4 Sikar India
19 H3 Sikaram mt Afgh.
54 B3 Sikasso Mali
77 F4 Sikeston U.S.A.
24 F2 Sikhote-Alin' mts Rus. Fed.
49 L6 Sikinos i. Greece
23 G4 Sikkim div. India
36 P4 Siksjö Sweden
33 E1 Sikuati Malaysia
45 C1 Sil r. Spain
31 C4 Silago Phil.
37 S9 Šilalė Lith.
82 D4 Silao Mex.
31 B4 Silay Phil.
43 H1 Silberberg h. Ger.
23 H4 Silchar India
16 B1 Şile Turkey
21 C2 Sileru r. India
22 E3 Silgarhi Nepal
48 C6 Siliana Tunisia
16 D3 Silifke Turkey
23 G3 Siling Co salt l. China
Silistat see Bozkır
49 M2 Silistra Bulg.
16 B1 Silivri Turkey
37 O6 Siljan l. Sweden
37 L8 Silkeborg Denmark
37 U7 Sillamäe Estonia
22 C5 Sillod India
59 J3 Silobela S. Africa
23 G3 Silong China
77 E6 Silsbee U.S.A.
36 U3 Siltaharju Fin.
19 F5 Sīlūp r. Iran
37 R9 Šilutė Lith.
17 H2 Silvan Turkey
22 C5 Silvassa India
68 B2 Silver Bay U.S.A.
73 E5 Silver City U.S.A.
68 C1 Silver Islet Can.
72 B3 Silver Lake U.S.A.
74 D4 Silver Lake l. CA U.S.A.
68 D2 Silver Lake l. MI U.S.A.
41 C5 Silvermine Mts h. Rep. of Ireland
74 D3 Silver Peak Range mts U.S.A.
80 E5 Silver Spring U.S.A.
74 C2 Silver Springs U.S.A.
8 C1 Silverton Austr.
39 D7 Silverton U.K.
69 F3 Silver Water Can.
84 E3 Silvituc Mex.
33 D2 Simanggang Malaysia
32 B1 Simao China
31 B3 Simara i. Phil.
69 H2 Simard, Lac l. Can.
17 L5 Sīmareh r. Iran
23 F4 Simaria India
16 B2 Simav Turkey
16 B2 Simav Dağları mts Turkey
56 C3 Simba Congo(Zaire)
Simbirsk see Ul'yanovsk
Simbor i. see Pānikoita
69 G4 Simcoe Can.
69 H3 Simcoe, Lake l. Can.
23 F5 Simdega India
56 D2 Simēn Mountains mts Eth.
33 A2 Simeulue i. Indon.
51 E6 Simferopol' Ukr.
23 E3 Simikot Nepal
89 B3 Simiti Col.
74 C4 Simi Valley U.S.A.
73 F4 Simla U.S.A.
47 L7 Şimleu Silvaniei Romania
42 E4 Simmerath Ger.
42 F5 Simmern (Hunsrück) Ger.
74 C4 Simmler U.S.A.
75 F4 Simmons U.S.A.
79 F7 Simms Bahamas
36 U3 Simojärvi l. Fin.
64 F4 Simonette r. Can.
65 J4 Simonhouse Can.
46 D7 Simplon Pass Switz.
6 D4 Simpson Desert Austr.
68 D1 Simpson I. i. Can.
74 D2 Simpson Park Mts mts U.S.A.
37 O9 Simrishamn Sweden
31 A5 Simunul i. Phil.
24 H2 Simushir, O. i. Rus. Fed.
21 A2 Sina r. India
33 A2 Sinabang Indon.
32 A5 Sinabung volc. Indon.
55 F2 Sinai reg. Egypt
42 C5 Sinai, Mont h. France
84 A1 Sinaloa div. Mex.
48 D3 Sinalunga Italy
27 C5 Sinan China
30 C4 Sinanju N. Korea
23 H5 Sinbyugyun Myanmar
16 F2 Sincan Turkey
89 B2 Sincé Col.
89 B2 Sincelejo Col.
79 D5 Sinclair, L. l. U.S.A.
64 E4 Sinclair Mills Can.
58 B2 Sinclair Mine Namibia
40 E2 Sinclair's Bay b. U.K.
22 D4 Sind r. India
31 B4 Sindañgan Phil.
33 C4 Sindangbarang Indon.
22 B4 Sindari India
46 D6 Sindelfingen Ger.
21 B2 Sindgi India
22 B4 Sindh div. Pak.
21 B3 Sindhnur India
16 B2 Sındırgı Turkey
22 D6 Sindkhed India
22 C5 Sindkheda India
30 C4 Sin-do i. China
50 J2 Sindor Rus. Fed.
23 F5 Sindri India
22 B3 Sind Sagar Doab lowland Pak.
50 J3 Sinegor'ye Rus. Fed.
49 M4 Sinekçi Turkey
45 B4 Sines Port.
45 B4 Sines, Cabo de pt Port.
36 T3 Sinettä Fin.
54 B4 Sinfra Côte d'Ivoire
55 F3 Singa Sudan
22 E3 Singahi India
30 D3 Sin'galp'a China
22 D2 Singa Pass pass India
32 B5 Singapore Sing.
11 M9 Singapore country Asia
32 B5 Singapore, Strait of chan. Indon./Sing.
33 E4 Singaraja Indon.
32 B2 Sing Buri Thai.
69 G3 Singhampton Can.
56 D4 Singida Tanz.
6 C2 Singkang Indon.
33 C2 Singkawang Indon.
32 A5 Singkil Indon.
8 H2 Singleton Austr.
Singora see Songkhla
30 D4 Sin'gye N. Korea
30 D3 Sinhŭng N. Korea
48 C4 Siniscola Sardinia Italy
48 G3 Sinj Croatia
6 C2 Sinjai Indon.
17 H3 Sinjār Iraq
17 H3 Sinjār, Jabal mt Iraq
17 K3 Sīnji Iran
55 F3 Sinkat Sudan
Sinkiang Uighur Aut. Region div. see
Xinjiang Uygur Zizhiqu
30 C4 Sinmi i. N. Korea
43 G4 Sinn Ger.
87 H2 Sinnamary Fr. Guiana
Sinneh see Sanandaj
49 N2 Sinoie, Lacul lag. Romania
51 E7 Sinop Turkey
30 D3 Sinpa N. Korea
30 E3 Sinp'o N. Korea
30 E3 Sinp'ung-dong N. Korea
30 D4 Sinp'yŏng N. Korea
30 D4 Sinsang N. Korea
43 G5 Sinsheim Ger.
33 D2 Sintang Indon.
77 D6 Sinton U.S.A.
89 A2 Sinú r. Col.
30 C3 Sinŭiju N. Korea
42 F4 Sinzig Ger.
31 B5 Siocon Phil.
46 J7 Siófok Hungary
46 C7 Sion Switz.
41 D3 Sion Mills U.K.
76 D3 Sioux Center U.S.A.
76 D3 Sioux City U.S.A.
76 D3 Sioux Falls U.S.A.
66 B3 Sioux Lookout Can.
31 B4 Sipalay Phil.
30 C2 Siping China
65 K3 Sipiwesk Can.
65 K3 Sipiwesk L. l. Can.
92 B4 Siple Coast coastal area Ant.
92 A4 Siple, Mt mt Ant.
22 C5 Sipra r. India
79 C5 Sipsey r. U.S.A.
33 A3 Sipura i. Indon.
83 H6 Siquia r. Nic.
31 B4 Siquijor Phil.
31 B4 Siquijor i. Phil.
22 B5 Sir r. Pak.
21 B3 Sira India
37 K7 Sira r. Norway
18 D5 Şir Abū Nu'āyr i. U.A.E.
Siracusa see Syracuse
64 E4 Sir Alexander, Mt mt Can.
17 G1 Şiran Turkey
69 H2 Siranda Lake l. Pak.
18 D5 Şīr Banī Yās i. U.A.E.
17 M3 Sīrdān Iran
6 D3 Sir Edward Pellew Group is Austr.
68 A3 Siren U.S.A.
19 F5 Sīrgān Iran
32 B1 Siri Kit Dam dam Thai.
18 D4 Sīrīz Iran
64 D2 Sir James McBrien, Mt mt Can.
Sirjan see Sa'īdābād
18 D4 Sirjan salt flat Iran
18 E5 Sirk Iran
22 E4 Sirmour India
17 J3 Şırnak Turkey
21 C2 Sironcha India
22 D4 Sironj India
21 B2 Sirpur India
74 C4 Sirretta Peak summit U.S.A.
18 D5 Sīrrī, Jazīreh-ye i. Iran
22 C3 Sirsa Haryana India
23 E4 Sirsa Uttar Pradesh India
64 F4 Sir Sanford, Mt mt Can.
21 A3 Sirsi Karnataka India
22 D3 Sirsi India
21 B2 Sirsilla India
55 D1 Sirte Libya
55 D1 Sirte, Gulf of g. Libya
21 A2 Sirur India
17 J2 Şirvan Turkey
37 T9 Širvintos Lith.
17 K4 Sīrwān r. Iraq
64 F4 Sir Wilfred Laurier, Mt mt Can.
48 G2 Sisak Croatia
32 C2 Sisaket Thai.
18 C4 Sīsakht Iran
84 E2 Sisal Mex.
58 E3 Sishen S. Africa
17 L2 Sisian Armenia
68 C2 Siskiwit Bay b. U.S.A.
32 B2 Sisŏphŏn Cambodia
74 B4 Sisquoc r. U.S.A.
76 D2 Sisseton U.S.A.
81 K1 Sisson Branch Reservoir Can.
19 F4 Sīstan reg. Iran
19 F4 Sīstan, Daryācheh-ye marsh Afgh.
22 C5 Sitamau India
31 A5 Sitangkai Phil.
22 E4 Sitapur India
49 M7 Siteia Greece
59 J3 Siteki Swaziland
49 K4 Sithonia pen. Greece
90 C1 Sitio da Abadia Brazil
90 D1 Sitio do Mato Brazil
64 B3 Sitka U.S.A.
22 B3 Sitpur Pak.
42 D4 Sittard Neth.
23 H4 Sittaung Myanmar
43 H1 Sittensen Ger.
39 H6 Sittingbourne U.K.
23 H5 Sittwe Myanmar
27 □ Siu A Chau i. H.K. China
23 F5 Siuri India
21 B4 Sivaganga India
21 B4 Sivakasi India
18 D4 Sivand Iran
16 F2 Sivas Turkey
16 B2 Sivaslı Turkey
17 G3 Siverek Turkey
17 G2 Sivrice Turkey
16 C2 Sivrihisar Turkey
59 H3 Sivukile S. Africa
55 E2 Siwa Egypt
22 D3 Siwalik Range mts India/Nepal
23 F4 Siwan India
22 C4 Siwana India
44 G5 Six-Fours-les-Plages France
26 E3 Si Xian China
68 E4 Six Lakes U.S.A.
41 D3 Sixmilecross U.K.
59 H2 Siyabuswa S. Africa
26 F3 Siyang China
17 M1 Siyäzän Azer.
26 C1 Siyitang China
18 D3 Sīyunī Iran
26 D1 Siziwang Qi China
Sjælland i. see Zealand
49 J3 Sjenica Yugo.
37 N9 Sjöbo Sweden
36 P2 Sjøvegan Norway
89 E2 S. Juan r. Venez.
51 E6 Skadovs'k Ukr.
36 E4 Skaftafell National Park Iceland
36 E5 Skaftárós est. Iceland
36 D3 Skagafjörður in. Iceland
37 M8 Skagen Denmark
37 L8 Skagerrak str. Denmark/Norway
72 B1 Skagit r. Can./U.S.A.
64 B3 Skagway U.S.A.
36 T1 Skaidi Norway
36 P2 Skaland Norway
36 O4 Skalmodal Sweden
37 L8 Skanderborg Denmark
81 E3 Skaneateles Lake l. U.S.A.
68 C2 Skanee U.S.A.
49 L5 Skantzoura i. Greece
37 N7 Skara Sweden
37 R7 Skärgårdshavet Nationalpark nat. park Fin.
37 M6 Skarnes Norway
47 K5 Skarżysko-Kamienna Pol.
36 R3 Skaulo Sweden
47 J6 Skawina Pol.
64 D3 Skeena r. Can.
64 D3 Skeena Mountains mts Can.
39 H4 Skegness U.K.
36 R4 Skellefteå Sweden
36 Q4 Skellefteälven r. Sweden
36 R4 Skelleftehamn Sweden
41 A6 Skellig Rocks is Rep. of Ireland
38 E4 Skelmersdale U.K.
41 E4 Skerries Rep. of Ireland
37 M7 Ski Norway
49 K5 Skiathos i. Greece
41 B6 Skibbereen Rep. of Ireland
36 R2 Skibotn Norway
38 D3 Skiddaw mt U.K.
37 L7 Skien Norway
47 K5 Skierniewice Pol.
54 C1 Skikda Alg.
38 G4 Skipsea U.K.
8 D4 Skipton Austr.
38 E4 Skipton U.K.
37 L8 Skive Denmark
36 E4 Skjálfandafljót r. Iceland
37 L9 Skjern Denmark
37 K6 Skjolden Norway
36 K5 Skodje Norway
36 T2 Skoganvarre Norway
41 F6 Skokholm Island i. U.K.
68 D4 Skokie U.S.A.
39 B6 Skomer Island i. U.K.
49 K5 Skopelos i. Greece
50 F4 Skopin Rus. Fed.
49 J4 Skopje Macedonia
51 F5 Skorodnoye Rus. Fed.
37 N7 Skövde Sweden
81 J2 Skowhegan U.S.A.
37 S8 Skrunda Latvia
64 B2 Skukum, Mt mt Can.
59 J2 Skukuza S. Africa
74 D3 Skull Peak summit U.S.A.
68 B5 Skunk r. U.S.A.
37 R8 Skuodas Lith.
37 N9 Skurup Sweden
37 P6 Skutskär Sweden
51 D5 Skvyra Ukr.
40 B3 Skye i. U.K.
49 L5 Skyros Greece
49 L5 Skyros i. Greece
92 B3 Skytrain Ice Rise ice feature Ant.
37 M9 Slagelse Denmark
36 Q4 Slagnäs Sweden
33 C4 Slamet, Gunung volc. Indon.
41 E4 Slane Rep. of Ireland
41 E5 Slaney r. Rep. of Ireland
50 D3 Slantsy Rus. Fed.
51 G5 Slashchevskaya Rus. Fed.
68 D1 Slate Is is Can.
48 G2 Slatina Croatia
49 L2 Slatina Romania
65 G2 Slave r. Can.
54 C4 Slave Coast coastal area Africa
64 G3 Slave Lake Can.
15 F1 Slavgorod Rus. Fed.
47 O2 Slavkovichi Rus. Fed.
49 H2 Slavonija reg. Croatia
49 H2 Slavonski Brod Croatia
51 C5 Slavuta Ukr.
51 D5 Slavutych Ukr.
28 B3 Slavyanka Rus. Fed.
51 F6 Slavyansk-na-Kubani Rus. Fed.
50 D4 Slawharad Belarus
46 H3 Sławno Pol.
39 G4 Sleaford U.K.
41 A5 Slea Head hd Rep. of Ireland
40 C3 Sleat pen. U.K.
40 C3 Sleat, Sound of chan. U.K.
66 E2 Sleeper Islands is Can.
68 D3 Sleeping Bear Dunes National Seashore res. U.S.A.
68 D3 Sleeping Bear Pt pt U.S.A.
51 H7 Sleptsovskaya Rus. Fed.
92 C3 Slessor Glacier gl. Ant.
77 F6 Slidell U.S.A.
41 A5 Slievanea h. Rep. of Ireland
41 D3 Slieve Anierin h. Rep. of Ireland
41 D5 Slieveardagh Hills h. Rep. of Ireland
41 C4 Slieve Aughty Mts h. Rep. of Ireland
41 D3 Slieve Beagh h. Rep. of Ireland/U.K.
41 C5 Slieve Bernagh h. Rep. of Ireland
41 D4 Slieve Bloom Mts h. Rep. of Ireland
41 B5 Slievecallan h. Rep. of Ireland
41 B3 Slieve Car h. Rep. of Ireland
41 F3 Slieve Donard h. U.K.
41 B4 Slieve Elva h. Rep. of Ireland
41 C3 Slieve Gamph h. Rep. of Ireland
41 C3 Slieve League h. Rep. of Ireland
41 B5 Slieve Mish Mts h. Rep. of Ireland
41 B5 Slieve Miskish Mts h. Rep. of Ireland
41 A3 Slieve More h. Rep. of Ireland
41 D4 Slieve na Calliagh h. Rep. of Ireland
41 D5 Slievenamon h. Rep. of Ireland
41 D2 Slieve Snaght mt Rep. of Ireland
40 B3 Sligachan U.K.
41 C3 Sligo Rep. of Ireland
41 C3 Sligo Bay b. Rep. of Ireland
37 Q8 Slite Sweden
49 M3 Sliven Bulg.
50 H2 Sloboda Rus. Fed.
50 J2 Slobodchikovo Rus. Fed.
49 M2 Slobozia Romania
64 F5 Slocan Can.
42 E1 Slochteren Neth.
50 C4 Slonim Belarus
42 C2 Slootdorp Neth.
42 D2 Sloten Neth.
42 D2 Slotermeer l. Neth.
7 F2 Slot, The chan. Solomon Is
39 G6 Slough U.K.
35 G4 Slovakia country Europe
34 G4 Slovenia country Europe
48 F1 Slovenj Gradec Slovenia
51 F5 Slov''yans'k Ukr.
46 H3 Słupsk Pol.
36 P4 Slussfors Sweden
50 C4 Slutsk Belarus
41 A4 Slyne Head hd Rep. of Ireland
13 M4 Slyudyanka Rus. Fed.
81 J3 Small Pt pt U.S.A.
67 H3 Smallwood Reservoir Can.
50 D4 Smalyavichy Belarus
47 N3 Smarhon' Belarus
58 E5 Smartt Syndicate Dam resr S. Africa
65 J4 Smeaton Can.
49 J2 Smederevo Yugo.
49 J2 Smederevska Palanka Yugo.
80 D4 Smethport U.S.A.
51 D5 Smila Ukr.
42 E2 Smilde Neth.
37 T8 Smiltene Latvia
64 G3 Smith Can.
74 C2 Smith U.S.A.
80 C6 Smith r. U.S.A.
62 C2 Smith Bay b. U.S.A.
64 D4 Smithers Can.
59 G5 Smithfield S. Africa
79 E5 Smithfield NC U.S.A.
72 E3 Smithfield UT U.S.A.
92 A3 Smith Glacier gl. Ant.
92 B2 Smith I. i. S. Shetland Is Ant.
81 E5 Smith I. i. MD U.S.A.
81 F6 Smith I. i. VA U.S.A.
80 D6 Smith Mountain Lake l. U.S.A.
64 D3 Smith River Can.
69 J3 Smiths Falls Can.
63 L2 Smith Sound str. Can./Greenland
74 C1 Smoke Creek Desert U.S.A.
64 F4 Smoky r. Can.
76 C4 Smoky r. U.S.A.
66 D3 Smoky Falls Can.
76 D4 Smoky Hills h. U.S.A.
64 G4 Smoky Lake Can.
36 K5 Smøla i. Norway
50 E4 Smolensk Rus. Fed.
50 E4 Smolenskaya Oblast' div. Rus. Fed.
49 L4 Smolyan Bulg.
28 C3 Smolyoninovo Rus. Fed.
66 D4 Smooth Rock Falls Can.
66 C3 Smoothrock L. l. Can.
65 H4 Smoothstone Lake l. Can.
36 T1 Smørfjord Norway
92 B3 Smyley I. i. Ant.
81 F5 Smyrna DE U.S.A.
79 C5 Smyrna GA U.S.A.
80 C4 Smyrna OH U.S.A.
81 J1 Smyrna Mills U.S.A.
38 C3 Snaefell h. U.K.
36 F4 Snæfell mt Iceland
64 A2 Snag Can.
72 D3 Snake r. U.S.A.
75 E2 Snake Range mts U.S.A.
72 D3 Snake River Plain plain U.S.A.
79 E7 Snap Pt pt Bahamas
64 G2 Snare Lake Can.
7 G6 Snares Is is N.Z.
36 N4 Snasa Norway
42 D1 Sneek Neth.
41 B6 Sneem Rep. of Ireland
58 F6 Sneeuberg mts S. Africa
67 H3 Snegamook Lake l. Can.
39 H5 Snettisham U.K.
12 K3 Snezhnogorsk Rus. Fed.
48 F2 Snežnik mt Slovenia
47 K4 Śniardwy, Jezioro l. Pol.
51 E6 Snihurivka Ukr.
40 B3 Snizort, Loch b. U.K.
72 B2 Snohomish U.S.A.
72 B2 Snoqualmie Pass U.S.A.
36 N3 Snøtinden mt Norway
65 J2 Snowbird Lake l. Can.
39 C4 Snowdon mt U.K.
39 D5 Snowdonia National Park U.K.
75 G4 Snowflake U.S.A.
81 F5 Snow Hill MD U.S.A.
79 E5 Snow Hill NC U.S.A.
65 J4 Snow Lake Can.
8 B2 Snowtown Austr.
72 D3 Snowville U.S.A.
8 G4 Snowy r. Austr.
8 G4 Snowy Mts mts Austr.
67 J3 Snug Harbour Nfld Can.
69 G3 Snug Harbour Ont. Can.
32 C2 Snuŏl Cambodia
77 D5 Snyder OK U.S.A.
77 C5 Snyder TX U.S.A.
57 E5 Soalala Madag.
57 E5 Soanierana-Ivongo Madag.
30 D6 Soan kundo i. S. Korea
89 B3 Soata Col.
40 B3 Soay i. U.K.
30 D6 Sobaek Sanmaek mts S. Korea
55 F4 Sobat r. Sudan
43 F5 Sobernheim Ger.
25 G7 Sobger r. Indon.
29 B8 Sobo-san mt Japan
87 K6 Sobradinho, Barragem de resr Brazil
87 K4 Sobral Brazil
So-chaoson-man g. see Korea Bay
51 F7 Sochi Rus. Fed.
30 D5 Sŏch'on S. Korea
5 M6 Society Islands is Pac. Oc.
90 C3 Socorro Brazil
89 B3 Socorro Col.
73 F5 Socorro U.S.A.
82 B5 Socorro, I. i. Mex.
20 D7 Socotra i. Yemen
32 C3 Soc Trăng Vietnam
45 E3 Socuéllamos Spain
74 D4 Soda Lake l. U.S.A.
36 U3 Sodankylä Fin.
22 D2 Soda Plains plain China/Jammu and Kashmir
72 E3 Soda Springs U.S.A.
37 P6 Söderhamn Sweden
37 P7 Söderköping Sweden
37 P7 Södertälje Sweden
55 E3 Sodiri Sudan
56 D3 Sodo Eth.
37 Q6 Södra Kvarken str. Fin./Sweden
59 H1 Soekmekaar S. Africa
42 D3 Soerendonk Neth.
43 G3 Soest Ger.
42 D2 Soest Neth.
8 G2 Sofala Austr.
49 K3 Sofia Bulg.
Sofiya see Sofia
36 W4 Sofporog Rus. Fed.
29 G10 Sōfu-gan i. Japan
89 B3 Sogamoso Col.
17 G1 Soğanlı Dağları mts Turkey
42 F2 Sögel Ger.
37 K7 Søgne Norway
37 J6 Sognefjorden in. Norway
31 C4 Sogod Phil.
26 A1 Sogo Nur l. China
50 H2 Sogra Rus. Fed.
26 A3 Sogruma China
16 C1 Söğüt Turkey
30 D7 Sŏgwip'o S. Korea
23 H3 Sog Xian China
55 F2 Sohâg Egypt
22 D5 Sohagpur India
39 H5 Soham U.K.
22 B2 Sohan r. Pak.
7 F2 Sohano P.N.G.
23 E5 Sohela India
22 D3 Sohna India
30 E3 Sŏho-ri N. Korea
30 C6 Sohŭksan i. S. Korea
42 C4 Soignes, Forêt de forest Belgium
42 C4 Soignies Belgium
36 T5 Soini Fin.
44 F2 Soissons France
22 C4 Sojat India
31 B4 Sojoton Point pt Phil.
51 C5 Sokal' Ukr.
30 E4 Sokch'o S. Korea
49 M6 Söke Turkey
51 G7 Sokhumi Georgia
54 C4 Sokodé Togo
27 □ Soko Islands is H.K. China
50 G3 Sokol Rus. Fed.
47 L4 Sokółka Pol.
54 B3 Sokolo Mali
43 L4 Sokolov Czech Rep.
28 C3 Sokolovka Rus. Fed.
47 L4 Sokołów Podlaski Pol.
54 C3 Sokoto Nigeria
54 C3 Sokoto r. Nigeria
51 C5 Sokyryany Ukr.
22 D3 Solan India
9 A7 Solander I. i. N.Z.
21 A2 Solāpur India
89 B2 Soledad Col.
74 B3 Soledad U.S.A.
89 E2 Soledad Venez.
84 C3 Soledad de Doblado Mex.
51 G6 Solenoye Rus. Fed.
39 F7 Solent, The str. U.K.
36 N3 Solfjellsjøen Norway
17 H2 Solhan Turkey
50 G3 Soligalich Rus. Fed.
39 F5 Solihull U.K.
12 G4 Solikamsk Rus. Fed.
12 G4 Sol'-Iletsk Rus. Fed.
42 F3 Solingen Ger.
58 A1 Solitaire Namibia
17 M1 Şollar Azer.
36 P5 Sollefteå Sweden
43 L3 Söllichau Ger.
43 H3 Solling h. Ger.
43 J3 Sollstedt Ger.
43 G4 Solms Ger.
50 F3 Solnechnogorsk Rus. Fed.
33 B3 Solok Indon.
84 E4 Sololá Guatemala
4 H5 Solomon Islands country Pac. Oc.
6 F2 Solomon Sea sea P.N.G./Solomon Is
68 B2 Solon Springs U.S.A.
25 E7 Solor, Kepulauan is Indon.
46 C7 Solothurn Switz.
50 E1 Solovetskiye Ostrova is Rus. Fed.
50 H3 Solovetskoye Rus. Fed.
48 G3 Šolta i. Croatia
18 C4 Solṭānābād Iran
19 E3 Solṭānābād Iran
19 E2 Solṭānābād Iran
43 H2 Soltau Ger.
50 D3 Sol'tsy Rus. Fed.
81 E3 Solvay U.S.A.
37 O8 Sölvesborg Sweden
40 E6 Solway Firth est. U.K.
57 C5 Solwezi Zambia
29 G6 Sōma Japan
16 A2 Soma Turkey
42 B4 Somain France
53 J5 Somalia country Africa
93 H3 Somali Basin sea feature Ind. Ocean
57 C4 Sombo Angola
49 H2 Sombor Yugo.
84 B2 Sombrerete Mex.
22 C4 Somdari India
81 J2 Somerest Junction U.S.A.
37 S6 Somero Fin.
78 C4 Somerset KY U.S.A.
68 E4 Somerset MI U.S.A.
80 D5 Somerset PA U.S.A.
59 F6 Somerset East S. Africa
63 J2 Somerset Island i. Can.

12 J2 Vise, O. *i.* Rus. Fed.
87 J4 Viseu Brazil
45 C2 Viseu Port.
21 C2 Vishakhapatnam India
37 U8 Viški Latvia
22 C5 Visnagar India
49 H3 Visoko Bos.-Herz.
48 B2 Viso, Monte *mt* Italy
46 C7 Visp Switz.
43 H2 Visselhövede Ger.
74 D5 Vista U.S.A.
90 A2 Vista Alegre Brazil
49 L4 Vistonida, Limni *lag.* Greece
89 C3 Vita *r.* Col.
22 B3 Vitakri Pak.
48 E3 Viterbo Italy
48 G2 Vitez Bos.-Herz.
86 E8 Vitichi Bol.
45 C2 Vitigudino Spain
7 H3 Viti Levu *i.* Fiji
24 D1 Vitim *r.* Rus. Fed.
24 D1 Vitimskoye Ploskogor'ye *plat.* Rus. Fed.
90 E3 Vitória Brazil
Vitoria *see* Vitoria-Gasteiz
90 E1 Vitória da Conquista Brazil
45 E1 Vitoria-Gasteiz Spain
44 D2 Vitré France
42 A4 Vitry-en-Artois France
44 G2 Vitry-le-François France
50 D4 Vitsyebsk Belarus
36 R3 Vittangi Sweden
48 F6 Vittoria *Sicily* Italy
48 E2 Vittorio Veneto Italy
94 F3 Vityaz Depth *depth* Pac. Oc.
45 C1 Viveiro Spain
59 H1 Vivo S. Africa
Vizagapatam *see* Vishakhapatnam
82 B3 Vizcaíno, Sierra *mts* Mex.
51 C7 Vize Turkey
21 C2 Vizianagaram India
50 J2 Vizinga Rus. Fed.
42 C3 Vlaardingen Neth.
47 L7 Vlădeasa, Vârful *mt* Romania
51 H7 Vladikavkaz Rus. Fed.
28 D3 Vladimir *Primorskiy Kray* Rus. Fed.
50 G3 Vladimir *Vladimir. Obl.* Rus. Fed.
28 C3 Vladimiro-Aleksandrovskoye Rus. Fed.
24 F2 Vladivostok Rus. Fed.
50 G4 Vlaimirskaya Oblast' *div.* Rus. Fed.
59 H2 Vlakte S. Africa
49 K3 Vlasotince Yugo.
58 D7 Vleesbaai *b.* S. Africa
42 C1 Vlieland *i.* Neth.
42 B3 Vlissingen Neth.
49 H4 Vlorë Albania
43 G2 Vlotho Ger.
46 G6 Vltava *r.* Czech Rep.
46 F5 Vöcklabruck Austria
50 F2 Vodlozero, Ozero *l.* Rus. Fed.
40 □ Voe U.K.
42 D4 Voerendaal Neth.
43 H4 Vogelsberg *h.* Ger.
48 C2 Voghera Italy
43 L4 Vogtland *reg.* Ger.
43 L5 Vohenstrauß Ger.
Vohimena, Cape *c. see* Vohimena, Tanjona
57 E6 Vohimena, Tanjona *c.* Madag.
43 G3 Vöhl Ger.
37 T7 Võhma Estonia
56 D4 Voi Kenya
54 B4 Voinjama Liberia
44 G4 Voiron France
37 L9 Vojens Denmark
49 H2 Vojvodina *div.* Yugo.
50 H3 Vokhma Rus. Fed.
50 D1 Voknavolok Rus. Fed.
72 F2 Volborg U.S.A.
91 B1 Volcán, Co del *mt* Chile
Volcano Bay *b. see* Uchiura-wan
Volcano Is *is see* Kazan-rettō
37 K5 Volda Norway
42 D2 Volendam Neth.
51 H6 Volga *r.* Rus. Fed.
68 B4 Volga *r.* U.S.A.
51 G6 Volgodonsk Rus. Fed.
51 H5 Volgograd Rus. Fed.
51 H5 Volgogradskaya Oblast' *div.* Rus. Fed.
46 G7 Völkermarkt Austria
50 E3 Volkhov Rus. Fed.
50 D3 Volkhov *r.* Rus. Fed.
42 E5 Völklingen Ger.
59 H3 Volksrust S. Africa
28 B3 Vol'no-Nadezhdinskoye Rus. Fed.
51 F6 Volnovakha Ukr.
13 L2 Volochanka Rus. Fed.
51 C5 Volochys'k Ukr.
51 F6 Volodars'ke Ukr.
51 J6 Volodarskiy Rus. Fed.
14 E1 Volodarskoye Kazak.
47 O5 Volodars'k-Volyns'kyy Ukr.
47 N5 Volodymyrets' Ukr.
51 C5 Volodymyr-Volyns'kyy Ukr.
50 F3 Vologda Rus. Fed.
50 G3 Vologodskaya Oblast' *div.* Rus. Fed.
51 F5 Volokonovka Rus. Fed.
49 K5 Volos Greece
50 D3 Volosovo Rus. Fed.
47 P2 Volot Rus. Fed.
51 F4 Volovo Rus. Fed.
51 H4 Vol'sk Rus. Fed.
54 B4 Volta, Lake *resr* Ghana
90 D3 Volta Redonda Brazil
48 F4 Volturno *r.* Italy
49 K4 Volvi, L. *l.* Greece
50 J4 Volzhsk Rus. Fed.
51 H5 Volzhskiy Rus. Fed.
57 E6 Vondrozo Madag.
50 G1 Vonga Rus. Fed.
36 F4 Vopnafjörður Iceland
36 F4 Vopnafjörður *b.* Iceland
50 B2 Vörå Fin.
47 M3 Voranava Belarus
50 J3 Vorchanka Rus. Fed.
50 E2 Vorenzha Rus. Fed.
12 H3 Vorkuta Rus. Fed.
37 S7 Vormsi *i.* Estonia
51 G5 Vorona *r.* Rus. Fed.
51 F5 Voronezh Rus. Fed.
51 F5 Voronezh *r.* Rus. Fed.
51 G5 Voronezhskaya Oblast' *div.* Rus. Fed.
50 G3 Voron'ye Rus. Fed.
Voroshilovgrad *see* Luhans'k
47 Q3 Vorot'kovo Rus. Fed.
51 E5 Vorskla *r.* Rus. Fed.
37 T7 Võrtsjärv *l.* Estonia
37 U8 Võru Estonia
19 H2 Vorukh Tajik.
58 E5 Vosburg S. Africa
44 H2 Vosges *mts* France
37 K6 Voss Norway
Vostochno-Sibirskoye More *sea see* East Siberian Sea
24 B1 Vostochnyy Sayan *mts* Rus. Fed.
28 D1 Vostok Rus. Fed.
92 C5 Vostok *Rus. Fed. Base* Ant.
5 M6 Vostok I. *i.* Kiribati
28 D2 Vostretsovo Rus. Fed.
12 G4 Votkinsk Rus. Fed.
90 C3 Votuporanga Brazil
42 C5 Vouziers France
44 E2 Voves France
50 J3 Voya *r.* Rus. Fed.
78 A1 Voyageurs Nat. Park *nat. park* U.S.A.
36 W4 Voynitsa Rus. Fed.
50 G2 Vozhega Rus. Fed.
50 F2 Vozhe, Ozero *l.* Rus. Fed.
51 D6 Voznesens'k Ukr.
28 C3 Vrangel' Rus. Fed.
13 V4 Vrangelya, O. *i.* U.S.A.
49 J3 Vranje Yugo.
49 M3 Vratnik *pass* Bulg.
49 K3 Vratsa Bulg.
49 H2 Vrbas Yugo.
48 G2 Vrbas *r.* Bos.-Herz.
59 H3 Vrede S. Africa
59 G3 Vredefort S. Africa
58 B6 Vredenburg S. Africa
58 C5 Vredendal S. Africa
42 C5 Vresse Belgium
21 B4 Vriddhachalam India
42 E1 Vries Neth.
37 O8 Vrigstad Sweden
49 J2 Vršac Yugo.
58 F3 Vryburg S. Africa
59 J3 Vryheid S. Africa
50 D2 Vsevolozhsk Rus. Fed.
49 J3 Vučitrn Yugo.
49 H2 Vukovar Croatia
12 G3 Vuktyl' Rus. Fed.
59 H3 Vukuzakhe S. Africa
48 F5 Vulcano, Isola *i.* Italy
75 F5 Vulture Mts *mts* U.S.A.
32 C3 Vung Tau Vietnam
37 U6 Vuohijärvi Fin.
36 U4 Vuolijoki Fin.
36 R3 Vuollerim Sweden
36 U3 Vuostimo Fin.
50 H4 Vurnary Rus. Fed.
57 D4 Vwawa Tanz.
22 C5 Vyara India
50 J3 Vyatka Rus. Fed.
50 J3 Vyatka *r.* Rus. Fed.
50 E4 Vyaz'ma Rus. Fed.
50 G3 Vyazniki Rus. Fed.
51 H5 Vyazovka Rus. Fed.
50 D2 Vyborg Rus. Fed.
50 J2 Vychegda *r.* Rus. Fed.
50 H2 Vychegodskiy Rus. Fed.
50 C4 Vyerkhnyadzvinsk Belarus
50 D4 Vyetryna Belarus
50 E2 Vygozero, Ozero *l.* Rus. Fed.
50 G4 Vyksa Rus. Fed.
51 D6 Vylkove Ukr.
47 L6 Vynohradiv Ukr.
50 E3 Vypolzovo Rus. Fed.
50 D3 Vyritsa Rus. Fed.
39 D5 Vyrnwy, Lake *l.* U.K.
51 F6 Vyselki Rus. Fed.
50 G4 Vysha Rus. Fed.
51 D5 Vyshhorod Ukr.
50 E3 Vyshnevolotskaya Gryada *ridge* Rus. Fed.
50 E3 Vyshniy-Volochek Rus. Fed.
46 H6 Vyškov Czech Rep.
51 D5 Vystupovychi Ukr.
50 F2 Vytegra Rus. Fed.

W

54 B3 Wa Ghana
42 D3 Waal *r.* Neth.
42 D3 Waalwijk Neth.
66 B3 Wabakimi L. *l.* Can.
64 G3 Wabasca Can.
64 G3 Wabasca *r.* Can.
68 E5 Wabash U.S.A.
68 E5 Wabash *r.* U.S.A.
68 A3 Wabasha U.S.A.
69 E1 Wabatongushi Lake *l.* Can.
56 E3 Wabē Gestro *r.* Eth.
56 E3 Wabē Shebelē Wenz *r.* Eth.
65 K4 Wabowden Can.
66 C2 Wabuk Pt *pt* Can.
67 G3 Wabush Can.
67 G3 Wabush L. *l.* Can.
74 C2 Wabuska U.S.A.
79 D6 Waccasassa Bay *b.* U.S.A.
43 H4 Wächtersbach Ger.
77 D6 Waco U.S.A.
19 G5 Wad Pak.
8 G4 Wadbilliga Nat. Park Austr.
55 D2 Waddān Libya
42 C1 Waddeneilanden *is* Neth.
42 C2 Waddenzee *chan.* Neth.
64 D4 Waddington, Mt *mt* Can.
42 C2 Waddinxveen Neth.
39 C7 Wadebridge U.K.
65 J4 Wadena Can.
76 E2 Wadena U.S.A.
42 E5 Wadern Ger.
21 A2 Wadgaon India
42 E5 Wadgassen Ger.
55 E3 Wadi el Milk *watercourse* Sudan
55 F2 Wadi Halfa Sudan
55 E3 Wadi Howar *watercourse* Sudan
55 F3 Wad Medani Sudan
74 C2 Wadsworth U.S.A.
30 B4 Wafangdian China
17 L7 Wafra Kuwait
43 G2 Wagenfeld Ger.
43 J2 Wagenhoff Ger.
63 K3 Wager Bay *b.* Can.
8 F3 Wagga Wagga Austr.
22 C2 Wah Pak.
74 □1 Wahiawa U.S.A.
43 H3 Wahlhausen Ger.
76 D3 Wahoo U.S.A.
76 D2 Wahpeton U.S.A.
75 F2 Wah Wah Mts *mts* U.S.A.
21 A2 Wai India
74 □1 Waialee U.S.A.
74 □1 Waialua U.S.A.
74 □1 Waialua Bay *b.* U.S.A.
74 □1 Waianae U.S.A.
74 □1 Waianae Ra. *mts* U.S.A.
9 D5 Waiau *r.* N.Z.
46 G7 Waidhofen an der Ybbs Austria
25 F7 Waigeo *i.* Indon.
9 E2 Waiharoa N.Z.
9 E2 Waiheke Island *i.* N.Z.
9 E2 Waihi N.Z.
9 E2 Waihou *r.* N.Z.
25 D7 Waikabubak Indon.
9 B6 Waikaia *r.* N.Z.
74 □1 Waikane U.S.A.
9 D5 Waikari N.Z.
9 E3 Waikato *r.* N.Z.
9 F2 Waikawa Pt *pt* N.Z.
8 B3 Waikerie Austr.
74 □1 Waikiki Beach *beach* U.S.A.
9 C6 Waikouaiti N.Z.
74 □2 Wailuku U.S.A.
9 D5 Waimakariri *r.* N.Z.
74 □1 Waimanalo U.S.A.
9 C4 Waimangaroa N.Z.
9 F3 Waimarama N.Z.
9 C6 Waimate N.Z.
74 □1 Waimea *HI* U.S.A.
74 □2 Waimea *HI* U.S.A.
22 D5 Wainganga *r.* India
25 E7 Waingapu Indon.
39 C7 Wainhouse Corner U.K.
65 G4 Wainwright Can.
62 C2 Wainwright *AK* U.S.A.
9 E3 Waiouru N.Z.
9 E3 Waipa *r.* N.Z.
9 B7 Waipahi N.Z.
74 □1 Waipahu U.S.A.
9 F3 Waipaoa *r.* N.Z.
9 B7 Waipapa Pt *pt* N.Z.
9 D5 Waipara N.Z.
9 F3 Waipawa N.Z.
9 F3 Waipukurau N.Z.
9 F3 Wairakei N.Z.
9 E4 Wairarapa, L. *l.* N.Z.
9 D4 Wairau *r.* N.Z.
9 F3 Wairoa N.Z.
9 F3 Wairoa *r. Hawke's Bay* N.Z.
9 E1 Wairoa *r. Northland* N.Z.
9 F3 Waitahanui N.Z.
9 B6 Waitahuna N.Z.
9 E2 Waitakaruru N.Z.
9 C6 Waitaki *r.* N.Z.
9 E3 Waitara N.Z.
9 E2 Waitoa N.Z.
9 E2 Waiuku N.Z.
9 B7 Waiwera South N.Z.
27 F5 Waiyang China
29 E6 Wajima Japan
56 E3 Wajir Kenya
29 D7 Wakasa-wan *b.* Japan
9 B6 Wakatipu, Lake *l.* N.Z.
65 H4 Wakaw Can.
29 D7 Wakayama Japan
76 D4 Wa Keeney U.S.A.
69 K3 Wakefield Can.
9 D4 Wakefield N.Z.
38 F4 Wakefield U.K.
68 C2 Wakefield *MI* U.S.A.
81 H4 Wakefield *RI* U.S.A.
80 E6 Wakefield *VA* U.S.A.
Wakeham *see* Kangiqsujuaq
4 H3 Wake Island *i.* Pac. Oc.
28 G4 Wakinosawa Japan
28 G2 Wakkanai Japan
59 J3 Wakkerstroom S. Africa
8 E3 Wakool Austr.
8 D3 Wakool *r.* Austr.
67 G2 Wakuach, Lac *l.* Can.
46 H5 Wałbrzych Pol.
8 H1 Walcha Austr.
46 E7 Walchensee *l.* Ger.
42 C4 Walcourt Belgium
46 H4 Wałcz Pol.
81 F4 Walden Montgomery U.S.A.
46 F6 Waldkraiburg Ger.
39 C7 Waldon *r.* U.K.
80 E5 Waldorf U.S.A.
92 C6 Waldron, C. *c.* Ant.
34 E3 Wales *div.* U.K.
6 E5 Walgett Austr.
92 A3 Walgreen Coast *coastal area* Ant.
56 C4 Walikale Congo(Zaire)
68 B4 Walker *IA* U.S.A.
76 E2 Walker *MN* U.S.A.
74 C2 Walker *r.* U.S.A.
58 C7 Walker Bay *b.* S. Africa
79 E7 Walker Cay *i.* Bahamas
74 C2 Walker Lake *l.* U.S.A.
92 A3 Walker Mts *mts* Ant.
74 C4 Walker Pass *pass* U.S.A.
58 A3 Walkerton Can.
76 C2 Wall U.S.A.
74 C2 Wallace U.S.A.
69 F4 Wallaceburg Can.
8 A2 Wallaroo Austr.
39 D4 Wallasey U.K.
8 F3 Walla Walla Austr.
72 C2 Walla Walla U.S.A.
43 H5 Walldürn Ger.
58 B5 Wallekraal S. Africa
8 G3 Wallendbeen Austr.
81 F4 Wallenpaupack, Lake *l.* U.S.A.
39 F6 Wallingford U.K.
81 G4 Wallingford U.S.A.
5 K6 Wallis and Futuna *terr.* Pac. Oc.
7 J3 Wallis, Îles *is* Pac. Oc.
81 F6 Wallops I. *i.* U.S.A.
72 C2 Wallowa Mts *mts* U.S.A.
40 □ Walls U.K.
65 H2 Walmsley Lake *l.* Can.
38 D3 Walney, Isle of *i.* U.K.
68 C5 Walnut U.S.A.
75 G4 Walnut Canyon National Monument *res.* U.S.A.
77 F4 Walnut Ridge U.S.A.
23 J3 Walong India
39 F5 Walsall U.K.
73 F4 Walsenburg U.S.A.
43 H2 Walsrode Ger.
21 C2 Waltair India
79 D5 Walterboro U.S.A.
79 C6 Walter F. George Res. *resr* U.S.A.
69 J3 Waltham Can.
78 C4 Walton *KY* U.S.A.
81 F3 Walton *NY* U.S.A.
57 B6 Walvis Bay Namibia
96 K7 Walvis Ridge *sea feature* Atl. Ocean
56 C3 Wamba Congo(Zaire)
22 B2 Wana Pak.
9 B6 Wanaka N.Z.
9 B6 Wanaka, L. *l.* N.Z.
27 E5 Wan'an China
69 G2 Wanapitei Lake *l.* Can.
81 F4 Wanaque Reservoir U.S.A.
8 C3 Wanbi Austr.
9 C6 Wanbrow, Cape *c.* N.Z.
26 C2 Wanda Shan *mts* China
60 R1 Wandel Sea *sea* Greenland
43 J4 Wandersleben Ger.
43 M2 Wandlitz Ger.
30 D6 Wando S. Korea
9 E3 Wanganui N.Z.
9 E3 Wanganui *r.* N.Z.
8 F4 Wangaratta Austr.
26 C3 Wangcang China
27 D4 Wangcheng China
43 F1 Wangerooge Ger.
43 F1 Wangerooge *i.* Ger.
30 A3 Wanghai Shan *h.* China
27 E4 Wangjiang China
27 C5 Wangmo China
30 E2 Wangqing China
22 B5 Wankaner India
56 E3 Wanlaweyn Somalia
43 G1 Wanna Ger.
27 E4 Wannian China
27 D7 Wanning China
26 E1 Wanquan China
42 D3 Wanroij Neth.
27 D6 Wanshan Qundao *is* China
9 F4 Wanstead N.Z.
39 F6 Wantage U.K.
69 G2 Wanup Can.
27 C4 Wan Xian China
27 C4 Wanxian China
26 C3 Wanyuan China
27 E4 Wanzai China
42 D4 Wanze Belgium
80 A4 Wapakoneta U.S.A.
68 B5 Wapello U.S.A.
66 C3 Wapikopa L. *l.* Can.
64 F4 Wapiti *r.* Can.
77 F4 Wappapello, L. *resr* U.S.A.
68 A5 Wapsipinicon *r.* U.S.A.
26 B3 Waqên China
18 C6 Waqr *well* S. Arabia
22 A4 Warah Pak.
21 B2 Warangal India
8 E4 Waranga Reservoir Austr.
22 E5 Waraseoni India
8 F5 Waratah B. *b.* Austr.
43 H3 Warburg Ger.
6 C4 Warburton Austr.
6 D4 Warburton *watercourse* Austr.
65 G2 Warburton Bay *l.* Can.
59 H3 Warden S. Africa
43 G1 Wardenburg Ger.
22 D5 Wardha India
22 D6 Wardha *r.* India
9 A6 Ward, Mt *mt Southland* N.Z.
9 B5 Ward, Mt *mt West Coast* N.Z.
64 D3 Ware Can.
81 G3 Ware U.S.A.
39 E7 Wareham U.K.
81 H4 Wareham U.S.A.
42 D4 Waremme Belgium
43 L1 Waren Ger.
43 F3 Warendorf Ger.
43 K1 Warin Ger.
32 C2 Warin Chamrap Thai.
9 E2 Warkworth N.Z.
38 F2 Warkworth U.K.
42 A4 Warloy-Baillon France
65 H4 Warman Can.
58 C4 Warmbad Namibia
59 H2 Warmbad S. Africa
39 E6 Warminster U.K.
81 F4 Warminster U.S.A.
42 C2 Warmond Neth.
74 D2 Warm Springs *NV* U.S.A.
80 D5 Warm Springs *VA* U.S.A.
58 D6 Warmwaterberg *mts* S. Africa
81 H3 Warner U.S.A.
72 B3 Warner Mts *mts* U.S.A.
79 D5 Warner Robins U.S.A.
86 F7 Warnes Bol.
22 D5 Warora India
8 D4 Warracknabeal Austr.
8 H3 Warragamba Reservoir Austr.
8 E5 Warragul Austr.
6 E4 Warrego *r.* Austr.
8 F1 Warren Austr.
69 G2 Warren Can.
77 E5 Warren *AR* U.S.A.
69 F4 Warren *MI* U.S.A.
76 D1 Warren *MN* U.S.A.
80 C4 Warren *OH* U.S.A.
80 D4 Warren *PA* U.S.A.
80 C4 Warrendale U.S.A.
41 E3 Warrenpoint U.K.
76 E4 Warrensburg *MO* U.S.A.
81 G3 Warrensburg *NY* U.S.A.
58 F4 Warrenton S. Africa
80 E5 Warrenton U.S.A.
54 C4 Warri Nigeria
9 C6 Warrington N.Z.
39 E4 Warrington U.K.
79 C6 Warrington U.S.A.
8 D5 Warrnambool Austr.
76 E1 Warroad U.S.A.
8 G1 Warrumbungle Ra. *mts* Austr.
47 K4 Warsaw Pol.
68 E5 Warsaw *IN* U.S.A.
76 E4 Warsaw *MO* U.S.A.
80 D3 Warsaw *NY* U.S.A.
80 E6 Warsaw *VA* U.S.A.
43 G3 Warstein Ger.
Warszawa *see* Warsaw
46 G4 Warta *r.* Pol.
6 F4 Warwick Austr.
39 F5 Warwick U.K.
81 F4 Warwick *NY* U.S.A.
81 H4 Warwick *RI* U.S.A.
73 E4 Wasatch Range *mts* U.S.A.
59 J4 Wasbank S. Africa
74 C4 Wasco U.S.A.
76 E2 Waseca U.S.A.
19 F5 Washap Pak.
68 C5 Washburn *IL* U.S.A.
81 J1 Washburn *ME* U.S.A.
76 C2 Washburn *ND* U.S.A.
68 B2 Washburn *WI* U.S.A.
22 D5 Wāshīm India
80 E5 Washington *DC* U.S.A.
79 D5 Washington *GA* U.S.A.
68 B5 Washington *IA* U.S.A.
68 C5 Washington *IL* U.S.A.
78 C4 Washington *IN* U.S.A.
76 F4 Washington *MO* U.S.A.
79 E5 Washington *NC* U.S.A.
81 F4 Washington *NJ* U.S.A.
80 C4 Washington *PA* U.S.A.
75 F3 Washington *UT* U.S.A.
72 B2 Washington *div.* U.S.A.
92 B5 Washington, C. *c.* Ant.
80 B5 Washington Court House U.S.A.
68 D3 Washington Island *i.* U.S.A.
63 M1 Washington Land *reg.* Greenland
81 H2 Washington, Mt *mt* U.S.A.
77 D5 Washita *r.* U.S.A.
39 H5 Wash, The *b.* U.K.
19 G5 Washuk Pak.
18 B5 Wasi' S. Arabia
17 L5 Wasit Iraq
66 E3 Waskaganish Can.
65 K3 Waskaiowaka Lake *l.* Can.
42 C2 Wassenaar Neth.
58 C3 Wasser Namibia
43 H4 Wasserkuppe *h.* Ger.
43 J5 Wassertrüdingen Ger.
74 C2 Wassuk Range *mts* U.S.A.
66 E4 Waswanipi, Lac *l.* Can.
25 E7 Watampone Indon.
81 G4 Waterbury *CT* U.S.A.
81 G2 Waterbury *VT* U.S.A.
65 H3 Waterbury Lake *l.* Can.
41 D5 Waterford Rep. of Ireland
80 D4 Waterford U.S.A.
41 E5 Waterford Harbour *harbour* Rep. of Ireland
41 C5 Watergrasshill Rep. of Ireland
42 C4 Waterloo Belgium
69 G4 Waterloo Can.
68 A4 Waterloo *IA* U.S.A.
81 H3 Waterloo *ME* U.S.A.
80 E3 Waterloo *NY* U.S.A.
68 C4 Waterloo *WV* U.S.A.
39 F7 Waterlooville U.K.
59 H1 Waterpoort S. Africa
68 C2 Watersmeet U.S.A.
64 G5 Waterton Lakes Nat. Park Can.
81 E3 Watertown *NY* U.S.A.
76 D2 Watertown *SD* U.S.A.
68 C4 Watertown *WV* U.S.A.
59 J2 Waterval-Boven S. Africa
8 B2 Watervale Austr.
81 J2 Waterville U.S.A.
65 G3 Waterways Can.
69 G4 Watford Can.
39 G6 Watford U.K.
76 C2 Watford City U.S.A.
65 J3 Wathaman *r.* Can.
43 J2 Wathlingen Ger.
80 E3 Watkins Glen U.S.A.
Watling I. *see* San Salvador
77 D5 Watonga U.S.A.
65 H4 Watrous Can.
56 C3 Watsa Congo(Zaire)
68 D5 Watseka U.S.A.
56 C4 Watsi Kengo Congo(Zaire)
65 J4 Watson Can.
64 D2 Watson Lake Can.
74 B3 Watsonville U.S.A.
40 E2 Watten U.K.
40 E2 Watten, Loch *l.* U.K.
65 J2 Watterson Lake *l.* Can.
64 F3 Watt, Mt *h.* Can.
39 H5 Watton U.K.
68 C2 Watton U.S.A.
6 D2 Watubela, Kepulauan *is* Indon.
6 E2 Wau P.N.G.
55 E4 Wau Sudan
68 D3 Waucedah U.S.A.
79 D7 Wauchula U.S.A.
68 D4 Waukegan U.S.A.
68 C4 Waukesha U.S.A.
68 B4 Waukon U.S.A.
68 C3 Waupaca U.S.A.
68 C4 Waupun U.S.A.
77 D5 Waurika U.S.A.
68 C3 Wausau U.S.A.
80 A4 Wauseon U.S.A.
68 C3 Wautoma U.S.A.
68 C4 Wauwatosa U.S.A.
39 J5 Waveney *r.* U.K.
68 A4 Waverly *IA* U.S.A.
80 B5 Waverly *OH* U.S.A.
79 C4 Waverly *TN* U.S.A.
80 E6 Waverly *VA* U.S.A.
42 C4 Wavre Belgium
68 E1 Wawa Can.
54 C4 Wawa Nigeria
68 E5 Wawasee, Lake *l.* U.S.A.
74 C3 Wawona U.S.A.
77 D5 Waxahachie U.S.A.
79 D6 Waycross U.S.A.
80 B6 Wayland *KY* U.S.A.
68 B5 Wayland *MO* U.S.A.
76 D3 Wayne U.S.A.
79 D5 Waynesboro *GA* U.S.A.
77 F6 Waynesboro *MS* U.S.A.
80 E5 Waynesboro *PA* U.S.A.
80 D5 Waynesboro *VA* U.S.A.
80 C5 Waynesburg U.S.A.
77 E4 Waynesville U.S.A.
77 D4 Waynoka U.S.A.
55 D3 Waza, Parc National de *nat. park* Cameroon
22 C2 Wazirabad Pak.
54 C3 W du Niger, Parcs Nationaux du *nat. park* Niger
66 B3 Weagamow L. *l.* Can.
39 H6 Weald, The *reg.* U.K.
38 E3 Wear *r.* U.K.
6 E3 Weary B. *b.* Austr.
77 D5 Weatherford U.S.A.
72 B3 Weaverville U.S.A.
69 G2 Webbwood Can.
66 C3 Webequie Can.
64 D3 Weber, Mt *mt* Can.
56 E3 Webi Shabeelle *r.* Somalia
81 H3 Webster *MA* U.S.A.
76 D2 Webster *SD* U.S.A.
68 A3 Webster *WV* U.S.A.
76 E3 Webster City U.S.A.
80 C5 Webster Springs U.S.A.
88 D8 Weddell I. *i.* Falkland Is
92 B2 Weddell Sea *sea* Ant.
8 D4 Wedderburn Austr.
43 H1 Weddel (Holstein) Ger.
72 B3 Weed U.S.A.
80 D4 Weedville U.S.A.
59 J4 Weenen S. Africa
42 F1 Weener Ger.
42 E2 Weerribben, Nationaal Park De *nat. park* Neth.
42 D3 Weert Neth.
8 F2 Weethalle Austr.
42 E3 Wegberg Ger.
47 K3 Węgorzewo Pol.
26 B2 Wei *r. Henan* China
26 D3 Wei *r. Shaanxi* China
26 E1 Weichang China
43 L4 Weida Ger.
43 K5 Weidenberg Ger.
43 L5 Weiden in der Oberpfalz Ger.
26 F2 Weifang China
30 B5 Weihai China
30 D2 Weihu Ling *mts* China
43 G4 Weilburg Ger.
43 K4 Weimar Ger.
26 C3 Weinan China
43 G5 Weinheim Ger.
27 B5 Weining China
43 H5 Weinsberg Ger.
6 E3 Weipa Austr.
65 L3 Weir River Can.
80 C4 Weirton U.S.A.
72 C2 Weiser U.S.A.
26 E3 Weishan China
26 E3 Weishan Hu *l.* China
26 E3 Weishi China
43 J5 Weißenburg in Bayern Ger.
43 K3 Weißenfels Ger.
79 C5 Weiss L. *l.* U.S.A.
58 C2 Weissrand Mts *mts* Namibia
43 G5 Weiterstadt Ger.
27 B5 Weixin China
26 B3 Weiyuan *Gansu* China
27 B4 Weiyuan *Sichuan* China
46 G7 Weiz Austria
27 C6 Weizhou Dao *i.* China
30 B3 Weizi China
46 J3 Wejherowo Pol.
65 K4 Wekusko Can.
65 K4 Wekusko Lake *l.* Can.
80 C6 Welch U.S.A.
81 H2 Weld U.S.A.
56 D2 Weldiya Eth.
74 C4 Weldon U.S.A.
56 D3 Welk'īt'ē Eth.
59 G3 Welkom S. Africa
69 H4 Welland Can.
39 G5 Welland *r.* U.K.
69 H4 Welland Canal *canal* Can.
21 C5 Wellawaya Sri Lanka
69 G4 Wellesley Can.
6 D3 Wellesley Is *is* Austr.
64 B2 Wellesley Lake *l.* Can.
81 H4 Wellfleet U.S.A.
42 D4 Wellin Belgium
39 G5 Wellingborough U.K.
8 G2 Wellington *N.S.W.* Austr.
8 B3 Wellington *S.A.* Austr.
9 E4 Wellington N.Z.
58 C6 Wellington S. Africa
39 D7 Wellington *Eng.* U.K.
39 E5 Wellington *Eng.* U.K.
72 F3 Wellington *CO* U.S.A.
77 D4 Wellington *KS* U.S.A.
74 C2 Wellington *NV* U.S.A.
80 B4 Wellington *OH* U.S.A.
77 C5 Wellington *TX* U.S.A.
75 G2 Wellington *UT* U.S.A.
88 A7 Wellington, I. *i.* Chile
8 F5 Wellington, L. *l.* Austr.
68 B5 Wellman U.S.A.
64 E4 Wells Can.
39 E6 Wells U.K.
72 D3 Wells *NV* U.S.A.
81 F3 Wells *NY* U.S.A.
80 E4 Wellsboro U.S.A.
9 E2 Wellsford N.Z.
64 E4 Wells Gray Prov. Park *res.* Can.
6 C4 Wells, L. *salt flat* Austr.
39 H5 Wells-next-the-Sea U.K.
80 B5 Wellston U.S.A.
80 E3 Wellsville U.S.A.
75 E5 Wellton U.S.A.
46 G6 Wels Austria
81 K2 Welshpool Can.
39 D5 Welshpool U.K.
43 M3 Welsickendorf Ger.
39 G6 Welwyn Garden City U.K.
43 H6 Welzheim Ger.
39 E5 Wem U.K.
59 H4 Wembesi S. Africa
64 F3 Wembley Can.
66 E3 Wemindji Can.
79 E7 Wemyss Bight Bahamas
26 F3 Wen *r.* China
72 B2 Wenatchee U.S.A.
27 D7 Wenchang China
27 F5 Wencheng China
54 B4 Wenchi Ghana
26 B4 Wenchuan China
43 K5 Wendelstein Ger.
43 F4 Wenden Ger.
75 F5 Wenden U.S.A.
30 B5 Wendeng China
56 D3 Wendo Eth.
72 D3 Wendover U.S.A.
69 F2 Wenebegon Lake *l.* Can.
27 C5 Weng'an China
27 E5 Wengyuan China
26 B4 Wenjiang China
27 F4 Wenling China
86 □ Wenman, Isla *i. Galapagos Is* Ecuador
68 C5 Wenona U.S.A.
27 B6 Wenshan China
39 H5 Wensum *r.* U.K.
43 J1 Wentorf bei Hamburg Ger.
8 C3 Wentworth Austr.
81 H3 Wentworth U.S.A.
26 B3 Wen Xian China
27 F5 Wenzhou China
43 L2 Wenzlow Ger.
59 G4 Wepener S. Africa
33 A1 We, Pulau *i.* Indon.
43 K2 Werben (Elbe) Ger.
58 E2 Werda Botswana
43 L4 Werdau Ger.
43 L2 Werder Ger.
43 F3 Werdohl Ger.
43 F3 Werl Ger.
43 L5 Wernberg-Köblitz Ger.
42 F3 Werne Ger.
64 C2 Wernecke Mountains Can.
43 J3 Wernigerode Ger.
43 H3 Werra *r.* Ger.
8 E4 Werribee Austr.
8 C3 Werrimull Austr.
8 H1 Werris Creek Austr.
43 H5 Wertheim Ger.
42 B4 Wervik Belgium
42 E3 Wesel Ger.
42 E3 Wesel-Datteln-Kanal *canal* Ger.
43 L1 Wesenberg Ger.
43 J2 Wesendorf Ger.
43 G1 Weser *chan.* Ger.
43 H2 Weser *r.* Ger.
43 G2 Wesergebirge *h.* Ger.
76 C4 Weskan U.S.A.
69 J3 Weslemkoon Lake *l.* Can.
81 K2 Wesley U.S.A.
67 K4 Wesleyville Can.
6 D3 Wessel, C. *c.* Austr.
6 D3 Wessel Is *is* Austr.
59 H3 Wesselton S. Africa
76 D2 Wessington Springs U.S.A.
68 C4 West Allis U.S.A.
92 A4 West Antarctica *reg.* Ant.
93 L5 West Australian Basin *sea feature* Ind. Ocean
93 L6 West Australian Ridge *sea feature* Ind. Ocean
22 B5 West Banas *r.* India
16 E5 West Bank *terr.* Asia
67 J3 West Bay Can.
77 F6 West Bay *b.* U.S.A.
68 C4 West Bend U.S.A.
23 F5 West Bengal *div.* India
69 E3 West Branch U.S.A.
80 D4 West Branch Susquehanna *r.* U.S.A.
39 F5 West Bromwich U.K.
81 H3 Westbrook U.S.A.
40 □ West Burra *i.* U.K.
39 E6 Westbury U.K.
8 F3 Westby Austr.
68 B4 Westby U.S.A.
94 E5 West Caroline Basin *sea feature* Pac. Oc.
81 F5 West Chester U.S.A.
81 G2 West Danville U.S.A.
69 F3 West Duck Island *i.* Can.
79 E7 West End Bahamas
74 D4 Westend U.S.A.
79 E7 West End Pt *pt* Bahamas
43 F4 Westerburg Ger.
42 F1 Westerholt Ger.
46 D3 Westerland Ger.
42 C3 Westerlo Belgium
81 H4 Westerly U.S.A.
65 H1 Western *r.* Can.
6 C4 Western Australia *div.* Austr.
58 D6 Western Cape *div.* S. Africa
55 E2 Western Desert *des.* Egypt
21 A2 Western Ghats *mts* India
8 E5 Western Port *b.* Austr.
52 C3 Western Sahara *terr.* Africa
5 K6 Western Samoa *country* Pac. Oc.
42 B3 Westerschelde *est.* Neth.
43 F1 Westerstede Ger.
43 F4 Westerwald *reg.* Ger.
88 D8 West Falkland *i.* Falkland Is
76 D2 West Fargo U.S.A.
68 D5 Westfield *IN* U.S.A.
81 G3 Westfield *MA* U.S.A.
81 K1 Westfield *ME* U.S.A.
80 D3 Westfield *NY* U.S.A.
42 E1 Westgat *chan.* Neth.
81 K2 West Grand Lake *l.* U.S.A.
43 J6 Westhausen Ger.
40 F3 Westhill U.K.
76 C1 Westhope U.S.A.
92 D5 West Ice Shelf *ice feature* Ant.
42 B3 Westkapelle Neth.
27 □ West Lamma Chan. *H.K.* China
80 B5 West Lancaster U.S.A.
9 B5 Westland National Park N.Z.
39 J5 Westleton U.K.
74 B3 Westley U.S.A.
80 B6 West Liberty *KY* U.S.A.
80 B4 West Liberty *OH* U.S.A.
40 E5 West Linton U.K.
40 B2 West Loch Roag *b.* U.K.
64 G4 Westlock Can.
69 G4 West Lorne Can.
42 C3 Westmalle Belgium
77 F5 West Memphis U.S.A.
80 E5 Westminster *MD* U.S.A.
79 D5 Westminster *SC* U.S.A.
80 C5 Weston U.S.A.
39 E6 Weston-super-Mare U.K.
81 F5 Westover U.S.A.
79 D7 West Palm Beach U.S.A.
77 F4 West Plains U.S.A.
77 F5 West Point *MS* U.S.A.
81 F4 West Point *NY* U.S.A.
69 J3 Westport Can.
9 C4 Westport N.Z.
41 B4 Westport Rep. of Ireland
74 A2 Westport U.S.A.
65 J4 Westray Can.
40 E1 Westray *i.* U.K.
69 G2 Westree Can.
42 F5 Westrich *reg.* Ger.
64 E4 West Road *r.* Can.
81 H2 West Stewartstown U.S.A.
42 D1 West-Terschelling Neth.
81 H4 West Tisbury U.S.A.
81 G2 West Topsham U.S.A.
81 G3 West Townshend U.S.A.
68 B4 West Union *IA* U.S.A.
80 B5 West Union *OH* U.S.A.
80 C5 West Union *WV* U.S.A.
68 D5 Westville U.S.A.
80 C5 West Virginia *div.* U.S.A.
74 C2 West Walker *r.* U.S.A.
74 B1 Westwood U.S.A.
8 F2 West Wyalong Austr.
72 E2 West Yellowstone U.S.A.
42 C2 Westzaan Neth.
25 E7 Wetar *i.* Indon.
64 G4 Wetaskiwin Can.
68 D2 Wetmore U.S.A.
43 G4 Wetter *r.* Ger.
43 K3 Wettin Ger.
43 G4 Wetzlar Ger.
6 E2 Wewak P.N.G.
41 E5 Wexford Rep. of Ireland
65 H4 Weyakwin Can.
68 C3 Weyauwega U.S.A.
39 G6 Weybridge U.K.
65 J5 Weyburn Can.
43 G2 Weyhe Ger.
39 E7 Weymouth U.K.
81 H3 Weymouth U.S.A.
42 E2 Wezep Neth.
9 F2 Whakatane N.Z.
9 F3 Whakatane *r.* N.Z.
32 A3 Whale B. *b.* Myanmar
64 B3 Whale B. *b.* U.S.A.
79 E7 Whale Cay *i.* Bahamas
65 L2 Whale Cove Can.
40 □ Whalsay *i.* U.K.
9 E2 Whangamata N.Z.
9 E3 Whangamomona N.Z.
9 E1 Whangarei N.Z.
66 E2 Whapmagoostui Can.
38 F4 Wharfe *r.* U.K.
69 F2 Wharncliffe Can.
65 J2 Wharton Lake *l.* Can.
68 A5 What Cheer U.S.A.
72 F3 Wheatland U.S.A.
68 C5 Wheaton U.S.A.
73 F4 Wheeler Peak *summit NM* U.S.A.
75 E2 Wheeler Peak *summit NV* U.S.A.
80 C4 Wheeling U.S.A.
91 E2 Wheelwright Arg.
38 E3 Whernside *h.* U.K.

72 B3 Whiskeytown-Shasta-Trinity Nat. Recreation Area res. U.S.A.
40 E5 Whitburn U.K.
69 H4 Whitby Can.
38 G3 Whitby U.K.
39 E5 Whitchurch U.K.
64 A2 White r. AK/Y.T. Can./U.S.A.
77 E4 White r. AR U.S.A.
75 G5 White r. AZ U.S.A.
72 E3 White r. CO U.S.A.
78 C4 White r. IN U.S.A.
68 D4 White r. MI U.S.A.
75 E2 White r. NV U.S.A.
76 C3 White r. SD U.S.A.
68 B2 White r. WV U.S.A.
67 J3 White Bay b. Can.
76 C2 White Butte mt U.S.A.
68 E4 White Cloud U.S.A.
64 F4 Whitecourt Can.
68 A2 Whiteface Lake l. U.S.A.
81 H2 Whitefield U.S.A.
69 G2 Whitefish Can.
72 D1 Whitefish MT U.S.A.
68 D3 Whitefish r. MI U.S.A.
65 H2 Whitefish Lake l. Can.
68 E2 Whitefish Pt pt U.S.A.
41 D5 Whitehall Rep. of Ireland
40 F1 Whitehall U.K.
81 G3 Whitehall NY U.S.A.
68 B3 Whitehall WV U.S.A.
38 D3 Whitehaven U.K.
41 F3 Whitehead U.K.
39 G6 Whitehill U.K.
64 B2 Whitehorse Can.
75 E1 White Horse Pass U.S.A.
39 F6 White Horse, Vale of v. U.K.
92 D4 White I. i. Ant.
9 F2 White I. i. N.Z.
77 E6 White L. l. LA U.S.A.
68 D4 White L. l. MI U.S.A.
6 C4 White, L. salt flat Austr.
81 H2 White Mountains mts U.S.A.
74 C3 White Mt Peak summit U.S.A.
55 F3 White Nile r. Sudan/Uganda
58 C1 White Nossob watercourse Namibia
75 E2 White Pine Range mts U.S.A.
81 G4 White Plains U.S.A.
66 C4 White River Can.
75 H5 Whiteriver U.S.A.
81 G3 White River Junction U.S.A.
75 E2 White River Valley v. U.S.A.
75 E2 White Rock Peak summit U.S.A.
73 F5 White Sands Nat. Mon. res. U.S.A.
80 B6 Whitesburg U.S.A.
12 E3 White Sea g. Rus. Fed.
65 K4 Whiteshell Prov. Park res. Can.
72 E2 White Sulphur Springs MT U.S.A.
80 C6 White Sulphur Springs WV U.S.A.
79 E5 Whiteville U.S.A.
54 B4 White Volta r. Ghana
68 C4 Whitewater U.S.A.
66 C3 Whitewater L. l. Can.
65 J4 Whitewood Can.
8 F4 Whitfield Austr.
39 J6 Whitfield U.K.
40 D6 Whithorn U.K.
9 E2 Whitianga N.Z.
81 K2 Whiting U.S.A.
39 C6 Whitland U.K.
38 F2 Whitley Bay U.K.
79 D5 Whitmire U.S.A.
69 H3 Whitney Can.
74 C3 Whitney, Mt mt U.S.A.
81 K2 Whitneyville U.S.A.
39 J6 Whitstable U.K.
6 E4 Whitsunday I. i. Austr.
8 E4 Whittlesea Austr.
39 G5 Whittlesey U.K.
8 F3 Whitton Austr.
65 H2 Wholdaia Lake l. Can.
75 F5 Why U.S.A.
8 A2 Whyalla Austr.
32 A1 Wiang Phran Thai.
32 B1 Wiang Sa Thai.
69 G3 Wiarton Can.
42 B3 Wichelen Belgium
77 D4 Wichita U.S.A.
77 D5 Wichita Falls U.S.A.
77 D5 Wichita Mts mts U.S.A.
40 E2 Wick U.K.
75 F5 Wickenburg U.S.A.
39 H6 Wickford U.K.
41 E5 Wicklow Rep. of Ireland
41 F5 Wicklow Head hd Rep. of Ireland
41 E5 Wicklow Mountains Rep. of Ireland
41 E4 Wicklow Mountains National Park Rep. of Ireland
39 E4 Widnes U.K.
30 D6 Wi-do i. S. Korea
43 G2 Wiehengebirge h. Ger.
42 F4 Wiehl Ger.
47 J5 Wieluń Pol.
Wien see Vienna
46 H7 Wiener Neustadt Austria
42 E2 Wierden Neth.
43 J2 Wieren Ger.
42 C2 Wieringermeer Polder reclaimed land Neth.
42 D2 Wieringerwerf Neth.
43 G4 Wiesbaden Ger.
43 L5 Wiesenfelden Ger.
43 J5 Wiesentheid Ger.
43 G5 Wiesloch Ger.
43 F1 Wiesmoor Ger.
43 H2 Wietze Ger.
43 H2 Wietzendorf Ger.
46 J3 Wieżyca h. Pol.
38 E4 Wigan U.K.
77 F6 Wiggins U.S.A.
39 F7 Wight, Isle of i. U.K.
65 H2 Wignes Lake l. Can.
39 F5 Wigston U.K.
38 D3 Wigton U.K.
40 D6 Wigtown U.K.
40 D6 Wigtown Bay b. U.K.
42 D3 Wijchen Neth.
42 E2 Wijhe Neth.
42 C3 Wijnegem Belgium
75 F4 Wikieup U.S.A.
69 G3 Wikwemikong Can.
72 C2 Wilbur U.S.A.
8 D1 Wilcannia Austr.
43 L2 Wildberg Ger.
65 J4 Wildcat Hill Wilderness Area res. Can.
74 D2 Wildcat Peak summit U.S.A.
59 H5 Wild Coast coastal area S. Africa
43 G2 Wildeshausen Ger.
68 C1 Wild Goose Can.
64 F4 Wildhay r. Can.
68 A2 Wild Rice Lake l. U.S.A.
46 E7 Wildspitze mt Austria
79 D6 Wildwood FL U.S.A.
81 F5 Wildwood NJ U.S.A.
59 H3 Wilge r. Free State S. Africa
59 H2 Wilge r. Gauteng/Mpumalanga S. Africa
92 C5 Wilhelm II Land reg. Ant.
80 C4 Wilhelm, Lake l. U.S.A.
6 E2 Wilhelm, Mt mt P.N.G.
43 G1 Wilhelmshaven Ger.
81 F4 Wilkes-Barre U.S.A.
92 B6 Wilkes Coast coastal area Ant.
92 B6 Wilkes Land reg. Ant.
65 H4 Wilkie Can.
92 B2 Wilkins Coast coastal area Ant.
92 B2 Wilkins Ice Shelf ice feature Ant.
72 B2 Willamette r. U.S.A.
39 D7 Willand U.K.
8 E2 Willandra Billabong r. Austr.
72 B1 Willapa B. b. U.S.A.
80 B4 Willard U.S.A.
81 F5 Willards U.S.A.
75 H5 Willcox U.S.A.
43 H3 Willebadessen Ger.
42 C3 Willebroek Belgium
83 L6 Willemstad Neth. Ant.
65 H3 William r. Can.
8 D4 William, Mt mt Austr.
75 F4 Williams AZ U.S.A.
74 A2 Williams CA U.S.A.
68 A5 Williamsburg IA U.S.A.
80 A6 Williamsburg KY U.S.A.
68 E3 Williamsburg MI U.S.A.
80 E6 Williamsburg VA U.S.A.
79 E7 Williams I. i. Bahamas
64 E4 Williams Lake Can.
67 H1 William Smith, Cap c. Can.
80 E3 Williamson NY U.S.A.
80 B6 Williamson WV U.S.A.
68 D5 Williamsport IN U.S.A.
80 E4 Williamsport PA U.S.A.
81 E5 Williamston U.S.A.
81 G3 Williamstown MA U.S.A.
81 F3 Williamstown NY U.S.A.
80 C5 Williamstown WV U.S.A.
81 G4 Willimantic U.S.A.
58 D5 Williston S. Africa
79 D6 Williston FL U.S.A.
76 C1 Williston ND U.S.A.
64 E3 Williston Lake l. Can.
39 D6 Williton U.K.
74 A2 Willits U.S.A.
76 E2 Willmar U.S.A.
64 F4 Willmore Wilderness Prov. Park res. Can.
64 D3 Will, Mt mt Can.
8 A1 Willochra r. Austr.
64 E4 Willow r. Can.
65 H5 Willow Bunch Can.
80 E4 Willow Hill U.S.A.
64 F2 Willow Lake l. Can.
58 E6 Willowmore S. Africa
68 C3 Willow Reservoir U.S.A.
74 A2 Willows U.S.A.
77 F4 Willow Springs U.S.A.
8 H1 Willow Tree Austr.
59 H6 Willowvale S. Africa
81 G2 Willsboro U.S.A.
6 C4 Wills, L. salt flat Austr.
8 B3 Willunga Austr.
8 B2 Wilmington Austr.
81 F5 Wilmington DE U.S.A.
79 E5 Wilmington NC U.S.A.
80 B5 Wilmington OH U.S.A.
81 G3 Wilmington VT U.S.A.
39 E4 Wilmslow U.K.
43 G4 Wilnsdorf Ger.
8 B1 Wilpena r. Austr.
43 H1 Wilseder Berg h. Ger.
76 D4 Wilson KS U.S.A.
79 E5 Wilson NC U.S.A.
92 B5 Wilson Hills h. Ant.
73 F4 Wilson, Mt mt CO U.S.A.
75 E2 Wilson, Mt mt NV U.S.A.
76 D4 Wilson Res. resr U.S.A.
81 H2 Wilsons Mills U.S.A.
8 F5 Wilson's Promontory pen. Austr.
8 F5 Wilson's Promontory Nat. Park Austr.
42 E2 Wilsum Ger.
68 B5 Wilton IA U.S.A.
81 H2 Wilton ME U.S.A.
42 D5 Wiltz Lux.
6 C4 Wiluna Austr.
39 J7 Wimereux France
8 D4 Wimmera r. Austr.
68 D5 Winamac U.S.A.
59 G4 Winburg S. Africa
39 E6 Wincanton U.K.
81 G3 Winchendon U.S.A.
66 E4 Winchester Can.
39 F6 Winchester U.K.
68 B6 Winchester IL U.S.A.
68 E5 Winchester IN U.S.A.
80 A6 Winchester KY U.S.A.
81 G3 Winchester NH U.S.A.
79 C5 Winchester TN U.S.A.
80 D5 Winchester VA U.S.A.
62 E3 Wind r. N.W.T. Can.
72 E3 Wind r. U.S.A.
76 C3 Wind Cave Nat. Park U.S.A.
38 E3 Windermere U.K.
38 E3 Windermere l. U.K.
57 B6 Windhoek Namibia
76 E3 Windom U.S.A.
6 E4 Windorah Austr.
75 H4 Window Rock U.S.A.
68 D4 Wind Pt pt U.S.A.
72 E3 Wind River Range mts U.S.A.
79 E6 Windrush r. U.K.
43 J5 Windsbach Ger.
8 H2 Windsor Austr.
67 J4 Windsor Nfld Can.
67 H5 Windsor N.S. Can.
69 F4 Windsor Ont. Can.
67 F4 Windsor Que. Can.
39 G6 Windsor U.K.
81 G4 Windsor CT U.S.A.
79 E5 Windsor NC U.S.A.
81 F3 Windsor NY U.S.A.
80 E6 Windsor VA U.S.A.
81 G3 Windsor VT U.S.A.
81 G4 Windsor Locks U.S.A.
83 M5 Windward Islands is Caribbean Sea
83 K5 Windward Passage chan. Cuba/Haiti
79 C5 Winfield AL U.S.A.
68 B5 Winfield IA U.S.A.
77 D4 Winfield KS U.S.A.
38 F3 Wingate U.K.
8 H1 Wingen Austr.
42 B3 Wingene Belgium
42 F6 Wingen-sur-Moder France
69 G4 Wingham Can.
66 C2 Winisk Can.
66 C2 Winisk r. Can.
66 C3 Winisk L. l. Can.
66 C3 Winisk River Provincial Park res. Can.
32 A2 Winkana Myanmar
65 K5 Winkler Can.
81 J2 Winn U.S.A.
54 B4 Winneba Ghana
68 C3 Winnebago, Lake l. U.S.A.
68 C3 Winneconne U.S.A.
72 C3 Winnemucca U.S.A.
74 C1 Winnemucca Lake l. U.S.A.
76 D3 Winner U.S.A.
77 E6 Winnfield U.S.A.
76 E2 Winnibigoshish L. l. U.S.A.
65 K5 Winnipeg Can.
65 K4 Winnipeg r. Can.
65 K4 Winnipeg, Lake l. Can.
65 J4 Winnipegosis Can.
65 J4 Winnipegosis, Lake l. Can.
81 H3 Winnipesaukee, L. l. U.S.A.
77 F5 Winnsboro U.S.A.
75 G4 Winona AZ U.S.A.
68 C2 Winona MI U.S.A.
68 B3 Winona MN U.S.A.
77 F5 Winona MS U.S.A.
81 G2 Winooski U.S.A.
81 G2 Winooski r. U.S.A.
42 F1 Winschoten Neth.
43 H2 Winsen (Aller) Ger.
43 J1 Winsen (Luhe) Ger.
39 E4 Winsford U.K.
75 G4 Winslow U.S.A.
81 G4 Winsted U.S.A.
79 D4 Winston-Salem U.S.A.
43 G3 Winterberg Ger.
79 D6 Winter Haven U.S.A.
81 J2 Winterport U.S.A.
74 B2 Winters U.S.A.
42 E3 Winterswijk Neth.
46 D7 Winterthur Switz.
59 H4 Winterton S. Africa
81 J1 Winterville U.S.A.
81 J2 Winthrop U.S.A.
6 E4 Winton Austr.
9 B7 Winton N.Z.
39 G5 Winwick U.K.
8 B3 Wirrabara Austr.
39 D4 Wirral pen. U.K.
8 C4 Wirrega Austr.
39 H5 Wisbech U.K.
81 J2 Wiscasset U.S.A.
43 H1 Wischhafen Ger.
68 C3 Wisconsin div. U.S.A.
68 B4 Wisconsin r. U.S.A.
68 C4 Wisconsin Dells U.S.A.
68 C4 Wisconsin, Lake l. U.S.A.
68 C3 Wisconsin Rapids U.S.A.
80 B6 Wise U.S.A.
40 E5 Wishaw U.K.
47 J4 Wisła r. Pol.
46 E4 Wismar Ger.
39 J7 Wissant France
68 B3 Wissota L. l. U.S.A.
64 D4 Wistaria Can.
59 H2 Witbank S. Africa
58 C2 Witbooisvlei Namibia
39 H6 Witham U.K.
39 G4 Witham r. U.K.
81 G2 Witherbee U.S.A.
38 H4 Withernsea U.K.
42 D1 Witmarsum Neth.
39 F6 Witney U.K.
59 J2 Witrivier S. Africa
42 C5 Witry-lès-Reims France
59 G5 Witteberg mts S. Africa
68 C3 Wittenberg U.S.A.
43 K2 Wittenberge Ger.
43 K1 Wittenburg Ger.
44 H3 Wittenheim France
43 J2 Wittingen Ger.
42 E5 Wittlich Ger.
43 F1 Wittmund Ger.
43 L1 Wittstock Ger.
6 E2 Witu Is is P.N.G.
57 B6 Witvlei Namibia
43 H3 Witzenhausen Ger.
30 D3 Wiwon N. Korea
46 J3 Władysławowo Pol.
47 J4 Włocławek Pol.
81 H2 Woburn Can.
8 F4 Wodonga Austr.
43 F6 Wœrth France
42 D5 Woëvre, Plaine de la plain France
43 G4 Wohra r. Ger.
42 E5 Woippy France
25 F7 Wokam i. Indon.
28 B1 Woken r. China
23 H4 Wokha India
39 G6 Woking U.K.
39 G6 Wokingham U.K.
68 D5 Wolcott IN U.S.A.
80 E3 Wolcott NY U.S.A.
43 M1 Woldegk Ger.
42 F1 Woldendorp Neth.
64 C2 Wolf r. Can.
68 C3 Wolf r. U.S.A.
72 D2 Wolf Creek U.S.A.
73 F4 Wolf Creek Pass pass U.S.A.
81 H3 Wolfeboro U.S.A.
69 J3 Wolfe I. i. Can.
43 L3 Wolfen Ger.
43 J2 Wolfenbüttel Ger.
43 H3 Wolfhagen Ger.
64 C2 Wolf Lake l. Can.
72 F1 Wolf Point U.S.A.
46 G7 Wolfsberg Austria
43 J2 Wolfsburg Ger.
42 F5 Wolfstein Ger.
67 H4 Wolfville Can.
86 □ Wolf, Volcán volc. Galapagos Is Ecuador
46 F3 Wolgast Ger.
46 G4 Wolin Pol.
88 C9 Wollaston, Islas is Chile
65 J3 Wollaston Lake Can.
65 J3 Wollaston Lake l. Can.
62 G3 Wollaston Peninsula Can.
8 H3 Wollongong Austr.
59 F3 Wolmaransstad S. Africa
43 K2 Wolmirstedt Ger.
8 C4 Wolseley Austr.
58 C6 Wolseley S. Africa
39 E5 Wolsingham U.K.
42 E2 Wolvega Neth.
39 E5 Wolverhampton U.K.
68 E3 Wolverine U.S.A.
42 C3 Wommelgem Belgium
42 F5 Womrather Höhe h. Ger.
8 E1 Wongalarroo Lake l. Austr.
8 G2 Wongarbon Austr.
23 G4 Wong Chu r. Bhutan
27 □ Wong Chuk Hang H.K. China
30 D5 Wŏnju S. Korea
8 F4 Wonnangatta Moroka Nat. Park Austr.
30 D4 Wŏnsan N. Korea
8 E5 Wonthaggi Austr.
6 D3 Woodah, Isle i. Austr.
39 J5 Woodbridge U.K.
80 E5 Woodbridge U.S.A.
64 G3 Wood Buffalo National Park Can.
72 B2 Woodburn U.S.A.
68 E4 Woodbury MI U.S.A.
81 F5 Woodbury NJ U.S.A.
80 A6 Wood Creek Lake l. U.S.A.
74 C2 Woodfords U.S.A.
74 C3 Woodlake U.S.A.
74 B2 Woodland U.S.A.
73 F4 Woodland Park U.S.A.
32 □ Woodlands Sing.
7 F2 Woodlark I. i. P.N.G.
6 D4 Woodroffe, Mt mt Austr.
72 E3 Woodruff U.S.A.
80 C5 Woodsfield U.S.A.
8 F5 Woodside Austr.
6 D3 Woods, L. salt flat Austr.
65 L5 Woods, Lake of the l. Can./U.S.A.
8 F4 Woods Pt Austr.
67 G4 Woodstock N.B. Can.
69 G4 Woodstock Ont. Can.
68 C4 Woodstock IL U.S.A.
80 D5 Woodstock VA U.S.A.
81 F5 Woodstown U.S.A.
81 G2 Woodsville U.S.A.
9 E4 Woodville N.Z.
80 E3 Woodville NY U.S.A.
77 E6 Woodville TX U.S.A.
77 D4 Woodward U.S.A.
38 E2 Wooler U.K.
6 D5 Woomera Austr.
81 H4 Woonsocket U.S.A.
80 C4 Wooster U.S.A.
43 J3 Worbis Ger.
58 C6 Worcester S. Africa
39 E5 Worcester U.K.
81 H3 Worcester U.S.A.
46 F7 Wörgl Austria
38 D3 Workington U.K.
39 F4 Worksop U.K.
42 D2 Workum Neth.
72 F2 Worland U.S.A.
43 L3 Wörlitz Ger.
42 C2 Wormerveer Neth.
43 G5 Worms Ger.
39 C6 Worms Head hd U.K.
58 B1 Wortel Namibia
43 G5 Wörth am Rhein Ger.
39 G7 Worthing U.K.
76 E3 Worthington U.S.A.
95 G5 Wotje i. Pac. Oc.
25 E7 Wotu Indon.
42 C3 Woudrichem Neth.
76 C3 Wounded Knee U.S.A.
42 F5 Woustviller France
25 E7 Wowoni i. Indon.
64 C3 Wrangell U.S.A.
64 C3 Wrangell I. i. U.S.A.
62 C4 Wrangell Mountains U.S.A.
40 C2 Wrath, Cape c. U.K.
76 C3 Wray U.S.A.
39 F5 Wreake r. U.K.
58 B4 Wreck Point pt S. Africa
43 J2 Wrestedt Ger.
39 E4 Wrexham U.K.
31 C4 Wright Phil.
72 F3 Wright U.S.A.
77 E5 Wright Patman L. l. U.S.A.
75 G6 Wrightson, Mt mt U.S.A.
64 E2 Wrigley Can.
46 H5 Wrocław Pol.
46 H4 Września Pol.
26 E2 Wu'an China
26 D2 Wubu China
30 D1 Wuchang Heilongjiang China
27 E4 Wuchang Hubei China
27 D6 Wuchuan Guangdong China
27 C4 Wuchuan Guizhou China
26 D1 Wuchuan Nei Monggol China
26 C2 Wuda China
26 D3 Wudang Shan mt China
26 C3 Wudang Shan mts China
30 A4 Wudao China
23 H2 Wudaoliang China
26 E2 Wudi China
27 B5 Wuding China
26 D2 Wuding r. China
26 B3 Wudu China
27 D4 Wufeng China
27 D5 Wugang China
26 C3 Wugong China
26 C2 Wuhai China
27 E4 Wuhan China
26 E3 Wuhe China
26 F4 Wuhu China
27 E6 Wuhua China
22 D2 Wüjang China
27 C6 Wujia China
27 C4 Wu Jiang r. China
54 C4 Wukari Nigeria
23 H3 Wulang China
22 C2 Wular L. l. India
30 B5 Wuleidao Wan l. China
26 F3 Wulian China
27 B4 Wulian Feng mts China
24 C4 Wuliang Shan mts China
25 F7 Wuliaru i. Indon.
27 C4 Wuling Shan mts China
27 C4 Wulong China
27 B5 Wumeng Shan mts China
27 C6 Wuming China
43 H1 Wümme r. Ger.
26 A4 Wungda China
27 E4 Wuning China
43 G3 Wünnenberg Ger.
43 L4 Wunsiedel Ger.
43 H2 Wunstorf Ger.
24 B4 Wuntho Myanmar
75 G4 Wupatki National Monument res. U.S.A.
27 E5 Wuping China
42 F3 Wuppertal Ger.
58 C6 Wupperthal S. Africa
26 C2 Wuqi China
26 E2 Wuqiao China
26 E2 Wuqing China
43 H5 Würzburg Ger.
43 L3 Wurzen Ger.
26 B3 Wushan Gansu China
26 C4 Wushan Sichuan China
26 D4 Wu Shan mts China
27 C4 Wusheng China
27 C6 Wushi China
43 H3 Wüstegarten h. Ger.
Wusuli Jiang r. see Ussuri
26 D2 Wutai China
26 D2 Wutai Shan mt China
6 E2 Wuvulu I. i. P.N.G.
26 E4 Wuwei Anhui China
26 B2 Wuwei Gansu China
26 F4 Wuxi Jiangsu China
26 C4 Wuxi Sichuan China
Wuxing see Huzhou
27 C6 Wuxu China
27 C6 Wuxuan China
26 D3 Wuyang China
27 F4 Wuyi China
24 E2 Wuyiling China
27 E5 Wuyi Shan mts China
27 E4 Wuyuan Jiangxi China
26 C1 Wuyuan Nei Monggol China
26 D2 Wuzhai China
26 D4 Wuzhen China
26 C2 Wuzhong China
27 D6 Wuzhou China
68 B5 Wyaconda r. U.S.A.
8 F2 Wyalong Austr.
69 F4 Wyandotte U.S.A.
68 C5 Wyanet U.S.A.
8 G2 Wyangala Reservoir Austr.
8 D4 Wycheproof Austr.
39 E6 Wye r. U.K.
39 F6 Wylye r. U.K.
39 J5 Wymondham U.K.
6 C3 Wyndham Austr.
77 F5 Wynne U.S.A.
62 G2 Wynniatt Bay b. Can.
65 J4 Wynyard Can.
68 C5 Wyoming IL U.S.A.
68 E4 Wyoming MI U.S.A.
72 E3 Wyoming div. U.S.A.
72 E3 Wyoming Peak summit U.S.A.
8 H2 Wyong Austr.
8 D3 Wyperfeld Nat. Park Austr.
38 E4 Wyre r. U.K.
81 E4 Wysox U.S.A.
47 K4 Wyszków Pol.
39 F5 Wythall U.K.
80 C6 Wytheville U.S.A.
81 J2 Wytopitlock U.S.A.

X

56 F2 Xaafuun Somalia
17 M1 Xaçmaz Azer.
58 E1 Xade Botswana
23 H3 Xagquka China
22 D1 Xaidulla China
23 G3 Xainza China
57 D6 Xai Xai Moz.
Xalapa see Jalapa Enríquez
25 C4 Xam Hua Laos
32 B1 Xan r. Laos
57 C6 Xanagas Botswana
26 B1 Xangd China
26 D1 Xangdin Hural China
57 B5 Xangongo Angola
17 L2 Xankändi Azer.
49 L4 Xanthi Greece
32 C2 Xan, Xé r. Vietnam
86 E6 Xapuri Brazil
17 M2 Xaraba Şähär Sayı i. Azer.
17 M2 Xärä Zirä Adası is Azer.
23 F3 Xarba La pass China
26 B1 Xar Burd China
26 F1 Xar Moron r. Nei Monggol China
26 D1 Xar Moron r. Nei Monggol China
45 F3 Xátiva Spain
57 C6 Xau, Lake l. Botswana
87 J6 Xavantes, Serra dos h. Brazil
32 C3 Xa Vo Đat Vietnam
80 B5 Xenia U.S.A.
30 A3 Xi r. China
30 F1 Xiachengzi China
27 D6 Xiachuan Dao i. China
26 B3 Xiahe China
26 E2 Xiajin China
27 E5 Xiajiang China
27 F5 Xiamen China
26 C3 Xi'an China
26 E3 Xiancheng China
26 C2 Xianchengbu China
27 C4 Xianfeng China
26 D3 Xiangcheng China
26 D3 Xiangfan China
26 D1 Xianghuang Qi China
32 B1 Xiangkhoang Laos
22 D3 Xiangquan He r. China
27 F4 Xiangshan China
27 D5 Xiangtan China
27 D5 Xiangxiang China
27 D4 Xiangyin China
27 F4 Xianju China
27 E4 Xianning China
27 E5 Xianxia Ling mts China
26 E2 Xian Xian China
26 C3 Xianyang China
27 F5 Xianyou China
27 C6 Xiaodong China
27 D4 Xiaogan China
24 E1 Xiao Hinggan Ling mts China
26 B4 Xiaojin China
23 H2 Xiaonanchuan China
27 F4 Xiaoshan China
27 E5 Xiaotao China
26 E2 Xiaowutai Shan mt China
26 E3 Xiao Xian China
27 B4 Xiaoxiang Ling mts China
26 D2 Xiaoyi China
27 F5 Xiapu China
30 A2 Xiawa China
26 D3 Xiayukou China
27 B5 Xichang China
26 B4 Xichong China
27 B6 Xichou China
26 D3 Xichuan China
27 B4 Xide China
89 D4 Xié r. Brazil
27 C6 Xieyang Dao i. China
26 E3 Xifei He r. China
27 C5 Xifeng Guizhou China
30 C2 Xifeng Liaoning China
26 C3 Xifengzhen China
15 G4 Xigazê China
26 C3 Xihan Shui r. China
26 B3 Xihe China
26 A1 Xi He watercourse China
26 B3 Xiji China
27 D6 Xi Jiang r. China
23 G2 Xijir China
23 G2 Xijir Ulan Hu salt l. China
26 B2 Xijishui China
26 D1 Xil China
30 B2 Xiliao r. China
27 B5 Xilin China
26 E1 Xilinhot China
26 D1 Xilin Qagan Obo Mongolia
26 A1 Ximiao China
27 F4 Xin'anjiang China
27 F4 Xin'anjiang Sk. resr China
59 K2 Xinavane Moz.
30 C3 Xinbin China
26 E3 Xincai China
27 F4 Xinchang China
26 A2 Xincheng Gansu China
27 C5 Xincheng Guangxi China
26 C2 Xincheng Ningxia China
26 C2 Xinchengbu China
27 D6 Xindu Guangxi China
26 B4 Xindu Sichuan China
27 E5 Xinfeng Guangdong China
27 E5 Xinfeng Jiangxi China
27 E6 Xinfengjiang Sk. resr China
27 E5 Xingan China
27 D5 Xing'an China
30 A4 Xingangzhen China
26 F1 Xingcheng China
27 E5 Xingguo China
15 H3 Xinghai China
26 D1 Xinghe China
26 F3 Xinghua China
27 F5 Xinghua Wan b. China
28 C2 Xingkai China
27 E5 Xingning China
27 D4 Xingou China
26 C3 Xingping China
27 B5 Xingren China
26 A3 Xingsagoinba China
26 D4 Xingshan China
26 E2 Xingtai China
87 H4 Xingu r. Brazil
87 H6 Xingu, Parque Indígena do nat. park Brazil
27 B4 Xingwen China
26 D2 Xing Xian China
26 D3 Xingyang China
27 B5 Xingyi China
27 E4 Xingzi China
27 D5 Xinhua China
26 B2 Xinhuacun China
27 C5 Xinhuang China
27 D6 Xinhui China
26 A2 Xining China
27 E4 Xinjian China
26 D3 Xinjiang China
24 A2 Xinjiang Uygur Zizhiqu div. China
26 C2 Xinjie China
27 B4 Xinjin Sichuan China
30 B4 Xinjin China
30 B1 Xinkai r. China
30 B3 Xinmin China
27 D5 Xinning China
27 A5 Xinping China
27 E5 Xinquan China
27 D5 Xinshao China
26 E3 Xintai China
27 D5 Xintian China
26 E4 Xin Xian Henan China
26 D2 Xin Xian Shanxi China
26 D3 Xinxiang China
27 D6 Xinxing China
26 E3 Xinyang Henan China
26 E3 Xinyang Henan China
26 D3 Xinye China
26 F3 Xinye r. China
27 D6 Xinyi Guangdong China
26 F3 Xinyi Jiangsu China
27 C7 Xinying China
27 E5 Xinyu China
26 D2 Xinzhou China
45 C1 Xinzo de Limia Spain
30 B3 Xiongyuecheng China
26 D3 Xiping Henan China
26 E3 Xiping Henan China
26 A3 Xiqing Shan mts China
87 K6 Xique Xique Brazil
27 C4 Xishui Guizhou China
27 E4 Xishui Hubei China
24 D2 Xi Ujimqin Qi China
27 F4 Xiuning China
27 C4 Xiushan China
27 E4 Xiushui China
27 E4 Xiu Shui r. China
27 C5 Xiuwen China
26 D3 Xiuwu China
30 B3 Xiuyan China
27 D6 Xiuying China
23 F3 Xixabangma Feng mt China
26 D3 Xixia China
26 E3 Xi Xian Henan China
26 D2 Xi Xian Shanxi China
26 C3 Xi Xiang China
27 E5 Xiyang Dao i. China
27 B5 Xiyang Jiang r. China
15 G3 Xizang Gaoyuan plat. China
24 B3 Xizang Zizhiqu div. China
30 A4 Xizhong Dao i. China
23 H3 Xoka China
32 C3 Xom An Lôc Vietnam
32 C3 Xom Duc Hanh Vietnam
26 F4 Xuancheng China
27 C4 Xuan'en China
26 C4 Xuanhan China
26 B2 Xuanhepu China
26 E1 Xuanhua China
32 C3 Xuân Lôc Vietnam
27 B5 Xuanwei China
26 D3 Xuchang China
17 M1 Xudat Azer.
56 E3 Xuddur Somalia
27 C5 Xuefeng Shan mts China
23 H2 Xugui China
23 E2 Xungba China
23 F3 Xungru China
26 C3 Xun He r. China
27 D6 Xun Jiang r. China
27 E5 Xunwu China
26 E3 Xun Xian China
26 C3 Xunyang China
26 C3 Xunyi China
27 D5 Xupu China
23 F3 Xuru Co salt l. China
26 E2 Xushui China
27 D6 Xuwen China
26 F3 Xuyi China
27 B4 Xuyong China
26 E3 Xuzhou China

Y

27 B4 Ya'an China
8 D3 Yaapeet Austr.
54 C4 Yabassi Cameroon
56 D3 Yabēlo Eth.
24 C1 Yablonovyy Khrebet mts Rus. Fed.
26 B2 Yabrai Shan mts China
26 B2 Yabrai Yanchang China
16 F5 Yabrūd Syria
30 E1 Yabuli China
89 C2 Yacambu, Parque Nacional nat. park Venez.
27 C7 Yacheng China
27 C5 Yachi He r. China
86 E6 Yacuma r. Bol.
21 B2 Yadgir India
71 K4 Yadkin r. NC U.S.A.
50 H4 Yadrin Rus. Fed.
28 G2 Yagishiri-tō i. Japan
18 D2 Yagman Turkm.
55 D3 Yagoua Cameroon
23 E3 Yagra China
23 H2 Yagradagzê Shan mt China
91 F1 Yaguari r. Uru.
Yaguarón r. see Jaguarão
32 B4 Yaha Thai.
16 D2 Yahşihan Turkey
16 E2 Yahyalı Turkey
19 H4 Yahya Wana Afgh.
29 F6 Yaita Japan
29 F7 Yaizu Japan
27 A4 Yajiang China
16 F3 Yakacık Turkey
19 G4 Yakhehal Afgh.
72 B2 Yakima U.S.A.
72 B2 Yakima r. U.S.A.
18 D3 Yakinish Iran
19 G2 Yakkabag Uzbek.
19 F4 Yakmach Pak.
54 B3 Yako Burkina
64 B3 Yakobi I. i. U.S.A.
28 C2 Yakovlevka Rus. Fed.
28 G3 Yakumo Japan
29 B9 Yaku-shima i. Japan
64 B3 Yakutat U.S.A.
64 B3 Yakutat Bay b. U.S.A.
13 O3 Yakutsk Rus. Fed.
51 E6 Yakymivka Ukr.
32 B4 Yala Thai.
69 F4 Yale U.S.A.
8 F5 Yallourn Austr.
27 A5 Yalong Jiang r. China
16 B1 Yalova Turkey
51 F6 Yalta Donets'k Ukr.
51 E6 Yalta Krym Ukr.
30 C3 Yalu Jiang r. China/N. Korea
30 C4 Yalujiang Kou river mouth N. Korea
16 C2 Yalvaç Turkey
28 G5 Yamada Japan
28 G5 Yamagata Japan
29 B9 Yamagawa Japan
29 B7 Yamaguchi Japan
12 H2 Yamal, Poluostrov pen. Rus. Fed.
65 G2 Yamba Lake l. Can.
89 C4 Yambi, Mesa de h. Col.
55 E4 Yambio Sudan
49 M3 Yambol Bulg.
12 J3 Yamburg Rus. Fed.
26 A2 Yamenzhuang China
29 G6 Yamizo-san mt Japan
37 V7 Yamm Rus. Fed.
54 B4 Yamoussoukro Côte d'Ivoire
72 E3 Yampa r. U.S.A.
51 D5 Yampil' Ukr.
22 E4 Yamuna r. India
22 D3 Yamunanagar India
23 G3 Yamzho Yumco l. China
26 D2 Yan r. China
13 P3 Yana r. Rus. Fed.
8 C4 Yanac Austr.
21 C2 Yanam India
26 C2 Yan'an China
86 D6 Yanaoca Peru
27 A5 Yanbian China
20 A5 Yanbu' al Baḥr S. Arabia
26 F3 Yancheng China
6 B5 Yanchep Austr.
26 C2 Yanchi China
26 D2 Yanchuan China
8 F3 Yanco Austr.
8 C1 Yanco Glen Austr.
8 E1 Yanda r. Austr.
54 B3 Yanfolila Mali
26 E1 Yang r. China
23 H3 Ya'ngamdo China
23 G3 Yangbajain China
26 D3 Yangcheng China
27 D6 Yangchun China
30 D4 Yangdok N. Korea
26 D1 Yanggao China
26 E2 Yanggu China
19 G2 Yangi-Nishan Uzbek.
19 G1 Yangirabad Uzbek.
27 D6 Yangjiang China
25 B5 Yangon Myanmar
26 D4 Yangping China
26 D2 Yangquan China
27 D5 Yangshan China
27 D5 Yangshuo China
27 E4 Yangtze r. China
26 F4 Yangtze, Mouth of the est. China
56 E2 Yangudi Nassa National Park Eth.
26 C3 Yang Xian China
30 E5 Yangyang S. Korea
26 E1 Yangyuan China
26 F3 Yangzhou China
27 C4 Yanhe China
23 E2 Yanhuqu China
30 E2 Yanji China
27 B4 Yanjin China
54 C4 Yankara National Park Nigeria
76 D3 Yankton U.S.A.
13 P2 Yano-Indigirskaya Nizmennost' lowland Rus. Fed.
21 C4 Yan Oya r. Sri Lanka
26 E1 Yanqing China
26 E2 Yanshan Hebei China
27 E4 Yanshan Jiangxi China
27 B6 Yanshan Yunnan China
26 E1 Yan Shan mts China
23 H2 Yanshiping China
30 E1 Yanshou China
13 P2 Yanskiy Zaliv g. Rus. Fed.
30 A5 Yantai China
47 J3 Yantarnyy Rus. Fed.
30 D2 Yantongshan China
27 A5 Yanyuan China
26 E3 Yanzhou China
54 D4 Yaoundé Cameroon
26 C3 Yao Xian China
25 F6 Yap i. Micronesia
89 D4 Yapacana, Co mt Venez.
25 F7 Yapen i. Indon.
25 F7 Yapen, Selat chan. Indon.
94 E5 Yap Tr. sea feature Pac. Oc.
82 C3 Yaqui r. Mex.
89 C2 Yaracuy r. Venez.
6 E4 Yaraka Austr.
50 H3 Yaransk Rus. Fed.
16 C3 Yardımcı Burnu pt Turkey
17 M2 Yardımlı Azer.

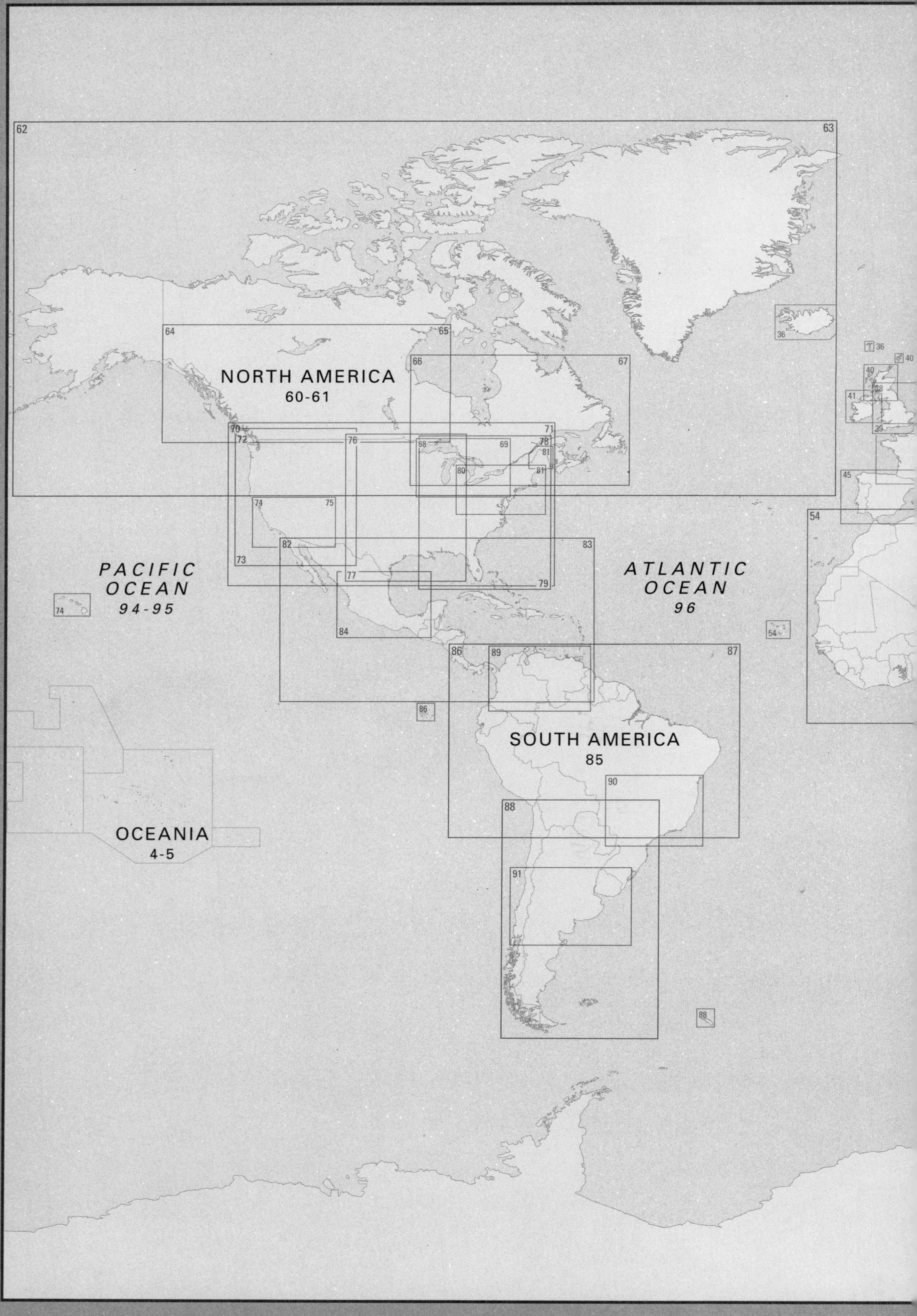

NORTH AMERICA
60-61

PACIFIC
OCEAN
94-95

ATLANTIC
OCEAN
96

SOUTH AMERICA
85

OCEANIA
4-5